VOYAGES IN DEVELOPMENT

VOYAGES IN DEVELOPMENT

SECOND CANADIAN EDITION

Spencer A. Rathus
THE COLLEGE OF NEW JERSEY

Christina M. Rinaldi
UNIVERSITY OF ALBERTA

NELSON

NELSON

Voyages in Development, Second Canadian Edition
by Spencer A. Rathus and Christina M. Rinaldi

Vice President, Editorial Higher Education:
Anne Williams

Publisher:
Lenore Taylor-Atkins

Marketing Manager:
Ann Byford

Developmental Editor:
Suzanne Simpson Millar

Photo Researcher:
Christine Elliott

Permissions Coordinator:
Christine Elliott

Production Project Manager:
Christine Gilbert

Production Service:
MPS Limited

Copy Editor:
Madelyn Odell

Proofreader:
Joan Templeton

Indexer:
Beverlee Day

Design Director:
Ken Phipps

Managing Designer:
Franca Amore

Interior Design:
Cathy Mayer

Cover Design:
Cathy Mayer

Cover Image:
Christopher T Stein/Getty Images

Compositor:
MPS Limited

Library and Archives Canada Cataloguing in Publication

Rathus, Spencer A.
[Childhood and adolescence]

Voyages in development / Spencer A. Rathus, The College of New Jersey, Christina M. Rinaldi, University of Alberta. — Second Canadian edition.

Revision of: Childhood and adolescence : voyages in development / Spencer A. Rathus, Christina M. Rinaldi. — 1st Canadian ed. — Toronto : Nelson Education, ©2009.

Includes bibliographical references and index.
ISBN 978-0-17-650222-5 (pbk.)

1. Child development—Textbooks. 2. Adolescence—Textbooks. I. Rinaldi, Christina M., 1970–, author II. Title. III. Title: Childhood and adolescence

HQ767.9.R347 2014
305.231   C2014-903864-X

ISBN-13: 978-0-17-650222-5
ISBN-10: 0-17-650222-X

To my mother
Angela
my first teacher

ABOUT THE AUTHORS

Spencer A. Rathus

Numerous personal experiences enter into Spencer Rathus's textbooks. For example, he was the first member of his family to go to college, and he found college textbooks to be cold and intimidating. Therefore, when his opportunity came to write college textbooks, he wanted them to be different—warm and encouraging, especially to students who were also the first generation in their families to be entering college. Rathus's first professional experience was in teaching high school English. Part of the task of the high school teacher is to motivate students and make learning fun. Through this experience he learned the importance of using humour and personal stories, which later became part of his textbook approach. Rathus wrote poetry and novels while he was an English teacher, and some of the poetry was published in poetry journals. The novels never saw the light of day (which is just as well, Rathus now admits in mock horror).

Rathus earned his Ph.D. in psychology and he entered clinical practice and teaching. He went on to publish research articles in journals such as *Adolescence, Behavior Therapy, Journal of Clinical Psychology, Behaviour Research and Therapy, Journal of Behavior Therapy and Experimental Psychiatry,* and *Criminology*. His research interests lie in the areas of human growth and development, psychological disorders, methods of therapy, and psychological assessment. Foremost among his research publications is the Rathus Assertiveness Schedule, which remains widely used in research and clinical practice. Rathus has since poured his energies into writing his textbooks, while teaching at Northeastern University, New York University, and currently at The College of New Jersey. His introductory psychology textbook, *Psychology: Concepts and Connections,* is soon to be in its 11th edition.

Rathus is proud of his family. His wife, Lois, is a successful author and a professor of art at The College of New Jersey. Their daughter, Allyn, obtained her M.A. from NYU's Steinhardt School, and is teaching in New York City. Their daughter, Jordan, completed her MFA in fine arts at Columbia University and is launching her career as a video artist. Their youngest daughter, Taylor, can dance the pants off both of them. Taylor completed her BFA at NYU's Tisch program in musical theatre and is lighting up the stage. Rathus's eldest daughter, Jill, has become a psychologist and teaches at C. W. Post College of Long Island University.

Photos courtesy of Spencer A. Rathus

The author is shown at various stages of development in these four photos.

Christina M. Rinaldi

Christina Rinaldi is a professor of educational psychology at the University of Alberta in Edmonton and a registered psychologist in both Alberta and Quebec. Since earning her Ph.D. in school/applied child psychology at McGill University, she has published research articles in journals such as *Early Childhood Research Quarterly*, *Eating Behaviors*, *Infant and Child Development*, and the *Journal of Adolescence and Youth*.

Dr. Rinaldi's professional experience working in schools, hospitals, and mental health settings has informed her research. Her research focuses on how parent–child relationships in early childhood and adolescence support social and emotional learning and development. She also studies the assessment of social functioning and how to support optimal social development. Her research has been funded by Social Sciences and Humanities Research Council of Canada (SSHRC) and the Alberta Centre for Child, Family, and Community Research (ACCFCR). She teaches undergraduate and graduate courses in learning and development in childhood, social development, adolescent development, and consultation in school and clinical child psychology. She presently serves on the Council of the College of Alberta Psychologists, and is on the Board of Directors of the Society for Safe and Caring Schools and Communities. Finally, Rinaldi values and cherishes the time spent with her family and friends. She especially enjoys playing and sharing quality time with her children, who never cease to amaze her and teach her something new each day.

BRIEF CONTENTS

CONTENTS

btrenkel/iStockphoto

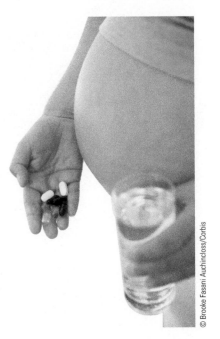

© Brooke Fasani Auchincloss/Corbis

TO COME

Part 3   Infancy

5   INFANCY: PHYSICAL DEVELOPMENT   155

WilliamJu/Thinkstock

© PM/Getty Images

Part 4 Early Childhood

TO COME

© Per Breiehagen/Getty Images

Diego Cervo/Shutterstock.com

Part 5 Middle Childhood

Wallenrock/Shutterstock.com

Monkey Business Images/Shutterstock.com

sanneberg/Shutterstock.com

Part 6 Adolescence (Online)

Palmer Kane LLC/Shutterstock.com

luchschen/Shutterstock.com

Corbis/Jupiterimages

PREFACE

My heart leaps up when I behold

A rainbow in the sky:

So was it when my life began;

So is it now I am a man;

So be it when I shall grow old,

Or let me die!

The Child is father of the Man;

And I could wish my days to be

Bound each to each by natural piety.

William Wordsworth, 1802

Yes, the child is father of the man and, no less certainly, the mother of the woman. In our children, we have the making of ourselves. In children, parents have the most impetuous, comical, ingratiating, delightful, and—at times—infuriating versions of themselves. It is hard to believe, but true, that the babies we hold in our hands at birth may someday be larger and stronger, more talented, and more insightful than we are.

Portraying the Fascination of Children: Personal and Scientific

Our goal in writing this book has been to capture the wonder of child and adolescent development, while portraying the field of development as the rigorous science it is. Our approach is designed to help motivate students by showing them the joy of observing children and adolescents. How can one hope to convey a true sense of development if one is blind to its marvels?

Voyages in Development evolved from our scientific interest and research in human growth and development and also from our experiences with our families and professional work. While our intention is to keep the tone of this text engaging and accessible, this book is rigorous in its reporting of research methods and science. On the other hand, the book is also "hands on"; it contains many applications, which range from preventing infant malnutrition and understanding why it is important to know about immunizations to helping children overcome enuresis and handling bullying in school.

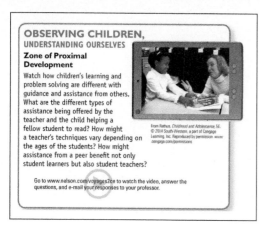

OBSERVING CHILDREN, UNDERSTANDING OURSELVES

Zone of Proximal Development

Watch how children's learning and problem solving are different with guidance and assistance from others. What are the different types of assistance being offered by the teacher and the child helping a fellow student to read? How might a teacher's techniques vary depending on the ages of the students? How might assistance from a peer benefit not only student learners but also student teachers?

Go to www.nelson.com/voyages2ce to watch the video, answer the questions, and e-mail your responses to your professor.

From Rathus, *Childhood and Adolescence, 5E.* © 2014 South-Western, a part of Cengage Learning, Inc. Reproduced by permission. www.cengage.com/permissions

Key Features

The second Canadian edition of *Voyages in Development* contains the following key features:

- A thorough and rigorous update.
- **Observing Children, Understanding Ourselves:** a video feature that enables students to observe different stages of development. There are 34 of these *Observing Children, Understanding Ourselves* videos throughout this edition. As they read each chapter, students can watch the videos by going to the text's website and can even take a quiz to test their comprehension of the concept.
- **Concept Reviews:** visual presentations of complex developmental concepts.
- **A Closer Look—Diversity:** interesting and timely topics that show how culture—especially diverse cultural backgrounds—influences the many aspects of child and adolescent development.
- **A Closer Look—Research:** features that offer expanded coverage of important research studies and also present research issues of great timeliness and interest.
- **A Closer Look—Real Life:** applications that enable readers to "take this book home with them"—to apply what they are learning with children and adults in their own lives.

A Thorough Update

This is an exciting time to be studying child and adolescent development. Every day, new research and new insights help us to better understand the mysteries and marvels of many aspects of development. Nearly 500 new citations refer the reader to research studies and broader documents, such as the federal government's most recent recommendations on childhood nutrition, healthy development during pregnancy, updated Canadian Physical Activity and Sedentary Behaviour Guidelines, relevant Canadian statistics throughout the text, an updated "10 Things You Need to Know about Immunizations," (see page 278) updated information on childhood disabilities and mental disorders in alignment with the *Diagnostic and Statistical Manual of Mental Disorders, Fifth Edition* (APA, 2013), recently published research on substance abuse, and brain and neuroscience in infancy through adolescence.

Chapter Previews

The second Canadian edition contains chapter preview sections that include *Major Topics, Features,* and *Truth or Fiction?* items. These previews help shape students' expectations and enhance the effectiveness of their learning by helping them create mental templates, or "advance organizers," into which they categorize the subject matter.

Chapter-by-Chapter Updates

Every chapter has undergone updating in terms of the coverage of topics and pedagogy. Following is a sampling of what is new:

Chapter 1—History, Theories, and Methods

- New subsection: "The Survey" in the section on methods of observation
- Updated Canadian immigration statistics

- New "A Closer Look—Research" feature: "Surveying High School Seniors' Attitudes toward Living Together before Getting Married"
- New "A Closer Look—Research" feature: "The Bell-and-Pad Method for Treating Bed-Wetting"
- New "A Closer Look—Research" feature: "Operant Conditioning of Vocalizations in Infants"
- New "Observing Children, Understanding Ourselves" video feature: "Zone of Proximal Development"
- Inclusion of Neuroscience and Dynamic Systems Theory
- New "A Closer Look—Research" feature: "The Conditioning of 'Little Albert': A Case Study in Ethics"
- Addition of James Marcia's research on identity development
- General updating: 21 new references

Chapter 2—Heredity and Conception

- New coverage of genetic transmission of hair colour
- New coverage of change in calcium ions as influencing movement of sperm
- New "A Closer Look—Diversity" feature: "LGBT Family Building"
- New "A Closer Look—Diversity" feature: "Where Are the Missing Chinese Girls?"
- New "Observing Children, Understanding Ourselves" video feature: "Twins"
- Expansion of niche-picking description
- New "A Closer Look— Research" feature: "Selecting the Sex of Your Child: Fantasy or Reality?"
- New contemporary perspectives and theories (codominance, epigenetics, and nature and nurture refocus)
- Canadian Cystic Fibrosis Association information
- Updated Canadian statistics related to prenatal development
- General updating: 11 new references

Chapter 3—Prenatal Development

- Updated United Nations information on fertility rates around the world
- New "A Closer Look—Diversity" feature: "Birth Rates around the World"
- New "A Closer Look—Real Life" feature: "Advice for Expectant Mothers"
- New "A Closer Look—Real Life" feature: "Advice for Expectant Fathers"
- New "A Closer Look— Real Life" feature: "Preventing One's Baby from Being Infected with HIV"
- New "Observing Children, Understanding Ourselves" video feature: "Antidepressants in Utero"
- Updated Health Canada guidelines on Healthy Pregnancy; HIV/AIDS, Rubella, and tobacco and alcohol use
- New "A Closer Look—Research" feature: "Can We Trust the Research on the Effects of Caffeine Taken during Pregnancy?"
- New "A Closer Look—Diversity" feature: "The Effects of Parents' Age on Children—Do Men Really Have All the Time in the World?"
- Updated information on fetal alcohol spectrum disorders
- Inclusion of sensitive periods of development
- Follow-up on the Canadian ice storm of 1998
- General updating: 31 new references

Chapter 4—Birth and the Newborn Baby: In the New World

- New "Observing Children, Understanding Ourselves" video feature: "Reflex Development in Infancy"

- Updated "A Closer Look—Diversity" feature: "Maternal and Infant Mortality around the World"
- New "A Closer Look—Research" feature: "Have We Found the Daddy Hormones?"
- New "Observing Children, Understanding Ourselves" video feature: "Early Learning"
- New coverage of hypnosis and biofeedback as methods to help women during childbirth
- Updated information on the use of the cesarean section and on vaginal birth after cesarean section (VBAC), as well as alternative birthing options for Canadian women
- Updated information from Save the Children on maternal and infant mortality around the world
- Expanded coverage of the kinds of maternal depression that may follow childbirth
- Updated information on sudden infant death syndrome (SIDS)
- General updating: 2 new references

Chapter 5—Infancy: Physical Development

- New coverage of infants living in poverty, how infant poverty varies with race and ethnicity, and the relationship of poverty to infant nutrition
- New "A Closer Look—Real Life" feature: "Food Timeline for the First Two Years"
- New "A Closer Look—Diversity" feature: "Wasting Away from Hunger," containing information from the World Hunger Organization
- New "Observing Children, Understanding Ourselves" video feature: "Early Gross Motor Development"
- New "Observing Children, Understanding Ourselves" video feature: "The Visual Cliff"
- New "A Closer Look—Research" feature: "Strategies for Studying the Development of Shape Constancy"
- A reference to Canada Health Agency report on "Attachment across cultures"
- Updated Canadian-based guidelines for breast-feeding
- General updating: 14 new references

Chapter 6—Infancy: Cognitive Development

- New "A Closer Look—Research" feature: "On Mirror Neurons and Really Early Childhood Imitation"
- New Language Development overview
- General updating: 4 new references

Chapter 7—Infancy: Social and Emotional Development

- New "Observing Children, Understanding Ourselves" video feature: "Early Attachment and Anxiety"
- Thoroughly revised and updated section on child abuse and neglect in Canada
- Thoroughly revised and updated section on day care
- Inclusion of research on fathers
- New "A Closer Look—Real Life" feature: "Prevention of Sexual Abuse of Children"
- New "A Closer Look—Research" feature: "How Child Abuse May Set the Stage for Psychological Disorders in Adulthood"

- New "Observing Children, Understanding Ourselves" video feature: "Emotional Development"
- New workforce statistics
- Canadian child care information
- General updating: 31 new references

Chapter 8—Early Childhood: Physical Development

- Revised "Observing Children, Understanding Ourselves" video feature: "Gross Motor Skills"
- Revised "Observing Children, Understanding Ourselves" video feature: "Fine Motor Skills"
- New coverage of the relationship between prenatal testosterone and handedness
- Updated coverage of healthy eating and *Canada's Food Guide*
- Updated Canadian obesity rates
- Updated coverage of major illnesses around the world
- Updated immunization schedule
- Updated "A Closer Look—Real Life" feature: "Ten Things You Need to Know about Immunizations"
- Updated "A Closer Look—Real Life" feature: "Protecting Children from Lead Poisoning"
- Expanded coverage of rough-and tumble play
- New coverage estimates for school-entry vaccinations
- Updated coverage of the leading causes of death for Canadian children
- New coverage of children's drawing and cognitive development
- Canadian Dental Association recommendations for oral health hygiene
- New information on how much sleep is needed at various ages
- New coverage of risk factors for developing encopresis
- Leading causes of injury and death in Canada
- General updating: 26 new references

Chapter 9—Early Childhood: Cognitive Development

- New coverage of Feuerstein theory was added
- New updated research and theories for theory of mind, memory, influence of TV
- New "A Closer Look—Research" feature: "Effects of Scaffolding on Children's Abilities to Recall and Retell Stories"
- Updated "A Closer Look—Real Life" feature: "Helping Children Use Television Wisely"
- New "Observing Children, Understanding Ourselves" video feature: "An Explosion in Vocabulary"
- Updated "A Closer Look—Diversity" feature: "Canada's Languages: A Multilingual Nation"
- New information on self-regulation
- Expanded preschool education for disadvantaged children
- Canadian bilingualism
- Information on Canadian and Aboriginal Head Start preschool programs
- General updating: 19 new references

Chapter 10—Early Childhood: Social and Emotional Development

- New "Observing Children, Understanding Ourselves" video feature: "Types of Play"
- New "Observing Children, Understanding Ourselves" video feature: "Early Childhood Play"

- Added review of hostile attribution bias in section on aggression
- New "A Closer Look—Research" feature: "Do You Have to Be Taught to Hate?"
- New information on parenting and fathers
- Updated coverage of the effects of media violence
- Expanded coverage of cultural stereotypes of "masculine" and "feminine" traits
- Updated coverage of biological factors in the development of gender differences
- General updating: 33 new references

Chapter 11—Middle Childhood: Physical Development

- New "Observing Children, Understanding Ourselves" video feature: "Childhood Obesity"
- Updated "A Closer Look—Real Life" feature: "Helping Overweight Children Manage Their Weight"
- New "Observing Children, Understanding Ourselves" video feature: "Middle Childhood: Gross Motor Skills"
- Updating of the section on overweight children
- New coverage of the Canadian physical exercise and guidelines for children
- New information on childhood disorder reflective of *DSM-V* updates
- Updated coverage of Canadian inclusive educational practices
- General updating: 11 new references

Chapter 12—Middle Childhood: Cognitive Development

- New "A Closer Look—Research" feature: "The Long-Term Effects of Good Teaching"
- New "Observing Children, Understanding Ourselves" video feature: "Rehearsal Strategies"
- New "A Closer Look—Real Life" feature: "Early Math Matters: Does a Child's Education in Math Need to Begin Prior to Kindergarten?"
- New "Observing Children, Understanding Ourselves" video feature: "Suggestibility"
- Expanded coverage of organization in long-term memory
- Updated section on theories of intelligence
- Updated discussion of intellectual disability to reflect *DSM-V* updates
- Updated discussion of the determinants of intellectual development
- Updated discussion of languages other than English that are most often spoken in the home in Canada
- Eyewitness memory has been updated but remains in this chapter
- New addition of the social side of language development
- Brief history on IQ
- Addition of domain theory
- Updated Canadian statistics and figures on bilingualism
- General updating: 21 new references

Chapter 13—Middle Childhood: Social and Emotional Development

- New "A Closer Look—Real Life" feature: "How to Answer a Seven-Year-Old's Questions about—Gulp—Sex"
- Revised "A Closer Look—Research" feature: "Is Bullying Murder?" with Canadian resources and studies cited

- New "Observing Children, Understanding Ourselves" video feature: "Self-Fulfilling Prophecies"
- New "A Closer Look—Research" feature: "When Doom Leads to... Doom"
- Expanded family type descriptions to include intergenerational, extended, and adoptive families
- Revised peer literature on peer rejection and popularity included with Canadian studies embedded throughout
- Revised Canadian divorce rates
- General updating: 24 new references

Chapter 14—Adolescence: Physical Development

- New "A Closer Look—Real Life" feature: "Schools and Adolescent Nutrition"
- New "Observing Children, Understanding Ourselves" video feature: "Puberty and Body Image"
- New "Observing Children, Understanding Ourselves" video feature: "Risk Taking"
- New "A Closer Look—Diversity" feature: "Gender, College Plans, Ethnicity, and Substance Abuse"
- Updated information on sexually transmitted infections (STIs) and HPV vaccine
- New information on brain structures and plasticity
- Inclusion of health figures
- General updating: 10 new references

Chapter 15—Adolescence: Cognitive Development

- New "A Closer Look—Diversity" feature: "Women in STEM Fields"
- Expanded and updated coverage of gender differences in cognitive abilities
- New "A Closer Look— Diversity" feature: "Ethnic Identity and Gender in Career Self-Efficacy Expectancies"
- Expanded discussion of sex differences in verbal/visual ability
- Updated Canadian information on dropping out of school
- General updating: 9 new references

Chapter 16—Adolescence: Social and Emotional Development

- New "A Closer Look—Real Life" feature: "Sexting: One More Way for Adolescents to Stay in Touch"
- New "A Closer Look—Research" feature: "Do Sexy TV Shows Encourage Sexual Behaviour in Teenagers and Lead to Teenage Pregnancy?"
- New "A Closer Look—Real Life" feature: "Sexual Health Education"
- New "Observing Children, Understanding Ourselves" video feature: "Development in Multiracial Individuals"
- New "Observing Children, Understanding Ourselves" video feature: "Peers and Domain Influences"
- New "A Closer Look—Diversity" feature: "Ethnicity, Gender, and Suicide"
- Revised and updated information on the origins of sexual orientation
- New information on adolescent sexual behaviour from Canadian data sources and reports
- Revised and updated information on the incidence of teenage pregnancy in Canada

- Revised material related to sexual orientation and gender identity
- Expanded and updated coverage of emerging adulthood
- General updating: 27 new references

Appendix B

- Current World Health Organization growth charts

What Carries through from Edition to Edition

The second Canadian edition of *Voyages in Development* continues to present cutting-edge topic coverage, emphasizing the latest findings and research in key areas. The text is organized chronologically. It begins with introductory theoretical material. Then it traces the physical, cognitive, and social and emotional sequences that characterize development from infancy through early and middle childhood to adolescence and emerging adulthood.

"Observing Children, Understanding Ourselves" Video Features

One of the themes of this text is how children learn by observation. College students and other adults also learn by observation. One of the best ways to learn about child development is to observe the behaviour of children. Unfortunately, many students do not have everyday access to children and therefore cannot observe for themselves how the many concepts and theories discussed in this textbook are embodied in the everyday lives of children.

All users of *Voyages in Development* will find the "Observing Children, Understanding Ourselves" feature integrated throughout the book. This feature showcases a series of observational videos that illustrate a wide range of topics. Each video is accompanied by Critical Thinking Questions in the text and a quick quiz can be taken online as part of watching the video. The second Canadian edition includes these videos:

- Chapter 1: "Zone of Proximal Development"
- Chapter 2: "Prenatal Assessment"
  "Twins"
- Chapter 3: "Antidepressants in Utero"
- Chapter 4: "Birth"
  "Reflex Development in Infancy"
  "Early Learning"
- Chapter 5: "Early Gross Motor Development"
  "The Visual Cliff"
  "Sensation and Perception in Infancy"
- Chapter 6: "Piaget's Sensorimotor Stage"
- Chapter 7: "Early Attachment and Anxiety"
  "Emotional Development"
  "Gender"
- Chapter 8: "Gross Motor Skills"
  "Fine Motor Skills"
- Chapter 9: "Piaget's Preoperational Stage"
  "An Explosion in Vocabulary"
- Chapter 10: "Types of Play"
  "Early Childhood Play"
  "Gender"

- Chapter 11: "Childhood Obesity"
      "Middle Childhood: Gross Motor Skills"
- Chapter 12: "Piaget's Concrete-Operational Stage"
      "Rehearsal Strategies"
      "Suggestibility"
- Chapter 13: "Self-Concept"
      "Self-Fulfilling Prophecies"
- Chapter 14: "Puberty and Body Image"
      "Risk Taking"
- Chapter 15 "Piaget's Formal-Operational Stage: Hypothetical
      Propositions"
- Chapter 16: "Development in Multiracial Individuals"
      "Peers and Domain Influences"

The *Observing Children, Understanding Ourselves* videos are available by going to www.nelsonbrain.com to access this textbook's CourseMate, where you will find an interactive ebook, flashcards, pre-lecture quizzes, section quizzes, exam practice, videos, and more.

Concept Reviews

Concept Reviews are more than simple summaries. They take complex developmental concepts, such as theories of intelligence, and present them in dynamic layouts that readily communicate the key concepts and the relationships among concepts. Many of them include photographs and figures as well as text. Here is a sampling of the Concept Reviews found in *Voyages in Development*:

- Concept Review 1.3: "Perspectives on Child Development"
- Concept Review 6.1: "The Six Substages of the Sensorimotor Stage, According to Piaget"
- Concept Review 14.2: "Five Stages of Female Development during Puberty"

"A Closer Look—Diversity" Features

These features address the most challenging issues related to the way children and adolescents are influenced by ethnic background, gender roles, sexual orientation, and age, in areas ranging from intellectual development to substance abuse. In many cases, cultural and ethnic factors affect the very survival of the child. This coverage helps students understand why parents of different backgrounds and genders rear their children and adolescents in certain ways, why children and adolescents from various backgrounds behave and think in different ways, and how the study of child and adolescent development is enriched by addressing those differences. Here are some examples of such topics:

- Chapter 2: "LGBT Family Building"
- Chapter 3: "The Effects of Parents' Age on Children—Do Men Really Have All the Time in the World?"
- Chapter 4: "Maternal and Child Mortality around the World" (the latest information from the Save the Children Organization)
- Chapter 8: "Gender Differences in Motor Activity"
- Chapter 15: "Ethnic Identity and Gender in Career Self-Efficacy Expectancies"

"A Closer Look—Research" Features

This research-focused feature expands the book's treatment of the ways in which researchers carry out their work. Examples of topics include

- Chapter 1: "Operant Conditioning of Vocalizations in Infants"
- Chapter 4: "Studying Visual Acuity in Neonates: How Well Can They See?"
- Chapter 5: "Strategies for Studying the Development of Shape Constancy"
- Chapter 6: "On Mirror Neurons and Really Early Childhood Imitation"
- Chapter 9: "Effects of Scaffolding on Children's Abilities to Recall and Retell Stories"

"A Closer Look—Real Life" Features

This feature enables readers to "take the book home with them"—that is, to apply what they are learning with children and adults in their own lives. Examples of topics include

- Chapter 3: "Advice for Expectant Fathers"
- Chapter 8: "Ten Things You Need to Know about Immunizations"
- Chapter 9: "Helping Children Use Television Wisely" (includes teaching children not to imitate the violence they observe in the media)

An Enhanced Pedagogical Package: PQ4R

PQ4R discourages students from believing that they are sponges who will automatically soak up the subject matter in the same way that sponges soak up water. The PQ4R method stimulates students to *actively* engage the subject matter. Students are encouraged to become *proactive* rather than *reactive*.

PQ4R is the abbreviation for *Preview, Question, Read, Review, Reflect, and Recite,* a method that is related to the work of educational psychologist Francis P. Robinson. PQ4R is more than the standard built-in study guide. It goes well beyond a few pages of questions and exercises that are found at the ends of the chapters of many textbooks. It is an integral part of every chapter. It flows throughout every chapter. It begins and ends every chapter, and it accompanies the student page by page.

Preview

Revised chapter previews include *Major Topics, Features,* and *Truth or Fiction?* items to help shape students' expectations. The previews enable students to create mental templates, or "advance organizers," into which they categorize the subject matter. The *Truth or Fiction?* items stimulate students to examine their own assumptions and prepare to delve into the subject matter by challenging folklore and common sense (which is often common *non*sense). *Truth or Fiction Revisited* sections in the chapter inform students whether or not they were correct in their assumptions. The *Major Topics* list outlines the material in the chapter, creating mental categories that guide the students' reading.

Following is a sample of challenging *Truth or Fiction?* items from various chapters.

T|F You can carry the genes for a deadly illness and not become sick yourself.

T|F More children die from sudden infant death syndrome (SIDS) than from cancer, heart disease, pneumonia, child abuse, HIV/AIDS, cystic fibrosis, and muscular dystrophy combined.

T|F Infants need to have experience crawling before they develop fear of heights.

T|F It is dangerous to awaken a sleepwalker.

T|F Three-year-olds usually say, "Daddy goed away" instead of "Daddy went away" because they *do* understand rules of grammar.

T|F Children who watch two to four hours of TV a day will see 8000 murders and another 100 000 acts of violence by the time they have finished elementary school.

Question

Devising questions about the subject matter, before reading it in detail, is another feature of the PQ4R method. Writing questions gives students goals: They attend class or read the text *in order to answer the questions.* Questions are strategically inserted in all primary sections of the text to help students use the PQ4R method most effectively. They are printed in **purple.** When students come to such a question, they can read the following material in order to answer it. And if they wish, they can also write the questions and answers in their notebooks, as Francis Robinson recommended.

Read

The first R in the PQ4R method stands for Read. Although students will have to read for themselves, they are not alone. The text helps by providing

- A *Major Topics* list that helps students organize the material in each chapter
- *Truth or Fiction?* items that stimulate students by challenging common knowledge and folklore
- Presentation of the subject matter in clear, stimulating prose
- A running glossary that defines key terms in the margin of the text, near where the terms first appear
- Development of concepts in an orderly fashion so that new concepts build on previously presented concepts

We have chosen a writing style that is "personal." It speaks directly to the student and employs humour and personal anecdotes designed to motivate and stimulate students.

Review

The second R in PQ4R stands for Review. Regular reviews of the subject matter help students learn. Therefore, reviews are incorporated into *Active Review* sections that follow all major sections in the text.

Active Reviews contain two types of items that foster active learning, retention, and critical thinking. First come fill-in-the-blank questions. In some of these, the student indicates which of two words or phrases in parentheses accurately completes a given statement. Other questions offer no such prompt; these items challenge students to *produce,* not simply *recognize,* the answer. For example, an *Active Review* from Chapter 2, "Heredity and Conception," includes the following items:

13. The sets of traits that we inherit are referred to as our (genotype or phenotype?).

14. The actual traits that we display at any point in time are the product of genetic and environmental influences and are called our (genotypes or phenotypes?).

15. Parents and children have a ___ percent overlap in their genetic endowments.

16. ___ (MZ) twins share 100 percent of their genes.

17. ___ (DZ) twins have a 50 percent overlap, as do other siblings.

Items are numbered, and answers are found at the end of the book.

Because reviewing the subject matter is so important, and because of the value of visual cues in learning, *Concept Reviews* are also found throughout the text (see page xxxvii of this Preface).

Reflect and Relate

Students learn more effectively when they *reflect* on (the third R in PQ4R is for Reflect), or *relate* to, the subject matter. Psychologists who study learning and memory refer to reflection on subject matter as *elaborative rehearsal.* One way for students to reflect on a subject is to *relate* it to things they already know about, whether the "subject" is academic material or events in their own lives. Reflecting on, or relating to, what they are learning makes it meaningful and easier to remember. It also makes it more likely that they will be able to *apply* the information to their own lives. Through effective reflection, students can embed material firmly in their memory so that rote repetition is unnecessary.

Because reflecting on the material is intertwined with relating to it, the second kind of item in each *Active Review* section is termed *Reflect & Relate.* Here is the *Reflect & Relate* item from an *Active Review* in Chapter 13 that follows a section on theories of social and emotional development in middle childhood:

> *Reflect & Relate:* Are you "responsible" for your own self-esteem, or does your self-esteem pretty much vary with the opinion that others have of you? Why is this an important question?

Recite

The PQ4R method recommends that students recite the answers to the questions aloud. Reciting answers aloud helps students remember them by means of repetition, by stimulating students to produce concepts and ideas they have learned, and by associating these ideas with spoken words and gestures.

A *Recite* section is found at the end of each chapter. These sections help students summarize the material, but they are active summaries. For this reason, the sections are termed *Recite—An Active Summary.* They are written in question-and-answer format. To provide a sense of closure, the Active Summaries repeat the questions found within the chapters. The answers are concise but include most of the key terms found in the text.

Themes

Voyages in Development continues to emphasize three themes:

- Human diversity in development
- Biology: neuroscience, evolution, genes, hormones, and behaviour
- Applications

Coverage of these themes is summarized as follows:

Human Diversity in Development

- Ecological circumstances that affect development (pp. 22–24)
- Study of students from different ethnic backgrounds and their environments in relationship to their happiness (p. 24)
- The sociocultural perspective and human diversity (pp. 26–27)

- Naturalistic observations in children of different cultures (p. 35)
- Ethnic differences in the incidence of bearing fraternal twins (p. 52)
- Ethnic differences in chromosomal and genetic disorders (p. 57)
- Birth rates around the world (p. 93)
- Cross-cultural differences in using a doula during delivery (p. 124)
- Maternal and infant mortality around the world (pp. 130–131)
- Socioeconomic status and nutrition (pp. 162–163)
- Differences in preference for breast-feeding (pp. 164–165)
- Ethnic differences in infant capacity to walk (pp. 172–173)
- Differences in babbling across cultures (p. 208)
- Two-word sentence development across different languages (pp. 212–213)
- Low-income families and levels of child attachment (p. 226)
- Attachment of Ugandan and Scottish infants (pp. 228–229)
- Social deprivation in a Guatemalan tribe (p. 236)
- Stranger anxiety across cultures (p. 251)
- Gender differences in personality (pp. 257–258)
- Cultural differences in rough-and-tumble play (p. 258)
- Gender differences in motor activity (p. 269)
- Cultural differences in the perception of handedness (pp. 272–273)
- Ethnicity and immunization (pp. 277–278)
- Differences in accidental death rate (pp. 280–282)
- Cross-cultural differences in sleeping arrangements (p. 283)
- Development of concepts of ethnicity and race (p. 310)
- Cultural and gender differences in authoritarian parenting and the effects on children (p. 331)
- Cross-cultural differences in effects of parental styles (p. 333)
- Individualism, collectivism, and patterns of child rearing (pp. 335–336)
- Fathers in Canada (p. 339)
- Gender differences in play (pp. 343–344)
- Cultural differences in empathy (pp. 344–345)
- Gender differences in effects of TV violence (pp. 350–351)
- Development of gender roles and gender differences (pp. 355–357)
- Possible gender differences in organization of the brain (pp. 358–359)
- Sex hormones (p. 359)
- Cross-cultural differences in gender identity, stability, and constancy (pp. 361–362)
- Ethnicity and percent of children and adolescents who are overweight (pp. 370–371)
- Gender differences and motor skills (pp. 377–378)
- Education for children with disabilities (pp. 384–386)
- Discrimination in standardized testing (pp. 406–407)
- Testing bias and culture-free tests (p. 422)
- Intellectual disability and giftedness (pp. 424–426)
- Socioeconomic and ethnic differences in IQ (pp. 425–426)
- Gender differences in self-concept (p. 442)
- Gender differences in self-esteem (p. 444)
- Gender differences in learned helplessness (p. 445)
- Effects of divorce across cultures (p. 449)
- Gender differences in coping with divorce (pp. 449–450)
- Gender differences in the development of friendships (p. 453)
- Differences in preparedness for school (p. 456)
- Sexism in the classroom (p. 460)
- Gender differences in the social impact of acne (pp. W14-9)
- Cultural impact of menarche (pp. W14-12–W14-13)
- Ethnicity and causes of death among adolescents (p. W14-22)

- Gender differences in anorexia nervosa (p. W14-26)
- Gender, college plans, ethnicity, and substance abuse (p. W14–34)
- Differences in formal-operational thought (p. W15-4)
- Gender differences in verbal ability (p. W15-9)
- Gender differences in visual-spatial ability (p. W15-9)
- Gender differences in mathematical ability (pp. W15-10–W15-11)
- Adolescent girls' vulnerability to stereotypes concerning female math ability (p. W15-11)
- Cross-cultural differences in moral development (p. W15-14–W15-15)
- Gender differences in moral development (p. W15-15–W15-16)
- Differences in postconventional thought (p. W15-16)
- Ethnic identity and gender in career self-efficacy expectancies (p. W15-23)
- Ethnicity and development of identity (pp. W16-7–W16-8)
- Gender and development of identity (pp. W16-8–W16-9)
- Ethnicity, gender, and adolescent friendships (pp. W16-13–W16-14)
- Differences in sexual orientation (pp. W16-19–W16-20)
- The origins of sexual orientation (pp. W16-21–W16-23)
- Ethnicity, gender, and juvenile delinquency (pp. W16-29–W16-30)
- Gender differences in delinquent behaviour (p. W16-29)
- Ethnicity, gender, and suicide (p. W16-32)

Biology: Neuroscience, Evolution, Genes, Hormones, and Behaviour

- Ethology (p. 21)
- The nature–nurture controversy (p. 31)
- Frequency of fraternal twins (p. 52)
- Chromosomal and genetic disorders (p. 57)
- Ethnic differences in chromosomal and genetic disorders (p. 58)
- The possible evolution of reflexes (p. 138)
- Pain as adaptive (p. 144)
- Nature and nurture in the development of the brain (pp. 169–170)
- Nature and nurture in motor development (pp. 173–174)
- Are humans prewired to prefer human stimuli to other stimuli? (pp. 176–177)
- Nature and nurture in perceptual development (pp. 184–185)
- Imitation as adaptive (pp. 197–198)
- Nature and nurture in language development (pp. 212–217)
- The nativist view of language development (p. 215)
- Nature and nurture in theories of attachment development (pp. 229–232)
- Genetic factors in handedness (p. 273)
- Evolutionary theory of aggression (p. 268)
- Genetic/hormonal factors in aggression (p. 268)
- Possible genetic influences on self-esteem (p. 352)
- Organization of the brain (pp. 358–359)
- Genetic factors in obesity (p. 372)
- Genetic factors in dyslexia (pp. 385–386)
- Genetic influences on intelligence (pp. 428–429)
- Possible genetic factors in conduct disorder (p. 462)
- Depression and serotonin (p. 465)
- The biology of puberty (pp. W14-5–W14-6)
- Hormonal regulation of the menstrual cycle (p. W14-12)
- Serotonin and eating disorders (p. W14-28)
- Genetic factors in eating disorders (p. W14-28)
- Biological factors in substance abuse (p. W14-35)

- Possible evolutionary factors in visual–spatial ability (p. W15-9)
- The origins of sexual orientation (pp. W16-21–W16-23)
- Biological effects of puberty (p. W16-24)

Applications

- Problems associated with the use of punishment (pp. 14–16)
- Ways of reversing infertility (p. 73)
- Choosing the gender of one's child (pp. 73–74)
- Maternal nutrition during pregnancy (pp. 92–93)
- Effects of maternal health problems on the embryo and fetus (pp. 96–100)
- Effects of environmental hazards on the embryo and fetus (p. 109)
- Using the Lamaze method to decrease fear and pain during delivery (p. 124)
- Using C-section to avoid disease transmission from mother to infant (pp. 124–125)
- How interaction, talking, and stimulation can help preterm infants develop (pp. 129–130)
- How a woman can work to get beyond postpartum depression (pp. 132–133)
- Understanding visual accommodation (p. 141)
- How to soothe an infant and ease crying (pp. 148–149)
- Teaching sign language to infants (pp. 209–210)
- "Motherese" (pp. 214–215)
- Establishing attachment (pp. 226–227)
- Preventing sexual abuse of children (pp. 239–240)
- How child abuse may lead to psychological disorders in adulthood (p. 242)
- Neurological differences in autistic children (pp. 244–245)
- Finding day care you and your child can live with (p. 248)
- How to comfort a child who doesn't know you (p. 251)
- Brain development and visual skills (p. 264)
- Right brain/left brain (p. 265)
- Plasticity of the brain (p. 265)
- Teaching a child to enjoy healthful food (pp. 275–276)
- Ten things you need to know about immunizations (p. 278)
- Assessing and minimizing the risk of lead poisoning (p. 280)
- What to do about bed-wetting (p. 287)
- Watching how children show (or don't show) conservation (pp. 298–299)
- Memory strategies (p. 316)
- Techniques for restricting children's behaviour (pp. 329–330)
- Helping children cope with fears (pp. 354–355)
- Piaget's theory applied to education (pp. 397–398)
- How teachers can help motivate students (pp. 406–407)
- Rehearsal strategies for memory (p. 410)
- How to ask children questions that elicit truthful answers (p. 410–411)
- How to help children with conduct disorders (p. 463)
- How parents and teachers can help children with mild depression (p. 465)
- How parents and teachers can help children with school phobia (pp. 468–469)
- Prevention of HIV/AIDS and other STIs (p. W14-21)
- Treatment and prevention of eating disorders (pp. W14-28–W14-29)
- Using different parenting styles to combat adolescent substance abuse (p. W14-33)
- Treatment and prevention of substance abuse (p. W14-35)
- How parents can help early adolescents in school (p. W15-19–W15-20)

Ancillaries

About the Nelson Education Teaching Advantage (NETA)

The **Nelson Education Teaching Advantage (NETA)** program delivers research-based instructor resources that promote student engagement and higher-order thinking to enable the success of Canadian students and educators. Be sure to visit Nelson Education's **Inspired Instruction** website at www.nelson.com/inspired to find out more about NETA. Don't miss the testimonials of instructors who have used NETA supplements and seen student engagement increase!

Instructor Resources

All NETA and other key instructor ancillaries are provided on the Instructor Companion Site at www.nelson.com/voyages2ce, giving instructors the ultimate tool for customizing lectures and presentations. Instructor materials can also be accessed through http://www.nelson.com/login and http://login.cengage.com.

NETA Test Bank: This resource was written by Karen McLaren. It includes over 2100 multiple-choice questions written according to NETA guidelines for effective construction and development of higher-order questions. The test bank was copyedited by a NETA-trained editor. Also included are matching, true/false, and essay questions with model answers.

The NETA Test Bank is available in a new, cloud-based platform. **Testing Powered by Cognero®** is a secure online testing system that allows you to author, edit, and manage test bank content from any place you have Internet access. No special installations or downloads are needed, and the desktop-inspired interface, with its drop-down menus and familiar, intuitive tools, allows you to create and manage tests with ease. You can create multiple test versions in an instant, and import or export content into other systems. Tests can be delivered from your learning management system, your classroom, or wherever you want. Testing Powered by Cognero for *Voyages in Development* can be accessed through http://www.nelson.com/login and http://login.cengage.com. Printable versions of the test bank in Word and PDF formats are available with the instructor resources for this textbook.

NETA Instructor's Manual: This resource was written by Jason Daniels, University of Alberta. It is organized according to the textbook chapters and addresses key educational concerns, such as typical stumbling blocks student face and how to address them. Other features include lecture topics, student exercises, and file and video suggestions.

NETA PowerPoint: Microsoft® PowerPoint® lecture slides for every chapter have been created by Patrice Esson, Sheridan College. Slides include many featuring key figures, tables, and photographs from *Voyages in Development*, Second Canadian Edition. In addition, instructor discussions are included in the Notes section, and embedded videos bring the content to life. NETA principles of clear design and engaging content have been incorporated throughout, making it simple for instructors to customize the deck for their courses.

Image Library: This resource consists of digital copies of figures, short tables, and photographs used in the book. Instructors may use these jpegs to customize the NETA PowerPoint or create their own PowerPoint presentations.

DayOne: Day One—Prof InClass is a PowerPoint presentation that instructors can customize to orient students to the class and their text at the beginning of the course.

Student Ancillaries

The more you study, the better the results. Make the most of your study time by accessing everything you need to succeed in one place. The *Voyages in Development* **CourseMate** includes:

- Interactive learning tools, including:
  - Pre-lecture quizzes
  - Interactive Flashcards
  - Videos: *Observing Children, Understanding Ourselves*
  - Video Quizzes: *Observing Development*
  - Glossary
  - … and more!

Visit NELSONbrain.com to start using **CourseMate**. Enter the Online Access Code from the card included with your text. If a code card is *not* provided, you can purchase instant access at NELSONbrain.com. Only new books include Access Codes.

Acknowledgments

This book is about human development. This section is about the development of this book. Its existence reflects the input and aid of a significant cast of characters.

First among these are my professional academic colleagues—the people who teach the course, the people who conduct the research. They know better than anyone else what's going on "out there"—out there in the world of children and adolescents, out there in the classroom. The book you hold in your hands would not have been what it is without their valuable insights and suggestions. Thank you to reviewers for this edition:

Wendy Ellis, *King's University College*

Ed Maruska, *Medicine Hat College*

Ann McDonald, *Fleming College*

Ulrich Mueller, *University of Victoria*

William L Roberts, *Thompson Rivers University*

Noella Surette, *Nova Scotia Community College*

With a group like this looking over your shoulder, it's difficult to make mistakes. But if any remain, we are responsible.

We acknowledge that the book you read would not have been what it is without the insights and suggestions of academic colleagues and students over the years. It also owes much to the fine editorial and production team at Nelson and assembled by Nelson: Lenore Taylor-Atkins, publisher; Suzanne Simpson Millar, developmental editor; Ann Byford, marketing manager; Sarah Fisher, editorial assistant; Christine Gilbert, production project manager; Christina Elliott, permissions researcher; and Daniela Glass, project manager, rights acquisition.

Major Topics

HISTORY, THEORIES, AND METHODS

Truth or Fiction?

T | F During the Middle Ages in Europe, children were often treated as miniature adults. **p. 6**

T | F Children come into the world as "blank tablets"—without inborn differences in intelligence and talents. **p. 6**

T | F Nail biting and smoking cigarettes are signs of conflict experienced during early childhood. **p. 9**

T | F Children should not be punished. **p. 16**

T | F Research with monkeys has helped psychologists understand the formation of attachment in humans. **p. 39**

T | F To learn how a person develops over a lifetime, researchers have tracked some individuals for more than 50 years. **p. 39**

This book has a story to tell. An important story. A remarkable story. It is your story. It is about the remarkable journey you have already taken through childhood. It is about the unfolding of your adult life. Billions have made this journey before. You have much in common with them. Yet you are unique, and things will happen to you, and because of you, that have never happened before.

Development of children, from a Canadian context, is what this book is about. In a very real sense, we cannot hope to understand ourselves as adults—we cannot catch a glimpse of the remarkable journeys we have taken—without understanding children. And for those of us who work with children or will be working with children, this understanding and appreciation of children and childhood is a critical part of professional training and development.

In this chapter, we explore some of the reasons for studying child development. We then take a brief tour of the history of child development. It may surprise you that until relatively recent times, people were not particularly sensitive to the ways in which children differ from adults. Next, we examine some controversies in child development, such as whether there are distinct stages of development. We see how theories help illuminate our observations and how theories help point the way toward new observations. Then we consider methods for the study of child development. Scientists have devised sophisticated methods for studying children, and ethics helps to determine what types of research are deemed proper and what types are deemed improper.

ziggy_mars/Thinkstock

1.1 What Is Child Development? Coming to Terms with Terms

QUESTION » What is child development? You have heard the word *child* all your life, so why bother to define it? We do so because words in common usage are frequently used inexactly. A **child** is a person experiencing the period of development from *infancy* to *puberty*—two other familiar words that are frequently used inexactly. The term **infancy** derives from Latin roots meaning "not speaking," and infancy is usually defined as the first two years of life, or the period of life before the development of *complex* speech. We stress the word *complex* because many children have a large vocabulary and use simple sentences before their second birthday.

Western researchers commonly speak of two other periods of development that lie between infancy and adolescence: early childhood and middle childhood. This book takes a western approach to understanding child development by presenting studies and statistics relevant to Canadian children and youth, using developmental definitions based in western education, health and psychological traditions. However, as we will explore "human development is a cultural process" (Rogoff, 2003, p. 3). Early childhood encompasses the ages from 2 to 5 years. Middle childhood generally is defined as the years from 6 to 12. For example, in Canadian society, the beginning of this period usually is marked by the child's entry into Grade 1. Because there is great cultural diversity in Canada, it important to question the generalizability of the research presented (who were the participants in the studies being referred to and does this generalize to other populations within Canada). To study development, we must also look further back to the origin of sperm and ova (egg cells), the process of conception, and the prenatal period. Yet this is not far enough to satisfy scientists. We also describe the mechanisms of heredity that give rise to traits in humans and other animals.

Development is the orderly appearance, over time, of physical structures, psychological traits, behaviours, and ways of adapting to the demands of life. The changes brought on by development are both *qualitative* and *quantitative*. Qualitative changes are changes in type or kind. Consider motor development. As we develop, we gain the abilities to lift our heads, sit up, crawl, stand, and walk. These changes are qualitative. However, within each of these qualitative changes are quantitative developments, or changes in *amount*. After babies begin to lift their heads, they lift them higher and higher. Soon after children walk, they begin to run. Then they gain the capacity to run faster.

Development occurs across many dimensions—biological, cognitive, social, emotional, and behavioural. Development is spurred by internal factors, such as genetics, and it is shaped by external factors, such as nutrition and culture.

The terms *growth* and *development* are not synonymous, although many people use them interchangeably. **Growth** is generally used to refer to changes in size or quantity, whereas development also refers to changes in quality. During the early days following conception, the fertilized egg cell develops rapidly. It divides repeatedly, and cells begin to take on specialized forms. However, it does not "grow" in that there is no gain in mass. Why? It has not yet become implanted in the uterus and therefore is without any external source of nourishment. Language development is the process by which the child's use of language becomes progressively more sophisticated and complex during the first few years of life. Vocabulary growth, by contrast, consists of the accumulation of new words and their meanings.

ziggy_mars/Thinkstock

Motor Development
This infant has just mastered the ability to pull herself up to a standing position. Soon she will be able to stand alone, and then she will begin to walk.

child A person undergoing the period of development from infancy through puberty.

infancy The period of very early childhood, characterized by lack of complex speech; the first two years after birth.

development The processes by which organisms unfold features and traits, grow, and become more complex and specialized in structure and function.

growth The processes by which organisms increase in size, weight, strength, and other traits as they develop.

Child development, then, is a field of study that tries to understand the processes that govern the appearance and growth of children's biological structures, psychological traits, behaviour, understanding, and ways of adapting to the demands of life.

Professionals from many fields are interested in child development. They include psychologists, educators, anthropologists, sociologists, nurses, and medical researchers, just to list a few. Each brings his or her own brand of expertise to the quest for knowledge. Intellectual cross-fertilization enhances the skills of developmentalists and enriches the lives of children.

Why Do We Study Child Development?

QUESTION » **Why do researchers study child development?** An important motive for studying child development is curiosity—the desire to learn about children. Curiosity may be driven by the desire to answer questions about development that remain unresolved. It may also be driven by the desire to have fun. (Yes, children and the study of children can be fun.) There are other motives as well:

To Gain Insight into Human Nature
For centuries, philosophers, scientists, and educators have argued over whether children are aggressive or loving, whether children are conscious and self-aware, whether they have a natural curiosity that demands to unravel the mysteries of the universe, or whether they merely react mechanically to environmental stimulation. The quest for answers has an impact on the lives of children, parents, educators, and others who interact with children.

To Gain Insight into the Origins of Adult Behaviour
How do we explain the origins of empathy in adults? Of antisocial behaviour? How do we explain the assumption of "feminine" and "masculine" behaviour patterns? The origins of special talents in writing, music, athletics, and math?

To Gain Insight into the Origins of Sex Differences and Gender Roles, and into the Effects of Culture on Development
How do gender roles—that is, culturally induced expectations for stereotypical feminine and masculine behaviour—develop? Are there sex differences in cognition and behaviour? If so, how do they develop?

To Gain Insight into the Origins of Learning
How do humans acquire language? Why is it easier to learn languages in early childhood than later in life? How do children interact with their environments to learn new things every day?

To Gain Insight into the Origins, Prevention, and Treatment of Developmental Concerns
Fetal alcohol syndrome, PKU (see Chapter 2), SIDS (see Chapter 4), Down syndrome, autism, hyperactivity, dyslexia, child abuse—these are but a few of the buzzwords that strike fear into parents and parents-to-be. A major focus in child development research is the search for the causes of such problems so that they can be prevented and/or treated.

To Optimize Conditions of Development
Most parents want to provide the best in nutrition and medical care so that their children will develop strong and healthy bodies. Parents want their

infants to feel secure with them. They want to ensure that major transitions, such as the transition from the home to the school, will be as stress-free as possible. Developmentalists therefore undertake research to learn about issues such as the following:

- The effects of various foods and chemicals on the development of the embryo
- The effects of parent–infant interaction immediately following birth on bonds of attachment
- The effects of bottle feeding versus breast feeding on mother–infant attachment and the baby's health
- The effects of day-care programs on parent–child bonds of attachment and on children's social and intellectual development
- The effects of various patterns of child rearing on the development of independence, competence, and social adjustment

The Development of Child Development

QUESTION » What views of children do we find throughout history? In ancient times and in the Middle Ages, children often were viewed as innately evil, and discipline was harsh. Legally, medieval children were treated as property and servants. They could be sent to the monastery, married without consultation, or convicted of crimes. Children were nurtured until they were seven years old, which was considered the "age of reason." Then they were expected to work alongside adults in the home and in the field. They ate, drank, and dressed as miniature adults. **TRUTH OR FICTION REVISITED:** Children were also treated as miniature adults throughout most of the Middle Ages. (For much of the Middle Ages, artists depicted children as small adults.) However, this means only that more was expected of them, not that they were given more privileges.

The transition to the study of development in modern times is marked by the thinking of philosophers such as John Locke and Jean-Jacques Rousseau. **TRUTH OR FICTION REVISITED:** The Englishman John Locke (1632–1704) believed that the child came into the world as a *tabula rasa*—a "blank tablet" or clean slate—that was written on by experience. Locke did not believe that inborn predispositions toward good or evil played an important role in the conduct of the child. Instead, he focused on the role of the environment or of experience. Locke believed that social approval and disapproval are powerful shapers of behaviour. Jean-Jacques Rousseau (1712–1778), a Swiss–French philosopher, reversed Locke's stance. Rousseau argued that children are inherently good and that, if allowed to express their natural impulses, they will develop into generous and moral individuals.

During the Industrial Revolution, family life came to be defined in terms of the nuclear unit of mother, father, and children, rather than the extended family. Children became more visible, fostering awareness of childhood as a

A View of Children as Perceived in the 1600s
Centuries ago, children were viewed as miniature adults. In this 17th-century painting, notice how the body proportions of the young princess (in the middle) are similar to those of her adult attendants.

© Erich Lessing/Art Resource, NY

special time of life. Still, children often laboured in factories from dawn to dusk through the early years of the 20th century.

In the 20th century, laws were passed to protect children from strenuous labour, to require that they attend school until a certain age, and to prevent them from getting married or being sexually exploited. Whereas children were once considered the property of parents to do with as they wished, laws now protect children from the abuse and neglect of parents and other caretakers. Juvenile courts see that children who break the law receive fair and appropriate treatment in the criminal justice system.

Young Child Labourers
Children often worked long days in factories up through the early years of the 20th century. A number of cultures in the world today still use child labour.

Pioneers in the Study of Child Development

Various thoughts about child development coalesced into a field of scientific study in the 19th and early 20th centuries. Many individuals, including Charles Darwin, G. Stanley Hall, and Alfred Binet, contributed to the emerging field.

Charles Darwin (1809–1882) is perhaps best known as the originator of the theory of evolution. But he also was one of the first observers to keep a *baby biography*, in which he described his infant son's behaviours in great detail. G. Stanley Hall (1844–1924) is credited with founding child development as an academic discipline. He adapted the questionnaire method for use with large groups of children so that he could study the "contents of children's minds." The Frenchman Alfred Binet (1857–1911), along with Theodore Simon, developed the first standardized intelligence test near the turn of the 20th century. Binet's purpose was to identify public-school children who were at risk of falling behind their peers in academic achievement. By the beginning of the 20th century, child development had emerged as a scientific field of study. Within a short time, major theoretical views of the developing child had begun to emerge, proposed by such developmentalists as Arnold Gesell, Sigmund Freud, John B. Watson, and Jean Piaget. We next describe their theories of child development and those of others.

Active Review

1. A child is a person experiencing the period of development from infancy to _____.

2. _____ is the orderly appearance, over time, of structures, traits, and behaviours.

3. The word *growth* is generally used to refer to changes in size or quantity, whereas the term _____ also refers to changes in quality.

Reflect & Relate: Do you believe that children are "wild"? That children must be "tamed"? Do you see dangers (to children) in answering yes to either question? Explain.

1.2 Historical Review of Theories of Child Development

"Give me a dozen healthy infants, well-formed, and my own specified world to bring them up in, and I'll guarantee to train them to become any type of specialist I might suggest—doctor, lawyer, merchant, chief, and, yes, even beggar and thief, regardless of their talents, penchants, tendencies, abilities, vocations, and the race of their ancestors" (Watson, 1924, p. 82).

John B. Watson, the founder of American **behaviourism**, viewed development in terms of learning. He generally agreed with Locke's idea that children's ideas, preferences, and skills are shaped by experience. There has been a long-standing nature–nurture debate in the study of children. In his theoretical approach to understanding children, Watson came down on the side of nurture—the importance of the physical and social environments—as found, for example, in parental training and approval. Watson's view turned upside down the history of approaches to understanding children. Nature, or the inherited, genetic characteristics of the child, had long been the more popular explanation of how children get to be what they are.

Four years after Watson sounded his call for the behavioural view, Arnold Gesell expressed the opposing idea that biological maturation was the main principle of development: "All things considered, the inevitability and surety of maturation are the most impressive characteristics of early development. It is the hereditary ballast which conserves and stabilizes growth of each individual infant" (Gesell, 1928, p. 378). Watson was talking largely about the behaviour patterns that children develop, whereas Gesell was focusing mainly on physical aspects of growth and development. Still, the behavioural and maturational perspectives lie at opposite ends of the continuum of theories of development. Many scientists fall into the trap of overemphasizing the importance of either nature or nurture at the risk of overlooking the ways in which nature and nurture interact. Just as a child's environments and experiences influence the development of his or her biological endowment, children often place themselves in environments that are harmonious with their personal characteristics. Children, for example, are influenced by teachers and other students. Nevertheless, because of the traits they bring to school with them, some children may prefer to socialize with other children and others with teachers. Still other children may prefer solitude.

What Are Theories of Child Development?

QUESTION » Why do we have theories? Child development is a scientific enterprise. Like other scientists, developmentalists seek to describe, explain, predict, and influence the events they study. When possible, descriptive terms and concepts are interwoven into **theories**. Theories are based on assumptions about behaviour, such as Watson's assumption that training outweighs talents and abilities or Gesell's assumption that the unfolding of maturational tendencies holds sway.

Theories enable us to derive explanations and predictions. For instance, a theory concerning the development of gender roles should allow us to predict how—and whether—children will acquire stereotypical feminine or masculine gender-typed behaviour patterns. A broad theory of the development of gender roles might apply to children from different cultural and racial backgrounds and, perhaps, to children with gay male and lesbian sexual orientations as well as to children with a heterosexual orientation. If observations cannot be explained by or predicted from a theory, we may need to revise or replace the theory.

Theories also enable researchers to influence events, as in working better with parents, teachers, nurses, and children themselves to promote the welfare of children. Psychologists may summarize and interpret theory and research on the effects of day care to help day-care workers provide an optimal child-care environment. Teachers may use learning theory to help children learn to read and write. Let us consider various theoretical perspectives on child development.

behaviourism John B. Watson's view that a science or theory of development must study observable behaviour only and investigate relationships between stimuli and responses.

theory A formulation of relationships underlying observed events. A theory involves assumptions and logically derived explanations and predictions.

The Psychoanalytic Perspective

QUESTION » What is the psychoanalytic perspective on child development? A number of theories fall within the psychoanalytic perspective. Each one owes its origin to Sigmund Freud and views children—and adults—as caught in conflict. Early in development, the conflict is between the child and the world outside. The expression of basic drives, such as sex and aggression, conflicts with parental expectations, social rules, moral codes, and even laws. However, the external limits—parental demands and social rules—are *internalized*; that is, they are brought inside. Once this happens, the conflict takes place between opposing *inner* forces. The child's observable behaviour, thoughts, and feelings reflect the outcomes of these hidden battles.

In this section, we explore Freud's theory of **psychosexual development** and Erik Erikson's theory of psychosocial development. Each is a **stage theory** that sees children as developing through distinct periods of life. Each suggests that the child's experiences during early stages affect the child's emotional and social life at the time and later on.

Sigmund Freud's Theory of Psychosexual Development

Sigmund Freud (1856–1939) focused on the emotional and social development of children and on the origins of psychological traits such as dependence, obsessive neatness, and vanity. Freud theorized three parts of the personality: the *id*, *ego*, and *superego*. The id is present at birth and is unconscious. It represents biological drives and demands instant gratification, as suggested by a baby's wailing. The ego, or the conscious sense of self, begins to develop when children learn to obtain gratification for themselves, without screaming or crying. The ego curbs the appetites of the id and makes plans that are in keeping with social conventions so that a person can find gratification yet avoid the disapproval of others. The superego develops throughout infancy and early childhood and brings inward the norms and morals of the child's caregivers and other members of the community. If the child misbehaves, the superego will flood him or her with guilt and shame.

According to Freud, childhood has five stages of psychosexual development: *oral, anal, phallic, latency,* and *genital.* If a child receives too little or too much gratification during a stage, the child can become *fixated* in that stage. For example, if the child is weaned early or breast-fed too long, the child may become fixated on *oral* activities such as nail biting or smoking, or even show a "sharp tongue" or "biting wit." **TRUTH OR FICTION REVISITED:** However, there is actually no research evidence that nail biting and smoking cigarettes are signs of conflict experienced during early childhood.

In the second stage, the *anal stage,* gratification is obtained through control and elimination of waste products. Excessively strict or permissive toilet training can lead to the development of anal-retentive traits, such as perfectionism and neatness, or anal-expulsive traits, such as sloppiness and carelessness. In the third stage, the *phallic stage,* parent–child conflict may develop over masturbation, which many parents treat with punishment and threats. It is normal for children to develop strong sexual attachments to the parent of the other sex during the phallic stage and to begin to view the parent of the same sex as a rival.

By age five or six, Freud believed, children enter a *latency stage* during which sexual feelings remain unconscious, children turn to schoolwork, and they typically prefer playmates of their own sex. The final stage of psychosexual development, the *genital stage,* begins with the biological changes that usher in adolescence. Adolescents generally desire sexual gratification through

Sigmund Freud
Sigmund Freud is the originator of psychoanalytic theory. He proposed five stages of psychosexual development and emphasized the importance of biological factors in the development of personality.

psychosexual development Freud's view that as children develop, they find sexual gratification through stimulating different parts of their bodies.

stage theory A theory of development characterized by hypothesizing the existence of distinct periods of life. Stages follow one another in an orderly sequence.

intercourse with a member of the other sex. Freud believed that oral or anal stimulation, masturbation, and male–male or female–female sexual activity are immature forms of sexual conduct that reflect fixations at early stages of development.

Evaluation   Freud's theory has had much appeal and was a major contribution to modern (early 20th century) thought. It is a rich theory of development, explaining the childhood origins of many traits and stimulating research on attachment, development of gender roles, and moral development. Freud's

Concept Review 1.1 Comparison of Freud's and Erikson's Stages of Development

Age	Freud's Stages of Psychosexual Development	Erikson's Stages of Psychosocial Development
Birth to 1 year 	**Oral Stage.** Gratification derives from oral activities such as sucking. Fixation leads to development of oral traits such as dependence, depression, and gullibility.	**Trust versus Mistrust.** The developmental task is to come to trust the key caregivers, primarily the mother, and the environment. It is desirable for the infant to connect the environment with inner feelings of satisfaction and contentment.
About 1 to 3 years	**Anal Stage.** Gratification derives from anal activities involving elimination. Fixation leads to development of anal-retentive traits (e.g., excessive neatness) or anal-expulsive traits (e.g., sloppiness).	**Autonomy versus Shame and Doubt.** The developmental task is to gain the desire to make choices and the self-control to regulate one's behaviour so that choices can be actualized.
About 3 to 6 years	**Phallic Stage.** Gratification derives from stimulation of the genital region. Fixation leads to development of phallic traits such as vanity.	**Initiative versus Guilt.** The developmental task is to add initiative—planning and attempting to achieve that which one has chosen. The preschooler is on the move and becomes proactive.
About 6 to 12 years 	**Latency Stage.** Sexual impulses are suppressed, allowing the child to focus on development of social and technological skills.	**Industry versus Inferiority.** The developmental task is to become absorbed in the development and implementation of skills, to master the basics of technology, to become productive.

views about the anal stage have influenced child-care workers to recommend that toilet training not be started too early or handled punitively.

Yet Freud's work has been criticized. For one thing, Freud developed his theory on the basis of contacts with patients (mostly women) who were experiencing emotional problems (Schultz & Schultz, 2012). He was also dealing with recollections of his patients' pasts, rather than observing children directly. Such recollections are subject to errors in memory.

Some of Freud's own disciples, including Erik Erikson and Karen Horney, believe that Freud placed too much emphasis on basic instincts and unconscious motives. They argue that people are motivated not only by drives

Concept Review 1.1 *(Continued)*

Age	Freud's Stages of Psychosexual Development	Erikson's Stages of Psychosocial Development
Adolescence 	**Genital Stage.** Sexual impulses reappear, with gratification sought through sexual relations with an adult of the other sex.	**Identity versus Role Diffusion.** The developmental task is to associate one's skills and social roles with the development of career goals. More broadly, the development of identity refers to a sense of who one is and what one believes in.
Young adulthood		**Intimacy versus Isolation.** The developmental task is to commit oneself to another person, to engage in a mature sexual love.
Middle adulthood		**Generativity versus Stagnation.** The developmental task is to appreciate the opportunity to "give back." Not only are generative people creative, but they also give encouragement and guidance to the younger generation, which may include their own children.
Late adulthood 		**Ego Integrity versus Despair.** The developmental task is to achieve wisdom and dignity in the face of declining physical abilities. Ego integrity also means accepting the time and place of one's own life cycle.

Patricia Malina/Shutterstock.com

LeventeGyori/Shutterstock.com

such as sex and aggression but also by social relationships and conscious desires to achieve, to have aesthetic experiences, and to help others. Most importantly for many who study child development and learning, there are few empirical studies supporting Freud's theoretical premises (Hayne, Garry, & Loftus, 2006).

Erik Erikson's Theory of Psychosocial Development

Erik Erikson (1902–1994) modified and expanded Freud's theory. Erikson's theory, like Freud's, focuses on the development of the emotional life and psychological traits. But Erikson also focuses on the development of self-identity and argues that social relationships are more important than sexual or aggressive instincts. Therefore, Erikson speaks of **psychosocial development** rather than of *psychosexual development*. Furthermore, it seemed to Erikson that he had developed his own personality through a series of conscious and purposeful acts. Consequently, he places greater emphasis on the ego, or the sense of self.

Erikson (1963) extended Freud's five developmental stages to eight to include the changing concerns throughout adulthood. Rather than labelling his stages after parts of the body, Erikson labelled stages after the **life crises** that the child (and then the adult) might encounter during that stage. Erikson's stages are compared with Freud's in Concept Review 1.1 on pages 10–11.

Erikson proposed that our social relationships and physical maturation give each stage its character. For example, the parent–child relationship and the infant's utter dependence and helplessness are responsible for the nature of the earliest stages of development. The six-year-old's capacity to profit from the school setting reflects the cognitive capacities to learn to read and to understand the basics of math—even the ability to sit still long enough to focus on schoolwork.

According to Erikson, early experiences affect future developments. With proper parental support early on, most children resolve early life crises productively. Successful resolution of each crisis bolsters their sense of identity—of who they are and what they stand for—and their expectation of future success.

Each stage in Erikson's theory carries a specific developmental task. Successful completion of this task depends heavily on the nature of the child's social relationships at each stage (see Concept Review 1.1).

Erikson's views, like Freud's, have influenced child rearing, early childhood education, and child therapy. For example, Erikson's views about an adolescent **identity crisis** have entered the popular culture and have affected the way many parents and teachers deal with teenagers. Some schools help students master the crisis by offering life-adjustment courses and study units on self-understanding in social studies and literature classes.

Evaluation Erikson's views are appealing in that they emphasize the importance of human consciousness and choice and minimize the role—and the threat—of dark, poorly perceived urges. They are also appealing because they portray us as prosocial and helpful, whereas Freud portrayed us as selfish and needing to be forced into compliance with social rules. There is also some empirical support for the Eriksonian view that positive outcomes of early life crises help put children on the path to positive development (Clark, 2010; Marcia, 2010). For example, infants who come to trust in their parents are more likely to achieve autonomy and ego identity later on. As well, Canadian developmental psychologist James Marcia expanded and refined Erikson's idea of identify formation in adolescence to include different identity statuses of psychosocial

Karen Horney
Horney, a follower of Freud, argued that Freud placed too much emphasis on sexual and biological determinants of behaviour while neglecting the importance of social factors.

psychosocial development
Erikson's theory, which emphasizes the importance of social relationships and conscious choice throughout the eight stages of development.

life crisis An internal conflict that attends each stage of psychosocial development. Positive resolution of early life crises sets the stage for positive resolution of subsequent life crises.

identity crisis According to Erikson, an adolescent period of inner conflict during which one examines one's values and makes decisions about one's life roles.

Erik Erikson

identity development: **identity diffusion**, **identity foreclosure**, **identity moratorium,** and **identity achievement** (Kroger & Marcia, 2011; Marcia, 2002). Marcia advanced Erikson's theory by arguing that adolescents explore and commit to identities from a variety of domains (vocational, relational, gender role). According to Marcia, identity develops based on two of Erikson's key terms—crisis/exploration and commitment (Muuss, 1996).

The Learning Perspective: Behavioural and Social Cognitive Theories

QUESTION » What is the learning perspective on child development? In this section, we discuss two types of learning—classical conditioning and operant conditioning—that have contributed to behaviourism and the understanding of development. We'll also see how the principles of learning have been used in behaviour modification to help children overcome behaviour disorders or cope with adjustment problems. Then we consider a more recent theory of learning that deals with children's cognitive processes and their overt behaviour—social cognitive theory.

We begin with John B. Watson's theory of behaviourism.

Behaviourism

John B. Watson argued that a scientific approach to development must focus on observable behaviour only, and not on things like thoughts, fantasies, and other mental images.

Classical conditioning is a simple form of learning in which an originally neutral **stimulus** comes to bring forth, or elicit, the response usually brought forth by a second stimulus as a result of being paired repeatedly with the second stimulus. In the bell-and-pad treatment for bed-wetting, psychologists repeatedly pair tension in the children's bladders with a stimulus that wakes them up (the bell). The children learn to respond to the bladder tension as if it were a bell—that is, they wake up (see Figure 1.1).

Behaviourists argue that a good deal of emotional learning is acquired through classical conditioning. For example, touching a hot stove is painful,

Erikson saw adolescence as a stage of life during which individuals develop—or fail to develop—a sense of identity.

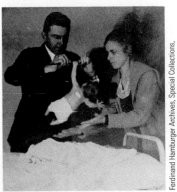

John B. Watson
Watson is shown here testing the grasping reflex of an infant. As a behaviourist, Watson believed that the environment is all-important in shaping development.

identity diffusion According to Marcia, the stage when adolescents are not committed to an identity and are not questioning who they are yet.

identity foreclosure According to Marcia, the stage at which adolescents are committed to ready-made values and goals, and have not yet experienced crisis or exploration.

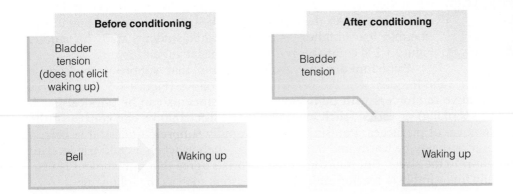

Before conditioning		After conditioning	
Bladder tension (does not elicit waking up)		Bladder tension	
Bell	Waking up		Waking up

Figure 1.1 ■ Schematic Representation of Classical Conditioning
Before conditioning, the bell elicits waking up. Bladder tension, a neutral stimulus, does not wake the infant. During conditioning, bladder tension always precedes urination, which in turn causes the bell to ring. After conditioning, bladder tension wakes the infant.

The Bell-and-Pad Method for Treating Bed-Wetting

During the 1930s, psychologists derived an ingenious method for helping five- and six-year-old children overcome bed-wetting from the behavioural perspective. Most children at this age wake up and go to the bathroom when their bladders are full. But bed-wetters sleep through bladder tension and reflexively urinate in bed. The psychologists' objective was to teach sleeping children with full bladders to wake up rather than wet their beds.

The psychologists placed a special pad beneath the sleeping child (Mowrer & Mowrer, 1938). When the pad was wet, an electrical circuit was closed, causing a bell to ring and the sleeping child to waken. After several repetitions, most children learned to wake up before they wet the pad. As behaviourists explain it, repeated association of bed-wetting and waking due to the alarm—that is, conditioning—caused the children to wake in response to the urge to urinate.

The so-called bell-and-pad method for treating bed-wetting is an exotic example of the application of learning theory in child development. Most applications of learning theory to development are found in everyday events. For example, children are not born knowing what the letters A and B sound like or how to tie their shoes. They learn these things. They are not born knowing how to do gymnastics. Nor are they born understanding the meanings of abstract concepts such as big, blue, decency, and justice. All these skills and knowledge are learned.

Reflect Does this application of learning theory to a developmental problem show that we can speak of learning in terms of what a young child does as well as in terms of what a child knows? What do you think? Explain.

Nina Leen/Time & Life Pictures/Getty Images

B. F. Skinner

Skinner, a behaviourist, developed principles of operant conditioning and focused on the role of reinforcement of behaviour.

identity moratorium According to Marcia, the stage at which adolescents are exploring but have not committed to self-chosen goals and values.

and one or two incidents may elicit a fear response when a child looks at a stove or considers touching it again.

In classical conditioning, children learn to associate stimuli so that a response made to one is then made in response to the other. But in **operant conditioning** (a different kind of conditioning), children learn to do something because of its effects. B. F. Skinner introduced the concept of **reinforcement**. Reinforcers are stimuli that increase the frequency of the behaviour they follow. Most children learn to adjust their behaviour to conform to social codes and rules in order to earn reinforcers, such as the approval of parents and teachers. Other children, ironically, may learn to misbehave, because misbehaviour also draws attention. Any stimulus that increases the frequency of the responses preceding it serves as a reinforcer. Most of the time, food, social approval, and attention serve as reinforcers.

Skinner distinguished between positive and negative reinforcers. **Positive reinforcers** increase the frequency of behaviours when they are *applied*. Food and approval usually serve as positive reinforcers. **Negative reinforcers** increase the frequency of behaviours when they are *removed*. Fear acts as a negative reinforcer in that its removal increases the frequency of the behaviours preceding it. For example, fear of failure is removed when students study for a quiz. Figure 1.2 ■ compares positive and negative reinforcers.

Punishments are aversive events that suppress or *decrease* the frequency of the behaviour they follow. (Figure 1.3 ■ compares negative reinforcers with punishments.) Punishments can be physical (such as spanking) or verbal (such as scolding or criticizing) or can consist of the removal of privileges. Punishments can rapidly suppress undesirable behaviour and may be warranted in emergencies, such as when a child tries to run out into the street. But many learning theorists agree that punishment is usually undesirable in rearing children, for reasons such as the following:

- Punishment does not in itself suggest an alternative, acceptable form of behaviour.

- Punishment tends to suppress undesirable behaviour only when its delivery is guaranteed. It does not take children long to learn that they

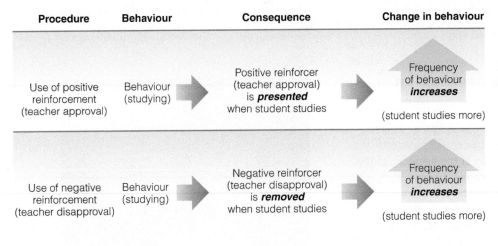

Procedure	Behaviour	Consequence	Change in behaviour
Use of positive reinforcement (teacher approval)	Behaviour (studying)	Positive reinforcer (teacher approval) **is presented** when student studies	Frequency of behaviour **increases** (student studies more)
Use of negative reinforcement (teacher disapproval)	Behaviour (studying)	Negative reinforcer (teacher disapproval) **is removed** when student studies	Frequency of behaviour **increases** (student studies more)

Figure 1.2 ■ Positive versus Negative Reinforcers

All reinforcers *increase* the frequency of behaviour. In these examples, teacher approval functions as a positive reinforcer when students study harder because of it. Teacher *disapproval* functions as a negative reinforcer when its *removal* increases the frequency of studying.

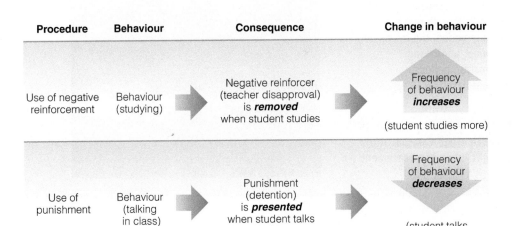

Procedure	Behaviour	Consequence	Change in behaviour
Use of negative reinforcement	Behaviour (studying)	Negative reinforcer (teacher disapproval) **is removed** when student studies	Frequency of behaviour **increases** (student studies more)
Use of punishment	Behaviour (talking in class)	Punishment (detention) **is presented** when student talks in class	Frequency of behaviour **decreases** (student talks less in class)

Figure 1.3 ■ Negative Reinforcers versus Punishments

Both negative reinforcers and punishments tend to be aversive stimuli. However, reinforcers increase the frequency of behaviour. Punishments decrease the frequency of behaviour. Negative reinforcers increase the frequency of behaviour when they are removed.

can "get away with murder" with one parent or one teacher but not with another.

- Punished children may withdraw from the situation. Severely punished children may run away, cut class, or drop out of school.
- Punishment can create anger and hostility. After being spanked by their parents, children may hit smaller siblings or destroy objects in the home.
- Punishment may generalize too far. The child who is punished severely for bad table manners may stop eating altogether. Such overgeneralization is more likely to occur when children do not know why they are being punished.
- Punishment may be imitated as a way of solving problems or coping with stress. Children learn by observing others. For example, children who are physically punished by their parents may act aggressively toward other children (Sim & Ong, 2005) or toward their own children when they become parents (Huesmann et al., 2006).

identity achievement According to Marcia, the stage after which adolescents have gone through identity crisis/exploration and have resolved identity issues and have self-chosen values and goals.

classical conditioning A simple form of learning in which one stimulus comes to bring forth the response usually elicited by a second stimulus by being paired repeatedly with the second stimulus.

stimulus A change in the environment that leads to a change in behaviour.

operant conditioning A simple form of learning in which an organism learns to engage in behaviour that is reinforced.

reinforcement The process of providing stimuli following a behaviour, which has the effect of increasing the frequency of the behaviour.

positive reinforcer A reinforcer that, when applied, increases the frequency of a behaviour.

negative reinforcer A reinforcer that, when removed, increases the frequency of a behaviour.

punishment An unpleasant stimulus that suppresses behaviour.

Operant Conditioning of Vocalizations in Infants

A classic study by psychologist Harriet Rheingold and her colleagues (1959) demonstrated how reinforcement and extinction can influence the behaviour of infants—in this case, vocalization. A researcher first observed the subjects, three-month-old infants, for about half an hour to record baseline (pre-experimental) measures of the frequency of their vocalizing. Infants averaged 13 to 15 vocalizations each. During the conditioning phase of the study, the researcher reinforced the vocalizations with social stimuli, such as encouraging sounds, smiles, and gentle touches. There was a significant increase in the frequency of vocalizing throughout this phase. By the end of an hour of conditioning spread over a two-day period, the average incidence of vocalizations had nearly doubled to 24 to 25 within a half-hour. During the extinction phase, as during the baseline period, the researcher passively observed each infant, no longer reinforcing vocalization. After two half-hour extinction periods, average vocalizing had returned to near baseline, 13 to 16 per half-hour.

Reflect Why is it of interest that the behaviour of infants can be influenced by operant conditioning? Can you think of any role this conditioning might play in attachment between parents and infants?

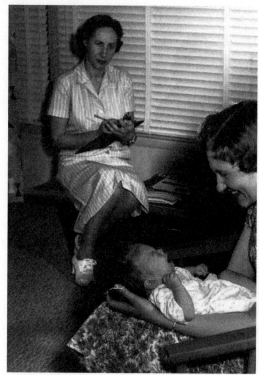

Courtesy of Dr. Arnold Rheingold

TRUTH OR FICTION REVISITED: Psychologists generally suggest that it is preferable to reward children for desirable behaviour rather than to punish them for unwanted behaviour. Sometimes by ignoring misbehaviour, we avoid reinforcing children for it.

We can teach children complex behaviours by **shaping**, or at first reinforcing small steps toward the behavioural goals. In teaching a two-year-old child to put on her own coat, it helps first to praise her for trying to stick her arm into a sleeve on a couple of occasions, then to praise her for actually getting her arm into the sleeve, and so on.

Operant conditioning is used every day in the socialization of young children. For example, as we will see in Chapter 10, parents and peers influence children to acquire gender-appropriate behaviours through the elaborate use of rewards and punishments. Thus, boys may ignore other boys when they play with dolls and housekeeping toys but play with boys when they use transportation toys.

Research suggests that when teachers praise and attend to appropriate behaviour and ignore misbehaviour, studying and classroom behaviour improve while disruptive and aggressive behaviours decrease (Carlson et al., 2011; Snyder et al., 2011). Teachers frequently use **time-out** from positive reinforcement to discourage misbehaviour. For example, misbehaviour might be punished by having the child remain in the classroom for a few minutes before being allowed to play with other children during recess. In using time-out in the home, parents might restrict children from watching television for a specified amount of time—say, ten minutes—if they misbehave. It is advisable to warn young children that they will have a time-out if they are misbehaving,

shaping A procedure for teaching complex behaviour patterns by reinforcing small steps toward the target behaviour.

time-out A behaviour-modification technique in which a child who misbehaves is temporarily removed from positive reinforcement.

and also to remind young children why they have been given a time-out. Otherwise, they may not reliably associate the time-out with misbehaviour.

Social Cognitive Theory

Behaviourists tend to limit their view of learning to the classical and operant conditioning of observable behaviour. **Social cognitive theorists**, such as Canadian-born psychologist Albert Bandura (1986, 2011), have shown that much of children's learning also occurs by observing parents, teachers, other children, and characters in the media. Children may need practice to refine their skills, but they can acquire the basic know-how through observation. Children can also let these skills *lie latent*. For example, children (and adults) are not likely to imitate aggressive behaviour unless they are provoked and believe that they are more likely to be rewarded than punished for aggressive behaviour.

In the view of behaviourists, learning occurs by mechanical conditioning. There is no reference to thought. In social cognitive theory, cognition plays a central role: Learning alters children's mental representation of the environment and affects their belief in their ability to change the environment. Children choose whether or not to engage in the behaviours they have learned. Their values and expectations of reinforcement affect whether they will imitate the behaviour they observe.

Social cognitive theorists see children as active. Children intentionally seek out or create environments in which reinforcers are available. The child with artistic ability may develop her skills by taking art lessons and by imitating her art teacher. In doing so, she creates an environment of social reinforcement in the form of praise from others. This reinforcement, in turn, influences the child's view of herself as a good artist.

Observational learning accounts for much human learning. It occurs when children observe how parents cook, clean, or repair a broken appliance. It takes place when children watch teachers solve problems on the blackboard or hear them speak a foreign language. Observational learning does not occur because of direct reinforcement. It occurs so long as children pay attention to the behaviour of others.

Evaluation of Learning Theories

Learning theories have done a fine job of enabling us to describe, explain, predict, and influence many aspects of children's behaviour. Psychologists and educators have developed many applications of conditioning and social cognitive theory. The use of the bell-and-pad method for bed-wetting is an example of behaviour modification that probably would not have been derived from any other theoretical approach. Behaviour modification has been used to help deal with autistic children, self-injurious children, and children showing temper tantrums and conduct disorders. Many of the teaching approaches used on educational TV shows are based on learning theory.

Yet learning-theory approaches to child development have been criticized. First, there is the theoretical question of whether the conditioning process in children is mechanical or whether it changes the ways in which children mentally represent the environment. In addition, learning theorists may underestimate the importance of maturational factors (Hergenhahn, 2009; Schultz & Schultz, 2012). Social cognitive theorists seem to be working on these issues. For example, they place more value on cognition and view children as being active, not as merely reacting mechanically to stimuli. Now let us turn to theories that place cognition at the heart of development.

Albert Bandura

Bandura and other social cognitive theorists showed that one way children learn is by observing others. Whereas behaviourists like John Watson and B. F. Skinner portrayed children as reactive to environmental stimuli, social cognitive theorists depict children as active learners who are capable of fashioning new environments. Here textbook author Christina Rinaldi poses with Bandura.

social cognitive theory A cognitively oriented learning theory that emphasizes the role of observational learning in determining behaviour.

The Cognitive Perspective

QUESTION » What is the cognitive perspective on child development? Cognitive theorists focus on children's mental processes. They investigate the ways in which children perceive and mentally represent the world, and how they develop thinking, logic, and problem-solving ability. One cognitive perspective is **cognitive-developmental theory**, advanced by Swiss biologist Jean Piaget (1896–1980). Another is information-processing theory.

Jean Piaget's Cognitive-Developmental Theory

During adolescence, Piaget studied philosophy, logic, and mathematics, but years later he took his Ph.D. in biology. In 1920 he obtained a job at the Binet Institute in Paris, where research on intelligence tests was being conducted. Piaget tried out items on children in various age groups. The task became boring, but then Piaget grew interested in children's *wrong* answers. Someone else might have shrugged them off and forgotten them, but Piaget realized that there were methods to his children's madness. Their wrong answers reflected consistent—though illogical—mental processes. Piaget looked into the patterns of thought that led to the wrong answers.

Piaget wrote dozens of books and articles on them, but his work was almost unknown in English-speaking countries until the 1950s. For one thing, Piaget's writing is difficult to understand, even to native speakers of French. (Piaget joked that he had the advantage of *not* having to read Piaget.) For another, Piaget's views differed from those of other theorists. Psychology in England and the United States was dominated by behaviourism and psychoanalysis, and Piaget's ideas had a biological-cognitive flavour. But today they are quite popular.

Behaviourists, such as John B. Watson, saw children as "blank slates" that are written upon by experience. Freud's psychoanalytic theory focused on personality and emotional development. Piaget, by contrast, was concerned with how children form concepts or mental representations of the world, and how they work with concepts to plan changes in the external world. But, like the behaviourists, he recognized that thoughts cannot be measured directly, so he tried to link his views on children's mental processes to observable behaviour.

Piaget believed that cognitive development largely depends on the maturation of the brain. He regarded maturing children as natural physicists who actively intend to learn about and take intellectual charge of their worlds. In the Piagetian view, children who squish their food and laugh enthusiastically are often acting as budding scientists. In addition to enjoying a response from parents, they are studying the texture and consistency of their food. (Parents, of course, often prefer that their children practice these experiments in the laboratory, not the dining room.)

Piaget's Basic Concepts Piaget used the concepts of *schemes, adaptation, assimilation, accommodation,* and *equilibration* to describe and explain cognitive development. Piaget defines the **scheme** as a pattern of action or a mental structure that is involved in acquiring or organizing knowledge. Babies are said to have sucking schemes, grasping schemes, and looking schemes. (Others call these *reflexes*.) Newborn babies suck things that are placed in their mouths, grasp objects placed in their hands, and visually track moving objects. Piaget would say that infants' schemes give meaning to objects. Infants are responding to objects as "things I can suck" versus "things I can't suck" and as "things I can grasp" versus "things I can't grasp." Among older children, a scheme may be the inclusion of an object in a class. For example, the mammal class, or concept, includes a group of animals that are warm-blooded and nurse their

Jean Piaget
Piaget's cognitive-developmental theory is a stage theory that focuses on the ways children adapt to the environment by mentally representing the world and solving problems. Piaget's early training as a biologist led him to view children as mentally assimilating and accommodating aspects of their environment.

cognitive-developmental theory The stage theory that holds that the child's abilities to mentally represent the world and solve problems unfold as a result of the interaction of experience and the maturation of neurological structures.

scheme According to Piaget, an action pattern or mental structure that is involved in the acquisition and organization of knowledge.

young. The inclusion of cats, apes, whales, and people in the mammal class involves schemes that expand the child's knowledge of the natural world.

Adaptation reflects the interaction between the organism and the environment. According to Piaget, all organisms adapt to their environment; it is a biological tendency. Adaptation consists of assimilation and accommodation, which occur throughout life. In biology, assimilation is the process by which food is digested and converted into the tissues that make up an animal. Cognitive **assimilation** is the process by which someone responds to new objects or events according to existing schemes or ways of organizing knowledge. Infants, for example, usually try to place new objects in their mouths to suck, feel, or explore them. Piaget would say that the child is assimilating (fitting) a new toy or object into the sucking-an-object scheme. Similarly, two-year-olds who refer to sheep and cows as "doggies" or "bowwows" can be said to be assimilating these new animals into the doggy (or bowwow) scheme.

Sometimes, a novel object or event cannot be made to fit (that is, it cannot be assimilated into an existing scheme). In that case, the scheme may be changed or a new scheme may be created to incorporate the new event. This process is called **accommodation**. Consider the sucking reflex. Within the first month of life, infants modify sucking behaviour as a result of their experience sucking various objects. The nipple on the bottle is sucked in one way, the thumb in a different way. Infants accommodate further by rejecting objects that are too large, taste bad, or have the wrong texture or temperature.

Piaget theorized that when children can assimilate new events into existing schemes, they are in a state of cognitive harmony, or equilibrium. When something that does not fit happens along, their state of equilibrium is disturbed and they may try to accommodate. The process of restoring equilibrium is termed **equilibration**. Piaget believed that the attempt to restore equilibrium is the source of intellectual motivation and lies at the heart of the natural curiosity of the child.

Piaget's Stages of Cognitive Development Piaget (1963) hypothesized that children's cognitive processes develop in an orderly sequence, or series, of stages. As with motor development, some children may be more advanced than others at particular ages, but the developmental sequence remains the same. Piaget identified four major stages of cognitive development: *sensorimotor*, *preoperational*, *concrete operational*, and *formal operational*. These stages are described in Concept Review 1.2 and are discussed in subsequent chapters.

Because Piaget's theory focuses on cognitive development, its applications are primarily in educational settings. Teachers following Piaget's views engage the child actively in solving problems. They gear instruction to the child's developmental level and offer activities that challenge the child to advance to the next level. For example, five-year-olds learn primarily through play and direct sensory contact with the environment. Early formal instruction using workbooks and paper may be less effective in this age group (Crain, 2000).

Evaluation Many researchers have found that Piaget may have underestimated the ages when children are capable of doing certain things. It also appears that cognitive skills may develop more gradually than Piaget thought and may not develop in distinct stages. But Piaget presented us with a view of children that is different from the psychoanalytic and behaviourist views, and he provided a strong theoretical foundation for researchers concerned with sequences in children's cognitive development. We shall see more of his theory in later chapters.

Information-Processing Theory

Another contemporary face of the cognitive perspective is information processing (Brigham et al., 2011; Siegler & Alibali, 2005; Schunk, 2012). Psychological thought has long been influenced by the status of the physical sciences

adaptation According to Piaget, an interaction between the organism and the environment that consists of two processes: assimilation and accommodation.

assimilation According to Piaget, the incorporation of new events or knowledge into existing schemes.

accommodation According to Piaget, the modification of existing schemes to permit the incorporation of new events or knowledge.

equilibration The creation of an equilibrium, or balance, between assimilation and accommodation as a way of incorporating new events or knowledge.

Concept Review 1.2 Jean Piaget's Stages of Cognitive Development

Stage	Approximate Age	Comments
Sensorimotor	Birth–2 years	At first, the child lacks language and does not use symbols or mental representations of objects. In time, reflexive responding ends, and intentional behaviour—such as making interesting stimulation last—begins. The child develops the object concept and acquires the basics of language.
Preoperational	2–7 years	The child begins to represent the world mentally, but thought is egocentric. The child does not focus on two aspects of a situation at once and therefore lacks conservation. The child shows animism, artificialism, and objective responsibility for wrongdoing.
Concrete operational	7–12 years	Logical mental actions—called operations—begin. The child develops conservation concepts, can adopt the viewpoints of others, can classify objects in series, and shows comprehension of basic relational concepts (such as one object being larger or heavier than another).
Formal operational	12 years and older	Mature, adult thought emerges. Thinking is characterized by deductive logic, consideration of various possibilities (mental trial and error), abstract thought, and the formation and testing of hypotheses.

Doug Goodman/Photo Researchers, Inc

of the day. For example, Freud's psychoanalytic theory was related to the development of the steam engine—which can explode when too much steam builds up—in the 19th century. Many of today's cognitive psychologists are influenced by computer science. Computers process information to solve problems. Information is encoded so that it can be accepted as input and then fed ("input") into the computer. Then it is placed in working memory (RAM) while it is manipulated. The information can be stored more permanently on a storage device, such as a hard drive. Many psychologists also speak of people as having working or short-term memory and a more permanent long-term memory (storage). If information has been placed in long-term memory, it must be retrieved before we can work on it again. To retrieve information from computer storage, we must know the code or name for the data file and the rules for retrieving data files. Similarly, note psychologists, we need cues to retrieve information from our own long-term memories, or the information may be lost to us.

Thus, many cognitive psychologists focus on information processing in people—the processes by which information is encoded (input), stored (in long-term memory), retrieved (placed in short-term memory), and manipulated to solve problems (output). Our strategies for solving problems are sometimes referred to as our "mental programs" or "software." In this computer metaphor, our brains are the "hardware" that runs our mental programs. Our brains—containing billions of brain cells called *neurons*—become our most "personal" computers.

When psychologists who study information processing contemplate the cognitive development of children, they are likely to speak in terms of the *size* of the child's short-term memory at a given age and of the *number of programs* a child can run simultaneously. Research suggests that these are indeed useful ways of talking about children (see Chapter 12).

The most obvious applications of information processing occur in teaching. For example, information-processing models alert teachers to the sequence of steps by which children acquire information, commit it to memory, and retrieve it to solve problems. Teachers who understand this sequence can provide experiences that give students practice with each stage.

The Biological Perspective

QUESTION » **What is the scope of the biological perspective?** The biological perspective is directly related to physical development—to gains in height and weight, development of the brain, and developments connected with hormones, reproduction, and heredity. For example, it is clear that during prenatal development, genes and sex hormones are responsible for the biological differentiation of female and male sex organs. However, biology is also intertwined with behaviour. In many species, including humans, sex hormones apparently "masculinize" or "feminize" the embryonic brain by creating tendencies to behave in stereotypical masculine or feminine ways. Testosterone, the male sex hormone, seems to be connected with feelings of self-confidence, high activity levels, and—the negative side—aggressiveness (Cooke & Shukla, 2011; Hines, 2011a; Zheng et al., 2011). Here we consider two biologically oriented theories of development: *ethology* and *developmental neuroscience*.

Ethology and Evolution: "Doing What Comes Naturally"

Ethology was heavily influenced by the 19th-century work of Charles Darwin and by the work of the 20th-century ethologists Konrad Lorenz and Niko Tinbergen (Washburn, 2007). **Ethology** is concerned with instinctive, or inborn, behaviour patterns—with how they help the organism adapt and how they have evolved.

The nervous systems of most, perhaps all, animals are "prewired" or "preprogrammed" to respond to some situations in specific ways. For example, birds raised in isolation from other birds build nests during the mating season, even if they have never seen a nest or seen another bird building one. Nest-building could not have been learned. Birds raised in isolation also sing the songs typical of their species. Salmon spawned in particular rivers swim out into the vast oceans and then, when mature, return to their own river of their origin to spawn. These behaviours are "built in," or instinctive. They are also referred to as inborn fixed action patterns (FAPs).

Evolution can work in wondrous ways. After the eggs of some species of Lake Tanganyika cichlids—mouth-brooding fish—are laid, both parents scoop them up and secure them from predators in their mouths. Fry swim out after hatching, but they often return to the mouth for protection during rest periods. The father is under the influence of "maternal" hormones during these days. Any fry that return to his mouth after his hormone levels have returned to "normal" become just another meal (Salzburger et al., 2008). Maternal hormones create a sensitive period during which the male parent behaves in a "motherly" fashion.

In Chapter 7, we will see that Konrad Lorenz treated the first year of life as a critical period for the development of social relationships, with consequences that last a lifetime. Infant–caregiver attachment is essential to the survival and social development of children. Lorenz viewed infant–caregiver attachment as a FAP that occurs over a time period when infants are particularly sensitive to parental attention and caring. During their critical period, geese develop an attachment to the first moving object they perceive. It is as if the image of the moving object becomes "imprinted" on them, so the process is called **imprinting**. We will see that John Bowlby and Mary Ainsworth extended Lorenz's view by studying stages of attachment in humans.

ethology The study of behaviours that are specific to a species—how these behaviours evolved, help the organism adapt, and develop during critical periods.

imprinting The process by which some animals exhibit the fixed action pattern (FAP) of attachment in response to a releasing stimulus. The FAP occurs during a critical period and is difficult to modify.

Evaluation Most theorists with an ethological perspective do not maintain that human behaviours are as mechanical as those of lower animals. Moreover, they tend to assume that instinctive behaviours can be modified through learning. But research into the ethological perspective suggests that instinct may play a role in human behaviour. Research evolving from the ethological theory perspective (no pun intended) has been termed evolutionary developmental psychology. Evolutionary developmental theorists are interested in the adaptive value and function of species-wide physical, cognitive, and social and emotional processes (Badcock, 2012). The questions that research seeks to answer are: What areas of human behaviour and development, if any, involve instincts? How do inborn tendencies and experience interact as a child develops? When and why does sex-segregated play occur during childhood?

Developmental Neuroscience

Neuroscience, or the science of the relations of the nervous system to development, learning, and behaviours is not a new theory; however, in recent years, due to strong scientific evidence emerging from brain research, we know more about how the brain shapes and influences children's development. Throughout this textbook, we will make references to the central nervous system's organization (neurons, glial cells, synapses) and brain structures (cerebral cortex, cerebellum, thalamus and hypothalamus, amygdala, hippocampus, corpus callosum, occipital lobe, brain stem and reticular formation, parietal lobe, temporal lobe, and frontal lobe) involved in child and adolescent development. Combining research from several disciplines such as neuroscience, biology, psychology, and health sciences, great advances have been made in explaining how the brain's neural organization and major structures are involved in learning and development (Schunk, 2012). These advances have been possible in recent decades due to advanced technology methods for conducting brain research, such as electroencephalographs (EEGs), positron emission tomography (PET) scans, magnetic resonance imagining (MRIs), and functional magnetic resonance imaging (fMRIs). What may seem like complex research has led to practical findings and applications that have helped us learn more about what is going on in the brains of babies (Blaze & Roth, 2013) and teenagers (Ganzel et al., 2013) in response to stressors in their environments. Of primary importance is the influence of genetics, environmental stimulation, nutrition, steroids, and teratogens (foreign agents that can damage the fetus or embryo). An excellent resource for explaining the fundamentals about brain development is an animated video entitled "Core Story of Brain Development," which can be found at the Alberta Health and Wellness website (www.albertafamilywellness.org).

The developmental neuroscience perspective advances our understanding of brain plasticity (see Chapter 8) and how the brain at certain ages of development can compensate for injuries to particular areas (Johnston et al., 2009). Neuroscience is also providing new evidence to help reconceptualize and explain behaviours and disorders, such as obesity (Fraser, 2013) and learning processes and difficulties (Meltzoff, Kuhl, Movellan, & Sejnowski, 2009; Schunk, 2012). Neuroscience theory and research is informing the role of early education, the complexity of cognitive processes (beyond the traditional theories of Piaget and information processing), and the intricacy of learning environments.

The Ecological Perspective

QUESTION » What is the ecological systems theory of child development? **Ecology** is the branch of biology that deals with the relationships between living organisms and their environment. The **ecological systems theory** of child development addresses aspects of psychological, social, and emotional

neuroscience The scientific study of the brain and nervous system.

ecology The branch of biology that deals with the relationships between living organisms and their environment.

ecological systems theory The view that explains child development in terms of the reciprocal influences between children and the settings that make up their environment.

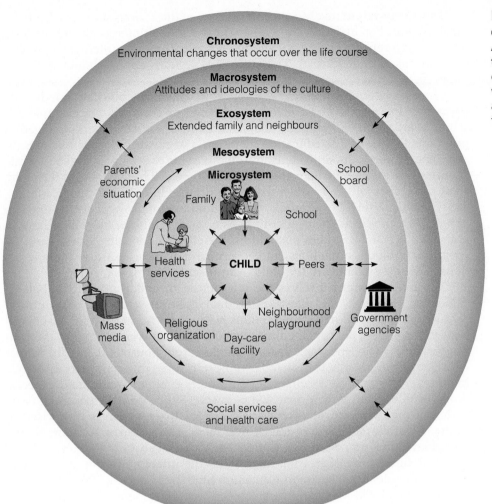

Figure 1.4 ■ **The Contexts of Human Development**
According to ecological systems theory, the systems within which children develop are embedded within larger systems. Children and these systems reciprocally influence each other.

development as well as aspects of biological development. Ecological systems theorists explain child development in terms of the interaction between children and the settings in which they live (Bronfenbrenner & Morris, 2006).

According to Urie Bronfenbrenner (1917–2005), we need to focus on the two-way interactions between the child and the parents, not just on maturational forces (nature) or parental child-rearing approaches (nurture). For example, some parents choose to feed newborns on demand, whereas others may decide to stick to feedings that occur four hours apart. Some babies, however, are more accepting than others, and some never become comfortable with a strict schedule. This is the point: Parents are a key part of the child's environment and have a major influence on the child, but even babies have inborn temperaments that affect the parents.

Bronfenbrenner (Bronfenbrenner & Morris, 2006) suggested that we can view the contexts of human development as a series of systems, each embedded in the next larger system. From narrowest to widest, these systems are the microsystem, the mesosystem, the exosystem, the macrosystem, and the chronosystem (see Figure 1.4 ■).

The **microsystem** involves the interactions of the child and other people in the immediate setting, such as the home, the school, or the peer group. Initially, the microsystem is small, involving care-giving interactions with the parents or others, usually at home. As children get older, they do more, with more people, in more places.

microsystem The immediate settings with which the child interacts, such as the home, the school, and the child's peers (from the Greek *mikros*, meaning "small").

The **mesosystem** involves the interactions of the various settings within the microsystem. For instance, the home and the school interact during parent–teacher conferences. The school and the larger community interact when children are taken on field trips. The ecological systems approach addresses the joint effect of two or more settings on the child.

The **exosystem** involves the institutions in which the child does not directly participate but which exert an indirect influence on the child. For example, the school board is part of the child's exosystem because board members put together programs for the child's education, determine what textbooks will be acceptable, and so forth. In similar fashion, the parents' workplaces and economic situations determine the hours during which they will be available to the child, what mood they will be in when they are with the child, and so on (Needlman, 2011; Tisdale, 2011). For example, poverty and unemployment create stress in parents, which affects their parenting. As a result, children may misbehave at home and in school. Studies that address the effects of housing, health care, TV programs, religious affiliations, and government agencies examine the interactions of the exosystem with the child (Kaminski & Stormshak, 2007).

The **macrosystem** involves the interaction of children with the beliefs, values, expectations, and lifestyles of their cultural settings. Cross-cultural studies examine children's interactions with their macrosystem. Macrosystems exist within a particular culture as well. For example, in Canada, the two-wage-earner family, the single-income single-parent household, and the family with one parent as sole breadwinner represent three different macrosystems. Each macrosystem has its characteristic lifestyle, set of values, and expectations (Bronfenbrenner & Morris, 2006; Lustig, 2011). Another pertinent issue is that of multiculturalism. The Canadian education system is comprised of students from a multitude of ethnicities, races, and cultures. A report by the Canadian Education Statistics Council acknowledged how literacy is influenced by the quality of instruction, as well the interconnection of language, culture, and identity (Canadian Education Statistics Council, 2009). Likewise, a U.S. study of 258 Mexican-American Grade 8-11 students found that those who perceived their environment to be multicultural found school to be easier, earned higher grades, and were more likely to stay in school (Tan, 1999).

The **chronosystem** considers the changes that occur over time. For example, the effects of divorce peak about a year after the event, and then children begin to recover (see Chapter 13). The breakup has more of an effect on boys than on girls and contributes to behavioural and academic problems in boys. The ecological approach broadens the strategies for intervention in problems, such as prevention of teenage pregnancy, child abuse, and juvenile offending, including substance abuse (Kaminski & Stormshak, 2007).

Evaluation   Ecological systems theory helps focus attention on the shifting systems with which children interact as they develop. The health of the infant requires relationships between parents and the health-care system, and the education of the child requires relationships between parents and schools. At the level of the exosystem, researchers look into the effects of parents' work lives, social support system agencies, transportation systems, shopping facilities, and so on. At the level of the macrosystem, we may compare child-rearing practices in Canada with those in other countries. We consider the role of culture further in our discussion of the sociocultural perspective.

The Sociocultural Perspective

QUESTION » What is the sociocultural perspective? The sociocultural perspective teaches that children are social beings who are affected by the cultures in which they live. Yes, we are affected by biochemical forces such as

mesosystem The interlocking settings that influence the child, such as the interaction of the school and the larger community when children are taken on field trips (from the Greek *mesos*, meaning "middle").

exosystem Community institutions and settings that indirectly influence the child, such as the school board and the parents' workplaces (from the Greek *exo*, meaning "outside").

macrosystem The basic institutions and ideologies that influence the child, such as the western ideals of freedom of expression and equality under the law (from the Greek *makros*, meaning "long" or "enlarged").

chronosystem The environmental changes that occur over time and have an impact on the child (from the Greek *chronos*, meaning "time").

neurotransmitters and hormones. We may be biologically "prewired" to form attachments and engage in other behaviours. Perhaps there are psychological tendencies to learn in certain ways, and maybe there are ways in which the psychological past affects the present. But, as noted within the ecological perspective, we are also affected by the customs, traditions, languages, and heritages of the societies in which we live.

The sociocultural perspective overlaps other perspectives on child development, but developmentalists use the term *sociocultural* in a couple of different ways. One way refers quite specifically to the *sociocultural theory* of the Russian psychologist Lev Semenovich Vygotsky (1896–1934). The other way broadly addresses the effect on children of human diversity, including such factors as ethnicity and gender.

Vygotsky's Sociocultural Theory

Whereas genetics is concerned with the biological transmission of traits from generation to generation, Vygotsky's (1978) theory is concerned with the transmission of information and cognitive skills from generation to generation. The transmission of skills involves teaching and learning, but Vygotsky does not view learning in terms of the conditioning of behaviour. Rather, he focuses on how the child's social interaction with adults, largely in the home, organizes a child's learning experiences in such a way that the child can obtain cognitive skills—such as computation or reading skills—and use them to acquire information. Like Piaget, Vygotsky sees the child's functioning as adaptive, and the child adapts to his or her social and cultural interactions.

The key concepts in Vygotsky's theory include the *zone of proximal development* and *scaffolding*. The word *proximal* means "nearby" or "close," as in the words *approximate* and *proximity*. The **zone of proximal development (ZPD)** is a range of tasks that a child can carry out with the help of someone who is more skilled. It is similar to an apprenticeship. Many developmentalists find that observing how a child learns when working with others provides more information about that child's cognitive abilities than does a simple inventory of knowledge. When learning with other people, the child tends to internalize— or bring inward—the conversations and explanations that help him or her gain the necessary skills (Vygotsky, 1962; Wass et al., 2011; Worthman, 2010). In other words, children not only learn the meanings of words from teachers but also learn ways of talking to themselves about solving problems within a cultural context (Murata & Fuson, 2006). Outer speech becomes inner speech. What was the teacher's becomes the child's. What was a social and cultural context becomes embedded within the child.

A *scaffold* is a temporary skeletal structure that enables workers to fabricate a building, bridge, or other more permanent structure. In Vygotsky's theory, teachers and parents provide children with problem-solving methods that serve as cognitive **scaffolding** while the child gains the ability to function independently. For example, a child's instructors may offer advice on sounding out letters and words that provide a

Lev Semenovich Vygotsky
Vygotsky is known for showing how social speech becomes inner speech and how "scaffolding" by others assists children in developing the cognitive skills to succeed.

zone of proximal development (ZPD) Vygotsky's term for the range of tasks that a child can carry out with the help of someone who is more skilled, frequently an adult who represents the culture in which the child develops.

scaffolding Vygotsky's term for temporary cognitive structures or methods of solving problems that help the child as he or she learns to function independently.

Archives of the History of American Psychology, The Center for the History of Psychology, The University of Akron

OBSERVING CHILDREN, UNDERSTANDING OURSELVES

Zone of Proximal Development

Watch how children's learning and problem solving are different with guidance and assistance from others. What are the different types of assistance being offered by the teacher and the child helping a fellow student to read? How might a teacher's techniques vary depending on the ages of the students? How might assistance from a peer benefit not only student learners but also student teachers?

From Rathus. *Childhood and Adolescence*, 5E. © 2014 South-Western, a part of Cengage Learning, Inc. Reproduced by permission. www .cengage.com/permissions

Go to www.nelson.com/voyages2ce to watch the video, answer the questions, and e-mail your responses to your professor.

Scaffolding
According to Vygotsky's theory, teachers and parents provide children with problem-solving methods that serve as cognitive scaffolding.

temporary support until reading "clicks" and the child no longer needs the device. Children may be offered scaffolding that enables them to use their fingers or their toes to do simple calculations. Eventually, the scaffolding is removed and the cognitive structures stand alone. A Puerto Rican study found that students also use scaffolding when they are explaining to one another how they can improve school projects, such as essay assignments (Guerrero & Villamil, 2000). The authors show that scaffolding can be mutual, not just unidirectional.

Evaluation   A good deal of research evidence supports Vygotsky's view that the presence of skilled adults helps children master tasks (Norton & D'Ambrosio, 2008). More-skilled children also play effective roles in teaching children (John-Steiner, 2007). Private speech appears to help children plan ways to carry out tasks and see them through. Among five-, seven-, and nine-year-olds who are given tasks with medium and high levels of difficulty, private speech facilitates task performance (Montero & De Dios, 2006). However, many teachers are unaware of the role of private speech in task performance, and some report that they discourage it when it distracts them—the teachers—or other children (Deniz, 2004).

Dynamic Systems Perspective

A relatively new theoretical approach is the **dynamic systems perspective** that emerged from the foundational work of Esther Thelen and Linda B. Smith (2006), as well as other theorists (Fischer & Bidell, 2006; Molenaar & Newell, 2010). Children's many systems (cognitive, social, physical) are all part of an integrated, dynamic system that considers time, nonlinear interactions of multiple subsystems, individuality, and uniqueness in how children solve problems and acquire skills and knowledge (Spencer et al., 2006). The dynamic systems perspective frames development as both continuous and stage-like (Fischer & Bidell, 2006). Looking ahead, research that uses dynamic systems theory perspective focuses on more of the *how* than the *what*—that is, how is change occurring rather than what is changing at any given moment (static view) (Molenaar & Newell, 2010; Spencer et al, 2012), leading developmental science into exciting territory.

The Sociocultural Perspective and Human Diversity

The field of child development focuses mainly on individuals and is committed to the dignity of the individual child. The sociocultural perspective asserts that we cannot understand individual children without awareness of the richness of their diversity (Pickren et al., 2012; Russo et al., 2012). For example, children diverge or differ in their ethnicity, gender, and socioeconomic status.

Children's **ethnic groups** involve their cultural heritage, their race, their language, and their common history. Canada's ethnic and cultural makeup is undergoing rapid change (see Figure 1.5 ■). The three largest visible minority groups are South Asians, Chinese, and Blacks, accounting for 61.3 percent of the visible minority population in 2011 (Statistics Canada, 2013). The cultural heritages, languages, and histories of ethnic minority groups are thus likely to have an increasing effect on the cultural life of Canadians. Yet the dominant cultures in Canada have often disparaged the traditions and languages of people from indigenous and ethnic minority groups. For example, there are ongoing debates as to how to educate children in the acquisition of a second language (Chapter 12), as well as how to acknowledge the rich traditions of the indigenous peoples to Canada.

Studying diversity is also important in helping ensure that children have appropriate educational experiences. Educators need to understand children's

dynamic systems perspective
View that children's physical, social, and cognitive development are all part of an integrated and actively changing system.

ethnic groups Groups of people distinguished by their cultural heritage, race, language, and common history.

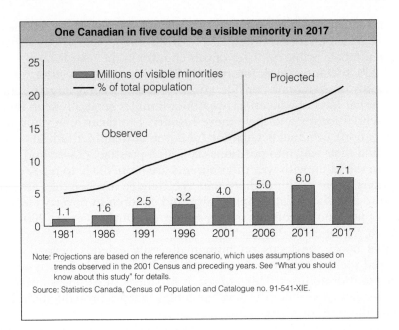

Figure 1.5 ■ **Future Trends of Ethnocultural diversity in Canada**

One Canadian in five could be a visible minority in 2017

Millions of visible minorities
% of total population

Observed
Projected

1.1 1.6 2.5 3.2 4.0 5.0 6.0 7.1
1981 1986 1991 1996 2001 2006 2011 2017

Note: Projections are based on the reference scenario, which uses assumptions based on trends observed in the 2001 Census and preceding years. See "What you should know about this study" for details.

Source: Statistics Canada, Census of Population and Catalogue no. 91-541-XIE.

family values and cultural expectations in order to teach them and guide their learning. Many professionals—teachers, psychologists, social workers, psychiatrists, and others—are called on to help children and families who are having problems in school or in the community. Professionals may need special training to identify the problems of children and families from ethnic minority groups and to treat them in culturally sensitive ways (Cardemil, 2008; DeSocio et al., 2008).

Throughout the text, we consider many issues that affect children from various ethnic groups. A few examples of these issues are bilingualism, ethnic differences in intelligence test scores, the prevalence of suicide among members of different ethnic minority groups, and patterns of child rearing among parents of various ethnic minority groups.

Gender is another aspect of human diversity. Gender is the psychological state of being male or being female, as influenced by cultural concepts of gender-appropriate behaviour. Unfortunately, females and males are often polarized by cultural expectations. Their differences may be exaggerated, as in the case of intellectual abilities. Males may very well differ from females in some respects, but history has created more burdens for women than for men as a result. Gender-role expectations affect children's self-esteem and limit their hopes and dreams for the future.

Historically, girls have been traditionally discouraged from pursuing careers in the sciences, politics, and business. Women today are making inroads into academic and vocational spheres—such as medicine, law, engineering, and the military—that were traditionally male preserves. Today, a majority of college and university students in Canada are female, but girls were not considered qualified for education until relatively recent times. In 1880 the medical school at Queen's University in Kingston, Ontario, was the first to admit females to its undergraduate courses, as recounted by Cataudella (1999). Queen's was also one of the first Canadian universities to exclude females and the last to re-admit females to their programs. Yet there remain many parts of the world, such as rural parts of Pakistan and Africa, where few if any women obtain an education (Smith et al., 2007). Opportunities for women are crucial to the development of girls. Opportunities for adults give children their sense of what is possible for them. Just as many children from ethnic minority groups wonder whether they can experience the rewards and opportunities they see in the dominant culture, so do girls wonder whether the career and social roles they admire are available to them. Many females question the representativeness of females in government, and whether there will be another female prime minister of this country in the near future.

A child's **socioeconomic status (SES)** is his or her position in society based mainly on economic considerations. A child's SES is largely connected with his or her level of education (wealthier families generally keep their children in school longer and have more resources to determine the quality of their education), eventual occupation (children in wealthier families are more likely to find their way into positions with high prestige, power, and income), and health (children with wealthier parents are more likely to receive all their vaccinations, to eat healthful diets, and to be tended to when they are ill). SES is therefore associated with opportunity, and children in poverty clearly have unequal opportunity to obtain society's rewards (Durham et al., 2007; Schutz et al., 2008; Victor et al., 2007).

In this book, the focus on human diversity extends beyond ethnicity, gender, and socioeconomic status to include children with various sexual orientations and disabilities. This approach broadens our understanding of all children as they experience the developmental changes brought about by quite different influences of heredity and experience.

Concept Review 1.3 summarizes similarities and differences among the perspectives on child development.

socioeconomic status (SES) Social position as determined mainly by level of income.

Concept Review 1.3 Perspectives on Child Development

Perspective or Theory	Core Concepts	Is Nature or Nurture More Important?	Is Development Viewed as Continuous or Discontinuous?	Is the Child Viewed as Active or Passive?
The Psychoanalytic Perspective				
Theory of psychosexual development (Sigmund Freud) 	Social codes channel primitive impulses, resulting in unconscious conflict.	Interaction of Maturation sets the stage for reacting to social influences.	Discontinuous: There are five stages of development, which express or repress sexual impulses in certain ways.	Passive: The child is largely at the mercy of older people and cultural modes of conduct.
Theory of psychosocial development (Erik Erikson) 	Children undergo life crises that are largely based on social relationships, opportunities, and expectations.	Interaction of nature and nurture: Maturation sets the stage for reacting to social influences and opportunities.	Discontinuous: There are eight stages of development, each of which involves a particular kind of life crisis.	Active: The child (or adult) makes conscious decisions about the formation of his or her own personality and behaviour.

Concept Review 1.3 Perspectives on Child Development *(Continued)*

Perspective or Theory	Core Concepts	Is Nature or Nurture More Important?	Is Development Viewed as Continuous or Discontinuous?	Is the Child Viewed as Active or Passive?
The Learning Perspective: Behavioural and Social Cognitive Theories				
Behaviourism (Ivan Pavlov, John B. Watson, B. F. Skinner)  Nina Leen/Time & Life Pictures/Getty Images	Behaviour is learned by association, as in classical and operant conditioning.	Nurture: Children are seen almost as blank tablets.	Continuous: Behaviour reflects the summation of conditioned responses.	Passive: Responses are learned by association and maintained by reinforcement.
Social cognitive theory (Albert Bandura and others)  Photo courtesy of Christina Rinaldi	Conditioning occurs, but children also learn by observing others and choose whether to display learned responses.	Emphasizes nurture but allows for the expression of natural tendencies.	Continuous.	Active: Children influence the environment even as the environment influences them.
The Cognitive Perspective				
Cognitive-developmental theory (Jean Piaget)  © Farrell Grehan/CORBIS	Children adapt to the environment by assimilating new events to existing mental structures and accommodating those structures.	Emphasizes nature but allows for influences of experience.	Discontinuous: Cognitive development follows an invariant sequence of four stages.	Active: Children are budding scientists who seek to understand and manipulate their worlds.
Information-processing theory (numerous theorists)	Children's cognitive functioning is compared to that of computers—how they input, manipulate, store, and output information.	Interaction of nature and nurture.	Continuous: The child's capacity for storing information and his or her ability to run multiple "programs" at once develop continuously.	Active: Children seek to obtain and manipulate information.

(Continued)

Concept Review 1.3 Perspectives on Child Development *(Continued)*

Perspective or Theory	Core Concepts	Is Nature or Nurture More Important?	Is Development Viewed as Continuous or Discontinuous?	Is the Child Viewed as Active or Passive?
The Biological Perspective				
Ethology and evolution (Charles Darwin, Konrad Lorenz, Niko Tinbergen)	Organisms are biologically "prewired" to develop certain adaptive responses during sensitive periods.	Emphasizes nature, but experience is also critical; e.g., imprinting occurs during a sensitive period but experience determines the object of imprinting.	Discontinuous: Certain kinds of learning are said to occur during sensitive periods, which are biologically determined.	Not indicated, although organisms respond automatically to FAPs.
The Ecological Perspective				
Ecological systems theory (Urie Bronfenbrenner)	Children's development occurs within interlocking systems, and development is enhanced by intervening in these systems.	Interaction of nature and nurture: Children's personalities and skills contribute to their development.	Not specifically indicated.	Active: Influences are bidirectional: Systems influence the child, and vice versa.
The Sociocultural Perspective				
Sociocultural theory (Lev Vygotsky)	Children internalize sociocultural dialogues in developing problem-solving skills.	Interaction of nature and nurture: Nurture is discussed in social and cultural terms.	Continuous: Children learn in the "zone" with experienced members of a culture, thereby accumulating knowledge and skills.	Both: Children seek to develop problem-solving abilities by internalizing cultural dialogues, but the dialogues originate externally.
Sociocultural perspective and human diversity (numerous theorists)	Children's development is influenced by sociocultural factors, such as ethnicity, gender, and SES.	Nurture.	Not specifically indicated.	Not indicated.
Dynamic systems perspective	Children's physical, cognitive, and social and emotional development make up an integrated system that is constantly adapting and changing.	Interaction of both nature and nurture.	Both continuous and discontinuous. While the system is constantly changing, stages development does occur, and children adapt their behaviours accordingly.	Children are active agents in their development.

Archives of the History of American Psychology, The Center for the History of Psychology, The University of Akron

Active Review

4. _____ are intended to enable us to explain, predict, and control events.

5. _____ hypothesized five stages of psychosexual development.

6. Erikson extended Freud's five stages of development to _____.

7. Behaviourism sees children's learning as mechanical and relies on classical and _____ conditioning.

8. According to _____, children assimilate new events to existing schemes or accommodate schemes to incorporate novel events.

9. Information-_____ theory focuses on the processes by which information is encoded, stored, retrieved, and manipulated.

10. The _____ systems theory explains child development in terms of the interaction between children and the settings in which they live.

11. Vygotsky's _____ theory is concerned with the transmission of information and cognitive skills from generation to generation.

Reflect & Relate: How have your ethnic background and your sex influenced your development? Consider factors such as race, country of origin, language, nutrition, values, and the dominant culture's reaction to people of your background.

1.3 Dominant Themes in Child Development

The discussion of theories of development reveals that developmentalists can see things in very different ways. Let us consider how they react to three of the most important debates in the field.

The Interplay of Nature–Nurture

QUESTION » **How do nature and nurture influence child development?** Think about your friends for a moment. Some may be tall and lanky, others short and stocky. Some are outgoing and sociable; others are more reserved and quiet. One may be a good athlete, another a fine musician. What made them this way? How much does inheritance have to do with it, and how much of a role does the environment play?

Researchers are continually trying to sort out the extent to which human behaviour is the result of **nature** (heredity) and of **nurture** (environmental influences). What aspects of behaviour originate in our **genes** and are biologically programmed to unfold in the child as time goes on, so long as minimal nutrition and social experience are provided? What aspects of behaviour can be traced largely to such environmental influences as nutrition and learning?

Scientists seek the natural causes of development in children's genetic heritage, the functioning of the nervous system, and maturation. Scientists seek the environmental causes of development in children's nutrition, cultural and family backgrounds, and opportunities to learn about the world, including cognitive stimulation during early childhood and formal education.

Some traditional theorists lean heavily toward natural explanations of development (e.g., cognitive-developmental and biological theorists), whereas others lean heavily toward environmental explanations (e.g., learning theorists). But today nearly all researchers would agree that nature and nurture play important roles in nearly every area of child development. Consider the

nature The processes within an organism that guide that organism to develop according to its genetic code.

nurture The processes external to an organism that nourish it as it develops according to its genetic code or that cause it to swerve from its genetically programmed course. Environmental factors that influence development.

genes The basic building blocks of heredity.

development of language. Language is based in structures found in certain areas of the brain. Thus, biology (nature) plays a vital role in language development. But children also come to speak the languages spoken by their caretakers. Parent–child similarities in accent and vocabulary provide additional evidence for the role of learning (nurture) in language development.

The Continuity–Discontinuity Theme

QUESTION » Is development continuous or discontinuous? Do developmental changes occur gradually (continuously), the way a seedling becomes a tree? Or do changes occur in major qualitative leaps (discontinuously) that dramatically alter our bodies and behaviour, the way a caterpillar turns into a butterfly?

Some developmentalists view human development as a continuous process in which the effects of learning mount gradually, with no major sudden qualitative changes. In contrast, other theorists believe that a number of rapid qualitative changes usher in new stages of development. Maturational theorists point out that the environment, even when enriched, profits us little until we are ready, or mature enough, to develop in a certain way. For example, newborn babies will not imitate their parents' speech, even when parents speak clearly and deliberately. Nor does aided practice in "walking" during the first few months after birth significantly accelerate the emergence of independent walking. Newborns are not ready to do these things.

Stage theorists such as Sigmund Freud and Jean Piaget saw development as discontinuous. They saw biological changes as providing the potential for psychological changes. Freud focused on the ways in which biological developments might provide the basis for personality development. Piaget believed maturation of the nervous system allowed cognitive development.

Certain aspects of physical development do occur in stages. For example, from the age of two years to the onset of puberty, children gradually grow larger. Then the adolescent growth spurt occurs, as rushes of hormones cause rapid biological changes in structure and function (as in the development of the sex organs) and in size. Psychologists disagree on whether developments in cognition occur in stages.

The Active–Passive Theme

QUESTION » Are children active (prewired to act on the world) or passive (shaped by experience)? Broadly speaking, all animals are active. But in the field of child development, the issue has a more specific meaning. Historical views of children as willful and unruly suggest that people have generally seen children as active—even if mischievous (at best) or evil (at worst). John Locke introduced a view of children as passive beings (blank tablets); experience "wrote" features of personality and moral virtue on them.

At one extreme, educators who view children as passive may assume that they must be motivated to learn by their instructors. Such educators are likely to provide a traditional curriculum with rigorous exercises in spelling, music, and math to promote absorption of the subject matter. They are also likely to apply a powerful system of rewards and punishments to keep children on the straight and narrow.

At the other extreme, educators who view children as active may assume that they have a natural love of learning. Such educators are likely to argue for open education and encourage children to explore an environment rich with learning materials. These educators are likely to listen to the children to learn

Stages of Physical Development
Certain aspects of physical development seem to occur in stages. Girls usually spurt in growth before boys. The girl and boy who are dancing are the same age.

Mark Richards/PhotoEdit Inc.

about their unique likes and talents and then support children as they pursue their own agendas.

These are extremes. Most educators would probably agree that children show individual differences and that some children require more guidance and external motivation than others. In addition, children can be active in some subjects and passive in others. Whether children who do not actively seek to master certain subjects are coerced tends to depend on how important the subject is to functioning in today's society, the age of the child, the attitudes of the parents, and many other factors.

Urie Bronfenbrenner (Bronfenbrenner & Morris, 2006) argued that we miss the point when we assume that children are entirely active or passive. Children are influenced by the environment, but children also influence the environment. The challenge is to observe the ways in which children interact with their settings. Albert Bandura (2006a, 2006b) also refers to the two-way influences between children and the environment.

These debates are theoretical. Scientists value theory for its ability to tie together observations and suggest new areas of investigation, but they also follow an **empirical** approach. That is, they engage in research methods, such as those described in the following section, to find evidence for or against various theoretical positions.

empirical Based on observation and experimentation.

Active Review

12. Researchers in child development try to sort out the effects of _____ (heredity) and nurture (environmental influences).

13. Learning theorists tend to see development as continuous, whereas stage theorists see development as _____.

Reflect & Relate: Consider the active–passive controversy. Do you see yourself as being active or passive? Explain.

1.4 How Do We Study Child Development?

What is the relationship between children's intelligence and their achievement? What are the effects of maternal use of aspirin and alcohol on the fetus? How can you rear children to become competent and independent? What are the effects of parental divorce on children? We all may have expressed opinions on questions such as these at one time or another. But scientists insist that such questions be answered by research. Strong arguments or references to authority figures are not evidence. Scientific evidence is obtained only by the scientific method.

The Scientific Method

QUESTION » **What is the scientific method?** The scientific method is a systematic way of forming and answering research questions. It enables scientists to test the theories discussed in the previous section. The scientific method consists of the following five steps.

Step 1: Forming a Research Question
Our daily experiences, theory, and even folklore help generate questions for research. Daily experience in using day-care centres may stimulate us to

The Scientific Method

wonder whether day care affects children's intellectual or social development or the bonds of attachment between children and parents. Reading about observational learning may suggest research into the effects of TV violence.

Step 2: Developing a Hypothesis

The second step is the development of a hypothesis. A **hypothesis** is a specific statement about behaviour that is tested through research. One hypothesis about day care might be that preschool children placed in day care will acquire greater skill in getting along with other children than will preschoolers who are cared for in the home. A hypothesis about TV violence might be that elementary-school children who watch more violent TV shows will behave more aggressively toward other children.

Step 3: Testing the Hypothesis

The third step is testing the hypothesis. Psychologists test the hypothesis through carefully controlled information-gathering techniques and research methods, such as **naturalistic observation**, the case study, correlation, and the experiment.

For example, we could introduce two groups of children—children who are in day care and children who are not in day care—to a new child in a college child-research centre and see how each group acts toward the new child. Concerning the effects of TV violence, we could have parents help us tally which TV shows their children watch and rate the shows for violent content. Then we could ask the children's teachers to report how aggressively the children act toward classmates. We could do some math to determine whether more aggressive children also watch more violence on TV. We describe research methods such as these later in the chapter.

Step 4: Drawing Conclusions

Scholars of development then draw conclusions from their research results. Those results may confirm a hypothesis or disconfirm a hypothesis.

Step 5: Publishing Findings

Scientists publish their research findings in professional journals and thus make their data available to scientists and the public at large for scrutiny. This gives other scientists the opportunity to review their data and conclusions to help determine their accuracy.

Now let us consider the information-gathering techniques and the research methods used by developmentalists. Then we will discuss ethical issues concerning research in child development.

Methods of Observation

QUESTION » What methods of observation do developmentalists use to gather information about children? Developmentalists use various methods to gather information. For example, they may ask children to keep diaries of their behaviour, ask teachers or parents to report on the behaviour of their children, or use interviews or questionnaires with children themselves. There are significant problems in asking children to report their behaviour or their experiences. For example, in court cases involving actual or suspected child sexual abuse, the testimony of children—the victims—has been challenged because of questions about children's memory and suggestibility. The concern is that, in the course of being prepared to testify, some children may have inaccurate memories or judgments implanted, either deliberately or inadvertently,

hypothesis A specific statement about behaviour that is tested by research.

naturalistic observation A method of scientific observation in which children (and others) are observed in their natural environments.

through the power of suggestion (Cossins, 2008). When possible, researchers directly observe children in the laboratory ("structured observations") or in the natural setting ("naturalistic observations"). Let us discuss two ways of gathering information: the naturalistic-observation method and the case-study method.

Naturalistic Observation

Naturalistic-observation studies of children are conducted in "the field"—that is, in the natural, or real-life, settings in which they happen. In field studies, investigators observe the natural behaviour of children in settings such as homes, playgrounds, and classrooms and try not to interfere with it. Interference could affect or "bias" the results. Researchers may try to "blend into the woodwork" by sitting quietly in the back of a classroom or may observe the class through a one-way mirror.

William H. Brown and his colleagues (2009) used naturalistic observation to study the activity levels of three- to five-year-olds in preschools. They found that the children spend 89 percent of their days in sedentary activity, 8 percent in light activity, and 3 percent in moderate to vigorous physical activity.

Naturalistic-observation studies have been done with children of different cultures. For example, researchers have observed the motor behaviour of Native American Hopi children who are strapped to cradle boards during the first year. They have observed language development in the United States, Mexico, Turkey, Kenya, and China—seeking universals that might suggest a major role for maturation in the acquisition of language skills. They have also observed the ways in which children are socialized in Russia, Israel, Japan, and other nations in an effort to determine what patterns of child rearing are associated with the development of behaviours such as attachment and independence.

The Case Study

Another way of gathering information about children is the case-study method. The **case study** is a carefully drawn account of the behaviour of an individual. Parents who keep diaries of their children's activities are involved in informal case studies. Case studies themselves often use a number of different kinds of information about children. In addition to direct observation, case studies may include questionnaires, **standardized tests**, and interviews with the child and his or her parents, teachers, and friends. Information gleaned from school and other records may be included. Scientists who use the case-study method take great pains to record all the relevant factors in a child's behaviour, and they are cautious in drawing conclusions about what leads to what.

Jean Piaget used the case-study method in carefully observing and recording the behaviour of children, including his own children (see Chapter 6). Sigmund Freud developed his psychoanalytic theory largely on the basis of case studies. Freud studied his patients in great depth and followed some of them for many years.

The Survey

Developmentalists conduct surveys to learn about behaviour and mental processes that cannot be observed in the natural setting or studied experimentally. They may employ questionnaires, as they did in the feature on high school students' attitudes toward living together without being married. When it comes to children, they may survey parents and teachers rather than the children themselves. They may personally interview people rather than distributing questionnaires. Researchers may also examine records,

case study A carefully drawn biography of the life of an individual.

standardized test A test of some ability or trait in which an individual's score is compared to the scores of a group of similar individuals.

Surveying High School Seniors' Attitudes toward Living Together before Getting Married

Living together with a partner without being married—cohabitation—was called "living in sin" a couple of generations ago. Yet more than half of today's marriages are preceded by the couple living together (Wilcox & Marquardt, 2011). The numbers of households consisting of an unmarried adults living together (i.e., common-law) in Canada has increased from 15 percent in 2006 to 16.7 percent in 2011 (Portraits of Families and Living Arrangements in Canada, Statistics Canada, 2012). More than half a million additional households consist of cohabiting same-sex couples. Some social scientists view cohabitation as a new stage of courtship.

The University of Michigan's "Monitoring the Future" research group has been surveying some 6000 students a year for nearly 40 years, and over those years, high school seniors' approval of cohabitation has changed markedly from a minority to a solid majority. As you can see in Figure 1.6 ■, about two-thirds of today's U.S. high school seniors believe that it is a good idea for couples to live together before getting married to test their compatibility, and the percentage continues to be on the rise.

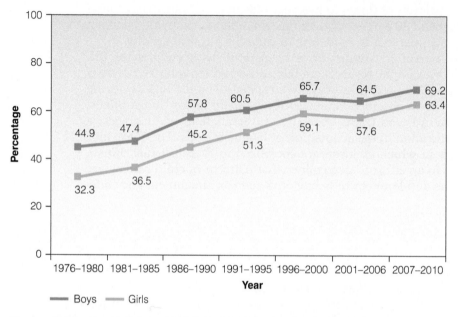

Figure 1.6 ■ **Percentage of High School Seniors Approving of Couples' Living Together before Marriage, by Period**

Source: Bachman, J. G., Johnston, L. D., & O'Malley, P. M. (2011). Monitoring the future: Questionnaire responses from the nation's high school seniors 2010. Survey Research Center. Institute for Social Research. Ann Arbor, MI: The University of Michigan.

---

correlation A relationship between variables in which one variable increases as a second variable also increases (a positive correlation) or decreases (a negative correlation).

variables Quantities that can vary from child to child or from occasion to occasion, such as height, weight, intelligence, and attention span.

correlation coefficient A number ranging from +1.00 to −1.00 that expresses the direction (positive or negative) and strength of the relationship between two variables.

such as hospital records, to determine factors such as the birth weight of children in different parts of the country or of children of different ethnic backgrounds.

Correlation: Putting Things Together

QUESTION » What does it mean to correlate information? Correlation is a mathematical method that researchers use to determine whether one behaviour or trait being studied is related to, or correlated with, another. Consider, for example, the **variables** of intelligence and achievement. These variables are assigned numbers such as intelligence test scores or academic grade averages. Then the numbers or scores are mathematically related and expressed as a correlation coefficient. A **correlation coefficient** is a number that varies between +1.00 and −1.00.

Positive correlation	Negative correlation
As one variable increases, the other variable increases.	As one variable increases, the other variable decreases.
A	**B**

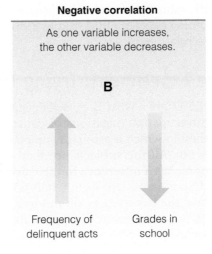

| Time spent studying | Grades in school | Frequency of delinquent acts | Grades in school |

Figure 1.7 ■ Examples of Positive and Negative Correlations

When two variables are correlated positively, one increases as the other increases. There is a positive correlation between the amount of time spent studying and grades, as shown in Part A. When two variables are correlated negatively, one increases as the other decreases. There is a negative correlation between the frequency of a child's delinquent acts and his or her grades, as shown in Part B. As delinquent behaviour increases, grades tend to decline.

Numerous studies report **positive correlations** between intelligence and achievement. In general, the higher children score on intelligence tests, the better their academic performance is likely to be. The scores attained on intelligence tests are positively correlated (about +0.60 to +0.70) with overall academic achievement.[1]

There is a **negative correlation** between children's school grades and their commission of delinquent acts. The higher a child's grades in school, the less likely the child is to engage in criminal behaviour. Figure 1.7 ■ illustrates positive and negative correlations.

Limitations of Correlational Information

Correlational information can reveal relationships between variables, but they do not show cause and effect. For example, children who watch TV shows with a lot of violence are more likely to engage in aggressive behaviour at home and in school. Thus, it may seem logical to assume that exposure to TV violence makes children more aggressive. But it could also be that children who are more aggressive to begin with prefer violent TV shows. In this case, another type of investigation has clarified the picture: Psychologists note that hundreds of *experiments* show that viewing violence increases aggressive behaviour (Anderson et al., 2010; Bushman & Anderson, 2007).

Similarly, studies in locations as far flung as the United States and China report that children (especially boys) in divorced families sometimes have more adjustment problems than children in intact families (Potter, 2010; Vélez et al., 2011). However, these studies do not show that divorce causes these adjustment problems. It could be that the same factors that led to divorce (such as parental disorganization or conflict) also led to adjustment problems among the children (Hetherington, 2006). Or, having a child with adjustment problems might put a strain on the parents' marriage and ultimately be a factor contributing to divorce.

When we study patterns of child rearing, we must also ask why parents choose to rear their children in certain ways. It is possible that the factors that lead parents to make these choices, such as the cultural environment, also influence the behaviour of the children. Thus, correlational research does not enable us to place clear "cause" and "effect" labels on variables. To investigate cause and effect, researchers turn to the experimental method. Nonetheless, there are benefits of correlation research. The most common is that finding

What Is the Relationship between Intelligence and Achievement?
Does the correlational method allow us to say that intelligence causes or is responsible for academic achievement? Why or why not?

positive correlation A relationship between two variables in which one variable increases as the other variable increases.

negative correlation A relationship between two variables in which one variable decreases as the other variable increases.

---

[1]Of course, +0.60 is the same as +.60. We insert the zero to help prevent the decimal point from getting lost.

relationships in correlation designs helps point us in the right direction when designing experimental studies aiming to draw conclusions about the cause of these relationships.

The Experiment: Trying Things Out

QUESTION » What is an experiment? The experiment is the preferred method for investigating questions of cause and effect. An **experiment** is a research method in which a group of subjects receives a **treatment** and another group does not. All the subjects are then observed to determine whether the treatment makes a difference in their behaviour.

Experiments are used when possible because they enable researchers to control the experiences of children and other subjects to determine the outcomes of a treatment. Experiments, like other research methods, are usually undertaken to test a hypothesis. For example, a researcher might hypothesize that exposure to TV violence causes aggressive behaviour in children. To test this hypothesis, she might devise an experiment in which some children are purposely exposed to TV violence and others are not. Remember that it is not enough to demonstrate that children who choose to watch more violent shows behave more aggressively; such evidence is only correlational. We review this research—correlational and experimental—in Chapter 10.

Independent and Dependent Variables

In an experiment to determine whether TV violence causes aggressive behaviour, subjects in the experimental group would be shown a TV program containing violence, and its effects on behaviour would be measured. TV violence would be considered an **independent variable**, a variable whose presence is manipulated by the experimenters so that its effects can be determined. The measured result, in this case the child's behaviour, is called a **dependent variable**. Its presence or level presumably depends on the independent variable.

Experimental and Control Groups

Experiments use experimental and control groups. Subjects in the **experimental group** receive the treatment, whereas subjects in the **control group** do not. Every effort is made to ensure that all other conditions are held constant for both groups of subjects. Holding other conditions constant gives us confidence that experimental outcomes reflect the treatments and not chance factors. In a study on the effects of TV violence on children's behaviour, children in the experimental group would be shown TV programs containing violence, and children in the control group would be shown programs that do not contain violence.

Random Assignment

Subjects should be assigned to experimental or control groups on a chance or random basis. We could not conclude much from an experiment on the effects of TV violence if the children were allowed to choose whether they would be in a group that watched a lot of TV violence or in a group that watched TV shows without violence. Children who chose to watch TV violence might have more aggressive tendencies to begin with! In an experiment on the effects of TV violence, we would therefore have to assign children randomly to view TV shows with or without violence, regardless of their personal preferences. As you can imagine, this would be difficult, if not impossible, to do in the child's own home. But such studies can be performed in laboratory settings, as we will see in Chapter 10.

Ethical and practical considerations also prevent researchers from doing experiments on the effects of many significant life circumstances, such as

experiment A method of scientific investigation that seeks to discover cause-and-effect relationships by introducing independent variables and observing their effects on dependent variables.

treatment In an experiment, a condition received by subjects so hat its effects may be observed.

independent variable In a scientific study, the condition that is manipulated (changed) so that its effects can be observed.

dependent variable In a scientific study, a measure of an assumed effect of an independent variable.

experimental group A group made up of subjects who receive a treatment in an experiment.

control group A group made up of subjects in an experiment who do not receive the treatment, but for whom all other conditions are comparable to those of subjects in the experimental group.

divorce and different patterns of child rearing. We cannot randomly assign some families to divorce or conflict and assign other families to "bliss." Nor can we randomly assign authoritarian parents to raising their children in a permissive manner, or vice versa. In some areas of investigation, we must be relatively satisfied with correlational evidence.

When experiments cannot ethically be performed on humans, researchers sometimes carry out experiments with animals and then generalize the findings to humans. For example, no researcher would separate human infants from their parents to study the effects of isolation on development. But experimenters have deprived monkeys of early social experience. Such research has helped psychologists investigate the formation of parent–child bonds of attachment (see Chapter 7). TRUTH OR FICTION REVISITED: Although it is true that research with monkeys has helped psychologists understand the formation of attachment in humans, ethics prevents investigators from carrying out this type of research with humans.

Longitudinal Research: Studying Development over Time

QUESTION » How do researchers study development over time? The processes of development occur over time, and researchers have devised different strategies for comparing children of one age to children (or adults) of other ages. In **longitudinal research**, the same children are observed repeatedly over time, and changes in development (such as gains in height or changes in approach to problem solving) are recorded. In **cross-sectional research**, children of different ages are observed and compared. It is assumed that when a large number of children are chosen at random, the differences found in the older age groups are a reflection of how the younger children will develop, given time.

Longitudinal Studies

Some ambitious longitudinal studies have followed the development of children and adults for more than half a century. One, the Fels Longitudinal Study, began in 1929. Children were observed twice a year in their homes and twice a year in the Fels Institute nursery school. From time to time, younger investigators dipped into the Fels pool of subjects, further testing, interviewing, and observing these individuals as they grew into adults. In this way, researchers have been able to observe, for example, the development of intelligence and of patterns of independence and dependence. They found, for example, that intelligence test scores at ages three and 18 were significantly related to intellectual and occupational status after the age of 26 (McCall, 1977). But the correlations were not high enough to allow long-term prediction for individual children.

The Terman Studies of Genius, also begun in the 1920s, tracked children with high IQ scores for more than half a century. TRUTH OR FICTION REVISITED: It is true that researchers have followed some subjects in developmental research for more than 50 years. Male subjects, but not female subjects, who obtained high IQ scores went on to high achievements in the professional world. Why the difference? Contemporary studies of women show that those with high intelligence generally match the achievements of men and suggest that women of the earlier era were held back by traditional gender-role expectations.

Most longitudinal studies span months or a few years, not decades. In Chapter 13, for example, we will see that briefer longitudinal studies have found that the children of divorced parents undergo the most severe adjustment problems within a few months of the divorce. By two or three years afterward, many children regain their equilibrium, as indicated by improved academic performance, social behaviour, and other measures (Hetherington, 2006; Moon, 2011).

longitudinal research The study of developmental processes by taking repeated measures of the same group of children at various stages of development.

cross-sectional research The study of developmental processes by taking measures of children of different age groups at the same time.

Longitudinal studies have drawbacks. For example, it can be difficult to enlist volunteers to participate in a study that will last a lifetime. Many subjects fall out of touch as the years pass; others die. Also, those who remain in the study tend to be more motivated than those who drop out. The researchers must be patient. To compare three-year-olds with six-year-olds, they must wait three years. In the early stages of such a study, the idea of comparing three-year-olds with 21-year-olds remains a distant dream. When the researchers themselves are middle-aged or older, they must hope that the candle of yearning for knowledge will be kept lit by a new generation of researchers.

Cross-Sectional Studies

Because of the drawbacks of longitudinal studies, most research that compares children of different ages is cross-sectional. In other words, most investigators gather data on what the "typical" six-month-old is doing by finding children who are six months old today. When they expand their research to the behaviour of typical 12-month-olds, they seek another group of children, and so on.

camilla$$/Shutterstock.com

Is Growing Up Using an iPad an Example of the Cohort Effect? Children and adults of different ages experience cultural and technological events specific to their age groups. Therefore, drawing conclusions based on cross-sectional research may be limited by the cohort effect.

A major challenge to cross-sectional research is the **cohort effect**. A cohort is a group of people born at about the same time. As a result, they experience cultural and other events unique to their age group. In other words, children and adults of different ages are not likely to have shared similar cultural backgrounds. People who are 70 years old today, for example, grew up largely without TV. (Really, there was a time when television did not exist!) People who are 60 years old today grew up before people landed on the Moon. Today's 50-year-olds did not spend their earliest years with *Sesame Street*. And today's children are growing up taking iPods and the Internet for granted. In fact, for today's children, Jennifer Lopez is an older woman.

Children of past generations also grew up with different expectations about gender roles and appropriate social behaviour. Women in the Terman study generally chose motherhood over careers because of the times. Today's girls are growing up with female role models who are astronauts, government officials, and athletes. Moreover, today the great majority of mothers are in the workforce, and their attitudes about women's roles have changed.

In other words, today's 80-year-olds are not today's five-year-olds as seen 75 years later. Today's 80-year-olds did not grow up with the Internet, social networking sites, cell phones, television, rock 'n' roll, or hip-hop. The times change, and their influence on children changes also. In longitudinal studies, we know that we have the same individuals as they have developed over 5, 25, even 50 years or more. In cross-sectional research, we can only hope that they will be comparable.

cohort effect Similarities in behaviour among a group of peers that stem from the fact that group members are approximately the same age.

cross-sequential research An approach that combines the longitudinal and cross-sectional methods by following individuals of different ages for abbreviated periods of time.

Cross-Sequential Research

Cross-sequential research combines the longitudinal and cross-sectional methods so that many of their individual drawbacks are overcome. In the cross-sequential study, the full span of the ideal longitudinal study is broken up into convenient segments (see Figure 1.8 ). Assume that we wish to follow the attitudes of children toward gender roles from the age of 4 through the age of 12. The typical longitudinal study would take eight years. However, we can divide this eight-year span in half by studying two samples of children (a cross-section) instead of one: four-year-olds and eight-year-olds. We would then interview, test, and observe each group at the beginning of the study (2014) and four years later (2018). By the time of the second observation

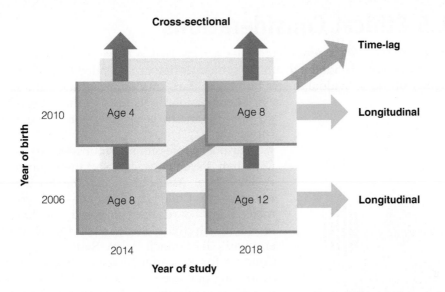

Cross-sectional

Year of birth

2010 — Age 4 — Age 8 → **Time-lag**
Age 8 → **Longitudinal**

2006 — Age 8 — Age 12 → **Longitudinal**

2014   2018

Year of study

Figure 1.8 ■ **Example of Cross-Sequential Research** Cross-sequential research combines three methods: cross-sectional, longitudinal, and time-lag. The child's age at the time of testing appears in the boxes. Vertical columns represent cross-sectional comparisons. Horizontal rows represent longitudinal comparisons. Diagonals represent time-lag comparisons.

period, the four-year-olds would have become eight years old, and the eight-year-olds would have turned 12.

An obvious advantage to this collapsed method is that the study is completed in four years rather than eight years. Still, the testing and retesting of samples provide some of the continuity of the longitudinal study. By observing both samples at the age of eight (this is called a **time-lag comparison**), we can also determine whether they are, in fact, comparable or whether the four-year difference in their birthdate is associated with a cohort effect—that is, cultural and other environmental changes that lead to different attitudes.

Concept Review 1.4 summarizes the major features of cross-sectional, longitudinal, and cross-sequential research.

time-lag comparison The study of developmental processes by taking measures of children of the same age group at different times.

Concept Review 1.4 Comparison of Cross-Sectional, Longitudinal, and Cross-Sequential Research

	Cross-Sectional Research	**Longitudinal Research**	**Cross-Sequential Research**
Description	Studies children of different ages at the same point in time	Studies the same children repeatedly over time	Breaks the span of a longitudinal study into children beginning at different ages
Advantages	Can be completed in a short period of time	Allows researchers to follow development over time	Can be completed in a shorter period of time than a longitudinal study but retains some of its continuity
	No dropouts or practice effects	Studies relationships between behaviour at earlier and later ages	Allows some comparison of behaviour at earlier and later ages
Disadvantages	Does not study development across time	Expensive Takes a long time to complete	Not completely longitudinal
	Cannot study the relationship between behaviour displayed at earlier and later ages	Subjects drop out, and dropouts may differ systematically from remaining subjects	More expensive than cross-sectional research
	Is prey to the cohort effect (subjects from different age groups may not be comparable)	Practice effects may occur	Some dropout effect (not as much as in longitudinal research)
			Some practice effects

1.5 Ethical Considerations

QUESTION » **What ethical guidelines are involved in research in child development?** Researchers adhere to ethical standards that are intended to promote the dignity of the individual, foster human welfare, and maintain scientific integrity. These standards also ensure that researchers do not use methods or treatments that harm subjects.

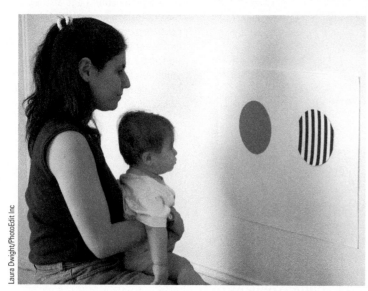

Various professional groups—such as the Canadian Psychological Association, American Psychological Association and the Society for Research in Child Development—and government review boards have proposed guidelines for research with children (such as the Canadian government's Tri-Council Policy Statement: Ethical Conduct for Research Involving Humans). The overriding purpose of these guidelines is to protect children from harm. These guidelines include the following:

- Researchers are not to use methods that may do physical or psychological harm (Axelin & Salanterä, 2008; Bersoff, 2008). In practice, this sort of issue boils down to exactly how much harm is being proposed and, sometimes, whether the value of the study outweighs the possible harm. For example, in using Mary Ainsworth's "strange situation" to study attachment between infants and caregivers, researchers separate infants from their caregivers for a while, often causing some distress. How much distress is too much? In Chapter 7, we will see that researchers have performed distressful or possibly distressful experiments with monkeys that they would not undertake with children.

- Children and their parents must be informed about the purposes of the research and about the research methods (Boccia et al., 2009; Salas et al., 2008). This allows participants to provide *informed consent* to the study. In most cases, it is the parent who becomes informed, and the child goes along with the parent's wishes. Is such a situation ethical?

- Children and their parents must provide voluntary consent to participate in the study (Boccia et al., 2009). Here we must consider what happens if the parent "volunteers" the child but the child seems unwilling. Eliminating reluctant children from a sample may systematically exclude certain kinds of children and lead to results that cannot be generalized to all children. Yet how much cajoling should a researcher do? And if parental consent is legally sufficient, should the researcher proceed with the child?

- Children and their parents may withdraw from the study at any time, for any reason (Bersoff, 2008). What should the researcher do if the child becomes tired or bored and starts crying or screeching, "I want to go home!"?

- Children and their parents should be offered information about the results of the study (Bersoff, 2008). Informing participants about the results is known as *debriefing*. The child, of course, may not be mature or experienced enough to understand the outcomes of the study, but the parent should be.

The Conditioning of "Little Albert": A Case Study in Ethics

In 1920 the behaviourist John B. Watson and his future wife, Rosalie Rayner, published a report (Watson & Rayner, 1920) of their demonstration that emotional reactions can be acquired through classical conditioning. The subject of their demonstration was an 11-month-old lad who has become known as "Little Albert." Albert was a phlegmatic fellow. He wasn't given to ready displays of emotion. But he did enjoy playing with a laboratory rat. Using a method that many psychologists subsequently criticized as being unethical, Watson startled Little Albert by clanging steel bars behind his head whenever the infant played with the rat. After repeated pairings, Albert showed fear of the rat even when the clanging was halted. Albert's fear also generalized to objects that were similar in appearance to the rat, such as a rabbit and the fur collar on a woman's coat. This study has become a hallmark in psychology, although Watson has also been criticized for not counterconditioning Albert's fear.

In counterconditioning, an object or situation that evokes a response opposed to a conditioned response is repeatedly associated with the feared object. A few years after the experiment with Little Albert, Mary Cover Jones, a protégé of Watson, carried out a mini-experiment in counterconditioning with a boy named Peter. Peter feared rabbits but enjoyed cookies. Unfortunately, these findings didn't do Albert any good. Albert's mother, distraught at the events that had occurred, removed her son from the laboratory.

Reflect Do you think Watson's experiment with Little Albert was ethical? Why or why not?"

- The identities of the children participating in a study are to remain *confidential* (Bersoff, 2008; Miller et al., 2008). Sometimes conflicts of interest or conflicts between principles may arise. What, for example, should researchers do if they acquire information from children that suggests they have been subjected to abuse? Whom do they inform, if anyone (Donner et al., 2008; Gorin et al., 2008)?

- Researchers should present their research plans to a committee of their colleagues and obtain the committee's approval before proceeding (Bersoff, 2008).

These guidelines present researchers (Canadian Psychological Association, 2000, Tri-Council Policy Statement: Ethical Conduct for Research Involving Humans, 2010) with a number of steps to consider in designing and implementing their research. But because they protect the welfare of children, the guidelines are valuable.

Active Review

14. The steps of the scientific method include formulating a research question, developing a _____, testing the hypothesis, drawing conclusions, and publishing results.

15. _____-observation studies are conducted in the real-life setting.

16. The _____ study is a carefully drawn account or biography of an individual child.

17. A correlational study describes relationships but does not reveal _____ and effect.

18. In an experiment, members of an experimental group receive a treatment, whereas members of a _____ group do not.

19. _____ research observes the same children repeatedly over time.

20. In cross-_____ research, children of different ages are observed and compared.

Reflect & Relate: How do you gather information about the behaviour and mental processes of other people? Which of the methods described in this section come closest to your own? Are your methods adequately scientific? Explain.

Recite an Active Summary

1.1 What Is Child Development? Coming to Terms with Terms

What is child development?

The field of child development attempts to advance knowledge of the processes that govern the development of children's physical structures, traits, behaviours, and cognitions. *Growth* consists of changes in size or quantity, whereas *development* also includes changes in quality.

Why do researchers study child development?

Researchers study child development to gain insight into human nature, the origins of adult behaviour, the origins of developmental problems, ways of optimizing development, and the effects of culture on development.

What views of children do we find throughout history?

Locke focused on the role of the environment, or experience, in development. Rousseau argued that children are good by nature, and if allowed to express their natural impulses, they would develop into moral and giving people. Darwin originated the modern theory of evolution and was one of the first observers to keep a baby biography. Hall founded child development as an academic discipline. Binet developed the first modern standardized intelligence test.

1.2 Historical Review of Theories of Child Development

Why do we have theories?

Theories are related sets of statements about events. Theories of development help us describe, explain, and predict development, and they enable researchers to influence development through education of caregivers and teachers.

What is the psychoanalytic perspective on child development?

Freud viewed children as caught in conflict. He believed that people undergo *oral, anal, phallic, latency,* and *genital* stages of psychosexual development. Too little or too much gratification in a stage can lead to fixation. Erikson's psychosocial theory sees social relationships as more important than sexual or aggressive impulses. Erikson extended Freud's five developmental stages to eight (to include adulthood) and named stages after life crises.

What is the learning perspective on child development?

Watson argued that scientists must address observable behaviour only, not mental activity. Behaviourism relies on two types of learning: classical conditioning and operant conditioning. In classical conditioning, one stimulus comes to elicit the same response as another by being paired repeatedly with it. In operant conditioning, children learn to engage in or to discontinue behaviour because of its effects (reinforcement or lack of reinforcement). Social cognitive theorists, such as Bandura, argue that much learning occurs by observing models and that children choose whether or not to engage in behaviours they have learned.

What is the cognitive perspective on child development?

Piaget saw children as actors on the environment, not reactors. He studied how children form mental representations of the world and manipulate them. Piaget's theory relies on the concepts of *schemes, adaptation, assimilation, accommodation,* and *equilibration.* He hypothesized that children's cognitive processes develop in an invariant series of stages: *sensorimotor, preoperational, concrete operational,* and *formal operational.* Information-processing theory deals with the ways in which children encode information, transfer it to working memory (short-term memory), manipulate it, place information in storage (long-term memory), and retrieve it from storage.

What is the scope of the biological perspective?

The biological perspective focuses on heredity and on developments such as the formation of sperm and ova, gains in height and weight, maturation of the nervous system and the brain, and the way hormones spur the changes of puberty. Ethology involves instinctive, or inborn, behaviour patterns, termed *fixed action patterns (FAPs).* Many FAPs, such as those involved in attachment, occur during a *sensitive period* of life. Advances in neuroscientific research in recent years are helping developmental psychologists learn more about child and adolescent behaviours.

What is the ecological systems theory of child development?

Bronfenbrenner's ecological theory explains development in terms of the *reciprocal interaction* between children and the settings in which development occurs. These settings are the *microsystem, mesosystem, exosystem, macrosystem,* and *chronosystem.*

What is the sociocultural perspective?

The sociocultural perspective emphasizes that children are social beings who are influenced by their cultural backgrounds. Vygotsky introduced the sociocultural concepts of *scaffolding* and the *zone of proximal development (ZPD).* Children internalize conversations and explanations that help them gain skills. Children learn ways of solving problems within a cultural context. The sociocultural perspective also addresses the richness of children's diversity, including their ethnicity and sex. Understanding the cultural heritages and historical problems of children from various ethnic groups is necessary for effective education and psychological intervention.

1.3 Dominant Themes in Child Development

How do nature and nurture influence child development?

Development would appear to reflect the interaction of nature (genetics) and nurture (nutrition, cultural and family backgrounds, and opportunities to learn about the world).

Is development continuous or discontinuous?

Maturational, psychoanalytic, and cognitive-developmental theorists see development as discontinuous (occurring in stages). Aspects of physical development, such as the adolescent growth spurt, do occur in stages. Learning theorists tend to see development as more continuous.

Are children active ("prewired" to act on the world) or passive (shaped by experience)?

Bronfenbrenner and Bandura do not see children as entirely active or entirely passive. They believe that children are influenced by the environment but that the influence is reciprocal.

1.4 How Do We Study Child Development?

What is the scientific method?

The scientific method is a systematic way of formulating and answering research questions that includes formulating a research question, developing a hypothesis, testing the hypothesis, drawing conclusions, and publishing results.

What methods of observation do developmentalists use to gather information about children?

Developmentalists use naturalistic observation, the case study, and the survey. Naturalistic observation is conducted in "the field"—in the actual settings in which children develop. The case study is a carefully drawn account or biography of the behaviour of a child. Information may be derived from diaries, observation, questionnaires, standardized tests, interviews, and public records. Surveys can be used to learn about behaviour and mental processes that cannot be observed in the natural setting or studied experimentally.

What does it mean to correlate information?

Correlation enables researchers to determine whether one behaviour or trait is related to another. A correlation coefficient can vary between +1.00 and −1.00. Correlational studies can reveal relationships but not cause and effect.

What is an experiment?

In an experiment, an experimental group receives a treatment (the independent variable) while another group (a control group) does not. Subjects are observed to determine whether the treatment has an effect.

How do researchers study development over time?

Longitudinal research studies the same children repeatedly over time. Cross-sectional research observes and compares children of different ages. A drawback to cross-sectional research is the cohort effect. Cross-sequential research combines the longitudinal and cross-sectional methods by breaking down the span of the ideal longitudinal study into convenient segments.

1.5 Ethical Considerations

What ethical guidelines are involved in research in child development?

Ethical standards are established to promote the dignity of the individual, foster human welfare, and maintain scientific integrity. Researchers are not to use treatments that may do harm. Subjects must participate voluntarily.

Key Terms

child   4
infancy   4
development   4
growth   4
behaviourism   8
theory   8
psychosexual development   9
stage theory   9
psychosocial development   12
life crisis   12
identity crisis   12
identity diffusion   13
identity foreclosure   13
identity moratorium   14
identity achievement   15
classical conditioning   15
stimulus   15
operant conditioning   15
reinforcement   15
positive reinforcer   15

negative reinforcer   15
punishment   15
shaping   16
time-out   16
social cognitive theory   17
cognitive-developmental theory   18
scheme   18
adaptation   19
assimilation   19
accommodation   19
equilibration   19
ethology   21
imprinting   21
neuroscience   22
ecology   22
ecological systems theory   22
microsystem   23
mesosystem   24
exosystem   24
macrosystem   24

chronosystem   24
zone of proximal development (ZPD)   25
scaffolding   25
dynamic systems perspective   26
ethnic groups   26
socioeconomic status (SES)   28
nature   31
nurture   31
genes   31
empirical   33
hypothesis   34
naturalistic observation   34
case study   35
standardized test   35
correlation   36
variables   36
correlation coefficient   36
positive correlation   37
negative correlation   37

Active Learning Resources

Go to **www.nelsonbrain.com** to access *Voyages in Development's* CourseMate, where you will find an interactive eBook, flashcards, Pre-Lecture Quizzes, Section Quizzes, Exam Practice, videos, and more.

btrenkel/iStockphoto

Major Topics

HEREDITY AND CONCEPTION

2

Truth or Fiction?

et's talk about the facts of life. Here are a few of them:

- People cannot breathe underwater (without special equipment).
- People cannot fly (without special equipment).
- Fish cannot learn to speak French or dance an Irish jig, even if you raise them in enriched environments and send them to finishing school.

We cannot breathe underwater or fly because we have not inherited gills or wings. Fish are similarly limited by their heredity. In this chapter, we explore heredity and conception. We could say that development begins long before conception. Development involves the origins of the genetic structures that determine that human embryos will grow arms rather than wings, lungs rather than gills, and hair rather than scales. Our discussion thus begins with an examination of the building blocks of heredity: genes and chromosomes. Then we describe the process of conception and find that the odds against any specific sperm uniting with an ovum are quite literally astronomical.

Monkey Business Images/Shutterstock.com

2.1 The Influence of Heredity on Development: The Nature of Nature

QUESTION » What is meant by heredity? Heredity defines one's nature—which is based on the biological transmission of traits and characteristics from one generation to another. Because of their heredity, fish cannot speak French or do a jig.

Heredity makes possible all things human. The structures we inherit make our behaviour possible *and* impose limits on it. The field within the science of biology that studies heredity is called **genetics**.

Genetic (inherited) influences are fundamental in the transmission of physical traits, such as height, hair texture, and eye colour. Genetics also appears to play a role in intelligence and in traits such as activity level, sociability, shyness, anxiety, empathy, effectiveness as a parent, happiness, and even interest in arts and crafts (Gregory et al., 2009; Ebstein et al., 2010; Knafo & Plomin, 2006a). Genetic factors are also involved in psychological problems such as schizophrenia, depression, and dependence on nicotine, alcohol, and other substances (Kendler et al., 2012; X. Li et al., 2012; van Haren et al., 2012).

Chromosomes and Genes

QUESTION » What are chromosomes and genes? The fundamental units of heredity are microscopic structures called chromosomes and genes. **Chromosomes** are rod-shaped structures found in cells. A normal human cell contains 46 chromosomes organized into 23 pairs. Each chromosome contains thousands of segments called genes. **Genes** are the biochemical materials that regulate the development of traits. Some traits, such as blood type, appear to be transmitted by a single pair of genes—one of which is derived from each parent. Other traits, referred to as **polygenic**, are determined by combinations of pairs of genes.

We have 20 000 to 25 000 genes in every cell of our bodies (Eyre et al., 2006). Genes are segments of large strands of **deoxyribonucleic acid (DNA)**. DNA takes the form of a double spiral, or helix, similar in appearance to a twisting ladder (see Figure 2.1 ■). In all living things, from one-celled animals to fish to people, the sides of the "ladder" consist of alternating segments of phosphate

heredity The transmission of traits and characteristics from parent to child by means of genes.

genetics The branch of biology that studies heredity.

chromosomes Rod-shaped structures that are composed of genes and found within the nuclei of cells.

gene The basic unit of heredity. Genes are composed of deoxyribonucleic acid (DNA).

polygenic Resulting from many genes.

deoxyribonucleic acid (DNA) Genetic material that takes the form of a double helix made up of phosphates, sugars, and bases.

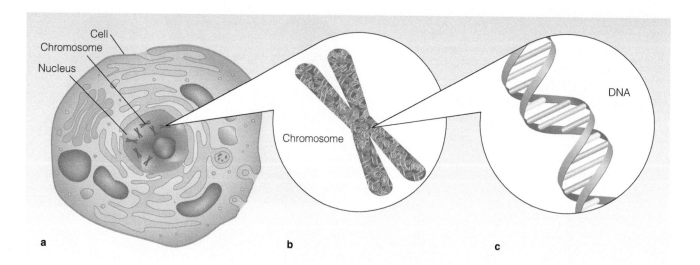

a   b   c

Figure 2.1 ■ The Double Helix of DNA
DNA consists of phosphate, sugar, and a number of bases. It takes the form of a double spiral, or helix.

and simple sugar. The "rungs" of the ladder are attached to the sugars and consist of one of two pairs of bases, either adenine with thymine (A with T) or cytosine with guanine (C with G). The sequence of the rungs is the genetic code that will cause the developing organism to grow arms or wings, skin or scales.

Mitosis and Meiosis

QUESTION » What happens during mitosis and meiosis? We begin life as a single cell, or **zygote**, that divides again and again. There are two types of cell division: mitosis and meiosis. **Mitosis** is the cell-division process by which growth occurs and tissues are replaced. Through mitosis, our genetic code is carried into new cells in our bodies. In mitosis, strands of DNA break apart, or "unzip." The double helix then duplicates. The DNA forms two camps on either side of the cell, and then the cell divides. Each incomplete rung combines with the appropriate "partner" element (that is, G combines with C, and A with T) to form a new complete ladder. The two resulting identical copies of the DNA strand move apart when the cell divides, each becoming a member of one of the newly formed cells. As a consequence, the genetic code is identical in new cells unless **mutations** occur through radiation or other environmental influences. Mutations are also believed to occur by chance, but not often.

Sperm and ova are produced through **meiosis**, or *reduction division*. In meiosis, the 46 chromosomes within the cell nucleus first line up into 23 pairs. The DNA ladders then unzip, leaving unpaired chromosome halves. When the cell divides, one member of each pair goes to each newly formed cell. As a consequence, each new cell nucleus contains only 23 chromosomes, not 46. Thus, a cell that results from meiosis has half the genetic material of a cell that results from mitosis.

When a sperm cell fertilizes an ovum, we receive 23 chromosomes from our father's sperm cell and 23 from our mother's ovum, and the combined chromosomes form 23 pairs (see Figure 2.2 ■). Twenty-two of the pairs are **autosomes**—pairs that look alike and possess genetic information concerning the same set of traits. The 23rd pair consists of the **sex chromosomes**, which look different from other chromosomes and determine our sex. We all receive an X sex chromosome (so called because of its X shape) from our mother. TRUTH OR FICTION REVISITED: It is true that your father determined whether you are a female or a male, by supplying either an X or a Y sex chromosome. If we

zygote A new cell formed from the union of a sperm and an ovum (egg cell); a fertilized egg.

mitosis The form of cell division in which each chromosome splits lengthwise to double in number. Half of each chromosome combines with chemicals to retake its original form and then moves to the new cell.

mutation A sudden variation in a heritable characteristic, such as by an accident that affects the composition of genes.

meiosis The form of cell division in which each pair of chromosomes splits and one member of each pair moves to the new cell. As a result, each new cell has 23 chromosomes.

autosome A member of a pair of chromosomes (with the exception of sex chromosomes).

sex chromosome A chromosome in the shape of a Y (male) or an X (female) that determines the sex of the child.

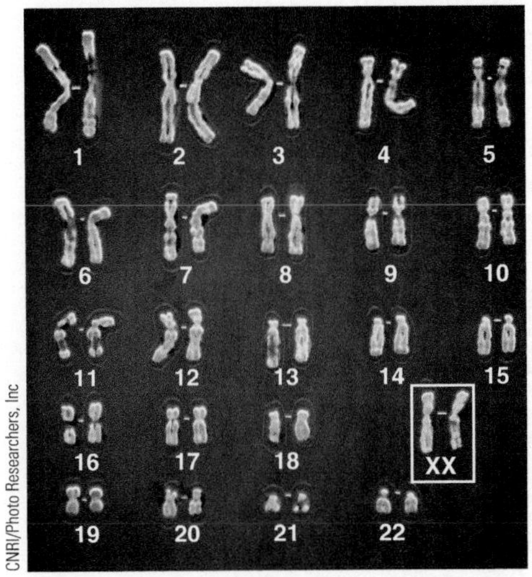

Female

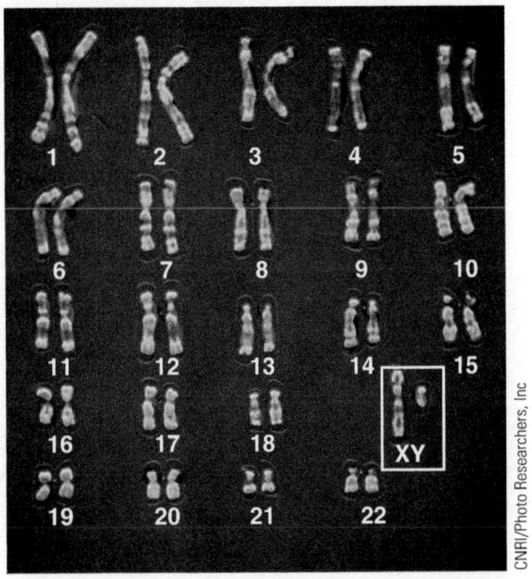

Male

Figure 2.2 ■ The 23 Pairs of Human Chromosomes
People normally have 23 pairs of chromosomes. Females have two X chromosomes, whereas males have an X and a Y sex chromosome.

receive another X sex chromosome from our fathers, we develop into females. If we receive a Y sex chromosome (named after its Y shape) from our fathers, we develop into males.

Identical and Fraternal Twins

QUESTION » **How are twins formed?** Now and then, a zygote divides into two cells that separate so that each subsequently develops into an individual, and those two individuals have the same genetic makeup. Such individuals are known as identical twins, or **monozygotic (MZ) twins**. If the woman produces two ova in the same month and each is fertilized by a different sperm cell, they develop into fraternal twins, or **dizygotic (DZ) twins**.

Twinning rates have been increasing in developed countries for two main reasons: increasing age of mothers and the use of assisted reproductive technologies (Davies et al., 2012; Kurosawa et al., 2012). As women reach the end of their child-bearing years, **ovulation** becomes less regular, resulting in a number of months when more than one ovum is released. Thus, the chances of twins increase with parental age (Hediger, 2011). Fertility drugs also increase the chances of multiple births by causing more than one ovum to ripen and be released during a woman's cycle (Hediger, 2011). About 12 000 multiple births are recorded in Canada each year (Government of Canada, 2014).

About two-thirds of twin pregnancies are DZ twins (NHS Choices, 2011). MZ twins occur with equal frequency in all ethnic groups (about three per 1000 pregnancies), but the incidence of DZ twins varies with age and race (Tong, Caddy, & Short, 1997).

DZ twins run in families. If a woman is a twin, if her mother was a twin, or if she has previously borne twins, the chances rise that she will bear twins (NHS Choices, 2011). Similarly, women who have borne several children have an increased likelihood of twins in subsequent pregnancies.

Dominant and Recessive Traits

QUESTION » **How do genes determine traits?** Traits are determined by pairs of genes. Each member of a pair of genes is referred to as an **allele**. When both of the alleles for a trait, such as hair colour, are the same, the person is said to be **homozygous** for that trait. (*Homo,* in this usage, derives from the Greek root meaning "same," not from the Latin root meaning "man.") When the alleles for a trait differ, the person is **heterozygous** for that trait.

Gregor Mendel (1822–1884), an Austrian monk, established a number of laws of heredity through his work with pea plants. Mendel realized that some traits result from an "averaging" of the genetic instructions carried by the parents. When the effects of both alleles are shown, there is said to be incomplete dominance or **codominance**. Mendel also discovered the "law of dominance." When a *dominant* allele is paired with a *recessive* allele, the trait determined by the dominant allele appears in the offspring. For example, the offspring from the crossing of purebred tall peas and purebred dwarf peas were tall, suggesting that tallness is dominant over dwarfism. We now know that many genes determine **dominant traits** or **recessive traits**.

TRUTH OR FICTION REVISITED: Brown eyes, for instance, are dominant over blue eyes. If one parent carries genes for only brown eyes, and if the other parent carries genes for only blue eyes, the children will have brown eyes. But brown-eyed parents can also carry recessive genes for blue eyes, as shown in Figure 2.3 ■. Similarly, the offspring of Mendel's crossing of purebred tall and purebred dwarf peas carried recessive genes for dwarfism.

---

monozygotic (MZ) twins Twins that derive from a single zygote that has split into two; identical twins. Each MZ twin carries the same genetic code.

dizygotic (DZ) twins Twins that derive from two zygotes; fraternal twins.

ovulation The release of an ovum from an ovary.

allele A member of a pair of genes.

homozygous Having two identical alleles.

heterozygous Having two different alleles.

codominance Condition of a trait that is neither dominant nor recessive in that it is expressed with another trait simultaneously

dominant trait A trait that is expressed.

recessive trait A trait that is not expressed when the gene or genes involved have been paired with dominant genes. Recessive traits are transmitted to future generations and expressed if they are paired with other recessive genes.

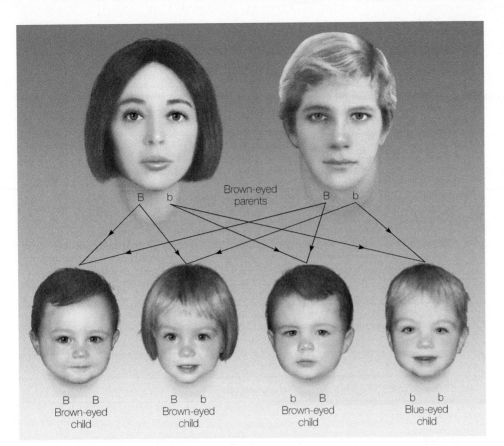

Figure 2.3 ■ **Transmission of Dominant and Recessive Traits**
Each of these two brown-eyed parents carries a gene for blue eyes. Their children have an equal chance of receiving a gene for brown eyes or a gene for blue eyes from each parent.

Brown-eyed parents

B b   B b

B B
Brown-eyed child

B b
Brown-eyed child

b B
Brown-eyed child

b b
Blue-eyed child

If the recessive gene from one parent combines with the recessive gene from the other parent, the recessive trait will be shown. As suggested by Figure 2.3, approximately 25 percent of the offspring of brown-eyed parents who carry recessive genes for blue eye colour will have blue eyes. Mendel found that 25 percent of the offspring of parent peas that carried recessive dwarfism were dwarfs. Table 2.1 ■ lists several other examples of dominant and recessive traits in humans.

People who bear one dominant gene and one recessive gene for a trait are said to be **carriers** of the recessive gene. In the cases of recessive genes that give rise to serious illnesses, carriers of those genes are fortunate to have dominant genes that cancel their effects. In the case of codominance, a common example often cited is the occurrence of individuals who may have the AB blood type. For instance, a person having the A allele and the B allele will have a blood type AB because both the A and B alleles are codominant with each other.

TRUTH OR FICTION REVISITED: It is true that you can carry the genes for a deadly illness and not become sick yourself. This occurs when genes for the illness are recessive, and dominant genes cancel their effects.

Chromosomal or genetic abnormalities can cause health problems. Some chromosomal disorders (such as Down syndrome) reflect abnormalities in the 22 pairs of autosomes; others (such as XYY syndrome) reflect abnormalities in the 23rd pair—the sex chromosomes. Some genetic abnormalities, such as cystic fibrosis, are caused by a single pair of genes; others are caused by combinations of genes. Diabetes mellitus, epilepsy, and peptic ulcers are **multifactorial problems**; that is, they reflect both a genetic predisposition *and* environmental contributors. Chromosomal and genetic abnormalities are discussed in the following sections.

carrier A person who carries and transmits characteristics but does not exhibit them.

multifactorial problems Problems that stem from the interaction of heredity and environmental factors.

TABLE 2.1

Examples of Dominant and Recessive Traits

Dominant Trait	Recessive Trait
Dark hair	Blonde hair
Dark hair	Red hair
Curly hair	Straight hair
Normal colour vision	Red-green colour blindness
Normal vision	Myopia (nearsightedness)
Farsightedness	Normal vision
Normal pigmentation	Deficiency of pigmentation in skin, hair and retina (albinism)
Normal sensitivity to touch	Extremely fragile skin
Normal hearing	Some forms of deafness
Dimples	Lack of dimpling
Type A blood	Type O blood
Type B blood	Type O blood
Tolerance of lactose	Lactose intolerance

2.2 Chromosomal and Genetic Abnormalities

People normally have 46 chromosomes. Children with more or fewer chromosomes usually experience health problems or behavioural abnormalities. A number of disorders have been attributed to defective genes.

Chromosomal Abnormalities

QUESTION » What kinds of disorders are caused by chromosomal abnormalities? Chromosomal abnormalities occur when children do not have the normal complement of 46 chromosomes. The risk of chromosomal abnormalities rises with the age of the parents (Park et al., 2010; Powrie et al., 2010). Although we commonly consider the age of the mother (see Table 2.2 ▪), the age of the

TABLE 2.2

Rates of Chromosomal Defect, by Maternal Age Group in Canada

Age Group	Rate	Risk
<20	0.10%	1 out of 1000
20–34	0.10%	1 out of 1000
35–39	0.27%	1 out of 370
40+	0.79%	1 out of 127

Source: Discharge Abstract Database, Canadian Institute for Health Information; Fichier des hospitalisations MED-ÉCHO, ministère de la Santé et des Services sociaux du Québec.

father apparently plays a role as well. For example, men who are 40 years of age and older are five to six times as likely as men below the age of 30 to have children with autistic disorders (Park et al., 2010; Powrie et al., 2010). Here we consider Down syndrome and sex-linked chromosomal abnormalities.

Down Syndrome

Down syndrome is usually caused by an extra chromosome on the 21st pair, resulting in 47 chromosomes. The probability of having a child with Down syndrome varies positively with the age of the parents: Older parents are more likely to bear children with the syndrome; for example, there is a one in 1650 chance for mother age 20 versus a one in 30 chance for mother aged 45 (Hook, 1981, www.mtsinai.on.ca/FamMedGen). The Canadian Down Syndrome Society describes Down syndrome as a naturally occurring chromosomal arrangement that occurs in approximately one in 800 births in Canada (www.cdss.ca).

A syndrome is a group of symptoms that characterize a disorder. Children with Down syndrome typically have a rounded face, a protruding tongue, a broad, flat nose, and a sloping fold of skin over the inner corners of the eyes (see Figure 2.4 ■). Some parents arrange for cosmetic surgery to alter the appearance of the eyes of children with Down syndrome to discourage their being stereotyped. More than 40 percent of children with Down syndrome have a congenital heart malformation (The Canadian Down Syndrome Society, 2009). Often persons with Down syndrome die from cardiovascular problems by middle age, although modern medicine has extended their lives appreciably. Children with the syndrome show deficits in cognitive development, including language development (Couzens et al., 2011), and in motor development (Virji-Babul et al., 2006). They encounter frequent disorders of the ear, nose, and throat, which also contribute to academic problems (Virji-Babul et al., 2006). Even so, Down syndrome varies widely in its expression.

Children with Down syndrome may often experience adjustment problems in school and in the community at large. Other children are not always sensitive to their needs and feelings and may poke fun at them. Children with Down syndrome and other problems also tend to need more attention from their parents. Parental response is variable; some parents are overwhelmed and a few are abusive, but many parents report that helping to meet the special needs of their children has contributed to their own self-esteem and self-worth (Gowers & Bryan, 2005).

Life for certain individuals with Down syndrome may include going to post-secondary schools, working, and getting married. The Canadian Down Syndrome Society advocates for individuals with Down syndrome to have the opportunities to be contributing members of their communities and the larger society (The Canadian Down Syndrome Society, 2009).

Sex-Linked Chromosomal Abnormalities

Several disorders stem from an abnormal number of sex chromosomes and are therefore said to be **sex-linked chromosomal abnormalities**. Most individuals with an abnormal number of sex chromosomes are infertile. Beyond that common finding, there are many differences, some of them associated with "maleness" or "femaleness" (Frühmesser & Kotzot, 2011; Heard & Turner, 2011).

George Doyle/Thinkstock

Figure 2.4 ■ Down Syndrome
The development and adjustment of children with Down syndrome are related to their acceptance by their families. Children with Down syndrome who are reared at home develop more rapidly and achieve higher levels of functioning than those who are reared in institutions.

Down syndrome A chromosomal abnormality characterized by intellectual disability and caused by an extra chromosome in the 21st pair.

sex-linked chromosomal abnormalities Abnormalities that are transmitted from generation to generation, carried by a sex chromosome, usually an X sex chromosome.

Approximately one male in 700–1000 has an extra Y chromosome. The Y chromosome is associated with maleness, and the extra Y sex chromosome apparently heightens male secondary sex characteristics. For example, XYY males are somewhat taller than average and develop heavier beards. For these kinds of reasons, males with XYY sex chromosomal structure were once referred to as "supermales." But the prefix *super* often implies superior, and it turns out that XYY males tend to have more problems than XY males. For example, they are often mildly delayed, particularly in language development. As part of their "excessive maleness," it was once thought that XYY males were given to aggressive criminal behaviour. When we examine prison populations, we find that the number of XYY males is "overrepresented" relative to their number in the population. However, it may be that the number of XYY males in prisons reflects their level of intelligence rather than aggressiveness.

About one male in 500 has **Klinefelter syndrome**, which is caused by an extra X sex chromosome (an XXY sex-chromosomal pattern). XXY males produce less of the male sex hormone **testosterone** than normal males. As a result, male primary and secondary sex characteristics, such as the testes, deepening of the voice, musculature, and the male pattern of body hair, do not develop properly. XXY males usually have enlarged breasts *(gynecomastia)* and usually exhibit mild intellectual disability, particularly in language skills (Frühmesser & Kotzot, 2011). XXY males are typically treated with testosterone replacement therapy, which can foster growth of sex characteristics and elevate mood, but the therapy does not reverse infertility.

About one female in 2500 has a single X sex chromosome and as a result develops what is called **Turner syndrome**. The external genitals of girls with Turner syndrome are normal, but their ovaries are poorly developed, and they produce little of the female sex hormone **estrogen**. Girls with this problem are shorter than average and infertile. Because of low estrogen production, they do not develop breasts or menstruate. Researchers have connected a specific pattern of cognitive deficits with low estrogen levels: problems in visual-spatial skills, mathematics, and nonverbal memory (Bray et al., 2011; Hong et al., 2011). Some studies find them to be more extroverted and more interested in seeking novel stimulation than other girls (e.g., Boman et al., 2006).

About one female in 1000 has an XXX sex chromosomal structure, *triple X syndrome*. Such girls are normal in appearance. However, they tend to show lower-than-average language skills and poorer memory for recent events. Development of external sexual organs appears normal enough, although there is increased incidence of infertility (N. R. Lee et al., 2011).

Our discussion of chromosomal and genetic abnormalities is summarized in Table 2.3 ■.

Genetic Abnormalities

QUESTION » What kinds of disorders are caused by genetic abnormalities? We will discuss several such disorders, beginning with phenylketonuria.

Phenylketonuria

The enzyme disorder **phenylketonuria (PKU)** is transmitted by a recessive gene and affects about one child in 8000. Therefore, if both parents possess the gene, PKU will be transmitted to one child in four (as in Figure 2.3). Two children in four will possess the gene but will not develop the disorder. These two, like their parents, will be carriers of the disease. One child in four will not receive the recessive gene. Therefore, he or she will not be a carrier.

Klinefelter syndrome A chromosomal disorder found among males that is caused by an extra X sex chromosome and is characterized by infertility and mild intellectual disability.

testosterone A male sex hormone produced mainly by the testes.

Turner syndrome A chromosomal disorder found among females that is caused by having a single X sex chromosome and is characterized by infertility.

estrogen A female sex hormone produced mainly by the ovaries.

phenylketonuria (PKU) A genetic abnormality in which phenylalanine builds up and causes intellectual disability.

Chromosomal and Genetic Disorders

Health Problem	Incidence	Comments	Treatment
CHROMOSOMAL DISORDERS			
Down syndrome www.cdss.ca	1 birth in 700–800 overall; risk increases with parental age.	A condition characterized by a third chromosome on the 21st pair. A child with Down syndrome has a characteristic fold of skin over the eye and intellectual disability.	No treatment, but educational programs are effective; syndrome is usually fatal, as a result of complications, by middle age.
Klinefelter syndrome www.klinefeltersyndrome.org	1 male in 500–900	A disorder affecting males that is characterized by an extra X sex chromosome and that is connected with underdeveloped male secondary sex characteristics and gynecomastia.	Hormone (testosterone) replacement therapy; special education.
Turner syndrome www.turnersyndrome.ca www.turner-syndrome-us.org	1 female in 2500	A disorder that affects females, characterized by single X-sex-chromosomal structure and associated with infertility, and problems in visual-spatial skills and mathematics.	Hormone (estrogen) replacement therapy; special education.
XXX syndrome www.triplo-x.org	1 female in 1000	A sex-chromosomal disorder that affects females and that is connected with mild intellectual disability.	Special education.
XYY syndrome www.aaa.dk/turner/engelsk/index .htm	1 male in 700–1000	A sex-chromosomal disorder that affects males—that is connected with heavy beards, tallness, and mild intellectual disability.	None.
GENETIC DISORDERS			
Cystic fibrosis www.cysticfibrosis.ca www.cff.org	1 birth in every 3600 children born in Canada	A genetic disease caused by a recessive gene in which the pancreas and lungs become clogged with mucus, impairing respiration and digestion.	Physical therapy to loosen mucus and prompt bronchial drainage; antibiotics for infections of respiratory tract; management of diet.
Duchenne muscular dystrophy www.mdausa.org	1 male birth in 3000–5000	A fatal sex-linked degenerative muscle disease caused by a recessive gene, usually found in males and characterized by loss of ability to walk during middle childhood or early adolescence.	None; usually fatal by adolescence because of respiratory infection or cardiovascular damage.
Hemophilia www.hemophilia.ca	1 male in 4000–10 000	A sex-linked disorder in which blood does not clot properly.	Transfusion of blood to introduce clotting factors.
Huntington disease www.hsc-ca.org	1 in 7000 Canadians	A fatal neurological disorder caused by a dominant gene; onset in adulthood.	None; usually fatal within 20 years of onset of symptoms.
Neural tube defects ibis-birthdefects.org/start/ntdfact.htm	1 birth in 1000	Disorders of the brain or spine in which part of the brain is missing, and spina bifida, in which part of the spine is exposed or missing.	None for anencephaly, which is fatal; surgery to close spinal canal in spina bifida.
Phenylketonuria (PKU) www.pkunetwork.org	1 birth in 8000–10 000	A disorder caused by a recessive gene in which children cannot metabolize the amino acid phenylalanine, which builds up in the form of phenylpyruvic acid and causes intellectual disability. PKU is diagnosable at birth.	Controlled by special diet, which can prevent intellectual disability.
Sickle-cell anemia www.ascaa.org	It is most common in West and Central Africa where as many as 25% of the people have sickle cell trait and 1–2% of all babies are born with a form of the disease	A blood disorder caused by a recessive gene that mainly people whose families come from Africa, the Caribbean, the Eastern Mediterranean, Middle East and Asia; deformed blood cells obstruct small blood vessels, decreasing their capacity to carry oxygen.	Transfusions to treat anemia and prevent strokes; antibiotics for infections; anesthetics; fatal to about half of those with disorder before adulthood.
Tay-Sachs disease www.ntsad.org	1 Jewish Canadian of Eastern European origin in 3000–3600	A fatal neurological disorder caused by a recessive gene that primarily afflicts Jews of Eastern European origin.	None; usually fatal by age 3–4.

Children with PKU cannot metabolize an amino acid called phenylalanine. As a consequence, the substance builds up in their bodies and impairs the functioning of the central nervous system. The results are serious: intellectual disability, psychological disorders, and physical problems. We have no cure for PKU, but it can be detected in newborn children through analysis of the blood or urine. Children with PKU who are placed on diets low in phenylalanine within three to six weeks after birth develop normally. The diet prohibits all meat, poultry, fish, dairy products, beans, and nuts. Fruits, vegetables, and some starchy foods are allowed (Dawson et al., 2011). Pediatricians recommend staying on the diet at least until adolescence, and some encourage staying on it for life.

Huntington Disease

Huntington disease (HD) is a fatal, progressive, degenerative disorder and is a dominant trait. Physical symptoms include uncontrollable muscle movements. Psychological symptoms include personality change and loss of intellectual functioning (Rickards et al., 2011). Because the onset of HD is delayed until middle adulthood, many individuals with the defect have borne children, only to discover years later that they and possibly half of their offspring will inevitably develop it. Fortunately, the disorder is rare—affecting about one Canadian in 7000 (Huntington Society of Canada). Medicines are helpful in treating some of the symptoms of HD, but they do not cure it.

Sickle-Cell Anemia

Sickle-cell anemia is caused by a recessive gene. Sickle-cell anemia is most common among people whose families come from Africa, the Caribbean, the Eastern Mediterranean, Middle East, and Asia. In sickle-cell anemia, red blood cells take on the shape of a sickle and clump together, obstructing small blood vessels and decreasing the oxygen supply. The lessened oxygen supply can impair cognitive skills and academic performance (Feig et al., 2011). Physical problems include painful and swollen joints, jaundice, and potentially fatal conditions such as pneumonia, stroke, and heart and kidney failure.

Tay-Sachs Disease

Tay-Sachs disease is also caused by a recessive gene. It causes the central nervous system to degenerate, resulting in death. The disorder is most commonly found among children in Jewish families of Eastern European background. About one in 30 Jewish North Americans from this background carries the recessive gene for Tay-Sachs. Children with the disorder progressively lose control over their muscles. They experience visual and auditory sensory losses, develop intellectual disability, become paralyzed, and die toward the end of early childhood, by about the age of five.

Cystic Fibrosis

Cystic fibrosis, also caused by a recessive gene, is the most common fatal hereditary disease affecting Canadian children and young adults. Approximately one in 3600 children born in Canada have cystic fibrosis (Canadian Cystic Fibrosis Society, 2013). Cystic fibrosis is a genetic disease, and occurs when a child inherits two abnormal genes, one from each parent. Approximately, one in 25 Canadians are carriers of the gene responsible for cystic fibrosis. Children with the disease suffer from excessive production of thick mucus that clogs the pancreas and lungs. Most victims die of respiratory infections in their 20s.

Huntington disease (HD) A fatal genetic neurological disorder whose onset is in middle age.

sickle-cell anemia A genetic disorder that decreases the blood's capacity to carry oxygen.

Tay-Sachs disease A fatal genetic neurological disorder.

cystic fibrosis A fatal genetic disorder in which mucus obstructs the lungs and pancreas.

Sex-Linked Genetic Abnormalities

Some genetic defects, such as **hemophilia**, are carried on only the X sex chromosome. For this reason, they are referred to as **sex-linked genetic abnormalities**. These defects also involve recessive genes. Females, who have two X sex chromosomes, are less likely than males to show sex-linked disorders, because the genes that cause the disorder would have to be present on both of a female's sex chromosomes for the disorder to be expressed. Sex-linked diseases are more likely to afflict sons of female carriers because males have only one X sex chromosome, which they inherit from their mothers.

One form of **muscular dystrophy**, Duchenne muscular dystrophy, is sex-linked. Muscular dystrophy is characterized by a weakening of the muscles, which can lead to wasting away, inability to walk, and sometimes death. Other sex-linked abnormalities include diabetes, colour blindness, and some types of night blindness.

Genetic Counselling and Prenatal Testing

QUESTION » How do health professionals determine whether children will have genetic or chromosomal abnormalities? It is now possible to detect the genetic abnormalities that are responsible for hundreds of diseases. In an effort to help parents inform and educate parents about various genetic disorders, **genetic counselling** is widely used. In fact, many Canadian hospitals have specific programs dealing with genetic counselling. One such program at Mount Sinai Hospital in Toronto is called the Prenatal and Diagnosis and Medical Genetics Program (www.mtsinai.on.ca/pdmg). Genetic counsellors compile information about a couple's genetic heritage to explore whether their children might develop genetic abnormalities. Couples who face a high risk of passing along genetic defects to their children sometimes decide to adopt children rather than conceive their own.

In addition, **prenatal** testing can indicate whether the embryo or fetus is carrying genetic abnormalities. Prenatal testing includes amniocentesis, chorionic villus sampling, ultrasound, and blood tests.

Amniocentesis

Amniocentesis is usually performed on the mother at about 14–16 weeks after conception, although many physicians perform the procedure earlier ("early amniocentesis"). In this method, the health professional uses a syringe (needle) to withdraw fluid from the amniotic sac (see Figure 2.5 ■). The fluid contains cells that are sloughed off by the fetus. The cells are separated from the amniotic fluid, grown in a culture, and then examined microscopically for genetic and chromosomal abnormalities.

Amniocentesis is very common among Canadian women who become pregnant after the age of 35, because the chances of Down syndrome increase dramatically as women approach or pass the age of 40. But women carrying the children of aging fathers may also wish to have amniocentesis. Amniocentesis can detect the presence of well over 100 chromosomal and genetic abnormalities in the fetus, including sickle-cell anemia, Tay-Sachs disease, **spina bifida**, muscular dystrophy, and Rh incompatibility. Women (or their partners) who carry or have a family history of any of these disorders are advised to have amniocentesis performed. If the test reveals the presence of a serious disorder, the parents may decide to abort the fetus, or they may decide to continue the pregnancy and prepare themselves to raise a child who has special needs.

hemophilia A genetic disorder in which blood does not clot properly.

sex-linked genetic abnormalities Abnormalities resulting from genes that are found on the X sex chromosome.

muscular dystrophy A chronic disease characterized by a progressive wasting away of the muscles.

genetic counselling Advice concerning the probabilities that a couple's children will show genetic abnormalities.

prenatal Before birth.

amniocentesis A procedure for drawing out and examining fetal cells sloughed off into amniotic fluid to determine whether various disorders are present.

spina bifida A neural tube defect that causes abnormalities of the brain and spine.

Figure 2.5 ■
Amniocentesis
Amniocentesis allows prenatal identification of certain genetic and chromosomal disorders via the examination of genetic material sloughed off by the fetus into the amniotic fluid. Amniocentesis also enables parents to learn the sex of their unborn child. Would you want to know?

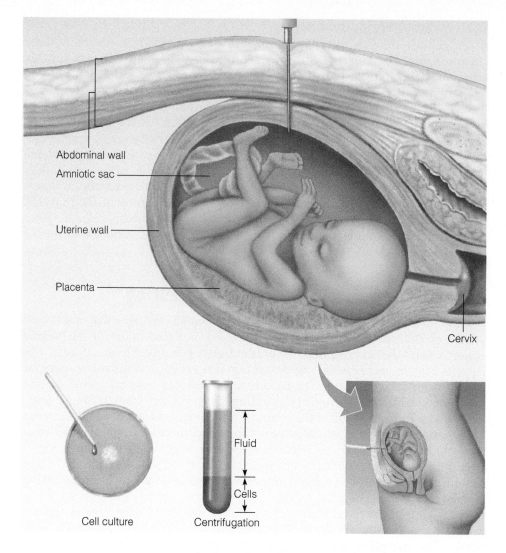

Abdominal wall
Amniotic sac
Uterine wall
Placenta
Cervix
Fluid
Cells
Cell culture
Centrifugation

Amniocentesis also permits parents to learn the sex of their unborn child through examination of the sex chromosomes, but most parents learn the sex of their baby earlier by means of ultrasound. Amniocentesis carries some risk of miscarriage (about one woman in 100 who undergo the procedure will miscarry), so health professionals do not conduct it to learn the sex of the child.

Chorionic Villus Sampling
Chorionic villus sampling (CVS) is similar to amniocentesis but offers the advantage of diagnosing fetal abnormalities earlier in pregnancy. CVS is carried out between the 9th and 12th weeks of pregnancy. A small syringe is inserted through the vagina into the **uterus**. The syringe gently sucks out a few of the threadlike projections (villi) from the outer membrane that envelops the amniotic sac and fetus. Results are available within days of the procedure. CVS has not been used as frequently as amniocentesis, because many studies have shown that CVS carries a slightly greater risk of spontaneous abortion.

The relative risks of amniocentesis and CVS are highly controversial. Some studies have suggested that the risks of the procedures are about equivalent (Simpson, 2000). However, there are two types of amniocentesis: "late" and

chorionic villus sampling A method for the prenatal detection of genetic abnormalities that samples the membrane enveloping the amniotic sac and fetus.

uterus The hollow organ within females in which the embryo and fetus develop.

"early," and there are also different types of CVS. More recent studies suggest that both amniocentesis and CVS increase the risk of miscarriage and that the risks might *not* be equal (Alfirevic et al., 2003; Philip et al., 2004). Another factor to consider, sad to say, is that some practitioners are better at carrying out these procedures than others. If you are considering having CVS or amnio-centesis, ask your doctor for the latest information about the risks of each procedure. Also ask around to make sure that your doctor is the right doctor to carry out the procedure.

Ultrasound

For more than half a century, the military has been using sonar to locate enemy submarines. Sonar sends high-frequency sound waves into the depths of the ocean, and the waves bounce back from objects such as submarines (and whales and schools of fish and the ocean floor) to reveal their presence. Within the past generation, health professionals have also introduced the use of (very!) high-frequency sound waves to obtain information about the fetus. The sounds waves are too high in frequency to be heard by the human ear and are called **ultrasound**. However, they are reflected by the fetus, and a computer can use the information to generate a picture (visual) of the fetus. The picture is referred to as a **sonogram**, a term derived from roots meaning "written with sound" (see Figure 2.6 ■).

Ultrasound is used in amniocentesis and CVS to better determine the position of the fetus. It helps the physician to make sure that the needle enters the sac surrounding the fetus and not the fetus itself—although a mistake will *not* be lethal to the fetus. Ultrasound is also used to locate fetal structures when intrauterine transfusions are necessary for the survival of a fetus with Rh disease.

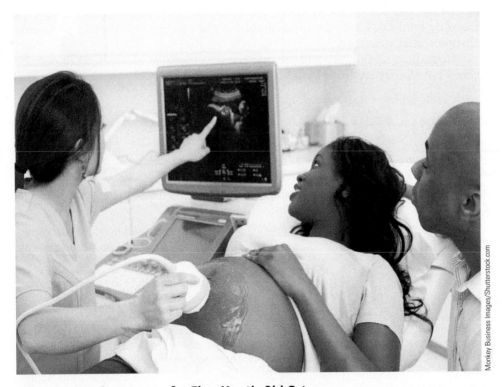

Monkey Business Images/Shutterstock.com

ultrasound Sound waves too high in pitch to be sensed by the human ear.

sonogram A procedure for using ultrasonic sound waves to create a picture of an embryo or fetus.

Figure 2.6 ■ Sonogram of a Five-Month-Old Fetus
In the ultrasound technique, sound waves are bounced off the fetus and provide a picture, called a sonogram, that enables professionals to detect various abnormalities.

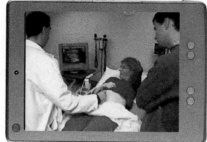
Ultrasound is used to track the growth of the fetus, to determine fetal age and sex, and to detect multiple pregnancies and structural abnormalities. Although ultrasound is beneficial for pregnant women whose fetuses are at risk of serious medical problems, it may not improve birth outcomes for women with low-risk pregnancies.

Blood Tests

Parental blood tests can reveal the presence of recessive genes for a variety of disorders, such as sickle-cell anemia, Tay-Sachs disease, and cystic fibrosis. When both parents carry genes for these disorders, the disorders can be detected in the fetus by means of amniocentesis or CVS.

Another kind of blood test, the **alpha-fetoprotein (AFP) assay**, is used to detect neural tube defects such as spina bifida and certain chromosomal abnormalities. Neural tube defects cause an elevation in the AFP level in the mother's blood. Elevated AFP levels also are associated with increased risk of fetal death. However, the mother's AFP level varies with other factors. For this reason, the diagnosis of a neural tube defect is confirmed by other methods of observation, such as amniocentesis or ultrasound.

A blood test administered as early as seven weeks into pregnancy can determine the sex of the fetus (Devaney et al., 2011). Health professionals examine fetal DNA found in the blood for the characteristic male or female chromosomal structure.

In the next section, we will see that our development is affected not only by genes but also by environmental influences.

alpha-fetoprotein (AFP) assay
A blood test that assesses the mother's blood level of alpha-fetoprotein, a substance that is linked to fetal neural tube defects.

Active Review

1. A normal human cell contains 46 _____, which are organized into 23 pairs.

2. Each chromosome contains thousands of genes, segments of _____ acid (DNA), which takes the form of a twisting ladder.

3. _____ is the cell-division process by which growth occurs and tissues are replaced.

4. Sperm and ova are produced through _____.

5. When a zygote divides into two cells that separate so that each develops into an individual, _____ (MZ) twins result.

6. When two ova are fertilized by different sperm cells, they develop into _____ (DZ) twins.

7. People who bear one dominant gene and one recessive gene for a trait are said to be _____ of the recessive gene.

8. In persons with _____, the 21st pair of chromosomes has an extra, or third, chromosome.

9. Phenylketonuria (PKU) is transmitted by a (dominant or recessive?) gene.

10. _____ anemia is caused by a recessive gene and is most common among people of African descent.

11. In the prenatal testing method of _____, fetal cells found in amniotic fluid are examined for genetic abnormalities.

12. The use of _____ can form a picture ("sonogram") of the fetus.

Reflect & Relate: Many methods of prenatal testing, including amniocentesis, some blood tests, and ultrasound, can enable parents to learn the sex of their fetus. If you were having such testing, would you want to know the sex of your fetus, or would you prefer to wait? Explain.

2.3 Heredity and the Environment: Considering the Interplay between Nature and Nurture

Now that we have studied heredity, we know why we have arms rather than wings and hairy skin rather than feathers. Well, perhaps not so hairy for many of us. But none of us is the result of heredity alone.

Reaction Range

QUESTION » **What is the difference between our genotypes and our phenotypes?** Heredity provides the biological basis for a **reaction range** in the expression of traits. Our inherited traits can vary in expression, depending on environmental conditions. In addition to inheritance, the development of our traits is influenced by nutrition, learning, exercise, and—unfortunately—accident and illness. A potential Shakespeare who is reared in poverty, seldom leaves his hometown, and is never taught to read or write will not create a *Hamlet*. Our traits and behaviours represent the interaction of heredity and environment. The sets of traits that we inherit from our parents are referred to as our **genotypes**. Our actual sets of traits are called our **phenotypes**. Our phenotypes develop because of both genetic and environmental influences. Another way to describe reaction range is that it is the range of phenotypic expression depending on different environments of different quality. Different people have different reaction ranges. That is, two different individuals might respond differently to the same environment, as well two siblings may each respond and react differently to their parents' divorce.

Canalization

Our genotypes lead to **canalization** of the development of various traits, both physical and—to some degree—psychological (Del Giudice et al., 2009). Environmental restrictions, such as scarcity of food, may prevent children from reaching heights within their reaction ranges. However, if food becomes more readily available, there is a tendency to "snap back" into the genetically determined "canal" (Crusio, 2006). Infant motor development is canalized in that the sequence of development is invariant: rolling over, sitting up, crawling, creeping, and so on. Similarly, the sequence of development of types of two-word utterances is invariant. The development of personality and intelligence is apparently less canalized, with the environment playing stronger roles.

Genetic-Environmental Correlation

There is also genetic-environmental correlation (Gottlieb, 2007; Narusyte et al., 2008). One of the problems in sorting out the influences of heredity and environment, or nature and nurture, is that genes in part determine the environments to which people are exposed. Developmental psychologist Sandra Scarr (1998) described three types of correlations between genetic and environmental influences, and they are related to the age of the individual.

Passive Correlation
Not only do children's biological parents contribute genes to their offspring, but they also intentionally and unintentionally place their offspring in certain kinds of environments. Just as artistically oriented parents are likely to transmit genes that predispose their children to having an interest in the arts,

reaction range The variability in the expression of inherited traits as they are influenced by environmental factors.

genotype The genetic form, or constitution, of a person as determined by heredity.

phenotype The actual form or constitution of a person as determined by heredity and environmental factors.

canalization The tendency of growth rates to return to genetically determined patterns after undergoing environmentally induced change.

they are also likely to expose their children to artistic activities, such as visits to museums and piano lessons. Athletic parents may enroll their children in soccer lessons and sports camps. These artistic and these athletic parents might also ridicule the interests of the other group, purposefully contributing to the development of their children's attitudes. This type of correlation is termed a **passive genetic-environmental correlation** because the children have no choice in the matter.

Evocative Correlation

An **evocative genetic-environmental correlation** exists because the child's genotype is connected with behaviours that evoke, or elicit, certain kinds of responses from others. These responses, in turn, become part of the social environment of the child. A sociable, active, even-tempered infant is likely to receive more positive social stimulation from caregivers and other people than a passive, socially withdrawn infant. A good-looking infant and child is likely to evoke more attentive and playful responses from others, including his or her mother, and possibly develop more skillful social behaviour as a result (Principe & Langlois, 2012). Teachers are more likely to befriend and smile at children who are interested in their subjects, pay attention, and avoid misbehaviour.

Genetic-Environmental Correlation

Both of these girls are athletic, but the one on the left immediately felt at home during a ballet class and chose to continue. The one on the right was not at all tempted by dance, but she enjoyed soccer and was competitive, so she joined her school's soccer team.

JHershPhoto/Shutterstock.com

gemenacom/iStockphoto

passive genetic-environmental correlation The correlation between the genetic endowment parents give their children and the environments in which they place their children.

evocative genetic-environmental correlation The correlation between the child's genetic endowment and the responses the child elicits from other people.

active genetic-environmental correlation The correlation between the child's genetic endowment and the choices the child makes about which environments they will seek.

niche-picking Choosing environmental conditions that foster one's genetically transmitted abilities and interests.

epigenesis The view that development reflects continual bidirectional exchanges between one's genotype and one's environmental conditions.

Active Correlation

As we mature, we are more likely to take an active, conscious role in choosing or creating our environments. This attitude is called an **active genetic-environmental correlation**. The intelligent, highly motivated child may ask to be placed in honours classes. The strong, coordinated, aggressive child may join athletic teams. The child or adolescent with less academic or athletic talent may choose to be a "loner" or join a deviant peer group in which friends reinforce his or her behaviours. At some point, children may ask caregivers to help them attend activities that enable them to pursue genetically inspired interests. Adolescents may also select after-school activities that are connected with their academic, artistic, or athletic interests. Choosing environments that allow us to develop inherited preferences is termed **niche-picking** (Groothuis & Trillmich, 2011; Scarr & McCartney, 1983).

The Epigenetic Framework

The relationship between genetic and environmental influences is not a one-way street. Instead, it is bidirectional. Even though our genes affect the development of our traits and behaviours, our traits and behaviours also prompt certain kinds of responses from other people and lead us to place ourselves in certain environments. These environments—specialized schools, after-school activities, museums, the theatre, certain films and television programs—all affect the manner in which genes are expressed. According to what developmentalists call **epigenesis**, or the *epigenetic framework* (see Figure 2.7 ■), our development reflects continuing bidirectional exchanges between our genetic heritages and the environments in which we find ourselves or place ourselves (Gottlieb, 2007; Groothuis & Trillmich, 2011). Especially important from a developmental perspective is the concept that the environment has an impact on gene expression not only during early childhood but also throughout development (Meaney, 2010).

Although the relationship between nature and nurture is complex, researchers have developed a number of strategies to help sort out the effects of heredity and of the environment on development.

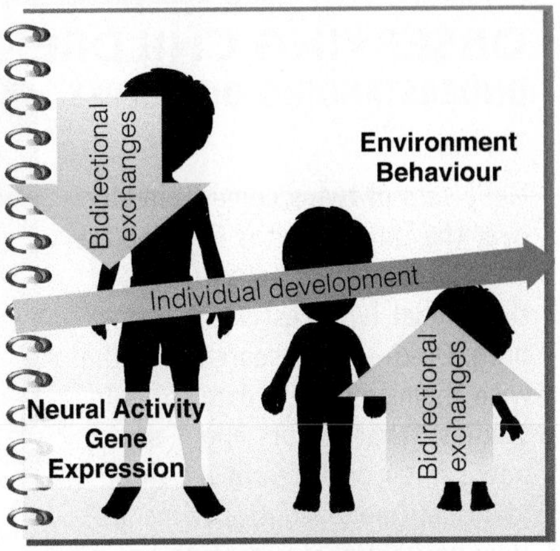

Kinship Studies: Are the Traits of Relatives Related?

QUESTION » How do researchers sort out the effects of genetics and environmental influences on development? To help sort out the effects of genetics and environmental influences on development, researchers study the distribution of a particular behaviour pattern among relatives who differ in degree of genetic closeness. The more closely people are related, the more genes they have in common. Parents and children have a 50 percent overlap in their genetic endowments, and so do siblings (brothers and sisters), on average. Aunts and uncles have a 25 percent overlap with nieces and nephews, and so do grandparents with their grandchildren. First cousins share 12.5 percent of their genetic endowment. Thus, if genes are implicated in a physical trait or behaviour pattern, people who are more closely related should be more likely to share the pattern. You probably look more like a parent or brother or sister than like a cousin, and you probably look very little like a stranger.

Figure 2.7 ■ The Epigenetic Framework
Development as a reflection of ongoing bidirectional exchanges between our genes and the environment.

Twin Studies: Looking in the Genetic Mirror

Monozygotic (MZ) twins share 100 percent of their genes, whereas dizygotic (DZ) twins have a 50 percent overlap, just as other siblings do. If MZ twins show greater similarity on some trait or behaviour than DZ twins, a genetic basis for the trait or behaviour is indicated.

MZ twins resemble each other more closely than DZ twins in physical and psychological traits. MZ twins are more likely to look alike, to be similar in height, and even to have similar cholesterol levels than DZ twins (Plomin, 2002). This finding holds even when the MZ twins are reared apart and the DZ twins are reared together (Bouchard & Loehlin, 2001). Other physical similarities between pairs of MZ twins may be more subtle, but they are also strong. For example, research shows that MZ twin sisters begin to menstruate about one to two months apart, whereas DZ twins begin to menstruate about a year apart. MZ twins are more alike than DZ twins in their blood pressure, brain wave patterns, speech patterns, gestures, and mannerisms (Bouchard & Loehlin, 2001; Plomin, 2002). Heredity even has an effect on their preference for coffee or tea (Luciano et al., 2005).

MZ twins resemble one another more strongly than DZ twins in intelligence; in personality traits such as sociability, anxiety, friendliness, conformity, and even happiness; and in the tendency to choose marriage over the single life (Hur, 2005; Johnson et al., 2004; McCrae et al., 2000). David Lykken and Mike Csikszentmihalyi (2001) suggested that we inherit a tendency to have a certain level of happiness. Despite the ups and downs of life, we tend to drift back to our usual levels of cheerfulness or irritability. It seems that our bank accounts, our levels of education, and our marital status are less influential than genes as contributors to happiness. Heredity is also a key contributor to psychological developmental factors such as cognitive functioning

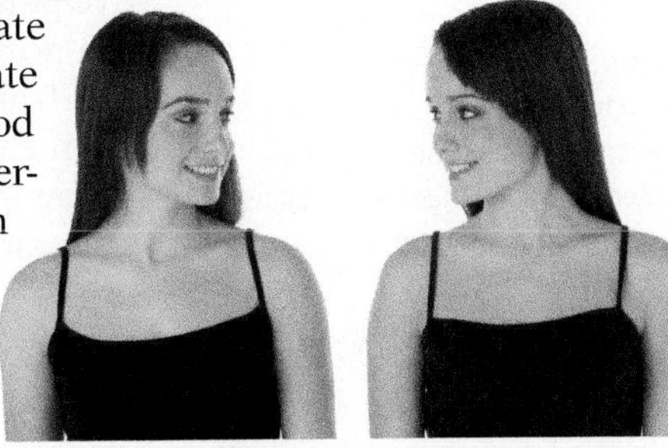

Twins
Monozygotic (MZ) twins, such as this pair of adolescents, share 100 percent of their genes. Dizygotic (DZ) twins, like other siblings, share 50 percent of their genes.

OBSERVING CHILDREN, UNDERSTANDING OURSELVES

Twins

Many sets of twins come from all over the United States to celebrate their likenesses and differences at the annual Twin Festival in Twinsburg, Ohio—and researchers gather with them to collect data for twin studies. What factors might affect how similar or different a pair of identical (monozygotic) twins are? How influential is parenting on children's behaviour? Why might genetics influence social attitudes?

From Rathus. *Childhood and Adolescence*, 5E. © 2014 South-Western, a part of Cengage Learning, Inc. Reproduced by permission. www.cengage.com/permissions

Go to www.nelson.com/voyages2ce to watch the video, answer the questions, and e-mail your responses to your professor.

and early signs of attachment (such as smiling, cuddling, and expressing fear of strangers) (Plomin, 2002). Twin studies show that at least half of the variation in the tendency to develop obesity is genetic (Hebebrand & Hinney, 2009). MZ twins are more likely than DZ twins to share psychological disorders such as **autism**, depression, schizophrenia, and even vulnerability to alcoholism (Belmonte & Carper, 2006; Lundstrom et al., 2012; Slane et al., 2012).

Of course, twin studies are not perfect. MZ twins may resemble each other more closely than DZ twins partly because they are treated more similarly. MZ twins frequently are dressed identically, and parents themselves sometimes have difficulty telling them apart.

One way to get around this problem is to find and compare MZ twins who were reared in different homes. Any similarities between MZ twins reared apart cannot be explained by a shared home environment and would appear to be largely a result of heredity. In the fascinating Minnesota Study of Twins Reared Apart (Bouchard et al., 1990; Haworth et al., 2009; Lykken, 2006), researchers have been measuring the physiological and psychological characteristics of 56 sets of MZ adult twins who were separated in infancy and reared in different homes. The MZ twins reared apart are about as similar as MZ twins reared together on a variety of measures of intelligence, personality, temperament, occupational and leisure-time interests, and social attitudes. These traits thus appear to have a genetic underpinning.

Adoption Studies

Adoption studies in which children are separated from their natural parents at an early age and reared by adoptive parents provide special opportunities for sorting out nature and nurture. As we will see in discussions of the origins of intelligence (see Chapter 12) and of various problem behaviours (see Chapters 10 and 13), psychologists look for the relative similarities between children and their adoptive and natural parents. When children who are reared by adoptive parents are nonetheless more similar to their natural parents in a trait, that is a powerful argument for a genetic role in the appearance of that trait.

Traits are determined by pairs of genes. One member of each pair comes from each parent, and they are joined in the process called *conception*. In the following section, we talk about the birds and the bees and the microscope to understand how conception works.

autism A developmental disorder characterized by failure to relate to others, communication problems, intolerance of change, and ritualistic behaviour (see Chapter 7).

Active Review

13. The sets of traits that we inherit are referred to as our (genotype or phenotype?).

14. The actual traits that we display at any point in time are the product of genetic and environmental influences and are called our (genotypes or phenotypes?).

15. Parents and children have a _____ percent overlap in their genetic endowments.

16. _____ (MZ) twins share 100 percent of their genes.

17. _____ (DZ) twins have a 50 percent overlap, as do other siblings.

Reflect & Relate: Do you know any sets of twins? Are they monozygotic or dizygotic? How are they alike? How do they differ?

2.4 Conception: Against All Odds

QUESTION » **What process unites the genes of the parents?** On a balmy day in October, Marta and her partner Jorge rush to catch the train to their jobs in the city. Marta's workday is outwardly the same as any other. Within her body, however, a drama is unfolding. Yesterday, hormones had caused an ovarian follicle to rupture, releasing its egg cell, or ovum. Like all women, Marta possessed all the ova she would ever have at birth, each encased in a follicle. How this particular follicle was selected to ripen and release its ovum this month remains a mystery. But for the next day or so, Marta will be capable of conceiving.

Yesterday morning, Marta had used her ovulation-timing kit, which showed that she was about to ovulate. That night, Marta and Jorge had made love, hoping that Marta would conceive. Jorge ejaculated hundreds of millions of sperm—a normal amount. Only a few thousand survived the journey through the cervix and uterus to the fallopian tube that contained the ovum, released just hours earlier. Of these, a few hundred remained to bombard the ovum. One succeeded in penetrating the ovum's covering, resulting in conception. From a single cell formed by the union of sperm and ovum, a new life began to form. The zygote is only about 1/70 of a centimetre across—a tiny beginning for the drama about to take place.

Marta is 37 years old. Four months into her pregnancy, Marta undergoes amniocentesis in order to check for the presence of chromosomal abnormalities, such as Down syndrome. (Down syndrome is more common among children born to women in their late 30s and older.) Amniocentesis also indicates the sex of the fetus. Although many parents prefer to know the sex of their baby before it is born, Marta and Jorge ask their doctor not to inform them. "Why ruin the surprise?" Jorge tells his friends. So Marta and Jorge are left to debate boys' names *and* girls' names for the next few months.

The process that brings together the genes from both parents is called **conception**—the union of an ovum and a sperm cell. Conception, from one perspective, is the beginning of a new human life. But conception is also the end of a fantastic voyage in which a single one of the several hundred thousand ova produced by the woman unites with one of the hundreds of millions of sperm produced by the man in the average ejaculate.

Ova

TRUTH OR FICTION REVISITED: At birth girls already have ova, but they are immature in form. The ovaries also produce the female hormones estrogen and progesterone. At puberty, in response to hormonal command, some ova begin to mature (see Figure 2.8 ■). Each month, one egg (occasionally more than one) is released from its ovarian follicle about midway through the menstrual cycle and enters a nearby **fallopian tube**. It might take three to four days for an egg to be propelled by small, hairlike structures called cilia and, perhaps, by contractions in the wall of the tube, along the several centimetres of the fallopian tube to the uterus. Unlike sperm, eggs do not propel themselves.

If the egg is not fertilized, it is discharged through the uterus and the vagina, along with the **endometrium** that had formed to support an embryo, in the menstrual flow. During a woman's reproductive years, only about 400 ova (that is, one in 1000) will ripen and be released.

In an early stage of development, egg cells contain 46 chromosomes. Each developing egg cell contains two X sex chromosomes. After meiosis, each ovum contains 23 chromosomes, one of which is an X sex chromosome.

Ova are much larger than sperm. Both the chicken egg and the 15-centimetre ostrich egg are just one cell, although the sperm of these birds are microscopic. Human ova are barely visible to the eye, but their bulk is thousands of times greater than that of sperm cells.

conception The union of a sperm cell and an ovum that occurs when the chromosomes of each of these cells combine to form 23 new pairs.

fallopian tube A tube through which ova travel from an ovary to the uterus.

endometrium The inner lining of the uterus.

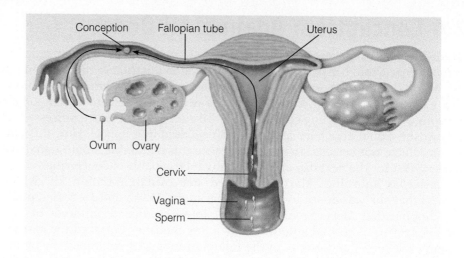

Figure 2.8 ■ Female Reproductive Organs
Conception is something of an obstacle course. Sperm must survive the pull of gravity and vaginal acidity, risk winding up in the wrong fallopian tube, and surmount other hurdles before they reach the ovum.

A CLOSER LOOK DIVERSITY

Where Are the Missing Chinese Girls?

It is no secret that most people in most cultures prefer that their child, or at least their first child, be a boy. According to traditional gender roles, boys carry on the business of the family and represent continuity of the lineage (Trent, 2011). They pass on the family name. In less developed nations such as China and India, especially in rural areas, sons also represent protection from neglect and poverty in the parents' later years. These attitudes are reflected in verses from the ancient Chinese *Book of Songs*, written some 3000 years ago:

When a son is born,
Let him sleep on the bed,
Clothe him with fine clothes,
And give him jade with which to play ...
When a daughter is born,
Let her sleep on the ground,
Wrap her in common wrappings,
And give broken tiles with which to play ...

When Mao Zedong took power in 1949, his Communist government replaced family support in old age with state support and also rejected male superiority. There remained a balance in the numbers of males and females in the population throughout most of the 1970s. But beginning in 1979, China attempted to gain control of its mushrooming population of more than a billion by enforcing strict limits on family size. One child per family is allowed in urban areas. A second child is usually allowed in rural areas after five

Chinese people show a preference for boys and, because they usually have just one chance to have a child, often use sex-selection techniques to guarantee having a child of the preferred sex.

years have passed, especially if the first child is a girl (Li, 2004). Because Chinese families, like the families of old, continue to prefer boys, the ratio of boys to girls began to change in response to the limitations on family size (Trent, 2011).

As shown in Table 2.4 ■, the desirability of having small families has generally caught on in the Chinese population. That is, the great majority of women interviewed in a recent survey expressed the desire to have either one or two children. However, there were some differences

Continued

Continued

Continued

● **TABLE 2.4**

Preferred Number of Children among Chinese Women (Percent Expressing Preference)

Age of Woman	Preferred Number of Children			
	0	1	2	3 or more
15–19	2.1	49	45	1.9
20–29	1.3	47	48	2.1
30–39	0.8	32	60	6.1
40–49	1.0	27	62	11.0
Area of Residence				
Urban	3.1	52	43	1.5
Rural	0.4	30	61	7.5
Level of Education				
Illiterate or semiliterate	0.4	17	67	14.0
Primary school	0.3	25	65	8.5
Secondary school	2.1	46	47	2.5
College	4.0	49	44	2.2

Note: Number of women interviewed: 39 344.
Source: National Family Planning and Reproductive Health Survey.
Ding & Hesketh (2006).

according to the woman's age, her area of residence, and her level of education. How would you account for them?

Since more boys than girls die in infancy, a "normal" ratio of boys to girls is about 106 to 100, which characterized China in the 1970s. The ratio was about 108.5 boys to 100 girls in the early 80s, then 111 to 100 in 1990, and 117 to 100 in 2000. It is now at least 120 boys for every 100 girls, and some estimates put it as high as 123 to 100 (Ding & Hesketh, 2006).

Therefore, a great shortage of Chinese women is being created, which may not be much of a problem for parents but will certainly be a problem for men seeking mates in future years. Chinese officials are concerned that the shortfall means that millions of men will have no prospect of getting married and settling down when they are of age. Thus, there will be an increased likelihood of social unrest, which can manifest itself as political dissent as well as ordinary crime (Trent, 2011).

Prenatal Sex Selection How do the Chinese have so many more sons than daughters? Once upon a time in places like China and India, much of the answer lay in infanticide—that is, killing unwanted female babies. Today, according to the International Planned Parenthood Federation, the main answer is the selective abortion of female fetuses, as identified by inexpensive, portable ultrasound scanners and backstreet abortion clinics. It is estimated that there are some 7 million abortions in China each year and that 70 percent of them are of females (Hesketh & Xing, 2006).

The director of China's National Population and Family Planning Commission admitted that the gender gap caused by the country's population policy has created a very serious challenge (Trent, 2011). However, China does not intend to loosen its constraints on population growth. Instead, the government will experiment with educational campaigns, penalties for sex-selective abortions, and bonuses for parents who have girls (Trent, 2011).

Reflect

- Do you think there are any circumstances under which a government, such as China's, has the right to limit family size? Why or why not?

- How would you explain the relationship between the number of children a Chinese woman desires and her age? Her area of residence (urban or rural)? Her level of education?

- What sources of error might distort the results in Table 2.4?

- Do you have a preference for boys or girls? What lengths would you go to in order to have a baby of your preferred sex?

Sperm Cells

Sperm cells develop through several stages. Like ova, in one early stage, each sperm cell contains 46 chromosomes, including one X and one Y sex chromosome. After meiosis, each sperm has 23 chromosomes. Half have X sex chromosomes, and the other half have Y sex chromosomes. Each sperm cell is about 1/200 of centimetre long, one of the smallest types of cells in the body. Sperm with Y sex chromosomes appear to swim faster than sperm with X sex chromosomes. TRUTH OR FICTION REVISITED: This is one of the reasons why 120–150 boys are conceived for every 100 girls. Male fetuses suffer a higher rate of **spontaneous abortion** than females, often during the first month of pregnancy. At birth, boys outnumber girls by a ratio of only 106 to

spontaneous abortion Unplanned, accidental abortion.

100. Boys also have a higher incidence of infant mortality, which further equalizes the numbers of girls and boys.

The 200–400 million sperm in the ejaculate may seem to be a wasteful investment because only one sperm can fertilize an ovum. But only one in 1000 sperm will ever approach an ovum. Millions deposited in the vagina flow out of the woman's body because of gravity. Normal vaginal acidity kills many more sperm. Many surviving sperm then have to swim against the current of fluid coming from the cervix (see Figure 2.8).

Sperm that survive these initial obstacles may reach the fallopian tubes 60–90 minutes after ejaculation. About half the sperm enter the wrong tube—that is, the tube without the egg. Perhaps 2000 enter the correct tube. Fewer still manage to swim the final 5 centimetres against the currents generated by the cilia that line the tube.

Although the journey of sperm is literally blind, it is apparently not random. **TRUTH OR FICTION REVISITED:** It is *not* true that sperm travel about at random inside the woman's reproductive tract, so that reaching the ovum is a matter of luck. Sperm cells are apparently attracted by the odour of a chemical secreted by ova. They seem to be "egged on" (pardon the pun) by a change in calcium ions that occurs when an ovum is released (Olson et al., 2011).

Of all the sperm swarming around the egg, only one enters (see Figure 2.9 ■). Ova are surrounded by a gelatinous layer that must be penetrated if fertilization is to occur. Many of the sperm that have completed their journey to the ovum secrete an enzyme that briefly thins the layer, but it still enables only one sperm to penetrate. Once a sperm cell has entered, the layer thickens, locking other sperm out. How this one sperm cell is "selected" is another biological mystery. Nevertheless, other sperm are unable to enter.

The chromosomes from the sperm cell line up across from the corresponding chromosomes in the egg cell. Conception finally occurs as the chromosomes combine to form 23 new pairs with a unique set of genetic instructions.

For couples who want children, few problems are more frustrating than the inability to conceive. Physicians often recommend that couples try to conceive on their own for six months before seeking medical assistance. The term *infertility* usually is not applied until the couple has failed to conceive for a year. We consider the problem of infertility next.

Figure 2.9 ■ Human Sperm Swarming around an Ovum in a Fallopian Tube
Fertilization normally occurs in a fallopian tube, not in the uterus. Thousands of sperm may wind up in the vicinity of an ovum, but only one fertilizes it. How this sperm cell is "selected" remains one of the mysteries of nature.

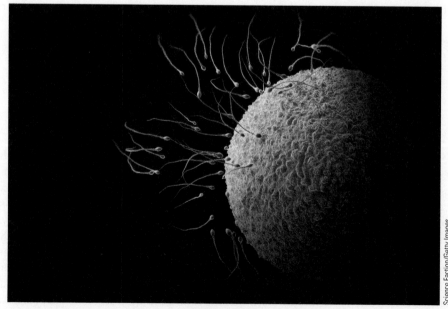

Science Faction/Getty Images

2.5 Infertility and Assisted Reproductive Technology

About one Canadian couple in six or seven (12–16 percent) has fertility problems (Bushnik, Cook, Yuzpe et al., 2012). Infertility was once viewed as a problem of the woman, but it turns out that the problem lies with the man in about 40 percent of cases.

Causes of Infertility

QUESTION » What are the causes of infertility? The following fertility problems are found in men (American Fertility Association, 2012a; www.myfertility.ca):

- Low sperm count
- Deformed sperm
- Poor ability of the sperm to swim to the ovum ("low sperm motility")
- Infectious diseases, such as sexually transmitted infections
- Chronic diseases, such as diabetes
- Injury of the testes
- An "autoimmune" response, in which the man's body attacks his own sperm as foreign agents

A low sperm count—or lack of sperm—is the most common infertility problem found in men. Men's fertility problems have a variety of causes: genetic factors, environmental poisons, diabetes, sexually transmitted infections (STIs), overheating of the testes (which happens now and then among athletes, such as long-distance runners), pressure (which can be caused by certain bicycle seats—have your doctor recommend a comfortable, safe seat), aging, and certain prescription and illicit drugs (American Fertility Association, 2012a).

TRUTH OR FICTION REVISITED: Yes, extensive athletic activity can contribute to infertility in the male. Sometimes the sperm count is adequate, but other factors (such as prostate or hormonal problems) can deform sperm or deprive them of their **motility**. Motility can also be impaired by the scar tissue from infections, such as STIs.

Women encounter the following major fertility problems (American Fertility Association, 2012a; www.myfertility.ca):

- Irregular ovulation, including failure to ovulate
- Declining hormone levels of estrogen and progesterone that occur with aging and may prevent the ovum from becoming fertilized or from remaining implanted in the uterus
- Inflammation of the tissue that is sloughed off during menstruation ("endometriosis")
- Obstructions or malfunctions of the reproductive tract, which are often caused by infections or diseases involving the reproductive tract

The most common problem in women is irregular ovulation or lack of ovulation. This problem can have many causes, including irregularities among the hormones that govern ovulation, stress, and malnutrition. So-called fertility drugs (such as *Clomiphene* and *Pergonal)* are made up of hormones that cause women to ovulate. These drugs may cause multiple births by stimulating more than one ovum to ripen during a month (Fertility drugs: Clomiphene citrate, 2010).

Infections may scar the fallopian tubes and other organs, impeding the passage of sperm or ova. Such infections include **pelvic inflammatory disease (PID)**. PID can result from any of a number of bacterial or viral infections,

motility Self-propulsion.

pelvic inflammatory disease (PID) An infection of the abdominal region that may have various causes and may impair fertility.

including the STIs gonorrhea and chlamydia. Antibiotics are usually helpful in treating bacterial infections, but infertility can be irreversible if the infection has gone without treatment for too long.

Endometriosis can obstruct the fallopian tubes, where conception normally takes place. This problem is clear enough. But endometriosis is also believed to somehow dampen the "climate" for conception; the mechanisms involved in this effect are not as well understood. Endometriosis has become a fairly frequent cause of infertility today, because so many women are delaying childbearing to further their educations and establish careers. What apparently happens is this: Each month tissue develops to line the uterus in case the woman conceives. This tissue, called the endometrium, is then normally sloughed off during menstruation. However, some of it backs up into the abdomen through the same fallopian tubes that would provide a duct for an ovum. Endometrial tissue then collects in the abdomen, where it can cause abdominal pain and reduce the chances of conception. Physicians may treat endometriosis with hormones that temporarily prevent menstruation or through surgery.

endometriosis Inflammation of endometrial tissue sloughed off into the abdominal cavity rather than out of the body during menstruation; the condition is characterized by abdominal pain and sometimes by infertility.

A CLOSER LOOK DIVERSITY

LGBT Family Building

Not only heterosexual couples want children. So do gay and lesbian singles. And so do couples who belong to the gay, lesbian, bisexual, and transgendered community.

Some gay and lesbian couples, of course, bring children from previous marriages or other kinds of relationships. But if they don't, and if they want children, they have to decide who these children will be and how to make it happen. Transgendered individuals who have had genital surgery are also sterile, so they cannot father or bear offspring.

Lesbians, of course, can conceive through sexual intercourse with a friend or confidant, but many prefer not to do so. Other methods of conception are assisted productive technologies such as at-home insemination, intrauterine insemination (IUI), in vitro fertilization (IVF), and reciprocal in vitro fertilization (RIVF) (American Fertility Association, 2012b). All these methods require obtaining donor sperm, from either a known or an anonymous source. IUI, known better perhaps as artificial insemination, is a low-technology method in which washed sperm are inserted directly into the uterus through a catheter. If IUI does not work, a woman may consider IVF. When both members of a lesbian couple are fertile, they sometimes choose to harvest the eggs from one partner, have them fertilized with donor sperm, and then insert the resulting embryos in the other partner, who may become pregnant through this process. The other partner may do the same. That's why this method is called *reciprocal* IVF. It permits both partners to play a role in bearing the child.

Gay males will need a surrogate mother to become impregnated by their sperm and carry the embryo and fetus to term. The two potential fathers' sperm is analyzed, and either the sperm with the strongest likelihood to impregnate the surrogate are selected, or the sperm may be mixed so that the fathers do not know which partner actu-

ally fathered the child. Of course, actual fatherhood usually becomes clear enough in terms of the child's appearance and behaviour as time goes on. DNA testing can also be used to make the determination. But both men played a role in the process, and as long as their relationship remains stable, they usually make no effort to precisely determine paternity.

The Infertility Awareness Association of Canada (www.iaac.ca) invites all individuals who have fertility questions or issues to be in touch with them—heterosexual couples, would-be single parents, and lesbian, gay, bisexual, and transgendered couples.

They've got each other. How do they go about building a family?

Reflect
- If you were receiving artificial insemination, would you want to know the identity of the sperm donor? Why or why not?
- How would you choose a sperm donor?
- If you were a partner in a gay male couple, would you consider mixing your sperm before attempting to impregnate a surrogate? Why or why not?
- If you were a partner in a lesbian couple, would you be interested in reciprocal IVF? Why or why not?

Helping People with Fertility Problems Become Parents

QUESTION » How are couples helped to have children? Let us now consider some of the methods that have been developed in recent years to help infertile couples bear children.

Artificial Insemination

Multiple ejaculations of men with low sperm counts can be collected and quick-frozen. The sperm can then be injected into the woman's uterus at the time of ovulation. This is one **artificial insemination** procedure. Sperm from men with low sperm motility can also be injected into their partners' uteruses, so that the sperm can begin their journey closer to the fallopian tubes. When a man has no sperm or an extremely low sperm count, his partner can be artificially inseminated with the sperm of a donor who resembles the man in physical traits. Women who want a baby but do not have a partner may also have artificial insemination. So may lesbian couples. The child then bears the genes of one of the parents—the mother.

In Vitro Fertilization

Have you heard the expression "test-tube baby"? Does it sound as though a baby develops in a test tube? **TRUTH OR FICTION REVISITED:** It is not true that test-tube babies are grown in a test tube. Does it sound as though a baby is conceived in a test tube? Not so—but close. In this method, which is more technically known as **in vitro fertilization (IVF)**, ripened ova are removed surgically from the mother and placed in a laboratory dish. The father's sperm are also placed in the dish. One or more ova are fertilized and then injected into the mother's uterus to become implanted.

In vitro fertilization may be appropriate when the fallopian tubes are blocked, because the ova need not travel through them. If the father's sperm are low in motility, they are sometimes injected directly into the ovum.

Several attempts may be needed to achieve pregnancy. Injecting several embryos into the uterus at once improves the odds. IVF remains costly but is otherwise routine—if not guaranteed.

Donor IVF

Donor IVF is used when a woman does not produce ova of her own but her uterus is apparently capable of providing an adequate environment to bring a baby to term. An ovum is harvested from another woman—the donor. It is fertilized in vitro, often by sperm from the partner of the recipient. Then, as in other cases of IVF, the fertilized ovum is placed directly into the uterus of the recipient. The embryo becomes implanted and undergoes the remainder of prenatal development in the recipient's uterus. This procedure is known as an **embryonic transplant**.

artificial insemination Injection of sperm into the uterus to fertilize an ovum.

in vitro fertilization (IVF) Fertilization of an ovum in a laboratory dish.

donor IVF The transfer of a donor's ovum, fertilized in a laboratory dish, to the uterus of another woman.

embryonic transplant The transfer of an embryo from the uterus of one woman to that of another.

A CLOSER LOOK | RESEARCH

Selecting the Sex of Your Child: Fantasy or Reality?

Folklore is replete with methods—and nonmethods—of sex selection. Some cultures advised coitus under the full moon to conceive boys. The Greek philosopher Aristotle suggested making love during a north wind to beget sons. A south wind would produce daughters. Sour foods were once suggested for parents desirous of having boys. Those who wanted girls were advised to consume sweets. Husbands who yearned to have boys might be advised to wear their boots to bed. It goes without saying that none of these methods worked (but we will say it anyhow).

Continued

These methods, or nonmethods, would supposedly lead to the conception of children of the desired sex. Methods applied after conception have also been used, such as the abortion of fetuses because of their sex. **TRUTH OR FICTION REVISITED:** Today, there is a reliable method for selecting the sex of your child prior to implantation: preimplantation genetic diagnosis (PGD). PGD was developed to detect genetic disorders, but it also enables health professionals to learn the sex of the embryo. In PGD, ova are fertilized in vitro, leading to conception of perhaps six to eight embryos. After a few days of cell division, a cell is extracted from each. The sex chromosomal structure of the cell is examined microscopically to determine whether the embryo is female or male. Embryos of the desired sex are implanted in the woman's uterus, where one or more can grow to term. PGD is medically invasive and expensive, and implantation cannot be guaranteed. Yet when implantation does occurs, the sex of the embryo is known.

Reflect Would you want to select the sex of your child? Explain.

Surrogate Mothers

In recent years, stories about **surrogate mothers** have filled the headlines. Surrogate mothers bring babies to term for other women who are infertile. (The word *surrogate* means "substitute.") Surrogate mothers may be artificially inseminated by the partners of infertile women, in which case the baby carries the genes of the father. But sometimes—as with 53-year-old singer-songwriter James Taylor and his 47-year-old wife—ova are surgically extracted from the biological mother, fertilized in vitro by the biological father, and then implanted in another woman's uterus, where the baby is carried to term. Surrogate mothers are usually paid fees and sign agreements to surrender the baby. (These contracts have been annulled in some states, however, so surrogate mothers cannot be forced to hand over their babies.) In the case of Taylor and his wife, the surrogate mother was a friend of the family, and she delivered twins.

Biologically, surrogate motherhood might seem the mirror image of the more common artificial insemination technique in which a fertile woman is artificially inseminated with sperm from a donor. But the methods are psychologically very different. For example, sperm donors usually do not know the identity of the women who have received their sperm, nor do they follow the child's prenatal development. Surrogate mothers, however, are involved throughout the course of prenatal development.

Ethical and legal dilemmas revolve around the fact that artificially inseminated surrogate mothers have a genetic link to their babies. If they change their minds and do not want to hand the babies over to the contractual parents, there can be legal struggles.

Adoption

Adoption is another way for people to obtain children. Despite occasional conflicts that pit adoptive parents against biological parents who change their minds about giving up their children, most adoptions result in the formation of loving families.

Many Canadians find it easier to adopt infants from other countries or infants with special needs. See Table 2.5 ■ for a listing of the various international adoptions in Canada from 2003 to 2005. Until the past generation, most adopted children were European Canadian babies adopted within a few days of birth. But the more widespread use of contraception and the decisions of many unwed mothers to keep their babies has contributed to a scarcity of Canadian babies. Today, greater numbers of adopted children are older, have spent some time in foster care, are of other races, have special needs, and/or were born in other countries (Gauthier et al., 2011; Schwam-Harris, 2008). Similarly, a generation or so ago, most adoptive parents were infertile, married European Canadian couples of secure socioeconomic status. Today, however, many adoption agencies allow more diversity in their

surrogate mother A woman who is artificially inseminated and carries to term a child who is then given to another woman, typically the spouse of the sperm donor.

TABLE 2.5

International Adoptions in Canada, Top 25 Countries

	2005	2004	2003
China	973	1001	1112
Haiti	115	159	150
United States	102	79	74
Republic of Korea	97	97	73
Russia	88	106	92
Philippines	70	62	58
India	41	37	10
Ukraine	39	16	23
Ethiopia	31	34	14
Taiwan	30	15	26
Jamaica	22	23	43
Thailand	21	40	38
Colombia	18	38	37
Pakistan	17	7	9
Ghana	15	12	11
Congo, Dem. Rep	11	8	X
Bulgaria	10	10	11
Liberia	10	10	X
Cambodia	10	14	23
Hong Kong	8	X	X
Guyana	8	14	19
Nigeria	6	X	X
Brazil	6	X	X
El Salvador	5	X	X
St. Vincent/Grenadines	5	X	X
Other Countries	113	183	297
Total	1871	1955	2180

X: From 0 to 4

Note: Due to privacy considerations, CIC has suppressed and replaced cells containing fewer than five cases with the notation "X." As a result, components may not sum to total indicated.

Source: Used with permission from Adoption Council of Canada. www.adoption.ca.

pool of adopting people; for example, they consider applications from older people and single people.

Although most adopted children and adoptive parents fare well, everything is relative. Adopted children are apparently less likely to be secure with their caregivers than biological children are (Gilmore, 2008). Everything else being equal, the younger the child at the time of adoption, the more smoothly the adoption seems to go (Klahr et al., 2011). Although adoptive parents of children from other races and ethnic backgrounds may make strong efforts to

AFP/Getty Images

Film actors Angelina Jolie and Brad Pitt have a family comprised of biological and adopted children.

"expose" their adoptive children to their cultures of origin, children adopted at younger ages acquire the language and customs of their adoptive parents more readily (Gauthier et al., 2011). Insecurities and anxiety are most likely to emerge in middle childhood, if they do emerge at all, because of increased understanding of what adoption means. One cause of problems for adopted children is that they often feel they were inexplicably rejected by their birth mother, which has detrimental effects on the development of a child's self-esteem (Klahr et al., 2011). Institutionalization prior to adoption, which can be a form of social deprivation, can heighten problems. Post-institutionalized children are at still greater risk of being insecure with the adoptive parents, and the insecurity can be found early (Chatham, 2008). One study found that such children had higher levels of cortisol (a stress hormone) than noninstitutionalized children in the presence of their mothers (Wismer Fries et al., 2008).

An aspect of adoption that is not often considered is its effects on the relinquishing mother (Aloi, 2009). These mothers frequently experience loss and guilt, along with wondering how their child is developing and adjusting.

In most of the next chapter, we will deal with issues on a smaller scale—beginning with the division of the single cell formed by the union of sperm cell and ovum into two cells, then four, and so on.

Active Review

18. The union of an ovum and a sperm cell is called _____.

19. Each month, an ovum is released from its follicle and enters a nearby _____ tube.

20. Low _____ count is the most common infertility problem in the male.

21. Failure to _____ is the most frequent infertility problem in women.

Reflect & Relate: What methods do people use to try to select the sex of their children? Do you believe it is right or proper to attempt to select the sex of one's child? Support your point of view.

Recite an Active Summary

2.1 The Influence of Heredity on Development: The Nature of Nature

What is meant by heredity?

Heredity defines one's nature, as determined by the biological transmission of traits and characteristics from one generation to another. Heredity is fundamental in the transmission of physical traits and is also involved in psychological traits, including psychological disorders.

What are chromosomes and genes?

Chromosomes are rod-shaped structures found in cell nuclei. People normally have 46 chromosomes organized into 23 pairs. Each chromosome contains thousands of genes—the biochemical materials that regulate the development of traits. Genes are segments of strands of DNA, which takes the form of a twisting ladder.

What happens during mitosis and meiosis?

In mitosis, strands of DNA break apart and are rebuilt in the new cell. Sperm and ova are produced by meiosis—or reduction division—and have 23 rather than 46 chromosomes.

How are twins formed?

If a zygote divides into two cells that separate and each develops into an individual, the result is monozygotic (MZ) twins, which are identical. If two ova are fertilized by different sperm cells, they develop into dizygotic (DZ) twins, which are fraternal. DZ twins run in families.

How do genes determine traits?

Traits are determined by pairs of genes. Mendel established laws of heredity and realized that some traits result from an "averaging" of the genetic instructions carried by the parents. However, genes can also be dominant (as in the case of brown eyes) or recessive (blue eyes). When recessive genes from both parents combine, the recessive trait is shown. People who bear one dominant gene and one recessive gene for a trait are carriers of the recessive gene. Some genetic abnormalities are caused by a single pair of genes, others by combinations of genes.

2.2 Chromosomal and Genetic Abnormalities

What kinds of disorders are caused by chromosomal abnormalities?

Chromosomal abnormalities become more likely as parents age. Intellectual disability is common in many such disorders. Down syndrome is caused by an extra chromosome on the 21st pair. Children with Down syndrome have characteristic facial features, including a downward-sloping fold of skin at the inner corners of the eyes, and various physical health problems. Disorders that arise from abnormal numbers of sex chromosomes are called sex-linked. These include XYY males and girls with a single X sex chromosome.

What kinds of disorders are caused by genetic abnormalities?

Phenylketonuria (PKU) is a metabolic disorder transmitted by a recessive gene. Huntington disease is a fatal progressive degenerative disorder and a dominant trait. Sickle-cell anemia is caused by a recessive gene and is most common among those of African descent. Tay-Sachs disease is a fatal disease of the nervous system that is caused by a recessive gene and is most common among children in Jewish families of Eastern European origin. Cystic fibrosis is caused by a recessive gene and is the most common fatal hereditary disease among European Canadians. Sex-linked genetic abnormalities are carried on only the X sex chromosome and include hemophilia, Duchenne muscular dystrophy, diabetes, and colour blindness.

How do health professionals determine whether children will have genetic or chromosomal abnormalities?

Prenatal testing procedures can determine the presence of various genetic and chromosomal abnormalities. Such tests include amniocentesis, chorionic villus sampling, ultrasound, and parental blood tests.

2.3 Heredity and the Environment: Considering the Interplay between Nature and Nurture

What is the difference between our genotypes and our phenotypes?

Our genotypes are the sets of traits that we inherit. However, inherited traits vary in expression, depending on environmental conditions. One's actual set of traits at a given point in time is one's phenotype.

How do researchers sort out the effects of genetics and environmental influences on development?

Researchers can study the distribution of a trait among relatives who differ in degree of genetic closeness. Parents and children have a 50 percent overlap in genes, as do brothers and sisters, with the exception of MZ twins, who have 100 percent overlap. MZ twins resemble each other more closely than DZ twins on physical and psychological traits, even when reared apart. If adopted children are closer to their natural parents than to their adoptive parents on a physical or psychological trait, that trait is likely to have a strong genetic basis.

2.4 Conception: Against All Odds

What process unites the genes of the parents?

The process is the union of a sperm and an ovum—conception. Fertilization normally occurs in a fallopian tube. If the egg is not fertilized, it is discharged. Men typically ejaculate hundreds of millions of sperm. More boys are conceived than girls, but male fetuses have a higher rate of spontaneous abortion. Chromosomes from the sperm cell align with chromosomes in the egg cell, combining to form 23 new pairs.

2.5 Infertility and Assisted Reproductive Technology

What are the causes of infertility?

Male fertility problems include low sperm count and motility, infections, and trauma to the testes. Female fertility problems include failure to ovulate, infections such as PID, endometriosis, and obstructions.

How are couples helped to have children?

Fertility drugs stimulate ovulation. Artificial insemination can be done with the sperm from multiple ejaculations of a man with a low sperm count or with the sperm of a donor. In vitro fertilization (IVF) can be used when the fallopian tubes are blocked. An embryo can also be transferred into a host uterus when the mother cannot produce ova.

Key Terms

heredity 50
genetics 50
chromosomes 50
gene 50
polygenic 50

deoxyribonucleic acid (DNA) 50
zygote 51
mitosis 51
mutation 51

meiosis 51
autosome 51
sex chromosome 51
monozygotic (MZ) twins 52
dizygotic (DZ) twins 52

Active Learning Resources

Go to **www.nelsonbrain.com** to access *Voyages in Development's* CourseMate, where you will find an interactive eBook, flashcards, Pre-Lecture Quizzes, Section Quizzes, Exam Practice, videos, and more.

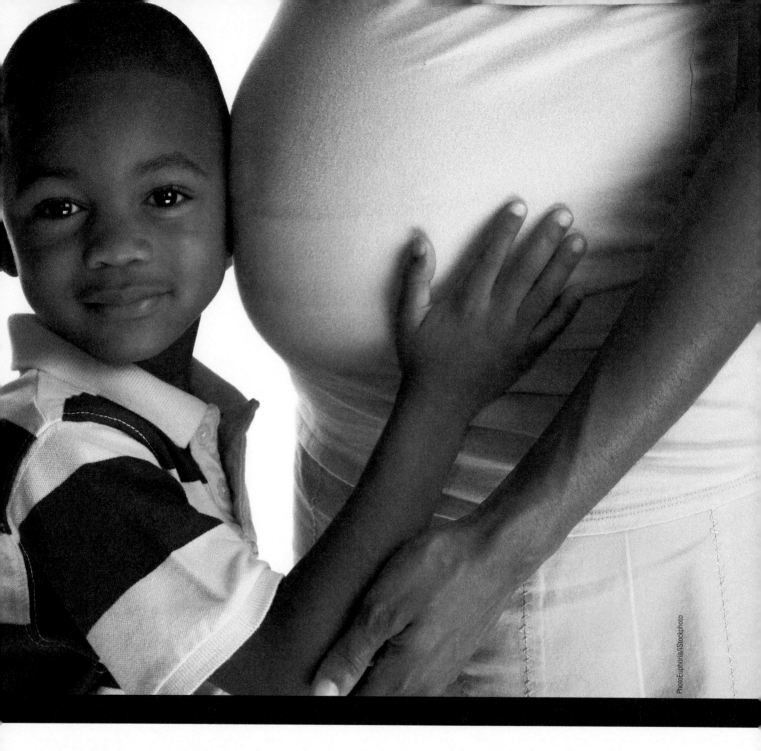

Major Topics

PRENATAL DEVELOPMENT

3

Truth or Fiction?

The most rapid and dramatic human developments are literally "out of sight." They take place in the uterus. Within nine months, a child develops from a nearly microscopic cell into a newborn about 50 centimetres long. Its weight increases a billionfold.

We can date pregnancy from the onset of the last menstrual period before conception, which makes the normal gestation period 280 days. We can also date pregnancy from the assumed date of fertilization, which normally occurs two weeks after the beginning of the woman's last menstrual cycle. With this accounting method, the gestation period is 266 days.

Soon after conception, the single cell formed by the union of sperm and egg begins to multiply—becoming two cells, then four, then eight, and so on. During the weeks and months that follow, tissues, organs, and structures begin to form, and the fetus gradually takes on the unmistakable shape of a human being. By the time a fetus is born, it consists of hundreds of billions of cells—more cells than there are stars in the Milky Way galaxy. Prenatal development is divided into three periods: the germinal stage (approximately the first two weeks), the embryonic stage (the third through the eighth weeks), and the fetal stage (the third month through birth). Health professionals also commonly speak of prenatal development in terms of three trimesters of three months each.

© Brooke Fasani Auchincloss/Corbis

3.1 The Germinal Stage: Wanderings

QUESTION » **What happens during the germinal stage of prenatal development?** Within 36 hours after conception, the zygote divides into two cells. It then divides repeatedly as it proceeds on its journey to the uterus. Within another 36 hours, it has become 32 cells. It takes the zygote three to four days to reach the uterus. The mass of dividing cells wanders about the uterus for another three to four days before it begins to become implanted in the uterine wall. Implantation takes another week or so. The period from conception to implantation is called the **germinal stage** (see Figure 3.1 ■).

A few days into the germinal stage, the dividing cell mass takes the form of a fluid-filled ball of cells called a **blastocyst**. A blastocyst already shows cell differentiation. Cells begin to separate into groups that will eventually become different structures. The inner part of the blastocyst has two distinct layers of cells that form a thickened mass of cells called the **embryonic disk**. These cells will become the embryo and eventually the fetus.

The outer part of the blastocyst, or **trophoblast**, at first consists of a single layer of cells. However, it rapidly differentiates into four membranes that will protect and nourish the embryo. One membrane produces blood cells until the embryo's liver develops and takes over this function. Then the membrane disappears. Another membrane develops into the **umbilical cord** and the blood vessels of the **placenta**. A third develops into the amniotic sac, and the fourth becomes the chorion, which will line the placenta.

Without Visible Means of Support ...

QUESTION » **If the dividing mass of cells is moving through a fallopian tube and then "wandering" through the uterus for another few days, how does it obtain any nourishment?** Although people are not chickens, the dividing cluster of cells that will become the embryo and then the fetus is at first nourished only by the yolk of the egg cell, just like a chick developing in an egg. **TRUTH OR FICTION REVISITED:** It is true that newly fertilized egg cells survive without

---

germinal stage The period of development between conception and the implantation of the embryo.

blastocyst A stage within the germinal period of prenatal development in which the zygote has the form of a sphere of cells surrounding a cavity of fluid.

embryonic disk The platelike inner part of the blastocyst that differentiates into the ectoderm, mesoderm, and endoderm of the embryo.

trophoblast The outer part of the blastocyst from which the amniotic sac, placenta, and umbilical cord develop.

umbilical cord A tube that connects the fetus to the placenta.

placenta An organ connected to the uterine wall and to the fetus by the umbilical cord. The placenta serves as a relay station between mother and fetus for the exchange of nutrients and wastes.

Figure 3.1 ■ The Ovarian Cycle, Conception, and the Early Days of the Germinal Stage
The zygote first divides about 36 hours after conception. Continuing division creates the hollow sphere of cells termed the blastocyst. The blastocyst normally becomes implanted in the wall of the uterus.

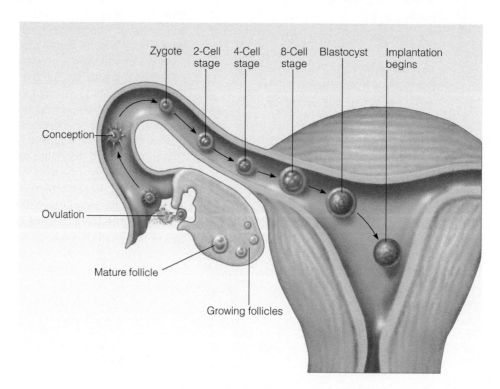

Zygote | 2-Cell stage | 4-Cell stage | 8-Cell stage | Blastocyst | Implantation begins

Conception

Ovulation

Mature follicle

Growing follicles

any nourishment from the mother for more than a week. They are nourished by the yolk of the ovum until they implant in the wall of the uterus. Therefore, the cluster makes no gain in mass. The blastocyst gains mass only when it receives nourishment from the outside. In order for that to happen, it must be implanted in the wall of the uterus.

Implantation may be accompanied by some bleeding, which is usually normal and results from the rupturing of small blood vessels that line the uterus.

Bleeding can also be a sign of miscarriage (also called spontaneous abortion). However, most women who experience implantation bleeding do not miscarry but go on to have normal pregnancies and normal babies. Miscarriage usually results from abnormalities in the developmental process. Many women miscarry early in pregnancy, but their menstrual flow appears about on schedule, so they may not even realize they had conceived. Nearly one-third of all pregnancies result in miscarriage, most of them occurring in the first three months (Miscarriage, 2007). Women who have miscarriages tend to experience a good deal of anxiety for several months afterward, and especially during the early months of subsequent pregnancies (Geller et al., 2004).

Active Review

1. A few days into the germinal stage, the dividing cell mass becomes a fluid-filled ball of cells that is called a _____.

2. The outer part of the blastocyst—called the_____—differentiates into membranes that will protect and nourish the embryo.

3. The dividing cluster of cells is nourished by the yolk of the ovum before _____.

Reflect & Relate: Nearly all of us have known—or have been—pregnant women. What early signs made the women suspect that they were pregnant? How do these signs fit with what was happening in their bodies?

3.2 The Embryonic Stage

QUESTION » What happens during the embryonic stage of prenatal development? The **embryonic stage** begins with implantation and covers the first two months, during which the major organ systems differentiate. Development follows two general trends: **cephalocaudal** (Latin for "head to tail") and **proximodistal** ("near to far"). The apparently oversized heads of embryos and fetuses at various stages of prenatal development show that growth of the head takes precedence over growth of the lower parts of the body (see Figure 3.2 ■). You can also think of the body as containing a central axis that coincides with the spinal cord. The growth of the organ systems in close proximity to this axis occurs earlier than the growth of the extremities, which are farther away (distant from the axis). Relatively early maturation of the brain and organ systems that lie near the central axis enables these organs to play important roles in the subsequent development of the embryo and fetus.

During the embryonic stage, the outer layer of cells of the embryonic disk, or **ectoderm**, develops into the nervous system, sensory organs, nails, hair, and teeth, and the outer layer of skin. At about 21 days, two ridges appear in the embryo and fold to make up the **neural tube**, which develops into the brain and spinal cord. The inner layer, or **endoderm**, forms the digestive and respiratory systems, the liver, and the pancreas. A bit later during the embryonic stage, the mesoderm, a middle layer of cells, becomes differentiated. The **mesoderm** develops into the excretory, reproductive, and circulatory systems, the muscles, the skeleton, and the inner layer of the skin.

embryonic stage The stage of prenatal development that lasts from implantation through the eighth week of pregnancy. It is characterized by the development of the major organ systems.

cephalocaudal From head to tail.

proximodistal From the inner part (or axis) of the body outward.

ectoderm The outermost cell layer of the newly formed embryo from which the skin and nervous system develop.

neural tube A hollowed-out area in the blastocyst from which the nervous system develops.

endoderm The inner layer of the embryo from which the lungs and digestive system develop.

mesoderm The central layer of the embryo from which the bones and muscles develop.

Figure 3.2 ■ Human Embryos and Fetuses at Various Stages of Development

Development proceeds in cephalocaudal and proximodistal directions. Development of the head takes precedence over development of the lower parts of the body, enabling the brain to participate in subsequent developments.

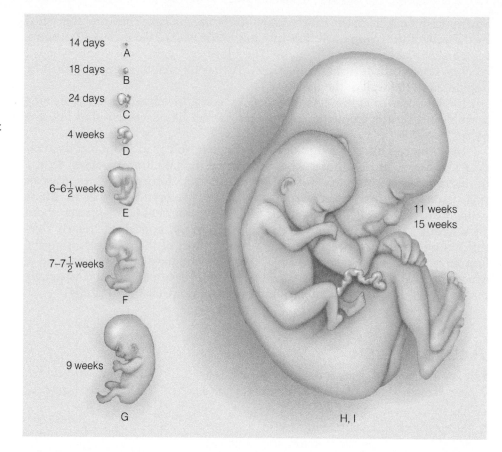

14 days — A
18 days — B
24 days — C
4 weeks — D
6–6½ weeks — E
7–7½ weeks — F
9 weeks — G
11 weeks
15 weeks
H, I

During the third week after conception, the head and blood vessels begin to form. **TRUTH OR FICTION REVISITED:** It is true that your heart started beating when you were only a few millimetres long and weighed only a few grams. The major organ systems develop within the first two months of pregnancy. The heart will continue to beat without rest every minute of every day for perhaps 80 or 90 years.

Arm buds and leg buds begin to appear toward the end of the first month. Eyes, ears, nose, and mouth begin to take shape. By this time, the nervous system, including the brain, has also begun to develop. In accordance with the principle of proximodistal development, the upper arms and legs develop before the forearms and lower legs. Next come hands and feet, followed at six to eight weeks by webbed fingers and toes. By the end of the second month, the limbs are elongating and separated. The webbing is gone. By this time, the embryo is looking quite human. The head has the lovely round shape of your own, and the facial features have become quite distinct. Bear in mind that all this detail is inscribed on an embryo that is only about 2.5 centimetres long and weighs only about a gram.

The nervous system develops rapidly because it will participate in enabling further developments. Before the end of the first month of embryonic development, the neural tube is producing about 400 million *neurons* per day. Neurons are also known as nerve cells, and they transmit information to other neurons, muscles, and glands. Once they have been produced, neurons travel to various parts of the brain, where they will develop to function as a variety of brain structures. In the fifth week, neurons form the cerebral hemispheres; the outer "bark" of the hemispheres is the cerebral cortex—the crowning glory of the brain—which the child will eventually use to perceive the itch from a mosquito bite, compose a concerto, or solve an algebraic equation. During the second month of embryonic development, the cells in the nervous system actually begin to "fire"—that is, to transmit messages. They do so by releasing countless chemicals called *neurotransmitters* into the fluid between neurons, muscles, and glands. These neurotransmitters are then taken up by receiving cells via structures that work like miniature docks. But at the beginning, much firing is probably random; much of the "content" of "messages" transmitted from neuron to neuron is anybody's guess. (No, the embryo isn't contemplating Chris Hadfield or Albert Einstein.)

By the end of the embryonic period, teeth buds have formed. The sensory organs—eyes, ears, and nose—are all taking shape. The embryo's kidneys are filtering acid from the blood, and its liver is producing red blood cells.

Sexual Differentiation

QUESTION » How do some babies develop into girls and others into boys? By five to six weeks, the embryo is only about a centimetre long. Nevertheless, nondescript sex organs already have formed, including the internal and external genital organs. Figure 3.3 ▄ shows changes in the internal organs. Both female and male embryos possess a pair of sexually undifferentiated gonads and two sets of primitive duct structures, the so-called Müllerian (female) ducts and Wolffian (male) ducts. At this stage of development, both the internal and the external genitals resemble primitive female structures.

By about the seventh week, the genetic code (XY or XX) begins to assert itself, causing sex organs to differentiate. Genetic activity on the Y sex chromosome causes the testes to begin to differentiate. Ovaries begin to differentiate if the Y chromosome is *absent*. By about four months after conception, males and females show distinct external genital structures.

Sex Hormones and Sexual Differentiation

Prenatal sexual differentiation requires hormonal influences as well as genetic influences. Male sex hormones—**androgens**—are critical in the development

androgens Male sex hormones.

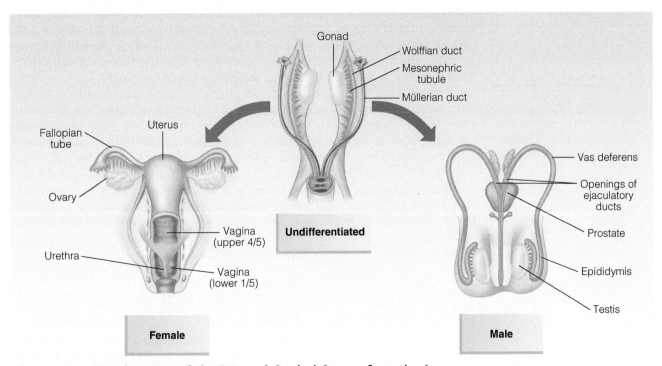

Figure 3.3 ▄ Development of the Internal Genital Organs from the Age of Five to Six Weeks after Conception.

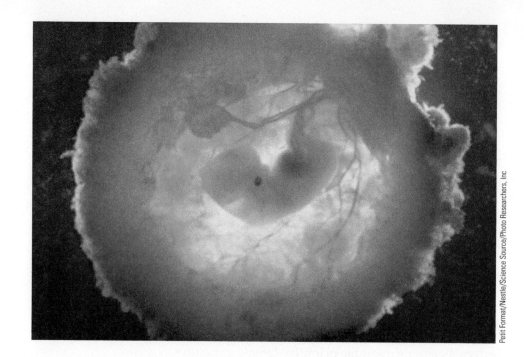

A Human Embryo at Seven Weeks
At this late point in the embryonic stage, the major organ systems except for the sex organs have already become differentiated.

of male genital organs. **TRUTH OR FICTION REVISITED:** Without androgens, all people—whether genetically female or male—would develop external sex organs that looked like those of females. However, apparent "females" with an XY sex chromosomal structure would be infertile (Goldman-Johnson et al., 2008; Lacham-Kaplan et al., 2008).

Once testes have developed in the embryo, they begin to produce androgens. The most important of these is **testosterone**. Testosterone spurs the differentiation of the male (Wolffian) duct system (see Figure 3.3) and remains involved in sexual development and activity for a lifetime. Each Wolffian duct develops into a complex maze of ducts and storage facilities for sperm. At about the eighth week of prenatal development, another androgen, dihydrotestosterone (DHT), spurs the formation of the external male genital organs, including the penis. Yet another testicular hormone, secreted somewhat later, prevents the Müllerian ducts from developing into the female duct system. That hormone is labelled Müllerian inhibiting substance (MIS).

Female embryos and fetuses do produce small amounts of androgens, but not normally enough to cause sexual differentiation along male lines. However, they do play important roles in the development of some secondary sexual characteristics in adolescence, such as the appearance of pubic and underarm hair. Androgens are also important in the sex drive of females for a lifetime (Morley & Perry, 2003; Nyunt et al., 2005). But in the female embryo and fetus, low levels of androgens are connected with degeneration of the Wolffian ducts and further development of female sexual organs. The Müllerian ducts develop into fallopian tubes, the uterus, and the inner part of the vagina. The presence of the female sex hormones is not necessary for these developments to occur, although they will become crucial in puberty.

The Amniotic Sac: A Shock Absorber

The embryo and fetus develop suspended within a protective **amniotic sac** in the uterus. The sac is surrounded by a clear membrane and contains **amniotic fluid**. The fluid serves as a kind of natural air bag, allowing the embryo and fetus to move around without injury. It also helps to maintain an even temperature.

testosterone A male sex hormone produced by the testes that promotes the development of male sexual characteristics and sperm.

amniotic sac The sac containing the fetus.

amniotic fluid Fluid within the amniotic sac that suspends and protects the fetus.

The Placenta: A Filtration System

QUESTIONS » How does the embryo get nourishment from its mother? How does it eliminate waste products? The answers involve the placenta and the umbilical cord. The placenta is a mass of tissue that permits the embryo (and, later on, the fetus) to exchange nutrients and wastes with the mother. The placenta is unique in origin. It grows from material supplied by both the mother and the embryo. The fetus is connected to the placenta by the umbilical cord. The mother is connected to the placenta by the system of blood vessels in the uterine wall.

In one of the more fascinating feats of prenatal engineering, it turns out that the mother and baby have separate circulatory systems. Her bloodstream is hers, and the embryo's bloodstream is the embryo's. The pancake-shaped placenta contains a membrane that acts as a filter: Only certain substances can pass through it. The membrane permits oxygen and nutrients to reach the embryo from the mother. It also permits carbon dioxide (which is the gas that you breathe out and plants "breathe" in) and waste products to pass to the mother from the child. Once the mother has these waste products, she eliminates them through her lungs and kidneys. This is the good part. It also happens that a number of harmful substances can sneak through the placenta. They include various "germs" (microscopic disease-causing organisms), such as the ones that cause syphilis (a bacterium called *Treponema pallidum*) and German measles (Oswal & Lyons, 2008). The good news here is that most pregnant women who are infected with HIV (the virus that causes AIDS) do not transmit it to the baby through the placenta during prenatal development (Lynch et al., 2011). HIV is more likely to be transmitted during childbirth, when the placenta can break down and the bloodstreams of mother and baby can mix (Lynch et al., 2011). But some drugs—aspirin, narcotics, alcohol, tranquilizers, and others—do cross the placenta and can affect the baby in various ways.

The placenta also secretes hormones that preserve the pregnancy, prepare the breasts for nursing, and stimulate the uterine contractions that prompt childbirth. Ultimately, the placenta passes from the woman's body after the child is delivered. For this reason, it is also called the afterbirth.

Active Review

4. The embryo and fetus develop within an _____ sac, which functions as a shock absorber, among other things.

5. Development follows two general trends: cephalocaudal and _____.

6. The (inner or outer?) layer of cells of the ectoderm develops into the nervous system, the sensory organs, and the outer layer of skin.

7. Without sex hormones, all embryos would develop the appearance of (males or females?).

8. The _____ permits the embryo to exchange nutrients and wastes with the mother.

9. The embryo and fetus are connected to the placenta by the _____.

Reflect & Relate: Are you surprised at how early the heart begins to beat and the size of the embryo at the time? Explain.

3.3 The Fetal Stage

QUESTION » What happens during the fetal stage of prenatal development? The **fetal stage** lasts from the beginning of the third month until birth. The fetus begins to turn and respond to external stimulation at about the ninth or tenth week. By the end of the first trimester, all the major organ systems have

fetal stage The stage of development that lasts from the beginning of the ninth week of pregnancy through birth.

formed. The fingers and toes are fully formed. The eyes can be clearly distinguished, and the sex of the fetus can be determined visually.

The second trimester is characterized by further maturation of fetal organ systems and dramatic gains in size. The brain continues to mature, contributing to the fetus's ability to regulate its own basic body functions. During the second trimester, the fetus advances from about 30 grams to 1 kilogram in weight and increases four to five times over in length, from about 8 centimetres to 36 centimetres. Soft, downy hair grows above the eyes and on the scalp. The skin turns ruddy because of blood vessels that show through the surface. (During the third trimester, fatty layers will give the skin a pinkish hue.)

By the end of the second trimester, the fetus opens and shuts its eyes, sucks its thumb, alternates between periods of wakefulness and sleep, and perceives light and sounds. **TRUTH OR FICTION REVISITED:** There are also sharp spasms of the diaphragm, or fetal hiccups, which may last for hours (ask a weary pregnant woman).

About half of babies who are born at 22–25 weeks of gestation survive. The survival rate is related to the quality of the medical care they receive (Rogowski et al., 2004).

During the third trimester, the organ systems of the fetus continue to mature. The heart and lungs become increasingly capable of sustaining independent life. The fetus gains about 2 kilograms and doubles in length. Newborn boys average about 3.4 kilograms, newborn girls about 3.2 kilograms.

During the seventh month, the fetus normally turns upside down in the uterus so that delivery will be head first. By the end of the seventh month, the fetus will have almost doubled in weight, gaining 800 grams, and will have increased another 5 centimetres in length. If the baby is born now, the chances of survival are nearly 90 percent. If the baby is born at the end of the eighth month, the odds are overwhelmingly in favour of survival.

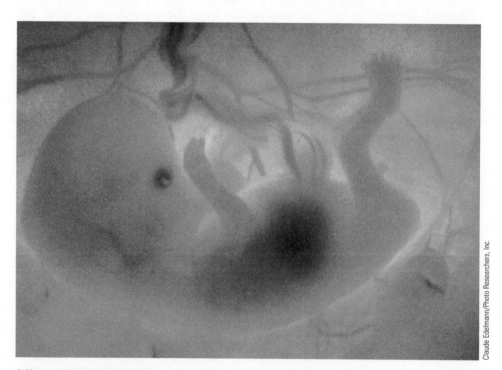

A Human Fetus at 12 Weeks
By the end of the first trimester, the formation of all major organ systems is complete. Fingers and toes are fully formed, and the sex of the fetus can be determined visually.

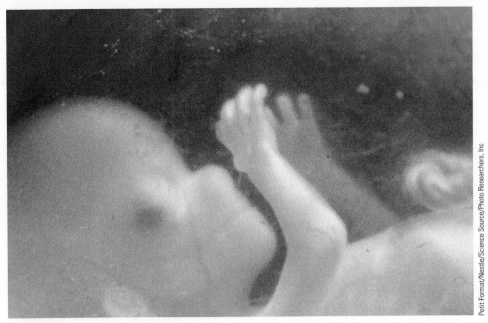

A Human Fetus at Four-and-a-Half Months
At this midway point between conception and birth, the fetus is covered with fine, downy hair called lanugo.

The mother usually feels the first fetal movements in the middle of the fourth month (Adolph & Berger, 2005). By 29–30 weeks, the mother gets her kicks; that is, the fetus moves its limbs so vigorously that the mother may complain of being kicked—often at 4 a.m. The fetus also turns somersaults, which the mother clearly feels.

Fetuses show different patterns of prenatal activity (de Vries & Hopkins, 2005). Slow squirming movements begin at about five or six months. Sharp jabbing or kicking movements begin at about the same time and increase in intensity until shortly before birth. As the fetus grows, it becomes cramped in the uterus, and movement is constricted. Many women become concerned that their fetuses are markedly less active during the ninth month than earlier, but most of the time this change is normal.

There are individual differences in level of fetal activity, but a Dutch study found no sex differences in fetal movement (de Medina et al., 2003). Moreover, prenatal activity predicts activity levels after birth. For instance, highly active fetuses show more advanced motor development after birth than their more lethargic counterparts (de Vries & Hopkins, 2005).

Concept Review 3.1 highlights key events during prenatal development.

Active Review

10. The fetal stage is characterized by _____ of organ systems and gains in size and weight.

11. Fetuses apparently discriminate sounds of different pitches during the _____ trimester of pregnancy.

12. Mothers usually detect fetal movements during the _____ month.

Reflect & Relate: During the fourth month, when the baby's movements can be detected, many women have the feeling that their babies are "alive." What is your view on when the baby is alive? What standard or standards are you using to form your opinion?

Concept Review 3.1 | Highlights of Prenatal Development

First Trimester

Period of the Ovum (Gestational Stage)

First 2 weeks

- Dividing cluster of cells enters and moves around the uterus, living off the yolk of the egg cell.
- Blastocyst becomes implanted in the wall of the uterus, possibly accompanied by implantation bleeding.

David M. Phillips/Photo Researchers, Inc

Embryonic Stage

3 weeks

- Head and blood vessels form.
- Brain begins to develop.

4 weeks

- Heart begins to beat and pump blood.
- Arm buds and leg buds appear.
- Eyes, ears, nose, and mouth form.
- Nerves begin to develop.
- Umbilical cord is functional.
- Embryo weighs a few grams and is less than a centimetre long.

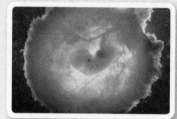

Petit Format/Nestle/Science Source/Photo Researchers, Inc

5–8 weeks

- Hands and feet develop with webbed fingers and toes.
- Undifferentiated sex organs appear.
- Teeth buds develop.
- Kidneys filter uric acid from the blood; liver produces blood cells.
- Bone cells appear.
- Head is half the length of the entire body.
- Embryo weighs about 2 grams and is 2.5 centimetres long.

Fetal Stage

9–12 weeks

- All major organ systems are formed.
- Fingers and toes are fully formed.
- Eyes can be clearly distinguished.
- Sex of fetus can be determined visually (e.g., by ultrasound).
- Mouth opens and closes; fetus swallows.
- Fetus responds to external stimulation.
- Fetus weighs about 30 grams and is about 8 centimetres long.

Concept Review 3.1 *(Continued)*

Second Trimester

13–16 weeks
- Mother detects fetal movement.
- Many reflexes are present.
- Fingernails and toenails form.
- Head is about one-fourth the length of the body.

17–20 weeks
- Hair develops on head.
- Fine, downy hair (lanugo) covers body.
- Fetus sucks its thumb and hiccups.
- Heartbeat can be heard when listener presses head against mother's abdomen.

21–24 weeks
- Eyes open and shut.
- Light and sounds can be perceived.
- Fetus alternates between periods of wakefulness and sleep.
- Skin looks ruddy because blood vessels show through the surface.
- Survival rate is low if fetus is born.
- Fetus weighs about 1 kilogram and is 36 centimetres long; growth rate is slowing down.

Third Trimester

25–28 weeks
- Organ systems continue to mature.
- Fatty layer begins to develop beneath the skin.
- Fetus turns head down in the uterus.
- Fetus cries, swallows, and sucks its thumb.
- Chances of survival are good if born now.
- Fetus weighs 1.5–2 kilograms and is about 40 centimetres long.

29 to 36–38 weeks
- Organ systems function well.
- Fatty layer continues to develop.
- Fetal activity level decreases in the weeks before birth as a result of crowding.
- Weight increases to an average of 3.2–3.4 kilograms; boys are about 200 grams heavier than girls; length increases to about 50 centimetres.

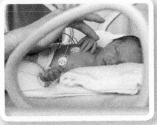

3.4 Environmental Influences on Prenatal Development

Yes, the fetus develops in a protective "bubble"—the amniotic sac. Nevertheless, the developing fetus is subject to many environmental hazards. Scientific advances have made us keenly aware of the types of things that can go wrong and what we can do to prevent these problems. In this section, we consider some of the environmental factors that have an effect on prenatal development.

Nutrition

QUESTION » **How does the nutrition of the mother affect prenatal development?** We quickly bring nutrition inside, but nutrition originates outside. Therefore, it is one environmental factor in prenatal (and subsequent) development.

It is a common misconception that fetuses "take what they need" from their mothers. If this were true, pregnant women would not have to be highly concerned about their diets. But malnutrition in the mother, especially during the last trimester when the fetus should be making rapid gains in weight, has been linked to low birth weight, prematurity, stunted growth, retardation of brain development, cognitive deficiencies, behavioural problems, and even cardiovascular disease (de Souza et al., 2011).

Fortunately, the effects of fetal malnutrition can sometimes be overcome by a supportive, care-giving environment. Experiments with children who suffered from fetal malnutrition show that enriched day-care programs enhance intellectual and social skills by five years of age (Ramey et al., 1999). Supplementing the diets of pregnant women who might otherwise be deficient in their intake of calories and protein also shows modest positive effects on the motor development of the women's infants (Morton, 2006).

On the other hand, maternal obesity is linked with a higher risk of **stillbirth** (Stillbirth Collaborative Research Network Writing Group, 2011; Tennant et al., 2011). Obesity during pregnancy also increases the likelihood of neural tube defects. In a study reported in *The Journal of the American Medical Association*, women who weighed 80–89 kilograms before pregnancy were about twice as likely as women who weighed 45–59 kilograms to bear children with neural tube defects; women who weighed 110 kilograms or more were four times more likely to have children with neural tube defects (Shaw et al., 1996). Note that these findings were for obese women only. Very tall women normally weigh more than shorter women, so the study's findings must be considered in terms of women's desirable weights for a given height. In Shaw's study, folic acid supplements did not appear to prevent neural tube defects in the babies of women who weighed more than 70 kilograms.

What Should a Pregnant Woman Eat?

Pregnant women need the following food elements to maintain themselves and to give birth to healthy babies: protein, which is heavily concentrated

stillbirth The birth of a dead fetus.

Birth Rates around the World

Let's have a look at some history and some pre-history— that is, some guesstimates of events that might have occurred before records were made. According to the U.S. Census Bureau, which was *not* distributing questionnaires at the time, some 5 million humans walked the Earth about 10 000 years ago. It took another 5000 years for that number to expand to 14 million. Skipping ahead 2000 years to the year 1, humans gained a stronger foothold on the planet, and the number increased tenfold, to some 170 million. By 1900, the population increased tenfold again, to about 1.7 billion. In 1950, estimates placed the number at about 2.5 billion, and today—with increases in the food supply, sanitary water supplies, and vaccinations—the number is estimated to be close to 7 billion.[1]

Therefore, we are in the middle of a population explosion, are we not? The answer depends on where you look. TRUTH OR FICTION REVISITED: For example, if you check out Table 3.1 ■, you will readily see that it is not true that parents in wealthy nations have more children. Parents need to have slightly in excess of two children to "reproduce themselves," because some children are lost to illness, accidents, or violence. The table shows that in countries such as Spain, Greece, Italy, Japan, Canada, Russia, and the United Kingdom, parents are not reproducing themselves.

Reflect

- How do the birth rates of countries where 30 percent or fewer of the population use modern means of contraception compare with those where 60 percent or more use modern means? What are the relationships between literacy and birth rate? Between education and birth rate?

- How would you judge whether a particular birth rate in a particular nation is a good thing or a bad thing? If it is a bad thing, what can be done about it? Explain your views.

- Why do parents in wealthier nations tend to have fewer children? What are your feelings about this? Explain your views.

- Does the information in Table 3.1 show cause and effect? Why or why not?

in red meat, fish, poultry, eggs, beans, milk, and cheese; vitamin A, which is found in milk and vegetables; vitamin B, which is found in wheat germ, whole grain breads, and liver; vitamin C, which is found in citrus fruits; vitamin D, which is derived from sunshine, fish-liver oil, and vitamin D–fortified milk; vitamin E, which is found in whole grains, some vegetables, eggs, and peanuts; iron, which is concentrated heavily in meat (especially liver), egg yolks, fish, and raisins; the trace minerals zinc and cobalt, which are found in seafood; calcium, which is found in dairy products; and, yes, calories. Research also demonstrates the importance of consuming folic acid, which is found in leafy green vegetables. Women who eat a well-rounded diet do not require food supplements, but most doctors recommend them, to be safe (de Souza et al., 2011). Pregnant women who take folic acid supplements reduce the risk of giving birth to babies with neural tube defects, which can cause paralysis and death (Giussani, 2011).

How Much Weight Should a Pregnant Woman Gain?

Malnutrition in the mother can adversely affect fetal development. Women who are too slender risk having preterm deliveries and low-birth-weight babies (Chen et al., 2009). Pregnant women who are adequately nourished are more likely to deliver babies of average or above-average size. Their infants are also less likely to develop colds and serious respiratory disorders.

---

[1]U.S. Census Bureau. Historical estimates of world population. www.census.gov/ipc/www/worldhis.html. Accessed February 14, 2012.

Fertility Rates and Related Factors around the World

Nation	Fertility Rate	Rate of Usage of Modern Methods of Contraception (%)	Literacy Rates (%)		Years of Education	
			Men	Women	Men	Women
Afghanistan	5.97	15	**	**	10	6
Brazil	1.80	77	90	90	14	14
Canada	1.69	72	**	**	15	16
China	1.56	84	97	91	11	12
Congo	4.44	13	**	**	11	10
Cuba	1.45	72	100	100	15	17
France	1.99	75	**	**	16	16
Germany	1.46	66	**	**	**	**
Greece	1.54	46	98	96	16	16
India	2.54	49	75	51	11	10
Iran	1.59	59	89	81	13	13
Iraq	4.54	33	86	70	11	9
Israel	2.91	52	**	**	15	16
Italy	1.48	41	99	99	16	17
Jamaica	2.26	66	81	91	13	14
Japan	1.42	44	**	**	15	15
Kenya	4.62	39	91	84	11	11
Mexico	2.23	67	95	92	13	14
Pakistan	3.20	19	69	40	8	6
Philippines	3.05	34	95	96	11	12
Russia	1.53	65	100	99	14	15
Saudi Arabia	2.64	**	90	81	15	14
Spain	1.50	62	98	97	16	17
United Kingdom	1.87	84	**	**	16	17
U.S.A.	2.08	73	**	**	16	17

Sources: United Nations. (2012). Department of Economic and Social Affairs. Economic and Social Development. Social Indicators. http://unstats.un.org/unsd/demographic/products/socind/default.htm, http://unstats.un.org/unsd/demographic/products/socind/childbearing.htm#tech Table 2d, Contraceptive preference, Table 4a, Literacy; Table 4e, School life expectancy.

**Missing information.

The slimmer a woman is before pregnancy, the more weight she is advised to gain during pregnancy. For example, a woman with a body mass index (BMI)[2] below 18.5 is advised to gain 13–18 kilograms

[2]The formula for calculating your BMI is [weight (kg)/height (metres)[2]]; that is, divide your weight (in kilograms) by your height (in metres) squared. For example, for a person who is 1.7 metres tall and weighs 65 kilograms, the BMI is [65/(1.7)^2] = 22.49.

Healthy Pregnancy

Promotion of healthy lifestyle has become increasingly important to Canadians in recent years. In fact, if you are pregnant or planning on becoming pregnant, Health Canada has a website especially for you (www.healthy pregnancy.gc.ca). This site offers up-to date information and covers many of the maternal and environmental influences on prenatal development. For women considering mother-hood, topics include alcohol and pregnancy, physical activity, folic acid, and smoking. For those who are already pregnant, additional topics include emotional health and healthy eating.

There was a time when expectant mothers were told to engage in as little physical activity as possible and to take it easy. Nowadays there is research indicating that women who are active during pregnancy may have reduced risk of gestational diabetes, hypertensive disease, and preterm birth (Mottola, Giroux, Gratton, Hammond, Hanley, Harris et al., 2010; Zhang, Solomon, Manson & Hu, 2006). In fact, physical activity during pregnancy has also been associated with enhanced psychological well-being (Gaston & Prapavessis, 2013). It comes as no surprise then that medical experts are encouraging expectant mothers to engage in some level of physical activity throughout their pregnancies. The types of activities pregnant women are suited to engage in varies, and women need to find activities they enjoy and are comfortable with. For instance, high-intensity sports and running may be replaced with walking, certain types of yoga, or aqua-fit activities. It is advised that women speak to their physicians about the type of activity they are interested in engaging in (or continuing to engage in) throughout their pregnancies.

How much weight women should gain during pregnancy is dictated by a woman's weight before pregnancy (Health Canada, 2010). The Public Health Agency of Canada recommends that women calculate their pre-pregnancy BMI and their recommended weight gain at healthcanada.gc.ca/pregnancy-calculator and then talk to their health-care provider. While there is a focus on tracking weight gain, the emphasis should be on eating a healthy balanced diet and getting the recommend daily intake from the four food groups detailed in Health Canada (2011), in addition to adding some physical activity to one's daily routine.

Reflect Are there social and cultural aspects that may contribute to a healthy lifestyle during pregnancy?

szefei/Shutterstock.com

(Rasmussen et al., 2009; see Table 3.2 ■). Women of normal weight, those with a BMI of 18.5–24.9, are advised to gain 11–16 kilograms. However, 44 percent of Canadian women are overweight or obese (Canadian Community Health Survey, 2012), and with these high rates of obesity, even for women entering pregnancy at normal weight, obesity is a risk factor (Bernier & Hanson, 2012). Women who are overweight (those with a BMI of 25.0–29.9) are advised to gain 7–11 kilograms. And obese women (those with a BMI above 30.0) are advised to limit their weight gain to 5–9 kilograms. Gaining weight gradually is most desirable.

● TABLE 3.2

Body Mass Index (BMI) and Weight Status

BMI	Weight Status
Below 18.5	Underweight
18.5–24.9	Normal weight
25.0–29.9	Overweight
30.0 and above	Obese

Source: NIH Publication no. 98-4083. Clinical Guidelines on the Identification, Evaluation, and Treatment of Overweight and Obesity in Adults: The Evidence Report. NHLBI (National Heart, Lung, and Blood Institute); 1998.

Teratogens and Health Problems of the Mother

QUESTIONS » What are teratogens? Does it matter when, during pregnancy, a woman is exposed to them? Most of what the mother does for the embryo is not only remarkable but also healthful. There are exceptions, however. Consider the case of teratogens. **Teratogens** (the word derives from frightening roots meaning "giving birth to monsters") are environmental agents that can harm the embryo or fetus. Teratogens include drugs that the mother ingests, such as thalidomide (connected with birth deformities) and alcohol, and substances that the mother's body produces, such as Rh-positive antibodies. Another class of teratogens is the heavy metals, such as lead and mercury, which are toxic to the embryo. Hormones are healthful in countless ways; for example, they help maintain pregnancy. However, excessive quantities of hormones are harmful to the embryo. If the mother is exposed to radiation, that radiation can harm the embryo. Then, of course, disease-causing organisms—also called pathogens—such as bacteria and viruses, are also teratogens. When it comes to pathogens, bigger is better for the embryo; that is, larger pathogens are less likely to pass through the placenta and affect the embryo. But smaller pathogens sneak through, including those that cause mumps, syphilis, measles, and chicken pox. Some disorders, such as toxemia, are not transmitted to the embryo or fetus but adversely affect the environment in which it develops.

Sensitive Periods in Prenatal Development

Exposure to particular teratogens is most harmful during **sensitive periods** that correspond to the times when organs are developing. **TRUTH OR FICTION REVISITED:** Therefore, the same disease organism or chemical agent that can do serious damage to a six-week-old embryo may have no or less of an effect on a four-month-old fetus. For example, the heart develops rapidly during the third to fifth weeks after conception. As you can see in Figure 3.4 ■, the heart is most vulnerable to certain teratogens at this time. The arms and legs, which develop later, are most vulnerable during the fourth through eighth weeks. Because the major organ systems differentiate during the embryonic stage, the embryo is generally more vulnerable to teratogens than the fetus. But many teratogens are harmful throughout the entire course of prenatal development. Understanding the effects of teratogens on the developing embryo and fetus is not simple. It depends on many additional factors, including duration and dose of teratogen exposure, the mother's genetic makeup, the age of developing embryo and fetus, as well as other negative influences.

Let us consider the effects of various health problems of the mother, beginning with sexually transmitted infections (STIs).

Sexually Transmitted Infections

The **syphilis** bacterium can cause miscarriage, stillbirth, or **congenital** syphilis. The symptoms of congenital syphilis include skin sores, a runny nose, which is sometimes bloody (and infectious), slimy patches in the mouth, inflamed bones in the arms and legs, swollen liver, jaundice, anemia, or a small head. Congenital syphilis can impair vision and hearing, damage the liver, or deform the bones and teeth. Untreated babies may develop intellectual

teratogens Environmental influences or agents that can damage the embryo or fetus.

sensitive period In this context, a period during which certain organs or structures are particularly vulnerable to a certain teratogen.

syphilis A sexually transmitted infection that can attack major systems.

congenital Present at birth; resulting from the prenatal environment.

Advice for Expectant Fathers

I got hungry while we were waiting for the contractions to get more frequent, and I made the mistake of bringing a tuna sandwich into the birthing room. My wife gave me a horrible look and threatened to throw up on me—and much worse—if I didn't get it out of there immediately.
—A former expectant father, now a father

First piece of advice: Unless your will is made out and your passage in this world has become weary, don't bring a tuna sandwich into the delivery room.

It's women who get pregnant, but these days it's often politically correct to say things like "We're pregnant"—especially when a father doesn't want to be left out of the process. But expectant fathers may not be sure that they are also pregnant. And they can indeed feel left out of the process. They can also have concerns about a pregnancy, and some fears. Following are some concerns expressed by expectant fathers, and some thoughts about responding to them.

1. *Will I be a good father? How will I know what to do?* "Women seem to take to motherhood naturally, but is fatherhood 'natural'?" One might counter, of course, that we can wonder whether motherhood is really so natural for women when they have typically been thrust into care-giving roles with dolls and with other people's children since early childhood. Think of parenting as a skill that can be learned, and if the father is motivated, he can acquire that skill.

2. *What if I die when they need me?* "I realized I was no longer the kid," said one expectant father. "I was going to have one. Suddenly my life didn't seem as open-ended." It's always good to think about our responsibilities toward others. Expectant fathers may be exaggerating the threats in their lives, but taking out an insurance policy is a good idea. A young father may find that a term life insurance policy fits into his financial picture quite well.

3. *Will she love the baby more than she loves me?* Perhaps, but that doesn't mean she'll love the father less. Having a baby creates a totally new configuration of attachments and emotions in a family. At the very least, it expands the potential for feelings of love. Many new fathers say things like "I never knew I had that much love in me." Your baby will form an attachment to you as well as to his or her mother, and the sum total of positive feelings you will be experiencing will most likely increase. Remember that your partner may also be wondering whether you will prefer the baby to her, especially if it's a daughter.

4. *How can I help during the pregnancy when I don't particularly understand women's medical issues?* A vast knowledge gap can emerge as the mother becomes well educated about pregnancy, childbirth, and parenting, and the father feels left out. The father can support the mother by trying to remain involved. For example, he can attend as many clinical visits as he can fit into his schedule, but he should not, perhaps, blow things out of proportion if he must miss some. He can also generally help by listening when his partner expresses her concerns, trying to understand them, and offering to help.

5. *Will I do what I'm supposed to do at the birth? Does she even really want me at the birth, or is she just being "politically correct" by including me?* Back to the tuna fish: You may have attended clinical visits and childbirth lessons with your partner, but you won't be the only person there to assist.

6. *But I don't even particularly like kids, so how am I going to feel about this one?* Since "this one" is, as the expression goes, "your own flesh and blood," you'll probably have rather positive feelings. Does that mean you'll never be annoyed when the baby cries at night or when your partner dotes on the baby? Not at all, but you'll be able to put these concerns into perspective.

7. *What do I do if it's a girl (boy)?* Many fathers worry that they won't provide a masculine enough role model for sons and that they won't have any idea what to do if it's a girl. "The fact of the matter is that I wanted a boy because I didn't know what I would do with a girl. But even so, I wasn't sure I wanted to have to toss around a football or a baseball with a boy. I never threw a football all that well, in truth. When we had a girl, I bonded with her immediately—she was very cute—and I found myself prepared to hug her. And I learned quickly enough that a large part of fatherhood is really about changing diapers, no matter how bad the smell."

Reflect Which of these concerns might you or a partner experience? Have you had—or has a partner had—any of these concerns? Why do you think many people, female and male, say things like "*We're* expecting a baby" these days?

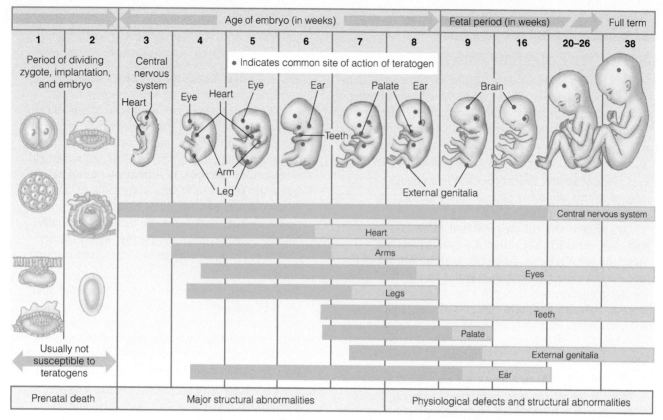

Figure 3.4 ■ **Sensitive Periods in Prenatal Development**

Knowledge of the sequence of prenatal development allows one to understand why specific teratogens are most harmful during certain periods of prenatal development. Major structural abnormalities are most likely to occur when teratogens strike during the embryonic period.

Source: National Institutes of Health. National Institute on Alcohol Abuse and Alcoholism. Pubs.niaaa.nih.gov. Accessed December 8, 2012.

disability or have seizures. Infected babies may show no symptoms when they are born, but they may develop symptoms within a few weeks if they are not treated.

HIV/AIDS (human immunodeficiency virus/acquired immunodeficiency syndrome) disables the body's immune system, leaving victims prey to a variety of fatal illnesses, including respiratory disorders and cancer. HIV/AIDS is lethal unless treated with a combination of antiviral drugs. Even then, the drugs do not work for everyone, and the eventual outcome remains in doubt (Rathus et al., 2014).

HIV can be transmitted by sexual relations, blood transfusions, sharing hypodermic needles while shooting up drugs, childbirth, and breast feeding. About one-fourth of babies born to HIV-infected mothers become infected themselves (Coovadia, 2004). During childbirth, blood vessels in the mother and baby rupture, allowing an exchange of blood and transmission of HIV. HIV is also found in breast milk. An African study found that the probability of transmission of HIV through breast milk was about one in six (16.2 percent) (Nduati et al., 2000).

Children from ethnic and racial minority groups are at greater risk of being infected with HIV. Canadian rates indicate that the average percentage of infants who were perinatally (during childbirth) infected with HIV during the 1984–2000 period (33.9 percent) was approximately six times greater than the average percentage infected between 2001 and 2008 (5.2 percent) (Public

HIV/AIDS HIV stands for a virus, human immunodeficiency virus, that cripples the body's immune system. AIDS stands for acquired immunodeficiency syndrome—the body's state when the immune system is weakened to the point where it is vulnerable to diseases that would otherwise be fought off.

Health Canada, 2009). While there has been a downward trend in HIV cases, this is not the case among Aboriginal women, as there has been an increase in the number of HIV cases among Aboriginal women of reproductive age (Public Health Canada, 2009).

The Flu

Although influenza ("the flu") primarily infects the mother's respiratory system, it has been suspected that flu may play a causal role in the development of fetal brain abnormalities and lead to problems such as autism and schizophrenia (Brown, 2006; Smith et al., 2007). Yet Limin Shi and Patterson (2005) studied the maternal and fetal tissues of laboratory animals for influenza virus and found that it appears only rarely to be transmitted to the fetuses of infected mothers. It may be that the effects of flu on the fetus are most likely to involve the mother's inflammatory response—for example, her secretion of high levels of substances such as corticosteroids and interleukin-6—to the virus (Limin Shi & Patterson, 2005; Smith et al., 2007). In recent years there has been an increased distribution of influenza vaccine (inactivated form), and distribution to pregnant women is deemed safe (Centers for Disease Control and Prevention, 2013).

Rubella

Rubella (German measles) is a viral infection. Women who are infected during the first 20 weeks of pregnancy stand at least a 20 percent chance of bearing children with birth defects such as deafness, intellectual disability, heart disease, or eye problems, including blindness (Food and Drug Administration, 2004; Rubella, 2009).

Many adult women had rubella as children and became immune in this way. Women who are not immune are best vaccinated before they become pregnant, although they can be inoculated during pregnancy, if necessary. Inoculation has led to a dramatic decline in the number of American children born with defects caused by rubella, from about 2000 cases in 1964–1965 to 21 in 2001 (Food and Drug Administration, 2004; Rubella, 2009). Canadians experience very low incidence of rubella and congenital rubella syndrome (0 to 0.6 per 100 000 live births) (Canadian Paediatric Society, 2004).

rubella A viral infection that can cause deafness, intellectual disability, heart disease, and eye problems in the embryo. Also called German measles.

A CLOSER LOOK REAL LIFE

Preventing One's Baby from Being Infected with HIV

Pregnant women who are infected with HIV or other STIs should discuss these conditions with their physicians. Measures can be taken that will help prevent their babies from being infected. The current recommendations concerning transmission of HIV from mother to baby include HAART, caesarean section (C-section), and formula feeding. HAART stands for highly active antiretroviral therapy—a combination of three drugs that reduce the amount of HIV in the bloodstream (Williams et al., 2009). C-sections help to prevent transmission of HIV to the baby because the baby is not exposed to the mother's blood to the extent that it is during vaginal delivery, when blood vessels rupture. HIV is also found in breast milk—hence the recommendation for formula feeding.

All in all, the combination of HAART, C-section, and formula feeding has reduced mother-to-infant transmission of HIV from about 25 percent to 1–2 percent (Coovadia, 2004).

For up-to-date information on HIV/AIDS, contact the Canadian HIV/AIDS Information Centre, 400-1565 Carling Avenue, Ottawa, ON K1Z 8R1, 1-877-999-7740 or (613) 725-3434. www.aidssida.cpha.ca. You can also log on to the website of the Centers for Disease Control and Prevention: www.cdc.gov.

Reflect What have you done—or what will you do—to try to protect your babies from being infected with HIV or with any other disease organism?

Pre-Eclampsia

Pre-eclampsia (sometimes referred to as toxemia) is a life-threatening disease, characterized by high blood pressure, that may afflict women late in the second or early in the third trimester (Bangal et al., 2012). Affected women often have **premature** or undersized babies. Pre-eclampsia is also a cause of pregnancy-related maternal deaths (Bangal et al., 2012). Pre-eclampsia appears to be linked to malnutrition, but the causes are unclear. Pregnant women who do not receive prenatal care are more likely than others to die from pre-eclampsia (Verlohren et al., 2012).

Rh Incompatibility

In **Rh incompatibility**, antibodies produced by the mother are transmitted to a fetus or newborn infant and cause brain damage or death. Rh is a blood protein that is found in the red blood cells of some individuals. Rh incompatibility occurs when a woman who does not have this factor—and is thus Rh negative—is carrying an Rh-positive fetus, which can happen if the father is Rh positive. The negative–positive combination occurs in about 10 percent of Canadian couples and becomes a problem in some pregnancies. Rh incompatibility does not affect a first child, because women will not have formed Rh antibodies. The chances of an exchange of blood are greatest during childbirth. If an exchange occurs, the mother produces Rh-positive antibodies to the baby's Rh-positive blood. These antibodies can enter the fetal bloodstream during subsequent deliveries, causing anemia, mental deficiency, or death.

If an Rh-negative mother is injected with Rh immunoglobulin within 72 hours after delivery of an Rh-positive baby, she will not develop the antibodies. A fetus or newborn child at risk of Rh disease may receive a blood transfusion to remove the mother's antibodies.

Drugs Taken by the Parents

QUESTION » **What are the effects of drugs taken by the mother on prenatal development?** Rh antibodies can be lethal to children, but many other substances can have harmful effects. In this section, we discuss the effects of various drugs on the unborn child—prescription drugs, over-the-counter drugs, and illegal drugs. Even commonly used medications, such as aspirin, can be harmful to the fetus. If a woman is pregnant or thinks she may be, it is advisable for her to consult her obstetrician before taking any drugs, not just prescription medications. A physician usually can recommend a safe and effective substitute for a drug that can potentially harm a developing fetus.

Accutane

Accutane (also known as isotretinoin, its generic name) is derived from vitamin A and is prescribed for difficult cases of acne that do not respond to other forms of treatment. It works by reducing the size of the oil glands in the skin, thus also reducing the amount of acne-causing bacteria present. It also helps prevent pores from clogging and has anti-inflammatory properties. However, Accutane is associated with numerous abnormalities during the first trimester of pregnancy, affecting the eyes and ears, brain, heart, and immune system (Fisher et al., 2008; Peterka et al., 2007). To avoid these outcomes, women are required to demonstrate via a pregnancy test that they are not pregnant when they begin or continue the drug, and it is recommended that they use two types of birth control during treatment. Not all women follow these precautions.

pre-eclampsia A life-threatening disease that can afflict pregnant women. It is characterized by high blood pressure.

premature Born before the full term of gestation. (Also referred to as *preterm*.)

Rh incompatibility A condition in which antibodies produced by the mother are transmitted to the child, possibly causing brain damage or death.

Thalidomide

Thalidomide was marketed in the 1960s as a treatment for insomnia and nausea—not specifically for pregnant women. It was available in Germany and England without prescription. Within a few years, more than 10 000 babies with missing or stunted limbs were born in these countries and elsewhere, as a result of their mothers' using thalidomide during pregnancy (Ances, 2002). Thalidomide is considered safe for people who are not pregnant and is used to treat disorders as varied as dermatological problems and Kaposi's sarcoma, a form of cancer that affects many people with HIV/AIDS.

Thalidomide provides a dramatic example of critical periods of vulnerability to various teratogens. The extremities undergo rapid development during the second month of pregnancy (see Figure 3.4). Thalidomide taken during this period almost invariably causes birth defects.

OBSERVING CHILDREN, UNDERSTANDING OURSELVES

Antidepressants in Utero

A researcher investigates whether prenatal exposure to prescription drugs, such as Prozac, will later result in impaired memory and cognition.

If prenatal exposure to Prozac negatively impacts cognitive functioning, how might this affect learning in childhood and adulthood? Do you think all pregnant women should avoid antidepressants, and why? What additional research is needed about taking prescription drugs during pregnancy?

Go to www.nelson.com/voyages2ce to watch the video, answer the questions, and e-mail your responses to your professor.

From Rathus. *Childhood and Adolescence*, 5E. © 2014 South-Western, a part of Cengage Learning, Inc. Reproduced by permission. www.cengage.com/permissions

Antibiotics

Several antibiotics may be harmful to the fetus. Tetracycline, which is frequently prescribed for bacterial infections, can lead to yellowed teeth and bone abnormalities (Teti & Zallone, 2009). Other antibiotics—aminoglycosides such as streptomycin—are strongly implicated in hearing loss (Hobbie et al., 2008; Steyger, 2008). Prenatal use of antibiotics also appears to increase the risk of childhood asthma (Murk et al., 2011).

Hormones

Women at risk for miscarriages have been prescribed hormones such as progestin and DES to help maintain their pregnancies. **Progestin** is chemically similar to male sex hormones and can masculinize the external sex organs of female embryos. Prenatal progestin has also been linked to aggressive behaviour and masculine-typed behaviours in females (Hines, 2011).

DES (diethylstilbestrol), a powerful estrogen, was given to many women during the 1940s and 1950s to help prevent miscarriage (Verloop et al., 2010), but it has caused cervical and testicular cancer in some of the offspring. Among daughters of DES users, about one in 1000 will develop cancer in the reproductive tract. Daughters are also more likely to have babies who are premature or have low birth weight. Daughters and sons of mothers who took DES have high rates of infertility and immune system disorders (Verloop et al., 2010).

Vitamins

Although pregnant women are often prescribed multivitamins to maintain their own health and to promote the development of their fetuses, too much of a good thing can be dangerous. High doses of vitamins A and D have been associated with central nervous system damage, small head size, and heart defects (Simpson et al., 2011). Nonetheless, Health Canada (2007) recommends that all women of child-bearing age take at least 0.4 mg of folic acid

thalidomide A sedative linked to birth defects, especially deformed or absent limbs.

progestin A hormone that is used to maintain pregnancy and can cause masculinization of the fetus.

DES Abbreviation for diethylstilbestrol, an estrogen that has been linked to cancer in the reproductive organs of children of women who used it when pregnant.

found in multivitamins. Folic acid supplements have reduced the number of neural tube deficits in infants (Berry et al., 1999). Health Canada's Healthy Pregnancy website (www.healthypregnancy.gc.ca) is one initiative aimed at promoting healthy prenatal development.

Heroin and Methadone

Maternal addiction to heroin or methadone is linked to low birth weight, prematurity, and toxemia. These narcotics readily cross the placental membrane, and the fetuses of women who use them regularly can become addicted (Hudak & Tan, 2012). **TRUTH OR FICTION REVISITED:** It is true that babies can be born addicted to narcotics and other substances used regularly by their mothers.

Addicted newborns may be given the narcotic or a substitute shortly after birth so that they will not suffer serious withdrawal symptoms. The drug is then withdrawn gradually. There are also behavioural effects. For example, infants exposed to heroin in utero show delays in motor and language development at the age of 12 months (Minnes et al., 2011).

Marijuana (Cannabis)

Smoking marijuana during pregnancy apparently poses a number of risks for the fetus, including slower fetal growth and low birth weight (Hayatbakhsh et al., 2012). These and the following risks are all proportional to the amount of marijuana smoked; that is, women who smoke more, or who inhale more secondary smoke (smoke from others who are smoking), place their fetuses at relatively greater risk. The babies of women who regularly used marijuana show increased tremors and startling, suggesting immature development of the nervous system (Minnes et al., 2011).

Research into the cognitive effects of maternal prenatal use of marijuana has yielded mixed results. Some studies suggest that there may be no impairment, but others suggest that cognitive skills, including learning and memory, may be impaired (Giussani, 2011). One study assessed the behaviour of ten-year-olds who had been exposed prenatally to maternal use of marijuana (Goldschmidt et al., 2000). The study included the children of 635 mothers, aged 18–42. Prenatal use of marijuana was significantly related to increased hyperactivity, impulsivity, and problems in paying attention (as measured by the Swanson, Noland, and Pelham checklist), increased delinquency (as measured by the Child Behaviour Checklist), and increased delinquency and aggressive behaviour (as measured by teacher report). The researchers hypothesized that the pathway between prenatal marijuana exposure and delinquency involves the effects of marijuana on attention, impairing the abilities to learn in school and to conform to social rules and norms. A Swedish study also suggests that fetal exposure to marijuana may impair systems in the brain that regulate emotional behaviour (Wang et al., 2004).

Researchers have found that maternal use of marijuana predisposes offspring to dependence on opiates (narcotics derived from the opium poppy). The fetal brain, like the adult brain, has cannabinoid receptors—called CB-1 receptors—and other structures that are altered by exposure to marijuana. The alterations make the individual more sensitive to the reinforcing properties of opiates, even in adulthood (Moreno et al., 2003). In any event, longitudinal research with 763 women recruited in the fourth month of pregnancy found that prenatal exposure to maternal marijuana smoking is a reasonably good predictor of whether the child will smoke marijuana at the age of 14 (Day et al., 2006).

Cocaine

There is little doubt that prenatal exposure to cocaine can harm the child. Pregnant women who abuse cocaine increase the risk of stillbirth, low birth weight, and birth defects (Stillbirth Collaborative Research Network Writing

Group, 2011). The infants are often excitable and irritable, or lethargic. The more heavily exposed to cocaine they are in utero, the more problems they have with jitteriness, concentration, and sleep (Bada et al., 2011; Bigsby et al., 2011). Lewis and colleagues (2004) compared 189 four-year-olds who had been exposed to cocaine in utero with 185 four-year-olds who had not, on the Clinical Evaluation of Language Fundamentals–Preschool (CELF-P) test. Children exposed to cocaine had much lower expressive language scores and somewhat lower receptive language scores. That is, their relative ability to express themselves was affected more than their ability to understand language. The study controlled for prenatal exposure to cigarette smoke, alcohol, and marijuana. There are suggestions that delays in cognitive development persist at ten years of age (Lewis et al., 2011).

A study of 473 six-year-olds by Delaney-Black and colleagues (2004) compared children who were exposed to cocaine in utero (204) with those who were not. The study found effects for the amount of cocaine used by the mother and the sex of the child. Boys were more likely to be affected than girls. According to teacher reports, boys whose mothers used cocaine regularly were likely to be rated as hyperactive, to be indifferent to their environment, and to show deficits in cognitive skills. The study controlled for maternal use of alcohol and illegal drugs other than cocaine while pregnant.

The studies with humans are correlational. That is, mothers are not randomly assigned to use cocaine; instead, they make the choice themselves. This problem is technically termed a selection factor. Thus, it may be that the same factors that lead mothers to use cocaine also affect their children. To overcome the selection factor, numerous experiments have been conducted with laboratory animals. In one study, randomly selected pregnant rats were given cocaine during days 12–21 of gestation, whereas control rats received no cocaine (Huber et al., 2001). The rat pups were then exposed to stressors such as cold-water swimming and tail flicks. The pups exposed to cocaine showed less tolerance of the stressors—as measured by behaviours such as tail twitches and convulsions—than control subjects. Another study found that such group differences in response to stressors endure into rat adulthood—that is, 90–120 days of age (J. O. Campbell et al., 2000).

Alcohol

No drug has meant so much to so many as alcohol. Alcohol is our dinner-time relaxant, our bedtime sedative, our cocktail-party social lubricant. We use alcohol to celebrate holy days, applaud our accomplishments, and express joyous wishes. Millions of adolescents assert their maturity with alcohol. Alcohol is used at least occasionally by the majority of high school and college students (L. D. Johnston et al., 2011). Alcohol even kills germs on surface wounds. Alcohol is the most frequently consumed teratogen (Streissguth, 1997).

However, because alcohol passes through the placenta, drinking by a pregnant woman poses risks for the embryo and fetus. Heavy prenatal alcohol exposure can be lethal to the fetus and neonate. It is also connected with deficiencies and deformities in growth (Kooistra et al., 2010; O'Leary et al., 2010). **Fetal alcohol spectrum disorder (FASD)** is the umbrella term used to refer to a group of specific diagnoses such as **fetal alcohol syndrome (FAS)**, partial fetal alcohol syndrome (pFAS), alcohol-related neurodevelopment disorder (ARND), and **fetal alcohol effects (FAE)** (FASD Fact Sheet, Government of Canada, 2007). Table 3.3 ▇ outlines some of the characteristics of people diagnosed with FASD. In Canada, about nine out of 1000 babies are born with FASD. FAS refers to individuals with the characteristic features (e.g., widely spaced eyes, an underdeveloped upper jaw, a flattened nose), stunted growth, and central nervous system impairment (Kerns, MacSween, Vander Wekken, & Gruppuso, 2010; Rasmussen, Beckert, McLennan,

fetal alcohol spectrum disorder (FASD) Umbrella term that refers to the different disabilities children of mothers who drank alcohol during pregnancy may experience. FASD is considered to be the result of preventable birth defects, and it is one of the most common sources of developmental delays.

fetal alcohol syndrome (FAS) A cluster of symptoms shown by children of women who drank during pregnancy, including characteristic facial features and intellectual disability.

fetal alcohol effect (FAE) A cluster of symptoms less severe than those of fetal alcohol syndrome shown by children of women who drank moderately during pregnancy.

Common Characteristics of People Diagnosed with FASD

Primary Disabilities	Secondary Effects
Physical birth defects	Difficulty communicating thoughts and inability to control behaviour
Facial abnormalities	
Physical health problems	Disrupted school experiences
Learning disabilities at school	Drug and alcohol abuse
Memory problems	Difficulty holding a job
Short attention span	Difficulty handling money
Difficulty communicating feelings in an appropriate manner	Interacting with others
	Inappropriate sexual behaviour
Difficulty understanding the consequences of actions	

Urichuk, & Andrew, 2010). There may be malformation of the limbs, poor coordination, and cardiovascular problems. A number of psychological characteristics connected with FAS appear to reflect dysfunction of the brain, including intellectual disability, hyperactivity, distractibility, lessened verbal fluency, and learning disabilities (Kooistra et al., 2010). There are deficits in speech and hearing, practical reasoning, and visual–motor coordination. The other diagnoses under the spectrum umbrella, pFAS, ARND, and FAE, denote those individuals who lack some or all of the facial features and growth deficiencies but still exhibit some of the neurobehavioural deficits (Chudley et al., 2005; Rasmussen et al., 2010).

Exciting research in diagnosis, prevention, and intervention is being conducted in Canada. The Canada Fetal Alcohol Spectrum Disorder Research Network (CanFASD) is Canada's comprehensive national FASD research network. The intervention team is led by Dr Jacqueline Pei from the University of Alberta. Information about the effects of FASD and evidence-based interventions can be found at www.KnowFASD.ca.

The facial irregularities of FAS diminish as the child moves into adolescence, and most children catch up in height and weight. But the intellectual, academic, and behavioural deficits of individuals with FAS persist. Academic and intellectual problems relative to peers range from verbal difficulties to deficiency in spatial memory (Guerrini et al., 2007). Studies find that the average academic functioning of adolescents and young adults with FAS is at the Grade 2 to 4 level. Maladaptive behaviours such as poor judgment, distractibility, and difficulty perceiving social cues are common (Schonfeld et al., 2005).

TRUTH OR FICTION REVISITED: It cannot be guaranteed that one glass of wine a day is harmless to the embryo and fetus. Although some health professionals allow pregnant women a glass of wine with dinner, research suggests that even moderate drinkers place their offspring at increased risk for brain, physical, central nervous system, and behavioural challenges. At present, Health Canada recommends that there is no safe time or safe amount of alcohol to drink when pregnant or when planning to become pregnant. Pregnant women who have as few as one or two drinks a day may be more likely to miscarry or have growth-delayed babies than pregnant women who do

Fetal Alcohol Syndrome (FAS)
The children of many mothers who drank alcohol during pregnancy exhibit FAS. This syndrome is characterized by developmental lags and such facial features as an underdeveloped upper jaw, a flattened nose, and widely spaced eyes.

Rick's Photography/Shutterstock.com

not drink (American Pregnancy Association, 2011). *There is no safe minimum amount of drinking during pregnancy.*

The reported effects of maternal drinking, like the effects of maternal use of cocaine, are based on correlational evidence. No researcher would randomly assign some pregnant women to drinking and others to abstention. However, researchers have randomly assigned experimental animals to intake of alcohol, and the results support the correlational evidence with humans. For example, research with animals reveals that exposure to alcohol during gestation is connected with retarded growth, facial malformations characteristic of FAS, deficiencies in the immune system, and structural and chemical differences in the central nervous system (O'Leary et al., 2010).

Caffeine

Many pregnant women consume caffeine in the form of coffee, tea, soft drinks, chocolate, and nonprescription drugs. The findings of research on caffeine's effects on the developing fetus have been inconsistent (Minnes et al., 2011). Some studies report no adverse findings, but others have found that pregnant women who take in a good deal of caffeine are more likely than nonusers to have a miscarriage or a low-birth-weight baby (Bakker et al., 2010). Because of such findings, many obstetricians recommend that pregnant women avoid caffeine or ingest low to moderate amounts.

A CLOSER LOOK | RESEARCH

Can We Trust the Research on the Effects of Caffeine Taken during Pregnancy?

Perhaps the best critiques of the literature on the effects of caffeine taken during pregnancy are by Lisa Signorello and Joseph McLaughlin (2004, 2008). They carefully reviewed 16 epidemiologic studies on caffeine and miscarriage, paying specific attention to the kinds of methodological problems that can lead to inaccurate results. These include selection factors in the sampling and problems in (1) women's recall of exactly how much caffeine they used, (2) measurement of the exposure to caffeine, and (3) timing of the loss of the embryo or the fetus. They concluded that each study was flawed, and there was no way to compare the results of the studies to one another—despite the fact that most studies reported a link between the intake of caffeine by the mother and the risk of miscarriage.

The recent investigation by Xiaoping Weng and his colleagues (2008) was described as a "prospective cohort study"—that is, a study that would predict future outcomes. However, most of the women included were first contacted and interviewed about their use of caffeine after

Svetlana Lukienko/Shutterstock.com

they had their miscarriages. Signorello and McLaughlin (2008) noted further that although Weng and his colleagues (2008) considered their study an experiment, it was not the researchers but the pregnant women who decided how much caffeine they would use. In a true experiment, the researchers control the independent variable—in this case, the intake of caffeine.

The evidence against the use of caffeine is flawed, so what can I advise? Simply this: Until we have better evidence, pregnant women should ask their obstetricians for their views about using caffeine during pregnancy (Bakker et al., 2010).

Reflect Do you know women who have drunk several cups of coffee or tea a day during pregnancy? Do you believe they were aware of the research linking caffeine and miscarriage? What did they say about it? If your obstetrician offers an opinion about the use of caffeine during pregnancy, will you ask what that opinion is based on? Why or why not?

Cigarettes

Cigarette smoke contains many ingredients, including the stimulant nicotine, the gas carbon monoxide, and hydrocarbons ("tars"), which are carcinogens. Fortunately, only the first two of these, nicotine and carbon monoxide, pass through the placenta and reach the fetus. That's the end of the fortunate news. Nicotine stimulates the fetus, but its long-term effects are uncertain. Carbon monoxide is toxic; it decreases the amount of oxygen available to the fetus. Oxygen deprivation is connected with cognitive and behavioural problems, including impaired motor development (Giussani, 2011). The cognitive difficulties include academic delays, learning disabilities, and intellectual disability. Not all children of smokers develop these problems, but many do not function as well as they would have if they had not been exposed to maternal smoking.

Pregnant women who smoke are likely to deliver smaller babies than non-smokers (Bernstein et al., 2005). In addition, their babies are more likely to be stillborn or to die soon after birth (Stillbirth Collaborative Research Network Writing Group, 2011). The combination of smoking and drinking alcohol places the child at greater risk of low birth weight than either practice alone (Spencer, 2006).

Maternal smoking may also have long-term negative effects on development. Children whose mothers smoke during pregnancy are more likely to show short attention spans, hyperactivity, lower cognitive and language scores, and poor grades (Secker-Walker & Vacek, 2003).

Okay—smoking during pregnancy poses significant threats to the fetus. So why do pregnant women do it? Are they ignorant of the risks to their children? Perhaps. Despite decades of public education efforts, there remain some women who are unaware that smoking will hurt the fetus. Most Canadian women are aware of the threat. Yet they say that they can't quit or that they can't suspend smoking until the baby is born. Why? Some claim they are under too much stress to stop smoking, although cigarette smoking actually contributes to stress; it's not a one-way ticket to relaxation. Others smoke to fight feelings of depression (nicotine is a stimulant and depression is, well, depressing), because "everybody" around them smokes (often, "everybody" translates into the partner), or because they just don't have the willpower (or perhaps we should say the "won't power") to deal with the withdrawal symptoms of quitting. Some parents simply deny that their smoking is likely to harm their children, despite knowledge to the contrary.

Second-hand smoke also holds dangers. Men who smoke are more likely to produce abnormal sperm. Babies of fathers who smoke have higher rates of birth defects and infant mortality, lower birth weights, and cardiovascular problems.

Environmental Hazards

QUESTION » **What are the effects of environmental hazards during pregnancy?** Mothers know when they are ingesting drugs, but there are many (many!) other substances in the environment that they may take in unknowingly. These are environmental hazards to which we are all exposed, and we refer to them collectively as pollution.

Prenatal exposure to heavy metals such as lead, mercury, and zinc threatens the development of children. Longitudinal research finds that newborns who have mildly elevated levels of lead in their umbilical cord blood show delayed mental development at one and two years of age (Heindel & Lawler, 2006). However, their cognitive functioning can improve if they are no longer exposed to lead in the home.

One study of the effects of prenatal exposure to lead recruited 442 children in Yugoslavia (Wasserman et al., 2000). Some of the children lived in a town with a smelter; the others did not. (Smelting—or the melting of lead-bearing scrap metal into metallic lead—is a major source of lead fume emissions.) The children received intelligence testing at the ages of three, four, five, and seven, using Wechsler and other scales. The researchers found that the children from the town with the smelter obtained somewhat lower intelligence test scores. It is conceivable, of course, that people who choose to live in a town without a smelter differ from those who are willing to cozy up to one.

Experiments with rodents support the correlational findings with humans. For example, mice exposed to lead in utero do not form memories as well as those that are free of prenatal exposure to lead (de Oliveira et al., 2001). Research with rats has found that prenatal exposure to lead decreases the levels of neurotransmitters (the chemical messengers of the brain) in all areas of the brain, but especially in the hippocampus. The hippocampus is involved in memory formation.

The devastating effects of mercury on the fetus were first recognized among the Japanese who lived around Minimata Bay. Industrial waste containing mercury was dumped into the bay and accumulated in the fish that were a major food source for local residents. Children born to women who had eaten the fish during pregnancy were often profoundly intellectually disabled and neurologically damaged (Mayes & Ward, 2003). Prenatal exposure to even small amounts of mercury and other heavy metals such as cadmium and chromium can produce subtle deficits in cognitive functioning and physical health (Heindel & Lawler, 2006).

Polychlorinated biphenyls (PCBs) are chemicals used in many industrial products. Like mercury, they accumulate in fish that feed in polluted waters. Newborns whose mothers had consumed PCB-contaminated fish from Lake Michigan were smaller and showed poorer motor functioning and less responsiveness than newborns whose mothers had not eaten these fish. Furthermore, even those PCB-exposed infants who appeared normal at birth showed deficits in memory at seven months and at four years of age (Jacobson et al., 1992).

An unfortunate natural experiment in the effects of prenatal exposure to PCBs took place in Taiwan during the late 1970s, when a group of people accidentally ingested contaminated rice. Children born to mothers who ate the rice had characteristic signs of PCB poisoning, including hyperpigmented skin. The researchers (Lai et al., 2001) had the opportunity to compare the cognitive development of 118 children born to exposed mothers with other children in the community. The children were all followed through the age of 12 and were tested with instruments including the Bayley Scale for Infant Development, the Chinese version of the Stanford–Binet IQ Test, and two nonverbal intelligence tests. The children of mothers who ate the contaminated rice scored lower than the control children on each of these measures throughout the observation period. It appears that prenatal exposure to PCBs has long-term harmful effects on cognitive development.

Experiments with mice show that fetal exposure to radiation in high doses can cause defects in a number of organs, including the eyes, central nervous system, and skeleton (e.g., Hossain et al., 2005). Pregnant women who were exposed to atomic radiation during the bombing of Hiroshima and Nagasaki in World War II gave birth to babies who were more likely to be intellectually disabled in addition to being physically deformed (Sadler, 2005). Pregnant women are advised to avoid unnecessary exposure to x-rays. (Ultrasound, which is not an x-ray, has not been shown to be harmful to the fetus [Park, 2008].)

The risks of radiation and other environmental agents to the embryo and fetus are summarized in Concept Review 3.2.

Concept Review 3.2 Risks of Various Agents to the Embryo and Fetus

Agent	Risks

Prescription Drugs*

Agent	Risks
Accutane (used to treat acne; repeated blood tests are required to show that one is not pregnant or encountering drug-related problems)	Stillbirth, malformation of limbs and organs. Do not use during pregnancy.
Bendectin	Cleft palate, malformation of the heart. Do not use.
Carbamazepine (and other anticonvulsant drugs)	Spina bifida. Do not use.
Diethylstilbestrol (DES; once used to help maintain pregnancy)	Cancer of the cervix or testes in offspring. (No longer available.)
Strong general anesthesia during labour (sedation that goes beyond normal medical practice)	Anoxia, asphyxiation, brain damage. Can request local anesthesia instead.
Progestin (a synthetic version of the natural hormone progesterone, which is sometimes used to help maintain pregnancy)	Masculinization of the sex organs of female embryos, possible development of "masculine" aggressiveness. Ask obstetrician.
Streptomycin (an antibiotic)	Deafness. Ask obstetrician about alternatives.
Tetracycline (an antibiotic)	Malformed bones, yellow teeth. Ask obstetrician about alternatives.
Thalidomide (several uses, including sedation)	Malformed or missing limbs. Do not use.

© Brooke Fasani Auchincloss/Corbis

Other Drugs

Agent	Risks
Alcohol	Fetal death, low birth weight, addiction, academic and intellectual problems, hyperactivity, distractibility, fetal alcohol syndrome (FAS), including characteristic facial features. Best not to drink alcohol during pregnancy.
Aspirin, ibuprofen	Bleeding, respiratory problems. Ask obstetrician about alternatives.
Caffeine (the stimulant found in coffee, tea, colas, chocolate)	Stimulates fetus (not necessarily a problem in itself); miscarriage and low birth weight are suspected. Ask obstetrician about latest information.
Cigarette smoke (the stimulant nicotine and carbon monoxide are transmitted through the placenta)	Stimulates fetus (not necessarily a problem in itself), premature birth, low birth weight, fetal death, academic problems, hyperactivity, and short attention span. Best not to smoke during pregnancy.

Rick's Photography/Shutterstock.com

Concept Review 3.2 *(Continued)*

Agent	Risks
Opiates—heroin, morphine, others	Low birth weight, premature birth, addiction, toxemia (pre-eclampsia). Avoid during pregnancy.
Marijuana	Tremors, startling, premature birth, birth defects, neurological problems. Avoid during pregnancy.

Vitamins†

Vitamin A (high doses)	Cleft palate, damage to the eyes.
Vitamin D (high doses)	Intellectual deficiency.

Pathogens (disease-causing agents)

HIV (the virus that causes AIDS)	Physical deformity and intellectual deficiency. Check with obstetrician about avoiding transmission to fetus and neonate.
Rubella (German measles)	Neurological impairment involving sensation and perception (vision, hearing), intellectual disability, heart problems, cataracts.
Syphilis (a sexually transmitted infection caused by the *Treponema pallidum* bacterium)	Infant mortality, seizures, intellectual disability, sensory impairment (vision, hearing), liver damage, malformation of bones and teeth. Possible to treat during pregnancy; ask obstetrician.

Environmental Hazards

Heavy metals (lead, mercury, zinc)	Intellectual deficiency, hyperactivity, stillbirth, problems in memory formation. Remain alert to your environment and adjust, if possible.
Paint fumes (heavy exposure)	Intellectual deficiency. Remain alert to your environment and adjust, if possible.
PCBs (polychlorinated biphenyls), dioxin, other insecticides and herbicides	Stillbirth, low birth weight, cognitive impairment, motor impairment. Remain alert to your environment and adjust, if possible.
X-rays	Deformation of organs. Ask obstetrician before having x-rays.

Biochemical Incompatibility with Mother

Rh antibodies	Infant mortality, brain damage. Mother can receive Rh immunoglobulin after delivery. Neonate may receive blood transfusion.

*Normally healthful, even life-saving drugs can be harmful to the embryo and fetus. Women should inform their physicians when they are pregnant, may be pregnant, or are planning to become pregnant.

†Adequate intake of vitamins is essential to the well-being of the mother and the embryo and fetus. Most obstetricians advise pregnant women to take vitamin supplements. However, too much of a good thing can be harmful. In brief, don't do "megavitamins." And when in doubt, ask your obstetrician.

Svetlana Lukienko/Shutterstock.com

Maternal Stress

QUESTION » **What are the apparent effects of maternal stress on the child?** Although pregnancy can be a time of immense gratification for women, it can also be a time of stress. The baby might be unplanned and unwanted. Parents might not have the financial resources or the room for the child. The mother might be experiencing physical discomforts because of the pregnancy.

How does a mother's emotional state affect her fetus? Emotions such as stress and anxiety are psychological feeling states, but they also have physiological components. For example, they are linked to the secretion of "stress hormones" such as adrenaline and corticosteroids. Adrenaline stimulates the mother's heart rate, respiratory rate, and other bodily functions. Hormones pass through the placenta and also have an effect on the fetus. For example, corticosteroids appear to decrease the growth of the placenta (Sawady et al., 2007). Extremes of anxiety have been shown to heighten the probabilities of low birth weight, prematurity, and miscarriage (Van den Bergh et al., 2005). However, injections of corticosteroids may help prevent certain types of brain injury in premature infants (Liu et al., 2008). Overall, there is strong evidence linking maternal stress during pregnancy to child behavioural problems (O'Connor, Heron, & Glover, 2002; Ramchandani, Richter, Norris, & Stein, 2010), difficult infant temperament (Davis & Sandman, 2010), cognitive development (LaPlante, Brunet, Schmitz, Clampi, & King, 2008), and later school performance (Li et al., 2013). Health Canada's *A Sensible Guide to a Healthy Pregnancy* (2007) addresses the issue of emotional well-being and encourages expectant mothers to relax during pregnancy and not to take on additional pressures or burdens if possible.

An interesting Canadian longitudinal study examining the effects of a natural disaster on prenatal maternal stress was conducted by researchers in Montreal. Suzanne King and David Laplante followed 150 children who were exposed in utero to a natural disaster (the 1998 Quebec ice storm). These authors suggest that a major stressful event (e.g., a natural disaster and aftermath) can have a negative impact on various child outcomes (e.g., cognitive, language, emotional functioning) (Dancause et al., 2011; King & Laplante, 2005; Laplante et al., 2004). While natural disasters are beyond anyone's control, this study reaffirms the importance of reducing maternal stress levels. However, in keeping with our nature and nurture theme, there are recent studies showing preliminary evidence for the interplay between genes and maternal prenatal stress and mood (Hill et al, 2013; Hompes et al., 2013). Advances in research methods and assessment will allow for growth in this area of study in the years to follow.

A CLOSER LOOK DIVERSITY

The Effects of Parents' Age on Children—Do Men Really Have All the Time in the World?

What if 30-year-old women started looking at 50-year-old men as damaged goods, what with their washed-up sperm, meaning those 50-year-olds might actually have to date (gasp!) women their own age? What if men, as the years passed, began to look with new eyes at Ms. Almost Right?

—Lisa Belkin

Former Canadian prime minister, Pierre Elliott Trudeau, fathered his last child in his 70s. It has been widely known that women's chances of conceiving children decline as they age. As noted by Belkin (2009), the traditional message has been "Women: you'd better hurry up. Men: you have all the time in the world."

Continued

Continued

Not so, apparently. True: From a biological vantage point, the 20s may be the ideal age for women to bear children. Teenage mothers have a higher incidence of infant mortality and children with low birth weight (Phipps et al., 2002; Save the Children, 2008). Early teens who become pregnant may place a burden on bodies that may not have matured enough to facilitate pregnancy and childbirth. Teenage mothers also are less educated and less likely to obtain prenatal care. These factors are associated with high-risk pregnancy (Berg et al., 2003).

CP PHOTO/staff

What about women older than 30? Women's fertility declines gradually until the mid-30s, after which it declines more rapidly. Women beyond their middle 30s may have passed the point at which their reproductive systems function most efficiently. Women possess all their ova in immature form at birth. Over 30 years, these cells are exposed to the slings and arrows of an outrageous environment of toxic wastes, chemical pollutants, and radiation, thus increasing the risk of chromosomal abnormalities such as Down syndrome (Behrman et al., 2000). Women who wait until their 30s or 40s to have children also increase the likelihood of having stillborn or preterm babies (Berg et al., 2003). But with adequate prenatal care, the risk of bearing a premature or unhealthy baby still is relatively small, even for older first-time mothers (Berg et al., 2003). This news should be encouraging for women who have delayed, or plan to delay, bearing children until their 30s or 40s.

Older fathers are more likely to produce abnormal sperm, leading to fertility problems (Belkin, 2009). But that's only the tip of the iceberg. University of Queensland researchers analyzed data from some 33 000 U.S. children and found that the older the father is at conception, the lower a child's score tends to be on tests of reading skills, reasoning, memory, and concentration. The ages of 29 and 30 are something of a turning point for men, because children conceived past these ages are at greater risk for the psychological disorders of schizophrenia and bipolar disorder (Perrin et al., 2007). Children born to men past 40 also have a greater risk of autism (Reichenberg et al., 2006).

RISKY BUSINESS?

Chance of autism spectrum disorder among 132 271 subjects, by paternal age:

6 in 10 000	**9** in 10 000
15- to 29-year-old fathers	30- to 39-year-old fathers
32 in 10 000	**52** in 10 000
40- to 49-year-old fathers	50- year-old fathers and older

Based on data from Reichenberg, A. et al. (2006). Advancing paternal age and autism. *Archives of General Psychiatry, 63*(9), 1026–1032.

These findings do not mean that the majority of children born to men past their reproductive "prime" will develop these problems, but it does mean that men's age, like women's age, is related to risks for their children. As noted by one of the researchers in schizophrenia, "It turns out the optimal age for being a mother is the same as the optimal age for being a father" (Malaspina, 2009).

Active Review

13. Mothers who ingest folic acid reduce their risk of giving birth to babies with _____ tube defects.

14. _____ are environmental agents that can harm the developing embryo or fetus.

15. Women (can or cannot?) be successfully treated for syphilis during pregnancy.

16. Toxemia is mainly characterized by high _____ pressure.

17. In _____ incompatibility, antibodies produced by the mother are transmitted to a fetus or newborn infant and cause brain damage or death.

18. _____ was once prescribed to help women maintain their pregnancies, but it caused cervical and testicular cancer in some of their children.

19. The babies of women who regularly used _____ during pregnancy have been found to show increased tremors and startling.

20. Heavy maternal use of alcohol is linked to _____ alcohol syndrome (FAS).

21. Women who smoke during pregnancy deprive their fetuses of _____, sometimes resulting in stillbirth or persistent academic problems.

22. Fetal exposure to the heavy metals lead and mercury can (slow or accelerate?) mental development.

Reflect & Relate: How will your knowledge of critical periods of prenatal development enable you to predict—and possibly prevent—the effects of various agents on the embryo and fetus? How difficult do you think it would be for you or someone you know to give up drinking alcohol or smoking during pregnancy? Would looking upon the "sacrifice" as temporary make it easier?

Recite an Active Summary

3.1 The Germinal Stage: Wanderings

What happens during the germinal stage of prenatal development?

During the germinal stage, the zygote divides repeatedly but does not gain in mass. It travels through a fallopian tube to the uterus, where it implants. It then takes the form of a blastocyst. Layers of cells form within the embryonic disk. The outer part of the blastocyst differentiates into membranes that will protect and nourish the embryo.

If the dividing mass of cells is moving through a fallopian tube and then "wandering" through the uterus for another few days, how does it obtain any nourishment?

Before implantation, the dividing cluster of cells is nourished by the yolk of the original egg cell. Once implanted in the uterine wall, it obtains nourishment from the mother.

3.2 The Embryonic Stage

What happens during the embryonic stage of prenatal development?

The embryonic stage lasts from implantation until the eighth week of development, during which the major organ systems differentiate. Development follows cephalocaudal and proximodistal trends. The outer layer of the embryonic disk develops into the nervous system, sensory organs, nails, hair, teeth, and skin. Two ridges form the neural tube, from which the nervous system develops. The inner layer forms the digestive and respiratory systems, liver, and pancreas. The middle layer becomes the excretory, reproductive, and circulatory systems, the muscles, the skeleton, and the inner layer of the skin. The heart begins to beat during the fourth week. Toward the end of the first month, arm and leg buds appear and the face takes shape. The nervous system has also begun to develop. By the end of the second month, limbs are elongating, facial features are becoming distinct, teeth buds have formed, the kidneys are working, and the liver is producing red blood cells.

How do some babies develop into girls and others into boys?

By five to six weeks, the embryo has undifferentiated sex organs that resemble female structures. Testes produce male sex hormones that spur development of male genital organs and the male duct system.

How does the embryo get nourishment from its mother? How does it eliminate waste products?

The embryo and fetus exchange nutrients and wastes with the mother through a mass of tissue called the placenta. The umbilical cord connects the fetus to the placenta. The germs that cause syphilis and rubella can pass through the placenta. Some drugs also pass through, including aspirin, narcotics, and alcohol.

3.3 The Fetal Stage

What happens during the fetal stage of prenatal development?

The fetal stage lasts from the end of the embryonic stage until birth. The fetus begins to turn at the ninth or tenth week. The second trimester is characterized by maturation of organs and gains in size. By the end of the second trimester, the fetus opens and shuts its eyes, sucks its thumb, alternates between wakefulness and sleep, and responds to light and sounds. During the third trimester, the heart and lungs become increasingly capable of sustaining independent life. The mother usually detects fetal movements during the fourth month. By the end of the second trimester, the fetus turns somersaults.

3.4 Environmental Influences on Prenatal Development

How does the nutrition of the mother affect prenatal development?

Malnutrition in the mother has been linked to low birth weight, prematurity, stunted growth, retardation of brain development, cognitive deficiencies, and behavioural problems. Folic acid reduces the risk of neural tube defects.

What are teratogens? Does it matter when, during pregnancy, a woman is exposed to them?

Teratogens are environmental agents that can harm the embryo and fetus. Exposure to particular teratogens is most harmful during critical periods—the times when certain organs are developing. The embryo is generally more vulnerable than the fetus because the major organ systems are differentiating. Women who contract rubella may bear children who suffer from deafness, intellectual disability, heart disease, or cataracts. Syphilis can cause miscarriage, stillbirth, or congenital syphilis. Babies can be infected with HIV in utero, during childbirth, or through breast-feeding. Toxemia is characterized by high blood pressure and is connected with preterm and/or undersized babies. In Rh incompatibility, antibodies produced by the mother are transmitted to a fetus or newborn infant and cause brain damage or death.

What are the effects of drugs taken by the mother on prenatal development?

Maternal use of Accutane is connected with numerous abnormalities in the embryo. Thalidomide causes missing or stunted limbs in babies. Tetracycline can cause yellowed teeth and bone problems. DES leads to high risk of cervical and testicular cancer. High doses of vitamins A and D are associated with nervous system damage and heart defects. Maternal addiction to narcotics is linked to low birth weight, prematurity, and toxemia, and fetuses can be born addicted themselves. Marijuana may cause tremors and startling in babies. Cocaine increases the risk of stillbirth, low birth weight, and birth defects. Maternal use of alcohol is linked to death of the fetus and neonate, malformations, growth deficiencies, and fetal alcohol spectrum disorder (FASD). Caffeine is associated with miscarriage and low birth weight. Maternal cigarette smoking is linked to low birth weight, stillbirth, and intellectual disability.

What are the effects of environmental hazards during pregnancy?

Prenatal exposure to heavy metals threatens cognitive development. Prenatal exposure to mercury is connected with neurological damage. Prenatal exposure to PCBs is associated with babies that are smaller, less responsive, and more likely to develop cognitive deficits. Fetal exposure to radiation can cause neural and skeletal problems.

What are the apparent effects of maternal stress on the child?

Maternal stress is linked to the secretion of hormones such as adrenaline, which pass through the placenta and affect the baby. Maternal stress may be connected with complications during pregnancy and labour, preterm or low-birth-weight babies, and irritable babies.

Key Terms

germinal stage 82
blastocyst 82
embryonic disk 82
trophoblast 82
umbilical cord 82
placenta 82
embryonic stage 83
cephalocaudal 83
proximodistal 83
ectoderm 83
neural tube 83
endoderm 83

mesoderm 83
androgens 85
testosterone 86
amniotic sac 86
amniotic fluid 86
fetal stage 87
stillbirth 92
teratogens 96
sensitive period 96
syphilis 96
congenital 96
HIV/AIDS 98

rubella 99
pre-eclampsia 100
premature 100
Rh incompatibility 100
thalidomide 101
progestin 101
DES 101
fetal alcohol spectrum disorders (FASD) 103
fetal alcohol syndrome (FAS) 103
fetal alcohol effect (FAE) 103

Active Learning Resources

Go to *Voyages in Development's* CourseMate at **www .nelsonbrain.com**, where you will find an interactive eBook, flashcards, Pre-Lecture Quizzes, Section Quizzes, Exam Practice, videos, and more.

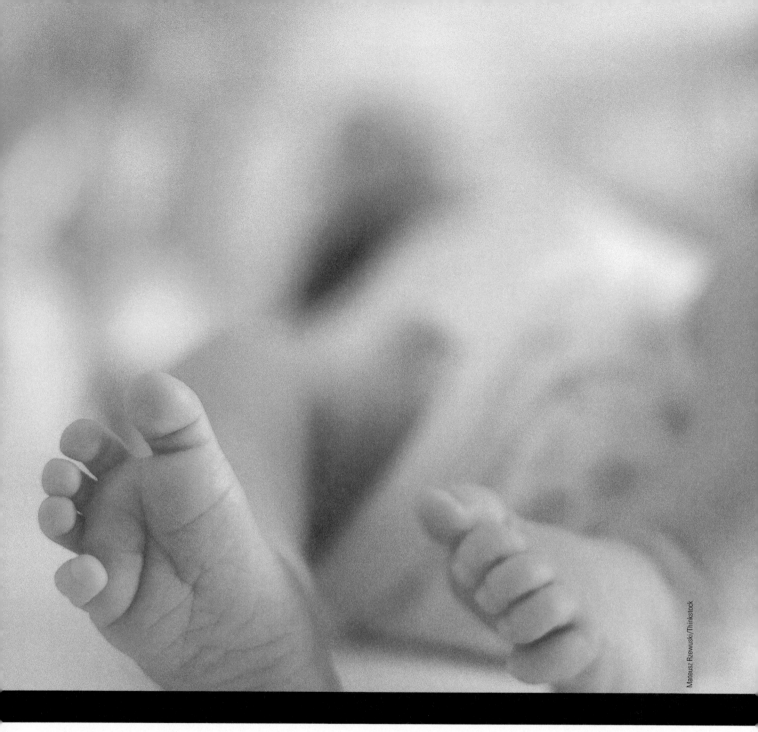

Mateusz Rzewuski/Thinkstock

Major Topics

BIRTH AND THE NEWBORN BABY:

In the New World

4

Truth or Fiction?

T | F The fetus signals its mother when it is ready to be born. **p. 118**

T | F After birth, babies are held upside down and slapped on the buttocks to stimulate independent breathing. **p. 121**

T | F The way that the umbilical cord is cut determines whether the baby's "belly button" will be an "innie" or an "outie." **p. 121**

T | F Women who give birth according to the Lamaze method do not experience pain. **p. 124**

T | F In Canada nearly 18 percent of births are by cesarean section. **p. 125**

T | F It is abnormal to feel depressed following childbirth. **p. 132**

T | F Parents must have extended early contact with their newborn children if adequate bonding is to take place. **p. 134**

T | F More children die from sudden infant death syndrome (SIDS) than from cancer, heart disease, pneumonia, child abuse, HIV/AIDS, cystic fibrosis, and muscular dystrophy combined. **p. 149**

During the last few weeks before she gave birth, Michele explained: "I couldn't get my mind off the pregnancy—what it was going to be like when I finally delivered Lisa. I'd had the amniocentesis, so I knew it was a girl. I'd had the ultrasounds, so all her fingers and toes had been counted, but I was still hoping and praying that everything would turn out all right. To be honest, I was also worried about the delivery. I had always been an A student, and I guess I wanted to earn an A in childbirth as well. Matt was understanding, and he was even helpful, but, you know, it wasn't him.

"My obstetrician was bending over backwards (she could bend—I couldn't) being politically correct and kept on talking about how *we* had gotten pregnant and about how *we* were going to have the baby. Toward the end there, I would have been thrilled if it had really been we. Or I would even have allowed Matt to do it all by himself. But the fact is it was *me*. And I was worrying about how I could even reach the steering wheel of the car in those days, much less deliver a perfect healthy child. On TV, of course, they do it without even disturbing their mascara, but I was living in the real world. And waiting, waiting, waiting. And, oh yes, did I mention waiting?"

Nearly all first-time mothers struggle through the last weeks of pregnancy and worry about the mechanics of delivery. Childbirth is a natural function, of course, but so many mothers have gone to classes to learn how to do what comes naturally! They worry about whether they'll get to the hospital or birthing centre on time ("Is there gas in the car?" "Is it snowing?"). They worry

Ronald Summers/Shutterstock.com

about whether the baby will start breathing on its own properly. They may wonder if they'll do it on their own or need a C-section. And they may worry about whether it will hurt, and how much, and when they should ask for anesthetics, and, well, how to earn that A.

Close to full **term**, Michele and other women are sort of front-loaded, and they feel bent out of shape. Guess what? They are. The weight of the fetus may also be causing backaches. Will they deliver the baby, or will the baby—by being born—deliver them from discomfort? "Hanging in and having Lisa was a wonderful experience," Michele said. "I think Matt should have had it."

4.1 Countdown ...

QUESTION » **What events occur just before childbirth begins?** Early in the last month of pregnancy, the head of the fetus settles in the pelvis. This is called dropping or lightening. Because lightening decreases pressure on the diaphragm, the mother may, in fact, feel lighter.

The first uterine contractions are called **Braxton-Hicks contractions** or false labour contractions. They are relatively painless and may be experienced as early as the sixth month of pregnancy. They tend to increase in frequency as the pregnancy progresses and may serve to tone the muscles that will be used in delivery. Although they may be confused with actual labour contractions, real labour contractions are more painful and regular and are also usually intensified by walking.

A day or so before labour begins, increased pelvic pressure from the fetus may rupture superficial blood vessels in the birth canal so that blood appears in vaginal secretions. The mucous tissue that had plugged the cervix and protected the uterus from infection becomes dislodged. At about this time, one woman in ten has a rush of warm liquid from the vagina. (Women tend to say their "water has broken.") This liquid is amniotic fluid, and its discharge means that the amniotic sac has burst. The amniotic sac usually does not burst until the end of the first stage of childbirth, as described later. Indigestion, diarrhea, an ache in the small of the back, and abdominal cramps are also common signs that labour is beginning.

TRUTH OR FICTION REVISITED: The fetus may actually signal the mother when it is "ready" to be born—that is, when it is mature enough to sustain life outside the uterus. The adrenal and pituitary glands of the fetus may trigger labour by secreting hormones (Snegovskikh et al., 2006).

Fetal hormones stimulate the placenta (which is a gland as well as a relay station for nutrition and wastes between mother and fetus) and the uterus to secrete **prostaglandins** (Plunkett et al., 2011; Snegovskikh et al., 2011). Prostaglandins are the main culprits when women experience uncomfortable cramping before or during menstruation; they also serve the function of exciting the muscles of the uterus to engage in labour contractions. As labour progresses, the pituitary gland releases **oxytocin**, another hormone. Oxytocin stimulates contractions that are powerful enough to expel the baby.

In this chapter, we discuss the events of childbirth and the characteristics of the **neonate**. Arriving in the new world may be a bit more complex than you had thought, and it may also be that neonates can do a bit more than you had imagined.

term The typical period of time between conception and the birth of a baby.

Braxton-Hicks contractions The first (usually painless) contractions of childbirth.

prostaglandins Hormones that stimulate uterine contractions.

oxytocin A pituitary hormone that stimulates labor contractions.

neonate A newborn child.

4.2 The Stages of Childbirth

Regular uterine contractions signal the beginning of childbirth. Developmentalists speak of childbirth as occurring in three stages.

The First Stage

QUESTION » What happens during the first stage of childbirth? In the first stage of childbirth, uterine contractions **efface** and **dilate** the cervix. This passageway needs to widen to about 10 centimetres to allow the baby to pass. Dilation of the cervix is responsible for most of the pain during childbirth. If the cervix dilates rapidly and easily, there may be little or no discomfort.

The first stage is the long stage. Among women undergoing their first deliveries, it may last from a few hours to more than a day. Half a day to a day is about average, but the first stage sometimes is much briefer and sometimes lasts up to a couple of days. Subsequent pregnancies take less time and may be surprisingly rapid—sometimes between one and two hours. The first contractions are not usually all that painful and are spaced 10–20 minutes apart. They may last from 20 to 40 seconds each.

As the process continues, the contractions become more powerful, frequent, and regular. Women are usually advised to go to the hospital or birthing centre when the contractions are four to five minutes apart. Until the end of the first stage of labour, the mother is frequently in a labour room with her partner or another companion.

If the woman is to be "prepped"—that is, if her pubic hair is to be shaved—it takes place now. The prep is intended to reduce the chances of infection during delivery and to facilitate the performance of an **episiotomy** (described later). A woman may be given an enema to prevent an involuntary bowel movement during labour. However, many women find prepping and enemas degrading and seek obstetricians who do not routinely perform them. In Canada the move towards more natural forms of childbirth has diminished or, in some cases, eliminated the prepping routine altogether.

During the first stage of childbirth, fetal monitoring may be used. One kind of monitoring is an electronic sensing device strapped around the woman's abdomen. It can measure the fetal heart rate as well as the frequency, strength, and duration of the mother's contractions. An abnormal heart rate alerts the medical staff to possible fetal distress so that appropriate steps can be taken, such as speeding up the delivery by such means as forceps or the vacuum extraction tube. The forceps is a curved instrument that fits around the baby's head and makes it possible to pull the baby out of the mother's body. The vacuum extraction tube relies on suction to pull the baby through the birth canal.

When the cervix is almost fully dilated, the head of the fetus begins to move into the vagina, or birth canal. This process is called **transition**. During transition, which lasts about 30 minutes or less, contractions usually are frequent and strong.

The Second Stage

QUESTION » What happens during the second stage of childbirth? The second stage of childbirth follows transition. This stage begins when the baby appears at the opening of the vagina (now referred to as the birth canal; see Figure 4.1 ▓). The second stage is briefer than the first stage. It may last minutes or a few hours and culminates in the birth of the baby. The woman may be taken to a delivery room for the second stage of childbirth.

The contractions of the second stage stretch the skin surrounding the birth canal farther and propel the baby farther along. The baby's head is said to have crowned when it begins to emerge from the birth canal. Once crowning has occurred, the baby normally emerges completely within minutes.

The physician, nurse, or midwife may perform an episiotomy once crowning takes place. The purpose of the episiotomy is to prevent random tearing

efface To thin.

dilate To widen or enlarge.

episiotomy A surgical incision in the area between the birth canal and the anus that widens the vaginal opening, preventing random tearing during childbirth.

transition The initial movement of the head of the fetus into the birth canal.

Figure 4.1 ■ The Stages of Childbirth

In the first stage, uterine contractions efface and dilate the cervix to about 10 centimetres so that the baby may pass. The second stage begins with movement of the baby into the birth canal and ends with the birth of the baby. During the third stage, the placenta separates from the uterine wall and is expelled through the birth canal.

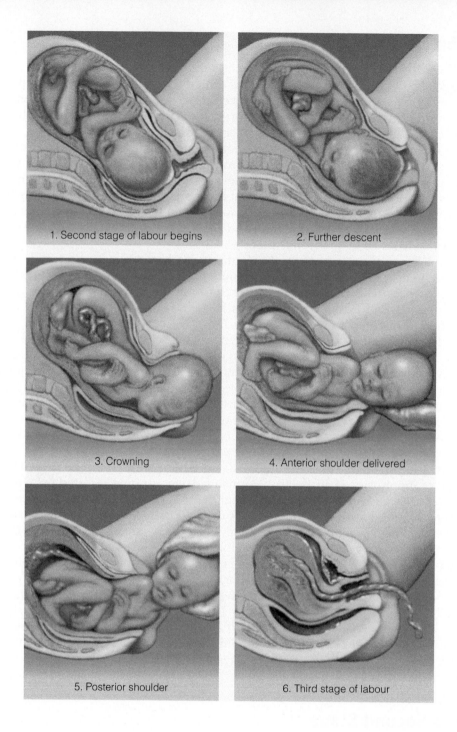

1. Second stage of labour begins

2. Further descent

3. Crowning

4. Anterior shoulder delivered

5. Posterior shoulder

6. Third stage of labour

when the area between the birth canal and the anus becomes severely stretched. Women are unlikely to feel the incision because the pressure of the crowning head tends to numb the region between the vagina and the anus. Like prepping and the enema, episiotomy is controversial and is not practised in Europe. The incision may cause itching and discomfort as it heals. The incidence of the use of episiotomy dropped from about 70 percent in 1983 to 19 percent in 2000 (Goldberg et al., 2002). Many health professionals believe that episiotomy is warranted when the baby's shoulders are wide or the baby's heart rate declines for a long period of time. But the strongest predictor of whether a practitioner will choose to use episiotomy is not the condition of the mother or the baby but rather whether the physician normally performs an episiotomy.

Whether or not the physician performs an episiotomy, the passageway into the world outside is a tight fit, and the baby squeezes through. Mothers may be alarmed at the visual results of the tight fit. Sometimes the baby's head and facial features are quite bent out of shape. The baby's head can wind up elongated, its nose can be flattened or pushed to the side, and the ears can be contorted—as though this little thing had gotten caught up in a prize-fight! Parents understandably wonder whether their baby's features will "pop up" properly or return to a more normal shape. Usually they need not worry.

Don't wait for the baby to be held upside down and slapped on the buttocks to spur breathing on its own. That happens in old movies but not in today's hospitals and birthing centres. Today, mucus is suctioned from the baby's mouth as soon as the head emerges from the birth canal, to clear any obstructions from the passageway for breathing. The procedure may be repeated when the baby has fully emerged. TRUTH OR FICTION REVISITED: Therefore, it is not true that newborn babies are held upside down and slapped on the buttocks to stimulate independent breathing.

When the baby is breathing adequately on its own, the umbilical cord is clamped and severed about 8 centimetres from the baby's body (see Figure 4.2 ■). At about 266 days after conception, mother and infant have finally become separate beings. The stump of the umbilical cord will dry and fall off on its own in about seven to ten days. There are exceptions. Spencer's (first author) daughter Allyn, nearly two at the time, yanked off the umbilical cord of her newborn sister Jordan, causing a crisis in the family but no particular harm to Jordan.

TRUTH OR FICTION REVISITED: It is not true that the way the umbilical cord is cut determines whether the baby's "belly button" will be an "innie" or an "outie." Your belly-button status—that is, whether you have an outie or an innie—is unrelated to the methods of your obstetrician.

You might think it would be nice for mother and baby to hang out for a while at this juncture, but the baby is frequently whisked away by a nurse, who performs various procedures—for example, footprinting the baby, supplying an ID bracelet, putting antibiotic ointment (erythromycin) or drops of silver nitrate into the baby's eyes to prevent bacterial infections, and giving the baby a vitamin K injection to help its blood clot properly if it bleeds (newborn babies do not manufacture vitamin K). While this goes on, the mother is in the third stage of labour.

The Third Stage

QUESTION » What happens during the third stage of childbirth? The third stage of labour is also referred to as the placental stage. It lasts from a few minutes to an hour or more. During this stage, the placenta separates from the wall of the uterus and is expelled through the birth canal along with fetal membranes.

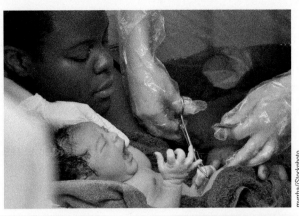

Figure 4.2 ■ A Clamped Umbilical Cord
The stump of the cord dries and falls off in about ten days.

OBSERVING CHILDREN, UNDERSTANDING OURSELVES

Birth

Lee delivers a healthy baby boy named Carter after labouring for more than nine hours.

What are the different birthing options available to expectant mothers? What are the stages of birth? If a baby scores low on the Apgar scale, what treatment options do parents and health-care providers have? Does the Apgar score predict the future health of a baby?

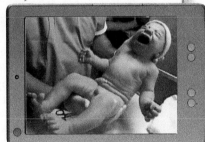

From Rathus. *Childhood and Adolescence*, 5E. © 2014 South-Western, a part of Cengage Learning, Inc. Reproduced by permission. www.cengage.com/permissions

Go to www.nelson.com/voyages2ce to watch the video, answer the questions, and e-mail your responses to your professor.

CHAPTER 4 BIRTH AND THE NEWBORN BABY

Bleeding is normal at this time. The uterus begins to shrink, although it will take some time for it to approximate its prepregnancy size. The obstetrician now sews the episiotomy, if one has been performed.

Active Review

1. The first uterine contractions are "false" and are called _____ contractions.

2. A day or so before delivery, about one woman in ten has a rush of _____ fluid from the vagina.

3. In the first stage of childbirth, uterine contractions cause the cervix to become effaced and _____.

4. _____ occurs when the cervix is almost fully dilated and the head of the fetus begins to move into the birth canal.

5. When the baby is breathing adequately, the _____ cord is clamped and severed.

6. During the third stage, the _____ separates from the uterine wall and is expelled.

Reflect & Relate: How do you feel about the routine performance of "prepping" and episiotomy? Why are these controversial and personal issues?

4.3 Methods of Childbirth

QUESTIONS » What methods of childbirth are in use today? What are their effects? Think of old movies in which a woman is giving birth in her home on the prairie, and a neighbour emerges heralding the good news to the anxious father and members of the community. Perhaps prairies have not hosted the majority of childbirths over the millennia, but childbirth was once a more intimate procedure that usually took place in the woman's home and involved her, perhaps a **midwife**, and her family. This pattern is followed in many less developed nations today, but only rarely in the developed nations. Contemporary Canadian childbirths usually take place in hospitals, where they are overseen by physicians who use sophisticated instruments and anesthetics to protect mother and child from complications and discomfort. There is no question that modern medicine has saved lives, but child bearing has also become more impersonal. Some argue that modern methods wrest from women control over their own bodies. They even argue that anesthetics have denied many women the experience of giving birth—although many or most women admit that they appreciate having the experience "muted." Let's consider methods for facilitating childbirth.

Anesthesia

Painful childbirth has historically been seen as the standard for women. But the development of modern medicine and effective anesthetics has led many people to believe that women need not experience discomfort during childbirth. Today, at least some **anesthesia** is used in most deliveries.

General anesthesia achieves its anesthetic effect by putting the woman to sleep by means of a barbiturate that is injected into a vein in the hand or arm. Other drugs in common use are tranquilizers, oral barbiturates, and narcotics. These drugs are not anesthetics per se, but they may reduce anxiety and the perception of pain without causing sleep.

General anesthesia can have negative effects on the infant, including abnormal patterns of sleep and wakefulness and decreased attention and social responsiveness shortly after birth. The higher the dose, the greater the effect. But there is mixed evidence about whether these anesthetics have long-term effects on the child (Landau & Yentis, 2011; Van Norman et al., 2011). Some of the variability has to do with the use of drugs by the physician, rather than with the drugs themselves.

midwife An individual who helps women in childbirth.

anesthesia A method that produces partial or total loss of the sense of pain.

Regional or local anesthetics deaden pain without putting the mother to sleep. In the pudendal block, the mother's external genitals are numbed by local injection. In the epidural block and the spinal block, anesthesia is injected into the spinal canal or spinal cord, temporarily numbing the body below the waist. Local anesthesia has minor depressive effects on the strength and activity levels of neonates shortly after birth, but when the drugs are administered properly, the effects have not been shown to linger (Torpy et al., 2011).

In contrast to the use of anesthesia, there is a trend toward **natural childbirth**. In natural childbirth, a woman uses no anesthesia. Instead, a woman is educated about the biological aspects of reproduction and delivery, encouraged to maintain physical fitness, and taught relaxation and breathing exercises.

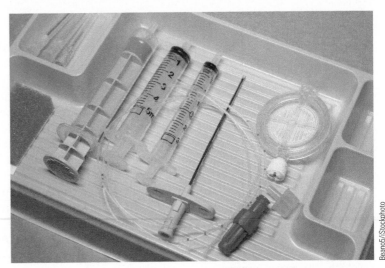

An Epidural Anesthesia Kit
An epidural "block" enables the woman giving birth to stay awake but feel no sensation in the pelvis or below.

Hypnosis and Biofeedback

Hypnosis has been used to help clients stick to diets, quit smoking, and undergo dental treatments with less discomfort. It has also been used with some success as an alternative to anesthesia during childbirth (Datta et al., 2010; Landolt & Milling, 2011). Mothers who use "HypnoBirthing" do not listen to someone telling them to sleep or stare at someone waving a watch on a cord in front of their eyes. Rather, they are encouraged to focus on relaxing scenes and to decrease their muscle tension. HypnoBirthing does not fully do away with pain, but, like some other contemporary psychological methods of childbirth, it puts the mother in charge and gives her "something to do" while she is delivering her baby.

Biofeedback is a method that provides the woman in labour with continuous information about what is happening with various bodily functions. Muscle tension and blood pressure are among the functions that can be targeted. Studies suggest that helping women reduce muscle tension may have some positive effects early in labour, but greater benefits have not so far been established (Loayza et al., 2011).

natural childbirth A method of childbirth in which women use no anesthesia and are educated about childbirth and strategies for coping with discomfort.

An Exercise Class for Pregnant Women
Years ago, the rule of thumb was that pregnant women were not to exert themselves. Today, it is recognized that exercise is healthful for pregnant women because it promotes cardiovascular fitness and increases muscle strength. Fitness and strength are assets during childbirth as well as at other times.

Prepared Childbirth

Most women who are pregnant for the first time expect pain and discomfort during childbirth. Certainly the popular media image of childbirth is one in which the woman sweats profusely and screams and thrashes in pain. When the French obstetrician Fernand Lamaze visited Russia, he discovered that many Russian women bore babies without anesthetics or pain. He studied their relaxation techniques and brought these to Western Europe, the United States, and Canada, where they became known as the **Lamaze method**, or prepared childbirth. Lamaze (1981) contended that women could engage in breathing and relaxation exercises that would lessen fear and pain if they were given something to do and distracted from discomfort.

In the Lamaze method, women do not go it alone. The mother-to-be attends Lamaze classes with a "coach"—most often her partner—who will aid her in the delivery room by massaging her, timing the contractions, offering social support, and coaching her in patterns of breathing and relaxation. The woman is taught to breathe in a specific way during contractions. As in HypnoBirthing and biofeedback, she is taught how to contract specific muscles in her body while remaining generally relaxed (Park, 2011). The idea is that she will be able to transfer this training to the process of childbirth by remaining generally at ease while her uterine muscles contract. The procedure tones muscles that will be helpful in childbirth (such as leg muscles) and enables her to minimize tension, conserve energy, and experience less anxiety.

The woman is also educated about the process of childbirth. The partner or another coach is integrated into the process. The woman receives more social support as a result. TRUTH OR FICTION REVISITED: It is not true that women who give birth according to the Lamaze method do not experience pain. But they apparently report less pain and ask for less medication when others, such as their partner, are present (Lothian, 2011).

Social support during labour can be provided by individuals other than a woman's partner. A mother, sibling, or friend can serve as a coach. Studies also demonstrate the benefit of continuous emotional support during labour by an experienced but nonprofessional female companion known as a doula (Guzikowski, 2006). Women with doulas appear to have shorter labours than women without doulas (Campbell et al., 2006).

Lamaze method A childbirth method in which women are educated about childbirth, learn to relax and breathe in patterns that conserve energy and lessen pain, and have a coach (usually the father) present during childbirth. Also termed prepared childbirth.

cesarean section A method of childbirth in which the neonate is delivered through a surgical incision in the abdomen. (Also spelled Caesarean.)

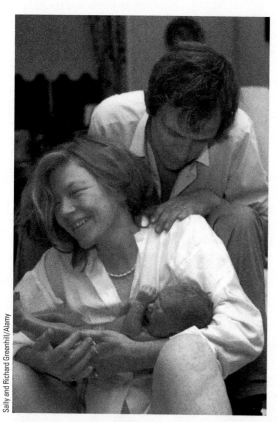

Partner in the Delivery Room
Today, the woman's partner is usually integrated into the process of childbirth. In this case, the father and mother take pride in "their" accomplishments of childbirth.

Cesarean Section

Many controversies surround the **cesarean section**. The first that comes to my mind involves its proper spelling. Years ago the term was spelled *Caesarean* section, after the Roman emperor Julius Caesar, who was thought to have been delivered in this manner. Now, however, the more common spelling is *cesarean*. In any event, the term is usually abbreviated *C-section*.

In a C-section, the physician delivers the baby by abdominal surgery. She or he cuts through the abdomen and the uterus and physically removes the baby. The incisions are then sewn up. Most health professionals encourage the mother to get up and walk around on the same day as the surgery, but make no mistake about it: Doing so is usually painful. When the C-section first came into common practice, it left visible scars in the abdomen. Physicians usually perform C-sections today in such a way that the incision is more or less hidden by the upper edge of the woman's pubic hair. This method is referred to as a "bikini cut," referring to the shape of the brief swimsuit.

Physicians prefer a C-section to vaginal delivery when they believe that normal delivery may threaten the mother or child or may simply be more difficult than desired. Typical indications for the C-section are a small pelvis in the mother, maternal weakness or fatigue (brought about, for example, by prolonged labour), or a baby that is too large or in apparent distress. C-sections are also performed when the physician wants to prevent the circulatory systems of the mother and baby from mixing, as might occur when there is bleeding during vaginal delivery. C-sections in such cases help prevent transmission of genital herpes or HIV, the virus that causes AIDS. The combination of anti-HIV drugs and C-section cuts the chance that an HIV-infected mother will transmit HIV to her baby to less than one in 50 (Coovadia, 2004). The physician may also perform a C-section when it appears that the baby is facing in the wrong direction. It is normal, and safest, for babies to be born head first. A C-section is indicated if the baby is going to be born sideways or "backwards"—that is, feet first. Some women ask for C-sections. Some want to avoid the pain of vaginal delivery; others want to control exactly when the baby will be born. This practice in particular has become controversial, especially with certain British papers using headlines like "too posh to push" in reference to elective C-sections of celebrity moms such as Britney Spears, Victoria Beckham, and Elizabeth Hurley. The Society of Obstetricians and Gynaecologists of Canada promotes natural childbirth and believes surgery should only occur when there are medical reasons for it.

As you can see from Figure 4.3 ■, the percentage of vaginal births among women who have had a C-section has also been declining, mainly because health professionals fear that the uterine incision (cut) made during the C-section may rupture during a subsequent vaginal delivery (Cunningham et al., 2011). Is "Once a C-section, always a C-section" the medical standard today?

To see what different Canadian Associations are saying, you may find the following websites as useful in shedding light on the debate:

- The Canadian Association of Midwives' position statement on elective cesarean section (www.canadianmidwives.org).
- Society of Obstetricians and Gynaecologists of Canada (www.sogc.org).
- Child Birth Connection (www.childbirthconnection.org).
- Canadian Medical Association Journal (www.cmaj.ca).
- Canadian Women's Health Network (www.cwhn.ca).

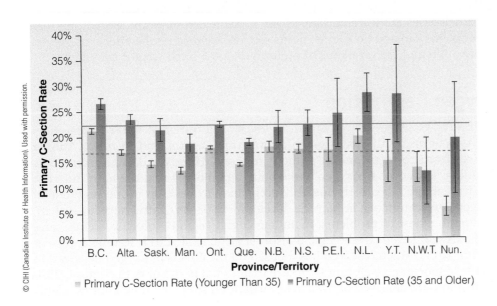

© CIHI (Canadian Institute of Health Information). Used with permission.

■ Primary C-Section Rate (Younger Than 35)   ■ Primary C-Section Rate (35 and Older)

Figure 4.3 ■ Primary Cesarean Section Rates, by Province/Territory, 2011–2012
Source: CIHI.

Home Birth

The overwhelming majority of Canadian women give birth in hospitals. In Canada, there are about nine maternal deaths for every 100 000 live births (Public Health Agency of Canada, 2011). In developing countries, where medical resources are scarce, as many as one woman in 11 will die in childbirth (Save the Children, 2011). Although the difference may be partly explained by women giving birth in hospitals, home delivery can be a reasonably safe option for healthy women who are believed to have little risk of complications, especially if they have given birth before. A certified nurse–midwife can assess a woman's risk for complications and her proximity to emergency medical care, and will usually do so before agreeing to assist with a home birth.

Home birth generally represents an effort by the mother to recapture childbirth as a warm family experience. It challenges the "obstetric view" of birth, which tends to medicalize the experience by making health professionals, rather than the mother, the primary actors in the drama. Some women also choose home birth because it decreases the cost of maternity care for women who have uncomplicated pregnancies and deliveries.

Active Review

7. _____ anesthesia achieves its anesthetic effect during childbirth by putting the woman to sleep.

8. In a(n) _____ block, anesthesia is injected into the spine, numbing the body below the waist.

9. _____ argued that women can learn to dissociate uterine contractions from pain and fear through breathing exercises and muscle-relaxation techniques.

10. A _____ is performed for various reasons, including when a baby is too large to pass through the woman's pelvis, when the mother or baby is in distress, and when there is a need to try to prevent transmission of genital herpes or HIV.

Reflect & Relate: If you were delivering a child, would you want to use anesthetic medication? Would you use the Lamaze method? Why or why not? If you were a prospective father, what would your thoughts be? What are the pros and cons of both methods?

4.4 Birth Problems

Although every delivery is most remarkable from the parents' point of view, most deliveries are unremarkable from a medical standpoint. Still, a number of problems can and do occur. In this section, we discuss the effects of oxygen deprivation and the problems of preterm and low-birth-weight neonates.

Oxygen Deprivation

QUESTION » What are the effects of oxygen deprivation at birth? Researchers use two terms to discuss oxygen deprivation: *anoxia* and *hypoxia*. **Anoxia** derives from roots meaning "without oxygen." **Hypoxia** derives from roots meaning "under" and "oxygen"—the point again being that the baby does not receive enough oxygen throughout pregnancy to develop properly. Prenatal oxygen deprivation can impair the development of the central nervous system, leading to a host of problems, including cognitive and motor problems, cerebral palsy, and even psychological disorders (Liu et al., 2011; Rennie & Rosenbloom, 2011). Much research has focused on the effects of oxygen deprivation on the hippocampus, a brain structure that is vital in memory formation. Children who were deprived of oxygen at birth often show the predicted problems

anoxia A condition characterized by lack of oxygen.

hypoxia A condition characterized by less oxygen than is required.

in learning and memory, and also problems in motor development and spatial relations (Hopkins-Golightly et al., 2003).

Oxygen deprivation can be caused by maternal disorders (such as diabetes), by immaturity of the baby's respiratory system, and by accidents, some of which involve pressure against the umbilical cord during birth. The fetus and emerging baby receive oxygen through the umbilical cord. Passage through the birth canal is tight, and the umbilical cord is usually squeezed during the process. If the squeezing is temporary, the effect is like holding one's breath for a moment, and no problems are likely to ensue. (In fact, slight oxygen deprivation at birth is not unusual, because the transition from receiving oxygen through the umbilical cord to breathing on its own may not take place immediately after the baby is born.) But if constriction of the umbilical cord is prolonged, developmental problems can result. Prolonged constriction is more likely during a **breech presentation**, or bottom-first presentation, when the baby's body may press the umbilical cord against the birth canal.

Fetal monitoring can help detect anoxia before it causes damage. A C-section can be performed if the fetus seems to be in distress.

Preterm and Low-Birth-Weight Infants

QUESTION » What risks are connected with being born prematurely or low in birth weight? Because the fetus makes dramatic gains in weight during the last weeks of pregnancy, prematurity and low birth weight usually go hand in hand. A baby is considered premature, or **preterm**, when birth occurs at or before 37 weeks of gestation, compared with the normal 40 weeks. A baby is considered to have a low birth weight when it weighs less than about 2500 grams. When a baby's birth weight is low, even though it is born at full term, it is referred to as being **small for dates**. As described in Chapter 3, mothers who smoke, use other drugs, or fail to receive proper nutrition place their babies at risk of being small for dates. Small-for-dates babies tend to remain shorter and lighter than their age-mates and show slight delays in learning and problems in attention as compared to age-mates (Heinonen et al., 2011). Preterm babies who survive are more likely than small-for-dates babies to achieve normal heights and weights.

About 7 percent of children are born preterm or low in birth weight, although the incidence varies in different racial and ethnic groups. However, among multiple births, even twins, the risk of having a preterm child rises to at least 50 percent (Kurosawa et al., 2012; Namiiro et al., 2012).

Risks Associated with Prematurity and Low Birth Weight

Neonates weighing between 1500 and 2500 grams are seven times more likely to die than infants of normal birth weight, whereas those weighing less than 1500 grams are nearly 100 times as likely to die (Nadeau et al., 2003; Strunk et al., 2012). But physical survival is only one issue connected with prematurity and low birth weight.

By and large, the lower a child's birth weight, the more poorly he or she fares on measures of neurological development and cognitive functioning throughout the school years (Pritchard et al., 2009; Rogers & Piecuch, 2009). Children whose birth weight was less than 750 grams fare less well at middle-school age than children whose birth weight was 750–1499 grams (Taylor et al., 2004). Both low-birth-weight groups perform more poorly than children whose birth weight was normal. There seem to be sex differences. The cognitive functioning and school achievement of girls with low birth weight seem to improve more rapidly than those of boys with low birth weight (Edwards et al., 2011; Munck et al., 2010).

There are also risks for motor development. One study compared 96 children with very low birth weight (VLBW) with normal-term children at 6, 9, 12,

breech presentation A position in which the fetus enters the birth canal buttocks first.

preterm Born at or before completion of 37 weeks of gestation.

small for dates A description of neonates who are unusually small for their age.

and 18 months, correcting for age according to the expected date of delivery (Jeng et al., 2000). The median age at which the full-term infants began to walk was 12 months, compared with 14 months for the VLBW infants. By 18 months of age, all full-term infants were walking, whereas 11 percent of the VLBW infants had not yet begun to walk.

The outcomes for low-birth-weight children are variable. One research group followed a group of 1338 Dutch individuals who were born in 1983 with either a gestational age of less than 32 weeks or a birth weight of less than 1500 grams (Walther et al., 2000). The children were assessed at the age of two years by their pediatricians, and at the ages of 5 and 9–14 years by teams of investigators, including teachers and parents. All in all, only 10 percent of the group could be characterized as having a severe disability at ages 9–14. However, many more children appeared to have mild to moderate problems in learning or behaviour.

Preschool experience appears to foster the cognitive and social development of VLBW children. Hoy and McClure (2000) compared a group of VLBW children who attended preschool with a group who did not and also with a group of normal-birth-weight children of the same age. The VLBW children who attended preschool outperformed the VLBW children who did not on measures of cognitive functioning and teacher ratings. They earned higher grades, worked harder, were more likely to participate in social interactions, and were more likely to be rated as "learns a lot." However, their performance on all measures was still exceeded somewhat by the normal-birth-weight children.

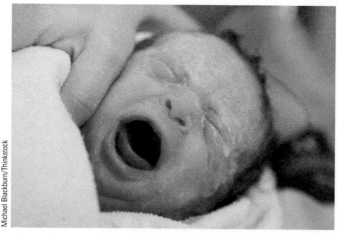

A Newborn Baby
This newborn shows lanugo and vernix, both characteristics of prematurity.

lanugo Fine, downy hair that covers much of the body of neonates, especially preterm babies.

vernix An oily, white substance that coats the skin of neonates, especially preterm babies.

respiratory distress syndrome A cluster of breathing problems, including weak and irregular breathing, to which preterm babies are particularly prone.

Signs of Prematurity

Preterm babies show characteristic signs of immaturity. They are relatively thin because they have not yet formed the layer of fat that gives so many full-term children their round, robust appearance. They often have fine, downy hair, referred to as **lanugo**, and an oily white substance on the skin known as **vernix**. Lanugo and vernix disappear within a few days or weeks. If the babies are born six weeks or more before full term, their nipples have not yet emerged. The testicles of boys born this early have not yet descended into the scrotum. After birth, however, the nipples develop further and the testes descend.

The muscles of preterm babies are immature. As a result, the babies' vital sucking and breathing reflexes are weak. The muscles of preterm babies may not be mature enough to sustain independent breathing. Also, the walls of the tiny air sacs in their lungs may tend to stick together because they do not yet secrete substances that lubricate the walls of the sacs. As a result, babies born more than a month before full term may breathe irregularly or suddenly stop breathing, evidence of a cluster of problems known as **respiratory distress syndrome**. About one baby in seven who is born one month early shows the syndrome. It is found more frequently among infants born still earlier. Respiratory distress syndrome causes a large percentage of neonatal deaths. Preterm infants with severe respiratory stress syndrome show poorer development in cognitive, language, and motor skills and more persistent neurological abnormalities over the first two years of development than infants with less severe respiratory distress and full-term infants. Injecting pregnant women at risk for delivering preterm babies with corticosteroids increases the babies' chances of survival (Murphy et al., 2011). These babies are less likely to have respiratory distress syndrome or severe lung disease. They are also less likely to need treatment with oxygen or mechanical help breathing.

Major strides have been made in helping low-birth-weight children survive. These techniques include increased prenatal use of steroids, decreased use of postnatal steroids, and C-section (Wilson-Costello et al., 2007). Still, low-birth-weight children who survive often have problems, including below-average achievement in language arts and mathematics and various physical, motor, perceptual, neurological, and behavioural impairments—even social shyness and timidity (Schmidt et al., 2008; Taylor et al., 2009).

Preterm infants with very low birth weights (under 1500 grams) are likely to show the greatest cognitive deficits and developmental delays. Still, medical advances in recent years have reduced the severity and incidence of handicaps among babies with very low birth weights.

Treatment of Preterm Babies

Because of their physical frailty, preterm infants usually remain in the hospital and are placed in **incubators**, which maintain a temperature-controlled environment and afford some protection from disease. The infants may be given oxygen, although excessive oxygen can cause permanent eye injury.

One might assume that parents would be more concerned about preterm babies than babies who have gone to full term and thus would treat them better. Ironically, this is not the case. Parents often do not treat preterm neonates as well as they treat full-term neonates. For one thing, preterm neonates are less attractive than full-term babies. Preterm infants usually do not have the robust, appealing appearance of many full-term babies. Their cries are more high pitched and grating, and they are more irritable (Bugental & Happaney, 2004; Gima et al., 2010). The demands of caring for preterm babies can be depressing to mothers (Holsti, 2010; Spittle et al., 2010). Mothers of preterm babies frequently report that they feel alienated from their babies and harbour feelings of failure, guilt, and low self-esteem (Baum et al., 2011; Vigod et al., 2010). They respond less sensitively to their infants' behaviour than mothers of full-term babies (Bugental & Happaney, 2004). Mothers of preterm infants also touch and talk to their infants less and hold them at a greater distance during feeding. Fear of hurting preterm babies can further discourage parents from handling them, but encouraging mothers to massage their preterm infants can help them cope with fear of handling their babies and with feelings of helplessness and hopelessness (Feijó et al., 2006).

After they come home from the hospital, preterm infants remain more passive and less sociable than full-term infants (Korja et al., 2011), so they demand less interaction with parents. However, when their parents do interact with them during the first year, they are more likely to poke at preterm babies, caress them, and talk to them, perhaps in an effort to prod them out of their passivity. Mothers of preterm babies report feeling overprotective toward them. This may in part explain why one-year-old preterm infants explore less and stay closer to their mothers than do full-term babies of the same age.

Preterm infants fare better when they have responsive and caring parents. Longitudinal research shows that preterm children who are reared in attentive and responsive environments attain higher intelligence test scores, have higher self-esteem, show more positive social skills, and have fewer behavioural and emotional problems in childhood than do preterm children reared in less responsive homes (Dieterich et al., 2004; Lawson & Ruff, 2004).

incubator A heated, protective container in which premature infants are kept.

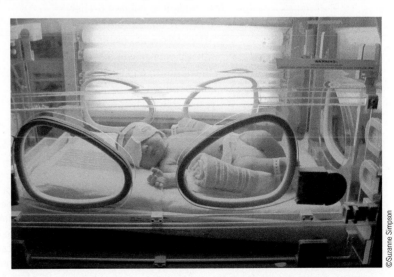
©Suzanne Simpson

Premature newborns typically spend a couple of days in an incubator at the hospital before they go home.

Intervention Programs

A couple of generations ago, preterm babies were left as undisturbed as possible. For one thing, concern was aroused by the prospect of handling such a tiny, frail creature. For another, preterm babies would not normally experience interpersonal

CHAPTER 4 BIRTH AND THE NEWBORN BABY

contact or other sources of external stimulation until full term. However, experiments carried out over the past two decades suggest that preterm infants profit from early stimulation just as full-term babies do. Preterm babies benefit from being cuddled, rocked, talked to, and sung to; from being exposed to recordings of their mothers' voices; and from having mobiles placed within view. Recent studies have shown the value of live and recorded music in the preterm infant's environment (Nordhov et al., 2012). Other effective forms of stimulation include massage (Ho, 2008) and "kangaroo care" (C. C. Johnston et al., 2011), in which the baby spends several hours a day lying skin to skin, chest to chest, with one of its parents, usually the mother. Kangaroo care provides olfactory sensations as well as tactile stimulation. Kangaroo care has been shown to decrease stress and pain in preterm infants, as measured, for example, by more rapid recovery from the "heel stick," a hospital procedure in which blood is drawn from the heel with a syringe (Johnston et al., 2011). Over the longer term, preterm infants exposed to stimulation tend to gain weight more rapidly, show fewer respiratory problems, and make greater advances in motor, intellectual, and neurological development than control preterm babies (Fucile & Gisel, 2010; Nordhov et al., 2010).

Other intervention programs help parents adjust to the birth and care of low-birth-weight infants. One such program involved 92 preterm infants at three sites (Als et al., 2003). The following factors contributed to superior cognitive and motor development in the infants and better adjustment in the parents: early discontinuation of intravenous feeding, hospitalization with intensive care for digestive and other problems, and individualized counselling to foster appreciation of the infant.

As you can see in the "A Closer Look—Diversity" feature, maternal and infant mortality remains a serious problem in many parts of the world.

A CLOSER LOOK DIVERSITY

Maternal and Infant Mortality around the World

Modern medicine has made vast strides in decreasing the rates of maternal and infant mortality, but the advances are not equally spread throughout the world. Save the Children, a nonprofit relief and development organization, tracks the likelihood that a woman will die in childbirth and that an infant will die during its first year (Table 4.1). The likelihood of maternal and infant mortality is connected with factors such as the percentage of births that are attended by trained people, the literacy rate of adult women (which is one measure of the level of education of women), and the participation of women in national government (which is one measure of the extent to which a society empowers women). Figure 4.4 ■ shows the various reasons why children die, according to a recent edition of "State of the World's Mothers" (Save the Children, 2011).

Why are maternal and infant mortality so low in Europe?

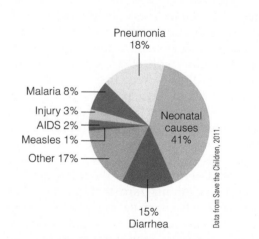

Figure 4.4 ■ Why Do Young Children Die?
Estimates show that pneumonia, diarrhea, and malaria remain the leading killers of children under age five worldwide. Together they account for 41 percent of child deaths. More than 40 percent of all under-five deaths occur in the first month of life. Most of these children could be saved by increasing coverage for known, affordable, and effective interventions. Ensuring proper nutrition is a critical aspect of prevention, because malnutrition contributes to more than a third of all child deaths.
Data from Save the Children, 2011.

Continued

Continued

Maternal and Child Mortality around the World as Related to Women's Life Expectancy and Number of Years of Education

Country	Lifetime Risk of Maternal Mortality (1 in number shown)	Percentage of Women Using Modern Contraception	Female Life Expectancy at Birth	Expected Number of Years of Formal Female Schooling	Child Mortality Rate per 1000 Live Births (from birth through 5 years of age)
Greece	31 800	46	82	17	3
Ireland	17 800	66	83	18	4
Italy	15 200	41	84	17	4
Poland	13 300	28	80	16	7
Japan	12 200	44	87	15	3
Spain	11 400	62	84	18	4
Sweden	11 400	65	83	16	3
Canada	5 600	72	83	16	6
United Kingdom	4 700	82	82	17	6
United States	2 100	68	82	17	8
Russia	1 900	52	74	15	12
China	1 500	86	75	12	19
Cuba	1 400	72	81	19	6
Mexico	500	67	79	14	17
Egypt	380	58	72	11	21
India	140	49	66	10	66
Afghanistan	11	16	45	5	199

Source: Save the Children (2011).

The safest place for a woman to deliver and for her baby to survive is Greece, where the chances of the woman dying are about 1 in 31 800, and where only three infants in 1000 die during the first year (Save the Children, 2011). Female life expectancy at birth in Greece is 82, and the average number of years of schooling is 17. In Afghanistan, one woman in 11 dies as a result of pregnancy, and 199 children of 1000 die during their first five years. In Afghan society, only 14 percent of births are attended by trained personnel, and female life expectancy at birth is 45. European countries in general are safest. One out of every 5600 women dies in pregnancy or childbirth in Canada.

Reflect How can you make certain that you—or those you care about—receive the health care needed during pregnancy and during childbirth?

Active Review

11. Prenatal _____ deprivation can impair the development of the central nervous system, leading to cognitive and motor problems and even psychological disorders.

12. A baby is considered _____ when birth occurs at or before 37 weeks of gestation.

13. A baby has a low _____ when it weighs less than 2500 grams.

14. Research suggests that it is (helpful or harmful?) to stimulate preterm infants.

Reflect & Relate: If you had a preterm infant, do you think you would want to handle him or her as much as possible, or would you tend to leave him or her alone? Explain.

4.5 The Postpartum Period

The term *postpartum* derives from roots meaning "after" and "birth." The **postpartum period** consists of the weeks following delivery, but there is no specific limit. "Parting is such sweet sorrow," Shakespeare has Juliet tell Romeo. The "parting" from the baby is also frequently a happy experience. The family's long wait is over. Concerns about pregnancy and labour are over, fingers and toes have been counted, and despite some local discomfort, the mother finds her "load" to be lightened—most literally. However, according to the American Psychiatric Association (APA, 2013), about 70 percent of new mothers have periods of tearfulness, sadness, and irritability that the Association refers to as the "baby blues" (p. 423). In this section, we discuss two issues of the postpartum period: maternal depression and bonding.

Maternal Depression

QUESTION » What mood problems do women experience during the postpartum period? These problems include the baby blues and more serious mood disorders ("postpartum-onset mood episodes"), which occasionally include "psychotic features" (American Psychiatric Association, 2013).

TRUTH OR FICTION REVISITED: Actually, it is normal to feel depressed following childbirth. The baby blues affect most women in the weeks after delivery (Canadian Mental Health Association, 2014). Baby blues and other postpartum mood problems are so common that they are statistically normal (Gavin et al., 2005). These problems are not limited to Canada or even to developed nations. They are far-flung, and researchers find them in China, Turkey, Guyana, Australia, and South Africa—with similar frequency (Bloch et al., 2006; Cohen et al., 2006). Researchers believe that the baby blues are so common because of hormonal changes that follow delivery (Kohl, 2004). Table 4.2 ■ shows the kinds of depression mothers might experience after delivery.

The baby blues last about ten days and are generally not severe enough to impair the mother's functioning. Don't misunderstand; the baby blues are seriously discomforting and not to be ignored, as in "Oh, you're just experiencing what most women go through." The point is that most women can handle the baby blues, even though they are pretty awful at times, partly because the women know that they are transient.

A minority of women, but perhaps as many as one in 5–10, encounter the more serious mood disorder frequently referred to as **postpartum depression (PPD)**. PPD begins about a month after delivery and may linger for weeks, even months. PPD is technically referred to as a major depressive disorder with postpartum onset. Like other major depressive disorders, it is characterized by serious sadness, feelings of hopelessness and helplessness, feelings of worthlessness, difficulty concentrating, and major changes in appetite (usually loss of appetite) and sleep patterns (frequently insomnia). There can also be severe fluctuations in mood, with women sometimes feeling elated. Some women show obsessive concern with the well-being of their babies at this time. PPD can also interfere with the mother–baby relationship in the short term.

Many researchers have suggested that PPD is caused by the interaction of psychological factors and physiological (mainly hormonal) factors, including a sudden drop in estrogen (Brummelte & Galea, 2010; Lokuge et al., 2011). Feelings of depression before getting pregnant or during pregnancy are a risk factor for PPD, as are concerns about all the life changes that motherhood creates, marital problems, and having a sick or unwanted baby. But the focus

postpartum period The time that immediately follows childbirth.

postpartum depression (PPD) Severe, prolonged depression that afflicts 10–20 percent of women after delivery and that is characterized by sadness, apathy, and feelings of worthlessness.

Kinds of Maternal Depression after Delivery

Type of Depression	Incidence	Symptoms	Comments
Baby blues	About 4 new mothers in 5	• Feeling let down • Crying for no apparent reason • Impatience, irritability, restlessness, anxiety	Occurs in first weeks and disappears on its own
Postpartum depression	About 1 new mother in 5	• Frequent sadness, crying, helplessness, despair, possible thoughts of suicide, anxiety, panic, feelings of inadequacy, guilt, shame • Changes in appetite • Insomnia or hypersomnia, fatigue • Lack of feeling for the baby—or excessive concern for the baby • Irritability • Difficulty concentrating • Frightening feelings, thoughts, images • Loss of interest in sex	Occurs within days of delivery or gradually during the first year
Postpartum psychosis	About 1 new mother in 1000	• Hallucinations • Severe insomnia • Agitation • Bizarre feelings or behaviour	Occurs within a few weeks after delivery; an emergency that requires help

today is on the contribution of physiological factors, because there are major changes in body chemistry during and after pregnancy and because women around the world seem to experience similar disturbances in mood, even when their life experiences and support systems are radically different (Cohen et al., 2006). But it is clear that stress can heighten symptoms of PPD (Brummelte & Galea, 2010; Hillerer et al., 2011).

According to the American Psychiatric Association (2013), postpartum mood episodes are accompanied by "psychotic features" in one woman in 500–1000. A psychotic feature may mean a break with reality. Mothers with these features may have delusional thoughts about the infant that place the infant at risk of injury or death. Some women experience delusions that the infant is possessed by the devil, and some have "command hallucinations" to kill the infant. That is, they experience a command to kill the infant as though it is coming from the outside—perhaps from a commanding person or some kind of divine or evil spirit—even though the idea originates within. But they may not be able to tell the difference, and the infant may be in serious jeopardy. Women with severe postpartum depression frequently have a history of psychological disorders and/or substance abuse (Comtois et al., 2008). Remember, too, that psychotic features are rare, and when they occur, they do not always place the baby at risk.

Women who experience milder forms of PPD usually profit from social support and a history of high self-esteem. They may benefit from counselling, even if counselling does little more than explain that many women encounter PPD and get over it. Drugs that increase estrogen levels or act as antidepressants may help. Most women get over PPD on their own, but with greater personal cost. At the very least, women should know that the problem is common and that it does not necessarily mean that there is something wrong with them or that they are failing to live up to their obligations.

Bonding

QUESTION » How critical is parental interaction with neonates in the formation of bonds of attachment? **Bonding**—that is, the formation of bonds of attachment between parents and their children—is essential to the survival and well-being of children. Since the publication of controversial research by Marshall Klaus and John Kennell in 1978, many have wondered about the answer to this question.

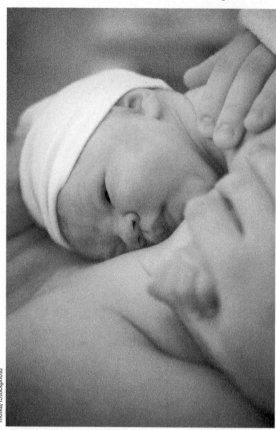

Are the first hours postpartum a special "maternal-sensitive" period for mother–baby bonding?

bonding The process of forming bonds of attachment between parent and child.

Klaus and Kennell argued that the first hours postpartum provided a special—even a necessary—opportunity for bonding between parents and neonates. They labelled these hours a "maternal-sensitive" period during which the mother is particularly disposed, largely because of hormone levels, to form a bond with the neonate. In their study, one group of mothers was randomly assigned to standard hospital procedure, in which their babies were whisked away to the nursery shortly after birth. Throughout the remainder of the hospital stay, the babies visited their mothers during feeding. The other group of mothers spent five hours a day with their infants during the hospital stay. The hospital staff encouraged and reassured the group of mothers who had extended contact. Follow-ups over two years suggested that extended contact benefited both the mothers and their children. Mothers with extended contact were more likely than control mothers to cuddle their babies, soothe them when they cried, and interact with them.

Critics note that the Klaus and Kennell studies are fraught with methodological problems. For example, we cannot separate the benefits of extended contact from benefits attributable to parents' knowledge that they were in a special group and from the extra attention the hospital staff gave them. In short, the evidence that the hours after birth are critical is tainted. Consider, too, the millions of solid adoptive parent–child relationships, in which parents did not have early access to their children.

Parent–child bonding has been shown to be a complex process involving desire to have the child; parent–child familiarity with one another's sounds, odours, and tastes; and parental caring. Serious maternal depression can delay bonding with newborns (Klier, 2006), but even so, a Dutch study found that mother–infant attachment appears to be normal by the age of 14 months (Tharner et al., 2012). A history of rejection by parents can interfere with women's bonding with their own children (Brockington, 2011).

TRUTH OR FICTION REVISITED: Despite the Klaus and Kennell studies, which made a brief splash a generation ago, it is not true that parents must have extended early contact with their newborn children if adequate bonding is to take place. Researchers now view the hours after birth as just one element—and not even an essential element—in a complex and prolonged bonding process.

Some Notes on Father–Newborn Bonding

An Australian study found that professionally employed new fathers are quite interested in seeking information about father–newborn bonding (Fletcher et al., 2008). The Internet surfing behaviour of a sample of 253 professionals revealed that the two parenting-related online topics that most interested them were baby games and father–infant bonding. They were significantly less interested in topics such as resuming sex after the delivery and breast feeding.

A Swedish study of ten fathers who were interviewed about a year after a child was born found that it was typical for fathers to feel overwhelmed at first, but that they were motivated to master parenting and to find a new "completeness" in their lives (Premberg et al., 2008). The fathers tended to bond with their babies by assigning them primary importance and spending time alone with them. The fathers reported that newborns generally provided feelings of happiness and warmth in the home, and they experienced a deeper relationship with their partner as a result. Can these findings be generalized to North America? Perhaps not; Sweden is an upper-middle-class country, with many affluent individuals, and the sample was not chosen entirely at random.

Research suggests that father–newborn bonding is affected by the father's relationship with the mother as well as by the father's own psychological well-being (Condon, 2006). As an example, many new mothers experience post-partum depression, which can compound the stress in a home that is already changed by the addition of a needy newborn. Stress can interfere with bonding as well as introduce its own challenges.

A CLOSER LOOK RESEARCH

Have We Found the Daddy Hormones?

Are oxytocin and vasopressin the "Daddy hormones"? Perhaps so, at least in meadow voles, which are a kind of tailless mouse, and sheep. These hormones are connected with the creation of mother–infant bonds in sheep, pair bonds in monogamous voles, and bonds of attachment between vole fathers and their young. Experimental research clearly shows that increasing vasopressin levels transform an indifferent male into a caring, monogamous, and protective mate and father (Insel, 2010).

Oxytocin and vasopressin are secreted by the pituitary gland, which secretes many hormones that are involved in reproduction and the nurturing of young. For example, prolactin regulates maternal behaviour in lower mammals and stimulates the production of milk in women. Oxytocin stimulates labour but is also involved in social recognition and bonding. Vasopressin enables the body to conserve water by inhibiting urine production when fluid levels are low; however,

David Chapman/Alamy

A Nest of Newborn Voles
The hormones oxytocin and vasopressin stimulate the formation of bonds of attachment in voles. Do they play a similar role in humans?

it is also connected with paternal behaviour patterns in some mammals. For example, male prairie voles form pair-bonds with female prairie voles after mating with them (McGraw & Young, 2010). Mating stimulates the secretion of vasopressin, and vasopressin causes the previously promiscuous male to sing "I only have eyes for you."

Given their effects on voles, we may wonder how oxytocin and vasopressin may be connected with the formation of bonds between men and women and between men and children. And will perfume makers soon be lacing new scents with the stuff?

Reflect In your own experience, and in the portrayals of males and females you see in the media, what are the apparent sex differences in "cuddling," parenting, and tendencies toward monogamy? To what extent do you think these differences result from cultural influences and to what extent from chemistry—that is, chemicals such as oxytocin and vasopressin? Explain.

Active Review

15. Research suggests that the (majority or minority?) of new mothers experience periods of depression.

16. Postpartum depression has been connected with a precipitous decline in the hormone _____.

17. Research (does or does not?) show that early parental interaction with neonates is critical in the formation of bonds of attachment.

Reflect & Relate: Pretend for a minute that you are visiting a friend who has just had a baby. She is weepy and listless and worries that she doesn't have the "right" feelings for a new mother. What would you say to her? Why?

4.6 Characteristics of Neonates

Many neonates come into the world looking a bit fuzzy, but even though they are utterly dependent on others, they are probably more aware of their surroundings than you had imagined. Neonates make rapid adaptations to the world around them. In this section, we see how health professionals assess the health of neonates and describe the characteristics of neonates.

Assessing the Health of Neonates

QUESTION » How do health professionals assess the health of neonates? The neonate's overall level of health is usually evaluated at birth according to the **Apgar scale**, developed by Virginia Apgar in 1953. Apgar scores are based on five signs of health, as shown in Table 4.3 ■. The neonate can receive a score of 0, 1, or 2 on each sign. The total Apgar score, therefore, can vary from 0 to 10. A score of 7 or higher usually indicates that the baby is not in danger. A score below 4 suggests that the baby is in critical condition and requires medical attention. By one minute after birth, most normal babies attain scores of 8–10 (Clayton & Crosby, 2006).

The acronym APGAR is commonly used as an aid in remembering the five criteria of the Apgar scale: A—the general **a**ppearance or colour of the neonate, P—the **p**ulse or heart rate, G—**g**rimace (a 1-point indicator of reflex irritability), A—general **a**ctivity level or muscle tone, and R—**r**espiratory effort, or rate of breathing.

The Brazelton Neonatal Behavioral Assessment Scale (**NBAS**), developed by pediatrician T. Berry Brazelton, measures neonates' reflexes and other behaviour patterns. The test screens neonates for behavioural and neurological problems by assessing four areas of behaviour: motor behaviour, including muscle tone and most reflexes, response to people, response to stress, adaptive behaviour, and control over physiological state. A low score on the NBAS may suggest neurological problems such as brain damage.

The NBAS was constructed to assess normal infants. Brazelton developed the Neonatal Intensive Care Unit Network Neurobehavioral Scale (**NNNS**) in collaboration with Barry Lester and Edward Tronick (2004) to help assess and consult with the parents of infants at risk—especially infants who have been exposed to parental substance abuse. Substances include but are not limited to cocaine, heroin, alcohol, methamphetamine, and polydrug abuse. The NNNS is administered in the presence of a parent and assesses infants' relative stability or instability in emotional states, overall irritability, signs of stress, response to various handling techniques, response to soothing efforts, responses to auditory and visual stimulation, and ability to soothe themselves (Boukydis & Lester, 2008). While the scale is being administered, the consultant has the

Apgar scale A measure of a newborn's health that assesses appearance, pulse, grimace, activity level, and respiratory effort.

NBAS Brazelton Neonatal Behavioral Assessment Scale.

NNNS Neonatal Intensive Care Unit Network Neurobehavioral Scale.

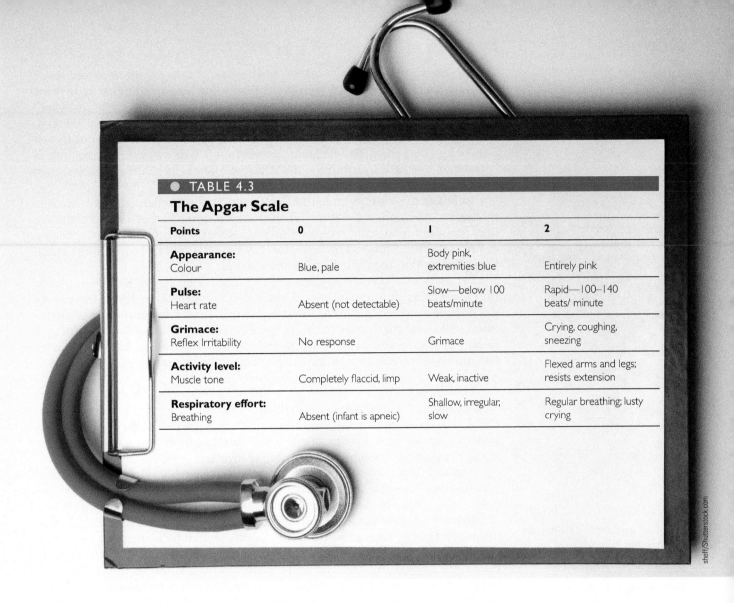

TABLE 4.3
The Apgar Scale

Points	0	1	2
Appearance: Colour	Blue, pale	Body pink, extremities blue	Entirely pink
Pulse: Heart rate	Absent (not detectable)	Slow—below 100 beats/minute	Rapid—100–140 beats/ minute
Grimace: Reflex Irritability	No response	Grimace	Crying, coughing, sneezing
Activity level: Muscle tone	Completely flaccid, limp	Weak, inactive	Flexed arms and legs; resists extension
Respiratory effort: Breathing	Absent (infant is apneic)	Shallow, irregular, slow	Regular breathing; lusty crying

opportunity to observe parent–infant interactions and suggest more effective child-rearing behaviour.

Infant Responses Assessed by the Neonatal Intensive Care Unit Network Neurobehavioral Scale (NNNS)

- Describe what events, handling, and movements caused the infant to change emotional states.
- Describe circumstances under which the infant cried or fussed during assessment.
- Describe how the consultant soothed the infant.
- Summarize ways in which the infant soothed himself or herself during the consultation.
- Describe how the infant responded to a bell or rattle.
- Describe how the infant responded to being cuddled.
- Describe signs of stress such as startles shown by the infant.
- Describe the causes or antecedents of these signs of stress.
- Describe the infant's quality of movement.
- Describe reflexes shown by the infant, especially those that were inadequate.
- Describe the infant's quality of sucking.

Source: Adapted from Boukydis & Lester (2008).

Reflexes

QUESTIONS » What are reflexes? What kinds of reflexes do neonates have?
If soon after birth you had been held gently for a few moments with your face down in comfortably warm water, you would not have drowned. Instead of breathing the water in, you would have exhaled slowly through the mouth and engaged in swimming motions. (We urge readers not to test babies for this reflex. The hazards are obvious.) This swimming response is "prewired"—innate or inborn—and it is just one of the many reflexes shown by neonates.

Reflexes are simple, unlearned, stereotypical responses that are elicited by certain types of stimulation. They do not require higher brain functions; they occur automatically, without thinking. Reflexes are the most complicated motor activities displayed by neonates. Neonates cannot roll over, sit up, reach for an object that they see, or raise their heads.

Let us return to our early venture into the water. If you had been placed into the water not a few moments but several months after birth, the results might have been very different—and disastrous. After a few months, the swimming reflex, like many others, ceases to exist. However, at 6–12 months of age, infants can learn how to swim voluntarily. In fact, the transition from reflexive swimming to learned swimming can be reasonably smooth with careful guided practice.

Many reflexes have survival value. Adults and neonates, for example, reflexively close their eyes when assaulted with a puff of air or sudden bright light. Other reflexes seem to reflect interesting facets of the evolution of the nervous system. The swimming reflex seems to suggest that there was a time when our ancestors profited from being born able to swim.

Pediatricians learn a good deal about the adequacy of neonates' **neural** functioning by testing their reflexes. The absence or weakness of a reflex may indicate immaturity (as in prematurity), slowed responsiveness (which can result from anesthetics used during childbirth), brain injury, or intellectual disability. Let us examine some of the reflexes shown by neonates.

The rooting and sucking reflexes are basic to survival. In the **rooting reflex**, the baby turns the head and mouth toward a stimulus that strokes the cheek, chin, or corner of the mouth. The rooting reflex facilitates finding the mother's nipple in preparation for sucking. Babies will suck almost any object that touches their lips. The sucking reflex grows stronger during the first days after birth and can be lost if not stimulated. As the months go on, reflexive sucking becomes replaced by voluntary sucking.

reflex An unlearned, stereotypical response to a stimulus.

neural Of the nervous system.

rooting reflex A reflex in which infants turn their mouths and heads in the direction of a stroking of the cheek or the corner of the mouth.

Dan Bryant Photography

Dan Bryant Photography

Dan Bryant Photography

The Rooting Reflex

The Moro Reflex

The Grasping Reflex

The Stepping Reflex

The Tonic-Neck Reflex

In the startle or **Moro reflex**, the back arches and the legs and arms are flung out and then brought back toward the chest, with the arms in a hugging motion. The Moro reflex occurs when a baby's position is suddenly changed or support for the head and neck is suddenly lost. It can also be elicited by making loud noises, by bumping the baby's crib, or by jerking the baby's blanket. In terms of our evolutionary history, the Moro reflex would probably have enhanced the survival of infants clinging to parents that regularly climbed trees. The Moro reflex is usually lost by six or seven months after birth (although similar movements can be found in adults who suddenly lose support). Absence of the Moro reflex can indicate immaturity or brain damage.

During the first few weeks following birth, babies show an increasing tendency to reflexively grasp fingers or other objects pressed against the palms of their hands. In this **grasping reflex**, or palmar reflex, they use four fingers only (the thumbs are not included). The grasping reflex is stronger when babies are startled. Most babies can support their own weight in this way. They can be literally lifted into the air as they reflexively cling with two hands. Some babies can actually support their weight with just one hand. (Please do not try this, however!) Absence of the grasping reflex may indicate depressed activity of the nervous system, which can stem from use of anesthetics during childbirth. The grasping reflex is usually lost by three to four months of age, and babies generally show voluntary grasping by five to six months.

One or two days after birth, babies show a reflex that mimics walking. When held under the arms and tilted forward so that the feet press against a solid surface, a baby will show a **stepping reflex** in which the feet advance one after the other. A full-term baby "walks" heel to toe, whereas a preterm infant is more likely to remain on tiptoe. The stepping reflex usually disappears by three or four months of age.

Moro reflex A reflex in which infants arch their back, fling out their arms and legs, and draw them back toward the chest in response to a sudden change in position.

grasping reflex A reflex in which infants grasp objects that cause pressure against their palms.

stepping reflex A reflex in which infants take steps when held under the arms and lean forward so that their feet press against the ground.

OBSERVING CHILDREN, UNDERSTANDING OURSELVES

Reflex Development in Infancy

Watch infants display a variety of reflexes.

What are the different reflexes present at birth? Which reflexes have survival value and which reflexes are considered primitive reflexes, and what is the difference between the two types? What happens to survival and primitive reflexes during a baby's first year?

Go to www.nelson.com/voyages2ce to watch the video, answer the questions, and e-mail your responses to your professor.

In the **Babinski reflex**, the neonate fans or spreads the toes in response to stroking of the foot from heel to toes. The Babinski reflex normally disappears toward the end of the first year, to be replaced by curling downward of the toes. Persistence of the Babinski reflex may suggest defects of the lower spinal cord, lagging development of nerve cells, or other disorders.

The **tonic-neck reflex** is observed when the baby is lying on its back and turns its head to one side. The arm and leg on that side extend, while the limbs on the opposite side flex. You can see why this reflex sometimes is known as the "fencing position."

Some reflexes, such as breathing and blinking the eye in response to a puff of air, remain with us for life. Others, such as the sucking and grasping reflexes, are gradually replaced by voluntary sucking and grasping after a number of months. Still others, such as the Moro and Babinski reflexes, disappear, indicating that the nervous system is maturing on schedule.

Sensory Capabilities

QUESTION » **How well do neonates see, hear, and so on?** In 1890 William James, one of the founders of modern psychology, wrote that the neonate must sense the world "as one great blooming, buzzing confusion." The neonate emerges from being literally suspended in a temperature-controlled environment to being—again, in James's words—"assailed by eyes, ears, nose, skin, and entrails at once." Let's describe the sensory capabilities of neonates. We'll see that James, for all his eloquence, probably exaggerated their disorganization.

Vision

Neonates can see, but they do not possess great sharpness of vision, or **visual acuity**. Visual acuity is expressed in numbers such as 20/20 and 20/200. 20/20 is ideal, meaning that you can see objects clearly at a distance of 20 feet (approximately 6 metres). Investigators estimate that neonates are nearsighted, with visual acuity in the neighborhood of 20/600 (Kellman & Arterberry, 2006). Neonates can best see objects that are about 18–23 centimetres away from their eyes (Braddick & Atkinson, 2011). Neonates also see best through the centres of their eyes. They do not have the peripheral vision of older children (Candy et al., 1998). To learn how psychologists measure the visual acuity of infants, see the nearby "A Closer Look—Research" feature.

Babinski reflex A reflex in which infants fan their toes when the undersides of their feet are stroked.

tonic-neck reflex A reflex in which infants turn their head to one side, extend the arm and leg on that side, and flex the limbs on the opposite side. Also known as the fencing position.

visual acuity Keenness or sharpness of vision.

A CLOSER LOOK RESEARCH

Studying Visual Acuity in Neonates—How Well Can They See?

How do psychologists determine the visual acuity of neonates? Naturally, they cannot ask babies to report how well they see, but psychologists can determine what babies are looking at and draw conclusions from this information.

One method of observing what a baby is looking at is by using a "looking chamber" of the sort employed in research by Robert Fantz and his colleagues (1975). In this chamber, the baby lies on its back, with two panels above. Each panel contains a visual stimulus. The researcher observes the baby's eye movements and records how much time is spent looking at each panel. A similar

strategy can be carried out in the baby's natural environment. Filtered lights and a movie or TV camera can be trained on the baby's eyes. Reflections from objects in the environment can then be recorded to show what the baby is looking at.

Neonates will stare at almost any nearby object for minutes—golf balls, wheels, checkerboards, bull's-eyes, circles, triangles, even lines (Maurer & Maurer, 1976). But babies have their preferences, as measured by the amount of time they spend fixating on (looking at) certain objects.

Continued

Continued

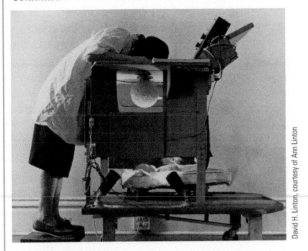

The Looking Chamber
This chamber makes it easier for the researcher to observe the baby's eye movements and to record how much time the baby spends looking at a visual stimulus.

David H. Linton, courtesy of Ann Linton

For example, they will spend more time looking at black and white stripes than at gray blobs. This fact suggests one strategy for measuring visual acuity in the neonate. As black and white stripes become narrower, they eventually take on the appearance of that dull gray blob. And, as the stripes are progressively narrowed, we can assume that babies continue to discriminate them as stripes only so long as they spend more time looking at them than at blobs.

Studies such as these suggest that neonates are very nearsighted. But we should remember that they, unlike older children and adults, are not motivated to "perform" in such experiments. If they were, they might show somewhat greater acuity.

Reflect What are the problems in studying the "preferences" of newborn children? How do researchers "get around" these problems? Are you confident that they are studying the preferences of newborns? Explain.

Neonates can visually detect movement, and many neonates can track movement the first day after birth. In fact, they appear to prefer (that is, they spend more time looking at) moving objects, rather than stationary ones (Kellman & Arterberry, 2006).

Visual accommodation consists of the self-adjustments made by the lens of the eye to bring objects into focus. If you hold your finger at arm's length and bring it gradually nearer, you will feel tension in your eyes as your lenses automatically foreshorten and thicken in an effort to keep the image in focus. When you move the finger away, the lens accommodates by lengthening and flattening to keep the finger in focus. Neonates show little or no visual accommodation; they see as if through a fixed-focus camera. Objects placed about 18–23 centimetres away are in clearest focus for most neonates, although this range can be somewhat expanded when lighting conditions are bright. Interestingly, this is about the distance of the face of an adult who is cradling a neonate in his or her arms. It has been speculated that this sensory capacity for gazing into others' eyes may promote attachment between neonates and caregivers. Visual accommodation improves dramatically during the first two months (Kavšek, et al., 2012; Kellman & Arterberry, 2006).

Now bring your finger toward your eyes, trying to maintain a single image of the approaching finger. If you do so, it is because your eyes turn inward, or converge on the finger, resulting in a crossed-eyed look and feelings of tension in the eye muscles (see Figure 4.5 ■). **Convergence** is made possible by coordination of the eye muscles. Neonates do not have the muscular control to converge their eyes on an object that is close to them. For this reason, one eye may be staring off to the side while the other fixates on an object straight ahead. Convergence does not occur until seven or eight weeks of age for near

visual accommodation The automatic adjustments made by the lenses of the eyes to bring objects into focus.

convergence The inward movement of the eyes as they focus on an object that is drawing nearer.

gmevi/Thinkstock

Figure 4.5 ■ Convergence of the Eyes
Neonates do not have the muscular control to converge their eyes on an object that is close to them. However, they do show some convergence for objects at intermediate viewing distances.

CHAPTER 4 BIRTH AND THE NEWBORN BABY **141**

objects, although neonates show some convergence for objects at intermediate distances (Kellman & Arterberry, 2006).

The degree to which neonates perceive colour remains an open question. The research problem is that colours vary in **intensity** (brightness), **saturation** (richness), and **hue**. For this reason, when babies appear to show preference for one colour over another, we cannot be certain that they are responding to the hue. They may be responding to the difference in brightness or saturation. So, you say, simply change hues and keep intensity and saturation constant. A marvelous idea—but easier said than done, unfortunately.

Physiological observations also cast doubt on the capacity of neonates to have highly developed colour vision. There are two types of cells in the retina of the eye that are sensitive to light: rods and cones. **Rods** transmit sensations of light and dark. **Cones** transmit sensations of colour. At birth, the cones are less well developed than the rods in structure.

Infants younger than one month of age do not show the ability to discriminate stimuli that differ in colour. Two-month-olds can do so, but they require large colour differences. By four months, infants can see most, if not all, of the colours of the visible spectrum (Kimura et al., 2010).

Even at birth, babies do not just passively respond to visual stimuli. Babies placed in the dark open their eyes wide and actively search the visual field (Braddick & Atkinson, 2011).

Hearing

Fetuses respond to sound months before they are born. Although myelination of the auditory pathways is not complete before birth, fetuses' middle and inner ears normally reach their mature shape and size before they are born. Normal neonates hear well, unless their middle ears are clogged with amniotic fluid (Zhiqi et al., 2010). Most neonates turn their heads toward unusual sounds, such as the shaking of a rattle.

Neonates have the capacity to respond to sounds of different **amplitude** and **pitch**. They are more likely to respond to high-pitched sounds than to low-pitched sounds (Homae et al., 2011). By contrast, speaking or singing to infants softly, in a relatively low-pitched voice, can have a soothing effect (Conrad et al., 2011; Volkova et al., 2006). This may explain the widespread practice in many cultures of singing lullabies to infants to promote sleep (Volkova et al., 2006).

The sense of hearing may play a role in the formation of affectional bonds between neonates and their mothers that goes well beyond the soothing potential of the mothers' voices. Research indicates that neonates prefer their mothers' voices to those of other women, but they do not show similar preferences for the voices of their fathers (DeCasper & Prescott, 1984; Freeman et al., 1993). It may be tempting to conclude that the human nervous system is prewired to respond positively to the voice of one's biological mother. However, neonates have already had several months of experience in the uterus, and for a good part of this time, they have been capable of sensing sounds. Because they are predominantly exposed to prenatal sounds produced by their mothers, learning appears to play a role in neonatal preferences.

There is fascinating evidence that neonates are particularly responsive to the sounds and rhythms of speech, although they do not show preferences for specific languages. Neonates can discriminate between different speech sounds, and they can discriminate between new sounds of speech and those that they have heard before (Gervain et al., 2011).

Smell: The Nose Knows—Early

Neonates can definitely discriminate distinct odours, such as those of onions and anise (licorice). They show more rapid breathing patterns and increased

intensity Brightness.

saturation Richness or purity of a colour.

hue Colour.

rods In the eye, rod-shaped receptors of light that are sensitive to intensity only. Rods permit black-and-white vision.

cones In the eye, cone-shaped receptors of light that transmit sensations of colour.

amplitude The maximum vibration of a sound wave. The higher the amplitude of sound waves, the louder they are.

pitch The highness or lowness of a sound, as determined by the frequency of sound waves.

bodily movement in response to powerful odours. They also turn away from unpleasant odours, such as ammonia and vinegar, as early as the first day after birth (Werner & Bernstein, 2001).

The nasal preferences of neonates are quite similar to those of older children and adults (Werner & Bernstein, 2001). When a cotton swab saturated with the odour of rotten eggs was passed beneath their noses, neonate infants spat, stuck out their tongues, wrinkled their noses, and blinked their eyes. However, they showed smiles and licking motions when presented with the odours of chocolate, strawberry, vanilla, butter, bananas, and honey.

Classic research by Aidan Macfarlane (1975, 1977) and others suggests that the sense of smell, like hearing, may provide a vehicle for mother–infant recognition and attachment. Macfarlane suspected that neonates may be sensitive to the smell of milk because, when held by the mother, they tend to turn toward her nipple before they have had a chance to see or touch it. In one experiment, Macfarlane placed nursing pads above and to the sides of neonates' heads. One pad had absorbed milk from the mother, and the other was clean. Neonates less than a week old spent more time turning to look at their mothers' pads than at the new pads.

Neonates also turn toward preferred odours. In the second phase of this research, Macfarlane suspended pads with milk from the neonates' mothers and from strangers to the sides of babies' heads. For the first few days following birth, the infants did not turn toward their mothers' pads. However, by the time they were one week old, they turned toward their mothers' pads and spent more time looking at them than at the strangers' pads. It appears that they learned to respond positively to the odour of their mothers' milk during the first few days. Afterward, a source of this odour received preferential treatment even when the infants were not nursing.

Breast-fed 15-day-old infants also prefer their mother's axillary (underarm) odour to odours produced by other lactating women and by nonlactating women. Bottle-fed infants do not show this preference (Cernoch & Porter, 1985; Porter et al., 1992). The investigators explain this difference by suggesting that breast-fed infants may be more likely than bottle-fed infants to be exposed to their mother's axillary odour; that is, mothers of bottle-fed infants usually remain clothed. Axillary odour, along with odours from breast secretions, might contribute to the early development of recognition and attachment (A. C. Lee et al., 2011).

Taste

Neonates are sensitive to different tastes, and their preferences, as suggested by their facial expressions in response to various fluids, appear to be similar to those of adults (Beauchamp & Mennella, 2011; Werner & Bernstein, 2001). Neonates swallow without showing any facial expression suggestive of a positive or negative response when distilled water is placed on their tongues). Sweet solutions are met with smiles, licking, and eager sucking, as shown in Figure 4.6a ■ (Rosenstein & Oster, 1988). Neonates discriminate among solutions with salty, sour, and bitter tastes, as suggested by reactions in the lower part of the face (Rosenstein & Oster, 1988). Sour fluids (see Figure 4.6b) elicit pursing of the lips, nose wrinkling, and eye blinking. Bitter solutions (see Figure 4.6c) stimulate spitting, gagging, and sticking out the tongue.

Sweet solutions have a calming effect on neonates (Fernandes et al., 2011). One study found that sweeter solutions increase the heart rate, suggesting heightened arousal, but also slow down the rate of sucking (Crook & Lipsitt, 1976). The researchers interpret this finding to suggest an effort to savour the sweeter solution—to make the flavour last. Although we do not know why infants ingest sweet foods more slowly, this difference could be adaptive in the sense of preventing overeating. Sweet foods tend to be high in calories; eating them slowly

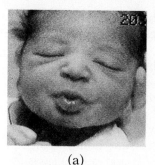 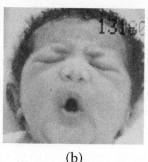 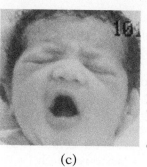

Rosenstein, D. S. & Oster, H. (1988). Differential facial responses to four basic tastes in newborns. CHILD DEVELOPMENT, 59, 1555–1568.

(a)   (b)   (c)

Figure 4.6 ■ Facial Expressions Elicited by Sweet, Sour, and Bitter Solutions
Neonates are sensitive to different tastes, as shown by their facial expressions when tasting (a) sweet, (b) sour, and (c) bitter solutions.

gives infants' brains more time to respond to bodily signals that they have eaten enough and thus should stop eating. Ah, to have the wisdom of a neonate!

Touch and Pain

The sense of touch is an extremely important avenue of learning and communication for babies. Not only do the skin senses provide information about the external world, but the sensations of skin against skin also appear to provide feelings of comfort and security that may be major factors in the formation of bonds of attachment between infants and their caregivers, as we will see in Chapter 7.

Neonates are sensitive to touch. Many reflexes—including the rooting, sucking, Babinski, and grasping reflexes—are activated by pressure against the skin.

It has been widely believed that neonates are not as sensitive to pain as older babies are. Considering the squeezing that takes place during childbirth, relative insensitivity to pain would seem to be adaptive. However, this belief has recently been challenged by health professionals (e.g., Royal Australasian College of Physicians, 2006). What would appear to be accurate enough is that neonates are not cognitively equipped to fret about pain that may be coming or to ruminate about pain they have experienced. But they are certainly conditionable. In other words, if they perceive themselves to be in a situation that has brought them pain in the past, we should not be surprised if they shriek—and shriek and shriek. Health professionals now recommend that neonates and older infants be given anesthetics if they are going to undergo uncomfortable procedures, such as circumcision.

Learning: Really Early Childhood "Education"

QUESTION » **Can neonates learn?** The somewhat limited sensory capabilities of neonates suggest that they may not learn as rapidly as older children do. After all, we must sense clearly those things we are to learn about. However, neonates seem capable of at least two basic forms of learning: classical conditioning and operant conditioning.

Classical Conditioning of Neonates

In classical conditioning of neonates, involuntary responses are conditioned to new stimuli. In a typical study (Lipsitt, 2002), neonates were taught to blink in response to a tone. Blinking (the unconditioned response) was elicited by a puff of air directed toward the infant's eye (the unconditioned stimulus). A tone was sounded (the conditioned stimulus) as the puff of air was delivered. After repeated pairings, sounding the tone caused the neonate to blink (the conditioned response). Thus neonates are equipped to learn that events peculiar to their own environments (touches or other conditioned stimuli) may mean that a meal is at hand—or, more accurately, at mouth. One neonate may learn that a light switched on overhead precedes a meal. Another may learn that feeding is preceded by the rustling of a carpet of thatched leaves. The conditioned stimuli are culture-specific; the capacity to learn is universal.

Operant Conditioning of Neonates

Operant conditioning, like classical conditioning, can take place in neonates. In an experiment by DeCasper and Fifer (1980), expectant mothers read the Dr. Seuss book *The Cat in the Hat* out loud twice daily during the final month and half of pregnancy. After birth, their babies were given special pacifiers: Sucking on them in one way would activate recordings of their mother reading *The Cat in the Hat*. Sucking them in another way would activate their mothers' reading another book—*The King, the Mice and the Cheese*—which was written in very different rhythms (see Figure 4.7 ■). In this example, the infants' sucking reflexes were modified through the reinforcement of hearing their mothers read a familiar story.

The younger the child, the more important it is that reinforcers be administered rapidly. Among neonates, it seems that reinforcers must be administered within one second after the desired behaviour is performed if learning is to occur. Infants aged six to eight months can learn if the reinforcer is delayed by two seconds, but if the delay is three seconds or more, learning does not take place (Millar, 1990). Although there are individual differences in conditionability in neonates, these differences do not correspond to differences in the complex cognitive abilities we refer to as intelligence later on.

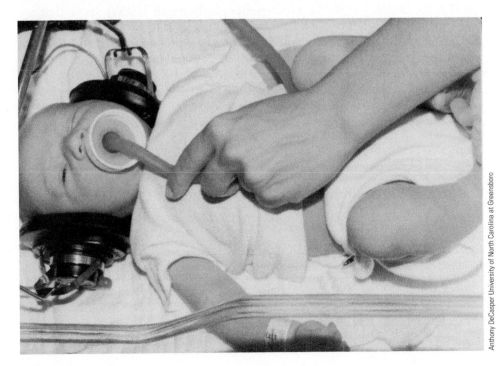

Figure 4.7 ■ A Neonate Sucking to Hear Her Mother's Voice

Anthony DeCasper University of North Carolina at Greensboro

Sleeping and Waking

QUESTION » **What patterns of sleep are found among neonates?** As adults, we spend about one-third of our time sleeping. Neonates greatly outdo us, spending two-thirds of their time, or about 16 hours per day, in sleep. And in one of life's basic challenges to parents, neonates do not sleep their 16 hours consecutively.

A number of different states of sleep and wakefulness have been identified in neonates and infants, as shown in Table 4.4 ■. Although individual babies differ in the amount of time they spend in each of these states, sleep clearly predominates over wakefulness in the early days and weeks of life.

Different infants require different amounts of sleep and follow different patterns of sleep, but virtually all infants distribute their sleeping throughout the day and night in a series of naps. The typical infant exhibits about six cycles of waking and sleeping in a 24-hour period. The longest nap typically approaches four-and-a-half hours, and the neonate is usually awake for a little more than one hour during each cycle.

This pattern of waking and sleeping changes rapidly and dramatically over the course of the years. Even after a month or so, the infant has fewer but longer sleep periods and usually takes longer naps during the night. Parents whose babies do not know the difference between night and day usually teach them the difference by playing with them during daytime hours, once feeding and caretaking chores have been carried out, and by putting them back to sleep as soon as possible when they awaken hungry during the night. Most parents do not require professional instruction in this method. At 3 A.M., parents are not likely to feel playful.

By the ages of about six months to a year, many infants begin to sleep through the night. Some infants start sleeping through the night even earlier (Salzarulo & Ficca, 2002). A number of infants begin to sleep through the night for a week or so and then revert to their wakeful ways again for a while.

REM and Non-REM Sleep

Sleep is not a consistent state. It can be divided into **rapid eye movement (REM) sleep** and **non–rapid eye movement (non-REM) sleep** (see Figure 4.8 ■). Studies with the **electroencephalograph (EEG)** show that we can subdivide non-REM sleep into four additional stages of sleep, each with its characteristic brain waves, but our discussion will be limited to REM and non-REM sleep. REM sleep is characterized by rapid eye movements that can be observed beneath closed lids. The EEG patterns produced during REM sleep resemble those of the waking state. For this reason, REM sleep is also called paradoxical sleep. However, we are difficult to awaken during REM sleep. About 80 percent of the time, adults who are roused during REM sleep

rapid eye movement (REM) sleep Periods of sleep during which we are likely to dream, as indicated by rapid eye movements.

non–rapid eye movement (non-REM) sleep Periods of sleep during which we are unlikely to dream.

electroencephalograph (EEG) An instrument that measures electrical activity of the brain.

● TABLE 4.4	
States of Sleep and Wakefulness in Infancy	
Quiet sleep (non-REM)	Regular breathing, eyes closed, no movement
Active sleep (REM)	Irregular breathing, eyes closed, rapid eye movement, muscle twitches
Drowsiness	Regular or irregular breathing, eyes open or closed, little movement
Alert inactivity	Regular breathing, eyes open, looking around, little body movement
Alert activity	Irregular breathing, eyes open, active body movement
Crying	Irregular breathing, eyes open or closed, thrashing of arms and legs, crying

report that they have been dreaming. Is the same true of neonates?

Note from Figure 4.8 that neonates spend about half their sleeping time in REM sleep. As they develop, the percentage of sleeping time spent in REM sleep declines. By six months or so, REM sleep accounts for only about 30 percent of the baby's sleep. By two to three years, REM sleep drops off to about 20–25 percent (Salzarulo & Ficca, 2002). There is a dramatic falling off in the total number of hours spent in sleep as we develop (Blumberg & Seelke, 2010). Figure 4.8 shows that most of the drop-off can be attributed to less REM sleep.

What is the function of REM sleep in neonates? Research with humans and other animals, including kittens and rat pups, suggests that the brain requires a certain amount of activity for the creation of proteins that are involved in the development of neurons and synapses (Blumberg & Seelke, 2010). Brain activity can be stimulated by internal or external sources. In older children and adults, external sources of stimulation are provided by activity, by a vast and shifting array of sensory impressions, and, perhaps, by thought processes during the waking state. The neonate, however, spends its brief waking periods largely isolated from the kaleidoscope of events of the world outside and is not likely to be lost in deep thought. Thus, in the waking state, the brain may not be provided with the needed stimulation. Perhaps the neonate compensates by spending relatively more time in REM sleep, which most closely parallels the waking state in terms of brain waves. While infants are in REM sleep, internal stimulation spurs the brain on to appropriate development. Preterm babies spend an even greater proportion of their time in REM sleep than full-term babies, perhaps—goes the argument—because they require relatively greater stimulation of the brain.

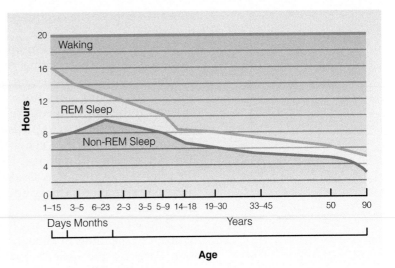

Figure 4.8 ■ REM Sleep and Non-REM Sleep

Neonates spend nearly 50 percent of their time sleeping in rapid eye movement (REM) sleep. The percentage of time spent in REM sleep drops off to 20–25 percent for two- to three-year-olds. Source: From Howard P. Roffwarg, Joseph N. Muzio, William C. Dement; "Ontogenetic Development of the Human Sleep-Dream Cycle"; *Science* (152/3722. April 29, 1966). Reprinted with permission from AAAS.

Crying

QUESTIONS » Why do babies cry? What can be done to soothe them? No discussion of the sleeping and waking states of the neonate would be complete without mentioning crying—a comment that parents will view as an understatement. We have known first-time parents who have attempted to follow an imaginary 11th commandment: "The baby shall not cry."

The main reason why babies cry seems to be simple enough. Studies suggest that a one-word answer often suffices: pain (Out et al., 2010).

Some parents have entered into conflict with hospital nurses who tell them not to worry when their babies are crying on the other side of the nursery's glass partition. Nurses often tell the parents that their babies must cry because crying helps clear their respiratory systems of fluids that linger from the amniotic sac and also stimulates the circulatory system.

On the other hand, let us consider some classic longitudinal research conducted by Silvia Bell and Mary Ainsworth (1972). These researchers followed the interactions of 26 mother–infant pairs and found that a consistent and prompt maternal response to crying is connected with decreases in crying. Close physical contact appears to be the most helpful maternal response (Douglas & Hill, 2011). Crying is apparently expressive initially, but as infants develop cognitively and learn that crying can lead to physical contact with a caregiver, it can become a form of communication. These findings appear to oppose the common view that responding to a crying baby "spoils" the baby.

At least some crying among babies seems to be universal. Some scholars have suggested that crying may be a primitive language, but it is not. Languages contain units and groupings of sounds that symbolize objects and events. Crying does not. Still, as noted by Bell and Ainsworth, crying appears to be both expressive and functional. Crying serves as an infant's expressive response to unpleasant feelings and also stimulates caretakers to do something to help. Crying thus communicates something, even though it is not a form of language. Crying may also communicate the identity of the crier across distance. Cries have multiple markers of individuality, and they may signal to parents and other caretakers the location of their infant in a group.

Before parenthood, many people wonder whether they will be able to recognize the meaning of their babies' cries, but it usually does not take them long. Parents typically learn to distinguish cries that signify hunger, anger, and pain. A sudden, loud, insistent cry associated with flexing and kicking of the legs may indicate colic—that is, pain resulting from gas or other sources of distress in the digestive tract. The baby may seem to hold its breath for a few moments, then gasp and begin to cry again. Crying from colic can be severe and persistent—lasting for hours, although cries generally seem to settle into a pattern after a while (Barr et al., 2005; Gudmundsson, 2010). Much to the relief of parents, colic tends to disappear by the third to sixth month, as a baby's digestive system matures.

Parents and other people, including children, have similar bodily responses to infant crying—increases in heart rate, blood pressure, and sweating (Reijneveld et al., 2004). Infant crying makes them feel irritated and anxious and motivates them to run to the baby to try to relieve the distress. The pitch of an infant's cries appears to provide information (Zeifman, 2004). Adults perceive high-pitched crying as more urgent, distressing, and sick sounding than low-pitched crying (Out et al., 2010).

Certain high-pitched cries, when prolonged, may signify health problems. For example, the cries of chronically distressed infants differ from those of normal infants in both rhythm and pitch. Patterns of crying may be indicative of such problems as chromosomal abnormalities, infections, fetal malnutrition, and exposure to narcotics (Douglas & Hill, 2011). A striking example of the link between crying and a health problem is the syndrome called *cri du chat*, French for "cry of the cat." This is a genetic disorder that produces abnormalities in the brain, atypical facial features, and a high-pitched, squeaky cry.

There are certain patterns of crying. For example, peaks of crying appear to be concentrated in the late afternoon and early evening (McGlaughlin & Grayson, 2001). Although some cries may seem extreme and random at first, they tend to settle into a pattern that is recognizable to most parents. Infants seem to produce about the same number of crying bouts during the first nine months or so, but the duration of the bouts grows briefer, by half, during this period (van IJzendoorn & Hubbard, 2000).

Soothing

Now that you are an expert on the causes and patterns of crying, you might be able to develop some ideas about how to soothe infants who are crying. As noted by Bell and Ainsworth (1972), physical contact with the infant is soothing. Sucking also seems to function as a built-in tranquilizer. Sucking on a pacifier decreases crying and agitated movement in neonates who have not yet had the opportunity to feed (Moon et al., 2011). Therefore, the soothing function of sucking need not be learned through experience. However, sucking (drinking) a sweet solution also appears to have a soothing effect (Stevens et al., 2005). (Can it be that even babies are programmed to enjoy "comfort food"?)

Parents find many other ways to soothe infants—patting, caressing and rocking, swaddling, and speaking to them in a soft voice. Parents then usually try to find the specific cause of the distress by offering a bottle or pacifier or checking the diaper. These responses to a crying infant are shown by parents in many cultures, such as those of Canada, the United States, France, and Japan.

Learning occurs quickly during the soothing process. Parents learn by trial and error what types of embraces and movements are likely to soothe their infants. And infants learn quickly that crying is followed by being picked up or other forms of intervention. Parents sometimes worry that if they pick up the crying baby quickly, they are reinforcing the baby for crying. In this way, they believe, the child may become spoiled and find it progressively more difficult to engage in self-soothing to get to sleep.

Fortunately, as infants mature and learn, crying tends to be replaced by less upsetting verbal requests for intervention. Among adults, of course, soothing techniques take very different forms—such as presenting a bouquet of flowers or admitting that one started the argument.

Soothing
How can a crying baby be soothed? Picking the baby up, talking to it quietly, patting, stroking, and rocking all seem to have calming effects.

4.7 Sudden Infant Death Syndrome (SIDS)

QUESTIONS » What is SIDS? What are the risk factors for SIDS? **TRUTH OR FICTION REVISITED:** It is true that more children die from sudden infant death syndrome (SIDS) than die from cancer, heart disease, pneumonia, child abuse, HIV/AIDS, cystic fibrosis, and muscular dystrophy combined (Lipsitt, 2003). **Sudden infant death syndrome (SIDS)**—also known as crib death—is a disorder of infancy that apparently strikes while the baby is sleeping. In the typical case, a baby goes to sleep, apparently in perfect health, and is found dead the next morning. There is no sign that the baby struggled or was in pain.

A Baby's Safe Sleep Environment

The incidence of SIDS has been declining, in part because some cases of SIDS have been reattributed to accidental suffocation. Even so, according to the Public Health Agency of Canada (2008), SIDS is the most common cause of death during the first year, and most of these deaths occur between two and five months of age (Käll & Lagercrantz, 2012). New parents frequently live in dread of SIDS and check regularly through the night to see whether their babies are breathing. It is not abnormal, by the way, for babies occasionally to suspend breathing for a moment.

sudden infant death syndrome (SIDS) The death, while sleeping, of apparently healthy babies who stop breathing for unknown medical reasons. Also called crib death.

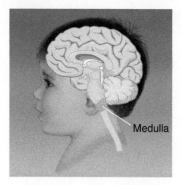

Figure 4.9 ■ The Medulla
Research by a team at the Children's Hospital Boston suggests that sudden infant death syndrome (SIDS) may be caused by a relatively low level of sensitivity of the medulla to the brain chemical serotonin.

Safe Sleep for Your Baby
Preventing sudden infant deaths in Canada

- Provide a **smoke-free** environment before and after your baby is born.
- **Breastfeeding** can protect your baby.
- Always place your baby on his or her **back to sleep**, at naptime and night time.
- Provide your baby with a **safe sleep** environment that has a firm surface and no pillows, comforters, quilts or bumper pads.
- Place your baby to sleep in a **crib, cradle, or bassinet next to your bed**.

Safe Sleep for Your Baby

medulla A part of the brain stem that regulates vital and automatic functions such as breathing and the sleep–wake cycle.

serotonin A neurotransmitter that is involved in the responsiveness of the medulla, emotional responses such as depression, and motivational responses such as hunger.

SIDS is more common among the following:

- Babies aged two to four months
- Babies who are put to sleep on their stomachs or their sides (sleeping prone decreases the oxygen supply to the brain [Wong et al., 2011])
- Premature and low-birth-weight infants
- Male babies
- Babies in families of lower socioeconomic status
- Bottle-fed babies (Hauck et al., 2011)
- Babies of teenage mothers
- Babies whose mothers smoked during or after pregnancy or whose mothers used narcotics during pregnancy

The Children's Hospital Boston Study

Perhaps the most compelling study to date was led by health professionals at the Children's Hospital Boston and published in *The Journal of the American Medical Association* (Paterson et al., 2006). This study focused on an area in the brainstem called the **medulla** (see Figure 4.9 ■), which is involved in basic functions such as breathing and sleep-and-wake cycles. Among other things, the medulla causes us to breathe if we are in need of oxygen. The researchers compared the medullas of babies who had died from SIDS with those of babies who had died at the same age from other causes. They found that the medullas of the babies who died from SIDS were less sensitive to the brain chemical **serotonin**, a chemical that helps keep the medulla responsive. The problem was particularly striking in the brains of the boys, which could account for the sex difference in the incidence of SIDS.

What precautions should *you* take to guard against SIDS if you are a new parent? Following are some suggestions from the American Academy of Pediatrics (2011):

- Place your baby to sleep on his back for every sleep.
- Place your baby to sleep on a firm sleep surface. To learn more about crib safety, visit the Consumer Product Safety Commission website at www.cpsc.gov.
- Keep soft objects, loose bedding, and any objects that could increase the risk of entrapment, suffocation, or strangulation out of the crib.
- Place your baby to sleep in the same room where you sleep but not in the same bed.
- Breastfeed as much and for as long as you can.
- Schedule and go to all well-child visits.
- Keep your baby away from smokers and places where people smoke.
- Do not let your baby get too hot.
- Offer a pacifier at nap time and bedtime.
- Do not use home cardiorespiratory monitors to help reduce the risk of SIDS.
- Do not use products that claim to reduce the risk of SIDS.

Perhaps within a few years we will have a screening test for SIDS and a method for preventing or controlling it. In the next chapter, we continue to follow physical development over the first two years.

Active Review

18. In Canada today, the neonate's overall level of health is usually evaluated at birth according to the _____ scale.

19. In the _____ reflex, the baby turns the head and mouth toward a stimulus that strokes the cheek, chin, or corner of the mouth.

20. Neonates are rather (nearsighted or farsighted?).

21. Neonates (do or do not?) prefer their mothers' voices to those of other women.

22. As babies mature, they spend a (greater or smaller?) percentage of their time sleeping in REM sleep.

23. _____ is the most common cause of death in infants between the ages of one month and one year.

Reflect & Relate: Have you or a family member had to adjust to the waking and sleeping patterns of a baby? Do you think it is normal to occasionally resent being awakened repeatedly through the night? Explain.

Recite an Active Summary

4.1 Countdown ...

What events occur just before childbirth begins?
The first uterine contractions are called Braxton-Hicks contractions or false labour contractions. A day or so before labour begins, some blood spotting can occur in vaginal secretions. At about this time, one woman in ten has a rush of amniotic fluid from the vagina. The initiation of labour may be triggered by secretion of hormones by the fetus. Maternal hormones stimulate contractions strong enough to expel the baby.

4.2 The Stages of Childbirth

What happens during the first stage of childbirth?
Childbirth begins with the onset of regular contractions of the uterus, which cause the cervix to become effaced and dilated. The first stage may last from a few hours to more than a day. During transition, the cervix is almost fully dilated and the head of the fetus moves into the birth canal.

What happens during the second stage of childbirth?
The second stage begins when the baby appears at the opening of the birth canal. It ends with the birth of the baby. Once the baby's head emerges from the mother's body, mucus is suctioned from its mouth so that breathing is not obstructed. When the baby is breathing on its own, the umbilical cord is clamped and severed.

What happens during the third stage of childbirth?
During this stage, the placenta separates from the uterine wall and is expelled along with fetal membranes.

4.3 Methods of Childbirth

What methods of childbirth are in use today? What are their effects?
General anesthesia puts the woman to sleep, but it decreases the strength of uterine contractions and lowers the responsiveness of the neonate. Regional or local anesthetics deaden pain in parts of the body without putting the mother to sleep. HypnoBirthing teaches mothers how to relax during childbirth and encourages focusing on pleasant imagery. Biofeedback provides a woman with information about what is happening in her body. Prepared childbirth teaches women to dissociate uterine contractions from pain and fear by associating other responses, such as relaxation, with contractions. A coach aids the mother in the delivery room. In a C-section, the baby is delivered surgically through the abdomen. C-sections are most likely to be recommended if the baby is large or in distress, or if the mother's pelvis is small or she is tired or weak. Herpes and HIV infections in the birth canal can be avoided by C-section. Home birth is generally safe for healthy women who have already borne children.

4.4 Birth Problems

What are the effects of oxygen deprivation at birth?
Prenatal oxygen deprivation can be fatal if prolonged; it can also impair development of the nervous system, leading to cognitive and motor problems.

What risks are connected with being born prematurely or low in birth weight?
A baby is preterm when birth occurs at or before 37 weeks of gestation. A baby has a low birth weight when it weighs less than 2500 grams. A baby who is low in birth weight but born at full term is said to be small for dates. The chances of having preterm babies rise with multiple births, such as twins. The risks associated with prematurity include infant mortality and delayed neurological and motor development. Preterm babies are relatively thin and often have vernix on the skin and lanugo. Sucking and breathing reflexes may be weak. The walls of air sacs in the lungs may stick together, leading to respiratory distress. Preterm babies usually remain in the hospital in incubators. Preterm infants profit from early stimulation just as full-term babies do.

Parents often do not treat preterm neonates as well as they treat full-term neonates, perhaps because preterm infants are less attractive and have irritating, high-pitched cries.

4.5 The Postpartum Period

What mood problems do women experience during the postpartum period?

Women may encounter the baby blues, postpartum depression, and postpartum psychosis. These problems are found around the world and probably reflect hormonal changes following birth, although stress can play a role. High self-esteem and social support help women manage these adjustment problems.

How critical is parental interaction with neonates in the formation of bonds of attachment?

It may not be. Early research by Klaus and Kennell suggested that the first few hours after birth present a "maternal-sensitive" period during which women's hormone levels particularly dispose them to "bond" with their neonates. However, the study confounded the effects of extra time with their babies with the effects of special attention from health professionals.

4.6 Characteristics of Neonates

How do health professionals assess the health of neonates?

The neonate's overall health is usually evaluated with the Apgar scale. The Brazelton Neonatal Behavioral Assessment Scale also screens neonates for behavioural and neurological problems.

What are reflexes? What kinds of reflexes do neonates have?

Reflexes are simple, unlearned, stereotypical responses that are elicited by specific stimuli. The rooting and sucking reflexes are basic to survival. Other key reflexes include the startle reflex, the grasping reflex, the stepping reflex, the Babinski reflex, and the tonic-neck reflex. Most reflexes disappear or are replaced by voluntary behaviour within months.

How well do neonates see, hear, and so on?

Neonates are nearsighted. Neonates visually detect movement, and many track movement. Fetuses respond to sound months before they are born. Neonates are particularly responsive to the sounds and rhythms of speech. The nasal preferences of neonates are similar to those of older children and adults. Neonates prefer sweet solutions and find them soothing. The sensations of skin against skin are also soothing and may contribute to the formation of bonds of attachment.

Can neonates learn?

Yes. Neonates are capable of classical and operant conditioning. For example, they can be conditioned to blink their eyes in response to a tone.

What patterns of sleep are found among neonates?

Neonates spend two-thirds of their time in sleep. Nearly all neonates distribute sleep through naps. Neonates spend about half their time sleeping in REM sleep, but as time goes on, REM sleep accounts for less of their sleep. REM sleep may be connected with brain development.

Why do babies cry? What can be done to soothe them?

Babies cry mainly because of pain and discomfort. Crying may communicate the identity of the crier across distance, as well as hunger, anger, pain, and the presence of health problems. Pacifiers help because sucking is soothing. Parents also try picking babies up, patting, caressing and rocking them, and speaking to them in a low voice.

4.7 Sudden Infant Death Syndrome (SIDS)

What is SIDS? What are the risk factors for SIDS?

SIDS is a disorder of infancy that apparently strikes while the baby is sleeping. SIDS is the most common cause of death in infants between the ages of one month and one year. SIDS is more common among babies who are put to sleep in the prone position, preterm and low-birth-weight infants, male infants, and infants whose mothers smoked during or after pregnancy or whose mothers used narcotics during pregnancy.

Key Terms

Active Learning Resources

Go to **www.nelsonbrain.com** to access *Voyages in Development's* CourseMate, where you will find an interactive eBook, flashcards, Pre-Lecture Quizzes, Section Quizzes, Exam Practice, videos, and more.

Aleph Studio/Shutterstock.com

Major Topics

INFANCY:
Physical Development

5

Truth or Fiction?

T | F   The head of the newborn child doubles in length by adulthood, but the legs increase in length by about five times. **p. 157**

T | F   Infants triple their birth weight within a year. **p. 158**

T | F   Breast-feeding helps prevent obesity later in life. **p. 164**

T | F   A child's brain reaches half its adult weight by the age of one year. **p. 168**

T | F   The cerebral cortex—the outer layer of the brain that is vital to human thought and reasoning—is only about 3 millimetres thick. **p. 168**

T | F   Native American Hopi infants spend the first year of life strapped to a board, yet they begin to walk at about the same time as children who are reared in other cultures. **p. 174**

T | F   Infants need to have experience crawling before they develop a fear of heights. **p. 178**

We are very keen observers of children—our own, that is. From our experiences as parents, we have derived the following basic principles of physical development:

- Just when you think your child has finally begun to make regular gains in weight, she or he will begin to lose weight or go for months without gaining an ounce.

- No matter how early your child sits up or starts to walk, your neighbour's child will do it earlier.

- Children first roll over when one parent is watching but will steadfastly refuse to repeat it when the other parent is called in.

- Children begin to get into everything before you get childproof latches on the cabinets.

- Every advance in locomotor ability provides your child with new ways to get hurt.

- Children display their most exciting developmental milestones when you don't have the camera rolling or can't get the video function of your smart phone to work.

More seriously, in this chapter, we discuss various aspects of physical development during the first two years. We examine changes in physical growth, the development of the brain and the nervous system, motor development, and the development and coordination of sensory and perceptual capabilities, such as vision and hearing.

Irina Rogova/Shutterstock.com

5.1 Physical Growth and Development

What a fascinating creature the newborn is: tiny, seemingly helpless, apparently oblivious to its surroundings, yet perfectly formed and fully capable of letting its caregivers know when it is hungry, thirsty, or uncomfortable. And what a fascinating creature is this same child two years later: running, climbing, playing, talking, hugging, and kissing.

It is hard to believe that only two short years can bring about such remarkable changes. It seems that nearly every day brings a new accomplishment. Yet, as we will see, not all infants share equally in the explosion of positive developments. Therefore, we will also be mentioning some developmental problems and what can be done about them.

Sequences of Physical Development: Head First?

QUESTION » **What are the sequences of physical development?** During the first two years, children make enormous strides in physical growth and development. In this section, we explore sequences of physical development, changes in height and weight, and nutrition. Three key sequences of physical development are cephalocaudal development, proximodistal development, and differentiation (see Concept Review 5.1).

Cephalocaudal Development

Development proceeds from the upper part of the head to the lower parts of the body. When we consider the central role of the brain, which is contained

Concept Review 5.1 Sequences of Physical Development

Cephalocaudal Development

Cephalocaudal means that development proceeds from the "head" to the "tail" or, in the case of humans, to the lower parts of the body. Cephalocaudal development gives the brain an opportunity to participate more fully in subsequent developments.

This photo shows that infants gain control over their hands and upper body before they gain control over their lower body.

Proximodistal Development

Proximodistal means that development proceeds from the trunk or central axis of the body outward. The brain and spine make up the central nervous system along the central axis of the body and are functional before the infant can control the arms and legs.

In this photo, you can see that the infant's arm is only slightly longer than her head. Compare this to the length of your own head and arm.

Differentiation

As children mature, physical reactions become less global and more specific. This infant engages in diffuse motor activity. Within a few months, he will be grasping for objects and holding onto them with a more and more sophisticated kind of grasp.

This photo shows that infants engage in diffuse motion before they begin to reach and grasp.

within the skull, the cephalocaudal sequence appears quite logical. The brain regulates essential functions, such as heartbeat. Through the secretion of hormones, the brain also regulates the growth and development of the body and influences basic drives, such as hunger and thirst.

The head develops more rapidly than the rest of the body during the embryonic stage. By eight weeks after conception, the head constitutes half the entire length of the embryo. The brain develops more rapidly than the spinal cord. Arm buds form before leg buds. Most newborn babies have a strong, well-defined sucking reflex, although their legs are spindly and their limbs move back and forth only in diffuse excitement or agitation. Infants can hold up their heads before they gain control over their arms, their torsos, and, finally, their legs. They can sit up before they can crawl and walk. When they first walk, they use their hands to hold onto a person or object for support.

The lower parts of the body, because they get off to a later start, must do more growing to reach adult size. **TRUTH OR FICTION REVISITED:** The head does double in length between birth and maturity, but the torso triples in length. The arms increase their length by about four times, but the legs and feet increase by about five times.

Proximodistal Development

Growth and development also proceed from the trunk outward—from the body's central axis toward the periphery. The proximodistal principle, too, makes sense. The brain and spinal cord follow a central axis down through the body, and it is essential that the nerves be in place before the infant can gain control over the arms and legs. Also, the life functions of the newborn baby—heartbeat, respiration, digestion, and elimination of wastes—are all carried out by organ systems close to the central axis. These must be in operation or ready to operate when the child is born.

In terms of motor development, infants gain control over their trunks and their shoulders before they can control their arms, hands, and fingers. They make clumsy swipes at objects with their arms before they can voluntarily grasp them with their hands. Infants can grab large objects before picking up tiny things with their fingers. Similarly, infants gain control over their hips and upper legs before they can direct their lower legs, feet, and toes.

Differentiation

As children mature, their physical reactions become less global and more specific. The tendency of behaviour to become more specific and distinct is called **differentiation**. If a neonate's finger is pricked or burned, he or she may withdraw the finger but also thrash about, cry, and show general signs of distress. Toddlers may also cry, show distress, and withdraw the finger, but they are less likely to thrash about wildly. Thus, the response to pain has become more specific. An older child or adult is also likely to withdraw the finger but is less likely to wail and show general distress.

Growth Patterns in Height and Weight: Heading toward the Greek Ideal?

QUESTION » What patterns of growth occur in infancy? The most dramatic gains in height and weight occur during prenatal development. Within a span of nine months, children develop from a zygote that is about 1/70 of a centimetre long to a neonate that is about 50 centimetres in length. Weight increases by a factor of billions.

differentiation The processes by which behaviours and physical structures become more specialized.

During the first year after birth, gains in height and weight are also dramatic, although not by the standards of prenatal gains. Infants usually double their birth weight in about five months and triple it by the first birthday (Kuczmarski et al., 2000). Their height increases by about 50 percent in the first year, so a child whose length at birth was 50 centimetres is likely to be about 75 centimetres tall at 12 months. **TRUTH OR FICTION REVISITED:** Thus, it is true that infants triple their birth weight within a year. The gain sounds dramatic, but keep in mind that their weight increases more than a billionfold in the nine months between conception and birth.

Growth in infancy has long been viewed as a slow and steady process. Growth charts in pediatricians' offices resemble the smooth, continuous curves shown in Appendix B. But research suggests that infants actually grow in spurts. About 90–95 percent of the time, they are not growing at all. One study measured the heights of infants throughout their first 21 months (Lampl et al., 1992). The researchers found that the infants remained the same size for 2 to 63 days and then shot up in length from 0.5–2.5 centimetres in less than 24 hours. Parents who swear that their infants sometimes consume enormous amounts of food and grow overnight may not be exaggerating.

Infants grow another 10–15 centimetres during the second year and gain another 2–3 kilograms. Boys generally reach half their adult height by their second birthday. Girls, however, mature more quickly than boys and are likely to reach half their adult height at the age of 18 months (Tanner, 1989). The growth rates of taller-than-average infants, as a group, tend to slow down. Those of shorter-than-average infants, as a group, tend to speed up. This is not to suggest that there is no relationship between infant and adult heights or that we all wind up in an average range. Tall infants, as a group, wind up taller than short infants, but (in most cases) not by as much as seemed likely during infancy.

Changes in Body Proportions

In rendering the human form, Greek classical sculptors followed the rule of the "golden section": The length of the head equals one-eighth the height of the body (including the head). This may be the ideal of human beauty, but the reality is that among adults, the length of the head actually varies from about one-eighth to one-tenth of the body's height. Among children, the head is proportionately larger (see Figure 5.1 ■).

Development proceeds in a cephalocaudal manner. A few weeks after conception, an embryo is almost all head. At the beginning of the fetal stage, the head is about half the length of the unborn child. In the neonate, it is about

Figure 5.1 ■ Changes in the Proportions of the Body
Development proceeds in a cephalocaudal direction. The head is proportionately larger among younger children.

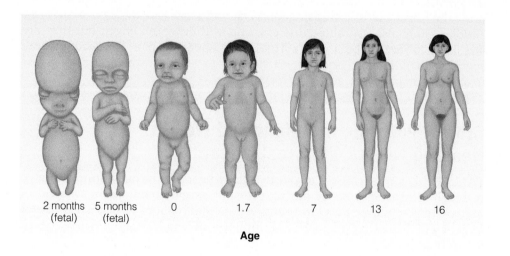

| 2 months (fetal) | 5 months (fetal) | 0 | 1.7 | 7 | 13 | 16 |

Age

one-fourth the length of the body. The head gradually diminishes in proportion to the rest of the body, even though it doubles in size by adulthood.

Among adults, the arms are nearly three times the length of the head. The legs are about four times as long—nearly half the length of the body. Among neonates, the arms and legs are about equal in length. Each is only about one and a half times the length of the head. By the first birthday, the neck has begun to lengthen visibly, as have the arms and legs. The arms grow more rapidly than the legs do at first (an example of the cephalocaudal trend), and by the second birthday, the arms are actually longer than the legs. The legs then grow more rapidly, soon catching up with and surpassing the arms in length.

We have described typical growth patterns. Most infants follow these patterns and thrive. Some, however, do not.

Failure to Thrive

QUESTION » What is failure to thrive? Haley is four months old. Her mother is breast-feeding her, as she puts it, "all the time," because Haley is not gaining weight. Not gaining weight for a while is normal enough, but Haley is also irritable and she feeds fitfully, sometimes refusing the breast entirely. Her pediatrician is evaluating her for a syndrome called **failure to thrive (FTT)**.

We live in one of the world's most bountiful nations. Few have trouble accessing food. Nevertheless, a number of infants, such as Haley, show FTT, which is a serious disorder that impairs growth in infancy and early childhood (Olsen et al., 2007). FTT is sometimes a fuzzy diagnosis. Olsen and his colleagues (2007) identify seven criteria for diagnosing FTT, including low weight for age and low body mass index (BMI). They found that 27 percent of infants meet one or more of these criteria during the first year of life, but this percentage is probably misleadingly high because most infants met only one of the standards.

Historically, researchers have spoken of biologically based (or "organic") FTT versus nonbiologically based ("nonorganic") FTT. The idea is that in organic FTT, an underlying health problem accounts for the failure to obtain or make use of adequate nutrition. Nonorganic FTT (abbreviated NOFTT in the research literature) apparently has psychological roots, social roots, or both (Jaffe, 2011). In either case, the infant does not make normal gains in weight and size.

Regardless of the cause or causes, feeding problems are central. Research has shown that infants with FTT tend to be introduced to solid and finger foods later than other children. As in Haley's case, they are more likely to be described as variable eaters and less often as being hungry (Wright & Birks, 2000). FTT is linked not only to slow physical growth but also to cognitive, behavioural, and emotional problems (Jaffe, 2011). For example, at the age of 2 to 12 months, infants with FTT express more negative feelings, vocalize less, and often refuse to make eye contact with adults (Steward, 2001). Another study found that at the age of eight-and-a-half, children who had been diagnosed with FTT at the median age of 20 months remained smaller, were less cognitively advanced, and were more emotionally and behaviourally disturbed than typical children (Dykman et al., 2001). They wind up shorter and lighter than their peers at the ages of 8 and 12 (Black et al., 2007; Drewett et al., 2006).

Many investigators believe that deficiencies in caregiver–child interaction play a key role in FTT (Benoit & Coolbear, 2004), leading to *reactive attachment disorder*. For example, compared with mothers of healthy infants, mothers of infants with FTT show fewer adaptive social interactions (they are less likely to "go with the flow") and fewer positive feelings toward their infants. The mothers also terminate feedings more arbitrarily (Robinson et al., 2001). Perhaps as a consequence, children with FTT are less likely than other children to

failure to thrive (FTT) A disorder of impaired growth in infancy and early childhood characterized by failure to gain weight within normal limits.

be securely attached to their mothers (Benoit & Coolbear, 2004). Why are the mothers of children with FTT less likely to help their children to feel secure? Many have a large number of children, an unstable home environment, or psychological problems of their own (Mackner et al., 2003).

Because FTT often results from a combination of factors, treatment may not be easy. Children with FTT need both nutritional support and attention to possible adjustment problems (Simonelli et al., 2005). It turns out that Haley's parents will profit from both personal counselling and advice on relating to Haley.

The condition **marasmus** is a form of FTT that is characterized by wasting away due to a diet low in essential nutrients. It typically appears in the first year of life. In some cases, a mother who is breast-feeding does not produce enough milk. Bottle feeding may also be inadequate. In any event, marasmus is life-threatening.

Catch-Up Growth

A child's growth can be slowed from its genetically predetermined course by many organic factors, including illness and dietary deficiency. However, once the problem is alleviated, the child's rate of growth frequently accelerates and returns to approximate the normal course from which it had been deflected (Parsons et al., 2011). The tendency to return to one's genetically determined pattern of growth is referred to as **canalization**. Once Haley's parents receive counselling and once Haley's FTT is overcome, Haley will put on weight rapidly and catch up to the norms for her age.

5.2 Nutrition: Fuelling Development

QUESTION » What are the nutritional needs of infants? The overall nutritional status of children in Canada is good compared with that of children in most other countries. However, the nutritional status of poor Canadian children varies. In comparison to other developed nations, Canada places third worst with respect to levels of child poverty (see Figure 5.2 ■; Save the Children, 2011, 2012). About a quarter of Aboriginal children in Canada live in poverty, compared to one in nine non-Aboriginal children (Save the Children 2012). Overall, the reported rate of child poverty is about one in seven children[1] (Conference Board of Canada, 2013). With programs like Save the Children–Canada, and provincially based initiatives (Breaking the Cycle–Ontario's Poverty Reduction Strategy, 2013), there are attempts to, tackle food insecurity issues; however, the need remains great. There are food banks across the country, and approximately 36.4 percent of those using food bank services are children and youth (Food Banks Canada, 2013). Canadian children have been targeted by programs such as Breakfast Club Canada, Food First Foundation, and Breakfast for Learning. Even so, infants and young children from low-income families are more likely than other children to display signs of poor nutrition, such as anemia and FTT (Bucholz et al., 2011; National Center for Children in Poverty, 2012).

marasmus A wasted, potentially lethal body condition caused by inadequate nutrition and characterized by painful thinness.

canalization The tendency of growth rates to return to genetically determined patterns after undergoing environmentally induced change.

---

[1]According to the *Low Income Lines 2010 to 2011* Report (Statistics Canada, 2012), the low-income cut-offs for individuals living in metropolitan areas (500 000 inhabitants or more) after-tax incomes are:

- one person: $19 307
- two persons: $23 498
- three persons: $29 260
- four persons: $36 504

Research suggests that, on average, families need an income equal to about two times the federal poverty level to meet their most basic needs.

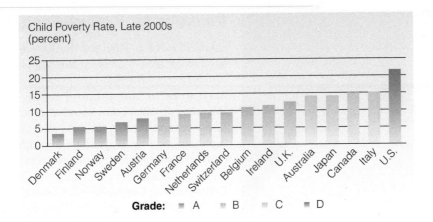

Figure 5.2 ■ **Child Poverty in Developed Nations across the World**
Source: © Conference Board of Canada. Used with permission.

Child Poverty Rate, Late 2000s (percent)

Grade: ■ A ■ B □ C ■ D

Denmark, Finland, Norway, Sweden, Austria, Germany, France, Netherlands, Switzerland, Belgium, Ireland, U.K., Australia, Japan, Canada, Italy, U.S.

From birth, infants should be fed either breast milk or an iron-fortified infant formula. Solid foods are often introduced at four to six months. During the first four months, the tongue-thrust reflex protects the infant from choking by pushing out solid substances. But between four and six months, the reflex diminishes gradually, giving solids a chance of being swallowed (Sears, 2009). At four to six months, the infant can also indicate hunger by leaning forward and fullness by turning away from food. Nevertheless, the American Academy of Pediatrics (2012) recommends that infants be fed breast milk throughout the first year and longer if possible (Meek, 2011). (For more information, visit the American Academy of Pediatrics at www.aap.org.) The first solid food is usually iron-enriched cereal, followed by strained fruits, then vegetables, and finally meats, poultry, and fish. Finger foods such as teething biscuits are introduced in the latter part of the first year.

A CLOSER LOOK | REAL LIFE

Food Timeline for the First Two Years[2]

All babies are unique individuals. Talk to your doctor or a registered dietitian about the nutrient-rich foods your baby needs and when to introduce them. The following are the usual age ranges for moving infants from breast milk to table foods:

- Birth to six months: Babies get all the nutrients they need from breast milk for the first six months.

- By six months: Even though most babies are ready to eat solid foods now, they will continue to get most of their calories, protein, vitamins, and minerals from breast milk. Introduce iron-fortified infant cereal such as rice and barley or pureed meats to help replenish iron reserves.

- By six to eight months: This is an appropriate time to begin pureed or mashed fruits and vegetables. Gradually introduce single-item foods one at a time. Watch carefully for any reactions such as diarrhea, vomiting, or unusual rashes.

- By seven to ten months: Babies are usually ready to begin feeding themselves with finger foods, such as dry cereal or teething biscuits. They also can begin to use a cup for water.

- By eight months to one year: At this stage, most infants are ready for soft or cooked table foods.

- From one to two years: Babies continue developing eating skills. They feed themselves and enjoy the same foods as the rest of the family. Choking on firm, round foods is a risk, so cut these foods into smaller squares (about 0.5 centimetre).

When in doubt, parents should check with a nurse, pediatrician or dietician. What is good for adults is not good for infants. Parents who are on low-fat, high-fiber diets to ward off cardiovascular problems, cancer, and other health problems should not assume that the same diet is healthful for infants.

---

[2]Adapted from Academy of Nutrition and Dietetics. (2012). *Getting Started on Eating Right*. www.eatright.org/Public/content.aspx?id=8044. Accessed February 17, 2012.

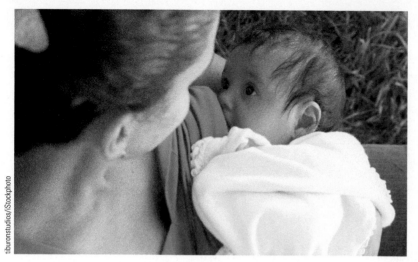

tiburonstudios/iStockphoto

Reasons to Breast-Feed

QUESTION » Why are mothers encouraged to breast-feed? What are the pros and cons of breast-feeding vs. bottle feeding? According to the Infant Feeding Joint Working Group, comprised of collaboration between Health Canada and national organizations such as the Canadian Paediatric Society's Nutrition and Gastroenterology Committee, Dietitians of Canada, Breastfeeding Committee for Canada, and the Public Health Agency of Canada, exclusive breast-feeding is the recommended global standard of feeding promoted by the World Health Organization for the first six months of life, with continued breast-feeding alongside other appropriate complementary foods up to two years of age or longer (World Health Organization, 2003).

Benefits of breast-feeding have been associated with infants' short- and long-term health (Horta, Bahl, Martines, & Victoria, 2007; Ip et al., 2007; Pound, Unger, & Canadian Paediatric Society, 2012). Breast-feeding has been correlated with enhanced cognitive development, and it may also protect against certain gastrointestinal infections, respiratory tract infections, and sudden infant death syndrome (Kramer et al., 2008; Quigley et al., 2012; Ip et al., 2007; Hauck, Thompson, Tanabe, Moon, & Vennemann, 2011).

Breast-feeding has become the norm in Canada. According to a report by Statistics Canada (Gionet, 2013), 89 percent of Canadian mothers breast-fed their babies in 2011–2012 (vs. 85 percent in 2003). The number of mothers exclusively breast-feeding until six months has also gone up (26 percent in 2011–2012 vs. 17 percent in 2003). The report also noted that the two main reasons for stopping breast-feeding were not enough milk and difficulty with breast-feeding technique.

In a Public Health Agency of Canada document entitled "Attachment Across Cultures" (www.attachmentacrosscultures.org/eindex.html), it is acknowledged that women's beliefs, values, and practices influence how they see their role in feeding and caring for their children.

A CLOSER LOOK · DIVERSITY

Wasting Away from Hunger

One in every seven or eight people in the world goes hungry (see Figure 5.3 ■). Protein-energy malnutrition (PEM) is the most severe form of malnutrition. Protein is essential for growth, and food energy translates into calories. Here are a few facts about children and hunger (World Hunger Organization, 2012):

- In the developing world (largely in Africa and Asia), about one child in three under age five has stunted growth, and more than 90 percent of the world's hungry children live on one of these two continents.
- Children who are "wasting" have a markedly increased risk of death. About 13 percent of children under age

five in the developing world are wasted, with 5 percent extremely wasted—some 26 million children.

- Almost 8 million children died of hunger in 2010.
- The main cause of hunger for children is poverty.
- Children may suffer from PEM before birth if their mother is malnourished.
- Malnutrition, also known as "the silent emergency," has contributed to about 60 percent of the 11 million deaths of children each year.
- Children with PEM suffer up to 160 days of illness per year.

Continued

Continued

In the condition known as **kwashiorkor**, the child may eat enough calories from starchy foods but does not take in enough protein. As a result, the body may metabolize its own reserves of protein, leading to enlargement of the stomach, swollen feet, a rash, and loss of hair (Ndekha, 2008). Irritability and lack of energy may follow.

The World Health Organization (2011) has issued step-by-step guidelines on the treatment of children with PEM in the clinical setting. These guidelines are being promoted for use worldwide by physicians, nurses, and all other frontline health workers. The guidelines for instruction include:

- Educating health workers on the extent and severity of PEM.
- Identifying children with severe malnutrition. Symptoms include hypoglycemia (shakiness resulting from low blood sugar levels), hypothermia, shock, dehydration, and severe anemia.

- Preparing appropriate feeding formulas and food supplements.
- Using antibiotics and other medicines to treat disease.
- Monitoring the child's intake of food and the child's waste products; preparing and using a weight chart.
- Monitoring the child's vital signs—pulse, respiration rate, and temperature—and being aware of signs of danger.
- Bathing the child.
- Involving mothers in care so that they can continue care at home, including feeding and play activities (for purposes of stimulation); providing mothers with comprehensive instructions at discharge.

The mortality rate of children with PEM can be as high as 50 percent, but with adequate care, the rates can be reduced to less than 5 percent. For more information, contact the Department of Nutrition for Health and Development, World Health Organization, 1211 Geneva, 27, Switzerland (phone: 141 22 791 2624/4342; fax: 141 22 791 4156).

Reflect What can you do to help alleviate PEM in developing nations?

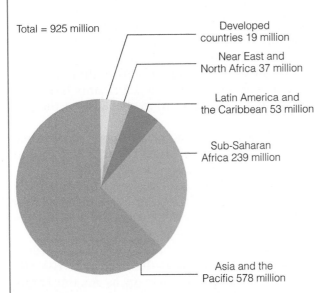

Total = 925 million

Developed countries 19 million

Near East and North Africa 37 million

Latin America and the Caribbean 53 million

Sub-Saharan Africa 239 million

Asia and the Pacific 578 million

Figure 5.3 ▪ Number of Hungry People in the World, 2012

Source: World Hunger Organization. (2012). *2012 World Hunger and Poverty Facts and Statistics*. World Hunger Organization Service. www.worldhunger.org/articles/Learn/world%20hunger%20facts%202002.htm. Accessed February 20, 2012.

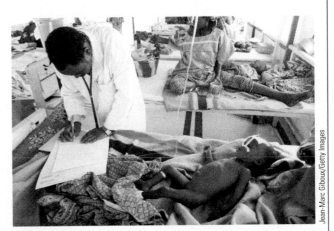

Jean-Marc Giboux/Getty Images

Kwashiorkor
In kwashiorkor, the enlargement of the stomach and other symptoms result from failure to take in adequate protein.

However, it is important to note that despite recommendations, 74 percent of Canadian women are not exclusively breast-feeding for the first six months. One hypothesis is that many women bottle-feed because they return to work after childbirth and are therefore unavailable (Guendelman et al., 2009). Their partners, extended families, nannies, or child-care workers give their children bottles during the day. Some mothers pump their milk and bottle it for their children's use when they are away. Some parents

kwashiorkor A form of protein-energy malnutrition in which the body may break down its own reserves of protein, resulting in enlargement of the stomach, swollen feet, and other symptoms.

bottle-feed because doing so enables both parents to share in feeding—around the clock. The father may not be equipped to breast-feed, but he can bottle-feed. Even though bottle feeding requires preparing formulas, some women find it to be less troublesome.

Colostrum is an early form of breast milk that is produced late in pregnancy and following childbirth. It is high in proteins and carbohydrates but low in fat, thus packing a high level of nutrients into a low volume. It also carries many of the mother's antibodies, boosting the early functioning of the baby's immune system. Observational research also suggests a protective effect of breast-feeding against obesity later in life (Arenz, Rückerl, Koletzko & von Kries, 2004, Ip et al., 2007).

Breast-feeding also has health benefits for the mother: It reduces the risk of early breast cancer and ovarian cancer, and it builds the strength of bones, which can reduce the likelihood of the hip fractures that result from osteoporosis following menopause. Breast-feeding also helps shrink the uterus and lessens weight retention after delivery (Baker et al., 2008). In addition, woman who breast-feed experience more rapid weight loss, and a quicker return to their pre-pregnancy weight (Pound, Unger, & Canadian Paediatric Society, 2012).

Human newborns also prefer human milk to formula. An interesting study recruited breast-fed and bottle-fed four-day-old infants as subjects and presented them with the odours of human milk and formula (Marlier & Schaal, 2005). Those who were breast-fed were presented with the odours of unfamiliar human milk—that is, milk from strangers. Preference was measured in terms of the direction in which the infants turned their heads and the intensity of their sucking movements. Although the responses of the infants were somewhat more complex than we are presenting here, they generally showed preference for human milk. Should this finding influence parents? The truth of the matter is that few formula-fed infants have been shown to refuse to eat (or develop a sour disposition) because of the type of food.

Breast-feeding has also been shown to help mothers respond more calmly to stress, as defined by stress-related bodily responses when presented with demanding mental arithmetic problems (Mezzacappa et al., 2005).

The advantages of feeding breast milk are summarized in Figure 5.4 ■.
TRUTH OR FICTION REVISITED: As noted in Figure 5.4, drinking breast milk is related to a better chance of avoiding obesity later in life. Perhaps this is because breast milk is lower in fat than whole milk.

There are, however, some disadvantages associated with breast-feeding. For example, breast milk is one of the bodily fluids that transmits HIV (the virus that causes AIDS). Researchers estimate that as many as one-third of the world's infants who have HIV/AIDS were infected in this manner (UNICEF, 2012). Alcohol, many drugs taken by the mother, and environmental hazards such as polychlorinated biphenyls (PCBs) can be transmitted to infants through breast milk. Therefore, breast milk is not always as pure as it would seem to be. Moreover, in order for breast milk to contain the necessary nutrients, the mother must be adequately nourished herself. In many cases, mothers in developing countries do not eat sufficiently well to pass along proper nutrition to their infants.

Another disadvantage is that in breast-feeding, the mother assumes sole responsibility for nighttime feedings. She also must weather the physical demands of producing and expelling milk, a tendency for soreness in the breasts, and the inconvenience of being continuously available to meet the infant's feeding needs.

Breast milk remains the ideal food for a baby, even if the mother smokes (Breastfeeding, 2006). Although nicotine may be present in breast milk, harmful effects on the infant have not been noted.

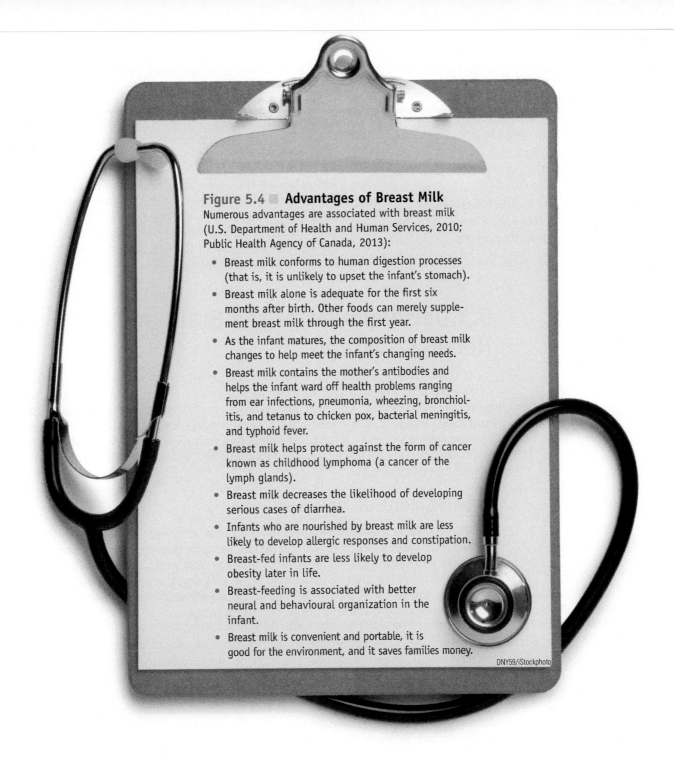

Figure 5.4 ■ Advantages of Breast Milk
Numerous advantages are associated with breast milk
(U.S. Department of Health and Human Services, 2010;
Public Health Agency of Canada, 2013):

- Breast milk conforms to human digestion processes
  (that is, it is unlikely to upset the infant's stomach).

- Breast milk alone is adequate for the first six
  months after birth. Other foods can merely supplement breast milk through the first year.

- As the infant matures, the composition of breast milk
  changes to help meet the infant's changing needs.

- Breast milk contains the mother's antibodies and
  helps the infant ward off health problems ranging
  from ear infections, pneumonia, wheezing, bronchiol-
  itis, and tetanus to chicken pox, bacterial meningitis,
  and typhoid fever.

- Breast milk helps protect against the form of cancer
  known as childhood lymphoma (a cancer of the
  lymph glands).

- Breast milk decreases the likelihood of developing
  serious cases of diarrhea.

- Infants who are nourished by breast milk are less
  likely to develop allergic responses and constipation.

- Breast-fed infants are less likely to develop
  obesity later in life.

- Breast-feeding is associated with better
  neural and behavioural organization in the
  infant.

- Breast milk is convenient and portable, it is
  good for the environment, and it saves families money.

DNY59/iStockphoto

The hormones prolactin and oxytocin are involved in breast-feeding. The word *prolactin* means in favour of ("pro") producing milk. By a few days after delivery, prolactin stimulates the mammary glands to produce milk. Oxytocin is secreted in response to suckling and stimulates the breasts to eject milk. When breast-feeding is discontinued, prolactin and oxytocin are no longer secreted, and lactation ends.

Women who have questions about breast-feeding can speak with lactation consultants at hospitals and consult La Leche League International (www.llli.org).

Active Review

1. Cephalocaudal development describes the processes by which development proceeds from the _____ to the lower parts of the body.

2. The _____ principle means that development proceeds from the trunk outward.

3. Infants usually double their birth weight in about _____ months and triple it by their first birthday.

4. Compared to mothers of healthy infants, mothers of infants with failure to thrive show fewer (positive or negative?) feelings toward their infants.

5. After illness or dietary deficiency, children show _____, which is a tendency to return to their genetically determined pattern of growth.

6. Breast milk contains _____ that can prevent problems such as ear infections, meningitis, tetanus, and chicken pox.

Reflect & Relate: How closely did your parents pay attention to your height and weight? Did they chart it? When did you begin to think that you were average (or above or below average) in height and weight? What effect did your size have on your self-concept and self-esteem?

5.3 Development of the Brain and Nervous System

Most students hearing about the nervous system for the first time often wonder what benefit to humans is it to have such a system. Who, after all, wants to be nervous? In reality, the nervous system is a system of **nerves** involved in heartbeat, visual–motor coordination, thought and language, and so on. The human nervous system is more complex than that of other animals. Although elephants and whales have heavier brains, our brains make up a larger proportion of our body weight.

Development of Neurons

QUESTIONS » What are neurons? How do they develop? The basic units of the nervous system are neurons. **Neurons** are cells that receive and transmit messages from one part of the body to another. The messages transmitted by neurons account for phenomena as varied as reflexes, the perception of an itch from a mosquito bite, the visual–motor coordination of a skier, the composition of a concerto, and the solution of a math problem.

People are born with about 100 billion neurons, most of which are in the brain. Neurons vary according to their functions and locations in the body. Some neurons in the brain are only a fraction of a centimetre in length, whereas neurons in the leg can grow over a metre long. Each neuron possesses a cell body, dendrites, and an axon (see Figure 5.5 ■). **Dendrites** are short fibres that extend from the cell body and receive incoming messages from thousands of adjoining transmitting neurons. The **axon** extends trunklike from the cell body and accounts for much of the difference in length among neurons. An axon can be over a metre long if it is carrying messages from the toes upward. Messages are released from axon terminals in the form of chemicals called **neurotransmitters**. These messages are then received by the dendrites of adjoining neurons, muscles, or glands. As the child matures, the axons of neurons grow in length, and the dendrites and axon terminals proliferate, creating vast interconnected networks for the transmission of complex messages.

Myelin

Many neurons are tightly wrapped with white, fatty **myelin sheaths** that give them the appearance of a string of white sausages. The high fat content of the myelin sheath insulates the neuron from electrically charged atoms in the

nerves Bundles of axons from many neurons.

neurons Nerve cells; cells found in the nervous system that transmit messages.

dendrites The rootlike parts of a neuron that receive impulses from other neurons.

axon A long, thin part of a neuron that transmits impulses to other neurons through small branching structures called axon terminals.

neurotransmitter A chemical substance that makes possible the transmission of neural impulses from one neuron to another.

myelin sheath A fatty, white substance that encases and insulates neurons, permitting more rapid transmission of neural impulses.

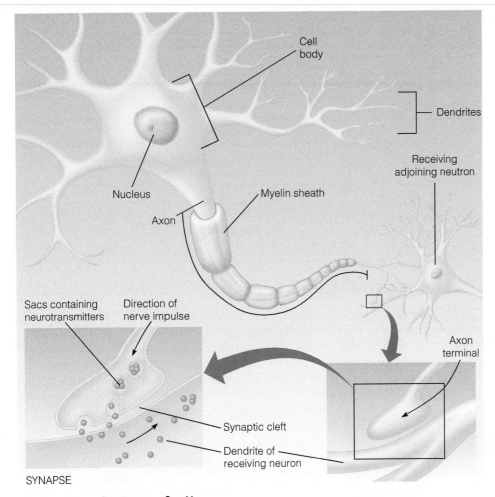

Figure 5.5 ■ Anatomy of a Neuron
"Messages" enter neurons through dendrites, are transmitted along the axon, and then are sent through axon terminals to muscles, glands, and other neurons. Neurons develop by means of proliferation of dendrites and axon terminals and through myelination.

fluids that encase the nervous system. In this way, leakage of the electric current being carried along the axon is minimized, and messages are conducted more efficiently.

The term **myelination** refers to the process by which axons are coated with myelin. Myelination is not complete at birth. Myelination is part of the maturation process that leads to the abilities to crawl and walk during the first year after birth. Incomplete myelination accounts for some of the helplessness of neonates. Myelination of the prefrontal matter of the brain continues into the second decade of life and is connected with advances in working memory and language ability (M. H. Johnson, 2011). Breakdown of myelin is believed to be associated with Alzheimer's disease, a source of cognitive decline that usually begins in middle or late adulthood.

In the disease **multiple sclerosis**, myelin is replaced by a hard, fibrous tissue that disrupts the timing of neural transmission, thus interfering with muscle control (Fancy et al., 2010). The disorder phenylketonuria (PKU) leads to intellectual disability by inhibiting the formation of myelin in the brain (Anderson & Leuzzi, 2010). Congenital infection with HIV has been shown to be connected with abnormalities in the formation of myelin and with cognitive and motor impairment, as measured by the Bayley Scales of Infant Development (Blanchette et al., 2001).

myelination The process by which axons are coated with myelin.

multiple sclerosis A disorder in which myelin is replaced by hard, fibrous tissue that impedes neural transmission.

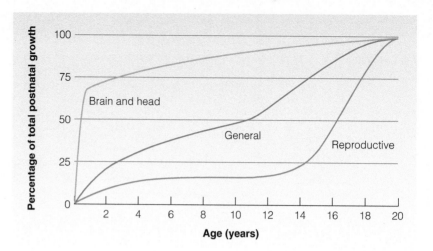

Figure 5.6 ■ Growth of Body Systems as a Percentage of Total Postnatal Growth

The brain of the neonate weighs about one-fourth of its adult weight. In keeping with the principle of cephalocaudal growth, the brain will triple in weight by the infant's first birthday, reaching nearly 70 percent of its adult weight.

medulla An oblong area of the hindbrain involved in heartbeat and respiration.

cerebellum The part of the hindbrain involved in muscle coordination and balance.

cerebrum The large mass of the forebrain, which consists of two hemispheres.

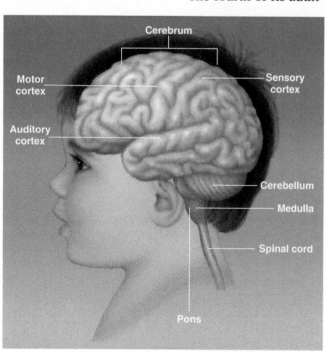

Figure 5.7 ■ Structures of the Brain

The convolutions of the cortex increase its surface area and, apparently, its intellectual capacity. (In this case, wrinkles are good.) The medulla is involved in vital functions such as respiration and heartbeat; the cerebellum is involved in balance and coordination.

Development of the Brain

QUESTIONS » What is the brain? How does the brain develop? The brain is the command centre of the developing organism. (If you like computer analogies, think of the brain as the central processing unit.) It contains neurons and provides the basis for physical, cognitive, and personal and social development.

The brain of the neonate weighs a little less than half a kilogram—nearly one-fourth of its adult weight. **TRUTH OR FICTION REVISITED:** In keeping with the principles of cephalocaudal growth, the brain reaches a good deal more than half its adult weight by the first birthday. It triples in weight, reaching nearly 70 percent of its adult weight (see Figure 5.6 ■). Let us look at the brain, as shown in Figure 5.7 ■, and discuss the development of the structures within.

Structures of the Brain

Many nerves that connect the spinal cord to higher levels of the brain pass through the **medulla** and the pons. The medulla is vital in the control of basic functions, such as heartbeat and respiration. The medulla is part of an area called the brain stem, which may be implicated in sudden infant death syndrome (SIDS; see Chapter 4).

Above the medulla lies the **cerebellum**, which is Latin for "little brain." The cerebellum helps the child maintain balance, control motor behaviour, and coordinate eye movements with bodily sensations.

The **cerebrum** is the crowning glory of the brain. It makes possible the breadth and depth of human learning, thought, memory, and language. Only in human beings does the cerebrum constitute such a large proportion of the brain. The surface of the cerebrum consists of two hemispheres—left and right—that become increasingly wrinkled as the child develops, coming to show ridges and valleys called fissures. This surface is the cerebral cortex. The wrinkles allow a great deal of surface area to be packed into the brain. **TRUTH OR FICTION REVISITED:** Yes, the cerebral cortex is only about 3 millimetres thick. Yet it is here that thought and reasoning occur. It is here that we display sensory information from the world outside and command our muscles to move.

Growth Spurts of the Brain

The brain makes gains in size and weight in different ways. One way is through the formation of neurons, a process completed by birth. The first major growth spurt of the brain occurs during the fourth and fifth months of prenatal development, when neurons proliferate. A second growth spurt in the brain occurs between the 25th week of prenatal development and the end of the second year after birth. Whereas the first growth spurt of the brain is due to the formation of neurons, the second growth spurt is due primarily to the proliferation of dendrites and axon terminals.

Brain Development in Infancy

There is a clear link between what infants can do and the myelination of areas within the brain. At birth, the parts of the brain involved in heartbeat and respiration, sleeping and arousal, and reflex activity are fairly well myelinated and functional.

Myelination of motor pathways allows neonates to show stereotyped reflexes, but otherwise neonates' physical activity tends to be random and badly organized. Myelination of the motor area of the cerebral cortex begins at about the fourth month of prenatal development. Myelin develops rapidly along the major motor pathways from the cerebral cortex during the last month of pregnancy and continues after birth. The development of intentional physical activity coincides with myelination as the unorganized movements of the neonate come under increasing control. Myelination of the nerves to muscles is largely developed by the age of two years, although research using magnetic resonance imaging (MRI) suggests that myelination continues into early adulthood and beyond (Silk & Wood, 2011).

Although neonates respond to touch and can see and hear quite well, the areas of the cortex that are involved in vision, hearing, and the skin senses are less well myelinated at birth. As myelination progresses and the interconnections between the various areas of the cortex thicken, children become increasingly capable of complex and integrated sensorimotor activities (Bartzokis et al., 2010).

Neonates whose mothers read *The Cat in the Hat* aloud during the last few weeks of pregnancy show a preference for this story (see Chapter 4). It turns out that myelination of the neurons involved in the sense of hearing begins at about the sixth month of pregnancy—coinciding with the period in which fetuses begin to respond to sound. Myelination of these pathways is developing rapidly at term and continues until about the age of four years.

Although the fetus shows some response to light during the third trimester, it is hard to imagine what use the fetus could have for vision. It turns out that the neurons involved in vision begin to myelinate only shortly before full term, but then they complete the process of myelination rapidly. Within a short five to six months after birth, vision has become the dominant sense.

Nature and Nurture in the Development of the Brain

QUESTION » How do nature and nurture affect the development of the brain? Development of the areas of the brain that control sensation and movement begins as a result of maturation, but sensory stimulation and physical activity during early infancy also spur their development. Sensory stimulation does not mean computer programs for infants, Baby Mozart, and electronic toys; it can consist of social interaction with caregivers, being held and spoken to, and the like. Therefore, experience interacts with the unfolding of the genetic code to produce the brain—and intellectual functioning—as seen by a snapshot at a given point in time (Posner & Rothbart, 2007; Syed et al., 2010).

Research with animals shows how sensory stimulation sparks growth of the cortex. Researchers have provided complex environmental exposure—in some cases, rat "amusement parks" with toys such as ladders, platforms, and boxes—to demonstrate the effects of enriched environments. In these studies, rats exposed to more complex environments develop heavier brains than control animals. The weight differences in part reflect more synapses per neuron than in other rats (B. J. Anderson, 2011). On the other hand, animals reared in darkness show shrinkage of the visual cortex, impaired vision, and impaired visual–motor coordination (B. J. Anderson, 2011; Salami et al., 2010). If they can't use it, they lose it.

Human brains also are affected by experience. Infants actually have more connections among neurons than adults do. Connections that are activated by experience survive; the others do not (Lewis, 2011). That is why brain **plasticity** (tendency of new parts of the brain to take up functions of injured parts) is greatest in the earliest period of development, meaning it can experience the greatest vulnerability but also the best capacity for recovery.

The great adaptability of the brain appears to be a double-edged sword. Adaptability enables us to develop different patterns of neural connections to meet the demands of different environments. However, lack of stimulation—especially during critical early periods of development (as we will see later)—can impair adaptability.

Brain nourishment, like early experience, plays a role in the brain's achieving what is permitted by the child's genes. Inadequate fetal nutrition, especially during the prenatal growth spurt of the brain, has several negative effects. These include smallness in the overall size of the brain, the formation of fewer neurons, and less myelination (Guerrini et al., 2007; Massaro et al., 2006).

Active Review

7. _____ are the basic units of the nervous system.

8. Each neuron possesses a cell body, dendrites, and a(n) _____.

9. The brain reaches nearly _____ percent of its adult weight by the first birthday.

10. The wrinkled part of the brain, called the _____, enables the child to maintain balance and to control physical behaviour.

Reflect & Relate: Are you surprised that there is such a close connection between experience and development of the brain? How does the information presented in this section fit with the adage "Use it or lose it"?

5.4 Motor Development: How Moving

QUESTIONS » What is motor development? How does it occur? "Zoe crawled so fast it seemed she was on high-octane fuel!" "Anthony was walking forward and backward by the age of 13 months."

These are the types of comments parents make about their children's motor development. Motor development involves the activity of muscles, leading to changes in posture, movement, and coordination of movement with the infant's developing sensory apparatus. Motor development includes some of the most fascinating changes in infants, in part because so much seems to happen so fast—and so much of it during the first year.

plasticity The tendency of new parts of the brain to take up the functions of injured parts

Like physical development, motor development follows cephalocaudal and proximodistal patterns and differentiation. Infants gain control of their heads and upper torsos before they can effectively use their arms. This trend illustrates cephalocaudal development. Infants also can control their trunks and shoulders before they can use their hands and fingers, demonstrating the proximodistal trend.

Lifting and Holding the Torso and Head: Heads Up

Neonates can move their heads slightly to the side. They can thus avoid suffocation if they are lying face down and their noses or mouths are obstructed by bedding. At about one month, infants can raise their heads. By about two months, they can also lift their chests while lying on their stomachs.

When neonates are held, their heads must be supported. But by three to six months of age, infants generally manage to hold their heads quite well, so that supporting the head is no longer necessary. Unfortunately, infants who can normally support their heads cannot do so when they are lifted or moved about in a jerky manner; thus infants who are handled carelessly can sustain neck injuries.

Control of the Hands: Getting a Grip on Things

The development of hand skills is a clear example of proximodistal development. Infants track (follow) slowly moving objects with their eyes shortly after birth, but they do not generally reach for them. They show a grasp reflex but do not reliably reach for the objects that appear to interest them. Voluntary reaching and grasping require visual–motor coordination. By about the age of three months, infants make clumsy swipes at objects, failing to grasp them, because their aim is poor or because they close their hands too soon or too late.

Between the ages of four and six months, infants become more successful at grasping objects (Daum et al., 2010; Heineman et al., 2010). However, they may not know how to let go of an object and may hold it indefinitely, until their attention is diverted and the hand opens accidentally. Four to six months is a good age for giving children rattles, large plastic spoons, mobiles, and other brightly coloured hanging toys that can be grasped but are harmless when they wind up in the mouth.

Grasping is reflexive at first. Voluntary grasping (holding) replaces reflexive grasping by the age of three to four months. Infants first use an **ulnar grasp**, in which they hold objects clumsily between their fingers and their palm (Butterworth et al., 1997). By the age of four to six months, they can transfer objects back and forth between hands. The oppositional thumb comes into play at about the age of 9 to 12 months. Use of the thumb gives infants the ability to pick up tiny objects in a **pincer grasp** (see Figure 5.8 ■). By about 11 months of age, infants can hold objects in each hand and inspect them in turn.

ulnar grasp A method of grasping objects in which the fingers close somewhat clumsily against the palm.

pincer grasp The use of the opposing thumb to grasp objects between the thumb and other fingers.

© Masterfile

Figure 5.8 ■ Pincer Grasp
Infants first hold objects between their fingers and palm. Once the oppositional thumb comes into play at about 9 to 12 months of age, infants are able to pick up tiny objects using what is termed a pincer grasp.

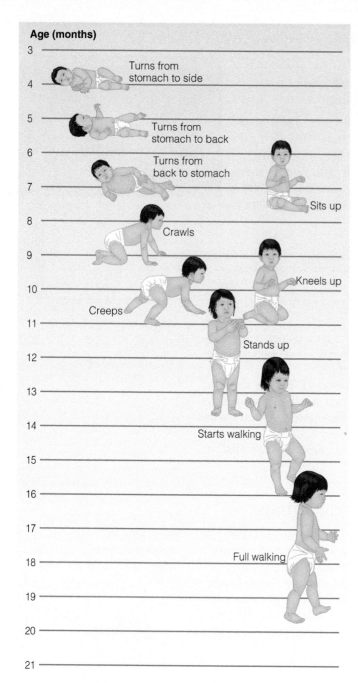

Age (months)

- 3
- 4 — Turns from stomach to side
- 5 — Turns from stomach to back
- 6
- 7 — Turns from back to stomach — Sits up
- 8 — Crawls
- 9 — Kneels up
- 10 — Creeps
- 11 — Stands up
- 12
- 13
- 14 — Starts walking
- 15
- 16
- 17
- 18 — Full walking
- 19
- 20
- 21

Figure 5.9 ■ Motor Development in Infancy
Motor development proceeds in an orderly sequence, but there is considerable variation in the timing of the marker events shown in this figure. An infant who is a bit behind will most likely develop without problems, and a precocious infant will not necessarily become a rocket scientist (or gymnast).

locomotion Movement from one place to another.

Between the ages of 5 and 11 months, infants adjust their hands in anticipation of grasping moving targets. They also gather information from the objects' movements to predict their future location and catch them (Wentworth et al., 2000). Think of the complex concepts it requires to explain this behaviour and how well infants perform it—without any explanation at all! Of course, we are not suggesting that infants solve problems in geometry and physics to grasp moving objects; that interpretation, as developmental psychologist Marshall M. Haith (1998) would describe it, would put a "cog in infant cognition."

Another aspect of visual–motor coordination is stacking blocks. On average, children can stack two blocks at 15 months, three blocks at 18 months, and five blocks at 24 months (Wentworth et al., 2000). At about 24 months of age, children can also copy horizontal and vertical lines.

Locomotion: Getting a Move On

Locomotion is movement from one place to another. Children gain the capacity to move their bodies through a sequence of activities that includes rolling over, sitting up, crawling, creeping, walking, and running (see Figure 5.9 ■). There is much variation in the ages at which infants first engage in these activities. Although the sequence mostly remains the same, some children skip a step. For example, an infant may creep without ever having crawled.

Most infants can roll over, from back to stomach and from stomach to back, by about the age of six months. They can also sit (and support their upper bodies, necks, and heads) for extended periods if they are aided by a person or placed in a seat with a strap, such as a high chair. By about seven months of age, infants usually begin to sit up by themselves.

At about eight or nine months, most infants begin to crawl, a motor activity in which they lie prone and use their arms to pull themselves along, dragging their bellies and feet behind. Creeping, a more sophisticated form of locomotion in which infants move themselves along up on their hands and knees, requires a good deal more coordination and usually appears a month or so after crawling (see Figure 5.10 ■).

There are fascinating alternatives to creeping. Some infants travel from one place to another by rolling over and over. Some lift themselves and swing their arms while in a sitting position, in effect dragging along on their buttocks. Still others do a "bear walk" in which they move on their hands and feet, without allowing their elbows and knees to touch the floor. And some, as noted, just crawl until they are ready to stand and walk from place to place while holding onto chairs, other objects, and people.

Standing overlaps with crawling and creeping. Most infants can remain in a standing position by holding on to something at the age of eight or nine months. At this age, they may also be able to walk a bit when supported by adults. Such walking is voluntary and does not have the stereotyped appearance of the stepping reflex described in Chapter 4. About two months later, they can pull themselves to a standing position by holding on to the sides of their cribs or other objects and can stand briefly without holding on. Soon afterward, they walk about unsteadily while holding on. By 12 to 30 months or so, they walk by themselves, earning them the name **toddler** (see Figure 5.11 ■). Attempts to master these new motor skills are often accompanied by signs of pleasure such as smiling, laughing, and babbling.

Toddlers soon run about, supporting their relatively heavy heads and torsos by spreading their legs in bow-legged fashion. Because they are top-heavy and inexperienced, they fall frequently. Some toddlers require consoling when they fall. Others spring right up and run on again with barely an interruption. Many toddlers are skillful at navigating steep and shallow slopes (Adolph et al., 2011). They walk down shallow slopes but prudently elect to slide or crawl down steep ones. Walking lends children new freedom. It enables them to get about rapidly and to grasp objects that were formerly out of reach. Give toddlers a large ball to toss and run after; it is about the least expensive and most enjoyable toy they can be given.

As children mature, their muscle strength, the density of their bones, and their balance and coordination improve (Metcalfe et al., 2005). By the age of two years, they can climb steps one at a time, placing both feet on each step. They can run well, walk backward, kick a large ball, and jump.

Cross-cultural studies highlight the variation of when infants are exposed to motor opportunities in their physical environments. Infant-rearing practices vary from culture to culture (e.g., Hopkins & Westra, 1988; Seymour, 1999). For example, the Kipsigis of Kenya and the West Indians of Jamaica actively promote physical and motor development early on, and their infants generally reach such motor milestones as sitting, walking, and running before European and European North American infants do (Allen & Alexander, 1990; Hopkins & Westra, 1988; Super, 1981). Although genetic factors may be involved in the earlier motor development, environmental factors also appear to play a role. African infants excel in areas of motor development in which they have received considerable stimulation and practice. For example, parents in Africa and in cultures of African origin, such as Jamaica, stress the development of sitting and walking and provide experiences, including stretching and massage, from birth that stimulate the development of these behaviours. From the second or third months, other activities are added, such as propping infants in a sitting position, bouncing them on their feet, and exercising the stepping reflex.

Figure 5.10 ■ Creeping
Creeping requires considerable coordination of arm and leg movements. Creeping usually appears a month or so after crawling.

Figure 5.11 ■ Walking
By 12 to 30 months or so, babies walk by themselves, earning them the name toddler.

Nature and Nurture in Motor Development

Research with humans and other species leaves little doubt that both maturation (nature) and experience (nurture) are involved in motor development (Muir, 2000; Pryce et al., 2001; Roncesvalles et al., 2005). Certain voluntary motor activities are not possible until the brain has matured in terms of myelination and the differentiation of the motor areas of the cortex. Although

toddler A child who walks with short, uncertain steps. Toddlerhood lasts from about 12 months to 30 months of age, thereby bridging infancy and early childhood.

CHAPTER 5 INFANCY: PHYSICAL DEVELOPMENT

Figure 5.12 ▪ A Hopi Infant Strapped to a Cradle Board

Researchers have studied Hopi children who are strapped to cradle boards during their first year to see whether their motor development is significantly delayed. Once released from their boards, Hopi children advance rapidly in their motor development, suggesting the important role of maturation in motor development.

the neonate shows stepping and swimming reflexes, these behaviours are controlled by more primitive parts of the brain. They disappear when cortical development inhibits some functions of the lower parts of the brain, and when they reappear, they differ in quality.

Infants also need some opportunity to experiment before they can engage in milestones such as sitting up and walking. Even so, many of these advances can apparently be attributed to maturation. **TRUTH OR FICTION REVISITED:** It is true that Native American Hopi infants spend their first year strapped to a board but begin to walk at about the same time as children who are reared in other cultures. In classic research, Wayne and Marsena Dennis (1940) reported on the motor development of Native American Hopi children who spent their first year strapped to a cradle board (see Figure 5.12 ▪). Although denied a full year of experience in locomotion, the Hopi infants gained the capacity to walk early in their second year, at about the same time as other children. Classic cross-cultural research (Hindley et al., 1966) reported that infants in five European cities began to walk at about the same time (generally, between 12 and 15 months), despite cultural differences in encouragement to walk.

On the other hand, evidence is mixed on whether specific training can accelerate the appearance of motor skills. For example, in a classic study with identical twins, Arnold Gesell (1929) gave one twin extensive training in hand coordination, block building, and stair climbing from early infancy. The other twin was allowed to develop on his own. At first, the trained twin had better skills, but as time passed, the untrained twin became just as skilled.

Although the appearance of motor skills can be accelerated by training (Zelazo & Müller, 2010), the effect seems slight. Practice in the absence of neural readiness has limited results. There is also little evidence that training leads to eventual superior motor skills.

Although being strapped to a cradle board did not delay the motor development of Hopi infants, Wayne Dennis (1960) reported that infants in an Iranian orphanage were significantly retarded in their motor development. In contrast to the Hopi infants, the institutionalized infants experienced extreme social and physical deprivation. Under these conditions, they grew apathetic, and all aspects of development suffered. But there is also a bright side to this tale of deprivation. The motor development of similar infants in a Lebanese orphanage accelerated dramatically in response to such minimal intervention as being propped up in their cribs and being given a few colourful toys (Sayegh & Dennis, 1965).

Nature provides the limits—the "reaction range"—for the expression of inherited traits. Nurture determines whether the child will develop skills that reach the upper limits of the range. Even a fundamental skill such as locomotion is determined by a complex interplay of maturational and environmental factors (Adolph et al., 2011). There may be little purpose in trying to train children to enhance their motor skills before they are ready. Once children are ready, however, teaching and practice do make a difference. One does not become an Olympic athlete without "good genes." But one also usually does not become an Olympic athlete without high-quality training. And because motor skills are important to the self-concepts of children, good teaching is all the more valuable.

Active Review

11. Infants can first raise their heads at about the age of _____ month(s).

12. Infants first use a(n) (ulnar or pincer?) grasp for holding objects.

13. Developmentalists assess infants' ability to stack blocks as a measure of their _____ motor coordination.

14. Infants (sit up or crawl?) before they (sit up or crawl?).

15. As children mature, their bones (increase or decrease?) in density.

16. Research reveals that both maturation and _____ play indispensable roles in motor development.

17. Arnold Gesell (did or did not?) find that extensive training in hand coordination, block building, and stair climbing gave infants enduring advantages over untrained infants in these skills.

Reflect & Relate: "When did your baby first sit up?" "When did he walk?" Why are people so concerned about when infants do what? Imagine that you are speaking to a parent who is concerned that her child is not yet walking at 14 months. What would you say to the parent? When should there be cause for concern?

5.5 Sensory and Perceptual Development: Taking In the World

QUESTION » **How do sensation and perception develop in the infant?** What a world we live in—green hills and reddish skies; rumbling trucks, murmuring brooks, and voices; the sweet and the sour; the acrid and the perfumed; the metallic and the fuzzy. What an ever-changing display of sights, sounds, tastes, smells, and touches! The pleasures of the world, and its miseries, are known to us through sensory impressions and the organization of these impressions into personal inner maps of reality. Our eyes, our ears, the sensory receptors in our noses and our mouths, our skin senses—these are our tickets of admission to the world.

In Chapter 4, we examined the sensory capabilities of the neonate. In this section, we see how infants develop the ability to integrate disjointed **sensations** into meaningful patterns of events termed **perceptions**. We see what captures the attention of infants, and we see how young children develop into purposeful seekers of information—selecting the sensory impressions they choose to capture. We focus on the development of vision and hearing because most of the research on sensory and perceptual development in infancy has been done in these areas.

We will see that many things that are obvious to us are not so obvious to infants. *You* may know that a coffee cup is the same whether you see it from above or from the side, but make no such assumptions about the infant's understanding. *You* may know that an infant's mother is the same size whether she is standing next to the infant or approaching from two blocks away, but do not assume that the infant agrees with you.

We cannot ask infants to explain why they look at some things and not at others. Nor can we ask them if their mother appears to be the same size whether she is standing close to them or far away. But investigators of childhood sensation and perception have devised clever methods to investigate these questions, and their findings provide us with fascinating insights into the perceptual processes of even the neonate. They reveal that many basic perceptual competencies are present early in life.

Development of Vision: The Better to See You With

Development of vision involves development of visual acuity or sharpness, development of peripheral vision (seeing things off to the sides while looking straight ahead), visual preferences, depth perception, and perceptual

sensation The stimulation of sensory organs, such as the eyes, ears, and skin, and the transmission of sensory information to the brain.

perception The process by which sensations are organized into a mental map of the world.

constancies—for example, knowing that an object remains the same object even though it may look different when seen from a different angle. (You knew that, didn't you?)

Development of Visual Acuity and Peripheral Vision

Newborns are extremely nearsighted, with vision beginning at about 20/600. The most dramatic gains in visual acuity are made between birth and six months of age, with acuity reaching about 20/50 (S. P. Johnson, 2011; Slater et al., 2010). Gains in visual acuity then become more gradual, approximating adult levels (20/20 in the best cases) by about three to five years of age. At present, pediatricians may use the Teller Acuity Test for Pediatric Visual Acuity, which is an infant vision screening tool that uses a series of cards with varying stripe widths on them and examines the infant's attention in response to the cards.

Neonates also have poor peripheral vision (Cavallini et al., 2002; Skoczenski, 2002). Adults can perceive objects that are nearly 90 degrees off to the side (i.e., directly to the left or right), although objects at these extremes are unclear. Neonates cannot perceive visual stimuli that are off to the side by an angle of more than 30 degrees, but their peripheral vision expands to an angle of about 45 degrees by the age of seven weeks. By six months of age, their peripheral vision is about equal to that of an adult.

Let us now consider the development of visual perception. In so doing, we will see that infants frequently prefer the strange to the familiar and will avoid going off the deep end—sometimes.

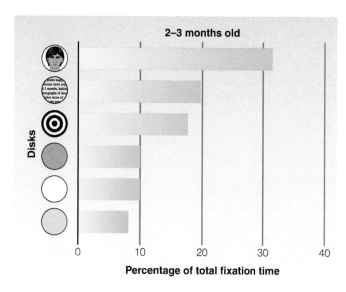

Figure 5.13 ■ **Preferences for Visual Stimuli in Two-Month-Olds**

Infants appear to prefer complex to simple visual stimuli. By the time they are two months old, they also tend to show preference for the human face. Researchers continue to debate whether the face draws attention because of its content (i.e., being a face) or because of its stimulus characteristics (complexity, arrangement, etc.).

Visual Preferences: How Do You Capture an Infant's Attention?

Neonates look at stripes longer than at blobs. This finding has been used in much of the research on visual acuity. Classic research found that by the age of 8 to 12 weeks, most infants also show distinct preferences for curved lines over straight lines (Fantz et al., 1975).

Robert Fantz (1961) wondered whether there was something intrinsically interesting about the human face that drew the attention of infants. To investigate this question, he showed two-month-old infants the six disks illustrated in Figure 5.13 ■. One disk contained a caricature of human features, another contained newsprint, and still another contained a bull's-eye. The remaining three disks were featureless but were coloured red, white, and yellow. In this study, the infants fixated significantly longer on the human face.

Some studies suggest that the infants in Fantz's (1961) study may have preferred the human face because it had a complex, intriguing pattern of dots (eyes) within an outline and not because it was a face. But other theorists, such as Michelle de Haan and Margrite Groen (2006), assert that "reading" faces is particularly important to infants because they do not understand verbal information as communicated through language. Thus, it would make evolutionary sense for them to orient toward the human face and perceive the differences between some facial expressions at very early ages.

Researchers therefore continue to investigate infants' preferences for the human face. They ask whether humans come into the world "prewired" to prefer human stimuli to other stimuli that are just as complex, and—if so—just what it is about human stimuli that draws attention. Some researchers—unlike de Haan and Groen—argue that neonates do not "prefer" faces because they are faces per se but because of the structure of their immature visual systems (Simion et al., 2001). A supportive study of 34 neonates found that the longer fixations on face-like stimuli resulted from a larger number of brief fixations (looks) rather than from a few prolonged fixations (Cassia et al., 2001). The infants' gaze, then, was sort of bouncing around from feature to feature rather than "staring" at the face in general. The researchers interpreted this finding to show that the stimulus properties of the visual object are more important than the fact that it represents a human face. Even so, of course, the "immature visual system" would be providing some "prewired" basis for attending to the face.

Learning clearly plays a role. Neonates can discriminate their mother's face from a stranger's after eight hours of mother–infant contact spread over four days (Bushnell, 2001). By three to five months of age, infants respond differently to happy, surprised, and sad faces (Muir & Hains, 1993). Moreover, infants as young as two months prefer attractive faces to unattractive faces (Ramsey et al., 2004). This preference is more deeply ingrained by six months of age (Ramsey et al., 2004). Do standards of attractiveness have an inborn component, or are they learned (very!) early?

Neonates appear to direct their attention to the edges of objects. This pattern persists for the first several weeks (S. P. Johnson, 2011). When they are given the opportunity to look at human faces, one-month-old infants tend to pay most attention to the "edges"—that is, the chin, an ear, or the hairline. Two-month-old infants move in from the edge, as shown in Figure 5.14 ■. They focus particularly on the eyes, although they also inspect other inner features, such as the mouth and nose (Aslin, 2012).

Some researchers (e.g., Haith, 1979) explain infants' tendencies to scan from the edges of objects inward by noting that for the first several weeks of life, infants seem to be essentially concerned with where things are. Their attention is captured by movement and sharp contrasts in brightness and shape, such as those that are found where the edges of objects stand out against their backgrounds. But by about two months of age, infants tend to focus on the *what* of things. They may locate objects by looking at their edges, but now they scan systematically within the boundaries of objects (Aslin, 2012).

Development of Depth Perception: On Not Going off the Deep End

Infants generally respond to cues for depth by the time they are able to crawl (six to eight months of age or so), and most have the good sense to avoid "going off the deep end"—that is, crawling off ledges and tabletops into open space (Campos et al., 1978).

In a classic study on depth perception, Eleanor Gibson and Richard Walk (1960) placed infants of various

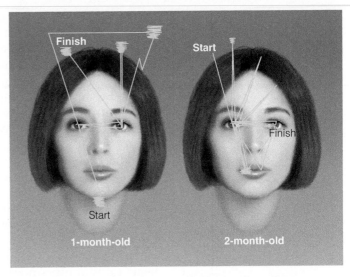

Figure 5.14 ■ Eye Movements of One- and Two-Month-Olds
One-month-olds direct their attention to the edges of objects. Two-month-olds "move in from the edge." When looking at a face, for example, they focus on the eyes and other inner features. How do researchers explain this change?

Source: Salapatek (1975).

OBSERVING CHILDREN, UNDERSTANDING OURSELVES

The Visual Cliff

This young explorer has the good sense not to crawl out onto a (visually) unsupported surface.

Do infants have to experience some of life's "bumps" before they avoid "going off the deep end," or does fear of heights "mature" at about the same time infants gain the ability to move around?

From Rathus. *Childhood and Adolescence*, 5E. © 2014 South-Western, a part of Cengage Learning, Inc. Reproduced by permission. www.cengage.com/permissions

Go to www.nelson.com/voyages2ce to watch the video, answer the questions, and e-mail your responses to your professor.

ages on a fabric-covered runway that ran across the center of a clever device called a visual cliff (see Observing Children, Understanding Ourselves, "The Visual Cliff"). The visual cliff is a sheet of Plexiglas that covers a cloth with a high-contrast checkerboard pattern. On one side, the cloth is placed immediately beneath the Plexiglas, and on the other, it is dropped about 1.2 metres below. Because the Plexiglas alone would easily support the infant, this is a visual cliff rather than an actual cliff. In the Gibson and Walk study, eight out of ten infants who had begun to crawl refused to venture onto the seemingly unsupported surface, even when their mothers beckoned encouragingly from the other side.

Psychologists can assess infants' emotional responses to the visual cliff long before infants can crawl. For example, Joseph Campos and his colleagues (1970) found that one-month-old infants showed no change in heart rate when placed face down on the "cliff." They apparently did not perceive the depth of the cliff. At two months, infants showed decreases in heart rate when so placed, which psychologists interpret as a sign of interest. But the heart rates of nine-month-olds accelerated on the cliff, which is interpreted as a fear response. The study appears to suggest that infants profit from some experience crawling about (and, perhaps, accumulating some bumps) before they develop fear of heights. The nine-month-olds, but not the two-month-olds, had had such experience. Other studies support the view that infants usually do not develop fear of heights until they can move around (Sorce et al., 2000; Witherington et al., 2010). Newly walking infants are highly reluctant to venture out onto the visual cliff, even when their mothers signal them to do so (Sorce et al., 2000; Witherington et al., 2010).

Infants' tendencies to avoid falling off a cliff are apparently connected with their body positions at the time (Franchak & Adolph, 2012). Infants generally sit before they crawl, and by nine months of age, we can think of most of them as experienced sitters. Crawling enters the picture at about nine months. Karen Adolph examined the behaviour of 19 nine-month-old infants who were on the edge of crawling as well as on the edge of a visual cliff. The infants were placed in a sitting or crawling position and enticed to reach out for an object over the cliff. The infants were more likely to avoid the cliff when they were sitting. This suggests that different postures involve the brain in different ways and that infants' avoidance of the cliff is connected with their posture. Adolph's findings bring into question the view that avoidance of the cliff depends on general knowledge, such as fear of heights, associations between perceived depth and falling, or awareness that the body cannot be supported in empty space.

TRUTH OR FICTION REVISITED: Actually, evidence is mixed on whether infants need to have experience crawling before they develop fear of heights. Some do not. This would appear to be a case in which survival might be enhanced by *not* having to learn from experience.

Development of Perceptual Constancies

It may not surprise you that a 30-centimetre ruler is the same length whether it is 60 centimetres or 2 metres away or that a door across the room is a rectangle whether it is closed or ajar. Awareness of these facts depends not on sensation alone but on the development of perceptual constancies. **Perceptual constancy** is the tendency to perceive an object to be the same, even though the sensations produced by the object may differ under various conditions.

Consider again the example of the ruler. When it is 60 centimetres away, its image, as focused on the retina, is a certain length. This length is the image's "retinal size." From 2 metres away, the 30-centimetre ruler is less than one-third as long in terms of retinal size, but we perceive it as being the same size because of size constancy. **Size constancy** is the tendency to perceive the same objects as being the same size even though their retinal sizes vary as a function of their

perceptual constancy The tendency to perceive objects as the same even though the sensations produced by them may differ when, for example, they differ in position or distance.

size constancy The tendency to perceive objects as being the same size even though the sizes of their images on the retina may differ as a result of distance.

distance. From 2 metres away, a 1-metre stick casts an image equal in retinal size to that of the 30-centimetre ruler at 60 centimetres, but—if recognized as a 1-metre stick—it is perceived as longer, again because of size constancy.

In a classic study of the development of size constancy, Thomas Bower (1974) conditioned two-and-a-half- to three-month-old infants to turn their heads to the left when shown a 30-centimetre cube from a distance of 90 centimetres. He then presented them with three experimental stimuli: (1) a 30-centimetre cube 2.7 metres away, whose retinal size was smaller than that of the original cube; (2) a 90-centimetre cube 90 centimetres away, whose retinal size was larger than that of the original cube; and (3) a 90-centimetre cube 2.7 metres away, whose retinal size was the same as that of the original cube. The infants turned their heads most frequently in response to the first experimental cube, even though its retinal image was only one-third the length of that to which they had been conditioned; this suggests that they had achieved size constancy. Later studies have confirmed Bower's finding that size constancy is present in early infancy. Some research suggests that even neonates possess rudimentary size constancy (Slater et al., 2010).

Shape constancy is the tendency to perceive an object as having the same shape even though, when the object is perceived from another angle, the shape projected onto the retina may change dramatically. When the top of a cup or a glass is seen from above, the visual sensations are in the shape of a circle. When the cup is seen from a slight angle, the sensations are elliptical, and when it is seen from the side, the retinal image is the same as that of a straight line. However, we still perceive the rim of the cup or glass as being a circle because of our familiarity with the object. In the first few months after birth, infants see the features of their caregivers, bottles, cribs, and toys from all different angles, so by the time they are four or five months old, a broad grasp of shape constancy seems to be established, at least under certain conditions (Slater et al., 2010). Strategies for studying the development of shape constancy are described in the "A Closer Look—Research" feature.

shape constancy The tendency to perceive objects as being the same shape even though the shapes of their images on the retina may differ when the objects are viewed from different positions.

A CLOSER LOOK RESEARCH

Strategies for Studying the Development of Shape Constancy

People are said to show shape constancy when they perceive objects as having the same shape even though, when viewed from another angle, the shape projected onto the retina may be very different. We can determine whether infants have developed shape constancy through the process of *habituation*, which involves paying less attention to a repeated stimulus.

Neonates tend to show a preference for familiar objects (Barrile et al., 1999). But once they are a few months old, infants show a preference for novel objects. They have become habituated to familiar objects, and—if we can take the liberty of describing their responses in adult terms—they are apparently bored by them. Certain bodily responses indicate interest in an object, including a slower heart rate (as with two-month-old infants placed face down on a visual cliff) and concentrated gazing. Therefore, when infants have become habituated to an object, their heart rates speed up moderately and they no longer show concentrated gazing.

Here, then, is the research strategy. Show an infant stimulus A for a prolonged period of time. At first, the heart rate will slow and the infant will focus on the object. But as time goes on, the heart rate will again rise to prestimulated levels and the infant's gaze will wander. Now show the infant stimulus B. If the heart rate again slows and the gaze again becomes concentrated, we can infer that stimulus B is perceived as a novel (different) object. But if the heart rate and pattern of gazing do not change, we can infer that the infant does not perceive a difference between stimuli A and B.

If stimuli A and B are actually the same object seen from different angles, what does it mean when the infant's heart rate and pattern of gazing do not change? We can assume this lack of change means that the infant perceives stimuli A and B to be the same—in this case, the same object. Therefore, we can conclude that the infant has developed shape constancy.

Continued

Continued

Using a strategy similar to that just described, Caron and his colleagues (1979) first habituated three-month-old infants to a square shown at different angles. The infants then were presented with one of two test stimuli: (1) the identical square, shown at an entirely new angle, or (2) a novel figure (a trapezoid), shown at the new angle. The two test stimuli projected identical trapezoidal images on the retina, even though their real shapes were different. Infants who were shown the square at the new angle showed little change in response. However, infants shown the trapezoid did show different responses. Therefore, it seems that infants perceived the trapezoid as novel, even though it cast the same retinal image as the square. But the infants were able to recognize the "real" shape of the square despite the fact that it cast a trapezoidal image on the retina. In other words, they showed shape constancy.

Reflect Can you think of examples of habituation in your own life?

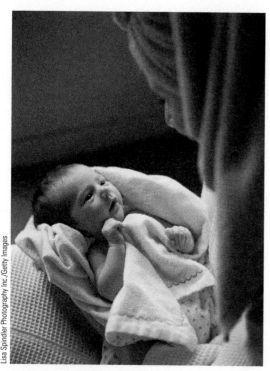

Lisa Spindler Photography Inc./Getty Images

Infants typically prefer the sound of their mother's voice and can discriminate the sounds of their parents' voices by the age of three-and-a-half months.

habituation A process in which one becomes used to a repeated stimulus and therefore pays less attention to it.

Development of Hearing: The Better to Hear You With

QUESTION » How does the sense of hearing develop in infancy? Neonates can crudely orient their heads in the direction of a sound (Burnham & Mattock, 2010). By 18 months of age, the accuracy of their sound-localizing ability approaches that of adults. Sensitivity to sounds increases in the first few months of life (Burnham & Mattock, 2010). As infants mature, the range of the pitch of the sounds they can sense gradually expands to include the adult's range of 20–20 000 cycles per second. The ability to detect differences in the pitch and loudness of sounds improves considerably throughout the preschool years. Auditory acuity also improves gradually over the first several years (Burnham & Mattock, 2010), although infants' hearing can be acute; many parents complain their napping infants awaken at the slightest sound. This is especially true if parents have been overprotective in attempting to keep their rooms as silent as possible. Infants who are normally exposed to a backdrop of moderate noise levels become habituated to them and are not likely to awaken unless there is a sudden, sharp noise.

By the age of one month, infants perceive differences between speech sounds that are highly similar. In a classic study relying on the **habituation** method, infants of this age could activate a recording of "bah" by sucking on a nipple (Eimas et al., 1971). As time went on, habituation occurred, as shown by decreased sucking in order to hear the "bah" sound. Then the researchers switched from "bah" to "pah." If the sounds had seemed the same to the infants, their lethargic sucking patterns would have continued. But the infants immediately sucked harder, suggesting that they perceived the difference. Other researchers have found that within another month or two, infants reliably discriminate between three-syllable words such as *marana* and *malana* (Kuhl et al., 2006).

Infants can discriminate the sounds of their parents' voices by three-and-a-half months of age. In classic research, infants of this age were oriented toward their parents as they reclined in infant seats. The experimenters played recordings of the mother's or father's voice while the parents themselves remained inactive (Brower & Wilcox, 2012; Spelke & Owsley, 1979). The infants reliably looked at the parent whose voice was being played.

Young infants are capable of perceiving most of the speech sounds present in the world's languages. But after exposure to their native language, infants gradually lose the capacity to discriminate those sounds that are not found in the native tongue (Werker et al., 2007, 2012). Before six months of age, for example, infants reared in an English-speaking environment could discriminate sounds found in Hindi (a language of India) and Salish (a Native American language). But by 10 to 12 months of age, they had lost the ability to do so, as shown in Figure 5.15 ■ (Werker, 1989).

Infants also learn at an early age to ignore small, meaningless variations in the sounds of their native language. Adults do this routinely. For example, if someone speaking your language has a head cold or a slight accent, you ignore the minor variations in the person's pronunciation and hear these variations as the same sound. But when you hear slight variations in the sounds of a foreign language, you might assume that each variation carries a different meaning, and so you hear the sounds as different.

Infants can screen out meaningless sounds as early as six months of age (Kuhl et al., 2006). Patricia Kuhl and her colleagues (1997) presented American and Swedish infants with pairs of sounds in either their own language or the other language. The infants were trained to look over their shoulder when they heard a difference in the sounds and to ignore sound pairs that seemed to be the same. The infants routinely ignored variations in sounds that were part of their language, because they apparently perceived these variations as the same sound. But they noticed slight variations in the sounds of the other language. Another study demonstrated the same ability in infants as young as two months (Marean et al., 1992). By their first birthday, many infants understand many words, and some may even say a word or two of their own.

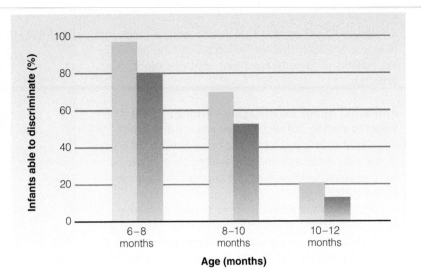

Figure 5.15 ■ Declining Ability to Discriminate the Sounds of Foreign Languages

Infants show a decline in the ability to discriminate sounds not found in their native language. Before six months of age, infants from English-speaking families could discriminate sounds found in Hindi (red bars) and Salish, a Native American language (blue bars). By 10 to 12 months of age, they could no longer do so.

Source: Werker (1989).

A CLOSER LOOK | REAL LIFE

Effects of Early Exposure to Garlic, Alcohol, and—Gulp—Veggies

Research shows that infants begin to learn about the flavours found in their cultures through breast milk, possibly even through amniotic fluid (Mennella et al., 2005). For example, psychologist Julie Mennella, of the Monell Chemical Senses Center, found that when women eat garlic, their infants suckle longer (Azar, 1998). It is not that the infants ingest more milk. Instead, they seem to be spending the extra time analyzing what they are tasting. They keep the milk in their mouths, pause, and perceive the flavours. Vanilla flavouring has a similar effect on suckling—increasing the duration.

Infants ingest amniotic fluid while they are still in the womb, and this fluid also acquires a distinct smell after a woman eats garlic, according to Mennella. It would appear that the fetus detects this change in its environment.

No Direct Road to Alcohol Abuse Does exposure to alcohol in the breast milk of mothers who drink create a disposition toward alcohol abuse in the infant? Mennella's research suggests that the truth may lie in the opposite direction. First of all, infants appear not to like the taste of alcohol in breast milk. Mennella (2001) found that infants aged two to five months drink less breast milk when the mother has recently drunk alcohol. In fact, they ingest more breast milk once the alcohol is out of the mother's system, apparently to compensate for the lessened calorie intake at the previous feeding.

A related study by Mennella and Garcia (2000) showed that early exposure to the odour of alcohol may also be something of a turnoff to infants. In this study, Mennella and Garcia compared the preferences of children who had been exposed to alcohol around the house during infancy with those of children who had not. All the children were about four to six years old at the time of testing. Children who had been exposed to alcohol early were significantly more likely than the other children to dislike the odour of a bottle containing alcohol.

Continued

Continued

We would not suggest that parents drink alcohol to discourage their children from drinking later on. But the findings do seem to contradict what one might have expected.

And What about Encouraging Children to Eat Their Veggies during Infancy?

Many parents understand the benefits of eating vegetables and bring out the jars of vegetable baby food when they are feeding their infants. Does early exposure to these foods encourage or discourage eating them?

Early exposure generally seems to have a positive effect on children's appetites for vegetables. Consider a study of four- to seven-month-old infants by Leann Birch and her colleagues (1998). The investigators repeatedly exposed infants to vegetables such as peas and green beans in the form of baby food to see whether the infants would subsequently eat more or less of them. Thirty-nine infants were fed the target foods once a day for ten consecutive days. During that period, their consumption of the vegetables doubled from an average of 35 grams to an average of 72 grams. Moreover, the infants became more likely to eat similar foods—that is, other vegetables. Julie Mennella and her colleagues have also found that the infants of mothers who eat more diverse diets are more willing to eat a variety of foods (cited in Azar, 1998). Moreover, studies of rodents, pigs, and sheep show that once they are weaned, young animals prefer the flavours to which they were exposed through their mothers' milk. Early

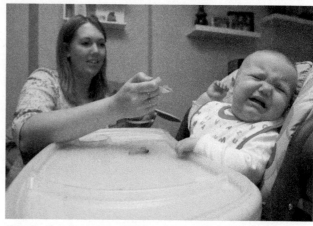
Leila Cutler/Alamy

How Do You Encourage Children to Eat Their Veggies?
Do you want to talk about cruel experimental treatments that skirt the edges of the ethical limits of the researchers? Try this one on for size. Leann Birch and her colleagues repeatedly exposed four- to seven-month-old infants to baby food consisting of vegetables. Actually, the "treatment" apparently had the effect of teaching the infants to like vegetables. In terms of what the experimenters measured, they found that the infants exposed to vegetables ate more of them during test trials.

exposure to the foods that are traditional within a culture may be a key to shaping an infant's food preferences.

Reflect Do you like vegetables? Can you trace your food preferences to early experiences in the home?

OBSERVING CHILDREN,
UNDERSTANDING OURSELVES

Sensation and Perception in Infancy

Vision is the least mature of a newborn's senses, but infants prefer patterns with strong contrasts and prefer human faces above other images. Here, two-month-old Giuseppina fixates on a drawing of a face.

How can a newborn's capacities for vision and hearing be considered adaptive? (Hint: Think about Carter's initial interaction with his mother in this video.)

Go to www.nelson.com/voyages2ce to watch the video, answer the questions, and e-mail your responses to your professor.

From Rathus. *Childhood and Adolescence*, 5E. © 2014 South-Western, a part of Cengage Learning, Inc. Reproduced by permission. www.cengage.com/permissions

---

Development of Coordination of the Senses: If I See It, Can I Touch It?

Neonates crudely orient their heads toward sounds and pleasant odours. In this way, they increase the probability that the sources of the sounds and odours will also be sensed through visual scanning. Young infants can also recognize that objects experienced by one sense (e.g., vision) are the same as those experienced through another sense (e.g., touch). This ability has been demonstrated in infants as young as one month (Bushnell, 1993). One experiment demonstrating such understanding in five-month-olds takes advantage of the fact that infants of this age tend to look longer at novel than at familiar sources of stimulation. Julie Féron and her colleagues (2006) first allowed five-month-old infants to handle (become manually familiar with) groups of either two or three objects, presented one by one, to their right hand. They were then shown visual displays of either two or three objects. The infants looked significantly longer at the group of objects that differed from the one with which they had become manually familiar, showing a transfer of information from the sense of touch to the sense of vision. Finally, in a series of experiments with nine-month-olds, it was found that infants recognize the correspondence between three-dimensional objects and their two-dimensional representations, even when these representations are not exact copies of the objects themselves (Jowkar-Baniani & Schmuckler, 2011).

The Active–Passive Controversy in Perceptual Development

QUESTION » Do children play an active or a passive role in perceptual development? Newborn children may have more sophisticated sensory capabilities than you expected. Still, their ways of perceiving the world are largely mechanical, or passive. The description of a stimulus capturing an infant's attention seems quite appropriate. Neonates seem to be generally at the mercy of external stimuli. When a bright light strikes, they attend to it. If the light moves slowly across the plane of their vision, they track it.

As time passes, broad changes occur in the perceptual processes of children, and the child's role in perception appears to become decidedly more active. Developmental psychologist Eleanor Gibson (1969, 1991) noted a number of these changes:

1. Intentional action replaces "capture" (automatic responses to stimulation). As infants mature and gain experience, purposeful scanning and exploration of the environment take the place of mechanical movements and passive responses to potent stimulation.

   Consider the scanning "strategies" of neonates. In a lighted room, neonates move their eyes mostly from left to right and back again. Mechanically, they sweep a horizontal plane. If they encounter an object that contrasts sharply with the background, their eye movements bounce back and forth against the edges. However, even when neonates awaken in a dark room, they show the stereotypical horizontal scanning pattern, with about two eye movements per second (Haith, 1990).

   The stereotypical quality of these initial scanning movements suggests that they are inborn. They provide strong evidence that the neonate is neurologically prewired to gather and seek visual information. They do not reflect what we would consider a purposeful, or intentional, effort to learn about the environment.

2. Systematic search replaces unsystematic search. Over the first few years of life, children become more active as they develop systematic ways of exploring the environment. They come to pay progressively more attention to details of objects and people and to make finer and finer discriminations.

3. Attention becomes selective. Older children become capable of selecting the information they need from the welter of confusion in the environment. For example, when older children are separated from their parents in a department store, they have the capacity to systematically scan for people of their parents' height, hair colour, vocal characteristics, and so on. They are also more capable of discriminating the spot where the parent was last seen. A younger child is more likely to be confused by the

welter of voices and faces and aisles and to be unable to extract essential information from this backdrop.

4. Irrelevant information becomes ignored. Older children gain the capacity to screen out, or deploy their attention away from, stimuli that are irrelevant to the task at hand. This might mean shutting out the noise of cars in the street or radios in the neighbourhood in order to focus on a book.

In short, children develop from passive, mechanical reactors to the world about them into active, purposeful seekers and organizers of sensory information. They develop from beings whose attention is diffuse and "captured" into people who make decisions about what they will attend to. This is a process that, like so many others, appears to depend on both maturation and experience.

Let us now screen out distractions and turn our attention to considering the importance of maturation (the development of nature) and experience (nurture) in perceptual development.

Nature and Nurture in Perceptual Development

QUESTION » What is the evidence for the roles of nature and nurture in perceptual development?

The Interplay between Nature and Nurture

Compelling evidence supports the idea that our inborn sensory capacities play a crucial role in our perceptual development. For one thing, neonates come into the world with a good number of perceptual skills. They can see nearby objects quite well, and their hearing is usually fine. They are also born with tendencies to track moving objects, to systematically scan the horizon, and to prefer certain kinds of stimuli. Preferences for different kinds of visual stimuli appear to unfold on schedule as the first months wear on. Sensory changes, like motor changes, appear to be linked to maturation of the nervous system.

For these reasons, it seems clear that we do have certain inborn ways of responding to sensory input—certain "categories" and built-in limits—that enable us to perceive certain aspects of the world of physical reality.

Evidence that experience plays a crucial role in perceptual development is also compelling. We could use any of hundreds of studies with children and other species to make the point, but let us limit our discussion to a couple of examples of research with kittens and human infants.

Children and lower animals have critical periods in their perceptual development. Failure to receive adequate sensory stimulation during these critical periods can result in permanent sensory deficits (Cascio, 2010; Greenough et al., 2002). For example, newborn kittens raised with a patch over one eye wind up with few or no cells in the visual area of the cerebral cortex that would normally be stimulated by light entering that eye. In effect, that eye becomes blind, even though sensory receptors in the eye itself may fire in response to light. On the other hand, when the eye of an adult cat is patched for the same amount of time, the animal does not lose vision in that eye. The critical period apparently has passed. Similarly, if health problems require that a child's eye must be patched for an extensive period of time during the first year, the child's visual acuity in that eye may be impaired.

Consider a study of visual acuity among 28 human infants who had been deprived of all patterned visual input by cataracts in one or both eyes until they were treated at one week to nine months of age (Maurer et al., 1999). Immediately following treatment, their visual acuity was no better than that of normal neonates, suggesting that their lack of visual experience had impaired their visual development. However, their visual acuity improved rapidly over the month following treatment. They showed some improvement in as little as one hour after visual input.

And so, with perceptual development, just as with other dimensions of development, nature and nurture play indispensable roles. Today, few developmentalists would subscribe to either extreme. Most agree that nature and nurture interact to shape perceptual development. Nature continues to guide the unfolding of the child's physical systems. Yet nurture continues to interact with nature in the development of these systems. We know that inborn physical structures, such as the nature of the cortex of the brain, place limits on our abilities to respond to the world. But we also know that experience continues to help shape our most basic physical structures. For example, sensorimotor experiences thicken the cortex of the brain. Sensory experiences are linked to the very development of neurons in the cortex, causing dendrites to proliferate and affecting myelination.

In the next chapter, we see how nature and nurture influence the development of thought and language in infants.

Active Review

18. At two months of age, infants tend to fixate longer on a (scrambled or real?) face.

19. Neonates direct their attention to the (centre or edges?) of objects.

20. Researchers have studied depth perception in infants through the use of the visual _____.

21. Research suggests that infants have developed size constancy by about _____ months.

22. As infants develop, they have (greater or less?) ability to screen out meaningless sounds in their native languages.

23. As time passes during infancy, one change in perceptual development is that intentional action replaces _____ (automatic responses to stimulation).

24. Research shows that both nature and _____ are essential to perceptual development.

Reflect & Relate: What do you think it would mean if infants came into the world "prewired" to prefer the human face to other, equally complex visual stimulation? Can you explain the evolutionary advantage that such prewiring would provide?

Recite an Active Summary

5.1 Physical Growth and Development

What are the sequences of physical development?

Three key sequences of physical development are cephalocaudal development, proximodistal development, and differentiation.

What patterns of growth occur in infancy?

Infants usually double their birth weight in five months and triple it by the first birthday. Height increases by about half in the first year. Infants grow another 10–15 centimetres in the second year and gain another 2–3 kilograms. The head gradually diminishes in proportion to the rest of the body.

What is failure to thrive?

Failure to thrive (FTT) is a serious disorder that impairs growth in infancy and early childhood. FTT can have

organic or nonorganic causes. Deficiencies in caregiver–child interaction may play a major role in FTT.

5.2 Nutrition: Fuelling Development

What are the nutritional needs of infants?

Infants require breast milk or an iron-fortified infant formula. Introduction of solid foods is recommended at six months. Caregivers are advised to gradually build up the baby's diet to include a variety of foods.

Why are mothers encouraged to breast-feed? What are the pros and cons of breast-feeding vs. bottle-feeding?

Breast-feeding is related to factors such as the mother's availability (most women work), knowledge of the advantages of breast-feeding, and the availability of alternatives to breast milk. Breast milk is tailored to human digestion, contains essential nutrients, provides the mothers' antibodies, helps protect against infant diarrhea, and is less likely than formula to cause allergies. However, some environmental toxins are found in breast milk.

5.3 Development of the Brain and Nervous System

What are neurons? How do they develop?

Neurons are cells that receive and transmit messages in the form of chemicals called neurotransmitters. As the child matures, axons grow in length, dendrites and axon terminals proliferate, and many neurons become wrapped in myelin, enabling them to function more efficiently.

What is the brain? How does the brain develop?

The brain is the command centre of the developing organism. The brain triples in weight by the first birthday, reaching nearly 70 percent of its adult weight. There are two major prenatal growth spurts: Neurons proliferate during the first growth spurt; the second spurt is due mainly to the proliferation of dendrites and axon terminals.

How do nature and nurture affect the development "of the brain?

Sensory and motor areas of the brain begin to develop because of maturation, but sensory stimulation and motor activity also spur development. Rats raised in enriched environments develop more dendrites and axon terminals. Malnutrition is related to a small brain, fewer neurons, and less myelination.

5.4 Motor Development: How Moving

What is motor development? How does it occur?

Motor development consists of developments in the activity of muscles and is connected with changes in posture, movement, and coordination. Children gain the ability to move their bodies through a sequence of activities that includes rolling over, sitting up, crawling, creeping, walking, and running. The sequence remains stable, but some children skip a step. Both maturation (nature) and experience (nurture) play indispensable roles in motor development. Infants need some opportunity for experimentation before they can engage in milestones such as sitting up and walking. Development of motor skills can be accelerated by training, but the effect is generally slight.

5.5 Sensory and Perceptual Development: Taking in the World

How do sensation and perception develop in the infant?

Neonates are nearsighted and have poor peripheral vision. Acuity and peripheral vision approximate adult levels by the age of six months. Neonates attend longer to stripes than to blobs, and by 8 to 12 weeks of age they prefer curved lines to straight lines. Two-month-old infants fixate longer on the human face than on other stimuli. Some researchers argue that neonates prefer faces not because they are faces but because they are complex images. Infants can discriminate their mother's face from a stranger's after about eight hours of contact. Neonates direct their attention to the edges of objects, but two-month-olds scan from the edges inward. Researchers study the development of depth perception by means such as the classic visual cliff apparatus. Most infants refuse to venture out over the visual cliff by the time they can crawl. Researchers have speculated that infants may need some experience crawling before they can develop fear of heights. Perceptual constancy is a tendency to perceive an object to be the same, even though it produces different sensations under different conditions. Size constancy appears to be present by two-and-a-half to three months of age; shape constancy develops by age four to five months.

How does the sense of hearing develop in infancy?

Neonates reflexively orient their heads toward a sound. By 18 months of age, infants locate sounds about as well as adults. Infants discriminate caregivers' voices by three-and-a-half months of age. Early infants can perceive most of the speech sounds throughout the languages of the world, but by 10 to 12 months of age, this ability lessens.

Do children play an active or a passive role in perceptual development?

Neonates seem to be at the mercy of external stimuli, but later on, intentional action replaces capture. Systematic search replaces unsystematic search, attention becomes selective, and irrelevant information gets ignored.

What is the evidence for the roles of nature and nurture in perceptual development?

Evidence shows that sensory changes are linked to maturation of the nervous system (nature) but that experience also plays a crucial role in perceptual development (nurture). For one thing, there are critical periods in the perceptual development of children and lower animals, such that sensory experience is required to optimize—or maintain—sensory capacities.

Key Terms

Active Learning Resources

Go to *Voyages in Development's* CourseMate at **www.nelsonbrain.com**, where you will find an interactive eBook, flashcards, Pre-Lecture Quizzes, Section Quizzes, Exam Practice, videos, and more.

WilliamJu/Thinkstock

Major Topics

INFANCY: Cognitive Development 6

Truth or Fiction?

T | F For two-month-old infants, "out of sight" is "out of mind." **p. 194**

T | F A one-hour-old infant may imitate an adult who sticks out his or her tongue. **p. 200**

T | F Psychologists can begin to measure intelligence in infancy. **p. 202**

T | F Infant crying is a primitive form of language. **p. 205**

T | F You can advance children's development of pronunciation by correcting their errors. **p. 213**

T | F Children are "prewired" to listen to language in such a way that they come to understand rules of grammar. **p. 216**

Laurent ... resumes his experiments of the day before. He grabs in succession a celluloid swan, a box, etc., stretches out his arm and lets them fall. He distinctly varies the position of the fall. Sometimes he stretches out his arm vertically, sometimes he holds it obliquely, in front of or behind his eyes, etc. When the object falls in a new position, he lets it fall two or three times more on the same place, as though to study the spatial relation; then he modifies the situation.

—Jean Piaget (1963 [1936])

Is this the description of a scientist at work? In a way, it is. Although Swiss psychologist Jean Piaget was describing his 11-month-old son Laurent, children of this age frequently act like scientists, performing what Piaget called "experiments in order to see."

In this chapter, we chronicle the developing thought processes of infants and toddlers—that is, their cognitive development. First we focus on the sensorimotor stage of cognitive development hypothesized by Piaget. Then we examine infant memory and imitation. We next explore individual differences in infant intelligence. Finally, we turn our attention to a remarkable aspect of cognitive development: language.

MNStudio/Shutterstock.com

6.1 Cognitive Development: Jean Piaget

Cognitive development focuses on the development of children's ways of perceiving and mentally representing the world. Piaget labelled children's concepts of the world **schemes.** He hypothesized that children try to use **assimilation** to absorb new events into existing schemes; and when assimilation does not enable them to make sense of novel events, children try to modify existing schemes through **accommodation**.

Piaget (1963 [1936]) hypothesized that children's cognitive processes develop in an orderly sequence, or series, of stages. As with motor and perceptual development, some children may be more advanced than others at particular ages, but the developmental sequence does not normally vary (Flavell et al., 2002; Siegler & Alibali, 2005). Piaget identified four major stages of cognitive development: sensorimotor, preoperational, concrete operational, and formal operational. In this chapter, we discuss the sensorimotor stage. (To refresh your memory go back to Chapter 1, pp. 18–19, for a review of Piaget's concepts.)

The Sensorimotor Stage (0–24 Months)

QUESTION » What is the sensorimotor stage of cognitive development? Piaget referred to the first two years of cognitive development as the sensorimotor stage, a time when children demonstrate these developments by means of sensory and motor activity. Although it may be difficult for us to imagine how we can develop and use cognitive processes in the absence of language, children do so in many ways.

During the sensorimotor stage, infants progress from responding to events with reflexes, or ready-made schemes, to goal-oriented behaviour that involves awareness of past events. During this stage, they come to form mental representations of objects and events, to hold complex pictures of past events in mind, and to solve problems by mental trial and error.

Piaget divided the sensorimotor stage into six substages, each of which is characterized by more complex behaviour than the preceding substage. But there is also continuity from substage to substage. Each substage can be characterized as a variation on a theme in which earlier forms of behaviour are repeated, varied, and coordinated.

Substage 1: Simple Reflexes (0–1 Month)

The first substage covers the first month after birth. It is dominated by the assimilation of sources of stimulation into inborn reflexes such as grasping, visual tracking, crying, sucking, and crudely turning the head toward a sound.

At birth, reflexes have a stereotypical, inflexible quality. But even within the first few hours, neonates begin to modify reflexes as a result of experience. For example, infants adapt (accommodate) patterns of sucking to the shape of the nipple and the rate of flow of fluid.

During the first month or so, infants apparently make no connection between stimulation perceived through different sensory modalities. They make no effort to grasp objects that they visually track. Crude turning toward sources of sounds and smells has a mechanical look about it that cannot be considered purposeful searching.

Substage 2: Primary Circular Reactions (1–4 Months)

The second substage, primary circular reactions, lasts from about one to four months of age and is characterized by the beginnings of the ability to coordinate various sensorimotor schemes. In this substage, infants tend to repeat

Simple Reflexes
At birth, neonates assimilate objects into reflexive responses. But even within hours after birth, neonates begin to modify reflexes as a result of experience. For example, they adapt sucking patterns to the shape of the nipple. (But don't be too impressed; porpoises are born swimming and "know" to rise to the surface of the ocean to breathe.)

Barbara Maurer/Stone/Getty Images

scheme According to Piaget, an action pattern (such as a reflex) or mental structure that is involved in the acquisition or organization of knowledge.

assimilation According to Piaget, the incorporation of new events or knowledge into existing schemes.

accommodation According to Piaget, the modification of existing schemes in order to incorporate new events or knowledge.

stimulating actions that first occurred by chance. For example, they may lift their arm repeatedly to bring it into view. A circular reaction is a behaviour that is repeated. **Primary circular reactions** focus on the infant's own body rather than on the external environment. Piaget noticed the following primary circular reaction in his son, Laurent:

> At 2 months 4 days, Laurent by chance discovers his right index finger and looks at it briefly. At 2 months 11 days, he inspects for a moment his open right hand, perceived by chance. At 2 months 17 days, he follows its spontaneous movement for a moment, then examines it several times while it searches for his nose or rubs his eye.
>
> At 2 months 21 days, he holds his two fists in the air and looks at the left one, after which he slowly brings it toward his face and rubs his nose with it, then his eye. A moment later the left hand again approaches his face; he looks at it and touches his nose. He recommences and laughs five or six times in succession while moving the left hand to his face. . . . He laughs beforehand but begins to smile again on seeing the hand.
>
> —Piaget (1963 [1936], pp. 96–97)

Thus, Laurent, early in the third month, visually tracks the behaviour of his hand, but his visual observations do not seem to influence their movement. At about two months 21 days, Laurent can apparently exert some control over his hands, because he seems to know when a hand is about to move (and entertain him). But the link between looking at and moving the hands remains weak. A few days later, however, his looking "acts" on the hands, causing them to remain in his field of vision. Sensorimotor coordination has been achieved. An action is repeated because it stimulates the infant.

In terms of assimilation and accommodation, the child is attempting to assimilate the motor scheme (moving the hand) into the sensory scheme (looking at it). But the schemes do not automatically fit. Several days of apparent trial and error pass, during which the infant seems to be trying to make accommodations so that the schemes will fit.

Goal-directed behaviour makes significant advances during the second substage. During the month after birth, infants visually track objects that contrast with their backgrounds, especially moving objects. But this ready-made behaviour is largely automatic, so that the infant is "looking and seeing." By the third month, infants may examine objects repeatedly and intensely, as Laurent did. It seems clear that the infant is no longer simply looking and seeing but is now "looking in order to see." And by the end of the third month, Laurent seems to be moving his hands in order to look at them.

Because Laurent (and other infants) repeat actions that enable them to see, cognitive-developmental psychologists consider sensorimotor coordination self-reinforcing. Laurent does not seem to be looking or moving his hands because these acts allow him to satisfy a more basic drive such as hunger or thirst. The desire to prolong stimulation may be just as basic.

Substage 3: Secondary Circular Reactions (4–8 months)

The third substage lasts from about four to eight months and is characterized by **secondary circular reactions**, in which patterns of activity are repeated because of their effect on the environment. In the second substage (primary circular reactions), infants are focused on their own bodies, as Piaget described in Laurent. In the third substage (secondary circular reactions), the focus shifts to objects and environmental events. Infants may now learn to pull strings in order to make a plastic face appear or to shake an object in order to hear it rattle.

Primary Circular Reactions
In the substage of primary circular reactions, infants repeat actions that involve their bodies. The three-month-old in this picture is also beginning to coordinate visual and sensorimotor schemes; that is, looking at the hand is becoming coordinated with holding it in the field of vision.

Secondary Circular Reactions
In the substage of secondary circular reactions, patterns of activity are repeated because of their effect on the environment. This infant shakes a rattle to produce an interesting sound.

primary circular reactions The repetition of actions that first occurred by chance and that focus on the infant's own body.

secondary circular reactions The repetition of actions that produce an effect on the environment.

Although infants in this substage track the trajectory of moving objects, they abandon their search when the object disappears from view. As we will see later in this chapter, the object concepts of infants are quite limited at these ages, especially the age at which the third substage begins.

Substage 4: Coordination of Secondary Schemes (8–12 Months)

In the fourth substage, infants no longer act simply to prolong interesting occurrences. Now they can coordinate schemes to attain specific goals. Infants begin to show intentional, goal-directed behaviour in which they differentiate between the means of achieving a goal and the goal or end itself. For example, they may lift a piece of cloth in order to reach a toy that they had seen a parent place under the cloth earlier. In this example, the scheme of picking up the cloth (the means) is coordinated with the scheme of reaching for the toy (the goal or end).

This example indicates that the infant has mentally represented the toy placed under the cloth. Consider another example. At the age of five months, one of Piaget's daughters, Lucienne, was reaching across her crib for a toy. As she did so, Piaget obscured the toy with his hand. Lucienne pushed her father's hand aside but, in doing so, became distracted and began to play with the hand. A few months later, Lucienne did not allow her father's hand to distract her from the goal of reaching the toy. She moved the hand firmly to the side and then grabbed the toy. The mental representation of the object appears to have become more persistent. The intention of reaching the object was also maintained, and so the hand was perceived as a barrier and not as another interesting stimulus.

During the fourth substage, infants also gain the capacity to copy actions that are not in their own repertoires. Infants can now imitate many gestures and sounds that they had previously ignored. The imitation of a new facial gesture implies that infants have mentally represented their own faces and can tell what parts of their faces they are moving through feedback from facial muscles. For example, when a girl imitates her mother sticking out her tongue, it would appear that she has coordinated moving her own tongue with feedback from muscles in the tongue and mouth. In this way, imitation suggests a great deal about the child's emerging self-concept.

Coordination of Secondary Schemes

During this substage, infants coordinate their behaviours to attain specific goals. This infant lifts the blanket to retrieve a toy that has been placed under the cloth.

Substage 5: Tertiary Circular Reactions (12–18 Months)

In the fifth substage, which lasts from about 12 to 18 months of age, Piaget looked on the behaviour of infants as characteristic of budding scientists. Infants now engage in **tertiary circular reactions**, or purposeful adaptations of established schemes to specific situations. Behaviour takes on a new experimental quality, and infants may vary their actions dozens of times in a deliberate trial-and-error fashion in order to learn how things work.

Piaget reported an example of tertiary circular reactions by his daughter Jacqueline. The episode was an experiment in which Piaget placed a stick outside Jacqueline's playpen, which had wooden bars (Piaget, 1963 [1936]). At

tertiary circular reactions The purposeful adaptation of established schemes to new situations.

first, Jacqueline grasped the stick and tried to pull it sideways into the playpen. The stick was too long and did not fit through the bars. Over a number of days of trial and error, however, Jacqueline discovered that she could bring the stick between the bars by turning it upright. In future presentations, she would immediately turn the stick upright and bring it in.

Jacqueline's eventual success with the stick was the result of overt trial and error. In the sixth substage, described next, the solution to problems is often more sudden, suggesting that children have manipulated the elements of the problems in their minds and engaged in mental trial and error before displaying the correct overt response.

Substage 6: Invention of New Means through Mental Combinations (18–24 Months)

The sixth substage lasts from about 18 to 24 months of age. It serves as a transition between sensorimotor development and the development of symbolic thought. External exploration is replaced by mental exploration.

Recall Jacqueline's trials with the stick. Piaget waited until his other children, Lucienne and Laurent, were 18 months old, and then he presented them with the playpen and stick problem. By waiting until 18 months, he could attribute differences in their performance to the age change instead of a possible warm-up effect from earlier tests. Rather than engaging in overt trial and error, the 18-month-old children sat and studied the situation for a few moments. Then they grasped the stick, turned it upright, and brought it into the playpen with little overt effort.

Jacqueline had at first failed with the stick. She then turned it every which way, happening on a solution almost by chance. Lucienne and Laurent solved the problem fairly rapidly, suggesting that they mentally represented the stick and the bars of the playpen and perceived that the stick would not fit through as it was. They must then have rotated the mental image of the stick until they perceived a position that would allow the stick to pass between the bars.

At about 18 months, children may also use imitation to symbolize, or stand for, a plan of action. Consider how Lucienne goes about retrieving a watch chain her father placed in a matchbox. It seems that symbolic imitation serves her as a way of thinking out loud:

> I put the chain back into the box and reduce the opening. [Lucienne] is not aware of [how to open and close] the match box. [She] possesses two preceding schemes: turning the box over in order to empty it of its contents, and sliding her fingers into the slit to make the chain come out. [She] puts her finger inside and gropes to reach the chain, but fails. A pause follows during which Lucienne manifests a very curious reaction....
>
> She looks at the slit with great attention. Then, several times in succession, she opens and shuts her mouth, at first slightly, then wider and wider! Apparently Lucienne understands the existence of a cavity.... [Lucienne then] puts her finger in the slit, and, instead of trying as before to reach the chain, she pulls so as to enlarge the opening. She succeeds and grasps the chain.
>
> —Piaget (1963 [1936], pp. 337–338)

Development of Object Permanence

QUESTIONS » What is object permanence? How does it develop? **Object permanence** is the recognition that an object or person continues to exist when it is out of sight. Your textbook continues to exist when you accidentally leave it

Tertiary Circular Reactions
In this substage, infants vary their actions in a trial-and-error fashion to learn how things work. This child is fascinated by the results of pulling on the end of a roll of toilet paper.

Carey Hope/Thinkstock

object permanence Recognition that objects continue to exist even when they are not seen.

in the library after studying for the big test, and an infant's mother continues to exist even when she is in another room. Your realization that your book exists, although out of view, is an example of object permanence. If an infant acts as though its mother no longer exists when she is out of sight, the infant does not have the concept of object permanence. The development of object permanence is tied into the development of infants' working memory and reasoning ability (Bell, 2012; Kibbe & Leslie, 2011).

Neonates show no tendency to respond to objects that are not within their immediate sensory grasp. By the age of two months, infants may show some surprise if an object (such as a toy duck) is placed behind a screen and then taken away so that when the screen is lifted, it is absent. However, they make no effort to search for the missing object. Through the first six months or so, when the screen is placed between the object and the infant, the infant behaves as though the object is no longer there (see Figure 6.1 ■). **TRUTH OR FICTION REVISITED:** It is true that "out of sight" is "out of mind" for two-month-old infants. Apparently, they do not yet reliably mentally represent objects they see.

There are some interesting advances in the development of the object concept by about the sixth month (Piaget's substage 3). For example, an infant at this age will tend to look for an object that has been dropped, behaviour that suggests some form of object permanence. There is also reason to believe that by this age, the infant perceives a mental representation (image) of an object, such as a favourite toy, in response to sensory impressions of part of the object. This is shown by the infant's reaching for an object that is partly hidden.

By 8 to 12 months of age (Piaget's substage 4), infants will seek to retrieve objects that have been completely hidden. But in observing his own children, Piaget (1963 [1936]) noted an interesting error known as the A-not-B error. Piaget repeatedly hid a toy behind a screen (A), and each time, his infant removed the screen and retrieved the toy. Then, as the infant watched, Piaget hid the toy behind another screen (B) in a different place. Still, the infant tried to recover the toy by pushing aside the first screen (A). It is as though the child

Figure 6.1 ■ Development of Object Permanence

To the infant who is in the early part of the sensorimotor stage, out of sight is truly out of mind. Once a sheet of paper is placed between the infant and the toy monkey (top two photos), the infant loses all interest in the toy. From evidence of this sort, Piaget concluded that the toy is not mentally represented. The bottom series of photos shows a child in a later part of the sensorimotor stage. This child does mentally represent objects and pushes through a towel to reach an object that has been screened from sight.

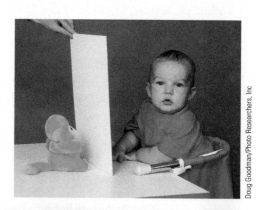

had learned that a certain motor activity would reinstate the missing toy. The child's concept of the object did not, at this age, extend to recognition that objects usually remain in the place where they have been most recently mentally represented.

But under certain conditions, nine- to ten-month-old infants do not show the A-not-B error. They apparently need a certain degree of maturation of the front lobes of the cerebral cortex, which fosters the development of working memory and attention (Cuevas & Bell, 2010). Also, if infants are allowed to search for the object immediately after seeing it hidden, the error often does not occur. But if they are forced to wait five or more seconds before looking, they are likely to commit the A-not-B error (Wellman et al., 1986).

Most children develop object permanence before they develop emotional bonds to specific caregivers. It seems logical that infants must have permanent representations of their mothers before they show distress at being separated from them. But wait, you say. Don't even three- or four-month-old infants cry when their mother leaves and then stop crying when she returns and picks them up? Doesn't this behaviour pattern show object permanence? Not necessarily. Infants appear to appreciate the comforts provided by their mothers and to express displeasure when these comforts end (such as when their mothers depart). The expression of displeasure frequently results in the reinstatement of pleasure (being held, fed, and spoken to). Therefore, infants may learn to engage in these protests when their mothers leave because of the positive consequences of protesting—not because they have developed object permanence.

Nevertheless, studies by Renee Baillargeon and her colleagues (Aguiar & Baillargeon, 1999; Wang et al., 2005) show that some rudimentary knowledge of object permanence may be present as early as two-and-a-half to three-and-a-half months. In one study, Baillargeon (1987) first showed three-and-a-half- and four-and-a-half-month olds the event illustrated in the top part of Figure 6.2 ■. A screen rotated back and forth through a 180-degree arc like a drawbridge. After several trials, the infants showed habituation; that is, they spent less time looking at the screen. Next, a box was placed in the path of the screen, as shown in the middle drawing of Figure 6.2. The infant could see the box at the beginning of each trial but could no longer see it when the screen reached the box. In one condition, labelled the "possible event," the screen stopped when it reached the box. In another condition, labelled the "impossible event," the screen rotated through a full 180-degree arc, as though the box were no longer behind it. (How could this happen? Unknown to the infant, a trapdoor was released, causing the box to drop out of the way.) The infants looked longer at the "impossible event" than at the "possible" one. (Infants look longer at unexpected events.) So it seems they were surprised that the screen did not stop when it reached the box. Therefore, children as young as three-and-a-half months of age realized that the box continued to exist when it was hidden. But why, then, do infants not actively look for hidden objects until about eight months of age? Perhaps, as Piaget suggested, *coordination of acts* (such as removing a barrier in order to reach a toy) does not occur until the later age.

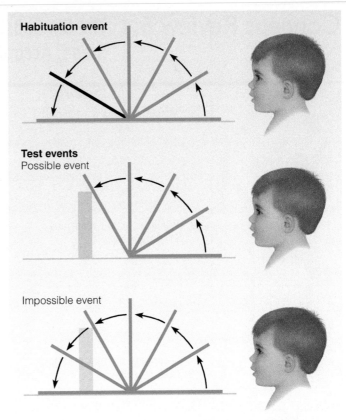

Figure 6.2 ■ Object Permanence before Four Months of Age?

Renee Baillargeon (1987) used the technique shown here to demonstrate that knowledge of object permanence may exist before four months of age. She first showed infants a screen rotated back and forth like a drawbridge (top drawing). After infants showed habituation, a box was placed in the path of the screen. The middle drawing shows a possible event—the screen stops when it reaches the box. The bottom drawing shows an impossible event—the screen rotates through a full 180-degree arc as though the box were no longer behind it. (The experimenter had removed it, unknown to the infant.) Infants looked longer at the impossible event, indicating they realized the box still existed even when hidden behind the screen.

Concept Review 6.1 — The Six Substages of the Sensorimotor Stage, According to Piaget

Substage	Comments
1. Simple reflexes (0–1 month)	Assimilation of new objects into reflexive responses. Infants "look and see." Inborn reflexes can be modified by experience.
2. Primary circular reactions (1–4 months)	Repetition of actions that may have initially occurred by chance but that have satisfying or interesting results. Infants "look in order to see." The focus is on the infant's body. Infants do not yet distinguish between themselves and the external world.
3. Secondary circular reactions (4–8 months)	Repetition of schemes that have interesting effects on the environment. The focus shifts to external objects and events. There is initial cognitive awareness that schemes influence the external world.
4. Coordination of secondary schemes (8–12 months)	Coordination of secondary schemes, such as looking and grasping to attain specific goals. There is the beginning of intentionality and means–end differentiation. We find imitation of actions not already in infants' repertoires.
5. Tertiary circular reactions (12–18 months)	Purposeful adaptation of established schemes to specific situations. Behaviour takes on an experimental quality. There is overt trial and error in problem solving.
6. Invention of new means through mental combinations (18–24 months)	Mental trial and error in problem solving. Infants take "mental detours" based on cognitive maps. Infants engage in deferred imitation and symbolic play. Infants' cognitive advances are made possible by mental representations of objects and events and the beginnings of symbolic thought.

oksix/Thinkstock

Lana K/Shutterstock.com

StockLite/Shutterstock.com

Ruth Jenkinson/Dorling Kindersley/Getty Images

Carey Hope/Thinkstock

Photo by Stephen Ausmus/Courtesy of the USDA

Evaluation of Piaget's Theory

QUESTION » What are the strengths and limitations of Piaget's theory of sensorimotor development? Piaget's theory remains a comprehensive model of infant cognition. Many of his observations of his own infants have been confirmed by others. The pattern and sequence of events he described have been observed among Canadian, American, European, African, and Asian infants (Werner, 1988). Still, research has raised questions about the validity of many of Piaget's claims (Siegler & Alibali, 2005).

For one thing, most researchers now agree that cognitive development is not as tied to discrete stages as Piaget suggested (Fuller, 2012; Siegler & Alibali, 2005). A stage theory requires that changes be discontinuous. In Piaget's theory, children's developing cognitive responses to the world would have to change relatively suddenly. Although later developments do seem to build on earlier ones, the process appears to be more gradual than discontinuous.

Second, Piaget emphasized the role of maturation, almost to the point of excluding adult and peer influences on cognitive development. However, these interpersonal influences have been shown to play roles in cognitive development (Chen & Hancock, 2011).

Third, Piaget appears to have underestimated infants' competence (Siegler & Alibali, 2005). For example, infants display object permanence earlier than he believed (Wang et al., 2005).

Another example of early infant competence is provided by studies on **deferred imitation**, which is imitation of an action that may have occurred hours, days, or even weeks earlier. The presence of deferred imitation suggests that children have mentally represented behaviour patterns. Piaget believed that deferred imitation appears at about 18 months, but others have found that infants show deferred imitation as early as nine months. In Meltzoff's (1988) study, nine-month-old infants watched an adult perform behaviours such as pushing a button to produce a beep. When given a chance to play with the same objects a day later, many infants imitated the actions they had witnessed.

Let us mention one final example of infant competence that occurs much earlier than Piaget predicted. Five-month-old infants may be able to grasp some basic computational concepts—more and less (see the "A Closer Look—Research" feature). In Piaget's view, this ability does not emerge until approximately two years of age.

Psychologists Andrew Meltzoff and M. Keith Moore (2002) assert bluntly that "the sensorimotor theory of infancy has been overthrown," but they admit that "there is little consensus on a replacement." Perhaps Piaget is not so readily replaced.

> **deferred imitation** The imitation of people and events that were encountered or experienced hours, days, or weeks in the past.

A CLOSER LOOK | RESEARCH

Counting in the Crib? Findings from a "Mickey Mouse Experiment"

Even during the first year, infants may have some ability to add and subtract (McCrink & Wynn, 2004; Wynn, 2002). Karen Wynn (1992) showed this ability with infants at five months of age. Her research method was based on the fact that infants look longer at unexpected (novel) events than at expected (familiar) events. If infants are able to engage in some basic addition and subtraction, then they should look longer at a "wrong" answer—that is, at an unexpected answer—than at an expected "correct" answer.

In her research, Wynn showed infants 10-centimetre-tall Mickey Mouse dolls. (Yes, this was a "Mickey Mouse experiment," literally.) One group of infants saw a single doll. Then a screen was raised, blocking the infants' view. Some behind-the-scenes manipulation occurred so that when the screen was removed, the infants were presented with either two dolls (the unexpected or "wrong" answer) or only one doll (the expected or "right" answer). They looked longer at the wrong answer. Another group of infants was initially shown two dolls. The screen was raised, and the infants watched while one doll was removed. But some manipulation took place behind the scenes again, so that when the screen was removed, the infants were shown

Continued

either one doll (the right answer) or two dolls (the wrong answer). The infants consistently looked longer at the two dolls—that is, at the wrong answer.

These results suggest that infants were responsive to some change in quantity—perhaps they showed some rudimentary sense of "more" or "less." But how do we know that the infants were aware of a difference in the number of objects? Can infants somehow calculate the change in number that was produced in the experiment?

To gain some insight into infants' abilities to "count," Wynn first presented a third group of infants with a single doll. She raised the screen and added one doll as the infants watched. Again, some behind-the-scenes manipulation took place so that when the screen was removed, the infants were presented with either two Mickeys (the right answer) or three Mickeys (the wrong answer) (see Figure 6.3 ■). In this phase of the research, the infants stared longer at the three Mickeys than at the two, which suggests that they might have somehow calculated the number of Mickeys that should have resulted from the researcher's manipulations. But again, we cannot say that the infants are adding per se. Other researchers suggest that the infants are more likely to be sensitive to simpler concepts of more and less (Gao et al., 2000).

Reflect Can you relate Wynn's methodology to the concept of habituation?

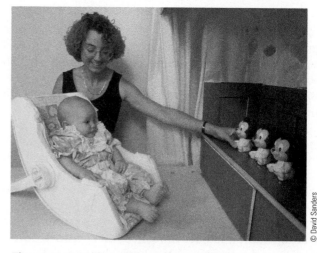

Figure 6.3 ■ Counting in the Crib?

Research by Karen Wynn suggests that five-month-old infants may know when simple computations—or demonstrations involving concepts of more and less—are done correctly. The research is made possible by the fact that infants stare longer at unexpected stimuli—in this case, at a "wrong answer." Wynn conducted her research by exposing infants to Mickey Mouse dolls. She then added or removed one or more dolls behind a screen as the infant watched her, removed the screen, and observed how long the infants gazed at "right" and at "wrong" answers.

Active Review

1. Piaget labelled children's concepts of the world as _____.

2. Children try to _____ new events into existing schemes.

3. Piaget's _____ stage spans the first two years of cognitive development.

4. Primary _____ reactions are characterized by repeating stimulating actions that occur by chance.

5. In _____ circular reactions, activity is repeated because of its effect on the environment.

6. _____ circular reactions are purposeful adaptations of established schemes to specific situations.

7. Object _____ is recognition that an object or person continues to exist when out of sight.

Reflect & Relate: How might an outside observer gather evidence that you and a friend or family member have mentally represented each other? How are you asked to demonstrate that you have mentally represented the subject matter in this textbook and in this course?

6.2 Information Processing

QUESTION » How do infants process information? The information-processing approach to cognitive development focuses on how children manipulate or process information coming in from the environment or already stored in the mind (Siegler & Alibali, 2005).

Infants' Memory

Many of the cognitive capabilities of infants—recognizing the faces of familiar people, developing object permanence, and, in fact, learning in any form—depend on one critical aspect of cognitive development: their memory (Bauer et al., 2010). Even neonates demonstrate memory for stimuli to which they have been exposed previously. Neonates adjust their rate of sucking to hear a recording of their mother reading a story she had read aloud during the last weeks of pregnancy (DeCasper & Fifer, 1980; DeCasper & Spence, 1991). Remember, too, that neonates who are breast-fed are able to remember and show recognition of their mother's unique odour (Cernoch & Porter, 1985).

Memory improves dramatically between two and six months of age and then again by 12 months (Pelphrey et al., 2004; Rose et al., 2011). The improvement may indicate that older infants are more capable than younger ones of encoding (i.e., storing) information, retrieving information already stored, or both (Hayne & Fagen, 2003). As reviewed in Chapter 5, brain growth and development is connected to increased memory capacity.

As infants' brains grow, their cognitive processing becomes more efficient (Case 1992, 1998). A common phrase is "Practice makes perfect," and in terms of memory acquisition, it makes sense. Neo-Piagetians like Robbie Case argue that assimilation is really practising schemes, and the practice leads to atomation. Working memory is then freed up and allows for accommodation. This description may be a simplification, but you can see how the Piaget's cognitive theory and the information processing theory are not mutually exclusive. Along these lines, the phenomenon of infantile amnesia (i.e., the inability of individuals to recall events from early childhood) has been hypothesized to be a result of rapid brain development during infancy, and it may prevent the regulation and ability to form long-lasting memories during this developmental stage (Josselyn & Frankland, 2012).

So what can infants recall? A series of studies by Carolyn Rovee-Collier and her colleagues (Giles & Rovee-Collier, 2011; Rovee-Collier, 1993) illustrates some of these developmental changes in infant memory (see Figure 6.4 ▪). One end of a ribbon was tied to a brightly coloured mobile suspended above the infant's crib. The other end was tied to the infant's ankle, so that when the infant kicked, the mobile moved. Infants quickly learned to increase their rate of kicking. To measure memory, the infant's ankle was again fastened to the mobile after a period of one or more days had elapsed. In one study, two-month-olds remembered how to make the mobile move after delays of up to three days, and three-month-olds remembered for more than a week (Greco et al., 1986).

Infant memory can be improved if infants receive a reminder before they are given the memory test (Bearce & Rovee-Collier, 2006). In one study that used a reminder ("priming"), infants were shown the moving mobile on the day before the memory test, but they were not allowed to activate it. Under these conditions, three-month-olds remembered how to move the mobile after a 28-day delay (Rovee-Collier, 1993).

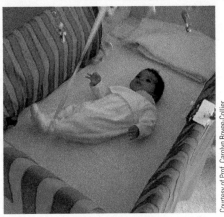

Figure 6.4 ▪ **Investigating Infant Memory**
In this technique, developed by Carolyn Rovee-Collier, the infant's ankle is connected to a mobile by a ribbon. Infants quickly learn to kick to make the mobile move. Two- and three-month-olds remember how to perform this feat after a delay of a few days. If they are given a reminder of simply viewing the mobile, their memory lasts for two to four weeks.

Imitation: Infant See, Infant Do?

Imitation is the basis for much of human learning. Deferred imitation—that is, the imitation of actions after a time delay—occurs as early as six months of age (Campanella & Rovee-Collier, 2005; Haley et al., 2010). To help them remember the imitated act, infants are usually permitted to practise it when they learn it. But in one study, 12-month-old infants were prevented from practising the behaviour they imitated. Even so, they were able to demonstrate it four weeks later, suggesting that they had mentally represented the act (Klein & Meltzoff, 1999).

Why might newborns possess some sort of imitation reflex? Answers lie in the realm of speculation. One possibility is that such a built-in response would contribute to the formation of caregiver–infant bonds and hence enhance the survival of the newborn (Meltzoff & Prinz, 2002). And as we have seen, some theorists speculate that the imitation reflex is made possible by "mirror neurons" that are found in human brains. Such neurons are maintained by evolutionary forces because they enhance the probability of survival as a result of caregiving (Rizzolatti et al., 2002; Oztop et al., 2006).

CHAPTER 6 INFANCY: COGNITIVE DEVELOPMENT

On Mirror Neurons and Really Early Childhood Imitation

Infants engage in deferred imitation as early as six months of age. But it turns out that infants can often imitate behaviour less than one hour after birth! Neonates only 0.7–71 hours old have been found to imitate adults who open their mouths or stick out their tongues (Meltzoff & Prinz, 2002; Rizzolatti et al., 2002; see Figure 6.5 ■).

Some studies have not found imitation in early infancy (Abravanel & DeYong, 1991; Subiaul et al., 2012), and one key factor may be the infants' age. The studies that find imitation generally have been done with very young infants—up to two weeks old—whereas the studies that do not find imitation have tended to use older infants. Therefore, the imitation of neonates is likely to be reflexive—and made possible by "mirror neurons." Thus, this early form of imitation disappears when reflexes are "dropping out" and re-emerges when it has a firmer cognitive footing.

TRUTH OR FICTION REVISITED: It is true that a one-hour-old infant may imitate an adult who sticks out his or her tongue. But such imitation is reflexive. That is, the infant is not observing the adult and then deciding to stick out his or her tongue.

Mirror Neurons

According to Giacomo Rizzolatti and Laila Craighero (2004), social organization and human culture, as we know them, are made possible by certain kinds of neurons that are present at birth. And these neurons, like so many other important psychological discoveries, were found by accident.

A research team in Parma, Italy, headed by Vittorio Gallese and including Giacomo Rizzolatti (Gallese et al., 1996), was recording the activity of individual neurons in monkey's brains as the animals reached for objects. One of the researchers reached for an object that had been handled by a monkey, and quite to his surprise, a neuron in the monkey's brain fired in the same way it had fired when the animal had picked up the object. The research team followed up the phenomenon and discovered many such neurons in the frontal lobes of their monkeys, just before the motor cortex, which they dubbed *mirror neurons*. These *mirror neurons* in monkeys, and in humans, are activated by performing a motor act or by observing another monkey or human engage in the same act (Cattaneo et al., 2010; see Figure 6.6 ■).

Mirror neurons in humans are also connected with emotions. Certain regions of the brain—particularly inthe frontal lobe—are

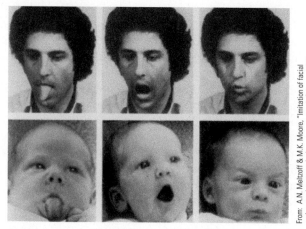

From: A.N. Meltzoff & M.K. Moore, "Imitation of facial and manual gestures by human neonates." *Science*, 1977, 198, 75–78.

Figure 6.5 ■ Imitation in Infants

These two- to three-week-old infants are imitating the facial gestures of an adult experimenter. How are we to interpret these findings? Can we say that the infants "knew" what the experimenter was doing and "chose" to imitate the behaviour, or is there an alternative explanation?

active when people experience emotions such as disgust, happiness, pain, and also when they observe another person experiencing an emotion (Rizzolatti & Fabbri-Destro, 2011). It thus appears that there is a neural basis for empathy—that is, the identification or vicarious experiencing of feelings in others based on the observation of visual and other cues.

It has also been suggested that mirror neurons are connected with the built-in human capacity to acquire language (Corballis, 2010). Mirror neurons are also apparently connected with observational learning and, perhaps, with gender differences in empathy (Shamay-Tsoory, 2011).

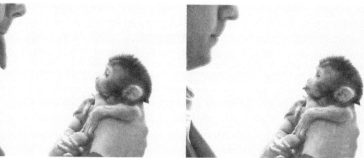

Evolution of Neonatal Imitation. Gross L, *PLoS Biology* Vol. 4/9/2006, e311 http://dx.doi.org/10.1371/journal.pbio.0040311

Figure 6.6 ■ A Newborn Rhesus Monkey Imitates Protrusion of the Tongue, a Feat Made Possible by Mirror Neurons, Not by Learning.

8. The _____-processing approach to cognitive development focuses on how children manipulate or process information.

9. _____ improves dramatically between the ages of two and six months.

10. The imitation of actions after a time delay is called _____ imitation.

Reflect & Relate: Why do adolescents and adults stick their tongues out at infants? (Why not ask a few—a few adolescents and adults, that is?)

6.3 Social Influences on Early Cognitive Development

QUESTION » **How do we apply Vygotsky's sociocultural theory to the cognitive development of infants?** Vygotsky's sociocultural theory talks about the transmission of skills from adults and older children to young children through teaching and learning. When we hear of teaching and learning, we may think of school, but Vygotsky also focused on infants' social interaction with adults, which at first normally takes place largely in the home. Vygotsky emphasized that children's cognitive development involves their internalizing skilled strategies from their joint problem solving with partners who are more skilled. These partners bring the intellectual tools of their society within the grasp of children in what Vygotsky called the *zone of proximal development*. During infancy, caregivers may provide such a zone by helping children play with blocks and picture books. We will see that children's receptive vocabulary exceeds their expressive vocabulary—that is, they can understand more than they can say—and adults who name objects in the environment and in picture books enhance infants' ability to think about these objects before they can talk about them (Daniels et al., 2007).

Adults frequently provide a learning situation in which they encourage their infants to try new things with their help. Then, as the infants show increasing ability to master tasks for themselves, the adults tend to permit the infants to do things by themselves, although they may continue to offer encouragement "from the sidelines." Adults may show a 16-month-old infant how to place blocks on top of one another to make a tower, but once the infant successfully copies the task, the adult typically allows the infant to do it by herself.

Julia Robinson and her colleagues (2008) studied the relationship between maternal *scaffolding* in low-income families and their preschoolers' ability to regulate their attention in a task that involved parent–child interaction. The maternal scaffolding differed largely according to the children's ability to remain task-oriented. Mothers of children who showed poor attention regulation were more likely to engage their children verbally, asking more strategic questions and providing hints and prompts. The children then engaged in a second task without their mothers' help. Those children whose mothers provided the highest amount of scaffolding performed best in the second, "child-alone" task.

Active Review

11. According to Vygotsky, children's cognitive development involves their _____ skilled approaches from joint problem solving with more skilled partners.

Reflect & Relate: Have you used scaffolding in playing with 12- to 24-month-olds? What did you do? What did the infant do?

6.4 Individual Differences in Cognitive Functioning among Infants

QUESTION » How do we measure individual differences in the development of cognitive functioning in infants? Cognitive development does not proceed in the same way or at the same pace for all infants (Rose et al., 2011). Efforts to understand the development of infant differences in cognitive development have relied on so-called scales of infant development or infant intelligence.

Measuring cognition or intelligence in infants is quite different from measuring it in adults. Infants cannot, of course, be assessed by asking them to explain the meanings of words, the similarity between concepts, or the rationales for social rules. One of the most important tests of intellectual development among infants contains very different kinds of items. It is the Bayley Scales of Infant Development (BSID), which was constructed in 1933 by psychologist Nancy Bayley and has since been revised (latest version published in 2005).

The Bayley II (Bayley, 2005) test, published by Pearson, currently consists of adaptive behaviour, cognitive, motor, language, and social-emotional development domains. The adaptive behaviour domain assesses some of the following: communication, community use, functional pre-academics, home living, health and safety, and leisure. The cognitive domain assesses sensorimotor development, exploration and manipulation, object relatedness, concept formation, memory, habituation, visual acuity, visual preference, and objection permanence, as well as other cognitive processes. On the language domain, both expressive (babbling, gesturing, vocabulary) and receptive (e.g., understanding of morphological markers) communication are assessed. The motor domain assesses (a) fine motor skills (e.g., motor planning, motor skills, prehension, manipulation, reaching, grasping) and (b) gross motor skills, such as standing, walking, and balance. A social-emotional domain was added to the third edition. For this domain, the early signs of social-emotional growth are assessed, such as self-regulation, use of emotions, and social interactions. The addition of an Adaptive scale and Social-Emotional scale to the Bayley-III reflects a growing a appreciation for a broader understanding of cognitive functioning.

TRUTH OR FICTION REVISITED: It is true that psychologists can begin to measure intelligence in infancy. However, they use items that differ quite a bit from the kinds of items used with older children and adults, and it remains unclear how well the results obtained in infancy predict intellectual functioning at later ages.

The Bayley Scales of Infant Development

The Bayley scales measure the infant's mental and motor development.

Testing Infants: Why and with What?

As you can imagine, it is no easy matter to test an infant. The items must be administered on a one-to-one basis by a patient tester, and it can be difficult to judge whether the infant is showing the targeted response. Why, then, do we test infants?

One reason is to screen infants for delays or areas of concern. A highly trained tester may be able to detect early signs of sensory or neurological problems, as suggested by development of visual–motor coordination. In addition to the Bayley scales, a number of tests have been developed to screen infants for such difficulties, including the Brazelton Neonatal Behavioral Assessment Scale (NBAS) and the Neonatal Intensive Care Unit Network Neurobehavioral Scale (NNNS) (see Chapter 4).

Instability of Intelligence Scores Attained in Infancy

QUESTION » How well do infant scales predict later intellectual performance? Researchers have also tried to use infant scales to predict development, but this effort has been less than successful. The answer is somewhat less than clear. One study found that scores obtained during the first year of life correlated only moderately with scores obtained a year later (Harris et al., 2005). Certain items on the Bayley scales appear to predict related intellectual skills later in childhood. For example, Bayley items measuring infant motor skills predict subsequent fine motor and visual–spatial skills at six to eight years of age (Siegel, 1992). Bayley language items also predict language skills at the same age (Siegel, 1992).

One study found that the Bayley scales and socioeconomic status were able to predict cognitive development among low-birth-weight children from 18 months to four years of age (Dezoete et al., 2003). But overall or global scores on the Bayley and other infant scales apparently do not predict school grades or IQ scores among schoolchildren very well (Colombo, 1993). Why do infant tests fail to do a good job of predicting IQ scores among school-age children? Aside from the possibility that intellectual functioning fluctuates between the preschool and school years, it may be that the sensorimotor test items used during infancy are not strongly related to the verbal and symbolic items used to assess intelligence at later ages.

The overall conclusion seems to be that the Bayley scales can identify gross lags in development and relative strengths and weaknesses. However, they are only moderate predictors of intelligence scores even one year later, and they are still poorer predictors of scores taken beyond longer stretches of time.

Use of Visual Recognition Memory: An Effort to Enhance Predictability

QUESTIONS » What is visual recognition memory? How is it used? In a continuing effort to find aspects of intelligence and cognition that might remain consistent from infancy through later childhood, a number of researchers have recently focused on visual recognition memory (Courage et al., 2004). **Visual recognition memory** is the ability to discriminate previously seen objects from novel objects. This procedure is based on habituation, as are many of the methods for assessing perceptual development (see Chapter 5).

Let us consider longitudinal studies of this type. Susan Rose and her colleagues (1992) showed seven-month-old infants pictures of two identical faces. After 20 seconds, the pictures were replaced with one picture of a new face and a second picture of the familiar face. The amount of time the infants spent looking at each of the faces in the second set of pictures was recorded. Some infants spent more time looking at the new face than at the older face, suggesting that they had better memory for visual stimulation. The children were given standard IQ tests yearly from ages one through six. It was found that the children with greater visual recognition memory later attained higher IQ scores.

Rose and her colleagues (2001) also showed that, from age to age, individual differences in capacity for visual recognition memory are stable. This finding is important because intelligence—the quality that many researchers seek to predict from visual recognition memory—is also theorized to be a

visual recognition memory The kind of memory shown in an infant's ability to discriminate previously seen objects from novel objects.

reasonably stable trait. Similarly, items on intelligence tests are age graded; that is, older children perform better than younger children, even as developing intelligence remains constant. So, too, with visual recognition memory. Capacity for visual recognition memory increases over the first year after birth (Rose et al., 2001).

A number of other studies have examined the relationship between either infant visual recognition memory or infant preference for novel stimulation (which is a related measure) and later IQ scores. In general, they show good predictive validity for broad cognitive abilities throughout childhood, including measures of intelligence and language ability (Heimann et al., 2006; S. A. Rose et al., 2004).

In sum, scales of infant development may provide useful data as screening devices, as research instruments, or simply as a way to describe the things that infants do and do not do. However, their predictive power as intelligence tests has so far been disappointing. Tests of visual recognition hold better promise as predictors of later intelligence.

Many parents today spend a good deal of time trying to teach their children skills that will enhance their intelligence testing scores. Any number of commercial products prey on parents' fears that their children might not measure up, and these products are found on the shelves of such stores as Toys "R" Us. Although these products themselves probably do no harm, parents might better spend their time reading to children, playing with them, and taking them on stimulating excursions. Even a supermarket provides ample opportunities for parents to talk about shapes and colours and temperatures and kinds of foods with their young children.

Now let us turn our attention to a fascinating aspect of cognitive development, the development of language. Language development boosts cognitive development, perhaps immeasurably, by enabling children to learn about, and talk about, things that have happened outside their immediate experience (DeLoache et al., 2009).

Active Review

12. The Bayley Scales of Infant Development consist of _____ development domains.

13. The Brazelton Neonatal Behavioral Assessment Scale is used to screen for sensory or _____ problems.

14. _____ recognition memory consists of an infant's ability to discriminate previously seen objects from novel objects.

Reflect & Relate: When you have observed infants, what kinds of behaviours have led you to think that one is "brilliant" or another one "dull"? How do your "methods" correspond to those used by researchers who attempt to assess intellectual functioning among infants?

6.5 Language Development

"The time has come," the Walrus said,
"To talk of many things
Of shoes—and ships—and sealing wax—
Of cabbages—and kings—
And why the sea is boiling hot—
And whether pigs have wings."
—Lewis Carroll, *Through the Looking-Glass*

Lewis Carroll wasn't quite telling the truth in his well-known children's book. The sea is not boiling hot—at least not in most places or at most times. Nor do walruses speak. At the risk of alienating walrus aficionados, we will assert that walruses neither speak nor use other forms of language to communicate. But children do. Children come "to talk of many things"—perhaps only rarely of sealing wax and cabbages, but certainly about things more closely connected with their environments and their needs. Children may be unlikely to debate "whether pigs have wings," but they do develop the language skills that will eventually enable them to do just that. Lewis Carroll enjoyed playing with language, and we will see that children join in that game. In physical development, the most dramatic developments come early—fast and furious—long before the child is born. Language does not come so early, and its development may not seem quite so fast and furious. Nevertheless, during the years of infancy, most children develop from creatures without language to little people who understand nearly all the things that are said to them and who relentlessly sputter words and simple sentences for all the world to hear. Though much of the world might think they have little of value to say, most parents find their utterances just priceless.

In this section, we first present an overview of language, trace language development from early crying and cooing through the production of two-word sentences. We then consider theoretical views of language development.

What Is Language?

Broadly speaking, language is the term we use to refer to the method of communication used by humans. There are different components to language and those who study the development of language tend to focus on the following key components: phonology, morphology, semantics, syntax, and pragmatics (Gleason & Ratner, 2013).

The first component, **phonology**, deals with the basic units of sound known as **phonemes** and the rules dictating the structure and sequence of speech sounds. Everyone figures out the sound patterns of their native language, and that is why children being reared in a home that speaks exclusively Thai will learn the rules needed to combine the basic sounds of Thai. A second component of language is **semantics**. Semantics refers to the meanings ascribed to words and clusters of words. Using semantics, children build their vocabularies. With word acquisition children rapidly begin to learn grammar, which is comprised of **morphology** and **syntax**. Morphology describes the process of using sounds to make words, using **morphemes** (the smallest unit of meaning in a language) to indicate tense, number, gender, and other meanings. Syntax refers to rules that stipulate the way words are to be arranged in sentences. Finally, there is **pragmatics**, which refers to the practical aspects of communication that can make communicating more or less effective, such as tone, nonverbal gestures, and social situations that may influence meaning. As we read about early language development during infancy, each of these key language components start to take shape.

Early Vocalizations

QUESTION » **What are prelinguistic vocalizations?** Children develop language according to an invariant sequence of steps, or stages, as outlined in Table 6.1. We begin with the **prelinguistic** vocalizations. True words are symbols of objects and events. Prelinguistic vocalizations, such as cooing and babbling, do not represent objects or events. **TRUTH OR FICTION REVISITED:** Actually, infant crying is not a primitive form of language. Cries do not represent objects or events.

phonology The understanding of how the basic units of sounds are combined.

phonemes Basic units of sounds.

semantics The meanings ascribed to words and clusters of words.

morphology The forming of words from sounds based on grammatical rules.

syntax Rules that stipulate the way words are to be arranged in sentences.

morpheme The smallest unit of meaning in a language.

pragmatics The practical aspects of communication, such as adaptation of language to fit the social situation.

prelinguistic Referring to vocalizations made by the infant before the development of language. (In language, words symbolize objects and events.)

● TABLE 6.1

What to Expect in Speech and Language Development

Approximate Age	Communication
Birth to 1 month	☐ Differential crying (different types of cries are detectable: hungry, tired) ☐ Throaty sounds; gurgles; may start to coo ☐ Looks to sounds ☐ Looks at people who speak
1 to 4 months	☐ Cooing ☐ Use of eye contact develops ☐ Listens and responds ☐ Imitation is present (e.g., imitates coos or facial expressions)
4 to 8 months	☐ Babbling ☐ Laughs ☐ Understands common words ☐ Vocalizes during play activities ☐ Enjoys playing games like "peek-a-boo"
8 to 12 months	☐ Imitation and turn-taking ☐ Use of proto words (e.g., Ma-ma-ma) ☐ Real words (may have about 2–6 real words)
12 to 18 months	☐ Average number of words is about 40 (range 0–347) ☐ Uses a variety of gestures (e.g., pointing, joint attention) ☐ Enjoys songs, rhymes, shorter stories ☐ Uses underextensions ☐ Uses overextensions ☐ Presence of holographic speech
18 to 30 months	☐ Uses telegraphic speech ☐ Vocabulary grows with an average of 170 words at 20 months of age ☐ Names objects to ask for them ☐ Speech is understood most of the time by family members ☐ Can produce most vowel sounds by about 21 months

Sources: Crowther (2006); www.children.gov.on.ca/htdocs/English/topics/earlychildhood/speechlanguage/brochure_speech.aspx; www.nidcd.nih.gov/health/voice/pages/speechandlanguage.aspx#6; http://firstwords.ca/wp-content/uploads/2010/06/MD-Checklist-PAD-EN1.pdf.

Newborn children, as parents are well aware, have an unlearned but highly effective form of verbal expression: crying and more crying. Crying is accomplished by blowing air through the vocal tract. There are no distinct well-formed sounds. Crying is about the only sound that infants make during the first month.

During the second month, infants begin **cooing**. Infants use their tongues when they coo. For this reason, coos are more articulated than cries. Coos are often vowel-like and may resemble extended "oohs" and "ahs." Cooing appears to be linked to feelings of pleasure or positive excitement. Infants tend not to coo when they are hungry, tired, or in pain.

Cries and coos are innate but can be modified by experience (Volterra et al., 2004). When parents respond positively to cooing by talking to their infants, smiling at them, and imitating them, cooing increases. Early parent-child "conversations," in which parents respond to coos and then pause as the infant coos, may foster infant awareness of taking turns as a way of verbally relating to other people.

By about eight months of age, cooing decreases markedly. Somewhere between six and nine months, children begin to babble. **Babbling** is the first vocalizing that sounds like human speech. In babbling, infants frequently combine consonants and vowels, as in *ba, ga*, and sometimes the much-valued *dada* (McCardle et al., 2009). At first, *dada* is purely coincidental (sorry, you dads), despite the family's jubilation over its appearance.

In verbal interactions between infants and adults, the adults frequently repeat the syllables produced by their infants. They are likely to say *dadada* or *bababa* instead of simply *da* or *ba*. Such redundancy apparently helps infants discriminate these sounds from others and further encourages them to imitate their parents (Elkind, 2007; Tamis-LeMonda et al., 2006).

After infants have been babbling for a few months, parents often believe that their children are having conversations with themselves. At 10 to 12 months, infants tend to repeat syllables, showing what linguists refer to as **echolalia**. Parents overhear them going on and on, repeating consonant-vowel combinations (ah-bah-bah-bah-bah), pausing, and then switching to other combinations.

Toward the end of the first year, infants are also using patterns of rising and falling **intonation** that resemble the sounds of adult speech. It may sound as though the infant is trying to speak the parents' language. Parents may think that their children are babbling in English or in whatever tongue is spoken in the home.

Development of Vocabulary

QUESTION » **How does vocabulary develop?** Vocabulary development consists of the child's learning the meanings of words. In general, children's **receptive vocabulary** development outpaces their **expressive vocabulary** development (Klee & Stokes, 2011). This means that at any given time, they can understand more words than they can use. One study, for example, found that 12-month-olds could speak an average of 13 words but could comprehend the meanings of 84 words (Tamis-LeMonda et al., 2006). Infants usually understand much of what others are saying well before they themselves utter any words at all. Their ability to segment speech sounds into meaningful units—or words—before 12 months is a good predictor of their vocabulary at 24 months (Newman et al., 2006).

The Child's First Words

Ah, that long-awaited first word! What a milestone! Sad to say, many parents miss it. They are not quite sure when their infants utter their first word, often because the first word is not pronounced clearly or because pronunciation varies from usage to usage.

cooing Prelinguistic, articulated vowel-like sounds that appear to reflect feelings of positive excitement.

babbling The child's first vocalizations that have the sounds of speech.

echolalia The automatic repetition of sounds or words.

intonation The use of pitches of varying levels to help communicate meaning.

receptive vocabulary The sum total of the words whose meanings one understands.

expressive vocabulary The sum total of the words that one can use in the production of language.

Babbling Here, There, and Everywhere

Babbling, like crying and cooing, appears to be inborn. Children from different cultures, where languages sound very different, all seem to babble the same sounds, including many they could not have heard (Oller, 2000). Deaf children whose parents use sign language babble with their hands and fingers, using repetitive gestures that resemble the vocal babbling of infants who can hear (Bloom, 1998; Koopmans-van Beinum et al., 2001).

Despite the fact that babbling is innate, it is readily modified by the child's language environment. One study followed infants growing up in French-, Chinese-, and Arabic-speaking households (Boysson-Bardies & Halle, 1994). At four to seven months of age, the infants began to use more of the sounds in their language environment; foreign phonemes began to drop out. The role that experience plays in language development is further indicated by the fact that the babbling of deaf infants never begins to approximate the sounds of the parents' language.

Reflect We say that babbling is innate. Yet as infants develop through the first year, they begin to babble sounds heard in the home, and foreign sounds begin to drop out. Why?

The first word—which represents *linguistic* speech—is typically spoken between 11 and 13 months, but a range of 8–18 months is normal (Klee & Stokes, 2011). First words tend to be brief, consisting of one or two syllables. Each syllable is likely to consist of a consonant followed by a vowel. Vocabulary acquisition is slow at first. It may take children three or four months to achieve a vocabulary of 10–30 words after the first word is spoken (de Villiers & de Villiers, 1999).

By about 18 months of age, children may be producing up to 50 words. Many of them are quite familiar, such as *no, cookie, mama, hi,* and *eat.* Others, such as *all gone* and *bye-bye,* may not be found in the dictionary, but they function as words. That is, they are used consistently to symbolize the same meaning.

More than half (65 percent) of children's first words make up "general nominals" and "specific nominals" (Hoff, 2006; Nelson, 1973). General nominals are similar to nouns in that they include the names of classes of objects (*car, ball*), animals (*doggy, cat*), and people (*boy, girl*). They also include both personal and relative pronouns (*she, that*). Specific nominals are proper nouns, such as *Daddy* and *Rover.* The attention of infants seems to be captured by movement. Words expressing movement are frequently found in early speech. Of children's first 50 words, the most common are names for people, animals, and objects that move (*Mommy, car, doggy*) or that can be moved (*dolly, milky*), action words (*bye-bye*), a number of modifiers (*big, hot*), and expressive words (*no, hi, oh*) (Tamis-LeMonda et al., 2006).

At about 18 to 22 months of age, there is a rapid burst in vocabulary acquisition (Tamis-LeMonda et al., 2006). The child's expressive vocabulary may increase from 50 to more than 300 words in just a few months. This vocabulary spurt could also be called a naming explosion, because almost 75 percent of the words added during this time are nouns. The rapid pace of vocabulary growth continues through the preschool years, with children acquiring an average of nine new words per day (Hoff, 2006).

Referential and Expressive Styles in Language Development

Some children prefer a referential approach in their language development, whereas others take a more expressive approach (Hoff, 2006; Nelson, 1981). Children who exhibit the **referential language style** use language primarily to label objects in their environments. Their early vocabularies consist mainly of nominals. Children who adopt an **expressive language style** use language primarily as a means for engaging in social interactions. Children with an expressive style use more pronouns and many words involved in social

referential language style Use of language primarily as a means for labelling objects.

expressive language style Use of language primarily as a means for engaging in social interaction.

routines, such as *stop*, *more*, and *all gone*. More children employ an expressive style than a referential style (Tamis-LeMonda et al., 2006), but most use a combination of the styles.

Why do some children prefer a referential style and others an expressive style? It may be that some children are naturally oriented toward objects, whereas others are primarily interested in social relationships. Nelson also found that the parents' ways of teaching children play a role. Some parents focus on labelling objects for children as soon as they notice their vocabularies expanding. Others are more oriented toward social interactions themselves, teaching their children to say *hi*, *please*, and *thank you*.

Overextension

Young children try to talk about more objects than they have words for (not so surprising—so do adults, now and then). To accomplish their linguistic feats, children often extend the meaning of one word to refer to things and actions for which they do not have words (Mayor & Plunkett, 2010). This process is called **overextension**. In classic research, Eve Clark (1973, 1975) studied diaries of infants' language development and found that overextensions are generally based on perceived similarities in function or form between the original object or action and the new one to which the first word is being extended. She provides the example of the word *mooi*, which one child originally used to designate the moon. The child then overextended *mooi* to designate all round objects, including the letter *o* and cookies and cakes.

Overextensions gradually pull back to their proper references as the child's vocabulary and ability to classify objects develop (Cohen & Brunt, 2009; Mayor & Plunkett, 2010). Consider the example of a child who first refers to a dog as a "bowwow." The word *bowwow* then becomes overextended to refer to horses, cats, and cows as well. In effect, *bowwow* comes to mean something akin to *familiar animal*. Next, the child learns to use the word *moo* to refer to cows. But *bowwow* still remains extended to horses and cats. As the child's vocabulary develops, she acquires the word doggy, so dogs and cats may now be referred to with either *bowwow* or *doggy*. Eventually, each animal has one or more correct names.

overextension Use of words in situations in which their meanings become extended or inappropriate.

A CLOSER LOOK | REAL LIFE

Teaching Sign Language to Infants

Jacqueline Turner is a Spanish language interpreter who lives in Oregon. When her daughter Riley was eight months old, she informed her mother that she wanted milk by pumping her fingers against her palm. She communicated her desire for more cereal by touching her fingertips. She also asked for her stuffed animals and a ball by using hand gestures—without saying a word.

Turner had taught Riley signs to communicate her wishes before she could speak. Why teach sign language to a baby who is not deaf? Turner believed that teaching signs to babies helps eliminate the frustration of not being able to verbally communicate.

For both children with normal hearing and deaf children, gesturing tends to develop ahead of words (Guidetti & Nicoladis, 2008). Babies can wave bye-bye to Grandma months before they can talk, for instance. The connection between sign language and the spoken language may

actually have evolved long ago, as evidenced by the relationship between children's actions and their inner, or private, speech (Bernardis et al., 2008). When they play with objects and gesture, their inner language is more complex (Guidetti & Nicoladis, 2008).

A researcher on children's language development, Elizabeth Bates (2004), noted that the development of sign language "has to do with how easily one can imitate and reproduce something with a great big fat hand as opposed to the mini, delicate hundreds of muscles that control the tongue .... You can also see somebody using a hand, which you can't do with a tongue." The areas in the brain that control the mouth and speech and the areas that control the hands and gestures overlap a great deal and develop together (Acredolo & Goodwyn, 2009; Guidetti & Nicoladis, 2008).

Teaching simple gestures, or signs, to babies before they can talk may affect the language and communication

Continued

process (Bernardis et al., 2008). It can also confer a host of related benefits, including increased vocabulary, a deeper parent–child bond, and enhanced self-esteem. Research by Linda Acredolo and Susan Goodwyn (2009) has perhaps drawn the most interest. They found that children in Grade 2 who had been encouraged to use their signing system during the second year had an advantage of 12 IQ points over children who did not use any such system.

Also intriguing has been the work of Joseph Garcia, author of Sign with Your Baby: How to Communicate with Infants Before They Can Speak. Garcia, an American Sign Language and early child development researcher, noticed that the hearing babies of deaf parents could communicate their needs and desires at a much earlier age than children of hearing parents. His research found that through signs, parent–infant communication could begin at eight months, rather than waiting for comprehensible speech to develop at 16–18 months.

Signing can apparently ease a toddler's transition to speaking by reducing the frustration of trying to pronounce words like toothbrush or to express concepts like needing a diaper changed. For instance, before Riley could speak, she used the sign for please to get a favourite toy or f a drink of milk more quickly.

For Turner, signing with a child is as much about empowerment as about communication. It provided Riley, and would provide other children, with another tool to get their needs met.

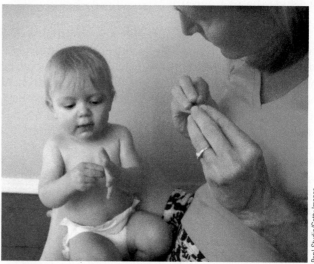

Signs of the Times?
Infants are apparently capable of learning some signs before they can speak. Does teaching infants sign language stimulate intellectual development, as some researchers suggest, or is it too early to sign off on this form of cognitive enrichment?

Reflect The article suggests that teaching one-year-olds to sign before they can speak accelerates their language development. Do you believe it is important to accelerate language development at such an early age? Why or why not?

Development of Sentences: Telegraphing Ideas

QUESTION » **How do infants create sentences?** The infant's first sentences are typically one-word utterances, but these utterances appear to express complete ideas and therefore can be thought of as sentences. Roger Brown (1973) called brief expressions that have the meanings of sentences **telegraphic speech**. When we write text messages, we use principles of syntax to cut out all the unnecessary words. "Home Tuesday" might stand for "I expect to be home on Tuesday." Similarly, only the essential words are used in children's telegraphic speech—in particular, nouns, verbs, and some modifiers.

Mean Length of Utterance

The **mean length of utterance (MLU)** is the average number of morphemes that communicators use in their sentences. As we learned earlier in this chapter, morphemes are the smallest units of meaning in a language. A morpheme may be a whole word or part of a word, such as a prefix or suffix. For example, the word *walked* consists of two morphemes: the verb *walk* and the suffix *-ed*, which changes the verb to the past tense. In Figure 6.7 ■, we see the relationship between chronological age and MLU for three children tracked by Roger Brown (1973, 1977): Lin, Victor, and Sarah.

The patterns of growth in MLU are similar for each child, showing swift upward movement broken by intermittent and brief regressions. Figure 6.7 also shows us something about individual differences. Lin was precocious compared to Victor and Sarah, extending her MLU at much earlier ages. However,

telegraphic speech Type of speech in which only the essential words are used.

mean length of utterance (MLU) The average number of morphemes used in an utterance.

as suggested earlier, the receptive language of all three children would have exceeded their expressive language at any given time. Also, Lin's earlier extension of MLU does not guarantee that she will show more complex expressive language than Victor and Sarah at maturity.

Let us now consider the features of two types of telegraphic speech: the holophrase and two-word sentences.

Holophrases

Holophrases are single words that are used to express complex meanings. For example, *Mama* may be used by the child to signify meanings as varied as "There goes Mama," "Come here, Mama," and "You are Mama." Most children readily teach their parents what they intend by augmenting their holophrases with gestures, intonations, and reinforcers. That is, they act delighted when parents do as requested and howl when they do not.

Infants are likely to combine single words with gestures as they undertake the transition from holophrases to two-word utterances (Tamis-LeMonda et al., 2006). For example, pointing can signify "there" before the word is used.

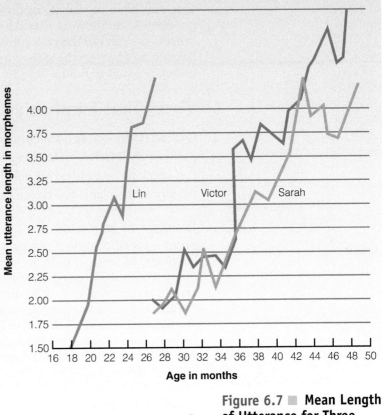

Figure 6.7 ■ Mean Length of Utterance for Three Children
Some children begin speaking earlier than others. However, the mean length of utterance (MLU) increases rapidly once speech begins.
Source: Brown (1973).

Two-Word Sentences

When the child's vocabulary consists of 50–100 words (usually somewhere between 18 and 24 months of age), telegraphic two-word sentences begin to appear (Saffran, 2009; Tamis-LeMonda et al., 2006). In the sentence "That ball," the words *is* and *a* are implied.

Two-word sentences, although brief and telegraphic, show understanding of syntax (Saffran, 2009; Slobin, 2001). The child will say "Sit chair," not "Chair sit," to tell a parent to sit in a chair. The child will say "My shoe," not "Shoe my," to show possession. "Mommy go" means Mommy is leaving, whereas "Go Mommy" expresses the wish for Mommy to go away.

6.6 Theories of Language Development: Can You Make a Houseplant Talk?

Since all normal humans talk but no house pets or house plants do, no matter how pampered, heredity must be involved in language. But since a child growing up in Japan speaks Japanese whereas the same child brought up in California would speak English, the environment is also crucial. Thus, there is no question about whether heredity or environment is involved in language, or even whether one or the other is "more important." Instead, … our best hope [might be] finding out how they interact.

—Steven Pinker (2007)

holophrase A single word that is used to express complex meanings.

Countless billions of children have learned the languages spoken by their parents and have passed them down, with minor changes, from generation to generation. But how do they do so? In discussing this question—and so many others—we refer to the possible roles of nature and nurture. Learning theorists have come down on the side of nurture, and those who point to a basic role for nature are said to hold a nativist view.

Views That Emphasize Nurture

QUESTION » How do learning theorists account for language development? Learning plays an obvious role in language development. Children who are reared in English-speaking homes learn English, not Japanese or Russian. Learning theorists usually explain language development in terms of imitation and reinforcement.

The Role of Imitation

From a social cognitive perspective, parents serve as **models**. Children learn language, at least in part, by observation and imitation. It seems likely that many vocabulary words, especially nouns and verbs (including irregular verbs), are learned by imitation.

But imitative learning does not explain why children spontaneously utter phrases and sentences that they have not heard (Tamis-LeMonda et al., 2006). Parents, for example, are unlikely to model utterances such as "Bye-bye sock" and "All gone Daddy," but children do say them.

And children sometimes steadfastly avoid imitating certain language forms suggested by adults, even when the adults are insistent. Note the following exchange between two-year-old Ben and a (very frustrated) adult (Kuczaj, 1982, p.48):

BEN: *I like these candy. I like they.*

ADULT: *You like them?*

BEN: *Yes, I like they.*

ADULT: *Say them.*

BEN: *Them.*

ADULT: *Say "I like them."*

BEN: *I like them.*

ADULT: *Good.*

BEN: *I'm good. These candy good too.*

ADULT: *Are they good?*

BEN: *Yes. I like they. You like they?*

Ben is not resisting the adult because of obstinacy. He does repeat "I like them" when asked to do so. But when given the opportunity afterward to construct the object *them*, he reverts to using the subjective form *they*. Ben is likely at this period in his development to use his (erroneous) understanding of syntax spontaneously to actively produce his own language, rather than just imitating a model.

models In learning theory, those whose behaviours are imitated by others.

A CLOSER LOOK DIVERSITY

Two-Word Sentences Here, There, and ...

Two-word sentences appear at about the same time in the development of all languages (Slobin, 2001). Also, the sequence of emergence of the types of two-word utterances—for example, first subject-verb ("Mommy go"), then verb-object ("Hit ball"), location ("Ball here"), and possession ("My ball")—is the same in languages as diverse as

Continued

English, Luo (an African tongue), German, Russian, and Turkish. This is an example of the point that language develops in a series of steps that appear to be invariant.

Dan Slobin interprets his findings to mean that the construction of sentences serves specific functions of communication in various languages. Slobin does not argue that there is an innate linguistic structure but rather that basic human processes of cognition, communication, and information processing are found across cultures (Slobin, 2001).

Reflect Which theory of language do Slobin's findings appear to support?

The Role of Reinforcement

B. F. Skinner (1957) conceded that prelinguistic vocalizations such as cooing and babbling may be inborn. But parents reinforce children for babbling that approximates the form of real words, such as *da*, which, in English, resembles *dog* or *daddy*. Children, in fact, do increase their babbling when it results in adults smiling at them, stroking them, and talking in response to their vocalizations. We have seen that as the first year progresses, children babble the sounds of their native tongues with increasing frequency, while foreign sounds tend to drop out. The behaviourist explains this pattern of changing frequencies in terms of reinforcement (of the sounds of the adults' language) and **extinction** (of foreign sounds). An alternative, nonbehavioural explanation is that children actively attend to the sounds in their linguistic environments and are intrinsically motivated to utter them.

From Skinner's perspective, children acquire their early vocabularies through **shaping**. That is, parents require that children's utterances be progressively closer to actual words before they are reinforced. In support of Skinner's position, research has shown that reinforcement accelerates the growth of vocabulary in children, especially children with learning disabilities (August et al., 2005; Kroeger & Nelson, 2006). Skinner viewed multiword utterances as complex stimulus-response chains that are also taught by shaping. As children's utterances increase in length, parents foster correct word order by uttering sentences to their children and reinforcing imitation. As with Ben, when children make grammatical errors, parents recast their utterances correctly. They reinforce the children for repeating them.

But recall Ben's refusal to be shaped into correct syntax. If the reinforcement explanation of language development were sufficient, parents' reinforcement would facilitate children's learning of syntax and pronunciation. We do not have such evidence. For one thing, parents are more likely to reinforce their children for the accuracy, or "truth value," of their utterances than for grammatical correctness (Brown, 1973). Parents, in other words, generally accept the syntax of their children's vocal efforts. The child who points down and says "The grass is purple" is not likely to be reinforced, despite correct syntax. But the enthusiastic child who shows her empty plate and blurts out "I eated it all up" is likely to be reinforced, despite the grammatical incorrectness of *eated*. Research confirms that, although parents tend to expand and rephrase their children's ungrammatical utterances more often than their grammatically correct ones, they do not overtly correct their children's errors (Bohannon & Stanowicz, 1988; Coley, 1993).

Also, selective reinforcement of children's pronunciation can backfire. Children whose parents reward proper pronunciation but correct poor pronunciation develop vocabulary more slowly than children whose parents are more tolerant about pronunciation (Nelson, 1973). TRUTH OR FICTION REVISITED: Actually, the evidence suggests that correcting children's pronunciation may slow their vocabulary development. Instead adults may repeat the correct pronunciations in responding, without having to overtly make a noted correction.

extinction The decrease and eventual disappearance of a response in the absence of reinforcement.

shaping In learning theory, the gradual building of complex behaviour patterns through reinforcement of successive approximations of the target behaviour.

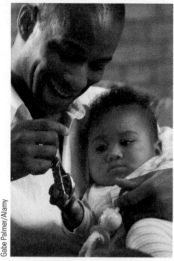

Gabe Palmer/Alamy

Fostering Language Development
Language growth in young children is enhanced when parents and caregivers engage the infant "in conversation" about activities and objects in the environment.

Learning theory also cannot account for the invariant sequences of language development and for children's spurts in acquisition. Even the types of two-word utterances emerge in a consistent pattern in diverse cultures. Although timing differs from child to child, the types of questions used, passive versus active sentences, and so on all emerge in the same order. It is unlikely that parents around the world teach language skills in the same sequence.

On the other hand, there is ample evidence that aspects of the child's language environment influence the development of language. Much of the research in this area has focused on the ways in which adults—especially mothers—interact with their children.

Enhancing Language Development

Studies show that language growth in young children is enhanced when mothers and other adults do the following things (Tamis-LeMonda et al., 2006):

- Use a simplified form of speech known as "infant-directed speech."
- Use questions that engage the child in conversation.
- Respond to the child's expressive language efforts in a way that is "attuned." For example, they relate their speech to the child's utterance by saying, "Yes, your doll is pretty" in response to the child's statement "My doll."
- Join the child in paying attention to a particular activity or toy.
- Gesture to help the child understand what they are saying.
- Describe aspects of the environment occupying the infant's current focus of attention.
- Read to the child.
- Talk to the child a great deal.

Infant-Directed Speech—Of "Yummy Yummy" and "Kitty Cats"

One fascinating way that adults attempt to prompt the language development of young children is through the use of baby talk or infant-directed speech, sometimes referred to as "motherese" (Meltzoff & Brooks, 2009). "Motherese" is actually a limiting term because grandparents, fathers, siblings, and unrelated people, including older children, also use varieties of infant-directed speech when talking to infants (Braarud & Stormark, 2008). Moreover, at least one study found that women (but not men) often talk to their pets as though they were infants (Prato-Previde et al., 2006). Infant-directed speech is used in languages as diverse as Arabic, English, Comanche, Italian, French, German, Xhosa (an African tongue), Japanese, Mandarin Chinese, and even a Thai sign language (Lee & Davis, 2010).

MNStudio/Shutterstock.com

Infant-Directed Speech
Mothers and others tend to speak slowly to infants, with careful enunciation. They also frequently use high-pitched speech and repetition.

Researchers have found that infant-directed speech has the following characteristics (Braarud & Stormark, 2008; Meltzoff & Brooks, 2009):

- Infant-directed speech is spoken more slowly than speech addressed to adults. It is spoken at a higher pitch, and there are distinct pauses between ideas.
- Sentences are brief, and adults make the effort to speak in a grammatically correct manner.
- Sentences are simple in syntax. The focus is on nouns, verbs, and just a few modifiers.

- Key words are put at the ends of sentences and are spoken in a higher and louder voice.
- Facial expression is encouraging (Shepard et al., 2012).
- The diminutive morpheme *y* is frequently added to nouns. *Dad* becomes *Daddy*, and *horse* becomes *horsey*.
- Adults repeat sentences several times, sometimes using minor variations, as in "Show me your nose." "Where is your nose?" "Can you touch your nose?" Adults also repeat children's utterances, often rephrasing them in an effort to expand children's awareness of their expressive opportunities. If the child says, "Baby shoe," the mother may reply, "Yes, that's your shoe. Shall Mommy put the shoe on baby's foot?"
- Infant-directed speech includes a type of repetition called reduplication. *Yummy* becomes *yummy yummy*. *Daddy* may alternate with *Da-da*.
- Much infant-directed speech focuses on naming objects (Meltzoff & Brooks, 2009). Vocabulary is concrete, referring to objects in the immediate environment. For example, stuffed lions may be called "kitties." Purposeful overextension is intended to avoid confusing the child by adding too many new labels.
- Objects may be overdescribed by being given compound labels. Rabbits may become "bunny rabbits," and cats may become "kitty cats." In this way parents may try to be sure that they are connecting with the child by using at least one label that the child will recognize.
- Parents speak for the children, as in "Is baby tired?" "Oh, we're so tired." "We want to take our nap now, don't we?" This parent is pretending to have a two-way conversation with the child. In this way, parents seem to be trying to help their children express themselves by offering children models of sentences they can use later on.
- Users of infant-directed speech stay a step ahead of the child. As children's vocabularies grow and their syntax develops, adults step up their own language levels—remaining just ahead of the child. In this way, adults seem to be encouraging the child to continue to play catch-up.

Thus adults and older children use a variety of strategies to communicate with young children and to draw them out. Does it work? Does infant-directed speech foster language development? Research supports its use. Infants as young as two days old prefer "baby talk," or infant-directed speech, over adult talk (Trevarthen, 2003; Weppelman et al., 2003). The short, simple sentences and high pitch are more likely to produce a response from the child and to enhance vocabulary development than are complex sentences and those spoken in a lower pitch. Children who hear their utterances repeated and recast do seem to learn from the adults who are modelling the new expressions (Trevarthen, 2003). Repetition of children's vocalizations also appears to be one method of reinforcing vocalizing.

Views That Emphasize Nature

QUESTION » What is the nativist view of language development? The nativist view holds that innate or inborn factors cause children to attend to and acquire language in certain ways. From this perspective, children bring an inborn tendency in the form of neurological "prewiring" to language learning (Pinker, 2007).

According to Steven Pinker and Ray Jackendoff (2005), the structures that enable humans to perceive and produce language evolved in bits and pieces. The individuals who possessed these "bits" and "pieces" were more likely to reach maturity and transmit their genes from generation to generation, because communication ability increased their chances of survival.

Psycholinguistic Theory

According to **psycholinguistic theory**, language acquisition involves an interaction between environmental influences—such as exposure to parental speech and reinforcement—and an inborn tendency to acquire language (Clancy & Finlay, 2001). Noam Chomsky (1988, 1990) and some others labelled this innate tendency a **language acquisition device (LAD)**. Evidence for an inborn tendency is found in the universality of human language abilities; in the regularity of the early production of sounds, even among deaf children; and in the invariant sequences of language development, regardless of which language the child is learning (Pinker, 2007).

The inborn tendency primes the nervous system to learn grammar. On the surface, languages differ a great deal in their vocabulary and grammar. Chomsky refers to these elements as the **surface structure** of language. However, the LAD serves children all over the world because languages share what Chomsky refers to as a "universal grammar"—an underlying **deep structure** or set of rules for transforming ideas into sentences. From Chomsky's perspective, children are genetically prewired to attend to language and to deduce the rules for constructing sentences from ideas. Consider an analogy with computers: According to psycholinguistic theory, the universal grammar that resides in the LAD is the basic operating system of the computer, and the particular language that a child learns to use is the word-processing program. **TRUTH OR FICTION REVISITED:** It is apparently true that children are prewired to listen to language in such a way that they come to understand rules of grammar.

Brain Structures Involved in Language

QUESTION » What parts of the brain are involved in language development? Many parts of the brain are involved in language development; however, some of the key biological structures that may provide the basis for the functions of the LAD appear to be based in the left hemisphere of the cerebral cortex for nearly all right-handed people and for two out of three left-handed people (Pinker, 2007).

Although both hemispheres of the brain are involved in the perception of speech, the sounds of speech elicit greater electrical activity in the left hemisphere of newborns than in the right hemisphere, as indicated by the activity of brain waves. In the left hemisphere of the cortex, the two areas most involved in speech are Broca's area and Wernicke's area (Dogil et al., 2002) (see Figure 6.8 ■). Even in the human fetus, Wernicke's area is usually larger in the left hemisphere than in the right. Damage to either area is likely to cause an **aphasia**—that is, a disruption in the ability to understand or produce language.

Broca's area is located near the section of the motor cortex that controls the muscles of the tongue, throat, and other areas of the face that are used when speaking. When Broca's area is damaged, people speak slowly and laboriously, with simple sentences—a pattern known as **Broca's aphasia**. Their ability to understand the speech of others is relatively unaffected, however. Wernicke's area lies near the auditory cortex and is connected to Broca's area by nerve fibres. People

Do Infants Have an Inborn Language Acquisition Device?
According to psycholinguistic theory, humans have an inborn "language acquisition device" that leads to commonalities in language development in all cultures. Babbling, for example, emerges at about the same time everywhere, and at about the same time, infants begin to sound as if they are babbling the sounds that occur in the language spoken in the home. Chomsky also hypothesizes that all languages have a universal grammar, regardless of how different they might seem.

psycholinguistic theory The view that language learning involves an interaction between environmental influences and an inborn tendency to acquire language. The emphasis is on the inborn tendency.

language acquisition device (LAD) In psycholinguistic theory, neural "prewiring" that facilitates the child's learning of grammar.

surface structure The superficial grammatical construction of a sentence.

deep structure The underlying meaning of a sentence.

aphasia A disruption in the ability to understand or produce language.

Broca's aphasia A form of aphasia caused by damage to Broca's area and characterized by slow, laborious speech.

with damage to Wernicke's area may show **Wernicke's aphasia**. Although they usually speak freely and with proper syntax, their abilities to comprehend other people's speech and to think of the words to express their own thoughts are impaired. Thus, Wernicke's area seems to be essential to understanding the relationships between words and their meanings.

A part of the brain called the angular gyrus lies between the visual cortex and Wernicke's area. The angular gyrus "translates" visual information, such as written words, into auditory information (sounds) and sends it on to Wernicke's area. It appears that problems in the angular gyrus can give rise to dyslexia, or serious impairment in reading, because it becomes difficult for the reader to segment words into sounds (Pugh et al., 2000).

The Sensitive Period

QUESTION » **What is meant by a sensitive period for language development?** Numerous researchers have suggested that language learning occurs during one or more **sensitive periods**, which begin at about 18 to 24 months of age and last until puberty (Bedny et al., 2012; Uylings, 2006). During these sensitive periods, neural development (as in the differentiating of brain structures) provides plasticity that facilitates language learning (Bates, 2001). Experience with language also alters the structure of the brain, although the exact relationships have not been discovered (Uylings, 2006).

Evidence for a sensitive period is found in recovery from brain injuries in some people. Injuries to the hemisphere that controls language (usually the left hemisphere) can impair or destroy the ability to speak (Wright et al., 2012). But before puberty, children suffering left-hemisphere injuries frequently recover a good deal of speaking ability. Lenneberg (1967) suggested that in young children, left-hemisphere damage may encourage the development of language functions in the right hemisphere. But adaptation ability wanes in adolescence, when brain tissue has reached adult levels of differentiation.

The best way to determine whether people are capable of acquiring language once they have passed puberty would be to run an experiment in which one or more children were reared in such severe isolation that they were not exposed to language until puberty. Of course, such an experiment could not be run because of ethical and legal barriers.

However, the disturbing case history of a girl named Genie offers insights into the issue of whether there is a sensitive period for language development (Siegal & Surian, 2012). Genie's father locked her in a small room at the age of 20 months and kept her there until she was 13. Her social contacts during this period were limited to her mother, who entered the room only to feed Genie, and to beatings by her father. When Genie was rescued, she weighed only about 27 kilograms, did not speak, was not toilet trained, and could barely stand. Genie was placed in a foster home, where she was exposed to English for the first time in nearly 12 years. Her language development followed the normal sequence of much younger children in a number of ways, but she never acquired the proficiency of children reared under normal circumstances. Five years after her liberation, Genie's language remained largely telegraphic. She still showed significant problems with syntax—for example, failing to reverse subjects and verbs to phrase spontaneous questions. She showed confusion concerning the use of the past tense (adding *-ed* to words) and had difficulty using negative helping verbs such as *isn't* and *haven't*.

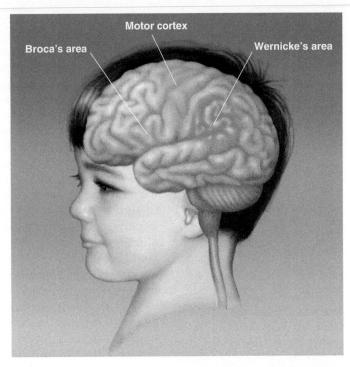

Figure 6.8 ■ Broca's and Wernicke's Areas of the Cerebral Cortex
Broca's area and Wernicke's area of (usually) the left hemisphere are most involved in speech. Damage to either area can produce an aphasia—an impairment in the ability to understand or produce language.

Wernicke's aphasia A form of aphasia caused by damage to Wernicke's area and characterized by impaired comprehension of speech and difficulty in attempting to produce the right word.

sensitive period In linguistic theory, the period from about 18 months to puberty when the brain is thought to be especially capable of learning language because of its plasticity.

CHAPTER 6 INFANCY: COGNITIVE DEVELOPMENT **217**

Genie's language development provides some support for the sensitive-period hypothesis, although her language problems might also be partly attributed to her years of malnutrition and abuse. She may have been intellectually disabled to begin with. Her efforts to acquire English after puberty were clearly laborious, and the results were substandard compared even to the language of many two- and three-year-olds.

Further evidence for the sensitive-period hypothesis is provided by a study of a deaf boy named Simon, who was observed from the ages of two-and-a-half to nine years (Newport, 1992). Researchers reported that Simon signed in **American Sign Language (ASL)** with correct grammar, even though he had been exposed to only grammatically incorrect ASL by his parents and their friends, who also were deaf. Simon's parents and their friends had not learned to sign until they were teenagers. At that age, people often learn languages imperfectly. But Simon showed early mastery of grammatical rules that his parents used incorrectly or not at all. Simon's deduction of these rules on his own supports the view that the tendency to acquire language is inborn, and it also provides evidence that such learning occurs most readily during a sensitive period early in life.

In sum, the development of language in infancy represents the interaction of environmental and biological factors. The child brings a built-in readiness to the task of language acquisition—whereas houseplants and other organisms do not. The child must also have the opportunity to hear spoken language and to interact verbally with others. In the next chapter, we will see how interaction with others affects the social development of the infant.

American Sign Language (ASL) The communication of meaning through the use of symbols that are formed by moving the hands and arms; the language used by some deaf people.

Active Review

15. _____ is the first vocalizing that sounds like human speech.

16. Children with a(n) _____ language style use language mainly to label objects.

17. Children try to talk about more objects than they have words for, which often results in _____ of the meanings of words.

18. _____ are single words that are used to express complex meanings.

19. The sequence of emergence of the different types of two-word utterances is (the same or different?) in diverse languages.

20. _____ theorists explain language development in terms of imitation and reinforcement.

21. According to _____ theory, language acquisition involves an interaction between environmental influences and an inborn tendency to acquire language.

22. Chomsky refers to this inborn tendency as a language _____ device (LAD).

23. Key biological structures that provide a basis for language are based in the (left or right?) hemisphere of the cerebral cortex for most people.

24. The brain areas most involved in speech are Broca's area and _____ area.

Reflect & Relate: Why are so many parents concerned with exactly when their children learn to talk?

Recite an Active Summary

6.1 Cognitive Development: Jean Piaget

What is the sensorimotor stage of cognitive development?

Piaget's sensorimotor stage is the first two years of cognitive development, during which changes are shown by means of sensory and motor activity. The first substage is dominated by the assimilation of stimulation into reflexes. In the second substage, primary circular reactions, infants repeat stimulating actions that occur by chance. In the third substage, secondary circular reactions, patterns of activity are repeated because of their effects. In the fourth substage, infants intentionally coordinate schemes to attain goals. In the fifth substage, tertiary circular reactions, infants purposefully adapt established schemes to specific situations. In the sixth substage, external exploration is replaced by mental exploration.

What is object permanence? How does it develop?

Object permanence is recognition that an object or person continues to exist when it is out of sight. Through the first six months or so, when a screen is placed between an object and an infant, the infant behaves as though the object is no longer there.

What are the strengths and limitations of Piaget's theory of sensorimotor development?

Evidence supports the pattern and sequence of events described by Piaget. However, cognitive development may not be tied to discrete stages as Piaget believed. Piaget also appears to have been incorrect about the ages at which infants develop various concepts.

6.2 Information Processing

How do infants process information?

Two means of doing so are memory and imitation. Older infants are more capable of encoding and retrieving information. Neonates reflexively imitate certain behaviours, such as sticking out the tongue. Infants later show deferred imitation, suggesting that they have mentally represented actions.

6.3 Social Influences on Early Cognitive Development

How do we apply Vygotsky's sociocultural theory to the cognitive development of infants?

Vygotsky stressed that cognitive development involves children's internalizing skilled strategies learned during joint problem solving with more skilled people—a *zone of proximal development*. During infancy, caregivers may provide such a zone by helping children gain skills with age-appropriate materials such as blocks and picture books.

6.4 Individual Differences in Cognitive Functioning among Infants

How do we measure individual differences in the development of cognitive functioning in infants?

Some infants develop cognitive functioning more rapidly than others. The Bayley Scales of Infant Development (BSID) have cognitive and motor domain items that can suggest early signs of sensory or neurological problems.

How well do infant scales predict later intellectual performance?

Certain BSID items predict intellectual skills later in childhood, but overall scores on such scales do not predict school grades accurately.

What is visual recognition memory? How is it used?

Visual recognition memory is the ability to discriminate previously seen objects from novel objects. It moderately predicts IQ scores in later childhood.

6.5 Language Development

What are prelinguistic vocalizations?

Prelinguistic vocalizations do not represent objects or events; they include crying, cooing, and babbling. Children from different cultures initially babble the same sounds.

How does vocabulary develop?

Receptive vocabulary development outpaces expressive vocabulary. The first word typically is spoken between 11 and 13 months of age. It may take another three or four months to achieve a vocabulary of 10–30 words. Children's first words are mostly nominals. Children with a referential language style use language mainly to label objects. Those with an expressive language style mainly seek social interactions. Infants often extend the meaning of a word to refer to things and actions for which they do not have words.

How do infants create sentences?

Infants' early sentences are telegraphic. Two-word sentences show an understanding of syntax. The kinds of two-word sentences are the same among children from diverse linguistic environments.

6.6 Theories of Language Development: Can You Make a Houseplant Talk?

How do learning theorists account for language development?

Learning theorists explain language development in terms of imitation and reinforcement. But children do not imitate sentences that are inconsistent with their grasp of grammar.

What is the nativist view of language development?

The nativist view holds that innate "prewiring" causes children to attend to and acquire language in certain ways. Chomsky asserts that learning language involves the interaction between experience and prewiring.

What parts of the brain are involved in language development?

For most people, key biological structures are based in the left hemisphere: Broca's area and Wernicke's area. Damage to either area may cause a characteristic aphasia.

What is meant by a *sensitive period* for language development?

Lenneberg proposed that plasticity of the brain provides a sensitive period for learning language that begins at about 18–24 months and lasts until puberty.

Key Terms

scheme   190
assimilation   190

accommodation   190
primary circular reactions   191

secondary circular reactions   191
tertiary circular reactions   192

Active Learning Resources

Go to *Voyages in Development's* CourseMate at **www
.nelsonbrain.com**, where you will find an interactive
eBook, flashcards, Pre-Lecture Quizzes, Section Quizzes,
Exam Practice, videos, and more.

Major Topics

INFANCY:
Social and Emotional Development

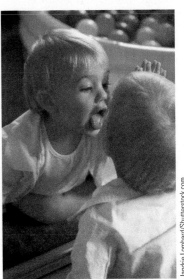

7

Truth or Fiction?

Any parent who has tried to complete a task (e.g., fill out federal tax returns, bake a soufflé, soothe another child) with a young child around can appreciate Spencer Rathus's personal account of the challenges of parenting his two-year-old daughter.

> At the age of two, my daughter Allyn almost succeeded at preventing publication of a book on which I was working. When I locked myself into my study, she positioned herself outside the door and called, "Daddy, oh Daddy." At other times she would bang on the door or cry. When I would give in (several times a day) and open the door, she would run in and say, "I want you to pick up me," and hold out her arms or climb into my lap. How would I ever finish the book?

In Rathus's case he had several options available to him. For example, he could write outside the home. But this solution had the drawback of distancing him from his family. Another solution was to ignore his daughter and let her cry. If he refused to reinforce crying, crying would become extinguished. (And research does suggest that ignoring crying discourages it [van Ijzendoorn & Hubbard, 2000].) There was only one problem with this solution. He didn't *want* to extinguish her efforts to get to him. Attachment, you see, is a two-way street.

Attachment is one of the key issues in the social and personality development of the infant. If this chapter had been written by the poet John Donne, it might have begun "No children are islands unto themselves." Children come into this world fully dependent on others for their survival and well-being.

This chapter is about some of the consequences of that absolute dependency. It is about the social relationships between infants and caregivers and about the development of the bonds of attachment that usually—but not always—bind them. It is about the behaviours of infants that prompt social and emotional responses from adults and about the behaviours of adults that prompt social and emotional responses from infants. It is also about infants' unique and different ways of reacting socially and emotionally.

Let us first consider the issue of attachment and the factors that contribute to its development. Next we examine some circumstances that interfere with the development of attachment: social deprivation, child abuse, and autism. Then we turn to a discussion of day care. Finally, we look at the development of emotions and personality in infancy, including the self-concept, temperament, and gender differences.

7.1 Attachment: Bonds That Endure

QUESTION » What is meant by "attachment"? **Attachment** is what most people refer to as affection or love. Mary Ainsworth (1989), one of the preeminent researchers on attachment, defines attachment as an emotional tie formed between one animal or person and another specific individual. Attachment keeps organisms together and tends to endure. John Bowlby believes that attachment is essential to the very survival of the infant (Ainsworth & Bowlby, 1991; Bowlby, 1988). He argues that babies are born with behaviours—crying, smiling, clinging—that elicit caregiving from parents.

Babies and children try to maintain contact with caregivers to whom they are attached. They engage in eye contact, pull and tug at them, and ask to be picked up. When they cannot maintain contact, infants show behaviours suggestive of **separation anxiety**. They may thrash about, fuss, cry, screech, or whine. Parents who are seeking a few minutes to attend to their own needs sometimes see these behaviours as manipulative, and in a sense, they are. That is, children learn that the behaviours achieve their desired ends. But what is wrong with "manipulating" a loved one to end distress?

Patterns of Attachment

QUESTION » What does it mean for a child to be "secure" or "insecure"? Mary Ainsworth and her colleagues (1978) identified various patterns of attachment. Broadly, infants show either **secure attachment** or insecure attachment. Ainsworth and other investigators have found that most infants, older children, and adults in North America are securely attached (Beebe et al., 2010; Zeanah et al., 2011).

Think of security in terms of what infants do. Ainsworth developed the strange-situation method as a way of measuring attachment (see Figure 7.1 ■). In this method, an infant is exposed to a series of separations and reunions with a caregiver (usually the mother) and a stranger who is a confederate of the researchers. In the strange situation, securely attached infants mildly protest their mother's departure, seek interaction upon reunion, and are readily comforted by her.

Hold on! This is science, and in the science of development we speak of insecurity as "insecure attachment." The two major types of insecure attachment are **avoidant attachment** and **ambivalent/resistant attachment**. Babies who show avoidant attachment are least distressed by their mothers' departure. They play without fuss when alone and ignore their mothers upon reunion. Ambivalent/resistant babies are the most emotional. They show severe signs of distress when their mothers leave and show ambivalence upon reunion by alternately clinging to their mothers and pushing them away. Additional categories of insecure attachment have been proposed, including **disorganized–disoriented attachment**. Babies exhibiting this pattern appear dazed, confused, or disoriented. They may show contradictory behaviours, such as moving toward the mother while looking away from her.

Mary D. Salter Ainsworth

Robert Marvin

attachment An affectional bond between individuals characterized by a seeking of closeness or contact and a show of distress upon separation.

separation anxiety Fear of being separated from a target of attachment, usually a primary caregiver.

secure attachment A type of attachment characterized by showing mild distress at leave-takings, seeking nearness to an attachment figure, and being readily soothed by this figure.

avoidant attachment A type of insecure attachment characterized by apparent indifference to the leave-takings of, and reunions with, an attachment figure.

ambivalent/resistant attachment A type of insecure attachment characterized by severe distress at the leave-takings of, and ambivalent behaviour at reunions with, an attachment figure.

disorganized–disoriented attachment A type of insecure attachment characterized by dazed and contradictory behaviours toward an attachment figure.

a
b
c
d

Mary D. S. Ainsworth via Bob Marvin

Figure 7.1 ■ The Strange Situation

These historic photos show a 12-month-old child in the strange situation. In (a), the child plays with toys, glancing occasionally at mother. In (b), the stranger approaches with a toy. While the child is distracted, mother leaves the room. In (c), mother returns after a brief absence. The child crawls to her quickly and clings to her when picked up. In (d), the child cries when mother again leaves the room. What pattern of attachment is this child showing?

Research indicates that securely attached infants and toddlers are happier, more sociable with unfamiliar adults, and more cooperative with parents; get along better with peers; and are better adjusted in school than insecurely attached children (Borelli et al., 2010; George et al., 2010). Insecure attachment in infancy predicts psychological disorders during adolescence (Lee & Hankin, 2009; Sroufe, 1998; Steele, 2005). Infants use the mother as a secure base from which to venture out and explore the environment (Belsky, 2006a). Secure attachment is also related to experiencing fewer negative emotions toward unfamiliar people (Mikulincer & Shaver, 2001), and it encourages children to explore interactions with new people. TRUTH OR FICTION REVISITED: Thus, infants who are securely attached to their mothers are likely to "stray" from them in the sense that they use them as a secure base for exploration of the environment.

Securely attached toddlers also have longer attention spans, are less impulsive, and are better at solving problems (Granot & Mayseless, 2001; Vando et al., 2008). At ages five and six, securely attached children are better liked by peers and teachers, are more competent, are less aggressive, and have fewer behaviour problems than insecurely attached children (Belsky, 2006a; Coleman, 2003).

The Attachment Q-set (AQS) is another measure that can be used to assess child attachment behaviour (Waters, 1995). The AQS consists of 90 individual statements that capture a range of child behaviour during interactions with their primary caregiver (e.g., "When child finds something new to play with, he carries it to mother or shows it to her from across the room"). Observers will place q-set items into nine piles of ten items each, ranging from *most characteristic* (pile 9) to *most uncharacteristic* (pile 1). Alternatively, to assess mothers' sensitivity, the Maternal Behavior Q-set (MBQS) may be used (Pederson, Moran, & Bento, 1999). The MBQS also consists of 90 statements regarding a mother's behaviour with her child, specifically behaviour reflecting reading of child cues and responding promptly and appropriately to those signals (e.g., "Interprets cues correctly according to baby's response"). Similar to the AQS, each statement is typed on a card and the cards are sorted into nine piles of ten statements each according to the degree to which they describe the mother. The cards are then sorted by the observers.

From Rathus. *Childhood and Adolescence,* 5E.
© 2014 South-Western, a part of Cengage Learning, Inc. Reproduced by permission. www.cengage.com/permissions

Establishing Attachment

QUESTION » What are the roles of the parents in the formation of bonds of attachment? Attachment can be used as a measure of the quality of care that infants receive (Belsky, 2006a; Sullivan et al., 2011). The parents of securely attached infants are more affectionate, cooperative, and predictable in their caregiving. They respond more sensitively to their infants' smiles, cries, and other social behaviours (Bigelow et al., 2010; Xue et al., 2010).

Researchers find evidence for the "intergenerational transmission of attachment" from mother to child (Hautamakl et al., 2010; Kazui et al., 2000). For example, the children of secure mothers showed the most secure patterns of attachment themselves, as assessed by various means. The children of secure mothers interacted positively both with their mothers and with strangers, so their pattern of attachment provided a secure base for exploration.

Providing economically stressed families with support services can enhance their involvement with their infants and increase secure attachment. In one study, low-income women received child-care information and social support from home visitors during pregnancy and through the child's third year (Spieker et al., 2005). The visitors first worked with the mothers on how they conceptualized their fetuses. Following childbirth, the home visitors helped the mothers accurately interpret their babies' cues and respond to them. They also encouraged mother–infant interaction and play, which by and large resulted in appropriate maternal responsiveness and secure attachment between infant and mother.

Insecure attachment occurs more often among infants whose mothers are mentally ill or abusive (Cicchetti et al., 2006; McCartney et al., 2004). It is found more often among infants whose mothers are slow to meet their needs or meet them coldly (Steele et al., 2003).

Siblings tend to develop similar attachment relationships with their mother (van IJzendoorn et al., 2000; O'Connor et al., 2011). The IJzendoorn study pooled data on sibling attachment from research groups in the United States, the Netherlands, and Canada to form 138 pairs of siblings. Children's security of attachment was assessed with the strange-situation procedure at 12–14 months. Maternal sensitivity to infants' needs was also observed. Broad sibling attachment relationships with the mother were found to be significantly alike (secure or insecure, but not necessarily the same kinds of insecurity). It was also found that siblings of the same gender are more likely to form similar attachment relationships with their mother than are girl–boy pairs. Mothers, that is, may behave differently with daughters and sons.

Although it is tempting to seek the sources of attachment in caregivers' behaviour and personalities, that is not the whole story. Security is also connected with the baby's temperament (Belsky, 2006a; Solmeyer & Feinberg, 2011). Babies who are more active and irritable and who display more negative emotion are more likely to develop insecure attachment. Such babies may elicit parental behaviours that are not conducive to the development of secure attachment. For example, mothers of children who may have difficulties self-soothing or settling down are less responsive to their children and report that they feel less emotionally close to them (Alink et al., 2008; Morrell & Steele, 2003). Caregivers respond to babies' behaviour, just as the babies respond to caregivers' behaviour. The processes of attachment are a two-way street.

Involvement of Fathers

TRUTH OR FICTION REVISITED: It is true that you can predict how strongly babies are attached to their fathers if you know how many diapers the fathers change each week. Gail Ross and her colleagues (1975) found that the more diapers the father changed, the stronger the attachment. There is no magical connection between diapers and love, but the number of diapers the father changes roughly reflects his involvement in child rearing.

How involved is the average father with his children? The brief answer in developed nations is more so than in the past. Recent census data (Statistics Canada, 2012) reports that 79.9 percent of Canadian children under the age of 14 live in two-parent homes (married or common law). Gender roles are blurring to some degree, and fathers, like mothers, can rear infants competently and sensitively (Grossmann et al., 2002). Mothers' and fathers' parenting contributes in similar *and* distinct ways to the promotion of children's optimal social and emotional outcomes (Grossmann et al., 2008; Newland & Coyl, 2010; Paquette & Brigas, 2010). Decades of research provide substantial evidence that responsive maternal involvement promotes children's positive social and emotional outcomes (Kiernan & Huerta, 2008). Early maternal sensitivity (warmth, responsiveness) is strongly associated with positive cognitive and behavioural outcomes in early childhood (Martin et al., 2010; Mattanah et al., 2005; NICHD Early Childcare Research Network, 2001). As well, engaging and stimulating maternal behaviours are associated with positive cognitive (Fagot & Gauvain, 1997; Hubbs-Tait et al., 2002) and behavioural outcomes (Zaslow et al., 2006). Overwhelmingly, most research has focused on maternal and not paternal patterns of parenting, thus our knowledge about father's impact on youngsters' social and emotional outcomes is largely derived from mother–child relationships (Downer, 2007; John & Halliburton, 2010). Conceptually and practically, one reason for taking a broader approach to studying parenting is that multiple, significant adults are often involved in socializing children. The role of fathers in the family system has evolved in recent decades; North American statistics indicate increased father involvement in primary-care activities (Marshall, 2006; Pleck, 2010). Additionally, the existing literature on fathers indicates that they uniquely influence child outcomes (Flouri, 2005; Lamb & Lewis, 2010; McWayne et al., 2013). In fact, fathers' parenting (warm, autonomy supportive) as well as strategies such as responsiveness and stimulation favours positive behavioural and cognitive child outcomes above and beyond mothers' parenting (Grossman et al., 2002; NICHD Early Childcare Research Network, 2005). Other studies have shown that father–child interactions differ qualitatively and quantitatively from mother–child interactions (Lucassen et al., 2011; Madigan et al., 2013). Mothers engage in far more interactions with their infants. Most fathers spend much less time on basic child-care tasks, such as feeding and diaper changing, than mothers do. Fathers are more likely to play with their children than to feed or clean them (Lucassen et al., 2011); however, father roles are gradually changing to reflect broader socio-economic changes (Paquette, Coyl-Shepperd, & Newland, 2013). Fathers more often than mothers engage in physical rough-and-tumble play, such as tossing their babies into the air and poking them. Mothers are more likely to play games like patty-cake and peekaboo and to play games involving toys (Lucassen et al., 2011).

Blend Images - Mike Kemp/Getty Images

Fathers and Attachment: The "Diaper Index"
The number of diapers a father changes reflects his involvement in child rearing. Children develop strong attachments to fathers as well as mothers, especially if the father interacts positively and affectionately with the child.

How strongly, then, do infants become attached to their fathers? The answer depends on the quality of the time that the father spends with the baby (R. A. Thompson et al., 2003), as well as whether fathers are present in the home and have contact with their offspring. The more affectionate the interaction between father and infant, the stronger the attachment (Lucassen et al., 2011). Infants under stress still seek out their mothers more than their fathers (Lamb et al., 1992). But when observed at their natural activities in the home and other familiar settings, they seek proximity and contact with their fathers about as often as with their mothers.

These parent–child interactions are dependent upon cultural practices. Canada and many countries nowadays are multicultural nations, so it is important to acknowledge that there is a wide variety of parent–child interactions beyond the typical western styles of interactions.

Stability of Attachment

Patterns of attachment tend to persist when care-giving conditions remain consistent (Beebe et al., 2010; Stupica et al., 2011). But attachment patterns can change when child care changes. Egeland and Sroufe (1981) followed a number of infants who were severely neglected and others who received high-quality care from 12 to 18 months of age. Attachment patterns remained stable (secure) for infants who received fine care. However, many neglected infants changed from insecurely to securely attached over the six-month period, sometimes because of a relationship with a supportive family member, sometimes because home life grew less tense. Children can also become less securely attached to caregivers when the quality of home life deteriorates (Levendosky et al., 2011).

Children adopted at various ages can become securely attached to adoptive parents (Niemann & Weiss, 2011; Pace & Zavattini, 2011). Children show resilience in their social and emotional development. Early insecurities can be overcome.

Early attachment patterns tend to endure into middle childhood, adolescence, and even adulthood (Ammaniti et al., 2005; Karavasilis et al., 2003). As Erik Erikson (1963) argued in *Childhood and Society*, positive relationships with caregivers may set the stage for positive relationships throughout life.

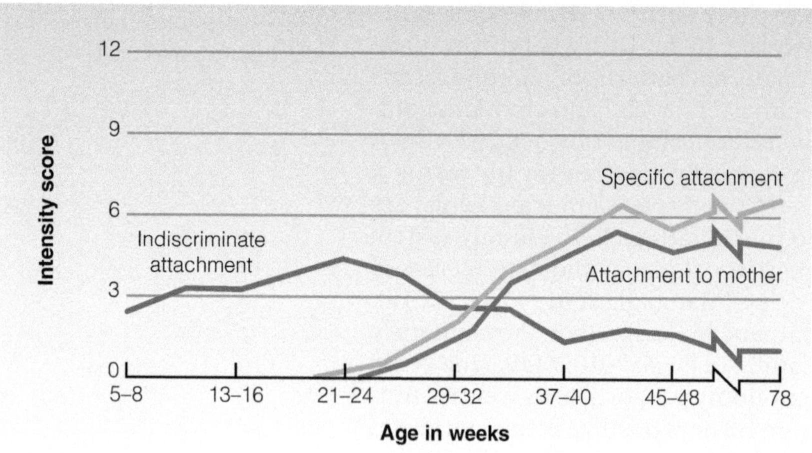

Stages of Attachment

QUESTION » What did Mary Ainsworth learn about the stages of attachment? Cross-cultural studies by Ainsworth (1967) and others have led to a theory of stages of attachment. In one study, Ainsworth tracked the attachment behaviours of Ugandan infants. Over a nine-month period, she noted their efforts to maintain contact with the mother, their protests when separated, and their use of the mother as a base for exploring the environment. At first, the Ugandan infants showed **indiscriminate attachment**. That is, they showed no particular preferences for the mother or another familiar caregiver. Specific attachment to the mother, as evidenced by separation anxiety and other behaviours, began to develop at about four months of age and grew to be intense by about seven months. Fear of strangers developed one or two months later.

In another study, shown in Figure 7.2 ■, Scottish infants showed indiscriminate attachment during the first six months or so after birth (Schaffer & Emerson, 1964). Then indiscriminate attachment waned. Specific attachments to the mother and other familiar caregivers intensified, as demonstrated by the

indiscriminate attachment The display of attachment behaviours toward any person.

Figure 7.2 ■ The Development of Attachment
During the first six months, infants tend to show indiscriminate attachment. Indiscriminate attachment then wanes while specific attachments grow intense and remain at high levels. Fear of strangers develops a month or so after the intensity of specific attachments begins to blossom. Adapted from Schaffer & Emerson (1964).

appearance of separation anxiety, and remained at high levels through the age of 18 months. **TRUTH OR FICTION REVISITED:** Fear of strangers, which is a normal part of the development of attachment, occurred a month or so after the intensity of specific attachments began to mushroom. Thus, in both this and the Ugandan study, fear of strangers followed separation anxiety and the development of specific attachments by a number of weeks.

Bowlby (1969) along with Ainsworth and her colleagues (1978) identified the following four phases of attachment:

1. The **initial-preattachment phase** lasts from birth to about three months and is characterized by indiscriminate attachment.

2. The **attachment-in-the-making phase** occurs at about three or four months and is characterized by preference for familiar figures.

3. The **clear-cut-attachment phase** occurs at about six or seven months and is characterized by intensified dependence on the primary caregiver, usually the mother.

4. Formation of a **reciprocal-relationship** (18 months to two years and onward) and is characterized by a better understanding of parents' comings and goings and ability to predict their return.

Most infants have more than one adult caregiver, however, and are likely to form multiple attachments—to the father, day-care providers, grandparents, and other caregivers, as well as to the mother. In most cultures, single attachments are the exception, not the rule.

Theories of Attachment

QUESTIONS » What are the various theories of attachment? How does each emphasize nature or nurture in its explanation of the development of attachment? Attachment, like so many other behaviour patterns, seems to develop as a result of the interaction of nature and nurture.

Cognitive View of Attachment

The cognitive view of attachment focuses on the contention that an infant must have developed some concept of object permanence before specific attachment becomes possible. In other words, if caregivers are to be missed when absent, the infant must perceive that they continue to exist. We have seen that infants tend to develop specific attachments at about the age of six or seven months. In support of the cognitive view, recall that rudimentary object permanence concerning physical objects develops somewhat earlier (see Chapter 6).

Behavioural View of Attachment: Caregiver as Reinforcer

Early in the 20th century, behaviourists argued that attachment behaviours are learned through conditioning. Caregivers feed their infants and tend to their other physiological needs. Thus, infants associate their caregivers with gratification and learn to approach them to meet their needs. From this perspective, a caregiver becomes a conditioned reinforcer.

Psychoanalytic Views of Attachment: Caregiver as Love Object

Psychoanalytic theorists view the development of attachment somewhat differently from behaviourists. The caregiver, usually the mother, becomes not just a "reinforcer" but also a love object that forms the basis for all later attachments.

In both the psychoanalytic and behaviourist views, the caregiver's role in gratifying the child's needs is crucial. Freud emphasized the importance of oral activities, such as eating, in the first year. Freud believed that the infant becomes emotionally attached to the mother during this time because she is the primary satisfier of the infant's needs for food and sucking.

initial-preattachment phase The first phase in the formation of bonds of attachment, lasting from birth to about three months of age and characterized by indiscriminate attachment.

attachment-in-the-making phase The second phase in the development of attachment, occurring at three or four months of age and characterized by preference for familiar figures.

clear-cut-attachment phase The third phase in the development of attachment, occurring at six or seven months of age and characterized by intensified dependence on the primary caregiver.

reciprocal-relationship phase The fourth phase in the development of attachment, occurring at 18 months to two years and onwards, and characterized by less separation protests and a better understanding of relationship duration beyond the immediate.

We will revisit Erik Erikson's theory of psychosocial development in later chapters, but the first two psychosocial stages of his developmental lifespan theory are pertinent to understanding attachment as well as self-concept (see page 253). Erikson described psychosocial development as a series of eight stages (listed in Chapter 1), and at each stage a particular challenge needs to be overcome. If these challenges are not properly resolved, they are likely to persist or cause problems. The two stages that apply to infancy and toddlerhood are

- Stage 1—trust versus mistrust (infancy)
- Stage 2—autonomy versus shame and doubt (toddler years)

The first stage (trust versus mistrust) is relevant to attachment theory in that it is the stage when infants learn whether or not they can trust the adults in their environment. Babies either learn that the world is a safe and predictable place (i.e., their primary needs are met), or they learn to mistrust their environment because their needs are not being met or are inconsistently dealt with. Erikson believed that the first year is critical for developing a sense of trust in the mother, which fosters attachment. Erikson wrote that the mother's general sensitivity to the child's needs, not just the need for food, fosters the development of trust and attachment.

The Harlows' View of Attachment: The Caregiver as a Source of Contact Comfort

Harry and Margaret Harlow (1966) conducted a series of classic experiments to demonstrate that feeding is not as critical to the attachment process as Freud suggested. In one study, the Harlows placed rhesus monkey infants in cages with two surrogate mothers (see Figure 7.3 ■). One "mother" was made from wire mesh, from which a baby bottle was extended. The other surrogate mother was made of soft, cuddly terry cloth. Infant monkeys spent most of their time clinging to the cloth mother, even though she did not offer food. The Harlows concluded that monkeys—and perhaps humans—have a need for **contact comfort** that is as basic as the need for food.

Harlow and Zimmerman (1959) found that a surrogate mother made of cloth could also serve as a comforting base from which an infant monkey could

contact comfort The pleasure derived from physical contact with another; a hypothesized need or drive for physical contact with another.

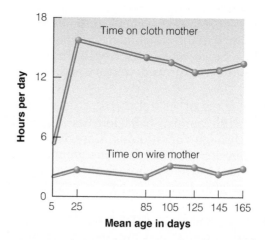

Figure 7.3 ■ Attachment in Infant Monkeys
Although this rhesus monkey infant is fed by the wire "mother," it spends most of its time clinging to the soft, cuddly, terry cloth "mother." It knows where to get a meal, but contact comfort is apparently more important than food in the development of attachment in infant monkeys (and infant humans?).
Adapted from Harlow & Harlow (1966), © Cengage Learning 2014.

explore its environment (see Figure 7.4 ■). Toys such as stuffed bears were placed in cages with infant rhesus monkeys and their surrogate mothers. When the infants were alone or had wire surrogate mothers for companions, they cowered in fear as long as the "bear monster" was present. But when the cloth mothers were present, the infants clung to them for a while and then explored the intruding "monster." With human infants, too, the bonds of mother–infant attachment appear to provide a secure base from which infants feel encouraged to explore their environments.

Ethological View of Attachment: Smiling and Imprinting

Ethologists note that for many animals, attachment is an inborn fixed action pattern (FAP). The FAP of attachment, like other FAPs, is theorized to occur in the presence of a species-specific releasing stimulus. According to John Bowlby, one component of the FAP of attachment in humans—and its releasing stimulus—is a baby's smile in response to a human voice or face (Ainsworth & Bowlby, 1991; Bowlby, 1988). Bowlby proposed that the baby's smile helps ensure survival by eliciting affection from caregivers. By two to three months of age, the human face begins to elicit a **social smile** in infants (Emde et al., 1976). The development of smiling seems to follow the same sequence throughout the world (Werner, 1988).

In many nonhuman animals, the FAP of attachment apparently occurs during a critical period of life. If it does not occur then, it may never do so. During this period, young animals can form an instinctive attachment to caregivers if the releasing stimuli are present. Waterfowl become attached to the first moving object they encounter during this period. The image of the moving object seems to become "imprinted" on the young animal, so this process is termed *imprinting*.

Ethologist Konrad Lorenz (1962, 1981) became well known when pictures of his "family" of goslings were made public (see Figure 7.5 ■). How did Lorenz acquire his family? He was present when the goslings hatched and during their critical period, and he allowed them to follow him. The critical period for geese and ducks begins when they first engage in locomotion and ends when they develop a fear of strangers. The goslings followed Lorenz persistently, ran to him when frightened, honked with distress at his departure, and tried to overcome barriers placed between them. If you substitute crying for honking, it all sounds rather human.

Figure 7.4 ■ Security

With its terry cloth surrogate mother nearby, this infant rhesus monkey apparently feels secure enough to explore the "bear monster" placed in its cage. But infants with wire surrogate mothers or no mother all cower in a corner when such "monsters" are introduced.

social smile A smile that occurs in response to a human voice or face.

Ethology, Ainsworth, and Bowlby

Now let us return full circle to Mary Ainsworth and John Bowlby (1991). At the beginning of a major retrospective article, they wrote that "the distinguishing characteristic of the theory of attachment that we have jointly developed is that it is an ethological approach to personality development." The theoretical aspects of their work developed almost by accident and have a broad base in the psychological and biological perspectives of their day.

Bowlby intended his contribution as an up-to-date version of psychoanalytic object-relations theory [developed largely by

OBSERVING CHILDREN, UNDERSTANDING OURSELVES

The Social Smile

The development of social smiling is another "endearing" quality of infants that solidifies the caregiver–infant bonds of attachment.

Is this infant smiling intentionally in reaction to another person, or is the smile instinctive? At what age do babies begin to show a social smile? What do researchers think a baby's facial expressions reflect?

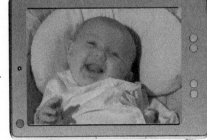

From Rathus. *Childhood and Adolescence*, 5E. © 2014 South-Western, a part of Cengage Learning, Inc. Reproduced by permission. www.cengage.com/permissions

Figure 7.5 ■ Imprinting: A Source of Attachment in Ethological Theory
Quite a following? Konrad Lorenz may not look like Mommy to you, but these goslings became attached to him because he was the first moving object they perceived and followed. This type of attachment process is referred to as imprinting.

Margaret Mahler], compatible with contemporary ethology [e.g., Lorenz] and evolution theory [e.g., Charles Darwin], supported by research, and helpful to clinicians in understanding and treating child and adult patients. Nevertheless, it was developmental psychologists rather than clinicians who first adopted attachment theory.

—Ainsworth & Bowlby (1991)

Yet theirs is not the attachment theory of Konrad Lorenz. True, there are what Bowlby believed to be "releasing stimuli," such as the human face and the crying, smiling, and clinging of infants. But caregiving in humans is largely learned, not inborn. Their ethological perspective is also informed by Bowlby's observations of rhesus monkeys (Suomi, 2005). Children and infants of many other species also try to maintain contact with caregivers to whom they have grown attached. When they cannot maintain contact, they show signs of distress—honking and flapping about in geese, whining and barking in dogs, crying and fussing in children.

Ainsworth and Bowlby (1991) wrote that the critical period for attachment in humans is extended for months or years (Upton & Sullivan, 2010). It involves learning and perceptual and cognitive processes. The type of attachment that develops is related to the quality of the caregiver–infant relationship. Caregiving itself and infant responsiveness, such as infant smiling, appear to spur the development of attachment. Theories of attachment are reviewed in Concept Review 7.1.

Concept Review 7.1 | Theories of Attachment

Theory	Characteristics
Cognitive theory (proponent: Alan Sroufe)	• Emotional development is connected with and relies on cognitive development. • Infant must have developed object permanence before attachment to a specific other becomes possible. • Infant must be able to discriminate familiar people from strangers to develop fear of strangers.
Behaviourism (proponent: John B. Watson)	• Caregiver is a conditioned reinforcer; attachment behaviours are learned through conditioning. • Caregivers meet infants' physiological needs; thus, infants associate caregivers with gratification. • Feelings of gratification associated with meeting needs generalize into feelings of security when the caregiver is present.
Psychoanalytic theory (proponents: Sigmund Freud, Erik Erikson, Margaret Mahler)	• Caregiver is a love object who forms the basis for future attachments. • Infant becomes attached to the mother during infancy because she primarily satisfies the infant's needs for food and sucking (Freud). • First year is critical in developing a sense of trust in the mother, which, in turn, fosters feelings of attachment (Erikson).
Contact comfort (proponents: Harry and Margaret Harlow)	• Caregiver is a source of contact comfort. • Experiments with rhesus monkeys suggest that contact comfort is more crucial to attachment than feeding is.
Ethological theory (proponents: Konrad Lorenz, Mary Ainsworth, John Bowlby)	• Attachment is an inborn fixed action pattern (FAP) that occurs in the presence of a species-specific releasing stimulus during a critical period of development (Lorenz).

Concept Review 7.1 (Continued)

Theory

Characteristics

- Waterfowl become attached to the first moving object they encounter (Lorenz).
- The image of the moving object becomes "imprinted" on the young animal (Lorenz).
- Caregiving in humans is elicited by infants' cries of distress (Bowlby).
- The human face is a releasing stimulus that elicits a baby's smile (Bowlby).
- Smiling helps ensure survival by eliciting caregiving and feelings of affection (Bowlby).
- Attachment in humans is a complex process that continues for months or years (Ainsworth).
- The quality of attachment is related to the quality of the caregiver–infant relationship (Ainsworth).
- Attachment in humans occurs in stages or phases (Ainsworth):

1. The initial-preattachment phase: birth to about three months; indiscriminate attachment
2. The attachment-in-the-making phase: three or four months; preference for familiar figures
3. The clear-cut-attachment phase: six or seven months; intensified dependence on the primary caregiver
4. The reciprocal-relationship phase: 18 months to two years and onward; characterized by a better understanding of parents' comings and goings and ability to predict their return

Active Review

1. Ainsworth defines _____ as an affectional tie that is formed between one animal or person and another specific individual.

2. One of Ainsworth's contributions to the field of child development is the _____ method of measuring attachment.

3. Broadly, infants have either secure attachment or _____ attachment.

4. Securely attached infants use the caregiver as a secure base from which to _____ the environment.

5. Ainsworth's study of Ugandan infants found that they at first show _____ attachment.

6. From the _____ perspective, a caregiver becomes a conditioned reinforcer.

7. The Harlows' research with monkeys suggests that _____ comfort is a key source of attachment.

8. Lorenz believed that attachment is an inborn _____ action pattern (FAP).

Reflect & Relate: To which caregiver are you most attached? Why?

7.2 When Attachment Fails

What happens when children are reared in group settings, such as some orphanages, where they have little or no contact with parents or other caregivers? What happens when parents neglect or abuse their children? In both cases, children's attachments may be impaired. Attachment may also fail in some children because of the development of autism spectrum disorders (ASDs). In this section, we consider the effect of social deprivation, child abuse, and ASDs on the development of attachment.

Social Deprivation

QUESTION » **What are the effects of social deprivation?** Studies of children reared in institutions where they receive little social stimulation from caregivers are limited in that they are correlational. In other words, family factors that led to the children's placement in institutions may also have contributed to their developmental problems. Ethical considerations prevent us from conducting experiments in which we randomly assign children to social deprivation. However, experiments of this kind have been undertaken with rhesus monkeys, and the results are consistent with those of the correlational studies of children. Let us first examine these animal experiments and then turn to the correlational research involving children.

Experiments with Monkeys

The Harlows and their colleagues conducted studies of rhesus monkeys that were "reared by" wire-mesh and terry-cloth surrogate mothers. In later studies, rhesus monkeys were reared without even this questionable "social" support. They were reared without seeing any other animal, whether monkey or human.

The Harlows (Harlow et al., 1971) found that rhesus infants reared in this most solitary confinement later avoided contact with other monkeys. They did not engage in the characteristic playful chasing and romping. Instead, they cowered in the presence of others and failed to respond to them. Nor did they attempt to fend off attacks by other monkeys. Rather, they sat in the corner, clutching themselves and rocking back and forth. Females who later bore children tended to ignore or abuse them.

Can the damage done by social deprivation be overcome? When monkeys deprived for six months or longer are placed with younger, three- to four-month-old females for a couple of hours a day, the younger monkeys make efforts to initiate social interaction with their deprived elders (see Figure 7.6 ■). Many of the deprived monkeys begin to play with the youngsters after a few weeks, and many of them eventually expand their social contacts to other rhesus monkeys of various ages (Suomi et al., 1972). Perhaps of greater interest is the related finding that socially withdrawn four- and five-year-old children make gains in their social and emotional development when they are provided with younger playmates (Furman et al., 1979; Rubin & Coplan, 2010).

Studies with Children

We cannot run on children experiments of the sort we have run with monkeys. Take a moment to consider why this is so. What practical problems would

Figure 7.6 ■ Monkey Therapists

In the left-hand photo, a three- to four-month-old rhesus monkey "therapist" tries to soothe a monkey that was reared in social isolation. The deprived monkey remains withdrawn. She clutches herself into a ball and rocks back and forth. The right-hand photo was taken several weeks later and shows that deprived monkeys given young "therapists" can learn to play and adjust to community life. Socially withdrawn preschoolers have similarly profited from exposure to peers.

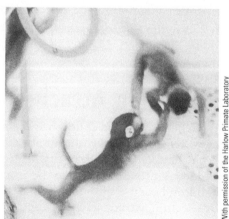

With permission of the Harlow Primate Laboratory

prevent running such studies? What ethical issues would stand in the way? Putting those questions aside for the moment, would you want to run such studies with children? Why or why not?

Studies with children have therefore been run with "found" participants—without random assignment to the home life or the institutional life. Institutionalized children whose material needs are met but who receive little social stimulation from caregivers exhibit problems in their physical, intellectual, social, and emotional development (Johnson & Gunnar, 2011; Phelps et al., 2012; Rutter, 2006). Spitz (1965) noted that many institutionalized children appear to develop a syndrome characterized by withdrawal and depression. They show progressively less interest in their world and become increasingly inactive. Some of them die.

In one institution, infants were maintained in separate cubicles for most of their first year to ward off infectious diseases (Provence & Lipton, 1962). Adults tended to them only to feed and change their diapers. As a rule, baby bottles were propped up in the infants' cribs. Attendants rarely responded to the babies' cries, and the infants were rarely played with or spoken to. By the age of four months, the infants in this institution showed little interest in adults. They rarely tried to gain their attention, even when in distress. A few months later, some of them sat withdrawn in their cribs and rocked back and forth, almost like the Harlows' monkeys. Language deficiencies were striking. As the first year progressed, little babbling was heard within the infants' cubicles. None were speaking even one word at 12 months.

Other studies conducted with samples of children who experienced profound institutional deprivation (e.g., sample of Romanian infants and children) show long-term deficits in specific key areas, such as quasi-autism, inattention/overactivity, and disinhibited attachment (Kreppner et al., 2007). In a study by Colvert and colleagues (2008) comparing Romanian adoptees from deprived institutional settings and within-United Kingdom adoptees on measures of **theory of mind** and executive functioning, the researchers found that the Romanian adoptees displayed deficits in theory of mind and executive functioning compared with the United Kingdom group. The longer the period of deprivation, the greater the deficits were, suggesting that many processes are affected by early deprivation, which is related to later social and emotional functioning.

Why do children whose basic needs of shelter and food are met show such dramatic deficiencies? Is it because they do not receive the love and affection of a human? Or is it because they do not receive adequate sensory or social stimulation?

The answer may depend, in part, on the age of the child. Classic studies by Leon Yarrow and his colleagues (Yarrow et al., 1971; Yarrow & Goodwin, 1973) suggest that deficiencies in sensory stimulation and social interaction may cause more problems than lack of love in infants who are too young to have developed specific attachments. However, once infants have developed specific attachments, separation from their primary caregivers can lead to problems.

In the first study, the development of 53 adopted children was followed over a ten-year period (Yarrow et al., 1971). The researchers compared the development of three subgroups: (1) children who were transferred to their permanent adoptive homes almost immediately after birth, (2) children who were given temporary foster mothers and then transferred to permanent adoptive homes before they were six months old, and (3) children who were transferred from temporary foster mothers to their permanent adoptive homes after they were six months old. At the age of ten, children in the first two groups showed no differences in social and emotional development. However, children in the third group showed significantly less ability to relate to other people. Perhaps their deficits resulted from being separated from their initial foster mothers after they had become attached to them.

theory of mind A commonsense understanding of how the mind works.

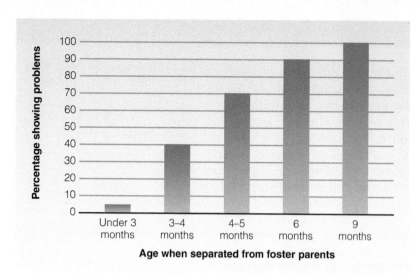

Figure 7.7 ■ **The Development of Adopted Children Separated from Temporary Foster Parents**

The older the child at the time of separation, the more likely it is that behavioural disturbances will occur.

Source: Data from Yarrow & Yarrow (1973).

In the second study, Yarrow and Goodwin (1973) followed the development of 70 adopted children who were separated from temporary foster parents between birth and the age of 16 months. The researchers found strong correlations between the age at which the children were separated and later feeding and sleeping problems, decreased social responsiveness, and extremes in attachment behaviours (see Figure 7.7 ■). Disturbed attachment behaviours included excessive clinging to the new mother and violent rejection of her. None of the children who were separated from their initial foster mothers before the age of three months showed moderate or severe disturbances. All the children who were separated at nine months or older did show such disturbances. Forty to 90 percent of the children separated between the ages of three and nine months showed moderate to severe disturbances. The incidence of problems increased as the age advanced.

The Yarrow studies suggest that babies in institutions, at least up to the age of three months or so, may require general sensory and social stimulation more than a specific relationship with a primary caregiver. After the age of three months, some disturbance is likely if there is instability in the care-giving staff. By the ages of six to nine months, disturbance seems to be guaranteed if there is instability in the position of primary caregiver. Fortunately, there is also evidence that children show some capacity to recover from early social deprivation.

The Capacity to Recover from Social Deprivation

Studies with animals and children show that early social deprivation is linked to developmental deficits. However, other studies suggest that infants also have powerful capacities to recover from deprivation.

Kagan and Klein (1973) reported that many children may be able to recover fully from 13 or 14 months of deprivation. The natives in an isolated Guatemalan village believe that fresh air and sunshine will make children ill. Thus, children are kept in windowless huts until they can walk. They are played with infrequently. During their isolation, the infants behave apathetically; they are physically and socially deficient when they start to walk. But by 11 years of age, they are alert, active, and as intellectually able as Canadian children of the same age.

A classic longitudinal study of children reared in orphanages also offers evidence of the ability of children to recover from social deprivation (Skeels, 1966). In this study, a group of 19-month-old, apparently intellectually deficient children were placed in the care of older institutionalized girls. The girls spent a great deal of time playing with, talking to, and nurturing them. Four years after being placed with the girls, the "intellectually deficient" children made dramatic gains in intelligence test scores, whereas children who remained in the orphanage showed declines in IQ.

The children placed in the care of the older girls also appeared to be generally well adjusted. By the time Skeels reported on their progress in 1966, most were married and were rearing children of their own who showed no intellectual or social deficits. Unfortunately, many of the children who had been left in the orphanage were still in some type of institutional setting. Few of them showed normal social and emotional development. Few were functioning as independent adults.

The good news is that many children who have been exposed to early social deprivation can catch up in their social and emotional development and lead normal adult lives if they receive individual attention and environmental stimulation (Rutter, 2006). The bad news is that society has not yet allocated the resources to give all children the opportunity to do so.

Child Abuse and Neglect

QUESTIONS » **What are the incidences of child abuse and neglect? What are their effects?** We have considered the results of rearing children in settings in which contact with parents is reduced or absent. But living with one's parents does not guarantee that a child will receive tender loving care. Sadly, there's no place like home—for violence, that is.

Some Facts about the Incidence of Child Abuse and Neglect

In Canada, measuring and reporting the actual rates of violence and abuse against children is limited to the official reports filed by police and from child services (Sinha, 2012), making the rates we report here likely an underestimation of actual values. However, all provinces and territories have mandatory laws requiring professionals (e.g., teachers, psychologists, nurses) working with children and also members of the general public to report suspected cases of abuse (Public Health Agency of Canada, 2010). First, consider the relationship between the abuser and the victim. Children under the age of nine are more likely to suffer a violent act at the hands of a family member (see Figure 7.8 ■). Other data (Child Maltreatment, 2010) reveal that four-fifths of victims (81 percent) were maltreated by a parent, and that more than one-third of victims were maltreated by the mother acting alone (37 percent). One child in five (19 percent) was maltreated by the father acting alone. **TRUTH OR FICTION REVISITED:** Approximately, twice as many children are maltreated by their mothers as by their fathers. Why do you think this is so? In addition, nearly one-fifth (19 percent) were maltreated by the parents acting together, and 13 percent of victims were maltreated by a perpetrator other than a parent.

Younger children suffer significant rates of victimization. About one quarter of victims (26 percent) were under the age of four (see Figure 7.9 ■). About a quarter (24 percent) were aged four to seven years. You might expect that older

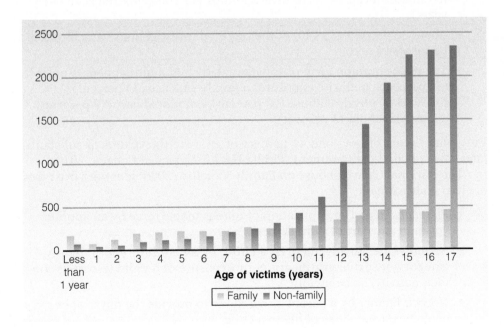

Figure 7.8 ■ Child and Youth Victims of Police-Reported Violent Crime, 2010
Incidences of reported violent crimes are more likely to be by a nonrelative as children get older.
Source: Statistics Canada.

Figure 7.9 ■ Age of Children in Maltreatment Investigations in Canada, 2008

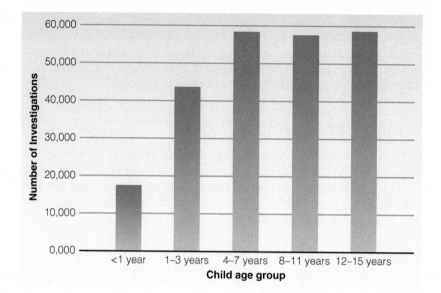

children would be more likely than younger children to be maltreated because they are more capable of "getting into trouble"; however, the Canadian data based on investigations of maltreatment demonstrate an even spread of maltreatment across age groups.

The various types of maltreatment are outlined below. Note that neglect is significantly more common than abuse. Neglect is, in effect, passive, whereas abuse is active. And nearly one child in ten is sexually abused. In the most recent Canadian Incidence Study of Reported Child Abuse & Neglect (CIS-2008), 235 842 cases of abuse were reported with the following results: 36 percent were substantiated, 8 percent were suspected, and 30 percent were unfounded. Consider the following incidence rates (i.e., the number of child maltreatment investigations conducted in a given year by child welfare agencies), as reported in the 2008 Canadian Incidence Study of Reported Child Abuse and Neglect (Public Health Agency of Canada, 2010):

- In 2008, 235 842 child maltreatment investigations were conducted in Canada (a rate of 39.16 investigations per 1000 children aged 0–15 years).

- About 36 percent (85 440) of the reported investigations were found to be substantiated.

- The most common form of substantiated child maltreatment is neglect (34 percent), tied with exposure to family violence (34 percent), followed by physical abuse (20 percent), emotional harm (9 percent), and sexual abuse (3 percent).

Fifty-one percent of boys and 41 percent of girls are the victims of substantiated cases of child maltreatment (Public Health Agency of Canada, 2010).

The National Clearinghouse on Family Violence (2006) identifies five types of child maltreatment:

- *Physical abuse:* The application of unreasonable force by an adult or youth to any part of a child's body.

- *Sexual abuse:* Involvement of a child, by an adult or youth, in any category of sexual gratification, or exposure of a child to sexual contact, activity, or behaviour.

- *Neglect:* Failure by a parent or caregiver to provide the physical or psychological necessities of life to a child.

The Three Forms of Child Neglect—Examples

Physical Neglect	Educational Neglect	Emotional Neglect
A 2-year-old who was found wandering in the street late at night, naked and alone.	An 11-year-old and a 13-year-old who were chronically truant.	Siblings who were subjected to repeated incidents of family violence between their mother and father.
An infant who had to be hospitalized for near-drowning after being left alone in a bathtub.	A 12-year-old whose parents permitted him to decide whether to go to school, how long to stay there, and in which activities to participate.	A 12-year-old whose parents permitted him to drink and use drugs.
Children who were living in a home contaminated with animal feces and rotting food.	A special education student whose mother refused to believe he needed help in school.	A child whose mother helped him shoot out the windows of a neighbour's house.

Source: Eric J. Mash & David A. Wolfe (2013). *Abnormal Child Psychology*, 5th edition. Belmont, CA: Cengage Learning.

- *Emotional harm:* Adult behaviour that harms a child psychologically, emotionally, or spiritually.
- *Exposure to family violence:* Circumstances that allow a child to be aware of violence occurring between a caregiver and his or her partner or between other family members.

Although blatant abuse is more horrifying, more injuries, illnesses, deaths, and long-term impacts result from neglect and exposure to family violence (Public Health Agency of Canada, 2010).

Table 7.1 ■ shows examples of three types of neglect.

Sexual Abuse of Children

No one knows how many children are sexually abused due to issues with reporting (Finkelhor et al., 2005a, 2005b; Public Health Agency of Canada, 2010). Although most sexually abused children are girls, one-quarter to one-third are boys (Child Maltreatment, 2010). Interviews with 8667 adults suggest that the prevalence of sexual abuse among boys is about 18 percent and among girls is 25 percent (Edwards et al., 2003). These estimates may underrepresent the actual prevalence because people may fail to report incidents due to faulty memory, shame, or embarrassment.

Sexual abuse of children ranges from exhibitionism, kissing, fondling, and sexual touching to oral sex and anal intercourse and, with girls, vaginal intercourse. Acts such as touching children's sexual organs while changing or bathing them, sleeping with children, and appearing nude before them are open to interpretation and often innocent (Haugaard, 2000).

A CLOSER LOOK REAL LIFE

Prevention of Sexual Abuse of Children

Many of us were taught by our parents never to accept a ride or an offer of candy from a stranger. However, many instances of sexual abuse are perpetrated by a familiar adult, often a family member or friend (Ullman, 2007). Prevention programs help children understand what sexual abuse is and how they can avoid it. In addition to learning to avoid strangers, children need to recognize the differences between acceptable touching, such as an affectionate embrace or pat on the head, and unacceptable or "bad" touching. Even elementary-school children can learn the distinction between "good touching" and "bad touching." School-based programs can help prepare children to handle

Continued

Continued

an actual encounter with a molester. Children who receive training are more likely to use strategies such as running away, yelling, or saying no when they are threatened by an abuser (Finkelhor, 2007). They are also more likely to report incidents to adults.

Researchers recognize that children can easily be intimidated or overpowered by adults or older children. Children may be unable to say no in a sexually abusive situation, even though they want to and know it is the right thing to do. Although children may not always be able to prevent abuse, they can be encouraged to tell someone about it. Most prevention programs emphasize teaching children messages such as "It's not your fault," "Never keep a bad or scary secret," and "Always tell your parents about this, especially if someone says you shouldn't tell them" (Finkelhor, 2007).

Children also need to be alerted to the types of threats they might receive for disclosing abuse. They are more likely to resist threats if they are reassured that they will be believed when they report the abuse, that their parents will continue to love them, and that they and their families will be protected from the molester.

In all provinces and territories, teachers and helping professionals are required to report suspected abuse to authorities. Tighter controls and better screening are needed to monitor the hiring of employees working with children. Administrators and teachers in preschool and daycare facilities also need to be educated to recognize the signs of sexual abuse and to report suspected cases.

What can you do if you suspect that a child has been victimized by sexual abuse? The National Clearinghouse on Family Violence (2006) offers the following guidelines:

- Act on the suspicion quickly (i.e., do not wait for days or weeks).
- Keep the best interest of the child in mind, and protect the child from any further harm (i.e., keep the child from returning to the abusive or neglectful situation).
- Write down what you have been told and by whom, as well as your observations and what you did.
- If the child had disclosed maltreatment, reassure him or her that it was right to do so, as he or she may have mixed feelings and/or feel loyalty to the perpetrator.
- Try to learn as much as you can about the situation and context, and find out if the child is currently ay risk (e.g., is experiencing ongoing exposure to the perpetrator), but do not interview the child about details; that is the responsibility of the child protective services (CPS).
- Contact the local CPS and report the situation. Provide identifying data and your contact information.
- In consultation with the CPS, consider immediate medical assessment/treatment of physical problems and referral to local emergency health services or sexual assault teams.
- Consider referral to a mental health professional for assessment/treatment of any psychological or psychiatric problems.
- Short-term and long-term safety plans for the child should be prepared in collaboration with the CPS.

Here are some Canadian resources:

- Centre of Excellence for Child Welfare (www.cecw-cepb.ca).
- Child Welfare League of Canada (www.cwlc.ca).
- First Nations Child Family Caring Society of Canada (www.fncfcs.com).
- National Clearinghouse on Family Violence (www.phac -aspc.gc.ca).

As well, provincial and territorial governments have explicit information for how to report suspected cases of abuse and neglect in their respective jurisdictions.

Reflect How would you attempt to teach a child the difference between "good touching" and "bad touching"?

Effects of Child Abuse and Neglect

Maltreated children show a high incidence of personal and social problems and psychological disorders (Sousa et al., 2011). In general, maltreated children are less securely attached to their parents. They are less intimate with their peers and are more aggressive, angry, and noncompliant than other children (Moylan et al., 2010). They rarely express positive emotions, have lower self-esteem, and show impaired cognitive functioning, leading to poorer performance in school (Sousa et al., 2011). When they reach adulthood, they are more likely to act aggressively toward their intimate partners (Gomez, 2011). As they mature, maltreated children are at greater risk for delinquency, academic failure, and substance abuse (Sousa et al., 2011).

Causes of Child Abuse and Neglect

A number of factors contribute to the probability that parents will abuse their children. They include situational stress, a history of child abuse in at least one of the parents' families of origin, lack of adequate coping and problem-solving skills, deficiency in child-rearing skills, unrealistic expectations of what a child should be able to do at a given developmental level, and substance abuse (Wolfe, 2011).

Stress has many sources, including such life changes as parental conflict and divorce or separation, the loss of a job, moving, and the birth of a new family member. Unemployment seems to be a particularly predisposing life change. Child abuse increases among the unemployed (Joshi et al., 2006).

Stress is created by crying infants themselves. Consequently, infants who are already in pain of some kind and relatively difficult to soothe may be more likely to be abused (Stupica et al., 2011). Abusive parents may find the cries of their infants particularly aversive, so the infants' crying may precipitate abusive behaviour (Schuetze et al., 2003). Ironically, mothers who are deeply depressed or using cocaine may neglect crying infants because they perceive the cries to be less aversive (Schuetze et al., 2003). Children who act disobediently, inappropriately, or unresponsively are at greater risk of abuse (Wolfe, 2011). Why? Parents tend to become frustrated and irritated when their children show prolonged signs of distress or misbehaviour. Abusive mothers are more likely than nonabusive mothers to assume that their children's misbehaviour is intentional, even when it is not. Within our culture, intentional misconduct is seen as more deserving of punishment than incidental misconduct. Abusive mothers also tend to believe that they have little control over their child's misbehaviour.

TRUTH OR FICTION REVISITED: It is true that child abusers have frequently been the victims of child abuse themselves (Ertem et al., 2000; White & Smith, 2004). Why does child abuse run in families? There are probably a number of reasons (White & Smith, 2004). One is that parents serve as role models for their children. As noted by Murray Straus (1995), "Spanking teaches kids that when someone is doing something you don't like and they won't stop doing it, you hit them." If children grow up observing their parents using violence as a means of coping with stress and feelings of anger, they are less likely to learn to diffuse their anger through techniques such as humour, verbal expression of feelings, reasoning, or even counting to 10 to let the anger pass.

Exposure to violence in their own homes may lead some children to accept family violence as a norm. They may see nothing wrong with it. Certainly, parents can find any number of "justifications" for violence—if they seek them. One is the adage "Spare the rod, spoil the child." Another is the belief that they are hurting their children "for their own good"—to discourage behaviour that is likely to get them into trouble.

Still another "justification" of child abuse is the sometimes cloudy distinction between the occasional swat on the rear end and spanking. Child abusers may argue that all parents hit their children (which is not true), and they may claim not to understand why outsiders are making such a fuss about private family behaviour. Child abusers who were subjected to abuse also may harbour the (incorrect) belief that "everyone does it."

The patterns of attachment of the perpetrators of child abuse have also been studied. One study, for example, found that nonfamilial perpetrators of sexual child abuse were significantly less likely to have a secure attachment style in their relationships (Jamieson & Marshall, 2000).

In any event, child abuse must be conceptualized and dealt with as a crime of violence. Whether or not child abusers happen to be victims of abuse themselves, child abusers are criminals, and children must be protected from them.

What to Do

Dealing with child abuse is a frustrating task. Social and human service agencies and the courts can find it difficult to distinguish between spanking and abuse, as many abusers do. Because of the belief in this country that parents have the right to rear their children as they wish, police and the courts have historically tried to avoid involvement in domestic quarrels and family disputes. However, the alarming incidence of child abuse has spawned new efforts at detection and prevention.

CHAPTER 7 INFANCY: SOCIAL AND EMOTIONAL DEVELOPMENT **241**

How Child Abuse May Set the Stage for Psychological Disorders in Adulthood

There is a significant correlation between child abuse and psychological disorders in adulthood. However, the causal connections have remained somewhat clouded. But now numerous studies suggest that two bodily systems are involved in the relationship between child abuse and psychological disorders in adulthood (Cirulli et al., 2009; Gillespie & Nemeroff, 2007). One is the autonomic nervous system (ANS), which is intimately involved in stress reactions and emotions such as anxiety and fear. The other system is the endocrine system, which consists of ductless glands that release hormones directly into the bloodstream. So-called stress hormones are released when the body is under stress. And child abuse is a prominent stressor.

Researchers assess the individual's responses to stress by measuring the quantities of stress hormones in bodily fluids, such as blood or saliva. One such hormone is the pituitary hormone ACTH, which, in a domino effect, stimulates the cortex (outer layer) of the adrenal glands to release corticosteroids, such as cortisol. Corticosteroids increase resistance to stress in ways such as promoting muscle development and causing the liver to release stored sugar, which makes more energy available in emergencies. The sympathetic division of the ANS goes into overdriveunder stress, as can be measured by the heart rate, the blood pressure, muscle tension, and sweating.

In one study, Christine Heim and her colleagues (2000) recruited 49 women (mean age 35 years). The sample was selected to have a high number of women who had suffered child abuse and were currently depressed. In interviews, 27 of the recruits reported that they had experienced physical and/or sexual abuse in childhood, whereas the other 22 had not. In addition, 23 of the group members were experiencing major depressive episodes at the time of the study, compared with 26 who were not. All the participants in the experiment were exposed to a stressor that other studies had shown to stimulate reactions of the endocrine system and the ANS. The women were given the task of making a speech in front of strangers; moreover, the speech would entail doing mental arithmetic. The women's levels of stress hormones and heart rates were measured while they anticipated and presented the speeches.

Results of the experiment are shown in Table 7.2 ▪, which reports the participants' blood levels of ACTH and cortisol and their heart rates. Looking at the women who did not experience child abuse (groups A and B), we see that the presence of depression did not make a significant difference. Now consider the two groups of women who had been abused as children (groups C and D). When they were subjected to the stressor, they were significantly more likely to show high blood levels of ACTH and cortisol than women who had not been abused as children (women in groups A and B). The women in group D showed the greatest hormonal and cardiac

● TABLE 7.2

Responses of Women with or without a History of Child Abuse to a Stressor

History of Child Abuse	Women Who Are Not Experiencing a Major Depressive Episode	Women Who Are Experiencing a Major Depressive Episode
Women with no history of child abuse	Group A: 12 women Endocrine system • ACTH peak: 4.7 parts/litre • Cortisol peak: 339 parts/litre Autonomic nervous system • Heart rate: 78.4 beats/minute	Group B: 10 women Endocrine system • ACTH peak: 5.3 parts/litre • Cortisol peak: 337 parts/litre Autonomic nervous system • Heart rate: 83.8 beats/minute
Women with a history of child abuse	Group C: 14 women Endocrine system • ACTH peak: 9.3 parts/litre • Cortisol peak: 359 parts/litre Autonomic nervous system • Heart rate: 82.2 beats/minute	Group D: 13 women Endocrine system • ACTH peak: 12.1 parts/litre • Cortisol peak: 527 parts/litre Autonomic nervous system • Heart rate: 89.7 beats/minute

Source: Adapted from Heim, C., et al (2000).

Continued

responses to the stressor, and these were women who (1) had been abused as children and (2) were undergoing a major depressive episode. The researchers concluded that child abuse leads to more reactive endocrine and autonomic nervous systems and that a combination of abuse and depression makes the body most reactive to stress.

These stress reactions exhaust the body. Women who were abused as children are apparently carrying a historic burden that makes their current burdens all the more unbearable.

Reflect What does biology contribute to our understanding of psychology? How can biological changes in childhood set the stage for psychological reactions in adulthood?

A number of techniques have been developed to help prevent child abuse. One approach focuses on strengthening parenting skills among the general population (Bugental et al., 2010). Parent-education classes in high school are an example of this approach.

Another approach targets groups at high risk for abuse, such as poor, single teen mothers (Joshi et al., 2006). In some programs, for example, home visitors help new parents develop skills in caregiving and home management (Duggan et al., 2004).

A third technique focuses on presenting information about abuse and providing support to families. For instance, many locales have violence prevention and child abuse and neglect hotlines. Private citizens who suspect child abuse and neglect may call for advice. Parents who are having difficulty controlling aggressive impulses toward their children are encouraged to call.

Another helpful measure is increased publicity about the magnitude of the child abuse problem. The public may also need more education about where an occasional swat on the behind ends and child abuse begins. Perhaps the format for such education could be something like this: "If you are doing such and such, make no mistake about it—you are abusing your child."

Autism Spectrum Disorders: Alone among the Crowd

QUESTION » What are autism spectrum disorders? **Autism spectrum disorders (ASDs)** are characterized by impaired communication skills, poor social interactions, and repetitive, stereotyped behaviour (Zimmerman, 2008) (see Table 7.3 ■). They tend to become evident by the age of three years and sometimes before the end of the first year. According to a CDC study, about one in every 152 children is affected with ASD (Rice, 2007). There are several variations of ASDs,

● TABLE 7.3

Characteristics of Autism Spectrum Disorders

Key Indicators	Other Indicators
• Does not babble, point, or make meaningful gestures by one year of age	• Has poor eye contact
	• Doesn't seem to know how to play with toys
• Does not speak one word by 16 months	• Excessively lines up toys or other objects
• Does not combine two words by two years	• Is attached to one particular toy or object
• Does not respond to name	• Doesn't smile
• Loses language or social skills	• At times seems to be hearing impaired

Source: Adapted from Strock (2004).

autism spectrum disorders (ASDs) Developmental disorders—including autism, Asperger's syndrome, Rett's disorder, and childhood disintegrative disorder—that are characterized by impaired communication skills, poor social interactions, and repetitive, stereotyped behaviour.

but autism is the major type and will be our focus here. Other forms of ASDs include

- Asperger's disorder: an ASD characterized by social deficits and stereotyped behaviour but without the significant cognitive or language delays associated with autism (Hoffman, 2009)
- Rett's disorder: an ASD characterized by a range of physical, behavioural, motor, and cognitive abnormalities that begin after a few months of apparently normal development
- Childhood disintegrative disorder: an ASD involving abnormal functioning and loss of previously acquired skills that begins after about two years of apparently normal development

Autism

Peter nursed eagerly, sat and walked at the expected ages. Yet some of his behaviour made us vaguely uneasy. He never put anything in his mouth. Not his fingers nor his toys—nothing ....

More troubling was the fact that Peter didn't look at us, or smile, and wouldn't play the games that seemed as much a part of babyhood as diapers. He rarely laughed, and when he did, it was at things that didn't seem funny to us. He didn't cuddle, but sat upright in my lap, even when I rocked him. But children differ and we were content to let Peter be himself. We thought it hilarious when my brother, visiting us when Peter was 8 months old, observed, "That kid has no social instincts, whatsoever." Although Peter was a first child, he was not isolated. I frequently put him in his playpen in front of the house, where the schoolchildren stopped to play with him as they passed. He ignored them, too.

It was Kitty, a personality kid, born two years later, whose responsiveness emphasized the degree of Peter's difference. When I went into her room for the late feeding, her little head bobbed up and she greeted me with a smile that reached from her head to her toes. And the realization of that difference chilled me more than the wintry bedroom.

Peter's babbling had not turned into speech by the time he was 3. His play was solitary and repetitious. He tore paper into long thin strips, bushel baskets of it every day. He spun the lids from my canning jars and became upset if we tried to divert him. Only rarely could I catch his eye, and then saw his focus change from me to the reflection in my glasses ....

[Peter's] adventures into our suburban neighborhood had been unhappy. He had disregarded the universal rule that sand is to be kept in sandboxes, and the children themselves had punished him. He walked around a sad and solitary figure, always carrying a toy airplane, a toy he never played with. At that time, I had not heard the word that was to dominate our lives, to hover over every conversation, to sit through every meal beside us. That word was autism.[1]

Peter, the boy with "no social instincts," was autistic. The word *autism* derives from the Greek *autos*, meaning "self." (An automobile is a self-driven method of moving from place to place.) **Autism** is four to five times more common among boys than girls. Perhaps the most poignant feature of autism is the child's utter aloneness (Georgiades et al., 2010). Autistic children do not show interest in social interaction and may avoid eye contact. Attachment to others is weak or absent.

autism An autism spectrum disorder characterized by extreme aloneness, communication problems, intolerance of change, and ritualistic behaviour.

---

[1]Adapted from Eberhardy (1967).

Other features of autism include communication problems, intolerance of change, and ritualistic or stereotypical behaviour (Georgiades et al., 2010). Parents of autistic children frequently report that they were "good babies." This usually means that they made few demands. However, as autistic children develop, they tend to shun affectionate contacts such as hugging, cuddling, and kissing.

Development of speech lags (Mackic-Magyar & McCracken, 2004). There is little babbling or communicative gesturing during the first year. Autistic children may show **mutism**, **echolalia**, and pronoun reversal, referring to themselves as "you" or "he." About half use language by middle childhood, but their speech is unusual and troubled (Zimmerman, 2008).

Autistic children become bound by ritual (Estes et al., 2011). Even slight changes in routines or the environment may cause distress. The teacher of a five-year-old autistic girl would greet her each morning with "Good morning, Lily, I am very, very glad to see you." Lily would ignore the greeting, but she would shriek if the teacher omitted even one of the *very*'s. This feature of autism is termed "preservation of sameness." When familiar objects are moved from their usual places, children with autism may throw tantrums or cry until the objects are restored. They may insist on eating the same food every day. Autistic children show deficits in peer play, imaginative play, imitation, and emotional expression. Many sleep less than their age-mates (Georgiades et al., 2010).

Some autistic children mutilate themselves, even as they cry out in pain. They may bang their heads, slap their faces, bite their hands and shoulders, or pull out their hair.

Causes of Autism Spectrum Disorders

Some theorists argue that children develop ASDs in response to parental rejection. From this viewpoint, autistic behaviour shuts out the cold outside world. But research evidence shows that the parents of autistic children are not deficient in child rearing (Landrigan, 2010).

Various lines of evidence suggest a key role for biological factors in autism. For example, very low birth weight and advanced maternal age may heighten the risk of autism (Maimburg & Væth, 2006). A role for genetic mechanisms is suggested by kinship studies (Kendler, 2010). For example, the concordance (agreement) rates for ASDs are about 60 percent among pairs of identical (monozygotic) twins, who fully share their genetic heritage, compared with about 10 percent for pairs of fraternal (dizygotic) twins, whose genetic codes overlap by only 50 percent (Kendler, 2010; Plomin et al., 1994). Twin status appears to increase susceptibility to the symptoms of autism, especially among males. Researchers suspect that multiple genes are involved in ASDs and interact with other factors—environmental and/or biological.

Investigation of biological factors has suggested neurological involvement. Many children with ASDs have abnormal brain wave patterns or seizures (Chonchaiya et al., 2012). Other researchers have found that, compared to others, the brains of children with ASDs have abnormal sensitivities to neurotransmitters such as serotonin, dopamine, acetylcholine, and norepinephrine (Bauman et al., 2006). Other researchers note unusual activity in the motor region of the cerebral cortex, and less activity in some other areas of the brain, including the frontal and temporal lobes and the limbic system (Fournier et al., 2010). Still other researchers link autism to disorders of the immune system, which they believe originate during prenatal development (Zimmerman, 2008).

Autism
The most poignant feature of autism is the child's utter aloneness. Autism is rather rare, but is more common in boys than in girls. Symptoms include communication problems, intolerance of any change, and ritualistic or stereotypical behaviour.

mutism Inability or refusal to speak.

echolalia The automatic repetition of sounds or words.

TRUTH OR FICTION REVISITED: While we are discussing biological factors in causation, let us delete one. It has been widely believed—it has almost achieved folklore status—that vaccines or the mercury preservative used in a number of vaccines, such as the measles-mumps-rubella (MMR) vaccine, can cause autism. We should note, rather strongly, that there is *no* scientific evidence for this view, regardless of whether or not it is widely held (Richler et al., 2006; Taylor, 2006).

All in all, it seems clear that we can consider autism a disease of the brain and that parents of children with autism should not blame themselves. Although it appears that heredity creates a vulnerability to autism, the conditions that interact with heredity to produce autistic behaviour remain unknown.

Treatment of Autism Spectrum Disorders

Treatment for ASDs is based largely on principles of learning, although investigation of biological approaches is also under way (Strock, 2004). Behaviour modification has been used to increase the child's ability to attend to others, to play with other children, and to discourage self-mutilation (Sigafoos et al., 2009).

Because children with ASDs show behavioural deficits, behaviour modification is used to help them develop new behaviour. **TRUTH OR FICTION REVISITED:** For example, many autistic children do respond to people as though they were furniture. They run around them rather than relating to them as people. But many autistic children can be taught to accept people as reinforcers—for example, by pairing praise with food treats (Drasgow et al., 2001). Praise can then be used to encourage speech and social play.

The most effective treatment programs focus on individualized instruction to correct behavioural, educational, and communication deficits. In a classic study conducted by O. Ivar Lovaas at UCLA (Lovaas et al., 1989), autistic children received more than 40 hours of one-to-one behaviour modification a week for at least two years. Significant intellectual and educational gains were reported for 9 of the 19 children (47 percent) in the program. The children who improved achieved normal scores on intelligence tests and succeeded in Grade 1. Only 2 percent of an untreated control group achieved similar gains. Somewhat less intensive educational programs have also yielded positive results with many autistic toddlers (Stahmer et al., 2004).

Biological approaches for the treatment of ASDs are under study. Drugs that enhance serotonin activity (selective serotonin reuptake inhibitors [SSRIs]), such as those used to treat depression, can help prevent self-injury, aggressive outbursts, depression and anxiety, and repetitive behaviour (Reiersen & Handen, 2011). Drugs that are usually used to treat schizophrenia—the "major tranquilizers"—are helpful with stereotyped behaviour, hyperactivity, and self-injury, but not with cognitive and language problems (Zimmerman, 2008).

Autistic behaviour generally continues into adulthood to one degree or another. Yet some children with autism go on to earn college degrees and function independently (Eaves & Ho, 2008). Others need continuous treatment, which may include institutionalized care.

We have been examining the development of attachment and some of the circumstances that may interfere with its development. In recent years, a lively debate has sprung up concerning the effects of day care on children's attachment and on their social and cognitive development. Let us turn now to a consideration of these issues.

9. The Harlows found that rhesus infants reared in isolation later (sought or avoided?) contact with other monkeys.

10. Spitz noted that many institutionalized children appear to develop a syndrome characterized by _____ and depression.

11. There are more cases of (physical abuse or neglect) in Canada?

12. Children with _____ do not show interest in social interaction, have communication problems, are intolerant of change, and display repetitive behaviour.

Reflect & Relate: What would you do if you learned that the child of a neighbour was being abused? What would you do if you were a teacher and learned that a child in your class was being abused?

7.3 Child Care

QUESTIONS » Does child care affect children's bonds of attachment with their parents? Does it affect their social, emotional, and cognitive development? Seeking a phrase that can strike fear into the hearts of thousands of Canadian parents? Try *day care*. Only a relatively small percentage of Canadian families still fit the conventional model where the father works and the mother stays at home and cares for the children. Nowadays most mothers, including those with infants, are in the workforce. The workforce participation rates for Canadian mothers with youngest child aged birth to two, three to five, and six to 15 are 69 percent, 75 percent, and 84 percent respectively (Human Resources and Skills Development Canada, 2012).

When the parents work outside the home, the children—at least young children—must be taken care of by others. What happens to them? Child care is under provincial and territory jurisdiction; therefore, the number of regulated child-care spaces is determined by both federal decisions and funding, as well as provincial funding and decision making. What does that mean for Canadian parents? It means there is great diversity in child-care quality and choices based on where you live, what resources you have access to (e.g., family supports, income, community supports), and provincial legislation).

Because so many families rely on nonparental care, parents, psychologists, educators, and other professionals are vitally concerned about the effects of child care. Let's examine some research findings.

- *Attachment.* Some studies find that infants placed in child care are more likely to be insecure (Aviezer & Sagi-Schwartz, 2008), but most infants, whether cared for in the home or in child care, are securely attached (Timmerman, 2006).

- *Social, emotional, and cognitive development.* Infants with day-care experience are more peer oriented and play at higher developmental levels. They are more independent, self-confident, outgoing, affectionate, and cooperative (Bekkhus et al., 2011; Gupta & Simonsen, 2010). High-quality child care—defined as richness of the learning environment and ratio of caregivers to children—is associated with greater language and cognitive skills (Belsky, 2009; Thompson, 2008).

- *Aggression.* About 17 percent of children placed in child care are rated as moderately more aggressive toward peers and adults than children reared at home by their mother (Belsky, 2001). Might the difference in part reflect competition for limited resources? **TRUTH OR FICTION REVISITED:** It therefore appears to be true that children who attend child-care programs behave more aggressively than children who do not, even though the increased aggressiveness of most of these children was not extreme.

Finding Child Care You (and Your Child) Can Live With

It is normal to be anxious. You are thinking about selecting a day-care centre or a private home for your child, and you have a lot at stake. So of course this is an anxiety-provoking task, but it may not be necessary to be overwhelmed. You can go about the task with a checklist that can guide your considerations. Above all: Don't be afraid to open your mouth and ask questions, even pointed, challenging questions. If the day-care provider does not like questions or if the provider does not answer them satisfactorily, *you want your child someplace else.* So much for the preamble. Here is the checklist.

1. Does the day-care centre have a licence? Who issued the licence? What did the day-care centre have to do to acquire the licence? (You can also call the licensing agency to obtain the answer to the last question.) Licenses need to be posted.

2. How many children are cared for by the centre? How many caregivers are there? Remember this nursery rhyme: "There was an old woman who lived in a shoe. She had so many children she didn't know what to do." All right, the rhyme is sexist and ageist and maybe even shoe-ist. But it suggests that it is important for caregivers not to be overburdened by too many children, especially infants. Know your provincial regulations for child-care services. Each province will have some sort of licensing standards and regulations. In Alberta for example, children under the age of 13 months require one primary caregiver for every three children. Children 13–18 months require one primary staff member for every four children. And the ratio for children 19–35 months one adult per six children.

3. Caregiver training is very important. Are child-care staff trained at the required provincial levels of certification? How were the caregivers hired? How were they trained? Did the centre check references? What were the minimum educational credentials? Did the centre check them out? Do the caregivers have any education or training in the behaviour and needs of children? Do the caregivers seem to be proactive and attempt to engage the children in activities and educational experiences? Or are they inactive unless a child cries or screams? Many child-care centres find one of their most challenging tasks is to find and keep qualified child-care workers, as the job is very demanding and the wages paid are not as competitive as in other fields.

4. Is the environment child-proofed and secure? Can children stick their fingers in electric sockets? Are toys and outdoor equipment in good condition? Are sharp objects within children's reach? Can anybody walk in off the street? What is the history of children being injured or otherwise victimized in this day-care centre? Is the day-care provider hesitant about answering any of these questions?

5. When are meals served? Snacks? What do they consist of? Will your child find them appetizing or go hungry? Some babies are placed in day care at six months or younger, and parents will need to know what formulas are used. Does the food prepared and/or served meet Canada's Food Guide for children needs? Are children fed (if infants, how often)? Do caregivers sit with children during meals?

6. Is it possible for you to meet the caregivers who will be taking care of your child? If not, why not?

7. With what children will your child interact and play?

8. Does the centre seem to have an enriching environment? Do you see books, toys, games, and educational objects strewn about? Do the toys, games, books, and activities suit the ages of all the children? Are they reflective of the multicultural context in which children live and of their own ethnic/racial/cultural backgrounds?

9. Check the facility and equipment. Are there facilities and objects such as swings and tricycles that will enhance your child's physical and motor development? Are children supervised when they play with these things, or are they pretty much left on their own?

10. Does the centre's schedule coincide with your needs?

11. Is the centre located conveniently for you? Does it appear to be in a safe location or to have adequate security arrangements? (Let us emphasize that you have a right to ask whether neighbourhood or other people can walk in unannounced to where the children are. It's a fair question. You can also ask what they would do if a stranger broke into the place.)

12. Are parents permitted to visit unannounced? They should be.

13. Do you like the overall environment and feel of the centre or home? Listen to your "gut."

Although we have listed many important items, this list is not exhaustive. In order for you to learn about child care and your provincial or territorial government's guidelines and checklists, visit their websites.

Reflect Which of the considerations in selecting a day-care centre are most important to you? Why?

Active Review

13. The (minority or majority?) of mothers in Canada work outside the home.

14. Infants with day-care experience play at (higher or lower?) developmental levels than do home-reared babies.

15. Belsky and his colleagues found that once children are in school, those who had spent more time in day care were rated by teachers, caregivers, and mothers as being (more or less?) aggressive toward other children.

Reflect & Relate: What are your concerns about placing children in day care? How do your concerns fit with the evidence on the effects of day care?

7.4 Emotional Development

QUESTIONS » What are emotions? How do they develop? Emotions colour our lives. We are green with envy, red with anger, blue with sorrow. We may experience purple passion or yellow cowardice. Positive emotions such as love can fill our days with pleasure. Negative emotions such as fear, depression, and anger can fill us with dread and make each day a chore.

An **emotion** is a state of feeling that has physiological, situational, and cognitive components. Physiologically, when emotions are strong, our hearts may beat more rapidly and our muscles may tense up. Situationally, we may feel fear in the presence of a threat and experience joy or relief in the presence of a loved one. Cognitively, fear is accompanied by the idea that we are in danger.

It is unclear how many emotions babies have, and they cannot tell us what they are feeling. We can only observe how they behave, including their facial expressions. Facial expressions appear to be universal in that they are recognized in different cultures around the world, so they are considered a reliable index of emotion.

Infants' initial emotional expressions appear to reflect two basic states of emotional arousal: a positive attraction to pleasant stimulation, such as the caregiver's voice or being held, and withdrawal from aversive stimulation, such as a sudden loud noise (Lagercrantz, 2010). By the age of two to three months, social smiling has replaced reflexive smiling. Social smiling is usually highly endearing to caregivers. At three to five months, infants laugh at active stimuli, such as repetitively touching their bellies or playing "Ah, boop!"

Carroll Izard's (2004; Izard et al., 2006) **differential emotions theory** proposes that infants are born with discrete emotional states. However, the timing of their appearance is linked to the child's cognitive development and social experiences. For example, Izard & Malatesta (1987) reported that two-month-old babies receiving inoculations showed distress, whereas older infants showed anger.

Izard claimed to have found many discrete emotions at the age of one month by using his Maximally Discriminative Facial Movement Scoring System. Figure 7.10 ■ shows four infant facial expressions that Izard believes are associated with the basic emotions of anger/rage, enjoyment/joy, fear/terror, and interest/excitement. Izard and his colleagues reported that facial expressions indicating interest, disgust, and pain are present at birth. They and others have observed expressions of anger and sadness at two months of age, expressions

emotion A state of feeling that has physiological, situational, and cognitive components.

differential emotions theory Izard's view that the major emotions are distinct at birth but emerge gradually in accord with maturation and the child's developing needs.

OBSERVING CHILDREN, UNDERSTANDING OURSELVES

Emotional Development

Observe one child's changes in emotional expression from birth through toddlerhood.

How do the cries of babies have survival value? How are the cries of infants less than two months of age different from those of older babies?

From Rathus. *Childhood and Adolescence*, 5E. © 2014 South-Western, a part of Cengage Learning, Inc. Reproduced by permission. www.cengage.com/permissions

Go to www.nelson.com/voyages2ce to watch the video, answer the questions, and e-mail your responses to your professor.

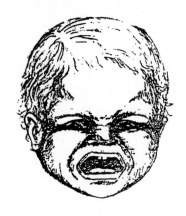

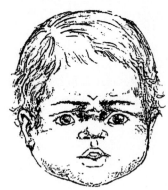

Figure 7.10 ■ Illustrations from Izard's Maximally Discriminative Facial Movement Scoring System What emotion do you think each of these infants is experiencing? Source: Izard, C. E. (1983). *Maximally discriminative facial movement scoring system*. Newark: University of Delaware Instructional Resources Center.

of surprise at four months, and expressions of fear at seven months (Izard & Malatesta, 1987). However, some researchers have suggested that this type of research is fraught with problems. First, observers cannot always accurately identify the emotions shown in slides or drawings of infant facial expressions. Second, we cannot know the exact relationship between a facial expression and an infant's inner feelings, which, of course, are private events. Even if the drawings accurately represent young infants' facial expressions, we cannot be certain that they express the specific emotions they would suggest if they were exhibited by older children and adults.

Emotional Development and Patterns of Attachment

Emotional development has been linked with various histories of attachment. In a longitudinal study of 112 children at ages 9, 14, 22, and 33 months, Kochanska (2001) studied the development of fear, anger, and joy using laboratory situations designed to evoke these emotions. Patterns of attachment were assessed using the strange-situation method. Differences in emotional development could first be related to attachment at the age of 14 months. Resistant children were most fearful and least joyful. Fear was their most powerful emotion. They frequently responded with distress even in episodes designed to evoke joy. When they were assessed repeatedly over time, it became apparent that securely attached children were becoming significantly less angry. By contrast, the negative emotions of insecurely attached children rose: Avoidant children grew more fearful, and resistant children became less joyful. At 33 months of age, securely attached children were less likely to show fear and anger, even when they were exposed to situations designed to elicit these emotions.

Enough disagreement. Let us focus on fear, an emotion that we can all agree is little fun. We focus on a common fear of infants: the fear of strangers.

Fear of Strangers

QUESTIONS » **What is fear of strangers? Is it normal?** When Spencer Rathus's daughter Jordan was one year old, he and her mother decided they had to get a nanny for a few hours a day so that they could teach, write, breathe, and engage in other life activities. They hired a graduate student in social work who had a mild, engaging way about her. She nurtured Jordan and played with her for about four months, during which time Jordan came to somewhat grudgingly accept her—most of the time. Still, Jordan was never completely comfortable with her and frequently let out a yowl as if buildings were collapsing around her, although the nanny did nothing except attempt to soothe her in a calm, consistent manner.

Jordan had a nanny *and* she had fear of strangers. Unfortunately, she met the nanny during the period when she had developed fear of strangers. The fear was eventually to subside, as these fears do, but during her entire encounter with the nanny, the nanny wondered what she was doing wrong. The answer, of course, was simple: She was existing, within sight of Jordan. Worse yet, Jordan's parents were not there to protect her from this vicious foe.

Was Jordan's response to her nanny "normal"? The answer is yes. Development of fear of strangers—sometimes termed **stranger anxiety**—is normal. Stranger anxiety appears at about six to nine months of age in many different cultures, including those of the United States, Great Britain, Guatemala, and Zambia (Smith, 1979). Canadian youngsters are no exception. By five or five months of age, infants smile more in response to their mothers than in response to strangers. At this age, infants may compare the faces of strangers and their mothers, looking back and forth. Somewhat older infants show marked distress by crying, whimpering, gazing fearfully, and crawling away. Fear of strangers may begin at about five to seven months, peak between 9 and 12 months, and decline in the second year or reach a second peak between 18 and 24 months and then decline in the third year (Peltola et al., 2009; Thompson & Limber, 1990).

Children who have developed fear of strangers show less distress in response to strangers when their mothers are present (Rapee, 2012). Babies are less likely to show fear of strangers when they are held by their mothers than when they are placed a metre or so away (Thompson & Limber, 1990). Children also are less likely to show fear of strangers when they are in familiar surroundings, such as their homes, than when they are in the laboratory (Brooker et al., 2011).

Social Referencing: What Should I Do Now?

QUESTIONS » What is social referencing? When does it develop? **Social referencing** is the seeking out of another person's perception of a situation to help us form our own view of it. Leslie Carver and Brenda Vaccaro (2007) suggest that social referencing requires three components: (1) looking at another, usually older individual in a novel, ambiguous situation; (2) associating that individual's emotional response with the unfamiliar situation; and (3) regulating one's own emotional response in accord with the response of the older individual. In an experiment, Carver and Vaccaro (2007) found that 12-month-old infants were quicker to mould their responses to those of an adult who displayed a negative emotion than to model their responses after those of an adult who exhibited a neutral or a positive emotion. Perhaps we are wired to respond to danger first and pleasure later.

Infants also display social referencing, as early as six months of age. They use a caregiver's facial expression or tone of voice as clues on how to respond (Hertenstein & Campos, 2004). In one study, eight-month-old infants were friendlier to a stranger when their mothers exhibited a friendly facial expression in the stranger's presence than when she looked worried (Boccia & Campos, 1989).

becky rockwood/Thinkstock

Emotional Regulation: Keeping on an Even Keel

QUESTION » What is emotional regulation? **Emotional regulation** consists of the ways in which young children control their own emotions (see Table 7.4  for an illustration of the development of emotional and behavioural milestones in infants and toddlers). Infants use emotional signals from an adult to help them cope with uncertainty. Another important feature of early emotional development is emotional regulation (Rothbart & Sheese, 2007). Even young

stranger anxiety A fear of unfamiliar people that emerges between six and nine months of age. Also called *fear of strangers*.

social referencing Using another person's reaction to a situation to form one's own assessment of it.

emotional regulation Techniques for controlling one's emotional states.

TABLE 7.4

The Development of Emotional and Behavioural Control in Infants and Toddlers

	Development of Emotional and Behavioural Control	Effects of the Environment
Infants	• Develop self-soothing and self-stimulating strategies • Develop arousal and sleep-wake patterns that relate to the environment • Begin voluntary efforts to control own motor activity and behaviours • Begin voluntary efforts to contact other people and objects and to engage in sustained interactions with them	• Chaotic, overstimulating, or under-stimulating environment impedes development of adaptive arousal and wake-sleep patterns • Caregiver warmth and responsiveness assists developmental of differentiated emotional responses • Caregiver warmth, consistency, and responsiveness to child's signals support feelings of security and development of awareness of control • Caregiver responsive interaction with infant establishes early understanding of social interaction and communication patterns (turn-taking, etc.)
Toddlers	• Experience more complex emotions • Develop early impulse control (can comply with simple directions and restrictions) • Develop language and increasing awareness of own desires (can form and carry out intentions) • Can regulate some types of activities by imitating others • Use social referencing to judge own actions and environmental events	• Caregiver sensitivity to child's needs and individual characteristics supports the development of inner control • Environments arranged for safe independent action and self-testing, with opportunities for positive experiences with objects and peers, support the development of inner control • Positive models of behaviour support the development of self-regulated control • Positive and responsive guidance that is consistent but respects autonomy and encourages responsibility and self-controls supports self-regulation

Source: Bronson (2000).

infants display certain behaviours to control unpleasant emotional states. They may look away from a disturbing event or suck their thumbs (Rothbart & Sheese, 2007). Caregivers play an important role in helping infants learn to regulate their emotions. Early in life, a two-way communication system develops in which the infant signals the caregiver that help is needed, and the caregiver responds. Claire Kopp (1989, p. 347) gave an example of how this interaction works:

> A 13-month-old, playing with a large plastic bottle, attempted to unscrew the cover, but could not. Fretting for a short time, she initiated eye contact with her mother and held out the jar. As her mother took it to unscrew the cover, the infant ceased fretting.

Research evidence suggests that the children of secure mothers are likely not only to be securely attached themselves but also to regulate their own emotions in a positive manner (Grolnick et al., 2006; Thompson & Meyer, 2007). A German longitudinal study (Zimmermann et al., 2001) related emotional regulation in adolescence with patterns of attachment during infancy, as assessed using the strange-situation method. Forty-one adolescents, aged 16 and 17 years, were placed in complex problem-solving situations with friends. It turned out that those adolescents who were secure as infants were most capable of regulating their emotions to interact cooperatively with their friends. Yet another study (Volling, 2001) addressed the relationship between attachment in infancy and emotional regulation in an interaction with a distressed sibling at the age of four. Of 45 preschoolers in the study, those who had an insecure-resistant infant–mother attachment at the age of one year engaged in more conflict with their siblings and showed greater hostility at the age of four.

Active Review

16. The (majority or minority?) of infants develop fear of strangers.

17. Social _____ is the seeking out of another person's perception of a situation to help us form our own view of it.

18. Emotional _____ consists of the ways in which young children control their own emotions.

Reflect & Relate: Have you ever found yourself in a novel situation and been uncertain what to do? How about when you entered adolescence or began your first college class? Did you observe other people's reactions to the situation in an effort to determine what to do? This behavior is termed social referencing. At what age do humans begin to use social referencing?

7.5 Personality Development

An individual's **personality** is his or her distinctive ways of responding to people and events. In this section, we examine important aspects of personality development in the infant years. First, we look at the emergence of the self-concept. We then turn to a discussion of temperament. Finally, we consider gender differences in behaviour.

The Self-Concept

QUESTIONS » What is the self-concept? How does it develop? The **self-concept** is the sense of self. It appears to emerge gradually during infancy. At some point, infants understand that the hand they are moving in and out of sight is "their" hand. At some point, they understand that their own bodies extend only so far and that at a certain point, external objects and the bodies of others begin.

At birth, we may find the world to be a confusing blur of sights, sounds, and inner sensations. Yet, the "we" may be missing, at least for a while. When our hands first come into view, there is little evidence we realize that that hand "belongs" to us and that we are somehow separate and distinct from the world outside.

Development of the Self-Concept

Psychologists have devised ingenious methods to assess the development of the self-concept among infants. One of these is the mirror technique. This technique involves the use of a mirror and a dot of rouge. Before the experiment begins, the researcher observes the infant for baseline data on how frequently the infant touches his or her nose. Then the mother places rouge on the infant's nose, and the infant is placed before a mirror. Not until about the age of 18 months do infants begin to touch their own noses when they look in the mirror (A. Campbell et al., 2000; Keller et al., 2005).

personality An individual's distinctive ways of responding to people and events.

self-concept One's impression of oneself; self-awareness.

Jandrie Lombard/Shutterstock.com

Self-Awareness

In the middle of the second year, infants begin to develop self-awareness, which has a powerful effect on social and emotional development.

Nose touching suggests that children recognize themselves and that they have a mental picture of themselves that enables them to perceive that the dot of rouge is an abnormality. Most two-year-olds can point to pictures of themselves, and they begin to use "I" or their own name spontaneously (Smiley & Johnson, 2006).

Self-awareness affects the infant's social and emotional development (Foley, 2006). Knowledge of the self permits the child to develop notions of sharing and cooperation. Self-awareness also makes possible the development of "self-conscious" emotions, such as embarrassment, envy, empathy, pride, guilt, and shame (Foley, 2006). One illustration of the development of these "self-conscious" emotions comes from a study by Deborah Stipek and her colleagues (1992). They found that children older than 21 months often seek their mother's attention and approval when they have successfully completed a task, whereas younger toddlers do not.

Temperament: Easy, Difficult, or Slow to Warm Up?

QUESTIONS » What types of temperament do we find among children? How do they develop? Each child has a characteristic way of reacting and adapting to the world. The term **temperament** refers to stable individual differences in styles of reaction that are present early in life. Many researchers believe that temperament forms the basic core of personality and that there is a strong genetic component to temperament (Elliot & Thrash, 2010; Zuckerman, 2011).

The child's temperament includes many aspects of behaviour. Alexander Thomas and Stella Chess, in their well-known New York Longitudinal Study, followed the development of temperament in 133 girls and boys from birth to young adulthood (Chess & Thomas, 1991; Thomas & Chess, 1989). They identified nine characteristics of temperament. Other researchers have identified other characteristics (e.g., Gartstein et al, 2003). These include

1. Activity level
2. Smiling/laughter
3. Regularity in child's biological functions, such as eating and sleeping
4. Approach or withdrawal from new situations and people
5. Adaptability to new situations
6. Sensitivity to sensory stimulation
7. Intensity of responsiveness
8. Quality of mood—generally cheerful or unpleasant
9. Distractibility
10. Attention span and persistence
11. Soothability
12. Distress shown when limitations occur

Types of Temperament

temperament Individual differences in styles of reaction that are present early in life.

Thomas and Chess (1989) found that from the first days of life, many of the children in their study could be classified into one of three types of temperament: "easy" (40 percent of their sample), "difficult" (10 percent), and "slow to

Types of Temperament

	Temperament Category		
	Easy	**Difficult**	**Slow to warm up**
Regularity of biological functioning	Regular	Irregular	Somewhat irregular
Response to new stimuli	Positive approach	Negative withdrawal	Negative withdrawal
Adaptability to new situations	Adapts readily	Adapts slowly or not at all	Adapts slowly
Intensity of reaction	Mild or moderate	Intense	Mild
Quality of mood	Positive	Negative	Initially negative; gradually more positive

Source: Based on Thomas, A., & Chess, S. (1989).

warm up" (15 percent). Only 65 percent of the children studied by Chess and Thomas fit into one of the three types of temperament. Some of the differences among these three types of children are shown in Table 7.5 ■. As you can see, the easy child has regular sleep and feeding schedules, approaches new situations (such as a new food, a new school, or a stranger) with enthusiasm and adapts easily to them, and is generally cheerful. It is obvious why such a child is relatively easy for parents to raise. Some children are more inconsistent and show a mixture of temperament traits. For example, a toddler may have a pleasant disposition but be frightened of new situations.

The difficult child, on the other hand, has irregular sleep and feeding schedules, is slow to accept new people and situations, takes a long time to adjust to new routines, and responds to frustrations with tantrums and loud crying. Parents find this type of child more difficult to deal with. The slow-to-warm-up child falls somewhere between the other two. These children have somewhat irregular sleep and feeding patterns and do not react as strongly as difficult children. They initially respond negatively to new experiences and adapt slowly, only after repeated exposure.

Stability of Temperament

How stable is temperament? **TRUTH OR FICTION REVISITED:** Children are not all born with the same temperament. Thomas and Chess found that many children have one of three kinds of temperament from the first days of life. Evidence also indicates that there is at least moderate consistency in the development of temperament from infancy onward (Elliot & Thrash, 2010; Zuckerman, 2011). The infant who is highly active and cries in novel situations often becomes a fearful toddler. An anxious, unhappy toddler tends to become an anxious, unhappy adolescent. The child who refuses to accept new foods during infancy may scream when getting the first haircut, refuse to leave a parent's side during the first day of kindergarten, and have difficulty adjusting to college as a young adult. Difficult children in general are at greater risk for developing psychological disorders and adjustment problems later in life (Pauli-Pott et al., 2003; Rothbart et al., 2004). A longitudinal study tracked the progress of infants with a difficult temperament from one-and-a-half through 12 years of age (Guerin et al., 1997). Temperament during infancy was assessed by the mother. Behaviour patterns were assessed by both parents

Differences in Temperament
Differences in temperament emerge in early infancy. The photo on the left shows the positive reactions of a five-month-old girl being fed a new food for the first time. The photo on the right shows the very different response of another girl of about the same age when she is introduced to a new food.

during the third year through the age of 12 and by teachers from the ages of 6 to 11. A difficult temperament correlated significantly with parental reports of behavioural problems from ages 3 to 12, including problems with attention span and aggression. Teachers concurred that children who had shown difficult temperaments during infancy were more likely to be aggressive later on and to have shorter attention spans.

Goodness of Fit: The Role of the Environment

The environment also affects the development of temperament. An initial biological predisposition toward a certain temperament may be strengthened or weakened by the parents' reaction to the child. Consider the following: Parents may react to a difficult child by becoming less available and less responsive (Schoppe-Sullivan et al., 2007). They may insist on imposing rigid care-giving schedules, which in turn can cause the child to become even more difficult to handle (Schoppe-Sullivan et al., 2007). This example illustrates a discrepancy, or poor fit, between the child's behaviour style and the parents' expectations and behaviours.

On the other hand, parents may respond in such a way as to modify a child's initial temperament in a more positive direction. Take the case of Carl, who in early life was one of the most difficult children in the New York Longitudinal Study:

> Whether it was the first solid foods in infancy, the beginning of nursery and elementary school, first birthday parties, or the first shopping trip, each experience evoked stormy responses, with loud crying and struggling to get away. However, his parents learned to anticipate Carl's reactions, knew that if they were patient, presented only one or a few new situations at a time, and gave him the opportunity for repeated exposure, Carl would finally adapt positively. Furthermore, once he adapted, his intensity of responses gave him a zestful enthusiastic involvement, just as it gave his initial negative reactions a loud and stormy character. His parents became fully aware that the difficulties in raising Carl were due to his temperament and not to their being "bad parents." The father even looked on his son's shrieking and turmoil as a sign of lustiness. As a result of this positive parent–child interaction, Carl never became a behaviour problem.
>
> —Chess & Thomas (1984, p. 263)

This example demonstrates **goodness of fit** between the behaviours of child and parent. A key factor is the parents' realization that their youngster's behaviour does not mean that the child is weak or deliberately disobedient, or that they are bad parents. This realization helps parents modify their attitudes and behaviours toward the child, whose behaviour may in turn change in the desired direction (Brook et al., 2009; Schoppe-Sullivan et al., 2007).

7.6 Gender Differences

QUESTION » How do infant girls and boys differ in behaviour? All cultures make a distinction between females and males and have beliefs and expectations about how they ought to behave. For this reason, a child's gender is a key factor in shaping her or his personality and other aspects of development.

Behaviour of Infant Girls and Boys

Girls tend to advance more rapidly in their motor development in infancy: They sit, crawl, and walk earlier than boys do (Matlin, 2008). Female and male infants are quite similar in their responses to sights, sounds, tastes, smells, and touch. Although a few studies have found that infant boys are more active and irritable than girls, others have not (Matlin, 2008). Girls and boys also are similar in their social behaviours. They are equally likely to smile at people's faces, for example, and do not differ in their dependency on adults (Maccoby & Jacklin, 1974; Matlin, 2008). One area in which girls and boys begin to differ early in life is their preference for certain toys and play activities. By 12–18 months of age, girls prefer to play with dolls, doll furniture,

dishes, and toy animals, whereas boys prefer transportation toys (trucks, cars, airplanes, and the like), tools, and sports equipment as early as 9–18 month of age (Berenbaum et al., 2008). On the other hand, gender differences that appear to show up later, such as differences in spatial relations skills, are not necessarily evident in infancy (Örnkloo & von Hofsten, 2007). By 24 months, both girls and boys appear to be quite aware of which behaviours are considered gender-consistent and which gender-inconsistent, as measured in terms of time spent looking at the "novel" (in this case, "gender-inconsistent," as dictated by cultural stereotypes) behaviour (Hill & Flom, 2007).

TRUTH OR FICTION REVISITED: Thus, it appears to be fiction that children play with gender-typed toys only after they have become aware of the gender roles assigned to them by society. It may well be the case that (most) girls prefer dolls and toy animals and that (most) boys prefer toy trucks and sports equipment before they have been socialized—even before they fully understand whether they themselves are female or male. Researchers continue to try to sort out the effects of nature and nurture in children's gender-related preferences.

goodness of fit Agreement between the parents' expectations of, or demands on, the child and the child's temperamental characteristics.

Adults' Behaviours toward Infant Girls and Boys

Adults respond differently to girls and boys. For example, in some studies, adults are presented with an unfamiliar infant who is dressed in boy's clothes and has a boy's name, whereas other adults are introduced to a baby who is dressed in girl's clothing and has a girl's name. (In reality, it is the same baby who simply is given different names and clothing.) When adults believe they are playing with a girl, they are more likely to offer "her" a doll; when they think the child is a boy, they are more likely to offer a football or a hammer. "Boys" also are encouraged to engage in more physical activity than are "girls" (Worell & Goodheart, 2006). Perhaps it is no wonder that infants labelled as "girls" are perceived as littler and softer (as well as nicer and more beautiful) than infants labelled as "boys."

Parents' Behaviours toward Sons and Daughters

Do parents treat infant sons and daughters differently? Yes, like the adults with the unfamiliar babies, parents are more likely to encourage rough-and-tumble play in their sons than in their daughters. Fathers are especially likely to do so (Eccles et al., 2000; Fagot et al., 2000). On the other hand, parents talk more to infant daughters than to infant sons. They smile more at daughters, are more emotionally expressive toward them, and focus more on feelings when talking to them (Blakemore & Hill, 2008; Matlin, 2008).

Adults Treat Infant Girls and Boys Differently

Perhaps the most obvious way in which parents treat their baby girls and boys differently is in their choice of clothing, toys, and room furnishings. If you met this infant, would you have any doubt as to his or her sex?

Perhaps the most obvious way in which parents treat their baby girls and boys differently is in their choice of clothing, room furnishings, and toys. Infant girls are likely to be decked out in a pink or yellow dress embellished with ruffles and lace, whereas infant boys wear blue or red (Cieraad, 2007). Parents also provide baby girls and boys with different bedroom decorations and toys. Examination of the contents of rooms of children found that boys' rooms were often decorated with animal themes and with blue bedding and curtains. Girls' rooms featured flowers, lace, ruffles, and pastel colours (Cieraad, 2007). Girls owned more dolls; boys had more vehicles, military toys, and sports equipment.

Other studies find that parents react favourably when their preschool daughters play with "toys for girls" and their sons play with "toys for boys." Parents and other adults show more negative reactions when girls play with toys for boys and when boys play with toys for girls (Martin et al., 2002; Worell & Goodheart, 2006). In general, fathers are more concerned than mothers that their children engage in activities viewed as "appropriate" for their gender.

Parents thus attempt to influence their children's behaviour during infancy and lay the foundation for development in early childhood. It is to that period of life that we turn next, in Chapter 8.

19. Psychologists devised the mirror technique to assess development of the self-_____.

20. The child's _____ consists of the stable individual differences in styles of reaction that are present very early in life.

21. The three basic types of temperament are easy, difficult, and _____ to warm up.

22. Girls prefer to play with dolls, whereas boys show a preference for playing with transportation toys as early as _____ months of age.

Reflect & Relate: Have you known infants who were easygoing or difficult? How did their temperaments affect their relationships with their parents?

Recite an Active Summary

7.1 Attachment: Bonds That Endure

What is meant by "attachment"?

An attachment is an enduring emotional tie between one animal or person and another specific individual. Children try to maintain contact with persons to whom they are attached.

What does it mean for a child to be "secure" or "insecure"?

Most infants in Canada are securely attached. In the strange situation, a securely attached infant mildly protests the mother's departure and is readily comforted by her. The two major types of insecure attachment are avoidant attachment and ambivalent/resistant attachment. Infants with avoidant attachment are least distressed by their mothers' departure. Infants with ambivalent/resistant attachment show severe distress when their mothers leave but are ambivalent upon reunion. Securely attached infants are happier, more sociable, and more cooperative. They use the mother as a secure base from which to explore the environment. At ages five and six, securely attached children are preferred by peers and teachers and are more competent.

What are the roles of the parents in the formation of bonds of attachment?

High-quality care contributes to security. Parents of securely attached infants are more likely to be affectionate and sensitive to their needs. Security of attachment is related to the infant's temperament as well as to caregivers' behaviour.

What did Mary Ainsworth learn about the stages of attachment?

The initial-preattachment phase lasts from birth to about three months and is characterized by indiscriminate attachment. The attachment-in-the-making phase occurs at about three or four months and is characterized by preference for familiar figures. The clear-cut-attachment phase occurs at about six or seven months and is characterized by dependence on the primary caregiver. The fourth stage, referred to as the reciprocal-relationship phase, begins at around 18 months to two years; it is characterized by a better understanding of parents' comings and goings.

What are the various theories of attachment? How does each emphasize nature or nurture in its explanation of the development of attachment?

Cognitive theorists suggest that an infant must develop object permanence before specific attachment is possible. Behaviourists suggest that infants become attached to caregivers because caregivers meet their bodily needs. Psychoanalysts suggest that the primary caregiver becomes a love object. The Harlows' experiments with monkeys suggest that contact comfort is a key to attachment. Ethologists view attachment as an inborn fixed action pattern (FAP), which occurs during a critical period in response to a releasing stimulus.

7.2 When Attachment Fails

What are the effects of social deprivation?

The Harlows found that rhesus infants reared in isolation confinement later avoided contact with other monkeys. Females who later had offspring tended to ignore or abuse them. Institutionalized children who receive little social stimulation encounter problems in development. Many exhibit withdrawal and depression. Deficiencies in sensory stimulation and social interaction may cause more problems than lack of love per se. Infants have considerable capacity to recover from deprivation.

What are the incidences of child abuse and neglect? What are their effects?

About one-quarter of children across the age groups reportedly experience some form of maltreatment or risk of maltreatment. Maltreated children are less intimate with peers and are more aggressive, angry, and noncompliant than other children. Child abuse and neglect may run in families because abusive parents serve as role models. Exposure to violence in the home may lead children to accept family violence as the norm. Some parents rationalize that they are hurting their children "for their own good"—to discourage problem behaviour.

What are autism spectrum disorders?

Autism spectrum disorders (ASDs) are characterized by impairment in communication skills and social interactions, and by repetitive, stereotyped behaviour. The most striking feature of autism is the child's aloneness. Other features include communication problems, intolerance of change, stereotypical behaviour, mutism, echolalia, and self-mutilation. Evidence suggests a role for biological factors in autism. Genetic studies find higher concordance rates for autism among monozygotic than among dizygotic twins. Researchers also suspect neurological involvement. Behaviour modification has been used to increase the child's attention to others and social play and to decrease self-mutilation. Aversive stimulation has been used to curtail self-injury. Researchers are studying the use of SSRIs and major tranquilizers.

7.3 Child Care

Does day care affect children's bonds of attachment with their parents? Does it affect their social, emotional, and cognitive development?

Infants with day-care experience are more independent, self-confident, outgoing, affectionate, and cooperative with peers and adults. Children in high-quality day care outperform children who remain in the home in cognitive skills. Children in day care are also more aggressive, but some aggression may indicate independence, not maladjustment.

7.4 Emotional Development

What are emotions? How do they develop?

Emotions are states of feeling that have physiological, situational, and cognitive components. Izard proposed that infants are born with several emotional states but that their appearance is linked to cognitive development and social experiences.

What is fear of strangers? Is it normal?

Fear of strangers is normal in that most infants develop it at about the age of six to nine months.

What is social referencing? When does it develop?

Infants display social referencing as early as six months of age, when they use caregivers' facial expressions or tones of voice for information on how to respond in novel situations.

What is emotional regulation?

Emotional regulation is emotional self-control. Caregivers help infants learn to regulate their emotions. The children of secure mothers are more likely to regulate their emotions positively.

7.5 Personality Development

What is the self-concept? How does it develop?

The self-concept is the sense of self. Findings using the mirror technique suggest that the self-concept develops by about 18 months of age. Self-awareness enables the child to develop concepts of sharing and cooperation and "self-conscious" emotions such as embarrassment, envy, empathy, pride, guilt, and shame.

What types of temperament do we find among children? How do they develop?

The term *temperament* refers to stable individual differences in styles of reaction to the world that are present early in life. These reactions include activity level, regularity, approach or withdrawal, adaptability, response threshold, response intensity, quality of mood, distractibility, attention span, and persistence. Thomas and Chess found that most infants can be classified as having an easy, difficult, or slow-to-warm-up temperament. Temperament remains moderately consistent from infancy through young adulthood.

7.6 Gender Differences

How do infant girls and boys differ in behaviour?

Female infants sit, crawl, and walk earlier than boys do. By 12 to 18 months of age, girls prefer to play with dolls and similar toys, whereas boys prefer transportation toys and gear.

Key Terms

Active Learning Resources

Go to *Voyages in Development's* CourseMate at **www
.nelsonbrain.com**, where you will find an interactive
eBook, flashcards, Pre-Lecture Quizzes, Section Quizzes,
Exam Practice, videos, and more.

Samuel Micut | Dreamstime.com

Major Topics

EARLY CHILDHOOD:
Physical Development

8

Truth or Fiction?

T | F   Some children are left-brained and others are right-brained. **p. 265**

T | F   Sedentary parents are more likely to have "couch potatoes" for children. **p. 268**

T | F   Julius Caesar, Michelangelo, Tom Cruise, and Oprah have something in common? (Hint: They don't all have book clubs.) **p. 272**

T | F   A disproportionately high percentage of math whizzes are left-handed. **p. 272**

T | F   Some diseases are normal. **p. 277**

T | F   Infections are the most common cause of death among children in Canada **p. 280**

T | F   It is dangerous to awaken a sleepwalker. **p. 285**

T | F   Competent parents toilet train their children by their second birthday. **p. 285**

Two-year-old Matteo is having lunch in his high chair. He is not without ambition. He begins by shoving fistfuls of hamburger into his mouth. He picks up his cup with both hands and drinks milk. Then he starts banging his spoon on his tray and his cup. He kicks his feet against the chair. He throws hamburger on the floor.

Compare Matteo's behaviour with that of Jacob, age three-and-a-half, who is getting ready for bed. Jacob carefully pulls his plastic train track apart and places each piece in the box. Then he walks to the bathroom, brings his stool over to the sink, and stands on it. He takes down his toothbrush and toothpaste, opens the cap, squeezes toothpaste on the brush, and begins to brush his teeth.

Matteo and Jacob are in early childhood, the years from two to six. These years are sometimes called the play years, and they include the preschool period, which usually ends at about age five, when most children enter kindergarten. During early childhood, physical growth is slower than it was in infancy. Children become taller and leaner, and by the end of early childhood they look more like adults than like infants. An explosion of motor skills occurs; children become stronger, faster, and better coordinated.

Language improves enormously, and children can carry on conversations with others. As cognitive skills develop, a new world of make believe or "pretend" play emerges. Curiosity and eagerness to learn are hallmarks of early childhood.

Physical and cognitive developments enable the child to emerge from total dependence on parents and caregivers to become part of the broader world outside the family. Peers take on an increasingly important role. Children develop a sense of their own abilities and shortcomings.

We learn about all these developments of early childhood—physical, cognitive, social, and emotional—in Chapters 8, 9, and 10.

Anetta/Shutterstock.com

8.1 Growth Patterns

In early childhood, physical and motor development proceeds by leaps and bounds—literally! While toddlers like Matteo are occupied with grasping, banging, and throwing things, three-year-olds like Jacob are busy manipulating objects and exercising their newly developing fine motor skills.

Height and Weight

QUESTION » What changes occur in height and weight during early childhood? Following the dramatic gains in height of the first two years, the growth rate slows (Kuczmarski et al., 2000). Girls and boys tend to gain about 5–8 centimetres in height per year throughout early childhood. Weight gains also remain fairly even, at about 2–3 kilograms per year (see Appendix B). Children become increasingly slender as they gain in height and lose some "baby fat." Boys as a group are only slightly taller and heavier than girls in early childhood. Noticeable variations in growth patterns also occur from child to child.

Development of the Brain

QUESTION » How does the brain develop during early childhood? The brain develops more quickly than any other organ in early childhood. At two years of age, for example, the brain already has attained 75 percent of its adult weight. By the age of five, the brain has reached 90 percent of its adult weight, even though the total body weight of the five-year-old is barely one-third of what it will be as an adult (Tanner, 1989).

The increase in brain size is due in part to the continuing process of myelination of nerve fibres (see Chapter 5). Completion of the myelination of the neural pathways that link the cerebellum to the cerebral cortex facilitates the development of fine motor skills (Allen et al., 2011; Fletcher, 2011). The cerebellum is involved in balance and coordination, and the young child's balancing abilities increase dramatically as myelination of these pathways nears completion.

Brain Development and Visual Skills

Brain development is also linked to improvements in the ability to attend to and process visual information (Seiler et al., 2011). These skills are critical in learning to read. The parts of the brain that enable the child to sustain attention and screen out distractions become increasingly myelinated between the ages of about four and seven (Nelson & Luciana, 2001). As a result, most children are ready to focus on schoolwork at these ages.

The speed with which children process visual information improves throughout childhood, reaching adult levels at the beginning of adolescence (Scherf et al., 2009; Seiler et al., 2011). The child's ability to scan visual material systematically also improves in early childhood. For example, researchers in one classic study presented children with pairs of pictures of similar-looking houses and asked the children whether or not the houses were identical (Vurpillot, 1968). Four-year-olds almost never showed thorough, systematic visual scanning of the features of the houses, but nine-year-olds often did so.

Right Brain, Left Brain?

It has become popular to speak of people as being "right-brained" or "left-brained." We have even heard it said that some instructional methods are aimed at the right brain (they are presented in an emotionally laden, aesthetic way), whereas others are aimed at the left brain (they are presented in a logical and straightforward manner).

The notion is that the hemispheres of the brain are involved in different kinds of intellectual and emotional functions and responses. Research does suggest that in right-handed individuals, the left hemisphere is relatively more involved in intellectual undertakings that require logical analysis and problem solving, language, and mathematical computation (Scull, 2010). The other hemisphere (usually the right hemisphere) is generally superior in visual–spatial functions (it is better at putting puzzles together), recognition of faces, discrimination of colours, aesthetic and emotional responses, understanding metaphors, and creative mathematical reasoning.

TRUTH OR FICTION REVISITED: Actually, it is not true that some children are left-brained and others are right-brained. Brain functions are not split up so precisely, as has been popularly believed. The functions of the left and right hemispheres overlap to some degree, and the hemispheres also tend to respond simultaneously when we focus our attention on one thing or another. They are aided in "cooperation" by the myelination of the **corpus callosum**—a thick bundle of nerve fibres that connects the hemispheres (Luders et al., 2010). Myelination of the corpus callosum proceeds rapidly during early and middle childhood and is largely complete by the age of eight. By that time, children can better integrate logical and emotional functioning.

Corpus callosum

The Corpus Callosum
The corpus callosum is a structure of the human brain that connects the left and right cerebral hemispheres.

Plasticity of the Brain

Many parts of the brain have specialized functions. Specialization enables our behaviour to be more complex. But specialization also means that injuries to certain parts of the brain can result in loss of these functions.

Fortunately, the brain also shows **plasticity** (M. V. Johnston et al., 2009). Plasticity means that the brain frequently can compensate for injuries to particular areas. This compensatory ability is greatest at about one to two years of age and then gradually declines, although it may not be completely gone, even in adulthood (Kolb & Gibb, 2007; Nelson et al., 2006). When we suffer damage to the areas of the brain that control language, we may lose the ability to speak or understand language. However, other areas of the brain may take over these functions in young children who suffer such damage. As a result, the children may dramatically regain the ability to speak or comprehend language (Nelson et al., 2006). In adolescence and adulthood, regaining such functions is much more difficult and may be all but impossible.

Two factors are involved in the brain's plasticity (Gauthier et al., 2009; Nelson et al., 2006). The first is "sprouting," or the growth of new dendrites. To some degree, new dendrites can allow for the rearrangement of neural circuits. The second factor is the redundancy of neural connections. In some cases, similar functions are found at two or more sites in the brain, although they are developed to different degrees. If one site is damaged, the other may be able to develop to perform the function.

corpus callosum The thick bundle of nerve fibres that connects the hemispheres of the brain.

plasticity The tendency of new parts of the brain to take up the functions of injured parts.

Active Review

1. Children gain about _____ centimetres in height per year throughout early childhood.

2. Weight gains average about _____ kilograms per year.

3. The _____ develops more rapidly than any other organ in early childhood.

4. _____ of the neural pathways that link the cerebellum to the cerebral cortex facilitates the development of fine motor skills.

5. The _____ is involved in balance and coordination.

6. Research suggests that in _____-handed individuals, the left hemisphere is relatively more involved in logical analysis and problem solving, language, and mathematical computation.

7. The _____ hemisphere of the cerebral cortex is usually superior in visual–spatial functions and emotional responses.

8. Because of its _____, the brain can often compensate for injuries to particular areas.

Reflect & Relate: Have you ever compared the growth of a child to the norms on a growth chart? What were you looking for? What were your concerns?

8.2 Motor Development

QUESTION » How do motor skills develop in early childhood? There is an explosion of motor skills in early childhood. As children's nervous systems mature, their movements become more precise and coordinated. The development of various gross and fine motor skills permits preschoolers to learn and discover new things about themselves and their environments. In the preschool years, children typically learn culture-specific motor skills such as riding a tricycle, ice skating, playing soccer with siblings, helping make dinner, and hopping for playing hopscotch.

Gross Motor Skills

gross motor skills Skills that employ the large muscles used in locomotion.

Between the ages of two and six, children make great strides in the development of **gross motor skills**, which involve the large muscles used in locomotion (see Table 8.1 ■). At about the age of three, children can balance on one foot. By age

● TABLE 8.1

Development of Gross Motor Skills in Early Childhood

2 Years (24–35 Months)	3 Years (36–47 Months)	4 Years (48–59 Months)	5 Years (60–71 Months)
• Runs well straight ahead	• Goes around obstacles while running	• Turns sharp corners while running	• Runs lightly on toes
• Walks up stairs, two feet to a step	• Walks up stairs, one foot to a step	• Walks down stairs, one foot to a step	• Jumps a distance of 1 metre
• Kicks a large ball	• Kicks a large ball easily	• Jumps from a height of 30 cm	• Catches a small ball, using hands only
• Jumps a distance of 10–36 cm	• Jumps from the bottom step	• Throws a ball overhand	• Hops 2–3 metres forward on each foot
• Throws a small ball without falling	• Catches a bounced ball, using torso and arms to form a basket	• Turns sharp corners while pushing and pulling toys	• Stands on one foot for 8–10 seconds
• Pushes and pulls large toys	• Goes around obstacles while pushing and pulling toys	• Hops on one foot, four to six hops	• Climbs actively and skillfully
• Hops on one foot, two or more hops	• Hops on one foot, up to three hops	• Stands on one foot for 3–8 seconds	• Skips on alternate feet
• Tries to stand on one foot	• Stands on one foot	• Climbs ladders	• Rides a bicycle with training wheels
• Climbs on furniture to look out of window	• Climbs preschool or childcare apparatus	• Rides a tricycle well	

Note: The ages are averages and are based on white, middle-class North American norms; there are individual variations and once again we highlight that other cultural experiences and activities also exist to promote motor development.

three or four, they can walk up stairs as adults do, by placing a foot on each step. By age four or five, they can skip and pedal a tricycle (Allen et al., 2011). They are better able to coordinate two tasks, such as singing and running at the same time, than are toddlers (Haywood & Getchell, 2008). In early childhood, children appear to acquire motor skills by teaching themselves and observing the behaviour of other children. The opportunity to play with other children seems more important than adult instruction at this age.

Throughout early childhood, girls and boys are not far apart in their motor skills. Girls are somewhat better at tasks requiring balance and precision of movement. Boys, on the other hand, show some advantage in throwing and kicking (Moreno-Briseño et al., 2010; Tzuriel & Egozi, 2010).

Individual differences are more impressive than sex differences throughout early and middle childhood. Some children develop motor skills earlier than others. Some are genetically predisposed to developing better coordination or more strength than others. Motivation and practice also are important in children's acquisition of motor skills. Motor experiences in infancy may affect the development of motor skills in early childhood. For example, children who have early crawling experience perform better than those who do not on tests of motor skills in early childhood (Haywood & Getchell, 2008).

OBSERVING CHILDREN, UNDERSTANDING OURSELVES

Gross Motor Skills

Although three-year-old Olivia can kick a ball, she has to use her torso and arms formed into a basket to catch a ball.

How do gross motor skills improve as children age? How does Olivia's attempt to catch a ball illustrate the proximodistal trend in motor development? How much individual variation is there in coordination of gross motor skills among children of the same age? Are there significant differences among the gross motor skills of boys and girls of the same age?

From Rathus. *Childhood and Adolescence*, 5E. © 2014 South-Western, a part of Cengage Learning, Inc. Reproduced by permission. www .cengage.com/permissions

Go to www.nelson.com/voyages2ce to watch the video, answer the questions, and e-mail your responses to your professor.

Physical Activity

Children spend quite a bit of time in physical activity in early childhood. One study found that they spend an average of more than 25 hours a week in large-muscle activity (D. W. Campbell et al., 2002). Two- to four-year-olds are more likely than four- to six-year-olds to engage in physically oriented play, such as grasping, banging, and mouthing objects (D. W. Campbell et al., 2002). Consequently, they need more space and less furniture in a preschool or day-care setting.

The level of motor activity begins to decline after two or three years of age. Children become less restless and are able to sit still longer (D. W. Campbell et al., 2002; Eaton et al., 2001). Between the ages of two and four, children in free play show an increase in sustained, focused attention. Although this is an exciting time for preschoolers to explore the world around them, with exploration and lack of supervision or proper childproofing accidental injuries may occur. According to Canadian government statistics, two children die from unintentional injuries and about 80 children need hospitalization on a daily basis (www .healthycanadians.gc.ca/kids-enfants/injury-blessure/index-eng.php).

Rough-and-Tumble Play
Play fighting and chasing activities—known as rough-and-tumble play—are found among young children in societies around the world.

Rough-and-Tumble Play

Rough-and-tumble play consists of a variety of energetic behaviours such as running, chasing, fleeing, wrestling, hitting with an open hand, laughing, and making faces. Rough-and-tumble play is not the same as aggressive behaviour. Aggression involves hitting with fists, pushing, taking, grabbing, and angry looks. Unlike aggression, rough-and-tumble play helps develop both physical and social skills in children (Cillessen & Bellmore, 2010; Pellis & Pellis, 2007). Most important for distinguishing rough-and-tumble play from aggression and dominance is the mutual understanding and enjoyment of the play partners (Flanders, Herman, & Paquette, 2012).

There are many identified benefits of social play, such as rough-and-tumble play—most notably, the positive associations with social competence (Rubin, 1982; Symons, 1978). Children are socialized through play about acceptable social norms, and also learn how to regulate impulses and arousal, how to read others' cues, and foster social skills (Carson et al., 1993; Edwards, 2000; Flanders et al., 2012).

In Western cultures there has been a focus on parent–child rough-and-tumble play (Paquette, 2004). While both mothers and fathers engage in rough-and-tumble play with their children, parents tend to engage in more rough-and-tumble play with their male children, and fathers engage in more rough-and-tumble play than mothers (Panksepp, Burgdorf, Turner, & Gordon, 2003). Children also engage in rough-and-tumble play with their peers during the preschool years, and this behaviour peaks between the ages of eight and ten (Carson, Burks, & Parke, 1993). In contrast, rough-and-tumble play with parents peaks at about age four (Pelligrini & Smith, 2008).

Play fighting and chasing activities are found during early childhood in societies around the world (Whiting & Edwards, 1988). But the particular form that rough-and-tumble play takes is influenced by culture and environment. For example, rough-and-tumble play among girls is quite common among the Pilaga Indians and the !Kung of Botswana but less common among girls in Canada. In Canada, rough-and-tumble play usually occurs in groups made up of the same sex. However, !Kung girls and boys engage in rough-and-tumble play together. And among the Pilaga, girls often are matched against the boys.

Individual Differences in Activity Level

Children differ widely in their activity levels. Some children are much more active than others.

TRUTH OR FICTION REVISITED: Sedentary parents are more likely to have "couch potatoes" for children. Physically active children are more likely to have physically active parents. In a study of four- to seven-year-olds (Moore et al., 1991), children of active mothers were twice as likely to be active as children of inactive mothers. Children of active fathers were 3.5 times as likely to be active as children of inactive fathers. More recently, studies have found support (both through longitudinal and cross-section study designs) for parental modelling of physical activity and positive associations with children's physical activity levels (Crawford et al., 2010; Jiménez-Pavón et al., 2012).

Several reasons may explain this relationship. First, active parents may serve as role models for activity. Second, sharing of activities by family members may play a role. Parents who are avid tennis players may involve their children in games of tennis from an early age. By the same token, couch-potato parents who prefer to view tennis on television rather than play it may be more likely to share this sedentary activity with their children. A third factor is that active parents may encourage and support their child's participation in physical activity. Finally, a tendency to be active or inactive may be transmitted genetically, as shown by evidence from kinship studies (see Chapter 2)

Canadian Physical Activity Guidelines and Canadian Sedentary Behaviour Guidelines

Canadian Physical Activity Guidelines (0–4 years)

For healthy growth and development:

- Infants (aged less than 1 year) should be physically active several times daily—particularly through interactive floor-based play.
- Toddlers (aged 1–2 years) and preschoolers (aged 3–4 years) should accumulate at least 180 minutes of physical activity *at any intensity* spread throughout the day, including:
  - A variety of activities in different environments
  - Activities that develop movements skills
  - Progressing toward at least 60 minutes of energetic play by 5 years of age
- More daily physical activity provides greater benefits.

Canadian Sedentary Behaviour Guidelines (0–4 years)

- For healthy growth and development, caregivers should minimize the time infants (aged less than 1 year), toddlers (aged 1–2 years), and preschoolers (aged 3–4 years) spend being sedentary during waking hours. This includes prolonged sitting or being restrained (e.g., stroller, high chair) for more than one hour at a time.
- For those under 2 years, screen time (e.g., TV, computer, electronic games) is not recommended.
- For children 2–4 years, screen time should be limited to under one hour per day; less is better.

Source: Canadian Society for Exercise Physiology, © 2012. Reproduced with permission. www.csep.ca/guidelines

(Saudino, 2012; Wood et al., 2008). Genetic and environmental factors apparently interact to determine a child's activity level.

Obesity is a national health concern, and rates of obesity in children aged two to five are estimated at 6.3 percent (Obesity in Canada, 2011). Health Canada endorses physical activity as part of a healthy lifestyle, and has guidelines aimed specifically at children and their families across settings (home, child care, preschool, and school). Table 8.2 ■ outlines the guidelines for physical activity and sedentary behaviour for children up to age four.

Parents, caregivers, and educators are encouraged to structure children's environments so as to optimize safe exploration, play, outdoor activities, and minimize screen time and overall sedentary behaviours.

A CLOSER LOOK DIVERSITY

Gender Differences in Motor Activity

QUESTION » Do girls and boys differ in their activity levels during early childhood? During early childhood, boys tend to be more active than girls, at least in some settings (Haywood & Getchell, 2008). Boys spend more time than girls in large-muscle activities. Boys tend to be more fidgety and distractible than girls and to spend less time focusing on tasks.

Why are boys more active and restless than girls? One theory is that boys of a given age are less mature physically than girls of the same age. Children tend to become less active as they develop. Therefore, the gender difference in activity level may be a maturational difference (Haywood & Getchell, 2008). However, parental encouragement and reward of motor activity in boys and discouragement of such behaviour in girls may be involved as well.

Boys also are more likely than girls to engage in rough-and-tumble play (Haywood & Getchell, 2008). What might account for this gender difference? Some psychologists suggest that the reasons are largely based in biology—having to do, especially, with the sex hormone testosterone. Others argue that the socializing influences of the family and culture at large promote play differences among girls and boys.

Reflect Why is it useful to know about gender differences in motor activity?

Fine Motor Skills

Fine motor skills develop gradually and lag behind gross motor skills (Fletcher, 2011). This is yet another example of the proximodistal trend in development (see Chapters 3 and 5). Fine motor skills involve the small muscles used in manipulation and coordination. Control over the wrists and fingers enables children to hold a pencil properly, dress themselves, and stack blocks (see Table 8.3 ■). Young children can labour endlessly in attempting to tie their shoelaces and get their jackets zipped. There are terribly frustrating (and funny) scenes of children alternating between steadfastly refusing to allow a parent to intervene and requesting the caregiver's help.

Fine motor skills become more refined with age for several reasons: typical neurological development, practice, and experience. While there are general developmental milestones of fine motor skills, there are still notably individual differences and variability in young children's fine motor skills due to exposure and practice (Bruni, 2006; Maraj & Bonertz, 2007) or cognitive development (Connor et al., 2006; Kalberg et al., 2006; Provost, Lopez, & Heimerl, 2007). For instance, children who have certain cognitive impairments (e.g., children with autism or fetal alcohol spectrum disorders) tend to show delays in fine motor skills (Connor et al., 2006; Provost et al., 2007).

Children's Drawings

QUESTION » Are children's scribbles the result of random motor activity? The development of drawing in young children is closely linked to the development of motor and cognitive skills. Children first begin to scribble during the second year. Initially, they seem to make marks for the sheer joy of it, and parents sometimes confuse their drawings with "messiness" (Jolley, 2010). Yet there is a method to them.

● TABLE 8.3

Development of Fine Motor Skills in Early Childhood

2 Years (24–35 Months)	3 Years (36–47 Months)	4 Years (48–59 Months)	5 Years (60–71 Months)
• Builds a tower of 6 cubes	• Builds a tower of 9 cubes	• Builds a tower of 10 or more cubes	• Builds 3 steps from 6 blocks, using a model
• Copies vertical and horizontal lines	• Copies circle and cross	• Copies square	• Copies triangle and star
• Imitates folding of paper	• Copies letters	• Prints simple words	• Prints first name and numbers
• Prints on an easel with a brush	• Holds crayons with fingers, not fist	• Imitates folding paper three times	• Imitates folding of square paper into a triangle
• Places simple shapes in correct holes	• Strings 4 beads using a large needle	• Uses pencil with correct hand grip	• Traces around a diamond drawn on paper
		• Strings 10 beads	• Laces shoes

Note: The ages are averages; there are individual variations.

fine motor skills Skills that employ the small muscles used in manipulation, such as those in the fingers.

Rhoda Kellogg (1959, 1970) studied more than 1 million drawings made by children. She found a meaningful pattern in the scribbles and identified 20 basic scribbles that she considered the building blocks of all art: vertical, horizontal, diagonal, circular, curving, waving or zigzagging lines, and dots (see Figure 8.1 ■).

Children go through four stages as they progress from making scribbles to drawing pictures: the *placement, shape, design,* and *pictorial stages* (see Figure 8.2 ■). Two-year-olds place their scribbles in various locations on the page (for example, in the middle of the page or near one of the borders). By age three, children are starting to draw basic shapes: circles,

Figure 8.1 ■ The 20 Basic Scribbles (Really)
By the age of two, children can scribble. Rhoda Kellogg identified these 20 basic scribbles as the building blocks of the young child's drawings.

©Suzanne Simpson Millar

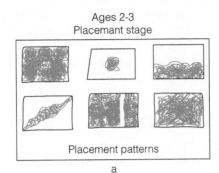

Ages 2-3
Placement stage

Placement patterns

a

Ages 3-4
Shape stage   Design stage

Ages 4-5
Pictorial stage

Diagrams   Combines   Aggregates   Early pictorial   Later pictorial

b   c   d   e   F

Suzanne Simpson Millar & Lenore-Taylor Atkins

Figure 8.2 ■ Four Stages in Children's Drawings
Children go through four stages in drawing pictures. (a) They first place their scribbles in various locations on the page. They then (b) draw basic shapes and (c, d) combine shapes into designs. Finally, (e, f) they draw recognizable objects.

Fine Motor Skills

Control over the wrists and fingers enables children to hold a pencil, play a musical instrument, and, as shown in this photograph, work with modelling clay.

squares, triangles, crosses, X's, and odd shapes. As soon as they can draw shapes, children begin to combine them in the design stage. Between ages four and five, the child reaches the pictorial stage, in which designs begin to resemble recognizable objects.

Children's early drawings tend to be symbolic of a broad category rather than specific. For example, a child might draw the same simple building whether she is asked to draw a school or a house (Tallandini & Valentini, 1991). Children between three and five years old usually do not start out to draw a particular thing. They are more likely to first see what they have drawn and then name it. As motor and cognitive skills improve beyond the age of five, children improve at copying figures and become able to draw an object they have in mind (Dağlıoğlu et al., 2010; Rübeling et al., 2011).

Handedness: On Being Right or ... Left?

QUESTIONS » When does handedness emerge? Are there any advantages or disadvantages to being left-handed? **TRUTH OR FICTION REVISITED:** Julius Caesar, Michelangelo, Tom Cruise, and Oprah do have something in common; they are all left-handed. Handedness emerges during infancy. By the age of two or three months, a rattle placed in the infant's hand is held longer with the right hand than with the left (Fitzgerald et al., 1991). By four months of age, most infants show a clear-cut right-hand preference in exploring objects using the sense of touch (Streri, 2002). Preference for grasping with the right or left hand increases markedly between the ages of 6 and 14 months (Ferre et al., 2010). Handedness becomes more strongly established during the early childhood years. Most people are right-handed, although studies vary as to how many are left-handed. Some people are ambidextrous—that is, they can use their right and left hands and arms equally effectively. Many professional baseball players have batted either "righty" or "lefty."

Left-Handedness: Is It Gauche to Be Left-Handed? Myths and Realities

Being a "lefty" has been commonly regarded as a deficiency or liability. The language still swarms with slurs on lefties. We speak of "left-handed compliments," of having "two left feet," and of strange events as "coming out of left field." The word *sinister* means "left-hand or unlucky side" in Latin. *Gauche* is a French word that literally means "left," although in English it is used to mean awkward or ill-mannered. The English word *adroit,* meaning "skillful," derives from the French *à droit,* literally translated as "to the right." Also consider positive usages such as "being righteous" or "being on one's right side."

Being left-handed is not gauche or sinister, but left-handedness may matter because it appears to be connected with language problems, such as dyslexia and stuttering, and with health problems, such as high blood pressure and epilepsy (Bryden et al., 2005; Lengen et al., 2009). Left-handedness is also apparently connected with psychological disorders, including schizophrenia and depression (van der Hoorn et al., 2009).

Yet there may be advantages to being left-handed. **TRUTH OR FICTION REVISITED:** A disproportionately high percentage of math whizzes are in fact left-handed (Kalbfleisch, 2008). In a series of studies, Michael O'Boyle and

Camilla Benbow (1990) related handedness to scores on math achievement tests among 12- and 13-year-olds. Twenty percent of the highest-scoring group was left-handed. Only 10 percent of the general population is left-handed, so it appears that left-handed children are more than proportionately represented among the most academically gifted.

Left-handedness (or use of both hands) also has been associated with success in athletic activities such as handball, fencing, boxing, basketball, and baseball (Flatt, 2008). Higher frequencies of left-handedness are found among musicians, architects, and artists as well (Flatt, 2008; O'Boyle & Benbow, 1990). Two of the greatest artists in history—Leonardo da Vinci and Michelangelo—were left-handed.

In the next section, we consider how it can be that left-handedness is associated with both talent and giftedness on the one hand (excuse the pun!) and with problems and deficits on the other.

Theories of Handedness

Handedness runs in families to some degree (Medland et al., 2009). In the English royal family, the Queen Mother, Queen Elizabeth II, Prince Charles, and Prince William are (or were) all left-handed (Rosenbaum, 2000).

On the other hand, identical (monozygotic) twins frequently differ in handedness (Sommer et al., 2002). Are MZ twins sometimes "mirror opposites" (Sommer et al., 2002)? If so, the disagreement on handedness among MZ twins would not contradict a role for genetics in handedness.

There also appears to be a relationship between prenatal testosterone and handedness. Girls developing in the uterus with male co-twins are less likely than girls developing in the uterus alone or with female co-twins to be left-handed, suggesting the possibility of "prenatal testosterone transfer" from the male co-twin to the female co-twin (Vuoksimaa et al., 2010).

In any case, handedness develops early. Ultrasound studies reveal that about 95 percent of fetuses suck their right thumbs rather than their left (Vuoksimaa et al., 2010).

Interestingly, handedness is also found in species other than humans—for example, chimpanzees and parrots (yes, parrots). It appears that hand preferences in chimpanzees are heritable but that environmental factors can modify inborn preferences (Hopkins, 2006).

In sum, left-handed children are not necessarily clumsier than right-handed children. They are somewhat more prone to allergies. Academically, left-handedness is associated with positive as well as negative outcomes. Because handedness may reflect the differential development of the hemispheres of the cortex, there is no point in struggling to write with the nondominant hand. After all, would training right-handed children to write with their left hands help them in math?

Active Review

9. (Girls or Boys?) are somewhat better at tasks requiring balance and precision of movement.

10. (Girls or Boys?) show some advantage in throwing and kicking.

11. Motor activity begins to (increase or decrease?) after two or three years of age.

12. During early childhood, (girls or boys?) tend to be more active.

13. Left-handed people have a (higher or lower?) incidence of language problems and psychological disorders than right-handed people.

Reflect & Relate: Think of left-handed people you know (perhaps including yourself). Do they seem to be awkward in any activities? Explain. Do you know anyone who was "changed" from a lefty to a righty? Why was the change made? How was it done? Was it successful? Explain.

"He just learned in school that potato chips are vegetables."

Food Aversions

Strong preferences—and aversions—for certain foods may develop in early childhood.

8.3 Nutrition

QUESTION » What are children's nutritional needs and their eating behaviour like in early childhood?

Nutritional Needs

As children move from infancy into early childhood, their nutritional needs change. They still need to consume the basic foodstuffs: proteins, fats, carbo-hydrates, minerals, and vitamins. But more calo-ries are required as children get older. For example, the average four- to seven-year-old needs about 1425 calories (for girls) and 1525 calories (for boys), compared with about 1250 calories (for girls) and 1350 calories (for boys) for the average two- to three-year-old, based on typical activity levels that would involve some physical activity (e.g., walking, play; Health Canada, 2014). However, they grow at a slower rate than infants. This means that in early childhood, children need fewer calories per kilogram of body weight.

Patterns of Eating

During the second and third years, a child's appetite typically decreases and becomes erratic, which often worries parents. But because the child is growing more slowly now, he or she needs fewer calories. Also, young children who eat less at one meal typically compensate by eating more at another. Children may develop strong (and strange) preferences for certain foods (Cooke & Wardle, 2005). As parents, we both have experienced pre-schoolers who at one time during their third year wanted to eat nothing but SpaghettiOs® (first author's daughter) and cinnamon toast (second author's daughter).

Using *Canada's Food Guide* (Health Canada, 2011) for the entire family is helpful since most children model and adapt the same eating patterns as their families. Unfortunately, many Canadian children (and adults) consume excessive amounts of sugar and salt, which can be harmful to their health. Infants seem to be born liking the taste of sugar, although they are fairly indifferent to salty tastes. Lucy Cooke and Jane Wardle (2005) found that girls like fruits and vegetables more than boys do. Boys like fatty and sugary foods, meat, and eggs more than girls do. Preference for both sweet and salty foods increases if children are repeatedly exposed to them during childhood. Parents also serve as role models in the development of food preferences. If a parent—especially the parent who usually prepares meals—displays an obvious dislike for vegetables, children may develop a similar dislike (Hannon et al., 2003). The message to parents is clear: The eating habits you help create will probably last.

Children eat according to the eating customs of their family, and these traditions are a valued aspect of their culture. Learning to appre-ciate a variety of foods as prepared by various ethnic and cultural groups is another way to engage and interest children in nutrition and eating (Health Canada, 2011). Kumar and Wandel (2006) studied nutrition chal-lenges among immigrant children and youth in Norway and discovered that breast-feeding and weaning practices, as well as the adoption of Western customs, are important variables when considering the nutrition practices of immigrant families.

Other helpful tips for parents and educators wanting to know more about preschoolers and nutrition can be found on Health Canada's website, where there are sample menus by age, as well as tips for planning meals for preschoolers and routines to help parents and caregivers establish healthy habits (see www.hc-sc.gc.ca/fn-an/food-guide-aliment/choose-choix/advice-conseil/child-enfant-eng.php).

What is the best way to get children to eat their green peas or spinach or other healthful foods they may dislike? (Notice that it is rarely dessert that the child refuses to eat.) One method is to encourage the child to taste tiny amounts of the food eight or ten times within a period of a few weeks so that it becomes more familiar. Familiarity with food may breed content, not contempt.

Table 8.4 ■, designed and published by Health Canada (2014), shows a healthful one-day diet for a three-year-old girl. It contains foods from all of the food groups but is low in fat. Portion sizes are contained, yet the child should not feel hungry throughout the day, because there are two planned snacks. There is emphasis on fruits, vegetables, whole grains, and lean meats or alternatives.

● TABLE 8.4

Sample One-Day Menu for Sophie, a 3-Year-Old Girl

| Foods | Amount | Number of Food Guide Servings | | | | | Oils and Fats |
		Vegetables and Fruit	Grain Products	Milk and Alternatives	Meat and Alternatives	
Breakfast						
Smoothie made with						
2% milk and	125 mL (1/2 cup)			1/2		
frozen berries	60 mL (1/4 cup)	1/2				
Whole grain cereal with	15 g		1/2			
2% milk	125 mL (1/2 cup)			1/2		
Snack						
Sliced banana	1/2	1/2				
Lunch						
Butternut squash soup	125 mL (1/2 cup)	1				
Tuna wrap made with						
half of a whole wheat tortilla,	1/2		1			
tuna,	38 g (1 1/4 oz)				1/2	
green peppers, and	60 mL (1/4 cup)	1/2				
mayonnaise	5 mL (1 tsp)					√

(Continued)

Foods	Amount	Number of Food Guide Servings				Oils and Fats
		Vegetables and Fruit	**Grain Products**	**Milk and Alternatives**	**Meat and Alternatives**	**Oils and Fats**
2% milk	125 mL (1/2 cup)			1/2		
Snack						
Cucumber slices with	60 mL (1/4 cup)	1/2				
dip	15 mL (1 Tbsp)					√
2% milk	125 mL (1/2 cup)			1/2		
Dinner						
Stir fry made with						
broccoli, carrots and cauliflower [frozen medley] and	125 mL (1/2 cup)	1				
chicken on	38 g (1 1/4 oz)				1/2	
cooked brown rice	125 mL (1/2 cup)		1			
Oil to cook stir fry	5 mL (1 tsp)					√
Roll with	1/2 (18 g)		1/2			
nonhydrogenated margarine	5 mL (1 tsp)					√
Total Food Guide Servings for the day		4	3	2	1	30 mL

Source: © All rights reserved. *Eating Well with Canada's Food Guide*. Health Canada, 2011. Reproduced with permission from the Minister of Health, 2014.

Active Review

14. During the second and third years, a child's appetite typically (increases or decreases?).

Reflect & Relate: Did you ever try to convince a two- or three-year-old to eat something? What did you do? What were the consequences?

8.4 Health and Illness

QUESTIONS » How healthy are children in Canada and in other countries? What are some of the illnesses and environmental hazards encountered during early childhood? Nearly all children get ill now and then. Some seem to be ill every other week or so. Most of these illnesses are minor, and children seem to eventually outgrow many of them, including ear infections. However, some illnesses are more serious. Fortunately, we have ways of preventing or curing a great many of them.

Minor Illnesses

Minor illnesses include respiratory infections, such as colds, and gastrointestinal upsets, such as nausea, vomiting, and diarrhea. **TRUTH OR FICTION REVISITED:** These diseases are normal—statistically speaking—in that most children come down with them. They typically last a few days or less and are not life threatening. Although diarrheal illness in Canada is usually mild, it is a leading killer of children in developing countries (UNICEF, 2006). Vaccines have been developed to fight the rotavirus, which is implicated in many cases of diarrhea (Patel et al., 2009).

Canadian children between the ages of one and three generally average eight to nine minor illnesses a year. Between the ages of four and ten, this drops to about four to six illnesses a year. Being ill can have some beneficial effects on children's development. It can lead to the creation of antibodies that may prevent them from coming down with the same illnesses later—say, in adulthood—when the illnesses can be more harmful.

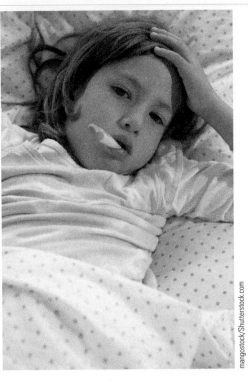

mangostock/Shutterstock.com

Major Illnesses

Let's travel around the world and consider some facts about illnesses that afflict children (Save the Children, 2011).

- Pneumonia kills more children under the age of five than AIDS, malaria, and measles combined—as many as 3 million children a year. This amounts to one under-five death in every three children. Antibiotics that vanquish bacterial pneumonia cost less than 30 cents a dose, but only 20 percent of children with pneumonia receive them.

- Diarrhea kills almost 2 million under-five children each year (Patel et al., 2009). The treatment to prevent children from dying from diarrhoea is **oral rehydration therapy** with salts that cost less than 50 cents a dose. But only 38 percent of children with diarrhea receive this therapy.

- Malaria, which is transmitted to people by mosquitoes, kills some 800 000 under-five children in sub-Saharan Africa annually. One of six childhood deaths in that part of the world is caused by malaria.

- Measles kills some 240 000 children each year. It is one of the world's leading causes of death that is preventable by vaccination.

- Malnutrition is connected with half of the deaths of children under the age of five. Poorly nourished children have lower resistance to infection and are thus more vulnerable to illnesses such as diarrhea and pneumonia.

Advances in immunization, along with the development of antibiotics and other medications, have dramatically reduced the incidence of serious and potentially fatal childhood diseases in Canada. Because most preschoolers and schoolchildren have been inoculated against major childhood illnesses such as rubella (German measles), measles, tetanus, mumps, whooping cough, diphtheria, and polio, these diseases no longer pose the threat they once did. Still, immunization in Canada is not universal. The recommended immunization schedule varies slightly from province to province and the different schedules are posted via provincial and territorial

oral rehydration therapy A treatment involving the administration of a salt and sugar solution to a child who is dehydrated from diarrhea.

Ten Things You Need to Know about Immunizations

1. Why your child should be immunized
Children need immunizations (shots) to protect them from dangerous childhood diseases. These diseases can have serious complications and can even kill children.

2. Diseases that childhood vaccines prevent
  * Diphtheria
  * Haemophilus influenzae type b (Hib disease, a major cause of bacterial meningitis)
  * Hepatitis A
  * Hepatitis B
  * Human Papillomavirus (HPV)
  * Measles
  * Meningococcus
  * Mumps
  * Pertussis (Whooping Cough)
  * Pneumococcus (causes bacterial meningitis and blood infections)
  * Polio
  * Rotavirus
  * Rubella (German Measles)
  * Tetanus (Lockjaw)
  * Varicella (Chicken pox)
  * Influenza (the flu)

3. Number of doses your child needs
The following vaccinations are recommended by age two and can be given over five visits to a doctor or health clinic:
  * 4 doses of diphtheria, tetanus, & pertussis vaccine (DTaP)
  * 3–4 doses of Hib vaccine (depending on the brand used)
  * 4 doses of pneumococcal vaccine
  * 3 doses of polio vaccine
  * 2 doses of hepatitis A vaccine
  * 3 doses of hepatitis B vaccine
  * 1 dose of measles, mumps, & rubella vaccine (MMR)
  * 2–3 doses of rotavirus vaccine (depending on the brand used)
  * 1 dose of varicella vaccine
  * 2–3 doses of influenza vaccine (6 months and older) (number of doses depends on child's birthday)

4. Like any medicine, there may be minor side effects.
Side effects can occur with any medicine, including vaccines. Depending on the vaccine, these can include slight fever, rash, or soreness at the site of injection. Slight discomfort is normal and should not be a cause for alarm. Your health-care provider can give you additional information.

5. It's extremely rare, but vaccines can cause serious reactions—weigh the risks!
Serious reactions to vaccines are extremely rare. The risks of serious disease from not vaccinating are far greater than the risks of serious reaction to a vaccination.

6. What to do if your child has a serious reaction
If you think your child is experiencing a persistent or severe reaction, call your doctor or get the child to a doctor right away. Write down what happened and the date and time it happened. Ask your doctor, nurse, or health clinic to note this in your child's medical file.

7. Why you should not wait to vaccinate
Children under five are especially susceptible to disease because their immune systems have not built up the necessary defences to fight infection. By immunizing on time (by age two), you can protect your child from disease and also protect others at school or child care.

8. Be sure to track your shots via a health record.
An immunization health record helps you and your health-care provider keep your child's vaccinations on schedule. If you move to another town, city, or province, having an accurate record might prevent your child from repeating vaccinations he or she has already had. A shot record should be started when your child receives his or her first vaccination and updated with each vaccination visit.

9. Can you get free vaccines?
Although this varies across provinces and territories, most vaccinations may be obtained free of charge from health clinics affiliated with regional health authorities.

10. More information is available:
At the website for Public Health Agency of Canada (www.phac-aspc.gc.ca), you can find personalized immunization schedules (by age or grade, province and territory). As well, there are reading materials, information on debunking myths, and research presented on the topic of vaccinations. Another useful site is Immunize Canada/Immunisation Canada (www.immunize.ca).

Reflect
  * Are you unclear about the meaning of any of the diseases these vaccinations protect against?
  * Do you know whether the children in your life have had every recommended vaccine?
  * Do you know what to do if a child has missed a vaccination?
  * Do you know what to do if you are unsure of the answer to any of these questions?

Sources: Centers for Disease Control and Prevention (2010), U.S. Department of Health and Human Services, *10 Things You Need to Know about Immunizations*, www.cdc.gov/vaccines/vac-gen/10-shouldknow.htm, accessed August 4, 2012; Immunize Canada, www.immunize.ca, accessed on June 15, 2014.

Routine Schedule for Children Beginning Immunization in Early Infancy (Starting at Two Months of Age), Ontario

Age at Vaccination: Completed months and years	DTaP-IPV-Hib	Pneu-C-13	Rot-1	Men-C-C	MMR	Var	MMRV	Men-C-ACYW	HB	HPV-4	Tdap	Inf
2 months old	X X	X	X									
4 months old	X X	X	X									
12 months old	X X	X		X	X							
15 months old						X						
18 months old	X X											
4–6 years	X						X					
Grade 7 students								X	X			
14–16 years old (10 years after 4–6 year old booster)											X	
Every year (in autumn)												X

Vaccine Antigen Abbreviations:

DTaP = diphtheria, tetanus, acellular pertussis; IPV = inactivated poliovirus; Hib = haemophilus influenzae type b; Pneu-C-13 = pneumococcal conjugate-13 valent; Rot-1 = rotavirus ORAL; MMR = measles, mumps, rubella; MMRV = measles, mumps, rubella, varicella; Men-C-C = meningococcal conjugate C; Men-C-ACYW = meningococcal conjugate ACYW-135; Var = varicella zoster; HA = hepatitis A; HB = hepatitis B; Tdap = tetanus, diphtheria, acellular pertussis; Td = tetanus, diphtheria; Inf = seasonal influenza; HPV-4 = human papillomavirus quadrivalent; Pneu-P-23 = pneumococcal polysaccharide-23 valent.

websites. Table 8.5 ▇ shows the immunization schedule for children in Ontario.

As well, a significant number of Canadian children younger than 18 years of age suffer from a chronic illness (Agency for Healthcare Research and Quality, 2004; Public Health Agency of Canada, 2009). The illnesses include such major disorders as arthritis, diabetes, cerebral palsy, and cystic fibrosis. Other chronic medical problems such as asthma and migraine headaches are less serious but still require extensive health care.

Although many major childhood diseases have been largely eradicated in industrialized nations, they remain fearsome killers of children in developing countries. Around the world, more than 13 million children die each year. Two-thirds of these children die of just six diseases: pneumonia, diarrhea, measles, tetanus, whooping cough, and tuberculosis (UNICEF, 2006). Air pollution from the combustion of fossil fuels for heating and cooking gives rise to many respiratory infections, which are responsible for nearly one death in five among children who are younger than five years of age (UNICEF, 2006). Diarrheal diseases are almost completely related to unsafe drinking water and a general lack of sanitation and hygiene. Children's immune systems and detoxification mechanisms are not as strong as those of adults, so they are more vulnerable to chemical, physical, and biological hazards in the water, soil, and air.

Lead is a particularly harmful pollutant. Many youngsters are exposed to lead in early childhood, often by eating chips of lead paint from their homes or by breathing in dust from the paint. Infants who are fed formula made with tap water also are at risk of lead poisoning, because the pipes that carry water into homes sometimes contain lead. Lead causes neurological damage and may result in lowered cognitive functioning and other developmental delays in early childhood. To help you assess and minimize the risks of lead poisoning in children younger than six years of age, see the nearby "A Closer Look—Real Life" feature.

Low-cost measures such as vaccines, antibiotics, and oral rehydration therapy could prevent most of these deaths. In oral rehydration therapy, a simple homemade salt and sugar solution is given to a child who is dehydrated from diarrhea. One promising finding is that most children in developing countries are now immunized against tuberculosis, measles, polio, diphtheria, tetanus, and whooping cough (UNICEF, 2006).

Accidents

TRUTH OR FICTION REVISITED: Infections are not the most common cause of death in early childhood in Canada (see Table 8.6 ■). Accidents are. But if you were to go back to the year 1900, you would certainly be correct if you had agreed that infections were the leading cause of death in early adulthood. In 1900[1] the five leading causes of death for children aged one to four were pneumonia (bacterial pneumonia is now usually treated successfully with antibiotics, and the symptoms of viral pneumonia are most often treated

A CLOSER LOOK REAL LIFE

Protecting Children from Lead Poisoning

People can get lead in their body if they put their hands (or other objects covered with lead dust) in their mouths, eat paint chips or soil that contains lead, or breathe in lead dust (especially during renovations that disturb painted surfaces). If the condition is not detected early, children with high levels of lead in their bodies can suffer from damage to the brain and nervous system, behavioural and learning problems (such as hyperactivity), delayed growth, hearing problems, and headaches.

Lead is found mainly in paint. Many homes built before the 1960s have lead-based paint. By the 1990s, all consumer paints made in Canada and the United States were lead-free.

Peeling, chipping, chalking, or cracking lead-based paint is a hazard and needs immediate attention. Lead-based paint may also be a hazard when found on surfaces

that children can chew or that get a lot of wear and tear. However, lead-based paint that is in good condition is usually not a hazard.

Consult your doctor for advice on testing your children. A simple blood test can detect high levels of lead. You can get your home checked in one of two ways: A paint inspection tells you the lead content of every different type of painted surface in your home. A risk assessment tells you whether there are any sources of serious lead exposure (such as peeling paint and lead dust). It also tells you what actions to take to address these hazards. Have qualified professionals do the work.

If you have a concern contact your local provincial Poison Control Centre, and for general enquiries, contact Health Canada (Email: Info@hc-sc.gc.ca; phone: 866-225-0709).

[1]As reported by Esther B. Clark (1950). Leading causes of childhood death. Palo Alto, CA: The Palo Alto Clinic, Department of Pediatrics. www.ncbi.nlm.nih.gov/pmc/articles/PMC1520569/pdf/califmed00241-0024 .pdf. Accessed August 4, 2012.

Leading Causes of Injury Death, Canada, 2008
Counts (Age-Specific Death Rate per 100 000)

Indicator	All ages			<1	1–9	10–14	15–19	20–39	40–64	65–79	80+
	Male	Female	MF								
All injuries[1]	9 807 (59.4)	5 414 (32.2)	15 221 (45.7)	43 (11.5)	141 (4.4)	119 (5.9)	676 (30.0)	3,312 (36.4)	5,230 (44.3)	1,969 (59.6)	3,731 (298.2)
Unintentional injuries	6,105 (37.0)	4 129 (24.6)	10 234 (30.7)	32 (8.6)	125 (3.9)	80 (4.0)	397 (17.6)	1,729 (19.0)	2,759 (23.4)	1,536 (46.5)	3,576 (285.8)
Motor vehicle traffic crashes	1 681 (10.2)	736 (4.4)	2 417 (7.3)	*	35 (1.1)	26 (1.3)	266 (11.8)	850 (9.3)	792 (6.7)	277 (8.4)	169 (13.5)
Falls	1 488 (9.0)	1 610 (9.6)	3 098 (9.3)	*	*	*	11 (0.5)	58 (0.6)	330 (2.8)	626 (18.9)	2,065 (165.1)
Poisonings	939 (5.7)	502 (3.0)	1,441 (4.3)	*	*	6 (0.3)	39 (1.7)	415 (4.6)	832 (7.1)	97 (2.9)	51 (4.1)
Suffocations	260 (1.6)	186 (1.1)	446 (1.3)	20 (5.4)	14 (0.4)	*	*	28 (0.3)	105 (0.9)	104 (3.1)	169 (13.5)
Drownings[2]	225 (1.4)	50 (0.3)	275 (0.8)	7 (1.9)	23 (0.7)	13 (0.6)	17 (0.8)	74 (0.8)	94 (0.8)	24 (0.7)	23 (1.8)
Fire and flame	163 (1.0)	112 (0.7)	275 (0.8)	*	25 (0.8)	7 (0.3)	8 (0.4)	44 (0.5)	101 (0.9)	59 (1.8)	29 (2.3)
Other unintentional injuries	1 349 (8.2)	933 (5.6)	2 282 (6.8)	*	28 (0.9)	21 (1.0)	54 (2.4)	260 (2.9)	505 (4.3)	349 (10.6)	1,070 (85.5)
Suicides	2,777 (16.8)	928 (5.5)	3 705 (11.1)	*	*	25 (1.2)	208 (9.2)	1,084 (11.9)	1,899 (16.1)	359 (10.9)	130 (10.4)
Homicides	452 (2.7)	123 (0.7)	575 (1.7)	8 (2.1)	13 (0.4)	8 (0.4)	58 (2.6)	275 (3.0)	177 (1.5)	27 (0.8)	9 (0.7)
Undetermined intent	457 (2.8)	233 (1.4)	690 (2.1)	*	*	*	10 (0.4)	218 (2.4)	389 (3.3)	47 (1.4)	15 (1.2)
Legal intervention/war	16 (0.1)	*	17 (0.1)	*	*	*	*	6 (0.1)	6 (0.1)	*	*

[1]All records where the external cause of injury is classified to the International Classification of Diseases, 10th Revision (ICD-10) (Chapter 20), except adverse effects due to drugs or medical care.

[2]Includes drownings in water transport events.

*Suppressed due to small number of cases or value of zero.

Source: Statistics Canada.

successfully), diarrhea (which is most often readily treated in developed countries today, although it remains deadly elsewhere), diphtheria (which is now prevented by vaccination), tuberculosis, and measles (also now prevented by vaccination).

Today, accidents now cause more deaths in early childhood than the other most frequent causes combined (Bloom et al., 2011; Kochanek et al., 2011; Statistics Canada, 2008). Motor vehicle accidents are the single most common cause of death in early childhood (ages one to nine), followed by other unintentional injuries (broad category), drowning, and fires.

Accidents also are the major killer of children in most other countries of the world, except for those developing nations still racked by high rates of malnutrition and disease. Injuries are responsible for nearly half the deaths of children two to six years of age and for more than half the deaths of children through the age of 14. Boys are more likely than girls to incur accidental injuries at all ages and in all socioeconomic groups.

Accidental injuries occur most often among low-income children. Poor children are five times as likely to die from fires and more than twice as likely to die in motor vehicle accidents (Kochanek et al., 2011). The high accident rate of low-income children may result partly from their living in dangerous housing and neighbourhoods. Parents from lower socioeconomic strata also are less likely than higher-income parents to take such preventive measures as using infant safety seats, fastening children's seat belts, installing smoke detectors, and having at hand the telephone number of a poison control centre. The families of children who are injured frequently may be more disorganized and under more stress than other families. Injuries often occur when family members are distracted and children have minimal supervision.

Prevention of Accidental Injury

Legislation has helped to reduce certain injuries in children. All provinces require child safety seats in automobiles, and their use has decreased deaths from automobile injuries. Most large cities in North America also require the installation of window guards in high-rise apartment buildings. In a number of countries, the risks of injury to children have been reduced because of legislation requiring manufacturers to meet safety standards for such items as toys and flammable clothing.

Mona Makela/Shutterstock.com

Automobile Safety
Automobile accidents are the most common cause of death in young children in Canada. All provinces require child-restraint seats in automobiles. These laws have contributed to a reduction in child deaths and injuries.

Active Review

15. The most frequent cause of death of children in Canada is _____.

16. Many children are exposed to _____ by eating chips of paint.

Reflect & Relate: What pollutants in your area are harmful to children? What can you do about them?

KidStock/Getty Images

transitional object A soft, cuddly object often carried to bed by a child to ease the separation from parents.

8.5 Sleep

QUESTIONS » How much sleep is needed during early childhood? What kinds of problems disrupt sleep? Children in the early years do not need as much sleep as infants. Most young children sleep 10–11 hours in a 24-hour period (National Sleep Foundation, 2012a) (see Table 8.7 ▇). A common pattern is 9–10 hours at night and a nap of one or two hours. In Canada, the young child's bedtime routine typically includes putting on pyjamas, brushing teeth, and being read a story. Many young children also take a so-called **transitional object**—such as a favoured blanket or a stuffed animal—to bed with them (Chamness, 2008). Children who sleep in bed with their parents are unlikely to use a transitional object (Goldberg & Keller, 2007).

How Much Sleep Do You Really Need?

Age	Sleep Needs
Newborns (0–2 months)	12–18 hours
Infants (3–11 months)	14–15 hours
Toddlers (1–3 years)	12–14 hours
Preschoolers (3–5 years)	11–13 hours
School-age children (5–10 years)	10–11 hours
Teens (10–17 years)	8.5–9.25 hours
Adults	7–9 hours

Source: National Sleep Foundation. Online by National Sleep Foundation. Reproduced with permission of National Sleep Foundation in the format Republish in a book via Copyright Clearance Center.

A CLOSER LOOK | RESEARCH

Cross-Cultural Differences in Sleeping Arrangements

The commonly accepted practice in middle-class Canadian families is for infants and children to sleep in separate beds and, when finances permit, in separate rooms from their parents. Historically, North American child-care experts have generally endorsed this practice. Sleeping in the same room, they have sometimes warned, can lead to problems such as the development of overdependence, difficulty of breaking the habit when the child gets older, and even accidental sexual stimulation of the child (National Sleep Foundation, 2011).

Nevertheless, bed sharing has been promoted as a means for facilitating breast feeding. In fact, co-sleeping or bed sharing is the most common sleeping arrangement throughout the world for mothers who are breast feeding (Young, 2006). Some health professionals are concerned that bed sharing can be dangerous for infants, because parents may roll onto them and crush or suffocate them (Weber et al., 2011).

In many other cultures, children commonly sleep with their mothers for the first few years of life, often in the same bed. The practice is found among 79 percent of preschool children in China (Huang et al., 2010). Co-sleeping occurs in cultures that are technologically advanced, such as Austria (Rothrauff et al., 2004) and Japan (Takahashi, 1990), as well as in those that are less technologically sophisticated, such as among the indigenous Sami people of Norway (Javo et al., 2004).

Surveys find that resistance to going to bed occurs regularly in 20–40 percent of North American infants and preschoolers (National Sleep Foundation, 2011), but it

Getting Their Z's
Traditionally in Canada, most parents believe that it is harmful or at least inappropriate for parents to sleep with their children. Parents in many other cultures are more relaxed about sleeping arrangements. Social norms vary.

seldom occurs in cultures that practise co-sleeping. Some psychologists believe that the resistance shown by some young Canadian children at bedtime is caused by the stress of separating from parents. This view is supported by the finding that young children who sleep with or near their parents are less likely to use transitional objects or to suck their thumbs at night than are children who sleep alone (Goldberg & Keller, 2007).

Reflect Would you (do you) allow your child to share your bed with you? Why or why not?

But we're not ending the discussion here because it sounds much too easy. As so many parents know, getting children to sleep can be a major challenge of parenthood. Many children resist going to bed or going to sleep. Getting to sleep late can be a problem because preschoolers tend not to make up fully for lost sleep (Kohyama et al., 2002). In the next section, we focus on sleep disorders.

Sleep Disorders

In this section, we focus on the sleep disorders of sleep terrors, nightmares, and sleepwalking.

Sleep Terrors and Nightmares

First, a few words about terms. **Sleep terrors** are more severe than the anxiety dreams we refer to as nightmares. For one thing, sleep terrors usually occur during deep sleep. **Nightmares** take place during lighter rapid eye movement (REM) sleep, when about 80 percent of normal dreams occur. In fact, nightmares sort of qualify as "normal" dreams because of their frequency, not because of desirability!

Deep sleep alternates with lighter, REM sleep. Sleep terrors tend to occur early during the night, when periods of deep sleep are longest. Nightmares tend to occur more often in the morning hours, when periods of REM sleep tend to lengthen (National Sleep Foundation, 2011). Children have several periods of REM sleep a night and may dream in each one of them. Don't be confused by the fact that sleep terrors are sometimes referred to as night terrors. The term *night terrors* always refers to sleep terrors, never to nightmares.

Sleep terrors usually begin in childhood or early adolescence and are outgrown by late adolescence. They are often (but not always) associated with stress, such as moving to a new neighbourhood, attending school for the first time, adjusting to parental divorce, or being caught up in a war zone (El Shakankiry, 2011). (Children are also more likely to have nightmares under stress.) Children with sleep terrors may wake suddenly with a surge in heart and respiration rates, talk incoherently, and thrash about. Children are not completely awake during sleep terrors and may fall back into more restful sleep. Fortunately, the incidence of sleep terrors wanes as children develop and spend less time in deep sleep. They are all but absent among adults.

Children who have frequent nightmares or sleep terrors may come to fear going to sleep. They may show distress at bedtime, refuse to get into their pajamas, and insist that the lights be kept on during the night. As a result, they can develop **insomnia**. Children with frequent nightmares or sleep terrors need their parents' understanding and affection. They also profit from a regular routine in which they are expected to get to sleep at the same time each night (El Shakankiry, 2011). Yelling at them over their "immature" refusal to have the lights out and return to sleep will not relieve their anxieties.

Sleepwalking

Sleepwalking, or **somnambulism**, is much more common among children than among adults. Like sleep terrors, sleepwalking tends to occur during deep sleep. Onset is usually between the ages of three and eight.

During medieval times, people believed that sleepwalking was a sign of possession by evil spirits. Psychoanalytic theory suggests that sleepwalking gives people the chance to express feelings and impulses they would inhibit while awake. But children who sleepwalk have not been shown to have any more trouble controlling impulses than other children do. Moreover, what children do when they sleepwalk is usually too boring to suggest exotic motivation.

sleep terrors Frightening dreamlike experiences that occur during the deepest stage of non-REM sleep, shortly after the child has gone to sleep.

nightmares Frightening dreams that occur during REM sleep, often in the morning hours.

insomnia One or more sleep problems, including difficulty falling asleep, difficulty remaining asleep during the night, and waking early.

somnambulism Sleepwalking.

They may rearrange toys, go to the bathroom, or go to the refrigerator and have a glass of milk. Then they return to their rooms and go back to bed. Their lack of recall in the morning is consistent with sleep terrors, which also occur during deep sleep. Sleepwalking episodes are brief; most tend to last no longer than half an hour.

There are some myths about sleepwalking—for example, that sleepwalkers' eyes are closed, that they will avoid harm, and that they will become violently agitated if they are awakened during an episode. All of these notions are false. Sleepwalkers' eyes are usually open, although they may not respond to on-looking parents. Children may incur injury when sleepwalking, just as they may when awake. TRUTH OR FICTION REVISITED: It is also not true that it is dangerous to awaken a sleepwalker. Children may be difficult to rouse when they are sleepwalking, just as during sleep terrors. But if they are awakened, they are more likely to show confusion and disorientation (again, as during sleep terrors) than violence.

Today, sleepwalking in children is assumed to reflect immaturity of the nervous system, not any acting out of dreams or psychological conflicts. As with sleep terrors, the incidence of sleepwalking drops as children develop. Parents may find it helpful to discuss persistent sleep terrors or sleepwalking with a health professional.

Active Review

17. Most two- to three-year-olds sleep about _____ hours at night and also have one nap during the day.

18. (Nightmares or Sleep terrors?) usually occur during deep sleep.

19. _____ is also referred to as somnambulism.

Reflect & Relate: Critical thinkers insist on evidence before they will accept beliefs, even widely held cultural beliefs. What are your attitudes toward children sleeping with their parents? Are your attitudes supported by research evidence? Explain.

8.6 Elimination Disorders

QUESTIONS » What are the elimination disorders? What can, or should, be done to help children gain control? The elimination of waste products occurs reflexively in neonates. As children develop, their task is to learn to inhibit the reflexes that govern urination and bowel movements. The process by which parents teach their children to inhibit these reflexes is referred to as toilet training. The inhibition of eliminatory reflexes makes polite conversation possible.

TRUTH OR FICTION REVISITED: It is not true that competent parents toilet train their children by their second birthday. Most Canadian children are toilet trained between the ages of three and four, although they normally have some "accidents" beyond those ages.

In toilet training, as in so many other areas of physical growth and development, maturation plays a crucial role, but so does cultural practice and expectations. During the first year, only an exceptional child can be toilet trained, even when parents devote a great deal of time and energy to the task. If parents wait until the third year to begin toilet training, the process usually runs smoothly.

An end to diaper changing is not the only reason parents are motivated to toilet train their children. Parents often experience pressure from grandparents, other relatives, and friends who point out that so-and-so's children were all toilet trained before the age of ___. (You fill in the blank. Choose a number

Comstock Images/Thinkstock

Toilet Training
If parents wait until the third year to begin toilet training, the process usually goes relatively rapidly and smoothly.

CHAPTER 8 EARLY CHILDHOOD: PHYSICAL DEVELOPMENT **285**

that will make most of us feel like inadequate parents!) Parents, in turn, may pressure their children to become toilet trained. And so toilet training can become a major arena for parent–child conflict. Children who do not become toilet trained within reasonable time frames are said to have enuresis, encopresis, or both.

Enuresis

Give it a name like *enuresis* (en-you-REE-sis), and suddenly it seems like a serious medical problem rather than a bit of an annoyance. **Enuresis** is the failure to control the bladder (urination) once the "normal" age for achieving control of the bladder has been reached. Conceptions of the normal age vary. The American Psychiatric Association (2012) is reasonably lenient on the issue and places the cut-off age at five years. The frequency of "accidents" is also an issue. The American Psychiatric Association (2012) does not consider such accidents enuresis unless the incidents occur at least twice a month for five- and six-year-olds or once a month for children who are older.

A night-time accident is referred to as **bed-wetting**. Night-time control is more difficult to achieve than daytime control. At night, children must first wake up when their bladders are full. Only then can they go to the bathroom.

About 10 percent of children wet their beds (Neveus, 2011), and the problem is about twice as common among boys as among girls. Nearly 15 percent of children five years and under wet their beds at night (Feldman & Canadian Paediatric Society Community Paediatrics Committee, 2005). The incidence drops as age increases. A study of 3344 Chinese children found that these children appeared to attain control a bit earlier: 7.7 percent obtained nocturnal urinary control by the age of two, 53 percent by the age of three, and 93 percent by the age of five (Liu et al., 2000b). Just as in Western studies, girls achieved control earlier than boys.

Causes of Enuresis

Enuresis usually has organic causes, such as infections of the urinary tract, kidney problems, or immaturity in development of the motor cortex of the brain (Robson, 2009). Thus, cases with different causes might clear up at different rates or profit from different kinds of treatment. In the case of immaturity of parts of the brain, administering no treatment at all might be in order.

Numerous psychological explanations of enuresis have also been advanced. Psychoanalytic theory suggests that enuresis is a way of expressing hostility toward parents (because of their harshness in toilet training) or a form of symbolic masturbation. These views are largely unsubstantiated. Learning theorists point out that enuresis is most common among children whose parents attempted to train them early. Early failures might have conditioned anxiety over attempts to control the bladder. Conditioned anxiety, then, prompts rather than inhibits urination.

Situational stresses seem to play a role. Children are more likely to wet their beds when they are entering school for the first time, when a sibling is born, and when they are ill. There may also be a genetic component; there is a strong family history in the majority of cases (Robson, 2009).

It has also been noted that bed-wetting tends to occur during the deepest stage of sleep. This is also the stage when sleep terrors and sleepwalking take place. For this reason, bed-wetting could be considered a sleep disorder. Like sleepwalking, bed-wetting could reflect immaturity of certain parts of the nervous system (Robson, 2009). Just as children outgrow sleep terrors and sleepwalking, they tend to outgrow bed-wetting (Mellon & Houts, 2006). In most cases, bed-wetting resolves itself by adolescence and usually by the age of eight.

enuresis Failure to control the bladder (urination) after the normal age for control has been reached.

bed-wetting Failure to control the bladder during the night.

What to Do about Bed-Wetting

Parents are understandably disturbed when their children continue to wet their beds long after most children stay dry through the night. Cleaning up is a hassle, and parents also often wonder what their child's bed-wetting "means"—what it means about the child and what it means about their own adequacy as parents.

Bed-wetting may "mean" only that the child is slower than most children to keep his or her bed dry through the night. Bed-wetting may mean nothing at all about the child's intelligence or personality or about the parents' capabilities. Certainly a number of devices (alarms) can be used to teach the child to awaken in response to bladder pressure (Behr, 2011; Bottomley, 2011; von Gontard, 2011). Medications also can be used to help the child retain fluids through the night (Bottomley, 2011). Before turning to these methods, however, parents may wish to consider the following suggestions:

- **Limit fluid intake late in the day.** Less pressure on the bladder makes it easier to control urinating, but do not risk depriving the child of liquids. On the other hand, it makes sense to limit fluid intake in the evening, especially at bedtime. Drinks with caffeine, such as colas, coffee, and tea, act as diuretics, making it more difficult to control urination, so it is helpful to cut down on them after lunch.

- **Wake the child during the night.** Waking the child at midnight or 1:00 in the morning may make it possible for him or her to go to the bathroom and urinate. Children may complain and say that they don't have to go, but often they will. Praise the child for making the effort.

- **Try a night-light.** Many children fear getting up in the dark and trying to find their way to the bathroom. A night-light can make the difference. If the bathroom is far from the child's bedroom, it may be helpful to place a chamber pot in the bedroom. The child can empty the pot in the morning.

- **Maintain a consistent schedule so that the child can form helpful bedtime and nighttime habits.** Having a regular bedtime not only helps ensure that your child gets enough sleep but also enables the child to get into a routine of urinating before going to bed and keeps the child's internal clock in sync with the clock on the wall. Habits can be made to work for the child rather than against the child.

- **Use a "sandwich" bed.** A sandwich bed? This is simply a plastic sheet, covered with a cloth sheet, covered with yet another plastic sheet, and then still another cloth sheet. If the child wets his or her bed, the top wet sheet and plastic sheet can be pulled off, and the child can get back into a comfortable, dry bed. In this way, the child develops the habit of sleeping in a dry bed. Moreover, the child learns how to handle his or her "own mess" by removing the wet sheets.

- **Have the child help clean up.** The child can throw the sheets into the wash and, perhaps, operate the washing machine. The child can make the bed, or at least participate. These behaviours are not punishments; they help connect the child to the reality of what is going on and what needs to be done to clean things up.

- **Reward the child's successes.** Parents risk becoming overly punitive when they pay attention only to the child's failures. Ignoring successes also causes them to go unreinforced. When the child has a dry night, or half of a dry night, make a note of it. Track successes on a calendar. Connect them with small treats, such as more TV time or time with you. Make a "fuss"—that is, a positive fuss. Also consider rewarding partial successes, such as the child's getting up after beginning to urinate so that there is less urine in the bed.

- **Show a positive attitude.** "Accentuate the positive." Talk with your child about "staying dry" rather than "not wetting." Communicate the idea that you have confidence that things will get better. (They almost always do.)

Reflect

- Why do so many parents "take it personally" when their children wet their beds?

- What do we mean when we say that children "outgrow" bed-wetting?

- How do you feel about giving a preschool child medicine to help curb bed-wetting? Explain.

Encopresis

Soiling, or **encopresis**, is lack of control over the bowels. Soiling, like enuresis, is more common among boys. However, the overall incidence of soiling is lower than that of enuresis. About 1–2 percent of children aged seven and eight have continuing problems controlling their bowels (Mellon, 2006; von Gontard, 2011).

Soiling, in contrast to enuresis, is more likely to occur during the day. Thus, it can be acutely embarrassing to the child, especially in school.

encopresis Failure to control the bowels after the normal age for bowel control has been reached. Also called soiling.

● TABLE 8.8

Risk Factors for Developing Encopresis

- Eating diets high in fat and sugar (junk food) and low in fibre.
- Not drinking enough water.
- Not exercising.
- Refusing to use the bathroom, especially public bathrooms.
- Having a history of constipation or painful experience during toilet training (ulcerative colitis or anal fissures). Note: Many children with encopresis have a history of painful defecation before 36 months of age.
- Having cognitive delays such as autism or intellectual deficiency.
- Having attention deficit disorders or difficulty focusing.
- Having conduct or oppositional disorders.
- Having obsessive compulsive disorders.
- Having a poor ability to identify physical sensations or symptoms.
- Having a chaotic, unpredictable life.

Source: Reprinted from Pediatric Nursing, 2011, Volume 37, Number 3, pp. 108. Reprinted with permission of the publisher, Jannetti Publications, Inc., East Holly Avenue/Box 56, Pitman, NJ 08071-0056; (856) 256-2300; FAX (856) 589-7463; Web site: www.pediatricnursing.net; For a sample copy of the journal, please contact the publisher.

Encopresis stems from both physical causes, such as constipation, and psychological factors. Risk factors for encopresis are shown in Table 8.8 ■. Soiling may follow harsh punishment of toileting accidents, especially in children who are already anxious or under stress. Punishment may cause the child to tense up on the toilet, when moving one's bowels requires that one relax the anal sphincter muscles. Harsh punishment also focuses the child's attention on soiling. The child then begins to ruminate about soiling, so that soiling, punishment, and worrying about future soiling become a vicious cycle.

We now leave our exploration of physical development in early childhood and begin, in the next chapter, an examination of cognitive development.

Active Review

20. In toilet training, maturation (does or does not?) play a crucial role.

21. Bed-wetting is more common among (girls or boys?).

22. A common physical cause of encopresis is _____.

Reflect & Relate: Why do you think so many parents become upset when their children are a bit behind others in toilet training? Do you think it is bad if it takes three or four years for a child to learn to use the toilet reliably? If so, why?

Recite an Active Summary

8.1 Growth Patterns

What changes occur in height and weight during early childhood?

Children gain about 5–8 centimetres in height and 2–3 kilograms in weight per year in early childhood.

How does the brain develop during early childhood?

The brain develops more quickly than any other organ in early childhood, in part because of myelination.

Myelination enhances children's ability to attend to and process visual information, enabling them to read and to screen out distractions.

8.2 Motor Development

How do motor skills develop in early childhood?

In the preschool years, children make great strides in the development of gross motor skills, which involve the large muscles. Girls are somewhat better at tasks requiring balance and precision; boys have some advantage in throwing and kicking. Fine motor skills develop gradually. After two or three years of age, children become less restless and are more able to sustain attention during play. Boys are more fidgety and distractible, perhaps because they are less mature physically.

Do girls and boys differ in their activity levels during early childhood?

Boys are found to engage in higher activity levels than girls in early childhood, especially in large-muscle activities.

Are children's scribbles the result of random motor activity?

Apparently not. Kellogg identified 20 scribbles that she considers the building blocks of art.

When does handedness emerge? Are there any advantages or disadvantages to being left-handed?

By six months, most infants show clear-cut hand preferences, which become still more established during early childhood. Being left-handed is apparently connected with language problems, some health problems, and some psychological disorders. But a high number of "math whizzes," athletes, and artists are left-handed.

8.3 Nutrition

What are children's nutritional needs and their eating behaviour like in early childhood?

The typical four- to seven-year-old needs about 1425 calories (for girls) and 1525 calories (for boys) a day, compared with about 1250 calories (for girls) and 1350 calories (for boys) for the average two- to three-year-old.

8.4 Health and Illness

How healthy are children in Canada and in other countries? What are some of the illnesses and environmental hazards encountered during early childhood?

The incidence of minor illnesses, such as colds, nausea and vomiting, and diarrhea, is high. Although diarrheal illness is usually mild in Canada, it is a leading killer of children in developing countries. Immunization and antibiotics reduce the incidence of serious childhood diseases.

8.5 Sleep

How much sleep is needed during early childhood? What kinds of problems disrupt sleep?

Most two- and three-year-olds sleep about 10 hours at night and nap during the day. Sleep terrors are more severe than nightmares. Sleep terrors and sleepwalking usually occur during deep sleep.

8.6 Elimination Disorders

What are the elimination disorders? What can, or should, be done to help children gain control?

Enuresis is the failure to control the bladder once a child has reached the "normal" age for doing so; the American Psychiatric Association places that age at five years. Encopresis (soiling) is lack of control over the bowels. Most Canadian children are toilet trained by about age three or four but continue to have "accidents" at night for another year or so. There are several strategies that can be used to help children with elimination control, such as maintaining a consistent schedule, rewarding children for success, and limiting fluid intake late in the day.

Key Terms

corpus callosum 265
plasticity 265
gross motor skills 266
fine motor skills 270
oral rehydration therapy 277

transitional object 282
sleep terrors 284
nightmares 284
insomnia 284
somnambulism 284

enuresis 286
bed-wetting 286
encopresis 287

Active Learning Resources

Go to *Voyages in Development's* CourseMate at www
.nelsonbrain.com, where you will find an interactive
eBook, flashcards, Pre-Lecture Quizzes, Section Quizzes,
Exam Practice, videos, and more.

© Per Breiehagen/Getty Images

Major Topics

EARLY CHILDHOOD:
Cognitive Development

9

Truth or Fiction?

T | F   A preschooler's having imaginary playmates is a sign of loneliness or psychological problems. **p. 295**

T | F   Two-year-olds tend to assume that their parents are aware of everything that is happening to them, even when their parents are not present. **p. 295**

T | F   "Because Mommy wants me to" may be a perfectly good explanation—for a three-year-old. **p. 296**

T | F   Children's levels of intelligence—not just their knowledge—are influenced by early learning experiences. **p. 304**

T | F   An academic preschool education provides children with advantages in school later on. **p. 306**

T | F   One- and two-year-olds are too young to remember past events. **p. 314**

T | F   During her third year, a girl explained that she and her mother had finished singing a song by saying, "We singed it all up." **p. 319**

T | F   Three-year-olds usually say "Daddy goed away" instead of "Daddy went away" because they do understand rules of grammar. **p. 319**

For those of you who work with young children, have young children of your own, or occasionally come in contact with young children, you will appreciate this next recollection by Spencer. He recounts how he was confused when his daughter Allyn, at the age of two-and-a-half, insisted that he continue to play "Billy Joel" on the stereo. Put aside the question of her taste in music. His problem stemmed from the fact that when Allyn asked for Billy Joel, the name of the singer, she could be satisfied only by the song "Moving Out." When "Moving Out" had ended and the next song, "The Stranger," had begun to play, she would insist that her dad play "Billy Joel" again. "That *is* Billy Joel," he would protest. "No, no," she would insist, "I want Billy Joel!"

Finally, it occurred to him that, for her, "Billy Joel" symbolized the song "Moving Out," not the name of the singer. Of course, his insistence that the second song was also "Billy Joel" could not satisfy her! She was conceptualizing Billy Joel as a property of a particular song, not as the name of a person who could sing many songs.

Children between the ages of two and four tend to show confusion between symbols and the objects they represent. They do not yet recognize that words are arbitrary symbols for objects and events and that people can use different words. They tend to think of words as inherent properties of objects and events.

In this chapter, we discuss cognitive development during early childhood. First, we examine Piaget's preoperational stage of cognitive development. Piaget viewed cognitive development largely in terms of maturation; however, in the section on Vygotsky's views on cognitive development, we will see that social and other factors foster cognitive development by placing children in "the zone," as Vygotsky might have put it. Next, we consider other factors in cognitive development, such as how children acquire a "theory of mind" and develop memory. Finally, we continue our exploration of language development.

Thinkstock Images/Thinkstock

9.1 Jean Piaget's Preoperational Stage (2–7 years)

QUESTION » How do children in the preoperational stage think and behave? According to Piaget, the **preoperational stage** of cognitive development lasts from about age two to age seven. Be warned: Any resemblance between the logic of a preschooler and your own may be purely coincidental!

Symbolic Thought

preoperational stage The second stage in Piaget's scheme, characterized by inflexible and irreversible mental manipulation of symbols.

symbolic play Play in which children make believe that objects and toys are other than what they are. Also termed *pretend play*.

Preoperational thought is characterized by the use of symbols to represent objects and relationships among them. Perhaps the most important symbolic activity of young children is language. But we will see that children's early use of language leaves something to be desired in the realm of logic.

Children begin to scribble and draw pictures in the early years. These drawings are symbols of objects, people, and events in children's lives. Symbolism is also expressed as symbolic or pretend play, which emerges during these years.

Symbolic or Pretend Play: "We Could Make Believe"

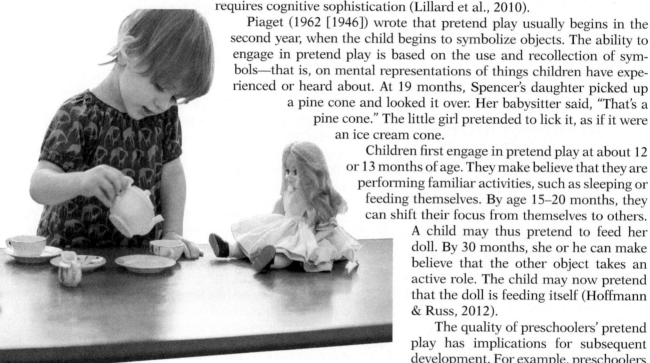

Children's **symbolic play**—the "let's pretend" type of play—may seem immature to busy adults meeting the realistic demands of the business world, but it requires cognitive sophistication (Lillard et al., 2010).

Piaget (1962 [1946]) wrote that pretend play usually begins in the second year, when the child begins to symbolize objects. The ability to engage in pretend play is based on the use and recollection of symbols—that is, on mental representations of things children have experienced or heard about. At 19 months, Spencer's daughter picked up a pine cone and looked it over. Her babysitter said, "That's a pine cone." The little girl pretended to lick it, as if it were an ice cream cone.

Children first engage in pretend play at about 12 or 13 months of age. They make believe that they are performing familiar activities, such as sleeping or feeding themselves. By age 15–20 months, they can shift their focus from themselves to others.

A child may thus pretend to feed her doll. By 30 months, she or he can make believe that the other object takes an active role. The child may now pretend that the doll is feeding itself (Hoffmann & Russ, 2012).

The quality of preschoolers' pretend play has implications for subsequent development. For example, preschoolers who engage in violent pretend play are less empathic, less likely to help other children, and more likely to engage in antisocial behaviour later on (Lillard et al., 2010). Preschoolers who engage in more elaborate pretend play are also more likely to do well in school later on (Hoffman & Russ, 2012). Solitary pretend play on the playground—when other children are available—may be suggestive of social maladjustment and low peer acceptance (Nelson et al., 2008). The quality of pretend play is also connected with preschoolers' creativity and their ability to relate to peers (Russ, 2006). Another interesting observation of how children make sense of the world around them is the sometimes-used is strategy of *magical thinking*. Children occasionally use

Symbolic Play

Symbolic play—also called pretend play—usually begins in the second year, when the child starts to form mental representations of objects. This two-and-a-half-year-old may engage in a sequence of play acts such as having a doll sit down at the table and offering it a make-believe cup of tea.

magical thinking (also referred to as *wishful thinking*) to explain occurrences that do not have realistic explanations (Subbotsky, 2004; Woolley, Phelps, Davis, & Mandell, 1999).

Imaginary friends are one example of pretend play. At age two, Spencer's daughter Allyn acquired an imaginary playmate named Loveliness. He told Allyn to do lots of things—move things from here to there, get food for him, and so on. At times, Allyn was overheard talking to Loveliness in her room. As many as 65 percent of preschoolers have such friends; they are more common among firstborn and only children (Honeycutt et al., 2011–2012; Lillard et al., 2010).

TRUTH OR FICTION REVISITED: It is not true that having imaginary playmates is a sign of loneliness or psychological problems. Having an imaginary playmate does not mean that the child is having difficulty in real relationships (Lillard et al., 2010). In fact, children with imaginary companions are less aggressive, more cooperative—they often nurture the imaginary friend—and more creative (Honeycutt et al., 2011–2012). They show greater ability to concentrate and are more advanced in language development.

As long as we are talking about play, let's note that some toys are called Transformers. In the following section, we see that the mental processes of children are also "transformers." (Clever transition to the next section.)

Operations: "Transformers" of the Mind

Operations are mental acts (or schemes) in which objects are changed or transformed and then can be returned to their original states. Mental operations are flexible and reversible.

Consider the example of planning a move in checkers. A move requires knowledge of the rules of the game. The child who plays the game well (as opposed to just making moves) is able to picture the results of the move—how, in its new position, the piece will support or be threatened by other pieces and how other pieces might be left undefended by the move. Playing checkers well requires that the child be able to picture, or focus on, different parts of the board and relationships between pieces at the same time. By considering several moves, the child shows flexibility. By picturing the board as it would be after a move, and then picturing it as it is, the child shows reversibility.

Having said all this, let's return to the fact that this section is about preoperational children—children who cannot yet engage in flexible and reversible mental operations. Young children's logic reflects the fact that their ability to perform operations is "under construction." The preoperational stage is thus characterized by features such as egocentrism, immature notions about what causes what, confusion between mental and physical events, and the ability to focus on only one dimension at a time.

Egocentrism: It's All about Me

Sometimes the attitude "It's all about me" is a sign of early childhood, not of selfishness. One consequence of one-dimensional thinking is egocentrism. **Egocentrism**, in Piaget's use of the term, does not mean that preoperational children are selfish (although, of course, they may be). It means that they do not understand that other people may have different perspectives on the world.

TRUTH OR FICTION REVISITED: Two-year-olds may, in fact, assume that their parents are aware of everything that is happening to them, even when their parents are not present. They may view the world as a stage that has been erected to meet their needs and amuse them. When Spencer asked Allyn—still at the age of two-and-a-half—to tell him about a trip to the store with her mother, she answered, "You tell me." It did not occur to her that her dad could not see the world through her eyes.

operations Flexible, reversible mental manipulations of objects, in which objects can be mentally transformed and then returned to their original states.

egocentrism Putting oneself at the centre of things such that one is unable to perceive the world from another person's point of view. Egocentrism is normal in early childhood but is a matter of choice, and rather intolerable, in adults. (Okay, we sneaked an editorial comment into a definition. Dr. Samuel Johnson did that too.)

Figure 9.1 ■ The Three-Mountains Test
Piaget used the three-mountains test to learn whether children at certain ages are egocentric or can take the viewpoints of others.

Piaget used the "three-mountains test" (see Figure 9.1 ■) to show that egocentrism literally prevents young children from taking the viewpoints of others. In this demonstration, the child sits at a table before a model of three mountains. The mountains differ in colour. One has a house on it, and another a cross at the summit.

Piaget then placed a doll elsewhere on the table and asked the child what the doll sees. The language abilities of very young children do not permit them to provide verbal descriptions of what can be seen from where the doll is situated, so they can answer in one of two ways. They can select a photograph taken from the proper vantage point, or they can construct another model of the mountains, as the doll would see them. The results of a classic experiment with the three-mountains test suggest that five- and six-year-olds usually select photos or build models that correspond to their own viewpoints (Laurendeau & Pinard, 1970).

Causality: Why? Because

Preoperational children's responses to questions such as "Why does the sun shine?" show other facets of egocentrism. At the age of two or so, children may answer that they do not know or change the subject. **TRUTH OR FICTION REVISITED:** Three-year-olds may report that they do things because they want to do them or "Because Mommy wants me to." In egocentric fashion, this explanation of behaviour is extended to inanimate objects. Children may think that the sun shines because it wants to shine or because someone (or something) else wants it to shine. In this case, the sun's behaviour is thought of as being caused by will—perhaps the sun's wish to bathe the child in its rays or the child's wish to remain warm. In either case, the answer puts the child at the centre of the conceptual universe. The sun becomes an instrument similar to a lightbulb.

Piaget labels this type of structuring of cause and effect **precausal**. Preoperational children believe that things happen for reasons and not by accident (Koslowski & Masnick, 2010). However, unless preoperational children know the natural causes of an event, their reasons are likely to have an egocentric flavour and not be based on science. Consider the question "Why does it get dark outside?" The preoperational child usually does not have knowledge of the earth's rotation and is likely to answer something like "So I can go to sleep."

Another example of precausal thinking is **transductive reasoning**. In transductive reasoning, children reason by going from one specific isolated event to another (Koslowski & Masnick, 2010). For example, a three-year-old may argue that she should go on her swings in the backyard because it is light outside or that she should go to sleep because it is dark outside. That is, separate specific events, daylight and going on the swings (or being awake), are thought of as having cause-and-effect relationships.

Preoperational children also show **animism** and **artificialism** in their attributions of causality. In animistic thinking, they attribute life and intentions to inanimate objects, such as the sun and the moon. ("Why is the moon gone during the day?" "It is afraid of the sun.") Artificialism assumes that environmental features such as rain and thunder have been designed and made by people (Baillargeon et al., 2010). In *Six Psychological Studies*, Piaget (1967 [1964]) wrote that "Mountains 'grow' because stones have been manufactured and then planted. Lakes have been hollowed out, and for a long time the child believes that cities are built [before] the lakes adjacent to them" (p. 28). Table 9.1 ■ lists other examples of egocentrism, animism, and artificialism. It is important to note that animism and artificialism are culturally influenced; therefore, the examples in Table 9.1 are not absolutes.

precausal A type of thought in which natural cause-and-effect relationships are attributed to will and other preoperational concepts—as in thinking that the sun sets because it is tired.

transductive reasoning Reasoning from the specific to the specific. (In deductive reasoning, one reasons from the general to the specific; in inductive reasoning, one reasons from the specific to the general.)

animism The attribution of life and intentionality to inanimate objects.

artificialism The belief that environmental features were made by people.

Highlights of Preoperational Thought

Type of Thought	Sample Questions	Typical Answers
Egocentrism (placing oneself at the centre of things such that one is unable to perceive the world from another's point of view)	Why does it get dark out?	So I can go to sleep.
	Why does the sun shine?	To keep me warm.
	Why is there snow?	For me to play in.
	Why is grass green?	Because that's my favourite colour.
	What are TV sets for?	To watch my favourite shows and cartoons.
Animism (attributing life and consciousness to physical objects)	Why do trees have leaves?	To keep them warm.
	Why do stars twinkle?	Because they're happy and cheerful.
	Why does the sun move in the sky?	To follow children and hear what they say.
	Where do boats go at night?	They sleep like we do.
Artificialism (assuming that environmental events are human inventions)	What makes it rain?	Someone emptying a watering can.
	Why is the sky blue?	Somebody painted it.
	What is the wind?	A man blowing.
	What causes thunder?	A man grumbling.
	How does a baby get in Mommy's tummy?	Just make it first. (How?) You put some eyes on it, then put on the head.

Confusion of Mental and Physical Events: On "Galaprocks" and Dreams That Are Real

What would you do if someone asked you to pretend you were a galaprock? Chances are you might inquire what a galaprock is and how it behaves. So might a five-year-old child. But a three-year-old might not think that such information is necessary (Gottfried et al., 2003). Have you seen horror movies in which people's dreams become real? It could be said that preoperational children tend to live in such worlds—although, for them, that world is normal and not horrible.

Young children can pretend to be galaprocks without knowing what they are because, according to Piaget, the preoperational child has difficulty making distinctions between mental and physical phenomena. Children between the ages of two and four show confusion between symbols and the things that they represent. Egocentrism contributes to the assumption that their thoughts exactly reflect external reality. They do not recognize that words are arbitrary and that people can use different words to refer to things. In *Play, Dreams, and Imitation in Childhood,* Piaget (1962 [1946]) asked a four-year-old child, "Could you call this table a cup and that cup a table?" "No," the child responded. "Why not?" "Because," explained the child, "you can't drink out of a table!"

Another example of the preoperational child's confusion of the mental and the physical is the tendency to believe that dreams are real. Dreams are cognitive events that originate within the dreamer but seem to be perceived through the dreamer's senses. These facts are understood by seven-year-olds, but many four-year-olds believe that dreams are real (Honig & Nealls, 2011). They think that their dreams are visible to others and that dreams come from the outside. It is as though they were watching a movie.

Focus on One Dimension at a Time: Mental Blinders

To gain further insight into preoperational thinking, consider these two problems: Imagine that you pour water from a low, wide glass into a tall, thin glass, as in Figure 9.2(b) ■. Now, does the tall, thin glass contain more than, less than, or the same amount of water as the low, wide glass? We won't keep you in suspense. If you said the same (with possible minor exceptions for spillage and evaporation), you are correct.

Now that you're on a roll, here's another problem. If you flatten a ball of clay into a pancake, do you wind up with more, less, or the same amount of clay? If you said the same, you are correct once more.

To arrive at the correct answers to these questions, you must understand the law of **conservation**, which holds that properties of substances such as volume, mass, and number remain the same—that is, they are conserved—even if you change their shape or arrangement.

Now, preoperational children are not conservationists. We don't mean that they throw out half-eaten meals (although they do so often enough). We mean that they tend to focus on only one aspect of a problem at a time.

Conservation requires the ability to focus on two aspects of a situation at once, such as height and width. The preoperational boy in Figure 9.2 focuses, or centres on, only one dimension at a time, a characteristic of thought that Piaget called **centration**. First, the boy is shown two low, wide glasses of water and agrees that they contain the same amount of water. Then, as he watches, water is poured from one of the low, wide glasses into a tall, thin glass. Asked which glass has more water, the boy points to the tall glass. Why? When he looks at the glasses, he is swayed by the fact that the water level in the tall glass is higher.

The preoperational child's failure to show conservation also comes about because of a characteristic of thought known as **irreversibility.** That is, the child does not realize that pouring water from the tall glass to the low, wide glass can be reversed, restoring things to their original condition.

conservation In cognitive psychology, the principle that properties of substances such as weight and mass remain the same (are conserved) when superficial characteristics such as their shapes or arrangement are changed.

centration Focusing on one dimension of a situation while ignoring others.

irreversibility Lack of recognition that actions can be reversed.

a b c

Figure 9.2 ■ Conservation

(a) The boy in this illustration agreed that the amounts of water in two identical containers are equal. (b) He then watched as water from one container was poured into a tall, thin container. (c) When asked whether the amounts of water in the two containers are now the same, he says no.

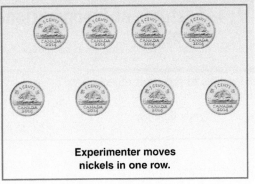

Child is shown two
rows of nickels.

Experimenter moves
nickels in one row.

Figure 9.3 ■ Conservation of Number

In this demonstration, we begin with two rows of nickels that are spread out equally, as shown in the left-hand part of the drawing. Then one row of nickels is spread out more, as shown on the right-hand side. We then ask the child, "Do the two rows still have the same number of nickels?" Do you think that a preoperational child will conserve the number of nickels or focus on the length of the longer row in arriving at an answer?

If all this sounds rather illogical, that is because it is illogical—or, to be precise, preoperational. But if you have any doubts concerning its accuracy, borrow a three-year-old and try the water experiment for yourself.

After you have tried the experiment with the water, try the following experiment on conservation of number. Make two rows with four nickels in each, the nickels located about a centimetre apart. As the three-year-old child is watching, increase the space between the nickels in the second row until they are about 2 centimetres apart, as shown in Figure 9.3 ■. Then ask the child which row has more nickels. What do you think the child will say? Why?

Class Inclusion

The term **class inclusion**, as we are using it here, does not refer to whether a class is open to children from diverse backgrounds. We are talking about an aspect of conceptual thinking that you most likely take for granted: including new objects or categories in broader mental classes or categories.

Class inclusion also requires children to focus on two aspects of a situation at once (Quinn, 2010). Class inclusion means that one category or class of things includes other subclasses. For example, the class "animals" includes the subclasses of dogs and cats.

In one of Piaget's class-inclusion tasks, the child is shown several objects from two subclasses of a larger class (see Figure 9.4 ■). For example, a four-year-old child is shown pictures of four cats and six dogs. She is asked whether there are more dogs or more animals. Now, she knows what dogs and cats are. She also knows that they are both animals. What do you think she will say? Preoperational children typically answer that there are more dogs than animals (Piaget, 1963 [1936]). That is, they do not show class inclusion.

Why do children make this error? According to Piaget, the preoperational child cannot think about the two subclasses and the larger class at the same time. Therefore, he or she cannot easily compare them. The child views dogs as dogs, or as animals, but finds it difficult to see them as both dogs and animals at once (Andrews et al., 2009; Fisher, 2010).

class inclusion The principle that one category or class of things can include several subclasses.

Figure 9.4 ■ Class Inclusion

A typical four-year-old child will say there are more dogs than animals in the example.

Concept Review 9.1 Features of Preoperational Cognition According to Piaget

Symbolic thought
- Child uses symbols to represent objects and relationships.
- Child engages in symbolic play.
- Symbolic play grows more frequent and complex.
- Child may have imaginary friend(s).
- Mental operations are inflexible and irreversible.

Egocentrism
- Child does not take viewpoint of others.
- Child may lack empathy for others.
- Piaget used the three-mountains test to assess egocentrism.

Precausal thinking
- Child believes things happen for a reason.
- Child engages in transductive reasoning ("Should sleep because it's dark outside").
- Child shows animism (attributes life and will to inanimate objects).
- Child shows artificialism (assumes environmental features are made by people).

Confusion of mental and physical events
- Child assumes thoughts reflect external reality.
- Child believes dreams are real.

Focus on one dimension at a time
- Child does not understand law of conservation.
- Child focuses on one dimension at a time.
- Child does not show appropriate class inclusion (may not include dogs as animals).

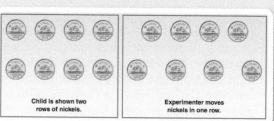

Child is shown two rows of nickels.

Experimenter moves nickels in one row.

Development of Concepts of Ethnicity and Race

North Americans are encouraged to be "colourblind" in matters of employment, housing, and other areas in which discrimination has historically occurred (Quintana et al., 2006). However, children, like adults, are not literally colourblind. Therefore, it is fascinating to see how children's concepts of race and ethnicity develop. Knowledge of the connection between cognitive development and the development of concepts about people from different ethnic and racial backgrounds suggests when it might be most useful to intervene to help children develop open attitudes toward people from different backgrounds.

From interviews of 500 African American, Asian American, Latin American, and Native American children, psychologists Stephen Quintana (1998, 2011) and L. Rabasca (2000) concluded that children undergo four levels of understanding of ethnicity and race. Between the ages of three and six, children generally think about racial differences in physical terms. They do not necessarily see race as a fixed or stable attribute. They may think that a person could change his or her race by means of surgery or tanning in the sun.

From the ages of six to ten, children generally understand that race is a matter of ancestry that affects not only physical appearance but also one's language, diet, and leisure activities. But understanding at this stage is literal, or concrete. For example, children believe that being Mexican American means that one speaks Spanish and eats Mexican-style food. Interethnic friendships are likely to develop among children of this age group.

From the ages of about 10 to 14, children tend to link ethnicity with social class. They become aware of connections between race and income, race and neighbourhood, and race and affirmative action. During adolescence, many individuals begin to take pride in their ethnic heritage and experience a sense of belonging to their ethnic group. They

If You Are Born White, Do You Remain White? If You Are Born Asian, Do You Remain Asian? If You Are Born ... According to research by Quintana, children between the ages of three and six tend to think about racial differences in physical terms. They do not necessarily see race as a fixed or stable attribute. They may think that people can change their race by means of surgery or sun tanning.

are less open to intergroup relationships than younger children are.

Quintana's research found that middle childhood and early adolescence (ages 6–14) are probably the best times to fend off the development of prejudice by teaching children about people from different cultural backgrounds. "That's when [children are] able to go beyond the literal meaning of the words and address their own observations about race and ethnicity," he noted (cited in Rabasca, 2000). Children at these ages also tend to be more open to forming relationships with children from different backgrounds (Quintana, 2011).

Reflect Why does Quintana suggest that early childhood might be too soon to try to prevent the development of prejudice? Do you agree? Explain.

Evaluation of Piaget

Piaget was an astute observer of the cognitive processes of young children. But more recent research questions the accuracy of his age estimates concerning children's failures (or apparent failures) to display certain cognitive skills. For example, the difficulty young children have with the three-mountains test may not be due to egocentrism (Miller, 2010). One can attribute much of the problem to the demands that this method makes on the child. The three-mountains test presents a lifeless scene, one devoid of people and human motives. By contrast, when children are asked to place a boy doll behind tabletop screens so that it cannot be "seen" by police dolls, three-and-a-half-year-olds succeed most of the time.

Language development may also play a role in tests of children's egocentrism and other aspects of cognitive development. Young children may not quite understand what is being asked of them in the three-mountains test, even though they may proceed to select the (wrong) photograph rather quickly (Miller, 2010). Let us give you an example. Spencer was interested in knowing whether his daughter, at age two years nine months, thought that her mother could see her from another room. "Can Mommy see you now?" Spencer asked. "Sure," said his daughter, "if she wants to." She thought her dad was asking whether her mother could have permission to see her, not whether her mother had the capacity to see her from behind a wall.

Newer studies indicate that the young child's understanding of causality is somewhat more sophisticated than Piaget believed (Meltzoff, 2007). Again, much depends on how the task is presented. When four- to seven-year-olds are asked the kind of open-ended questions that Piaget used (such as "Where did the ocean come from?"), they give artificialistic responses, such as "The ocean comes from sinks." But when asked direct questions ("Do you think people made the oceans?"), most will correctly respond that people do not make natural things such as oceans or flowers, but they do make objects such as cups and TVs (Meltzoff, 2010; Miller, 2010).

The demands of the standard conservation task may also present a misleading picture of the child's knowledge. Piaget and other experimenters filled identical beakers with the same amount of water and then poured water from one of the beakers into a beaker of another shape. Before pouring the water, the experimenter typically asked the child whether both beakers have the same amount of water and instructed the child to watch the pouring carefully. In doing so, perhaps the experimenter is "leading the witness"—that is, leading the child to expect a change.

Active Review

1. According to Piaget, _____ play is based on the use of symbols.

2. _____ are mental acts in which objects are changed or transformed and can then be returned to their original states.

3. Piaget used the three-mountains test to show that preoperational children are _____.

4. The type of thinking in which children attribute will to inanimate objects is termed _____ thinking.

5. In _____ reasoning, children reason from one specific event to another.

6. The law of _____ holds that properties of substances such as volume, mass, and number remain the same even when their shape or arrangement changes.

7. Preoperational children focus on (how many?) _____ dimension(s) of a problem at once.

Reflect & Relate: Preoperational children focus on one dimension of a problem at a time. Do we as adults sometimes focus on one dimension of a situation at a time? If you injure someone in an accident, should you be held responsible? (Note the two elements: the injury and the fact that it is accidental.) Most people would probably say, "An accident is an accident." But what if a utility injures 8 million people in a nuclear accident? Should it be held responsible? (That is, does the enormity of the damage affect responsibility?)

9.2 Vygotsky's Views on Early Childhood Cognitive Development

QUESTION » What are Vygotsky's views on some of the factors that influence cognitive development in early childhood? One of the most important factors is scaffolding, Lev Vygotsky's concept of social supports for cognitive development, as we see in this section. Other factors, as we see in the following section, are familial and social—the home environment, preschool education, and television.

Scaffolding and the Zone of Proximal Development

Parental responsiveness and interaction with the child are key ingredients in the child's cognitive development. One component of this social interaction is scaffolding (see Chapter 1). A scaffold is a temporary structure used for holding workers during building construction. Similarly, cognitive scaffolding is temporary support provided by a parent or teacher to a learning child. The guidance provided by the adult decreases as the child gains skill and becomes capable of carrying out the task on her or his own (Daniels, 2010; Egan, 2009).

A related concept is Vygotsky's zone of proximal development (ZPD). Adults or older children can best guide the child through this zone by gearing their assistance to the child's capabilities. Human neurobiology underlies cognitive development in early childhood, but key forms of children's cognitive activities develop through interaction with older, more experienced individuals who teach and guide them within appropriate learning environments such as schools and shops (Daniels, 2010).

A CLOSER LOOK RESEARCH

Effects of Scaffolding on Children's Abilities to Recall and Retell Stories

According to Vygotsky, children's cognitive development is promoted by scaffolding—that is, by interaction with older, more knowledgeable people, often their caregivers, who teach and guide them. Researchers have studied the relationships between such interactions of children and adults and the children's ability to retell and remember stories.

In an experiment by K. Alison Clarke-Stewart and Robert Beck (1999), 31 five-year-olds observed a videotaped film segment with their mothers, talked about it with their mothers, and then retold the story to a researcher. Clarke-Stewart and Beck found that the quality of the stories, as retold by the children, was related to the scaffolding strategies their mothers had used. Children whose mothers focused the children's attention on the tape, asked their children to talk about it, and discussed the feelings of the characters told better stories than children whose mothers did not use such scaffolding strategies and children in a control group who did not discuss the story at all. Children's understanding of the characters' emotional states was most strongly connected with the number of questions the mother asked and her correction of their misunderstandings of what they saw.

In a longitudinal study, Catherine Haden and her colleagues (2001) observed 21 mother–child pairs as they engaged in specially constructed tasks when the children were 30, 36, and 42 months of age. They analyzed the children's recall of their performance one day and three weeks

afterward at all three ages. It turned out that the children best recalled those aspects of the tasks they had both worked on and discussed with their mothers. Recall under these circumstances exceeded recall when the activities were (1) handled jointly but talked about only by the mother or (2) handled jointly but not discussed.

In sum, scaffolding within a zone of proximal development promotes children's learning and memory.

Reflect Did your caregivers ever watch TV with you and discuss what you saw? What types of things did they say or ask? Did any of your teachers in elementary school use scaffolding after you watched a film or video in class? What did they do?

Temych/Shutterstock.com

Scaffolding
Children's cognitive development is promoted by scaffolding—that is, their interaction with older, more knowledgeable people. Research shows that children better recall and retell stories when their caregivers focus their attention on them, prod children to talk about them, and discuss the feelings of the characters.

9.3 Other Factors in Early Childhood Cognitive Development: The Home Environment, Preschool, and Screen Time

There are many factors in cognitive development in early childhood. Some of them reflect the views of Piaget or Vygotsky, but they have developed as topics of their own.

The Effect of the Home Environment

QUESTION » How does the home environment affect the cognitive development of children? Bettye Caldwell and her colleagues (e.g., Bradley, Caldwell, & Corwyn, 2003) developed a measure for evaluating children's home environments labelled, appropriately enough, HOME—an acronym for Home Observation for the Measurement of the Environment. With this method, researchers directly observe parent–child interaction in the home. The HOME inventory contains six scales, as shown in Table 9.2 ■. The HOME inventory items are better predictors of young children's later IQ scores than is social class, mother's IQ, or infant IQ scores (Bradley, 2006; Totsika & Sylva, 2004). Longitudinal research shows that the home environment is also related to occupational success as an adult (Huesmann et al., 2006).

TRUTH OR FICTION REVISITED: It is true that early learning experiences affect children's levels of intellectual functioning. In a longitudinal study, Caldwell and her colleagues observed children from poor and working-class families over a period of years, starting at six months of age. The HOME inventory was used at the early ages, and standard IQ tests were given at ages three and four. The children of mothers who were emotionally and verbally responsive, who were involved with their children, and who provided

---

● TABLE 9.2

Scales of the HOME Inventory

Scale	Sample Items
Parental emotional and verbal responsiveness	• The parent spontaneously vocalizes to the child during the visit. • The parent responds to the child's vocalizations with vocal or other verbal responses.
Avoidance of restriction and punishment	• The parent does not shout at the child. • The parent does not interfere with the child's actions or restrict the child's movements more than three times during the visit.
Organization of the physical environment	• The child's play environment seems to be safe and free from hazards.
Provision of appropriate play materials	• The child has a push or a pull toy. • The child has one or more toys or pieces of equipment that promote muscle activity. • The family provides appropriate equipment to foster learning.
Parental involvement with child	• The parent structures the child's play periods. • The parent tends to keep the child within her or his visual range and looks at the child frequently.
Opportunities for variety in daily stimulation	• The child gets out of the house at least four times a week. • The parent reads stories to the child at least three times a week.

appropriate play materials and a variety of daily experiences during the early years showed advanced social and language development even at six months of age (Parks & Bradley, 1991). These children also attained higher IQ scores at ages three and four and higher achievement test scores at age seven. Other studies support the view that being responsive to preschoolers, stimulating them, and encouraging independence are connected with higher IQ scores and greater school achievement later on (Bradley, 2006; Bradley & Corwyn, 2006). Molfese and her colleagues (1997) found that the home environment was the single most important predictor of scores on IQ tests among children ages three to eight.

The Home Environment
The home environment of the young child is linked to intellectual development and later academic achievement. Key aspects of the home environment include the parents' involvement and encouragement of the child, the availability of toys and learning materials, and the variety of experiences to which the child is exposed.

Early Childhood Education

QUESTION » How do preschool educational programs affect children's cognitive development? What kinds of preschools are available? Why do parents choose them? How important are academic experiences in early childhood? Do they facilitate cognitive development? Research suggests that preschool education enables children to get an early start on achievement in school (Frede & Ackerman, 2007).

Affluent parents may fret about whether their youngsters will gain admittance to the most prestigious and challenging preschools—such as quality child care and preschool programs in their areas—because these early preschool experiences may shape their later school experiences and then, often, to a successful post-secondary career. Some preschools and child-care settings offer *academic programs,* in which teachers structure learning experiences and the curricula take children, step by step, through learning letters, numbers, shapes and colours, and other academic competencies. The intention is to give children a running start for achievement in a challenging kindergarten and a challenging elementary school.

Other preschools are more *child-centred.* In these settings, teachers provide a variety of activities. Children are permitted to choose those that interest them the most. Although academic-type learning may occur, the child is more likely to set the pace and acquire whatever academic skills are available through play. The input of parents tends to be more accepted and even desired in child-centred programs, whereas parental views may be seen as counter-productive in more structured academic programs (Burgess & Fleet, 2009).

Preschool Education for Economically Disadvantaged Children

Children growing up in poverty generally perform less well on standardized intelligence tests, and they are at greater risk for school failure (Caputo, 2003; Stipek & Hakuta, 2007; Whitehouse, 2006). This topic is a complex one. Some would argue that intelligence tests may be insensitive and biased against children from diverse backgrounds who may not have had the same breadth of experiences or opportunities to learn what certain cognitive tests measures (Flanagan, Ortiz, & Alfonso, 2007). Alternatively, dynamic assessment offers an alternative form of assessment, one which incorporates the opportunity to test for children's potential by diminishing the focus on knowledge of culturally learned information. For example, with dynamic assessment children may be prompted, provided with feedback, and actually testing so that problem

Head Start

Preschoolers enrolled in Head Start programs have made dramatic increases in readiness for elementary school and in intelligence test scores. Head Start and similar programs also can have long-term effects on educational and employment outcomes.

solving can be assessed (Feuerstein et al., 1979, 1980). An example is Feuerstein's Learning Potential Assessment Device, in which children are taught new knowledge with the guidance of an adult (teacher or parent) who can provide hints (Feuerstein et al., 1980). Sound familiar? It should, as this approach aligns with Vygotsky's sociocultural theory of cognitive development.

To reach children of varying cultural and disadvantaged backgrounds, a number of preschool programs in Canada were started. While the programs and services offered by Head Start programs across the country vary, they typically include services such as preparation for the school, Aboriginal culture and traditions (if program is for Aboriginal children and families), parent support groups and classes, and health nutrition and physical development. Children in these programs typically are exposed to letters and words, numbers, books, exercises in drawing, pegs and pegboards, puzzles, and toy animals and dolls, in addition to other materials and activities that middle-class children can usually take for granted. Many programs encourage parental involvement in the program itself.

In Canada, the federal government established Aboriginal Head Start in 1995 to support child development and school readiness initiatives for Aboriginal children living in urban centres and large northern communities. The main objectives of these locally run programs are to support culture and language, education, health promotion, nutrition, social support, and parent education and involvement (Health Canada, 2011a).

In Ontario, three major reports dealing with early childhood development, entitled *The Early Years: Reversing the Brain Drain* (McCain & Mustard, 1999), the *Early Years Report II: Putting Science into Action* (McCain, Mustard, & Shanker, 2007), and *The Early Years 3 Study* (McCain, Mustard, & McCuaig, 2011), have been published. These reports examine the strength of provincial-level community initiatives in early childhood development programs that provide support to parents in the following ways:

- Providing good advice and support on nourishment, nurturing, and stimulation for young children through play-based learning;
- Providing support to parents of young children;
- Offering nonparental care (day care), which supports early child development and parenting capacity; and
- Improving the community's capacity to support early child development programs (*The Early Years: Reversing the Brain Drain*, p. 115).

A key conclusion from these reports is that parents need and want nonparental care to varying degrees. What McCain and Fraser (1999) recommended for Ontario are (a) early childhood development and parenting centres that are available and accessible for all families, (b) improved maternity/parental leaves, (c) family-friendly work places, and (d) tax incentives for development of new centres in communities.

TRUTH OR FICTION REVISITED: It is true that an academic preschool can provide children with advantages in school. Studies of Head Start show that environmental enrichment can enhance the cognitive development of economically disadvantaged children (Zhai et al., 2011). The initial effects can be dramatic. In the Milwaukee Project, poor children of low-IQ mothers were provided with enriched day care from the age of six months. By the late preschool years, their IQ scores averaged about 121, compared with an average of 95 for children from similar backgrounds who did not receive day care (Garber, 1988). In addition to positively influencing IQ scores, Head Start and similar programs also lead to gains in school readiness tests and achievement tests (Fuhs & Day, 2011). Programs that involve and educate parents are particularly beneficial (Stipek & Hakuta, 2007).

Preschool intervention programs can have long-term effects on life outcomes for poor children (Reynolds et al., 2011). During the elementary and high school years, graduates of preschool programs are less likely to have been left back or placed in classes for slow learners. They are more likely to graduate from high school, go on to college, and earn higher incomes. They are also less likely to become involved in substance abuse or other areas of delinquent behaviour, or to be unemployed or on welfare in adulthood (Reynolds et al., 2011).

A contributor to the cycle of poverty and risk is the incidence of pregnancy among single teenage girls. Pregnancy may alter the course of and levels of completion of formal education, so these children are likely reared by mothers with less formal education than older mothers. Some researchers have found that girls from preschool education programs are less likely to become single mothers (Doyle et al., 2009). Girls who attended preschool intervention programs became pregnant as frequently as matched controls, but they were more likely to return to school after giving birth.

Educators recognize that academic environments in the preschool years benefit advantaged as well as disadvantaged children (Hyson et al., 2006). On the other hand, excessive pressure to achieve during the preschool years, especially on the part of middle-class parents, may impair children's learning and social–emotional development.

Television and Screen Time

QUESTION » What are the effects of television on children's cognitive development? How many people do you know who do not have a TV? Canadian children aged 2 to 11 spend an average of 15.5 hours a week watching television. (Statistics Canada, 2001). In the United States, by the time children turn three, the average child already watches two to three hours of television a day (Palmer, 2003).

Television has great potential for teaching a variety of cognitive skills, social behaviours, and attitudes. In Chapter 10, we will explore the effects of television on children's social behaviours and attitudes (uh-oh). Here, we focus on television's effect on cognitive development in early childhood. In many ways, television provides children with an important window on the outside world and on the cognitive skills required to succeed in that world.

Educational Television

Television, in general, has been shown to have mixed effects on children's development. For example, no relationship has been found between general viewing and language development in children under the age of two (Zimmerman et al., 2007). However, educational television might have superior effects.

"At its best," notes Fisch (2004), "educational television can provide children with a window to new experiences, enrich academic knowledge, enhance attitudes and motivation, and nurture social skills." In the United States, the Children's Television Act requires that networks devote a number of hours per week to educational television. Many, but not all, of the resultant programs have been shown to have mild to moderate positive effects on preschoolers' cognitive development, and more so with girls than with boys (Calvert & Kotler, 2003). Why is this relevant for Canadians? Because the reality is that Canadians access American programming, and that U.S. shows make up a good portion of what is broadcast in Canada. Even though the Canadian Broadcasting Act requires Canadian content in programming, Canadians are nonetheless exposed to a great deal of non-Canadian material. Hence, we have included studies conducted with American children here.

"Street" Smart?

Sesame Street is viewed regularly by an estimated 50–60 percent of children in the United States between the ages of two and three years. Research shows that regular viewing of the program improves children's cognitive and language skills.

Sesame Street is the most successful children's educational TV program. Begun in 1969, *Sesame Street* had the goal of promoting the intellectual growth of preschoolers, particularly those of lower socioeconomic status. Large-scale evaluations of the effects of the program have concluded that regular viewing increases children's learning of numbers, letters, and cognitive skills such as sorting and classification (Linebarger & Piotrowski, 2010). These effects are found for black and white children, for girls and boys, and for children in urban, suburban, and rural settings.

What about the effects of watching television on other aspects of cognitive behaviour in the young child? Characters on *Sesame Street* talk out differences and do not fight with one another. Therefore, it is not surprising that most research indicates that exposure to such educational programs as *Sesame Street* may increase impulse control and concentration among preschoolers (Cole et al., 2003). In fact, a joint project by Israelis and Palestinians is under way to bring a Middle Eastern version of *Sesame Street* to the region, in the hope that it may contribute to a more peaceful interaction between the groups (Lampel & Honig, 2006).

We can argue about just how much good a program like *Sesame Street* does, but few would argue that it does any harm. Marie Evans Schmidt and her colleagues (Schmidt & Anderson, 2007; Schmidt et al., 2009) conclude that educational television can have positive benefits but that "entertainment television" can be harmful. Suggested guidelines for helping children use television wisely are presented in the "A Closer Look—Real Life" feature.

A CLOSER LOOK REAL LIFE

Helping Children Use Television Wisely

Overall, television appears to have some positive effects on cognitive development. But there is more to life than television. Let us share some ideas on how parents can help their children reap the benefits of television without allowing it to take over their lives.

General Suggestions

• Encourage children to watch educational programming.

• Help children choose among cartoon shows. Not all are filled with violence. *Toopy and Binoo*, *Roll Play*, and *Max and Ruby* may help foster intellectual and social development.

Continued

František Czanner/Thinkstock

Continued

- Encourage your children to sit with you when you are watching educational programming.
- If your child is spending too much time in front of the tube, keep a chart with the child of his or her total activities, including TV, homework, and play with friends. Discuss what to eliminate and what to substitute.
- Set a weekly viewing limit.
- Rule out TV at certain times, such as before breakfast and on school nights.
- Make a list of alternative activities—riding a bicycle, reading a book, working on a hobby.
- Encourage the entire family to choose a program before turning the TV set on. Turn the set off when the show is over.

Coping with Violence

- Watch at least one episode of programs the child watches to see how violent they are.
- When viewing TV together, discuss the violence with the child. Talk about why the violence happened and how painful it is. Discuss how conflict can be resolved without violence.
- Explain to the child how violence on TV shows is faked.
- Encourage children to watch programs with characters who cooperate with, help, and care for each other. Such programs can influence children in a positive way.

Applying TV to Real Life

- Ask children to compare what they see on the screen with people, places, and events they know firsthand, have read about, or have studied in school.

- Tell children what is real and what is make-believe on TV—including the use of stunt people, dream sequences, and animation.
- Explain to the child your values with regard to sex, alcohol, and drugs.

Understanding Advertising

- Explain to children that the purpose of advertising is to sell products.
- On shopping trips, let children see that toys that look big, fast, and exciting on the screen are disappointingly small and slow close up.
- Talk to the child about nutrition. If the child can read package labels, allow her or him to choose a breakfast cereal from those in which sugar levels are low.

Reflect Have you seen television used as a baby-sitter? What risks are there in doing this?

© KidStock/Blend Images/Getty Images

TV, TV Everywhere—How Do We Teach Children to Stop to Think?
Parents can have a positive effect on children's cognitive processing of the information they glean from TV programs and commercials.

Commercials

Critics are concerned that the cognitive limitations of young children make them particularly susceptible to commercials, which can be misleading and even harmful. Preschoolers do not understand the selling intent of advertising, and they often are unable to tell the difference between commercials and program content (Kundanis & Massaro, 2004; Palmer, 2003). Exposure to commercials does not make the child a sophisticated consumer. In fact, children who are heavy TV viewers are more likely than light viewers to believe commercial claims.

Commercials that encourage children to choose nutritionally inadequate foods—such as sugared breakfast cereals, candy, and fast foods—are harmful to children's nutritional beliefs and diets. Young children do not understand that sugary foods are detrimental to health, nor do they understand disclaimers in ads that, for example, caution that sugared cereals should be part of a balanced breakfast (Palmer, 2003; Pine & Nash, 2002).

The Couch-Potato Effect

Watching television, of course, is a sedentary activity. Parents might prefer that their children spend more time exercising, but television also functions as an engrossing babysitter. However, research in the United States, England, and even China shows that preschool children who watch more television are more likely to be overweight than peers who watch less television (Jordan & Robinson, 2008). The number of hours watching television is a stronger predictor of being overweight than diet (Jago et al., 2005)!

This research is correlational, to be sure; that is, children choose (or are allowed) to watch more or less television. They are not randomly assigned to view various amounts of television. Thus, it may be that the same factors that lead them to choose more television also lead them to put on more body fat. On the other hand, there may be little harm (and much good!) in encouraging children to spend more time in physical activity.

According to a Canadian Paediatric Society position statement (Lipnowski, LeBlanc, & Canadian Paediatric Society, 2012), children under the age of two should have no screen time (e.g. TV, computer, electronic games), and children between the ages of two and four should have no more than one hour per day.

Active Review

8. Cognitive _____ is temporary support provided by a parent or teacher to a child who is learning to perform a task.

9. Caldwell and her colleagues found that the children of parents who are emotionally and verbally _____ show advanced social and language development.

10. Molfese and her colleagues found that the _____ was the single most important predictor of scores on IQ tests among children.

11. Head Start programs (can or cannot?) significantly enhance the cognitive development of economically disadvantaged children.

Reflect & Relate: What was your early home environment like? How do you think it would have appeared in terms of the factors listed in Table 9.2? How can you use the information in this section to create a home environment for your own children? How much television did you watch as a child? Can you think of things you learned by watching television? Can you imagine developing in a world without television? Explain.

9.4 Theory of Mind: What Is the Mind? How Does It Work?

QUESTION » What are children's ideas about how the mind works? Adults appear to have a commonsense understanding of how the mind works. This understanding, known as a **theory of mind**, allows us to explain and predict behaviour by referring to mental processes. For example, we understand that we can acquire knowledge through our senses or through hearsay. We understand the distinction between external and mental events and between how things appear and how they really are. We are able to infer the perceptions, thoughts, and feelings of others. We understand that mental states affect behaviour.

Piaget might have predicted that preoperational children are too egocentric and too focused on misleading external appearances to have a theory of mind. But research has shown that even preschool-age children can accurately predict and explain human action and emotion in terms of mental states. They are beginning to understand where knowledge comes from. And they have a rudimentary ability to distinguish appearance from reality (Wellman, 2010). Let us consider these developments.

False Beliefs: Just Where Are Those Crayons?

theory of mind A commonsense understanding of how the mind works.

One important indication of the young child's understanding that mental states affect behaviour is the ability to understand false beliefs. This concept involves children's ability to separate their beliefs from those of another

a   b   c

Figure 9.5 ▪ False Beliefs
John Flavell and his colleagues showed preschoolers a videotape in which a girl named Cathy found crayons in a bag (a). When Cathy left the room, a clown entered, removed the crayons from the bag, hid them in a drawer (b), and filled the bag with rocks (c). When asked whether Cathy thought there would be rocks or crayons in the bag, most three-year-olds said "rocks." Most four-year-olds correctly answered "crayons," showing the ability to separate their own beliefs from someone who has false beliefs about a situation.

person who has false knowledge of a situation. It is illustrated in a study of three-year-olds by Louis Moses and John Flavell (1990). The children were shown a videotape in which a girl named Cathy found some crayons in a bag. When Cathy left the room briefly, a clown entered the room. The clown removed the crayons from the bag, hid them in a drawer, and put rocks in the bag instead. When Cathy returned, the children were asked whether Cathy thought there were going to be rocks or crayons in the bag. Most of the three-year-olds incorrectly answered "rocks," demonstrating their difficulty in understanding that the other person's belief would be different from their own (see Figure 9.5 ▪). But by the age of four to five years, children do not have trouble with this concept and correctly answer "crayons" (Flavell, 1993). By the ages of four and five, children in North America and China are also starting to understand that beliefs may be held with differing degrees of certainty (Tardif et al., 2005).

Another intriguing demonstration of the false-belief concept comes from studies of children's ability to deceive others. For example, Sodian and her colleagues (1991) asked children to hide a toy truck driver in one of five cups in a sandbox so that another person could not find it. The child was given the opportunity to deceive the other person by removing real trails in the sand and creating false ones. Once again, four-year-olds acted in ways that were likely to mislead the other person. Younger children did not.

The ability to understand false beliefs is related to the development of executive functioning, including working memory, ability to pay sustained attention to problems, and self-control (Flynn et al., 2004; Razza & Blair, 2009).

Origins of Knowledge: Where Does It Come From?

Another aspect of theory of mind is how we acquire knowledge. By age three, most children begin to realize that people gain knowledge about a thing by looking at it (Pratt & Bryant, 1990). By age four, children understand that particular senses provide information about certain qualities of an object; that is, they recognize that we come to know an object's colour through our eyes, but its weight by feeling it (O'Neill & Chong, 2001). In one study, three-, four-, and five-year-olds learned about the contents of a toy tunnel in three different ways (O'Neill & Gopnik, 1991). They saw the contents, were told about them, or felt them. The children then were asked what was in the tunnel and how they knew. Although four- and five-year-olds had no trouble identifying the sources of their knowledge, the three-year-olds did. For example, after feeling but not seeing a ball in the tunnel, a number of three-year-olds told the experimenter that they could tell it was a blue ball. They did not realize that it was impossible to discover the ball's colour just by feeling it.

The Appearance–Reality Distinction: Appearances Are More Deceiving at Some Ages Than at Others

One of the most important things children must acquire in developing a theory of mind is a clear understanding of the difference between real events, on the one hand, and mental events, fantasies, and misleading appearances, on the other hand (Flavell et al., 2002; Leerkes et al., 2008). This is known as the **appearance–reality distinction**.

Piaget's view was that children do not differentiate reality from appearances or mental events until the age of seven or eight. But more recent studies have found that children's ability to distinguish between the two emerges in the preschool years. Children as young as three can distinguish between pretended actions and real actions, between pictures of objects and the actual objects, and between toy versions of an object and the real object (Cohen, 2006; Wellman, 2002). By the age of four, children make a clear distinction between real items (such as a cup) and imagined items (such as an imagined cup or an imagined monster) (Leerkes et al., 2008).

Despite these accomplishments, preoperational children still show some difficulties in recognizing the difference between reality and appearances, perhaps because children of this age still have only a limited understanding of **mental representations**. They have trouble understanding that a real object or event can take many forms in our minds (Abelev & Markman, 2006). In a study by Marjorie Taylor and Barbara Hort (1990), children aged three to five were shown a variety of objects that had misleading appearances, such as an eraser that looked like a cookie. The children initially reported that the eraser looked like a cookie. But once they learned that it was actually an eraser, they tended to report that it looked like an eraser, ignoring its cookie-like appearance. Apparently, the children could not mentally represent the eraser as both being an eraser and looking like a cookie.

Three-year-olds also apparently cannot understand changes in their mental states. In one study (Gopnik & Slaughter, 1991), three-year-olds were shown a crayon box. They consistently said they thought crayons were inside. The box was opened, revealing birthday candles, not crayons. When the children were asked what they had thought was in the box before it was opened, they now said "candles."

Children aged two-and-a-half to three also find it difficult to understand the relationship between a scale model and the larger object or space that it represents (DeLoache & Sharon, 2005; Ware et al., 2006). Perhaps this is because the child cannot conceive that the model can be two things at once: both a representation of something else and an object in its own right.

appearance–reality distinction The difference between real events on the one hand and mental events, fantasies, and misleading appearances on the other hand.

mental representations The mental forms that a real object or event can take.

Active Review

12. Moses and Flavell used crayons and a clown to learn whether preschoolers can understand _____ beliefs.

13. By age three, most children begin to realize that people gain knowledge about things through the _____.

Reflect & Relate: Think of research on the origins of knowledge—on where knowledge comes from. Can you relate this area of research to arguments we might find among adults about sources of knowledge, such as experience versus revelation?

9.5 Development of Memory: Creating Documents, Storing Them, Retrieving Them

QUESTION » What sorts of memory skills do children possess in early childhood? Even newborns have some memory skills, and memory improves substantially throughout the first two years of life.

Memory Tasks: Recognition and Recall

Two of the basic tasks used in the study of memory are recognition and recall. Recognition is the easiest type of memory task. For this reason, multiple-choice tests are easier than fill-in-the-blank or essay tests. In a recognition test, one simply indicates whether a presented item has been seen before or which of a number of items is paired with a stimulus (as in a multiple-choice test). Children are capable of simple recognition during early infancy; they recognize their mother's nursing pads, her voice, and her face. To test recognition memory in a preschooler, you might show the child some objects and then present those objects along with somenew ones. The child is then asked which objects you showed her the first time.

Recall is more difficult than recognition. In a recall task, children must reproduce material from memory without having it in front of them. If someone asks you to name the capital of Nunavut, that is a test of recall. A recall task for a preschooler might consist of showing her some objects, taking them away, and asking her to name the objects from memory.

When preschoolers are presented with objects, words, or TV shows, they typically recognize more, later on, than they can recall (Schneider, 2010). In fact, younger preschoolers are almost as good as older ones at recognizing objects they have seen. But they are not nearly as good at recall (Schneider, 2010). In Figure 9.6 ■, compare the abilities of three- and four-and-a-half-year-olds to recognize and recall various objects from a life-size playhouse (Jones et al., 1988). (We will discuss the "activities" part of this figure later.)

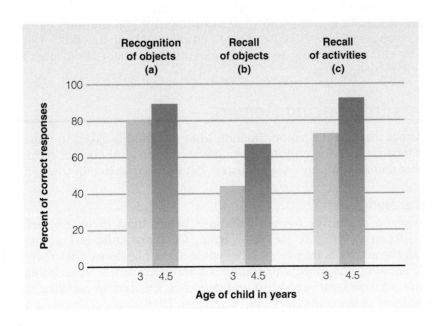

Figure 9.6 ■ Recognition and Recall Memory
Preschoolers can recognize previously seen objects (a) better than they can recall them (b). They also are better at recalling their activities (c) than at recalling objects (b). Older preschoolers have better memories than younger ones.
Source: Jones et al. (1988).

Competence of Memory in Early Childhood

Until recently, most studies of children's memory were conducted in laboratory settings. The tasks had little meaning for the children. The results appeared to show that the memories of young children are deficient relative to those of older children. But parents often tell you that their children have excellent memories for events. It turns out that they are right. Children, like adults, frequently remember what they *want* to remember. More recently, psychologists have focused their research on children's memory for meaningful events and activities.

TRUTH OR FICTION REVISITED: It is not true that one- and two-year-olds are too young to remember past events. Children as young as 11-and-a-half months can remember organized sequences of events they have just experienced (Schneider, 2010). Even after a delay of six weeks, 16-month-old children can re-enact a sequence of events they experienced only one time, such as placing a ball in a cup, covering it with another cup, and shaking the resulting "rattle" (Schneider, 2010). By the age of four, children can remember events that occurred at least a year and a half earlier (Schneider, 2010).

Katherine Nelson and Robyn Fivush (2004) report the results of studies in which children aged two to five are interviewed to study their memory for recurring events in their lives, such as having dinner, playing with friends, and going to birthday parties. Even three-year-olds can present coherent, orderly accounts of familiar events. Furthermore, young children seem to form **scripts**, which are abstract, generalized accounts of these repeated events. For example, in describing what happens during a birthday party, a child might say, "You play games, open presents, and eat cake." Details of particular events often are omitted. However, an unusual experience, such as a devastating hurricane, may be remembered in detail for many years (Bauer & Fivush, 2010).

Young children begin forming scripts after experiencing an event only once. The script becomes more elaborate with repeated experiences. As might be expected, older preschoolers form detailed scripts more quickly than younger preschoolers (Schneider, 2010).

Even though children as young as one and two years clearly can remember events, these memories seldom last into adulthood. This memory of specific events—known as **autobiographical memory** or *episodic memory*—appears to be linked to the development of language skills. It is facilitated by children's talking with their parents and others about past events (Bauer & Fivush, 2010).

Childhood Memory
Despite his youth, this boy will most likely remember this traumatic experience in detail for years to come.

Factors Influencing Memory

The factors that affect memory include what the child is asked to remember, the interest level of the child, the availability of retrieval cues or reminders, and what memory measure we are using. Let us discuss each of these in turn.

Types of Memory

Preschoolers' memories for activities are better than their memories for objects. Return to Figure 9.6 once again. Compare children's accuracy in recalling the activities they engaged in while in the playhouse with their accuracy in recalling the objects they used. Children are better at recalling their activities, such as washing a shirt and chopping ice, than at recalling specific objects, such as shirts and icepicks (Schneider, 2010).

scripts Abstract generalized accounts of familiar repeated events.

autobiographical memory The memory of specific episodes or events.

Children also find it easier to remember events that follow a logical order than events that do not occur in a particular order. For instance, three- and five-year-olds have a better memory for the activities involved in making pretend cookies out of Play-Doh (you put the ingredients in the bowl, then mix the ingredients, then roll out the dough, and so on) than for the activities involved in sand play, which can occur in any order (Bauer & Fivush, 2010).

Interest Level

There is nothing new about the idea that we pay more attention to the things that interest us. The world is abuzz with signals, and we tend to remember those to which we pay attention. Attention opens the door to memory.

Interest level and motivation also contribute to memory among young children (Schneider, 2010). Research consistently shows that (most) preschool boys are more interested in playing with toys such as cars and weapons, whereas (most) preschool girls are more interested in playing with dolls, dishes, and teddy bears. Later, the children typically show better recognition and recall for the toys in which they were interested (Martin & Ruble, 2004).

Retrieval Cues

To retrieve information (a file) from your computer's storage, you have to remember its name or some part of it. Then you can use a Find routine. The name is the retrieval cue. In the same way, we need retrieval cues to find things in our own memories.

Although young children can remember a great deal, they depend more than older children do on cues provided by adults to help them retrieve their memories. Consider the following interchange between a mother and her two-year-old child (Hudson, 1990, p. 186).

MOTHER: What did we look for in the grass and in the bushes?

CHILD: Easter bunny.

MOTHER: Did we hide candy eggs outside in the grass?

CHILD: (nods)

MOTHER: Remember looking for them? Who found two? Your brother?

CHILD: Yes, brother.

Preschoolers whose parents elaborate on the child's experiences and ask questions that encourage the child to contribute information to the narrative remember an episode better than children whose parents simply provide reminders (Nelson & Fivush, 2004). Parental assistance is more important under some conditions than others. For example, when four-year-olds are internally motivated to remember items needed to prepare their own sack lunches, they do equally well with or without parental coaching. But when the task is simply to recall a series of items, they do better with parental assistance (Schneider, 2010).

Types of Measurement

What we find is in part determined by how we measure it. Children's memory is often measured or assessed by asking them to say what they remember. But verbal reports, especially from preschoolers, appear to underestimate children's memory (Schneider, 2010). In one longitudinal study, children's memory for certain events was tested at age two-and-a-half and again at age four. Most of the information recalled at age four had not been mentioned at age two-and-a-half, which indicates that when they were younger, the children remembered much more than they reported (Fivush & Hammond, 1990).

What measures might be more accurate than a verbal report? When preschoolers are allowed to use dolls to re-enact an event, their recall exceeds that exhibited when they give a verbal report of the event (Schneider, 2010).

Memory Strategies: Remembering to Remember

When adults and older children are trying to remember things, they use strategies to help their memory. One common strategy is mental repetition, or **rehearsal**. If you are trying to remember a new friend's phone number, for example, you might repeat it several times. Another strategy is to organize things to be remembered into categories. Many students outline textbook chapters to prepare for an exam. Organizing information in a meaningful way makes it easier to learn and remember. Similarly, if you are going to buy some things at the grocery store, you might mentally group together items that belong to the same category: dairy items, produce, household cleaners, and so on.

Helping Young Children Remember

Memory functioning in early childhood—and at other ages—is aided when adults provide cues to help children remember. Adults can help by elaborating on the child's experiences and asking questions that encourage the child to contribute information.

rehearsal Repetition—mental, behavioural, or both.

But preschool children generally do not appear to use memory strategies on their own initiative. Most young children do not spontaneously engage in rehearsal until about five years of age (Labrell & Ubersfeld, 2004). They also rarely group objects into related categories to help them remember. By about age five, many children have learned to verbalize information silently to themselves—counting mentally rather than aloud.

Even very young children use some simple and concrete memory aids to help them remember. They look, point, and touch when trying to remember. For example, in a study by Judith DeLoache and her colleagues (1985), 18- to 24-month-old children observed as the experimenter hid a Big Bird doll under a pillow. Then they were given attractive toys to play with and, after a short period of time, were asked to find the hidden object. During the play interval, the children frequently looked or pointed at the hiding place or repeated the name of the hidden object. These behaviours suggest the beginning of the use of strategies to prompt the memory.

Young children also can be taught to successfully use strategies they might not use on their own. Six-year-old children who are trained to rehearse show improvement in their ability to recall items on a memory test (Schneider, 2010). Similarly, having preschoolers sort objects into categories enhances memory (Howe, 2006; Lange & Pierce, 1992). Even three- and four-year-olds will use rehearsal and labelling if they are instructed to try to remember something (Schneider, 2010).

The preschooler's use of memory strategies is not nearly as sophisticated as that of the school-age child. Children's use of memory strategies and understanding of how memory works advance greatly in middle childhood.

Active Review

14. Children are capable of simple (recognition or recall?) during infancy.

15. Memory for events in one's life is referred to as _____ memory.

16. Preschoolers' memories for activities are (better or worse?) than their memories for objects.

17. Interest level is (positively or negatively?) connected with ability to remember.

18. Using mental repetition to remember is termed _____.

Reflect & Relate: How do you prepare for a test? How do you remember lists of new vocabulary words, for example? What strategies do your textbook authors use to help you remember the subject matter in this course?

9.6 Language Development: Why "Daddy Goed Away"

QUESTION » What language developments occur during early childhood? Children's language skills grow dramatically during the preschool years. By the fourth year, children are asking adults and each other questions, taking turns talking, and engaging in lengthy conversations (Hoover et al., 2011). Some milestones of language development that occur during early childhood are listed in Table 9.3 ■. Let's consider a number of them.

Development of Vocabulary: Words, Words, and More Words

The development of vocabulary proceeds at an extraordinary pace during early childhood. Preschoolers learn an average of nine new words per day (Rodriguez & Tamis-LeMonda, 2011; Tomasello, 2010). But how can this be possible when each new word has so many potential meanings? Consider the following example. A toddler observes a small black dog running through the park. His older sister points to the animal and says "doggy." The word *doggy* could mean this particular dog, or all dogs, or all animals. It could refer to one part of the dog (such as its tail) or to its behaviour (running, barking) or to its characteristics (small, black) (Waxman & Lidz, 2006). Does the child consider all these possibilities before determining what *doggy* actually means?

Studies have generally shown that word learning, in fact, does not occur gradually but is better characterized as a **fast-mapping** process, in which the

● TABLE 9.3		
Development of Language Skills in Early Childhood		
Age	**Characteristics**	**Typical Sentences**
2½ years	• There is a rapid increase in vocabulary, with new additions each day. • There is no babbling. • Intelligibility is still not very good. • Child uses 2 or 3 words in sentences. • Child uses plurals. • Child uses possessives. • Child uses past tense. • Child uses some prepositions.	Two cups. Sarah's car. It broke. Keisha in bed.
3 years	• Child has vocabulary of some 1000 words. • Speech nears 100% intelligibility. • Articulation of *l* and *r* is frequently faulty. • Child uses 3 or 4 words in sentences. • Child uses yes–no questions. • Child uses *wh* questions. • Child uses negatives. • Child embeds one sentence within another.	Will I go? Where is the doggy? I not eat yucky peas. That's the book Mommy buyed me.
4 years	• Child has vocabulary of 1500–1600 words. • Speech is fluent. • Articulation is good except for *sh, z, ch,* and *j* sounds. • Child uses 5 or 6 words in sentences. • Child coordinates two sentences.	I went to Allie's and I had cookies.

fast mapping A process of quickly determining a word's meaning, which facilitates children's vocabulary development.

Vocabulary Development
When this adult points to the goat and says "goat," the child assumes that "goat" refers to the whole animal, rather than to its horns, fur, size, or colour. This bias, known as the whole-object assumption, helps children acquire a large vocabulary in a relatively short period of time.

child quickly attaches a new word to its appropriate concept (Tomasello, 2010). The key to fast mapping seems to be that children are equipped with early cognitive biases, or constraints, that lead them to prefer certain meanings over others (Waxman & Lidz, 2006).

One bias that children have is assuming that words refer to whole objects and not to their component parts or their characteristics, such as colour, size, or texture (Tomasello, 2010). This inclination is known as the **whole-object assumption**. In the example given at the beginning of the section, this bias would lead the young child to assume that "doggy" refers to the dog rather than to its tail, its colour, or its barking.

Children also seem to hold the bias that objects have only one label. Therefore, novel terms must refer to unfamiliar objects and not to familiar objects that already have labels. This is the **contrast assumption**, which is also known as the mutual exclusivity assumption (Bloom, 2002; Waxman & Lidz, 2006). How might this bias help children figure out the meaning of a new word? Suppose that a child is shown two objects, one of which has a known label ("doggy") and one of which is an unknown object. Let us further suppose that an adult now says, "Look at the lemur." If the child assumes that "doggy" and "lemur" each can refer to only one object, the child will correctly figure out that "lemur" refers to the other object and is not just another name for "doggy." This bias facilitates children's learning of words (Homer & Nelson, 2005; Waxman & Lidz, 2006).

Development of Grammar: Toward More Complex Language

Somewhat similar to the naming explosion in the second year is a "grammar explosion" that occurs during the third year (Rodriguez & Tamis-LeMonda, 2011). Children's sentence structure expands to include the words missing in telegraphic speech. During the third year, children usually add to their vocabulary an impressive array of articles (*a, an, the*), conjunctions (*and, but, or*), possessive adjectives (*your, her*), pronouns (*she, him, one*), and prepositions (*in, on, over, around, under, through*). Usually between the ages of three and four, children show knowledge of rules for combining phrases and clauses into complex sentences. An early example of a complex sentence is "You goed and Mommy goed, too." Table 9.4 ■ lists some interesting examples of one child's use of language during the third year.

Overregularization

One of the more intriguing language developments—**overregularization**—is apparently based on the simple fact that children acquire grammatical rules as they learn language. At young ages, they tend to apply these rules rather strictly, even in cases that call for exceptions (Zapf & Smith, 2009). Consider the formation of the past tense and plurals in English. We add *-d* or *-ed* to regular verbs and *-s* to regular nouns. Thus, *walk* becomes *walked* and *doggy* becomes *doggies*. But then there are irregular verbs and irregular nouns. For example, *sit* becomes *sat* and *go* becomes *went*. *Sheep* remains *sheep* (plural) but *child* becomes *children*.

At first, children learn a small number of these irregular constructions by imitating their parents. Two-year-olds tend to form them correctly temporarily. Then they become aware of the syntactic rules for forming the

whole-object assumption The assumption that words refer to whole objects and not to their component parts or characteristics.

contrast assumption The assumption that objects have only one label. Also known as the mutual exclusivity assumption (if a word means one thing, then it cannot mean another).

overregularization The application of regular grammatical rules (e.g., to create past tense and plurals) to irregular verbs and nouns.

Examples of Allyn's Speech during the Third Year

- Objecting to something said to her: "No, that is not a good talk to say. I don't like that."

- Describing her younger sister: "Jordan is very laughy today."

- On the second floor of her home: "This is not home. This is upstairs."

- Objecting to her father's departure: "Stay here for a couple of whiles."

- Directing her father to turn up the stereo: "Make it a big louder, not a small louder."

- Use of the plural number: "I see two policemans."

- Use of the past tense: "I goed on the choo-choo."

- Requesting a nickel: "Give me another money."

- Explaining that she and her mother are finished singing a song: "We singed it all up."

- Requesting an empty cup: "Give me that. I need it to drink nothing."

- Use of the possessive case: "That car is blue, just like us's."

- When she wants her father to hold her: "I want you to pick up me."

- Directing her father to turn on the stereo: "Push the button and make it too loud." (A minute later): "Make it more louder."

- Refusing to answer a question: "I don't want you to ask that to me."

- Confessing what she did with several coins: "I taked those money and put it on the shelf."

Courtesy of Spencer A. Rathus

past tense and plurals in English. As a result, they tend to make charming errors (Tomasello, 2010). **TRUTH OR FICTION REVISITED:** It is true that a two-and-a-half-year-old girl—(Spencer's daughter)—said, "We singed it all up" after she and her mother had finished singing a song. Some three- to five-year-olds are more likely to say, "Mommy sitted down" than "Mommy sat down." They are likely to talk about the "sheeps" they "seed" on the farm and about all the "childs" they ran into at the playground. **TRUTH OR FICTION REVISITED:** It is also true that a three-year-old is likely to say "Daddy goed away" rather than "Daddy went away" because the child *does* understand rules of grammar. The child is correctly applying a rule for forming the past tense of regular verbs, but applying it to an irregular verb.

Some parents recognize that their children were forming the past tense of irregular verbs correctly and that they then began to make errors. And some of these parents become concerned that their children are "slipping" in their language development and attempt to correct them. However, overregularization reflects accurate knowledge of grammar—not faulty language development. (Really.) In another year or two, *mouses* will be boringly transformed into *mice,* and Mommy will no longer have "sitted down." Parents might as well enjoy overregularization while they can.

In a classic experiment designed to show that preschool children are not just clever mimics in their formation of plurals but have actually grasped rules of grammar, Berko (1958) showed children pictures of nonexistent animals (see Figure 9.7 ■). She first showed them a single animal and said, "This is a wug." Then she showed them a picture of two animals and said, "Now there are two of them. There are two _____," asking the children to finish the sentence. Ninety-one percent of the children said "wugs," providing the proper plural of the bogus word.

Figure 9.7 ■ Wugs

Wugs? Why not? Many bright, sophisticated college students have not heard of "wugs." What a pity. Here are several wugs—actually, make-believe animals used in a study to learn whether preschool children can use rules of grammar to form the plurals of unfamiliar nouns.

This is a wug.   **Now there are two of them.**   **There are two _____.**

OBSERVING CHILDREN,
UNDERSTANDING OURSELVES

An Explosion In Vocabulary

After the age of two, children's vocabularies seem to explode as they rapidly acquire new words.

What strategies do they use to make pronunciation easier? What is a grammatical morpheme? What is overregularization?

From Rathus. *Childhood and Adolescence*, 5E. © 2014 South-Western, a part of Cengage Learning, Inc. Reproduced by permission. www.cengage.com/permissions

Go to www.nelson.com/voyages2ce to watch the video, answer the questions, and e-mail your responses to your professor.

Asking Questions

Children's first questions are telegraphic and characterized by a rising pitch (which signifies a question mark in English) at the end. "More milky?" for example, can be translated into "May I have more milk?" or "Would you like more milk?" or "Is there more milk?" depending on the context. It is usually toward the latter part of the third year that the *wh* questions appear. Consistent with the child's general cognitive development, certain *wh* questions (*what, who,* and *where*) appear earlier than others (*why, when, which,* and *how*) (Tomasello, 2010). *Why* is usually too philosophical for a two-year-old, and *how* is too involved. Two-year-olds are also likely to be now-oriented, so *when* is of less than immediate concern. By the fourth year, most children are spontaneously producing *why, when,* and *how* questions. These *wh* words are initially tacked on to the beginnings of sentences. "Where Mommy go?" can stand for "Where is Mommy going?" or "Where did Mommy go?" or "Where will Mommy go?", and its meaning must be derived from context. Later on, the child will add the auxiliary verbs *is, did,* and *will* to indicate whether the question concerns the present, past, or future.

Passive Sentences

Passive sentences, such as "The food is eaten by the dog," are difficult for two- and three-year-olds to understand, so young preschoolers almost never produce them. In a fascinating study of children's comprehension (Strohner & Nelson, 1974), two- to five-year-olds used puppets and toys to act out a number of sentences that were read to them. Two- and three-year-olds in the study made errors in acting out passive sentences (e.g., "The car was hit by the truck") 70 percent of the time. Older children had less difficulty interpreting the meanings of passive sentences correctly. However, most children usually do not produce passive sentences spontaneously even at the ages of five and six.

Pragmatics: Preschoolers Can Be Practical

Pragmatics in language development consists of the practical aspects of communication. Children are showing pragmatism when they adjust their speech to fit the social situation (Nelson, 2006). For example, children show greater formality in their choice of words and syntax when they are role-playing high-status figures, such as teachers or physicians, in their games. They also say "please" more often when making requests of high-status people. Children

pragmatics The practical aspects of communication, such as adaptation of language to fit the social situation

also show pragmatism in their adoption of infant-directed speech when they address a younger child.

Pragmatism provides another example of the ways in which cognitive and language development are intertwined. Preschoolers tend to be egocentric; therefore, a two-year-old telling another child "Gimme my book," without specifying which book, may be assuming that the other child knows what she herself knows. She is also probably overestimating the clearness of her communication and how well she is understood. Once children can perceive the world through the eyes of others, however, they advance in their abilities to make themselves understood to others. Now the child recognizes that the other child will require a description of the book or of its location to carry out the request. Between the ages of three and five, egocentric speech gradually disappears and there is rapid development of pragmatic skills. The child's conversation shows increasing sensitivity to the listener, as, for example, by taking turns talking and listening.

Language and Cognition

Language and cognitive development are strongly interwoven (Tomasello, 2010). For example, the child gradually gains the capacity to discriminate between animals on the basis of distinct features, such as size, patterns of movement, and the sounds they make. At the same time, the child also is acquiring words that represent broader categories, such as *mammal* and *animal*.

But it's chicken-and-egg time. Which comes first? Does the child first develop concepts and then acquire the language to describe them, or does the child's increasing language ability lead to the development of new concepts?

Does Cognitive Development Precede Language Development?

Jean Piaget (1976) believed that cognitive development precedes language development. He argued that children must first understand concepts before they can use words that describe the concepts. Object permanence emerges toward the end of the first year. Piaget believed that words that relate to the disappearance and appearance of people and objects (such as *all gone* and *bye-bye*) are used only after the emergence of object permanence.

From Piaget's perspective, children learn words in order to describe classes or categories that they have already created. Children can learn the word *doggy* because they have perceived the characteristics that distinguish dogs from other things.

Some studies support the notion that cognitive concepts may precede language. For example, the vocabulary explosion that occurs at about 18 months of age is related to the child's ability to group a set of objects into categories, such as "dolls" and "cars" (Quinn, 2010). Young children may need to experience an action themselves or by observation in order to learn the meaning of a verb (Pulverman et al., 2006).

A CLOSER LOOK DIVERSITY

Canada's Languages: A Multilingual Nation

Learning a second language is common for Canadian children. Canada's two official languages are English and French, but Canada has a large number of language groups, as revealed by the 2011 census. The majority of Canadians (58 percent) listed English as the language spoken at home, 18 percent listed French, and just 3.7 percent listed both French and English. The remaining languages range from other language only (6.5 percent) to other languages in combination with English and French (Statistics Canada, 2012a).

Continued

In contemporary Canadian society, learning more than one language and being bilingual is seen as an asset. However, this has not always been the case. Drawing conclusions from language-based research in the 1950s and 1960s led to erroneous conclusions about the pros and cons of bilingual or multilingual education. Present-day research confirms what many multilingual nations around the world already know—that learning more than one language can be enriching, not restrictive in the long term. But understanding bilingual or multilingual language acquisition is complex (Bialystok & Herman, 1999).

Canadian bilingualism researcher Ellen Bialystok, a professor of psychology at York University, is interested in issues of bilingualism and relationships with cognitive development, language proficiency, and reading. Her work has great practical relevance for many Canadian children who are growing up in multicultural settings. While there are some noted benefits of bilingualism (e.g., it speeds up the development of cognitive functions dealing with attention and inhibition), bilingual education is affected by cultural communities (Bialystok, 2001, 2011; Bialystok et al., 2009; Bialystok, McBride-Chang, & Luk, 2005). The reasons parents choose bilingual education are varied. In Alberta, for example, bilingual schools are quite common, and parents have an opportunity to send their children to publicly funded schools that offer nonofficial language instruction in Cree, Hebrew, Ukrainian, or Chinese, for example. This educational approach allows for cultural stability for children where second language acquisition can include the child's native language (e.g., Chinese) as well

as one of Canada's official languages. However, instruction in other nonofficial languages is not always possible or readily available.

Let's turn our attention to the issue of French immersion. Students who attend French immersion programs tend to do as well (or better) in main subject areas as their English-only-program peers (Allen, 2004; Genesee & Jared, 2008; Holobow, Genesee, & Lambert, 1991; Turnbull, Hart, & Lapkin, 2003). There have been many explanations put forth for this finding. It has been suggested that French-immersion students are more likely to be from high-socio-economic backgrounds and more likely to have parents with postsecondary education. However, even when these factors are controlled for, French-immersion students outperform their English-only-instructed peers on certain reading achievement tests. There are also other issues to consider. For example, selection and attrition in French immersion programs may influence reading performance as well. An additional caution put forth by language researchers is that looking for global advantages or universal effects of bilingualism may be misleading (Bruck & Genesee, 1995). From a practical perspective, being able to function well in one or both of Canada's official languages is a realistic goal for many Canadian children when supported by their communities (parents, teachers, administrators, and governments).

Reflect If you had a school-age child in your care, how would you go about deciding if you would place him or her in an immersion school?

Does Language Development Precede Cognitive Development?

Although many theorists argue that cognitive development precedes language development, others reverse the causal relationship and claim that children create cognitive classes in order to understand things that are labelled by words (Dodd & Crosbie, 2010; Horst et al., 2009). When children hear the word *dog*, they try to understand it by searching for characteristics that separate dogs from other things. Research with four-and-a-half-year-olds shows that descriptions of events can prompt children to create categories in which to classify occurrences (Nazzi & Gopnik, 2000).

The Interactionist View: Outer Speech and Private (Inner) Speech

Today, most developmentalists find something of value in each of these cognitive views (Rakison & Oakes, 2003; Waxman & Lidz, 2006). In the early stages of language development, concepts often precede words, so that many of the infant's words describe classes that have already developed. Later, however, language is not merely the servant of thought; language influences thought.

Vygotsky also made key contributions to our understanding of the relationships between concepts and words (Guajardo et al., 2008). Vygotsky believed that during most of the first year, vocalizations and thought are separate. But during the second year, thought and speech—cognition and language—usually combine forces. "Speech begins to serve intellect and thoughts begin to be spoken" (Vygotsky, 1962, p. 43). Usually during the second year, children discover that objects have labels. Learning labels becomes more active, more self-directed. At some point, children ask what new words mean. Learning new words clearly fosters the creation of new categories and classes. An interaction develops in which classes are filled with labels for new things, and labels nourish the blossoming of new classes.

Vygotsky's concept of **private speech** (also called *inner speech*) is a key feature of his position. At first, according to Vygotsky, children's thoughts are spoken aloud. You can overhear the three-year-old giving herself instructions as she plays with toys. At this age, her vocalizations may serve to regulate her behaviour. But language gradually becomes internalized. What was spoken aloud at ages four and five becomes an internal dialogue by age six or seven. This internal dialogue, or private speech, is the ultimate binding of language and thought. Private speech is involved in the development of planning and self-regulation, and facilitates learning. Vygotsky's ideas about the self-regulative function of language have inspired psychological treatment approaches for children with problems in self-control. For example, children with hyperactivity can be taught to use self-directed speech to increase their self-control (Crain, 2000).

Language is thus connected not only with thought but also with the social and emotional development of the young child. We turn to these areas of development in Chapter 10.

private speech Vygotsky's concept of the ultimate binding of language and thought. Private speech originates in vocalizations that may regulate the child's behaviour and become internalized by age six or seven.

Active Review

19. Word learning does not occur gradually but is better characterized as a fast-_____ process.

20. The _____-object assumption refers to the fact that young children assume that words refer to whole objects and not to their component parts or to their characteristics, such as color or texture.

21. Young children tend to assume that objects have (how many?) label(s).

22. Young children have the _____ assumption, which holds that novel terms must refer to unfamiliar objects and not to familiar objects that already have labels.

23. Vygotsky's concept of _____ speech refers to the fact that what was spoken aloud at ages four and five becomes an internal dialogue by age six or seven.

Reflect & Relate: What are some of the new words you are learning by reading this book? Do the words you chose to list have a single meaning or multiple meanings? How does their number of meanings affect your acquisition of these words? (Consider the examples *conservation*, *scaffold*, and *mapping*.)

Recite an Active Summary

9.1 Jean Piaget's Preoperational Stage (2–7 Years)

How do children in the preoperational stage think and behave?

Piaget's preoperational stage lasts from about age two to age seven and is characterized by the use of symbols to represent objects and relationships. Pretend play is based on the use and recollection of symbols or on mental representations of things. By 30 months, children can pretend that objects are active. Preoperational thinking is characterized by egocentrism, precausal thinking, confusion between mental and physical events, and ability to focus on only one dimension at a time. Young children's thinking about causality is egocentric, animistic, and artificialistic. In transductive reasoning, children reason by going from one instance of an event to another. Preoperational children have difficulty distinguishing between mental and physical events. Egocentrism contributes to their belief that their thoughts reflect reality. The law of conservation holds that properties of substances such as volume, mass, and number stay the same (are conserved) even if their shape or arrangement changes. Conservation requires focusing on two aspects of a situation at once.

9.2 Vygotsky's Views on Early Childhood Cognitive Development

What are Vygotsky's views on some of the factors that influence cognitive development in early childhood?

Some of the most important factors include scaffolding and the zone of proximal development, as envisioned by Vygotsky. Others include social and family factors such as the home environment, preschool education, and television. The children of responsive parents who provide appropriate play materials and stimulating experiences show gains in social and language development. Head Start and similar programs enhance economically disadvantaged children's cognitive development, academic skills, and readiness for school.

9.3 Other Factors in Early Childhood Cognitive Development: The Home Environment, Preschool, and Screen Time

How does the home environment affect the cognitive development of children?

Factors such as parental responsiveness, avoidance of restriction and punishment, organization of the physical environment, and provision of proper play materials and opportunities for variety all promote cognitive development.

How do preschool educational programs affect children's cognitive development?

Preschool programs, such as Head Start and similar programs, not only increase readiness for school but also decrease the likelihood of future juvenile delinquency and teenage pregnancy.

What are the effects of television on children's cognitive development?

Television programs such as *Sesame Street* can enhance children's cognitive development, but children need to be made aware of the pitfalls of violent shows and commercials.

9.4 Theory of Mind: What Is the Mind? How Does It Work?

What are children's ideas about how the mind works?

As children's theory of mind develops, children come to understand that there are distinctions between external and mental events and between appearances and realities. By age three, most children begin to realize that people gain knowledge through the senses. By age four, children understand which sense is needed to provide information about qualities such as colour (vision) and weight (touch). Although Piaget believed that children do not differentiate reality from appearances or mental events until the age of seven or eight, research reveals that preschoolers can do so.

9.5 Development of Memory: Creating Documents, Storing Them, Retrieving Them

What sorts of memory skills do children possess in early childhood?

Preschoolers recognize more items than they can recall. Autobiographical memory is linked to language skills. By the age of four, children can remember events that occurred a year and a half earlier. Young children seem to form scripts, which are abstract, generalized accounts of events. Factors affecting memory include what the child is asked to remember, interest level and motivation, the availability of retrieval cues, and the memory measure being used. Preschoolers engage in behaviours such as looking, pointing, and touching when trying to remember. Preschoolers can be taught to use strategies such as rehearsal and grouping of items, which they might not use on their own.

9.6 Language Development: Why "Daddy Goed Away"

What language developments occur during early childhood?

Preschoolers acquire about nine new words per day. Word learning often occurs rapidly through fast mapping. During the third year, children usually add articles, conjunctions, possessive adjectives, pronouns, and prepositions. Between the ages of three and four, children combine phrases and clauses into complex sentences. Preschoolers tend to overregularize irregular verbs and noun forms as they acquire rules of grammar. Piaget believed that children learn words in order to describe classes or categories they have created. Other theorists argue that children create classes to understand things that are labeled by words. Vygotsky believed that during most of the first year, vocalizations and thought are separate. But usually during the second year, cognition and language combine forces. To Vygotsky, private speech is the ultimate binding of language and thought.

Key Terms

Active Learning Resources

NELSON
brain
.com

Go to *Voyages in Development's* CourseMate at **www .nelsonbrain.com**, where you will find an interactive eBook, flashcards, Pre-Lecture Quizzes, Section Quizzes, Exam Practice, videos, and more.

Diego Cervo/Shutterstock.com

Major Topics

EARLY CHILDHOOD: Social and Emotional Development

10

Truth or Fiction?

T | F   Parents who are restrictive and demand mature behaviour wind up with rebellious children, not mature children. **p. 329**

T | F   There is no point in trying to reason with a four-year-old. **p. 330**

T | F   Firstborn children are more highly motivated to achieve than later-born children. **p. 337**

T | F   Children who are physically punished are more likely to be aggressive. **p. 349**

T | F   Children who watch two to four hours of TV a day will see 8000 murders and another 100 000 acts of violence by the time they have finished elementary school. **p. 350**

T | F   Children mechanically imitate the aggressive behaviour they view in the media. **p. 351**

T | F   The most common fear among preschoolers is fear of social disapproval. **p. 353**

T | F   A two-and-a-half-year-old may know that she is a girl but still think that she can grow up to be a daddy. **p. 361**

Jeremy and Jessica are both two-and-a-half years old. They are standing at the water table in the preschool classroom. Jessica is filling a plastic container with water and spilling it out. She watches the water splash down the drain. Jeremy watches and then goes to get another container. He, too, fills his container with water and spills it out. The children stand side by side. They empty and refill their plastic pails; they glance at each other and exchange a few words. They continue playing like this for several minutes, until Jessica drops her pail and runs off to ride the tricycle. Soon after, Jeremy also loses interest and finds something else to do.

Meanwhile, four-and-a-half-year-olds Melissa and Mike are building in the block corner, making a huge rambling structure that they have decided is a spaceship. They talk animatedly as they work, negotiating who should be captain of the ship and who should be the space alien. Mike and Melissa take turns adding blocks. They continue to build, working together and talking as they play.

These observations illustrate some of the changes that occur in social development during early childhood. Toddlers often spend time watching and imitating each other, but they do not interact very much. Older preschoolers are more likely to take turns, work cooperatively toward a goal, and share. Also, through play children learn social rules, such as who has greater power in social exchanges (known as a dominance hierarchy). They often engage in fantasy play that involves adopting adult roles.

In this chapter, we explore social and emotional development in early childhood. We consider the roles played by parents, siblings, and peers. We examine child's play, helping and sharing, and aggression. Then we look at personality and emotional development. We begin with the development of the self-concept, move on to Erikson's stage of initiative versus guilt, and explore the changing nature of children's fears. Finally, we discuss the development of gender roles and gender differences in behaviour.

Shooter Bob Square Lenses/Shutterstock.com

10.1 Influences on Development: Parents, Siblings, and Peers

Young children usually spend most of their time within the family. Most parents attempt to foster certain behaviours in their children. They want them to develop a sense of responsibility and conform to family routines. They want them to develop into well-adjusted individuals. They want them to acquire social skills. In other words, they want to ensure healthy social and emotional development. How do parents go about trying to achieve these goals? What part do siblings play? How do children's peers influence social and emotional development?

Dimensions of Child Rearing

QUESTION » **What are the dimensions of child rearing?** Parents have different approaches to rearing their children. Investigators of parental patterns of child rearing in Western cultures have found it useful to classify them according to two broad dimensions: warmth–coldness, and restrictiveness–permissiveness (Baumrind, 1989, 2005). Warm parents and cold parents can be either restrictive or permissive. It is important to note that child-rearing practices are greatly influenced by cultural practices as well. Providing parents with information about effective parenting practices is an essential part of healthy family development.

Acceptance and Parental Involvement (Warmth–Coldness)
Warm parents are affectionate toward their children. They tend to hug and kiss them and smile at them frequently. Warm parents are caring and supportive of their children. They generally behave in ways that communicate their enjoyment in being with the children. Parents who engage in warm exchanges are less likely than parents with colder tendencies to use physical discipline (Holden et al., 2011).

Parents who tend to be cold may not enjoy being with their children and may have few feelings of affection for them. They are likely to complain about their children's behaviour, saying that the children are naughty or have "minds of their own." In contrast, parents with a warmer style may also say that their children have "minds of their own," but they are frequently proud of and entertained by their children's stubborn behaviour. Even when they are irked by it, they usually focus on attempting to change it, instead of rejecting the children.

It requires no stretch of the imagination to conclude that it is better to be warm than cold toward children. The children of parents who are warm and accepting are more likely to develop internalized standards of conduct—a moral sense or conscience (Bender et al., 2007; Lau et al., 2006). Parental warmth also is related to the child's social and emotional well-being (Holden et al., 2011).

Where does parental warmth come from? Some of it reflects parental beliefs about how to best rear children, and some of it reflects parents' tendencies to imitate the behaviour of their own parents. But research by E. Mavis Hetherington and her colleagues (Feinberg et al., 2001) suggests that genetic factors may be involved as well.

Parental Control (Restrictiveness–Permissiveness)
Parents must generally decide how restrictive they will be. How will they respond when children make excessive noise, play with dangerous objects, damage property, mess up their rooms, hurt others, go nude, or masturbate? Parents who are restrictive tend to impose rules and to watch their children closely.

TRUTH OR FICTION REVISITED: It is not true that parents who are strict and demand mature behaviour wind up with rebellious children. Consistent control and firm enforcement of rules can have positive consequences for the child, particularly when combined with strong support and affection (Grusec & Sherman, 2011). This parenting style is termed the *authoritative style*. On the other hand, if "restrictiveness" means physical punishment, interference, or intrusiveness, it can have negative effects, such as disobedience, rebelliousness, and lower levels of cognitive development (Grusec & Sherman, 2011; Rudy & Grusec, 2006).

Permissive parents impose few, if any, rules and supervise their children less closely. They allow their children to do what is "natural"—make noise, treat toys carelessly (although they may also extensively childproof their homes to protect their children and the furniture), and experiment with their own bodies. They may also allow their children to show some aggression, intervening only when another child is in danger. Parents may be permissive for different reasons. Some parents believe that children need the freedom to express their natural urges. Others may simply be uninterested and uninvolved.

Cross-cultural research suggests that the permissive parenting style is connected with higher self-esteem and adjustment, compared with other parenting styles, in Spain and Brazil (Martínez et al., 2003). The investigators suggested that these cultures may be somewhat more "laid back" than "Anglo-Saxon" cultures and that there is a better fit between indulgence of children and their adjustment in Latin American cultures.

How Parents Set (or Enforce) Boundaries

QUESTION » What techniques do parents use to restrict their children's behaviour? Regardless of their general approaches to child rearing, most (if not all) parents impose boundaries now and then, even if only when they are teaching their children not to run into the street or touch a hot stove. These methods may range in from positive to less healthy ways of setting limits. Parents tend to use the methods of induction, power assertion, and withdrawal of love. See Table 10.1 ■ for examples of how parents and caregivers support emotional and behavioural development in children.

● TABLE 10.1

The Development of Emotional and Behavioural Control in Preschoolers

Development of Emotional and Behavioural Control	Effects of the Environment
• Increasingly capable of true internal control of emotions and behaviour	• Caregiver guidance techniques and styles that support responsibility, inner control, and positive interactions with others support the development of self-regulation
• Needs less continuous adult support and guidance to maintain control (shifting from external to internal control)	• Adult and peer modelling influence children's patterns of interaction, self-control, and developing standards for appropriate behaviour
• More interest in interacting with other children and being accepted by them	• Opportunities for positive interactions with peers (e.g., adult monitoring of peer interactions, mediating disputes, if necessary, in a problem-solving way, and an expressed value for cooperative interactions) increase positive self-regulation
• Capable of cooperative interactions with peers	
• Able to use internalized rules, strategies, and plans to guide behaviour (though not necessarily consciously)	
• Internalizing standards for appropriate behaviour and emotional expression	
• Can use language to assist and guide self-regulation	

Source: Bronson (2000).

Inductive Techniques

Inductive methods aim to impart knowledge that will enable children to produce desirable behaviour in similar situations. The main inductive technique is "reasoning," or explaining why one kind of behaviour is good and another is not. Reasoning with a one- or two-year-old can be basic. "If you touch the hot stove—it hurts!" qualifies as reasoning with toddlers. "It hurts!" is an explanation, although a brief one. TRUTH OR FICTION REVISITED: Thus, there *is* a point in trying to reason with a four-year-old. The inductive approach helps the child understand moral behaviour and fosters prosocial behaviour such as helping and sharing (Grusec & Sherman, 2011).

Inductive Reasoning
Inductive methods for enforcing limits or restrictions attempt to teach children the principles they should use in guiding their own behaviour. This mother is using the inductive technique of reasoning.

Power-Assertive Methods

Power-assertive methods include physical punishment and denial of privileges. Parents often justify physical punishment with sayings such as "Spare the rod, spoil the child." Parents may insist that power assertion is necessary because their children are noncompliant. However, the use of power-assertive methods is related to parental authoritarianism as well as to children's behaviour (Roopnarine et al., 2006; Rudy & Grusec, 2006). Parental power assertion is associated with lower acceptance by peers, poorer grades, and higher rates of antisocial behaviour in children. The more parents use power-assertive techniques, the less children appear to develop internal standards of moral conduct. Parental punishment and rejection are often linked with aggression and delinquency (Bosmans et al., 2011; Grusec & Sherman, 2011).

Recently, Baumrind (2013) has challenged the notion that all power-assertive tactics by parents are indeed equivalent and detrimental. She argues that there are distinctions within the range of power-assertive techniques parents may use, and stresses that physical and coercive methods are detrimental, whereas imposing consequences may be not be problematic when accompanied by reasoning, negotiation, and explanation.

Withdrawal of Love

Some parents control children by threatening them with withdrawal of love. They isolate or ignore misbehaving children. Because most children need parental approval and contact, loss of love can be more threatening than physical punishment. Withdrawal of love may foster compliance, but it may also instill guilt and anxiety (Grusec & Sherman, 2011).

Preschoolers more readily comply when asked to do something than when asked to stop doing something (Kochanska et al., 2001). One way to manage children who are doing something wrong or inappropriate is to involve them in something else.

Parenting Styles: How Parents Transmit Values and Standards

QUESTION » **What parenting styles are involved in the transmission of values and standards?** Traditional views of the ways in which children acquire values and standards for behaviour focus on parenting styles. Psychologist Diana Baumrind (1989, 1991b) studied the relationship between parenting styles and the development of competent behaviour in young children. She used

inductive Characteristic of disciplinary methods, such as reasoning, that try to teach an understanding of the principles behind parental demands.

Baumrind's Patterns of Parenting

Parental Style	Parental Behaviour Patterns	
	Restrictiveness and Control	Warmth and Responsiveness
Authoritative	High	High
Authoritarian	High	Low
Permissive–Indulgent	Low	High
Rejecting–Neglecting	Low	Low

Source: Based on Baumrind, D. (1989) Rearing component in children. In W. Damon (Ed.) *Child development today and tomorrow* (pp. 349–378). San Francisco: Jossey-Bass.

the dimensions of warmth–coldness and restrictiveness–permissiveness. She developed a grid of four parenting styles based on whether parents are high or low on each of the two dimensions, as seen in Table 10.2 ■.

Authoritative Parents

The parents of the most capable children are rated as high in both parental behaviour patterns listed in Table 10.2. They make strong efforts to control their children (i.e., they are highly restrictive), and they make strong demands for maturity. However, they also reason with their children and show them strong support and feelings of love. Baumrind applies the label **authoritative** to these parents to suggest that they have a clear vision of what they want their children to do but they also respect their children and provide them with warmth.

Compared to other children, the children of authoritative parents tend to show self-reliance and independence, high self-esteem, high levels of activity and exploratory behaviour, and social competence. They are highly motivated to achieve and do well in school (Grusec & Sherman, 2011). With regard to attachment, researchers have found the authoritative parenting style to be positively associated with secure attachment in children (Karavasilis, Doyle, & Markiewicz, 2003; Nair & Murray, 2005).

Authoritarian Parents

"Because I say so" could be the motto of parents whom Baumrind labels **authoritarian**. These parents tend to look on obedience as a high virtue. Authoritarian parents believe in strict guidelines for determining what is right and wrong. They demand that their children accept these guidelines without question. Like authoritative parents, they are controlling. Unlike authoritative parents, their enforcement methods rely on coercion. Moreover, authoritarian parents do not communicate well with their children. They do not show respect for their children's viewpoints, and most researchers find them to be generally cold and rejecting. However, among some ethnic groups—such as Egyptians living in Canada—authoritarianism reflects cultural values, and these authoritarian parents are also warm and reasonably flexible (Grusec, 2002; Rudy & Grusec, 2006). When families immigrate to societies with different values, they tend to bring their own values with them—as Arabic speaking parents tend to bring authoritarian attitudes to Australia (Renzaho et al., 2011).

In Baumrind's research, the sons of authoritarian parents were relatively hostile and defiant and the daughters were low in independence and dominance

authoritative A child-rearing style in which parents are restrictive and demanding, yet communicative and warm.

authoritarian A child-rearing style in which parents demand submission and obedience from their children but are not very communicative and warm.

(Baumrind, 1989). Other researchers have found that children of authoritarian parents are less competent socially and academically than children of authoritative parents. Children of authoritarian parents also tend to be conflicted, anxious, and irritable. They are less friendly and spontaneous in their social interactions (Grusec, 2002; Shuster et al., 2012). As adolescents, they may be conforming and obedient or, on the other hand, aggressive (Shuster et al., 2012).

Permissive Parents

Baumrind found two types of parents who are permissive, as opposed to restrictive. One type is labelled permissive–indulgent and the other rejecting–neglecting. **Permissive–indulgent** parents are rated low in their attempts to control their children and in their demands for mature behaviour. They are easygoing and unconventional. Their brand of permissiveness is accompanied by high nurturance (warmth and responsiveness).

Rejecting–neglecting parents also are rated low in their demands for mature behaviour and in their attempts to control their children. But unlike indulgent parents, they are low in warmth and responsiveness.

The neglectful parenting style is associated with poor outcomes for children. By and large, the children of neglectful parents are the least competent, responsible, and mature and the most prone to problem behaviours. Children of permissive–indulgent parents, like those of neglectful parents, show less competence in school and more deviant behaviour (such as misconduct and substance abuse) than children of more restrictive, controlling parents.

permissive–indulgent A child-rearing style in which parents are not controlling and restrictive but are warm.

rejecting–neglecting A child-rearing style in which parents are neither restrictive and controlling nor supportive and responsive.

Permissive Parents
Some parents are considered permissive and demand little of their children in terms of mature behaviour or control. Permissive-indulgent parents still provide plenty of warmth and support for their children, whereas rejecting-neglecting parents tend to neglect or ignore their children.

Zoe/Image Source

But children from permissive–indulgent homes, unlike those from neglectful homes, are fairly high in social competence and self-confidence (Baumrind, 1991a).

Effects of the Situation and the Child on Parenting Styles

QUESTION » **How do the situation and the child influence parenting styles?** Parenting styles are not just a one-way street—from parent to child. Parenting styles also depend partly on the situation and partly on the characteristics of the child (Grusec, 2006; Grusec & Sherman, 2011). Parenting research acknowledges the notion of mutuality in parent–child relations. That is, the parent–child relationship is a bidirectional one. Recent theorizing asserts that mutuality (a bidirectional process) has become a key factor in explaining parent–child interactions (Azak & Raeder, 2013; Lollis & Kuczynski, 1997).

One example of how the situation affects the parenting style is that parents are more likely to use power-assertive techniques for dealing with aggressive behaviour than for dealing with social withdrawal (Casas et al., 2006; Lipman et al., 2006). Parents prefer power assertion over induction when they believe that children understand the rules they have violated, are capable of acting appropriately, and are responsible for their bad behaviour. Stressful life events, marital discord, and emotional problems all contribute to parental use of power assertion.

Baumrind's research suggests that we can make an effort to avoid some of the pitfalls of being authoritarian or overly permissive. Some recommended techniques that parents can use to help control and guide their children's behaviour are listed in Table 10.3 ▪.

Influence of Siblings

QUESTION » **How do siblings influence social and emotional development in early childhood?** One of Christina's uncles—who was two at the time—"placed" a large rock in his infant brother's crib, while his younger brother was still sleeping in it. Fortunately, both survived. They literally lived to laugh about it.

● TABLE 10.3

Advice for Parents in Guiding Young Children's Behaviour

Do ...	Don't ...
• Reward good behaviour with praises, smiles, and hugs.	• Pay attention only to a child's misbehaviour.
• Give clear, simple, realistic rules appropriate to the child's age.	• Issue too many rules or enforce them haphazardly.
• Enforce rules with reasonable consequences.	• Try to control behaviour solely in the child's domain (such as thumb sucking), which can lead to frustrating power struggles.
• Ignore annoying behaviour such as whining and tantrums.	• Nag, lecture, shame, or induce guilt.
• Childproof the house, putting dangerous and breakable items out of reach. Then establish limits.	• Yell or spank.
• Be consistent.	• Be overly permissive.

Siblings

Siblings make a unique contribution to one another's social, emotional, and cognitive development.

Despite the uncle's limitations as a sibling during toddlerhood, children make tremendous advances in social skills and behaviour during early childhood (Underwood & Rosen, 2011). Their play increasingly involves other children. They learn how to share, cooperate, and comfort others. But young children, like adults, can be aggressive as well as loving and helpful.

Based on the 2011 Canadian Census (Statistics Canada, 2013), the average number of children per Canadian family is 1.1. Of Canadian families with children, most have at least two children; however, an increasing rise in one-child families or in blended families is occurring in Western countries. In many cases, children spend more time with their siblings in the early years than they spend with their parents. Siblings make a unique contribution to one another's social, emotional, and cognitive development (McHale et al., 2006). They serve many functions, including giving physical care, providing emotional support and nurturance, offering advice and direction, serving as role models, providing social interaction that helps develop social skills, and making demands and imposing restrictions (Abuhatoum & Howe, 2013; Holden et al., 2011). They also advance each other's cognitive development, as shown in research concerning false beliefs and the theory of mind (see Chapter 9).

In early childhood, when siblings spend a great deal of time together, their interactions are often emotionally loaded and marked by both positive aspects (cooperation, teaching, nurturance) and negative aspects (conflict, control, competition) (Howe et al., 2012; Parke & Buriel, 2006). By and large, older siblings are more nurturant, but also more dominating, than younger siblings. Younger siblings are more likely to imitate older siblings and to accept their direction. For example, at the age of two, Christina's daughter raced onto the soccer field and attempted to intercept play to the surprise of her brother and his five-year-old team mates. She was convinced she was part of Team Blizzard, and was not pleased when her mother quickly escorted her back to her spectator blankie on the sidelines.

However, older siblings may also imitate younger siblings, especially when parents remark "how cute" the baby is being in front of the older child. At the age of two years five months, Spencer's daughter Allyn would pretend that she could not talk every once in a while, just like her five-month-old sister Jordan.

In many cultures (including this one, laments Christina's mother, a firstborn), older girls are given the chore of caring for younger siblings (Underwood & Rosen, 2011). Younger siblings frequently turn to older sisters when the mother is unavailable. ("They still do," notes Christina's mother.)

Parents often urge their children to stop fighting among themselves, and there are times when these conflicts look deadly (and occasionally they are). It is important to note, however, that garden-variety conflict among siblings can have positive outcomes. (Really!) It appears that conflict between siblings enhances their social competence, their development of self-identity (who they are and what they stand for), and their ability to rear their own children in a healthful manner (Ross et al., 2006). When adults look back on their childhood conflicts with their siblings, their memories of them are often positive.

As siblings move from early childhood through middle childhood and into adolescence, their relationships change in at least two ways (Underwood & Rosen, 2011). First, as siblings grow more competent and their developmental statuses become similar, their relationship becomes more egalitarian. In other words, as later-born siblings grow older and become more self-sufficient, they need and accept less nurturance and direction from older siblings. Second, sibling relationships become less intense as children grow older. The exercise of power and the amount of conflict decline. The extent of warmth and closeness diminishes somewhat as well, although the attachment between siblings remains fairly strong throughout adolescence.

Other factors also affect the development of sibling relationships. For example, there is more conflict between siblings in families in which the parents treat the children differently (Scharf et al., 2005). Conflict between siblings also is greater when the relationships between the parents or between the parents and children is not as harmonious (Kim et al., 2006; Rinaldi & Howe, 2003).

Adjusting to the Birth of a Sibling

The birth of a sister or brother is often a source of stress for young children because of changes in family relationships and the environment. When a new baby comes into the home, the mother pays relatively more attention to the baby and spends much less time in playful activities with the older child. No wonder the child may feel displaced and resentful of the affection lavished on the newborn. These feelings are reflected, for example, in the comments of a three-year-old who worried that his new sister would take all his mother's love and not leave enough for him.

individualist A person who defines herself or himself in terms of personal traits and gives priority to her or his own goals.

collectivist A person who defines herself or himself in terms of relationships to other people and groups and gives priority to group goals.

A CLOSER LOOK DIVERSITY

Individualism, Collectivism, and Patterns of Child Rearing

Much of the research on parenting styles has been done with middle-class Western families. But parenting styles must be viewed within the context of particular cultures (Renzaho et al., 2011; Shuster et al., 2012). Socialization methods that appear authoritarian or punitive by middle-class standards may be used more frequently among poor families from ethnic minority groups to prepare children to cope with the hazards of daily life. Placing a high value on unquestioned obedience might be considered overly restrictive in a quiet middle-class neighbourhood, but unquestioned obedience might well be warranted now and then in a more dangerous, inner-city environment. Poor families in other countries also tend to use authoritarian child-rearing styles.

A study by Kobayashi-Winata and Power (1989) compared the child-rearing practices of middle-class Japanese and American parents whose children ranged in age from four to seven. In both groups of families, the most compliant children had parents who provided opportunities for appropriate behaviour and who used relatively little punishment. But American parents were more likely to rely on

external punishments such as sending children to their room, whereas Japanese parents more often used verbal commands, reprimands, and explanations (see Table 10.4 ■).

These differences in disciplinary practices apparently reflect cultural differences. Cross-cultural research reveals that people in many Western cultures tend to be individualistic (Becker et al., 2012). In contrast, many people from cultures in Africa, Asia, and Central and South America tend to be collectivistic (Becker et al., 2012).

Individualists tend to define themselves in terms of their personal identities and to give priority to their personal goals (Hartung et al., 2010; Triandis, 2005). When asked to complete the statement "I am ...," they are likely to respond in terms of their personality traits ("I am outgoing," "I am artistic") or their occupations ("I am a nurse," "I am a systems analyst"). In contrast, **collectivists** tend to define themselves in terms of the groups to which they belong and to give priority to the group's goals (Berry & Triandis, 2006; Triandis, 2005). They feel complete in terms of their relationships with others (see Figure 10.1 ■). They are more likely than individualists to conform to

Continued

Continued

● TABLE 10.4

Cultural Values and Child-Rearing Techniques in North America and Japan

Culture	Parental Value	Child-Rearing Practices
North American middle class	• Early socialization • Independence • Individualism	• Expect child to follow more rules • Listen to child's opinion • Use external punishment (e.g., send child to his or her room)
Japanese middle class	• Group harmony • Dependence on others • Conformity	• Make fewer demands • Be more indulgent • Use verbal commands • Use reprimands and explanations

group norms and judgments (Berry & Triandis, 2006; Hartung et al., 2010). When asked to complete the statement "I am ...," they are more likely to respond in terms of their families, gender, or nation ("I am a father," "I am a Buddhist," "I am Japanese").

It must be noted, however, that individuals from within the same country can belong to different "cultures" in terms of individualistic and collectivistic tendencies. In Lebanon, for example, Ayyash-Abdo (2001) found that college students who spoke French or English were more likely to be individualistic than those who spoke mainly Arabic. Traditional Islamic values were also connected with collectivism.

Other studies reveal additional differences in the child-rearing techniques of American and Far Eastern parents that appear to foster the American emphasis on early socialization and independence and the Chinese focus on group harmony and dependence on others (Chen & Eisenberg, 2012).

Reflect

• Do you think it is better to raise a child to be individualistic or collectivistic? Explain.

• We all belong to subcultures within Canada. Would you characterize your subculture as mainly individualistic or collectivistic? Explain.

• The culture of Canada is said to value "rugged individualism." Is that always true? Explain.

• Can you make the case that a culture or subculture is individualistic in some ways but collectivistic in others? Explain.

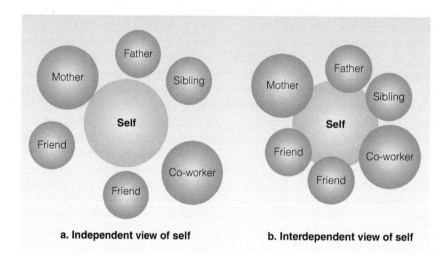

a. Independent view of self   b. Interdependent view of self

Figure 10.1 ■ The Self in Relation to Others from the Perspectives of Individualists and Collectivists

(a) To an individualist, the self is separate from other people. (b) To a collectivist, the self is complete only in terms of relationships to other people. Are there differences in the ways in which people in individualistic and collectivistic cultures rear their children?
Source: Based on Markus & Kitayama (1991).

Children show a mixture of negative and positive reactions to the birth of a sibling. These include **regression** to babyish behaviours, such as increased clinging, crying, and toilet accidents. Anger and naughtiness may increase as well. But the same children often show increased independence and maturity, insisting on feeding or dressing themselves and helping to take care of the baby (Underwood & Rosen, 2011).

What can parents do to help a young child cope with the arrival of a new baby? For one thing, they can prepare the child by explaining in advance what is to come. For example, one item on the agenda of those who run sibling preparation classes in many locales is to reduce **sibling rivalry** when a new child is born into a family (Stanford University School of Medicine, 2012). Parental support is extremely important as well. Children show less distress following the birth of a sibling when the parents spend time with them, give them encouragement, and praise them (Kavcic & Zupancic, 2005).

Birth Order: Not Just Where in the World But Also Where in the Family

QUESTION » What does the research say about the effects of being a firstborn or an only child? Interestingly, both Spencer and Christina are only children. We experienced what we imagine are most of the advantages and, yes, draw-backs of being an only child. First and perhaps foremost, we each were the little king and queen in our respective households. A petty tyrant at best, and at worst, Spencer enjoyed all the resources his family had to offer: a relatively good allowance (with which he bought a comic book a day—Superman did nothing that escaped his young attention) and lots of parental attention. He never knew that his family was poor because he got most of what he wanted. Like Spencer, Christina's experience of being an only child allowed her to get a lot of parental attention. Although surrounded by many close cousins and friends, she enjoyed relating to adults, sometimes more so than to other children. And there were times when she had sibling envy—she wanted an older sister, one to lend her cool clothes and play Charlie's Angels. In Spencer's case, he recalls being lonely at home and wished that he had a sister or a brother. But these are the experiences of only two individuals, and it is difficult to know how accurately they are recalled. So let's be more scientific about it. *Question: What does the research say about the effects of being a firstborn or an only child?*

Many differences in personality and achievement have been observed among firstborn and only children compared with later-born children. TRUTH OR FICTION REVISITED: It is true that firstborn children, as a group, are more highly motivated to achieve than later-born children (Silles, 2010), especially to master the subject matter or other tasks at hand (Carette et al., 2011). As a group, firstborn and only children perform better academically and are more cooperative (Healy & Ellis, 2007). They are also helpful (maybe), adult-oriented (more true for Spencer), and less aggressive (possibly, it's not easy to recall) (Beck et al., 2006; Silles, 2010). They obtain higher standardized test scores, including SAT scores (Zajonc, 2001). An adoptee study found that first-reared children, regardless of their biological birth order, were more conscientious than later-reared children (Beer & Horn, 2000). As part of their achievement orientation, firstborn children also see themselves as being more in control of their successes (Phillips & Phillips, 2000). On the negative side, firstborn and only children show greater anxiety and are less self-reliant (hmmm … we wonder).

Interviews with the parents of 478 children ranging in age from three to nine years found that firstborn children are more likely than later-born

regression A return to behaviours characteristic of earlier stages of development.

sibling rivalry Jealousy or rivalry among brothers and sisters.

children to have imaginary playmates (Bouldin & Pratt, 1999). Spencer's first-born daughter, Allyn, had the imaginary playmate Loveliness. His second-born (Jordan) and third-born (Taylor) may have been too busy coping with older siblings to have imaginary playmates.

Later-born children may learn to act aggressively to compete for the attention of their parents and older siblings (Silles, 2010). They also contend with the fact that they do not come first. Perhaps for that reason, their self-concepts tend to be lower than those of firstborn or only children. But the social skills they acquire from dealing with their family position seem to translate into greater popularity with peers. They tend to be more rebellious, liberal, and agreeable than firstborn children—factors connected with their popularity (Beck et al., 2006; Zweigenhaft & Von Ammon, 2000).

Differences in personality and achievement among firstborn and later-born children may be linked to contrasting styles in parenting. Firstborn children start life as only children. For a year or more, they receive the full attention of parents. Even after other children come along, parents still tend to relate more often to the first child. Parents continue to speak at levels appropriate for the firstborn. Parents impose tougher restrictions on firstborn children and make greater demands of them. Parents are more highly involved in their activities. Firstborn children are often recruited to help teach younger siblings (Zajonc, 2001). As we can testify, being asked to teach something (often) prompts one to learn something about it.

By and large, parents are more relaxed and flexible with later-born children. Children are aware of the greater permissiveness often given to later-born children and may complain about it. (Endlessly.) Why are parents more indulgent with later-born children? They have probably gained some self-confidence in child rearing. They see that the firstborn child is turning out just fine. (All right, the firstborn child usually turns out to be just fine, and sometimes "just fine" needs to be qualified as "just fine much of the time.") Parents may therefore assume that later-born children will also turn out, well, just fine.

There is also a more negative interpretation of parents' relative "relaxation" in rearing later-born children. Parents have just so many resources, in terms of time, energy, and, yes, money. As new children come along, they dilute the resources, so not as much can be devoted to each of them.

Peer Relationships

QUESTION » How do peers influence social and emotional development in early childhood? The importance of **peers** in the development of the young child is widely recognized. As children move into the preschool years, they spend more time in the company of other children. Peer interactions serve many functions. Children learn social skills in the peer group—sharing, helping, taking turns, dealing with conflict. They learn how to lead and how to follow. Physical and cognitive skills develop through peer interactions. Peers also provide emotional support (Bukowski et al., 2011; Grusec & Sherman, 2011).

Infants first show positive interest in one another at about six months of age. If they are placed on the floor facing one another, they will smile, occasionally imitate one another, and often touch one another. Social interaction increases over the next few months, but during the first year, contacts between infants tend to be brief. In the second year, children show more interest in each other and interact by playing with each other's toys. But they still show relatively little social interaction (Bukowski et al., 2011). By about two years of age, however, children imitate one another's play and engage in social games such as follow the leader (Bukowski et al., 2011; Underwood & Rosen, 2011). By the age of two, children have preferences for a few particular playmates.

peers Children of the same age. (More generally, people of similar background and social standing.)

The preference of toddlers for certain other children is an early sign of friendship (Gleason & Hohmann, 2006; Sherwin-White, 2006). Friendship extends beyond casual interactions. It is characterized by shared positive experiences and feelings of attachment (Gleason & Hohmann, 2006). Even early friendships can be fairly stable. One- to six-year-olds tend to maintain their friendships from one year to the next, some for as long as three years (Rubin et al., 2006). On the other hand, parental conflict can spill over into peer conflict. Children of fighting parents are less tolerant of the bumps and bruises of peer relationships (Du Rocher Schudlich et al., 2004).

Preschool children behave somewhat differently toward their friends than toward ordinary playmates. Friends, compared with other children, show higher levels of interaction, helpful behaviour, and smiling and laughing and more frequent cooperation and collaboration (Rubin et al., 2006). Conflicts between young friends are less intense and are resolved more readily than other conflicts.

What are children's conceptions of friendships? When preschoolers are asked what they like about their friends, they typically mention the toys and activities they share (Gleason & Hohmann, 2006). Children in early elementary school usually report that their friends are the children with whom they do things and have fun (Gleason & Hohmann, 2006). Not until late childhood and adolescence do friends' traits and notions of trust, communication, and intimacy become key aspects of friendship.

Friendship

Friendship takes on different meanings as children develop. Preschoolers focus on sharing toys and activities. Five- to seven-year-olds report that friends are children with whom they have fun. Sharing confidences becomes important in late childhood and adolescence.

A CLOSER LOOK | DIVERSITY

What about Dads?

Over the past two centuries, forces such as urbanization, industrialization, and government-funded child-support programs have contributed to the changing roles of mother and fathers in families. Social scientists believe that fathers play a significant role in children's development and view responsible fatherhood as providing children with financial support, caregiving (feeding and bathing children, tucking them in, reading to them, spending time with them), and emotional support (Underwood & Rosen, 2011).

According to Canadian data, multiple, significant adults are often involved in raising children (Statistics Canada, 2012d). In fact, about 80 percent of children aged 14 and under live in two-parent families (married or common-law) (Statistics Canada, 2012d). The role of fathers in the family system has evolved in recent decades; North American statistics indicate increased father involvement in primary care activities (Marshall, 2006; Pleck, 2010). Additionally, studies that included fathers indicate that they uniquely influence child outcomes (Flouri, 2005; Lamb & Lewis, 2010; McWayne et al., 2013). We know that fathers' parenting

(warm, autonomy supportive) as well as strategies such as responsiveness and stimulation favours positive behavioural and cognitive child outcomes above and beyond mothers' parenting (Grossman et al., 2002; NICHD Early Childcare Research Network, 2005). Martin and colleagues (2010) reported that fathers' supportiveness mattered most when mothers' supportiveness was low. In sum, we are only beginning to outline the specific ways that fathers contribute to children's overall development and well-being.

Reflect

- Does it surprise you that 80 percent of children under the age of 14 live in two-parent households?

- What are some of the ways that fathers contribute to children's development? Is it different from the ways in which mothers contribute?

- You're up, guys: What types of "father figures," other than your biological father, did you have when you were a child? What type of influence did these father figures have on you?

Active Review

1. Investigators of child rearing find it useful to classify parents according to two dimensions: warmth–coldness and _____.

2. _____ methods of enforcing restrictions attempt to give children knowledge that will enable them to generate desirable behaviour patterns in similar situations.

3. _____ parents are both warm and restrictive.

4. _____ parents believe that obedience is a virtue for its own sake.

5. _____-born children tend to be the most highly motivated to achieve.

Reflect & Relate: Where do you fit into your family of origin? Are you a firstborn or only child? Were you born later? How do your own development and personality compare to the stereotypes discussed in this section?

10.2 Social Behaviour: In the World, among Others

During the early childhood years, children make tremendous strides in the development of social skills and behaviour. Their play activities increasingly involve other children. They learn how to share, cooperate, and comfort others. But young children, like adults, are complex beings. They can be aggressive at times, as well as loving and helpful. Some key developments in early childhood are the ability to control negative emotions and behaviours, to talk about mental states, to take perspectives, to carry out various roles in dramatic play, to internalize standards of behaviour, and to follow prosocial rules. In the following section, we will see how these developments take place.

Play—Child's Play, That Is

dramatic play Play in which children enact social roles; made possible by the attainment of symbolic thought. A form of pretend play.

QUESTION » **What does the research show about child's play?** While children play, researchers work to understand just how they do so. They have found that play has many characteristics. It is meaningful, pleasurable, voluntary, and internally motivated (Elkind, 2007). Play is fun! But play also serves many important functions in the life of the young child (Elkind, 2007). Play helps children develop motor skills and coordination. It contributes to social development because children learn to share play materials, take turns, and try on new roles through **dramatic play**. It supports the development of such cognitive qualities as curiosity, exploration, symbolic thinking, and problem solving. Play may even help children learn to control impulses (Elkind, 2007).

Play and Cognitive Development

Play contributes to and expresses milestones in cognitive development. Jean Piaget (1962 [1946]) identified four kinds of play, each characterized by increasing cognitive complexity:

- *Functional play.* Beginning in the sensorimotor stage, the first kind of play involves repetitive motor activity, such as rolling a ball or running and laughing.
- *Symbolic play.* Also called pretend play, imaginative play, or dramatic play, symbolic play emerges toward the end of the sensorimotor stage and increases during early childhood. In symbolic play, children create settings and characters and scripts (Kavanaugh, 2006).
- *Constructive play.* Constructive play is common in early childhood. Children use objects or materials to draw something or make something, such as a tower of blocks.
- *Formal games.* The most complex form of play, according to Piaget, involves formal games with rules. These include board games, which are sometimes enhanced or invented by children, and games involving motor skills, such as marbles and hopscotch, ball games involving sides or teams, and video games. Such games may involve social interaction as well as physical activity and rules. People play such games for a lifetime.

Mildred Parten, whom we discuss next, focused on the social dimensions of play.

Associative Play
Associative play is a form of social play in which children interact and share toys.

Parten's Types of Play

In classic research on children's play, Mildred Parten (1932) observed the development of six categories of play among two- to five-year-old nursery school children: unoccupied play, solitary play, onlooker play, parallel play, associative play, and cooperative play (see Table 10.5 ■). Unoccupied play, solitary play, and onlooker play are considered types of **nonsocial play**—that is, play in which children do not interact socially. Nonsocial play occurs more often in two- and three-year-olds than in older preschoolers. Parallel play, associative play, and cooperative play are considered **social play**. In each case, children are influenced by other children as they play. Parten found that associative play and cooperative play become common by age five. They are more likely to be found among older and more experienced preschoolers (Bukowski et al., 2011). Girls are somewhat more likely than boys to engage in social play (Underwood & Rosen, 2011).

But there are exceptions to these age trends in social play. Nonsocial play can involve educational activities that foster cognitive development. In fact, many four- and five-year-olds spend a good deal of time in parallel constructive play. For instance, they may work on puzzles or build with blocks near other children. Parallel constructive players are frequently perceived by teachers to be socially skillful and are popular with their peers. Some toddlers are also more capable of social play than one might expect, given their age. Two-year-olds who have older siblings or a great deal of group experience may engage in advanced forms of social play.

nonsocial play Forms of play (solitary play or onlooker play) in which play is not influenced by the play of nearby children.

social play Play in which children interact with others and are influenced by their play. Examples include parallel play, associative play, and cooperative play.

CHAPTER 10 EARLY CHILDHOOD: SOCIAL AND EMOTIONAL DEVELOPMENT

Parten's Categories of Play

Category	Nonsocial or Social?	Description
Unoccupied play	Nonsocial	Children do not appear to be playing. They may engage in random movements that seem to be without a goal. Unoccupied play appears to be the least frequent kind of play in nursery schools.
Solitary play	Nonsocial	Children play with toys by themselves, independently of the children around them. Solitary players do not appear to be influenced by children around them. They make no effort to approach them.
Onlooker play	Nonsocial	Children observe other children who are at play. Onlookers frequently talk to the children they are observing and may make suggestions, but they do not overtly join in.
Parallel play	Social	Children play with toys similar to those of surrounding children. However, they treat the toys as they choose and do not directly interact with other children.
Associative play	Social	Children interact and share toys. However, they do not seem to share group goals. Although they interact, individuals still treat toys as they choose. The association with the other children appears to be more important than the nature of the activity. They seem to enjoy each other's company.
Cooperative play	Social	Children interact to achieve common, group goals. The play of each child is subordinated to the purposes of the group. One or two group members direct the activities of others. There is also a division of labour, with different children taking different roles. Children may pretend to be members of a family, animals, space monsters, and all sorts of creatures.

Source: Based on Parten, M. B. (1932). Social participation among pre-school children. *The Journal of Abnormal and Social Psychology, 27*(3), 243–269.

decentration Simultaneous focusing (centring) on more than one aspect or dimension of a problem or situation.

Learning Through Play: A Vygotskian Perspective

We have discussed Lev Vygotsky's sociocultural theory of cognitive development in other chapters. It is fitting to discuss Vygostky's influence on early childhood educators' understanding of play as well. Both researchers and practitioners adhering to a Vygotskian approach would argue that play has a key purpose in the lives of children. In particular, play (1) creates a zone of proximal development, (2) eases the separation of thought from actions and objects, (3) aids the development of self-regulation, (4) impacts motivation, and (5) helps **decentration** (Bordova & Leong, 2007). One fascinating conclusion is that play allows children to grow by engaging in higher levels of attention, symbolizing, and problem solving. Play is serious business.

OBSERVING CHILDREN, UNDERSTANDING OURSELVES

Early Childhood Play

Observe different types of play for children in different developmental stages.

What are the four categories of play, from least to most social? At ages four to five, what types of play appear and what skills are needed to participate?

From Rathus. Childhood and Adolescence, 5E. © 2014 South-Western, a part of Cengage Learning, Inc. Reproduced by permission. www.cengage.com/permissions

Go to www.nelson.com/voyages2ce to watch the video, answer the questions, and e-mail your responses to your professor.

Gender Differences in Play

Lisa Serbin and her colleagues (2001) explored infants' visual preferences for gender-stereotyped toys using the time-honoured assumption that infants spend more time looking at objects that are of greater interest. They found that both girls and boys showed significant preferences for gender-stereotyped toys by 18 months of age. Other research reveals that infants show visual preferences for gender-stereotyped toys as early as three to eight months of age (Alexander et al., 2009). Although preferences for gender-typed toys are well developed by the ages of 15 to 36 months, girls are more likely to stray from the stereotypes (Bussey & Bandura, 1999; Underwood & Rosen, 2011). Girls ask for and play with "boys' toys" such as cars and trucks more often than boys choose dolls and other "girls' toys." "Cross-role" activities may reflect the greater prestige of "masculine" activities and traits in Canadian culture. Therefore, a boy playing with "girls' toys" might be seen as taking on an inferior role. A girl playing with "boys' toys" might be considered to have a desire for power or esteem.

Girls and boys differ not only in toy preferences but also in their choice of play environments and activities. During the preschool and early elementary school years, boys prefer vigorous physical outdoor activities such as climbing, playing with large vehicles, and rough-and-tumble play (Underwood & Rosen, 2011). In middle childhood, boys spend more time than girls in play groups of five or more children and in competitive play. Girls are more likely than boys to engage in arts and crafts, domestic play, running, and chasing, with minimal physical contact (Boulton, 1996; Pelligrini & Smith, 1998). Girls' activities are more closely directed and structured by adults (A. Campbell et al., 2002).

Why do children show these early preferences for gender-stereotyped toys and activities? Biological factors may play a role—for example, boys' slightly greater strength and activity levels and girls' slightly greater physical maturity and coordination. But there are also psychosocial factors; adults treat girls and boys differently. They provide gender-stereotyped toys and room furnishings and encourage gender typing in play and household chores (Leaper, 2011). Children, moreover, tend to seek out information on which kinds of toys and play are "masculine" or "feminine" and then to conform to the label (Martin & Dinella, 2011; Martin & Ruble, 2004).

Some studies find that children who "cross the line" by showing interest in toys or activities considered appropriate for the other gender are often teased, ridiculed, rejected, or ignored by their parents, teachers, other adults, and peers. Boys are more likely than girls to be criticized (Zosuls et al., 2011).

A Girl Enjoying a Game of Hockey
Although preferences for gender-typed toys are well established by the age of three, girls are more likely to stray from the stereotypes, as in this photograph of a girl playing hockey.

Whom Do You Want to Play With?
During early and middle childhood, children tend to prefer the company of children of their own gender. Why?

Another well-documented finding is that children begin to prefer playmates of the same gender by the age of two. Girls develop this preference somewhat earlier than boys (Hay et al., 2004). The tendency strengthens during middle childhood.

Two factors may be involved in the choice of the gender of playmates in early childhood. One is that boys' play is more oriented toward dominance, aggression, and rough play (Hines, 2011b). The second is that boys are not very responsive to girls' polite suggestions. Boys may avoid girls because they see them as inferior (Caplan & Larkin, 1991).

Prosocial Behaviour: It Could Happen! And It Does

QUESTION » How does prosocial behaviour develop? Spencer's wife recalls always trying to help others in early childhood. She remembers sharing her toys, often at her own expense. She had many sad times when toys or favours she gave were not returned or when toys were broken by others.

Prosocial behaviour, sometimes known as *altruism,* is behaviour intended to benefit another without expectation of reward. Prosocial behaviour includes helping and comforting others in distress, sharing, and cooperating.

Even in the first year of life, children begin to share. They spontaneously offer food and objects to others (Markova & Legerstee, 2006). In the second year, children continue to share objects, and they also begin to comfort distressed companions and help others with tasks and chores (Knafo & Plomin, 2006b).

By the preschool and early school years, children frequently engage in prosocial behaviour. Some types of prosocial behaviour occur more often than others. One study observed four- and seven-year-olds at home and found that helping occurred more often than sharing, affection, and reassuring (Grusec, 1991). Research suggests that the development of prosocial behaviour is linked to the development of other capabilities in the young child, such as empathy and taking the perspective of others.

What can adults do to support the development of prosocial behaviours? Primary adults in the lives of children have a critical role to play in fostering prosocial behaviours. Adult behaviours that have been found to support prosocial behaviour are empathic caregiving, prosocial modelling, and the provision of clear rules when negative or coercive behaviours are used (Brosnon, 2000). Furthermore, adults (parents, caregivers, educators) can coach children through appropriate sibling or peer interactions. Modelling is an excellent tool for adults to use—whether they are modelling or communicating about caring actions and values, using prosocial reasoning to explain and guide behaviour, or employing positive reinforcement of prosocial behaviours (while avoiding physical punishment and criticism) (Bronson, 2000). Finally, empowering children by assigning them age- and skill-appropriate social responsibilities is a recommended educational strategy.

Empathy: "I Feel Your Pain"

Empathy is sensitivity to the feelings of others. It is the ability to understand and share another person's feelings and is connected with sharing and cooperation. A survey of American and Japanese mothers of preschoolers found that both groups reported that cooperativeness and interpersonal sensitivity were the most desirable characteristics in young children (Olson et al., 2001).

From infancy, children respond emotionally when others are in distress (Strayer & Roberts, 2004). Infants frequently begin to cry when they hear other children crying, although this early agitated response may be largely reflexive. Even so, crying might signal an early development in empathy.

prosocial behaviour Behaviour intended to benefit another without expectation of reward.

empathy Ability to share another person's feelings.

Empathy appears to promote prosocial behaviour and to decrease aggressive behaviour, and these links are evident by the second year (Hastings et al., 2000; Strayer & Roberts, 2004). During the second year, many children approach other children and adults who are in distress and try to help them. They may hug a crying child or tell the child not to cry. Toddlers who are rated as emotionally unresponsive to the feelings of others are more likely to behave aggressively throughout the school years (Olson et al., 2000).

Girls show more empathy than boys (Strayer & Roberts, 2004). It is unclear whether this gender difference reflects socialization of girls to be attuned to the emotions of others or genetic factors, although some researchers argue that prenatal exposure to testosterone has a suppressive effect on empathy (Hines, 2011a).

Perspective Taking: Standing in Someone Else's Shoes

According to Piaget, children in the preoperational stage tend to be egocentric; that is, they tend not to be able to see things from the vantage points of others. Various cognitive abilities, such as being able to take another person's perspective, are related to knowing when someone is in need or distress. Perspective-taking skills improve with age, and so do prosocial skills. Among children of the same age, those with better developed perspective-taking ability also show more prosocial behaviour and less aggressive behaviour (Hastings et al., 2000).

Influences on Prosocial Behaviour

Yes, altruistic behaviour is usually defined as prosocial behaviour that occurs in the absence of rewards or the expectation of rewards. Nevertheless, prosocial behaviour is influenced by rewards and punishments. Observations of nursery school children show that the peers of children who are cooperative, friendly, and generous respond more positively to them than they do to children whose behaviour is self-centred (Grusec & Sherman, 2011). Children who are rewarded in this way for acting prosocially are likely to continue these behaviours (Grusec & Sherman, 2011).

Some children at early ages are made responsible for doing household chores and caring for younger siblings. They are taught helping and nurturance skills, and their performances are selectively reinforced by other children and adults. Children who are given such tasks are more likely to show prosocial behaviours than children who do not have such responsibilities (Bremner et al., 2010).

There is evidence that children can acquire sharing behaviour by observing models who help and share. In one experiment in sharing, 29- to 36-month-olds were more likely to share toys with playmates who first shared toys with them (Levitt et al., 1985). The children appeared to model—and reciprocate—the sharing behaviour of their peers.

It seems that children's prosocial behaviour is influenced by the kinds of interactions they have with their parents. For example, prosocial behaviour and empathy are enhanced in children who are securely attached to their parents and in children whose mothers show a high degree of empathy (Strayer & Roberts, 2004).

Parenting styles also affect the development of prosocial behaviour. Prosocial behaviour is fostered when parents use inductive techniques such as explaining how behaviour affects others ("You made Josh cry. It's not nice to hit"). Parents of prosocial children are more likely to expect mature behaviour from their children. They are less likely to use power-assertive techniques of discipline (Strayer & Roberts, 2004).

Do You Have to Be Taught to Hate?

In the musical *South Pacific,* Lieutenant Cable sings, "You've got to be taught [to] hate ... people whose skin is a diff'rent shade. You've got to be taught before you are six or seven or eight [to] hate all the people your relatives hate!"

It is widely assumed that children learn racial prejudices at home, but the evidence has been less than clear. No clear, consistent relationship has been found between the expressed, or explicit, racial attitudes of white parents and the racial attitudes of their children (Castelli et al., 2009). Yet in early childhood, children show preferences for playing with members of their own ethnic group and are more likely to ascribe positive traits to their own ethnic group (Castelli et al., 2007). The attitudes of children and their parents' attitudes toward people of other races can differ, although there is apparently some overlap when the children strongly identify with their parents (Sinclair et al., 2005).

Because of the inconsistency of findings with expressed or explicit attitudes, some recent research has turned to the assessment of implicit attitudes, as shown, for example, in body language in the presence of the other persons—body posture, eye contact, and the like (Hofmann et al., 2008). Are young children sensitive to these nonverbal behaviours and their implications? Research suggests that preschoolers correctly interpret what it means for adults of different races to lean toward one another or back away when they are interacting, and to maintain or avoid eye contact (Castelli et al., 2008).

In a recent study, Luigi Castelli and his colleagues (2009) recruited 72 middle-class Italian families living in northern Italy. Confidentiality was guaranteed. In each family, the mother, the father, and a biological child (36 girls and 36 boys with a mean age of 58 months participated).

Children were assessed individually in their kindergartens. They were shown two drawings, one of a white preschooler and one of a black preschooler, and they were asked which of the two they would prefer to play with. Two out of three children (67 percent) said they would prefer the white playmate. Then the children were given eight cards, one at a time, with a single trait written on each. Four were positive (*nice, happy, clean, likable*); four were negative (*ugly, sad, dirty, bad*). The experimenter asked the child to assign each card to either the white child or the black child. As a result, each pictured child could obtain a score between 0 and 4 on positive traits, and the same on negative traits. As shown in Figure 10.2 ■, positive traits were more likely to be attributed to the white child and negative traits to the black child.

The parents were tested on scales of explicit (intentional) and implicit (unconscious) prejudice. Results on the explicit scale (the Blatant-Subtle Prejudice Scale) showed that the parents tended to express nonprejudiced—even quite egalitarian—attitudes toward black people. However, results on the implicit scale found that fathers and mothers both showed a good deal of implicit prejudice.

Statistical techniques revealed that there was a statistically significant association between children's choices and their mothers' implicit racial attitudes. There was no connection with the mothers' explicit attitudes. There was no relationship between children's behaviours and their fathers' explicit or implicit attitudes. In terms of assigning positive or negative traits to the white and black children, the greater the mothers' implicit prejudice, the fewer positive traits and the more negative traits their children attributed to the black child. We should note, however, that although the correlations between the mothers' implicit attitudes and their children's choices were too high to be due to chance, they were only of the magnitudes 0.29, 0.339, and 0.352. Positive correlations, as noted in Chapter 1, can range from 0.00 to 1.00. The correlations found in the present study must be considered mild, not even moderate.

Reflect What can we conclude from this study? Is there a relationship between young children's racial attitudes and the implicit racial attitudes of their mothers? How strong is that relationship? Can you think of other factors in the development of racial preferences?

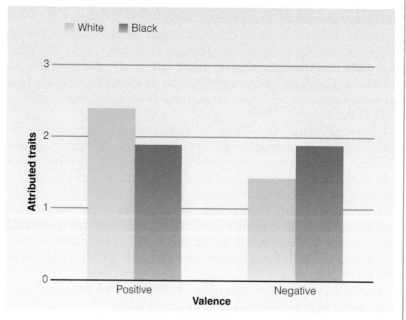

Figure 10.2 ■ Mean Number of Positive and Negative Traits Attributed to the White Child and to the Black Child
Source: Castelli et al. (2009).

Development of Aggression: The Dark Side of Social Interaction

QUESTION » **How does aggression develop?** Children, like adults, are complex beings. Not only can they be loving and altruistic, but they can also be aggressive. Some children, of course, are more aggressive than others. Aggression consists of behaviour intended to cause pain or hurt to another person.

Although there are many definitions of aggression, the two common features are the intention to harm by the aggressor and that a victim is hurt (Underwood & Rosen, 2011). Aggression has been categorized as either proactive (i.e., unprovoked aggression to obtain a desired outcome) or reactive aggression, which is defensive and retaliatory in nature (Dodge & Coie, 1987). Further, aggression may take several forms—it may be physical, verbal, or relational (Buss, 1961; Crick, 1996). Physical aggression involves physically aggressive acts such as hitting, kicking, biting, or destroying another person's property. Verbal aggression involves the use of hostile language, threats, name-calling, and put-downs. Finally, relational aggression involves aggressive acts that destroy an individual's peer relationships through exclusion, gossip, spreading rumours, and manipulation.

Aggressive behaviour, like other social behaviours, seems to follow developmental patterns. For one thing, the aggression of preschoolers is frequently instrumental or possession-oriented (Persson, 2005). That is, young children tend to use aggression to obtain the toys and things they want, such as a favoured seat at the table or in the car. But older preschoolers are more likely to resolve their conflicts over toys by sharing than by fighting (Caplan et al., 1991). Anger and aggressive behaviour in preschoolers usually cause other preschoolers to reject them (Morine et al., 2011).

By age six or seven, aggression becomes hostile and person-oriented. Children taunt and criticize each other and call each other names; they also attack one another physically.

Aggressive behaviour appears to be generally stable and predictive of a wide variety of social and emotional difficulties in adulthood (Mesman et al., 2001; Nagin & Tremblay, 2001). Boys are more likely than girls to show aggression from childhood through adulthood, a finding that has been documented in many cultures (Frieze & Li, 2010). Typically, boys engage in more physical forms of aggression than girls (Dodge et al., 2006). Olson and her colleagues (2000) found that toddlers who were perceived as difficult and defiant were more likely to behave aggressively throughout the school years. A longitudinal study of more than 600 children found that aggressive eight-year-olds tended to remain more aggressive than their peers 22 years later, at age 30 (Eron et al., 1991). Aggressive children of both genders were more likely to have criminal convictions as adults, to abuse their spouses, and to drive while drunk.

Theories of Aggression

QUESTION » **What causes aggression in children?** What causes some children to be more aggressive than others? Aggression in childhood appears to result from a complex interplay of biological factors and environmental factors such as reinforcement and modelling.

Evolutionary Theory

Is aggression "natural"? According to evolutionary theory, more individuals are produced than can find food and survive into adulthood. Therefore, there is a struggle for survival. Individuals who possess characteristics that give them an advantage in this struggle are more likely to reach reproductive maturity and contribute their genes to the next generation. In many species, then, whatever genes are linked to aggressive behaviour are more likely to be transmitted to new generations (Ray, 2012). Nonetheless, for most children levels of aggression decline from infancy to early childhood to middle childhood.

Biological Factors

Evidence suggests that genetic factors may be involved in aggressive behaviour, including criminal and antisocial behaviour (Bezdjian et al., 2011). Jasmine Tehrani and Sarnoff Mednick (2000) report that there is a greater concordance (agreement) rate for criminal behaviour between monozygotic (MZ) twins, who fully share their genetic code, than between dizygotic (DZ) twins, who, like other brothers and sisters, share only half of their genetic code. Physical aggression has been estimated to be about 60 percent heritable (Moffitt, 2005).

If genetics is involved in aggression, genes may do their work at least in part through the male sex hormone testosterone. Testosterone is apparently connected with feelings of self-confidence, high activity levels, and—the negative side—aggressiveness (Bezdjian et al., 2011; Underwood, 2011). Males are more aggressive than females, and males have higher levels of testosterone than females. Studies show, for example, that 9- to 11-year-old boys with conduct disorders are likely to have higher testosterone levels than their less aggressive peers (Booth et al., 2003; Chance et al., 2000). Research with same-gender female DZ twins and opposite-gender female DZ twins suggests that fetal exposure to male sex hormones (in this case, from a male fraternal twin) may heighten aggressiveness (Cohen-Bendahan et al., 2005).

Cognitive Factors

Aggressive boys are more likely than nonaggressive boys to incorrectly interpret the behaviour of other children as potentially harmful (Dodge et al., 2002). This bias may make the aggressive child quick to respond aggressively in social situations. Research with primary schoolchildren finds that children who believe in the legitimacy of aggression are more likely to behave aggressively when they are presented with social provocations (Underwood & Rosen, 2011). Children who demonstrate *hostile attribution bias* (HAB—not to be confused with the Montreal Canadiens professional hockey team nickname, the Habs) tend to have higher rates of aggressive peer interactions (Crick & Dodge, 1996; Dodge, 2006). What is a hostile attribution bias? Let's consider the following scenario: If a child accidentally spills her apple juice on her classmate, and the classmate interprets this behaviour as intentional, when the intent is unclear, this is described as HAB.

Aggressive children are also often found to be lacking in empathy and in the ability to see things from the perspective of other people (Hastings et al., 2000). They fail to conceptualize the experiences of their victims, so they are less likely to inhibit their aggressive impulses.

Social Learning

Social cognitive explanations of aggression focus on the role of environmental factors, such as reinforcement and observational learning. Children, like adults, are most likely to be aggressive when they are frustrated in attempts to gain something they want, such as attention or a toy. When children repeatedly push, shove, and hit in order to grab toys or break into line, other children usually let them have their way (Kempes et al., 2005). Children who are thus rewarded for acting aggressively are likely to continue to use aggressive means, especially if they do not have alternative means of achieving their ends.

Aggressive children may associate with peers who value their aggression and encourage it (Stauffacher & DeHart, 2006). Aggressive children have often been rejected by less aggressive peers, a fact that decreases their motivation to please less aggressive children and reduces their opportunity to learn social skills (Morine et al., 2011).

Parents may also encourage aggressive behaviour, sometimes inadvertently. Gerald Patterson (2005) studied families in which parents use coercion as the primary means for controlling children's behaviour. In a typical pattern, parents threaten, criticize, and punish a "difficult" or "impossible" child. The child then responds by whining, yelling, and refusing to comply until the parents give in. Both parents and child are relieved when the cycle ends. Thus, when the child misbehaves again, the parents become yet more coercive and the child yet more defiant, until parents or child gives in. A study with 407 five-year-olds found that the Patterson model predicts aggressive behaviour in both genders (Eddy et al., 2001).

Children learn not only from the effects of their own behaviour but also from observing the behaviour of others. They may model the aggressive behaviour of their peers, their parents, or their communities at large (Underwood, 2011). Children are more apt to imitate what their parents do than to heed what they say. If adults say they disapprove of aggression but smash furniture or hit each other when frustrated, children are likely to develop the notion that this is the way to handle frustration.

TRUTH OR FICTION REVISITED: It is true that children who are physically punished are more likely to be aggressive themselves (Patterson, 2005). Physically aggressive parents serve as models for aggression and also stoke their children's anger.

Media Influences

Real people are not the only models of aggressive behaviour in children's lives. A classic study by Bandura and his colleagues (1963) suggested that televised models had a powerful influence on children's aggressive behaviour. One group of preschool children observed a film of an adult model hitting and kicking an inflated Bobo doll, whereas a control group saw an aggression-free film. The experimental and control children were then left alone in a room with the same doll as hidden observers recorded their behaviour. The children who had observed the aggressive model showed significantly more aggressive behaviour toward the doll themselves (see Figure 10.3 ■). Many children imitated bizarre attack behaviours devised for the model in this experiment—behaviours that they would not have thought up themselves.

The children exposed to the aggressive model also showed aggressive behaviour patterns that had not been modelled. Therefore, observing the model not only led to imitation of modelled behaviour patterns but also apparently **disinhibited** previously learned aggressive responses. The results were similar whether children observed human or cartoon models on film.

The Bandura study was a setup—an experimental setup, to be sure, but still a setup. It turns out that television is one of children's major sources of informal observational learning. It also turns out that television is a fertile source of aggressive models throughout much of the world (Villani, 2001). Children are routinely exposed to scenes of murder, beating, and sexual

disinhibit To stimulate a response that has been suppressed (inhibited) by showing a model engaging in that response without aversive consequences.

Figure 10.3 ■ **Photos from Albert Bandura's Classic Experiment in the Imitation of Aggressive Models**

Research by Albert Bandura and his colleagues showed that children frequently imitate the aggressive behaviour they observe. In the top row, an adult model strikes a clown doll. The second and third rows show a boy and a girl imitating the aggressive behaviour.

assault—just by turning on the TV set. **TRUTH OR FICTION REVISITED:** It is true that children who watch two to four hours of TV a day will see 8000 murders and another 100 000 acts of violence by the time they have finished elementary school (Christakis & Zimmerman, 2007; Eron, 1993). Are children less likely to be exposed to violence when their watching is restricted to G-rated movies? No. Virtually all G-rated animated films have scenes of violence. Other media that contain violence include movies, rock music and music videos, advertising, video games, and the Internet (Villani, 2001).

In any event, most organizations of health professionals agree that media violence does contribute to aggression (Holland, 2000; Villani, 2001). This relationship has been found for girls and boys of different ages, social classes, ethnic groups, and cultures. Consider the following ways in which depictions of violence make such a contribution (Anderson et al., 2010; Bushman & Anderson, 2007):

- *Observational learning.* Children learn from observation. TV violence supplies models of aggressive "skills," which children may acquire. Children tend to imitate the aggressive behaviour they see in the media (see Figure 10.3).

- *Disinhibition.* Punishment inhibits behaviour. Conversely, media violence may disinhibit aggressive behaviour, especially when media characters "get away" with violence or are rewarded for it.

- *Increased arousal.* Media violence and aggressive video games increase viewers' level of arousal; that is, television "works them up." We are more likely to be aggressive under high levels of arousal.

- *Priming of aggressive thoughts and memories.* Media violence "primes" or arouses aggressive ideas and memories.

- *Habituation.* We become "habituated to," or used to, repeated stimuli. Repeated exposure to TV violence may decrease viewers' sensitivity to real violence.

- Children who see a lot of violence are more likely to view violence as an effective way of settling conflicts. Children exposed to violence are more likely to assume that violence is acceptable.
- Viewing violence can decrease the likelihood that one will take action on behalf of a victim when violence occurs.
- Viewing violence may lead to real-life violence. Children exposed to violent programming at a young age are more likely to be violent themselves later in life.

The Canadian Paediatric Society (Lipnowski, 2012) urges Canadian children to watch less television and be more active. Here are some specific recommendations to help parents curb their children's TV viewing habits:

- Limit daily TV viewing to one hour for preschoolers.
- Try to watch television with children.
- Turn off the television during meals, when visitors arrive, and during study time.
- Allow older children to plan their weekly viewing schedule in advance.
- Help children understand the difference between fantasy and real-life situations.
- Support media literacy education in the schools.

There is no simple one-to-one connection between observing media violence and behaving aggressively in real life. **TRUTH OR FICTION REVISITED:** Therefore, it is not true that children mechanically imitate the aggressive behaviour they view in the media. But exposure to violence in the media increases the probability of violence in viewers in several ways.

Violent video games are also connected with aggressive behaviour, including juvenile delinquency (Dubow et al., 2010). Playing violent video games increases aggressive thoughts and behaviour in the laboratory (Anderson et al., 2010). However, males are more likely than females to act aggressively after playing violent video games and are more likely to see the world as a hostile place. Students who obtain higher grades are less likely to behave aggressively following exposure to violent video games. Thus, cultural stereotyping of males and females, possible biological gender differences, and moderating variables such as academic achievement figure into the effects of media violence.

There is apparently a circular relationship between exposure to media violence and aggressive behaviour (Anderson et al., 2010; Bushman & Anderson, 2009; see Figure 10.4 ■). Yes, TV violence and violent video games contribute to aggressive behaviour, but aggressive youngsters are also more likely to seek out this kind of "entertainment."

The family constellation also affects the likelihood that children will imitate the violence they see on TV. Studies find that parental substance abuse, physical punishments, and father absence contribute to the likelihood of aggression in early childhood (Bendersky et al., 2006; Chang et al., 2003; Roelofs et al., 2006). Parental rejection further increases the likelihood of aggression in children (Eron, 1982; Hoffman & Edwards, 2004). These family factors suggest that the parents of aggressive children are absent or unlikely to help young children understand that the kinds of socially inappropriate behaviours they see in the media are not for them. A harsh home life may also confirm the TV viewer's vision of the world as a violent place and further encourage reliance on television for companionship. In Chapter 9, we saw how parents can help children understand that the violence they view in the media is not real and is not to be imitated.

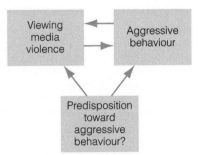

Figure 10.4 ■ Violence in the Media and Aggressive Behaviour
What are the connections between viewing media violence and engaging in aggressive behaviour? Does exposure to media violence cause aggressive behaviour? Do aggressive children prefer to tune in to violent shows or play violent video games? Or do other factors, such as personality traits, predispose some children both to seek out media violence and to behave aggressively?

Active Review

6. In _____ play, children play with toys by themselves.

7. In _____ play, children interact and share toys.

8. Preschoolers tend to prefer to play with children of the (other or same?) gender.

9. _____ is another term for prosocial behaviour.

10. Preschoolers tend to (admire or reject?) aggressive peers.

11. Aggressive behaviour is linked with the hormone _____.

12. _____ theorists explain aggressive behaviour in terms of reinforcement and observational learning.

13. Observing aggression in the media tends to (inhibit or disinhibit?) aggressive behaviour in children.

Reflect & Relate: Do you believe that violence in the media causes aggression? (What does the word *cause* mean?) Media violence is everywhere—not only in R-rated films but also in G-rated films and in video games. There are connections between media violence and aggression, but not everyone who witnesses media violence behaves aggressively. How, then, do we explain the connections between violence in the media and aggression?

10.3 Personality and Emotional Development

In the early childhood years, children's personalities start becoming more defined. Their sense of self—who they are and how they feel about themselves—continues to develop and becomes more complex. They begin to acquire a sense of their own abilities and their increasing mastery of the environment. As they move out into the world, they also face new experiences that may cause them to feel fearful and anxious. Let's explore some of these facets of personality and emotional development.

The Self

QUESTION » How does the self develop during early childhood? The sense of self, or the self-concept, emerges gradually during infancy. Infants and toddlers visually begin to recognize themselves and differentiate themselves from other individuals, such as their parents.

In the preschool years, children continue to develop their sense of self. Almost as soon as they begin to speak, they describe themselves in terms of certain categories, such as age groupings (baby, child, adult) and gender (girl, boy). These self-definitions that refer to concrete external traits have been called the **categorical self**.

Children as young as three years are able to describe themselves in terms of behaviours and internal states that appear to occur frequently and are fairly stable over time (Rosen & Patterson, 2011). For example, in response to the question "How do you feel when you're scared?" young children frequently respond, "Usually like running away" (Eder, 1989). Or, in answer to the question "How do you usually act around grown-ups?" a typical response might be "I mostly been good with grown-ups." Thus, even preschoolers seem to understand that they have stable characteristics that endure over time.

One aspect of the self-concept is self-esteem, the value or worth that people attach to themselves. Children who have a good opinion of themselves during the preschool years are more likely to show secure attachment and have parents who are attentive to their needs (Roisman & Groh, 2011). They also are more likely to engage in prosocial behaviour (Grusec & Sherman, 2011).

categorical self Definitions of the self that refer to concrete external traits.

Preschool children begin to make evaluative judgments about two different aspects of themselves by the age of four (Underwood & Rosen, 2011). One of these aspects is their cognitive and physical competence (e.g., being good at puzzles, counting, swinging, tying shoes), and the second is their social acceptance by peers and parents (e.g., having lots of friends, being read to by Mom) (Piek et al., 2006). But preschoolers do not yet make a clear distinction between different areas of competence. For example, a child of this age is not likely to report being good in school but poor in physical skills. Either one is "good at doing things" or one is not (Harter, 2012).

During middle childhood, personality traits become increasingly important in children's self-definitions. Children then are also able to make judgments about their self-worth in many different areas of competence, behavioural conduct, appearance, and social relations.

Initiative versus Guilt

As preschool children continue to develop a separate sense of themselves, they increasingly move out into the world and take the initiative in learning new skills. Erik Erikson refers to these early childhood years as the stage of initiative versus guilt.

Children in this stage strive to achieve independence from their parents and master adult behaviours. They are curious, try new things, and test themselves. These qualities are illustrated in the following account of a day in the life of a five-year-old:

> In a single day, he decided to see how high he could build his blocks, invented a game that consisted of seeing who could jump the highest on his parents' bed, and led the family to a new movie containing a great deal of action and violence. (Crain, 2000)

During these years, children learn that not all of their plans, dreams, and fantasies can be realized. Adults prohibit children from doing certain things, and children begin to internalize these adult rules. Fear of violating the rules may cause the child to feel guilty and may curtail efforts to master new skills. Parents can help children develop and maintain a healthy sense of initiative by encouraging their attempts to learn and explore and by not being unduly critical and punitive.

Fears: The Horrors of Early Childhood

QUESTION » What sorts of fears do children have in the early years? In Erik Erikson's view, fear of violating parental prohibitions can be a powerful force in the life of a young child. Both the frequency and the content of fears change as children move from infancy into the preschool years. The number of fears seems to follow a predictable course, peaking between two-and-a-half and four years of age and then tapering off (Muris & Field, 2011).

The preschool period is marked by a decline in fears of loud noises, falling, sudden movement, and strangers. **TRUTH OR FICTION REVISITED:** Fear of social disapproval is not the most common fear among preschoolers. Preschoolers are most likely to have fears that revolve around animals, imaginary creatures, the dark, and personal safety (Muris & Field, 2011). The fantasies of young children frequently involve stories they

are told and media imagery. Frightening images of imaginary creatures can persist. Many young children are reluctant to have the lights turned off at night for fear that these creatures may harm them in the dark. Imaginary creatures also threaten personal safety.

But real objects and situations also cause many children to fear for their personal safety, such as lightning, thunder and other loud noises, the dark, high places, sharp objects and being cut, blood, unfamiliar people, strange people, stinging and crawling insects, and other animals.

During middle childhood, children's fears become more realistic. They grow less fearful of imaginary creatures, but fears of bodily harm and injury remain fairly common. Children become more fearful of failure and criticism in school and in social relationships (Muris & Field, 2011).

Girls report more fears and higher levels of anxiety than boys (Muris & Field, 2011). Whether these findings reflect actual differences in fears and anxieties or differences in the willingness of girls and boys to report "weaknesses" is a matter of debate.

A CLOSER LOOK REAL LIFE

Helping Children Cope with Fears

A number of methods have been developed to help children cope with fears. Professionals who work with children today are most likely to use such behaviour modification methods as desensitization, operant conditioning, and participant modelling (Gordon et al., 2007). Each method is based on principles of learning.

Desensitization Desensitization exposes children gradually to the sources of their fears while they are engaging in behaviour that is incompatible with fear (Gordon et al., 2007). Fear includes bodily responses such as rapid heart rate and respiration rate. Thus, doing things that reduce the heart and respiration rates is incompatible with fear.

In a classic study, Mary Cover Jones (1924) used a form of desensitization along with counterconditioning to eliminate a fear of rabbits in a two-year-old boy named Peter. Desensitization consisted of bringing a rabbit gradually closer to Peter. Fear was counterconditioned in that as the rabbit was being brought closer, the boy was experiencing pleasure from munching away merrily on candy and cookies. Peter cast a wary eye in the rabbit's direction, but he continued to eat. Jones suspected that if she brought the rabbit too close too quickly, the cookies left on Peter's plate and those already eaten might have decorated the walls. But gradually the animal could be brought nearer without upsetting the boy. Eventually, Peter could eat cookies and touch the rabbit at the same time. Jones gave the child a treat. Having the child play with a game or favourite toy or asking the child to

talk about a favourite book or TV hero is another way of relaxing the child.

Operant Conditioning In operant conditioning, children are guided to desirable behaviours and then reinforced for engaging in them. When behaviour modification is used in the classroom, good behaviour is reinforced and misbehaviour is ignored.

Parents and other adults use operant techniques all the time. They may teach children how to draw letters of the alphabet by guiding their hand and saying "Good!" when the desired result is obtained. When children fear touching a dog, parents frequently take their hands and guide them physically in petting the animal. Then they say something reinforcing, such as "Look at that big girl/boy petting that doggy!" or "Isn't the puppy nice and soft?" (Ollendick & Seligman, 2006).

Participant Modelling In participant modelling, children first observe live models or filmed or taped models (ideally, children similar in age) engaging in the behaviour that evokes fear. Then they imitate the behaviour of the models. In an often-cited experiment on participant modelling, Bandura and his colleagues (1969) found that participant modelling helped people who were afraid of snakes. Figure 10.5 ■ shows children and adults in the Bandura study who imitated unafraid models.

Reflect How can you apply the methods discussed in this feature to a "grown-up" fear you might have?

Continued

Continued

Albert Bandura

Figure 10.5 ■ **Participant Modelling**
Participant modelling helps children overcome fears through principles of observational learning. In these photos, children with a fear of snakes observe and then imitate models who are unafraid. As another example, parents often try to convince children that something tastes good by eating it in front of them and saying "Mmm!"

Active Review

14. Self-definitions that refer to concrete external traits are called the _____ self.

15. Self-_____ is the value or worth that people attach to themselves.

16. Children who are _____ attached tend to have high self-esteem.

17. Erikson referred to early childhood as the stage of _____ versus guilt.

18. Early childhood fears tend to revolve around personal _____.

19. (Boys or Girls?) report more fears and higher levels of anxiety.

Reflect & Relate: Do you remember any fears you had during early childhood? Have they faded over the years?

10.4 Development of Gender Roles and Gender Differences

QUESTIONS » What are stereotypes and gender roles? How do they develop?

> I am woman, hear me roar …
> I am strong
> I am invincible
> I am woman

These lyrics are from the song 1970s "I Am Woman" by Helen Reddy and Ray Burton. They capture our attention because they run counter to the stereotype of the woman as vulnerable and in need of a man's protection. The stereotype of the vulnerable woman, like all stereotypes, is a fixed, oversimplified, and often distorted idea about a group of people—in this case, women. The stereotype of the chivalrous, protective man is also a stereotype. Fast forward four decades, and does the 21st century find its equivalent "roar" song in Katy Perry's anthem "Roar"? She sings "'Cause I am a champion, and you're gonna hear me roar."

Cultural stereotypes of males and females involve broad expectations of behaviour that we call **gender roles** (Leaper & Bigler, 2011). Researchers who investigate people's perceptions of gender differences in personality tend to find groups of "masculine" and "feminine" traits such as those listed in Table 10.6 ▪.

Gender-role stereotypes appear to develop through a series of stages. First, children learn to label the genders. At about two to two-and-a-half years of age, children can distinguish between pictures of girls and boys (Fagot & Leinbach, 1993). By age three, they display knowledge of gender stereotypes for toys, clothing, work, and activities (Campbell et al., 2004). Children of this age generally agree that boys play with cars and trucks, help their fathers, and tend to hit others. They also agree that girls play with dolls, help their mothers, and do not hit others (Cherney et al., 2006).

Showing distress apparently becomes gender typed so that preschoolers judge it to be acceptable for girls. One study found that preschool boys but not girls were rejected by their peers when they showed distress (Walter & LaFreniere, 2000).

Children become increasingly traditional in their stereotyping of activities, occupational roles, and personality traits between the ages of three

---

● TABLE 10.6

Cultural Stereotypes of "Masculine" and "Feminine" Traits—Are They Accurate?

Masculine	Feminine
Adventurous	Affectionate
Aggressive	Agreeable
Assertive	Appreciative
Capable	Artistic
Coarse	Cautious
Confident	Dependent
Courageous	Emotional
Determined	Fearful
Disorderly	Fickle
Enterprising	Gentle
Hardheaded	Kind
Independent	Nurturant
Intelligent	Patient
Pleasure-seeking	Prudish
Quick	Sensitive
Rational	Sentimental
Realistic	Shy
Reckless	Softhearted
Sensation-seeking	Submissive
Scientific	Suggestible
Stern	Talkative
Tough	Unambitious

Sources: Amanatullah & Morris, 2010; Guzzetti, 2010; Lippa, 2010; Schmitt et al., 2012.

gender role A complex cluster of traits and behaviours that are considered stereotypical of females (or of males).

and nine or ten (Miller et al., 2006). Traits such as "cruel" and "repairs broken things" are viewed as masculine, and traits such as "often is afraid" and "cooks and bakes" are seen as feminine. A study of 55 middle-class, primarily European American children, ages 39–84 months, found that they considered men to be more competent in traditionally masculine-typed occupations (such as occupations in science and transportation) and women to be more competent in traditionally feminine-typed occupations (such as nursing and teaching) (Levy et al., 2000). The children equated competence with income: They believed that men earned more money in the masculine-typed jobs but that women earned more in the feminine-typed jobs.

Stereotyping levels off or declines beyond the preschool years (Martin & Ruble, 2004). Older children and adolescents become somewhat more flexible in their perceptions of males and females (Sinno & Killen, 2009). They retain the broad stereotypes but also perceive similarities between the genders and recognize that there are individual differences. They are more capable of recognizing the arbitrary aspects of gender categories and more willing to try behaviours that typify the other gender. But even though North American children appear to be used to the idea that both mothers and fathers "belong" in the workplace, they find it less acceptable for fathers to remain in the home (Sinno & Killen, 2009).

Children and adolescents show some chauvinism by perceiving their own gender in a somewhat better light. For example, girls perceive other girls as nicer, more hardworking, and less selfish than boys. Boys, on the other hand, think that they are nicer, more hardworking, and less selfish than girls (Matlin, 2008; Miller et al., 2006).

Gender Differences

QUESTION » How do females and males differ in their cognitive, social, and emotional development? Clearly, females and males are anatomically different. If they weren't, none of us would be here. But according to the gender-role stereotypes we have just examined, people believe that they also differ in their behaviours, personality characteristics, and abilities.

Gender differences in infancy are small and rather inconsistent. In this chapter, we have reviewed gender differences during early childhood. Young girls and boys display some differences in their choices of toys and play activities, even by 13 months of age (van de Beek et al., 2009). Boys engage in more rough-and-tumble play and also are more aggressive. Girls tend to show more empathy and to report more fears. Girls show greater verbal ability than boys, whereas boys show greater visual–spatial ability than girls.

Theories of the Development of Gender Differences

QUESTION » What are the origins of gender differences in behaviour? Like mother, like daughter; like father, like son—at least often, if not always. Why is it that little girls (often) grow up to behave according to the cultural stereotypes of what it means to be female? Why is it that little boys (often) grow up to behave like male stereotypes? Let's have a look at various explanations of the development of gender differences.

hurricanehank/Thinkstock

Gender Stereotyping?
Does this woman fit the feminine stereotype? Why or why not?

The Roles of Evolution and Heredity

According to evolutionary psychologists, gender differences were fashioned by natural selection in response to problems in adaptation that were repeatedly encountered by humans over thousands of generations (Buss, 2009; Ray, 2012; Schmitt, 2008). The story of the survival of our ancient ancestors is recorded in our genes. Genes that bestow attributes that increase an organism's chances of surviving to produce viable offspring are most likely to be transmitted to future generations. We thus possess the genetic codes for traits that helped our ancestors survive and reproduce. These traits include structural gender differences, such as those found in the brain, and differences in body chemistry, such as hormones.

Consider a gender difference. Males tend to place relatively more emphasis on physical appearance in mate selection than females do, whereas females tend to place relatively more emphasis on personal factors such as intelligence, stability, and financial status (Furnham, 2009). Why? Evolutionary psychologists believe that evolutionary forces favour the survival of women who seek status in their mates and the survival of men who seek physical allure, because these preferences provide reproductive advantages.

Evolution has also led to the development of the human brain. As we will see in the next section, the organization of the brain apparently plays a role in gender typing.

Organization of the Brain

The organization of the brain is largely genetically determined, and one thing that affects it is prenatal exposure to sex hormones (Collins et al., 2000; Maccoby, 2000). The hemispheres of the brain are specialized to perform certain functions. In most people, the left hemisphere is more involved in language skills, whereas the right hemisphere is specialized to carry out visual–spatial tasks.

Both males and females have a left hemisphere and a right hemisphere. They also share other structures in the brain, but the question is whether they use them in quite the same way. Consider the hippocampus, a brain structure that is involved in the formation of memories and in relaying incoming sensory information to other parts of the brain (Ohnishi et al., 2006). Matthias Riepe and his colleagues (Grön et al., 2000) have studied the ways in which humans and rats use the hippocampus when they are navigating mazes. Males use the hippocampus in both hemispheres when they are navigating (Grön et al., 2000). Females, however, rely on the hippocampus in the right hemisphere in concert with the right prefrontal cortex—an area of the brain that evaluates information and makes plans. Researchers have also found that females tend to rely on landmarks when they are finding their way ("Go a block past Ollie's Noodle Shop, turn left, and go to the corner past Café Lalo"). Men rely more on geometry, as in finding one's position in terms of coordinates or on a map ("You're on the corner of Eleventh Avenue and 57th Street, and you want to get to Seventh Avenue and 55th Street, so ...") (Grön et al., 2000).

Some psychological activities, such as the understanding and production of language, are regulated by structures in the left hemisphere—particularly Broca's area and Wernicke's area. But emotional and aesthetic responses, along with some other psychological activities, are more or less regulated in the right hemisphere. Brain-imaging research suggests that the left and right hemispheres of males may be more specialized than those of females (Shaywitz & Shaywitz, 2003). If the brain hemispheres of women "get along better" than those of men—that is, if they better share the regulation of various cognitive activities—we may have an explanation why women frequently outperform men in language tasks that involve some spatial organization, such as spelling, reading, and enunciation. Yet men, with more specialized spatial-relations skills, could be expected to generally outperform women at visualizing objects in space and reading maps.

Sex Hormones

Researchers suggest that the development of gender differences in personality, along with the development of anatomical gender differences, may be related to prenatal levels of sex hormones. Although results of many studies that tried to correlate prenatal sex hormone levels with subsequent gender-typed play have been mixed, a study of 212 pregnant women conducted by Bonnie Auyeung and her colleagues (2009) found that fetal testosterone was related to masculine- or feminine-typed play at the age of eight-and-a-half years. Other studies show that children display gender-typed preferences—with boys preferring transportation toys and girls preferring dolls—as early as the age of 13 months (Knickmeyer et al., 2005). Another study investigated the gender-typed visual preferences of 30 human infants at the early ages of three to eight months (Alexander et al., 2009). The researchers assessed interest in a toy truck and in a doll by using eye-tracking technology to indicate the direction of visual attention. Girls showed a visual preference for the doll over the truck (that is, they made a greater number of visual fixations on the doll), and boys showed a visual preference for the truck.

The gender differences in activity preferences of children are also found in rhesus monkeys. For example, male rhesus juveniles and boys are more likely than female rhesus juveniles and girls to engage in rough-and-tumble play (Wallen & Hassett, 2009). Researchers also introduced wheeled toys and plush toys into a 135-member rhesus monkey troop and found that male monkeys, like boys, showed consistent, strong preferences for the wheeled toys, whereas female monkeys, like girls, showed greater flexibility in preferences, sometimes playing with the plush toy and sometimes playing with the wheeled toy (Hassett et al., 2008). Do these cross-species findings suggest that such preferences in humans can develop without human gender-typed socialization experiences?

Let us also consider psychological views of the development of gender differences.

Social Cognitive Theory

Social cognitive theorists pay attention both to the roles of rewards and punishments (reinforcement) in gender typing and to the ways in which children learn from observing others and then decide what behaviours are appropriate for them. Children learn much about what society considers "masculine" or "feminine" by observing and imitating models of the same gender. These models may be their parents, other adults, children, and even TV characters.

The importance of observational learning was shown in a classic experiment conducted by Kay Bussey and Albert Bandura (1984). In this study, children obtained information on how society categorizes behaviour patterns

OBSERVING CHILDREN,
UNDERSTANDING OURSELVES

Gender

When asked "What doll takes care of the babies?" young children typically respond in a stereotyped manner by pointing to the female doll.

If a child is reared without gender-typed toys in the household or if the child's parents avoid giving the child gender-typed messages about what kinds of behaviours are appropriate, how might that child's views on gender differ from those of his or her classmates? Are classmates likely to respond flexibly to his or her views of gender?

From Rathus. *Childhood and Adolescence*, 5E. © 2014 South-Western, a part of Cengage Learning, Inc. Reproduced by permission. www .cengage.com/permissions

Go to www.nelson.com/voyages2ce to watch the video, answer the questions, and e-mail your responses to your professor.

by observing how often they were performed either by men or by women. While children of ages two to five observed them, female and male adult role models exhibited different behaviour patterns, such as choosing a blue or a green hat, marching or walking across a room, and repeating different words. Then the children were given a chance to imitate the models. Girls were twice as likely to imitate the woman's behaviour as the man's, and boys were twice as likely to imitate the man's behaviours as the woman's.

Socialization also plays a role in gender typing. Parents, teachers, other adults—even other children—provide children with information about the gender-typed behaviours they are expected to display (Sabattini & Leaper, 2004). Boys are encouraged to be independent, whereas girls are more likely to be restricted and given help. Boys are allowed to roam farther from home at an earlier age and are more likely to be left unsupervised after school (Leaper, 2011).

Fathers are more likely than mothers to communicate norms for gender-typed behaviours to their children (Leaper, 2011). Mothers are usually less demanding. Fathers tend to encourage their sons to develop instrumental behaviour (behaviour that gets things done or accomplishes something) and their daughters to develop warm, nurturant behaviour. Fathers are likely to cuddle daughters. By contrast, they are likely to toss their sons into the air and use hearty language with them, such as "How're yuh doin', Tiger?" and "Hey you, get your keister over here." Being a nontraditionalist, Spencer would toss my young daughters into the air, which raised objections from relatives who criticized him for being too rough. This, of course, led him to modify his behaviour. (He learned to toss his daughters into the air when the relatives were not around!)

Maternal employment is associated with less polarized gender-role concepts for girls and boys (Powlishta, 2004; Sabattini & Leaper, 2004). The daughters of employed women also have higher educational and career aspirations than the daughters of unemployed women, and they are more likely to choose careers that are nontraditional for women.

Let us now consider two cognitive approaches to gender typing: cognitive-developmental theory and gender-schema theory.

Cognitive-Developmental Theory

Lawrence Kohlberg (1966) proposed a cognitive-developmental view of gender typing. According to this perspective, children play an active role in gender

Acquiring Gender Roles
What psychological factors contribute to the acquisition of gender roles? Psychoanalytic theory focuses on the concept of identification. Social cognitive theory focuses on imitation of the behaviour patterns of same-sex adults and reinforcement by parents and peers.

Vicki Reid/Thinkstock

Kathy Sloane/Photo Researchers, Inc.

typing (Martin & Ruble, 2004). They form concepts about gender and then fit their behaviour to the concepts. These developments occur in stages and are entwined with general cognitive development.

According to Kohlberg, gender typing involves the emergence of three concepts: gender identity, gender stability, and gender constancy. The first step in gender typing is attaining **gender identity**. Gender identity is the knowledge that one is male or female. At two years, most children can say whether they are boys or girls. By the age of three, many children can discriminate anatomical gender differences (Bem, 1989; Campbell et al., 2004). By five or six, children can identify the gender of adults based on waist-to-hip ratios—that is, the more similar the girth of the waist and that of the hips, the more likely the children are to judge the person to be a man (K. L. Johnson et al., 2010).

At around age four or five, most children develop the concept of **gender stability**, according to Kohlberg. They recognize that people retain their gender for a lifetime. Girls no longer believe they can grow up to be daddies, and boys no longer think they can become mommies. **TRUTH OR FICTION REVISITED:** Because most two-and-a-half-year-olds have not developed gender stability, a girl of this age may know that she is a girl but still think she can grow up to be a daddy.

Kohlberg believes that by the age of five to seven years, most children develop the more sophisticated concept of **gender constancy**. Children with gender constancy recognize that gender does not change, even if people modify their dress or behaviour. A woman who cuts her hair short remains a woman. A man who dons an apron and cooks dinner remains a man. According to cognitive-developmental theory, once children have established the concepts of gender stability and constancy, they seek to behave in ways that are consistent with their gender (Martin & Ruble, 2004).

Cross-cultural studies have found that the concepts of gender identity, gender stability, and gender constancy emerge in the order predicted by Kohlberg (Zosuls et al., 2011). But children may achieve gender constancy earlier than Kohlberg stated. More important, Kohlberg's theory cannot account for the age at which gender-typed preferences for toys emerges. Girls show preferences for dolls and soft toys, and boys for hard transportation toys, as early as three to eight months of age (Alexander et al., 2009)!

Gender-Schema Theory

Sandra Bem's **gender-schema theory** proposes that children use gender as one way of organizing their perceptions of the world (Martin & Dinella, 2011). A gender schema is a cluster of concepts about male and female physical traits, behaviours, and personality traits. For example, consider the dimension of strength–weakness. Children learn that strength is linked to the male gender-role stereotype and weakness to the female stereotype. They also learn that some dimensions, such as strength–weakness, are more relevant to one gender than to the other—in this case, to males. A boy will learn that the strength he displays in weight training or wrestling affects the way others perceive him. But most girls do not find this trait to be important to others, unless they are competing in gymnastics, tennis, swimming, or other sports. A girl is likely to find that gentleness and neatness are more important in the eyes of others than strength.

From the viewpoint of gender-schema theory, gender identity alone can inspire "gender-appropriate" behaviour. As soon as children understand the labels "girl" and "boy," they seek information concerning gender-typed traits and try to live up to them. A boy may fight back when provoked because boys are expected to do so. A girl may be gentle and kind because that is expected

gender identity Knowledge that one is female or male. Also, the name of the first stage in Kohlberg's cognitive-developmental theory of the assumption of gender roles.

gender stability The concept that one's gender is a permanent feature.

gender constancy The concept that one's gender remains the same despite superficial changes in appearance or behaviour.

gender-schema theory The view that one's knowledge of the gender schema in one's society (the behaviour patterns that are considered appropriate for men and women) guides one's assumption of gender-typed preferences and behaviour patterns.

of girls. Both boys' and girls' self-esteem will depend on how they measure up to the gender schema.

Studies indicate that children do possess information according to a gender schema. For example, boys show better memory for "masculine" toys, activities, and occupations, whereas girls show better memory for "feminine" toys, activities, and occupations (Martin & Ruble, 2004). However, gender-schema theory does not answer the question of whether biological forces also play a role in gender typing.

The previous three chapters lay the groundwork for the next major period in development: the middle childhood years. We will explore those years in the next three chapters, beginning with physical development in Chapter 11.

Concept Review 10.1 Theories of the Development of Gender Differences

Nature and Gender Typing

Deals with the roles of evolution, heredity, and biology in gender typing

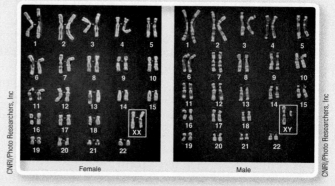

Female   Male

Perspective	Key Points	Comments
Evolution and heredity	Psychological gender differences were fashioned by natural selection in response to challenges that humans faced repeatedly over thousands of generations.	Evolutionary theorists believe that gender differences in aggression are natural. They suggest that a woman's allure is strongly connected with her age and health, which are markers of reproductive capacity, but the value of men as reproducers is also connected with factors that create a stable environment for child rearing.
Sex hormones	Sex hormones may prenatally "masculinize" or "feminize" the brain by creating predispositions consistent with gender roles.	Male rats are generally superior to females in maze-learning ability, a task that requires spatial skills. Aggressiveness appears to be connected with testosterone.

Nature and Gender Typing

Deals with theories in psychology—for example, learning theory and cognitive theory—and related research

Perspective	Key Points	Comments
Social cognitive theory	Children learn what is "masculine" and what is "feminine" by observational learning.	Parents and others tend to reinforce children for gender-appropriate behaviour.
Cognitive-developmental theory	Gender typing is connected with the development of the concepts of gender identity, gender stability, and gender constancy.	Research evidence shows that children develop gender-typed preferences and behaviours before the development of gender stability and gender constancy.
Gender-schema theory	Cultures tend to organize social life around polarized gender roles. Children accept these scripts and try to behave in accord with them.	Research evidence suggests that polarized female–male scripts pervade our culture. For example, children tend to distort their memories to conform to the gender schema.

Active Review

20. Cultural stereotypes of males and females involve broad expectations for behaviour that are called gender _____.

21. Brain imaging suggests that the hemispheres of the brain are more specialized in (males or females?).

22. (Mothers or Fathers?) are more likely to communicate norms for gender-typed behaviours to children.

23. Kohlberg proposes that the emergence of three concepts guides gender typing: gender identity, gender stability, and gender _____.

24. Gender-_____ theory proposes that children blend their self-concepts with the gender schema of their culture.

Reflect & Relate: Do you see yourself as being traditionally feminine or traditionally masculine? Have the gender roles and stereotypes of our culture created opportunities or conflicts for you? Or both? Explain.

Recite an Active Summary

10.1 Influences on Development: Parents, Siblings, and Peers

What are the dimensions of child rearing?

Parental approaches to child rearing can be classified according to the independent dimensions of warmth–coldness and restrictiveness–permissiveness. Consistent control and firm enforcement of rules can have positive consequences for the child.

What techniques do parents use to restrict their children's behaviour?

Parents tend to use inductive methods, power assertion, and withdrawal of love to enforce rules. Inductive methods rely on "reasoning," or explaining why one sort of behaviour is good and another is not.

What parenting styles are involved in the transmission of values and standards?

The main methods are authoritative, authoritarian, and permissive. Authoritative parents are restrictive but warm and tend to have the most competent and achievement-oriented children. Authoritarian parents are restrictive and cold. The sons of authoritarian parents tend to be hostile and defiant; daughters are low in independence. Children of neglectful parents show the least competence and maturity.

How do the situation and the child influence parenting styles?

Parents tend to prefer power-assertive techniques when they believe that children understand the rules they have violated and are capable of acting appropriately. Stress contributes to the use of power assertion.

How do siblings influence social and emotional development in early childhood?

Siblings provide caregiving, emotional support, advice, role models, social interaction, restrictions, and cognitive stimulation. However, they are also sources of conflict, control, and competition. Younger siblings usually imitate older siblings.

What does the research say about the effects of being a firstborn or an only child?

Firstborn and only children are generally more highly motivated to achieve, more cooperative, more helpful, more adult-oriented, and less aggressive. Later-born children tend to be more aggressive, to have lower self-esteem, and to have greater social skills with peers.

How do peers influence social and emotional development in early childhood?

Children learn social skills from peers—such as sharing, helping, taking turns, and coping with conflict. Peers foster the development of physical and cognitive skills and provide emotional support. Preschoolers' friendships are characterized by shared activities and feelings of attachment.

10.2 Social Behaviour: In the World, among Others

What does the research show about child's play?

Play is meaningful, pleasurable, and internally motivated and develops motor, social, and cognitive skills. It may help children deal with conflict and anxiety. Parten followed the development of six categories of play among two- to five-year-olds: unoccupied play, solitary play, onlooker play, parallel play, associative play, and cooperative play. Children show preferences for gender-stereotyped toys by 15–30 months of age. Boys' toys commonly include transportation toys (cars and trucks) and weapons; girls' toys more often include dolls. Boys in early childhood prefer vigorous outdoor activities and rough-and-tumble play. Girls are more likely to engage in arts and crafts. Preferences for toys may involve the interaction of biological factors and socialization.

How does prosocial behaviour develop?

Prosocial behaviour—altruism—begins to develop in the first year, when children begin to share. Development of prosocial behaviour is linked to the development of empathy and perspective taking. Girls show more empathy than boys do.

How does aggression develop?

The aggression of preschoolers is frequently instrumental or possession-oriented. By age six or seven, aggression becomes hostile and person-oriented. Aggressive behaviour appears to be generally stable and predictive of problems in adulthood.

What causes aggression in children?

Genetic factors may be involved in aggressive behaviour. Genes may be expressed in part through the male sex hormone testosterone. Impulsive and relatively fearless children are more likely to be aggressive. Aggressive boys are more likely than nonaggressive boys to incorrectly assume that other children mean them ill. Social cognitive theory suggests that children become aggressive as a result of frustration, reinforcement, and observational learning. Aggressive children are often rejected by less aggressive peers. Children who are physically punished are more likely to behave aggressively. Observing aggressive behaviour teaches aggressive skills, disinhibits the child, and habituates children to violence.

10.3 Personality and Emotional Development

How does the self develop during early childhood?

Self-definitions that refer to concrete external traits are called the categorical self. Children as young as three years can describe themselves in terms of characteristic behaviours and internal states. Secure attachment and competence contribute to the development of self-esteem.

What sorts of fears do children have in the early years?

Preschoolers are most likely to fear animals, imaginary creatures, and the dark; the theme involves threats to personal safety. Girls report more fears than boys do.

10.4 Development of Gender Roles and Gender Differences

What are stereotypes and gender roles? How do they develop?

A stereotype is a fixed conventional idea about a group. Females are stereotyped as dependent, gentle, and home-oriented. Males are stereotyped as aggressive, self-confident, and independent. Cultural expectations of females and males are called gender roles.

How do females and males differ in their cognitive, social, and emotional development?

Males tend to excel in math and spatial-relations skills, whereas girls tend to excel in verbal skills. Stereotypical gender preferences for toys and play activities are in evidence at an early age. Males are more aggressive than females. The magnitude and origins of all these gender differences are under debate.

What are the origins of gender differences in behaviour?

Male sex hormones are connected with greater maze-learning ability in rats and with aggressiveness. Social cognitive theorists explain the development of gender-typed behaviour in terms of observational learning and socialization. According to Kohlberg's cognitive-developmental theory, gender typing involves the emergence of three concepts: gender identity, gender stability, and gender constancy. According to gender-schema theory, preschoolers attempt to conform to the cultural gender schema.

Key Terms

Active Learning Resources

Go to *Voyages in Development's* CourseMate at **www
.nelsonbrain.com**, where you will find an interactive
eBook, flashcards, Pre-Lecture Quizzes, Section Quizzes,
Exam Practice, videos, and more.

Major Topics

MIDDLE CHILDHOOD:
Physical Development

Truth or Fiction?

T | F   Children outgrow "baby fat." **p. 370**

T | F   The typical North American child is exposed to about 10 000 food commercials each year. **p. 372**

T | F   Most Canadian children are physically fit. **p. 378**

T | F   Hyperactivity is caused by chemical food additives. **p. 382**

T | F   Stimulants are often used to treat children who are hyperactive. **p. 383**

T | F   Some children who are intelligent and are provided with enriched home environments cannot learn how to read or do simple math problems. **p.384**

It is six-year-old Jessica's first day of school. During recess, she runs to the climbing apparatus in the schoolyard and climbs to the top. As she reaches the top, she announces to the other children, "I'm coming down." She then walks to the parallel bars, goes halfway across, lets go, and tries again.

Steve and Mike are eight-year-olds. They are riding their bikes up and down the street. Steve tries riding with no hands on the handlebars. Mike starts riding fast, standing up on the pedals. Steve shouts, "Boy, you're going to break your neck!"[1]

Middle childhood is a time for learning many new motor skills. Success in both gross and fine motor skills reflects children's increasing physical maturity, their opportunities to learn, and personality factors such as their persistence and self-confidence.

Competence in motor skills enhances children's self-esteem and their acceptance by their peers.

In this chapter, we examine physical and motor development during middle childhood. We also discuss children with certain disorders.

David Fischer/Digital Vision/Getty Images

---

[1]Adapted from Rowen (1973).

11.1 Growth Patterns

QUESTION » What patterns of growth occur in middle childhood? Gains in height and weight are fairly steady throughout middle childhood. But notable variations in growth patterns also occur from child to child. Following the growth trends begun in early childhood, boys and girls continue to gain a little over 5 centimetres in height per year during the middle childhood years. This pattern of gradual gains does not vary significantly until children reach the adolescent **growth spurt** (see Appendix B). The average gain in weight between the ages of 6 and 12 is about 2–3 kilograms a year. During these years, children continue to become less stocky and more slender (Kuczmarski et al., 2000).

Most deviations from average height and weight figures are quite normal. Individual differences are more marked in middle childhood than they were earlier. For example, most three-year-olds are within 4–5 kilograms and 10 centimetres of one another. But by the age of ten, children's weights may vary by as much as 14–16 kilograms, and their heights may vary by as much as 15 centimetres.

As bones lengthen and broaden and muscles strengthen, many children want to engage in more exercise. Because their muscles are adjusting to a growing skeleton, children may experience aches and stiffness that have been dubbed "growing pains," especially in the legs (Evans et al., 2006; Marcolin et al., 2009).

Between the ages of 6 and 12, children lose their primary teeth, and the permanent teeth grow in. Because the permanent teeth grow in at full size, they may at first seem too large for the child's face, but the facial bones "catch up," widening and lengthening the face so that the teeth and face once again come "into proportion."

Brain Development

The brain undergoes its most dramatic growth during prenatal development and infancy. Myelination of axons continues to occur during middle childhood and, apparently, into young adulthood. Growth of the volume and weight of the brain decelerates, although there are overall gains in size and weight. The frontal part of the brain is most highly involved in the so-called "executive functions" of planning and self-regulation. And it is here that dramatic developments take place in middle childhood (Bell et al., 2007). We can think of executive functioning as having several aspects: deployment of attention, cognitive flexibility, self-regulation, goal setting, and information processing. Information processing is connected with "fluid reasoning," or the ability to think logically and solve problems in novel situations. Neuroscientific research suggests that the child's gaining of control over his or her attentional processes emerges in infancy and develops rapidly in early childhood. However, cognitive flexibility, goal setting, and information processing (fluid reasoning) appear to undergo an important period of development during the ages of seven to nine and to be relatively mature by about the age of 12, thus setting the stage for the cognitive advances of adolescence (Anderson, 2002; Ferrer et al., 2009).

Nutrition and Growth

In middle childhood, average body weight doubles. Children also expend a good deal of energy as they engage in physical activity and play. To fuel this growth and activity, children need to eat more than they did in the preschool years. Children in middle childhood also have varying energy requirements largely determined by age, gender, and activity levels (i.e., sedentary, low activity, or active). For example, your typical eight- to nine-year-old female needs 1600 calories per day, while a male of that age requires 1750; the average

growth spurt A period during which growth advances at a dramatically rapid rate compared with other periods.

ten- to eleven-year-old female requires 1800 calories a day, and a male of that age requires 2000 calories per day (Health Canada, 2014).

Nutrition involves much more than calories, as we will see in our discussion of children struggling with weight issues. *Canada's Food Guide* (Public Health Agency of Canada, 2011a) suggests it is healthful to eat fruits and vegetables, fish, poultry, lean meats, legumes, and whole grains, and to limit intake of fats, sugar, and starches. However, the food offered to children in some schools and elsewhere tends to be heavy on sugar, animal fats, and salt (Childhood obesity, 2011). In addition, food portions have grown over the past couple of decades, particularly for salty snacks, desserts, soft drinks, fruit drinks, French fries, poutine, hamburgers, cheeseburgers, and fast foods (Childhood obesity, 2011).

Fast-food restaurants offer the largest portions and the most fattening foods. The National Bureau of Economic Research (NBER) found that for Grade 9 students, having a fast-food restaurant within 0.1 mile (0.16 kilometres) of their school is connected with a 5.2 percent increase in their obesity rate (Currie et al., 2009). The NBER found no association between fast-food restaurants and obesity rate when the restaurant is 0.25 or 0.5 mile (0.4 or 0.8 kilometres) away.

Nutrition and social class are also connected. Consider two studies with African American mothers and daughters. Daughters living at the poverty line were likely to be fed diets high in fats and fast foods (Miklos et al., 2004). Middle-class mothers, however, were concerned about the weight of their daughters and encouraged physical activity as a means of weight control. Middle-class mothers also tended to limit their daughters' consumption of snack foods and sugar-laden carbonated beverages. Instead, they encouraged their daughters to drink water (V. J. Thompson et al., 2003).

Gender Similarities and Differences in Physical Growth

Boys continue to be slightly heavier and taller than girls through the age of nine or ten (see Appendix B). Girls then begin their adolescent growth spurt and surpass boys in height and weight until about age 13 or 14. At that time, boys are approaching the peak of their adolescent growth spurt, and they become taller and heavier than girls (Högler et al., 2008; Wehkalampi et al., 2008).

The steady gain in height and weight during middle childhood is accompanied by an increase in muscular strength for both girls and boys (Högler et al., 2008; Wehkalampi et al., 2008). The relative proportion of muscle and fatty tissue is about the same for boys and girls in early middle childhood. But this begins to change at about age 11, as males develop relatively more muscle tissue and females develop more fatty tissue.

Vision and Hearing

In middle childhood, some 30 percent of children in Western countries are myopic, or nearsighted (Russo, Semeraro, Romano, Mastropasqua, Dell'Omo & Costagliola, 2014). Myopia is readily treated with corrective lenses. The incidence of myopia tends to increase into young adulthood, when some 60 percent of the population has difficulty bringing distant objects into focus. Laser surgery is typically reserved for more serious vision problems with children, and there can be complications (Daoud et al., 2009). An experiment found some psychological benefits for children who wear contact lenses. In the study, 237 children 8–11 years old were assigned at random to wear glasses, and 237 were assigned to wear soft contact lenses (Walline et al., 2009). The study lasted for three years. At the end of the experiment, there were no differences in children's global self-worth; however, the children who wore the contact lenses rated their physical appearance, athletic competence, and social acceptance significantly higher.

Children 6–12 years old are not as likely as younger children to come down with ear infections, because the Eustachian tube, which runs down from the inner ear to the throat, elongates and narrows as children grow. As a result, bacteria and infected fluids cannot move so readily from the throat to the ear. Children with frequent ear infections are more likely to experience headaches—including migraines—hay fever, and asthma (Lateef et al., 2009). Ear infections can also lead to hearing loss and difficulty acquiring language (Vohr et al., 2008).

11.2 Overweight Children

QUESTIONS » How many children in Canada are overweight? Why are they overweight? According to a Joint Report from the Public Health Agency of Canada and the Canadian Institute for Health Information (Public Health Agency of Canada, 2011a) the prevalence of obesity in children aged 6–17 is 8.6 percent. Data from the Canadian Health Measures Survey (Roberts, Shields, de Groh, Aziz, & Gilbert, 2012), which used World Health Organization cut-offs, indicates that 19.7 percent of children between the ages of 5 and 11 qualify as overweight, and 13.1 percent are obese (see Table 11.1 ▪). Prevalence rates vary by source due to different methods of reporting—self-reports versus actual weight measurements. Consider some facts about childhood overweight and obesity (Basics about childhood obesity, 2011):

- Over the past 20 years, the prevalence of obesity among children has doubled.
- Children who are obese are more likely to have high blood pressure and high cholesterol (as children!).
- Children who are obese are more likely to have diabetes.
- Obesity is more prevalent among boys than girls.
- Children with obesity are more likely to have breathing problems and asthma, joint problems, fatty liver disease, gallstones, and acid reflux—all in childhood.
- **TRUTH OR FICTION REVISITED:** Although parents often assume that heavy children will "outgrow" "baby fat," most overweight children become overweight adults.

In North America, most overweight children become overweight adults (Basics about childhood obesity, 2011; Obesity in Canada, 2011). By contrast, only about 40 percent of normal-weight boys and 20 percent of normal-weight girls become overweight adults. However, similar samples of Japanese and Swiss children apparently did not mostly become overweight adults (Funatogawa et al., 2008; Junod, 2008). Perhaps there is greater social pressure to slim down as one develops in those cultures.

Overweight children, despite the stereotype, are usually far from jolly. Research suggests that heavy children are often rejected by their peers or are the objects of derision (Basics

OBSERVING CHILDREN,
UNDERSTANDING OURSELVES

Childhood Obesity

Being overweight puts children at risk for later health problems such as diabetes, high blood pressure, and heart disease.

Why are so many children overweight? Does being overweight in childhood predict being overweight in adulthood?

From Rathus. *Childhood and Adolescence*, 5E. © 2014 South-Western, a part of Cengage Learning, Inc. Reproduced by permission. www.cengage.com/permissions

Go to www.nelson.com/voyages2ce to watch the video, answer the questions, and e-mail your responses to your professor.

Percentage Distribution of Children and Adolescents, by BMI Category, Age Group and Sex, Household Population Aged 5 to 17, 2009 to 2011

	Thinness			Normal weight			Overweight			Obesity		
		95% confidence interval			95% confidence interval			95% confidence interval			95% confidence interval	
	%	from	to	%	from	to	%	from	to	%	from	to
Total	**2.2^E**	**1.1**	**4.1**	**66.4**	**62.8**	**69.8**	**19.8**	**16.6**	**23.4**	**11.7**	**9.9**	**13.7**
Age group (years)												
5 to 11	F	...	...	65.5	61.7	69.2	19.7	16.4	23.4	13.1	10.5	16.3
12 to 17	F	...	...	67.2	60.2	73.6	19.9	15.0	25.8	10.2	7.3	14.1
Boys	F	...	...	62.3	56.3	68.0	19.4	15.1	24.4	15.1	12.6	17.9
Age group (years)												
5 to 11	F	...	...	59.0	51.9	65.7	19.8	14.8	26.0	19.5	15.5	24.1
12 to 17	F	...	...	65.6	55.3	74.6	18.9^E	12.6	27.5	10.7*	7.5	15.0
Girls	1.0^E	0.6	1.6	70.8	64.6	76.3	20.2	15.8	25.6	8.0†	5.7	11.1
Age group (years)												
5 to 11	1.5^E	0.7	3.1	72.6†	69.8	75.2	19.6	16.1	23.6	6.3†,^{E}	4.1	9.8
12 to 17	F	...	...	69.0	58.5	77.9	20.9	14.9	28.6	9.6^E	6.0	15.1

This table displays the results of percentage distribution of children and adolescents thinness, normal weight, overweight, obesity, %, and 95% confidence interval, calculated using "from" and "to" units of measure (appearing as column headers).
*Significantly different from ages 5 to 11 ($p < 0.05$).
†Significantly different from boys ($p < 0.05$).
^{E}Use with caution.
F Too unreliable to be published.
... Not applicable.
Source: 2009 to 2011 Canadian Health Measures Survey. Statistics Canada.

about childhood obesity, 2011). They usually perform poorly in sports, which can bestow prestige on slimmer children (Salvy et al., 2008). As overweight children approach adolescence, they become even less popular because they are less likely to be found sexually attractive. It is no surprise, then, that overweight children have poorer body images than children of normal weight (Storch et al., 2007). Overweight adolescents are also more likely to be depressed and anxious than peers who are normal in weight (Kirkcaldy et al., 2002).

Children who are overweight are at greater risk for a number of physical health problems in childhood and later in life (Childhood obesity, 2011; Obesity in Canada, 2011). Among these are high blood pressure, hardening of the arteries (atherosclerosis), type 2 diabetes, fatty liver disease, ovary disorders, and abnormal breathing patterns during sleep. Being overweight in childhood can accelerate the development of heart disease, which can lead to heart attacks or stroke in adulthood. The dramatically increased prevalence of overweight in childhood might even reverse the contemporary increase in life expectancy, such that overweight youth have less healthy and shorter lives than their parents. As Daniels (2006) notes, this would be the first reversal in increasing longevity to occur in modern life.

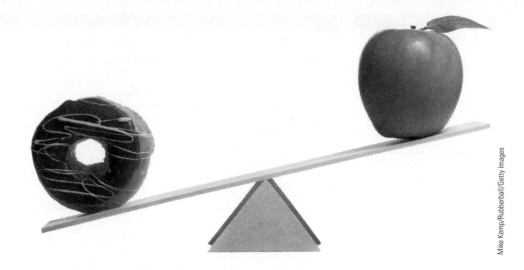

Causes of Being Overweight

Evidence from kinship studies, including twin studies, and adoption studies shows that heredity plays a role in being overweight (Childhood obesity, 2011). Some people inherit a tendency to burn up extra calories, whereas others inherit a tendency to turn extra calories into fat.

But there is nothing one can do about one's heredity. Other factors that contribute to child overweight and obesity include consuming sugar drinks and less healthful food at school, the advertising of fattening foods, variation in diets at child-care centres, lack of regular physical activity (and for low-income children, lack of community places in which to play or exercise), limited access to healthful affordable foods, availability of "high-energy" (translation: high-sugar) drinks, large portion sizes (supersizing), lack of breastfeeding, and TV and other media (couch-potato syndrome) (Zimmerman & Bell, 2010).

Children who have more fat cells than other children feel hungry sooner, even if they are the same weight. Perhaps possessing more fat cells means that more signals are transmitted to the hypothalamus in the brain. Children (and adults) who are overweight and those who were once overweight usually have more fat cells than individuals who have weighed less. This abundance is no blessing. Overweight in childhood may cause adolescent or adult dieters to feel persistent hunger, even after they have levelled off at a weight they prefer (Guerdjikova et al., 2007).

Evidence that genetic and physiological factors are involved in weight does not mean that the environment is without influence. Family, peers, and other environmental factors also play roles in children's eating habits (Overweight and obesity, 2011). Overweight parents, for example, may be models of poor exercise habits, may encourage overeating, and may keep unhealthy foods in the house.

The amount of television watching also affects children's weight (Schumacher & Queen, 2007). Children who watch television extensively during the middle childhood years are more likely to become overweight as adolescents (Schumacher & Queen, 2007). The influence of TV watching is at least threefold (Stephenson & Banet-Weiser, 2007). First, children tend to consume snacks while watching. Second, television bombards children with commercials for fattening foods, such as candy and potato chips. Third, watching television is a sedentary activity. We burn fewer calories sitting than engaging in physical activity. Children who are heavy TV viewers are less physically active overall. **TRUTH OR FICTION REVISITED:** It is true that North American children are exposed to about 10 000 food commercials per year—the bulk of them for fast foods (such as those sold at Burger King and Pizza Hut), highly sweetened cereals, soft drinks, and candy bars (Overweight and obesity, 2011).

Stressors and emotional reactions can also prompt children to eat (Schumacher & Queen, 2007). Overeating may occur in response to severe stresses, such as that inflicted by bickering in the home, parental divorce, or the birth of a sibling. Family celebrations and arguments are quite different, but both can lead to overeating or breaking a diet. Efforts to curb food intake also may be hampered by negative feeling states, such as anxiety and depression (Overweight and obesity, 2011). The rule of thumb here seems to be something like this: If life is awful, try chocolate (or French fries, or pizza, or whatever).

In summary, the main determinants of obesity are heredity, diet, physical activity, sedentary behaviours and screen time, socioeconomic factors, and community-level factors (Obesity in Canada, 2011).

For some suggestions on how parents can help their children (and themselves) live a healthier lifestyle, see the "A Closer Look—Real Life" feature.

A CLOSER LOOK | REAL LIFE

Helping Overweight Children Manage Their Weight

Health-conscious parents not only want to be slimmer themselves but also are more aware of the health benefits their children gain by avoiding being overweight. However, losing weight is a difficult problem in self-control for children and adults alike. Nevertheless, childhood is the best time to prevent or reverse obesity because it is easiest to promote a lifetime pattern of healthful behaviours during childhood (Childhood obesity facts, 2011).

Methods such as improving nutritional knowledge, reducing calories, introducing exercise, and modifying behaviour show promise for helping children lose excess weight (Strategies and solutions, 2011).

Behavioural methods involve tracking the child's calorie intake and weight, keeping the child away from temptations, setting a good example, and systematically using praise and other rewards. The most successful weight-loss programs for children combine exercise, decreased caloric intake, behaviour modification, and emotional support from parents. Here are some suggestions:

- Teach children about nutrition—calories, protein, vitamins, minerals, fibre, food groups, and so on. Indicate which foods may be eaten without concern (such as green vegetables) and which foods should be eaten only sparingly (cakes, cookies, soft drinks sweetened with sugar, and so on). Check out *Canada's Food Guide* on Health Canada's website (www.hc-sc.gc.ca/fn-an/food-guide-aliment/index-eng.php).

- Do not insist that the entire family sit down at the same time for a large meal.

- Allow children to eat only when they are hungry.

- Allow children to stop eating when they feel full.

- Prepare low-calorie snacks for your child to eat throughout the day. Children who feel deprived may binge.

- Do not cook, eat, or display fattening foods when the child is at home. The sight and aroma of such foods can be tantalizing.

- Involve the child in more activities. When children are busy, they are less likely to think about food. (And physical activity burns calories.)

- If you take your child food shopping, try to avoid the market aisles with ice cream, cake, and candy.

- Ask relatives and friends not to offer fattening or empty calorie treats when you visit.

- Do not allow snacking while engaged in screen time (TV, digital devices) or while playing, reading, or engaging in any other activity. Allowing children to snack while watching TV or using digital devices makes eating a mindless habit.

- Involve the child in exercise, such as swimming or prolonged bicycle riding. Exercise will burn calories, increase the child's feelings of competence and self-esteem, improve cardiovascular condition, and possibly promote lifetime exercise habits.

- Reward the child for steps in the right direction, such as eating less or exercising more. Praise is a powerful reward, but children also respond to tangible rewards such as a new toy.

- Do not assume that it is a catastrophe if the child slips and goes on a binge. Talk with the child about what triggered the binge to avert similar problems in the future.

Continued

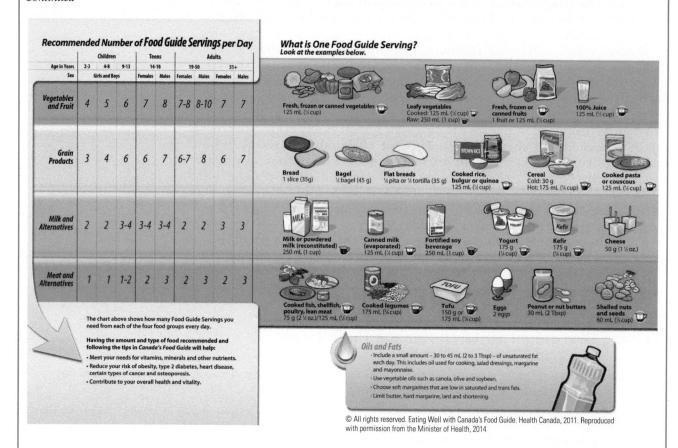

Recommended Number of *Food Guide Servings* per Day

	Children			Teens		Adults			
Age in Years	2-3	4-8	9-13	14-18		19-50		51+	
Sex	Girls and Boys			Females	Males	Females	Males	Females	Males
Vegetables and Fruit	4	5	6	7	8	7-8	8-10	7	7
Grain Products	3	4	6	6	7	6-7	8	6	7
Milk and Alternatives	2	2	3-4	3-4	3-4	2	2	3	3
Meat and Alternatives	1	1	1-2	2	3	2	3	2	3

The chart above shows how many Food Guide Servings you need from each of the four food groups every day.

Having the amount and type of food recommended and following the tips in *Canada's Food Guide* will help:
- Meet your needs for vitamins, minerals and other nutrients.
- Reduce your risk of obesity, type 2 diabetes, heart disease, certain types of cancer and osteoporosis.
- Contribute to your overall health and vitality.

What is One Food Guide Serving?
Look at the examples below.

Vegetables and Fruit
- Fresh, frozen or canned vegetables — 125 mL (½ cup)
- Leafy vegetables — Cooked: 125 mL (½ cup) Raw: 250 mL (1 cup)
- Fresh, frozen or canned fruits — 1 fruit or 125 mL (½ cup)
- 100% Juice — 125 mL (½ cup)

Grain Products
- Bread — 1 slice (35g)
- Bagel — ½ bagel (45 g)
- Flat breads — ½ pita or ½ tortilla (35 g)
- Cooked rice, bulgur or quinoa — 125 mL (½ cup)
- Cereal — Cold: 30 g Hot: 175 mL (¾ cup)
- Cooked pasta or couscous — 125 mL (½ cup)

Milk and Alternatives
- Milk or powdered milk (reconstituted) — 250 mL (1 cup)
- Canned milk (evaporated) — 125 mL (½ cup)
- Fortified soy beverage — 250 mL (1 cup)
- Yogurt — 175 g (¾ cup)
- Kefir — 175 g (¾ cup)
- Cheese — 50 g (1 ½ oz.)

Meat and Alternatives
- Cooked fish, shellfish, poultry, lean meat — 75 g (2 ½ oz.)/125 mL (½ cup)
- Cooked legumes — 175 mL (¾ cup)
- Tofu — 150 g or 175 mL (¾ cup)
- Eggs — 2 eggs
- Peanut or nut butters — 30 mL (2 Tbsp)
- Shelled nuts and seeds — 60 mL (¼ cup)

Oils and Fats
- Include a small amount – 30 to 45 mL (2 to 3 Tbsp) – of unsaturated fat each day. This includes oil used for cooking, salad dressings, margarine and mayonnaise.
- Use vegetable oils such as canola, olive and soybean.
- Choose soft margarines that are low in saturated and trans fats.
- Limit butter, hard margarine, lard and shortening.

- Remind the child that tomorrow is a new day and a new start.
- If you and your children are overweight, consider losing weight together. It is more effective for overweight children and their parents to diet and exercise together than for children to go it alone.

For further information and activities for active and healthy living, refer to the Canadian Physical Activity Guidelines (www.csep.ca).

Reflect

- You believe that a friend's or relative's child is dangerously obese, but the parent thinks it's normal or just "baby fat." What do you do?
- Imagine yourself about to visit a relative or friend whose self-esteem is wrapped up in spreading appealing but fattening food around during visits. How can you prevent your children from overeating? Must you stay home or go somewhere else?
- You are concerned about your child's weight, and you learn that he or she has been sneaking "forbidden" foods. What do you do?

CountryStyle/iStockphoto

Being overweight runs in families. We don't know precisely why, but heredity tends to play a role, and so do environmental factors.

Active Review

1. Gains in height and weight are generally (abrupt or steady?) throughout middle childhood.

2. Children gain about _____ centimetres in height per year during middle childhood.

3. Children gain about _____ kilograms a year during middle childhood.

4. (Boys or Girls?) are slightly heavier and taller through the age of nine or ten.

5. Boys begin to become more muscular than girls at about the age of _____.

6. About _____ percent of Canadian children are obese.

7. Children (do or do not?) tend to outgrow "baby fat."

8. Being overweight (does or does not?) run in families.

Reflect & Relate: What were your gains in height and weight like in middle childhood? Were they "average" or below or above average? Think of people you know who were overweight as children: Did they "outgrow" it?

11.3 Childhood Asthma

QUESTION » What is childhood asthma? Asthma is an allergy-type respiratory disorder characterized by spasms in the lungs, difficulty breathing, wheezing, often coughing (dry hacking), and a feeling of tightness in the chest that prevents the sufferer from getting enough air (NHLBI, 2011). The wheezing can be severe enough to disturb sleep and speech. A study of more than a million children reported by more than 300 health centres around the world found that the prevalence of wheezing ranged from 2.4 percent in Jodhpur, India, to 37.6 percent in Costa Rica for six- to seven-year-olds, and from 0.8 percent in Tibet to 32.6 percent in Wellington, New Zealand, for 13- to 14-year-olds (Lai et al., 2009). The researchers found that, by and large, childhood asthma is more likely to be found in more affluent nations. However, the problem tended to be more serious in poorer nations.

Some children die from severe attacks of asthma, as do some adults. Just as asthma tends to be more severe in poor nations, it is more likely to be lethal among poorer Americans.

What factors increase the risk of developing asthma? A Canadian study mailed questionnaires to the mothers of more than 26 000 children to find the answers (Martel et al., 2008). Children who had previously had respiratory infections and skin irritations (dermatitis) were at higher risk of developing asthma. Other determinants of asthma included male gender, administration of oxygen after birth, prescription of antibiotics during the first six months, asthma in the father or in siblings, maternal asthma during pregnancy, use of antibiotics during pregnancy, and maternal receipt of public assistance. Protective factors included the use of nasal steroids during pregnancy, breast feeding, day-care attendance, and, surprisingly, having pets in the home. In sum, risk factors seem to be previous respiratory or allergy problems, a family history of asthma, and lower socioeconomic status (SES). It is doubtful that pets in the home actually protect children from asthma. It is more likely that parents with fewer allergies are more likely to have pets.

The National Institutes of Health lists medicines for treating asthma (NHLBI, 2011). Nasal corticosteroids block reaction to allergens and reduce airway constriction. Other medicines include cromolyn sodium and nedocromil, immunomodulators, leukotriene modifiers, and bronchodilators (LABAs) (NHLBI, 2011). Parents are also typically advised to try to remove dust, dander, mites, and other sources of respiratory irritation from the home as much as possible. Some children "outgrow" asthma, meaning that symptoms tend to improve in some children when they reach adolescence and young adulthood (Li, 2009). For some, the symptoms do not return; for others, they may return after some years have passed.

11.4 Motor Development

QUESTION » What changes in motor development occur in middle childhood? The school years are marked by increases in the child's speed, strength, agility, and balance (Kopp, 2011). These developments, in turn, lead to more skilful performance of motor activities, such as skipping.

Gross Motor Skills

Throughout middle childhood, children show steady improvement in their ability to perform various gross motor skills (Kopp, 2011). School-age children are usually eager to participate in group games and athletic activities that require the movement of large muscles, such as catching and throwing balls. As seen in Concept Review 11.1, children are hopping, jumping, and climbing by age six or so, and by age six or seven, they are usually capable of pedaling and balancing on a bicycle. By the ages of eight to ten, children are showing the balance, coordination, and strength that allow them to engage in gymnastics and team sports.

Concept Review 11.1 Development of Motor Skills during Middle Childhood

Age	Skills
Gross Motor Skills	
6 years	• Hops, jumps, climbs
7 years	• Balances on and pedals a bicycle
8 years	• Has good body balance
9 years	• Engages in vigorous bodily activities, especially team sports such as baseball, football, volleyball, and basketball
10 years	• Balances on one foot for 15 seconds; catches a fly ball
12 years	• Displays some awkwardness as a result of asynchronous bone and muscle development
Fine Motor Skills	
6–7 years	• Ties shoelaces • Throws ball by using wrist and finger release • Holds pencil with fingertips • Follows simple mazes • May be able to hit a ball with a bat
8–9 years	• Spaces words when writing • Writes and prints accurately and neatly • Copies a diamond shape correctly • Swings a hammer well • Sews and knits • Shows good hand–eye coordination

David Fischer/Digital Vision/Getty Images

Jupiterimages/Thinkstock

During these years, the muscles are growing stronger, and the pathways that connect the cerebellum to the cortex are becoming increasingly myelinated. Experience also plays an indispensable role in refining many sensorimotor abilities, especially at championship levels, but individual differences that seem inborn are also present. Some people, for example, have better visual acuity or better depth perception than others. For reasons such as these, they will have an edge in playing in the outfield or hitting a golf ball.

One of the most important factors in athletic performance is **reaction time**, or the amount of time required to respond to a stimulus. Reaction time is basic to the child's timing of a swing of the bat to meet the ball. Reaction time is basic to adjusting to a fly ball or hitting a tennis ball. Reaction time is also involved in children's responses to cars and other (sometimes deadly) obstacles when they are riding their bicycles or running down the street.

Reaction time gradually improves (i.e., decreases) from early childhood to about age 18 (Kopp, 2011). However, individual differences can be large (Largo et al., 2001). Reaction time begins to increase again in the adult years. Even so, 75-year-olds still outperform children. Baseball and volleyball may be "child's play," but, everything else being equal, adults respond to the ball more quickly.

OBSERVING CHILDREN, UNDERSTANDING OURSELVES

Middle Childhood: Gross Motor Skills

Observe children ages 6–11 expressing their gross motor control.

What are some gross motor skills that affect a child's athletic abilities? Although older children tend to use gross motor skills more efficiently than younger children, why might this not always be true? What activities may help a child develop his or her gross motor skills?

Go to www.nelson.com/voyages2ce to watch the video, answer the questions, and e-mail your responses to your professor.

From Rathus. *Childhood and Adolescence,* 5E. © 2014 South-Western, a part of Cengage Learning, Inc. Reproduced by permission. www .cengage.com/permissions

Fine Motor Skills

By the age of six or seven years, children can usually tie their shoelaces and hold their pencils as adults do (see Concept Review 11.1). Their abilities to fasten buttons, zip zippers, brush their teeth, wash themselves, coordinate a knife and fork, and use chopsticks all develop in the early school years and improve during childhood (Abdelaziz et al., 2001; Beilei et al., 2002).

Gender Similarities and Differences in Motor Development

QUESTION » Are there gender differences in motor skills? Throughout middle childhood, boys and girls perform similarly in most motor activities. Boys show slightly greater overall strength and, in particular, more forearm strength, which aids them in swinging a bat or throwing a ball (Butterfield & Loovis, 1993).

Girls, on the other hand, show somewhat greater limb coordination and overall flexibility, which is valuable in dancing, balancing, and gymnastics (Abdelaziz et al., 2001; Cratty, 1986). Girls with a certain type of physique seem particularly well suited to gymnastics. Those who are short, lean, and small-boned make the best gymnasts, according to Olympic coaches, because they displace gravity most effectively. This may explain why female gymnasts are considered old for the sport by the time they reach their late teens. By then, they have often grown taller and their body contours have filled out (Erlandson et al., 2008).

reaction time The amount of time required to respond to a stimulus

At puberty, gender differences in motor performance favouring boys become progressively greater (Dorfberger et al., 2009). What factors might account for the development of gender differences in physical performance? The slight gender differences in motor performance prior to puberty are not large enough to be attributed to biological variables. (The one exception may be throwing, a skill in which boys excel from an early age.) Boys are more likely than girls to receive encouragement, support, and opportunities for participation in sports (Geary, 1998). Even during the preschool years, parents emphasize physical activity in boys more than in girls. By middle childhood, boys are involved in competitive games and in games of longer duration. They also engage in more vigorous activity on average than girls (A. M. Thompson et al., 2003).

At puberty, when boys begin to excel in such areas as running, the long jump, sit-ups, and grip strength, boys' greater size and strength confer a biological advantage. But some environmental factors that operated in middle childhood may assume even greater importance in puberty. "Tomboy" behaviour in girls is less socially accepted in adolescence than it was in middle childhood. Therefore, girls may become less interested in participating in athletic activities and may be less motivated to do well in the ones they do pursue (Geary, 1998; Vu et al., 2006). By the ages of 12 and 13, girls are less likely than boys to perceive themselves as competent (Barnett et al., 2008), and self-perception of competence predicts the extent of participation in sports (Papaioannou et al., 2006).

In any event, physical activity decreases with age between middle childhood and adolescence in both genders (R. A. Thompson et al., 2003). Physical activities become increasingly stereotyped by children as being masculine (e.g., football) or feminine (e.g., dance) (Meaney et al., 2002).

Exercise and Fitness

QUESTIONS » Are children in Canada physically fit? If not, why not? The health benefits of exercise for both adults and children are well known. Exercise reduces the risk of heart disease, stroke, diabetes, and certain forms of cancer (Erwin et al., 2012; Singh et al., 2012). Exercise confers psychological benefits as well. Physically active children and adolescents have a better self-image and better coping skills than those who are inactive (Physical activity and health, 2011).

Canadian adults are becoming more conscientious about exercising and staying fit. TRUTH OR FICTION REVISITED: However, most children in Canada are not physically fit. A majority of Canadian children do not meet the Canadian physical activity level guidelines (see www.csep.ca/guidelines) set by the Canadian Society for Exercise Physiology (2012).

What are some possible reasons for this decline in fitness? Again, one obvious culprit is sedentary behaviours such as watching television. Students who watch relatively little television have less body fat and are more physically fit than those who watch for several hours per day (Physical activity and health, 2011).

Cardiac and muscular fitness, in both childhood and adulthood, is developed by participation in continuous exercise, such as running, walking quickly, swimming laps, bicycling, or jumping rope for intervals of several minutes at a time. However, schools and parents tend to focus on sports such as baseball and football, which are less apt to promote fitness (Schumacher & Queen, 2007).

Children with high levels of physical activity are more likely to have school officials and parents who encourage their children to exercise and who actively exercise themselves (Physical activity and health, 2011). How, then, can more

PHYSICAL ACTIVITY LEVELS

D-

THIS YEAR'S GRADE HAS IMPROVED FROM AN F TO A D- BECAUSE NEW, NATIONALLY REPRESENTATIVE DATA HAVE BECOME AVAILABLE ON 3- TO 4-YEAR-OLDS IN CANADA, an age group that the Report Card has not been able to include within the assessment of this indicator. The new data reveal that the majority of 3- to 4-year-olds are meeting the Canadian Physical Activity Guidelines for the Early Years. It is important to note that <u>no improvement</u> has been observed in the physical activity levels of 5- to 17-year-olds. Only 5% of them are meeting the Canadian Physical Activity Guidelines for Children and Youth.

The D- grade reflects the balance between one age group that is doing well (3- to 4-year-olds) and 2 age groups (5- to 11-year-olds and 12- to 17-year-olds) that are doing very poorly. The grade for this indicator has not been in the D range since 2006.

YEAR	2005	2006	2007	2008	2009	2010	2011	2012	2013
GRADE	D	D	F	F	F	F	F	F	D-

BENCHMARK	› % of children and youth who meet the Canadian Physical Activity Guidelines (3- to 4-year-olds: at least 180 minutes of physical activity at any intensity every day; 5- to 17-year-olds: at least 60 minutes of moderate- to vigorous-intensity physical activity every day).

A 81–100% **D** 21–40%
B 61–80% **F** 00–20%
C 41–60%

Active Healthy Kids Canada (2013). Are We Driving Our Kids to Unhealthy Habits? *The 2013 Active Healthy Kids Canada Report Card on Physical Activity for Children and Youth.* Toronto: Active Healthy Kids Canada. The 2013 Report Card, and a summary of its findings, are available online at www.activehealthykids.ca.

children be motivated to engage in regular physical activity? Here are some ideas for parents:

- Engage in family outdoor activities that promote fitness: walking, swimming, bicycling, skating.
- Reduce the amount of time spent watching television.
- Encourage outdoor play during daylight hours after school.
- Do not assume that your child gets sufficient exercise by participating in a team sport. Many team sports involve long periods of inactivity.

Organized sports for children are enormously popular, but many children lose their enthusiasm and drop out. Participation in sports declines as middle childhood progresses (Schumacher & Queen, 2007). Why? Sometimes parents or coaches push children too hard, too early, or too quickly. If competition is stressed, children may feel frustrated or inferior; they are sometimes injured. Parents are

5% of 5- to 17-year-olds in Canada meet the Canadian Physical Activity Guidelines for Children and Youth, which recommend at least 60 minutes of daily MVPA (2009-11 CHMS).

40% of 5- to 17-year-olds in Canada accumulate at least **60 minutes** of MVPA at least **3 days per week** (2009-11 CHMS).

75% accumulate at least **30 minutes** of daily MVPA on **3 or more days of the week** (2009-11 CHMS).

advised not to place excessive demands for performance on their children. Let them progress at their own pace. Encourage them to focus on the fun and health benefits of physical activity and sports, not on winning.

Active Review

9. During middle childhood, children show (abrupt or steady?) improvement in gross motor skills.

10. By the age of about _____, children show the balance, coordination, and strength that allow them to engage in gymnastics and team sports.

11. Reaction time gradually (increases or decreases?) from early childhood to about age 18.

12. (Boys or Girls?) tend to show greater overall strength.

13. (Boys or Girls?) show somewhat greater coordination and flexibility.

14. Most children in Canada tend to be physically (fit or unfit?).

Reflect & Relate: When did you become "good at" things such as riding a bicycle, skating, or team sports? Did these activities provide you with an opportunity for fulfillment and social approval, or were they a source of anxiety? Did you approach these activities with pleasure or shy away from them? Explain.

11.5 Disorders That Affect Learning

Certain disorders are most apt to be noticed in the middle childhood years, when the child enters school. The school setting requires that a child sit still, pay attention, and master a number of academic skills. But some children have difficulty with one or more of these demands. Table 11.2 ■ lists several disorders that can affect a child's learning, especially in school. We will consider attention-deficit/hyperactivity disorder, learning disabilities, and communication disorders in greater depth.

Attention-Deficit/Hyperactivity Disorder (AD/HD)

Nine-year-old Eddie presents a challenge for his teacher. His teacher complains that he is so restless and fidgety that the rest of the class cannot concentrate on their work. He hardly ever sits still. He is in

● TABLE 11.2

Types of Disorders That Affect Learning

Overall intellectual functioning	• Intellectual deficiency (Chapter 12)
Learning disabilities	• Reading disability (dyslexia) (this chapter)
	• Mathematics disability (dyscalculia) (this chapter)
	• Disorder of written expression (this chapter)
Speech disorders	• Articulation disorders (this chapter)
	• Voice disorders (this chapter)
	• Fluency disorders (this chapter)
Physical disabilities	• Visual impairment (this chapter)
	• Hearing impairment (this chapter)
	• Paralysis
Social and emotional disorders	• Attention-deficit/hyperactivity disorder (this chapter)
	• Autism spectrum disorders (Chapter 7)
	• Conduct disorders (Chapter 13)
	• Childhood depression (Chapter 13)
	• Childhood anxiety (Chapter 13)

constant motion, roaming the classroom and talking to other children while they are working. He has been suspended repeatedly for outrageous behaviour, most recently swinging from a fluorescent light fixture, from which he was unable to get himself down. His mother reports that Eddie has been a problem since he was a toddler. By the age of three he had become unbearably restless and demanding. He has never needed much sleep and always awakened before anyone else in the family, making his way downstairs and wrecking things in the living room and kitchen. Once, at the age of four, he unlocked the front door and wandered into traffic; thankfully, he was rescued by a passer-by.

Psychological testing shows Eddie to be average in academic ability, but to have a "virtually nonexistent" attention span. He shows no interest in television or in games or toys that require some concentration. He is unpopular with peers and prefers to ride his bike alone or to play with his dog. He has become disobedient at home and at school and has stolen small amounts of money from his parents and classmates.

Eddie has been treated with methylphenidate (Ritalin), but it was discontinued because it had no effect on his disobedience and stealing. However, it did seem to reduce his restlessness and increase his attention span at school.

—Adapted from Spitzer et al. (2002)

QUESTION » **How does run-of-the-mill failure to "listen" to adults differ from attention-deficit/hyperactivity disorder?** Many parents think that their children do not pay enough attention to them—that they tend to run around as the whim strikes and to do things in their own way. Some inattention, especially at early ages, is to be expected. In **attention-deficit/hyperactivity disorder (AD/HD)**, however, the child shows developmentally inappropriate or excessive inattention, impulsivity, and **hyperactivity** (Bruchmüller et al., 2012). A more thorough list of symptoms is given in Table 11.3 ■. The degree of hyperactive behaviour is crucial, because many normal children are labelled overactive and fidgety from time to time. In fact, if talking too much were the sole criterion for AD/HD, the label would have applied to many of us as children.

The onset of AD/HD occurs by age 12. According to the American Psychiatric Association (2013), the behaviour pattern must have persisted for at least six months for the diagnosis to be made. The hyperactivity and restlessness of children with AD/HD impair their ability to function in school. They simply cannot sit still. They also have difficulty getting along with others. Their disruptive and noncompliant behaviour often elicits punishment from parents. AD/HD is quite common. It is diagnosed in about 5 percent of school-age children and is one of the most common causes of childhood referrals to mental health clinics. AD/HD is many times more commonly diagnosed in boys than in girls (Coles et al., 2012; Nussbaum, 2012).

Some psychologists and educators argue that AD/HD is overdiagnosed (Bruchmüller et al., 2012). That is, many children who do not toe the line in school tend to be diagnosed with AD/HD and are medicated to encourage more acceptable behaviour. Research does suggest that those who diagnose children with AD/HD tend to be "suggestible." That is, they are more likely to diagnose children with the disorder when they are given other sources of information—for example, teachers and parents—to the effect that the children do not adequately control their behaviour (Bruchmüller et al., 2012).

attention-deficit/hyperactivity disorder (AD/HD) A behaviour disorder characterized by excessive inattention, impulsiveness, and hyperactivity

hyperactivity Excessive restlessness and overactivity; one of the primary characteristics of attention-deficit/hyperactivity disorder (AD/HD). Not to be confused with misbehaviour or with high activity levels that are normal during childhood.

BSIP SA/Alamy

A Boy with Attention-Deficit/ Hyperactivity Disorder
Children with hyperactive tendencies are continually on the go, as if their "motors" are constantly running. The psychological disorder we refer to as hyperactivity is not to be confused with the normal high energy levels of children. However, it is sometimes—sometimes—difficult to tell where one ends and the other begins.

Behaviours Connected with Attention-Deficit/Hyperactivity Disorder (AD/HD)

Category	Behaviour
Inattention	• Easily distracted from tasks and activities • Doesn't pay attention to instructions and details • Does not complete work in class or homework • Does not organize tasks and activities • Loses pencils, books, homework assignments
Hyperactivity	• Fidgets in seat in class • Walks around or leaves classroom suddenly during assignments and activities • Sleeps restlessly • Runs around persistently, "like a motor" • Has difficulty playing quietly • Talks excessively
Impulsiveness	• Acts first, thinks second • Goes from one thing to another without completing assignments or activities • "Calls out" in class • Does not wait his or her turn

Source: Adapted from American Psychological Association.

Causes of AD/HD

QUESTION » **What are the causes of AD/HD?** Because AD/HD is characterized in part by excessive motor activity, many theorists focus on possible physical causes. For one thing, AD/HD tends to run in families for both girls and boys with the disorder (Martel et al., 2011). Some researchers suggest that there may be a genetic component to the disorder (Martel et al., 2011). If so, such a genetic component might involve the manner in which children process the brain messenger dopamine (Mazei-Robison et al., 2005; Walitza et al., 2006). Brain-imaging studies support the probability that many genes are involved and that they affect the regulation of dopamine (Walitza et al., 2006).

AD/HD is also found to coexist with other psychological disorders and problems, ranging most commonly from oppositional defiant disorder and anxiety disorders to mood disorders and tics (Biederman et al., 2007; Hasler et al., 2007). Brain-imaging studies have found that the brain chemistry of children who have AD/HD differs in certain respects from that of children who have AD/HD plus other disorders, such as serious mood disorders. This raises the prospect that different causes and treatments will be discovered for various groups of children with AD/HD.

In the 1970s, it was widely believed—because of the arguments and anecdotes of Benjamin Feingold—that artificial food colourings and (benzoate) food preservatives were largely responsible for hyperactivity. Feingold then introduced what was dubbed the "Feingold diet," which removed all such chemicals from foods and, according to Feingold and a few researchers, reduced hyperactivity in children who used the diet. TRUTH OR FICTION REVISITED: Over the years, however, studies of the use of the Feingold diet have yielded conflicting results, and researchers generally agree that food colouring and preservatives are not responsible for the epidemic of AD/HD (Cruz & Bahna, 2006).

Researchers suggest that AD/HD is caused by inhibitory processes that do not work efficiently; that is, children who have AD/HD do not inhibit, or control, impulses that most children are capable of controlling (Hale et al., 2011; Shimoni et al., 2012). But inhibition is defined in somewhat different ways by different theorists. We may distinguish between inhibition that is under the executive control of the brain (a sort of cognitive–neurological inhibition) and inhibition that is normally motivated by emotions such as anxiety and fear (for example, anxiety about disappointing a teacher or fear of getting poor grades). AD/HD probably does not reflect failure to respond to feelings of anxiety or fear. The disorder is more likely to result from a lack of executive control, but the precise nature of this control—its possible neurological aspects, for example—remains poorly understood.

Treatment and Outcome

QUESTION » Why are children who have AD/HD treated with stimulants? TRUTH OR FICTION REVISITED: Stimulants such as Ritalin, which increase the activity of the nervous system, are often used to treat hyperactive children; in fact, they are the most widespread treatment for AD/HD. It may seem ironic that stimulants are used for children who are already overly active. The rationale is that the activity of the hyperactive child stems from inability of the cerebral cortex to inhibit more primitive areas of the brain (Pearson & Crowley, 2012). The drugs block the reuptake (reabsorption) of two neurotransmitters in the brain: dopamine and noradrenaline. Keeping more of these neurotransmitters active has the effect of stimulating the cerebral cortex and facilitating cortical control of primitive areas of the brain.

Children with AD/HD who are given stimulants show increased attention span, improved cognitive and academic performance, and a reduction in disruptive, annoying, and aggressive behaviours (Pearson & Crowley, 2012). The use of stimulants is controversial, however. Some critics argue that stimulants suppress gains in height and weight, do not contribute to academic gains, and lose effectiveness over time. Another concern is that stimulants are overused or misused in an attempt to control normal high activity levels of children at home or in the classroom. Supporters of stimulant treatment argue that many children who have AD/HD are helped by medication. They counter that the suppression of growth appears to be related to the dosage of the drug and that low doses seem to be about as effective as large doses (Evans et al., 2001).

Cognitive behavioural therapy also shows some promise in treating children with AD/HD. This approach attempts to increase the child's self-control and problem-solving abilities through modeling, role-playing, and self-instruction. A Spanish study found that it was possible to teach many children with AD/HD to "stop and think" before giving in to angry impulses and behaving in an aggressive manner (Miranda & Presentacion, 2000). However, the Multimodal Treatment Study sponsored by the National Institute of Mental Health found that stimulant medication was more effective than cognitive behavioural therapy (Greene & Ablon, 2001; Whalen, 2001). Hinshaw (2006) argues that cognitive behavioural programs for children should use clear rewards and behavioural contingencies, and they should involve parents and teachers. Waxmonsky (2005) suggests that children may fare better with medication, whereas adolescents and adults with AD/HD may be able to profit more from cognitive behavioural therapy.

Some children "outgrow" AD/HD, but longitudinal studies have found that at least two-thirds of children with AD/HD continue to exhibit one or more of the core symptoms in adolescence and adulthood (Barkley, 2004; Nigg et al., 2004). Problems in attention, conduct, hyperactivity, and learning frequently continue.

stimulants Drugs that increase the activity of the nervous system.

Learning Disabilities

QUESTION » **What are learning disabilities?** Nelson Rockefeller served as vice president of the United States under Gerald Ford. He was intelligent and well educated. And yet, despite the best of tutors, he could never master reading. Rockefeller suffered from **dyslexia**. **TRUTH OR FICTION REVISITED:** It is true that some children who are intelligent and who are provided with enriched home environments cannot learn how to read or do simple math problems (Ferrer et al., 2010). Many such children have learning disabilities.

Dyslexia is one type of **learning disability**. The term *learning disabilities* refers to a group of disorders characterized by inadequate development of specific academic, language, and speech skills (see Concept Review 11.2). Children with learning disabilities may have problems in math, writing, or reading. Some have difficulty in articulating sounds of speech or in understanding spoken language. Others have problems in motor coordination. Children are usually considered to have a learning disability when they are performing below the level expected for their age and level of intelligence and when there is no evidence of other handicaps such as vision or hearing problems, intellectual disability, or socioeconomic disadvantage (Ferrer et al., 2010). However, some psychologists and educators, such as Frank Vellutino (Vellutino et al., 2004), argue that too much emphasis is placed on the discrepancy between intelligence and reading achievement.

dyslexia A reading disorder characterized by problems such as letter reversals, mirror reading, slow reading, and reduced comprehension (from the Greek roots *dys*, meaning "bad," and *lexikon*, meaning "of words").

learning disabilities A group of disorders characterized by inadequate development of specific academic, language, and speech skills

Concept Review 11.2 Kinds of Learning Disabilities

Dyslexia (difficulty reading)

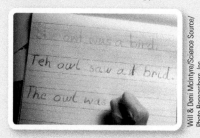
Will & Deni McIntyre/Science Source/ Photo Researchers, Inc

- Reading ability is substantially less than what one would expect considering the individual's age, level of intelligence, and educational background.
- The difficulty in reading interferes with the individual's scholastic achievement or daily living.
- If there is also a sensory or perceptual defect, the reading problems are worse than one would expect with it.

Disorder of written expression

- Makes mistakes in spelling that exceed what one would expect considering the individual's age, level of intelligence, and educational experiences.
- Makes errors in grammar and punctuation; shows difficulty organizing paragraphs.
- Shows anxiety and frustration when attempting to write—for example, breaking pencils and tearing up assignments.
- Typically concurrent with dyslexia.

Dyscalculia (difficulty in mathematics)

- Mathematical ability is substantially less than what one would expect considering the individual's age, level of intelligence, and educational background.
- The math problem interferes with the individual's scholastic achievement or daily living.
- If there is also a sensory or perceptual defect, the problems in mathematics are worse than one would expect with it.

Source: Adapted from Learning Disabilities Association of America (www.ldanatl.org) and National Center for Learning Disabilities (www.ncld.org). Accessed December 6, 2012.

Specific learning disorder is a neurodevelopmental disorder, which is typically first noticed during the school-age years (Diagnostic and Statistical Manual of Mental Disorders, 2013). Children with learning disabilities frequently display various problems. They are more likely than other children to have AD/HD (Schulte-Körne et al., 2006), and as they mature, they are more likely to develop schizophrenia as adolescents or adults (Maneschi et al., 2006). They do not communicate as well with their peers, have poorer social skills, show more behaviour problems in the classroom, and are more likely to experience emotional problems (Frith, 2001; Lyon et al., 2003).

For most children who have learning disabilities, the problem persists through life. But with early recognition and appropriate remediation, many individuals can learn to overcome or compensate for their learning disability (Vellutino et al., 2004).

Dyslexia

It has been estimated that dyslexia affects anywhere from 5 percent to 17.5 percent of children (Shaywitz, 1998). Most studies show that dyslexia is much more common in boys than in girls. Figure 11.1 ■ is a writing sample from a dyslexic child.

In childhood, treatment of dyslexia focuses on remediation (Bakker, 2006; Tijms, 2007). Children are given highly structured exercises to help them become aware of how to blend sounds to form words, such as identifying word pairs that rhyme and pairs that do not rhyme. Later in life, the focus tends to be on accommodation rather than on remediation. For example, college students with dyslexia may be given extra time to do the reading involved in taking tests. Interestingly, college students with dyslexia are frequently excellent at word recognition. Even so, they continue to show problems in decoding new words.

Origins of Dyslexia   QUESTION » **What are the origins of dyslexia?** Current views of dyslexia focus on the ways in which sensory and neurological problems may contribute to reading problems we find in dyslexic individuals, but first let's note that genetic factors appear to be involved in dyslexia. Dyslexia runs in families. It has been estimated that 25–65 percent of children who have one dyslexic parent are dyslexic themselves (Plomin & Walker, 2003). About 40 percent of the siblings of children with dyslexia are also dyslexic.

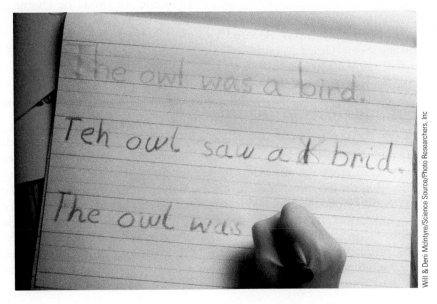

Figure 11.1 ■ A Writing Sample from a Dyslexic Child
Dyslexic children have trouble perceiving letters in their correct orientation. They may perceive letters upside down (confusing *w* with *m*) or reversed (confusing *b* with *d*). This perceptual difficulty may lead to rotations or reversals in their writing, as shown in the sample.

Will & Deni McIntyre/Science Source/Photo Researchers, Inc

Genetic factors may give rise to neurological problems. The problems can involve "faulty wiring" or circulation problems in the left hemisphere of the brain, which is usually involved in language functions (Arduini et al., 2006). The circulation problems result in less oxygen than is desirable. A part of the brain called the angular gyrus lies in the left hemisphere between the visual cortex and Wernicke's area. The angular gyrus "translates" visual information, such as written words, into auditory information (sounds) and sends it on to Wernicke's area. Problems in the angular gyrus may give rise to reading problems by making it difficult for the reader to associate letters with sounds (Grigorenko, 2007; Shaywitz et al., 2006b). Other researchers find evidence that brain abnormalities that pose a risk for schizophrenia also pose a risk for dyslexia, suggesting an overall vulnerability to cognitive deficits (Leonard et al., 2008; Steinbrink et al., 2008).

Some researchers report evidence that dyslexic children have difficulty controlling their eye movements (Boden & Giaschi, 2007), but most researchers today focus on dyslexic individuals' "phonological processing"—that is, the ways in which they make, or do not make, sense of sounds. It was once thought that dyslexic children hear as well as other children, but now it seems that they may not discriminate sounds as accurately as other children do (Bergmann & Wimmer, 2008; Halliday & Bishop, 2006). As a result, *b*'s and *d*'s and *p*'s, for example, may be hard to tell apart at times, creating confusion that impairs reading ability (Boada & Pennington, 2006; Shaywitz et al., 2006a).

We also have the **double-deficit hypothesis** of dyslexia, which suggests that dyslexic children have neurologically based deficits both in *phonological processing* and in *naming speed* (Sawyer, 2006; Vukovic & Siegel, 2006). Therefore, not only do they have difficulty sounding out a *b* as a *b*, but it also takes them longer than other children to name or identify a *b* when they attempt to do so.

Other Learning Disabilities

Other learning disabilities include mathematics disorder and disorder of written expression. *Mathematics disorder* is diagnosed in children who have severe deficiencies in arithmetic skills. They may have problems understanding basic mathematical terms or operations, such as addition and subtraction; decoding mathematical symbols such as + and =; or learning multiplication tables. The problem may become apparent during Grade 1 but often is not recognized until about Grade 2 or 3. Children with *disorder of written expression* have grossly deficient writing skills. The deficiency may be characterized by errors in spelling, grammar, or punctuation, or by difficulty in composing sentences and paragraphs. Severe writing difficulties generally become apparent by age seven (Grade 2), although milder cases may not be recognized until the age of ten (Grade 5) or later.

Communication Disorders

QUESTION » What are communication disorders? **Communication disorders** are persistent problems in understanding or producing language. They include expressive language disorder, mixed receptive/expressive language disorder, phonological disorder, and stuttering. Each of these disorders interferes with academic or occupational functioning or ability to communicate socially.

Expressive language disorder is impairment in the use of spoken language, such as slow vocabulary development, errors in tense, difficulty recalling words, and problems producing sentences of appropriate length and complexity for the individual's age. Children who are affected may also have a phonological (articulation) disorder, compounding their speech problems.

double-deficit hypothesis The theory of dyslexia that suggests that dyslexic children have biological deficits in two areas: *phonological processing* (interpreting sounds) and *naming speed* (for example, identifying letters—such as *b* versus *d*, or *w* versus *m*).

communication disorders Persistent problems in understanding or producing language.

Mixed receptive/expressive language disorder is characterized by difficulties both understanding and producing speech. There may be difficulty understanding words or sentences. In some cases, children have trouble understanding certain word types (such as words expressing differences in quantity—*large, big,* or *huge*), spatial terms (such as *near* or *far*), or sentence types (such as sentences that begin with the word *unlike*). Other cases are marked by difficulty understanding simple words or sentences.

Phonological disorder is a persistent difficulty articulating the sounds of speech, in the absence of defects in the oral speech mechanism or neurological impairment. Children with the disorder may omit, substitute, or mispronounce certain sounds—especially *ch, f, l, r, sh,* and *th,* which most children articulate properly by the time they reach the early school years. It may sound as if they are uttering "baby talk." Children with more severe cases have problems articulating sounds usually mastered during the preschool years: *b, m, t, d, n,* and *h.* Speech therapy is often helpful, and mild cases often resolve themselves by about the age of eight.

Stuttering is a disturbance in the ability to speak fluently with appropriate timing of speech sounds. The lack of normal fluency must be inappropriate for the person's age in order to justify the diagnosis. Stuttering usually begins between two and seven years of age and affects about one child in 100. It is characterized by one or more of the following: (a) repetitions of sounds and syllables; (b) prolongations of certain sounds; (c) interjections of inappropriate sounds; (d) broken words, such as pauses occurring within a spoken word; (e) blocking of speech; (f) circumlocutions (substitutions of alternative words to avoid problematic words); (g) an excess of physical tension when emitting words; and (h) repetitions of monosyllabic whole words (for example, "I-I-I-I am glad to meet you"). Stuttering occurs in three times as many males as females. Most children who stutter—upwards of 80 percent—overcome the problem without any treatment, typically before age 16.

What causes stuttering? Although the question is still unresolved, most researchers believe that genetic and environmental influences interact in producing stuttering (Grigorenko, 2009). Brain scans reveal abnormal patterns of neural activity in the basal ganglia of the brain (Giraud et al., 2008; Lu et al., 2009). Stuttering also appears to have an emotional component. Children who stutter tend to be more emotionally reactive than non-stutterers; when faced with stressful or challenging situations, they become more upset or excited (Karrass et al., 2006). Social anxiety, or overconcern with how others see them, may also contribute to the problem (Mulcahy et al., 2008; Schultz & Heimberg, 2008).

Mainstreaming
Today, most students with mild disabilities spend at least part of their school day in regular classrooms. The goals of mainstreaming include providing broader educational opportunities for students with disabilities and fostering interactions with children without disabilities.

Treatment of communication disorders is generally approached with specialized speech therapy or fluency training and with psychological counselling for anxiety or other emotional problems. The Institute for Stuttering Treatment and Research (www.istar.ualberta.ca) at the University of Alberta in Edmonton, Alberta, focuses on treatment to children who stutter, research in the area of stuttering, and offers advanced professional development to for speech and language pathologists.

Educating Children with Learning and Communication Disorders

QUESTION » Why is inclusion still debated? Special educational programs have been created to meet the needs of schoolchildren who have mild to moderate disorders. These include learning disabilities, communication disorders, emotional disturbance, mild intellectual deficiency, and physical disabilities such as blindness, deafness, or paralysis. Evidence is mixed on whether placing children with disabilities in separate classes can also stigmatize them and segregate them from other children. Special-needs classes also negatively influence teacher expectations. Both the teacher and the students themselves come to expect very little. This negative expectation becomes a self-fulfilling prophecy, and the exceptional students' achievements suffer. In Canada the process of **inclusion** and educating students with exceptionalities is different from the American system. The Constitution Act of 1982 (which includes the Canadian Charter or Rights and Freedom) includes the rights of peoples with disabilities. Another unique feature of the Canadian system is that all provinces and territories have their own Education or School Act governing education within its jurisdiction. Despite having individual provinces and territories overseeing special education services, all educational policy must follow the Charter of Rights (Smith & Foster, 1996). For information about inclusive educational practices in your province check out your provincial or territorial Ministry of Education.

Research evidence on inclusion is mixed. Some studies suggest that children with disabilities achieve more when they are included in regular classrooms. Other studies suggest that many children with disabilities find regular classrooms overwhelming. Clearly, interpreting the research related to this topic is not simple. One confounding factor that muddies our interpretation of inclusion research is the amount of support and resources different school districts receive for implementing full inclusion models. Universal design for learning and differentiated learning are two approaches that have been successfully used to help with inclusive educational practice (Specht, 2013). The Canadian Research Centre on Inclusive Education at Western University is a network of researchers, practitioners, and community partners interested in studying and promoting inclusive education. The centre supplies sources of information for understanding inclusive education in a Canadian context.

Our discussion of problems in learning and communication leads us into an investigation of cognitive development in middle childhood and the conditions that influence it. We address this topic in Chapter 12.

inclusion Most students with mild disabilities spend at least part of their school day in regular classrooms. The goals of inclusion include providing broader educational opportunities for students with exceptionalities and fostering interactions with other children of varying abilities.

Active Review

15. Children with _____ (AD/HD) show developmentally inappropriate or excessive inattention, impulsivity, and hyperactivity.

16. AD/HD is more common among (boys or girls?).

17. AD/HD (does or does not?) tend to run in families.

18. Children with AD/HD are likely to be treated with (stimulants or tranquilizers?).

19. Learning _____ are a group of disorders characterized by inadequate development of specific academic, language, and speech skills.

20. Difficulty learning to read is called _____.

21. Current views of dyslexia focus on the ways in which _____ problems contribute to the perceptual problems we find in dyslexic children.

22. Stuttering (does or does not?) tend to run in families.

Reflect & Relate: Did you have an inclusive classrooms in your grade school? How were students with disabilities treated by other students? How were they treated by teachers? Do you believe that inclusion was helpful for them?

Recite an Active Summary

11.1 Growth Patterns

What patterns of growth occur in middle childhood?

Children tend to gain a little over 5 centimetres in height and 2–3 kilograms in weight per year during middle childhood. Children become more slender. Boys are slightly heavier and taller than girls through the age of nine or ten, when girls begin the adolescent growth spurt. At around age 11, boys develop relatively more muscle tissue, and females develop more fatty tissue.

11.2 Overweight Children

How many children in Canada are overweight? Why are they overweight?

About one-quarter of Canadian children fall into the overweight and obese categories, and the prevalence of being overweight and obese has been increasing. Overweight children usually do not outgrow "baby fat." During childhood, heavy children are often rejected by their peers. Heredity plays a role in being overweight. Children with high numbers of fat cells feel food-deprived sooner than other children. Overweight parents may encourage overeating by keeping fattening foods in the home. Sedentary habits also foster being overweight.

11.3 Childhood Asthma

What is childhood asthma?

Asthma is an allergy-type respiratory disorder characterized by spasms in the lungs, difficulty breathing, wheezing, often coughing (dry hacking), and a feeling of tightness in the chest that prevents the sufferer from getting enough air. Treatments for asthma include nasal steroids and bronchodilators.

11.4 Motor Development

What changes in motor development occur in middle childhood?

Middle childhood is marked by increases in speed, strength, agility, and balance. Children show regular improvement in gross motor skills and are often eager to participate in athletic activities, such as ball games that require movement of large muscles. Muscles grow stronger, and pathways that connect the cerebellum to the cortex become more myelinated. Reaction time gradually decreases. Fine motor skills also improve; most six- to seven-year-olds tie their shoelaces and hold pencils as adults do.

Are there gender differences in motor skills?

Boys have slightly greater overall strength, whereas girls have better coordination and flexibility, which are valuable in dancing, balancing, and gymnastics. Boys generally receive more encouragement than girls to excel in athletics.

Are children in Canada physically fit? If not, why not?

Most children in the Canada are not physically fit. One reason is the amount of time they spend in sedentary behaviour such as watching television and playing digital games.

11.5 Disorders that Affect Learning

How does run-of-the-mill failure to "listen" to adults differ from attention-deficit/hyperactivity disorder?

Attention-deficit/hyperactivity disorder (AD/HD) involves lack of attention, impulsivity, and hyperactivity. AD/HD impairs children's ability to function in school. AD/HD tends to be overdiagnosed and overmedicated.

What are the causes of AD/HD?

AD/HD runs in families and often coexists with other problems. Abnormalities may suggest brain damage. Children with AD/HD do not inhibit impulses that most children control, suggesting poor executive control in the brain.

Why are children who have AD/HD treated with stimulants?

Stimulants are used to stimulate the cerebral cortex to inhibit more primitive areas of the brain. Stimulants increase the attention span and academic performance of children with AD/HD, but there are side effects, and the medications may be used too often. Cognitive behavioural therapy can also help teach children self-control.

What are learning disabilities?

Learning disabilities are characterized by inadequate development of specific academic, language, and speech skills. Children may be diagnosed with a learning disability when their performance is below that expected for their age and level of intelligence. Learning disabilities tend to persist.

What are the origins of dyslexia?

Current views of dyslexia focus on the ways in which neurological problems may contribute to perceptual problems. Genetic factors appear to be involved because dyslexia runs in families. The double-deficit hypothesis suggests that dyslexic children have neurologically based deficits in phonological processing and in naming speed.

What are communication disorders?

Communication disorders are persistent problems in understanding or producing language. They include expressive language disorder, mixed receptive/expressive language disorder, phonological disorder, and stuttering.

Why is inclusion still debated?

Research on inclusion is mixed. Some studies suggest that children with disabilities achieve more when they are included. Other studies suggest that many children with disabilities find regular classrooms overwhelming.

Clearly, interpreting the research related to this topic is not simple. One confounding factor that muddies our interpretation of inclusion research is the amount of support and resources different school districts receive for implementing full inclusion models. Universal design for learning and differentiated learning are two approaches that have been successfully used to help with inclusive educational practice.

Key Terms

growth spurt   368
reaction time   377
attention-deficit/hyperactivity
     disorder (AD/HD)   381

hyperactivity   381
stimulants   383
dyslexia   384
learning disabilities   384

double-deficit hypothesis   386
communication disorders   386
inclusion   388

Active Learning Resources

Go to *Voyages in Development's* CourseMate at **www .nelsonbrain.com**, where you will find an interactive eBook, flashcards, Pre-Lecture Quizzes, Section Quizzes, Exam Practice, videos, and more.

Monkey Business Images/Shutterstock.com

Major Topics

MIDDLE CHILDHOOD:
Cognitive Development

12

Truth or Fiction?

Did you hear the one about the judge who pounded her gavel and yelled, "Order! Order in the court!"? "A hamburger and French fries, Your Honour," responded the defendant. Or how about this one? "I saw a man-eating lion at the zoo." "Big deal! I saw a man eating snails at a restaurant." Or how about, "Make me a glass of chocolate milk!"? "Poof! You're a glass of chocolate milk." These children's jokes are based on ambiguities in the meanings of words and phrases. Most seven-year-olds find the joke about order in the court funny and can recognize that the word *order* has more than one meaning. The jokes about the man-eating lion and chocolate milk strike most children as funny at about the age of 11, when they can understand ambiguities in grammatical structure.

Children make enormous strides in their cognitive development during the middle childhood years. Their thought processes and language become more logical and more complex. In this chapter, we follow the course of cognitive development in middle childhood. First, we continue our discussion of Piaget's cognitive-developmental view from Chapter 9, also reflecting on cognitive-developmental views of moral development. We then consider the information-processing approach that has been stimulated by our experience with the computer. We next explore the development of intelligence, ways of measuring it, and the roles of heredity and environment in shaping it. Finally, we turn to the development of language.

mediaphotos/Thinkstock

12.1 Piaget: The Concrete-Operational Stage

QUESTION » **What is meant by the stage of concrete operations?** According to Piaget, the typical child is entering the stage of **concrete operations** by the age of seven. In the stage of concrete operations, which lasts until about the age of 12, children show the beginnings of the capacity for adult logic. However, their thought processes, or operations, generally involve tangible objects rather than abstract ideas. This is why we refer to their thinking as "concrete."

The thinking of the concrete-operational child is characterized by **reversibility** and flexibility. Consider adding the numbers 2 and 3 to get 5. Adding is an operation. The operation is reversible in that the child can then subtract 2 from 5 to get 3. There is flexibility in that the child can also subtract 3 from 5 to get the number 2. To the concrete-operational child, adding and subtracting are not just rote activities. The concrete-operational child recognizes that there are relationships among numbers—that operations can be carried out according to rules. This understanding lends concrete-operational thought flexibility and reversibility.

Concrete-operational children are less egocentric than preoperational children. Their abilities to take on the roles of others and to view the world and themselves from other peoples' perspectives are greatly expanded. They recognize that people see things in different ways because of different situations and different sets of values.

Compared with preoperational children, who can focus on only one dimension of a problem at a time, concrete-operational children can engage in **decentration**; that is, they can focus on multiple parts of a problem at once. Decentration has implications for conservation and other intellectual undertakings.

Conservation

Concrete-operational children show understanding of the laws of conservation. The seven-year-old girl in Figure 12.1 ■ would say that the flattened ball still has the same amount of clay. If asked why, she might reply, "Because you can roll it up again like the other one." This answer shows reversibility.

concrete operations The third stage in Piaget's scheme, characterized by flexible, reversible thought concerning tangible objects and events.

reversibility According to Piaget, recognition that processes can be undone, leaving things as they were before. Reversibility is a factor in conservation of the properties of substances.

decentration Simultaneous focusing (centring) on more than one aspect or dimension of a problem or situation.

Figure 12.1 ■ Conservation of Mass
This girl is in the concrete-operational stage of cognitive development. She has rolled two clay balls. In the photo on the left, she agrees that both have the same amount (mass) of clay. In the photo on the right, she (gleefully) flattens one clay ball. When asked whether the two pieces still have the same amount of clay, she says yes.

© Judy Allen Biggs

The concrete-operational girl knows that objects can have several properties or dimensions. Things that are tall can also be heavy or light. Things that are red can also be round or square, or thick or thin. Knowledge of this principle enables the girl to decentre and to avoid focusing on only the diameter of the clay pancake. By attending to both the height and the width of the clay, she recognizes that the loss in height compensates for the gain in width.

Children do not necessarily develop conservation in all kinds of tasks simultaneously. Conservation of mass usually develops first, followed by conservation of weight and conservation of volume. Piaget theorized that the gains of the concrete-operational stage are so tied to specific events that achievement in one area does not necessarily transfer to achievement in another.

OBSERVING CHILDREN, UNDERSTANDING OURSELVES

Piaget's Concrete-Operational Stage

Children in Piaget's concrete-operational stage not only can understand that both glasses contain the same amount of water no matter what the shape of the glass is but also can explain why.

What is the concrete-operational stage of cognitive development? How is this child demonstrating reliance on concrete operations?

From Rathus. *Childhood and Adolescence*, 5E. © 2014 South-Western, a part of Cengage Learning, Inc. Reproduced by permission. www.cengage.com/permissions

Go to www.nelson.com/voyages2ce to watch the video, answer the questions, and e-mail your responses to your professor.

Transitivity

Question of the day: If your parents are older than you are and you are older than your children, are your parents older than your children? (How do you know?)

We have posed some tough questions in this book, but the one about your parents is a real ogre. The answer, of course, is yes. But how did you arrive at this answer? If you said yes simply on the basis of knowing that your parents are older than your children (e.g., 58 and 56 compared with 5 and 3), your answer did not require concrete-operational thought. One aspect of concrete-operational thought is the principle of **transitivity**: If A exceeds B in some property (say, age or height) and if B exceeds C, then A must also exceed C.

Researchers can assess whether or not children understand the principle of transitivity by asking them to place objects in a series, or order, according to some property or trait, such as lining up one's family members according to age, height, or weight. Placing objects in a series is termed **seriation**. Let's consider some examples with preoperational and concrete-operational children.

Piaget frequently assessed children's abilities at seriation by asking them to place ten sticks in order of size. Children who are four or five years of age usually place the sticks in a random sequence or in small groups, as in small, medium, or large. Six- to seven-year-old children, who are in transition between the preoperational and concrete-operational stages, may place the sticks in the proper sequence. However, they usually do so by trial and error, rearranging their series a number of times. In other words, they are capable of comparing two sticks and deciding that one is longer than the other, but their overall perspective seems limited to the pair they are comparing at the time and does not seem to encompass the entire array.

But consider the approach of seven- and eight-year-olds who are capable of concrete operations. They go about the task systematically, usually without error. They look over the array of ten sticks and then select either the longest or the shortest and place it at the point from which they will build their series. Then they select the next longest (or next shortest) and continue in this fashion until the task is complete.

Knowledge of the principle of transitivity enables concrete-operational children to go about their task unerringly. They realize that if stick A is longer

transitivity The principle that if A is greater than B in a property and B is greater than C, then A is greater than C.

seriation Placing objects in an order or series according to a property or trait.

Figure 12.2 ■ A Grid for Demonstrating the Development of Seriation

To classify these 49 leaves, children must be able to focus on two dimensions at once: size and lightness. They must also recognize that if quantity A of a particular property exceeds quantity B and quantity B exceeds quantity C, then quantity A must also exceed quantity C. This relationship is called the *principle of transitivity*.

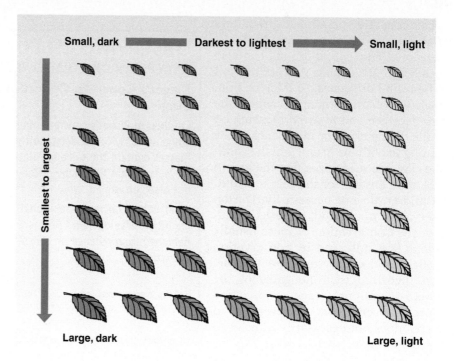

Small, dark   **Darkest to lightest**   Small, light

Smallest to largest

Large, dark   Large, light

than stick B and stick B is longer than stick C, then stick A is also longer than stick C. After putting stick C in place, they need not double-check to make sure it will be shorter than stick A; they know it will be.

Concrete-operational children also have the decentration capacity that enables them to seriate in two dimensions at once. Consider a seriation task used by Piaget and his long-time colleague, Barbel Inhelder. In this test, children are given 49 leaves and asked to classify them according to size and brightness (from small to large and from dark to light) (see Figure 12.2 ■). As the grid is completed from left to right, the leaves become lighter. As it is filled in from top to bottom, the leaves become larger. Preoperational six-year-olds can usually order the leaves according to size or brightness, but not both simultaneously. But concrete-operational children of age seven or eight can work with both dimensions at once and fill in the grid properly.

A number of researchers have argued that children can seriate earlier than Piaget believed and that Piaget's results reflected the demand characteristics of his experiments (De Leeuw et al., 2004; Siegler & Alibali, 2005). This may be so, but the sequence of developments in seriation and transitivity seems to have been captured fairly well by Piaget.

Class Inclusion

Another example of an operation is **class inclusion**, which we learned about in Chapter 9. In the example in Chapter 9 (p. 299), a four-year-old was shown pictures of four cats and six dogs. When asked whether there were more dogs or more animals, she said more dogs. This preoperational child apparently could not focus on the two subclasses (dogs and cats) and the larger class (animals) at the same time. But concrete-operational children can focus on two dimensions (in this case, classes and subclasses) at the same time. Therefore, they are more likely to answer the question about the dogs and the animals correctly (Chapman & McBride, 1992; Deneault & Ricard, 2006). Their thought still remains concrete in that they will give you the correct answer if you ask them about dogs and animals (or daffodils and flowers), but not if you attempt

class inclusion The principle that one category or class of things can include several subclasses.

to phrase the question in terms of abstract symbols, such as A, B1, and B2. As with other areas of cognitive development, researchers have taken issue with Piaget's views of the ages at which class-inclusion skills develop. They have argued that language continues to pose hazards for the children being tested. Aspects of concrete-operational thinking are summarized in Concept Review 12.1.

Applications of Piaget's Theory to Education

QUESTION » Can we apply Piaget's theory of cognitive development to educational practices? It seems that we can (Crain, 2000; Mayer, 2008). Piaget pointed out some applications himself. First, Piaget believed that learning

Concept Review 12.1 Aspects of Concrete-Operational Thinking

Conservation

Concrete-operational children show conservation of mass and number.

As you may remember, the girl on the right shows conservation of the mass of the clay. Refer to Figure 9.3 (p. 299), showing the experiment using pennies to test conservation of number. A concrete-operational child will conserve number and say that both panels have the same number of nickels. Preoperational children will say that the wider row has "more."

© Judy Allen Biggs

Child is shown two rows of nickels. | Experimenter moves nickels in one row.

Hemera Technologies/Thinkstock

Seriation

A concrete-operational child understands the principle of transitivity (if A > B and B > C, then A > C). Therefore, the child can place the sticks in order from longest to shortest.

Class Inclusion

Here are ten animals, including six dogs. When asked whether there are more dogs or more animals, the preoperational child, focusing on one aspect of the problem at a time, may see that there are more dogs than cats and say "dogs." The concrete-operational child is more likely to recognize that the class "animals" includes both "dogs" and "cats" and thus will answer "animals."

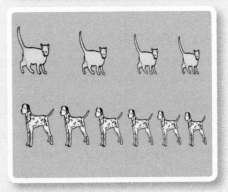

CHAPTER 12 MIDDLE CHILDHOOD: COGNITIVE DEVELOPMENT

involves active discovery. Kamii, Lewis, and Kirklad (2001) examined the usefulness of manipulatives (e.g., tanagrams, counters, cards used in games) in helping children acquire logio-mathematical knowledge. They noted that a rigid use of manipulatives—without the possibility of exploration and problem solving and minimal teacher intervention. If a child is struggling with a problem, the authors recommend that a simpler problem be given (and allowing them to work through that one) rather than pointing out the "missing step" to the child. Other researchers (e.g., Carbonneau, Marley, & Selig, 2013; Marley & Carbonneau, 2014; Sherman & Bisanz, 2009) have also found that instructional strategies that incorporate the use of manipulatives in math have positive results. However, Carbonneau and colleagues do caution that the use of manipulatives is dependent on other factors such as level of instructional guidance, the particular mathematical concept being taught, the developmental stage of students, and amount of instructional time. Therefore, teachers should not simply try to impose knowledge on the child but, rather, should find interesting and stimulating materials.

Second, instruction should be geared to the child's level of development. When teaching a concrete-operational child about fractions, for example, the teacher should not just lecture but should allow the child to divide concrete objects into parts. Third, Piaget believed that learning to take into account the perspectives of others is a key ingredient in the development of both cognition and morality. Accordingly, he thought that teachers should promote group discussions and interactions among their students.

Evaluation of Piaget's Theory

Although Piaget's theory has led many psychologists to recast their concepts of children, it has also met with criticism on several grounds. As noted in Chapters 6 and 9, some researchers have shown that Piaget underestimated children's abilities. Modified task demands suggest that children are capable of conservation and other concrete-operational tasks earlier than Piaget believed. Cognitive skills may develop more independently and continuously than Piaget thought—not in stages. For example, conservation does not arrive all at once. Children develop conservation for mass, weight, and volume at different ages. The onset of conservation can be seen in terms of the gradual accumulation of problem-solving abilities instead of suddenly changing cognitive structures (Flavell et al., 2002). However, the sequences of development—which are at the core of Piaget's theory—still appear to remain the same. In sum, Piaget's theoretical edifice has been rocked, but it has not been dashed to rubble.

In the next section, we revisit Piaget and examine his views on children's decisions about right and wrong. Then we consider the views of Lawrence Kohlberg on the same topic.

Active Review

1. Concrete-operational children are (more or less?) egocentric than preoperational children.

2. The principle of _____ holds that if A exceeds B and B exceeds C, then A must exceed C.

3. Class _____ involves the ability to recognize that one class of things (A) can include subclasses (B₁ and B₂).

Reflect & Relate: Logan becomes angry that Harper wants to break off their relationship and beats her so badly that she must remain in the hospital for six months. Jacob makes a mistake at the nuclear energy plant where he works, causing a nuclear accident in which a great deal of radiation is released, killing 300 people within a week and shortening the lives of more than a million people because of cancer. Which person has done something naughtier: Logan or Jacob? Explain your viewpoint. (Now you are ready to read the next section.)

12.2 Moral Development: The Child as Judge

Moral development is a complex issue with both cognitive and behavioural aspects. On a cognitive level, moral development concerns the basis on which children make judgments that an act is right or wrong. In this section, we examine the contributions of Jean Piaget and Lawrence Kohlberg to our understanding of children's moral development.

Piaget and Kohlberg argued that moral reasoning exhibits the same cognitive-developmental pattern around the world. The moral considerations that children weigh at a given age are likely to reflect the values of the social and cultural settings in which they are being reared. However, moral reasoning is also theorized to reflect the orderly unfolding of cognitive processes (Lapsley, 2006). Moral reasoning is related to the child's overall cognitive development.

Piaget's Theory of Moral Development

QUESTION » How does Piaget view the development of moral reasoning? For years, Piaget observed children playing games such as marbles and making judgments on the seriousness of the wrongdoing of characters in stories. On the basis of these observations, Piaget (1932) concluded that children's moral judgments develop in two major overlapping stages: moral realism and autonomous morality.

The Stage of Moral Realism

The first stage is usually referred to as the stage of **moral realism**—also termed **objective morality**. During this stage, which emerges at about the age of five, children consider behaviour to be correct when it conforms to authority or to the rules of the game. When asked why something should be done in a certain way, the five-year-old may answer, "Because that's the way to do it" or "Because my Mommy says so."

At about the age of five, children perceive rules as embedded in the structure of things. Rules, to them, reflect ultimate reality—hence the term *moral realism*. Rules and right and wrong are seen as absolute. They are not seen as deriving from people's efforts to meet social needs.

Another consequence of viewing rules as embedded in the fabric of the world is **immanent justice**, or automatic retribution. Immanent justice reasoning consists of thinking that negative experiences are punishment for prior misdeeds, even when realistic causal links are absent (Callan et al., 2006). Five- or six-year-old children who lie or steal usually believe that they will be found out or at least punished for their acts. If they trip and scrape their knees, they may assume that this accident represents punishment for a transgression.

TRUTH OR FICTION REVISITED: It is true that you are guilty in the eyes of a five-year-old even if your behaviour was an accident. Preoperational children tend to focus on only one dimension at a time. Therefore, they judge the wrongness of an act only in terms of the amount of damage done, not in terms of the intentions of the wrongdoer. Children in the stage of moral realism are tough judges indeed. They do not excuse the person who harms by accident. As an illustration, consider children's response to Piaget's story about the broken cups. Piaget told children a story in which one child breaks 15 cups accidentally and another child breaks one cup deliberately. Which child is naughtier? Which should be punished more? Children in the stage of moral realism typically say that the child who did the most damage is naughtier and should be punished more. The amount of damage is more important than the wrongdoer's intentions (Piaget, 1932).

Fuse/Thinkstock

Moral Realism
It looks bad, but Mom asked her to find the car keys. Mom wasn't thinking of having her go through her purse, however. If the girl breaks things or drops them on the floor in the effort, is she being "bad"? Children in the stage of moral realism might well say "yes," because they focus on the damage done, not on the intentions of the wrongdoer.

moral realism According to Piaget, the stage during which children judge acts as moral when they conform to authority or to the rules of the game. Morality at this stage is perceived as embedded in the structure of the universe.

objective morality The perception of morality as objective—that is, as existing outside the cognitive functioning of people; a characteristic of Piaget's stage of moral realism.

immanent justice The view that retribution for wrongdoing is a direct consequence of the wrongdoing, reflecting the belief that morality is embedded within the structure of the universe.

The Stage of Autonomous Morality

Piaget found that when children reach the ages of 9–11, they begin to show **autonomous reality**. Their moral judgments tend to become more self-governed. Children come to view social rules as arbitrary agreements that can be changed. Children no longer automatically view obedience to authority figures as right. They realize that circumstances can require breaking rules.

Children who show autonomous morality are capable of flexible operational thought. They can focus simultaneously on multiple dimensions, so they consider not only social rules but also the motives of the wrongdoer.

Children in this stage also show a greater capacity to take the point of view of others—to empathize with them. Decentration and increased empathy prompt children to weigh the intentions of the wrongdoer more heavily than the amount of damage done. The child who broke one cup deliberately may be seen as more deserving of punishment than the child who broke 15 cups accidentally. Children become capable of considering mitigating circumstances. Accidents are less likely to be considered crimes.

Piaget assumed that autonomous morality usually develops as a result of cooperative peer relationships. But he also believed that parents could help foster autonomous morality by creating egalitarian relationships with their children and explaining the reasons for social rules. As we will see in the next section, knowledge of social rules is also a key factor in Lawrence Kohlberg's theory of moral development.

Kohlberg's Theory of Moral Development

QUESTION » How does Kohlberg view the development of moral reasoning? Lawrence Kohlberg (1981, 1985) advanced the cognitive-developmental theory of moral development by elaborating on the kinds of information children use and on the complexities of moral reasoning. Before we discuss Kohlberg's views, read the following tale, which Kohlberg used in his research, and answer the questions that follow.

> In Europe a woman was near death from a special kind of cancer. There was one drug that the doctors thought might save her. It was a form of radium that a druggist in the same town had recently discovered. The drug was expensive to make, but the druggist was charging 10 times what the drug cost him to make. He paid $200 for the radium and charged $2000 for a small dose of the drug. The sick woman's husband, Heinz, went to everyone he knew to borrow the money, but he could only get together about $1000, which was half of what it cost. He told the druggist that his wife was dying and asked him to sell it cheaper or let him pay later. But the druggist said: "No, I discovered the drug and I'm going to make money from it." So Heinz got desperate and broke into the man's store to steal the drug for his wife.
>
> —Kohlberg (1969)

Kohlberg emphasized the importance of being able to view the moral world from the perspective of another person (Krebs & Denton, 2005; Lapsley & Hill, 2008). Look at this situation from Heinz's perspective. What do you think? Should Heinz have tried to steal the drug? Was he right or wrong? As you can see from Table 12.1 ■, the issue is more complicated than a simple yes or no. Heinz is caught in a moral dilemma in which legal or social rules (in this case, laws against stealing) are pitted against a strong human need (Heinz's desire to save his wife). According to Kohlberg's theory, children and adults arrive at yes or no answers for different reasons. These reasons can be classified according to the level of moral development they reflect.

autonomous morality The second stage in Piaget's cognitive-developmental theory of moral development. In this stage, children base moral judgments on the intentions of the wrongdoer more so than on the amount of damage done. Social rules are viewed as agreements that can be changed.

Kohlberg's Levels and Stages of Moral Development

Stage of Development	Examples of Moral Reasoning that Support Heinz's Stealing the Drug	Examples of Moral Reasoning that Oppose Heinz's Stealing the Drug
Level I: Preconventional—Typically Begins in Early Childhood[a]		
Stage 1: Judgments guided by obedience and the prospect of punishment (the consequences of the behaviour)	It is not wrong to take the drug. Heinz did try to pay the druggist for it, and it is only worth $200, not $2000.	Taking things without paying is wrong because it is against the law. Heinz will get caught and go to jail.
Stage 2: Naively egoistic, instrumental orientation (things are right when they satisfy people's needs)	Heinz ought to take the drug because his wife really needs it. He can always pay the druggist back.	Heinz should not take the drug. If he gets caught and winds up in jail, it won't do his wife any good.
Level II: Conventional—Typically Begins in Middle Childhood		
Stage 3: Good-boy/good-girl orientation (moral behaviour helps others and is socially approved)	Stealing is a crime, so it is bad, but Heinz should take the drug to save his wife or else people would blame him for letting her die.	Stealing is a crime. Heinz should not just take the drug because his family will be dishonoured and they will blame him.
Stage 4: Law-and-order orientation (moral behavior is doing one's duty and showing respect for authority)	Heinz must take the drug to do his duty to save his wife. Eventually, he has to pay the druggist for it, however.	If we all took the law into our own hands, civilization would fall apart, so Heinz should not steal the drug.
Level III: Postconventional—Typically Begins in Adolescence[b]		
Stage 5: Contractual, legalistic orientation (one must weigh pressing human needs against society's need to maintain social order)	This thing is complicated because society has a right to maintain law and order, but Heinz has to take the drug to save his wife.	I can see why Heinz feels he has to take the drug, but laws exist for the benefit of society as a whole and cannot simply be cast aside.
Stage 6: Universal ethical principles orientation (people must follow universal ethical principles and their own conscience, even if it means breaking the law)	In this case, the law comes into conflict with the principle of the sanctity of human life. Heinz must take the drug because his wife's life is more important than the law.	If Heinz truly believes that stealing the drug is worse than letting his wife die, he should not take it. People have to make sacrifices to do what they think is right.

[a]Tends to be used less often in middle childhood.
[b]May not develop at all.

Children (and adults) are faced with many moral dilemmas. Consider cheating in school. When children fear failing a test, they may be tempted to cheat. Different children may decide not to cheat for different reasons. One child may simply fear getting caught. A second child may decide that it is more important to live up to her moral principles than to get the highest possible grade. In each case, the child's decision is not to cheat. However, the cognitive processes behind each decision reflect different levels of reasoning.

As a stage theorist, Kohlberg argued that the developmental stages of moral reasoning follow the same sequence in all children. Children progress at different rates, and not all children (or adults) reach the highest stage. But children must experience Stage 1 before they enter Stage 2, and so on. According to Kohlberg, there are three levels of moral development and two stages within each level.

Let us return to Heinz and see how responses to the questions we have posed can reflect different levels and stages of moral development.

The Preconventional Level

At the **preconventional level**, children base their moral judgments on the consequences of their behaviour. For instance, Stage 1 is oriented toward obedience and punishment. Good behaviour means being obedient, which enables one to avoid punishment. According to Stage 1 reasoning, Heinz could be

preconventional level According to Kohlberg, a period during which moral judgments are based largely on expectations of rewards or punishments.

urged to steal the drug because he did ask to pay for it first. But he could also be urged not to steal the drug so that he will not be sent to jail (see Table 12.1).

In Stage 2, good behaviour allows people to satisfy their own needs and, perhaps, the needs of others. A Stage 2 reason for stealing the drug is that Heinz's wife needs it. Therefore, stealing the drug—the only way of attaining it—is not wrong. A Stage 2 reason for not stealing the drug is that Heinz's wife might die even if he does so. Thus, he might wind up in jail needlessly.

In a study of American children aged seven through 16, Kohlberg (1963) found that Stage 1 and 2 types of moral judgments were offered most frequently by seven- and ten-year-olds. There was a steep falling off of Stage 1 and 2 judgments after age ten.

The Conventional Level

In the **conventional level** of moral reasoning, right and wrong are judged by conformity to conventional (family, religious, societal) standards of right and wrong. According to the Stage 3 "good-boy/good-girl" orientation, it is good to meet the needs and expectations of others. Moral behaviour is what is "normal"—what the majority does. From the Stage 3 perspective, Heinz should steal the drug because that is what a "good husband" would do. It is "natural" or "normal" to try to help one's wife. Or Heinz should not steal the drug because "good people do not steal." Stage 3 judgments also focus on the role of sympathy—on the importance of doing what will make someone else feel good or better.

In Stage 4, moral judgments are based on rules that maintain the social order. Showing respect for authority and duty is valued highly. From this perspective, one could argue that Heinz must steal the drug because it is his duty to save his wife. He would pay the druggist when he could. Or one could argue that Heinz should not steal the drug because he would be breaking the law. He might also be contributing to the breakdown of the social order. Many people do not develop beyond the conventional level.

Kohlberg (1963) found that Stage 3 and 4 types of judgments emerge during middle childhood. They are all but absent among seven-year-olds. However, they are reported by about 20 percent of ten-year-olds (and by higher percentages of adolescents). Developmental critics of Kohlberg's approach argue that moral reasoning can be achieved earlier than what Kohlberg initially proposed, and Kohlberg underestimated children's cognitive abilities (Turiel, 1983, 1998, 2002).

A domain theory approach to moral development frames morality as a universal domain, whereby prescriptive and formal rules are applied to solve concrete moral dilemmas and problems (Keefer, 2006). Domain theorists argue that moral values and knowledge are neutral and free of cultural norms and personal beliefs (Keefer, 2006). Studies conducted with young children using creative methodologies including questioning and interviewing were able to distinguish between moral transgressions versus social personal opinion (Rest et al., 1999; Nucci, 2001).

The Postconventional Level

At the **postconventional level**, moral reasoning is based on the person's own moral standards. If this level of reasoning develops at all, it is found among adolescents and adults (see Table 12.1).

In Chapter 15, we discuss the postconventional level in depth. We include Carol Gilligan's research showing that although girls' moral judgments have frequently been considered inferior to boys', girls actually consider more factors in arriving at their judgments of right and wrong. We also evaluate Kohlberg's theory and see that other theorists are proposing major modifications.

conventional level According to Kohlberg, a period during which moral judgments largely reflect social rules and conventions.

postconventional level According to Kohlberg, a period during which moral judgments are derived from moral principles and people look to themselves to set moral standards.

4. Piaget believed that children's moral judgments develop in two stages: moral realism and _____ morality.

5. Preoperational children judge the wrongness of an act in terms of the (amount of damage done or intentions of the wrongdoer?).

6. In Kohlberg's _____ level, children base their moral judgments on the consequences of their behaviour.

7. At the _____ level, right and wrong are judged by conformity to conventional (family, religious, societal) standards of right and wrong.

Reflect & Relate: Do you believe that Heinz should have taken the drug without paying? Why or why not? What does your reasoning suggest about your level of moral development?

12.3 Information Processing: Learning, Remembering, Problem Solving

QUESTION » **What is the difference between Piaget's view of cognitive development and the information-processing approach?** Whereas Piaget looked on children as budding scientists, psychologists who view cognitive development in terms of **information processing** see children (and adults) as akin to computer systems. Sort of. Children, like computers, obtain information (input) from the environment, store it, retrieve it, manipulate it, and then respond to it overtly (output). One goal of the information-processing approach is to learn how children store, retrieve, and manipulate information—how their "mental programs" develop. Information-processing theorists also study the development of children's strategies for processing information (Courage & Cowan, 2009; Pressley & Hilden, 2006).

Although something may be gained from thinking of children as computers, children, of course, are not computers. Children are self-aware and capable of creativity and intuition.

In the following sections, we discuss these key elements in information processing:

- *Development of selective attention*—development of children's abilities to focus on the elements of a problem and find solutions
- *Development of the capacity for storage and retrieval of information*—development of the capacity of memory and of children's understanding of the processes of memory and how to strengthen and use memory
- *Development of strategies for processing information*—development of the ability to solve problems (for example, by finding the correct formula and applying it)

Development of Selective Attention

A key cognitive process is the ability to pay attention to relevant features of a task. The ability to focus one's attention and screen out distractions advances steadily through middle childhood (Li et al, 2009; Passow et al., 2013; Waszak et al., 2010; Rubia et al., 2006). Preoperational children who are engaged in problem solving tend to focus (or centre) their attention on one element of the problem at a time—a major reason why they lack conservation. Concrete-operational children, by contrast, can attend to multiple aspects of the problem at once, which enables them to conserve number, volume, and so on.

A seminal experiment by Strutt and colleagues (1975) illustrates how selective attention and the ability to ignore distraction develop during middle

information processing The view in which cognitive processes are compared to the functions of computers. The theory deals with the input, storage, retrieval, manipulation, and output of information. The focus is on the development of children's strategies for solving problems— their "mental programs."

Figure 12.3 ■ Development of the Ability to Ignore Distractions

Strutt and his colleagues demonstrated how the ability to ignore distraction develops during middle childhood. The effect of irrelevant dimensions on sorting speed was determined by subtracting the speed of the sort in the no-irrelevant-dimension condition from the speed in the other two conditions. As shown here, irrelevant information interfered with sorting ability for all age groups, but older children were less affected than younger ones.

Source: Strutt et al. (1975).

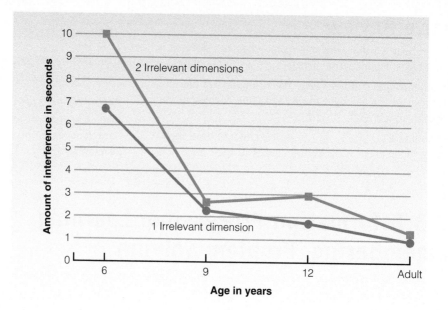

childhood. The researchers asked children between 6 and 12 years of age to sort a deck of cards as quickly as possible on the basis of the figures depicted on each card (e.g., circle versus square). In one condition, only the relevant dimension (form) was shown on each card. In another condition, a dimension not relevant to the sorting also was present (e.g., a horizontal or vertical line in the figure). In a third condition, two irrelevant dimensions were present (e.g., a star above or below the figure, in addition to a horizontal or vertical line in the figure). As seen in Figure 12.3 ■, the irrelevant information interfered with sorting ability for all age groups, but older children were much less affected than younger children. In the next section, we will learn more about how children gain the ability to store and retrieve information.

Developments in the Storage and Retrieval of Information

QUESTION » **What is meant by the term memory?** Keep in mind that the word **memory** is not a scientific term, even though psychologists and other scientists may use it for the sake of convenience. Psychologists usually use the term to refer to the processes of storing and retrieving information. Many, but not all, psychologists divide memory functioning into three major processes or structures: sensory memory, working memory (short-term memory), and long-term memory (see Figure 12.4 ■).

Sensory Memory

When we look at an object and then blink our eyes, the visual impression of the object lasts for a fraction of a second in what is called **sensory memory** or the **sensory register**. Then the "trace" of the stimulus decays. The concept of sensory memory applies to all the senses. For example, when we are introduced to somebody, the trace of the sound of the name also decays, but as we will see in the next section, we can maintain the name in memory by focusing on it.

Working Memory (Short-Term Memory)

When children focus their attention on a stimulus in the sensory register, it tends to be retained in **working memory** (also called *short-term memory*) for

memory The processes by which we store and retrieve information.

sensory memory The structure of memory that is first encountered by sensory input. Information is maintained in sensory memory for only a fraction of a second.

sensory register Another term for sensory memory.

working memory The structure of memory that can hold a sensory stimulus for up to 30 seconds after the trace decays. Also called "short-term memory."

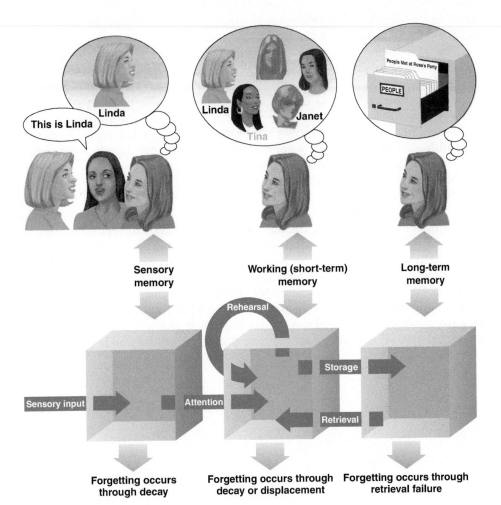

Figure 12.4 ■ **The Structure of Memory**
Many psychologists divide memory into three processes, or "structures." Sensory information enters the registers of sensory memory, where memory traces are held briefly before decaying. If we attend to the information, much of it is transferred to working memory (also called short-term memory), where it may decay or be displaced if it is not transferred to long-term memory. We usually use rehearsal (repetition) or elaborative strategies to transfer memories to long-term memory. Once in long-term memory, memories can be retrieved through appropriate search strategies. But if information is organized poorly or if we cannot find cues to retrieve it, it may be "lost" for all practical purposes.

up to 30 seconds after the trace of the stimulus decays. The ability to maintain information in short-term memory depends on cognitive strategies and on the basic capacity to continue to perceive a vanished stimulus. Memory function in middle childhood seems largely adultlike in organization and strategies and shows only gradual improvement in a quantitative sense through early adolescence (Swanson & Alloway, 2012).

Auditory stimuli can be maintained longer in short-term memory than can visual stimuli. For this reason, one strategy for promoting memory is to **encode** visual stimuli as sounds, or auditory stimulation. Then the sounds can be repeated out loud or mentally. For example, in Figure 12.4, mentally repeating the sound of Linda's name helps the other girl remember it; that is, the sounds can be **rehearsed**.

Capacity of Short-Term Memory   The basic capacity of short-term memory can be described in terms of the number of "bits" or chunks of information that can be kept in memory at once. To remember a new phone number, for example, one must keep seven chunks of information in short-term memory simultaneously; that is, one must rehearse them consecutively.

Classic research shows that the typical adult can keep about seven chunks of information—plus or minus two—in short-term memory at a time (Miller, 1956). As measured by the ability to recall digits, the typical five- to six-year-old can work on two chunks of information at a time. The ability to recall a series of digits improves throughout middle childhood, and adolescents can keep

encode To transform sensory input into a form that is more readily processed.

rehearse Repeat.

about seven chunks of information in short-term memory at the same time (Silva et al., 2012; Towse et al., 2010).

The information-processing view focuses on children's capacity for memory and their use of cognitive strategies, such as the way in which they focus their attention (Swanson & Alloway, 2012). Certain Piagetian tasks require several cognitive strategies instead of one. Young children often fail at such tasks because they cannot simultaneously hold many pieces of information in their short-term memories. Put another way, preschoolers can solve problems that have only one or two steps, whereas older children can retain information from earlier steps as they proceed to subsequent steps.

But how do young children remember the alphabet, which is 26 chunks of information? TRUTH OR FICTION REVISITED: It is not true that learning the alphabet requires keeping 26 chunks of information in mind at once. Children usually learn the alphabet by **rote learning**—simple associative learning based on repetition. After the alphabet is repeated many, many times, M triggers the letter N, N triggers O, and so on. The typical three-year-old who has learned the alphabet by rote will not be able to answer the question "What letter comes after N?" However, if you recite "H, I, J, K, L, M, N" with the child and then pause, the child is likely to say, "O, P." The three-year-old probably will not realize that he or she can find the answer by using the cognitive strategy of reciting the alphabet, but many five- or six-year-olds will.

rote learning Learning by repetition.

The Long-Term Effects of Good Teaching

Just the title of this Closer Look—"The Long-Term Effects of Good Teaching"—will stimulate arguments. Who, some readers will want to know, can say what makes a good teacher? We all have memories of teachers we would consider "good" and of teachers we would think of as not so good. But what do we look at when we make our judgments? Do we look at how likeable the teacher was? How helpful and empathic? Or do we ask ourselves whether we learning something? And what else do we consider?

Many psychologists and educators believe that it is difficult to measure "good teaching" objectively (Lowrey, 2012). Yet a team of economists—not educators—tried to do precisely that, and one of the outcomes they looked at was admittedly financial—what students earned over the years. But they didn't just decide that students who went on to earn more had had better teachers in elementary and high school. Rather, for the sake of the study, they defined good teachers as those who raised students' scores on standardized achievement tests. Economist Raj Chetty and his colleagues (2012) tracked elementary and high school students over a period of 20 years and found that "good teachers" not only raise test scores but also contribute to lasting academic and financial gains for the students. They labelled such teaching "value-added" teaching, and, as Figure 12.5 ■

shows, there is a strong correlation between value-added teaching and financial outcome at age 28. (The relatively low dollar amounts reflect the times during which data were gathered.) Value-added teaching even lowered the risk of unwanted teenage pregnancy. One commentator summarized the data as showing that "having a good Grade 4 teacher" increases the likelihood that a student will go on to college by 25 percent, lowers the risk of teen pregnancy by 25 percent, and boosts the student's lifetime income by an average of $25 000 (Kristof, 2012a).

Some readers also object to the notion of "teaching for the test." If we are talking about tests that are given to a particular class, or to a particular grade in a single school district, that objection is perfectly understandable. But if we are talking about standardized achievement tests, does the objection carry a bit less weight? After all, if those tests measure achievement at all, isn't it a good thing if teachers' students show greater achievement on those tests? In any event, the association between "good teaching" and life outcomes seems clear enough: Not only do students who have "value-added" teachers score better on those tests; they are also likely to make more money throughout their lifetimes.

The authors of the study did not claim that value-added teachers were the most likeable teachers. A next step would seem to be to study the behaviour of

Continued

Continued

value-added teachers to discover what types of things they are doing and whether there are principles of effective teaching that might be applied more widely.

Reflect Looking back to Grades 4 through 8, how would you describe your favourite teachers? Which teachers helped you learn the most? How did they do so?

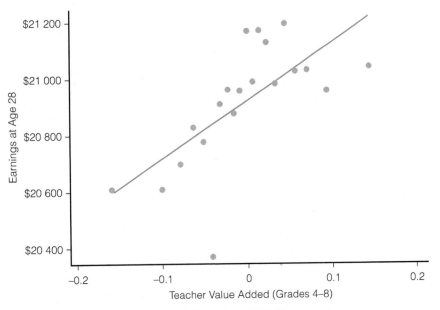

Figure 12.5 ■ The Long-Term Impact of Teachers
Teaching that raises students' standardized achievement test scores also raises their lifetime incomes and lowers the risk of teenage pregnancy.
Source: Chetty et al. (2012).

Long-Term Memory

Think of your **long-term memory** as a vast storehouse of information containing names, dates, places, what Harry did to you in Grade 2, and what Alexa said about you when you were 12. Long-term memories may last days, years, or, for practical purposes, a lifetime.

There is no known limit to the amount of information that can be stored in long-term memory. From time to time it may seem that we have forgotten, or lost, a long-term memory, such as the names of elementary or high school classmates. But it is more likely that we simply cannot find the proper cues to help us retrieve the information. It is "lost" in the same way as when we misplace an object but know that it is still in the house. It remains there somewhere for the finding.

How is information transferred from short-term memory to long-term memory? Rehearsal is one method. Older children are more likely than younger children to use rehearsal (Cowan et al., 2010; Silva et al., 2012).

OBSERVING CHILDREN, UNDERSTANDING OURSELVES

Rehearsal Strategies

See how children start to improve their own memory using rehearsal strategies.

What are some different strategies that children use to retain information?

From Rathus. *Childhood and Adolescence*, 5E. © 2014 South-Western, a part of Cengage Learning, Inc. Reproduced by permission. www.cengage.com/permissions

Go to www.nelson.com/voyages2ce to watch the video, answer the questions, and e-mail your responses to your professor.

long-term memory The memory structure capable of relatively permanent storage of information.

But pure rehearsal, with no attempt to make information meaningful by linking it to past learning, is no guarantee that the information will be stored permanently.

A more effective method than simple rehearsal is to purposefully relate new material to well-known information. Relating new material to well-known material is an **elaborative strategy**. English teachers encourage children to use new vocabulary words in sentences to help them remember them. This is an example of an elaborative strategy. In this way, children are building extended **semantic codes** that will help them retrieve the words' meanings in the future.

Before we proceed to the next section, here's a question for you. Which of the following words is spelled correctly: *retreival* or *retrieval*? The spellings sound alike, so an acoustic code for reconstructing the correct spelling would not be any help. But a semantic code, such as the spelling rule "i before e except after c," would enable you to reconstruct the correct spelling: retrieval. This is why children are taught rules and principles. Of course, whether these rules are retrieved in the appropriate situation is another issue.

Organization in Long-Term Memory

As children's knowledge of concepts advances, the storehouse of their long-term memory becomes gradually organized according to categories. Preschoolers tend to organize their memories by grouping objects that share the same function (Cowan et al., 2010). "Toast" may be grouped with "peanut butter sandwich" because both are edible. Only during the early elementary school years are toast and peanut butter likely to be joined under the concept of food.

When items are correctly categorized in long-term memory, children are more likely to recall accurate information about them (Figure 12.6 ■). For instance, do you "remember" whether whales breathe underwater? If you did not know that whales are mammals or if you knew nothing about mammals, a

elaborative strategy A method for increasing retention of new information by relating it to well-known information.

semantic code A code based on the meaning of information.

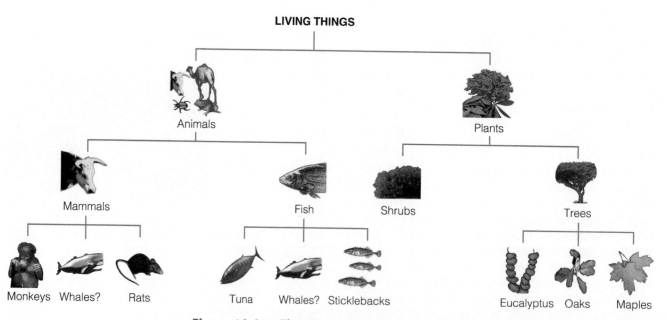

Figure 12.6 ■ The Categorical Structure of Long-Term Memory
Where are whales filed in the cabinets of children's memory? Do whales breathe underwater? Are they warm-blooded? Do they nurse their young? A child's classification of the whale concept will provide answers to these questions.

correct answer might depend on some remote instance of rote learning. If children have incorrectly classified whales as fish, they might search their "memories" and construct the incorrect answer that whales breathe underwater. Correct categorization, in sum, expands children's knowledge and enables them to retrieve information more readily.

But it has also been shown that when the knowledge of children in a particular area surpasses that of adults, the children have a superior capacity to store and retrieve related information. For example, children who are chess experts are superior to adult amateurs at remembering where chess pieces have been placed on the board (Gelman, 2010).

Development of Recall Memory

Recall memory involves retrieval of information from memory. As children develop, their capacity for recalling information increases (Cowan et al., 2010; Gathercole & Alloway, 2008). Improvement in memory is linked to their ability to quickly process (i.e., scan and categorize) information. Children's memory is a good overall indicator of their cognitive ability (Cowan et al., 2010; Towse et al., 2008).

In an experiment on categorization and memory, researchers placed objects that fell into four categories (furniture, clothing, tools, fruit) on a table before Grade 2 and Grade 4 students (Hasselhorn, 1992). The children were allowed three minutes to arrange the pictures as they wished and to remember as many as they could. The Grade 4 students were more likely to categorize and recall the pictures than the Grade 2 students.

Research also reveals that children are more likely to accurately recall information when they are strongly motivated to do so (Baltazar et al., 2012; Roebers et al., 2001). Fear of poor grades can encourage recall even in middle childhood. The promise of rewards also helps.

A CLOSER LOOK RESEARCH

Children's Eyewitness Testimony

Jean Piaget distinctly "remembered" an attempt to kidnap him from his baby carriage as he was being wheeled along the Champs Élysées. He recalled the excited throng, the abrasions on the face of the nurse who rescued him, the police officer's white baton, and the flight of the assailant. Although they were graphic, Piaget's memories were false. Years later, the nurse admitted that she had made up the tale.

Children are often called on to testify about events they have seen or experienced, often involving child abuse. But how reliable is children's testimony?

Even preschoolers can recall and describe personally experienced events, although the accounts may be sketchy (Bruck et al., 2006; Goodman et al., 2011). However, there are many individual differences. Consequently, the child witness is typically asked questions to prompt information. But such questions may be "leading"—that is,

How Reliable is Children's Eyewitness Testimony?
This question remains hotly debated. By age 10 or 11, children may be no more suggestible than adults. The findings for younger children are inconsistent, however.

they may suggest an answer. For example, "What happened at school?" is not a leading question, but "Did your teacher touch you?" is.

Can children's testimony be distorted by leading questions? It appears that by the age of 10 or 11, children are no more suggestible than adults, but younger children are more prone to being misled (Bruck et al., 2006; Goodman et al., 2011).

One hotly debated question is whether children can be led into making false reports of abuse. There is no simple answer to this question, as illustrated by a study carried out by Gail Goodman and her colleagues (Goodman et al., 2011; Goodman & Clarke-Stewart, 1991). They interviewed five- and seven-year-old girls following a routine medical check-up that included genital and anal exams for half the girls. Most of thechildren who experienced genital and anal touching failed to mention it when simply asked what happened

Continued

during the exam. But when asked specific leading questions ("Did the doctor touch you there?"), 31 of 36 girls mentioned the experience. Of the 36 girls who did not have genital and anal exams, none reported any such experience when asked what happened during the exam. When asked the leading questions, however, three girls falsely reported being touched in these areas. This illustrates the dilemma faced by investigators of sexual abuse: Children may not reveal genital contact until specifically asked, but asking may influence some children to give a false report.

Research indicates that repeated questioning may lead children to make up events that never happened to them (Goodman et al., 2011). In one study, preschoolers were questioned each week for 11 weeks about events that either had or had not happened to them (Ceci, 1993). By the 11th week, 58 percent of the children reported at least one false event as true.

What, then, are investigators to do when the only witnesses to criminal events are children? Maggie Bruck and her colleagues (2006) recommended that interviewers avoid leading or suggestive questions to minimize influencing the child's response. It might also be useful to ask the child whether he or she actually saw what happened or merely heard about it. Young children do not always make this distinction by themselves.

Reflect There are problems in children's eyewitness testimony. What would be lost if we did not allow children's eyewitness testimony? Give examples.

Development of Metacognition and Metamemory

QUESTION » What do children understand about the functioning of their cognitive processes and, more particularly, their memory? Children's knowledge and control of their cognitive abilities is termed **metacognition**. The development of metacognition is shown by having the ability to formulate problems, being aware of the processes required to solve a problem, activating cognitive strategies, maintaining focus on the problem, and checking answers.

When Grade 6 student decides which homework assignments to do first, memorizes her geography for tomorrow's test, and then tests herself to see what she needs to study more, she is displaying metacognition. Teaching students metacognitive skills improves their performance in reading and other areas of education (Flavell et al., 2002; Stright et al., 2001).

Metamemory is one aspect of metacognition. It more specifically refers to children's awareness of the functioning of their memory. Older children show greater insight into how memory works (Towse et al., 2008). For example, young elementary school students frequently announce that they have memorized educational materials before they have actually done so. Older students are more likely to assess their knowledge accurately (Cowan et al., 2010; Towse et al., 2008). As a result, older children store and retrieve information more effectively than younger children (Siegler & Alibali, 2005; Silva et al., 2012).

Older children also show more knowledge of strategies that can be used to facilitate memory. Preschoolers generally use rehearsal if someone else suggests that they do, but not until about the age of six or seven do children use rehearsal on their own (Flavell et al., 2002). Older elementary school children also become better at adapting their memory strategies to fit the characteristics of the task at hand (Cowan et al., 2010; Towse et al., 2008).

As children develop, they also are more likely to use selective rehearsal to remember important information. That is, they exclude the meaningless mass of perceptions milling about them by confining rehearsal to what they are trying to remember. Selectivity in rehearsal is found more often among adults than among ten-year-olds (Karatekin, 2004).

If you are trying to remember a new phone number, you know that you should rehearse it several times or write it down before setting out to do

metacognition Awareness of and control of one's cognitive abilities, as shown by the intentional use of cognitive strategies in solving problems.

metamemory Knowledge of the functions and processes involved in one's storage and retrieval of information (memory), as shown by the use of cognitive strategies to retain information.

math problems. However, five-year-olds, asked whether it would make a difference if they jotted the number down before or after doing the math problems, do not reliably report that doing the problems first would matter. Ten-year-olds, however, are aware that new mental activities (the math problems) can interfere with old ones (memorizing the telephone number) and usually suggest jotting the number down before doing the math problems.

Your metamemory is, of course, advanced to the point where you recognize that it would be poor judgment to read this book while watching *reality TV* or fantasizing about your next vacation, isn't it?

Active Review

8. The ability to screen out distractions (increases or decreases?) through middle childhood.

9. When children focus on stimuli, they can keep them in _____ memory for up to 30 seconds.

10. Children can remember visual stimuli longer when they _____ it as sounds.

11. Repetition of sounds or other stimuli is known as _____ learning.

12. _____ rehearsal consists of relating new information to things that are already known.

13. _____ is awareness of the functioning of one's own memory processes.

Reflect & Relate: How is information transferred from short-term memory to long-term memory? How is the process analogous to placing information in a computer's "memory" into a computer's "storage" device? What happens if you forget to "save" information in the computer's memory?

12.4 Intellectual Development, Creativity, and Achievement

QUESTION » What is intelligence? At an early age, we gain impressions of how intelligent we are compared to other family members and schoolmates. We think of some people as having more **intelligence** than others. We associate intelligence with academic success, advancement on the job, and appropriate social behaviour (Mayer, 2011). It was towards the end of the 19th century and beginning of the 20th century that psychologists and researchers became interested in trying to measure intelligence in humans. Why? Mainly because the development of universal public education in Europe and North America prompted administrators in the educational systems to identify and screen students for appropriate programming.

Despite our sense of familiarity with the concept of intelligence, intelligence cannot be seen, touched, or measured physically. For this reason, intelligence is subject to various interpretations. Theories about intelligence are some of the most controversial issues in psychology today.

Psychologists generally distinguish between achievement and intelligence. **Achievement** is what a child has learned, the knowledge and skills that have been gained by experience. Achievement involves specific content areas, such

intelligence A complex and controversial concept, defined by David Wechsler as "[the] capacity ... to understand the world [and the] resourcefulness to cope with its challenges." Intelligence implies the capacity to make adaptive choices (from the Latin *inter*, meaning "among," and *legere*, meaning "to choose").

achievement That which is attained by one's efforts and presumed to be made possible by one's abilities.

as English, history, and math. Educators and psychologists use achievement tests to measure what children have learned in academic areas. The strong relationship between achievement and experience seems obvious. We are not surprised to find that a student who has taken Spanish but not French does better on a Spanish achievement test than on a French achievement test.

The meaning of intelligence is more difficult to pin down (Nisbett, 2009). Most psychologists would agree that intelligence provides the cognitive basis for academic achievement. Intelligence is usually perceived as a child's underlying competence or learning ability, whereas achievement involves a child's acquired competencies or performance. Most psychologists also would agree that many of the competencies underlying intelligence manifest themselves during middle childhood, when most children are first exposed to formal schooling. Psychologists disagree, however, about the nature and origins of a child's underlying competence or learning ability.

12.5 Theories of Intelligence

Let's consider some theoretical approaches to intelligence. Then we will see how researchers and practitioners actually assess intellectual functioning.

Factor Theories

QUESTION » What are "factor theories" of intelligence? Many investigators have viewed intelligence as consisting of one or more major mental abilities, or **factors** (Willis et al., 2011). In 1904, the British psychologist Charles Spearman suggested that the various behaviours that we consider intelligent have a common, underlying factor: *g*, or "general intelligence." He thought that *g* represented broad reasoning and problem-solving abilities. He supported this view by noting that people who excel in one area generally show the capacity to excel in others. But he also noted that even the most capable people seem more capable in some areas—perhaps in music or business or poetry—than in others. For this reason, he also suggested that *s*, or "specific capacities," accounts for a number of individual abilities (Lubinski, 2004).

This view seems to make sense. Most of us know children who are good at math but poor in English, or vice versa. Nonetheless, some link—*g*—seems to connect different mental abilities. Few, if any, people surpass 99 percent of the population in one mental ability yet are surpassed by 80 percent or 90 percent of the population in other abilities.

To test his views, Spearman developed **factor analysis**, a statistical technique that enables researchers to determine which items on tests seem to be measuring the same things. Researchers continue to find a key role for *g* in performance on many intelligence tests. Jackson and Rushton (2006) claim that *g* underlies scores on the verbal and quantitative parts of the Scholastic Aptitude Test (SAT), although we can also note that it would be absurd to argue that education has nothing to do with SAT scores. A number of researchers (S. B. Kaufman et al., 2012) connect *g* with academic achievement and *working memory*—that is, the ability to keep various elements of a problem in mind at once. Contemporary psychologists continue to speak of the extent to which a particular test of intellectual ability measures *g* (S. B. Kaufman et al., 2012).

The American psychologist Louis Thurstone (1938) used factor analysis and concluded that intelligence consists of several specific factors, which he termed *primary mental abilities*, including visual–spatial abilities, perceptual speed, numerical ability, ability to learn the meanings of words, ability to bring to mind the right word rapidly, and ability to reason. Thurstone suggested, for

factor A condition or quality that brings about a result—in this case, "intelligent" behaviour. A cluster of related items, such as those found on an intelligence or personality test.

factor analysis A statistical technique that enables researchers to determine the relationships among a large number of items, such as test items.

Figure 12.7 ■ Sternberg's Triarchic Theory of Intelligence

Robert Sternberg views intelligence as three-pronged—as having analytical or componential, creative or experiential, and practical or contextual aspects.

Analytic intelligence (Information Processing Component - academic ability)
Abilities to solve problems, compare and contrast, judge, evaluate, and criticize

Creative intelligence (Experimental Component - creativity and insight)
Abilities to invent, discover, suppose, and theorize

Practical intelligence (Contextual Component - "street smarts")
Abilities to adapt to the demands of one's environment and apply knowledge in practical situations

example, that an individual might be able to rapidly develop lists of words that rhyme but might not be particularly able to solve math problems.

The Triarchic Theory of Intelligence

QUESTION » **What is Sternberg's triarchic model of intelligence?** Psychologist Robert Sternberg (Sternberg & Kaufman, 2011) constructed a three-pronged, or **triarchic**, theory of intelligence, which is similar to a view proposed by the Greek philosopher Aristotle. The three prongs of Sternberg's theory are analytical intelligence, creative intelligence, and practical intelligence (see Figure 12.7 ■).

One component of Sternberg's triarchic model is the *contextual or practical component.* That is, intelligent behaviour is highly dependent on the context. Both Aristotle and Sternberg speak of practical intelligence, or "street smarts." Practical intelligence enables people to adapt to the demands of their environment, including the social environment.

A second component to Sternberg's model is termed the *creative or experiential component.* Here Sternberg was interested in (a) novelty, creativity, and insight; and (b) automatization. Providing children with relatively novel tasks and assessing how they perform and solve these tasks provides psychologists and educators with practical information. Psychologists who believe that creativity is separate from analytical intelligence (academic ability) find only a moderate relationship between academic ability and creativity (Simonton, 2000). However, to Sternberg, creativity is a basic facet of intelligence. Creative intelligence is defined by the abilities to cope with novel situations and to profit from experience. Creativity allows us to relate novel situations to familiar situations (i.e., to perceive similarities and differences) and fosters adaptation. Sternberg also believes, however, that there is some usefulness in the automatization of everyday routines and practices as well. Psychologists who believe that creativity is separate from analytical intelligence (academic ability) find only small to moderate relationships between academic ability and creativity (Kim, 2005). However, to Sternberg, creativity is a basic facet of intelligence.

A third component of the triarchic model is the *information processing component*, also sometimes referred to as *analytical intelligence*. This component enables us to solve problems and acquire new knowledge. Information processing theorists such as Sternberg believe that how we process stimuli and cues, generate strategies to solve problems evaluate these strategies, and implement a strategy and evaluate the outcome (do we learn from our mistakes or do we repeat them?) tells us a great deal about our intellectual potential.

triarchic Governed by three. Descriptive of Sternberg's view that intellectual functioning has three aspects: analytical intelligence, creative intelligence, and practical intelligence.

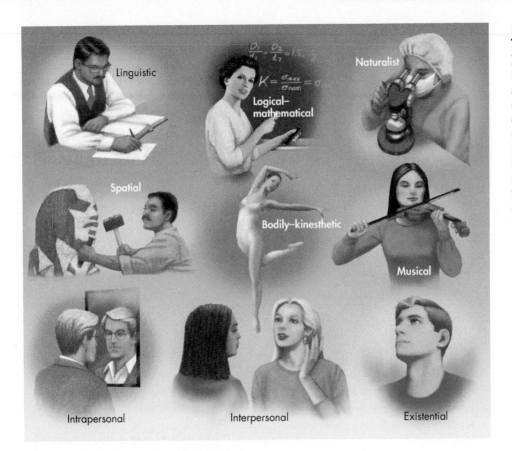

Figure 12.8 ■ **Gardner's Theory of Multiple Intelligences**
Howard Gardner argued that there are many intelligences, not just one, including bodily talents as expressed through dancing or gymnastics. Each "intelligence" is presumed to have its neurological base in a different part of the brain. Each is an inborn talent that must be developed through educational experiences if it is to be expressed.

The Theory of Multiple Intelligences

QUESTION » What is meant by multiple intelligences? Psychologist Howard Gardner (1983; Davis et al., 2011), like Robert Sternberg, believes that intelligence—or intelligences—reflects more than academic ability. Gardner refers to each kind of intelligence in his theory as "an intelligence" because the kinds differ in quality (see Figure 12.8 ■). He also believes that intelligences are based in different parts of the brain.

Three of Gardner's intelligences are familiar enough: verbal ability, logical–mathematical reasoning, and spatial intelligence (visual–spatial skills). But Gardner also includes bodily–kinesthetic intelligence (as shown by dancers and gymnasts), musical intelligence, interpersonal intelligence (as shown in empathy and ability to relate to others), and personal knowledge (self-insight). Occasionally, individuals show great "intelligence" in one area—such as the genius of the young Mozart with the piano or that of the island girl who can navigate her small boat to hundreds of islands by observing the changing patterns of the stars—without notable abilities in other areas. Naturalist intelligence refers to the ability to look at natural events, such as various kinds of animals and plants or the stars above, and develop insights into their nature and the laws that govern their behaviour. Existential intelligence involves dealing with the larger philosophical issues of life. According to Gardner, one can compose symphonies or advance mathematical theory yet be average in, say, language and personal skills. (Aren't some academic "geniuses" foolish or cumbersome in their personal lives?)

Critics of Gardner's view agree that people function more intelligently in some areas of life than others. They also agree that many people have special talents, such as bodily–kinaesthetic talents, even if their overall intelligence is average. But they question whether such special talents are "intelligences"

(Neisser et al., 1996). Language skills, reasoning ability, and the ability to solve math problems seem to be more closely related than musical or gymnastic talent to what most people mean by intelligence.

The various theories of intelligence are reviewed in Concept Review 12.2. We do not yet have the final word on the nature of intelligence, but we would

Concept Review 12.2 Theories of Intelligence

Theory	Basic Information	Comments
General versus specific factors (main proponent: Charles Spearman) 	• Spearman created factor analysis to study intelligence. • There is strong evidence for the general factor (*g*) in intelligence. • *s* factors are specific abilities, skills, and talents.	• The concept of *g* remains in use today—a century later.
Primary mental abilities (proponent: Louis Thurstone) 	• Thurstone used factor analysis. • There are many "primary" abilities. • All abilities and factors are academically oriented.	• Other researchers (e.g., Guilford) claim to have found hundreds of factors. • The more factors that are claimed, the more they overlap.
Triarchic theory (proponent: Robert Sternberg) 	• Intelligence is three-pronged—with analytical, creative, and practical components. • Analytical intelligence is analogous to academic ability.	• The theory coincides with the views of Aristotle. • Critics do not view creativity as a component of intelligence.
Multiple intelligences (proponent: Howard Gardner) 	• Gardner theorized distinct "intelligences." • Intelligences include academic intelligences, personal and social intelligences, talents, and philosophical intelligences. • The theory posits different bases in the brain for different intelligences.	• Proponents continue to expand the number of "intelligences." • Critics see little value in theorizing "intelligences" rather than aspects of *intelligence*. • Most critics consider musical and bodily skills to be special talents, not "intelligences."

Archives of History of American Psychology. The Center for History of Psychology, The University of Akron.

George Skadding/Time & Life Pictures/Getty Images

Robert Sternberg/Tufts University

© 2003 J. Gardner

like to share with you David Wechsler's definition of intelligence. Wechsler is the originator of the most widely used series of contemporary intelligence tests, and he defined intelligence as "[the] capacity of an individual to understand the world [and the] resourcefulness to cope with its challenges" (Wechsler, 1975, p. 139). To Wechsler, intelligence involves accurate representation of the world and effective problem solving (adapting to one's environment, profiting from experience, selecting the appropriate formulas and strategies, and so on).

Emotional Intelligence and Social Intelligence

Psychologists Peter Salovey and John Mayer developed the theory of emotional intelligence, which holds that social and emotional skills are a form of intelligence, just as academic skills are (Brackett et al., 2011; Kihlstrom & Cantor, 2011; Mayer et al., 2011). Emotional intelligence and social intelligence bear a resemblance to two of Gardner's intelligences—awareness of one's inner feelings and sensitivity to the feelings of others. It also involves control or regulation of one's emotions.

The theory suggests that self-awareness and social awareness are best learned during childhood. Failure to develop emotional intelligence is connected with childhood depression and aggression. Moreover, childhood experiences may even mould the brain's emotional responses to life's challenges.

To illustrate social intelligence, Goleman (2006) described how an American commander prevented a confrontation between his troops and an Iraqi mob by ordering the troops to point their rifles at the ground and smile. Although there was a language barrier, the aiming of the weapons downward and the smiles were a form of universal communication that was understood by the Iraqis, who then smiled back. Conflict was avoided. According to Goleman, the commander had shown social intelligence—the ability to read the Iraqis' social concerns and solve the social problem by coming up with a useful social response. Like emotional intelligence, social intelligence corresponds to one of Gardner's intelligences, and critics question whether it brings anything new to the table (Landy, 2006).

Measurement of Intellectual Development

QUESTION » How do we measure intellectual development? There may be disagreements about the nature of intelligence, but thousands of intelligence tests are administered by psychologists and educators every day (Urbina, 2011).

The Stanford–Binet Intelligence Scale (SBIS) and the Wechsler scales for preschool children, school-age children, and adults are the most widely used and respected intelligence tests. The SBIS and Wechsler scales yield scores called **intelligence quotients**. TRUTH OR FICTION REVISITED: An IQ is in fact a score on a test. The concept of intelligence per se is more difficult to define. The SBIS and Wechsler scales have been carefully developed and revised over the years. Each of them has been used to make vital educational decisions about children. In many cases, children whose test scores fall below or above certain scores require individualized program plans or adapted curriculum in order to meet their particular needs (i.e., intellectual disabilities, giftedness).

It must be noted just as emphatically that each test has been accused of discriminating against ethnic minorities (such as Aboriginal children and ESL children in Canada), immigrants, and the children of the socially and economically

intelligence quotient (IQ) Originally, a ratio obtained by dividing a child's score (or "mental age") on an intelligence test by his or her chronological age. In general, a score on an intelligence test.

disadvantaged (Beiser & Gotwiec, 2000; Harris et al., 2003; Maynard et al., 2005). Because of the controversy surrounding IQ tests, no single test should be used to make important decisions about a child. Decisions about children should be made only after a battery of tests is administered by a qualified psychologist, in consultation with parents and teachers.

The Stanford–Binet Intelligence Scale

The SBIS originated in the work of Alfred Binet and Theodore Simon, in France, over a century ago. The French public school system sought an instrument to identify children who were unlikely to profit from the regular classroom so that they could receive special attention. The Binet–Simon scale came into use in 1905. Since then, it has undergone revision and refinement.

The Binet–Simon scale yielded a score called a **mental age (MA)**. The MA shows the intellectual level at which a child is functioning. A child with an MA of six is functioning, intellectually, like the average six-year-old child. In taking the test, children earned months of credit for each correct answer. Their MA was determined by adding the months of credit they attained.

Lewis Terman adapted the Binet–Simon scale for use with children. Because Terman carried out his work at Stanford University, he renamed the test the Stanford–Binet Intelligence Scale. The first version of the SBIS was published in 1916. The SBIS yielded an intelligence quotient, or IQ, rather than an MA. The SBIS today can be used with children from the age of two onward up to adults. Table 12.2 ■ shows the kinds of items that define typical performance at various ages.

The IQ indicates the relationship between a child's mental age and his or her actual or **chronological age (CA)**. The ratio reflects the fact that the same

● TABLE 12.2

Items Similar to Those on the Stanford-Binet Intelligence Scale

Age	Item
2 years	1. Children show knowledge of basic vocabulary words by identifying parts of a doll, such as the mouth, ears, and hair. 2. Children show counting and spatial skills along with visual–motor coordination by building a tower of four blocks to match a model.
4 years	1. Children show word fluency and categorical thinking by filling in the missing words when they are asked questions such as "Father is a man; mother is a _____?" "Hamburgers are hot; ice cream is _____?" 2. Children show comprehension by answering correctly when they are asked questions such as "Why do people have automobiles?" and "Why do people have medicine?"
9 years	1. Children can point out verbal absurdities, as in this question: "In an old cemetery, scientists unearthed a skull that they think was that of George Washington when he was only five years of age. What is silly about that?" 2. Children display fluency with words, as shown by answering these questions: "Can you tell me a number that rhymes with snore?" and "Can you tell me a colour that rhymes with glue?"
Adult	1. Adults show knowledge of the meanings of words and conceptual thinking by correctly explaining the differences between word pairs, such as "sickness and misery," "house and home," and "integrity and prestige." 2. Adults show spatial skills by correctly answering questions such as "If a car turned to the right to head north, in what direction was it heading before it turned?"

mental age (MA) The accumulated months of credit that a person earns on the Stanford–Binet Intelligence Scale.

chronological age (CA) A person's age.

MA score has different meanings for children of different ages; that is, an MA of eight is an above-average score for a six-year-old but a below-average score for a ten-year-old. David Wechsler introduced the concept of the *deviation IQ*, which is based on an individual's score in relation to those of her or his age-mates.

The IQ is computed by the formula IQ = (Mental Age/Chronological Age) × 100, or

$$IQ = \frac{Mental\ Age\ (MA)}{Chronological\ Age\ (CA)} \times 100$$

According to this formula, a child with an MA of 6 and a CA of 6 has an IQ of 100. Children who can handle intellectual problems and older children have IQs above 100. For instance, an eight-year-old who does as well on the SBIS as the average ten-year-old will have an IQ of 125. Children who do not answer as many items correctly as other children of their age will have MAs that are lower than their CAs. Their IQ scores will be below 100.

TRUTH OR FICTION REVISITED: It is true that two children can answer exactly the same items on an intelligence test correctly, yet one can be above average in intelligence and the other below average. The children would have different ages, and the younger of the two would be considered more intelligent.

Today, IQ scores on the SBIS are derived by comparing children's and adults' performances with those of other people of the same age. People who get more items correct than average receive IQ scores above 100, and people who answer fewer items correctly receive below 100.

The Wechsler Scales

David Wechsler (1975) developed a series of scales for use with school-age children (Wechsler Intelligence Scale for Children; WISC), younger children (Wechsler Preschool and Primary Scale of Intelligence; WPPSI), and adults (Wechsler Adult Intelligence Scale; WAIS). These tests have been repeatedly revised. For example, the current version of the WISC is the WISC-IV, and it is available in both Spanish and English. For example, the WISC and the WISC-IV are available in both Spanish and English. The latest edition, the WISC-V, was published in 2014.

The Wechsler scales group test questions into subtests (such as those shown in Table 12.3 ■). Each subtest measures a different intellectual task. For this reason, the test compares a person's performance on one type of task (such as defining words) with her or his performance on another (such as using blocks to construct geometric designs). The Wechsler scales thus suggest children's strengths and weaknesses and provide overall measures of intellectual functioning.

Wechsler described some subtests as measuring verbal tasks and others as assessing performance tasks. In general, verbal subtests require knowledge of verbal concepts, whereas performance subtests require familiarity with spatial-relations concepts (see Figure 12.9 ■). Wechsler's scales make it possible to compute verbal and performance IQs. College students who are not technically oriented often obtain higher verbal than performance IQ scores.

Figure 12.10 ■ indicates the labels that Wechsler assigned to various IQ scores and the approximate percentages of the population who attain IQ scores at those levels. As you can see, most children's IQ scores cluster around the average. Only about 5 percent of the population obtain IQ scores above 130 or below 70.

Kinds of Items Found on the Wechsler Intelligence Scales

Verbal Items	Nonverbal–Performance Items
Information: "What is the capital of Canada?" "Who was Shakespeare?"	Picture completion: Pointing to the missing part of a picture.
Comprehension: "Why do we have postal codes?" "What does 'A stitch in time saves 9' mean?"	Picture arrangement: Arranging cartoon pictures in sequence so that they tell a meaningful story.
Arithmetic: "If 3 candy bars cost 25 cents, how much will 18 candy bars cost?"	Block design: Copying pictures of geometric designs using multi-coloured blocks.
Similarities: "How are good and bad alike?" "How are peanut butter and jelly alike?"	Object assembly: Putting pieces of a puzzle together so that they form a meaningful object.
Vocabulary: "What does *canal* mean?"	Coding: Rapid scanning and drawing of symbols that are associated with numbers.
Digit span: Repeating a series of numbers, presented by the examiner, forward and backward.	Mazes: Using a pencil to trace the correct route from a starting point to home.

Note: The items for verbal subtests are similar but not identical to actual test items on the Wechsler intelligence scales.

Figure 12.9 ■ Performance Items on an Intelligence Test

This figure shows a number of items that resemble those found on the Wechsler Intelligence Scale for Children.

Picture arrangement

These pictures tell a story, but they are in the wrong order. Put them in the right order so that they tell a story.

Picture completion

What part is missing from this picture?

Block design

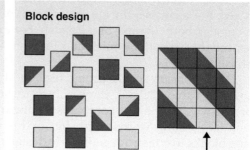

Put the blocks together to make this picture.

Object assembly

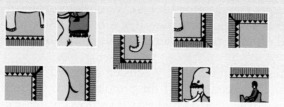

Put the pieces together as quickly as you can.

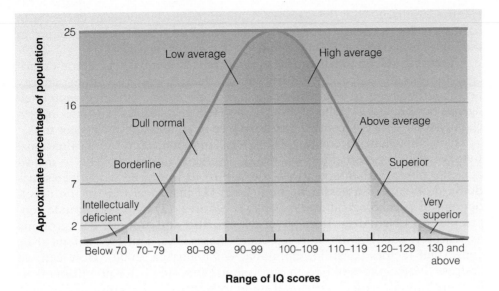

The Testing Controversy

QUESTION » Many psychologists and educators consider standard intelligence tests to be culturally biased. What is that controversy about?

> I was almost one of the testing casualties. At 15 I earned an IQ test score of 82, three points above the track of the special education class. Based on this score, my counsellor suggested that I take up brick-laying because I was "good with my hands." My low IQ, however, did not allow me to see that as desirable.
>
> —Robert Williams (1974, p. 32)

This testimony, offered by African American psychologist Robert Williams, echoes the sentiments of many psychologists. Most psychologists and educational specialists consider intelligence tests to be at least somewhat biased against certain minority groups and members of lower social classes (Daley & Onwuegbuzie, 2011; Suzuki et al., 2011). To fill in a bit more historical background, let's note that during the 1920s intelligence tests were used to prevent many Europeans and others from immigrating to the United States. For example, testing pioneer H. H. Goddard assessed 178 newly arrived immigrants at Ellis Island and claimed that most of the Hungarians, Italians, and Russians were "feeble-minded." It was apparently of little concern to Goddard that these immigrants, by and large, did not understand English—the language in which the tests were administered! Because of a history of abuse of intelligence testing, some states have outlawed the use of IQ tests as the sole standard for placing children in special-education classes. In Canada, our practices are somewhat different; however, we too often use information gleaned from intelligence tests to help make educational recommendations. In fact, we have often used American norms (because Canadian norms were nonexistent or not readily available) in calculating subscale scores on the Wechsler scales.

Supporters of standard intelligence tests point out that they appear to do a good job of measuring Spearman's *g* (Frey & Detterman, 2004) and cognitive skills that are valued in modern high-tech societies (Maynard et al., 2005). The vocabulary and arithmetic subtests on the Wechsler scales, for example, clearly reflect achievement in language arts and computational ability. Although the broad types of achievement measured by these tests reflect intelligence, they might also reflect cultural familiarity with the concepts required to answer questions correctly. In particular, the tests seem to reflect middle-class European American culture in the United States (Daley & Onwuegbuzie, 2011; Suzuki et al., 2011).

If scoring well on intelligence tests requires a certain type of cultural experience, the tests are said to have a **cultural bias**. Children reared in certain minority neighbourhoods could be at a disadvantage, not because of differences in intelligence but because of cultural differences (Helms, 2006). For this reason, psychologists have tried to construct **culture-free** or culture-fair intelligence tests.

It is important to conduct culturally competent and fair evaluations. Inappropriate assessment of culturally diverse students can lead to misdiagnosis, misguided interventions, or failure to intervene when necessary. Some problems in assessment stem from (1) historical bias in the development of psychological assessment procedures; (2) disproportionate representation of children from diverse linguistic and cultural backgrounds as research participants or researchers themselves; and (3) ecological or contextual factors (Castillo, Quintana, & Zamarripa, 2000). How can we address these sources of bias in our system? One step is for practitioners to become familiar with professional standards for assessing culturally diverse children. Notably, psychologists should (a) assess their own cultural self-knowledge and cultural competence; (b) review and, where appropriate, include key elements in culturally competent assessment; (c) be aware of the strengths and limitations of assessment instruments, scales, and inventories; (d) research and implement alternate assessment strategies; and (e) be sensitive to the continuing evolution of intellectual assessment (Rodriguez, 2000). Ideally, psychologists should become familiar with the primary cultural characteristics of the child as part of the assessment process. In addition, they should evaluate proficiency in the child's native language and in English (or French if it is the instructional language) if possible.

Some tests do not rely on expressive language at all. For example, Cattell's (1949) Culture-Fair Intelligence Test evaluates reasoning ability through the child's comprehension of the rules that govern a progression of geometric designs, as shown in Figure 12.11 ■.

Culture-free tests have not lived up to their promise. First, children from middle-class backgrounds still outperform children from lower-class on them (Daley & Onwuegbuzie, 2011; Suzuki et al., 2011). Children from the middle-class, for example, are more likely to have basic familiarity with materials such as blocks and pencils and paper. They are more likely than disadvantaged children to have arranged blocks into various designs (practice relevant to the Cattell test). Second, culture-free tests do not predict academic success as well as other intelligence tests, and scholastic aptitude remains the central concern of educators.

Might there be no such thing as a culture-free intelligence test? Motivation to do well, for example, might be a cultural factor. Because of lifestyle

cultural bias A factor hypothesized to be present in intelligence tests that bestows an advantage on test takers from certain cultural or ethnic backgrounds but that does not reflect true intelligence.

culture-free Descriptive of a test in which cultural biases have been removed. On such a test, test takers from different cultural backgrounds would have an equal opportunity to earn scores that reflect their true abilities.

Figure 12.11 ■ Sample Items from Cattell's Culture-Fair Intelligence Test
Culture-fair tests attempt to exclude items that discriminate on the basis of cultural background rather than intelligence.

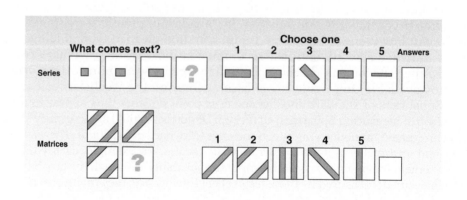

differences, some children from low-income families might not share the motivation of middle-class children to succeed on tests (Daley & Onwuegbuzie, 2011; Suzuki et al., 2011).

Patterns of Intellectual Development

QUESTION » **Putting test scores aside, how does intelligence develop?** Sometimes you have to run rapidly to stay in the same place—at least in terms of taking intelligence tests. The "average" taker of an intelligence test obtains an IQ score of 100. However, that person must answer more questions correctly as childhood progresses in order to obtain the same score. Even though his or her intelligence is "developing" at a typical pace, he or she continues to obtain the same score.

Rapid advances in intellectual functioning occur during childhood. Within a few years, children gain the ability to symbolize experiences and manipulate symbols to solve increasingly complex problems. Their vocabularies leap, and their sentences become more complex. Their thought processes become increasingly logical and abstract, and they gain the capacity to focus on two or more aspects of a problem at once.

Intellectual growth seems to occur in at least two major spurts. The first growth spurt occurs at about the age of six. This spurt coincides with entry into a school system and also with the shift from preoperational to concrete-operational thought (Rose & Fischer, 2011). The school experience may begin to help crystallize intellectual functioning at this time. The second spurt occurs at about age 10 or 11.

Once they reach middle childhood, however, children appear to undergo relatively more stable patterns of gains in intellectual functioning, although there are still spurts (Deary et al., 2004). As a result, intelligence tests gain greater predictive power. In a classic study by Marjorie Honzik and colleagues (1948), intelligence test scores at the age of nine correlated strongly (+0.90) with scores at the age of ten and more moderately (+0.76) with scores at the age of 18. Scores at age 11 even show a moderate to high relationship with scores at the age of 77 (Deary et al., 2004).

Despite the increased predictive power of intelligence tests during middle childhood, individual differences exist. In the classic Fels Longitudinal Study (see Figure 12.12 ■), two groups of children (Groups 1 and 3) made reasonably

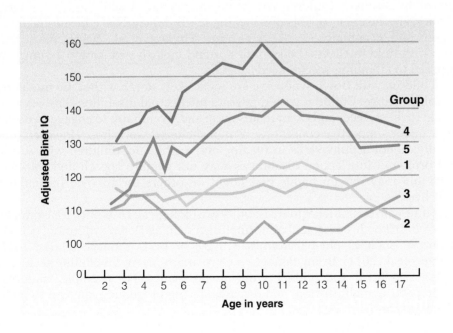

Figure 12.12 ■ Five Patterns of Change in IQ Scores for Children in the Fels Longitudinal Study
In the Fels Longitudinal Study, IQ scores remained stable between the ages of two-and-a-half and 17 for only one of five groups—Group 1. Please Note: While there was change, this was in rank-order, not intelligence.
Source: McCall et al. (1973).

consistent gains in intelligence test scores between the ages of 10 and 17, whereas three groups showed declines. Group 4, children who had shown the most intellectual promise at age ten, went on to show the most precipitous decline, although they still wound up in the highest 2–3 percent of the population (McCall et al., 1973). Many factors influence changes in intelligence test scores, including changes in the child's home environment, social and economic circumstances, educational experiences, and even intake of B vitamins such as folic acid (Deary et al., 2004).

Although intelligence test scores change throughout childhood, many children show reasonably consistent patterns of below-average or above-average performance. In the next section, we discuss children who show consistent patterns of extreme scores—low and high.

Differences in Intellectual Development

QUESTION » How do children differ in their intellectual development? The average IQ score in Canada is close to 100. About half the children in Canada obtain IQ scores in the broad average range from 90 to 110 (see Figure 12.10). Nearly 95 percent score between 70 and 130. But what of the other 5 percent? Children who obtain IQ scores below 70 are generally labelled "intellectually disabled" or as exhibiting intellectual disabilities. The Canadian Association for Community Living endorses the following terminology: intellectual disabilities or developmental disabilities. Children who score 130 and above are usually labelled "gifted." These labels—these verbal markers of extreme individual differences—lead to certain expectations of children. Ironically, the labels can place heavy burdens on both children and parents.

Intellectual Disability

According to the American Association on Intellectual and Developmental Disabilities (AAIDD, 2012), "Intellectual disability is characterized by significant limitations both in intellectual functioning and in adaptive behaviour as expressed in conceptual, social, and practical adaptive skills, which are apparent prior to the age of 18."

Most of the children (more than 80 percent) with intellectual disabilities are mildly disabled. Children with mild intellectual disabilities, as the term implies, are the most capable of adjusting to the demands of educational institutions and, eventually, to society at large (Hodapp et al., 2011). Many children with mild intellectual disabilities attend inclusive education settings, as opposed to attending special-needs classes.

Children with Down syndrome are most likely to fall within the moderate disability range. Children with moderate intellectual disabilities can learn to speak; to dress, feed, and clean themselves; and, eventually, to engage in useful work under supportive conditions, as in a sheltered workshop. However, they usually do not acquire skills in reading and arithmetic. Children with severe and profound intellectual disabilities may not acquire speech and self-help skills and may remain highly dependent on others for survival throughout their lives.

Some causes of intellectual disability are biological. Disability, for example, can stem from chromosomal abnormalities, such as Down syndrome; genetic disorders, such as phenylketonuria (PKU); or brain damage (Haier, 2011; Hodapp et al., 2011). Brain damage can have many origins, including accidents during childhood and problems during pregnancy. For example, maternal alcohol abuse, malnutrition, and diseases during pregnancy can lead to intellectual disability in the fetus.

There is also **cultural–familial disability**, in which the child is biologically normal but does not develop age-appropriate behaviours at the normal pace because of social isolation of one kind or another. For example, the later-born children of impoverished families may have little opportunity to interact with adults or play with stimulating toys. As a result, they may not develop sophisticated language skills or the motivation to acquire the kinds of knowledge that are valued in a technologically oriented society.

Naturally, we wish to encourage all children to develop to the maximum of their capacities. As a rule of thumb, keep in mind that IQs are scores on tests. They are not perfectly reliable, which means that they can and do change somewhat from testing to testing. Thus, it is important to focus on children's current levels of achievement in the academic and self-help skills we wish to impart; by doing so, we can try to build these skills gradually and coherently, step by step.

Children with cultural–familial disability can change dramatically when enriched learning experiences are provided, especially at early ages. Head Start programs, for example, have enabled many children at risk for cultural–familial disability to function at above-average levels.

cultural–familial disability Substandard intellectual performance that is presumed to stem from lack of opportunity to acquire the knowledge and skills considered important within a cultural setting.

A CLOSER LOOK DIVERSITY

Socioeconomic and Ethnic Differences in IQ

What is your own ethnic background? Are there any stereotypes about how people from your ethnic background perform in school or on IQ tests? If so, what is your reaction to these stereotypes? Why?

Research suggests that differences in IQ exist among socioeconomic and ethnic groups (Beiser & Gotowiec, 2000; Noble et al., 2012; Noble & Farah, 2013; McLoyd, 1998; Rouse, Brooks-Gunn, & McLanahan, 2005; Wright, Taylor, & Ruggiero, 1996). Children from lower-income families obtain IQ scores some 10–15 points lower than those obtained by children from the middle and upper classes. African American children tend to obtain IQ scores below those obtained by their European American counterparts (Daley & Onwuegbuzie, 2011; Nisbett, 2009). According to American studies, Latin American and Native American children also tend to score below the norms for European Americans (Daley & Onwuegbuzie, 2011; Nisbett, 2009). Native children scored significantly lower IQ scores (using the Wechsler scales) than their non-Native counterparts (Beiser & Gotowiec, 2000). In a Canadian study of Inuit children of Arctic Quebec using a less culturally biased non-verbal intelligence test (in this study, the Raven's Coloured Progressive Matrices), the children fared better than the U.S. norms and about the same as their southern Quebec counterparts (Wright, Taylor & Ruggiero, 1996). There have been noted ethnic differences in psychological research, and so the question that is asked frequently is "Why?" The answer is still researched and debated today. Intelligence, race, and genetics are controversial topics in psychology (Sternberg, Grigorenko, & Kidd, 2005; Templer, 2006).

Several studies of IQ have confused social class with ethnicity because larger proportions of children from certain minority groups come from lower socioeconomic backgrounds (Nisbett, 2009). When we limit our observations to particular ethnic groups, we still find an effect for social class. That is, middle-class European Americans outscore lower-class European Americans. Middle-class African Americans, Latin Americans, and Native Americans also outscore their less affluent counterparts. However, in the study by Beiser and Gotowiec (2000) that found differences between IQ scores of Native and non-Native children, when biopsychosocial variables (e.g., maternal and child health, socioeconomic status, English-language skills, and parental attitudes toward school) were controlled for, the differences disappeared. Sternberg and Grigorenko (2006) argue that intelligence cannot be interpreted apart from its cultural context.

Research has also suggested possible cognitive differences between Asians and Caucasians. Youth of Asian descent, for example, frequently outscore youth of European backgrounds on achievement tests in math and science, including the math portion of the SAT (Nisbett, 2009; Suzuki et al., 2011). Asian Americans are more likely than European Americans, African Americans, and Latin Americans to graduate from high school and complete college. Asian Americans are highly overrepresented in competitive U.S. colleges and universities (Suzuki et al., 2011).

Attributions for success may also be involved. Research shows that Asian students and their mothers tend to

Continued

CHAPTER 12 MIDDLE CHILDHOOD: COGNITIVE DEVELOPMENT

attribute academic successes to hard work (Randel et al., 2000). American mothers, in contrast, are more likely to attribute children's academic successes to "natural" ability (Sternberg & Kaufman, 2011). Asians are more likely to believe that they can work to make good scores happen.

Because Asian Americans have suffered discrimination in blue-collar careers, they have come to emphasize the value of education (Nisbett, 2009). In Japan, emphasis on succeeding through hard work is illustrated by the increasing popularity of cram schools, or *juku*, which prepare Japanese children for entrance exams to private schools and colleges (Ruiz & Tanaka, 2001). More than half of Japanese schoolchildren are enrolled in these schools, which meet after the regular school day. Parental encouragement and supervision, in combination with peer support for academic achievement, partially explain the superior performances (Nisbett, 2009).

Robert Sternberg and his colleagues (2005) argue that as long as there remains a dispute about what intelligence *is*, the attempt to relate intelligence to ethnicity makes no sense.

Reflect

- If the members of one ethnic group are smarter, on average, than the members of another ethnic group, does that make them "better"?

Who's Smart?
Asian children and Asian American children frequently outscore other American children on intelligence tests. Can we attribute the difference to genetic factors or to Asian parents' emphasis on acquiring cognitive skills?

- To say that one ethnic group is genetically smarter than another, do we have to be able to point to the genes that are responsible? Explain.

- Do you think we should be conducting research into the relationships between ethnicity and intelligence? Explain.

Giftedness

Giftedness involves more than excellence on the tasks posed by standard intelligence tests. In determining who is gifted, most educators include children who have outstanding abilities; who are capable of high performance in a specific academic area, such as language or mathematics; or who show creativity, leadership, distinction in the visual or performing arts, or bodily talents, such as in gymnastics and dancing (Reis & Renzulli, 2011).

Creativity and Intellectual Development

QUESTION » What is creativity? To illustrate something about the nature of creativity, let us ask you a rather ordinary question: What does the word *duck* mean? Now let us ask you a somewhat more interesting question: How many meanings can you find for the word *duck*? Arriving at a single correct answer to the question might earn you points on an intelligence test. Generating many answers to the question, as we will see, may be a sign of creativity as well as of the knowledge of the meanings of words.

Creativity is the ability to do things that are novel and useful. Creative children and adults can solve problems to which there are no pre-existing solutions, no tried and tested formulas (Kaufman & Plucker, 2011). Creative children share a number of qualities (Kaufman & Plucker, 2011; Sternberg, 2006):

- They take chances. (They may use sentence fragments in essays, and they may colour outside the lines in their colouring books.)
- They refuse to accept limitations and try to do the impossible.
- They appreciate art and music (which sometimes leaves them out among their peers).

creativity The ability to generate novel solutions to problems; a trait characterized by flexibility, ingenuity, and originality.

- They use the materials around them to make unique things.
- They challenge social norms. (Creative children are often independent and nonconformist, but independence and nonconformity do not necessarily make a child creative. Creative children may be at odds with their teachers because of their independent views. Faced with the task of managing large classes, teachers often fall into preferences for quiet, submissive, "good" children.)
- They take unpopular stands (which sometimes gives them the appearance of being oppositional, when they are expressing their genuine ideas and feelings).
- They examine ideas that other people accept at face value. (They come home and say, "_____ said that yada yada. What's that all about?")

A professor of Spencer's once remarked that there is nothing new under the sun, only new combinations of existing elements. Many psychologists agree. They see creativity as the ability to make unusual, sometimes remote, associations to the elements of a problem to generate new combinations. An essential aspect of a creative response is the leap from the elements of the problem to the novel solution. A predictable solution is not creative, even if it is hard to reach.

What Is the Relationship between Creativity and Intelligence?

The answer to this question depends on how one defines intelligence. If one accepts Sternberg's triarchic model, creativity is one of three aspects of intelligence (along with analytical thinking and practical intelligence). From this perspective, creativity overlaps with intelligence. **TRUTH OR FICTION REVISITED:** From other perspectives, however, it is not necessarily true that highly intelligent children are creative.

Some scientists argue that creativity and innovation require high levels of general intelligence (Heilman et al., 2003), but the tests we use to measure intelligence and creativity tend to show only a moderate relationship between global intelligence test scores and measures of creativity (Simonton, 2006; Sternberg & Williams, 1997). In terms of Gardner's theory of multiple intelligences, we can note that some children who have only average intellectual ability in some areas, such as logical analysis, can excel in areas that are considered more creative, such as music or art.

Considering two different kinds of thinking may help shed some light on this issue. In **convergent thinking**, thought is limited to present facts; the problem solver narrows his or her thinking to find the best solution. (A child uses convergent thinking to arrive at the right answer to a multiple-choice question or to a question on an intelligence test.)

Creative thinking tends to be divergent rather than convergent (Vartanian et al., 2003). In **divergent thinking**, the child associates freely to the elements of the problem, allowing "leads" to run a nearly limitless course. (Children use divergent thinking when they are trying to generate ideas to answer an essay question or to find keywords to search on the Internet.) Tests of creativity determine how flexible, fluent, and original a person's thinking is. Here, for example, is an item from a test used by Getzels and Jackson (1962) to measure associative ability, a factor in creativity: "Write as many meanings as you can for each of the following words: (a) duck; (b) sack; (c) pitch; (d) fair." Those who write several meanings for each word, rather than only one, are rated as potentially more creative.

Another measure of creativity might ask children to produce as many words as possible that begin with T and end with N within a minute. Still another item might give people a minute to classify a list of names in

convergent thinking A thought process that attempts to focus on the single best solution to a problem.

divergent thinking A thought process that attempts to generate multiple solutions to problems; free and fluent association to the elements of a problem.

What Is Creativity?
How is creativity related to intelligence?

CHAPTER 12 MIDDLE CHILDHOOD: COGNITIVE DEVELOPMENT **427**

as many ways as possible. In how many ways can you classify the following group of names?

Martha   Paul   Jeff   Sally   Pablo   Joan

Sometimes arriving at the right answer involves both divergent and convergent thinking. When presented with a problem, a child may first use divergent thinking to generate many possible solutions to the problem. Convergent thinking may then be used to select likely solutions and reject others.

Intelligence tests such as the Stanford–Binet and Wechsler scales require children to focus in on the single right answer. On intelligence tests, ingenious responses that differ from the designated answers are marked wrong. Tests of creativity, by contrast, are oriented toward determining how flexible and fluent one's thinking can be. Such tests include items such as suggesting improvements or unusual uses for a familiar toy or object, naming things that belong in the same class, producing words that are similar in meaning, and writing different endings for a story.

Determinants of Intellectual Development

QUESTION » What are the roles of nature (heredity) and nurture (environmental influences) in the development of intelligence? No research strategy for attempting to ferret out genetic and environmental determinants of IQ is flawless (McLafferty, 2006; Moore, 2007). Still, a number of ingenious approaches have been devised. The evidence provided through these approaches is instructive.

Genetic Influences

Various strategies have been devised for research into genetic factors, including kinship studies and studies of adopted children.

If heredity is involved in human intelligence, then closely related people ought to have more similar IQs than distantly related or unrelated people, even when they are reared separately. Figure 12.13 ■ shows the averaged results of more than 100 studies of IQ and heredity in humans (McGue et al., 1993; Plomin & Spinath, 2004; Plomin et al., 2008). The IQ scores of identical (monozygotic, MZ) twins are more alike than the scores for any other pairs, even when the twins have been reared apart. The average correlation for MZ twins reared together is +0.85; for those reared apart, it is +0.67. Correlations between the IQ scores of fraternal (dizygotic, DZ) twins, siblings, and parents and children are generally comparable, as is their degree of genetic relationship. The correlations tend to vary from about +0.40 to +0.59. Correlations between the IQ scores of children and their natural parents (+0.48) are higher than those between children and their adoptive parents (+0.18). TRUTH OR FICTION REVISITED: Actually, adopted children are more similar in intelligence to their biological parents than to their adoptive parents, which is suggestive of the role of genetic factors in intellectual functioning.

All in all, studies suggest that the **heritability** of intelligence is between 40 percent and 60 percent (Haworth et al., 2009; Sternberg & Kaufman, 2011). In other words, about half of the difference between your IQ score and the IQ scores of other people can be explained in terms of genetic factors.

Let's return to Figure 12.13. Note that genetic pairs (such as MZ twins) reared together show higher correlations between IQ scores than similar genetic pairs (such as other MZ twins) who were reared apart. This finding holds for MZ twins, siblings, parents, children, and unrelated people. For this reason, the same group of studies that suggests that heredity plays a role in determining IQ scores also suggests that the environment plays a role.

When children are separated from their biological parents at early ages, one can argue that strong relationships between their IQ scores and those of their natural parents reflect genetic influences. Strong relationships between

heritability The degree to which the variations in a trait from one person to another can be attributed to, or explained by, genetic factors.

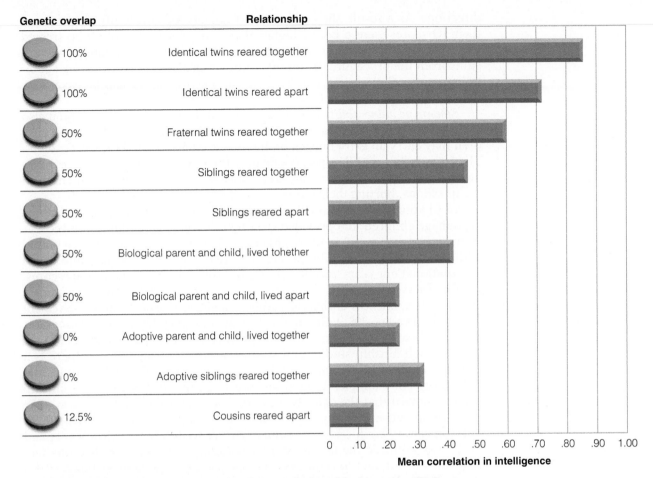

Genetic overlap	Relationship
100%	Identical twins reared together
100%	Identical twins reared apart
50%	Fraternal twins reared together
50%	Siblings reared together
50%	Siblings reared apart
50%	Biological parent and child, lived tohether
50%	Biological parent and child, lived apart
0%	Adoptive parent and child, lived together
0%	Adoptive siblings reared together
12.5%	Cousins reared apart

0 .10 .20 .30 .40 .50 .60 .70 .80 .90 1.00

Mean correlation in intelligence

Figure 12.13 ■ Findings of Studies of the Relationship between IQ Scores and Heredity

The data represent a composite of several studies. By and large, correlations are higher between people who are more closely related, yet people who are reared together have more similar IQ scores than people who are reared apart. Such findings suggest that both genetic and environmental factors contribute to IQ scores.

their IQs and those of their adoptive parents, on the other hand, might reflect environmental influences. Classic projects involving adopted children in Colorado, Texas, and Minnesota (Scarr, 1993; Sternberg & Kaufman, 2011; Turkheimer, 1991) have found a stronger relationship between the IQ scores of adopted children and their biological parents than between the IQ scores of adopted children and their adoptive parents.

These studies, then, also point to a genetic influence on intelligence. Nevertheless, the environment also has an impact.

Environmental Influences

Studies of environmental influences on IQ use several research strategies, including discovering situational factors that affect IQ scores, exploring children's ability to rebound from early deprivation, and exploring the effects of positive early environments.

In some cases, we need look no further than the testing situation to explain some of the discrepancy between the IQ scores of middle-class children and those of children from economically disadvantaged backgrounds. In one study (Zigler et al., 1982), the examiner simply made children as comfortable as possible during the test. Rather than being cold and impartial, the examiner was warm and friendly, and care was taken to see that the children understood the directions. As a result, the children's test anxiety was markedly reduced and their IQ scores were 6 points higher than those for a control group treated in a more indifferent manner. Disadvantaged children made relatively greater gains from the procedure. By doing nothing more than making testing conditions more optimal for all children, we can narrow the IQ gap between low-income and middle-class children.

Stereotype vulnerability is another aspect of the testing situation, and it also affects test scores. For example, African American and Latin American children may carry an extra burden on intelligence tests (Inzlicht & Good, 2006). They may worry that they risk confirming their group's negative stereotype by doing poorly. Their concern may create anxiety, which can distract them from the questions, hurting their scores.

In Chapter 7, we discussed a longitudinal study of intellectually disabled orphanage children that provided striking evidence that children can recover from early deprivation. In the orphanage, 19-month-old children were placed with surrogate mothers who provided a great deal of intellectual and social stimulation. Four years later, the children showed dramatic gains in IQ scores.

Children whose parents are responsive and provide appropriate play materials and varied experiences during the early years obtain higher IQ and achievement test scores (Bradley, 2006). Graduates of Head Start and other preschool programs show significant gains in later educational outcomes (Phillips & Styfco, 2007).

Although kinship studies and studies of adoptees suggest that there is a genetic influence on intelligence, they also suggest a role for environmental influences. For example, an analysis of a large number of twin and kinship studies showed that the older twins and other siblings become, the less alike they are on various measures of intelligence and personality (Nisbett, 2009). This appears to be due to increasing exposure to different environments and experiences outside the family. Many psychologists believe that heredity and environment interact to influence intelligence (Daley & Onwuegbuzie, 2011; Haier, 2011). An impoverished environment may prevent some children from living up to their potential. An enriched environment may encourage others to realize their potential, minimizing possible differences in heredity.

Perhaps we need not be concerned with how much of a person's IQ is due to heredity and how much is due to environmental influences. Psychology has traditionally supported the dignity of the individual. It might be more appropriate for us to try to identify children of all races whose environments place them at high risk for failure and to do what we can to enrich those environments.

Active Review

14. Spearman suggested that the behaviours we consider intelligent have a common factor, which he labelled _____.

15. Gardner argues for the existence of _____ intelligences, each of which is based in a different area of the brain.

16. The IQ indicates the relationship between a child's _____ age and chronological age.

17. The Wechsler scales have subtests that assess _____ tasks and performance tasks.

18. If scoring well on an IQ test requires a certain type of cultural experience, then the tests are said to have a cultural _____.

19. The first spurt in intellectual growth occurs at about the age of _____.

20. Children of lower socioeconomic status in North America obtain IQ scores some _____ points lower than those obtained by middle- and upper-class children.

21. Children tend to use (convergent or divergent?) thinking when they are thinking creatively.

22. Studies find that there is a stronger relationship between the IQ scores of adopted children and their (adoptive or biological?) parents, than between the IQ scores of adopted children and their (adoptive or biological?) parents.

Reflect & Relate: As you look back on your own childhood, can you point to any kinds of family or educational experiences that seem to have had an impact on your intellectual development? Would you say that your background, overall, was deprived or enriched? In what ways?

12.6 Language Development

QUESTION » How does language develop in middle childhood? Children's ability to understand and use language becomes increasingly sophisticated in middle childhood. Children learn to read as well.

Vocabulary and Grammar

By the age of six, the child's vocabulary has expanded to 10 000 words, give or take a few thousand. By seven to nine years of age, most children realize that words can have different meanings, and they become entertained by riddles and jokes that require semantic sophistication. (Remember the jokes at the beginning of the chapter?) By the age of eight or nine, children are able to form "tag questions," in which the question is tagged on to the end of a declarative sentence (Weckerly et al., 2004). "You want more ice cream, don't you?" and "You're sick, aren't you?" are examples of tag questions.

Children also make subtle advances in articulation and in their capacity to use complex grammar. For example, preschool-age children have difficulty understanding passive sentences, such as "The truck was hit by the car," but children in the middle years have less difficulty interpreting the meanings of passive sentences (Aschermann et al., 2004).

During these years, children develop the ability to use connectives, as illustrated by the sentence "I'll eat my spinach, but I don't want to." They also learn to form indirect object–direct object constructions, such as "She showed her sister the toy."

Pragmatic Language Skills

Children who have acquired the phonology, morphology, syntax, and semantics of a language have basically acquired linguistic competence (Bryant, 2013). However, living in a social world means that children must do much more. For example, they also need to acquire communicative competence—that is, mastering how to use language appropriately across various social contexts (e.g., classroom, home, friend's house) and with different people (parents, peers, teachers). As children move from early childhood and into middle childhood, they continue to refine their ability to make requests, use conversational skills (taking turns, staying on topic), and give and respond to feedback advances. While these skills are seen in preschoolers, it is during middle childhood that children's pragmatic skill growth shows their ability to provide more feedback and support for conversations. In order to excel in the area of communicative competence, children require practice and support. Parents and educators can encourage and provide opportunities for students to practise speaking in different contexts and with different audiences (e.g., peers, adults) (Aukrust, 2004). At school, students can receive feedback and learn about social rules of language (Burdelski, 2010).

Reading Skills

QUESTION » What cognitive skills are involved in reading? Reading is a complex activity that depends on perceptual, cognitive, and linguistic processes (Smolka & Eviatar, 2006). It relies on skills in the integration of visual and auditory information. Accurate awareness of the sounds in the child's language is an extremely important factor in subsequent reading achievement (Caravolas & Bruck, 2000; Dufva et al., 2001). Reading also requires the ability to make basic visual discriminations (Levinthal & Lleras, 2007). In reading, for example, children must "mind their *p*'s and *q*'s." That is, in order to recognize letters, children must be able to perceive the visual differences between letters such as *b* and *d,* and *p* and *q.*

During the preschool years, neurological maturation and experience combine to enable most children to make visual discriminations between different letters with relative ease. Those children who can recognize and name the letters of the alphabet by kindergarten age are better readers in the early school grades (Kirby, Parrila, & Pfeiffer, 2003; Siegler & Alibali, 2005).

How do children become familiar with their own written languages? More and more today, children are being exposed to TV programs such as *Sesame Street* and multimedia software promoting reading skills, but these are relatively newer means of exploration. Children are also exposed to books, street signs, names of stores and restaurants, and the writing on packages, especially at the supermarket. Some children, of course, have more books in the home than others do. Children from affluent homes where books and other sources of stimulation are plentiful learn to read more readily than children from impoverished homes. But regardless of income level, reading storybooks with parents in the preschool years helps prepare a child for reading (Dockett et al., 2006; Raikes et al., 2006). Children who read at home during the school years also show better reading skills in school and more positive attitudes toward reading.

Methods of Teaching Reading

When they read, children integrate visual and auditory information (they associate what they see with sounds), whether they are using the whole-language approach or the phonetic method. The **whole-language approach** emphasizes the use and recognition of words in everyday situations and in books. The word-recognition method requires that children associate visual stimuli such as *cat* and *Robert* with the sound combinations that produce the spoken words "cat" and "Robert." This capacity is usually acquired by rote learning, or extensive repetition.

In the **phonetic method**, children first learn to associate written letters and letter combinations (such as *ph* or *sh*) with the sounds they are meant to indicate. Then they sound out words from left to right, decoding them. The phonetic method has the obvious advantage of giving children skills that they can use to decode (read) new words (Bastien-Toniazzo & Jullien, 2001; Murray, 2006). However, some children learn more rapidly at early ages through the word-recognition method. The phonetic method can also slow them down when it comes to familiar words. Most children and adults, in fact, tend to read familiar words by the word-recognition method (regardless which method was used in their original training) and to make some effort to sound out new words.

Which method works? Controversy rages over this issue, and we cannot resolve it here. But let us note that some words in English can be read only by the word-recognition method—consider the words *one* and *two.* This method is useful when it comes to words such as *danger, stop, poison,* and the child's name, because it helps provide children with a basic **sight vocabulary**. But children must also acquire decoding skills so that they can read new words on their own.

whole-language approach A method for learning to read in which children come to recognize words in a variety of contexts through repeated exposure to them.

phonetic method A method for learning to read in which children decode the sounds of words via their knowledge of the sounds of letters and letter combinations.

sight vocabulary Words that are immediately recognized on the basis of familiarity with their overall shapes, rather than decoded.

12.7 Bilingualism

QUESTION » What does research reveal about the advantages and disadvantages of bilingualism? Most people throughout the world speak two or more languages. Most countries have minority populations whose languages differ

Size and percentage of the population that reported speaking a language other than English or French at home, alone or in combination with English or French by type of use of these languages, Canada, 2011

Language(s) Spoken at Home	Number	Percentage
A language "other" than English or French only[1]	2 145 250	32.4
An "other" language most often with English spoken on a regular basis	1 342 860	20.3
An "other" language most often with French spoken on a regular basis	143 990	2.2
English most often with or without an "other" language than French (equally or on a regular basis)	2 515 935	37.9
French most often with or without an "other" language than English (equally or on a regular basis)	276 740	4.2
Other combinations[2]	205 620	3.1
Total	6 630 395	100.0

Notes:
1. The category "Language other than English or French only" also includes persons speaking another language most often and those speaking it on a regular basis (less than 5 percent combined).
2. The category "Other combinations" mainly comprises cases where three languages or more are spoken at home.
Source: Statistics Canada, Census of Population, 2011.

from the national tongue. Nearly all Europeans are taught English and the languages of neighbouring nations. Consider the Netherlands. Dutch is the native tongue, but all children are also taught French, German, and English and are expected to become fluent in each of them.

Although we have already reviewed some of the literature regarding learning a second language in Chapter 9, we will review some additional information about second language acquisition here as well. About 5.8 million Canadians report they are bilingual in the two official languages. Even though English and French are the two official languages of Canada, Canadians are speaking many other languages in the home. In fact, two-thirds of the population speaking a nonofficial language at home are also doing so in combination with either English or French (see Table 12.4 ■ and Figure 12.14 ■; Statistics Canada, 2012).

A century ago, it was widely believed that children reared in bilingual homes were delayed in their cognitive development. The theory was that mental capacity is limited, so people who stored two linguistic

Figure 12.14 ■ Population growth in number of persons who reported speaking one of the top 25 immigrant languages most often at home, Canada 2006–2011

Source: Statistics Canada.

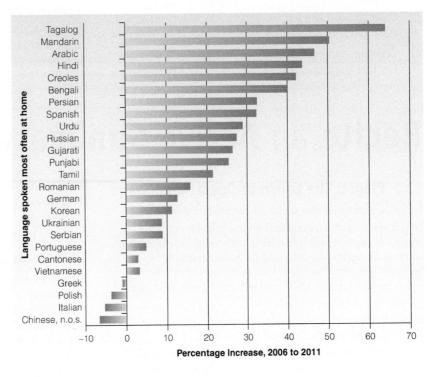

systems were thought to be taxing their mental abilities (Barac & Bialystok, 2011). Bilingual children do show some differences from monolingual children; this may be largely because the vocabularies used at home and in the school are not identical (Bialystok et al., 2010). **TRUTH OR FICTION REVISITED:** It is not true, however, that **bilingual** children have more academic problems than children who speak only one language (Barac & Bialystok, 2011). There is some "mixing" of languages by bilingual children (Gonzalez, 2005), but they can generally separate the two languages from an early age. At least half of the children in an American sample of children who spoke Spanish at home were proficient in both languages (Shin & Bruno, 2003).

Today most linguists consider it advantageous for children to be bilingual because knowledge of more than one language contributes to the complexity of the child's cognitive processes (Barac & Bialystok, 2011). For example, bilingual children are more likely to understand that the symbols used in language are arbitrary. Monolingual children are more likely to think, erroneously, that the word *dog* is somehow intertwined with the nature of the beast. Bilingual children therefore have somewhat more cognitive flexibility.

Bilingualism

Most people throughout the world speak two or more languages. It was once thought that children reared in bilingual homes were deficient in their cognitive and language development, but today most linguists consider it advantageous for children to be bilingual.

bilingual Using or capable of using two languages with nearly equal or equal facility.

Active Review

23. Reading relies on skills in the integration of _____ and auditory information.

24. In using the _____ method of reading, children associate written letters and letter combinations (such as *ph* or *sh*) with the sounds they indicate.

25. Bilingual children generally (can or cannot?) separate the two languages at an early age.

26. Today most linguists consider it a(n) (advantage or disadvantage?) to be bilingual.

Reflect & Relate: Did you grow up speaking a language other than English in your home? If so, what special opportunities and problems were connected with the experience?

Recite an Active Summary

12.1 Piaget: The Concrete-Operational Stage

What is meant by the stage of concrete operations?

In the stage of concrete operations, children begin to show the capacity for adult logic with tangible objects. Concrete-operational thinking is characterized by reversibility, flexibility, and decentration. Concrete-operational children show understanding of conservation, transitivity, and class inclusion.

Can we apply Piaget's theory of cognitive development to educational practices?

Piaget believed that learning involves active discovery. Thus, teachers should not impose knowledge on the child

but instead find materials to interest and stimulate the child. Instruction should be geared to the child's level of development.

12.2 Moral Development: The Child as Judge

How does Piaget view the development of moral reasoning?

Piaget posited two stages of moral development: moral realism and autonomous morality. The earlier stage emerges at about the age of five; in this stage, the child judges behaviour as right when it conforms to rules. Five-year-olds see rules as embedded in the structure of things and believe in immanent justice. Preoperational children focus on one dimension at a time—in this case, the amount of damage and not the intentions of the wrongdoer. Children begin to show autonomous morality in middle childhood. At that time, they view social rules as agreements that can be changed.

How does Kohlberg view the development of moral reasoning?

Kohlberg believed that there are three levels of moral development and two stages within each level. In the preconventional level, children base moral judgments on the consequences of behaviour. In the conventional level, right and wrong are judged in terms of conformity to conventional standards. In the postconventional level, moral reasoning is based on one's own values.

12.3 Information Processing: Learning, Remembering, Problem Solving

What is the difference between Piaget's view of cognitive development and the information-processing approach?

Information-processing theorists aim to learn how children store, retrieve, and manipulate information—how their "mental programs" develop. One key cognitive process is selective attention—attending to the relevant features of a task—which advances steadily through middle childhood.

What is meant by the term memory?

Memory refers to the storage and retrieval of information. Many psychologists divide memory functioning into three major processes: sensory memory, working memory, and long-term memory. Maintenance of information in working memory depends on cognitive strategies such as encoding and rehearsing stimuli. Older children process information more efficiently. There is no known limit to the capacity of long-term memory. Information is transferred from short-term memory to long-term memory by rehearsal and elaboration. Children organize their long-term memory into categories. Correct categorization expands knowledge and allows for efficient retrieval.

What do children understand about the functioning of their cognitive processes and, more particularly, their memory?

Awareness and conscious control of cognitive abilities is termed metacognition, as evidenced by the ability to formulate problems, awareness of how to solve them, use of rules and strategies, ability to remain focused, and ability to check answers. Metamemory consists of people's awareness of the workings of their memory. By age six or seven, children know how to use rehearsal to remember things.

12.4 Intellectual Development, Creativity, and Achievement

What is intelligence?

Intelligence provides the basis for academic achievement. It is a child's underlying competence or learning ability.

12.5 Theories of Intelligence

What are "factor theories" of intelligence?

Spearman suggested that the behaviours we consider intelligent have a common underlying factor: g. But s, or specific capacities, accounts for some individual abilities. Thurstone used factor analysis to define several primary mental abilities.

What is Sternberg's triarchic model of intelligence?

Sternberg proposes a three-pronged theory of intelligence, including analytical intelligence (academic ability), creative intelligence, and practical intelligence ("street smarts").

What is meant by multiple intelligences?

Gardner believes that people have multiple "intelligences," each based in a different part of the brain. Some of these—verbal ability, logical–mathematical reasoning, and spatial intelligence—involve academic ability. Others—for example, bodily–kinesthetic intelligence, musical intelligence, interpersonal intelligence, and personal knowledge—strike other psychologists as special talents, not intelligences.

How do we measure intellectual development?

The SBIS assumes that intelligence increases with age, so older children must answer more items correctly than younger children to obtain a comparable score—which Binet termed a *mental age (MA)*. Comparing a child's MA with his or her chronological age (CA)—that is, computing MA/CA—yields an *intelligence quotient (IQ)*. The average IQ score is defined as 100. Wechsler introduced the concept of the *deviation IQ*, which is based on an individual's score in relation to those of her or his age-mates. The Wechsler scales group test questions into subtests that measure different types of intellectual tasks. Some tasks are mainly verbal, whereas others rely more on spatial-relations skills.

Many psychologists and educators consider standard intelligence tests to be culturally biased. What is that controversy about?

Many psychologists and educational specialists believe that intelligence tests are at least somewhat biased against members of certain minority group and the lower social classes. In addition to underlying competence, they reflect knowledge of the language and culture in which the test is given.

Putting test scores aside, how does intelligence develop?

During middle childhood, thought processes become more logical and abstract. Children gain the capacity to focus on two or more aspects of a problem at once. The first intellectual spurt occurs at about the age of six and coincides with entry into school. The second spurt occurs at age 10 or 11. Intelligence tests gain greater predictive power during middle childhood.

How do children differ in their intellectual development?

The term *intellectual disability* refers to limitations in intellectual functioning that are characterized by an IQ score no higher than 70–75. Some causes of intellectual disability are biological, but cultural–familial disability also occurs. Giftedness involves outstanding abilities, high performance in a specific academic area (such as language or mathematics), leadership, distinction in the arts, or bodily talents. Children identified as gifted tend to be successful as adults.

Children of a lower socio-economic status or disadvantaged backgrounds obtain lower IQ scores than children from more affluent backgrounds. As a group, children from most ethnic minority households score lower than those from a European background, but those from an Asian background tend to outscore those from a European background.

What is creativity?

Creativity is the ability to do things that are novel and useful. Creative children take chances, refuse to accept limitations, and appreciate art and music. The relationship between intelligence test scores and measures of creativity are only moderate. Children use mainly convergent thinking to arrive at the correct answers on intelligence tests. Creative thinking tends to be divergent rather than convergent.

What are the roles of nature (heredity) and nurture (environmental influences) in the development of intelligence?

The closer the genetic relationship between people, the more alike their IQ scores. The IQ scores of adopted children are more like those of their biological parents than those of their adoptive parents. Research also finds situational influences on IQ scores, including motivation, familiarity with testing materials, and the effects of enriched environments.

12.6 Language Development

How does language develop in middle childhood?

In middle childhood, language use becomes more sophisticated, including understanding that words can have multiple meanings. There are advances in articulation and use of grammar. Additionally, children become more proficient in the social art of conversation, better known as pragmatics or communicative competence.

What cognitive skills are involved in reading?

Reading relies on skills in the integration of visual and auditory information. During the preschool years, neurological maturation and experience combine to enable most children to make visual discriminations between letters with relative ease.

12.7 Bilingualism

What does research reveal about the advantages and disadvantages of bilingualism?

Research shows that children can generally separate two languages from an early age and that most Canadians who first spoke another language in the home also speak English well. Knowledge of more than one language expands children's knowledge of different cultures.

Key Terms

concrete operations   394
reversibility   394
decentration   394
transitivity   395
seriation   395
class inclusion   396
moral realism   399
objective morality   399
immanent justice   399
autonomous morality   400
preconventional level   401
conventional level   402
postconventional level   402
information processing   403
memory   404

sensory memory   404
sensory register   404
working memory   404
encode   405
rehearse   405
rote learning   406
long-term memory   407
elaborative strategy   408
semantic code   408
metacognition   411
metamemory   411
intelligence   412
achievement   412
factor   413
factor analysis   413

triarchic   414
intelligence quotient (IQ)   417
mental age (MA)   418
chronological age (CA)   418
cultural bias   422
culture-free   422
cultural–familial disability   425
creativity   426
convergent thinking   427
divergent thinking   427
heritability   428
whole-language approach   432
phonetic method   432
sight vocabulary   432
bilingual   434

Active Learning Resources

Go to **www.nelsonbrain.com** to access *Voyages in Development's* CourseMate, where you will find an interactive eBook, flashcards, Pre-Lecture Quizzes, Section Quizzes, Exam Practice, videos, and more.

sanneberg/Shutterstock.com

Major Topics

MIDDLE CHILDHOOD:
Social and Emotional Development

13

Truth or Fiction?

T | F   Children's self-esteem rises throughout middle childhood. **p. 444**

T | F   Parents who are in conflict should stay together "for the sake of the children." **p. 451**

T | F   In middle childhood, popular children tend to be attractive and relatively mature for their age. **p. 452**

T | F   Teachers who have higher expectations of students may elicit greater achievements from them. **p. 459**

T | F   Some children—like some adults—blame themselves for all the problems in their lives, whether they deserve the blame or not. **p. 465**

T | F   It is better for children with school phobia to remain at home until the origins of the problem are uncovered and resolved. **p. 468**

A university student taking a child development course had a conversation with a nine-year-old girl named Hannah:

Student: Hannah, how was school today?
Hannah: Oh, it was all right. I don't like it a lot.
Student: How come?
Hannah: Taylor and Hunter won't talk to me. I told Taylor I thought her dress was very pretty, and she pushed me out of the way. That made me so mad.
Student: That wasn't nice of them.
Hannah: No one is nice except for Kate. At least she talks to me.

Here is part of a conversation between a different university student and her nine-year-old cousin, Madison:

Madison: My girlfriend Heather in school has the same glasses as you. My girlfriend, no, not my girlfriend—my friend—my friend picked them up yesterday from the doctor, and she wore them today.
Student: What do you mean—not your girlfriend, but your friend? Is there a difference?
Madison: Yeah, my friend. 'Cause Chloe is my girlfriend.
Student: But what's the difference between Heather, your friend, and Chloe, your girlfriend?
Madison: Well, Chloe is my best friend, so she's my girlfriend. Heather isn't my best friend, so she's just a friend. (Adapted from Rowen, 1973)

Between the ages of six and 12, the child's social world expands. As illustrated by the remarks of these nine-year-old girls, peers take on greater importance and friendships deepen (Hamm, 2000). Entry into school exposes the child to the influence of teachers and to a new

omgimages/Thinkstock

peer group. Relationships with parents change as children develop greater independence. Some children face adjustments resulting from the divorce and remarriage of parents. During these years, major advances occur in children's ability to understand themselves. Their knowledge of social relationships and their skill in developing such relationships increase as well (Collins, 1984; Davis, 2001). Some children, unfortunately, develop problems during these years, although some are able to cope with life's stresses better than others.

In this chapter, we discuss each of these areas. First, we examine major theories of social and emotional development in the middle years. Next, we examine the development of self-concept and the development of relationships with parents and peers. Then we turn to the influences of the school. Finally, we look at some of the social and emotional problems that can arise in middle childhood.

13.1 Theories of Social and Emotional Development in Middle Childhood

QUESTION » What are some features of social and emotional development in middle childhood?

Middle childhood is one of the least studied and yet one of the most exciting periods of life. Imagine a 5-year-old girl going to kindergarten for her first day of formal school. Now imagine this same girl at 12 years when she goes to secondary school. At 5 years, she is a cute child still anxious about separating from her parents as they leave her at the school. By 12 she will have grown into a young woman with secondary sex characteristics. In addition to starting school, she is likely to have experienced other institutional settings without her parents, settings in which she will have been exposed to a variety of peers and adults as well as many opportunities to learn new skills. Each of these new institutional settings (e.g., primary school, scouting, recreational programs, music lessons, etc.) will provide her with a series of new life experiences—experiences that will encourage the development of intellectual and interpersonal competencies, and introduce the child to new social roles in which [social approval] is based upon competence and performance.

—Jacqueline Eccles and her colleagues (2006, p. 325)

As noted by Eccles and her colleagues (2006), the major theories of personality have had less to say about this age group than about the other periods of childhood and adolescence. Nevertheless, common threads emerge. These include the development of skills, the importance of interpersonal relationships, and the expansion of self-understanding.

Psychoanalytic Theory

Is it possible that children have taken such an emotional beating from conflict over weaning in the oral stage, conflict over toilet training in the anal stage, and conflict over masturbation in the phallic stage that by the time they hit middle childhood, they repress it all and enter the **latency stage**, during which psychosexual impulses are hidden? Sigmund Freud believed that it was quite possible and that by making sexual feelings unconscious, children could focus on developing intellectual, social, and other culturally valued skills.

Erik Erikson agreed with Freud that the major developmental task of middle childhood is the acquisition of cognitive and social skills, but he did not suggest that children were sweeping five to six years of emotional turmoil under the rug

latency stage In Freud's psychoanalytic theory, the fourth stage of psychosexual development, characterized by repression of sexual impulses and development of skills.

to make it happen (Eccles et al., 2006). Erikson labelled the middle childhood years the stage of **industry versus inferiority**. Children who are able to master the various tasks and challenges of the middle years develop a sense of industry, or competence. He believed that children who have difficulties in school or with peer relationships during this period may develop a sense of inferiority.

Social Cognitive Theory

Social cognitive theory focuses on the continued importance of rewards and modelling in middle childhood. During these years, children depend less on external rewards and punishments and increasingly regulate their own behaviour.

How do children acquire moral and social standards for judging their own behaviour? One mechanism is direct reward and punishment. Parents may praise a child when she shares her toys with her younger brother. In time, she incorporates the importance of sharing into her own value system. Another mechanism is modelling. Children in the middle years are exposed to an increasing variety of models. Not only parents but also teachers, other adults, peers, and TV characters, and the heroine in a story can serve as models (Grusec, 2011; Richert et al., 2011). The parents' educational level also influences children's hopes and expectations. Longitudinal research shows that the educational level of the parents when the child is eight years old predicts the educational and occupational success of the child some 40 years later (Dubow et al., 2009).

Cognitive-Developmental Theory and Social Cognition

QUESTION » **What is the relationship between social cognition and perspective taking?** According to Piaget, middle childhood coincides with the stage of concrete operations and is partly characterized by a decline in egocentrism and an expansion of the capacity to view the world and oneself from other people's perspectives. This cognitive advance enhances the child's intellectual functioning and affects the child's social relationships (Slaughter, 2011).

Social cognition consists of the development of children's knowledge about the social world. It focuses on the child's understanding of the relationship between the self and others. A key aspect of the development of social cognition is the ability to assume the role or perspective of another person (Bengtsson & Arvidsson, 2011; Killen & Smetana, 2010). Robert Selman and his colleagues (Selman & Dray, 2006) devised a method to study the development of perspective-taking skills in childhood. Selman presented children with a social dilemma such as the following:

> Holly is an eight-year-old girl who likes to climb trees. She is the best tree climber in the neighbourhood. One day while climbing down from a tall tree, she falls off the bottom branch but does not hurt herself. Her father sees her fall. He is upset and asks her to promise not to climb trees anymore. Holly promises. Later that day, Holly and her friends meet Sean. Sean's kitten is caught up in a tree and can't get down. Something has to be done right away, or the kitten may fall. Holly is the only one who climbs trees well enough to reach the kitten and get it down, but she remembers her promise to her father.

The children then were asked a series of questions designed to test their ability to take the role of another person (e.g., "How will Holly's father feel if he finds out she climbed the tree?"). Based on the children's responses to these questions, Selman (1976) described five levels of perspective-taking skills in childhood (see Table 13.1 ■).

industry versus inferiority The fourth stage of psychosocial development in Erikson's theory, occurring in middle childhood. Mastery of tasks leads to a sense of industry, whereas failure produces feelings of inferiority.

social cognition Development of children's understanding of the relationship between the self and others.

Levels of Perspective Taking

Level	Approximate Age (years)[a]	What Happens
0	3–6	Children are egocentric and do not realize that other people have perspectives different from their own. A child of this age will typically say that Holly will save the kitten because she likes kittens and that her father will be happy because he likes kittens, too. The child assumes that everyone feels as she does.
1	5–9	Children understand that people in different situations may have different perspectives. The child still assumes that only one perspective is "right." A child might say that Holly's father would be angry if he did not know why she climbed the tree. But if she told him why, he would understand. The child recognizes that the father's perspective may differ from Holly's because of lack of information. But once he has the information, he will assume the "right" (i.e., Holly's) perspective.
2	7–12	The child understands that people may think or feel differently because they have different values or ideas. The child also recognizes that others are capable of understanding the child's own perspective. Therefore, the child is better able to anticipate the reactions of others. The typical child of this age might say that Holly knows that her father will understand why she climbed the tree and that he therefore will not punish her.
3	10–15	The child finally realizes that both she and another person can consider each other's point of view at the same time. The child may say something similar to this: Holly's father will think that Holly shouldn't have climbed the tree. But once he has heard her side of the story, he would feel that she was doing what she thought was right. Holly realizes that her father will consider how she felt.
4	12 and above	The child realizes that mutual perspective taking does not always lead to agreement. The perspectives of the larger social group also must be considered. A child of this age might say that society expects children to obey their parents and therefore that Holly should realize why her father might punish her.

Source: Selman (1976).
[a]Ages may overlap.

Research supports Selman's developmental progression in perspective taking (De Lisi, 2005; Mischo, 2005; Nakkula & Nikitopoulos, 2001). Children with better perspective-taking skills tend to be more skilled at negotiating peer relations (Selman & Dray, 2006; Smith & Rose, 2011; Visser et al., 2009).

OBSERVING CHILDREN, UNDERSTANDING OURSELVES

Self-Concept

At age four-and-a-half, Christopher describes himself by listing objects and possessions in his house.

What do you think is this child's self-concept? How does the self-concept develop over time? When do children begin to incorporate personal traits into their self-descriptions?

From Rathus. *Childhood and Adolescence*, 5E.
© 2014 South-Western, a part of Cengage Learning, Inc. Reproduced by permission. www.cengage.com/permissions

Go to www.nelson.com/voyages2ce to watch the video, answer the questions, and e-mail your responses to your professor.

Development of the Self-Concept in Middle Childhood

QUESTION » How does the self-concept develop during middle childhood? In early childhood, children's self-concepts, or self-definitions, focus on concrete external traits, such as appearance, activities, and living situations. But as children undergo the cognitive developments of middle childhood, their more abstract internal traits, or personality characteristics, begin to play a role in their self-definition. Social relationships and group memberships take on significance (Bukowski et al., 2011; Rosen & Patterson, 2011).

An investigative method called the Twenty Statements Test bears out this progression and also highlights the relationships between the self-concept and general cognitive development. According to this method, children are given a sheet of paper with the question "Who am I?" and 20 spaces in which to write answers. Consider the answers of a nine-year-old boy and an 11-year-old girl:

The nine-year-old boy: "My name is Bruce C. I have brown eyes. I have brown hair. I have brown eyebrows. I'm 9 years old. I LOVE? sports. I have 7 people in my family. I have great? eye site. I have lots! of friends. I live on 1923 Pinecrest Drive. I'm going on 10 in September. I'm a boy. I have a uncle that is almost 7 feet tall. My school is Pinecrest. My teacher is Mrs. V. I play hockey! I'm also the smartest boy in the class. I LOVE! food. I love fresh air. I LOVE school."

The eleven-year-old girl: "My name is A. I'm a human being. I'm a girl. I'm a truthful person. I'm not pretty. I do so-so in my studies. I'm a very good cellist. I'm a very good pianist. I'm a little bit tall for my age. I like several boys. I like several girls. I'm old fashioned. I play tennis. I am a very good musician. I try to be helpful. I'm always ready to be friends with anybody. Mostly I'm good, but I lose my temper. I'm not well liked by some girls and boys. I don't know if boys like me or not."

—Montemayor & Eisen (1977, pp. 317–318)

Only the nine-year-old gives his age and address, discusses his family, and focuses on physical traits, such as eye colour, in his self-definition. The nine-year-old mentions his likes, which can be considered rudimentary psychological traits, but they are tied to the concrete, as would be expected of a concrete-operational child.

Both children list their competencies. The 11-year-old's struggle to bolster her self-esteem—her insistence on her musical abilities despite her qualms about her attractiveness—shows a greater concern with internal traits, psychological characteristics, and social relationships.

Research also finds that females are somewhat more likely than males to define themselves in terms of the groups to which they belong (Madson & Trafimow, 2001). A Chinese study found that children with siblings are more likely than only children to define themselves in terms of group membership (Wang et al., 1998).

self-esteem The sense of value or worth that people attach to themselves.

Self-Esteem

QUESTION » **How does self-esteem develop during middle childhood?** One of the most critical aspects of self-concept is **self-esteem**, the value or worth that people attach to themselves. A positive self-image is crucial to psychological adjustment (Rosen & Patterson, 2011).

As children enter middle childhood, their self-concepts become more differentiated and they are able to evaluate their self-worth in many different areas (Rosen & Patterson, 2011). Preschoolers do not generally make a clear distinction between different areas of competence. They are either "good at doing things" or not. At one time, it was assumed that before age eight, children could differentiate between only two broad facets of self-concept. One involved general competence, and the other involved social

Children's self-esteem tends to decline during middle childhood, in part because they come to evaluate their physical appearance and their performance in academic and social domains more realistically.

acceptance (Harter, 2006). It was also believed that an overall, or general, self-concept did not emerge until the age of eight. But research indicates that even as early as five to seven years of age, children are able to make judgments about their performance in seven different areas: physical ability, physical appearance, peer relationships, parent relationships, reading, mathematics, and general school performance. They also display an overall, or general, self-concept (Harter, 2006).

TRUTH OR FICTION REVISITED: Children's self-esteem actually declines throughout middle childhood, reaching a low point at about age 12 or 13. Then it increases during adolescence (Harter, 2006). What accounts for the decline? Because young children are egocentric, their initial self-concepts may be unrealistic. As children become older, they compare themselves with other children and adjust their self-concepts. For most children, the comparison results in a more critical self-appraisal and the consequent decline in self-esteem.

Do girls or boys have a more favourable self-image? The answer depends on the area. Girls tend to have more positive self-concepts regarding reading, general academics, and helping others than boys do, whereas boys tend to have more positive self-concepts in math, physical ability, and physical appearance (Tobin et al., 2010; Underwood & Rosen, 2011). Cross-cultural studies in China (Dai, 2001), Finland (Lepola et al., 2000), and Germany (Tiedemann, 2000) also find that girls tend to have higher self-concepts in writing, and boys in math.

Why do girls and boys differ in their self-concepts? Socialization and gender stereotypes appear to affect the way females and males react to their achievements. For example, girls predict that they will do better on tasks that are labelled "feminine," and boys predict better performance for themselves when tasks are labelled "masculine" (Jacobs et al., 2005; Rathus et al., 2011).

Authoritative parenting apparently contributes to children's self-esteem (Chan & Koo, 2011; Supple & Small, 2006). Children with a favourable self-image tend to have parents who are restrictive, involved, and loving. Children with low self-esteem are more likely to have authoritarian or rejecting–neglecting parents.

Authoritative Parenting and Self-Esteem
Research suggests that parental demands for mature behaviour, imposition of restrictions, and warmth help children develop behaviour patterns that are connected with self-esteem.

High self-esteem in children is related to their closeness to parents, especially as found in father–son and mother–daughter relationships (Fenzel, 2000). Close relationships between parents are also associated with positive self-concepts in children (DeHart et al., 2006).

Peers also play a role in children's self-esteem (Nesdale & Lambert, 2007). Social acceptance by peers is related to self-perceived competence in academic, social, and athletic domains (Cillessen & Bellmore, 2011). Parents and classmates have an equally strong effect on children's sense of self-worth in the middle years. Friends and teachers have relatively less influence in shaping self-esteem but are also important (Harter, 2006).

Self-esteem appears to have a genetic component, which would contribute to its stability. A Japanese study found that the concordance (agreement) rate for self-esteem is higher among identical (MZ) twins than fraternal (DZ) twins (Kamakura et al., 2007). A longitudinal British study found that both genetic and environmental factors appear to contribute to the stability of children's self-esteem (Neiss et al., 2006). Most children will encounter failure, but high self-esteem may contribute to the belief that they can master adversity. Low self-esteem may become a self-fulfilling prophecy: Children with low self-esteem may not carve out much to boast about.

Learned Helplessness

One outcome of low self-esteem in academics is known as **learned helplessness**. Learned helplessness is an acquired belief that one is unable to obtain the rewards that one seeks. "Helpless" children tend to quit following failure, whereas children who believe in their own ability tend to persist in their efforts or change their strategies (Zimmerman, 2000). One reason for this difference is that helpless children believe that success is due more to ability than to effort and they have little ability in a particular area. Consequently, persisting in the face of failure seems futile (Bandura et al., 2001; Sutherland et al., 2004). "Helpless" children typically perform more poorly in school and on standardized tests of intelligence and achievement (Goldstein & Brooks, 2005).

Gender Differences in Learned Helplessness

It is unclear whether girls or boys exhibit more learned helplessness in middle childhood, but a gender difference does emerge in mathematics (Simpkins et al., 2006). Researchers have found that even when girls are performing as well as boys in math and science, they have less confidence in their ability (Hall, 2012). Why? Parents' expectations that children will do well (or poorly) in a given area influence both the children's self-perceptions and their performance. Parents tend to hold the stereotyped view that girls have less math ability than boys, regardless of their own daughter's actual performance in math.

Active Review

1. Erikson labels middle childhood the stage of _____ versus inferiority.

2. According to Piaget, middle childhood coincides with the stage of _____ operations.

3. A key aspect of the development of social cognition is the ability to take the _____ of another person.

4. Children's self-esteem (increases or decreases?) during middle childhood.

5. (Authoritarian or Authoritative?) parenting contributes to high self-esteem in children.

Reflect & Relate: Are you "responsible" for your own self-esteem, or does your self-esteem pretty much vary with the opinion that others have of you? Why is this an important question?

13.2 The Family

QUESTION » What kinds of influences does the family exert during middle childhood? In middle childhood, the family continues to play a key role in socializing the child, even though peers, teachers, and other outsiders begin to play a greater role (Carr, 2011; Grusec, 2011). In this section, we look at developments in parent–child relationships during the middle years. We also consider the effects of different family environments: the family environment provided by lesbian and gay parents, adoptive parents, and the experience of living in families with varying marital arrangements. While we don't cover all family types and configurations, they do exist—from multigenerational families comprised of extended family members, to families where grandparents are primary guardians, to foster families. Families come in all shapes and sizes.

Parent–Child Relationships

Parent–child interactions focus on some new concerns during the middle childhood years, including school-related matters, assignment of chores, and peer activities (Maughan, 2011).

learned helplessness An acquired (hence, learned) belief that one is unable to control one's environment.

Children spend less time with their parents during middle childhood than they did in early childhood, and they need fewer reminders about do's and don'ts.

During the middle years, parents do less monitoring of children's activities and provide less direct feedback than they did in the preschool years. In middle childhood, children do more monitoring of their own behaviour. Although the parents still retain control over the child, control is gradually transferred from parent to child, a process known as **coregulation** (Maughan, 2011). Children no longer need to be constantly reminded of do's and don'ts as they begin to internalize the standards of their parents.

Children and parents spend less time together in middle childhood than in the preschool years. But as in early childhood, children spend more of this time with their mothers than with their fathers (Grusec, 2011). Mothers' interactions with school-age children continue to revolve around care-giving and household tasks, whereas fathers are relatively more involved in recreational activities, when they are involved, especially with sons. But here, too, mothers may actually spend more time (Wolfenden & Holt, 2005).

In the later years of middle childhood (ages 10–12), children evaluate their parents more critically than they did in the early years (Denham et al., 2011; Grusec, 2011). This shift in perception may reflect the child's developing cognitive ability to view relationships in more complex ways (De Goede et al., 2009). Throughout middle childhood, however, children rate their parents as their best source of emotional support, rating them higher than friends (Denham et al., 2011).

According to the Adoption Council of Canada (n.d.), almost one in five Canadians is somehow connected to adoption either through the role of the adoptee, adoptive parents, birth parents, adoptive family members, or birth relatives. Adults may welcome new members to their families through adoption for a variety of different reasons. Children may be adopted domestically through provincial social and human services, through private agencies, or through international adoption. As outlined by Grotevant and McDermott (2014), there are many social and biological factors to consider, such the characteristics of the child at the time of adoption (age, health), characteristics of parents (marital status, ethnicity and nationality in relation to adoptive child), and reasons for adoption (e.g., abandonment, removal following abuse, death of parents) in understanding children's development and well-being over time. As we briefly mentioned in Chapter 7, there are studies that have found that children adopted at different ages (early vs. later in childhood) form positive attachment relationships with their adoptive parents (Niemann & Weiss, 2011; Pace & Zavattini, 2011).

Lesbian and Gay Parents

QUESTION » What are the effects of having lesbian or gay parents? "Where did you get that beautiful necklace?" Spencer asked the little girl in the pediatrician's office. "From my Moms," she answered. It turned out that her family consisted of two women, each of whom had a biological child, one girl and one boy.

In 2011, 0.8 percent of couple families (with and without children) were same-sex couples (Statistics Canada, 2012). Research on **lesbian** and **gay** parenting has fallen into two general categories: the general adjustment of children and whether the children of lesbian and gay parents are more likely than other children to be lesbian or gay themselves. Research by Charlotte Patterson

coregulation A gradual transferring of control from parent to child, beginning in middle childhood.

lesbian A female who is interested romantically and sexually in other females.

gay A male who is interested romantically and sexually in other males. (Can also refer to lesbians.)

and colleagues (2006; Patterson & Farr, 2011; Farr, Forssell, Patterson, 2010) has generally found that the psychological adjustment of children of lesbian and gay parents—whether conceived by intercourse or donor insemination, or adopted—is comparable to that of children of heterosexual parents. Despite the stigma attached to same-sex partnerships, lesbians and gay men frequently create and sustain positive family relationships (Lamb, 2012; Lick et al., 2011; Tasker & Granville, 2011).

An earlier review article by Tasker (2005) confirms that children with lesbian or gay parents are comparable to children with heterosexual parents on psychological development outcomes. However Tasker also underscores that variations in family form, children's awareness of lesbian and gay relationships, heterosexism, and homophobia are important issues for children. A good Canadian resource is Egale Canada (http://egale.ca-), whose purpose is to advance equality and justice for lesbian, gay, bisexual, and trans-identified people and their families.

Being reared by lesbian or gay parents has not been shown to influence children's adjustment or their sexual orientation.

Now let's consider the sexual orientation of the children of lesbian and gay parents. In doing so, we begin a generation back with the research of psychiatrist Richard Green. In a classic study, Green (1978) observed 37 children and young adults, 3–20 years old, who were being reared—or had been reared—by lesbians or **transsexuals**. All but one of the children reported or recalled preferences for toys, clothing, and friends (male or female) that were typical for their gender and age. All of the 13 older children who reported sexual fantasies or sexual behaviour were heterosexually oriented. In a subsequent study, Green and his colleagues (1986) compared the children of European American mothers who were currently single, 50 of whom were lesbians and 40 heterosexual. Boys from the two groups showed no significant differences in intelligence test scores, sexual orientation, gender-role preferences, relationships with family and peer groups, or adjustment to life with a single parent. Girls showed slight differences, including somewhat more flexibility in gender roles. Green concluded that the mother's sexual orientation had no connection with parental fitness. A study by Patterson and her colleagues (Farr et al., 2010) suggested that many adoption agencies now agree with Green's conclusions.

Another review by Patterson (2003) addressed the personal and social development of children who have lesbian and gay parents. Patterson found that the sexual orientation of the children was generally heterosexual. When parents had gotten divorced and created families with same-gender partners because of their sexual orientations, their children experienced a period of adjustment that entailed some difficulties—as do children when heterosexual parents get divorced. Children who are adopted by lesbian or gay parents tend to be well adjusted. The point here—reinforcing Green's findings—is that wanting the child is more important to the child's adjustment than the sexual orientation of the parents.

Generation X or Generation Ex?

QUESTION » What happens to children whose parents get divorced? To many in Canada, the 2000s are the period of "Generation X." However, it may be more accurate to think of our time as that of "Generation Ex"—that is, a generation characterized by ex-wives and ex-husbands. Their children are also a part of Generation Ex, which is large and growing continuously. The total divorce rate, by the 30th wedding anniversary was 40.7 per 100 marriages in 2008—an

transsexual A person who sees himself or herself as a person of the other gender and who may undergo hormone treatments and/or cosmetic surgery to achieve the appearance of being a member of the other gender.

Generation Ex: Ex-Husband, Ex-Wife, Ex-Family, Ex-Security
About 40 percent of Canadian marriages end in divorce, and divorce turns life topsy-turvy for children. Younger children tend to erroneously blame themselves for the dissolution of the family, but children in middle childhood come to see things more accurately. Children of divorced parents tend to develop problems, many of which fade as time passes. Should parents in conflict stay together for the sake of the children? The answer seems to be that the children will not be better off if the parents continue to fight in front of them.

increase from 36 percent in 1998—and the divorce rate varies depending how long couples have been together (Statistics Canada, 2011).

Divorce may be tough on parents; it may be even tougher on children (Kim, 2011; Moon, 2011). The automatic aspects of family life cease being automatic. No longer do children eat with both parents. No longer do they go to ball games, the movies, or Disneyland with both of them. No longer do they curl up with them on the sofa to watch TV. No longer do they kiss both at bedtime. The parents are now often supporting two households, which results in fewer resources for the children (Lansford, 2009). Children lose other things besides family life. Sometimes the losses are minor, but many children who live with their mothers scrape by—or fail to scrape by—at the poverty level or below. Some children move from spacious houses into cramped apartments or from a desirable neighbourhood to one where they are afraid to walk the streets. The mother who was once available may become an occasional visitor—spending more time at work and placing the kids in day care for extended periods of time.

In considering the effects of divorce on family members—both children and adults—we must ask whether the effects are due to divorce or to "selection factors" (Amato, 2006; Lansford, 2009). For example, are the effects on children due to divorce per se, or are they due to marital conflict, to inadequate parental problem-solving ability, or to changes in financial status? Also, do children undergo a temporary crisis and gradually adjust, or do stressors persist indefinitely? For example, three years after the divorce, feelings of sadness, shock, disbelief, and desire for parental reunion tend to decline, but even ten years later, children tend to harbour anger toward the parent they hold responsible for the breakup.

A CLOSER LOOK REAL LIFE

How to Answer a Seven-Year-Old's Questions about—Gulp—Sex

Daddy, where do babies come from?

Why are you asking me? Ask your mother.

Most children do not find it easy to talk to their parents about sex. Only about one-quarter of the children in a national survey had done so (National Campaign to Prevent Teen Pregnancy, 2003). Children usually find it easier to approach their mothers than their fathers (Guttmacher Institute, 2007).

Yet most children are curious about where babies come from, about how girls and boys differ, and the like. Adults who avoid these issues convey their own uneasiness about sex and may teach children that sex is something to be ashamed of.

Adults need not be sex experts to talk to their children about sex. They can surf the Internet to fill gaps in their knowledge or find books written for parents to read to their children. They can admit they do not know all the answers.

Here are some pointers (Rathus et al., 2014):

- Be approachable. Be willing to discuss sex.
- Provide accurate information. The six-year-old who wants to know where babies mature within the mother should not be told "in Mommy's tummy." It's wrong and isn't cute; the "tummy" is where food is digested. The child may worry that the baby is going to be digested. The child should be told, instead, "In Mommy's uterus" and can be shown diagrams if he or she wants specifics.
- Teach children the correct names of their sex organs and that the "dirty words" others use to refer to the sex organs are not acceptable in most social settings. Avoid using words like *pee pee* or *private parts* to describe sex organs.

Reflect How do you feel about the advice offered in this feature? Would you follow it? Why or why not?

Parents who get divorced are often in conflict about many things, and one of them typically involves how to rear the children (Amato, 2006; Lansford, 2009). Because the children often hear their parents fighting over child rearing, the children may come to blame themselves for the split. Young children, who are less experienced than adolescents, are more likely to blame themselves. Young children also worry more about uncharted territory—the details of life after the breakup. Adolescents are relatively more independent and have some power to control their day-to-day lives.

Most children live with their mothers after a divorce (Amato, 2006). Some fathers remain fully devoted to their children despite the split, but others tend to spend less time with their children as time goes on. This pattern is especially common when fathers create other families, such that the children of their new partners are competing with their biological children (Angarne-Lindberg et al., 2009). Not only does the drop-off in paternal attention deprive children of activities and social interactions, but it also saps their self-esteem: "Why doesn't Daddy love me anymore? What's wrong with me?"

There is no question that divorce has challenging effects on children. Children whose parents divorce are more likely to have conduct disorders, lower self-esteem, drug abuse, and poor grades in school (Kim, 2011; Moon, 2011). Their physical health may decline, at least temporarily (Moon, 2011). There are individual differences, but by and large, the fallout for children is worst during the first year after the breakup. Children tend to rebound after a couple of years or so (Malone et al., 2004).

A parental breakup is connected with a decline in the quality of parenting. A longitudinal study by E. Mavis Hetherington and her colleagues (Hetherington, 2006; Hetherington et al., 1989) tracked the adjustment of children who were four years old at the time of the divorce; the follow-ups occurred two months, one year, two years, and six years after the divorce. The investigators found that the organization of family life deteriorates. The family is more likely to eat meals pickup style, as opposed to sitting together. Children are less likely to get to school or to sleep on schedule. Divorced mothers have a more difficult time setting limits and enforcing restrictions on sons' behaviour. Divorced parents are significantly less likely to show the authoritative behaviours that foster competence. They make fewer demands for mature behaviour, communicate less, and show less nurturance and warmth. Their disciplinary methods become inconsistent.

Cross-cultural studies show that children of divorced parents in other cultures experience problems similar to those experienced by such children in North America (Boey et al., 2003). A study in China matched 58 children of divorced parents with 116 children from intact families according to gender, age, and social class. Children of divorced parents were more likely than the other children to make somatic complaints ("My stomach hurts," "I feel nauseous"), demonstrate lower social competence, and behave aggressively (Liu et al., 2000a). Another Chinese study found that divorce impairs the quality of parent–child relationships, interferes with concern over the children's education, and creates financial hardships (Sun, 2001). A third Chinese study showed that divorce compromises the academic and social functioning of both Chinese and North American children (Zhou et al., 2001).

A study of children and their mothers in Botswana, Africa, had similar results (Maundeni, 2000). Divorce led to economic hardship for most mothers and children. Lack of money made some children feel inferior to other children. Financial worries and feelings of resentment and betrayal led to social and emotional problems among both children and mothers.

Back in North America, boys seem to have a harder time than girls coping with divorce, and they take a longer time to recover (Grych, 2005; Malone et al., 2004). In the Hetherington study, boys whose parents were divorced showed more social, academic, and conduct problems than boys whose parents were married. These problems sometimes persisted for six years. Girls, by contrast, tended to regain normal functioning within two years.

K. Alison Clarke-Stewart and her colleagues (2000) compared the well-being of children in families headed by a separated or divorced mother with the well-being of about 170 children reared in intact families. As a group, the children who were being reared in two-parent families exhibited fewer problematic behaviours, more social skills, and higher IQ test scores. They were more securely attached to their mothers. But then the researchers factored in the mother's level of education, her socioeconomic status, and her psychological well-being. Somewhat surprisingly, the differences between the children in the two groups (one-parent versus intact families) almost vanished. The researchers concluded that at least in this study, it was not the parental breakup per se that caused the problems among the children. Instead, the difficulties were connected with the mother's psychological status (such as feelings of depression), income, and level of education (Hammen, 2003). The father's psychological status, of course, is frequently a factor that leads to marital conflict and divorce (Angarne-Lindberg et al., 2009; El-Sheikh et al., 2009).

By and large, research shows that the following types of support help children cope with divorce: social support from the immediate family, support from the extended family, support of friends, membership in a religious community, communication among family members, and financial security (Angarne-Lindberg et al., 2009; Greeff & Van Der Merwe, 2004).

Some children of divorced parents profit from psychological treatment (Bonkowski, 2005). Many treatment programs include parents. The usefulness of a program that includes the mother was studied with 240 children, ages 9–12 (Wolchik et al., 2000). The program addressed the quality of the mother–child relationship, ways of disciplining the child, ways of coping with interparental conflict, and the nature of the father–child relationship. Children were also helped to handle stressors (by thinking of them as difficult but not impossible) and to not blame themselves. The children showed improved adjustment at the completion of the program and at a six-month follow-up.

In Canada, there are programs for families in transition, either through specific programs in the community or through resources available through schools, health centres, or different professional groups (e.g., psychologists, social workers, pediatricians). In a report by Clark and the Canadian Pediatric Society Mental Health and Developmental Disabilities Committee (2013), it was recommended that effective parenting, managing parent–child relationships, and managing and strengthening relationships between parents helps children adjust to loss and change.

Life in Stepfamilies: His, Hers, Theirs, and ...

Most divorced people remarry, usually while the children are young. According to the 2011 Canadian Census, 12.6 percent of couples with children were stepfamilies (Statistics Canada, 2012).

The rule of thumb about the effects of living in stepfamilies is that there is no rule of thumb (Harvey & Fine, 2011). Living in a stepfamily may have no measurable psychological effects (Ganong & Coleman, 2003). Stepparents may claim stepchildren as their own and become intimately involved in their well-being (Marsiglio, 2004). In that case, children frequently report that they are content with the outcome of the divorce (Angarne-Lindberg et al., 2009). But there are also some risks to living in stepfamilies. Stepchildren appear to be at greater risk of being physically abused by stepparents than by biological parents (Adler-Baeder, 2006). Infanticide (killing infants) is a rarity in North America, but according to American statistics the crime occurs 60 times as often in stepfamilies as in families with biological kinship (Daly & Wilson, 2000). There is a significantly higher incidence—by a factor of eight—of sexual abuse by stepparents than by natural parents.

"All Right, We Fight—Should We Remain Married 'for the Sake of the Children'?"

QUESTION » What is best for the children? Should parents in conflict remain together for their children's sake? Let's have it out at once. We are going to address this issue from a psychological perspective only. Many readers believe—for moral or religious reasons—that marriage and family life must be permanent, no matter what. Readers will have to consider the moral and religious aspects of divorce in the light of their own value systems.

So—from a purely psychological perspective—what should bickering parents do? The answer seems to depend largely on how they behave in front of the children. Research shows that parental bickering—especially severe fighting—is linked to the same kinds of problems that children experience when their parents get separated or divorced (Furstenberg & Kiernan, 2001; Troxel & Matthews, 2004). Moreover, when children are exposed to adult or marital conflict, they display a biological "alarm reaction": Their heart rate, blood pressure, and sweating rise sharply (El-Sheikh et al., 2009). The bodily response is even stronger when children blame themselves for parental conflict, as is common among younger children.

One study analyzed data from 727 children, ages four to nine years, from intact families and followed up on them six years later, when many of the families had gone through separation or divorce (Morrison & Coiro, 1999). Both separation and divorce were associated with increases in behaviour problems in children, regardless of the amount of conflict between the parents. However, in the marriages that remained intact, high levels of marital conflict were associated with yet more behaviour problems in the children. What's the message? Although separation and divorce are related to adjustment problems in children, the outcome can be worse for children when conflicted parents stay together.

Because of the stresses experienced by children caught up in marital conflict, E. Mavis Hetherington and her colleagues suggest that divorce can be a positive alternative to harmful family functioning (Hetherington, 1989; Wallerstein et al., 2005). **TRUTH OR FICTION REVISITED:** From a psychological perspective, when parents in severe conflict stay together "for the sake of the children," the children experience chronic stress.

Active Review

6. During the middle years, parents do (more or less?) monitoring of children's activities and provide less direct feedback than they did in the preschool years.

7. The children of lesbian and gay parents are most likely to be (heterosexual or homosexual?) in their sexual orientation.

8. Children of divorced parents most often experience (upward or downward?) movement in financial status.

9. Most children of divorced parents live with their (mothers or fathers?).

10. (Boys or Girls?) seem to have a harder time coping with divorce.

Reflect & Relate: Have you known children whose families have gone through a divorce? What were the effects on the children?

13.3 Peer Relationships

QUESTION » What is the influence of peers during middle childhood? Families exert the most powerful influences on a child during his or her first few years. But as children move into middle childhood, their activities and interests become directed farther away from home. Peers take on increasing importance in middle childhood. This is easily mirrored in popular culture—through books (e.g., the *Harry Potter* series) and TV shows (e.g., *Phineas & Ferb*)—where children are usually involved in adventures with their friends. Let us explore the ways in which peers socialize one another. Then we will examine factors in peer acceptance and rejection. Finally, we will see how friendships develop.

Peers as Socialization Influences

Peer relationships are a major part of growing up. Peers exert powerful socialization influences and pressures to conform (Eivers et al., 2012). Even highly involved parents can provide children only with experience relating to adults. Children profit from experience relating to peers because peers have interests and skills that reflect being part of the same generation as the child. Peers differ as individuals, however. For all these reasons, peer experiences broaden children (Bukowski, Buhrmester, & Underwood, 2011; Molinari & Corsaro, 2000).

Peers guide children and afford practice in sharing and cooperating, in relating to leaders, and in coping with aggressive impulses, including their own. Peers can be important confidants (Dunn et al., 2001). Peers, like parents, help children learn what types of impulses—affectionate, aggressive, and so on—they can safely express and with whom. Children who are at odds with their parents can turn to peers as sounding boards. They can compare feelings and experiences they would not bring up in the home. When children share troubling ideas and experiences with peers, they often learn that friends have similar concerns. They realize that they are normal and are not alone (Barry & Wentzel, 2006).

Peer Acceptance and Rejection

Acceptance or rejection by peers is of major importance in childhood because problems with peers affect adjustment later on (Wentzel et al., 2004). What are the characteristics of popular and of rejected children?

TRUTH OR FICTION REVISITED: Popular children tend to be attractive and relatively mature for their age, although attractiveness seems to be more important for girls than for boys (Langlois et al., 2000). Socially speaking, popular children are friendly, nurturant, cooperative, helpful, and socially skillful (Chen et al., 2001; Xie et al., 2006). This type of popular child is called *popular–prosocial* and is the most common type of popular (Cillessen & Bellmore, 2010; Puckett, Aikins, & Cillessen, 2008). Another subtype of popular children is termed *popular–antisocial* children. This group comprises physically aggressive children (e.g., children who push or shove others) and relationally aggressive children (e.g., children who may exclude, gossip, and spread rumours about others to improve their own social standing); despite exhibiting aggressive behaviours, they are often perceived as popular by peers (Lease, Kennedy, & Axelrod, 2002; Vaillancourt & Hymel, 2006). Popular children have higher self-esteem than other children, which tends to reflect success in academics or valued extracurricular activities such as sports (Chen et al., 2001). Later-born children are more likely to be popular than firstborns, perhaps because they tend to be more sociable (Beck et al., 2006).

Children who demonstrate a lack of prosocial behaviours and engage in negative social behaviours are more likely to be rejected by peers. Children who show behavioural and learning problems, who are aggressive, and who

Peer Rejection
Few things are as painful as rejection by one's peers in middle childhood. Children may be rejected if they look unusual or unattractive, lack valued skills, or are aggressive.

disrupt group activities are more likely to be rejected by peers (Boivin et al., 2005). These children are identified as *rejected–aggressive* children, and usually lack the social skills needed to interpret cues from others and acting out when frustrated (Dempsey et al., 2006; Hoza et al., 2005). However, aggressive children who are also highly popular may be excused for their aggressive ways (A. J. Rose et al., 2004). Moreover, aggressive children are more likely to seek out aggressive friends (A. J. Rose et al., 2004).

Although pressure to conform to group norms and standards can be powerful, most children who are rejected seem to remain on that path. That is, they tend to remain lonely—on the fringes of the group (Klima & Repetti, 2008; Wentzel et al., 2004). Fortunately, interventions such as training in social skills seem to help increase children's popularity (Cashwell et al., 2001).

Development of Friendships

QUESTION » How do children's concepts of friendship develop? In the preschool years and the early years of middle childhood, friendships are based on geographical closeness or proximity. Friendships are relatively superficial—quickly formed and easily broken. What matters are activity levels, shared activities, and who has the swing set or sandbox. Children through the age of seven usually report that their friends are the children with whom they share activities (Berndt, 2004; Gleason et al., 2005). There is little reference to friends' traits.

Between the ages of 8 and 11, children increasingly recognize the importance of friends meeting each other's needs and possessing desirable traits (Ellis & Zarbatany, 2007). Children at these ages are more likely to say that friends are nice to one another and share interests as well as things. During these years, children increasingly pick friends who are similar to themselves in behaviour and personality. Trustworthiness, mutual understanding, and a willingness to share personal information characterize friendships in middle childhood and beyond (Rotenberg et al., 2004; Ullrich-French & Smith, 2009). Girls tend to develop closer friendships than boys (Ellis & Zarbatany, 2007; Rodkin & Ahn, 2009). Girls are more likely to seek confidants—girls with whom they can share their innermost feelings.

Robert Selman (1980) described five stages in children's changing concepts of friendship (see Table 13.2 ▉). The stages correspond to the five levels of perspective-taking skills discussed earlier in the chapter.

Friends behave differently with each other than they do with other children. School-age friends are more verbal, attentive, expressive, relaxed, and mutually responsive to each other during play than are children who are only acquaintances (Cleary et al., 2002). Cooperation occurs more readily between friends than between other groupings, as might be expected. But intense competition can also occur among friends, especially among boys. When conflicts occur between friends, they tend to be less intense and are resolved in ways that maintain positive social interaction (Bowker et al., 2011).

In one study, 696 children in Grade 4 and 5 responded to 30 hypothetical situations involving conflict with a friend (Rose & Asher, 1999). It was found that those children who responded to conflict by seeking revenge were least likely to have friendships or close friendships. Gender differences were also found. Girls were generally more interested in resolving conflicts than boys were.

Children in middle childhood typically will tell you that they have more than one "best" friend (Bukowski et al., 2011). One study found that nine-year-olds reported having an average of four best friends (Lewis & Feiring, 1989). Best friends tend to be more alike than other friends.

omgimages/Thinkstock

Friendship, Friendship ... A Perfect "Blendship"?
Children's concepts of friendship develop over time. In middle childhood, friendship is generally seen in terms of what children do for each other. These children are beginning to value loyalty and intimacy.

CHAPTER 13 MIDDLE CHILDHOOD: SOCIAL AND EMOTIONAL DEVELOPMENT **453**

Stages in Children's Concepts of Friendship

Stage	Name	Approximate Age (Years)[a]	What Happens
0	Momentary physical interaction	3–6	Children remain egocentric and unable to take one another's point of view. Thus, their concept of a friend is one who likes to play with the same things they do and who lives nearby.
1	One-way assistance	5–9	Children realize that their friends may have different thoughts and feelings than they do, but they place their own desires first. They view a friend as someone who does what they want them to do.
2	Fair-weather cooperation	7–12	Friends are viewed as doing things for one another (reciprocity), but the focus remains on each individual's self-interest rather than on the relationship per se.
3	Intimate and mutual sharing	10–15	The focus is on the relationship itself, rather than on the individuals separately. The function of friendship is viewed as mutual support over a long period of time, rather than concern about a given activity or self-interest.
4	Autonomous interdependence	12 and above	Children (as well as adolescents and adults) understand that friendships grow and change as people change. They realize that they may need different friends to satisfy different personal and social needs.

Source: Selman (1980).
[a]Ages may overlap.

In middle childhood, boys tend to play in larger groups than girls. Children's friendships are almost exclusively with others of the same gender, continuing the trend of gender segregation (Pfaff, 2010). Contact with members of the other gender is strongly discouraged by peers. For example, a study of 10- and 11-year-old American children from different cultural backgrounds found that those who crossed the "gender boundary" were especially unpopular with their peers (Sroufe et al., 1993).

Active Review

11. As children move into middle childhood, their activities and interests become directed (closer to or farther away from?) the home.

12. Popular children tend to be attractive and relatively (mature or immature?) for their age.

13. (First-born or Later-born?) children are more likely to be popular.

14. During middle childhood, contact with members of the other sex is (encouraged or discouraged?) by peers.

Reflect & Relate: Do you remember what your attitudes were toward playing with children of your own gender and children of the other gender? Did these attitudes change? Do you remember when, and what you were thinking at the time?

13.4 The School

QUESTION » What are the effects of the school on children's social and emotional development? The school exerts a powerful influence on many aspects of the child's development. Schools, like parents, set limits on behaviour, make demands for mature behaviour, attempt to communicate, and are oriented toward nurturing positive physical, social, and cognitive development. Schools, like parents, have a direct influence on children's IQ scores, achievement motivation, and career aspirations (Aber et al., 2007; Woolfolk, 2013). Like the family, schools influence social and moral development (Killen & Smetana, 2010).

Schools are also competitive environments, and children who do too well—and students who do not do well enough—can suffer from the resentment or the low opinion of others. An Italian study placed 178 male and 182 female eight- to nine-year-old elementary school students in competitive situations (Tassi et al., 2001). It was found that when the students were given the task of trying to outperform one another, competition led to social rejection by students' peers. On the other hand, when the students were simply asked to do the best they could, high rates of success led to admiration by one's peers.

In this section, we consider children's transition to school and then examine the effects of the school environment and of teachers.

Entry into School: Getting to Know You

An increasing number of children attend preschool. About half have had some type of formal prekindergarten experience, often part-time (Ebert & Culyer, 2011; Woolfolk, 2013). But most children first experience full-time schooling when they enter kindergarten or Grade 1. Children must master many new tasks when they start school. They have to meet new academic challenges, learn new school and teacher expectations, and fit into a new peer group. They must learn to accept extended separation from their parents and develop increased attention, self-control, and self-help skills.

You may be surprised to know that kindergarten is not mandatory for children in all provinces. For example, in Alberta parents may choose not to place their child into a half-day kindergarten program. In contrast, in New Brunswick and Nova Scotia kindergarten is compulsory. In Canada, parents have the choice of placing their children in half-day programs, full-day programs, and also in preschool or junior kindergarten programs based on where they live.

What happens to children during the transition from home or preschool to elementary school may be critical for their eventual success or failure in their educational experience. This is particularly true for low-income children. Families of children living in poverty may be less able to supply both the material and the emotional supports that help the child adjust successfully to school (Slavin, 2012; Woolfolk, 2013).

How well prepared are children to enter school? Discussions of school readiness must consider at least three critical factors:

1. The diversity and inequity of children's early life experiences
2. Individual differences in young children's development and learning
3. The degree to which schools establish reasonable and appropriate expectations of children's capabilities when they enter school

Cheryl Casey/Shutterstock.com

Unfortunately, some children enter school less well prepared than others. In one study (Chira, 1991), nearly half the teachers thought that children entered school less ready to learn than had children five years earlier. Most of the teachers said that children often lacked the language skills needed to succeed. This report and others (Ebert & Culyer, 2011; Woolfolk, 2013) concluded that poor health care and nutrition and lack of adequate stimulation and support by parents place many children at risk for academic failure even before they enter school.

The average school reports that between 10 percent and 20 percent of incoming kindergartners had difficulty adjusting to kindergarten (Buyse et al., 2011; Slavin, 2012). Adjusting to the academic demands of school was reported to be the area of greatest difficulty. Children from families with low socioeconomic status had a harder time adjusting than other children, particularly in academics. Children who enter school with deficits in language and math skills generally continue to show deficits in these areas during at least the first years of school (Ebert & Culyer, 2011; Woolfolk, 2013).

Magnuson and colleagues (2004) found that children who attended a centre or school-based preschool program in the year before school entry performed better on assessments of reading and math skills upon beginning kindergarten, after controlling for a host of family background and other factors that might be associated with selection into early education programs and relatively high academic skills. This advantage persisted into the spring of kindergarten and Grade 1.

Another area of increasing concern for educators is social and emotional functioning, also termed as the fourth "r" (the "relationship" factor) because it is often overlooked in educational settings; however, it is clearly an area that warrants serious attention (Hymel et al., 2006). To date, the vast majority of school readiness research has concentrated on academic outcomes. However social-emotional development may be as important, if not more so, than traditional forms of school readiness (e.g., analytical intelligence; Hymel et al., 2006; Snow, 2006).

The School Environment: Setting the Stage for Success or ...

QUESTION » **What are the characteristics of a good school?** Research summaries (Slavin, 2012; Woolfolk, 2013) indicate that an effective school has the following characteristics:

- An active, energetic principal
- An atmosphere that is orderly but not oppressive
- Empowerment of teachers—that is, teachers participating in decision making
- Teachers who have high expectations that children will learn
- A curriculum that emphasizes academics
- Frequent assessment of student performance
- Empowerment of students—that is, students participating in setting goals, making classroom decisions, and engaging in cooperative learning activities with other students

Certain aspects of the school environment are important as well. One key factor is class size. Smaller classes permit students to receive more individual attention and to express their ideas more often (Ebert & Culyer, 2011). Smaller classes lead to increased achievement in mathematics and reading in the early primary grades. Smaller classes are particularly useful in teaching the "basics"—reading, writing, and arithmetic—to elementary school students who are at risk for academic failure (Ebert & Culyer, 2011; Woolfolk, 2013).

Is Bullying Murder?

I was called really horrible, profane names very loudly in front of huge crowds of people, and my schoolwork suffered at one point," she said. "I didn't want to go to class. And I was a straight-A student, so there was a certain point in my high school years where I just couldn't even focus on class because I was so embarrassed all the time. I was so ashamed of who I was.

—Lady Gaga (quoted in Kristof, March, 2012)

Eleven-year-old Michael Wilson committed suicide in 2011. His family found him with a plastic bag tied around his head (Nurwisah, 2011).

Michael had had muscular dystrophy. He struggled to walk around the block or climb the stairs. He used a walker to get by in school. A 12-year-old mugged him, after his iPhone, and a few months before his death, Michael said, "If I have to go back to that school, I'll kill myself." And he did.

Amanda Cummings, 15, liked animals, poetry, and Katy Perry's music. She committed suicide by jumping in front of a bus. She was being bullied, both in person and on Facebook, by fellow students in her high school on New York's Staten Island (Flegenheimer, 2012).

Dawn-Marie Wesley, 14, of Mission, British Columbia, hanged herself shortly after three teenage girls called her. Wesley's suicide note indicated peers had threatened her and she believed death was her only escape (CBC News Canada, 2002).

A Korean court sentenced two teenagers to prison for bullying another student until he committed suicide (Hancocks, 2012).

According to *Bullying and Suicide* (2009),

- Victims of bullying are at least twice as likely to commit suicide as other children.
- At least half of the suicides by children and teens are related to bullying.
- The group most vulnerable to committing suicide as a result of bullying appears to be 10–14-year-old girls.
- Approximately 30 percent of students say they are either bullies or victims of bullying.
- Some 160 000 U.S. students refuse to go to school each day as a consequence of fear of being bullied.

All in all, it is estimated that 10 percent of students in North America have been exposed to extreme bullying, and that 70–75 percent of students overall have been bullied (Li, 2007). Bullying has devastating effects on the school atmosphere. It transforms the perception of school from a safe place into a violent place (Batsche & Porter, 2006). Bullying also impairs adjustment to middle school,

© Ray Tamarra/Contributor/Getty Images

Lady Gaga may be a superstar now, but bullying led her to have serious self-doubts in school.

where bullying is sometimes carried out by older children against younger children (Scheithauer et al., 2006).

Boys are more likely than girls to engage in bullying behaviours, but many girls engage in bullying as well (Holt et al., 2009; Q. Li et al., 2012). Those who bully have some things in common. Their achievement tends to be lower than average, such that peer approval or deference might be more important to them than academics (Perren & Alsaker, 2006). Children who bully are more likely to come from homes of lower socioeconomic status with parental violence (Pereira et al., 2004).

Bullying is frequently associated with diagnoses of conduct disorder, oppositional defiant disorder, attention-deficit/hyperactivity disorder, and depression (Li et al., 2012). Individuals who bully are also more likely to have personality problems, such as assuming that others are out to harm them when they're not. Bullying is intentional and targeted.

Cyberbullying Some children are bullied electronically rather than in person. Amanda Cummings was bullied on Facebook as well as in person. They receive threatening

Continued

Continued

messages from fellow students by means of electronic technology such as computers, cell phones, or iPads (Mishna et al., 2009). This phenomenon is referred to as *cyberbullying*. At least one student in six has experienced cyberbullying (Schneider et al., 2012). Although cyberbullying might seem to provide a "comfortable" distance between the bully and the victim, its effects can be devastating—because of the pervasiveness and the far reach of the technology. Cases of severe anxiety, including school phobia and refusal, depression, lowered self-esteem, and suicide, have been reported (Mishna et al., 2009). As in other forms of bullying, the majority of cyberbullies are male, and most victims do not report the incidents (Li et al., 2012).

Is there a "cure" for bullying? School systems and families have a stake in controlling bullying, and sometimes setting strict limits on bullies is helpful. But, as noted, much—or most—bullying goes unreported, sometimes because children are embarrassed to admit they are being bullied and sometimes because they fear retaliation by those who are engaging in bullying behaviours (Li et al., 2012). Many children simply learn to accommodate or avoid those who bully until they are out of school (Li et al., 2012). Then the victim and the bully go their separate ways.

Canadians are taking the lead in anti-bullying prevention, intervention, research and education. Debra Pepler sity established Promoting Relationships and Eliminating from York University and Wendy Craig at Queens UniverVio-lence (PREVNet)—a network of Canadian researchers and child/youth-focused national organizations with the vision of eliminating aggression and promoting healthy relationships. PREVNet is funded through the Networks of Centres of Excellence. Within PREVNet, Canadian researchers and education advocates have begun a dialogue to promote safe and healthy relationships for all Canadian children and youth. As Pepler and Craig (2000) point out, the following messages about bullying need to be communicated:

- Bullying is wrong and hurtful.
- Bullying is a relationship problem.
- Promoting relationships and eliminating violence are everyone's responsibility.

For in-depth discussion of these key messages, visit PREVNet.ca.

Reflect
- Were you ever bullied in school? If so, how did you handle it?
- What should teachers and school officials do about bullies?
- What should parents tell their children about bullies?

Teachers: Setting Limits, Making Demands, Communicating Values, and—Oh, Yes—Teaching

The influence of the schools is mainly due to teachers. Teachers, like parents, set limits, make demands, communicate values, and foster development. Teacher–student relationships are more limited than parent–child relationships, but teachers still have the opportunity to serve as powerful role models and dispensers of reinforcement. After all, children spend several hours each weekday in the presence of teachers.

Teacher Influences on Student Performance

Many aspects of teacher behaviour are related to student achievement (Ebert & Culyer, 2011). Achievement is enhanced when teachers expect students to master the curriculum, allocate most of the available time to academic activities, and manage the classroom environment effectively. Students learn more in classes when they are actively instructed or supervised by teachers than when they work on their own. The most effective teachers ask questions, give personalized feedback, and provide opportunities for drill and practice, as opposed to straight lecturing.

Student achievement also is linked to the emotional climate of the classroom (Ebert & Culyer, 2011). Students do not do as well when teachers rely heavily on criticism, ridicule, threats, or punishment. Achievement is high in classrooms that have a pleasant, friendly atmosphere, but not in classrooms with extreme teacher warmth.

Teacher Expectations

There is a saying that "You find what you're looking for." Consider the so-called **Pygmalion effect** in education. In Greek mythology, the amorous sculptor Pygmalion breathed life into a beautiful statue he had carved. Similarly, in the musical *My Fair Lady,* a reworking of the Pygmalion legend, Henry Higgins fashions a great lady from the lower-class Eliza Doolittle.

Teachers also try to bring out positive traits that they believe dwell within their students. TRUTH OR FICTION REVISITED: A classic experiment by Robert Rosenthal and Lenore Jacobson (1968) suggested that teacher expectations can become **self-fulfilling prophecies**. As reported in their classic *Pygmalion in the Classroom,* Rosenthal and Jacobson (1968) first gave students a battery of psychological tests. Then they informed teachers that a handful of the students, although average in performance to date, were about to blossom forth intellectually in the current school year.

Now, in fact, the tests had indicated nothing in particular about the "chosen" children. These children had been selected at random. The purpose of the experiment was to determine whether changing teacher expectations could affect student performance. As it happened, the identified children made significant gains in intelligence test scores.

In subsequent research, however, results have been mixed. Some studies have found support for the Pygmalion effect (Madon et al., 2001). Others have not. A review of 18 such experiments found that the Pygmalion effect was most pronounced when the procedure for informing teachers of the potential in the target student had the greatest credibility (Raudenbusch, 1984). A fair conclusion seems to be that teacher expectations sometimes, but not always, affect students' motivation, self-esteem, expectations for success, and achievement.

These findings have serious implications for children from ethnic minority and low-income families. There is some indication that teachers expect less academically from children in these groups (Ebert & Culyer, 2011; Woolfolk, 2008). Teachers with lower expectations for certain children may spend less time encouraging and interacting with them.

What are some of the ways in which teachers can help motivate all students to do their best? Anita Woolfolk (2008) suggests the following:

- Make the classroom and the lesson interesting and inviting.
- Ensure that students can profit from social interaction.
- Make the classroom a safe and pleasant place.
- Recognize that students' backgrounds can give rise to diverse patterns of needs.
- Help students take appropriate responsibility for their successes and failures.
- Encourage students to perceive the links between their own efforts and their achievements.
- Help students set attainable short-term goals.

OBSERVING CHILDREN, UNDERSTANDING OURSELVES

Self-Fulfilling Prophecies

Learn how powerful self-fulfilling prophecies can be and which children are most likely to be affected.

What is a self-fulfilling prophecy?

What is the difference between a positive and a negative self-fulfilling prophecy? In what situations are self-fulfilling prophecies found? What two subgroups of students seem to be most strongly influenced by self-fulfilling prophecies?

From Rathus. *Childhood and Adolescence,* 5E. © 2014 South-Western, a part of Cengage Learning, Inc. Reproduced by permission. www.cengage.com/permissions

Go to www.nelson.com/voyages2ce to watch the video, answer the questions, and e-mail your responses to your professor.

Pygmalion effect A self-fulfilling prophecy; an expectation that is confirmed because of the behaviour of those who hold the expectation.

self-fulfilling prophecy An event that occurs because of the behaviour of those who expect it to occur.

Waiting to Be Called On
Who is the teacher most likely to call on? Some studies say that teachers may favour the boy and call on him before the girl, especially in math, science, and technology classes.

Sexism in the Classroom

Although girls were systematically excluded from formal education for centuries, today we might not expect to find **sexism** among teachers. Teachers, after all, are generally well educated. They are also trained to be fair-minded and sensitive to the needs of their young charges in today's changing society.

However, we may not have heard the last of sexism in our schools. Researchers (Gruber & Fineran, 2007; Sadker, 2011; Sadker et al., 2009) have recently found that:

- Many teachers pay less attention to girls than to boys, especially in math, science, and technology classes.
- Many girls are subjected to **sexual harassment**—unwelcome verbal or physical conduct of a sexual nature—from male classmates, and many teachers minimize the harmfulness of harassment and ignore it.
- Some school textbooks still stereotype or ignore women, more often portraying males as the shakers and movers in the world.

In a widely cited study, Myra and David Sadker (1994) observed students in Grade 4, 6, and 8 classes in four U.S. states and the District of Columbia. Teachers and students were European American and African American, urban, suburban, and rural. In almost all cases, the findings were depressingly similar. Boys generally dominated classroom communication, whether the subject was math (a traditionally "masculine" area) or language arts (a traditionally "feminine" area). Despite the stereotype that girls are more likely to talk or even chatter, boys were eight times more likely than girls to call out answers without raising their hands. So far, it could be said, we have evidence of a gender difference, but not of sexism. However, teachers were less than impartial in responding to boys and girls when they called out. Teachers, male and female, were significantly more likely to accept calling out from boys. Girls were significantly more likely, as the song goes, to receive "teachers' dirty looks"—or to be reminded that they should raise their hands and wait to be called on. Boys, it appears, are expected to be impetuous, but impetuous girls are reprimanded for "unladylike behaviour." Sad to say, until they saw tapes of themselves, the teachers generally were unaware that they were treating girls and boys differently.

Some observers note that primary and secondary teachers tend to give more active teaching attention to boys than to girls, especially in math and technology courses (Bell & Norwood, 2007; Crocco & Libresco, 2007; Koch, 2007). They call on boys more often, ask them more questions, talk to and listen to them more, give them lengthier directions, and praise and criticize them more often.

Others argue the exact opposite—that we are not connecting with our boys early enough. In early child and elementary school programs, most teachers are females, and boys have very few role models. In fact, there is growing concern by some researchers and professionals that boys struggle in early education (Gurian, 2005; Kindlon & Thomson, 2002; Pollack, 2002; Sadker & Sadker, 2002). Rather than see is this matter as a "girls versus boys" issue, it would be more helpful to view education as providing all students (male or female) with opportunities to learn and express themselves in a safe and caring environment. Easier said than done, right?

sexism Discrimination or bias against people on the basis of their gender.

sexual harassment Unwelcome verbal or physical conduct of a sexual nature.

Active Review

15. Children from families with (high or low?) socioeconomic status have a more difficult time adjusting to school.

16. (Smaller or Larger?) classes facilitate learning during middle childhood.

17. An experiment by Rosenthal and Jacobson suggests that teacher expectations can become _____ prophecies.

18. (Boys or Girls?) tend to be favoured by teachers in the classroom.

Reflect & Relate: Do you remember what it was like for you to enter school at kindergarten or Grade 1? Did you experience some adjustment problems? What were they?

13.5 Social and Emotional Problems

QUESTION » What kinds of social and emotional problems do children encounter in middle childhood? What can we do about them? Many school-aged children suffer from emotional or behavioural problems that could benefit from professional treatment (Denham et al., 2011). But most of them are unlikely to receive help. What are some of the more common psychological problems of middle childhood? In previous chapters, we examined attention-deficit/hyperactivity disorder (AD/HD) and learning disabilities. Here, we focus on those problems more likely to emerge during middle childhood: conduct disorders, depression, and anxiety. We use the terminology in the *Diagnostic and Statistical Manual of Mental Disorders*, Fifth Edition (DSM-5) of the American Psychiatric Association (2013) because it is the most widely used index of psychological disorders.

Conduct Disorders

> David is a 16-year-old high school dropout. He has just been arrested for the third time in two years for stealing video equipment and computers from people's homes. Acting alone, David was caught in each case when he tried to sell the stolen items. In describing his actions in each crime, David expressed defiance and showed a lack of remorse. In fact, he bragged about how often he had gotten away with similar crimes.
>
> —Adapted from Halgin & Whitbourne (1993, p. 335)

David has a **conduct disorder**. Children with conduct disorders, like David, persistently break rules or violate the rights of others. They exhibit behaviours such as lying, stealing, setting fires, truancy, cruelty to animals, and fighting (American Psychiatric Association, 2013). To receive this diagnosis, children must engage in the behaviour pattern (presence of specific range of criteria) for at least 12 months, with at least one criterion from a list of 15 present in the past six months. Conduct disorders typically emerge by eight years of age and are much more prevalent in boys (Nock et al., 2006).

Children with conduct disorders are often involved in sexual activity, and they often smoke, drink, and engage in other substance abuse (American Psychiatric Association, 2013). They have a low tolerance for frustration and may have temper flare-ups. They tend to blame other people for the trouble they get into (Schultz & Shaw, 2003). They believe that they are misunderstood and treated unfairly. Their academic achievement is usually below grade level, but intelligence is usually at least average. Many children with conduct disorders also are diagnosed with ADHD (Chronis et al., 2007; Drabick et al., 2004; Hudziak, 2001).

conduct disorders Disorders marked by persistent breaking of the rules and violations of the rights of others.

Origins of Conduct Disorders

Conduct disorders may have a genetic and physiological component (Subbarao et al., 2008). They are more likely to be found in the biological parents than in the adoptive parents of adopted children who have such problems (Rhee & Waldman, 2009). Other contributors include antisocial family members, deviant peers, inconsistent discipline, parental insensitivity to the child's behaviour, physical punishment, and family stress (Kilgore et al., 2000; Straus, 2000; Subbarao et al., 2008).

A CLOSER LOOK RESEARCH

When *Doom* Leads to ... Doom

Dylan Klebold and Eric Harris were engrossed in violent video games for hours at a time. They were particularly keen on a game named *Doom*. Harris had managed to reprogram *Doom* so that he, the player, became invulnerable and had an endless supply of weapons. He would "mow down" all the other characters in the game. His program caused some of the characters to ask God why they had been shot as they lay dying. Later on, Klebold and Harris asked some of their shooting victims at Columbine High School in Colorado whether they believed in God. One of the killers also referred to his shotgun as Arlene, the name of a character in *Doom* (Saunders, 2003).

Michael Carneal was also a fan of *Doom*—and of another video game, *Redneck Revenge*. He showed up at school one morning with a semiautomatic pistol, two shotguns, and two rifles. He aimed them at people in a prayer group. Before he was finished, three of them lay dead and five were wounded. Although Carneal had had no appreciable experience with firearms, authorities noted that his aim was uncannily accurate. He fired just once at each person's head, as one would do to rack up points in a video game—especially a game that offers extra points for head shots.

Middle childhood, the ages of 6–12, is a prime time for initiating participation in violent video games such as *Doom*. In Chapter 10, we noted that the debate about whether violence in media such as films, television, and video games fuels violence in the real world has been going on for more than 40 years. Research strongly suggests that media violence is a risk factor for increasing emotional arousal, aggressive behaviour, and violent thoughts (Bushman & Gibson, 2011). Moreover, it tends to desensitize observers to violence, possibly contributing to the development of conduct disorders in children in middle childhood.

One reason to be particularly concerned about violent video games is that they require audience participation (Power, 2011). Players don't just watch; they *participate*.

Monkey Business Images/Shutterstock.com

Research with children aged 8–12 who have conduct disorders shows that they are less likely than other children to experience arousal of the sympathetic division of the autonomic nervous system when they inflict pain on others in the real world or in video games (Anderson et al., 2010). Sympathetic arousal is connected with emotions such as anxiety, guilt, and shame—emotions that children with conduct disorders, especially boys, are less likely to experience (Bushman & Gibson, 2011). A study of mostly 10- to 11-year-olds with conduct disorders suggests that these children are therefore more likely to apply what they learn in violent video games, because they are less likely to be inhibited by the discomfort of others (van Baardewijk et al., 2009).

Reflect

- Why is it that some, but not all, children react violently to violent video games?

- For debate: Should violent video games be censored?

- Have you ever played a violent video game? What were its effects on you?

- Why do you think violent video games are more appealing to boys than to girls?

A study of 123 African American boys and girls pointed toward relationships among parental discipline, parental monitoring, and conduct problems (Kilgore et al., 2000). The researchers found that coercive parental discipline and poor parental monitoring of children at age four-and-a-half were reliable predictors of conduct problems for boys and girls at age six. The families were poor, and the parents had no choice but to send the children to schools with many peers who had conduct disorders. However, once socioeconomic status and school choice were taken into account, parental discipline and monitoring were the strongest predictors of conduct disorders. These findings are consistent with research on European American, more advantaged boys, which suggests that family processes are stronger predictors of conduct disorders than ethnicity.

Treatment of Conduct Disorders

The treatment of conduct disorders is challenging, but it seems that cognitive-behavioural techniques involving parent training hold promise (Cavell, 2001; Kazdin, 2000; Sukhodolsky et al., 2005). Children with conduct disorders profit from interventions in which their behaviour is monitored closely, there are consequences (such as time-outs) for unacceptable behaviour, physical punishment is avoided, and positive social behaviour is rewarded. That is, rather than just targeting noncompliant behaviour, it is useful to attend to children when they are behaving properly and to reward them for doing so (Cavell, 2001).

Other approaches include teaching aggressive children methods for coping with feelings of anger that will not violate the rights of others. One promising cognitive-behavioural method teaches children social skills and how to use problem solving to manage interpersonal conflicts (Webster-Stratton et al., 2001). Desirable social skills include asking other children to stop annoying behaviour rather than hitting them. Children are also taught to "stop and think" before engaging in aggressive behaviour. They are encouraged to consider the outcomes of their behaviour and find acceptable ways to reach their goals.

Childhood Depression

QUESTION » What is depression? What can we do about it?

> Kristin, an 11-year-old, feels "nothing is working out for me." For the past year she has been failing in school, although she previously had been a B student. She has trouble sleeping, feels tired all the time, and has started refusing to go to school. She cries easily and thinks her peers are making fun of her because she is "ugly and stupid." Her mother recently found a note written by Kristin that said she wanted to jump in front of a car "to end my misery."
>
> —Adapted from Weller & Weller (1991, p. 655)

Childhood is the happiest time of life, correct? Not necessarily. Many children are happy enough—protected by their parents and unencumbered by adult responsibilities. From the perspective of aging adults, their bodies seem made of rubber and free of aches. Their energy is apparently boundless.

Yet many children, like Kristin, are depressed. Children with depression may feel sad, blue, down in the dumps. They may show poor appetite, insomnia, lack of energy and inactivity, loss of self-esteem, difficulty concentrating, loss of interest in people and activities they usually enjoy, crying, feelings of hopelessness and helplessness, and thoughts of suicide (American Psychiatric Association, 2013).

But many children do not recognize depression in themselves until the age of seven or so. Part of the problem is cognitive developmental. The capacity for concrete operations apparently contributes to children's abilities to perceive internal feeling states (Glasberg & Aboud, 1982).

When children cannot report their feelings, depression is inferred from behaviour. Depressed children in middle childhood engage in less social activity and have poorer social skills than peers (American Psychiatric Association, 2013). In some cases, childhood depression is "masked" by conduct disorders, physical complaints, academic problems, and anxiety.

About 3 percent of children under age 13 and 5.6 percent of 13- to 18-year-olds report being depressed (Costello et al., 2006). Depression occurs equally often in girls and boys during childhood but is more common among women later in life. Depressed children frequently continue to have depressive episodes as adolescents and adults.

Origins of Depression

The origins of depression are complex and varied. Psychological and biological explanations have been proposed.

Some social cognitive theorists explain depression in terms of relationships between competencies (knowledge and skills) and feelings of self-esteem. Children who gain academic, social, and other competencies usually have high self-esteem. Perceived low levels of competence are linked to helplessness, low self-esteem, and depression. Longitudinal studies of primary schoolchildren have found that problems in academics, socializing, physical appearance, and sports can predict feelings of depression (Kistner, 2006). Conversely, self-perceived competence in these areas is negatively related to feelings of depression; that is, competence appears to "protect" children from depression. Children who have not developed competencies because of lack of opportunity, inconsistent parental reinforcement, and so on, may develop feelings of helplessness and hopelessness. Stressful life events, daily hassles, and poor problem-solving ability also give rise to helplessness and hopelessness. These ideas, in turn, trigger depression (Kendler et al., 2011). In contrast, social support and self-confidence tend to protect children from depression. Some competent children might not give themselves credit because of excessive parental expectations. Or children may be perfectionistic themselves. Perfectionistic children may be depressed because they cannot meet their own standards.

Children in elementary school are likely to be depressed because of situational stresses, such as family problems. Among middle school children, however, we find cognitive contributors to depression. For example, a study of 582 Chinese children from Hong Kong secondary schools found that cognitive distortions, such as minimizing accomplishments and blowing problems out of proportion, are associated with feelings of depression (Leung & Poon, 2001). A European study found that ruminating about problems (going over them again and again—and again), blaming oneself for

Childhood depression can have many origins, including feelings of failure and helplessness, losses, self-blame for problems that are not of one's own making—and, possibly, genetic factors.

things that are not one's fault, and blowing problems out of proportion are linked with depression (Garnefski et al., 2001).

The tendency to blame oneself (internal attribution) or others (external attribution) is called a child's **attributional style**. Certain attributional styles can contribute to helplessness and hopelessness and hence to depression (Cohen et al., 2011).

TRUTH OR FICTION REVISITED: It is true that some children blame themselves for all the problems in their lives, whether they deserve any blame or not. Research shows that children who are depressed are more likely to attribute their failures to internal, stable, and global factors—factors they are relatively helpless to change (Cohen et al., 2011; Cole et al., 2011). Helplessness triggers depression. Consider the case of two children who do poorly on a math test. John thinks, "I'm a jerk! I'm just no good in math! I'll never learn." Jim thinks, "That test was tougher than I thought it would be. I'll have to work harder next time." John is perceiving the problem as global (he's "a jerk") and stable (he'll "never learn"). Jim perceives the problem as specific rather than global (related to the type of math test the teacher makes up) and as unstable rather than stable (he can change the results by working harder). In effect, John thinks "It's me" (an internal attribution), whereas Jim thinks "It's the test" (an external attribution). Depressed children tend to explain negative events in terms of internal, stable, and global causes. As a result, they, like John, are more likely than Jim to be depressed.

There is also evidence of genetic factors in depression (Kendler et al., 2011). For example, the children of depressed parents are at greater risk for depression and other disorders. A Norwegian study of 2794 twins estimated that the heritability of depression in females is 49 percent and in males is 25 percent (Orstavik et al., 2007). On a neurological level, evidence suggests that depressed children (and adults) "underutilize" the neurotransmitter **serotonin** (Vitiello, 2006).

Treatment of Depression

Parents and teachers can do a good deal to alleviate relatively mild feelings of depression among children. They can involve children in enjoyable activities, encourage the development of skills, offer praise when appropriate, and point out when children are being too hard on themselves. But if feelings of depression persist, treatment is called for.

Psychotherapy for depression tends to be mainly cognitive behavioural these days, and it is often straightforward. Children (and adolescents) are encouraged to do enjoyable things and build social skills. They are made aware of their tendencies to minimize their accomplishments, catastrophize their problems, and overly blame themselves for shortcomings (e.g., Kendall, 2011).

We noted that many depressed children underutilize the neurotransmitter serotonin. Antidepressant medication (selective serotonin reuptake inhibitors, or SSRIs), such as Luvox, Prozac, and Zoloft, increase the action of serotonin in the brain and are some-times used to treat childhood depression. Studies of their effectiveness yield a mixed review, ranging from something like "deadly dangerous" to "often effective" (Vitiello, 2006). Although SSRIs are often effective, the U.S. Food and Drug Administration has warned that there may be a link between their use and suicidal thinking in children (Henry et al., 2011).

Childhood depression is frequently accompanied by anxiety (Kendler et al., 2011), as we will see in the next section. Social and emotional problems that tend to emerge in middle childhood are summarized in Concept Review 13.1.

attributional style The way in which one is disposed toward interpreting outcomes (successes or failures), as in tending to place blame or responsibility on oneself or on external factors.

serotonin A neurotransmitter that is involved in mood disorders such as depression.

Problem	Behaviour Patterns	Comments
Conduct disorders 	• Precocious sexual activity and substance abuse • Truancy, stealing, lying, and aggression	More common in boys Child blames others for problems Probably connected with genetic factors Other contributors—antisocial family members, deviant peers, inconsistent discipline, physical punishment, and family stress Tends to be stable throughout adolescence and into adulthood Frequently accompanied by ADHD
Childhood depression 	• Feelings of sadness, poor appetite, insomnia, lack of energy and inactivity, loss of self-esteem, difficulty concentrating, loss of interest in people and activities, crying, feelings of hopelessness and helplessness, and thoughts of suicide • Can be masked by conduct disorders, physical complaints, academic problems, and anxiety	Occurs about equally in both genders Connected with lack of competencies (knowledge and skills) Connected with situational stresses, such as divorce Connected with feelings of helplessness and hopelessness Connected with cognitive factors such as perfectionism, rumination, minimization of achievements, blowing problems out of proportion, and a negative attributional style—internal, stable, and global attributions for failures Possibly connected with genetic factors Connected with "underutilization" of the neurotransmitter serotonin Frequently accompanied by anxiety
Childhood anxiety 	• Persistent, excessive worrying • Fear of the worst happening • Anxiety inappropriate for child's developmental level • Physical symptoms such as stomachaches, nausea, and vomiting • Nightmares • Concerns about death and dying	More common in girls Genetic factors implicated Frequently develops after stressful life events, such as divorce, illness, death of relative or pet, or change of schools or homes Often overlaps with—but not the same as—school refusal Frequently accompanied by depression

Image credits: Stockbyte/Thinkstock; Galina Barskaya/Shutterstock.com; Brian McEntire/Thinkstock

Childhood Anxiety

generalized anxiety disorder (GAD) An anxiety disorder in which anxiety is present continuously and is unrelated to the situation.

Children show many kinds of anxiety disorders, and these disorders are accompanied by depression in 50–60 percent of children (Kendler et al., 2011; Vallance & Garralda, 2011). Yet many children show anxiety disorders, such as **generalized anxiety disorder (GAD)**, in the absence of depression

(Rubin et al., 2011). Other anxiety disorders shown by children include **phobias** such as **separation anxiety disorder (SAD)** and stage fright (Rubin et al., 2011).

A cross-cultural study compared anxiety disorders and obsessive-compulsive disorders in 862 German children and 975 Japanese children between the ages of 8 and 12 (Essau et al., 2004). The German children were significantly more likely to report generalized anxiety, separation anxiety, social phobias, and **obsessive-compulsive disorder (OCD)**. The Japanese children were more likely to report physical complaints and phobias in the realm of bodily injury. In both nations, girls were more likely than boys to report anxieties.

Separation Anxiety
School phobia is often a form of separation anxiety. This boy is afraid to be separated from his mother. He imagines that something terrible will happen to her (or to him) when they are apart. Many mornings he complains of a tummy ache or of being too tired to go to school.

Separation Anxiety Disorder

QUESTION » What is separation anxiety disorder? It is normal for children to show anxiety when they are separated from their caregivers. Separation anxiety is a normal feature of the child–caregiver relationship and begins during the first year. But the sense of security that is usually provided by bonds of attachment encourages children to explore their environments and become progressively independent of caregivers.

Separation anxiety disorder affects an estimated 4–5 percent of children and young adolescents (American Psychiatric Association, 2013). The disorder occurs most often in girls and is often associated with school refusal (Vallance & Garralda, 2011). It also frequently occurs together with social anxiety (Ferdinand et al., 2006). The disorder may persist into adulthood, leading to an exaggerated concern about the well-being of one's children and spouse and to difficulty tolerating any separation from them.

SAD is diagnosed when separation anxiety is persistent and excessive, when it is inappropriate for the child's developmental level, and when it interferes with activities or development tasks—most important, attending school. Six-year-olds ought to be able to enter Grade 1 without anxiety-related nausea and vomiting and without dread that they or their parents will come to harm. Children with SAD tend to cling to their parents and follow them around the house. They may voice concerns about death and dying and insist that someone stay with them while they are falling asleep. They may complain of nightmares, stomachaches, and nausea and vomiting on school days. They may plead with their parents not to leave the house, or they may throw tantrums.

SAD may occur before middle childhood, preventing adjustment to day care or nursery school. In adolescence, refusal to attend school is often connected with academic and social problems, in which case the label of SAD does not apply. SAD usually becomes a significant problem in middle childhood because that is when children are expected to adjust to school.

SAD frequently develops after a stressful life event, such as an illness, the death of a relative or pet, or a change of schools or homes. Alison's problems followed the death of her grandmother:

> Alison's grandmother died when Alison was 7 years old. Her parents decided to permit her … to view her grandmother in the open coffin. Alison took a tentative glance from her father's arms across the room, then asked to be taken out of the room. Her 5-year-old sister took a leisurely close-up look, with no apparent distress.

phobia An irrational, excessive fear that interferes with one's functioning.

separation anxiety disorder (SAD) An extreme form of normal separation anxiety that is characterized by anxiety about separating from parents; SAD often takes the form of school refusal.

obsessive-compulsive disorder (OCD) A disorder characterized by obsessions (recurring thoughts or images that seem beyond control) and compulsions (irresistible urges to repeat an act).

Alison had been concerned about death for two or three years by this time, but her grandmother's passing brought on a new flurry of questions: "Will I die?" "Does everybody die?" and so on. Her parents tried to reassure her by saying, "Grandma was very, very old, and she also had a heart condition. You are very young and in perfect health. You have many, many years before you have to start thinking about death."

Alison also could not be alone in any room in her house. She pulled one of her parents or her sister along with her everywhere she went. She also reported nightmares about her grandmother and, within a couple of days, insisted on sleeping in the same room with her parents. Fortunately, Alison's fears did not extend to school. Her teacher reported that Alison spent some time talking about her grandmother, but her academic performance was apparently unimpaired.

Alison's parents decided to allow Alison time to "get over" the loss. Alison gradually talked less and less about death, and by the time 3 months had passed, she was able to go into any room in her house by herself. She wanted to continue to sleep in her parents' bedroom, however. So her parents "made a deal" with her. They would put off the return to her own bedroom until the school year had ended (a month away), if Alison would agree to return to her own bed at that time. As a further incentive, a parent would remain with her until she fell asleep for the first month. Alison overcame the anxiety problem in this fashion with no additional delays.

—Author's files

Separation Anxiety Disorder, School Phobia, and School Refusal

QUESTION » **What are the connections among separation anxiety disorder, school phobia, and school refusal?** SAD is similar to but not the same as school phobia. SAD is an extreme form of separation anxiety. It is characterized by anxiety about separating from parents and may be expressed as **school phobia**—which means fear of school—or refusal to go to school (which can be based on fear or other factors). Separation anxiety—fear—is not the basis of all instances of school refusal (Bernstein & Layne, 2006). Some children refuse school because they perceive it as unpleasant, unsatisfying, or hostile—and sometimes it is. Some children are concerned about doing poorly in school or being asked to answer questions in class (in which case, they might be suffering from the social phobia of stage fright). High parental expectations to perform may heighten concern. Other children may refuse school because of problems with classmates (Kearney, 2007).

Treatment of School Phobia or School Refusal

QUESTION » **What can we do about school phobia or school refusal?** **TRUTH OR FICTION REVISITED:** It is usually not better for children with school phobia to remain at home until the origins of the problem are uncovered and resolved. A phobia is an irrational or overblown fear—out of proportion to any danger in the situation. Therefore, one need not protect the child from school phobia. Most professionals agree that the first rule in the treatment of school phobia is this: Get the child back into school. The second rule: Get the child back into school. The third rule: You guessed it. Even without any investigation of the "meanings" of the child's refusal to attend school, many of the "symptoms" of the disorder disappear once the child is back in school on a regular basis.

Put it this way: There is nothing wrong with trying to understand why a child refuses to attend school. Knowledge of the reasons for refusal can help parents and educators devise strategies for helping the child adjust. But should such understanding precede insistence that the child return to school? Perhaps not. Here are some things parents can do to get a child back into school:

school phobia Fear of attending school, marked by extreme anxiety at leaving parents.

- Do not give in to the child's demands to stay home. If the child complains of being tired or ill, tell the child he or she may feel better at school and can rest there if necessary.
- Discuss the problem with the child's teacher, principal, and school nurse. (Gain the cooperation of school professionals.)
- If there is a specific school-related problem, such as an overly strict teacher, help the child find ways to handle the situation. (Finding ways to handle such problems can be accomplished while the child is in school. Not all such problems need to be ironed out before the child returns to school.)
- Reward the child for attending school. (Yes, parents shouldn't "have to" reward children for "normal" behaviour, but do you want the child in school or not?)

What if these measures don't work? How can professionals help? A variety of therapeutic approaches have been tried, and it appears that cognitive-behavioural approaches are the most effective (Kendall et al., 2004; Turner, 2006; Valderhaug et al., 2004). One cognitive-behavioural method is counterconditioning to reduce the child's fear. (As described in Chapter 10, Mary Cover Jones used counterconditioning to reduce Peter's fear of rabbits.) Other cognitive-behavioural methods include systematic desensitization, modelling, cognitive restructuring, and the shaping and rewarding of school attendance.

When possible, the children's parents are taught to apply cognitive-behavioural methods. One study assessed the effectiveness of family-based group cognitive-behavioural treatment (FGCBT) for anxious children (Shortt et al., 2001). It included 71 children between the ages of six and ten who were diagnosed with SAD, generalized anxiety (anxiety that persisted throughout the day), or social phobia (e.g., stage fright). The children and their families were assigned at random to FGCBT or to a ten-week waiting list ("We'll get to you in ten weeks"), which was the control group. The effectiveness of the treatment was evaluated after treatment and at a 12-month follow-up. The researchers found that nearly 70 percent of the children who had completed FGCBT were no longer diagnosable with anxiety disorders, compared with 6 percent of the children on the waiting list. Even at the 12-month follow-up, 68 percent of the treated children remained diagnosis free.

Antidepressant medication has been used—often in conjunction with cognitive-behavioral methods—with a good deal of success (Murphy et al., 2000; Pine et al., 2001; Walkup et al., 2001). Antidepressants can have side effects, however, such as abdominal discomfort (Burke & Baker, 2001). Moreover, some professionals fear that antidepressants can trigger suicidal thoughts in children (Mosholder, 2004). However, drugs in themselves do not teach children how to cope with situations. Many health professionals suggest that the drugs—in this case, antidepressants—are best used only when psychological treatments have proved ineffective (Masi et al., 2001).

Daniel Pine and his colleagues (2001) reported a study on the treatment of 128 anxious children, ages 6–17 years. Like those in the Shortt study, they were diagnosed with a social phobia (such as stage fright), SAD, or GAD. All the children had received psychological treatment for three weeks without improvement. The children were assigned at random to receive an antidepressant (fluvoxamine) or a placebo (a "sugar pill") for eight weeks. Neither the children, their parents, their teachers, nor the evaluators knew which child had received which treatment. After eight weeks, the children's anxiety was evaluated. Forty-eight of 63 children (76 percent) who had received the antidepressant improved significantly, compared with 19 of 65 children (29 percent) who had received the placebo.

It seems unfortunate to end our study of middle childhood right after discussing social and emotional problems. Most children in developed nations come through middle childhood quite well—in good shape to take on the challenges and dramas of adolescence.

Active Review

19. Conduct disorders are more likely to be found among the (biological or adoptive?) parents of adopted children who have conduct disorders.

20. Self-perceived competence appears to (protect children from or make children vulnerable to?) feelings of depression.

21. Depressed children tend to (underutilize or overutilize?) the neurotransmitter serotonin in the brain.

22. Separation _____ disorder is similar to but not exactly the same as school phobia.

23. Separation anxiety (is or is not?) the basis of all instances of school refusal.

Reflect & Relate: Have you known children who have conduct disorders, depression, or separation anxiety disorder (or school phobia)? Do you have any thoughts about the origins of the problems? Were the problems treated? What happened to the children?

Recite an Active Summary

13.1 Theories of Social and Emotional Development in Middle Childhood

What are some features of social and emotional development in middle childhood?

Social development in middle childhood involves the development of skills, changes in interpersonal relationships, and the expansion of self-understanding. Freud viewed the period as the latency stage; Erikson saw it as the stage of industry versus inferiority. Social cognitive theorists note that children now depend less on external rewards and punishments and that they increasingly regulate their own behaviour. Cognitive-developmental theory notes that concrete operations enhance social development.

What is the relationship between social cognition and perspective taking?

In middle childhood, children become more capable of taking the role or perspective of another person. Selman theorizes that children move from egocentricity to seeing the world through the eyes of others in five stages.

How does the self-concept develop during middle childhood?

In early childhood, children's self-concepts focus on concrete external traits. In middle childhood, children begin to include abstract internal traits. Social relationships and group membership assume greater importance.

How does self-esteem develop during middle childhood?

In middle childhood, competence and social acceptance contribute to self-esteem, but self-esteem tends to decline because the self-concept becomes more realistic. Authoritative parenting fosters self-esteem.

What is learned helplessness? How does it develop in middle childhood?

Learned helplessness is the acquired belief that one cannot obtain rewards. "Helpless" children tend not to persist in the face of failure. Girls tend to feel more helpless in math than boys do, largely because of gender-role expectations.

13.2 The Family

What kinds of influences does the family exert during middle childhood?

In middle childhood, the family continues to play a key role in socialization. Parent–child interactions focus on school-related issues, chores, and peers. Parents do less monitoring of children; coregulation develops.

What are the effects of having lesbian or gay parents?

By and large, children of lesbian and gay parents develop the same as children of heterosexual parents. The sexual orientation of these children is generally heterosexual.

What happens to children whose parents get divorced?

Divorce disrupts children's lives and usually lowers the family's financial status. Children are likely to greet divorce with sadness, shock, and disbelief. Children of divorced parents fare better when parents cooperate on child rearing. Children's adjustment is related to the mother's coping ability.

What is best for the children? Should parents in conflict remain together for their children's sake?

In terms of the child's psychological adjustment, the answer seems to be "Not necessarily." Children appear to suffer as much from marital conflict as from divorce per se.

13.3 Peer Relationships

What is the influence of peers during middle childhood?

Peers take on increasing importance and exert pressure to conform. Peer experiences also broaden children. Peers afford practice in developing social skills, sharing, relating to leaders, and coping with aggressive impulses. Popular children tend to be attractive and mature for their age.

How do children's concepts of friendship develop?

Early in middle childhood, friendships are based on proximity. Between the ages of 8 and 11, children become more aware of the value of friends as meeting each other's needs and having traits such as loyalty. At this age, peers tend to discourage contact with members of the other gender.

13.4 The School

What are the effects of the school on children's social and emotional development?

Schools make demands for mature behaviour and nurture positive physical, social, and cognitive development. Readiness for school is related to children's early life experiences, individual differences in development and learning, and the schools' expectations.

What are the characteristics of a good school?

An effective school has an energetic principal, an orderly atmosphere, empowerment of teachers and students, high expectations for children, and solid academics. Teachers' expectations can become self-fulfilling prophecies. Many girls suffer from sexism and sexual harassment in school. Math and science are generally stereotyped as masculine, and language arts as feminine.

13.5 Social and Emotional Problems

What kinds of social and emotional problems do children encounter in middle childhood? What can we do about them?

Children with conduct disorders persistently break rules or violate the rights of others. There may be a genetic component to such disorders, but sociopathic models in the family, deviant peers, and inconsistent discipline all contribute. Parental training in cognitive-behavioural methods holds promise for treating these disorders.

What is depression? What can we do about it?

Depressed children tend to complain of poor appetite, insomnia, lack of energy, and feelings of worthlessness. Depressed children tend to blame themselves excessively for shortcomings. Psychotherapy tends to make children aware of their tendencies to minimize their accomplishments and to overly blame themselves for shortcomings. Antidepressants are sometimes helpful but remain controversial.

What is separation anxiety disorder?

Separation anxiety disorder (SAD) is diagnosed when separation anxiety is persistent and excessive and interferes with daily life. Children with SAD tend to cling to parents and may refuse to attend school.

What are the connections among separation anxiety disorder, school phobia, and school refusal?

SAD is an extreme form of otherwise normal separation anxiety and may take the form of school phobia. But children can refuse school for other reasons, including finding school to be unpleasant or hostile.

What can we do about school phobia or school refusal?

The most important aspect of treatment is to insist that the child attend school. Cognitive-behavioural therapy and medication may also be useful.

Key Terms

latency stage   440
industry versus inferiority   441
social cognition   441
self-esteem   443
learned helplessness   445
coregulation   446
lesbian   446
gay   446

transsexual   447
Pygmalion effect   459
self-fulfilling prophecy   459
sexism   460
sexual harassment   460
conduct disorders   461
attributional style   465
serotonin   465

generalized anxiety disorder
   (GAD)   466
phobia   467
separation anxiety disorder
   (SAD)   467
obsessive-compulsive disorder
   (OCD)   467
school phobia   468

Active Learning Resources

Go to **www.nelsonbrain.com** to access *Voyages in Development's* CourseMate, where you will find an interactive eBook, flashcards, Pre-Lecture Quizzes, Section Quizzes, Exam Practice, videos, and more.

ANSWER KEY TO ACTIVE REVIEWS

CHAPTER 1

1. Puberty
2. Development
3. Development
4. Theories
5. Freud
6. Eight
7. Operant
8. Piaget
9. Processing
10. Ecological
11. Sociocultural
12. Nature
13. Discontinuous
14. Hypothesis
15. Naturalistic
16. Case
17. Cause
18. Control
19. Longitudinal
20. Sectional

CHAPTER 2

1. Chromosomes
2. Deoxyribonucleic
3. Mitosis
4. Meiosis
5. Monozygotic, identical
6. Dizygotic, fraternal
7. Carriers
8. Down syndrome
9. Recessive
10. Sickle-cell
11. Amniocentesis
12. Ultrasound
13. Genotype
14. Phenotype
15. 50
16. Monozygotic, identical
17. Dizygotic, fraternal
18. Conception, fertilization
19. Fallopian
20. Sperm
21. Ovulate

CHAPTER 3

1. Blastocyst
2. Trophoblast
3. Implantation
4. Amniotic
5. Proximodistal
6. Outer
7. Females
8. Placenta
9. Umbilical cord
10. Maturation
11. Third
12. Fourth
13. Neural

14. Teratogens
15. Can
16. Blood
17. Rh
18. DES
19. Marijuana
20. Fetal
21. Oxygen
22. Slow

CHAPTER 4

1. Braxton-Hicks
2. Amniotic
3. Dilated
4. Transition
5. Umbilical
6. Placenta
7. General
8. Epidural, spinal
9. Lamaze
10. Cesarean section, C-section
11. Oxygen
12. Preterm
13. Birth weight
14. Helpful
15. Majority
16. Estrogen
17. Does not
18. Apgar
19. Rooting
20. Nearsighted
21. Do
22. Smaller
23. Sudden infant death syndrome (SIDS)

CHAPTER 5

1. Head, brain
2. Proximodistal
3. Five
4. Positive
5. Canalization
6. Antibodies
7. Neurons
8. Axon
9. 70
10. Cerebellum
11. One
12. Ulnar
13. Visual
14. Sit up, crawl
15. Increase
16. Experience, practice, nurture
17. Did not
18. Real
19. Edges
20. Cliff
21. 2 to 3

22. Greater
23. Capture
24. Nurture

CHAPTER 6

1. Schemes
2. Assimilate
3. Sensorimotor
4. Circular
5. Secondary
6. Tertiary
7. Permanence
8. Information
9. Memory
10. Deferred
11. Internalizing
12. Social-emotional
13. Neurological
14. Visual
15. Babbling
16. Referential
17. Overextension
18. Holophrases
19. The same
20. Learning
21. Psycholinguistic
22. Acquisition
23. Left
24. Wernicke's

CHAPTER 7

1. Attachment
2. Strange situation
3. Insecure
4. Explore
5. Indiscriminate
6. Behavioural, behaviourist, learning
7. Contact
8. Fixed
9. Avoided
10. Withdrawal
11. Neglect
12. Autism, autism spectrum disorders
13. Majority
14. Higher
15. More
16. Majority
17. Referencing
18. Regulation
19. Concept
20. Temperament
21. Slow
22. 12 to 18

CHAPTER 8

1. 5 to 8
2. 2 to 3

3. Brain
4. Myelination
5. Cerebellum
6. Right
7. Right
8. Plasticity
9. Girls
10. Boys
11. Decrease
12. Boys
13. Higher
14. Decreases
15. Automobile accidents
16. Lead
17. 10
18. Sleep terrors
19. Sleep walking
20. Does
21. Boys
22. Constipation

CHAPTER 9

1. Symbolic, pretend
2. Operations
3. Egocentric
4. Animistic
5. Transductive
6. Conservation
7. One
8. Scaffolding
9. Responsive
10. Home environment
11. Can
12. False
13. Senses
14. Recognition
15. Autobiographical, episodic
16. Better
17. Positively
18. Rehearsal, rote rehearsal, rote learning
19. Mapping
20. Whole
21. One
22. Contrast
23. Inner

CHAPTER 10

1. Restrictiveness– permissiveness
2. Inductive
3. Authoritative
4. Authoritarian
5. First
6. Solitary
7. Associative
8. Same
9. Altruism

10. Reject
11. Testosterone
12. Social cognitive, social learning
13. Disinhibit
14. Categorical
15. Esteem
16. Securely
17. Initiative
18. Safety
19. Girls
20. Roles, role stereotypes
21. Males
22. Fathers
23. Constancy
24. Schema

CHAPTER 11

1. Steady
2. 5
3. 2 to 3
4. Boys
5. 11
6. 25
7. Do not
8. Does
9. Steady
10. 8 to 10
11. Decreases
12. Boys
13. Girls
14. Unfit
15. Attention-deficit/ hyperactivity disorder
16. Boys
17. Does
18. Stimulants
19. Disabilities, disorders
20. Dyslexia
21. Neurological
22. Does

CHAPTER 12

1. Less
2. Transitivity
3. Inclusion
4. Autonomous
5. The amount of damage done
6. Preconventional
7. Conventional
8. Increases
9. Working, short-term
10. Encode, rehearse
11. Rote
12. Elaborative
13. Metamemory
14. g
15. Multiple
16. Mental
17. Verbal
18. Bias
19. 6
20. 10 to 15
21. Divergent
22. Biological, Adoptive
23. Visual
24. Phonetic
25. Can
26. Advantage

CHAPTER 13

1. Industry
2. Concrete
3. Perspective, viewpoint
4. Decreases
5. Authoritative
6. Less
7. Heterosexual
8. Downward
9. Mothers
10. Boys
11. Farther away from
12. Mature
13. Later-born
14. Discouraged
15. Low
16. Smaller
17. Self-fulfilling
18. Boys
19. Biological
20. Protect children from
21. Underutilize
22. Anxiety
23. Is not

CHAPTER 14

1. Stress
2. Feedback
3. Sex
4. Growth
5. Asynchronous
6. Epiphyseal
7. Estrogen
8. Boys
9. Boys
10. Cortex
11. Frontal
12. More
13. Male
14. Injuries and poisonings
15. Anorexia nervosa
16. Purging
17. Do
18. Perfectionism, obsessiveness, depression
19. Abuse
20. Abstinence, withdrawal
21. Alcohol
22. Nicotine

CHAPTER 15

1. Formal
2. Egocentrism
3. Superior
4. Superior
5. Sex
6. Postconventional
7. Positive
8. More
9. Drop
10. Girls
11. More
12. Boys
13. Realistic, practical, conventional
14. Gender
15. Efficacy
16. Homework, paid and unpaid work

CHAPTER 16

1. Identity, ego identity
2. Moratorium
3. Achievement
4. Physical attractiveness, appearance
5. Mothers
6. Do
7. Increases
8. Their own
9. Masturbation
10. Gay or lesbian
11. Hormones
12. Less
13. Peer
14. Status
15. More
16. More
17. Common
18. Depression, helplessness, hopelessness
19. Does
20. Marriage
21. Job
22. Emerging

WHO GROWTH CHARTS FOR CANADIAN CHILDREN AND YOUTH BY SEX

The curves in Figures B.1 ■, B.2 ■, B.3 ■, and B.4 ■ indicate the percentiles for weight and length at different ages. Lines labelled 97, 85, 50, 5, and 3 show the height and weight of children who are taller and heavier than 97 percent, 85 percent, 50 percent, 5 percent, or 3 percent of children of a particular age. Lines marked 50 indicate the height and weight of the average child of a given age. That is, half of their age-mates are shorter and lighter, and half are heavier and taller.

GIRLS

BIRTH TO 24 MONTHS: GIRLS
Length-for-age and Weight-for-age percentiles

NAME: _____

DOB: _____ RECORD # _____

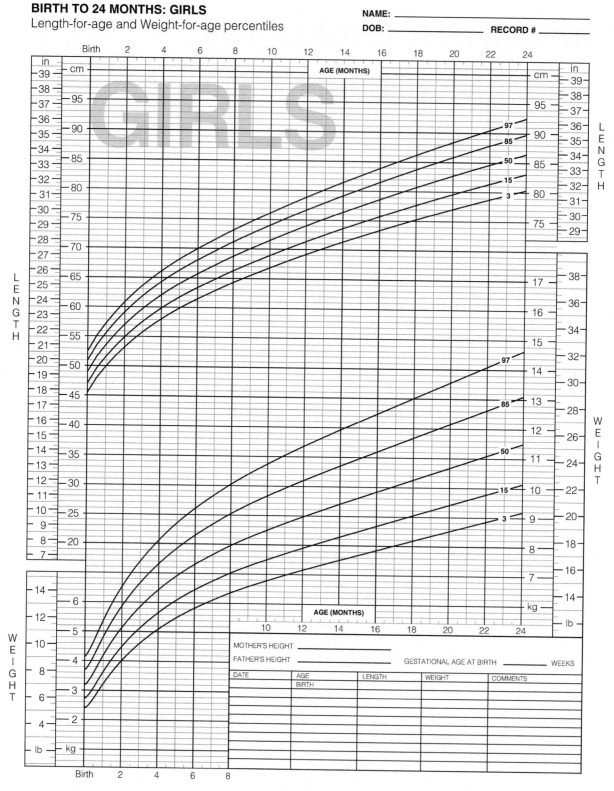

SOURCE: Based on World Health Organization (WHO) Child Growth Standards (2006) and WHO Reference (2007) and adapted for Canada by Canadian Paediatric Society, Canadian Pediatric Endocrine Group, College of Family Physicians of Canada, Community Health Nurses of Canada and Dietitians of Canada.

© Dietitians of Canada, 2014. Chart may be reproduced in its entirety (i.e., no changes) for non-commercial purposes only. **www.whogrowthcharts.ca**

Figure B.1 ■ **Growth Chart for Weight and Height from Birth to Age 2 Years (Girls)**

BOYS

BIRTH TO 24 MONTHS: BOYS
Length-for-age and Weight-for-age percentiles

NAME: _____

DOB: _____ RECORD # _____

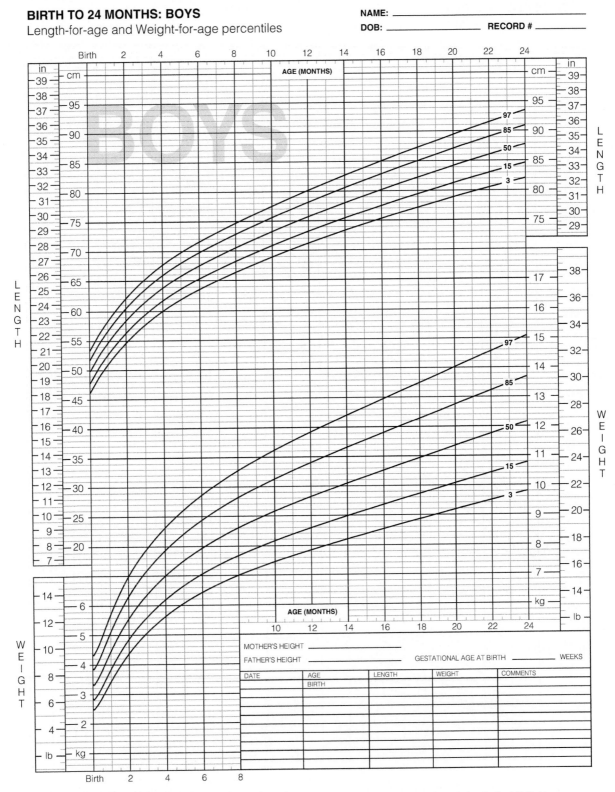

SOURCE: Based on World Health Organization (WHO) Child Growth Standards (2006) and WHO Reference (2007) and adapted for Canada by Canadian Paediatric Society, Canadian Pediatric Endocrine Group, College of Family Physicians of Canada, Community Health Nurses of Canada and Dietitians of Canada.

© Dietitians of Canada, 2014. Chart may be reproduced in its entirety (i.e., no changes) for non-commercial purposes only. **www.whogrowthcharts.ca**

Figure B.2 ■ **Growth Chart for Weight and Height from Birth to Age 2 Years (Boys)**

2 TO 19 YEARS: GIRLS
Height-for-age and Weight-for-age percentiles

NAME: _____

DOB: _____ RECORD # _____

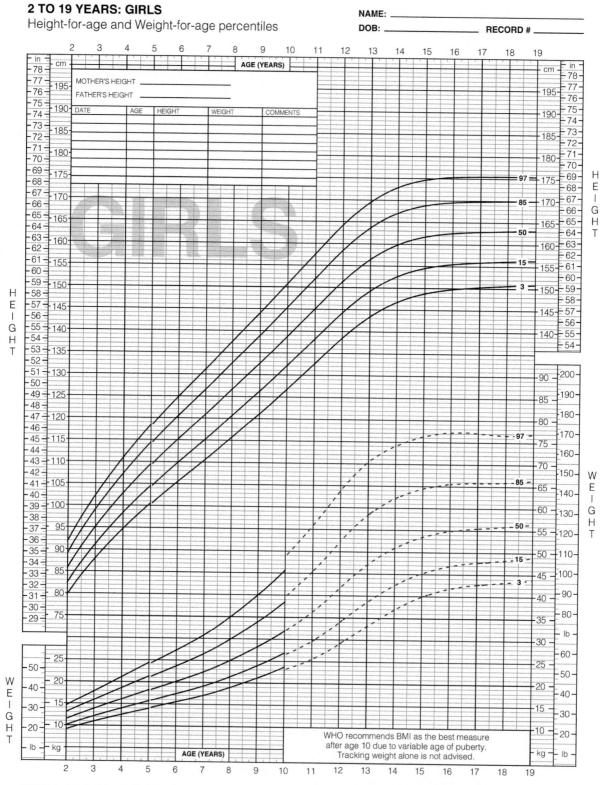

Figure B.3 ■ **Growth Chart for Weight and Height from 2 to 19 Years (Girls)**

BOYS

2 TO 19 YEARS: BOYS
Height-for-age and Weight-for-age percentiles

NAME: _____

DOB: _____   RECORD # _____

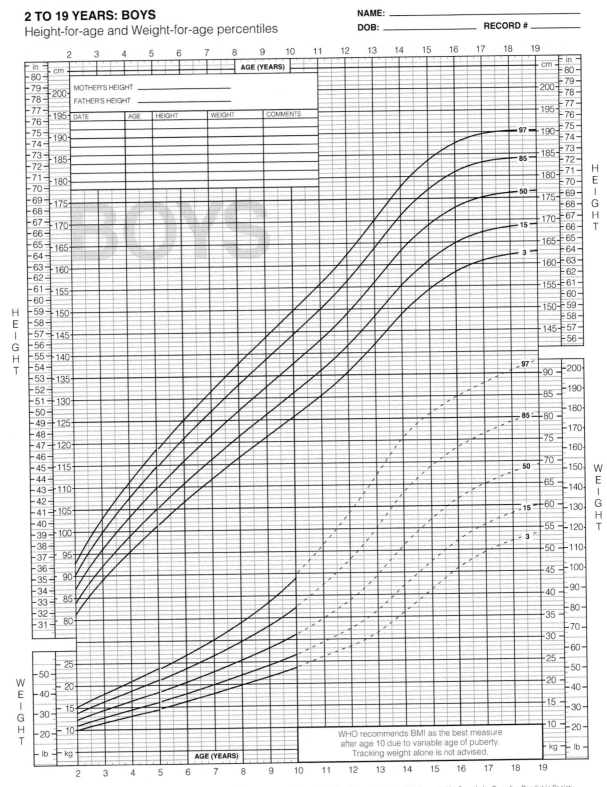

SOURCE: The main chart is based on World Health Organization (WHO) Child Growth Standards (2006) and WHO Reference (2007) adapted for Canada by Canadian Paediatric Society, Canadian Pediatric Endocrine Group (CPEG), College of Family Physicians of Canada, Community Health Nurses of Canada and Dietitians of Canada. The weight-for-age 10 to 19 years section was developed by CPEG based on data from the US National Center for Health Statistics using the same procedures as the WHO growth charts.

© Dietitians of Canada, 2014. Chart may be reproduced in its entirety (i.e., no changes) for non-commercial purposes only. **www.whogrowthcharts.ca**

Figure B.4 ■ **Growth Chart for Weight and Height from 2 to 19 Years (Boys)**

GLOSSARY

abstinence syndrome A characteristic cluster of symptoms that results from a sudden decrease in the level of usage of a substance. p. W14-30

accommodation According to Piaget, the modification of existing schemes to permit the incorporation of new events or knowledge. p. 19

achieved ethnic identity The final stage of ethnic identity development; similar to the identity achievement status. p. W16-8

achievement That which is attained by one's efforts and presumed to be made possible by one's abilities. p. 412

active genetic-environmental correlation The correlation between the child's genetic endowment and the choices the child makes about which environments they will seek. p. 64

adaptation According to Piaget, an interaction between the organism and the environment that consists of two processes: assimilation and accommodation. p. 19

adolescence A transitional period between childhood and adulthood, usually seen as being bounded by puberty at the lower end and by the assumption of adult responsibilities at the upper end. p. W14-4

allele A member of a pair of genes. p. 52

alpha-fetoprotein (AFP) assay A blood test that assesses the mother's blood level of alpha-fetoprotein, a substance that is linked to fetal neural tube defects. p. 62

ambivalent/resistant attachment A type of insecure attachment characterized by severe distress at the leave-takings of, and ambivalent behaviour at reunions with, an attachment figure. p. 224

American Sign Language (ASL) The communication of meaning through the use of symbols that are formed by moving the hands and arms; the language used by some deaf people. p. 218

amniocentesis A procedure for drawing out and examining fetal cells sloughed off into amniotic fluid to determine whether various disorders are present. p. 59

amniotic fluid Fluid within the amniotic sac that suspends and protects the fetus. p. 86

amniotic sac The sac containing the fetus. p. 86

amplitude The maximum vibration of a sound wave. The higher the amplitude of sound waves, the louder they are. p. 142

androgens Male sex hormones. p. 85

anesthesia A method that produces partial or total loss of the sense of pain. p. 122

animism The attribution of life and intentionality to inanimate objects. p. 296

anorexia nervosa An eating disorder characterized by irrational fear of weight gain, distorted body image, and severe weight loss. p. W14-26

anoxia A condition characterized by lack of oxygen. p. 126

Apgar scale A measure of a newborn's health that assesses appearance, pulse, grimace, activity level, and respiratory effort. p. 136

aphasia A disruption in the ability to understand or produce language. p. 216

appearance–reality distinction The difference between real events on the one hand and mental events, fantasies, and misleading appearances on the other hand. p. 312

artificial insemination Injection of sperm into the uterus to fertilize an ovum. p. 73

artificialism The belief that environmental features were made by people. p. 296

assimilation According to Piaget, the incorporation of new events or knowledge into existing schemes. p. 19

assimilation According to Piaget, the incorporation of new events or knowledge into existing schemes. p. 19

asynchronous growth Imbalanced growth, such as the growth that occurs during the early part of adolescence and causes many adolescents to appear gawky. p. W14-7

attachment An affectional bond between individuals characterized by a seeking of closeness or contact and a show of distress upon separation. p. 224

attachment-in-the-making phase The second phase in the development of attachment, occurring at three or four months of age and characterized by preference for familiar figures. p. 229

attention-deficit/hyperactivity disorder (AD/HD) A behaviour disorder characterized by excessive inattention, impulsiveness, and hyperactivity. p. 381

attributional style The way in which one is disposed toward interpreting outcomes (successes or failures), as in tending to place blame or responsibility on oneself or on external factors. p. 465

authoritarian A child-rearing style in which parents demand submission and obedience from their children but are not very communicative and warm. p. 331

authoritative A child-rearing style in which parents are restrictive and demanding, yet communicative and warm. p. 331

autism A developmental disorder characterized by failure to relate to others, communication problems, intolerance of change, and ritualistic behaviour. p. 66

autism spectrum disorders (ASDs) Developmental disorders—including autism, Asperger's syndrome, Rett's disorder, and childhood disintegrative disorder—that are characterized by impaired communication skills, poor social interactions, and repetitive, stereotyped behaviour. p. 243

autobiographical memory The memory of specific episodes or events. p. 314

autonomous morality The second stage in Piaget's cognitive-developmental theory of moral development. In this stage, children base moral judgments on the intentions of the wrongdoer more so than on the amount of damage done. Social rules are viewed as agreements that can be changed. p. 400

autosome A member of a pair of chromosomes (with the exception of sex chromosomes). p. 51

avoidant attachment A type of insecure attachment characterized by apparent indifference to the leave-takings of, and reunions with, an attachment figure. p. 224

axon A long, thin part of a neuron that transmits impulses to other neurons through small branching structures called axon terminals. p. 166

babbling The child's first vocalizations that have the sounds of speech. p. 207

Babinski reflex A reflex in which infants fan their toes when the undersides of their feet are stroked. p. 140

bed-wetting Failure to control the bladder during the night. p. 286

behaviourism John B. Watson's view that a science or theory of development must study observable behaviour only and investigate relationships between stimuli and responses. p. 8

bilingual Using or capable of using two languages with nearly equal or equal facility. p. 434

bisexual A person who is attracted physically and emotionally to both males and females. p. W16-19

blastocyst A stage within the germinal period of prenatal development in which the zygote has the form of a sphere of cells surrounding a cavity of fluid. p. 82

bonding The process of forming bonds of attachment between parent and child. p. 134

Braxton-Hicks contractions The first (usually painless) contractions of childbirth. p. 118

breech presentation A position in which the fetus enters the birth canal buttocks first. p. 127

Broca's aphasia A form of aphasia caused by damage to Broca's area and characterized by slow, laborious speech. p. 216

bulimia nervosa An eating disorder characterized by cycles of binge eating and vomiting as a means of controlling weight gain. p. W14-27

canalization The tendency of growth rates to return to genetically determined patterns after undergoing environmentally induced change. p. 63

carrier A person who carries and transmits characteristics but does not exhibit them. p. 53

case study A carefully drawn biography of the life of an individual. p. 35

categorical self Definitions of the self that refer to concrete external traits. p. 352

centration Focusing on one dimension of a situation while ignoring others. p. 298

cephalocaudal From head to tail. p. 83

cerebellum The part of the hindbrain involved in muscle coordination and balance. p. 168

cerebrum The large mass of the forebrain, which consists of two hemispheres. p. 168

cesarean section A method of childbirth in which the neonate is delivered through a surgical incision in the abdomen. (Also spelled *Caesarean*.) p. 124

child A person undergoing the period of development from infancy through puberty. p. 4

chorionic villus sampling A method for the prenatal detection of genetic abnormalities that samples the membrane enveloping the amniotic sac and fetus. p. 60

chromosomes Rod-shaped structures that are composed of genes and found within the nuclei of cells. p. 50

chronological age (CA) A person's age. p. 418

chronosystem The environmental changes that occur over time and have an impact on the child (from the Greek *chronos*, meaning "time"). p. 24

class inclusion The principle that one category or class of things can include several subclasses. p. 299

classical conditioning A simple form of learning in which one stimulus comes to bring forth the response usually elicited by a second stimulus by being paired repeatedly with the second stimulus. p. 13

clear-cut-attachment phase The third phase in the development of attachment, occurring at six or seven months of age and characterized by intensified dependence on the primary caregiver. p. 229

clique A group of five to ten individuals who hang around together and share activities and confidences. p. W16-14

clitoris A female sex organ that is highly sensitive to sexual stimulation but is not directly involved in reproduction. p. W14-11

codominance Condition of a trait that is neither dominant nor recessive in that it is expressed with another trait simultaneously. p. 52

cognitive-developmental theory The stage theory that holds that the child's abilities to mentally represent the world and solve problems unfold as a result of the interaction of experience and the maturation of neurological structures. p. 18

cohort effect Similarities in behaviour among a group of peers that stem from the fact that group members are approximately the same age. p. 40

collectivist A person who defines herself or himself in terms of relationships to other people and groups and gives priority to group goals. p. 335

commitment A stable investment in one's goals, values, and beliefs. p. W16-5

communication disorders Persistent problems in understanding or producing language. p. 386

conception The union of a sperm cell and an ovum that occurs when the chromosomes of each of these cells combine to form 23 new pairs. p. 67

concrete operations The third stage in Piaget's scheme, characterized by flexible, reversible thought concerning tangible objects and events. p. 394

conduct disorders Disorders marked by persistent breaking of the rules and violations of the rights of others. p. 461

cones In the eye, cone-shaped receptors of light that transmit sensations of colour. p. 142

congenital Present at birth; resulting from the prenatal environment. p. 96

conservation In cognitive psychology, the principle that properties of substances such as weight and mass remain the same (are conserved) when superficial characteristics such as their shapes or arrangement are changed. p. 298

contact comfort The pleasure derived from physical contact with another; a hypothesized need or drive for physical contact with another. p. 230

contrast assumption The assumption that objects have only one label. Also known as the mutual exclusivity assumption (if a word means one thing, then it cannot mean another). p. 318

control group A group made up of subjects in an experiment who do not receive the treatment, but for whom all other conditions are comparable to those of subjects in the experimental group. p. 38

conventional level According to Kohlberg, a period during which moral judgments largely reflect social rules and conventions. p. 401

convergence The inward movement of the eyes as they focus on an object that is drawing nearer. p. 141

convergent thinking A thought process that attempts to focus on the single best solution to a problem. p. 427

cooing Prelinguistic, articulated vowel-like sounds that appear to reflect feelings of positive excitement. p. 207

coregulation A gradual transferring of control from parent to child, beginning in middle childhood. p. 446

corpus callosum The thick bundle of nerve fibres that connects the hemispheres of the brain. p. 265

correlation A relationship between variables in which one variable increases as a second variable also increases (a positive correlation) or decreases (a negative correlation). p. 36

correlation coefficient A number ranging from +1.00 to –1.00 that expresses the direction (positive or negative) and strength of the relationship between two variables. p. 36

creativity The ability to generate novel solutions to problems; a trait characterized by flexibility, ingenuity, and originality. p. 426

cross-sectional research The study of developmental processes by taking measures of children of different age groups at the same time. p. 39

cross-sequential research An approach that combines the longitudinal and cross-sectional methods by following individuals of different ages for abbreviated periods of time. p. 40

crowd A large, loosely organized group of people who may or may not spend much time together and who are identified by the activities of the group. p. W16-14

cultural bias A factor hypothesized to be present in intelligence tests that bestows an advantage on test takers from certain cultural or ethnic backgrounds but that does not reflect true intelligence. p. 422

cultural–familial disability Substandard intellectual performance that is presumed to stem from lack of opportunity to acquire the knowledge and skills considered important within a cultural setting. p. 425

culture-free Descriptive of a test in which cultural biases have been removed. On such a test, test takers from different cultural backgrounds would have an equal opportunity to earn scores that reflect their true abilities. p. 422

cystic fibrosis A fatal genetic disorder in which mucus obstructs the lungs and pancreas. p. 58

decentration Simultaneous focusing (centring) on more than one aspect or dimension of a problem or situation. p. 342

deep structure The underlying meaning of a sentence. p. 216

deferred imitation The imitation of people and events that were encountered or experienced hours, days, or weeks in the past. p. 197

dendrites The rootlike parts of a neuron that receive impulses from other neurons. p. 166

deoxyribonucleic acid (DNA) Genetic material that takes the form of a double helix made up of phosphates, sugars, and bases. p. 50

dependent variable In a scientific study, a measure of an assumed effect of an independent variable. p. 38

DES Abbreviation for diethylstilbestrol, an estrogen that has been linked to cancer in the reproductive organs of children of women who used it when pregnant. p. 101

development The processes by which organisms unfold features and traits, grow, and become more complex and specialized in structure and function. p. 4

differential emotions theory Izard's view that the major emotions are distinct at birth but emerge gradually in accord with maturation and the child's developing needs. p. 249

differentiation The processes by which behaviours and physical structures become more specialized. p. 157

dilate To widen or enlarge. p. 119

disinhibit To stimulate a response that has been suppressed (inhibited) by showing a model engaging in that response without aversive consequences. p. 349

disorganized–disoriented attachment A type of insecure attachment characterized by dazed and contradictory behaviours toward an attachment figure. p. 224

divergent thinking A thought process that attempts to generate multiple solutions to problems; free and fluent association to the elements of a problem. p. 427

dizygotic (DZ) twins Twins that derive from two zygotes; fraternal twins. p. 52

dominant trait A trait that is expressed. p. 52

donor IVF The transfer of a donor's ovum, fertilized in a laboratory dish, to the uterus of another woman. p. 73

double-deficit hypothesis The theory of dyslexia that suggests that dyslexic children have biological deficits in two areas: *phonological processing* (interpreting sounds) and *naming speed* (for example, identifying letters—such as *b* versus *d*, or *w* versus *m*). p. 386

Down syndrome A chromosomal abnormality characterized by intellectual disability and caused by an extra chromosome in the 21st pair. p. 55

dramatic play Play in which children enact social roles; made possible by the attainment of symbolic thought. A form of pretend play. p. 340

dynamic systems perspective View that children's physical, social, and cognitive development are all part of an integrated and actively changing system. p. 26

dyslexia A reading disorder characterized by problems such as letter reversals, mirror reading, slow reading, and reduced comprehension (from the Greek roots *dys*, meaning "bad," and *lexikon*, meaning "of words"). p. 384

echolalia The automatic repetition of sounds or words. p. 207

ecological systems theory The view that explains child development in terms of the reciprocal influences between children and the settings that make up their environment. p. 22

ecology The branch of biology that deals with the relationships between living organisms and their environment. p. 22

ectoderm The outermost cell layer of the newly formed embryo from which the skin and nervous system develop. p. 83

efface To thin. p. 119

ego identity According to Erikson, one's sense of who one is and what one stands for. p. W16-4

egocentrism Putting oneself at the centre of things such that one is unable to perceive the world from another person's point of view. p. 295

elaborative strategy A method for increasing retention of new information by relating it to well-known information. p. 408

electroencephalograph (EEG) An instrument that measures electrical activity of the brain. p. 146

embryonic disk The platelike inner part of the blastocyst that differentiates into the ectoderm, mesoderm, and endoderm of the embryo. p. 82

embryonic stage The stage of prenatal development that lasts from implantation through the eighth week of pregnancy. It is characterized by the development of the major organ systems. p. 83

embryonic transplant The transfer of an embryo from the uterus of one woman to that of another. p. 73

emotion A state of feeling that has physiological, situational, and cognitive components. p. 249

emotional regulation Techniques for controlling one's emotional states. p. 251

empathy Ability to share another person's feelings. p. 344

empirical Based on observation and experimentation. p. 33

encode To transform sensory input into a form that is more readily processed. p. 405

encopresis Failure to control the bowels after the normal age for bowel control has been reached. Also called *soiling*. p. 287

endoderm The inner layer of the embryo from which the lungs and digestive system develop. p. 83

endometriosis Inflammation of endometrial tissue sloughed off into the abdominal cavity rather than out of the body during menstruation; the condition is characterized by abdominal pain and sometimes by infertility. p. 72

endometrium The inner lining of the uterus. p. 67

enuresis Failure to control the bladder (urination) after the normal age for control has been reached. p. 286

epigenesis The view that development reflects continual bidirectional exchanges between one's genotype and one's environmental conditions. p. 64

epiphyseal closure The process by which the cartilage that separates the long end (epiphysis) of a bone from the main part of the bone turns to bone. p. W14-9

episiotomy A surgical incision in the area between the birth canal and the anus that widens the vaginal opening, preventing random tearing during childbirth. p. 119

equilibration The creation of an equilibrium, or balance, between assimilation and accommodation as a way of incorporating new events or knowledge. p. 19

estrogen A female sex hormone produced mainly by the ovaries. p. 56

ethnic groups Groups of people distinguished by their cultural heritage, race, language, and common history. p. 26

ethnic identity A sense of belonging to an ethnic group. p. W16-8

ethnic identity search The second stage of ethnic identity development; similar to the moratorium identity status. p. W16-8

ethology The study of behaviours that are specific to a species—how these behaviours evolved, help the organism adapt, and develop during critical periods. p. 21

evocative genetic-environmental correlation The correlation between the child's genetic endowment and the responses the child elicits from other people. p. 64

exosystem Community institutions and settings that indirectly influence the child, such as the school board and the parents' workplaces (from the Greek *exo*, meaning "outside"). p. 24

experiment A method of scientific investigation that seeks to discover cause-and-effect relationships by introducing independent variables and observing their effects on dependent variables. p. 33

experimental group A group made up of subjects who receive a treatment in an experiment. p. 38

exploration Active questioning and searching among alternatives in the quest to establish goals, values, and beliefs. p. W16-5

expressive language style Use of language primarily as a means for engaging in social interaction. p. 208

expressive vocabulary The sum total of the words that one can use in the production of language. p. 207

extinction The decrease and eventual disappearance of a response in the absence of reinforcement. p. 213

factor A condition or quality that brings about a result—in this case, "intelligent" behaviour. A cluster of related items, such as those found on an intelligence or personality test. p. 413

factor analysis A statistical technique that enables researchers to determine the relationships among a large number of items, such as test items. p. 413

failure to thrive (FTT) A disorder of impaired growth in infancy and early childhood characterized by failure to gain weight within normal limits. p. 159

fallopian tube A tube through which ova travel from an ovary to the uterus. p. 67

fast mapping A process of quickly determining a word's meaning, which facilitates children's vocabulary development. p. 317

feedback loop A system in which glands regulate each other's functioning through a series of hormonal messages. p. W14-6

fetal alcohol effect (FAE) A cluster of symptoms less severe than those of fetal alcohol syndrome shown by children of women who drank moderately during pregnancy. p. 103

fetal alcohol spectrum disorder (FASD) Umbrella term that refers to the different disabilities children of mothers who drank alcohol during pregnancy may experience. FASD is considered to be the result of preventable birth defects, and it is one of the most common sources of developmental delays. p. 103

fetal alcohol syndrome (FAS) A cluster of symptoms shown by children of women who drank during pregnancy, including characteristic facial features and intellectual disability. p. 103

fetal stage The stage of development that lasts from the beginning of the ninth week of pregnancy through birth. p. 87

fine motor skills Skills that employ the small muscles used in manipulation, such as those in the fingers. p. 270

foreclosure An identity status that characterizes those who have made commitments without considering alternatives; according to Marcia, the stage at which adolescents are committed to ready-made values and goals, and have not yet experienced crisis or exploration. p. W16-4

formal operations The fourth stage in Piaget's cognitive-developmental theory, characterized by the capacity for flexible, reversible operations concerning abstract ideas and concepts, such as symbols, statements, and theories. p. W15-4

gay A person who is physically and emotionally attracted to someone of the same sex. The word gay can refer to both males and females, but is commonly used to identify males only. p. W16-19

gender constancy The concept that one's gender remains the same despite superficial changes in appearance or behaviour. p. 361

gender identity A person's internal sense or feeling of being male or female, which may or may not be the same as one's biological sex; also, the name of the first stage in Kohlberg's cognitive-developmental theory of the assumption of gender roles. p. W16-20

gender role A complex cluster of traits and behaviours that are considered stereotypical of females (or of males). p. 356

gender stability The concept that one's gender is a permanent feature. p. 361

genderqueer Used to describe individuals who perceive their gender to be neither that of a male or female but outside of the gender binary. p. W16-20

gender-schema theory The view that one's knowledge of the gender schema in one's society (the behaviour patterns that are considered appropriate for men and women) guides one's assumption of gender-typed preferences and behaviour patterns. p. 361

gene The basic unit of heredity. Genes are composed of deoxyribonucleic acid (DNA). p. 50

generalized anxiety disorder (GAD) An anxiety disorder in which anxiety is present continuously and is unrelated to the situation. p. 466

genes The basic building blocks of heredity. p. 31

genetic counselling Advice concerning the probabilities that a couple's children will show genetic abnormalities. p. 59

genetics The branch of biology that studies heredity. p. 50

genital stage In Freud's psychoanalytic theory, the fifth and final stage of psychosexual development, in which gratification is attained through sexual intercourse with a person of the other gender. p. 440

genotype The genetic form, or constitution, of a person as determined by heredity. p. 63

germinal stage The period of development between conception and the implantation of the embryo. p. 82

goodness of fit Agreement between the parents' expectations of, or demands on, the child and the child's temperamental characteristics. p. 257

grasping reflex A reflex in which infants grasp objects that cause pressure against their palms. p. 139

gray matter Neural tissue, especially of the brain and spinal cord, that contains cell bodies and their dendrites and forms most of the cortex of the brain. p. W14-18

gross motor skills Skills that employ the large muscles used in locomotion. p. 266

growth The processes by which organisms increase in size, weight, strength, and other traits as they develop. p. 4

growth spurt A period during which growth advances at a dramatically rapid rate compared with other periods. p. 368

gynecomastia Enlargement of breast tissue in males. p. W14-9

habituation A process in which one becomes used to a repeated stimulus and therefore pays less attention to it. p. 180

hallucinogenics Drugs that give rise to hallucinations. p. W14-31

hemophilia A genetic disorder in which blood does not clot properly. p. 59

heredity The transmission of traits and characteristics from parent to child by means of genes. p. 50

heritability The degree to which the variations in a trait from one person to another can be attributed to, or explained by, genetic factors. p. 428

heterozygous Having two different alleles. p. 52

HIV/AIDS *HIV* stands for human immunodeficiency virus, the virus that causes AIDS. *AIDS* stands for acquired immunodeficiency syndrome, a condition that cripples the body's immune system, making the person vulnerable to diseases that would not otherwise be as threatening. p. W14-19

holophrase A single word that is used to express complex meanings. p. 211

homozygous Having two identical alleles. p. 52

hue Colour. p. 142

Huntington disease (HD) A fatal genetic neurological disorder whose onset is in middle age. p. 58

hyperactivity Excessive restlessness and overactivity; one of the primary characteristics of attention-deficit/hyperactivity disorder (AD/HD). Not to be confused with misbehaviour or with high activity levels that are normal during childhood. p. 381

hypothalamus A pea-sized structure above the pituitary gland that is involved in the regulation of body temperature, motivation (such as hunger, thirst, sexual desire), and emotion. p. W14-6

hypothesis A specific statement about behaviour that is tested by research. p. 34

hypoxia A condition characterized by less oxygen than is required. p. 126

identity achievement An identity status that characterizes those who have explored alternatives and have developed commitments. p. W16-4

identity achievement According to Marcia, the stage after which adolescents have gone through identity crisis/exploration and have resolved identity issues and have self-chosen values and goals. p. 15

identity crisis A turning point in development during which one examines one's values and makes decisions about life roles; according to Erikson, an adolescent period of inner conflict during which one examines one's values and makes decisions about one's life roles. p. W16-4

identity diffusion An identity status that characterizes those who have made no commitments and are not in the process of exploring alternatives; according to Marcia, the stage when adolescents are not committed to an identity and are not questioning who they are yet. p. W16-5

identity moratorium According to Marcia, the stage at which adolescents are exploring but have not committed to self-chosen goals and values. p. 14

imaginary audience The belief that others around us are as concerned with our thoughts and behaviours as we are; one aspect of adolescent egocentrism. p. W15-7

immanent justice The view that retribution for wrongdoing is a direct consequence of the wrongdoing, reflecting the belief that morality is embedded within the structure of the universe. p. 399

imprinting The process by which some animals exhibit the fixed action pattern (FAP) of attachment in response to a releasing stimulus. The FAP occurs during a critical period and is difficult to modify. p. 21

in vitro fertilization (IVF) Fertilization of an ovum in a laboratory dish. p. 73

inclusion Most students with mild disabilities spend at least part of their school day in regular classrooms. The goals of inclusion include providing broader educational opportunities for students with exceptionalities and fostering interactions with other children of varying abilities. p. 388

incubator A heated, protective container in which premature infants are kept. p. 129

independent variable In a scientific study, the condition that is manipulated (changed) so that its effects can be observed. p. 38

indiscriminate attachment The display of attachment behaviours toward any person. p. 228

individualist A person who defines herself or himself in terms of personal traits and gives priority to her or his own goals. p. 335

inductive Characteristic of disciplinary methods, such as reasoning, that try to teach an understanding of the principles behind parental demands. p. 330

industry versus inferiority The fourth stage of psychosocial development in Erikson's theory, occurring in middle childhood. Mastery of tasks leads to a sense of industry, whereas failure produces feelings of inferiority. p. 441

infancy The period of very early childhood, characterized by lack of complex speech; the first two years after birth. p. 4

information processing The view in which cognitive processes are compared to the functions of computers. The theory deals with the input, storage, retrieval, manipulation, and output of information. The focus is on the development of children's strategies for solving problems—their "mental programs." p. 403

initial-preattachment phase The first phase in the formation of bonds of attachment, lasting from birth to about three months of age and characterized by indiscriminate attachment. p. 229

insomnia One or more sleep problems, including difficulty falling asleep, difficulty remaining asleep during the night, and waking early. p. 284

intelligence A complex and controversial concept, defined by David Wechsler as "[the] capacity ... to understand the world [and the] resourcefulness to cope with its challenges." Intelligence implies the capacity to make adaptive choices (from the Latin *inter*, meaning "among," and *legere*, meaning "to choose"). p. 412

intelligence quotient (IQ) Originally, a ratio obtained by dividing a child's score (or "mental age") on an intelligence test by his or her chronological age. In general, a score on an intelligence test. p. 417

intensity Brightness. p. 142

intonation The use of pitches of varying levels to help communicate meaning. p. 207

irreversibility Lack of recognition that actions can be reversed. p. 298

juvenile delinquency Conduct in a child or adolescent characterized by illegal activities. p. W16-29

Klinefelter syndrome A chromosomal disorder found among males that is caused by an extra X sex chromosome and is characterized by infertility and mild intellectual disability. p. 56

kwashiorkor A form of protein-energy malnutrition in which the body may break down its own reserves of protein, resulting in enlargement of the stomach, swollen feet, and other symptoms. p. 163

labia The major and minor lips of the female genitalia. p. W14-11

Lamaze method A childbirth method in which women are educated about childbirth, learn to relax and breathe in patterns that conserve energy and lessen pain, and have a coach (usually the father) present during childbirth. Also termed prepared childbirth. p. 124

language acquisition device (LAD) In psycholinguistic theory, neural "prewiring" that facilitates the child's learning of grammar. p. 216

lanugo Fine, downy hair that covers much of the body of neonates, especially preterm babies. p. 128

larynx The part of the throat that contains the vocal cords. p. W14-9

latency stage In Freud's psychoanalytic theory, the fourth stage of psychosexual development, characterized by repression of sexual impulses and development of skills. p. 440

learned helplessness An acquired (hence, learned) belief that one is unable to control one's environment. p. 445

learning disabilities A group of disorders characterized by inadequate development of specific academic, language, and speech skills. p. 384

lesbian A female who is attracted physically and emotionally to other females p. W16-19

life crisis An internal conflict that attends each stage of psychosocial development. Positive resolution of early life crises sets the stage for positive resolution of subsequent life crises. p. 12

locomotion Movement from one place to another. p. 172

longitudinal research The study of developmental processes by taking repeated measures of the same group of children at various stages of development. p. 39

long-term memory The memory structure capable of relatively permanent storage of information. p. 407

macrosystem The basic institutions and ideologies that influence the child, such as the western ideals of freedom of expression and equality under the law (from the Greek *makros*, meaning "long" or "enlarged"). p. 24

mammary glands Glands that secrete milk. p. W14-9

marasmus A wasted, potentially lethal body condition caused by inadequate nutrition and characterized by painful thinness. p. W14-9

mean length of utterance (MLU) The average number of morphemes used in an utterance. p. 210

medulla A part of the brain stem that regulates vital and automatic functions such as breathing and the sleep–wake cycle. p. 150

meiosis The form of cell division in which each pair of chromosomes splits and one member of each pair moves to the new cell. As a result, each new cell has 23 chromosomes. p. 51

memory The processes by which we store and retrieve information. p. 404

menarche The onset of menstruation. p. W14-11

menopause The cessation of menstruation, typically occurring between ages 48 and 52. p. W14-23

mental age (MA) The accumulated months of credit that a person earns on the Stanford–Binet Intelligence Scale. p. 418

mental representations The mental forms that a real object or event can take. p. 312

mesoderm The central layer of the embryo from which the bones and muscles develop. p. 83

mesosystem The interlocking settings that influence the child, such as the interaction of the school and the larger community when children are taken on field trips (from the Greek *mesos*, meaning "middle"). p. 24

metacognition Awareness of and control of one's cognitive abilities, as shown by the intentional use of cognitive strategies in solving problems. p. 411

metamemory Knowledge of the functions and processes involved in one's storage and retrieval of information (memory), as shown by the use of cognitive strategies to retain information. p. 411

microsystem The immediate settings with which the child interacts, such as the home, the school, and the child's peers (from the Greek *mikros*, meaning "small"). p. 23

midwife An individual who helps women in childbirth. p. 122

mitosis The form of cell division in which each chromosome splits lengthwise to double in number. Half of each chromosome combines with chemicals to retake its original form and then moves to the new cell. p. 51

models In learning theory, those whose behaviours are imitated by others. p. 212

monozygotic (MZ) twins Twins that derive from a single zygote that has split into two; identical twins. Each MZ twin carries the same genetic code. p. 52

moral realism According to Piaget, the stage during which children judge acts as moral when they conform to authority or to the rules of the game. Morality at this stage is perceived as embedded in the structure of the universe. p. 399

moratorium An identity status that characterizes those who are actively exploring alternatives in an attempt to form an identity. p. W16-4

Moro reflex A reflex in which infants arch their back, fling out their arms and legs, and draw them back toward the chest in response to a sudden change in position. p. 139

morpheme The smallest unit of meaning in a language. p. 205

morphology The forming of words from sounds based on grammatical rules. p. 205

motility Self-propulsion. p. 71

multifactorial problems Problems that stem from the interaction of heredity and environmental factors. p. 53

multiple sclerosis A disorder in which myelin is replaced by hard, fibrous tissue that impedes neural transmission. p. 167

muscular dystrophy A chronic disease characterized by a progressive wasting away of the muscles. p. 59

mutation A sudden variation in a heritable characteristic, such as by an accident that affects the composition of genes. p. 51

mutism Inability or refusal to speak. p. 245

myelin sheath A fatty, white substance that encases and insulates neurons, permitting more rapid transmission of neural impulses. p. 166

myelination The process by which axons are coated with myelin. p. 167

natural childbirth A method of childbirth in which women use no anesthesia and are educated about childbirth and strategies for coping with discomfort. p. 123

naturalistic observation A method of scientific observation in which children (and others) are observed in their natural environments. p. 34

nature The processes within an organism that guide that organism to develop according to its genetic code. p. 31

NBAS Brazelton Neonatal Behavioral Assessment Scale. p. 136

negative correlation A relationship between two variables in which one variable decreases as the other variable increases. p. 37

negative reinforcer A reinforcer that, when removed, increases the frequency of a behaviour. p. 15

neonate A newborn child. p. 118

nerves Bundles of axons from many neurons. p. 166

neural Of the nervous system. p. 138

neural tube A hollowed-out area in the blastocyst from which the nervous system develops. p. 83

neurons Nerve cells; cells found in the nervous system that transmit messages. p. 166

neuroscience The scientific study of the brain and nervous system. p. 22

neurotransmitter A chemical substance that makes possible the transmission of neural impulses from one neuron to another. p. 166

niche-picking Choosing environmental conditions that foster one's genetically transmitted abilities and interests. p. 64

nightmares Frightening dreams that occur during REM sleep, often in the morning hours. p. 284

NNNS Neonatal Intensive Care Unit Network Neurobehavioral Scale. p. 136

nocturnal emission Emission of seminal fluid while asleep. p. W14-9

non–rapid eye movement (non-REM) sleep Periods of sleep during which we are unlikely to dream. p. 146

nonsocial play Forms of play (solitary play or onlooker play) in which play is not influenced by the play of nearby children. p. 341

nurture The processes external to an organism that nourish it as it develops according to its genetic code or that cause it to swerve from its genetically programmed course. Environmental factors that influence development. p. 31

object permanence Recognition that objects continue to exist even when they are not seen. p. 193

objective morality The perception of morality as objective—that is, as existing outside the cognitive functioning of people; a characteristic of Piaget's stage of moral realism. p. 399

obsessive-compulsive disorder (OCD) A disorder characterized by obsessions (recurring thoughts or images that seem beyond control) and compulsions (irresistible urges to repeat an act). p. 467

operant conditioning A simple form of learning in which an organism learns to engage in behaviour that is reinforced. p. 15

operations Flexible, reversible mental manipulations of objects, in which objects can be mentally transformed and then returned to their original states. p. 295

oral rehydration therapy A treatment involving the administration of a salt and sugar solution to a child who is dehydrated from diarrhea. p. 277

osteoporosis A condition involving the progressive loss of bone tissue. p. W14-23

overextension Use of words in situations in which their meanings become extended or inappropriate. p. 209

overregularization The application of regular grammatical rules (e.g., to create past tense and plurals) to irregular verbs and nouns. p. 318

ovulation The release of an ovum from an ovary. p. 52

oxytocin A pituitary hormone that stimulates labor contractions. p. 118

passive genetic-environmental correlation The correlation between the genetic endowment parents give their children and the environments in which they place their children. p. 64

peers Children of the same age. (More generally, people of similar background and social standing.) p. 338

pelvic inflammatory disease (PID) An infection of the abdominal region that may have various causes and may impair fertility. p. 71

perception The process by which sensations are organized into a mental map of the world. p. 175

perceptual constancy The tendency to perceive objects as the same even though the sensations produced by them may differ when, for example, they differ in position or distance. p. 178

permissive–indulgent A child-rearing style in which parents are not controlling and restrictive but are warm. p. 332

personal fable The belief that our feelings and ideas are special and unique and that we are invulnerable; one aspect of adolescent egocentrism. p. W15-8

personality An individual's distinctive ways of responding to people and events. p. 253

phenotype The actual form or constitution of a person as determined by heredity and environmental factors. p. 63

phenylketonuria (PKU) A genetic abnormality in which phenylalanine builds up and causes intellectual disability. p. 56

phobia An irrational, excessive fear that interferes with one's functioning. p. 467

phonemes Basic units of sounds. p. 205

phonetic method A method for learning to read in which children decode the sounds of words via their knowledge of the sounds of letters and letter combinations. p. 432

phonology The understanding of how the basic units of sounds are combined. p. 205

pincer grasp The use of the opposing thumb to grasp objects between the thumb and other fingers. p. 171

pitch The highness or lowness of a sound, as determined by the frequency of sound waves. p. 142

pituitary gland The body's "master gland," which is located in the lower central part of the brain and which secretes many hormones essential to development, such as oxytocin, prolactin, and growth hormone. p. W14-6

placenta An organ connected to the uterine wall and to the fetus by the umbilical cord. The placenta serves as a relay station between mother and fetus for the exchange of nutrients and wastes. p. 82

plasticity The tendency of new parts of the brain to take up the functions of injured parts p. 170

polygenic Resulting from many genes. p. 50

positive correlation A relationship between two variables in which one variable increases as the other variable increases. p. 37

positive reinforcer A reinforcer that, when applied, increases the frequency of a behaviour. p. 15

postconventional level According to Kohlberg, a period during which moral judgments are derived from moral principles and people look to themselves to set moral standards. p. 402

postpartum depression (PPD) Severe, prolonged depression that afflicts 10–20 percent of women after delivery and that is characterized by sadness, apathy, and feelings of worthlessness. p. 132

postpartum period The time that immediately follows childbirth. p. 132

pragmatics The practical aspects of communication, such as adaptation of language to fit the social situation. p. 205

precausal A type of thought in which natural cause-and-effect relationships are attributed to will and other preoperational concepts—as in thinking that the sun sets because it is tired. p. 296

preconventional level According to Kohlberg, a period during which moral judgments are based largely on expectations of rewards or punishments. p. 401

pre-eclampsia A life-threatening disease that can afflict pregnant women. It is characterized by high blood pressure. p. 100

prelinguistic Referring to vocalizations made by the infant before the development of language. (In language, words symbolize objects and events.) p. 205

premature Born before the full term of gestation. (Also referred to as *preterm*.) p. 100

prenatal Before birth. p. 59

preoperational stage The second stage in Piaget's scheme, characterized by inflexible and irreversible mental manipulation of symbols. p. 294

preterm Born at or before completion of 37 weeks of gestation. p. 127

primary circular reactions The repetition of actions that first occurred by chance and that focus on the infant's own body. p. 191

primary sex characteristics The structures that make reproduction possible. p. W14-6

private speech Vygotsky's concept of the ultimate binding of language and thought. Private speech originates in vocalizations that may regulate the child's behaviour and become internalized by age six or seven. p. 323

progestin A hormone that is used to maintain pregnancy and can cause masculinization of the fetus. p. 101

prosocial behaviour Behaviour intended to benefit another without expectation of reward. p. 344

prostaglandins Hormones that stimulate uterine contractions. p. 118

proximodistal From the inner part (or axis) of the body outward. p. 83

psycholinguistic theory The view that language learning involves an interaction between environmental influences and an inborn tendency to acquire language. The emphasis is on the inborn tendency. p. 216

psychosexual development Freud's view that as children develop, they find sexual gratification through stimulating different parts of their bodies. p. 9

psychosocial development Erikson's theory, which emphasizes the importance of social relationships and conscious choice throughout the eight stages of development. p. 12

puberty The biological stage of development characterized by changes that lead to reproductive capacity. Puberty signals the beginning of adolescence. p. W14-5

punishment An unpleasant stimulus that suppresses behaviour. p. 15

Pygmalion effect A self-fulfilling prophecy; an expectation that is confirmed because of the behaviour of those who hold the expectation. p. 459

rapid eye movement (REM) sleep Periods of sleep during which we are likely to dream, as indicated by rapid eye movements. p. 146

reaction range The variability in the expression of inherited traits as they are influenced by environmental factors. p. 63

reaction time The amount of time required to respond to a stimulus. p. 377

receptive vocabulary The sum total of the words whose meanings one understands. p. 207

recessive trait A trait that is not expressed when the gene or genes involved have been paired with dominant genes. Recessive traits are transmitted to future generations and expressed if they are paired with other recessive genes. p. 52

reciprocal relationship phase The fourth phase in the development of attachment, occurring at 18 months to two years and onwards, and characterized by less separation protests and a better understanding of relationship duration beyond the immediate. p. 229

reciprocity The principle that actions have mutual effects and that people depend on one another to treat each other morally. p. W15-13

referential language style Use of language primarily as a means for labelling objects. p. 208

reflex An unlearned, stereotypical response to a stimulus. p. 138

regression A return to behaviours characteristic of earlier stages of development. p. 337

rehearsal Repetition—mental, behavioural, or both. p. 316

reinforcement The process of providing stimuli following a behaviour, which has the effect of increasing the frequency of the behaviour. p. 15

rejecting–neglecting A child-rearing style in which parents are neither restrictive and controlling nor supportive and responsive. p. 332

respiratory distress syndrome A cluster of breathing problems, including weak and irregular breathing, to which preterm babies are particularly prone. p. 128

reversibility According to Piaget, recognition that processes can be undone, leaving things as they were before. Reversibility is a factor in conservation of the properties of substances. p. 394

Rh incompatibility A condition in which antibodies produced by the mother are transmitted to the child, possibly causing brain damage or death. p. 100

rods In the eye, rod-shaped receptors of light that are sensitive to intensity only. Rods permit black-and-white vision. p. 142

rooting reflex A reflex in which infants turn their mouths and heads in the direction of a stroking of the cheek or the corner of the mouth. p. 138

rote learning Learning by repetition. p. 406

rubella A viral infection that can cause deafness, intellectual disability, heart disease, and eye problems in the embryo. Also called German measles. p. 99

saturation Richness or purity of a colour. p. 142

scaffolding Vygotsky's term for temporary cognitive structures or methods of solving problems that help the child as he or she learns to function independently. p. 25

scheme According to Piaget, an action pattern (such as a reflex) or mental structure that is involved in the acquisition or organization of knowledge. p. 18

school phobia Fear of attending school, marked by extreme anxiety at leaving parents. p. 468

scripts Abstract generalized accounts of familiar repeated events. p. 314

secondary circular reactions The repetition of actions that produce an effect on the environment. p. 191

secondary sex characteristics Physical indicators of sexual maturation—such as changes to the voice and growth of bodily hair—that do not directly involve reproductive structures. p. W14-6

secular trend A historical trend toward increasing adult height and earlier puberty. p. W14-7

secure attachment A type of attachment characterized by showing mild distress at leave-takings, seeking nearness to an attachment figure, and being readily soothed by this figure. p. 224

sedatives Drugs that soothe or quiet restlessness or agitation. p. W14-30

self-concept One's impression of oneself; self-awareness. p. 253

self-efficacy expectations One's beliefs that he or she can handle the requirements of a situation. p. W15-21

self-esteem The sense of value or worth that people attach to themselves. p. 443

self-fulfilling prophecy An event that occurs because of the behaviour of those who expect it to occur. p. 459

semantic code A code based on the meaning of information. p. 408

semantics The meanings ascribed to words and clusters of words. p. 205

semen The fluid that contains sperm and substances that nourish and help transport sperm. p. W14-9

sensation The stimulation of sensory organs, such as the eyes, ears, and skin, and the transmission of sensory information to the brain. p. 175

sensitive period In linguistic theory, the period from about 18 months to puberty when the brain is thought to be especially capable of learning language because of its plasticity. p. 217

sensitive period A period during which certain organs or structures are particularly vulnerable to a certain teratogen. p. 86

sensory memory The structure of memory that is first encountered by sensory input. Information is maintained in sensory memory for only a fraction of a second. p. 404

sensory register Another term for sensory memory. p. 404

separation anxiety Fear of being separated from a target of attachment, usually a primary caregiver. p. 224

separation anxiety disorder (SAD) An extreme form of normal separation anxiety that is characterized by anxiety about separating from parents; SAD often takes the form of school refusal. p. 467

seriation Placing objects in an order or series according to a property or trait. p. 395

serotonin A neurotransmitter that is involved in the responsiveness of the medulla, emotional responses such as depression, and motivational responses such as hunger. p. 150

sex chromosome A chromosome in the shape of a Y (male) or an X (female) that determines the sex of the child. p. 51

sexism Discrimination or bias against people on the basis of their gender. p. 460

sex-linked chromosomal abnormalities Abnormalities that are transmitted from generation to generation, carried by a sex chromosome, usually an X sex chromosome. p. 55

sex-linked genetic abnormalities Abnormalities resulting from genes that are found on the X sex chromosome. p. 59

sexual harassment Unwelcome verbal or physical conduct of a sexual nature. p. 460

sexual orientation A person's affection and sexual attraction to other persons. p. W16-19

shape constancy The tendency to perceive objects as being the same shape even though the shapes of their images on the retina may differ when the objects are viewed from different positions. p. 179

shaping In learning theory, the gradual building of complex behaviour patterns through reinforcement of successive approximations of the target behaviour. p. 213

sibling rivalry Jealousy or rivalry among brothers and sisters. p. 337

sickle-cell anemia A genetic disorder that decreases the blood's capacity to carry oxygen. p. 58

sight vocabulary Words that are immediately recognized on the basis of familiarity with their overall shapes, rather than decoded. p. 432

size constancy The tendency to perceive objects as being the same size even though the sizes of their images on the retina may differ as a result of distance. p. 178

sleep terrors Frightening dreamlike experiences that occur during the deepest stage of non-REM sleep, shortly after the child has gone to sleep. p. 284

small for dates A description of neonates who are unusually small for their age. p. 127

social cognition Development of children's understanding of the relationship between the self and others. p. 441

social cognitive theory A cognitively oriented learning theory that emphasizes the role of observational learning in determining behaviour. p. 17

social play Play in which children interact with others and are influenced by their play. Examples include parallel play, associative play, and cooperative play. p. 341

social referencing Using another person's reaction to a situation to form one's own assessment of it. p. 251

social smile A smile that occurs in response to a human voice or face. p. 231

socioeconomic status (SES) Social position as determined mainly by level of income. p. 28

somnambulism Sleepwalking. p. 284

sonogram A procedure for using ultrasonic sound waves to create a picture of an embryo or fetus. p. 61

spina bifida A neural tube defect that causes abnormalities of the brain and spine. p. 59

spontaneous abortion Unplanned, accidental abortion. p. 69

stage theory A theory of development characterized by hypothesizing the existence of distinct periods of life. Stages follow one another in an orderly sequence. p. 9

standardized test A test of some ability or trait in which an individual's score is compared to the scores of a group of similar individuals. p. 35

status offences Offences considered illegal only when performed by minors, such as truancy and underage drinking. p. W16-29

stepping reflex A reflex in which infants take steps when held under the arms and lean forward so that their feet press against the ground. p. 139

stillbirth The birth of a dead fetus. p. 92

stimulants Drugs that increase the activity of the nervous system. p. 383

stimulus A change in the environment that leads to a change in behaviour. p. 15

stranger anxiety A fear of unfamiliar people that emerges between six and nine months of age. Also called *fear of strangers*. p. 251

substance dependence A persistent pattern of use of a substance that is accompanied by physiological addiction. p. W14-29

substance use disorders A persistent pattern of use of a substance characterized by frequent intoxication and impairment of physical, social, and/or emotional well-being. p. W14-29

sudden infant death syndrome (SIDS) The death, while sleeping, of apparently healthy babies who stop breathing for unknown medical reasons. Also called crib death. p. 149

surface structure The superficial grammatical construction of a sentence. p. 216

surrogate mother A woman who is artificially inseminated and carries to term a child who is then given to another woman, typically the spouse of the sperm donor. p. 74

symbolic play Play in which children make believe that objects and toys are other than what they are. Also termed *pretend play*. p. 294

syntax Rules that stipulate the way words are to be arranged in sentences. p. 205

syphilis A sexually transmitted infection that can attack major systems. p. 96

Tay-Sachs disease A fatal genetic neurological disorder. p. 58

telegraphic speech Type of speech in which only the essential words are used. p. 210

temperament Individual differences in styles of reaction that are present early in life. p. 254

teratogens Environmental influences or agents that can damage the embryo or fetus. p. 96

term The typical period of time between conception and the birth of a baby. p. 118

tertiary circular reactions The purposeful adaptation of established schemes to new situations. p. 192

testosterone A male sex hormone produced by the testes that promotes the development of male sexual characteristics and sperm. p. 56

thalidomide A sedative linked to birth defects, especially deformed or absent limbs. p. 101

theory A formulation of relationships underlying observed events. A theory involves assumptions and logically derived explanations and predictions. p. 8

theory of mind A commonsense understanding of how the mind works p. 235

time-lag comparison The study of developmental processes by taking measures of children of the same age group at different times. p. 41

time-out A behaviour-modification technique in which a child who misbehaves is temporarily removed from positive reinforcement. p. 16

toddler A child who walks with short, uncertain steps. Toddlerhood lasts from about 12 months to 30 months of age, thereby bridging infancy and early childhood. p. 173

tolerance Habituation to a drug such that increasingly higher doses are needed to achieve similar effects. p. W14-30

tonic-neck reflex A reflex in which infants turn their head to one side, extend the arm and leg on that side, and flex the limbs on the opposite side. Also known as the fencing position. p. 140

transductive reasoning Reasoning from the specific to the specific. (In deductive reasoning, one reasons from the general to the specific; in inductive reasoning, one reasons from the specific to the general.) p. 296

transition The initial movement of the head of the fetus into the birth canal. p. 119

transitional object A soft, cuddly object often carried to bed by a child to ease the separation from parents. p. 282

transitivity The principle that if A is greater than B in a property and B is greater than C, then A is greater than C. p. 395

transsexual A person who experiences intense personal and emotional discomfort with his or her assigned birth gender and may undergo treatment (e.g., hormones and/or surgery) to transition genders. p. W16-20

treatment In an experiment, a condition received by subjects so that its effects may be observed. p. 38

triarchic Governed by three. Descriptive of Sternberg's view that intellectual functioning has three aspects: analytical intelligence, creative intelligence, and practical intelligence. p. 414

trophoblast The outer part of the blastocyst from which the amniotic sac, placenta, and umbilical cord develop. p. 82

Turner syndrome A chromosomal disorder found among females that is caused by having a single X sex chromosome and is characterized by infertility. p. 56

two-spirit An Aboriginal person who identifies as two-spirit rather than as lesbian, gay, bisexual, or transgender. p. W16-20

ulnar grasp A method of grasping objects in which the fingers close somewhat clumsily against the palm. p. 171

ultrasound Sound waves too high in pitch to be sensed by the human ear. p. 61

umbilical cord A tube that connects the fetus to the placenta. p. 82

unexamined ethnic identity The first stage of ethnic identity development; similar to the diffusion or foreclosure identity status. p. W16-8

uterus The hollow organ within females in which the embryo and fetus develop. p. 60

utopian Referring to an ideal vision of society. p. W15-5

variables Quantities that can vary from child to child or from occasion to occasion, such as height, weight, intelligence, and attention span. p. 36

vernix An oily, white substance that coats the skin of neonates, especially preterm babies. p. 128

visual accommodation The automatic adjustments made by the lenses of the eyes to bring objects into focus. p. 141

visual acuity Keenness or sharpness of vision. p. 140

visual recognition memory The kind of memory shown in an infant's ability to discriminate previously seen objects from novel objects. p. 203

Wernicke's aphasia A form of aphasia caused by damage to Wernicke's area and characterized by impaired comprehension of speech and difficulty in attempting to produce the right word. p. 217

whole-language approach A method for learning to read in which children come to recognize words in a variety of contexts through repeated exposure to them. p. 432

whole-object assumption The assumption that words refer to whole objects and not to their component parts or characteristics. p. 318

working memory The structure of memory that can hold a sensory stimulus for up to 30 seconds after the trace decays. Also called short-term memory. p. 404

zone of proximal development (ZPD) Vygotsky's term for the range of tasks that a child can carry out with the help of someone who is more skilled, frequently an adult who represents the culture in which the child develops. p. 25

zygote A new cell formed from the union of a sperm and an ovum (egg cell); a fertilized egg. p. 51

REFERENCES

AAIDD. (2012). What is the AAIDD definition of intellectual disability? http://www.aaidd.org/intellectualdisabilitybook/content_7473.cfm?navID=366.

Aalsma, M. C., Lapsley, D. K., & Flannery, D. J. (2006). Personal fables, narcissism, and adolescent adjustment. *Psychology in the Schools, 43*(4), 481–491.

Abdelaziz, Y. E., Harb, A. H., & Hisham, N. (2001). *Textbook of Clinical Pediatrics.* Philadelphia: Lippincott Williams & Wilkins.

Abelev, M., & Markman, E. (2006). Young children's understanding of multiple object identity: Appearance, pretense and function. *Developmental Science, 9*(6), 590–596.

Aber, J. L., Bishop-Josef, S. J., Jones, S. M., McLearn, K. T., & Phillips, D. A. (Eds.). (2007). Child development and social policy: Knowledge for action. APA Decade of Behavior volumes. Washington, DC: American Psychological Association.

Abravanel, E., & DeYong, N. G. (1991). Does object modeling elicit imitative-like gestures from young infants? *Journal of Experimental Child Psychology, 52,* 22–40.

Abuhatoum, S., & Howe, N. (2013). Power in sibling conflict during early and middle childhood. *Social Development, 22*(4), 738–754.

Academy of Nutrition and Dietetics. (2012). *Getting Started on Eating Right.* http://www.eatright.org/Public/content.aspx?id=8044. Accessed February 17, 2012.

Acredolo, L., & Goodwyn, S. (2009). *Baby signs* (3rd ed.). New York: McGraw-Hill.

Active Healthy Kids Canada. (2009). *Active kids are fit to learn. Report card on physical activity for children and youth—2009.* Toronto, ON.

Adams, G. R., Berzonsky, M. D., & Keating, L. (2006). Psychosocial resources in first-year university students: The role of identity processes and social relationships. *Journal of Youth and Adolescence, 35*(1), 81–91.

Adler-Baeder, F. (2006). What do we know about the physical abuse of stepchildren? A review of the literature. *Journal of Divorce & Remarriage, 44*(3–4), 67–81.

Adolph, K. E., & Berger, S. E. (2005). Physical and motor development. In M. H. Bornstein & M. E. Lamb (Eds.), *Developmental science: An advanced textbook* (5th ed.) (pp. 223–281). Hillsdale, NJ: Erlbaum.

Adolph, K. E., Berger, S. E., & Leo, A. J. (2011). Developmental continuity? Crawling, cruising, and walking. *Developmental Science, 14*(2), 306–318.

Adoption Council of Canada. (n.d.). Myths and Realities. http://www.adoption.ca/myths-and-realities. Accessed June 23, 2014.

Agency for Healthcare Research and Quality. (2004, April). Chronic illnesses. In *Child Health Research Findings,* Program Brief, AHRQ Publication 04-P011. Rockville, MD: Agency for Healthcare Research and Quality. Available at http://www.ahrq.gov/research/childfind/chfchrn.htm.

Agrawal, A., Silberg, J. L., Lynskey, M. T., Maes, H. H., & Eaves, L. J. (2010). Mechanisms underlying the lifetime co-occurrence of tobacco and cannabis use in adolescent and young adult twins. *Drug and Alcohol Dependence, 108*(1–2), 49–55.

Aguiar, A., & Baillargeon, R. (1999). 2.5-month-old infants' reasoning about when objects should and should not be occluded. *Cognitive Psychology, 39*(2), 116–157.

Ainsworth, M. D. S. (1967). *Infancy in Uganda: Infant care and the growth of love.* Baltimore, MD: Johns Hopkins University Press.

Ainsworth, M. D. S. (1989). Attachments beyond infancy. *American Psychologist, 44,* 709–716.

Ainsworth, M. D. S., Blehar, M. C., Waters, E., & Wall, S. (1978). *Patterns of attachment: A psychological study of the Strange Situation.* Hillsdale, NJ: Erlbaum.

Ainsworth, M. D. S., & Bowlby, J. (1991). An ethological approach to personality development. *American Psychologist, 46*(4), 333–341.

Alamian, A., & Paradis, G. (2012). Individual and social determinants of multiple chronic disease behavioral risk factors among youth. *BMC Public Health, 12,* 224.

Alberts, A., Elkind, D., & Ginsberg, S. (2007). The personal fable and risk-taking in early adolescence. *Journal of Youth and Adolescence, 36*(1), 71–76.

Alexander, G. M., Wilcox, T., & Woods, R. (2009). Sex differences in infants' visual interest in toys. *Archives of Sexual Behavior, 38*(3), 427–433.

Alfirevic, Z., Sundberg, K., & Brigham, S. (2003). Amniocentesis and chorionic villus sampling for prenatal diagnosis. *Cochrane Database of Systematic Reviews.* doi:10.1002/14651858.CD003252.

Ali, M. M., & Dwyer, D. S. (2011). Estimating peer effects in sexual behavior among adolescents. *Journal of Adolescence, 34*(1), 183–190.

Alink, L. R. A., et al. (2008). Maternal sensitivity moderates the relation between negative discipline and aggression in early childhood. *Social Development, 18*(1), 99–120.

Allen, G., et al. (2011). Functional neuroanatomy of the cerebellum. In A. S. Davis (Ed.). *Handbook of pediatric neuropsychology.* New York: Springer.

Allen, J. P., & Antonishak, J. (2008). Adolescent peer influences: Beyond the dark side. In M. J. Prinstein & K. A. Dodge (Eds.). *Understanding peer influence in children and adolescents* (pp. 141–160). New York: Guilford.

Allen, M. (2004). Does French immersion improve reading achievement? *Canadian Social Trends.* Ottawa, ON: Statistics Canada.

Allen, M. C., & Alexander, G. R. (1990). Gross motor milestones in preterm infants: Correction for degree of prematurity. *Journal of Pediatrics, 116,* 955–959.

Allison, C. M., & Hyde, J. S. (2011). Early menarche: Confluence of biological and contextual factors. *Sex Roles,* doi:10.1007/s11199-011-9993-5.

Aloi, J. A. (2009). Nursing the disenfranchised: Women who have relinquished an infant for adoption. *Journal of Psychiatric and Mental Health Nursing, 16*(1), 27–31.

Als, H., et al. (2003). A three-center, randomized, controlled trial of individualized developmental care for very low birth weight preterm infants: Medical, neurodevelopmental, parenting, and caregiving effects. *Journal of Developmental and Behavioral Pediatrics, 24*(6), 399–408.

Amanatullah, E. T., & Morris, M. W. (2010). Negotiating gender roles: Gender differences in assertive negotiating are mediated by women's fear of backlash and attenuated when negotiating on behalf of others. *Journal of Personality and Social Psychology, 98*(2), 256–267.

Amato, P. R. (2006). Marital discord, divorce, and children's well-being: Results from a 20-year longitudinal study of two generations. In A. Clarke-Stewart & J. Dunn (Eds.), *Families count: Effects on child and adolescent development. The Jacobs Foundation series on adolescence* (pp. 179–202). New York: Cambridge University Press.

America's Children. (2007). Centers for Disease Control and Prevention. National Center for Health Statistics. Childstats.gov. *America's children: Key* national indicators of well-being, 2007. Adolescent births. Indicator Fam6: Birth Rates for Females Ages 15–17 by Race and Hispanic Origin, 1980–2005. Available at http://www.childstats.gov/americaschildren/famsoc6.asp.

American Academy of Pediatrics. (2011). SIDS and other sleep-related infant deaths: Expansion of recommendations for a safe infant sleeping environment. *Pediatrics, 128*(5), e1341–e1367.

American Academy of Pediatrics. (2012). Breastfeeding initiatives. http://www2.aap.org/breastfeeding/faqsbreastfeeding.html. Accessed July 28, 2012.

American Fertility Association. (2012a). Infertility: Causes and treatments. Available at http://www.theafa.org/family-building/infertility-causes-treatments.

American Fertility Association. (2012b). *LGBT Family Building.* Available at http://www.theafa.org/family-building/lgbt-family-building.

American Lung Association. (2010). *Smoking.* Retrieved from http://www.lungusa.org/stop-smoking/about-smoking/health-effects/smoking.html.

American Pregnancy Association. (2011). Alcohol and pregnancy: What you should know. http://www.americanpregnancy.org/pregnancyhealth/alcohol.html. Accessed February 14, 2012.

American Psychiatric Association. (2012). DSM-5: The future of psychiatric diagnosis. http://www.dsm5.org/Pages/Default.aspx.

American Psychiatric Association. (2013). Diagnostic and Statistical Manual of the Mental Disorders-5th edition (DSM-5). Washington, DC: American Psychiatric Association.

Ammaniti, M., Speranza, A. M., & Fedele, S. (2005). Attachment in infancy and in early and late childhood: A longitudinal study. In K. A. Kerns & R. A. Richardson (Eds.), *Attachment in middle childhood* (pp. 115–136). New York: Guilford.

Amsel, E. (2011). Hypothetical thinking in adolescence: Its nature, development, and applications. In E. Amsel, & J. Smetana (Eds.), *Adolescent vulnerabilities and opportunities* (pp. 86–116). New York: Cambridge University Press.

Ances, B. M. (2002). New concerns about thalidomide. *Obstetrics & Gynecology, 99,* 125–128.

Andersen, A. E., & Ryan, G. L. (2009). Eating disorders in the obstetric and gynecologic patient population. *Obstetrics and Gynecology, 114*(6), 1353–1367.

Anderson, B. J. (2011). Plasticity of gray matter volume: The cellular and synaptic plasticity that underlies volumetric change. *Developmental Psychobiology, 53*(5), 456–465.

Anderson, C. A., et al. (2010). Violent video game effects on aggression, empathy, and prosocial behavior in Eastern and Western countries: A meta-analytic review. *Psychological Bulletin, 136*(2), 151–173.

Anderson, P. (2002). Assessment and development of executive function (EF) during childhood. *Child Neuropsychology, 8*(2), 71–82.

Anderson, P. J., & Leuzzi, V. (2010). White matter pathology in phenylketonuria. *Molecular Genetics and Metabolism, 99*(Suppl.), S3–S9.

Andreano, J. M., & Cahill, L. (2009). Sex influences on the neurobiology of learning and memory. *Learning and Memory, 16,* 248–266.

Andrews, G., Halford, G. S., Murphy, K., & Knox, K. (2009). Integration of weight and distance information in young children: The role of relational complexity. *Cognitive Development, 24*(1), 49–60.

Angarne-Lindberg, T., Wadsby, M., & Bertero, C. (2009). Young adults with childhood experience of divorce: Disappointment and contentment. *Journal of Divorce & Remarriage, 50*(3), 172–184.

Anthis, K. (2006). Possible selves in the lives of adult women: A short-term longitudinal study. In C. Dunkel & J. Kerpelman (Eds.), *Possible selves: Theory, research and applications* (pp. 123–140). Hauppauge, NY: Nova Science Publishers.

Anthis, K. S., Dunkel, C. S., & Anderson, B. (2004). Gender and identity status differences in late adolescents' possible selves. *Journal of Adolescence, 27*(2), 147–152.

Anzengruber, D., et al. (2006). Smoking in eating disorders. *Eating Behaviors, 7*(4), 291–299.

Arbuthnot, J., & Gordon, D. A. (1988). Crime and cognition: Community applications of sociomoral reasoning development. *Criminal Justice and Behavior, 15*(3), 379–393.

Archambault, I., Janosz, M., Fallu, J-S., & Pagani, L. S. (2009). Student engagement and its relationship with early high school dropout. *Journal of Adolescence, 32*(3), 651–670.

Archer, S. L., & Grey, J. A. (2009). The sexual domain of identity. *Identity: An International Journal of Theory and Research, 9*(1), 33–62.

Arduini, R. G., Capellini, S. A., & Ciasca, S. M. (2006). Comparative study of the neuropsychological and neuroimaging evaluations in children with dyslexia. *Arquivos de Neuro-Psiquiatría, 64*(2-B), 369–375.

Arenz, S. R., Rûkerl, B. Koletzko, & von Kries, R. (2004). Breast-feeding and childhood obesity—systematic review. *International Journal of Obesity, 28,* 1247–1256.

Arnett, J. J. (1999). Adolescent storm and stress, reconsidered. *American Psychologist, 54*(5), 317–326.

Arnett, J. J. (2000). Emerging adulthood. *American Psychologist, 55*(5), 469–480.

Arnett, J. J. (2007). Socialization in emerging adulthood: From the family to the wider world, from socialization to self-socialization. In J. E. Grusec & P. D. Hastings (Eds.), *Handbook of socialization: Theory and research* (pp. 208–231). New York: Guilford.

Arnett, J. J. (2011). Emerging adulthood. In L. A. Jensen (Ed.), *Bridging cultural and developmental approaches to psychology: New syntheses in theory, research and policy* (pp. 255–275). New York: Oxford University Press.

Arnett, J. J. (2012). New horizons in research on emerging and young adulthood. *Early Adulthood in a Family Context: National Symposium on Family Issues, 2*(5), 231–244.

Arnett, J. J., & Brody, G. H. (2008). A fraught passage: The identity challenges of African American emerging adults. *Human Development, 51*(5–6), 291–293.

Aschermann, E., Gülzow, I., & Wendt, D. (2004). Differences in the comprehension of passive voice in German- and English-speaking children. *Swiss Journal of Psychology, 63*(4), 235–245.

Aslin, R. N. (2012). Infant eyes: A window on cognitive development. *Infancy: Special Issue: Advances in Eye Tracking in Infancy Research, 17*(1), 126–140.

Aspy, C. B., et al. (2007). Parental communication and youth sexual behaviour. *Journal of Adolescence, 30*(3), 449–466.

Athenstaedt, U., Mikula, G., & Bredt, C. (2008). Gender role self-concept and leisure activities of adolescents. *Sex Roles, 60*(5–6), 399–409.

August, D., Carlo, M., Dressler, C., & Snow, C. (2005). The critical role of vocabulary development for English language learners. *Learning Disabilities Research & Practice, 20*(1), 50–57.

Aukrust, V. (2004). Talk about talk with young children. *Journal of Child Language, 31,* 177–201.

Auyeung, B., et al. (2009). Fetal testosterone predicts sexually differentiated childhood behavior in girls and in boys. *Psychological Science, 20*(2), 144–148.

Aviezer, O., & Sagi-Schwartz, A. (2008). Attachment and non-maternal care: Towards contextualizing the quantity versus quality debate. *Attachment and Human Development, 10*(3), 275–285.

Axelin, A., & Salanterä, S. (2008). Ethics in neonatal pain research. *Nursing Ethics, 15*(4), 492–499.

Ayyash-Abdo, H. (2001). Individualism and collectivism: The case of Lebanon. *Social Behavior and Personality, 29*(5), 503–518.

Azak, S., & Raeder, S. (2013). Trajectories of parenting behavior and maternal depression. *Infant Behavior and Development, 36*(3), 391–402.

Azar, B. (1998). What predicts which foods we eat? A genetic disposition for certain tastes may affect people's food preferences. *APA Monitor, 29,* 1.

Bachman, J. G., Johnston, L. D., & O'Malley, P. M. (2011). *Monitoring the future: Questionnaire responses from the nation's high school seniors 2010.* Survey Research Center. Institute for Social Research. Ann Arbor, MI: The University of Michigan.

Bachman, J. G., Safron, D. J., Sy, S. R., & Schulenberg, J. E. (2003). Wishing to work: New perspectives on how adolescents' part-time work intensity is linked to educational disengagement, substance use, and other problem behaviours. *International Journal of Behavioral Development, 27*(4), 301–315.

Bada, H. S., et al. (2011). Preadolescent behavior problems after prenatal cocaine exposure: Relationship between teacher and caretaker ratings (Maternal Lifestyle Study). *Neurotoxicology and Taratology, 33*(1), 78–87.

Badcock, P. B. (2012). Evolutionary systems theory: A unifying meta-theory of psychological science. *Review of General Psychology, 16*(1), 10–23.

Bagley, C., & D'Augelli, A. R. (2000). Suicidal behaviour in gay, lesbian, and bisexual youth. *British Medical Journal, 320,* 1617–1618.

Bailey, J. M. (2003). *The man who would be queen: The science of gender-bending and transsexualism.* Washington, DC: Joseph Henry Press.

Baillargeon, R. (1987). Object permanence in 3½- and 4½-month-old infants. *Developmental Psychology, 23,* 655–664.

Baillargeon, R., Li, J., Gertner, Y., & Wu, D. (2010). In U. Goswami (Ed.), *The Wiley–Blackwell handbook of childhood cognitive development.* (2nd ed.) (pp. 11–48). Chichester, West Sussex, UK: Wiley–Blackwell.

Baker, B., Birch, L., Trost, S., & Davison, K. (2007). Advanced pubertal status at age 11 and lower physical activity in adolescent girls. *The Journal of Pediatrics, 151*(5), 488–493.

Baker, J. L., et al. (2008). Breastfeeding reduces postpartum weight retention. *American Journal of Clinical Nutrition, 88*(6), 1543–1551.

Bakker, D. J. (2006). Treatment of developmental dyslexia: A review. *Pediatric Rehabilitation, 9*(1), 3–13.

Bakker, R., et al. (2010). Maternal caffeine intake from coffee and tea, fetal growth, and the risks of adverse birth outcomes: The Generation R Study. *The American Journal of Clinical Nutrition, 91*(6), 1691–1698.

Ball, J., Lohaus, A., & Miebach, C. (2006). Psychological adjustment and school achievement during transition from elementary to secondary school. *Zeitschrift für Entwicklungs-psychologie und Pädagogische Psychologie, 38*(3), 101–109.

Ballweg, Rachel. (2001). *Can you be too rich or too thin? Well and Good, no. 3.* Retrieved from: http://www.uihealthcare.com/wellandgood/2001issue3/eatingdisorders.htm.

Baltazar, N. C., Shutts, K., & Kinzler, K. D. (2012). Children show heightened memory for threatening social actions. *Journal of Experimental Child Psychology.* http://dx. doi.org/10.1016/j.jecp.2011.11.003.

Bandura, A. (1986). *Social foundations of thought and action: A social-cognitive theory.* Englewood Cliffs, NJ: Prentice Hall.

Bandura, A. (2006a). Going global with social cognitive theory: From prospect to paydirt. In S. I. Donaldson, D. E. Berger & K. Pezdek (Eds.), *Applied psychology: New frontiers and rewarding careers* (pp. 53–79). Hillsdale, NJ: Erlbaum.

Bandura, A. (2006b). Toward a psychology of human agency. *Perspectives on Psychological Science, 1*(2), 164–180.

Bandura, A. (2011). The social and policy impact of social cognitive theory. In M. M. Mark, S. I. Donaldson, & B. Campbell (Eds.). *Social psychology and evaluation.* (pp. 33–71). New York: Guilford Press.

Bandura, A., Barbaranelli, C., Vittorio Caprara, G., & Pastorelli, C. (2001). Self-efficacy beliefs as shapers of children's aspirations and career trajectories. *Child Development, 72*(1), 187–206.

Bandura, A., Blanchard, E. B., & Ritter, B. (1969). The relative efficacy of desensitization and modeling approaches for inducing behavioral, affective, and cognitive changes. *Journal of Personality and Social Psychology, 13,* 173–199.

Bandura, A., Ross, S. A., & Ross, D. (1963). Imitation of film-mediated aggressive models. *Journal of Abnormal and Social Psychology, 66,* 3–11.

Bangal, V. B., Giri, P. A., & Mahajan, A. S. (2012). Maternal and foetal outcome in pregnancy induced hypertension: A study from rural tertiary care teaching hospital in India. *International Journal of Biomedical Research, 2*(12), 595–599.

Barac, R., & Bialystok, E. (2011). Cognitive development in bilingual children. *Language Teaching, 44,* 36–54.

Bardick, A. D., Bernes, K. B., Magnusson, K. C., & Witko, K. D. (2006). Junior high school students' career plans for the future. *Journal of Career Development, 32,* 250–271.

Barkley, R. A. (2004). Adolescents with attention-deficit/hyperactivity disorder: An overview of empirically based treatments. *Journal of Psychiatric Practice, 10*(1), 39–56.

Barr, R. G., Paterson, J. A., MacMartin, L. M., Lehtonen, L., & Young, S. N. (2005). Prolonged and unsoothable crying bouts in infants with and without colic. *Journal of Developmental & Behavioral Pediatrics, 26*(1), 14–23.

Barrile, M., Armstrong, E. S., & Bower, T. G. R. (1999). Novelty and frequency as determinants of newborn preference. *Developmental Science, 2*(1), 47–52.

Barry, C. M., & Wentzel, K. R. (2006). Friend influence on prosocial behavior: The role of motivational factors and friendship characteristics. *Developmental Psychology, 42*(1), 153–163.

Bartzokis, G., et al. (2010). Lifespan trajectory of myelin integrity and maximum motor speed. *Neurobiology of Aging, 31*(9), 1554–1562.

Basics about childhood obesity. (2011). Centers for Disease Control and Prevention. http://www.cdc.gov/obesity/childhood/basics.html. Accessed August 18, 2012.

Bastien-Toniazzo, M., & Jullien, S. (2001). Nature and importance of the logographic phase in learning to read. *Reading and Writing, 14*(1–2), 119–143.

Bates, E. (2001). Plasticity, localization and language development. In S.T. Parker, J. Langer & C. Milbrath (Eds.), *Biology and knowledge revisited* (pp. 205–254). London: Routledge.

Bates, E. (2004). In J. Berck, *Before baby talk, signs and signals. The New York Times* online.

Batsche, G. M., & Porter, L. J. (2006). Bullying. In G. G. Bear & K. M. Minke (Eds.), *Children's needs III: Development, prevention, and intervention* (pp. 135–148). Washington, DC: National Association of School Psychologists.

Bauer, K. A., et al. (2009). Acne vulgaris and steroid acne. In R. Fife, S. Schrager & S. B. Schrager (Eds.), *The ACP handbook of women's health* (pp. 337ff.). Philadelphia: ACP Press.

Bauer, P. J., & Fivush, R. (2010). Context and consequences of autobiographical memory development. *Cognitive Development, 25*(4), 303–308.

Bauer, P., San Souci, P., & Pathman, T. (2010). Infant memory. *Wiley Interdisciplinary Reviews: Cognitive Science, 1,* 267–277.

Baum, N., Weidberg, Z., Osher, Y., & Kohelet, D. (2011). No longer pregnant, not yet a mother: Giving birth prematurely to a very low birth weight baby. *Qualitative Health Research.* doi:10.1177/1049732311422899.

Bauman, M. L., Anderson, G., Perry, E., & Ray, M. (2006). Neuroanatomical and neurochemical studies of the autistic brain: Current thought and future directions. In S. O. Moldin & J. L. R. Rubenstein (Eds.), *Understanding autism: From basic neuroscience to treatment* (pp. 303–322). Boca Raton, FL: CRC Press.

Baumrind, D. (1989). Rearing competent children. In W. Damon (Ed.), *Child development today and tomorrow.* San Francisco: Jossey-Bass.

Baumrind, D. (1991a). The influence of parenting style on adolescent competence and substance use. *Journal of Early Adolescence, 11,* 56–95.

Baumrind, D. (1991b). Parenting styles and adolescent development. In J. Brooks-Gunn, R. Lerner & A. C. Petersen (Eds.), *Encyclopedia of adolescence.* New York: Garland.

Baumrind, D. (2005). Taking a stand in a morally pluralistic society: Constructive obedience and responsible dissent in moral/character education. In L. Nucci (Ed.), *Conflict, contradiction, and contrarian elements in moral development and education* (pp. 21–50). Mahwah, NJ: Erlbaum.

Baumrind, D. (2013). Is a pejorative view of power assertion in the socialization process justified? *Review of General Psychology, 17*(4), 420–427.

Bayley, N. (2005). *Bayley Scales of Infant and Toddler Development* (3rd ed.) (Bayley-III). San Antonio, TX: Pearson.

Bearce, K. H., & Rovee-Collier, C. (2006). Repeated priming increases memory accessibility in infants. *Journal of Experimental Child Psychology, 93*(4), 357–376.

Beauchamp, G. K., & Mennella, J. A. (2011). Flavor perception in human infants: Development and functional significance. *Digestion, 83*(Suppl. 1), 1–6.

Beck, E., Burnet, K. L., & Vosper, J. (2006). Birth-order effects on facets of extraversion. *Personality and Individual Differences, 40*(5), 953–959.

Becker, M., et al. (2012). Culture and the distinctiveness motive: Constructing identity in individualistic and collectivistic contexts. *Journal of Personality and Social Psychology.* doi:10.1037/a0026853.

Bedny, M., Pascual-Leone, A., Dravida, S., & Saxe, R. (2012). A sensitive period for language in the visual cortex: Distinct patterns of plasticity in congenitally versus late blind adults. *Brain and Language*, in press.

Beebe, B., et al. (2010). The origins of 12-month attachment: A microanalysis of 4-month mother-infant interaction. *Attachment & Human Development, 12*(1–2), 3–141.

Beer, J. M., & Horn, J. M. (2000). The influence of rearing order on personality development within two adoption cohorts. *Journal of Personality, 68*(4), 789–819.

Behr, A. M. (2011). Disorders of elimination: Nocturnal enuresis. *Guide to pediatric urology and surgery in clinical practice*, Part 1 (pp. 121–140.) doi:10.1007/978-1-84996-366-4_12.

Behrman, R. E., Kliegman, R. M., & Jenson, H. B. (2000). *Nelson review of pediatrics* (2nd ed.). Philadelphia: Saunders.

Beilei, L., Lei, L., Qi, D., & von Hofsten, C. (2002). The development of fine motor skills and their relations to children's academic achievement. *Acta Psychologica Sinica, 34*(5), 494–499.

Beiser, M., & Gotowiec, A. (2000). Accounting for native/non-native differences in IQ scores. *Psychology in the Schools, 37*(3), 237–252.

Bekkhus, M., Rutter, M., Maughan, B., & Borge, A. I. H. (2011). The effects of group daycare in the context of paid maternal leave and high-quality provision. *European Journal of Developmental Psychology, 8*(6), 681–696.

Belkin, L. (2009, April 5). Your old man. *The New York Times Magazine*.

Bell, J. H., & Bromnick, R. D. (2003). The social reality of the imaginary audience: A ground theory approach. *Adolescence, 38*(150), 205–219.

Bell, K. N., & Norwood, K. (2007). Gender equity intersects with mathematics and technology: Problem-solving education for changing times. In D. M. Sadker & E. S. Silber (Eds.), *Gender in the classroom: Foundations, skills, methods, and strategies across the curriculum* (pp. 225–258). Mahwah, NJ: Erlbaum.

Bell, M. A. (2012). A psychobiological perspective on working memory performance at 8 months of age. *Child Development, 83*(1), 251–265.

Bell, M. A., Wolfe, C. D., & Adkins, D. R. (2007). Frontal lobe development during infancy and childhood. In D. Coch et al. (Eds.), *Human behavior, learning, and the developing brain* (pp. 247–276). New York: Guilford.

Bell, S. M., & Ainsworth, M. D. S. (1972). Infant crying and maternal responsiveness. *Child Development, 43*(4), 1171–1190.

Belmonte, M. K., & Carper, R. A. (2006). Monozygotic twins with Asperger syndrome: Differences in behaviour reflect variations in brain structure and function. *Brain and Cognition, 61*(1), 110–121.

Belsky, J. (2001). Emanuel Miller Lecture: Developmental risks (still) associated with early child care. *Journal of Child Psychology and Psychiatry and Allied Disciplines, 42*(7), 845–859.

Belsky, J. (2006a). Determinants and consequences of infant–parent attachment. In L. Balter & C. S. Tamis-LeMonda (Eds.), *Child psychology: A handbook of contemporary issues* (2nd ed.) (pp. 53–77). New York: Psychology Press.

Belsky, J. (2009). Classroom composition, childcare history and social development: Are childcare effects disappearing or spreading? *Social Development, 18*(1), 230–238.

Bem, S. L. (1989). Genital knowledge and gender constancy in preschool children. *Child Development, 60*, 649–662.

Bender, H. L., et al. (2007). Use of harsh physical discipline and developmental outcomes in adolescence. *Development and Psychopathology, 19*(1) 227–242.

Bendersky, M., Bennett, D., & Lewis, M. (2006). Aggression at age 5 as a function of prenatal exposure to cocaine, gender, and environmental risk. *Journal of Pediatric Psychology, 31*(1), 71–84.

Bengtsson, H., & Arvidsson, A. (2011). The impact of developing social perspective-taking skills on emotionality in middle and late childhood. *Social Development, 20*(2), 353–375.

Benoit, D., & Coolbear, J. (2004). Disorders of attachment and failure to thrive. In L. Atkinson & S. Goldberg (Eds.), *Attachment issues in psychopathology and intervention* (pp. 49–64). Hillsdale, NJ: Erlbaum.

Berenbaum, S. A., Martin, C. L., Hanish, L. D., Briggs, P. T., & Fabes, R. A. (2008). Sex differences in children's play. In J. B. Becker et al. (Eds.). *Sex differences in the brain* (pp. 275–290). New York: Oxford University Press.

Berg, C. J., Chang, J., Callaghan, W. M., & Whitehead, S. J. (2003). Pregnancy-related mortality in the United States, 1991–1997. *Obstetrics and Gynecology, 101*, 289–296.

Bergmann, J., & Wimmer, H. (2008). A dual-route perspective on poor reading in a regular orthography: Evidence from phonological and orthographic lexical decisions. *Cognitive Neuropsychology, 25*(5), 653–676.

Berko, J. (1958). The child's learning of English morphology. *Word, 14*, 150–177.

Bernardis, P., et al. (2008). Manual actions affect vocalizations of infants. *Experimental Brain Research, 184*(4), 599–603.

Berndt, T. J. (1992). Friendship and friends' influence in adolescence. *Current Directions in Psychological Science, 1*, 156–159.

Berndt, T. J. (2004). Friendship and three A's (aggression, adjustment, and attachment). *Journal of Experimental Child Psychology, 88*(1), 1–4.

Berndt, T. J., & Perry, T. B. (1990). Distinctive features and effects of early adolescent friendships. In R. Montemayor, G. R. Adams & T. P. Gullotta (Eds.), *From childhood to adolescence: A transitional period?* Newbury Park, CA: Sage.

Bernier, J., Hanson, Y., & Barber, T. (2012). *Weight expectations: Experiences and needs of overweight and obese pregnant women and their health care providers*. Halifax, NS: Atlantic Centre of Excellence for Women's Health.

Bernstein, G. A., & Layne, A. E. (2006). Separation anxiety disorder and generalized anxiety disorder. In M. K. Dulcan & J. M. Wiener (Eds.), *Essentials of child and adolescent psychiatry* (pp. 415–439). Washington, DC: American Psychiatric Publishing.

Bernstein, I. M., et al. (2005). Maternal smoking and its association with birth weight. *Obstetrics & Gynecology, 106*, 986–991.

Berry, J. W., & Triandis, H. C. (2006). Culture. In K. Pawlik & G. d'Ydewalle (Eds.), *Psychological concepts: An international historical perspective* (pp. 47–62). Hove, England: Psychology Press/Taylor & Francis.

Berry, R. J., Li, Z., Erickson, J. D., Li, S., Moore, C. A., Wang, H., Mulinare, J., Zhao, P., Wong, L.-Y. C., Gindler, J., Hong, S.-X., & Correa, A. (1999). Prevention of neural-tube defects with folic acid in China. *New England Journal of Medicine, 341*, 1485–1490.

Bersoff, D. N. (Ed.) (2008). *Ethical conflicts in psychology* (4th ed.). Washington, DC: American Psychological Association.

Berzonsky, M. D. (2004). Identity style, parental authority, and identity commitment. *Journal of Youth and Adolescence, 33*(3), 213–220.

Berzonsky, M. D. (2005). Ego identity: A personal standpoint in a postmodern world. *Identity, 5*(2), 125–136.

Berzonsky, M. D., & Kuk, L. S. (2005). Identity style, psychosocial maturity, and academic performance. *Personality and Individual Differences, 39*(1), 235–247.

Bezdjian, S., Tuvblad, C., Raine, A., & Baker, L. A. (2011). The genetic and environmental covariation among psychopathic personality traits, and reactive and proactive aggression in children. *Child Development, 82*(4), 1267–1281.

Bialystok, E. (2001). *Bilingualism in development: Language, literacy, and cognition*. New York: Cambridge University Press.

Bialystok, E. (2011). Coordination of executive functions in monolingual and bilingual children. *Journal of Experimental Child Psychology, 110,* 461–468.

Bialystok, E., Carik, F. I. M., Green, D. W., & Gollan, T. H. (2009). Bilingual minds. *Psychological Science in the Public Interest, 10,* 89–129. doi:10.1177/1529100610387084

Bialystok, E., & Herman, J. (1999). Does bilingualism matter for early literacy? *Bilingualism: Language and Cognition, 2*(1), 35–44.

Bialystok, E., Luk, G., Peets, K. F., & Yang, S. (2010). Receptive vocabulary differences in monolingual and bilingual children. *Bilingualism: Language and Cognition, 13,* 525–531.

Bialystok, E., McBride-Chang, C., & Luk, G. (2005). Bilingualism, language proficiency, and learning to read in two writing systems. *Journal of Educational Psychology, 97*(4), 580–590.

Biederman, J., et al. (2007). Effect of comorbid symptoms of oppositional defiant disorder on responses to atomoxetine in children with ADHD: A meta-analysis of controlled clinical trial data. *Psychopharmacology, 190*(1), 31–41.

Bigelow, A. E., et al. (2010). Maternal sensitivity throughout infancy: Continuity and relation to attachment security. *Infant Behavior and Development, 33*(1), 50–60.

Bigsby, R., et al. (2011). Prenatal cocaine exposure and motor performance at 4 months. *The American Journal of Occupational Therapy, 65*(5), e60–e68.

Birch, L. L., Gunder, L., Grimm-Thomas, K., & Laing, D. G. (1998). Infants' consumption of a new food enhances acceptance of similar foods. *Appetite, 30*(3), 283–295.

Biro, F. M. (2008). Normal growth and development. In G. B. Slap (Ed.), *Adolescent Medicine* (pp. 3ff.). Philadelphia: Elsevier Health Sciences.

Black, M. M., et al. (2007). Early intervention and recovery among children with failure to thrive. *Pediatrics, 120*(1), 59–69.

Blake, S. M., Ledsky, R., Goodenow, C., Sawyer, R., Lohrmann, D., & Windsor, R. (2003). Condom availability programs in Massachusetts high schools: Relationships with condom use and sexual behavior. *American Journal of Public Health, 93,* 955–962.

Blakemore, J. E. O., & Hill, C. A. (2008). The Child Gender Socialization Scale: A measure to compare traditional and feminist parents. *Sex Roles, 58*(3–4), 192–207.

Blanchette, N., Smith, M. L., Fernandes-Penney, A., King, S., & Read, S. (2001). Cognitive and motor development in children with vertically transmitted HIV infection. *Brain and Cognition, 46*(1–2), 50–53.

Blaze, J., & Roth, T. L. (2013). Exposure to caregiver maltreatment alters expression levels of epigenetic regulators in the medial prefrontal cortex. *International Journal of Developmental Neuroscience, 31,* 804–810.

Bloch, M., Rotenberg, N., Koren, D., & Ehud, K. (2006). Risk factors for early postpartum depressive symptoms. *General Hospital Psychiatry, 28*(1), 3–8.

Bloom, B., Cohen, R. A., & Freeman, G. (2011). Summary health statistics for U.S. children: National Health Interview Survey, 2010. National Center for Health Statistics. *Vital Health Statistics 10*(250). http://www.cdc.gov/nchs/data/series/sr_10/sr10_250.pdf. Accessed August 4, 2012.

Bloom, L. (1998). Language acquisition in its developmental context. In W. Damon (Ed.), *Handbook of child psychology* (5th ed.), Vol. 2. New York: Wiley.

Bloom, P. (2002). Mind reading, communication, and the learning of names for things. *Mind and Language, 17*(1–2), 37–54.

Blumberg, M. S., & Seelke, A. M. H. (2010). The form and function of infant sleep: From muscle to neocortex. In M. S. Blumberg, J. H. Freeman, & S. R. Robinson (Eds.), *Oxford handbook of developmental behavioral neuroscience* (pp. 391–423). New York: Oxford University Press.

Blumenthal, H., et al. (2011). Elevated social anxiety among early maturing girls. *Developmental Psychology, 47*(4), 1133–1140.

Boada, R., & Pennington, B. F. (2006). Deficient implicit phonological representations in children with dyslexia. *Journal of Experimental Child Psychology, 95*(3), 153–193.

Boccia, M., & Campos, J. J. (1989). Maternal emotional signals, social referencing, and infants' reactions to strangers. In N. Eisenberg (Ed.), *New directions for child development,* No. 44, *Empathy and related emotional responses.* San Francisco: Jossey-Bass.

Boccia, M. L., Campbell, F. A., Goldman, B. D., & Skinner, M. (2009). Differential recall of consent information and parental decisions about enrolling children in research studies. *Journal of General Psychology, 136*(1), 91–108.

Boden, C., & Giaschi, D. (2007). M-stream deficits and reading-related visual processes in developmental dyslexia. *Psychological Bulletin, 133*(2), 346–366.

Boehnke, K., Silbereisen, R. K., Eisenberg, N., Reykowski, J., & Palmonari, A. (1989). The development of prosocial motivation: A cross-national study. *Journal of Cross-Cultural Psychology, 20,* 219–243.

Boekeloo, B. O., & Howard, D. E. (2002). Oral sexual experience among young adolescents receiving general health examination. *American Journal of Health Behavior, 26,* 306–314.

Boey, C. C. M., Omar, A., & Phillips, J. A. (2003). Correlation among academic performance, recurrent abdominal pain and other factors in year-6 urban primary-school children in Malaysia. *Journal of Paediatrics and Child Health, 39*(5), 352–357.

Bohannon, J. N., III, & Stanowicz, L. (1988). The issue of negative evidence: Adult responses to children's language errors. *Developmental Psychology, 24,* 684–689.

Bohon, C., Garber, J., & Horowitz, J. L. (2007). Predicting school dropout and adolescent sexual behavior in offspring of depressed and nondepressed mothers. *Journal of the American Academy of Child & Adolescent Psychiatry, 46*(1), 15–24.

Boivin, M., Vitaro, F., & Poulin, F. (2005). Peer relationships and the development of aggressive behavior in early childhood. In R. E. Tremblay, W. W. Hartup & J. Archer (Eds.), *Developmental origins of aggression* (pp. 376–397). New York: Guilford.

Boman, U. W., Hanson, C., Hjelmquist, E., & Möller, A. (2006). Personality traits in women with Turner syndrome. *Scandinavian Journal of Psychology, 47*(3), 219–223.

Bonkowski, S. (2005). Group work with children of divorce. In G. L. Greif & P. H. Ephross (Eds.), *Group work with populations at risk* (2nd ed.) (pp. 135–145). New York: Oxford University Press.

Bonn-Miller, M. O., Zvolensky, M. J., & Bernstein, A. (2007). Marijuana use motives: Concurrent relations to frequency of past 30-day use and anxiety sensitivity among young adult marijuana smokers. *Addictive Behaviors, 32*(1) 49–62.

Boom, J., Wouters, H., & Keller, M. (2007). A cross-cultural validation of stage development: A Rasch re-analysis of longitudinal socio-moral reasoning data. *Cognitive Development, 22*(2), 213–229.

Booth, A., Johnson, D. R., Granger, D. A., Crouter, A. C., & McHale, S. (2003). Testosterone and child and adolescent adjustment: The moderating role of parent–child relationships. *Developmental Psychology, 39*(1), 85–98.

Bordova, E., & Leong, D. J. (2007). *Tools of the mind: The Vygotskian Approach to Early Childhood Education.* Upper Saddle Rover, NJ: Pearson.

Borelli, J., et al. (2010). Attachment and emotion in school-aged children. *Emotion, 10*(4). 475–485.

Boskind-White, M., & White, W. C. (1983). *Bulimarexia: The binge/purge cycle.* New York: Norton.

Bosmans, G., Braet, C., Beyers, W., Leeuwen, K. V., & Vlierberghe, L. V. (2011). Parents' power assertive discipline and internalizing problems in adolescents: The role of attachment. *Parenting: Science and Practice, 11,* 34–55.

Bottomley, G. (2011). Treating nocturnal enuresis in children in primary care. *Practitioner, 23*(6), 2–3.

Bouchard, T. J., Jr., & Loehlin, J. C. (2001). Genes, evolution, and personality. *Behavior Genetics, 31*(3), 243–273.

Bouchard, T. J., Jr., Lykken, D. T., McGue, M., Segal, N. L., & Tellegen, A. (1990). Sources of human psychological differences: The Minnesota study of twins reared apart. *Science, 250,* 223–228.

Boukydis, C. F. Z., & Lester, B. M. (2008). Mother–infant consultation during drug treatment: Research and innovative clinical practice. *Harm Reduction Journal, 5,* 6. Available at http://www.harmreductionjournal.com/content/5/1/6. Accessed March 3, 2009.

Bouldin, P., & Pratt, C. (1999). Characteristics of preschool and school-age children with imaginary companions. *Journal of Genetic Psychology, 160*(4), 397–410.

Boulton, M. J. (1996). A comparison of 8- and 11-year-old girls' and boys' Participation in specific types of rough-and-tumble play and aggressive fighting: Implications for functional hypotheses. *Aggressive Behavior, 22,* 271–287.

Bower, T. G. R. (1974). *Development in infancy.* San Francisco: Freeman.

Bowker, J. C., Thomas, K. K., Norman, K. E., & Spencer, S. V. (2011). Mutual best friend involvement. *Journal of Youth and Adolescence, 40*(5), 545–555.

Bowlby, J. (1969). Disruption of affectional bonds and its effects on behavior. *Canada's Mental Health Supplement, 59,* 12.

Bowlby, J. (1988). *A secure base.* New York: Basic Books.

Boysson-Bardies, B. de, & Halle, P. A. (1994). Speech development: Contributions of cross-linguistic studies. In A. Vyt et al. (Eds.), *Early child development in the French tradition: Contributions from current research.* Hillsdale, NJ: Erlbaum.

Braarud, H. C., & Stormark, K. M. (2008). Prosodic modification and vocal adjustments in mothers' speech during face-to-face interaction with their two- to four-month-old infants: A double video study. *Social Development, 17*(4), 1074–1084.

Brackett, M. A., Rivers, S. E., & Salovey, P. (2011). Emotional intelligence: Implications for personal, social, academic, and workplace success. *Social & Personality Psychology, 5*(1), 88–103.

Braddick, O., & Atkinson, J. (2011). Development of human visual function. *Vision Research, 51*(13), 1588–1609.

Bradley, R. H. (2006). The home environment. In N. F. Watt et al. (Eds.), *The crisis in youth mental health: Critical issues and effective programs,* Vol. 4, *Early intervention programs and policies, Child psychology and mental health* (pp. 89–120). Westport, CT: Praeger/Greenwood.

Bradley, R. H., Caldwell, B. M., & Corwyn, R. F. (2003). The child care HOME inventories: Assessing the quality of family child care homes. *Early Childhood Research Quarterly, 18*(3), 294–309.

Bradley, R. H., & Corwyn, R. F. (2006). The family environment. In L. Balter & C. S. Tamis-LeMonda (Eds.), *Child psychology: A handbook of contemporary issues* (2nd ed.) (pp. 493–520). New York: Psychology Press.

Bramen, J. E., et al. (2011). Puberty influences medial temporal lobe and cortical gray matter maturation differently in boys than girls matched for sexual maturity. *Cerebral Cortex, 21*(3), 636–646.

Bravender, T., et al. (2010). Classification of eating disturbance in children and adolescents: Proposed changes for the DSM-V. *European Eating Disorders Review, 18*(2), 79–89.

Bray, S., Dunkin, B., Hong, D. S., & Reiss, A. L. (2011). Reduced functional connectivity during working memory in Turner syndrome. *Cerebral Cortex, 21*(11), 2471–2481.

Breaking the Cycle–Ontario's Poverty Reduction Strategy. (2013). Available at http://www.children.gov.on.ca/htdocs/English/breakingthecycle/index.aspx.

Breastfeeding. (2006). Centers for Disease Control and Prevention. Department of Health and Human Services. Available at http://www.cdc.gov/breastfeeding/faq/index.htm. Accessed July 16, 2007.

Breastfeeding. (2010). U.S. Department of Health and Human Services: http://www.womenshealth.gov/breastfeeding. Accessed February 17, 2012.

Brigham, N. B., Yoder, P. J., Jarzynka, M. A., & Tapp, J. (2011). The sequential relationship between parent attentional cues and attention to objects in young children with autism. *Journal of Autism and Developmental Disorders, 40*(2), 200–208).

Brockington, I. (2011). Maternal rejection of the young child: Present status of the clinical syndrome. *Psychopathology, 44*(5), 329–336.

Bronfenbrenner, U., & Morris, P. A. (2006). The bioecological model of human development. In R. M. Lerner & W. Damon (Eds.), *Handbook of child psychology* (6th ed.), Vol. 1, *Theoretical models of human development* (pp. 793–828). Hoboken, NJ: Wiley.

Bronson, M. B. (2000). *Self-regulation in early childhood: Nature & Nurture.* New York: Guilford.

Brook, J. S., et al. (2009). Psychosocial antecedents and adverse health consequences related to substance use. *American Journal of Public Health, 99*(3), 563–568.

Brooker, R. J., et al. (2011). The association between infants' attention control and social inhibition is moderated by genetic and environmental risk for anxiety. *Infancy, 16*(5), 490–507.

Brower, T., & Wilcox, T. (2012). Shaking things up: Young infants' use of sound information for object individuation. *Infant Behavior and Development, 35*(2), 323–327.

Brown, A. S. (2006). Prenatal infection as a risk factor for schizophrenia. *Schizophrenia Bulletin, 32*(2), 200–202.

Brown, B. B., Mounts, N., Lamborn, S. D., & Steinberg, L. (1993). Parenting practices and peer group affiliation in adolescence. *Child Development, 64,* 467–482.

Brown, G. L., Mangelsdorf, S. C., Neff, C., Schoppe-Sullivan, S. J., & Frosch, C. A. (2009). Young children's self-concepts: Associations with child temperament, mothers' and fathers' parenting, and triadic family interaction. *Merrill-Palmer Quarterly, 55*(2), 184–216.

Brown, L. M., & Gilligan, C. (1993). *Meeting at the crossroads: Women's psychology and girls' development.* Cambridge, MA: Harvard University Press.

Brown, R. (1973). *A first language: The early stages.* Cambridge, MA: Harvard University Press.

Brown, R. (1977). Introduction. In C. A. Snow & C. Ferguson (Eds.), *Talking to children.* New York: Cambridge University Press.

Browning, J. R., Hatfield, E., Kessler, D., & Levine, T. (2000). Sexual motives, gender, and sexual behavior. *Archives of Sexual Behavior, 29*(2), 135–153.

Bruchmüller, K., Margraf, J., & Schneider, S. (2012). Is ADHD diagnosed in accord with diagnostic criteria? Overdiagnosis and influence of client gender on diagnosis. *Journal of Consulting and Clinical Psychology, 80*(1), 128–138.

Bruck, M., Ceci, S. J., & Principe, G. F. (2006). The child and the law. In K. Renninger, I. E. Sigel, W. Damon & R. M. Lerner (Eds.), *Handbook of child psychology* (6th ed.), Vol. 4, *Child psychology in practice* (pp. 776–816). Hoboken, NJ: Wiley.

Bruck, M., & Genesee, F. (1995). Phonological awareness in young second language learners. *Journal of Child Language, 22,* 307–324.

Brummelte, S., & Galea, L. A. M. (2010). Depression during pregnancy and postpartum: Contribution of stress and ovarian hormones. *Progress in Neuro-Psychopharmacology and Biological Psychiatry, 34*(5), 766–776.

Brun, C. C., et al. (2009). Sex differences in brain structure in auditory and cingulate regions. *NeuroReport: For Rapid Communication of Neuroscience Research, 20*(10), 930.

Bruni, M. (2006). *Fine motor skills in children with Down syndrome: A guide for parents and professionals* (2nd ed.). Bethesda, MA: Woodbine House.

Brunner, R., Parzer, P., & Resch, F. (2005). Involuntary hospitalization of patients with anorexia nervosa: Clinical issues and empirical findings. *Fortschritte der Neurologie, Psychiatrie, 73*(1), 9–15.

Bryant, J. B. (2013). Language in social context: Development of communicative competence. In J. B. Gleason & N. Bernstein Ratner (Eds.), *The development of language* (8th ed.). NewYork, NY: Pearson.

Bryden, P. J., Bruyn, J., & Fletcher, P. (2005). Handedness and health: An examination of the association between different handedness classifications and health disorders. *Laterality: Asymmetries of Body, Brain and Cognition, 10*(5), 429–440.

Buchanan, C. M., & Hughes, J. (2009). Construction of social reality during early adolescence: Can expecting storm and stress increase real or perceived storm and stress? *Journal of Research on Adolescence, 19*(2), 261–285.

Bucholz, E. M., Desai, M. M., & Rosenthal, M. S. (2011). Dietary intake in Head Start vs non-Head Start preschool-aged children: Results from the 1999–2004 National Health and Nutrition Examination Survey. *Journal of the American Dietetic Association, 111*(7), 1021–1030.

Budney, A. J., Vandrey, R. G., Hughes, J. R., Moore, B. A., & Bahrenburg, B. (2007). Oral delta-9-tetrahydrocannabinol suppresses cannabis withdrawal symptoms. *Drug and Alcohol Dependence, 86*(1), 22–29.

Bugental, D. B., & Happaney, K. (2004). Predicting infant maltreatment in low-income families: The interactive effects of maternal attributions and child status at birth. *Developmental Psychology, 40*(2), 234–243.

Bugental, D. B., et al. (2010). A cognitive approach to child abuse prevention. *Psychology of Violence, 1*(Suppl.), 84–106.

Bukowski, W. M., Buhrmester, D., & Underwood, M. K. (2011). Peer relations as a developmental context. In M. K. Underwood & L. H. Rosen (Eds.), *Social development: Relationships in infancy, childhood, and adolescence* (pp. 153–179). New York: Guilford.

Bukowski, W. M., Hoza, B., & Boivin, M. (1993b). Popularity, friendship, and emotional adjustment during early adolescence. In B. Laursen (Ed.), *New directions in child development*, No. 60, *Close friendships in adolescence*. San Francisco: Jossey-Bass.

Bull, R., Espy, K. A., Wiebe, S. A., Sheffield, T. D., & Nelson, J. M. (2011). Using confirmatory factor analysis to understand executive control in preschool children: Sources of variation in emergent mathematics achievement. *Developmental Science, 14*(4), 679–692.

Bullying and suicide. (2009). http://www .bullyingstatistics.org/content/bullying -and-suicide.html. Accessed March 1, 2012.

Bunting, L., & McAuley, C. (2004). Teenage pregnancy and motherhood: The contribution of support. *Child and Family Social Work, 9*(2), 207–215.

Burdelski, M. (2010). Socializing politeness routines: Action, other-orientation, and embodiment in a Japanese preschool. *Journal of Pragmatics, 42*, 1606–1621.

Burgess, J., & Fleet, A. (2009). Frameworks for change: Four recurrent themes for quality in early childhood education initiatives. *Asia-Pacific Journal of Teacher Education, 37*(1), 45–61.

Burke, J. M., & Baker, R. C. (2001). Is fluvoxamine safe and effective for treating anxiety disorders in children? *Journal of Family Practice, 50*(8), 719.

Burnham, D., and Mattock, K. (2010). Auditory development. In J. G. Bremner & T. D. Wachs (Eds.). *The Wiley-Blackwell handbook of infant development*, Vol. 1 (2nd ed.). Wiley-Blackwell, Oxford, UK. doi:10.1002/9781444327564.ch3

Bushman, B. J., & Anderson, C. A. (2007). Measuring the strength of the effect of violent media on aggression. *American Psychologist, 62*(3), 253–254.

Bushman, B. J., & Anderson, C. A. (2009). Comfortably numb: Desensitizing effects of violent media on helping others. *Psychological Science, 20*(3), 273–277.

Bushman, B. J., & Gibson, B. (2011). Violent video games cause an increase in aggression long after the game has been turned off. *Social Psychological and Personality Science, 2*(1), 29–32.

Bushnell, E. W. (1993, June). *A dual-processing approach to cross-modal matching: Implications for development.* Paper presented at the Society for Research in Child Development, New Orleans, LA.

Bushnell, I. W. R. (2001). Mother's face recognition in newborn infants: Learning and memory. *Infant and Child Development, 10*(1–2), 67–74.

Bushnik T., Cook, J. L., Yuzpe, A. A., et al. (2012). Estimating the prevalence of infertility in Canada. *Human Reproduction, 27*, 738–746.

Buss, A. H. (1961). *The psychology of aggression.* New York: Wiley.

Buss, D. M. (2009). How can evolutionary psychology successfully explain personality and individual differences? *Perspectives on Psychological Science, 4*(4), 359–366.

Bussey, K., & Bandura, A. (1984). Influence of gender constancy and social power on sex-linked modeling. *Journal of Personality and Social Psychology, 47*, 1292–1302.

Bussey, K., & Bandura, A. (1999). Social cognitive theory of gender development and differentiation. *Psychological Review, 106*(4), 676–713.

Butterfield, S. A., & Loovis, E. M. (1993). Influence of age, sex, balance, and sport participation on development of throwing by children in grades K–8. *Perceptual and Motor Skills, 76*, 459–464.

Butterworth, G., Verweij, E., & Hopkins, B. (1997). The development of prehension in infants: Halverson revisited. *British Journal of Developmental Psychology, 15*(2), 223–236.

Buyse, E., Verschueren, K., & Doumen, S. (2011). Preschoolers' attachment to mother and risk for adjustment problems in kindergarten: Can teachers make a difference? *Social Development, 20*(1), 33–50.

Bynum, M. S. (2007). African American mother–daughter communication about sex and daughters' sexual behavior: Does college racial composition make a difference? *Cultural Diversity & Ethnic Minority Psychology, 13*(2), 151–160.

Cabrera, N. J., & Bradley, R. H. (2012). Latino fathers and their children. *Child Development Perspectives, 6*(3), 232–238.

Callan, M. J., Ellard, J. H., & Nicol, J. E. (2006). The belief in a just world and immanent justice reasoning in adults.

Personality and Social Psychology Bulletin, 32(12), 1646–1658.

Calvert, S. L., & Kotler, J. A. (2003). Lessons from children's television: The impact of the Children's Television Act on children's learning. *Journal of Applied Developmental Psychology, 24*(3), 275–335.

Calvete, E. (2007). Justification of violence beliefs and social problem-solving as mediators between maltreatment and behavior problems in adolescents. *The Spanish Journal of Psychology, 10*(1), 131–140.

Camarena, P. M. (1991). Conformity in adolescence. In R. M. Lerner, A. C. Petersen & J. Brooks-Gunn (Eds.), *Encyclopedia of adolescence.* New York: Garland.

Campanella, J., & Rovee-Collier, C. (2005). Latent learning and deferred imitation at 3 months. *Infancy, 7*(3), 243–262.

Campbell, A., Shirley, L., & Caygill, L. (2002). Sex-typed preferences in three domains: Do two-year-olds need cognitive variables? *British Journal of Psychology, 93*(2), 203–217.

Campbell, A., Shirley, L., Heywood, C., & Crook, C. (2000). Infants' visual preference for sex-congruent babies, children, toys and activities: A longitudinal study. *British Journal of Developmental Psychology, 18*(4), 479–498.

Campbell, D. A., Lake, M. F., Falk, M., & Backstrand, J. R. (2006). A randomized control trial of continuous support in labor by a lay doula. *Journal of Obstetric, Gynecologic, and Neonatal Nursing, 35*(4), 456–464.

Campbell, D. W., Eaton, W. O., & McKeen, N. A. (2002). Motor activity level and behavioural control in young children. *International Journal of Behavioral Development, 26*(4), 289–296.

Campbell, J. O., Bliven, T. D., Silver, M. M., Snyder, K. J., & Spear, L. P. (2000). Effects of prenatal cocaine on behavioral adaptation to chronic stress in adult rats. *Neurotoxicology and Teratology, 22*(6), 845–850.

Campbell, S. B., et al. (2004). The course of maternal depressive symptoms and maternal sensitivity as predictors of attachment security at 36 months. *Development and Psychopathology, 16*(2), 231–252.

Campos, J. J., Hiatt, S., Ramsey, D., Henderson, C., & Svejda, M. (1978). The emergence of fear on the visual cliff. In M. Lewis & L. Rosenblum (Eds.), *The origins of affect.* New York: Plenum.

Campos, J. J., Langer, A., & Krowitz, A. (1970). Cardiac responses on the visual cliff in prelocomotor human infants. *Science, 170*, 196–197.

Canadian Community Health Survey. (2012). *Overweight and obese adults (self-reported), 2012.* Ottawa, ON.

Canadian Down Syndrome Society. (2009). What is Down syndrome? http://www.cdss.ca/information/ general-information/what-is-down -syndrome.html. Accessed July 17, 2014.

Canadian Education Statistics Council. (2009). Key factors to support literacy success in school-aged populations: A literature review. Council of Minsters of Education. Toronto, ON.

Canadian Institutes of Health Research, Natural Sciences and Engineering Research Council of Canada, and Social Sciences and Humanities Research Council of Canada. (2010). Tri-Council Policy Statement: Ethical Conduct for Research Involving Humans, December 2010.

Canadian Mental Health Association. (2014). *Postpartum depression.* Available at http://www.cmha .ca/mental_health/postpartum -depression/#.U8gHL1bFT-t

Canadian Paediatric Society. (2004). *Canadian Paediatric Surveillance Program, 2004 Results.* Ottawa, ON: Author.

Canadian Psychological Association. (2000). *Canadian Code of Ethics for Psychologists* (3rd ed.). Ottawa: Author.

Canadian Society for Exercise Physiology. (2012). Canadian physical activity, and sedentary behaviour guidelines, http://www.csep.ca/english/ view.asp?x=949.

Candy, T. R., Crowell, J. A., & Banks, M. S. (1998). Optical, receptoral, and retinal constraints on foveal and peripheral vision in the human neonate. *Vision Research, 38*(24), 3857–3870.

Caplan, M., Vespo, J., Pedersen, J., & Hale, D. F. (1991). Conflict and its resolution in small groups of one- and two-year-olds. *Child Development, 62,* 1513–1524.

Caplan, P. J., & Larkin, J. (1991). The anatomy of dominance and self-protection. *American Psychologist, 46,* 536.

Capron, C., Thérond, C., & Duyme, M. (2007). Brief report: Effect of menarcheal status and family structure on depressive symptoms and emotional/ behavioural problems in young adolescent girls. *Journal of Adolescence, 30*(1), 175–179.

Caputo, R. K. (2003). Head Start, other preschool programs, and life success in a youth cohort. *Journal of Sociology and Social Welfare, 30*(2), 105–126.

Caravolas, M., & Bruck, M. (2000). Vowel categorization skill and its relationship to early literacy skills among first-grade Quebec-French children. *Journal of Experimental Child Psychology, 76*(3), 190–221.

Carbonneau, K. J., Marley, S. C., & Selig, J. P. (2013). A meta-analysis of the efficacy of teaching mathematics with concrete manipulatives. *Journal of Educational Psychology, 105*(2), 380–400.

Cardemil, E. V. (2008). Culturally sensitive treatments. *Culture & Psychology, 14*(3), 357–367.

Carette, B., Anseel, F., & Van Yperen, N. W. (2011). Born to learn or born to win? Birth order effects on achievement goals. *Journal of Research in Personality, 45*(5), 500–503.

Carlson, J. S., Tiret, H. B., Bender, S. L., & Benson, L. (2011). The influence of group training in the Incredible Years Teacher Classroom Management Program on preschool teachers' classroom management strategies. *Journal of Applied School Psychology, 27*(2), 134–154.

Caron, A. J., Caron, R. F., & Carlson, V. R. (1979). Infant perception of the invariant shape of objects varying in slant. *Child Development, 50,* 716–721.

Carr, A. (2011). Social and emotional development in middle childhood. In D. Skuse, H. Bruce, L. Dowdney, & D. Mrazek (Eds.). *Child psychology and psychiatry: Frameworks for practice* (2nd ed.) (pp. 56–61). Hoboken, NJ: Wiley.

Carroll, J. S., et al. (2007). So close, yet so far away: The impact of varying marital horizons on emerging adulthood. *Journal of Adolescent Research, 22*(3), 219–247.

Carson, J., Burks, V., & Parke, R. D. (1993). Parent-child physical play: Determinants and consequences. In K. MacDonald (Ed.,), *Children's play in society* (pp. 197–220). Albany, NY: State University of New York Press.

Carver, L. J., & Vaccaro, B. G. (2007). 12-month-old infants allocate increased neural resources to stimuli associated with negative adult emotion. *Developmental Psychology, 43*(1), 54–69.

Casas, J. F., et al. (2006). Early parenting and children's relational and physical aggression in the preschool and home contexts. *Journal of Applied Developmental Psychology, 27*(3), 209–227.

Cascio, C. J. (2010). Somatosensory processing in neurodevelopmental disorders. *Journal of Neurodevelopmental Disorders, 2*(2), 62–69.

Case, R. (1992). *The mind's staircase.* Hillsdale, NJ: Erlbaum.

Case, R. (1998). The development of central conceptual structures. In D. Kuhn & R. Siegler (Eds.), *Handbook of child psychology: Vol. 2. Cognition, perception and language* (5th ed.). New York: Wiley.

Cashwell, T. H., Skinner, C. H., & Smith, E. S. (2001). Increasing second-grade students' reports of peers' prosocial behaviors via direct instruction, group reinforcement, and progress feedback: A replication and extension. *Education and Treatment of Children, 24*(2), 161–175.

Cassia, V. M., Simion, F., & Umilta, C. (2001). Face preference at birth: The role of an orienting mechanism. *Developmental Science, 4*(1), 101–108.

Castelli, L., De Amicis, L., & Sherman, S. J. (2007). The loyal member effect: On the preference for ingroup members who engage in exclusive relations with the ingroup. *Developmental Psychology, 43,* 1347–1359.

Castelli, L., De Dea, C., & Nesdale, D. (2008). Learning social attitudes: Children's sensitivity to the nonverbal behaviors of adult models during interracial interactions. *Personality and Social Psychology Bulletin, 34,* 1504–1513.

Castelli, L., Zogmaister, C., & Tomelleri, S. (2009). The transmission of racial attitudes within the family. *Developmental Psychology, 45*(2), 586–591.

Castillo, E. M., Quintana, S. M., Zamarripa, M. X. (2000). Cultural and linguistic issues. In E. S. Shapiro & T. R. Kratochwill (Eds.), *Conducting school-based assessments of child and adolescent behavior* (pp. 274–308). New York: Guilford Press.

Cataudella, J. (1999). When women came to Queen's. *Canadian Medical Association Journal, 161*(5), 575–576.

Cattaneo, L., Sandrini, M., & Schwarzbach, J. (2010). State-dependent TMS reveals a hierarchical representation of observed acts in the temporal, parietal, and premotor cortices. *Cerebral Cortex, 20*(9), 2252–2258.

Cattell, R. B. (1949). *The culture-fair intelligence test.* Champaign, IL: Institute for Personality and Ability Testing.

Catterall, J. (2011). The societal benefits and costs of school dropout recovery. *Education Research International,* Article ID 957303. doi:10.1155/2011/957303.

Cavallini, A., et al. (2002). Visual acuity in the first two years of life in healthy term newborns: An experience with the Teller Acuity Cards. *Functional Neurology: New Trends in Adaptive and Behavioral Disorders, 17*(2), 87–92.

Cavell, T. A. (2001). Updating our approach to parent training. I. The case against targeting noncompliance. *Clinical Psychology: Science and Practice, 8*(3), 299–318.

CBC News Canada. (March 26, 2002). BC girl convicted in school bullying tragedy. Retrieved from http://www.cbc.ca/news/canada/b -c-girl-convicted-in-school-bullying -tragedy-1.308111

Ceci, S. J. (1993, August). *Cognitive and social factors in children's testimony.* Master lecture presented at the meeting of the American Psychological Association, Toronto.

Celizic, M. (2009, March 10). *With child porn charges being leveled, some say laws are behind the times.* www .TODAYShow.com contributor.

Centers for Disease Control and Prevention. (2010). U.S. Department of Health and Human Services. *10 Things You Need to Know about Immunizations.* http://www.cdc.gov/vaccines/ vac-gen/10-shouldknow.htm. Accessed August 4, 2012.

Centers for Disease Control and Prevention. (2013). Seasonal flu vaccine safety for pregnant women. http://www.cdc .gov/flu/protect/vaccine/qa_vacpregnant .htm. Accessed January 13, 2014.

Cernoch, J., & Porter, R. (1985). Recognition of maternal axillary odors by infants. *Child Development, 56,* 1593–1598.

Chamness, J. A. (2008). Taking a pediatric sleep history. *Pediatric Annals, 37*(7), 502–508.

Chan, T. W., & Koo, A. (2011). Parenting style and youth outcomes in the UK. *European Sociological Review, 27*(3), 385–399.

Chance, S. E., Brown, R. T., Dabbs, J. M., Jr., & Casey, R. (2000). Testosterone, intelligence and behavior disorders in young boys. *Personality and Individual Differences, 28*(3), 437–445.

Chandler, M. J., Lalonde, C. E., Sokol, B. W., & Hallett, D. (2003). Personal persistence, identity, and suicide: A study of Native and non-Native North American adolescents. *Monographs for the Society for Research in Child Development*, serial No. 273, Vol. 68, No. 2.

Chandra, A., et al. (2008). Does watching sex on television predict teen pregnancy? Findings from a national longitudinal survey of youth. *Pediatrics, 122*(5), 1047–1054.

Chang, L., Schwartz, D., Dodge, K., & McBride-Chang, C. (2003). Harsh parenting in relation to child emotion regulation and aggression. *Journal of Family Psychology, 17*(4), 598–606.

Chapman, M., & McBride, M. C. (1992). Beyond competence and performance: Children's class inclusion strategies, superordinate class cues, and verbal justifications. *Developmental Psychology, 28*, 319–327.

Chatham, M. L. (2008). Early predictors of disinhibited attachment behaviors among internationally adopted children. *Dissertation Abstracts International: Section B: The Sciences and Engineering, 69*(3-B), 1985.

Chehil, S., & Kutcher, S. (2012). Suicide risk assessment. In *Suicide risk management* (pp. 56–87). Hoboken, NJ: Wiley.

Chen, A., et al. (2009). Maternal obesity and the risk of infant death in the United States. *Epidemiology, 20*(1), 74–81.

Chen, X., & Eisenberg, N. (2012). Understanding cultural issues in child development: Introduction. *Child Development Perspectives, 6*(1), 1–4.

Chen, X., Chen, H., & Kaspar, V. (2001). Group social functioning and individual socioemotional and school adjustment in Chinese children. *Merrill-Palmer Quarterly, 47*(2), 264–299.

Chen, Z., & Hancock, J. E. (2011). Cognitive development. In A. S. Davis (Ed.). *Handbook of pediatric neuropsychology*. New York: Springer.

Cherney, I. D., Harper, H. J., & Winter, J. A. (2006). Nouveaux jouets: Ce que les enfants identifient comme "jouets de garcons" et "jouets de filles." *Enfance, 58*(3), 266–282.

Chess, S., & Thomas, A. (1984). *Origins and evolution of behavior disorders: From infancy to early adult life.* New York: Brunner/Mazel.

Chess, S., & Thomas, A. (1991). Temperament. In M. Lewis (Ed.), *Child and adolescent psychiatry: A comprehensive textbook*. Baltimore: Williams & Wilkins.

Chetty, R., Friedman, J. N., & Rockoff, J. E. (2012). The long-term impacts of teachers: Teacher value-added and student outcomes in adulthood. http://obs.rc.fas.harvard.edu/chetty/value_added.pdf.

Child Maltreatment. (2010). U.S. Department of Health and Human Services, Administration for Children and Families, Administration on Children, Youth and Families, Children's Bureau. (2011). *Child Maltreatment 2010.* Available from http://www.acf.hhs.gov/programs/cb/stats_research/index.htm#can.

Childhood obesity. (2011). http://aspe.hhs.gov/health/reports/child_obesity. Accessed August 18, 2012.

Childhood obesity facts. (2011). Centers for Disease Control and Prevention. http://www.cdc.gov/healthyyouth/obesity/facts.htm. Accessed March 1, 2012.

Chiou, W-B., & Wan, C-S. (2006). Sexual self-disclosure in cyberspace among Taiwanese adolescents: Gender differences and the interplay of cyberspace and real life. *CyberPsychology & Behavior, 9*(1), 46–53.

Chira, S. (1991, December 8). Report says too many aren't ready for school. *New York Times*, p. B18.

Chomsky, N. (1988). *Language and problems of knowledge.* Cambridge, MA: MIT Press.

Chomsky, N. (1990). On the nature, use, and acquisition of language. In W. G. Lycan (Ed.), *Mind and cognition.* Oxford: Blackwell.

Chonchaiya, W., et al. (2012). Increased prevalence of seizures in boys who were probands with the fMRI premutation and co-morbid autism spectrum disorder. *Human Genetics, 131*(4), 581–589.

Christakis, D. A., & Zimmerman, F. J. (2007). Violent television viewing during preschool is associated with antisocial behavior during school age. *Pediatrics, 120*(5), 993–999.

Chronis, A. M., et al. (2007). Maternal depression and early positive parenting predict future conduct problems in young children with attention-deficit/hyperactivity disorder. *Developmental Psychology, 43*(1), 70–82.

Chudley, A. E., Conry, J., Cook, J. L., Loock, C., Rosales, T., & LeBlanc, N. (2005). Fetal alcohol spectrum disorder: Canadian guidelines for diagnosis. *The Canadian Medical Association Journal, 172*, 1–21.

Cicchetti, D., Rogosch, F. A., & Toth, S. L. (2006). Fostering secure attachment in infants in maltreating families through preventive interventions. *Development and Psychopathology, 18*(3), 623–649.

Cieraad, I. (2007). Gender at play: Décor differences between boys' and girls' bedrooms. In E. Casey & L. Martens (Eds.), *Gender and consumption* (pp. 197–218). London: Ashgate.

Cillessen, A. H. N., & Bellmore, A. D. (2010). Social skills and social competence in interactions with peers. In P. K. Smith, & C. H. Hart (Eds.). *The Wiley-Blackwell handbook of childhood social development* (2nd ed.). Oxford, UK: Wiley-Blackwell. doi:10.1002/9781444390933.ch21.

Ciro, D., et al. (2005). Lesbian, gay, bisexual, sexual-orientation questioning adolescents seeking mental health services: Risk factors, worries, and desire to talk about them. *Social Work in Mental Health, 3*(3), 213–234.

Cirulli, F., et al. (2009). Early life stress as a risk factor for mental health. *Neuroscience & Biobehavioral Reviews, 33*(4), 573–585.

Clancy, B., & Finlay, B. (2001). Neural correlates of early language learning. In M. Tomasello & E. Bates (Eds.), *Language development: The essential readings.* Malden, MA: Blackwell.

Clark, B., & Canadian Pediatric Society Mental Health and Developmental Disabilities Committee (2013). *Pediatric Health 18*(7), 373–377.

Clark, E. V. (1973). What's in a word? On the child's acquisition of semantics in his first language. In E. Moore (Ed.), *Cognitive development and the acquisition of language.* New York: Academic Press.

Clark, E. V. (1975). Knowledge, context, and strategy in the acquisition of meaning. In D. P. Date (Ed.), *Georgetown University roundtable on language and linguistics.* Washington, DC: Georgetown University Press.

Clark, J. J. (2010). Life as a source of theory: Erik Erikson's contributions, boundaries, and marginalities. In T. W. Miller (Ed.). *Handbook of stressful transitions across the lifespan, Part 1* (pp. 59–83). New York: Springer Science+Business Media, LLC.

Clarke-Stewart, K. A., & Beck, R. J. (1999). Maternal scaffolding and children's narrative retelling of a movie story. *Early Childhood Research Quarterly, 14*(3), 409–434.

Clarke-Stewart, K. A., Vandell, D. L., McCartney, K., Owen, M. T., & Booth, C. (2000). Effects of parental separation and divorce on very young children. *Journal of Family Psychology, 14*(2), 304–326.

Clayton, R., & Crosby, R. A. (2006). Measurement in health promotion. In R. A. Crosby, R. J. DiClemente & L. F. Salazar (Eds.), *Research methods in health promotion* (pp. 229–259). San Francisco: Jossey-Bass.

Cleary, D. J., Ray, G. E., LoBello, S. G., & Zachar, P. (2002). Children's perceptions of close peer relationships: Quality, congruence and meta-perceptions. *Child Study Journal, 32*(3), 179–192.

Clément, R., Michaud, C., & Noels, K. A. (1998). Effets acculturatifs du support social en situation de contact intergroup. [Acculturative effects of social support in an intergroup contact situation]. *Revue Québecoise de Psychologie, 19*, 189–210.

Coelho, D. P. (2011). Encopresis: A medical and family approach. *Pediatric Nursing, 37*(3), 107–112.

Cohen, D. (Ed.). (2006). *The development of play.* New York: Routledge.

Cohen, J. R., Young, J. F., & Abela, J. R. Z. (2011). Cognitive vulnerability to depression in children. *Cognitive Therapy and Research.* doi:10.1007/s10608-011-9431-6.

Cohen, L. B., & Brunt, J. (2009). Early word learning and categorization: Methodological issues and recent empirical evidence. In J. Colombo, P. McCardle & L. Freud (Eds.), *Infant pathways to language: Methods, models, and research disorders* (pp. 245–266). New York: Psychology Press.

Cohen, L. S., et al. (2006). Relapse of major depression during pregnancy in women who maintain or discontinue antidepressant treatment. *Journal of the American Medical Association, 295*(5), 499–507.

Cohen-Bendahan, C. C. C., Buitelaar, J. K., van Goozen, S. H. M., Orlebeke, J. F., & Cohen-Kettenis, P. T. (2005). Is there an effect of prenatal testosterone on aggression and other behavioral traits? A study comparing same-sex and opposite-sex twin girls. *Hormones and Behavior, 47*(2), 230–237.

Colby, A., Kohlberg, L. G., J., & Lieberman, M. (1983). A longitudinal study of moral judgment. *Monographs of the Society for Research in Child Development, 48*(4, Serial No. 200).

Cole, C., et al. (2003). The educational impact of Rechov Sumsum/Shara'a Simsim: A Sesame Street television series to promote respect and understanding among children living in Israel, the West Bank, and Gaza. *International Journal of Behavioral Development, 27*(5), 409–422.

Cole, D. A., et al. (2011). A longitudinal study of cognitive risks for depressive symptoms in children and young adolescents. *Journal of Early Adolescence, 3*(6), 782–816.

Coleman, P. K. (2003). Perceptions of parent–child attachment, social self-efficacy, and peer relationships in middle childhood. *Infant and Child Development, 12*(4), 351–368.

Coles, E. K., Slavec, J., Bernstein, M., & Baroni, E. (2012). Exploring the gender gap in referrals for children with ADHD and other disruptive behavior disorders. *Journal of Attention Disorders, 16*, 101–108.

Coley, J. D. (1993, March). *Parental feedback to child labeling as input to conceptual development.* Paper presented at the meeting of the Society for Research in Child Development, New Orleans, LA.

Collaer, M. L., & Hill, E. M. (2006). Large sex difference in adolescents on a timed line judgment task: Attentional contributors and task relationship to mathematics. *Perception, 35*(4), 561–572.

Collins, R. L., et al. (2004). Watching sex on television predicts adolescent initiation of sexual behavior. *Pediatrics, 114*(3), e280–e289.

Collins, R. L., et al. (2010). Off-premise alcohol sales policies, drinking, and sexual risk among people living with HIV. *American Journal of Public Health, 100*(10), 1890–1892.

Collins, W. A. (1984). Conclusion: The status of basic research on middle childhood. In W. A. Collins (Ed.), *Development during middle childhood: The years from six to twelve.* Washington, DC: National Academy Press.

Collins, W. A., & Laursen, B. (2006). Parent–adolescent relationships. In P. Noller & J. A. Feeney (Eds.), *Close relationships: Functions, forms and processes* (pp. 111–125). Hove, England: Psychology Press/Taylor & Francis.

Collins, W. A., Maccoby, E. E., Steinberg, L., Hetherington, E. M., & Bornstein, M. H. (2000). Contemporary research on parenting: The case for nature and nurture. *American Psychologist, 55*(2), 218–232.

Colombo, J. (1993). *Infant cognition.* Newbury Park, CA: Sage.

Colvert, E., Rutter, M., Kreppner, J., Beckett, C., Castle, J., Groothues, C., Hawkins, A., Stevens, S., & Sonuga-Barke, E. J. S. (2008). Do theory of mind and executive function deficits underlie the adverse outcomes associated with profound early deprivation? Findings from the English and Romanian adoptees study. *Journal of Abnormal Child Psychology. 36*(7), 1057–1068.

Commons, M. L., Galaz-Fontes, J. F., & Morse, S. J. (2006). Leadership, cross-cultural contact, socio-economic status, and formal operational reasoning about moral dilemmas among Mexican non-literate adults and high school students. *Journal of Moral Education, 35*(2), 247–267.

Comtois, K. A., Schiff, M. A., & Grossman, D. C. (2008). Psychiatric risk factors associated with postpartum suicide attempt in Washington State, 1992–2001. *American Journal of Obstetrics and Gynecology, 199*(2), 120. e1–120.e5.

Condon, J. (2006). What about dad? Psychosocial and mental health issues for new fathers. *Australian Family Physician, 35*(9), 657–752.

Conference Board of Canada. (2014). How Canada Performs. http://www .conferenceboard.ca/hcp/details/society/ child-poverty.aspx. Retrieved February 23, 2014.

Connolly, J., & McIsaac, C. (2011). Romantic relationship in adolescence. In M. K. Underwood & L. H. Rosen (Eds.), *Social development: Relationships in infancy, childhood and adolescence.* New York, NY: Guilford.

Connolly, J., Craig, W., Goldberg, A., & Pepler, D. (2004). Mixed-gender groups, dating, and romantic relationships in early adolescence. *Journal of Research on Adolescence, 14*(2), 185–207.

Connolly, J., Furman, W., & Konarski, R. (2000). The role of peers in the emergence of heterosexual romantic relationships in adolescence. *Child Development, 71*(5), 1395–1408.

Connor, P. D., Sampson, P. D., Streissguth, A. P., Bookstein, F. L., & Barr, H. M. (2006). Effects of prenatal alcohol exposure on fine motor coordination and balance: A study of two adult samples. *Neuropsychologia, 44*(5), 744–751.

Conrad, N. J., Walsh, J. A., Allen, J. M., & Tsang, C. D. (2011). Examining infants' preferences for tempo in lullabies and playsongs. *Canadian Journal of Experimental Psychology/Revue canadienne de psychologie expérimentale, 65*(3), 168–172.

Cooke, B. M., & Shukla, D. (2011). Double helix: Reciprocity between juvenile play and brain development. *Developmental Cognitive Neuroscience, 1*(4), 459–470.

Cooke, L. J., & Wardle, J. (2005). Age and gender differences in children's food preferences. *British Journal of Nutrition, 93*, 741–746.

Cooper, J., Appleby, L., & Amos, T. (2002). Life events preceding suicide by young people. *Social Psychiatry and Psychiatric Epidemiology, 37*(6), 271–275.

Coovadia, H. (2004). Antiretroviral agents: How best to protect infants from HIV and save their mothers from AIDS. *New England Journal of Medicine, 351*(3), 289–292.

Copeland, A. L., Martin, P. D., Geiselman, P. J., Rash, C. J., & Kendzor, D. E. (2006). Smoking cessation for weight-concerned women: Group vs. individually tailored, dietary, and weight-control follow-up sessions. *Addictive Behaviors, 31*(1), 115–127.

Copeland, W., et al. (2010). Do the negative effects of early pubertal timing on adolescent girls continue into young adulthood? *American Journal of Psychiatry, 167*(10), 1218–1225.

Corballis, M. C. (2010). Mirror neurons and the evolution of language. *Brain and Language, 112*(1), 25–35.

Corporate Planning & Policy Directorate Natural Sciences & Engineering Research Council of Canada. (2010). Women in Science and Engineering in Canada, 2010. Ottawa, ON.

Cossins, A. (2008). Children, sexual abuse, and suggestibility: What laypeople think they know and what the literature tells us. *Psychiatry, Psychology and Law, 15*(1), 153–170.

Costello, E. J. (2007). Psychiatric predictors of adolescent and young adult drug use and abuse. *Drug and Alcohol Dependence, 88*, S1–S3.

Costello, E. J., Erkanli, A., & Angold, A. (2006). Is there an epidemic of child or adolescent depression? *Journal of Child Psychology & Psychiatry, 47*(12), 1263–1271.

Costello, E. J., Sung, M., Worthman, C., & Angold, A. (2007). Pubertal maturation and the development of alcohol use and abuse. *Drug and Alcohol Dependence, 88*, S50–S59.

Costigan, C. L., Cauce, A. M., & Etchison, K. (2007). Changes in African American mother–daughter relationships during adolescence: Conflict, autonomy, and warmth. In B. J. R. Leadbeater & N. Way (Eds.), *Urban girls revisited: Building strengths* (pp. 177–201). New York: New York University Press.

Courage, M. L., Howe, M. L., & Squires, S. E. (2004). Individual differences in 3.5-month-olds' visual attention: What do they predict at 1 year? *Infant*

Behavior and Development, 27(1), 19–30.

Courage, M., & Cowan, N. (2009). *The development of memory in infancy and childhood.* New York: Psychology Press.

Couzens, D., Cuskelly, M., & Haynes, M. (2011). Cognitive development and Down Syndrome: Age-related change on the Stanford-Binet Test (Fourth Edition). *American Journal on Intellectual and Developmental Disabilities, 116*(3), 181–204.

Cowan, N., et al. (2010). With development, list recall includes more chunks, not just larger ones. *Developmental Psychology, 46*(5), 1119–1131.

Crain, W. C. (2000). *Theories of development: Concepts and applications* (4th ed.). Englewood Cliffs, NJ: Prentice Hall.

Cratty, B. (1986). *Perceptual and motor development in infants and children* (3rd ed.). Englewood Cliffs, NJ: Prentice Hall.

Crawford, D., Cleland, V., Timperio, A., Slamon, J., Andrianopoulos, N., Roberst, R., Giles-Corti, B., Baur, L., & Ball, K. (2010). The longitudinal influence of home and neighborhood environments on children's body mass index and physical activity over 5 years: The LSN study. *International Journal of Obesity, 34,* 1177–1187.

Crick, N. R. (1996). The role of overt aggression, relational aggression, and prosocial behavior in the prediction of children's future social adjustment. *Child Development, 67,* 2317–2327.

Crick, N. R., & Dodge, K. A. (1996). Social information-processing mechanisms on reactive and proactive aggression. *Child Development, 67,* 993–1002.

Crocco, M. S., & Libresco, A. S. (2007). Citizenship education for the 21st century—A gender inclusive approach to social studies. In D. M. Sadker & E. S. Silber (Eds.), *Gender in the classroom: Foundations, skills, methods, and strategies across the curriculum* (pp. 119–164). Mahwah, NJ: Erlbaum.

Crocetti, E., Rubini, M., Berzonsky, M. D., & Meeus, W. (2009). Brief report: The Identity Style Inventory—Validation in Italian adolescents and college students. *Journal of Adolescence, 32*(2), 425–433.

Crook, C. K., & Lipsitt, L. P. (1976). Neonatal nutritive sucking: Effects of taste stimulation upon sucking rhythm and heart rate. *Child Development, 47,* 518–522.

Crosnoe, R. (2011). Schools, peers, and the big picture of adolescent development. In E. Amsel, & J. Smetana (Eds.), *Adolescent vulnerabilities and opportunities* (pp. 182–204). New York: Cambridge University Press.

Crow, S. J., Mitchell, J. E., Roerig, J. D., & Steffen, K. (2009). What potential role is there for medication treatment in anorexia nervosa? *International Journal of Eating Disorders, 42*(1), 1–8.

Crowther, I. (2006). *Child development: A primer.* Toronto, ON: Nelson.

Crusio, W. E. (2006). Inheritance of behavioral and neuroanatomical phenotypical variance. *Behavior Genetics, 36*(5), 723–731.

Cruz, N. V., & Bahna, S. L. (2006). Do foods or additives cause behavior disorders? *Psychiatric Annals, 36*(10), 724–732.

Csikszentmihalyi, M., & Larson, R. (1984). *Being adolescent.* New York: Basic Books.

Cuevas, K., & Bell, M. A. (2010). Developmental progression of looking and reaching performance on the A-not-B task. *Developmental Psychology, 46*(5), 1363–1371.

Cunningham, F. G., et al. (2011). National Institutes of Health Consensus Development Conference Statement: Vaginal birth after cesarean section: New insights, March 8–10, 2010. *Obstetric Anesthesia Digest, 31*(3), 140–142.

Currie, J., DellaVigna, S., Moretti, E., & Pathania, V. (2009). *The effect of fast food restaurants on obesity.* National Bureau of Economic Research (NBER). NBER Working Paper No. W14721.

CWTAFacts. (2013). Canadians send 71.5 billion text messages in first nine months of 2013. Retrieved from http://cwta.ca/communique/archive/76#canadians-send-71-5-billion-text-messages-in-first-nine-months-of-2012 on July 2, 2014.

Cybermentors. (2014). Available at http://www.cybermentors.ca. Accessed May 21, 2014.

Cystic Fibrosis Canada. (2014). What is cystic fibrosis? http://www.cysticfibrosis.ca/about-cf/what-is-cystic-fibrosis. Accessed January 8, 2014.

Dağlioğlu, H. E., et al. (2010). Examination of human figure drawings by gifted and normally developed children at preschool period. *Elementary Education Online, 9*(1), 31–43.

Dai, D. Y. (2001). A comparison of gender differences in academic self-concept and motivation between high-ability and average Chinese adolescents. *Journal of Secondary Gifted Education, 13*(1), 22–32.

Daley, C. E., & Onwuegbuzie, A. J. (2011). Race and intelligence. In R. J. Sternberg & S. J. Kaufman (Eds.), *The Cambridge handbook of intelligence* (pp. 293–308). New York: Cambridge University Press.

Daly, M., & Wilson, M. (2000). Genetic ties may be factor in violence in stepfamilies. *American Psychologist, 55*(6), 679–680.

Damon, W. (1991). Adolescent self-concept. In R. M. Lerner, A. C. Petersen & J. Brooks-Gunn (Eds.), *Encyclopedia of adolescence.* New York: Garland.

Dancause, K. N., Laplante, D. P., Oremus, C., Fraser, S., Brunet, A., & King, S. (2011). Disaster-related prenatal maternal stress influences birth outcomes: Project ice storm. *Early Human Development, 87*(12), 813–820.

Daniels, H. (2010). Vygotsky and psychology. In U. Goswami (Ed.), *The Wiley–Blackwell handbook of childhood cognitive development.* (2nd ed.) (pp. 673–696). Chichester, West Sussex, UK: Wiley–Blackwell.

Daniels, H., et al. (Eds.). (2007). *The Cambridge companion to Vygotsky.* New York: Cambridge University Press.

Daniels, S. R. (2006). The consequences of childhood overweight and obesity. *The Future of Children, 16*(1), 47–67.

Daoud, Y., et al. (2009). Refractive surgery in children: Treatment options, outcomes, and controversies. *American Journal of Ophthalmology, 147*(4), 573–582.

Datta, S., Kodali, B. S., & Segal, S. (2010). Non-pharmacological methods for relief of labor pain. *Obstetric anesthesia handbook* (pp. 85–93). doi:10.1007/978-0-387-88602-2_7.

Daum, M. M., Prinz, W., & Aschersleben, G. (2010). Perception and production of object-related grasping in 6-month-olds. *Journal of Experimental Child Psychology, 108*(4), 810–818.

Davies, M. J., et al. (2012). Reproductive technologies and the risk of birth defects. *New England Journal of Medicine, 366,* 1803–1813.

Davis, E. P., & Sandman, C. A. (2010). The timing of prenatal exposure to maternal cortisol and psychosocial stress is associated with human infant cognitive development. *Child Development, 81,* 31–48.

Davis, H. A. (2001). The quality and impact of relationships between elementary school students and teachers. *Contemporary Educational Psychology, 26*(4), 431–453.

Davis, K., Christodoulou, J., Seider, S., & Gardner, H. (2011). The theory of multiple intelligences. In R. J. Sternberg & S. J. Kaufman (Eds.), *The Cambridge handbook of intelligence* (pp. 485–503). New York: Cambridge University Press.

Dawood, K., Bailey, J. M., & Martin, N. G. (2009). Genetic and environmental influences on sexual orientation. In Y-K. Kim (Ed.), *Handbook of behavior genetics* (pp. 269–279). New York: Springer.

Dawson, C., et al. (2011). Dietary treatment of phenylketonuria: The effect of phenylalanine on reaction time. *Journal of Inherited Metabolic Disease, 34*(2), 449–454.

Dawson, T. L. (2002). New tools, new insights: Kohlberg's moral judgement stages revisited. *International Journal of Behavioral Development, 26*(2), 154–166.

Day, N. L., Goldschmidt, L., & Thomas, C. A. (2006). Prenatal marijuana exposure contributes to the prediction of marijuana use at age 14. *Addiction, 101*(9), 1313–1322.

Deary, I. J., Whiteman, M. C., Starr, J. M., Whalley, L. J., & Fox, H. C. (2004). The impact of childhood intelligence on later life: Following up the Scottish mental surveys of 1932 and 1947. *Journal of Personality and Social Psychology, 86*(1), 130–147.

DeCasper, A. J., & Fifer, W. P. (1980). Of human bonding: Newborns prefer their mothers' voices. *Science, 208,* 1174–1176.

DeCasper, A. J., & Prescott, P. A. (1984). Human newborns' perception of male voices: Preference, discrimination, and reinforcing value. *Developmental Psychobiology, 17,* 481–491.

DeCasper, A. J., & Spence, M. J. (1991). Auditorially mediated behavior during the perinatal period: A cognitive view. In M. J. Weiss & P. R. Zelazo (Eds.), *Infant attention* (pp. 142–176). Norwood, NJ: Ablex.

Deep, A. L., et al. (1999). Sexual abuse in eating disorder subtypes and control women: The role of comorbid substance dependence in bulimia nervosa. *International Journal of Eating Disorders, 25*(1), 1–10.

DeHart, T., Pelham, B. W., & Tennen, H. (2006). What lies beneath: Parenting style and implicit self-esteem. *Journal of Experimental Social Psychology, 42*(1), 1–17.

Del Giudice, M., Manera, V., & Keysers, C. (2009). Programmed to learn? The ontogeny of mirror neurons. *Developmental Science, 12*(2), 50–363.

De Goede, I. H. A., Branje, S. J. T., & Meeus, W. H. J. (2009). Developmental changes and gender differences in adolescents' perceptions of friendships. *Journal of Adolescence,* in press. doi:10.1016/j.adolescence.2009.03.002.

De Haan, M., & Groen, M. (2006). Neural bases of infants' processing of social information in faces. In P. J. Marshall & N. A. Fox (Eds.), *The development of social engagement: Neurobiological perspectives. Series in affective science* (pp. 46–80). New York: Oxford University Press.

Delaney-Black, V., et al. (2004). Prenatal cocaine: Quantity of exposure and gender influences on school-age behavior. *Developmental and Behavioral Pediatrics, 25*(4), 254–263.

De Leeuw, E., Borgers, N., & Smits, A. (2004). Pretesting questionnaires for children and adolescents. In S. Presser et al. (Eds.), *Methods for testing and evaluating survey questionnaires.* Hoboken, NJ: Wiley.

De Lisi, R. (2005). A lifetime of work using a developmental theory to enhance the lives of children and adolescents. *Journal of Applied Developmental Psychology, 26*(1), 107–110.

DeLoache, J. S., Cassidy, D. J., & Brown, A. L. (1985). Precursors of mnemonic strategies in very young children's memory. *Child Development, 56,* 125–137.

DeLoache, J. S., Ganea, P. A., & Jaswal, V. K. (2009). Early learning through language. In J. Colombo, P. McCardle & L. Freud (Eds.), *Infant pathways to language: Methods, models, and research disorders* (pp. 119–140). New York: Psychology Press.

DeLoache, J. S., & Sharon, T. (2005). Symbols and similarity: You can get too much of a good thing. *Journal of Cognition and Development, 6*(1), 33–49.

De Medina, P. G. R., Visser, G. H. A., & Huizink, J. K. (2003). Fetal behaviour does not differ between boys and girls. *Early Human Development, 73*(2), 17.

Dempsey, J. P., Fireman, G. D., & Wang, E. (2006). Transitioning out of peer victimization in school children: Gender and behavioral characteristics. *Journal of Psychopathology and Behavioral Assessment, 28 ,* 271–280.

Deneault, J., & Ricard, M. (2006). The assessment of children's understanding of inclusion relations: Transitivity, asymmetry, and quanitification. *Journal of Cognition and Development, 7*(4), 551–570.

Denham, S., et al. (2011). Emotions and social development in childhood. In P. K. Smith, & C. H. Hart (Eds.). *The Wiley–Blackwell handbook of childhood social development* (pp. 413–433). Chichester, West Sussex, UK: Wiley-Blackwell.

Deniz, C. B. (2004). Early childhood teachers' beliefs about and self-reported practices toward children's private speech. *Dissertation Abstracts International Section A: Humanities and Social Sciences, 64*(9-A), 3185.

Dennis, W. (1960). Causes of retardation among institutional children: Iran. *Journal of Genetic Psychology, 96,* 47–59.

Dennis, W., & Dennis, M. G. (1940). The effect of cradling practices upon the onset of walking in Hopi children. *Journal of Genetic Psychology, 56,* 77–86.

de Oliveira, F. S., Viana, M. R., Antoniolli, A. R., & Marchioro, M. (2001). Differential effects of lead and zinc on inhibitory avoidance learning in mice. *Brazilian Journal of Medical and Biological Research, 34*(1), 117–120.

DeSimone, J. (2006). Academic performance and part-time employment among high school seniors. *Topics in Economic Analysis & Policy, 6*(1), Article 10.

DeSocio, J., Elder, L., & Puckett, S. (2008). Bridging cultures for Latino children. *Journal of Child and Adolescent Psychiatric Nursing, 21*(3), 146–153.

de Souza, A. S., Fernandes, F. S., & do Carmo, M. (2011). Effects of maternal malnutrition and postnatal nutritional rehabilitation on brain fatty acids, learning, and memory. *Nutrition Reviews, 69*(3), 132–144.

Devaney, S. A., Palomaki, G. E., Scott, J. A., & Bianchi, D. W. (2011). Noninvasive fetal sex determination using cell-free fetal DNA: A systematic review and analysis. *New England Journal of Medicine, 306*(6), 627–636.

De Villiers, J. G., & de Villiers, P. A. (1999). Language development. In M. H. Bornstein & M. E. Lamb (Eds.), *Developmental psychology: An advanced textbook* (4th ed.) (pp. 313–373). Mahwah, NJ: Erlbaum.

De Vries, J. I. P., & Hopkins, B. (2005). Fetal movements and postures: What do they mean for postnatal development? In B. Hopkins & S. P. Johnson (Eds.), *Prenatal development of postnatal functions. Advances in infancy research* (pp. 177–219). Westport, CT: Praeger/Greenwood.

Dezoete, J. A., MacArthur, B. A., & Tuck, B. (2003). Prediction of Bayley and Stanford–Binet scores with a group of very low birth-weight children. *Child: Care, Health and Development, 29*(5), 367–372.

Diagnostic and statistical manual of mental disorders. (2013). Fifth Edition (DSM-5). American Psychiatric Association. Washington, DC.

Diamond, L. M. (2006). What we got wrong about sexual identity development: Unexpected findings from a longitudinal study of young women. In A. M. Omoto & H. S. Kurtzman (Eds.), *Sexual orientation and mental health: Examining identity and development in lesbian, gay, and bisexual people* (pp. 73–94). *Contemporary perspectives on lesbian, gay, and bisexual psychology.* Washington, DC: American Psychological Association.

Dick, D. M., Prescott, C. A., & McGue, M. (2009). The genetics of substance use and substance use disorders. In Y-K. Kim (Ed.), *Handbook of behavior genetics* (pp. 433–453). New York: Springer.

Dieterich, S. E., Hebert, H. M., Landry, S. H., Swank, P. R., & Smith, K. E. (2004). Maternal and child characteristics that influence the growth of daily living skills from infancy to school age in preterm and term children. *Early Education and Development, 15*(3), 283–303.

DiIorio, C., McCarty, F., Denzmore, P., & Landis, A. (2007). The moderating influence of mother–adolescent discussion on early and middle African-American adolescent sexual behavior. *Research in Nursing & Health, 30*(2), 193–202.

Dindia, K., & Allen, M. (1992). Sex differences in self-disclosure: A meta-analysis. *Psychological Bulletin, 112,* 106–124.

Ding, Q. J., & Hesketh, T. (2006). Family size, fertility preferences, and sex ratio in China in the era of the one child family policy: Results from National Family Planning and Reproductive Health Survey. *British Medical Journal, 333*(7564), 371–373.

Dockett, S., Perry, B., & Whitton, D. (2006). Picture storybooks and starting school. *Early Child Development and Care, 76*(8), 835–848.

Dodd, B., & Crosbie, S. (2010). Language and cognition. In U. Goswami (Ed.), *The Wiley–Blackwell handbook of childhood cognitive development.* (2nd ed.) (pp. 604–625). Chichester, West Sussex, UK: Wiley–Blackwell.

Dodge, K. A. (2006). Translational science in action: Hostile attribution style and the development of aggressive behavior problems. *Development and Psychopathology, 18,* 791–814.

Dodge, K. A., & Coie, J. D. (1987). Social information-processing factors in reactive and proactive aggression in children's peer groups. *Journal of Personality and Social Psychology, 53,* 1146–1158.

Dodge, K. A., Coie, J. D., & Lyman, D. (2006). Aggression and antisocial behavior in youth. In W. Damon (Series Ed.) & N. Eisenberg (Vol. Ed.), *Handbook of child psychology: Vol. 3. Social, emotional, and personality development* (pp. 719–788). Hoboken, NJ: Wiley.

Dodge, K. A., Laird, R., Lochman, J. E., Zelli, A., & Conduct Problems Prevention Research Group U.S. (2002). Multidimensional latent-construct analysis of children's social information processing patterns: Correlations with aggressive behavior problems. *Psychological Assessment, 14*(1), 60–73.

Dogil, G., et al. (2002). The speaking brain: A tutorial introduction to fMRI experiments in the production of speech, prosody, and syntax. *Journal of Neurolinguistics, 15*(1), 59–90.

Donner, M. B., VandeCreek, L., Gonsiorek, J. C., & Fisher, C. B. (2008). Balancing confidentiality: Protecting privacy and protecting the public. *Professional Psychology: Research and Practice, 39*(3), 369–376.

Donohue, B. C., Karmely, J., & Strada, M. J. (2006). Alcohol and drug abuse. In M. Hersen (Ed.), *Clinician's handbook of child behavioral assessment* (pp. 337–375). San Diego, CA: Elsevier Academic Press.

Donohue, K. F., Curtin, J. J., Patrick, C. J., & Lang, A. R. (2007). Intoxication level and emotional response. *Emotion, 7*(1), 103–112.

Donovan, D. M., & Wells, E. A. (2007). "Tweaking 12-Step": The potential role of 12-step self-help group involvement in methamphetamine recovery. *Addiction, 102*(Suppl. 1), 121–129.

Dorfberger, S., Adi-Japha, E., & Karni, A. (2009). Sex differences in motor performance and motor learning in children and adolescents: An increasing male advantage in motor learning and consolidation phase gains. *Behavioural Brain Research, 198*(1), 165–171.

Douglas, P. S., & Hill, P. S. (2011). The crying baby: What approach? *Current Opinion in Pediatrics, 23*(5), 523–529.

Downer, J. (2007). *Father involvement during early childhood.* In R. C. Pianta, M. J. Cox, & K. L. Snow (Eds.), *School readiness and the transition to kindergarten in the era of accountability* (pp. 329–354). Baltimore, MD: Brookes.

Doyle, O., et al. (2009). Investing in early human development. *Economics & Human Biology, 7*(1), 1–6.

Drabick, D. A. G., Gadow, K. D., Carlson, G. A., & Bromet, E. J. (2004). ODD and ADHD symptoms in Ukrainian children: External validators and comorbidity. *Journal of the American Academy of Child and Adolescent Psychiatry, 43*(6), 735–743.

Drasgow, E., Halle, J. W., & Phillips, B. (2001). Effects of different social partners on the discriminated requesting of a young child with autism and severe language delays. *Research in Developmental Disabilities, 22*(2), 125–139.

Drewett, R. F., Corbett, S. S., & Wright, C. M. (2006). Physical and emotional development, appetite and body image in adolescents who failed to thrive as infants. *Journal of Child Psychology and Psychiatry, 47*(5), 524–531.

DuBois, D. L., & Hirsch, B. J. (1990). School and neighborhood friendship patterns of blacks and whites in early adolescence. *Child Development, 61,* 524–536.

Dubow, E. F., Boxer, P., & Huesmann, L. R. (2009). Long-term effects of parents' education on children's educational and occupational success: Mediation by family interactions, child aggression, and teenage aspirations. *Merrill-Palmer Quarterly, 55*(3), 224–249.

Dubow, E. F., et al. (2010). Exposure to conflict and violence across contexts: Relations to adjustment among Palestinian children. *Journal of Clinical Child and Adolescent Psychology, 39*(1), 103–116.

Dufva, M., Niemi, P., & Voeten, M. J. M. (2001). The role of phonological memory, word recognition, and comprehension skills in reading development: From preschool to grade 2. *Reading and Writing, 14*(1–2), 91–117.

Duggan, A., et al. (2004). Evaluating a statewide home visiting program to prevent child abuse in at-risk families of newborns: Fathers' participation and outcomes. *Child Maltreatment: Journal of the American Professional Society on the Abuse of Children, 9*(1), 3–17.

Dumont, M., Leclerc, D., & McKinnon, S. (2009). Consequences of part-time work on the academic and psychosocial adaptation of adolescents. *Canadian Journal of School Psychology, 24*(1), 58–75.

Dunn, J., Davies, L. C., O'Connor, T. G., & Sturgess, W. (2001). Family lives and friendships: The perspectives of children in step-, single-parent, and nonstep families. *Journal of Family Psychology, 15*(2), 272–287.

Dunn, M. G., & Mezzich, A. C. (2007). Development in childhood and adolescence: Implications for prevention research and practice. In P. Tolan, J. Szapocznik & S. Sambrano (Eds.), *Preventing youth substance abuse: Science-based programs for children and adolescents* (pp. 21–40). Washington, DC: American Psychological Association.

Durham, R. E., et al. (2007). Kindergarten oral language skill: A key variable in the intergenerational transmission of socioeconomic status. *Research in Social Stratification and Mobility, 25*(4), 294–305.

Durkin, S. J., Paxton, S. J., & Sorbello, M. (2007). An integrative model of the impact of exposure to idealized female images on adolescent girls' body satisfaction. *Journal of Applied Social Psychology, 37*(5), 1092–1117.

Du Rocher Schudlich, T. D., Shamir, H., & Cummings, E. M. (2004). Marital conflict, children's representations of family relationships, and children's dispositions towards peer conflict strategies. *Social Development, 13*(2), 171–192.

Dweck, C. S. (2007). Is math a gift? Beliefs that put females at risk. In S. J. Ceci & W. M. Williams (Eds.), *Why aren't more women in science: Top researchers debate the evidence* (pp. 47–55). Washington, DC: American Psychological Association.

Dykman, R. A., Casey, P. H., Ackerman, P. T., & McPherson, W. B. (2001). Behavioral and cognitive status in school-aged children with a history of failure to thrive during early childhood. *Clinical Pediatrics, 40*(2), 63–70.

Eaton, W. O., McKeen, N. A., & Campbell, D. W. (2001). The waxing and waning of movement: Implications for psychological development. *Developmental Review, 21*(2), 205–223.

Eaves, L. C., & Ho, H. H. (2008). Young adult outcome of autism spectrum disorder. *Journal of Autism and Developmental Disorders, 38*(4), 739–747.

Eberhardy, F. (1967). The view from "the couch." *Journal of Child Psychological Psychiatry, 8,* 257–263.

Ebert, E. S., & Culyer, R. C. (2011). *School: An introduction to education* (2nd ed.). Belmont, CA: Cengage.

Ebstein, R., Israel, S., Chew, S., Zhong, S., & Knafo, A. (2010). Genetics of human social behavior. *Neuron, 65*(6), 831–844.

Eccles, J. S., et al. (2000). Gender-role socialization in the family: A longitudinal approach. In T. Eckes & H. M. Trautner (Eds.), *The developmental social psychology of gender* (pp. 333–360). Mahwah, NJ: Erlbaum.

Eccles, J. S., Roeser, R., Vida, M., Fredricks, J., & Wigfield, A. (2006). Motivational and achievement pathways through middle childhood. In L. Balter & C. S. Tamis-LeMonda (Eds.), *Child psychology: A handbook of contemporary issues* (2nd ed.) (pp. 325ff). New York: Psychology Press.

Ecuyer-Dab, I., & Robert, M. (2004). Spatial ability and home-range size: Examining the relationship in Western men and women *(Homo sapiens)*. *Journal of Comparative Psychology, 118*(2), 217–231.

Eddy, J. M., Leve, L. D., & Fagot, B. I. (2001). Coercive family processes: A replication and extension of Patterson's Coercion Model. *Aggressive Behavior, 27*(1), 14–25.

Eder, R. A. (1989). The emergent personologist: The structure and content of 3½-, 5½-, and 7½-year-olds' concepts of themselves and other persons. *Child Development, 60,* 1218–1228.

Edwards, C. P. (2000). Children's play in cross-cultural perspective: A new look at the Six Cultures study. *Cross-Cultural Research, 34*(4), 318–338.

Edwards, J., et al. (2011). Developmental coordination disorder in school-aged children born very preterm and/or at very low birth weight: A systematic review. *Journal of Developmental Behavioral Pediatrics, 32*(9), 678–687.

Edwards, V. J., Holden, G. W., Felitti, V. J., & Anda, R. F. (2003). Relationship between multiple forms of childhood maltreatment and adult mental health in community respondents: Results from the Adverse Childhood Experiences study. *American Journal of Psychiatry, 160*(8), 1453–1460.

Effinger, J. M., & Stewart, D. G. (2012). Classification of co-occurring depression and substance abuse symptoms predicts suicide attempts in adolescents. *Suicide and Life-Threatening Behavior, 42*(4), 353–358.

Egan, B. A. (2009). Learning conversations and listening pedagogy: The relationship in student teachers' developing professional identities. *European Early Childhood Education Research Journal, 17*(1), 43–56.

Egeland, B., & Sroufe, L. A. (1981). Attachment and early maltreatment. *Child Development, 52,* 44–52.

Egerton, A., Allison, C., Brett, R. R., & Pratt, J. A. (2006). Cannabinoids and prefrontal cortical function: Insights from preclinical studies. *Neuroscience & Biobehavioral Reviews, 30*(5), 680–695.

Eimas, P. D., Sigueland, E. R., Juscyk, P., & Vigorito, J. (1971). Speech perception in infants. *Science, 171,* 303–306.

Eisenberg, M. E., Neumark-Sztainer, D., & Paxton, S. J. (2006). Five-year change in body satisfaction among adolescents. *Journal of Psychosomatic Research, 61*(4), 521–527.

Eisenberg, N., Hertz-Lazarowitz, R., & Fuchs, I. (1990). Prosocial moral judgment in Israeli kibbutz and city children: A longitudinal study. *Merrill-Palmer Quarterly, 36,* 273–285.

Eivers, A. R., Brendgen, M., Vitaro, F., & Borge, A. I. H. (2012). Concurrent and longitudinal links between children's and their friends' antisocial and prosocial behavior in preschool. *Early Childhood Research Quarterly, 27*(1), 137–146.

Elias, M. J., Zins, J. E., Graczyk, P. A., & Weissberg, R. P. (2003). Implementation, sustainability, and scaling of social-emotional and academic innovations in public schools. *School Psychology Quarterly, 32,* 303–319.

Elkind, D. (1967). Egocentrism in adolescence. *Child Development, 38,* 1025–1034.

Elkind, D. (1985). Egocentrism redux. *Developmental Review, 5,* 218–226.

Elkind, D. (2007). *The power of play: How spontaneous imaginative activities lead to happier, healthier children.* Cambridge, MA: Da Capo Press.

Elliot, A. J., & Thrash, T. M. (2010). Approach and avoidance temperament as basic dimensions of personality. *Journal of Personality, 78*(3), 865–906.

Ellis, W., & Zarbatany, L. (2007). Explaining friendship formation and friendship stability. *Merrill-Palmer Quarterly, 53*(1), 79–104.

Ellison, N. B., Steinfield, C., & Lampe, C. (2007). The benefits of Facebook "friends": Social capital and college students' use of online social network sites. *Journal of Computer-Mediated Communication, 12*(4), 1143–1168.

Else-Quest, N. M., & Grabe, S. (2012). The political is personal: Measurement and application of nation-level indicators of gender equity in psychological research. *Psychology of Women Quarterly, 36*(2), 131–144.

Else-Quest, N. M., Hyde, J. S., & Linn, M. C. (2010). Cross-national patterns of gender differences in mathematics: A meta-analysis. *Psychological Bulletin, 136*(1), 103–127.

El Shakankiry, H. M. (2011). Sleep physiology and sleep disorders in childhood. *Nature and Science of Sleep, 3,* 101–114.

El-Sheikh, M., et al. (2009). Marital conflict and children's externalizing behavior: Interactions between parasympathetic and sympathetic nervous system activity: V. Discussion. *Monographs of the Society for Research in Child Development, 74*(1), 56–69.

Embry, D., Hankins, M., Biglan, A., & Boles, S. (2009). Behavioral and social correlates of methamphetamine use in a population-based sample of early and later adolescents. *Addictive Behaviors, 34,* 343–351.

Emde, R. N., Gaensbauer, T. J., & Harmon, R. J. (1976). *Emotional expression in infancy: A biobehavioral study.* New York: International Universities Press.

Employment and Social Development Canada. (2014). Family Life—Marriage. http://www4.hrsdc .gc.ca/.3ndic.1t.4r@-eng.jsp?iid=78. Accessed June 3, 2014.

Engels, R. (2009). Early pubertal maturation and drug use: Underlying mechanisms. *Addiction, 104*(1), 67–68.

Erikson, E. H. (1963). *Childhood and society.* New York: Norton.

Erikson, E. H. (1968). *Identity: Youth and crisis.* New York: Norton.

Erikson, E. H. (1975). *Life history and the historical moment.* New York: Norton.

Erlandson, M. C., et al. (2008). Growth and maturation of adolescent female gymnasts, swimmers, and tennis players. *Medicine & Science in Sports & Exercise, 40*(1), 34–42.

Eron, L. D. (1982). Parent–child interaction, television violence, and aggression of children. *American Psychologist, 37,* 197–211.

Eron, L. D. (1993). Cited in T. DeAngelis (1993), It's baaack: TV violence, concern for kid viewers, *APA Monitor, 24*(8), 16.

Eron, L. D., Huesmann, L. R., & Zelli, A. (1991). The role of parental variables in the learning of aggression. In D. J. Pepler & K. H. Rubin (Eds.), *The development and treatment of childhood aggression.* Hillsdale, NJ: Erlbaum.

Ertem, I. O., Leventhal, J. M., & Dobbs, S. (2000). Intergenerational continuity of child physical abuse: How good is the evidence? *Lancet, 356,* 814–819.

Erwin, H., Fedewa, A., Belghle, A., & Ahn, S. (2012). A quantitative review of physical activity, health, and learning outcomes associated with classroom-based physical activity interventions. *Journal of Applied School Psychology, 28*(1), 14–36.

Essau, C. A., Sakano, Y., Ishikawa, S., & Sasagawa, S. (2004). Anxiety symptoms in Japanese and in German children. *Behaviour Research and Therapy, 42*(5), 601–612.

Estes, A., et al. (2011). Basal ganglia morphometry and repetitive behavior in young children with autism spectrum disorder. *Autism Research, 4*(3), 212–220.

Evans, A., et al. (2006). "Growing pains" in young children. *The Foot, 16*(3), 120–124.

Evans, S. W., et al. (2001). Dose–response effects of methylphenidate on ecologically valid measures of academic performance and classroom behavior in adolescents with ADHD. *Experimental and Clinical Psychopharmacology, 9*(2), 163–175.

Eyre, T. A., et al. (2006). The HUGO gene nomenclature database, 2006 updates. *Nucleic Acids Research, 34,* Database issue D319–D321.

Fagot, B. I., & Gauvain, M. D. (1997). Mother-child problem solving: Continuity through the early childhood years. *Developmental Psychology, 33,* 480–488.

Fagot, B. I., & Leinbach, M. D. (1993). Gender-role development in young children: From discrimination to labeling. *Developmental Review, 13,* 205–224.

Fagot, B. I., Rodgers, C. S., & Leinbach, M. D. (2000). Theories of gender socialization. In T. Eckes & H. M. Trautner (Eds.), *The developmental social psychology of gender* (pp. 65–89). Mahwah, NJ: Erlbaum.

Fancy, S. P. J., et al. (2010). Overcoming remyelination failure in multiple sclerosis and other myelin disorders. *Experimental Neurology, 225*(1), 18–23.

Fantz, R. L. (1961). The origin of form perception. *Scientific American, 204,* 66–72.

Fantz, R. L., Fagan, J. F., III, & Miranda, S. B. (1975). Early visual selectivity. In L. B. Cohen & P. Salapatek (Eds.), *Infant perception: From sensation to cognition,* Vol. 1. New York: Academic Press.

Farr, R. H., Forssell, S. L., & Patterson, C. J. (2010). Parenting and child development in adoptive families: Does parental sexual orientation matter? *Applied Developmental Science, 14*(3), 164–178.

Farrer, L. A., et al. (2009). Association of variants in MANEA with cocaine-related behaviors. *Archives of General Psychiatry, 66*(3), 267–274.

Feig, S. A., Segel, G. B., & Morimoto, K. (2011). Sickle cell anemia. In S. Yazdani, S. A. McGhee, & E. R. Stiehm (Eds.). *Chronic complex diseases of childhood* (pp. 235–240). Boca Raton, FL: Brown Walker Press.

Feijó, L., et al. (2006). Mothers' depressed mood and anxiety levels are reduced after massaging their preterm infants.

Infant Behavior & Development, 29(3), 476–480.

Feinberg, M. E., Neiderhiser, J. M., Howe, G., & Hetherington, E. M. (2001). Adolescent, parent, and observer perceptions of parenting: Genetic and environmental influences on shared and distinct perceptions. *Child Development, 72*(4), 1266–1284.

Feiring, C. (1993, March). *Developing concepts of romance from 15 to 18 years.* Paper presented at the meeting of the Society for Research in Child Development, New Orleans, LA.

Feldman, M., & Canadian Paediatric Society Community Paediatrics Committee. (2005). Management of primary nocturnal enuresis. *Paediatric Child Health, 10*(10), 611–614.

Fenzel, L. M. (2000). Prospective study of changes in global self-worth and strain during the transition to middle school. *Journal of Early Adolescence, 20*(1), 93–116.

Ferdinand, R. F., Bongersa, I. L., van der Ende, J., van Gastela, W., Tick, N., Utens, E., et al. (2006). Distinctions between separation anxiety and social anxiety in children and adolescents. *Behaviour Research and Therapy, 44*, 1523–1535.

Fernandes, A., Campbell-Yeo, M., & Johnston, C. C. (2011). Procedural pain management for neonates using nonpharmacological strategies: Part 1: Sensorial interventions. *Advances in Neonatal Care, 11*(4), 235–241.

Féron, J., Gentaz, E., & Streri, A. (2006). Evidence of amodal representation of small numbers across visuo-tactile modalities in 5-month-old infants. *Cognitive Development, 21*(2), 81–92.

Ferre, C. L., Babik, I., & Michel, G. F. (2010). Development of infant prehension handedness: A longitudinal analysis during the 6- to 14-month age period. *Infant Behavior and Development, 33*(4), 492–502.

Ferrer, E., O'Hare, E. D., & Bunge, S. A. (2009). Fluid reasoning and the developing brain. *Frontiers in Neuroscience, 3*(1), 46–51.

Ferrer, E., Shaywitz, B. A., Holahan, J. M., Marchione, K., & Shaywitz, S. E. (2010). Uncoupling of reading and IQ over time: Empirical evidence for a definition of dyslexia. *Psychological Science, 21*(1), 93–101.

Feuerstein, R., Rand, Y., & Hoffman, M. B. (1979). *The dynamic assessment of retarded performers: The learning potential assessment device: Theory, instruments and techniques.* Baltimore, MD: University Park Press.

Feuerstein, R., Rand, Y., Hoffman, M. B., & Miller, R. (1980). *Instrumental enrichment: An intervention program for cognitive modifiability.* Baltimore, MD: University Park Press.

Finkelhor, D. (2007). Prevention of sexual abuse through educational programs directed toward children. *Pediatrics, 120*(3), 640–645.

Finkelhor, D., Cross, T. P., & Cantor, E. N. (2005a). The justice system for juvenile victims: A comprehensive model of case flow. *Trauma, Violence, & Abuse, 6*(2), 83–102.

Finkelhor, D., Ormrod, R., Turner, H., & Hamby, S. L. (2005b). The victimization of children and youth: A comprehensive, national survey. *Child Maltreatment: Journal of the American Professional Society on the Abuse of Children, 10*(1), 5–25.

Fisch, S. M. (2004). *Children's learning from educational television: Sesame Street and beyond.* Mahwah, NJ: Erlbaum.

Fischer, K. W. (1980). A theory of cognitive development: The control and construction of hierarchies of skills. *Psychological Review, 87*(6), 477–531.

Fischer, K. W., & Bidell, T. (2006). Dynamic development of action and thought. In R. M. Lerner (Ed.), *Handbook of child psychology: Vol 1. Theoretical models of human development* (6th ed., pp. 313–399). Hoboken NJ: Wiley.

Fisher, A. V. (2010). What's in the name? On how rocks and stones are different from bunnies and rabbits. *Journal of Experimental Child Psychology, 105*(3), 198–212.

Fisher, B., Rose, N. C., & Carey, J. C. (2008). Principles and practice of teratology for the obstetrician. *Clinical Obstetrics and Gynecology, 51*(1), 106–118.

Fisher, L. D., Gushue, G. V., & Cerrone, M. T. (2011). The influences of career support and sexual identity on sexual minority women's career aspirations. *Career Development Quarterly, 59*(5), 441–454.

Fishman, H. C. (2006). Juvenile anorexia nervosa: Family therapy's natural niche. *Journal of Marital & Family Therapy, 32*(4), 505–514.

Fitzgerald, H. E., et al. (1991). The organization of lateralized behavior during infancy. In H. E. Fitzgerald, B. M. Lester & M. W. Yogman (Eds.), *Theory and research in behavioral pediatrics.* New York: Plenum.

Fivush, R., & Hammond, N. R. (1990). Autobiographical memory across the preschool years: Toward reconceptualizing childhood amnesia. In R. Fivush & J. A. Hudson (Eds.), *Knowing and remembering in young children.* Cambridge: Cambridge University Press.

Flanagan, D. P., Ortiz, S. O., & Alfonso, V. C. (2007). *Essentials of cross-battery assessment* (2nd ed.). New York: Wiley.

Flanders, J., Herman, K. N., & Paquette, D. (2012). Tough-and-tumble play and the cooperation-competition dilemma: Evolutionary and developmental perspectives on the development of social competence. In D. Narvaez, J. Panksepp, A. Schore, & T. Gleason (Eds.), *Evolution, early experience and human development: From research to practice and policy.* New York, NY: Oxford University Press.

Flatt, A. E. (2008). Is being left-handed a handicap? The short and useless answer is "yes and no." *Proceedings of the Baylor University Medical Center, 21*(3), 304–307.

Flavell, J. H. (1993). Young children's understanding of thinking and consciousness. *Current Directions in Psychological Science, 2*, 40–43.

Flavell, J. H., Miller, P. H., & Miller, S. A. (2002). *Cognitive development* (4th ed.). Upper Saddle River, NJ: Prentice Hall.

Flegenheimer, M. (2012, January 3). Accusations of bullying after death of a teenager. *New York Times*, A21.

Fletcher, K. L. (2011). Neuropsychology of early childhood (3 to 5 years old). In A. S. Davis (Ed.). *Handbook of pediatric neuropsychology.* New York: Springer.

Fletcher, R., et al. (2008). The evaluation of tailored and web-based information for new fathers. *Child: Care, Health & Development, 34*(4), 439–446.

Florsheim, P. (Ed.). (2003). *Adolescent romantic relations and sexual behavior: Theory, research, and practical implications.* Mahwah, NJ: Erlbaum.

Flouri, E. (2005). *Fathering and child outcomes.* New York: Wiley.

Flouri, E., & Buchanan, A. (2003). The role of father involvement and mother involvement in adolescents' psychological well-being. *British Journal of Social Work, 33*(3), 399–406.

Flynn, E., O'Malley, C., & Wood, D. (2004). A longitudinal, microgenetic study of the emergence of false belief understanding and inhibition skills. *Developmental Science, 7*(1), 103–115.

Foley, G. M. (2006). Self and social–emotional development in infancy: A descriptive synthesis. In G. M. Foley & J. D. Hochman (Eds.), *Mental health in early intervention: Achieving unity in principles and practice* (pp. 139–173). Baltimore, MD: Paul H. Brookes.

Food and Drug Administration. (2004, July 20). *Decreasing the chance of birth defects.* Available at http://www.fda.gov/fdac/features/996_bd.html.

Food Banks Canada. (2013). Hunger Count 2013. Toronto: Food Banks Canada.

Forbush, K., Heatherton, T. F., & Keel, P. K. (2007). Relationships between perfectionism and specific disordered eating behaviors. *International Journal of Eating Disorders, 40*(1), 37–41.

Fortenberry, J. D., Schick, V., Herbenick, D., Sanders, S. A., Dodge, B., & Reece, M. (2010). Sexual behaviors and condom use at last vaginal intercourse: A national sample of adolescents ages 14 to 17 years. *Journal of Sexual Medicine, 7*(suppl 5), 305–314.

Foster-Clark, F. S., & Blyth, D. A. (1991). Peer relations and influences. In R. M. Lerner, A. C. Petersen & J. Brooks-Gunn (Eds.), *Encyclopedia of adolescence.* New York: Garland.

Fournier, K. A., Hass, C. J., Naik, S. K., Lodha, N., & Cauraugh, J. H. (2010). Motor coordination in autism spectrum disorder: A synthesis and meta-analysis. *Journal of Autism and Developmental Disorders, 40*(10), 1227–1240.

Fox, A., Harrop, C., Trower, P., & Leung, N. (2009). A consideration of developmental egocentrism in anorexia nervosa. *Eating Behaviors, 10*(1), 10–15.

Franchak, J. M., & Adolph, K. E. (2012). What infants know and what they do: Perceiving possibilities for walking through openings. *Developmental Psychology.* doi:10.1037/a0027530.

Fraser, S. (2013). Junk: Overeating and obesity and the neuroscience of addiction. *Addiction Research and Theory, 21*(6), 496–506.

Frede, E., & Ackerman, D. J. (2007). *Preschool curriculum decision-making: Dimensions to consider.* Rutgers University: National Institute for Early Education Research.

Freeman, M. S., Spence, M. J., and Oliphant, C. M. (1993, June). *Newborns prefer their mothers' low-pass filtered voices over other female filtered voices.* Paper presented at the meeting of the American Psychological Society, Chicago.

Freud, A. (1969). Adolescence as a developmental disturbance. In G. Caplan & S. Lebovici (Eds.), *Adolescence, Psychosocial perspectives* (pp. 5–10). New York: Basic Books.

Freud, S. (1964 [1933]). *The standard edition of the complete psychological works of Sigmund Freud.* James Strachy (trans.). Oxford: Macmillan.

Frey, M. C., & Detterman, D. K. (2004). Scholastic assessment or *g*? The relationship between the scholastic assessment test and general cognitive ability. *Psychological Science, 15*(6), 373–378.

Frieze, I. H., & Li, M. Y. (2010). Gender, aggression, and prosocial behavior. *Handbook of Gender Research in Psychology, 4,* 311–335.

Frith, U. (2001). What framework should we use for understanding developmental disorders? *Developmental Neuropsychology, 20*(2), 555–563.

Frühmesser, A., & Kotzot, D. (2011). Chromosomal variants in Klinefelter syndrome. *Sexual Development, 5*(3), 109–123.

Fucile, S., & Gisel, E. G. (2010). Sensorimotor interventions improve growth and motor function in preterm infants. *Neonatal Network: The Journal of Neonatal Nursing, 29*(6), 359–366.

Fuhs, M. W., & Day, J. D. (2011). Verbal ability and executive functioning development in preschoolers at Head Start. *Developmental Psychology, 47*(2), 404–416.

Fuligni, A. J., & Eccles, J. S. (1993). Perceived parent–child relationships and early adolescents' orientation toward peers. *Developmental Psychology, 29,* 622–632.

Fuller, T. (2012). Is scientific theory change similar to early cognitive development? Gopnik on science and childhood. *Philosophical Psychology.* doi:10.1080/09515089.2011.625114.

Funatogawa, K., Funatogawa, T., & Yano, E. (2008). Do overweight children necessarily make overweight adults? Repeated cross sectional annual nationwide survey of Japanese girls and women over nearly six decades. *British Medical Journal, 337,* a802. doi:10.1136/bmj.a802.

Furman, W., & Buhrmester, D. (1992). Age and sex differences in perceptions of networks of personal relationships. *Child Development, 63,* 103–115.

Furman, W., Rahe, D., & Hartup, W. W. (1979). Social rehabilitation of low-interactive preschool children by peer intervention. *Child Development, 50,* 915–922.

Furnham, A. (2009). Sex differences in mate selection preferences. *Personality and Individual Differences, 47,* 262–267.

Furstenberg, F. F., & Kiernan, K. E. (2001). Delayed parental divorce: How much do children benefit? *Journal of Marriage and the Family, 63*(2), 446–457.

Gallese, V., Fadiga, L., Fogassi, L., & Rizzolatti, G. (1996). Action recognition in the premotor cortex. *Brain, 119*(2), 593–609.

Ganong, L. H., & Coleman, M. (2003). Studying stepfamilies. In L. H. Ganong & M. Coleman (Eds.), *Stepfamily relationships: Development, dynamics, and interventions* (pp. 1–24). New York: Springer.

Ganzel, B. L., Kim, P., Gilmore, H., Tottenham, N., & Temple, E. (2013). Stress and the healthy adolescent brain: Evidence for the neural embedding of life events. *Development and Psychopathology, 25,* 879–889.

Gao, F., Levine, S. C., & Huttenlocher, J. (2000). What do infants know about continuous quantity? *Journal of Experimental Child Psychology, 77*(1), 20–29.

Garber, H. L. (1988). *The Milwaukee Project: Preventing mental retardation in children at risk.* Washington, DC: American Association on Mental Retardation.

Gardini, G. G., et al. (2009). Respiratory function in patients with stable anorexia nervosa. *Chest, 136*(5), 1356–1363.

Gardner, H. (1983). *Frames of mind: The theory of multiple intelligences.* New York: Basic Books.

Garnefski, N., Kraaij, V., & Spinhoven, P. (2001). De relatie tussen cognitieve copingstrategieen en symptomen van depressie, angst en suiecidaliteit. *Gedrag and Gezondheid: Tijdschrift voor Psychologie and Gezondheid, 29*(3), 148–158.

Garner, J., & Thomas, M. (2011). The role and contribution of nurture groups in secondary schools: Perceptions of children, parents, and staff. *Emotional and Behavioural Difficulties, 16*(2), 207–224.

Gartstein, M. A., Slobodskaya, H. R., & Kinsht, I. A. (2003). Cross-cultural differences in temperament in the first year of life: United States of America (U.S.) and Russia. *International Journal of Behavioral Development, 27*(4), 316–328.

Gaser, C., & Schlaug, G. (2003). Brain structures differ between musicians and nonmusicians. *Journal of Neuroscience, 23*(27), 9240–9245.

Gaston, A., & Prapavessis, H. (2013). Tired, moody and pregnant? Exercise may be the answer. *Psychology & Health, 28,* 1353–1369.

Gathercole, S. E., & Alloway, T. P. (2008). *Working memory and learning.* Thousand Oaks, CA: Sage Publications.

Gau, S. S. F., et al. (2007). Psychiatric and psychosocial predictors of substance use disorders among adolescents. Longitudinal study. *British Journal of Psychiatry, 190*(1), 42–48.

Gaudet, S., Clément, R., & Deuzeman, K. (2005). Daily hassles, ethnic identity and psychological adjustment among Lebanese Canadians. *International Journal of Psychology, 40*(3), 157–168.

Gauthier, J. L., et al. (2009). Uniform signal redundancy of parasol and midget ganglion cells in primate retina. *Journal of Neuroscience, 29*(14), 4675–4680.

Gauthier, K., Genesee, F., Dubois, M. E., & Kasparian, K. (2011). Communication patterns between internationally adopted children and their mothers: Implications for language development. *Applied Psycholinguistics,* doi:10.1017/S0142716411000725.

Gavin, L., et al. (2009, July 17). Sexual and reproductive health of persons aged 10–24 years—United States, 2002–2007. *Morbidity and Mortality Weekly Report, 58*(27), 1–58. Available at http://www.cdc.gov/mmwr/preview/mmwrhtml/ss5806a1.htm.

Gavin, N. I., et al. (2005). Perinatal depression: A systematic review of prevalence and incidence. *Obstetrics & Gynecology, 106,* 1071–1083.

Geary, D. C. (1998). *Male, female: The evolution of human sex differences.* Washington, DC: American Psychological Association.

Geller, P. A., Kerns, D., & Klier, C. M. (2004). Anxiety following miscarriage and the subsequent pregnancy: A review of the literature and future directions. *Journal of Psychosomatic Research, 56*(1), 35–45.

Gelman, S. (2010). Modules, theories, or islands of expertise? Domain specificity in socialization. *Child Development, 81*(3), 715–719.

Genesee, F., & Jared, D. (2008). Literacy development in early French immersion programs. *Canadian Psychology, 49*(2), 140–147.

George, M. R. W., Koss, K. J., McCoy, K. P., Cummings, E. M., & Davies, P. T. (2010). *Advances in School Mental Health Promotion, 3*(4), 51–62.

Georgiades, S., et al. (2010). Phenotypic overlap between core diagnostic features and emotional/behavioral problems in preschool children with autism spectrum disorder. *Journal of Autism and Developmental Disorders, 41*(10), 1321–1329.

Gervain, J., Berent, I., & Werker, J. F. (2011). Binding at birth: The newborn brain detects identity relations and sequential position in speech. *Journal of Cognitive Neuroscience.* doi:10.1162/jocn_a_00157.

Gesell, A. (1928). *Infancy and human growth.* New York: Macmillan.

Gesell, A. (1929). Maturation and infant behavior patterns. *Psychological Review, 36*, 307–319.

Getzels, J. W., & Jackson, P. W. (1962). *Creativity and intelligence.* New York: Wiley.

Gibson, E. J. (1969). *Principles of perceptual learning and development.* New York: Appleton-Century-Crofts.

Gibson, E. J. (1991). *An odyssey in learning and perception.* Cambridge, MA: MIT Press.

Gibson, E. J., & Walk, R. D. (1960). The visual cliff. *Scientific American, 202*, 64–71.

Giles, A., & Rovee-Collier, C. (2011). Infant long-term memory for associations formed during mere exposure. *Infant Behavior and Development, 34*(2), 327–338.

Gillespie, C. F., & Nemeroff, C. B. (2007). Corticotropin-releasing factor and the psychobiology of early-life stress. *Current Directions in Psychological Science, 16*(2), 85–89.

Gilligan, C. (1977). In a different voice: Women's conceptions of self and morality. *Harvard Educational Review, 47*, 481–517.

Gilligan, C. (1982). *In a different voice.* Cambridge, MA: Harvard University Press.

Gilligan, C. (2011). *Resistance refined, patriarchy defined: Carol Gilligan reflects on her journey from difference to resistance.* Malden, MA: Polity Press.

Gillooly, J. B. (2004). Making menarche positive and powerful for both mother and daughter. *Women & Therapy, 27*(3–4), 23–35.

Gilmore, K. (2008). Birth mother, adoptive mother, dying mother, dead mother. In E. L. Jurist et al. (Eds.), *Mind to mind: Infant research, neuroscience, and psychoanalysis* (pp. 373–397). New York: Other Press.

Gima, H., Ohgi, S., Fujiwara, T., & Abe, K. (2010). Stress behavior in premature infants with periventricular leukomalacia. *Journal of Physical Therapy Science, 22*(2), 109–115.

Gionet, L. (2013). Breastfeeding trends in Canada. Health at a Glance. Statistics Canada Catalogue no. 82-624-X, http://www.statcan.gc.ca/pub/82 -624-x/2013001/article/11879-eng .htm#n7.

Giussani, D. A. (2011). The vulnerable developing brain. *Proceedings of the National Academy of Sciences, 108*(7), 2641–2642.

Glasberg, R., & Aboud, F. (1982). Keeping one's distance from sadness: Children's self-reports of emotional experience. *Developmental Psychology, 18*, 287–293.

Gleason, J. B., & Ratner, N. B. (2013). *The development of language* (8th ed.). New York: NY: Pearson.

Gleason, K. A., Jensen-Campbell, L. A., & Ickes, W. (2009). The role of empathic accuracy in adolescents' peer relations and adjustment. *Personality and Social Psychology Bulletin, 35*(8), 997–1011.

Gleason, T. R., Gower, A. L., Hohmann, L. M., & Gleason, T. C. (2005). Temperament and friendship in preschool-aged children. *International Journal of Behavioral Development, 29*(4), 336–344.

Gleason, T. R., & Hohmann, L. M. (2006). Concepts of real and imaginary friendships in early childhood. *Social Development, 15*(1), 128–144.

Goldberg, J., Holtz, D., Hyslop, T., & Tolosa, J. E. (2002). Has the use of routine episiotomy decreased? Examination of episiotomy rates from 1983 to 2000. *Obstetrics and Gynecology, 99*(3), 395–400.

Goldberg, W. A., & Keller, M. A. (2007). Co-sleeping during infancy and early childhood: Key findings and future directions. *Infant and Child Development, 16*(4), 457–469.

Goldman-Johnson, D. R., de Kretser, D. M., & Morrison, J. R. (2008). Evidence that androgens regulate early developmental events, prior to sexual differentiation. *Endocrinology, 149*(1), 5–14.

Goldschmidt, L., Day, N. L., & Richardson, G. A. (2000). Effects of prenatal marijuana exposure on child behavior problems at age 10. *Neurotoxicology and Teratology, 22*(3), 325–336.

Goldstein, E. B. (2005). *Cognitive psychology: Connecting mind, research, and everyday experience.* Belmont, CA: Wadsworth.

Goldstein, S., & Brooks, R. B. (2005). *Handbook of resilience in children.* New York: Kluwer Academic/Plenum.

Goleman, D. (2006). *Social intelligence.* New York: Bantam Books.

Gomez, A. M. (2011). Testing the cycle of violence hypotheses: Child abuse and adolescent dating violence as predictors of intimate partner violence in young adulthood. *Youth & Society, 43*(1), 171–192.

Gonzalez, V. (2005). Cultural, linguistic, and socioeconomic factors influencing monolingual and bilingual children's cognitive development. In V. Gonzalez & J. Tinajero (Eds.), *Review of research and practice*, Vol. 3 (pp. 67–104). Mahwah, NJ: Erlbaum.

González, Y. S., Moreno, D. S., & Schneider, B. H. (2004). Friendship expectations of early adolescents in Cuba and Canada. *Journal of Cross-Cultural Psychology, 35*(4), 436–445.

Goodman, G. S., & Clarke-Stewart, A. (1991). Suggestibility in children's testimony: Implications for sexual abuse investigations. In J. Doris (Ed.), *The suggestibility of children's recollections.* Washington, DC: American Psychological Association.

Goodman, G. S., Pipe, M-E., & McWilliams, K. (2011). Children's eyewitness testimony: Methodological issues. In B. Rosenfeld & S. D. Penrod (Eds.), *Research methods in forensic psychology* (pp. 257–282). Hoboken, NJ: Wiley.

Gooren, L. (2006). The biology of human psychosexual differentiation. *Hormones and Behavior, 50*(4), 589–601.

Gopnik, A., & Slaughter, V. (1991). Young children's understanding of changes in their mental states. *Child Development, 62*, 98–110.

Gordon, J., King, N. J., Gullone, E., Muris, P., & Ollendick, T. H. (2007). Treatment of children's night-time fears: The need for a modern randomised controlled trial. *Clinical Psychology Review, 27*(1), 98–113.

Gorin, S., Hooper, C., Dyson, C., & Cabral, C. (2008). Ethical challenges in conducting research with hard-to-reach families. *Child Abuse Review, 17*(4), 275–287.

Gottfried, G. M., Hickling, A. K., Totten, L. R., Mkroyan, A., & Reisz, A. (2003). To be or not to be a galaprock: Preschoolers' intuitions about the importance of knowledge and action for pretending. *British Journal of Developmental Psychology, 21*(3), 397–414.

Gottlieb, B. H., Still, E., & Newby-Clark, I. R. (2007). Types and precipitants of growth and decline in emerging adulthood. *Journal of Adolescent Research, 22*(2), 132–155.

Gottlieb, G. (2007). Developmental neurobehavioral genetics: Development as explanation. In B. C. Jones & P. Mormède (Eds.), *Neurobehavioral genetics: Methods and applications* (2nd ed.) (pp. 17–27). Boca Raton, FL: CRC Press.

Gottlieb, G. (2007). Probabilistic epigenesis. *Developmental Science, 19*(1), 1–11.

Gottschalk, L. J. (2007). Carol Gilligan—Psychologist, feminist, educator, philosopher. *Behavioral & Social Sciences Librarian, 26*(1), 65–90.

Government of Canada. (2007). *FASD Fact Sheet.*

Government of Canada. (2014). Multiple births. http://www.canadiensensante .gc.ca/health-sante/pregnancy-grossesse /multiples-eng.php. Accessed July 16, 2014.

Gowers, S. G., & Bryan, C. (2005). Families of children with a mental disorder. In N. Sartorius et al. (Eds.), *Families and mental disorders: From burden to empowerment* (pp. 127–159). Hoboken, NJ: Wiley.

Graber, J. A., Seeley, J. R., Brooks-Gunn, J., & Lewinsohn, P. M. (2004). Is pubertal timing associated with psychopathology in young adulthood? *Journal of the American Academy of Child and Adolescent Psychiatry, 43*(6), 718–726.

Granot, D., & Mayseless, O. (2001). Attachment security and adjustment to school in middle childhood. *International Journal of Behavioral Development, 25*(6), 530–541.

Greco, C., Rovee-Collier, C., Hayne, H., Griesler, P., & Early, L. (1986). Ontogeny of early event memory: II. Encoding and retrieval by 2- and 3-month-olds. *Infant Behavior and Development, 9*, 461–472.

Greeff, A. P., & Van Der Merwe, S. (2004). Variables associated with resilience in divorced families. *Social Indicators Research, 68*(1), 59–75.

Green, M. A., et al. (2009). Eating disorder behaviors and depression: A minimal relationship beyond social comparison, self-esteem, and body dissatisfaction. *Journal of Clinical Psychology.* doi:10.1002/jclp.20586.

Green, R. (1978). Sexual identity of 37 children raised by homosexual or transsexual parents. *American Journal of Psychiatry, 135,* 692–697.

Green, R., Mandel, J. B., Hotvedt, M. E., Gray, J., & Smith, L. (1986). Lesbian mothers and their children: A comparison with solo parent heterosexual mothers and their children. *Archives of Sexual Behavior, 15,* 167–184.

Greene, R. W., & Ablon, J. S. (2001). What does the MTA study tell us about effective psychosocial treatment for ADHD? *Journal of Clinical Child Psychology, 30*(1), 114–121.

Greenough, W. T., Black, J. E., & Wallace, C. S. (2002). Experience and brain development. In M. H. Johnson, Y. Munakata & R. O. Gilmore (Eds.), *Brain development and cognition: A reader* (2nd ed.) (pp. 186–216). Malden, MA: Blackwell.

Gregory, A. M., Light-Häusermann, J. H., Rijsdijk, F., & Eley, T. C. (2009). Behavioral genetic analyses of prosocial behavior in adolescents. *Developmental Science, 12*(1), 165–174.

Grigorenko, E. L. (2007). Triangulating developmental dyslexia: Behavior, brain, and genes. In D. Coch, G. Dawson & K. W. Fischer (Eds.), *Human behavior, learning, and the developing brain: Atypical development* (pp. 117–144). New York: Guilford.

Grigorenko, E. L. (2009). Speaking genes or genes for speaking? Deciphering the genetics of speech and language. *Journal of Child Psychology and Psychiatry, 50*(1–2), 116–125.

Grolnick, W. S., McMenamy, J. M., & Kurowski, C. O. (2006). Emotional self-regulation in infancy and toddlerhood. In L. Balter & C. S. Tamis-LeMonda (Eds.), *Child psychology: A handbook of contemporary issues* (2nd ed.) (pp. 3–25). New York: Psychology Press.

Grolnick, W. S., Price, C. E., Beiswenger, K. L., & Sauck, C. C. (2007). Evaluative pressure in mothers. *Developmental Psychology, 43*(4), 991–1002.

Grön, G., Wunderlich, A. P., Spitzer, M., Tomczak, R., & Riepe, M. W. (2000). Brain activation during human navigation: Gender-different neural networks as substrate of performance. *Nature Neuroscience, 3*(4), 404–408.

Groothuis, T. G. G., & Trillmich, F. (2011). Unfolding personalities: The importance of studying ontogeny. *Developmental Psychobiology, 53*(6), 641–655.

Gross, L. (2006). Evolution of Neonatal Imitation. *PLoS Biol, 4*(9): e311. doi:10.1371journal.pbio.0040311.

Grossmann, K., et al. (2002). The uniqueness of the child–father attachment relationship: Fathers' sensitive and challenging play as a pivotal variable in a 16-year longitudinal study. *Social Development, 11*(3), 307–331.

Grossmann, K., Grossman, K. E., Kindler, H., & Zimmerman, P. (2008). A wider view of attachment exploration: The influence of mothers and fathers on the development of psychological security to infancy to young adulthood. In J. Cassidy & P. R. Shaver (Eds.), *Handbook of attachment: Theory, research and clinical applications* (2nd ed., pp. 880–905). New York: Guilford.

Grotevant, H. D., & McDermott, J. M. (2014). Adoption: Biological and social processes linked to adaptation. *The Annual Review of Psychology, 65,* 235–265.

Grov, C., Bimbi, D. S., Nanin, J. E., & Parsons, J. T. (2006). Race, ethnicity, gender, and generational factors associated with the coming-out process among gay, lesbian, and bisexual individuals. *The Journal of Sex Research, 43*(2), 115–121.

Gruber, J. E., & Fineran, S. (2007). The impact of bullying and sexual harassment on middle and high school girls. *Violence Against Women, 13*(6), 627–643.

Grusec, J. E. (1991). Socializing concern for others in the home. *Developmental Psychology, 27,* 338–342.

Grusec, J. E. (2002). Parenting socialization and children's acquisition of values. In M. H. Bornstein (Ed.), *Handbook of parenting* (2nd ed.), Vol. 5, *Practical issues in parenting* (pp. 143–167). Mahwah, NJ: Erlbaum.

Grusec, J. E. (2006). The development of moral behavior and conscience from a socialization perspective. In M. Killen & J. G. Smetana (Eds.), *Handbook of moral development* (pp. 243–265). Mahwah, NJ: Erlbaum.

Grusec, J. E. (2011). Socialization processes in the family: Social and emotional development. *Annual Review of Psychology, 62,* 243–269.

Grusec, J. E., & Sherman, A. (2011). Prosocial behavior. In M. K. Underwood, & L. H. Rosen (Eds.), *Social development: Relationships in infancy, childhood, and adolescence* (pp. 263–288). New York: Guilford.

Grych, J. H. (2005). Interparental conflict as a risk factor for child maladjustment: Implications for the development of prevention programs. *Family Court Review, 43*(1), 97–108.

Guajardo, N. R., Snyder, G., & Petersen, R. (2008). Relationships among parenting practices, parental stress, child behaviour, and children's social-cognitive development. *Infant and Child Development, 18*(1), 37–60.

Gudmundsson, G. (2010). Infantile colic is a pain syndrome. *Medical Hypotheses, 75*(6), 528–529.

Guendelman, S., et al. (2009). Juggling work and breastfeeding. *Pediatrics, 123*(1), e38–e46.

Guerdjikova, A. I., McElroy, S. L., Kotwal, R., Stanford, K., & Keck, P. E., Jr. (2007). Psychiatric and metabolic characteristics of childhood versus adult-onset obesity in patients seeking weight management. *Eating Behaviors, 8*(2), 266–276.

Guerin, D. W., Gottfried, A. W., & Thomas, C. W. (1997). Difficult temperament and behaviour problems: A longitudinal study from 1.5 to 12 years. *International Journal of Behavioral Development, 21*(1), 71–90.

Guerrero, M. C. M., & Villamil, O. S. (2000). Activating the ZPD: Mutual scaffolding in L2 peer revision. *Modern Language Journal, 84*(1), 51–68.

Guerrini, I., Thomson, A. D., & Gurling, H. D. (2007). The importance of alcohol misuse, malnutrition and genetic susceptibility on brain growth and plasticity. *Neuroscience & Biobehavioral Reviews, 31*(2), 212–220.

Guidetti, M., & Nicoladis, E. (2008). Gestures and communicative development. *First Language, 28*(2), 107–115.

Gupta, N. D., & Simonsen, M. (2010). Non-cognitive child outcomes and universal high quality child care. *Journal of Public Economics, 94*(1–2), 30–43.

Gurian, M., & Stevens, K. (2005). *The minds of boys: Saving our sons from falling behind in school and life.* San Francisco, CA: Jossey-Bass.

Gushue, G. V., & Whitson, M. L. (2006). The relationship of ethnic identity and gender role attitudes to the development of career choice goals among black and Latina girls. *Journal of Counseling Psychology, 53*(3), 379–385.

Guttmacher Institute. (2007, June 8). Available at http://www.guttmacher.org

Guttmacher Institute. (2012). Facts on American teens' sources of information about sex. http://www.guttmacher.org/pubs/FB-Teen-Sex-Ed.html. Accessed May 6, 2012.

Guzikowski, W. (2006). Doula—a new model of delivery (continuous, non-professional care during the delivery). *Ceska Gynekologie, 71*(2), 103–105.

Guzzetti, B. J. (2010). Feminist perspectives on the new literacies. In E. A. Baker & D. J. Leu (Eds.), *The new literacies* (pp. 242–264). New York: Guilford.

Haden, C. A., Ornstein, P. A., Eckerman, C. O., & Didow, S. M. (2001). Mother–child conversational interactions as events unfold: Linkages to subsequent remembering. *Child Development, 72*(4), 1016–1031.

Hagenauer, M. H., Perryman, J. I., Lee, T. M., & Carskadon, M. A. (2009). Adolescent changes in the homeostatic and circadian regulation of sleep. *Developmental Neuroscience, 31*(4), 276–284.

Haier, R. J. (2011). Biological basis of intelligence. In R. J. Sternberg & S. J. Kaufman (Eds.), *The Cambridge handbook of intelligence* (pp. 351–370). New York: Cambridge University Press.

Haith, M. M. (1979). Visual cognition in early infancy. In R. B. Kearsly & I. E. Sigel (Eds.), *Infants at risk: Assessment of cognitive functioning.* Hillsdale, NJ: Erlbaum.

Haith, M. M. (1990). Progress in the understanding of sensory and perceptual processes in early infancy. *Merrill-Palmer Quarterly, 36,* 1–26.

Haith, M. M. (1998). Who put the cog in infant cognition? Is rich interpretation too costly? *Infant Behavior and Development, 21*(2), 167–179.

Hale, J. B., et al. (2011). Executive impairment determines ADHD medication response. *Journal of Learning Disabilities, 44*(2), 196–212.

Haley, D. W., Grunau, R. E., Weinberg, J., Keidar, A., & Oberlander, T. F. (2010). *Infant Behavior and Development, 33*(2), 219–234.

Halgin, R. P., & Whitbourne, S. K. (1993). *Abnormal psychology.* Fort Worth, TX: Harcourt Brace Jovanovich.

Hall, G. S. (1904). *Adolescence: Its psychology and its relations to physiology, anthropology, sociology, sex, crime, religion, and education,* Vol. I. New York: D. Appleton & Company.

Hall, J. (2012). Gender issues in mathematics. *Journal of Teaching and Learning, 8*(1), 59–72.

Halliday, L. F., & Bishop, D. V. M. (2006). Auditory frequency discrimination in children with dyslexia. *Journal of Research in Reading, 29*(2), 213–228.

Halpern, D. (2012). *Sex differences in cognitive abilities* (4th ed.). New York: Psychology Press.

Halpern, R. (2005). Book review: Examining adolescent leisure time across cultures: New Directions for child and adolescent development, No. 99. *Journal of Adolescent Research, 20*(4), 524–525.

Hamm, J. V. (2000). Do birds of a feather flock together? The variable bases for African American, Asian American, and European American adolescents' selection of similar friends. *Developmental Psychology, 36*(2), 209–219.

Hammack, P. L., & Cohler, B. J. (2009). *The story of sexual identity.* New York: Oxford University Press.

Hammen, C. (2003). Social stress and women's risk for recurrent depression. *Archives of Women's Mental Health, 6*(1), 9–13.

Hancocks, P. (2012, February 20). 2 teens sent to prison for S. Korean bullying suicide. CNN U.S.

Hanna, A. C., & Bond, M. J. (2006). Relationships between family conflict, perceived maternal verbal messages, and daughters' disturbed eating symptomatology. *Appetite, 47*(2), 205–211.

Hannon, P., Bowen, D. J., Moinpour, C. M., & McLerran, D. F. (2003). Correlations in perceived food use between the family food preparer and their spouses and children. *Appetite, 40*(1), 77–83.

Harel, Z. (2008). Dysmenorrhea in adolescents. *Annals of the New York Academy of Sciences, 1135,* 185–195.

Harlow, H. F., & Harlow, M. K. (1966). Learning to love. *American Scientist, 54,* 244–272.

Harlow, H. F., Harlow, M. K., & Suomi, S. J. (1971). From thought to therapy: Lessons from a primate laboratory. *American Scientist, 59,* 538–549.

Harlow, H. F., & Zimmermann, R. R. (1959). Affectional responses in the infant monkey. *Science, 130*(3373), 421–432.

Harris, J. G., Tulsky, D. S., & Schultheis, M. T. (2003). Assessment of the non-native English speaker: Assimilating history and research findings to guide clinical practice. In D. S. Tulsky et al. (Eds.), *Clinical interpretation of the WAIS–III and WMS–III* (pp. 343–390). San Diego, CA: Academic Press.

Harris, S. R., Megens, A. M., Backman, C. L., & Hayes, V. E. (2005). Stability of the Bayley II Scales of Infant Development in a sample of low-risk and high-risk infants. *Developmental Medicine & Child Neurology, 47*(12), 820–823.

Hart, D., Burock, D., London, B., & Atkins, R. (2003). Prosocial tendencies, antisocial behavior, and moral development. In A. Slater & G. Bremner (Eds.), *An introduction to developmental psychology* (pp. 334–356). Malden, MA: Blackwell.

Harter, S. (1988). *The self-perception profile for adolescents.* Unpublished manual, University of Denver.

Harter, S. (1990). Self and identity development. In S. S. Feldman & G. R. Elliott (Eds.), *At the threshold: The developing adolescent.* Cambridge, MA: Harvard University Press.

Harter, S. (1999). *The construction of the self.* New York: Guilford.

Harter, S. (2006). The Self. In K. A. Renninger, I. E. Sigel, W. Damon & R. M. Lerner (Eds.), *Handbook of child psychology* (6th ed.), Vol. 4, *Child psychology in practice* (pp. 505–570). Hoboken, NJ: Wiley.

Harter, S. (2012). *The construction of the self: Developmental and sociocultural foundations* (2nd ed.). New York: Guilford.

Harter, S., & Monsour, A. (1992). Developmental analysis of conflict caused by opposing attributes in the adolescent self-portrait. *Developmental Psychology, 28,* 251–260.

Harter, S., Waters, P. L., Whitesall, N. R., & Kastelic, D. (1998). Level of voice among female and male high school students: Relational context, support and gender orientation. *Developmental Psychology, 34*(5), 892–901.

Harter, S., & Whitesell, N. R. (2003). Beyond the debate: Why some adolescents report stable self-worth over time and situation, whereas others report changes in self-worth. *Journal of Personality, 71*(6), 1027–1058.

Hartung, P. J., Fouad, N. A., Leong, F. T. L., & Hardin, E. E. (2010). Individualism–collectivism. *Journal of Career Assessment, 18*(1), 34–45.

Hartup, W. W. (1993). Adolescents and their friends. In B. Laursen (Ed.), *Close friendships in adolescence* (pp. 3–22). San Francisco: Jossey-Bass.

Harvey, J. H., & Fine, M. A. (2011). *Children of divorce.* New York: Routledge, Taylor & Francis Group.

Hasler, G., et al. (2007). Familiality of factor analysis-derived YBOCS dimensions in OCD-affected sibling pairs from the OCD Collaborative Genetics Study. *Biological Psychiatry, 61*(5), 617–625.

Hasselhorn, M. (1992). Task dependency and the role of typicality and metamemory in the development of an organizational strategy. *Child Development, 63,* 202–214.

Hassett, J. M., Siebert, E. R., & Wallen, K. (2008). Sex differences in rhesus monkey toy preferences parallel those of children. *Hormones and Behavior, 54*(3), 359–364.

Hastings, P. D., Zahn-Waxler, C., Robinson, J., Usher, B., & Bridges, D. (2000). The development of concern for others in children with behavior problems. *Developmental Psychology, 36*(5), 531–546.

Hauck, F. R., et al. (2011). Breastfeeding and reduced risk of sudden infant death syndrome: A meta-analysis. *Pediatrics, 128*(1), 103–110.

Haugaard, J. J. (2000). The challenge of defining child sexual abuse. *American Psychologist, 55*(9), 1036–1039.

Hautamakl, A., et al. (2010). Transmission of attachment across three generations. *European Journal of Developmental Psychology, 7*(5), 618–634.

Haworth, C. M. A., et al. (2009). A twin study of the genetics of high cognitive ability selected from 11,000 twin pairs in six studies from four countries. *Behavior Genetics, 39*(4), 359–370.

Hay, C., & Evans, M. M. (2006). Violent victimization and involvement in delinquency: Examining predictions from general strain theory. *Journal of Criminal Justice, 34*(3), 261–274.

Hay, D. F., Payne, A., & Chadwick, A. (2004). Peer relations in childhood. *Journal of Child Psychology and Psychiatry, 45*(1), 84–108.

Hayatbakhsh, M. R., et al. (2012). Birth outcomes associated with cannabis use before and during pregnancy. *Pediatric Research, 71*(2), 215–219.

Hayne, H., & Fagen, J. W. (Eds.). (2003). *Progress in infancy research,* Vol. 3. Mahwah, NJ: Erlbaum.

Hayne, H., Garry, M., & Loftus, E. F. (2006). On the continuing lack of scientific evidence for repression. *Behavioral and Brain Sciences, 29*(5), 521–522.

Haywood, K. M., & Getchell, N. (2008). *Lifespan motor development* (5th ed.). Champaign, IL: Human Kinetics.

He, C., et al. (2009). Genome-wide association studies identify loci associated with age at menarche and age at natural menopause. *Nature Genetics, 41,* 724–728.

Health Canada. (2007). The sensible guide to a healthy pregnancy, www.healthypregnancy.gc.ca.

Health Canada. (2011). Aboriginal Head Start on Reserve program. Retrieved from http://www.hc-sc.gc.ca/fniah-spnia/famil/develop/ahsor-papar-eng.php.

Health Canada. (2011). Eating well with Canada's food guide. Ottawa, ON. Cat: H164-38/1-2011E-PDF.

Health Canada. (2013). National Aboriginal youth suicide prevention strategy (NAYSPS). Ottawa, ON.

Health Canada. (2014). Estimated Energy Requirements. Available at http://www.hc-sc.gc.ca/fn-an/food -guide-aliment/basics-base/1_1_1-eng .php. Accessed June 23, 2014.

Healy, M. D., & Ellis, B. J. (2007). Birth order, conscientiousness, and openness to experience: Tests of the family-niche model of personality using a within-family methodology. *Evolution and Human Behavior, 28*(1), 55–59.

Heard, E., & Turner, J. (2011). Function of the sex chromosomes in mammalian fertility. *Cold Spring Harbor Perspectives in Biology,* doi:10.1101/cshperspect. a002675.

Hebebrand, J., & Hinney, A. (2009). Environmental and genetic risk factors in obesity. *Child and Adolescent Psychiatric Clinics of North America, 18*(1), 83–94.

Hediger, M. L. (2011). Pregnancy, prenatal care, weight, and maternal age. In G. B. Louis & R. W. Platt (Eds.). *Reproductive and perinatal epidemiology* (pp. 85–100). New York: Oxford University Press.

Heilman, K. M., Nadeau, S. E., & Beversdorf, D. O. (2003). Creative innovation: Possible brain mechanisms. *Neurocase, 9*(5), 369–379.

Heim, C., et al. (2000). Pituitary–adrenal and autonomic responses to stress in women after sexual and physical abuse in childhood. *Journal of the American Medical Association, 284,* 592–597.

Heimann, M., et al. (2006). Exploring the relation between memory, gestural communication, and the emergence of language in infancy: A longitudinal study. *Infant and Child Development, 15*(3), 233–249.

Heindel, J. J., & Lawler, C. (2006). Role of exposure to environmental chemicals in developmental origins of health and disease. In P. Gluckman & M. Hanson (Eds.), *Developmental origins of health and disease* (pp. 82–97). New York: Cambridge University Press.

Heineman, K. R., Middelburg, K. J., & Hadders-Algra, M. (2010). Development of adaptive motor behavior in typically developing infants. *Acta Paediatrica, 99*(4), 618–624.

Heinonen, K., et al. (2011). Trajectories of growth and symptoms of attention-deficit/hyperactivity disorder in children: A longitudinal study. *BMC Pediatrics, 11*(84). doi:10.1186/ 1471-2431-11-84.

Helms, J. E. (2006). Fairness is not validity or cultural bias in racial-group assessment: A quantitative perspective. *American Psychologist, 61*(8), 845–859.

Helwig, C. C. (2006). Rights, civil liberties, and democracy across cultures. In M. Killen & J. G. Smetana (Eds.), *Handbook of moral development* (pp. 185–210). Mahwah, NJ: Erlbaum.

Henry, A., Kisicki, M. D., & Varley, C. (2011). Efficacy and safety of antidepressant drug treatment in children and adolescents. *Molecular Psychiatry.* doi:10.1038/mp.2011.150.

Henry, K. L., Knight, K. E., & Thornberry, T. P. (2012). School disengagement as a predictor of dropout, delinquency, and problem substance abuse during adolescence and early adulthood. *Journal of Youth and Adolescence, 41*(2), 156–166.

Henzi, S. P., et al. (2007). Look who's talking: Developmental trends in the size of conversational cliques. *Evolution and Human Behavior, 28*(1), 66–74.

Herbenick, D., Reece, M., Schick, V., Sanders, S. A., Dodge, B., & Fortenberry, J. D. (2010a). Sexual behavior in the United States: Results from a national probability sample of males and females ages 14 to 94. *Journal of Sexual Medicine, 7*(suppl 5), 255–265.

Herbenick, D., Reece, M., Schick, V., Sanders, S. A., Dodge, B., & Fortenberry, J. D. (2010b). Sexual behaviors, relationships, and perceived health among adult women in the United States: Results from a national probability sample. *Journal of Sexual Medicine, 7*(suppl 5), 277–290.

Herbenick, D., Reece, M., Schick, V., Sanders, S. A., Dodge, B., & Fortenberry, J. D. (2010c). An event-level analysis of the sexual characteristics and composition among adults ages 18 to 59: Results from a national probability sample in the United States. *Journal of Sexual Medicine, 7*(suppl 5), 346–361.

Hergenhahn, B. R. (2009). *An introduction to the history of psychology* (6th ed.). Belmont, CA: Wadsworth.

Hershberger, S. L., & D'Augelli, A. R. (2000). Issues in counseling lesbian, gay, and bisexual adolescents. In R. M. Perez, K. A. De-Bord & K. J. Bieschke (Eds.), *Handbook of counseling and psychotherapy with lesbian, gay, and bisexual clients* (pp. 225–247). Washington, DC: American Psychological Association.

Hertenstein, M. J., & Campos, J. J. (2004). The retention effects of an adult's emotional displays on infant behavior. *Child Development, 75*(2), 595–613.

Hesketh, T., & Xing, Z. W. (2006). Abnormal sex ratios in human populations: Causes and consequences. *Proceedings of the National Academy of Sciences, 103,* 13271–13275.

Hetherington, E. M. (1989). Coping with family transition: Winners, losers, and survivors. *Child Development, 60,* 1–14.

Hetherington, E. M. (2006). The influence of conflict, marital problem solving and parenting on children's adjustment in nondivorced, divorced and remarried families. In A. Clarke-Stewart & J. Dunn (Eds.), *Families count: Effects on child and adolescent development, The Jacobs Foundation series on adolescence* (pp. 203–237). Cambridge, UK: Cambridge University Press.

Hetherington, E. M., Stanley-Hagan, M., & Anderson, E. R. (1989). Marital transitions: A child's perspective. *American Psychologist, 44,* 303–312.

Hilborn, R. (2006). 2005 Statistics: Second year of decline in intercountry adoption. http://www.familyhelper.net/ news/060817stat.html. Accessed July 17, 2014.

Hill, J., Breen, G., Quinn, J., Tibu, F., Sharp, H., & Pickles, A. (2013). Evidence for interplay between genes and maternal stress in utero: Monoamine oxidase A polymorphism moderates effects of life events during pregnancy on infant negative emotionality at 5 weeks. *Genes, Brain and Behavior, 12,* 388–396.

Hill, N. E., & Taylor, L. C. (2004). Parental school involvement and children's academic achievement: Pragmatics and issues. *Current Directions in Psychological Science, 13,* 161–164.

Hill, N. E., & Tyson, D. F. (2009). Parental involvement in middle school: A meta-analytic assessment of the strategies that promote achievement. *Developmental Psychology, 45*(3), 740–763.

Hill, S. E., & Flom, R. (2007). 18- and 24-month-olds' discrimination of gender-consistent and inconsistent activities. *Infant Behavior & Development, 30*(1), 168–173.

Hillerer, K. M., Neumann, I. D., & Slattery, D. A. (2011). From stress to postpartum mood and anxiety disorders: How chronic peripartum stress can impair maternal adaptations. *Neuro-Endocrinology.* doi:10.1159/000330445.

Hills, A. P., & Byrne, N. M. (2011). An overview of physical growth and maturation. In J. Jürimäe, A. P. Hills, & T. Jürimäe (Eds.), *Cytokines, growth mediators and physical activity in children during puberty* (pp. 1–13). Basel, Switzerland: S. Karger.

Hindley, C. B., Filliozat, A. M., Klackenberg, G., Nicolet-Neister, D., & Sand, E. A. (1966). Differences in age of walking for five European longitudinal samples. *Human Biology, 38,* 364–379.

Hines, M. (2011a). Prenatal endocrine influences on sexual orientation and on sexually differentiated childhood behavior. *Frontiers in Neuroendocrinology, 32*(2), 170–182.

Hines, M. (2011b). Gender development and the human brain. *Annual Review of Neuroscience, 34,* 69–88.

Hinshaw, S. P. (2006). Treatment for children and adolescents with attention-deficit/hyperactivity disorder. In P. C. Kendall (Ed.), *Child and adolescent therapy: Cognitive-behavioral procedures* (3rd ed.) (pp. 82–113). New York: Guilford.

Ho, Y. (2008). *The effects of massage therapy on weight gain, length of stay and motor development in preterm very low birth weight infants: A pilot randomised controlled trial.* Thesis, Hong Kong Polytechnic University.

Hobbie, S. N., et al. (2008). Genetic analysis of interactions with eukaryotic rRNA identify the mitoribosome as target in aminoglycoside ototoxicity. *Proceedings of the National Academy of Sciences, 105,* 20888–20893.

Hodapp, R. M., Griffin, M. M., Burke, M. M., & Fisher, M. H. (2011). Intellectual disabilities. In R. J. Sternberg & S. J. Kaufman (Eds.), *The Cambridge handbook of intelligence* (pp. 193–209). New York: Cambridge University Press.

Hoff, E. (2006). Language experience and language milestones during early childhood. In K. McCartney & D. Phillips (Eds.), *Blackwell handbook of early childhood development., Blackwell handbooks of developmental psychology* (pp. 233–251). Malden, MA: Blackwell.

Hoffman, K. L., & Edwards, J. N. (2004). An integrated theoretical model of sibling violence and abuse. *Journal of Family Violence, 19*(3), 185–200.

Hoffman, L. (2009). Asperger's syndrome and autistic disorder: Clearly differentiating the diagnostic criteria. *American Journal of Psychiatry, 166*(2), 235ff.

Hoffmann, J., & Russ, S. (2012). Pretend play, creativity, and emotion regulation in children. *Psychology of Aesthetics, Creativity, and the Arts, 6*(2), 175–184.

Hofmann, W., Gschwendner, T., Castelli, L., & Schmitt, M. (2008). Impulsive and reflective determinants of interracial interaction behavior: The moderating role of situationally available control resources. *Group Processes and Intergroup Behaviors, 11*, 69–87.

Högler, W., et al. (2008). Sex-specific developmental changes in muscle size and bone geometry at the femoral shaft. *Bone, 42*(5), 982–989.

Holden, G. W., Vittrup, B., & Rosen, L. H. (2011). Families, parenting and discipline. In M. K. Underwood & L. H. Rosen (Eds.), *Social development: Relationships in infancy, childhood, and adolescence* (pp. 127–152). New York: Guilford.

Holland, J. J. (2000, July 25). *Groups link media to child violence.* Available at http://www.ap.org

Holland, J. L. (1997). *Making vocational choices: A theory of vocational personalities and work environments* (3rd ed.). Odessa, FL: Psychological Assessment Resources.

Holloway, J. H. (2004). *Part-time work and student achievement.* Alexandria VA: Association for Supervision and Curriculum Development. Available at http://www.ascd.org/publications/ed_lead/200104/holloway.html.

Holobow, N., Genesee, F., & Lambert, W. (1991). The effectiveness of a foreign language immersion program for children from different ethnic and social class backgrounds: Report 2. *Applied Psycholinguistics, 12*, 179–198.

Holsen, I., Kraft, P., & Roysamb, E. (2001). The relationship between body image and depressed mood in adolescence: A 5-year longitudinal panel study. *Journal of Health Psychology, 6*(6), 613–627.

Holsti, L. (2010). A preventive care program for very preterm infants improves infant behavioural outcomes and decreases anxiety and depression in caregivers. *Journal of Physiotherapy, 56*(4), 277.

Holt, M. K., Kantor, G. K., & Finkelhor, D. (2009). Parent/child concordance about bullying involvement and family characteristics related to bullying and peer victimization. *Journal of School Violence, 8*(1), 42–63.

Homae, F., Watanabe, H., Nakano, T., & Taga, G. (2011). Functional development in the human brain for auditory pitch processing. *Human Brain Mapping.* doi:10.1002/hbm.21236.

Homer, B. D., & Nelson, K. (2005). Seeing objects as symbols and symbols as objects: Language and the development of dual representation. In B. D. Homer & C. S. Tamis-LeMonda (Eds.), *The development of social cognition and communication* (pp. 29–52). Mahwah, NJ: Erlbaum.

Hompes, T., Izzi, B., Gellens, E., Morreels, M., Fieuws, S., Pexsters, A., et al. (2013). Investigating the influence of maternal cortisol and emotional state during pregnancy on the DNA methylation status of the glucocorticoid receptor gene (NR3C1) promoter region in cord blood. *Journal of Psychiatric Research, 47*, 880–891.

Honeycutt, J. M., Pecchioni, L., Keaton, S. A., & Pence, M. E. (2011–2012). Developmental implications of mental imagery in childhood imaginary companions. *Imagination, Cognition and Personality, 31*(1–2), 79–98.

Hong, D. S., Dunkin, B., & Reiss, A. L. (2011). Psychosocial functioning and social cognitive processing in girls with Turner syndrome. *Journal of Developmental & Behavioral Pediatrics, 32*(7), 512–520.

Honig, A. S., & Nealls, A. L. (2011). What do young children dream about? *Early Child Development and Care, 182*(6), 771–795.

Honzik, M. P., Macfarlane, J. W., & Allen, L. (1948). The stability of mental test performance between two and eighteen years. *Journal of Experimental Education, 17*, 309–324.

Hook, E. B. (1981). Rates of chromosomal abnormalities at different maternal ages. *Obstetrics & Gynecology, 53*, 282–285.

Hoover, J. R., Sterling, A. M., & Storkel. (2011). Speech and language development. In A. S. Davis (Ed.). *Handbook of pediatric neuropsychology.* New York: Springer.

Hopkins, B., & Westra, T. (1988). Maternal handling and motor development: An intracultural study. *Genetic, Social, and General Psychology Monographs, 14*, 377–420.

Hopkins, W. D. (2006). Comparative and familial analysis of handedness in great apes. *Psychological Bulletin, 132*(4), 538–559.

Hopkins-Golightly, T., Raz, S., & Sander, C. J. (2003). Influence of slight to moderate risk for birth hypoxia on acquisition of cognitive and language function in the preterm infant: A cross-sectional comparison with preterm-birth controls. *Neuropsychology, 17*(1), 3–13.

Horst, J. S., et al. (2009). Toddlers can adaptively change how they categorize: Same objects, same session, two different categorical distinctions. *Developmental Science, 12*(1), 96–105.

Horta, B. L., Bahl, R., Martines, J. C., & Victora, C. G. (2007). *Evidence on the long-term effects of breastfeeding: Systematic reviews and meta-analyses* (Report). Geneva: World Health Organization. Retrieved from http://whqlibdoc.who.int/publications/2007/9789241595230_eng.pdf.

Hossain, M., Chetana, M., & Devi, P. U. (2005). Late effect of prenatal irradiation on the hippocampal histology and brain weight in adult mice. *International Journal of Developmental Neuroscience, 23*(4), 307–313.

Howe, M. L. (2006). Developmentally invariant dissociations in children's true and false memories: Not all relatedness is created equal. *Child Development, 77*(4), 1112–1123.

Howe, N., Recchia, H., Porta, S. D., & Funamoto, A. (2012). "The driver doesn't sit, he stands up like the Flintstones!": Sibling teaching during teacher-directed and self-guided tasks. *Journal of Cognition and Development, 13*(2), 208–231.

Hoy, E. A., & McClure, B. G. (2000). Preschool experience: A facilitator of very low birthweight infants' development? *Infant Mental Health Journal, 21*(6), 481–494.

Hoza, B., Gerdes, A. C., Hinshaw, S. P., Bukowski, W. M., Gold, J. A., & Kraemer, H. C. (2005). What aspects of peer relationship are impaired in children with attention-deficit disorder? *Journal of Consulting and Clinical Psychology, 73*, 411–423.

Huang, B., Biro, F. M., & Dorn, L. D. (2009). Determination of relative timing of pubertal maturation through ordinal logistic modeling. *Journal of Adolescent Health,* in press.

Huang, X-N., et al. (2010). Co-sleeping and children's sleep in China. *Biological Rhythm Research, 41*(3), 169–181.

Hubbard, T. K. (2009). The paradox of "natural" heterosexuality with "unnatural" women. *Classical World, 102*(3), 249–258.

Hubbs-Tait, L., Culp, A. M., Culp, R. E., & Miller, C. E. (2002). Relation of maternal cognitive stimulation, emotional support, and intrusive behavior during Head Start to children's kindergarten cognitive abilities. *Child Development, 73*, 110–131.

Huber, J., Darling, S., Park, K., & Soliman, K. F. A. (2001). Altered responsiveness to stress and NMDA following prenatal exposure to cocaine. *Physiology and Behavior, 72*(1–2), 181–188.

Hudak, M. L., & Tan, R. C. (2012). Neonatal drug withdrawal. *Pediatrics, 129*(2), e540–e560.

Hudson, J. A. (1990). The emergence of autobiographical memory in mother–child conversation. In R. Fivush & J. A. Hudson (Eds.), *Knowing* and remembering in young children. Cambridge: Cambridge University Press.

Hudziak, J. J. (2001). Latent class analysis of ADHD and comorbid symptoms in a population sample of adolescent female twins. *Journal of Child Psychology and Psychiatry and Allied Disciplines, 42*(7), 933–942.

Huesmann, L. R., Dubow, E. F., Eron, L. D., & Boxer, P. (2006). Middle childhood family contextual factors as predictors of adult outcomes. In A. C. Huston & M. N. Ripke (Eds.), *Middle childhood: Contexts of development*. Cambridge, UK: Cambridge University Press.

Human Resources and Skills Development Canada. (2012). Public investment in early childhood education and care in Canada–2010. Gatineau, QC. Catalogue no. HS64-18/2012E.

Hur, Y. (2005). Genetic and environmental influences on self-concept in female pre-adolescent twins: Comparison of Minnesota and Seoul data. *Twin Research and Human Genetics, 8*(4), 291–299.

Hurd, N. M., Sanchez, B., Zimmerman, M. A., & Caldwell, C. H. (2012). Natural mentors, racial identity, and educational attainment among African American adolescents: Exploring pathways to success. *Child Development, 83*(4), 1196–1212.

Hyde, J. S., Lindberg, S. M., Linn, M. C., Ellis, A. B., & Williams, C. C. (2008). Gender similarities characterize math performance. *Science, 321*, 494–495.

Hyde, J. S., & Mertz, J. E. (2009). Gender, culture, and mathematics performance. *Proceedings of the National Academy of Sciences, 106*, 8801–8807.

Hymel, S., Schonert-Reichl, K. A., & Miller, L. D. (2006). Reading,'riting, 'rithmetic and relationships: Considering the social side of education. *Exceptionality Education Canada, 16*, 149–192.

Hyson, M., Copple, C., & Jones, J. (2006). Early childhood development and education. In K. A. Renninger, I. E. Sigel, W. Damon & R. M. Lerner (Eds.), *Handbook of child psychology* (6th ed.), Vol. 4, *Child psychology in practice* (pp. 3–47). Hoboken, NJ: Wiley.

IJzendoorn, M. H. van, & Hubbard, F. O. A. (2000). Are infant crying and maternal responsiveness during the first year related to infant–mother attachment at 15 months? *Attachment and Human Development, 2*(3), 371–391.

IJzendoorn, M. H. van, Moran, G., Belsky, J., Pederson, D., Bakermans-Kranenburg, M. J., & Kneppers, K. (2000). The similarity of siblings' attachments to their mother. *Child Development, 71*(4), 1086–1098.

Inhelder, B., & Piaget, J. (1959). *The early growth of logic in the child: Classification and seriation*. New York: Harper & Row.

Insel, T. R. (2010). The challenge of translation in social neuroscience: A review of oxytocin, vasopressin, and affiliative behavior. *Neuron, 65*(6), 768–779.

Institute for Sexual Minority Studies and Services. (2014). Together we can … empower youth to embrace who they are. Available at http://www.ismss .ualberta.ca/sites/dev.ismss.ualberta.ca/ files/iSMSSbrochure.pdf. Accessed July 3, 2014.

Inzlicht, M., & Good, C. (2006). How environments can threaten academic performance, self-knowledge, and sense of belonging. In S. Levin & C. van Laar (Eds.), *Stigma and group inequality: Social psychological perspectives. The Claremont symposium on Applied Social Psychology* (pp. 129–150). Mahwah, NJ: Erlbaum.

Ip, S., Chung, M., Raman, G., Chew, P., Magula, N., DeVine, D., Trikalinos, T., & Lau, J. (2007). Breastfeeding and Maternal and Infant Health Outcomes in Developed Countries. Evidence Report/Technology Assessment No. 153 (Prepared by Tufts-New England Medical Center Evidence-based Practice Center, under Contract No. 290-02-0022). AHRQ Publication No. 07-E007. Rockville, MD: Agency for Healthcare Research and Quality.

Ito, M. (2008). Cited in T. Lewin (2008, November 19). Study finds teenagers' Internet socializing isn't such a bad thing. *New York Times*.

Ito, M., Robinson, L., Horst, H. A., Pascoe, C. J., & Bittanti, M. (2009). *Living and learning with new media: Summary of findings from the Digital Youth Project*. Cambridge, MA: MIT Press.

Izard, C. E. (1983). *Maximally discriminative facial movement scoring system*. Newark: University of Delaware Instructional Resources Center.

Izard, C. E. (2004). The generality–specificity issue in infants' emotion responses: A comment on Bennett, Bendersky, and Lewis (2002). *Infancy, 6*(3), 417–423.

Izard, C. E., & Malatesta, C. Z. (1987). Perspectives on emotional development. I. Differential emotions theory of early emotional development. In J. D. Osofsky (Ed.), *Handbook of infant development* (2nd ed.). New York: Wiley.

Izard, C. E., Youngstrom, E. A., Fine, S. E., Mostow, A. J., & Trentacosta, C. J. (2006). Emotions and developmental psychopathology. In D. Cicchetti & D. J. Cohen (Eds.), *Developmental psychopathology*, Vol. 1, *Theory and method* (2nd ed.) (pp. 244–292). Hoboken, NJ: Wiley.

Jackson, D. N., & Rushton, J. P. (2006). Males have greater g: Sex differences in general mental ability from 100,000 17- to 18-year-olds on the Scholastic Assessment Test. *Intelligence, 34*(5), 479–486.

Jackson, L. A., et al. (2009). Self-concept, self-esteem, gender, race, and information technology use. *CyberPsychology & Behavior, 12*(4), 437–440.

Jacobs, J. E., Davis-Kean, P., Bleeker, M., Eccles, J. S., & Malanchuk, O. (2005). "I can, but I don't want to": The impact of parents, interests, and activities on gender differences in math. In A. M. Gallagher & J. C. Kaufman (Eds.), *Gender differences in mathematics: An integrative psychological approach* (pp. 246–263). New York: Cambridge University Press.

Jacobson, J. L., Jacobson, S. W., Padgett, R. J., Brumitt, G. A., & Billings, R. L. (1992). Effects of prenatal PCB exposure on cognitive processing efficiency and sustained attention. *Developmental Psychology, 28*, 297–306.

Jaffe, A. C. (2011). Failure to thrive: Current clinical concepts. *Pediatrics in Review, 32*(3), 100–108.

Jago, R., Baranowski, T., Baranowski, J. C., Thompson, D., & Greaves, K. A. (2005). BMI from 3–6 y of age is predicted by TV viewing and physical activity, not diet. *International Journal of Obesity, 29*(6), 557–564.

Jamieson, S., & Marshall, W. L. (2000). Attachment styles and violence in child molesters. *Journal of Sexual Aggression, 5*(2), 88–98.

Jarvis, B. (1993, May 3). Against the great divide. *Newsweek*, p. 14.

Javo, C., Ronning, J. A., & Heyerdahl, S. (2004). Child-rearing in an indigenous Sami population in Norway: A cross-cultural comparison of parental attitudes and expectations. *Scandinavian Journal of Psychology, 45*(1), 67–78.

Jeng, S-F., Yau, K-I. T., Liao, H-F., Chen, L-C., & Chen, P-S. (2000). Prognostic factors for walking attainment in very low-birthweight preterm infants. *Early Human Development, 59*(3), 159–173.

Jiménez-Pavón, D., Fernández-Alvira, J. M., te Velde, S. J., Brug, J., Bere, E. , Jan, N., Kovacs, E., Androutsos, O., Manios, Y., De Bourdeaudhuij, I., & Moreno, L. A. (2012). Associations of parental education and parental physical activity (PA) with children's PA: The ENERGY cross-sectional study. *Preventive Medicine, 55*, 310–314.

John, A., Halliburton, A. L., & Humphrey, J. (2013). Child-mother and child-father play interaction patterns with preschoolers. *Early Child Development and Care, 183*(3–4), 483–497.

Johnson, D. A., & Gunnar, M. R. (2011). Growth failure in institutionalized children. *Monographs of the Society for Research in Child Development, 76*(4), 92–126.

Johnson, K. L., Lurye, L. E., & Tassinary, L. G. (2010). Sex categorization among preschool children: Increasing utilization of sexually dimorphic cues. *Child Development, 81*(5), 1346–1355.

Johnson, M. H. (2011). *Developmental cognitive neuroscience* (3rd ed.). Chichester, West Sussex, UK: Wiley-Blackwell.

Johnson, S. P. (2011). Development of visual perception. *WIREs Cognitive Science, 2*, 515–528. doi:10.1002/wcs.128.

Johnson, W., & Bouchard, T. J., Jr. (2007). Sex differences in mental abilities: g masks the dimensions on which they lie. *Intelligence, 35*(1), 23–39.

Johnson, W., et al. (2012). A changing pattern of childhood BMI growth during the 20th century: 70 years of data from the Fels Longitudinal Study. *The*

American Journal of Clinical Nutrition, 95(5), 1136–1143.

Johnson, W., McGue, M., Krueger, R. F., & Bouchard, T. J., Jr. (2004). Marriage and personality: A genetic analysis. *Journal of Personality and Social Psychology, 86*(2), 285–294.

Johnson-Laird, P. (2010). Deductive reasoning. *Wiley Interdisciplinary Reviews: Cognitive Science, 1*(1), 8–17.

John-Steiner, V. P. (2007). Vygotsky on thinking and speaking. In H. Daniels et al. (Eds.), *The Cambridge companion to Vygotsky* (pp. 136–152). New York: Cambridge University Press.

Johnston, C. C., Campbell-Yeo, M., & Fillon, F. (2011). Paternal vs maternal kangaroo care for procedural pain in preterm neonates: A randomized crossover trial. *Archives of Pediatrics and Adolescent Medicine, 165*(9), 792–796.

Johnston, L. D., O'Malley, P. M., Bachman, J. G., & Schulenberg, J. E. (2009). *Monitoring the Future national results on adolescent drug use: Overview of key findings, 2008* (NIH Publication No. 09-7401). Bethesda, MD: National Institute on Drug Abuse.

Johnston, L. D., O'Malley, P. M., Bachman, J. G., & Schulenberg, J. E. (December 14, 2011). Marijuana use continues to rise among U.S. teens, while alcohol use hits historic lows. University of Michigan News Service: Ann Arbor, MI. Retrieved 03/15/2012 from http://www.monitoringthefuture.org.

Johnston, M. V., et al. (2009). Plasticity and injury in the developing brain. *Brain and Development, 31*(1), 1–10.

Jolley, R. P. (2010). *Children and pictures; Drawing and understanding.* Chichester, West Sussex, UK: Wiley-Blackwell.

Jones, D. C., & Crawford, J. K. (2006). The peer appearance culture during adolescence: Gender and body mass variations. *Journal of Youth and Adolescence, 35*(2), 257–269.

Jones, D. C., Swift, D. J., & Johnson, M. A. (1988). Nondeliberate memory for a novel event among preschoolers. *Developmental Psychology, 24,* 641–645.

Jones, D. J., Hussong, A. M., Manning, J., & Sterrett, E. (2008). Adolescent alcohol use in context: The role of parents and peers among African American and European American youth. *Cultural Diversity and Ethnic Minority Psychology, 14*(3), 266–273.

Jones, M. C. (1924). Elimination of children's fears. *Journal of Experimental Psychology, 7,* 381–390.

Jones, R. M., Dick, A. J., Coyl-Shepherd, D. D., & Ogletree, M. (2012). Antecedents of the male adolescent identity crisis. *Youth and Society.* doi:10.1177/0044118X12438904.

Jordan, A. B., & Robinson, T. N. (2008). Children, television viewing, and weight status: Summary and recommendations from an expert panel meeting. *The Annals of the American Academy of Political and Social Science, 615*(1), 119–132.

Jordan, N. C., Kaplan, D., Ramineni, C., & Locuniak, M. N. (2009). Early math matters: Kindergarten number competence and later mathematics outcomes, *Developmental Psychology, 45*(3), 850–867.

Jorgensen, G. (2006). Kohlberg and Gilligan: Duet or duel? *Journal of Moral Education, 35*(2), 179–196.

Joshi, P. T., Salpekar, J. A., & Daniolos, P. T. (2006). Physical and sexual abuse of children. In M. K. Dulcan & J. M. Wiener (Eds.), *Essentials of child and adolescent psychiatry* (pp. 595–620). Washington, DC: American Psychiatric Publishing.

Josselyn, S. A., & Frankland, P. W. (2012). Infantile amnesia: A neurogenic hypothesis. *Learning & Memory, 19,* 423–433.

Jowkar-Baniani, G & Schmuckler, M. A. (2011). Picture perception in infants: Generalization from two-dimensional to three-dimensional displays. *Infancy, 16*(2), 211–226.

Junod, A. F. (2008). Overweight children do not necessarily become overweight adults. *Swiss Medical Review, 4*(174), 2175.

Kaestle, C. E., & Allen, K. R. (2011). The role of masturbation in healthy sexual development: Perceptions of young adults. *Archives of Sexual Behavior, 40*(5), 983–994.

Kagan, J., & Klein, R. E. (1973). Cross-cultural perspectives on early development. *American Psychologist, 28,* 947–961.

Kaiser Family Foundation, Holt, T., Greene, L., & Davis, J. (2003). *National Survey of Adolescents and Young Adults: Sexual health knowledge, attitudes, and experiences.* Menlo Park, CA: Henry J. Kaiser Family Foundation.

Kalberg, W. O., Provost, B., Tollison, S. J., Tabachnick, B. G., Robinson, L. K., Hoyme, H. E., Trujillo, P. M., Buckley, D., Aragon, A. S., & May, P. A. (2006). Comparison of motor delays in young children with fetal alcohol syndrome to those with prenatal alcohol exposure and with no prenatal alcohol exposure. *Alcoholism: Clinical and Experimental Research, 30,* 2037–2045.

Kalbfleisch, M. L. (2008). Neuroscientific investigator of high mathematical ability: An interview with Michael W. O'Boyle. *Roeper Review, 30*(3), 153–157.

Kalil, A., Ziol-Guest, K. M., & Coley, R. L. (2005). Perceptions of father involvement patterns in teenage-mother families: Predictors and links to mothers' psychological adjustment. *Family Relations, 54*(2), 197–211.

Käll, A., & Lagercrantz, H. (2012). Highlights in this issue. *Acta Paediatrica, 101*(1). doi:10.1111/j.1651-2227.2011.02524.x.

Kamakura, T., Ando, J., & Ono, Y. (2007). Genetic and environmental effects of stability and change in self-esteem during adolescence. *Personality and Individual Differences, 42*(1), 181–190.

Kamii, C., Lewis, B. A., & Kirkland, L. (2001). Manipulatives: When are they useful? *Journal of Mathematical Behaviour, 20,* 21–31.

Kaminski, R. A., & Stormshak, E. A. (2007). Project STAR: Early intervention with preschool children and families for the prevention of substance abuse. In P. Tolan, J. Szapocznik & S. Sambrano (Eds.), *Preventing youth substance abuse: Science-based programs for children and adolescents* (pp. 89–109). Washington, DC: American Psychological Association.

Karatekin, C. (2004). Development of attentional allocation in the dual task paradigm. *International Journal of Psychophysiology, 52*(1), 7–21.

Karavasilis, L., Doyle, A. B., & Markiewicz, D. (2003). Associations between parenting style and attachment to mother in middle childhood and adolescence. *International Journal of Behavioral Development, 27*(2), 153–164.

Karrass, J., et al. (2006). Relation of emotional reactivity and regulation to childhood stuttering. *Journal of Communication Disorders, 39*(6), 402–423.

Karwautz, A., et al. (2001). Individual-specific risk factors for anorexia nervosa: A pilot study using a discordant sister-pair design. *Psychological Medicine, 31*(2), 317–329.

Kaufman, J. C., & Plucker, J. A. (2011). Intelligence and creativity. In R. J. Sternberg & S. J. Kaufman (Eds.), *The Cambridge handbook of intelligence* (pp. 771–783). New York: Cambridge University Press.

Kaufman, S. B., Reynolds, M. R., Liu, X., Kaufman, A. S., & McGrew, K. S. (2012). Are cognitive g and academic achievement g one and the same g? *Intelligence.* http://dx.doi.org/10.1016/j.intell.2012.01.009.

Kavanaugh, R. D. (2006). Pretend play. In B. Spodek & O. N. Saracho (Eds.), *Handbook of research on the education of young children* (2nd ed.) (pp. 269–278). Mahwah, NJ: Erlbaum.

Kavcic, T., & Zupancic, M. (2005). Sibling relationship in early/middle childhood: Trait- and dyad-centered approach. *Studia Psychologica, 47*(3), 179–197.

Kavšek, M., Yonas, A., & Granrud, C. E. (2012). Infants' sensitivity to pictorial depth cues: A review and meta-analysis of looking studies. *Infant Behavior and Development, 35*(1), 109–128.

Kaye, W. H., et al. (2004). Genetic analysis of bulimia nervosa: Methods and sample description. *International Journal of Eating Disorders, 35*(4), 556–570.

Kazdin, A. E. (2000). Treatments for aggressive and antisocial children. *Child and Adolescent Psychiatric Clinics of North America, 9*(4), 841–858.

Kazui, M., Endo, T., Tanaka, A., Sakagami, H., & Suganuma, M. (2000). Intergenerational transmission of attachment: Japanese mother–child dyads. *Japanese Journal of Educational Psychology, 48*(3), 323–332.

Kearney, C. A. (2007). School absenteeism and school refusal behavior in youth: A contemporary review. *Clinical Psychology Review, 28*(3), 451–471.

Keefer, M. W. (2006). A critical comparison of classical and domain theory: Some implications for character education. *Journal of Moral Education, 35*(3), 369–386.

Keller, H., Kärtner, J., Borke, J., Yovsi, R., & Kleis, A. (2005). Parenting styles and the development of the categorical self: A longitudinal study on mirror self-recognition in Cameroonian Nso and German families. *International Journal of Behavioral Development, 29*(6), 496–504.

Kellman, P. J., & Arterberry, M. E. (2006). Infant visual perception. In D. Kuhn et al. (Eds.), *Handbook of child psychology*, Vol. 2, *Cognition, perception, and language* (6th ed.) (pp. 109–160). Hoboken, NJ: Wiley.

Kellogg, R. (1959). *What children scribble and why.* Oxford: National Press.

Kellogg, R. (1970). Understanding children's art. In P. Cramer (Ed.), *Readings in developmental psychology today.* Del Mar, CA: CRM.

Kelly, K. M., Jones, W. H., & Adams, J. M. (2002). Using the Imaginary Audience Scale as a measure of social anxiety in young adults. *Educational and Psychological Measurement, 62*(5), 896–914.

Kempes, M., Matthys, W., de Vries, H., & van Engeland, H. (2005). Reactive and proactive aggression in children: A review of theory, findings and the relevance for child and adolescent psychiatry. *European Child & Adolescent Psychiatry, 14*(1), 11–19.

Kendall, P. C. (2011). *Child and adolescent therapy: Cognitive-behavioral procedures* (4th ed.). New York: Guilford.

Kendall, P. C., Safford, S., Flannery-Schroeder, E., & Webb, A. (2004). Child anxiety treatment: Outcomes in adolescence and impact on substance use and depression at 7.4-year follow-up. *Journal of Consulting and Clinical Psychology, 72,* 276–287.

Kendler, K. S. (2010). Advances in our understanding of genetic risk factors for autism spectrum disorders. *American Journal of Psychiatry, 167*(11), 1291–1293.

Kendler, K. S., et al. (2011). The impact of environmental experiences on symptoms of anxiety and depression across the life span. *Psychological Science, 22*(1), 1343–1352.

Kendler, K. S., et al. (2012). Recent advances in the genetic epidemiology and molecular genetics of substance use disorders. *Nature Neuroscience, 15,* 181–189.

Kerns, K., MacSween, J., Vander Wekken, S., & Gruppuso, V. (2010). Investigating the efficacy of an attention training programme in children with foetal alcohol spectrum disorder. *Developmental Neurorehabilitation, 13*(6), 413–422.

Khurana, A., Cooksey, E. C., & Gavazzi, S. M. (2011). Juvenile delinquency and teenage pregnancy. *Psychology of Women Quarterly, 35*(2), 282–289.

Kiang, L., Yip, T., Gonzales-Backen, M., Witkow, & Fuligni, A. J. (2006). Ethnic identity and the daily psychological wellbeing of adolescents from Mexican and Chinese backgrounds. *Child Development, 77*(5), 1338–1350.

Kibbe, M. M., & Leslie, A. M. (2011). What do infants remember when they forget? Location and identity in 6-month-olds' memory for objects. *Psychological Science, 22*(12), 1500–1505.

Kiernan, K. E., & Huerta, M. C. (2008). Economic deprivation, maternal depression, parenting, and children's cognitive and emotional development in early childhood. *The British Journal of Sociology, 59*(4), 783–806.

Kihlstrom, J. F., & Cantor, N. (2011). Social intelligence. In R. J. Sternberg & S. J. Kaufman (Eds.), *The Cambridge handbook of intelligence* (pp. 564–581). New York: Cambridge University Press.

Kilgore, K., Snyder, J., & Lentz, C. (2000). The contribution of parental discipline, parental monitoring, and school risk to early-onset conduct problems in African American boys and girls. *Developmental Psychology, 36*(6), 835–845.

Killen, M., & Smetana, J. G. (2010). Future directions: Social development in the context of social justice. *Social Development, 19*(3), 642–657.

Kim, E. H., et al. (2012). Depression mediates the relationship between obsessive–compulsive symptoms and eating disorder symptoms in an inpatient sample. *Journal of Obsessive–Compulsive and Related Disorders, 1*(1), 62–68.

Kim, H. S. (2011). Consequences of parental divorce for child development. *American Sociological Review, 76*(3), 487–511.

Kim, J., & Cicchetti, D. (2009). Mean-level change and intraindividual variability in self-esteem and depression among high-risk children. *International Journal of Behavioral Development, 33*(3), 202–214.

Kim, J-Y., McHale, S. M., Osgood, D. W., & Crouter, A. C. (2006). Longitudinal course and family correlates of sibling relationships from childhood through adolescence. *Child Development, 77*(6), 1746–1761.

Kim, K. H. (2005). Can only intelligent people be creative? A meta-analysis. *Journal of Secondary Gifted Education, 16*(2–3), 57–66.

Kimmons, J., et al. (2009). Fruit and vegetable intake among adolescents and adults in the United States: Percentage meeting individualized recommendations. *The Medscape Journal of Medicine, 11*(1), 26.

Kimura, et al. (2010). Infants' recognition of objects using canonical color. *Journal of Experimental Child Psychology, 105*(3), 256–263.

Kindlon, D., & Thompson, M. (2002). Thorns among roses: The struggle of young boys in early education. In *The Jossey-Bass reader on gender in education* (pp. 151–181). San Francisco, CA: Jossey-Bass.

King, M. (2008). A systematic review of mental disorder, suicide, and deliberate self harm in lesbian, gay and bisexual people. *BMC Psychiatry, 8,* 70. doi:10.1186/1471-244X-8-70.

King, R. (2000). Interview comments in L. Frazier (2000, July 16), The new face of HIV is young, black. *Washington Post,* p. C01.

King, S., & Laplante, D. (2005). The effects of parental maternal stress in children's cognitive development: Project Ice Storm. *Stress, 8,* 35–45.

Kinsey, A. C., Pomeroy, W. B., & Martin, C. E. (1948). *Sexual behavior in the human male.* Philadelphia: W. B. Saunders.

Kinsey, A. C., Pomeroy, W. B., Martin, C. E., & Gebhard, P. H. (1953). *Sexual behavior in the human female.* Philadelphia: W. B. Saunders.

Kirby, D. B., et al. (2007). Sex and HIV education programs: Their impact on sexual behaviors of young people throughout the world. *Journal of Adolescent Health, 40*(3), 206–217.

Kirby, J. R., Parrila, R. K., & Pfeiffer, S. L. (2003). Naming speed and phonological awareness as predictors of reading development. *Journal of Educational Psychology, 95*(3), 453–464.

Kirchler, E., Pombeni, M. L., & Palmonari, A. (1991). Sweet sixteen . . . Adolescents' problems and the peer group as source of support. *European Journal of Psychology of Education, 6,* 393–410.

Kirkcaldy, B. D., Shephard, R. J., & Siefen, R. G. (2002). The relationship between physical activity and self-image and problem behaviour among adolescents. *Social Psychiatry and Psychiatric Epidemiology, 37*(11), 544–550.

Kirke, D. M. (2009). Gender clustering in friendship networks. *Methodological Innovations Online, 4,* 23–36.

Kistner, J. (2006). Children's peer acceptance, perceived acceptance, and risk for depression. In T. E. Joiner, J. S. Brown & J. Kistner (Eds.), *The interpersonal, cognitive, and social nature of depression* (pp. 1–21). Mahwah, NJ: Erlbaum.

Kiuru, N., et al. (2012). Best friends in adolescence show similar educational careers in early adulthood. *Journal of Applied Developmental Psychology, 33*(2), 102–111.

Kjelsås, E., Bjornstrom, C., & Götestam, K. G. (2004). Prevalence of eating disorders in female and male adolescents (14–15 years). *Eating Behaviors, 5*(1), 13–25.

Klahr, A. M., McGue, M., Iacono, W. G., & Burt, S. A. (2011). The association between parent–child conflict and adolescent conduct problems over time: Results from a longitudinal adoption study. *Journal of Abnormal Psychology, 120*(1), 46–56.

Klee, T., & Stokes, S. F. (2011). Language development. In D. Skuse et al. (Eds.). *Child psychology and psychiatry: Frameworks for practice* (2nd ed.) (pp. 45–50). Chichester, UK: John Wiley.

Klein, P. J., & Meltzoff, A. N. (1999). Long-term memory, forgetting and deferred imitation in 12-month-old infants. *Developmental Science, 2*(1), 102–113.

Klier, C. M. (2006). Mother–infant bonding disorders in patients with postnatal depression: The Postpartum Bonding Questionnaire in clinical practice. *Archives of Women's Mental Health, 9*(5), 289–291.

Klima, T., & Repetti, R. L. (2008). Children's peer relations and their psychological adjustment. *Merrill-Palmer Quarterly, 54*(2), 151–178.

Klimstra, T. A., et al. (2012). Associations of identity dimensions with Big Five personality domains and facets. *European Journal of Personality.* doi:10.1002/per.1853.

Knafo, A., & Plomin, R. (2006a). Parental discipline and affection and children's prosocial behavior: Genetic and environmental links. *Journal of Personality and Social Psychology, 90*(1), 147–164.

Knafo, A., & Plomin, R. (2006b). Prosocial behavior from early to middle childhood: Genetic and environmental influences on stability and change. *Developmental Psychology, 42*(5), 771–786.

Knickmeyer, R., et al. (2005). Gender-typed play and amniotic testosterone. *Developmental Psychology, 41*, 517–528.

Kobayashi-Winata, H., & Power, T. G. (1989). Childrearing and compliance: Japanese and American families in Houston. *Journal of Cross-Cultural Psychology, 20*, 333–356.

Koch, J. (2007). A gender-inclusive approach to science education. In D. M. Sadker & E. S. Silber (Eds.), *Gender in the classroom: Foundations, skills, methods, and strategies across the curriculum* (pp. 205–223). Mahwah, NJ: Erlbaum.

Kochanek, K. D., et al. (2011). Deaths: Preliminary data for 2009. *National Vital Statistics Reports, 59*(4), Table 7. Hyattsville, MD: National Center for Health Statistics.

Kochanska, G. (2001). Emotional development in children with different attachment histories: The first three years. *Child Development, 72*(2), 474–490.

Kochanska, G., Coy, K. C., & Murray, K. T. (2001). The development of self-regulation in the first four years of life. *Child Development, 72*(4), 1091–1111.

Kohl, C. (2004). Postpartum psychoses: Closer to schizophrenia or the affective spectrum? *Current Opinion in Psychiatry, 17*(2), 87–90.

Kohlberg, L. (1963). Moral development and identification. In H. W. Stevenson (Ed.), *Child psychology: 62nd yearbook of the National Society for the Study of Education.* Chicago: University of Chicago Press.

Kohlberg, L. (1966). Cognitive stages and preschool education. *Human Development, 9*, 5–17.

Kohlberg, L. (1969). Stage and sequence: The cognitive-developmental approach to socialization. In D. A. Goslin (Ed.), *Handbook of socialization theory and research.* Chicago: Rand McNally.

Kohlberg, L. (1981). *The meaning and measurement of moral development.* Worcester, MA: Clark University Press.

Kohlberg, L. (1985). *The psychology of moral development.* San Francisco: Harper & Row.

Kohlberg, L., & Kramer, R. (1969). Continuities and discontinuities in childhood and adult moral development. *Human Development, 12*, 93–120.

Kohyama, J., Shiiki, T., Ohinata-Sugimoto, J., & Hasegawa, T. (2002). Potentially harmful sleep habits of 3-year-old children in Japan. *Journal of Developmental and Behavioral Pediatrics, 23*(2), 67–70.

Kolb, B., & Gibb, R. (2007). Brain plasticity and recovery from early cortical injury. *Developmental Psychobiology, 49*(2), 107–118.

Konijn, E. A., Bijvank, M. N., & Bushman, B. J. (2007). I wish I were a warrior: The role of wishful identification in the effects of violent video games on aggression in adolescent boys. *Developmental Psychology, 43*(4), 1038–1044.

Kooistra, L., et al. (2010). Differentiating attention deficit in child with fetal alcohol spectrum disorder or attention-deficit-hyperactivity disorder. *Developmental Medicine & Child Neurology, 52*(2), 205–211.

Koopmans-van Beinum, F. J., Clement, C. J., & van den Dikkenberg-Pot, I. (2001). Babbling and the lack of auditory speech perception: A matter of coordination? *Developmental Science, 4*(1), 61–70.

Kopp, C. B. (1989). Regulation of distress and negative emotions: A developmental view. *Developmental Psychology, 25*, 343–354.

Kopp, C. B. (2011). Development in the early years: Socialization, motor development, and consciousness. *Annual Review of Psychology, 62*, 165–187.

Korja, R., Latva, R., & Lehtonen, L. (2011). The effects of preterm birth on mother-infant interaction and attachment during the infant's first two years. *ACTA Obstetrica et Gynecologica Scandinavica.* doi:10.1111/j.1600-0412.2011.01304.x.

Koslowski, B., & Masnick, A. (2010). Causal reasoning and explanation. In U. Goswami (Ed.), *The Wiley–Blackwell handbook of childhood cognitive development.* (2nd ed.) (pp. 377–398). Chichester, West Sussex, UK: Wiley–Blackwell.

Kramer, M. S., Aboud, F., Mironova, E., Vanilovich, I., Platt, R. W., Matush, L., Igumnov, S., Fombonne, E., Bogdanovich, N., Ducruet, T., Collet, J. P., Chalmers, B., Hodnett, E., Davidovsky, S., Skugarevsky, O., Trofimovich, O., Kozlova, L., Shapiro, S., & Promotion of Breastfeeding Intervention Trial (PROBIT) Study Group (2008). Breastfeeding and child cognitive development: New evidence from a large randomized trial. *Archives of General Psychiatry, 65*(5), 578–584.

Krebs, D. L., & Denton, K. (2005). Toward a more pragmatic approach to morality: A critical evaluation of Kohlberg's model. *Psychological Review, 112*(3), 629–649.

Krebs, D. L., & Denton, K. (2006). Explanatory limitations of cognitive-developmental approaches to morality. *Psychological Review, 113*(3), 672–675.

Kreppner, J. M., Rutter, M., Beckett, C., Castle, J., Colvert, E.,Groothues, C., Hawkins, A., O'Connor, T. G., Stevens, S. E., & Sonuga-Barke, E. J. S. (2007). What predicts normality and impairment following profound early institutional deprivation? A longitudinal examination through childhood. *Developmental Psychology, 43*, 931–946.

Kristof, N. D. (2012, January 11). The value of teachers. *New York Times*, p. A7.

Kristof, N. D. (2012, March 1). Born to not get bullied. *New York Times*, p. A31.

Kroeger, K. A., & Nelson, W. M., III. (2006). A language programme to increase the verbal production of a child dually diagnosed with Down syndrome and autism. *Journal of Intellectual Disability Research, 50*(2), 101–108.

Kroger, J., & Marcia, J. E. (2011). The identity statuses: The origins, meanings, and interpretations. In S. J. Schwartz, K. Luyckx, V. L. Vignoles (Eds.), *Handbook of identity theory and research* (Vols. 1 and 2, pp. 31–53). New York, NY: Springer.

Kuczaj, S. A., II. (1982). On the nature of syntactic development. In S. A. Kuczaj, II (Ed.), *Language development*, Vol. 1, *Syntax and semantics.* Hillsdale, NJ: Erlbaum.

Kuczmarski, R. J., et al. (2000, December 4). *CDC growth charts: United States.* Advance Data from Vital and Health Statistics, No. 314. Hyattsville, MD: National Center for Health Statistics.

Kuhl, P. K., et al. (1997). Cross-language analysis of phonetic units in language addressed to infants. *Science, 277*(5326), 684–686.

Kuhl, P. K., et al. (2006). Infants show a facilitation effect for native language phonetic perception between 6 and 12 months. *Developmental Science, 9*(2), F13–F21.

Kumar, B., & Wandel, M. (2006). Nutritional challenges among immigrant children and youth in Norwat. In L. D. Adams & A. Kirova (Eds.), *Global migration and education: Schools, children, and families* (pp. 67–81). Mahwah, NJ: Lawrence Erlbaum.

Kundanis, R., & Massaro, D. W. (2004). Televisual media for children are more interactive. *American Journal of Psychology, 117*(4), 643–648.

Kuo, P-H., et al. (2010). Genome-wide linkage scans for major depression in individuals with alcohol dependence. *Journal of Psychiatric Research, 44*(9), 616–619.

Kurosawa, K., Masuno, M., & Kuroki, Y. (2012). Trends in occurrence of twin births in Japan. *American Journal of Medical Genetics Part A, 158A*(1), 75–77.

Labouvie-Vief, G. (2006). Emerging structures of adult thought. In J. J. Arnett & J. L. Tanner (Eds.), *Emerging adults in America* (pp. 59–84). Washington, DC: American Psychological Association.

Labrell, F., & Ubersfeld, G. (2004). Parental verbal strategies and children's capacities at 3 and 5 years during a memory task. *European Journal of Psychology of Education, 19*(2), 189–202.

Lacham-Kaplan, O., Chy, H., & Trounson, A. (2008). Testicular cell conditioned medium supports differentiation of embryonic stem cells into ovarian structures containing oocytes. *Stem Cells, 24*(2), 266–273.

Lachance, J. A., & Mazzocco, M. M. M. (2006). A longitudinal analysis of sex difference in math and spatial skills in primary school age children. *Learning and Individual Differences, 16*, 195–216.

Lagercrantz, H. (2010). Basic consciousness of a newborn. *Seminars in Perinatology, 34*(3), 201–206.

Lai, C. K., et al. (2009). Global variation in the prevalence and severity of asthma symptoms: Phase three of the International Study of Asthma and Allergies in Childhood (ISAAC). *Thorax, 64*(6), 476–483.

Lai, T. J., Guo, Y. I., Guo, N-W., & Hsu, C. C. (2001). Effect of prenatal exposure to polychlorinated biphenyls on cognitive development in children: A longitudinal study in Taiwan. *British Journal of Psychiatry, 178*(Suppl. 40), S49–S52.

Lalumière, M. L., Blanchard, R., & Zucker, K. J. (2000). Sexual orientation and handedness in men and women: A meta-analysis. *Psychological Bulletin, 126*(4), 575–592.

Lam, T. H., Shi, H. J., Ho, L. M., Stewart, S. M., & Fan, S. (2002). Timing of pubertal maturation and heterosexual behavior among Hong Kong Chinese adolescents. *Archives of Sexual Behavior, 31*(4), 359–366.

Lamaze, F. (1981). *Painless childbirth.* New York: Simon & Schuster.

Lamb, M. E. (2012). Mothers, father, families, and circumstances: Factors affecting children's adjustment. *Applied Developmental Science, 16*(2), 98–111.

Lamb, M. E., & Lewis, C. (2010). The development and significance of father-child relationships in two-parent families. In M. E. Lamb (Ed.), *The role of the father in child development* (5th ed., pp. 94–153). Hoboken, NJ: Wiley.

Lamb, M. E., Sternberg, K. J., & Prodromidis, M. (1992). Nonmaternal care and the security of infant–mother attachment: A reanalysis of the data. *Infant Behavior and Development, 15*, 71–83.

Lamers, C. T. J., Bechara, A., Rizzo, M., & Ramaekers, J. G. (2006). Cognitive function and mood in MDMA/THC users, THC users and non-drug using controls. *Journal of Psychopharmacology, 20*(2), 302–311.

Lampel, J., & Honig, B. (2006). Let the children play: Muppets in the middle of the Middle East. In J. Lampel, J. Shamsie & T. K. Lant (Eds.), *Strategic perspectives on entertainment and media.* Mahwah, NJ: Erlbaum.

Lampl, M., Veldhuis, J. D., & Johnson, M. L. (1992). Saltation and stasis: A model of human growth. *Science, 258*, 801–803.

Landau, R., & Yentis, S. (2011). Maternal–fetal conflicts: Cesarean delivery on maternal request. In G. A. Van Norman, et al. (Eds.), *Clinical ethics in anesthesiology.* (pp. 49–54). New York: Cambridge University Press.

Landolt, A. S., & Milling, L. S. (2011). The efficacy of hypnosis as an intervention for labor and delivery pain: A comprehensive methodological review. *Clinical Psychology Review, 31*(6), 1022–1031.

Landrigan, P. J. (2010). What causes autism? Exploring the environmental contribution. *Current Opinion in Pediatrics, 22*(2), 219–225.

Landy, F. J. (2006). The long, frustrating, and fruitless search for social intelligence: A cautionary tale. In K. R. Murphy (Ed.), *A critique of emotional intelligence: What are the problems and how can they be fixed?* (pp. 81–123). Mahwah, NJ: Erlbaum.

Lange, G., & Pierce, S. H. (1992). Memory-strategy learning and maintenance in preschool children. *Developmental Psychology, 28*, 453–462.

Lange, R. A., & Hillis, L. D. (2010). Sudden death in cocaine abusers. *European Heart Journal, 31*(3), 271–273.

Langlois, J. H., et al. (2000). Maxims or myths of beauty? A meta-analytic and theoretical review. *Psychological Bulletin, 126*(3), 390–423.

Lansford, J. E., et al. (2009). Social network centrality and leadership status: Links with problem behaviors and tests of gender differences. *Merrill-Palmer Quarterly, 55*(1), 1–25.

Laplante, D., et al. (2004). Stress during pregnancy affects intellectual and linguistic functioning in human toddlers. *Pediatric Research, 56*, 400–410.

LaPlante, D., Brunet, A., Schmitz, N., Clampi, A., & King, S. (2008). Project Ice Storm: Prenatal maternal stress affects cognitive and linguistic functioning in 5- 1/2–year-old children. *Journal of the American Academy of Child & Adolescent Psychiatry, 47*, 1063–1072.

Lapsley, D. K. (2006). Moral stage theory. In K. Killen & J. G. Smetana (Eds.), *Handbook of moral development* (pp. 37–66). Mahwah, NJ: Erlbaum.

Lapsley, D. K., & Hill, P. L. (2008). On dual processing and heuristic approaches to moral cognition. *Journal of Moral Education, 37*(3), 313–332.

Largo, R. H., et al. (2001). Neuromotor development from 5 to 18 years. Part 1: Timed performance. *Developmental Medicine and Child Neurology, 43*(7), 436–443.

Larson, R., & Richards, M. H. (1991). Daily companionship in late childhood and early adolescence: Changing developmental contexts. *Child Development, 62*, 284–300.

Lateef, T. M., et al. (2009). Headache in a national sample of American children: Prevalence and comorbidity. *Journal of Child Neurology, 24*(5), 536–543.

Laturi, C. A., et al. (2010). Treatment of adolescent gynecomastia. *Journal of Pediatric Surgery, 45*(3), 650–654.

Lau, A. S., Litrownik, A. J., Newton, R. R., Black, M. M., & Everson, M. D. (2006). Factors affecting the link between physical discipline and child externalizing problems in Black and White families. *Journal of Community Psychology, 34*(1), 89–103.

Lau, M., et al. (2009). Dating and sexual attitudes in Asian-American adolescents. *Journal of Adolescent Research, 24*(1), 91–113.

Laurendeau, M., & Pinard, A. (1970). *The development of the concept of space in the child.* New York: International Universities Press.

Lawson, K., & Ruff, H. A. (2004). Early focused attention predicts outcome for children born prematurely. *Journal of Developmental & Behavioral Pediatrics, 25*(6), 399–406.

Leahey, E., & Guo, G. (2001). Gender differences in mathematical trajectories. *Social Forces, 80*(2), 713–732.

Leaper, C. (2011). More similarities than differences in contemporary theories of social development? A plea for theory bridging. *Advances in Child Development and Behavior, 40*, 337–378.

Leaper, C., & Bigler, R. S. (2011). Gender. In M. K. Underwood & L. H. Rosen (Eds.), *Social development: Relationships in infancy, childhood, and adolescence* (pp. 289–315). New York: Guilford.

Leaper, C., Farkas, T., & Brown, C. S. (2012). Adolescent girls' experiences and gender-related beliefs in relation to their motivation in math/science and English. *Journal of Youth and Adolescence, 41*(3), 268–282.

Lease, A. M., Kennedy, C. A., & Axelrod, J. L. (2002). Children's social construction of popularity. *Social Development, 11*, 87–109.

Lee, A., & Hankin, B. L. (2009). Insecure attachment, dysfunctional attitudes, and low self-esteem predicting prospective symptoms of depression and anxiety during adolescence. *Journal of Clinical Child and Adolescent Psychology, 38*(2), 219–231.

Lee, A. C., He, J., & Ma, M. (2011). Olfactory marker protein is crucial for functional maturation of olfactory sensory neurons and development of mother preference. *The Journal of Neuroscience, 31*(8), 2974–2982.

Lee, N. R., Lopez, K. C., Adeyemi, E. I., & Giedd, J. N. (2011). Sex chromosome aneuploidies: A window for examining the effects of the X and Y chromosomes on speech, language, and social development. In D. J. Fidler (Ed.), *Early development in neurogenetic disorders* (pp. 141–171). New York: Elsevier.

Lee, S. A. S., & Davis, B. L. (2010). Segmental distribution patterns of English infant- and adult-directed speech. *Journal of Child Language, 37*, 767–791.

Leerkes, E. M., Paradise, M. J., O'Brien, M., Calkins, S. D., & Lange, G. (2008). Emotion and cognition processes in preschool children. *Merrill-Palmer Quarterly, 54*(1), 102–124.

Lengen, C., et al. (2009). Anomalous brain dominance and the immune system: Do left-handers have specific immunological patterns? *Brain and Cognition, 69*(1), 188–193.

Lenneberg, E. H. (1967). *Biological foundations of language.* New York: Wiley.

Lenroot, R. K., et al. (2009). Differences in genetic and environmental influences on the human cerebral cortex associated with development during childhood and adolescence. *Human Brain Mapping, 30*(1), 163–173.

Leonard, C. M., et al. (2008). Identical neural risk factors predict cognitive deficit in dyslexia and schizophrenia. *Neuropsychology, 22*(2), 147–158.

Lepola, J., Vaurus, M., & Maeki, H. (2000). Gender differences in the development of academic self-concept of attainment from the 2nd to the 6th grade: Relations with achievement and perceived motivational orientation. *Psychology: The Journal of the Hellenic Psychological Society, 7*(3), 290–308.

Lester, B. M., & Tronick, E. Z. (2004). *NICU Network Neurobehavioral Scale (NNNS) manual.* Baltimore, MD: Brookes.

Leung, P., Curtis, R. L., Jr., & Mapp, S. C. (2010). Incidences of sexual contacts of children: Impacts of family characteristics and family structure from a national sample. *Children and Youth Services Review, 32*(5), 650–656.

Leung, P. W. L., & Poon, M. W. L. (2001). Dysfunctional schemas and cognitive distortions in psychopathology. *The Journal of Child Psychology and Psychiatry and Allied Disciplines, 42*, 755–765.

Levendosky, A. A., Bogat, G. A., Huth-Bocks, A. C., Rosenblum, K., & von Eye, A. (2011). *Journal of Clinical Child & Adolescent Psychology, 40*(3), 398–410.

Leventhal, T., Graber, J. A., & Brooks-Gunn, J. (2001). Adolescent transitions to young adulthood: Antecedents, correlates, and consequences of adolescent employment. *Journal of Research on Adolescence, 11*(3), 297–323.

Levinthal, B. R., & Lleras, A. (2007). The unique contributions of retinal size and perceived size on change detection. *Visual Cognition, 15*(1), 101–105.

Levitt, M. J., Weber, R. A., Clark, M. C., & McDonnell, P. (1985). Reciprocity of exchange in toddler sharing behavior. *Developmental Psychology, 21*, 122–123.

Levy, G. D., Sadovsky, A. L., & Troseth, G. L. (2000). Aspects of young children's perceptions of gender-typed occupations. *Sex Roles, 42* (11–12), 993–1006.

Lewis, B. A., et al. (2004). Four-year language outcomes of children exposed to cocaine in utero. *Neurotoxicology and Teratology, 26*(5), 617–627.

Lewis, B. A., et al. (2011). The effects of prenatal cocaine on language development at 10 years of age. *Neurotoxicology and Teratology, 33*(1), 17–24.

Lewis, M., & Feiring, C. (1989). Early predictors of childhood friendship. In T. J. Berndt & G. W. Ladd (Eds.), *Peer relationships in child development.* New York: Wiley.

Lewis, S. (2011). Development: Pruning the dendritic tree. *Nature Reviews Neuroscience, 12*, 493.

Li, J. (2004). Gender inequality, family planning, and maternal and child care in a rural Chinese county. *Social Science & Medicine, 59*, 659–708.

Li, J., Robinson, M., Malacova, E., Jacoby, P., Foster, J., & Van Eekelen, A. (2013). Maternal life stress events in pregnancy link to children's school achievement at age 10 years.

Li, J. T. (2009). *Childhood asthma.* Available at http://www.mayoclinic.com/health/outgrow-asthma/AN01973.

Li, Q. (2007). New bottle but old wine: A research of cyberbullying in schools. *Computers in Human Behavior, 23*(4), 1777–1791.

Li, Q., Cross, D., & Smith, P. K. (2012). *Cyberbullying in the global playground.* Chichester, West Sussex, UK: Wiley–Blackwell.

Li, S-C., Hämmerer, D., Müller, V., Hommel, B., & Lindenberger, U. (2009). Lifespan development of stimulus-response conflict cost: Similarities and differences between maturation and senescence. *Psychological Research, 73*, 777–785.

Li, X., McGue, M., & Gottesman, I. I. (2012). Two sources of genetic liability to depression: Interpreting the relationship between stress sensitivity and depression under a multifactorial polygenic model. *Behavior Genetics, 42*(2), 268–277.

Lick, D. J., Schmidt, K. M., & Patterson, C. J. (2011). The Rainbow Families Scale (RFS): A measure of experiences among individuals with lesbian and gay parents. *Journal of Applied Measurement, 12*(3), 222–241.

Lillard, A., Pinkham, A. M., & Smith, E. (2010). Pretend play and cognitive development. In U. Goswami (Ed.), *The Wiley–Blackwell handbook of childhood cognitive development.* (2nd ed.) (pp. 285–311). Chichester, West Sussex, UK: Wiley–Blackwell.

Limin Shi, N. T., & Patterson, P. H. (2005). Maternal influenza infection is likely to alter fetal brain development indirectly: The virus is not detected in the fetus. *International Journal of Developmental Neuroscience, 23*(2–3), 299–305.

Linebarger, D. L., & Piotrowski, J. T. (2010). Structure and strategies in children's educational television: The roles of program type and learning strategies in children's learning. *Child Development, 81*(5), 1582–1597.

Lipman, E. L., et al. (2006). Testing effectiveness of a community-based aggression management program for children 7 to 11 years old and their families. *Journal of the American Academy of Child & Adolescent Psychiatry, 45*(9), 1085–1093.

Lipnowski, S., & Canadian Paediatric Society Healthy Active Living and Sports Medicine Committee (2012). Healthy active living: Physical activity guidelines for children and adolescents. *Paediatric Child Health, 17*(4), 209–210.

Lipnowksi, S., LeBlanc, C. M. A., & Canadian Pediatric Society (2012). Healthy Active Living and Sports Medicine Committee. *Pediatric Child Health, 17*(4), 1–10.

Lippa, R. A. (2010). Sex differences in personality traits and gender-related occupational preferences across 53 nations: Testing evolutionary and social-environmental theories. *Archives of Sexual Behavior, 39*(3), 619–636.

Lipsitt, L. P. (2002). Early experience and behavior in the baby of the twenty-first century. In J. Gomes-Pedro et al. (Eds.), *The infant and family in the twenty-first century* (pp. 55–78). London: Brunner-Routledge.

Lipsitt, L. P. (2003). Crib death: A biobehavioral phenomenon? *Current Directions in Psychological Science, 12*(5), 164–170.

Liu, J., et al. (2008). The role of antenatal corticosteroids for improving the maturation of choroid plexus capillaries in fetal mice. *Pediatrics, 167*(10), 1209–1212.

Liu, W., et al. (2011). Protective effects of hydrogen on fetal brain injury during maternal hypoxia. *Intracerebral Hemorrhage Research, 111*(3), 307–311.

Liu, X., et al. (2000a). Behavioral and emotional problems in Chinese children of divorced parents. *Journal of the American Academy of Child and Adolescent Psychiatry, 39*(7), 896–903.

Liu, X., Sun, Z., Uchiyama, M., Li, Y., & Okawa, M. (2000b). Attaining nocturnal urinary control, nocturnal enuresis, and behavioral problems in Chinese children aged 6 through 16 years. *Journal of the American Academy of Child and Adolescent Psychiatry, 39*(12), 1557–1564.

Loayza, I. M., Sola, I., & Prats, C. J. (2011). *Biofeedback for pain management during labor.* John Wiley: The Cochrane Library.

Lochman, J. E., Wells, K. C., & Murray, M. (2007). The Coping Power Program: Preventive intervention at the middle school transition. In P. Tolan, J. Szapocznik & S. Sambrano (Eds.), *Preventing youth substance abuse: Science-based programs for children and adolescents* (pp. 185–210). Washington, DC: American Psychological Association.

Lock, J., Couturier, J., & Agras, W. S. (2006). Comparison of long-term outcomes in adolescents with anorexia nervosa treated with family therapy. *Journal of the American Academy of Child & Adolescent Psychiatry, 45*(6), 666–672.

Lohmann, R. I. (2004). Sex and sensibility: Margaret Mead's descriptive and rhetorical ethnography. *Reviews in Anthropology, 33*(2), 111–130.

Lokuge, S., Frey, B. N., Foster, J. A., Soares, C. N., & Steiner, M. (2011). Depression in women: Windows of vulnerability and new insights into the link between estrogen and serotonin. *Journal of Clinical Psychiatry, 72*(11), e1563–e1569.

Lollis, S., & Kuczynski, L. (1997). Beyond one hand clapping: Seeing bidirectionality in parent-child relations. *Journal of Personal Relationships, 14*, 441–461.

Lorenz, K. (1962). *King Solomon's ring.* London: Methuen.

Lorenz, K. (1981). *The foundations of ethology.* New York: Springer-Verlag.

Lothian, J. A. (2011). Lamaze breathing. *The Journal of Perinatal Education, 20*(2), 118–120.

Lovaas, O. I., Smith, T., & McEachin, J. J. (1989). Clarifying comments on the young autism study: Reply to Schapler, Short, and Mesibov. *Journal of Consulting and Clinical Psychology, 57*, 165–167.

Lowrey A. (2012, January 6). Big study links good teachers to lasting gain. *New York Times*, p. A1.

Lubinski, D. (2004). Introduction to the special section on cognitive abilities: 100 years after Spearman's (1904) "'General Intelligence,' Objectively Determined and Measured." *Journal of Personality and Social Psychology, 86*(1), 96–111.

Lucassen, N., et al. (2011). The association between paternal sensitivity and infant–father attachment security: A meta-analysis of three decades of research. *Journal of Family Psychology, 25*(6), 986–992.

Luciano, M., Kirk, K. M., Heath, A. C., & Martin, N. G. (2005). The genetics of tea and coffee drinking and preference for source of caffeine in a large community sample of Australian twins. *Addiction, 100*(10), 1510–1517.

Luders, E., Thompson, P. M., & Toga, A. W. (2010). The development of the corpus callosum in the healthy human brain. *The Journal of Neuroscience, 30*(33), 10985–10990.

Lundstrom, S., et al. (2012). Autism spectrum disorders and autisticlike traits. *Archives of General Psychiatry, 69*(1), 46–52.

Lustig, S. L. (2011). Chaos and its influence on children's development: An ecological perspective. In G. W. Evans, & T. D. Wachs (Eds.). *Decade of behavior (science conference)* (pp. 239–251). Washington, DC: American Psychological Association.

Lykken, D. T. (2006). The mechanism of emergenesis. *Genes, Brain & Behavior, 5*(4), 306–310.

Lykken, D. T., & Csikszentmihalyi, M. (2001). Happiness: Stuck with what you've got? *Psychologist, 14*(9), 470–472.

Lynam, D. R., Caspi, A., Moffitt, T. E., Loeber, R., & Stouthamer-Loeber, M. (2007). Longitudinal evidence that psychopathy scores in early adolescence predict adult psychopathy. *Journal of Abnormal Psychology, 116*(1), 155–165.

Lynch, J. B., et al. (2011). The breadth and potency of passively acquired human immunodeficiency virus Type 1-specific neutralizing antibodies do not correlate with the risk of infant infection. *Journal of Virology, 85*(11), 5252–5261.

Lynne, S. D., Graber, J. A., Nichols, T. R., Brooks-Gunn, J., & Botvin, G. J. (2007). Links between pubertal timing, peer influences, and externalizing behaviors among urban students followed through middle school. *Journal of Adolescent Health, 40*(2), 181.e7–181.e13.

Lyon, G. R., Shaywitz, S. E., & Shaywitz, B. A. (2003). A definition of dyslexia. *Annals of Dyslexia, 53*, 1–14.

Maccoby, E. E. (2000). Perspectives on gender development. *International Journal of Behavioral Development, 24*(4), 398–406.

Maccoby, E. E., & Jacklin, C. N. (1974). *The psychology of sex differences.* Stanford, CA: Stanford University Press.

Macfarlane, A. (1975). Olfaction in the development of social preferences in the human neonate. In M. A. Hofer (Ed.), *Parent–infant interaction.* Amsterdam: Elsevier.

Macfarlane, A. (1977). *The psychology of childbirth.* Cambridge, MA: Harvard University Press.

Mackic-Magyar, J., & McCracken, J. (2004). Review of autism spectrum disorders: A research review for practitioners. *Journal of Child and Adolescent Psychopharmacology, 14*(1), 17–18.

Mackner, L. M., Black, M. M., & Starr, R. H., Jr. (2003). Cognitive development of children in poverty with failure to thrive: A prospective study through age 6. *Journal of Child Psychology and Psychiatry and Allied Disciplines, 44*(5), 743–751.

Maclean, A. M., Walker, L. J., & Matsuba, M. K. (2004). Transcendence and the moral self: Identity integration, religion, and moral life. *Journal for the Scientific Study of Religion, 43*(3), 429–437.

Madigan, S., Atkinson, L, Laurin, K., & Benoit, D. (2013). Attachment and internalizing behavior in early childhood: A meta-analysis. *Developmental Psychology, 49*(4), 672–689.

Madon, S., et al. (2001). Am I as you see me or do you see me as I am? Self-fulfilling prophecies and self-verification. *Personality and Social Psychology Bulletin, 27*(9), 1214–1224.

Madson, L., & Trafimow, D. (2001). Gender comparisons in the private, collective, and allocentric selves. *Journal of Social Psychology, 141*(4), 551–559.

Magnuson, K. A., Meyers, M. K., Ruhm, C. J., & Waldfogel, J. (2004). Inequality in preschool education and school readiness. *American Educational Research Journal, 41*(1), 115–157.

Maimburg, R. D., & Væth, M. (2006). Perinatal risk factors and infantile autism. *Acta Psychiatrica Scandinavica, 114*(4), 257–264.

Malaspina, D. (2009). Cited in L. Belkin (2009, April 5), Your old man, *The New York Times Magazine.*

Malekoff, A. (2004). *Group work with adolescents* (2nd ed.). New York: Guilford.

Malone, P. S., et al. (2004). Divorce and child behavior problems: Applying latent change score models to life event data. *Structural Equation Modeling, 11*(3), 401–423.

Maneschi, M. L., Maddalena, F., & Bersani, G. (2006). The role of genetic factors in developmental dyslexia. Convergence between schizophrenia and other psychiatric disorders. *Rivista di Psichiatria, 41*(2), 81–92.

Maraj, B., & Bonertz, C. M. (2007). Verbal-motor learning in children with Down syndrome. *Journal of Sports & Exercise Psychology, 29*(pS108).

Marcia, J. E. (1991). Identity and self-development. In R. M. Lerner, A. C. Petersen & J. Brooks-Gunn (Eds.), *Encyclopedia of adolescence.* New York: Garland.

Marcia, J. E. (2002). Adolescence, identity, and the Bernardone family. *Identity: An International Journal of Theory and Research, 2*(3), 199–209.

Marcia, J. E. (2010). Life transitions and stress in the context of psychosocial development. In T. W. Miller (Ed.). *Handbook of stressful transitions across the lifespan, Part 1* (pp. 19–34). New York: Springer Science+Business Media, LLC.

Marcolin, A. L. V., Cardin, S. P., & Magalhães, C. S. (2009). Muscle strength assessment among children and adolescents with growing pains and joint hypermobility. *Revista Brasileira de Fisioterapia, 13*(2). doi:10.1590/S1413-35552009005000006.

Marean, G. C., Werner, L. A., & Kuhl, P. K. (1992). Vowel categorization by very young infants. *Developmental Psychology, 28*, 396–405.

Markova, G., & Legerstee, M. (2006). Contingency, imitation, and affect sharing: Foundations of infants' social awareness. *Developmental Psychology, 42*(1), 132–141.

Markovits, H., & Lortie-Forgues, H. (2011). Conditional reasoning with false premises facilitates the transition between familiar and abstract reasoning. *Child Development, 82*(2), 646–660.

Markus, H., & Kitayama, S. (1991). Culture and the self. *Psychological Review, 98*(2), 224–253.

Marlatt, G. A. (2010). Update on harm-reduction policy and intervention research. *Annual Review of Clinical Psychology, 6*, 591–606.

Marley, S. C., & Carbonneau, K. J. (2014). Theoretical perspectives and empirical evidence relevant to classroom instruction with manipulatives. *Educational Psychology Review, 26*, 1–7.

Marlier, L., & Schaal, B. (2005). Human newborns prefer human milk: Conspecific milk odor is attractive without postnatal exposure. *Child Development, 76*(1), 155–168.

Marshall, K. (2006). Converging gender roles. *Perspectives, 7* (No. 75-001-XIE). Ottawa, Ontario: Statistics Canada. Retrieved from http://www.statcan.gc.ca/bsolc/olc-cel/olc-cel?lang=eng&catno=75-001-X20061079268.

Marsiglio, W. (2004). When stepfathers claim stepchildren: A conceptual analysis. *Journal of Marriage and Family, 66*(1), 22–39.

Martel, M. M., et al. (2011). The dopamine receptor D4 gene (DRD4) moderates family environmental effects on ADHD. (2011). *Journal of Abnormal Child Psychology, 39*(1), 1–10.

Martel, M-J., et al. (2008). Determinants of the incidence of childhood asthma: A two-stage case-control study. *American Journal of Epidemiology.* doi:10.1093/aje/kwn309.

Martin, A., Ryan, R. M., & Brooks-Gunn, J. (2010). When fathers' supportiveness matters most: Maternal and paternal parenting and children's school readiness. *Journal of Family Psychology, 24,* 145–155.

Martin, C. L., & Dinella, L. M. (2011). Congruence between gender stereotypes and activity preference in self-identified tomboys and non-tomboys. *Archives of Sexual Behavior.* doi:10.1007/s10508-011-9786-5.

Martin, C. L., & Ruble, D. (2004). Children's search for gender cues: Cognitive perspectives on gender development. *Current Directions in Psychological Science, 13*(2), 67–70.

Martin, C. L., Ruble, D. N., & Szkrybalo, J. (2002). Cognitive theories of early gender development. *Psychological Bulletin, 128*(6), 903–933.

Martin, J., & Sokol, B. (2011). Generalized others and imaginary audience: A neo-Meadian approach to adolescent egocentrism. *New Ideas in Psychology, 29*(3), 364–375.

Martinez, G., Abma, J., & Copen, C. (2010). *Educating teenagers about sex in the United States.* NCHS data brief no. 44. Hyattsville, MD: National Center for Health Statistics.

Martinez, G., Copen, C. E., & Abma, J. C. (2011). Teenagers in the United States: Sexual activity, contraceptive use, and childbearing, 2006–2010. National Survey of Family Growth. National Center for Health Statistics. *Vital and Health Statistics, 23*(31).

Martínez, I., Musitu, G., Garcia, J. F., & Camino, L. (2003). A cross-cultural analysis of the effects of family socialization on self-concept: Spain and Brazil. *Psicologia Educação Cultura, 7*(2), 239–259.

Masi, G., Mucci, M., & Millepiedi, S. (2001). Separation anxiety disorder in children and adolescents: Epidemiology, diagnosis, and management. *CNS Drugs, 15*(2), 93–104.

Massaro, A. N., Rothbaum, R., & Aly, H. (2006). Fetal brain development: The role of maternal nutrition, exposures and behaviors. *Journal of Pediatric Neurology, 4*(1), 1–9.

Mathews, T. J., & MacDorman, M. F. (2007). Infant mortality statistics from the 2004 period linked birth/infant death data set. *National Vital Statistics Reports, 55*(14). Hyattsville, MD: National Center for Health Statistics.

Matlin, M. W. (2008). *The psychology of women* (8th ed.). Belmont, CA: Thomson/Wadsworth.

Mattanah, J. F., Pratt, M. W., Cowan, P. A., & Cowan, C. P. (2005). Authoritative parenting, parental scaffolding of long-division mathematics, and children's academic competence in fourth grade. *Applied Developmental Psychology, 26,* 85–106.

Mau, W. C., & Lynn, R. (2000). Gender difference in homework, and test scores in mathematics, reading and science at tenth and twelfth grade. *Psychology, Evolution, & Gender, 2*(2), 119–125.

Maughan, B. (2011). Family and systemic influences. In D. Skuse, H. Bruce, L. Dowdney, & D. Mrazek (Eds.). *Child psychology and psychiatry: Frameworks for practice* (2nd ed.) (pp. 1–7). Hoboken, NJ: Wiley.

Maundeni, T. (2000). The consequences of parental separation and divorce for the economic, social and emotional circumstances of children in Botswana. *Childhood: A Global Journal of Child Research, 7*(2), 213–223.

Maurer, D. M., & Maurer, C. E. (1976, October). Newborn babies see better than you think. *Psychology Today,* pp. 85–88.

Maurer, D. M., Lewis, T. L., Brent, H. P., & Levin, A. V. (1999). Rapid improvement in the acuity of infants after visual input. *Science, 286*(5437), 108–110.

Mayer, J. D., Salovey, P., Caruso, D. R., & Cherkasskiy, L. (2011). Emotional intelligence. In R. J. Sternberg & S. J. Kaufman (Eds.), *The Cambridge handbook of intelligence* (pp. 528–549). New York: Cambridge University Press.

Mayer, R. E. (2011). Intelligence and achievement. In R. J. Sternberg & S. J. Kaufman (Eds.), *The Cambridge handbook of intelligence* (pp. 738–747). New York: Cambridge University Press.

Mayer, S. J. (2008). Dewey's dynamic integration of Vygotsky and Piaget. *Education and Culture, 24*(2), Article 3. Available at http://docs.lib.purdue.edu/eandc/vol24/iss2/art3.

Mayes, L. C., & Ward, A. (2003). Principles of neurobehavioral teratology. In D. Cicchetti & E. Walker (Eds.), *Neurodevelopmental mechanisms in psychopathology* (pp. 3–33). New York: Cambridge University Press.

Maynard, A. E., Subrahmanyam, K., & Greenfield, P. M. (2005). Technology and the development of intelligence: From the loom to the computer. In R. J. Sternberg & D. D. Preiss (Eds.), *Intelligence and technology: The impact of tools on the nature and development of human abilities. The educational psychology series* (pp. 29–53). Mahwah, NJ: Erlbaum.

Mayor, J., & Plunkett, K. (2010). A neurocomputational account of taxonomic responding and fast mapping in early word learning. *Psychological Review, 117*(1), 1–31.

Mazei-Robison, M. S., Couch, R. S., Shelton, R. C., Stein, M. A., & Blakely, R. D. (2005). Sequence variation in the human dopamine transporter gene in children with attention deficit hyperactivity disorder. *Neuropharmacology, 49*(6), 724–736.

McCain, M. N., Mustard, J. F., & McCuaig, K. (2011). Early years study 3: Making decisions, taking action. Toronto: Margaret & Wallace McCain Family Foundation.

McCain, M., & Mustard, J. F. (1999). Early years study: Reversing the real brain drain. Toronto, ON: Ontario

McCain, M., Mustard, J. F., & Shanker, S. (2007). Early years study 2: Putting science into action. Toronto, ON: Council for Early Childhood Development.

McCall, R. B. (1977). Childhood IQ's as predictors of adult educational and occupational status. *Science, 197*(4302), 482–483.

McCall, R. B., Applebaum, M. I., & Hogarty, P. S. (1973). *Developmental changes in mental performance.* Monographs of the Society for Research in Child Development, 38(3, ser. 150).

McCardle, P., Colombo, J., & Freud, L. (2009). Measuring language in infancy. In J. Colombo, P. McCardle & L. Freud (Eds.), *Infant pathways to language: Methods, models, and research disorders* (pp. 1–12). New York: Psychology Press.

McCartney, K., Owen, M. T., Booth, C. L., Clarke-Stewart, K. A., & Vandell, D. L. (2004). Testing a maternal attachment model of behavior problems in early childhood. *Journal of Child Psychology and Psychiatry, 45*(4), 765–778.

McCarty, C., Prawitz, A. D., Derscheid, L. E., & Montgomery, B. (2011). Perceived safety and teen risk taking in online chat sites. *Cyberpsychology, Behavior, and Social Networking, 14*(3), 169–174.

McCauley, J. L., Ruggiero, K. L., Resnick, H. S., & Kilpatrick, D. G. (2010). Incapacitated, forcible, and drug/alcohol-facilitated rape in relation to binge drinking, marijuana use, and illicit drug use: A national survey. *Journal of Traumatic Stress, 23*(1), 132–140.

McCrae, R. R., et al. (2000). Nature over nurture: Temperament, personality, and life span development. *Journal of Personality and Social Psychology, 78*(1), 173–186.

McCrink, K., & Wynn, K. (2004). Large-number addition and subtraction by 9-month-old infants. *Psychological Science, 15*(11), 776–781.

McGlaughlin, A., & Grayson, A. (2001). Crying in the first year of infancy: Patterns and prevalence. *Journal of Reproductive and Infant Psychology, 19*(1), 47–59.

McGraw, L. A., & Young, L. J. (2010). The prairie vole: An emerging model organism for understanding the social brain. *Trends in Neuroscience, 33*(2), 103–109.

McGreal, C. (2009, July 20). Teen pregnancy and disease rates rose sharply during Bush years, agency finds. *The Guardian*. Available at http://www.guardian.co.uk/world/2009/jul/20/bush-teen-pregnancy-cdc-report.

McGue, M., Bouchard, T. J., Jr., Iacono, W. G., & Lykken, D. T. (1993). Behavioral genetics of cognitive ability: A life-span perspective. In R. Plomin & G. E. McClearn (Eds.), *Nature, nurture & psychology* (pp. 59–76). Washington, DC: American Psychological Association.

McHale, S. M., Kim, J-Y., & Whiteman, S. D. (2006). Sibling relationships in childhood and adolescence. In P. Noller & J. A. Feeney (Eds.), *Close relationships: Functions, forms and processes* (pp. 127–149). New York: Psychology Press/Taylor & Francis.

McKay, A. (2004). Oral sex among teenagers: Research, discourse, and education. *The Canadian Journal of Human Sexuality*, 201–203.

McKay, A. (2004). Sexual health education in the schools: Questions and answers. *The Canadian Journal of Human Sexuality, 13*(3/4), 129–142.

McKay, A., Pietrusiak, M. A., & Holowaty, P. (1998). Parents' opinions and attitudes toward sexuality education in the schools. *The Canadian Journal of Human Sexuality, 6*, 29–28.

McLafferty, C. L., Jr. (2006). Examining unproven assumptions of Galton's nature–nurture paradigm. *American Psychologist, 61*(2), 177–178.

McLoyd, V. C. (1998). Socioeconomic disadvantage and child development. *American Psychologist, 53*(2), 185–204.

McWayne, C., Downer, J. T., Campos, R., & Harris, D. (2013). Father involvement during early childhood and its association with children's early learning: A meta-analyses. *Early Education & Development, 24*(6), 898–922.

Meaney, K. S., Dornier, L. A., & Owens, M. S. (2002). Sex-role stereotyping for selected sport and physical activities across age groups. *Perceptual and Motor Skills, 94*(3), 743–749.

Meaney, M. J. (2010). Epigenetics and the biological definition of Gene x Environment interactions. *Child Development, 81*, 41–79.

Medland, S. E., et al. (2009). Genetic influences on handedness: Data from 25,732 Australian and Dutch twin families. *Neuropsychologia, 47*(2), 330–337.

Meek, J. Y. (Ed.). (2011). *American Academy of Pediatrics New Mother's Guide to Breastfeeding* (2nd ed.). New York: Bantam Books.

Mellon, M. W. (2006). Enuresis and encopresis. In G. G. Bea, & K. M. Minke (Eds.), *Children's needs III: Development, prevention, and intervention* (pp. 1041–1053). Washington, DC: National Association of School Psychologists.

Mellon, M. W., & Houts, A. C. (2006). Nocturnal enuresis. In J. E. Fisher & W. T. O'Donohue (Eds.), *Practitioner's guide to evidence-based psychotherapy* (pp. 432–441). New York: Springer Science/Business Media.

Meltzoff, A. N. (1988). Infant imitation and memory: Nine-month-olds in immediate and deferred tests. *Child Development, 59*(1), 217–225.

Meltzoff, A. N. (2007). Infants' causal learning: Intervention, observation, imitation. In A. Gopnik & L. Schulz (Eds.), *Causal learning: Psychology, philosophy, and computation* (pp. 37–47). New York: Oxford University Press.

Meltzoff, A. N. (2010). Social cognition and the origins of imitation, empathy, and theory of mind. In U. Goswami (Ed.), *The Wiley–Blackwell handbook of childhood cognitive development.* (2nd ed.) (pp. 49–75). Chichester, West Sussex, UK: Wiley–Blackwell.

Meltzoff, A. N., & Brooks, R. (2009). Social cognition and language: The role of gaze following in early word learning. In J. Colombo, P. McCardle, & L. Freund (Eds.), *Infant pathways to language: Methods, models, and research disorders* (pp. 169–194). New York: Psychology Press.

Meltzoff, A. N., Kuhl, P. K., Movellan, J., & Sejnowski, T. J. (2009). Foundations for a new science of learning. *Science, 325*, 284–288.

Meltzoff, A. N., & Prinz, W. (Eds.). (2002). *The imitative mind: Development, evolution, and brain bases.* New York: Cambridge University Press.

Mendelsohn, F., & Warren, M. (2010). Anorexia, bulimia, and the female athlete triad: Evaluation and management. *Endocrinology and Metabolism Clinics of North America, 39*(1), 155–167.

Mendez, L. M. R. (2000). Gender roles and achievement-related choices: A comparison of early adolescent girls in gifted and general education programs. *Journal for the Education of the Gifted, 24*(2), 149–169.

Mennella, J. A. (2001). Regulation of milk intake after exposure to alcohol in mothers' milk. *Alcoholism: Clinical and Experimental Research, 25*(4), 590–593.

Mennella, J. A., & Garcia, P. L. (2000). Children's hedonic response to the smell of alcohol: Effects of parental drinking habits. *Alcoholism: Clinical & Experimental Research, 24*(8), 1167–1171.

Mennella, J., Turnbull, B., Ziegler, P., & Martinez. H. (2005). Infant feeding practices and early flavor experiences in Mexican infants. *Journal of the American Dietetic Association, 105*(6), 908–915.

Mercken, L., Steglich, C., Knibbe, R., & Vries, H. (2012). Dynamics of friendship networks and alcohol use in early and mid-adolescence. *Journal of Studies in Alcohol and Drugs, 73*(1), 99–110.

Mesman, J., Bongers, I. L., & Koot, H. M. (2001). Preschool developmental pathways to preadolescent internalizing and externalizing problems. *Journal of Child Psychology and Psychiatry and Allied Disciplines, 42*(5), 679–689.

Metcalfe, J. S., et al. (2005). Development of somatosensory-motor integration: An event-related analysis of infant posture in the first year of independent walking. *Developmental Psychobiology, 46*(1), 19–35.

Meyer, P. (2009). Evaluation and management of gynecomastia. *Revue Médicale Suisse, 5*(198), 783–787.

Mezzacappa, E. S., Kelsey, R. M., & Katkin, E. S. (2005). Breast feeding, bottle feeding, and maternal autonomic responses to stress. *Journal of Psychosomatic Research, 58*(4), 351–365.

Miklos, E. A., Brahler, C. J., Baer, J. T., & Dolan, P. (2004). Dietary deficiencies and excesses: A sample of African American mothers and daughters eligible for nutrition assistance programs. *Family and Community Health, 27*(2), 123–129.

Mikulincer, M., & Shaver, P. R. (2001). Attachment theory and intergroup bias: Evidence that priming the secure base schema attenuates negative reactions to out-groups. *Journal of Personality and Social Psychology, 81*(1), 97–115.

Millar, W. S. (1990). Span of integration for delayed-reward contingency learning in 6- to 8-month-old infants. In A. Diamond (Ed.), *The development and neural bases of higher cognitive functions.* New York: New York Academy of Sciences.

Miller, C. F., Trautner, H. M., & Ruble, D. N. (2006). The role of gender stereotypes in children's preferences and behavior. In L. Balter & C. S. Tamis-LeMonda (Eds.), *Child psychology: A handbook of contemporary issues* (2nd ed.) (pp. 293–323). New York: Psychology Press.

Miller, F. A., Christensen, R., Giacomini, M., & Robert, J. S. (2008). Duty to disclose what? Querying the putative obligation to return research results to participants. *Journal of Medical Ethics, 34*(3), 210–213.

Miller, G. A. (1956). The magical number seven, plus or minus two: Some limits on our capacity to process information. *Psychological Review, 63*, 81–97.

Miller, P. H. (2010). In U. Goswami (Ed.), *The Wiley–Blackwell handbook of childhood cognitive development.* (2nd ed.) (pp. 649–672). Chichester, West Sussex, UK: Wiley–Blackwell.

Miniño, A. M. (2010). Mortality among teenagers aged 12–19 years: United States, 1999–2006. Centers for Disease Control and Prevention. NCHS data brief. Number 37, May 2010. http://www.cdc.gov/nchs/data/databriefs/db37.htm. Accessed September 19, 2012.

Minnes, S., Lang, A., & Singer, L. (2011). Prenatal tobacco, marijuana, stimulant, and opiate exposure: Outcomes and practice implications. *Addiction Science & Clinical Practice, 6*(1), 57–70.

Miranda, A., & Presentacion, M. J. (2000). Efectos de un tratamiento cognitivo-conductual en ninos con trastorno por deficit de atencion con hiperactividad, agresivos y no agresivos: Cambio clinicamente significativo. *Infancia y Aprendizaje, 92*, 51–70.

Miscarriage. (2007, January 11). Available at http://www.nlm.nih.gov/medlineplus/ency/article/001488.htm. Accessed February 23, 2007.

Mischo, C. (2005). Promoting perspective coordination by dilemma discussion. The effectiveness of classroom group discussion on interpersonal negotiation strategies of 12-year-old students. *Social Psychology of Education, 8*(1), 41–63.

Mishna, F., Saini, M., & Solomon, S. (2009). Ongoing and online: Children and youth's perceptions of cyber bullying. *Children and Youth Services Review*, in press.

Mishra, G. D., Cooper, R., Tom, S. E., & Kuh, D. (2009). Early life circumstances and their impact on menarche and menopause. *Women's Health, 5*(2), 175–190.

Miyake, Y., et al. (2010). Neural processing of negative word stimuli concerning body image in patients with eating disorders: An fMRI study. *NeuroImage, 50*(3), 1333–1339.

Moffitt, T. E. (2005). The new look at behavioural genetics in developmental psychopathology: Gene-environment interplay in antisocial behaviors. *Psychological Bulletin, 131*, 533–554.

Molenaar, P. C. M., & Newell, K. M. (Eds.). (2010). Individual pathways of change: Statistical models for analyzing learning and development. Washington DC: American Psychological Association.

Molfese, V. J., DiLalla, L. F., & Bunce, D. (1997). Prediction of the intelligence test scores of 3- to 8-year-old children by home environment, socioeconomic status, and biomedical risks. *Merrill-Palmer Quarterly, 43*(2), 219–234.

Molinari, L., & Corsaro, W. A. (2000). Le relazioni amicali nella scuola dell'infanzia e nella scuola elementare: Uno studio longitudinale. *Eta Evolutiva, 67*, 40–51.

Montemayor, R., & Eisen, M. (1977). The development of self-conceptions from childhood to adolescence. *Developmental Psychology, 13*, 314–319.

Montero, I., & De Dios, M. J. (2006). Vygotsky was right. An experimental approach to the relationship between private speech and task performance. *Estudios de Psicología, 27*(2), 175–189.

Moon, M. (2011). The effects of divorce on children: Married and divorced parents' perspectives. *Journal of Divorce & Remarriage, 52*(5), 344–349.

Moon, R. Y., et al. (2011). Pacifier use and SIDS: Evidence for a consistently reduced risk. *Maternal and Child Health Journal*. doi:10.1007/s10995-011-0793-x.

Moore, D. S. (2007). A very little bit of knowledge: Re-evaluating the meaning of the heritability of IQ. *Human Development, 49*(6), 347–353.

Moore, L. L., et al. (1991). Influence of parents' physical activity levels on activity levels of young children. *Journal of Pediatrics, 118*, 215–219.

Moreno, M., Trigo, J. M., Escuredo, L., Rodriguez de Fonseca, F., & Navarro, M. (2003). Perinatal exposure to Delta-sup-9tetrahydrocannabinol increases presynaptic dopamine D-sub-2 receptor sensitivity: A behavioral study in rats. *Pharmacology, Biochemistry and Behavior, 75*(3), 565–575.

Moreno-Briseño, P., et al. (2010). Sex-related differences in motor learning and performance. *Brain and Behavioral Functions, 6*, 74.

Morine, K. A., et al. (2011). Relational aggression in preschool students: An exploration of the variables of sex, age, and siblings. *Child Development Research*. doi:10.1155/2011/931720.

Morley, J. E., & Perry, H. M., III. (2003). Androgens and women at the menopause and beyond. *Journals of Gerontology, Series A: Biological Sciences and Medical Sciences, 58A*(5), 409–416.

Morrell, J., & Steele, H. (2003). The role of attachment security, temperament, maternal perception, and care-giving behavior in persistent infant sleeping problems. *Infant Mental Health Journal, 24*(5), 447–468.

Morrison, D. R., & Coiro, M. J. (1999). Parental conflict and marital disruption: Do children benefit when high-conflict marriages are dissolved? *Journal of Marriage and the Family, 61*(3), 626–637.

Morrison, E. S. (1980). *Growing up sexual*. New York: Van Nostrand Co.

Morton, S. M. B. (2006). Maternal nutrition and fetal growth and development. In P. Gluckman & M. Hanson (Eds.), *Developmental origins of health and disease* (pp. 98–129). New York: Cambridge University Press.

Moses, L. J., & Flavell, J. H. (1990). Inferring false beliefs from actions and reactions. *Child Development, 61*, 929–945.

Moshman, D. (2011). *Adolescent rationality and development: Cognition, morality, and identity* (3rd ed.). New York: Psychology Press.

Mosholder, A. D. (2004). Cited in G. Harris (2004, September 24), *Warnings called likely on drug risk for suicide*. Available at http://www.nytimes.com.

Mottola, M. F., Giroux, I., Gratton, R., Hammond, J. A., Hanley, A., Harris, S., et al. (2010). Nutrition and exercise prevents excess weight gain in overweight pregnant women. *Medicine and Science in Sports and Exercise, 42*, 265–272.

Mowrer, O. H., & Mowrer, W. M. (1938). Enuresis—A method for its study and treatment. *American Journal of Orthopsychiatry, 8*, 436–459.

Moylan, C. A., et al. (2010). The effects of child abuse and exposure to domestic violence on adolescent internalizing and externalizing behavior problems. *Journal of Family Violence, 25*(1), 53–63.

Muir, D. W., & Hains, S. M. J. (1993). Infant sensitivity to perturbations in adult facial, vocal, tactile, and contingent stimulation during face-to-face interactions. In B. de Boysson-Bardies, S. de Schonen, P. W. Jusczyk, P. F. MacNeilage & J. Morton (Eds.), *Changes in speech and face processing in infancy: A glimpse at developmental mechanisms of cognition*. Dordrecht, Netherlands: Kluwer Academic.

Muir, G. D. (2000). Early ontogeny of locomotor behaviour: A comparison between altricial and precocial animals. *Brain Research Bulletin, 53*(5), 719–726.

Mulcahy, K., et al. (2008). Social anxiety and the severity and typography of stuttering in adolescents. *Journal of Fluency Disorders, 33*(4), 6–19.

Munck, P., et al. (2010). Cognitive outcome at 2 years of age in Finnish infants with very low birth weight born between 2001 and 2006. *Acta Paediatrica, 99*(3), 359–366.

Murata, A., & Fuson, K. (2006). Teaching as assisting individual constructive paths within an interdependent class learning zone: Japanese first graders learning to add using 10. *Journal for Research in Mathematics Education, 37*(5), 421–456.

Muris, P., & Field, A. P. (2011). The "normal" development of fear. In W. K. Silverman, & A. P. Field (Eds.), *Anxiety disorders in children and adolescents* (pp. 76–89). New York: Cambridge University Press.

Murk, W., Risnes, K. R., & Bracken, M. B. (2011). Prenatal or early-life exposure to antibiotics and risk of childhood asthma: A systematic review. *Pediatrics, 127*(6), 1125–1138.

Murphy, K. E., et al. (2011). Maternal side-effects after multiple courses of antenatal corticosteroids (MACS): The three-month follow-up of women in the Randomized Controlled Trial of MACS for Preterm Birth Study. *Journal of Obstetrics and Gynecology, Canada, 33*(9), 909–921.

Murphy, T. K., Bengtson, M. A., Tan, J. Y., Carbonell, E., & Levin, G. M. (2000). Selective serotonin reuptake inhibitors in the treatment of paediatric anxiety disorders: A review. *International Clinical Psychopharmacology, 15*(Suppl. 2), S47–S63.

Murray, B. (1998). Survey reveals concerns of today's girls. *APA Monitor, 29*(10).

Murray, B. A. (2006). Hunting the elusive phoneme: A phoneme-direct model for learning phoneme awareness. In K. A. Dougherty Stahl & M. C. McKenna (Eds.), *Reading research at work: Foundations of effective practice* (pp. 114–125). New York: Guilford.

Muuss, R. E. (1996). *Theories of adolescence* (6th ed.). Toronto, ON: McGraw Hill.

Muzzatti, B., & Agnoli, F. (2007). Gender and mathematics: Attitudes and stereotype threat susceptibility in Italian children. *Developmental Psychology, 43*(3), 747–759.

Nadeau, L., et al. (2003). Extremely premature and very low birthweight infants: A double hazard population? *Social Development, 12*(2), 235–248.

Nagin, D. S., & Tremblay, R. E. (2001). Parental and early childhood predictors of persistent physical aggression in boys from kindergarten to high school. *Archives of General Psychiatry, 58*(4), 389–394.

Naimi, T., Nelson, D., & Brewer, R. (2010). The intensity of binge alcohol consumption among U.S. adults. *American Journal of Preventive Medicine, 38*(2), 201–207.

Nair, H., & Murray, A. D. (2005). Predictors of attachment security in preschool children from intact and divorced families. *The Journal of Genetic Psychology, 166*, 245–263.

Nakkula, M. J., & Nikitopoulos, C. E. (2001). Negotiation training and interpersonal development: An exploratory study of early adolescents in Argentina. *Adolescence, 36*(141), 1–20.

Namiiro, F. B., Mugalu, J., McAdams, R. M., & Ndeezi, G. (2012). Poor birth weight recovery among low birth weight/preterm infants following hospital discharge in Kampala, Uganda. *BMC Pregnancy and Childbirth, 12*(1). doi:0.1186/1471-2393-12-1.

Narusyte, J., et al. (2008). Testing different types of genotype–environment correlation: An extended children-of-twins model. *Developmental Psychology, 44*(6), 1591–1603.

National Campaign to Prevent Teen and Unplanned Pregnancy. (2012a). Preventing unplanned and teen pregnancy: Why it matters. http://www.thenationalcampaign.org/why-it-matters/default.aspx. Accessed September 17, 2012.

National Campaign to Prevent Teen and Unplanned Pregnancy. (2012b). *Counting it up: The public costs of teen childbearing: Key data.* Washington, DC: National Campaign to Prevent Teen and Unplanned Pregnancy. Available from http://www.thenationalcampaign.org/costs/pdf/counting-it-up/key-data.pdf. Accessed September 26, 2012.

National Campaign to Prevent Teen Pregnancy. (2003, September 30). *Teens say parents most influence their sexual decisions: New polling data and "Tips for Parents" released.* Available at http://www.teenpregnancy.org/about/announcements/pr/2003/release9_30_03.asp.

National Center for Children in Poverty. (2012, February). *Basic facts about low-income children, 2010.* The Trustees of Columbia University in the City of New York: http://www.nccp.org/publications/pub_1049.html. Accessed February 17, 2012.

National Center for Education Statistics (2011). Digest of Education Statistics. Bachelor's, master's, and doctor's degrees conferred by degree-granting institutions, by sex of student, 2009–2010. http://nces.ed.gov/programs/digest/d11/tables/dt11_290.asp. Accessed September 18, 2012.

National Center for Education Statistics. (2007, June). *Dropout rates in the United States: 2005.* Available at http://nces.ed.gov/pubs2007/dropout05. Accessed July 20, 2007.

National Center for Education Statistics. (2010). *The condition of education 2010.* Washington, DC: Author. Available at http://nces.ed.gov/pubsearch/pubsinfo.asp?pubid=2010028. Accessed September 26, 2012.

National Clearinghouse on Family Violence. (2006). *Child maltreatment in Canada: Overview paper.* Prepared by S. Jack, C. Munn, C. Cheng, & H. MacMillan. Ottawa: Public Health Agency of Canada.

National Mathematics Advisory Panel. (2008). *Foundations for success: The final report of the National Mathematics Advisory Panel.* Washington, DC: U.S. Department of Education.

National Sleep Foundation. (2011). Children and sleep. http://www.sleepfoundation.org/article/sleep-topics/children-and-sleep. Accessed February 22, 2012.

National Sleep Foundation. (2012a). Children and sleep. http://www.sleepfoundation.org/article/sleep-topics/children-and-sleep. Accessed December 10, 2012.

National Sleep Foundation. (2012b). Adolescent sleep needs and patterns. http://www.sleepfoundation.org/article/hot-topics/adolescent-sleep-needs-and-patterns. Accessed December 10, 2012.

Nazzi, T., & Gopnik, A. (2000). A shift in children's use of perceptual and causal cues to categorization. *Developmental Science, 3*(4), 389–396.

Ndekha, M. (2008). Kwashiorkor and severe acute malnutrition in childhood. *The Lancet, 371*(9626), 1748.

Nduati, R., et al. (2000). Effect of breastfeeding and formula feeding on transmission of HIV-1. *Journal of the American Medical Association, 283*, 1167–1174.

Needlman, R. (2011). Chaos and its influence on children's development: An ecological perspective. *Journal of Developmental Behavioral Pediatrics, 32*(3), 275.

Neiss, M. B., Sedikides, C., & Stevenson, J. (2006). Genetic influences on level and stability of self-esteem. *Self and Identity, 5*(3), 247–266.

Neisser, U., et al. (1996). Intelligence: Knowns and unknowns. *American Psychologist, 51*, 77–101.

Nelson, C. A., & Luciana, M. (Eds.). (2001). *Handbook of developmental cognitive neuroscience.* Cambridge, MA: MIT Press.

Nelson, C. A., de Haan, M., & Thomas, K. M. (2006). *Neuroscience of cognitive development: The role of experience and the developing brain.* Hoboken, NJ: Wiley.

Nelson, K. (1973). *Structure and strategy in learning to talk.* Monographs for the Society for Research in Child Development, 38(1–2, ser. 149).

Nelson, K. (1981). Individual differences in language development: Implications for development of language. *Developmental Psychology, 17*, 170–187.

Nelson, K. (2006). Advances in pragmatic developmental theory: The case of language acquisition. *Human Development, 49*(3), 184–188.

Nelson, K., & Fivush, R. (2004). The emergence of autobiographical memory: A social cultural developmental theory. *Psychological Review, 111*(2), 486–511.

Nelson, L. J., Hart, C. H., & Evans, C. A. (2008). Solitary-functional play and solitary-pretend play: Another look at the construct of solitary-active behavior using playground observations. *Social Development, 17*(4), 812–831.

Nesdale, D., & Lambert, A. (2007). Effects of experimentally manipulated peer rejection on children's negative affect, self-esteem, and maladaptive social behavior. *International Journal of Behavioral Development, 31*(2), 115–122.

Neveus, T. (2011). Nocturnal enuresis. *Pediatric Nephrology, 26*, 1207–1214.

Newland, L. A., & Coyl, D. D. (2010). Father's role as attachment figures: An interview with Sir Richard Bowlby. *Early Child Development and Care, 180*(1), 25–32.

Newman, K., Harrison, L., Dashiff, C., & Davies, S. (2008). Relationships between parenting styles and risk behaviors in adolescent health: An integrative literature review. *Revista Latino-Americana de Enfermagem, 16*(1). doi:10.1590/S0104-11692008000100022.

Newman, R., Ratner, N. B., Jusczyk, A. M., Jusczyk, P. W., & Dow, K. A. (2006). Infants' early ability to segment the conversational speech signal predicts later language development: A retrospective analysis. *Developmental Psychology, 42*(4), 643–655.

Newport, E. L. (1992, June). *Critical periods and creolization: Effects of maturational state and input on the acquisition of language.* Paper presented at the meeting of American Psychological Society, San Diego, CA.

Nguyen, H. V., et al. (2012). Risky sex: Interactions among ethnicity, sexual sensation seeking, sexual inhibition, and sexual excitation. *Archives of Sexual Behavior,* doi:10.1007/s10508-012-9904-z.

NHLBI (National Heart Lung and Blood Institute). (2011). http://www.nhlbi.nih.gov/health/health-topics/topics/asthma. Accessed August 18, 2012.

NHS Choices. (2011). Do twins run in families? Available at http://www.nhs.uk/chq/pages/2550.aspx. Accessed January 9, 2012.

NICHD Early Childcare Research Network. (2001). Nonmaternal care and family factors in early development: An overview of the NICHD Study of Early Child Care. *Journal of Applied Developmental Psychology, 22*, 457–492.

NICHD Early Childcare Research Network. (2005). Predicting individual differences in attention, memory, and planning in first graders from experience at home, childcare, and school. *Developmental Psychology, 41*, 99–114.

Niemann, S., & Weiss, S. (2011). Attachment behavior and children adopted internationally at six months post adoption. *Adoption Quarterly, 14*(4), 246–267.

Niemeier, H. M., Raynor, H. A., Lloyd-Richardson, E. E., Rogers, M. L., & Wing, R. R. (2006). Fast food consumption and breakfast skipping: Predictors of weight gain from adolescence to adulthood in a nationally representative sample. *Journal of Adolescent Health, 39*(6), 842–849.

Nigg, J. T., Goldsmith, H. H., & Sachek, J. (2004). Temperament and attention deficit hyperactivity disorder: The development of a multiple pathway model. *Journal of Clinical Child and Adolescent Psychology, 33*(1), 42–53.

Nisbett, R. E. (2009). *Intelligence and how to get it*. New York: Norton.

Noble, K., Houston, S. M., Kan, E., & Sowell, E. R. (2012). Neural correlates of socioeconomic status in the developing human brain. *Developmental Science, 15*(4), 516–527.

Noble, K. G., & Farah, M. J. (2013). Neurocognitive consequences of socioeconomic disparities: The intersection of cognitive neuroscience and public health. *Developmental Science, 16*(5), 639–640.

Nock, M. K., Kazdin, A. E., Hiripi, E., & Kessler, R. C. (2006). Prevalence, subtypes, and correlates of DSM-IV conduct disorder in the National Comorbidity Survey Replication. *Psychological Medicine, 36*, 699–710.

Nolen-Hoeksema, S., Stice, E., Wade, E., & Bohon, C. (2007). Reciprocal relations between rumination and bulimic, substance abuse, and depressive symptoms in female adolescents. *Journal of Abnormal Psychology, 116*(1), 198–207.

Nordhov, S. M., et al. (2010). Early intervention improves cognitive outcomes for preterm infants: Randomized controlled trial. *Pediatrics, 126*(5), e1088–e1094.

Nordhov, S. M., et al. (2012). Early intervention improves behavioral outcomes for preterm infants: Randomized controlled trial. *Pediatrics, 129*(1), e9–e16.

Norton, A., & D'Ambrosio, B. S. (2008). ZPC and ZPD: Zones of teaching and learning. *Journal for Research in Mathematics Education, 39*(3), 220–246.

Novotny, R., et al. (2011). Puberty, body fat, and breast density in girls of several ethnic groups. *American Journal of Human Biology, 23*(3), 359–365.

Nowinski, J. (2007). *The identity trap: Saving our teens from themselves*. New York: AMACOM.

Nucci, L. (2001). *Education in the moral domain*. Cambridge: Cambridge University Press.

Nucci, L. P., & Gingo, M. (2010). The development of moral reasoning. In U. Goswami (Ed.), *The Wiley-Blackwell handbook of childhood cognitive development* (2nd ed.) (pp. 420–455). Hoboken, NJ: Wiley.

Nurwisah, R. (2011, September 29). Mitchell Wilson suicide: Disabled boy's death raises bullying concerns. *Huffington Post Canada*.

Nussbaum, N. L. (2012). ADHD and female specific concerns: A review of the literature and clinical implications. *Journal of Attention Disorders, 16*, 87–100.

Nutrition Facts. (2012). Centers for Disease Control and Prevention. http://www.cdc.gov/healthyyouth/nutrition/facts.htm.

Nyunt, A., et al. (2005). Androgen status in healthy premenopausal women with loss of libido. *Journal of Sex & Marital Therapy, 31*(1), 73–80.

O'Boyle, M. W., & Benbow, C. P. (1990). Handedness and its relationship to ability and talent. In S. Coren (Ed.), *Left-handedness: Behavior implications and anomalies*. Amsterdam: North-Holland.

O'Connor, K. A., et al. (2011). The puzzle of sibling attachment non-concordance. *Psychology Presentations*, Paper 32. http://ir.lib.uwo.ca/psychologypres/32.

O'Connor, T. G., Heron J., & Glover, V. P. D. (2002). Antenatal anxiety predicts child behavioral/emotional problems independently of postnatal depression. *Journal of the American Academy of Child & Adolescent Psychiatry, 41*, 1470–1477.

O'Dea, J. A. (2006). Self-concept, self-esteem and body weight in adolescent females: A three-year longitudinal study. *Journal of Health Psychology, 11*(4), 599–611.

O'Donnell, L., et al. (2003). Long-term influence of sexual norms and attitudes on timing of sexual initiation among urban minority youth. *Journal of School Health, 23*(2), 68–75.

Ogden, C. L., et al. (2012). Prevalence of obesity and trends in body mass index among U.S. children and adolescents, 1999–2010. *Journal of the American Medical Association, 307*(5), 483–490.

Ohalete, N. (2007). Adolescent sexual debut: A case for studying African American father–adolescent reproductive health communication. *Journal of Black Studies, 37*(5), 737–752.

Ohnishi, T., Matsuda, H., Hirakata, M., & Ugawa, Y. (2006). Navigation ability dependent neural activation in the human brain: An fMRI study. *Neuroscience Research, 55*(4), 361–369.

O'Leary, C. M., et al. (2010). Prenatal alcohol exposure and risk of birth defects. *Pediatrics, 126*(4), e843–e850.

Ollendick, T. H., & Seligman, L. D. (2006). Anxiety disorders. In C. Gillberg, R. Harrington & H-C. Steinhausen (Eds.), *A clinician's handbook of child and adolescent psychiatry* (pp. 144–187). New York: Cambridge University Press.

Oller, D. K. (2000). *The emergence of the speech capacity*. Mahwah, NJ: Erlbaum.

Olsen, E. M., et al. (2007). Failure to thrive: The prevalence and concurrence of anthropometric criteria in a general infant population. *Archives of Disease in Childhood, 92*, 109–114.

Olson, S. D., Fauci, L. J., & Suarez, S. S. (2011). Mathematical modeling of calcium signaling during sperm hyperactivation. *Molecular Human Reproduction, 17*(8), 500–510.

Olson, S. L., Bates, J. E., Sandy, J. M., & Lanthier, R. (2000). Early developmental precursors of externalizing behavior in middle childhood and adolescence. *Journal of Abnormal Child Psychology, 28*(2), 119–133.

Olson, S. L., Kashiwagi, K., & Crystal, D. (2001). Concepts of adaptive and maladaptive child behavior: A comparison of U.S. and Japanese mothers of preschool-age children. *Journal of Cross-Cultural Psychology, 32*(1), 43–57.

O'Neill, D. K., & Chong, S. C. F. (2001). Preschool children's difficulty understanding the types of information obtained through the five senses. *Child Development, 72*(3), 803–815.

O'Neill, D. K., & Gopnik, A. (1991). Young children's ability to identify the sources of their beliefs. *Developmental Psychology, 27*, 390–397.

Örnkloo, H., & von Hofsten, C. (2007). Fitting objects into holes: On the development of spatial cognition skills. *Developmental Psychology, 43*(2), 404–416.

Orstavik, R. E., Kendler, K. S., Czajkowski, N., Tambs, K., & Reichborn-Kjennerud, T. (2007). Genetic and environmental contributions to depressive personality disorder in a population-based sample of Norwegian twins. *Journal of Affective Disorders, 99*(1–3), 181–189.

Osuch, J. R., et al. (2010). Association of age at menarche with adult leg length and trunk height: Speculations in relation to breast cancer risk. *Annals of Human Biology, 37*(1), 76–85.

Oswal, S., & Lyons, G. (2008). Syphilis in pregnancy. *Continuing Education in Anaesthesia, Critical Care & Pain, 8*(6), 224–227.

Out, D., et al. (2010). Intended sensitive and harsh caregiving responses to infant crying: The role of cry pitch and perceived urgency in an adult twin sample. *Child Abuse & Neglect, 34*(11), 863–873.

Overweight and obesity. (2011). http://www.cdc.gov/obesity/childhood/problem.html. Accessed August 18, 2012.

Oztop, E., Kawato, M., & Arbib, M. (2006). Mirror neurons and imitation: A computationally guided review. *Neural Networks, 19*(3), 254–271.

Pace, C. S., & Zavattini, G. C. (2011). "Adoption and attachment theory": The attachment models of adoptive mothers and the revision of attachment patterns of their late-adopted children. *Child: Care, Health and Development, 37*(1), 82–88.

Page, K. (1999, May 16). The graduate. *Washington Post Magazine, 152,* 18, 20.

Palla, G., Barabási, A-L., & Vicsek, T. (2007). Quantifying social group evolution. *Nature, 446*(7136), 664–667.

Palmer, E. J. (2005). The relationship between moral reasoning and aggression, and the implications for practice. *Psychology, Crime & Law, 11*(4), 353–361.

Palmer, E. L. (2003). Realities and challenges in the rapidly changing televisual media landscape. In E. L. Palmer & B. M. Young (Eds.), *The faces of televisual media: Teaching, violence, selling to children* (2nd ed.) (pp. 361–377). Mahwah, NJ: Erlbaum.

Panksepp, J., Burgdorf, J.,Turner, C., & Gordon, N. (2003). Modeling ADHD-type arousal with unilateral frontal cortex damage in rates and beneficial effects of play therapy. *Brain & Cognition, 52*(1), 97–105.

Papadopoulos, F. C., Ekbom, A., Brandt, L., & Ekselius, L. (2009). Excess mortality, causes of death and prognostic factors in anorexia nervosa. *British Journal of Psychiatry, 194,* 10–17.

Papaioannou, A., Bebetsos, E., Theodorakis, Y., Christodoulidis, T., & Kouli, O. (2006). Causal relationships of sport and exercise involvement with goal orientations, perceived competence and intrinsic motivation in physical education: A longitudinal study. *Journal of Sports Sciences, 24*(4), 367–382.

Paquette, D. (2004). Theorizing the father-child relationship: Mechanism and developmental outcomes. *Human Development, 47*(4), 193–219.

Paquette, D., & Bigras, M. (2010). The risky situation: A procedure for assessing the father-child activation relationship. *Early Child Development and Care, 180,* 33–50.

Paquette, D., Coyl-Shepperd, D. D., & Newland, L. A. (2013). Fathers and development: New areas for exploration. *Early Child Development and Care, 183*(6), 735–745.

Park, J. S. (2008). Is diagnostic ultrasound harmful to the fetus? *Journal of the Korean Medical Association, 51*(9), 823–830.

Park, M. (2011, August 12). Hypno-Birthing: Relax while giving birth? CNN. http://www.cnn.com/2011/HEALTH/08/12/hypnobirth.pregnancy. Accessed March 1, 2012.

Park, Y., Kwon, J. Y., Kim, Y. H., Kim, M., & Shin, J. C. (2010). Maternal age-specific rates of fetal chromosomal abnormalities at 16–20 weeks' gestation in Korean pregnant women greater than or equal to 35 years of age. *Fetal Diagnosis and Therapy, 27*(4), 214–221.

Parke, R. D., & Buriel, R. (2006). Socialization in the family: Ethnic and ecological perspectives. In N. Eisenberg, W. Damon & R. M. Lerner (Eds.), *Handbook of child psychology* (6th ed.), Vol. 3, *Social, emotional, and personality development* (pp. 429–504). Hoboken, NJ: Wiley.

Parks, P., & Bradley, R. (1991). The interaction of home environment features and their relation to infant competence. *Infant Mental Health Journal, 12,* 3–16.

Parsons, H. G., George, M. A., & Innis, S. M. (2011). Growth assessment in clinical practice: Whose growth curve? *Current Gastroenterology Reports, 13*(3), 286–292.

Parten, M. B. (1932). Social participation among preschool children. *Journal of Abnormal and Social Psychology, 27,* 243–269.

Passell, P. (1992, August 9). Twins study shows school is a sound investment. *New York Times,* p. A14.

Passow, S., Muller, M., Westerhausen, R. Hugdahl, K., Wartenburger, I., Heekeren, H. R., Lindenberger, U., & Li, S-C (2013). Development of attentional control of verbal auditory perception from middle to late childhood: Comparison to Healthy aging. *Developmental Psychology, 49*(10), 1982–1993.

Pastor, J., et al. (2007). Makin' homes: An urban girl thing. In B. J. R. Leadbeater & N. Way (Eds.), *Urban girls revisited: Building strengths* (pp. 75–96). New York: New York University Press.

Patel, M. M., et al. (2009). Broadening the age restriction for initiating rotavirus vaccination in regions with high rotavirus mortality: Benefits of mortality reduction versus risk of fatal intussusception. *Vaccine, 27*(22), 2916–2922.

Patenaude, J., Niyonsenga, T., & Fafard, D. (2003). Changes in students' moral development during medical school: A cohort study. *Canadian Medical Association Journal, 168*(7), 840–844.

Paterson, D. S., et al. (2006). Multiple serotonergic brainstem abnormalities in sudden infant death syndrome. *Journal of the American Medical Association, 296,* 2124–2132.

Patrick, M. E., O'Malley, P. M., Johnston, L. D., Terry-McElrath, Y. M., & Schulenberg, J. E. (2012). HIV/AIDS risk behaviors and substance abuse by young adults in the United States. *Prevention Science, 13*(5), 532–538.

Patterson, C. J. (2003). Children of lesbian and gay parents. In L. D. Garnets & D. C. Kimmel (Eds.), *Psychological perspectives on lesbian, gay, and bisexual experiences* (2nd ed.) (pp. 497–548). New York: Columbia University Press.

Patterson, C. J. (2006). Children of lesbian and gay parents. *Current Directions in Psychological Science, 15*(5), 241–244.

Patterson, C. J., & Farr, R. H. (2011). Coparenting among lesbian and gay couples. In J. P. McHale, & K. M. Lindahl (Eds.). *Coparenting: A conceptual and clinical examination of family systems* (pp. 127–146). Washington, DC: American Psychological Association.

Patterson, G. R. (2005). The next generation of PMTO models. *The Behavior Therapist, 28*(2), 27–33.

Pauli-Pott, U., Mertesacker, B., & Beckmann, D. (2003). Ein Fragebogen zur Erfassung des fruhkindlichen Temperaments im Elternurteil. *Zeitschrift für Kinder- und Jugendpsychiatrie und Psychotherapie, 31*(2), 99–110.

Paus, T. (2013). How environment and genes shape the adolescent brain. *Hormones and Behavior, 64,* 195–202.

Paus, T., Bernard, M., Chakravarty, M. M., Davy Smith, G., Gillis, J., Lourdusamy, A., Leonard, G., Mrelka, M. G., Pavlidis, P. Perron, M., Pike, G. B., Richer, L., Schumann, G., Timpson, N., Toro, R., Veillette, S., & Pausova, Z. (2012). KCTD8 gene and brain growth in adverse intra-uterine environment: A genome wide association study. *Cerebral Cortex, 22,* 2634–2642.

Paus, T., Toro, R., Leonard, G., Lerner, J., Lerner, R. M., Perron, M., Pike, G. B., Richer, L., Steinberg, L., Veillette, S., & Pausova, Z. (2008). Morphological properties of the action-observation cortical network in adolescents with low and high resistance to peer influence. *Social Neuroscience, 3,* 303–316.

Pearson, G. S., & Crowley, A. A. (2012). Attention deficit hyperactivity disorder. In E. L. Yearwood, G. S. Pearson, & J. A. Newland, *Child and adolescent behavioral health* (pp. 139–152). Chichester, West Sussex, UK: Wiley-Blackwell.

Pederson, D. R., Moran, G., & Bento, S. (1999). *Manual—Maternal Behavior Q-sort Version 3.1.* London, ON: University of Western Ontario.

Peeters, M. W., et al. (2005). Genetic and environmental causes of tracking in explosive strength during adolescence. *Behavior Genetics, 35*(5), 551–563.

Pellegrini, A. D., & Smith, P. K. (1998). The development of play during childhood: Forms and possible functions. *Child Psychology and Psychiatry Review, 3,* 51–57.

Pelligrini, A. D., & Smith, P. K. (2008). Physical activity play: The nature and function of a neglected aspect of play. *Child Development, 69*(3), 577–598.

Pellis, S. M., & Pellis, V. V. (2007). Rough-and-tumble play and the development of the social brain. *Current Directions in Psychological Science, 16*(2), 95–98.

Peltola, M. J., Leppänen, J. M., Mäki, S., & Hietanen, J. K. (2009). Emergence of enhanced attention to fearful faces between 5 and 7 months of age. *Social Cognitive and Affective Neuroscience.* doi:10.1093/scan/nsn046.

Pepler, D. J., & Craig, W. M. (2000). *Making a difference in bullying* (Report #60). Toronto, ON: York University, LaMarsh Institute. Retrieved December 5, 2006, from http://www.arts.yorku.ca/lamarsh/pdf/Making_a_Difference_in _Bullying.pdf.

Pereira, B., Mendonça, D., Neto, C., Valente, L., & Smith, P. K. (2004). Bullying in Portuguese schools. *School Psychology International, 25*(2), 241–254.

Perrault, S. (2013). Police-reported youth Crime Severity Indexes, Canada, 2002–2012. Statistics Canada, Catalogue no. 85-002-x. Ottawa, ON, Canada.

Perren, S., & Alsaker, F. D. (2006). Social behavior and peer relationships of victims, bully-victims, and bullies in kindergarten. *Journal of Child Psychology and Psychiatry, 47*(1), 45–57.

Perrin, M. C., Brown, A. S., & Malaspina, D. (2007, August 21). Aberrant epigenetic regulation could explain the relationship of paternal age to schizophrenia. *Schizophrenia Bulletin online.* Available at http://schizophreniabulletin .oxfordjournals.org/cgi/content/abstract/ sbm093v1.

Persike, M., & Seiffge-Krenke, I. (2011). Competence in coping with stress in adolescents from three regions of the world. *Journal of Youth and Adolescence.* doi:10.1007/s10964-011-9719-6.

Persson, G. E. B. (2005). Developmental perspectives on prosocial and aggressive motives in preschoolers' peer interactions. *International Journal of Behavioral Development, 29*(1), 80–91.

Peterka, M., Likovsky, Z., & Peterkova, R. (2007). Environmental risk and sex ratio in newborns. *Congenital Diseases and the Environment, 23*, 295–319.

Peterson, C. B., et al. (2009). Personality dimensions in bulimia nervosa, binge eating disorder, and obesity. *Comprehensive Psychiatry, 51*(1), 31–36.

Pfaff, N. (2010). Gender segregation in pre-adolescent peer groups as a matter of class. *Childhood, 17*(1), 43–60.

Phelps, R., Eisert, D., Schulz, S., & Augustyn, M. (2012). Attached to a diagnosis: The quandary of social deficits and reactive attachment disorder. *Journal of Developmental and Behavioral Pediatrics. 33*(1), 84–86.

Philip, J., et al. (2004). Late first-trimester invasive prenatal diagnostic results of an international randomized trial. *Obstetrics & Gynecology, 103*(6), 1164–1173.

Phillips, A. S., & Phillips, C. R. (2000). Birth-order differences in self-attributions for achievement. *Journal of Individual Psychology, 56*(4), 474–480.

Phillips, D. A., & Styfco, S. J. (2007). Child development research and public policy: Triumphs and setbacks on the way to maturity. In J. L. Aber et al. (Eds.), *Child development and social policy: Knowledge for action. APA Decade of Behavior volumes* (pp. 11–27). Washington, DC: American Psychological Association.

Phinney, J. S. (1989). Stages of ethnic identity in minority group adolescents. *Journal of Early Adolescence, 9*, 34–49.

Phinney, J. S. (1992). The multigroup ethnic identity measure: A new scale for use with adolescents and young adults with diverse groups. *Journal of Adolescent Research, 12*, 156–176.

Phinney, J. S. (2006). Ethnic identity exploration in emerging adulthood. In J. J. Arnett & J. L. Tanner (Eds.), *Emerging adults in America: Coming of age in the 21st century* (pp. 117–134). Washington, DC: American Psychological Association.

Phinney, J. S., & Alipuria, L. L. (2006). Multiple social categorization and identity among multiracial, multiethnic, and multicultural individuals: Processes and implications. In R. J. Crisp & M.

Hewstone (Eds.), *Multiple social categorization: Processes, models and applications* (pp. 211–238). New York: Psychology Press.

Phinney, J. S., & Chavira, P. (1992). Ethnic identity and self-esteem: An exploratory longitudinal study. *Journal of Adolescence, 15*, 1–11.

Phipps, M. G., Blume, J. D., & DeMonner, S. M. (2002). Young maternal age associated with increased risk of postneonatal death. *Obstetrics and Gynecology, 100*, 481–486.

Physical activity and health. (2011). Centers for Disease Control and Prevention. http://www.cdc.gov/ physicalactivity/everyone/health/index .html. Accessed August 18, 2012.

Piaget, J. (1932). *The moral judgment of the child.* London: Kegan Paul.

Piaget, J. (1962). *Play, dreams, and imitation in childhood.* New York: Norton. (Originally published in 1946.)

Piaget, J. (1963). *The origins of intelligence in children.* New York: Norton. (Originally published in 1936.)

Piaget, J. (1967). In D. Elkind (Ed.), *Six psychological studies.* New York: Random House. (Originally published in 1964.)

Piaget, J. (1972). Intellectual evolution from adolescence to adulthood. *Human Development, 15*, 1–12.

Piaget, J. (1976). *The grasp of consciousness: Action and concept in the young child.* Cambridge, MA: Harvard University Press.

Pickren, W. E., Marsella, A. J., Leong, F. T. L., & Leach, M. M. (2012). Playing our part: Crafting a vision for a psychology curriculum marked by multiplicity. In F. T. L. Leong, W. E. Pickren, M. M. Leach, & A. J. Marsella (Eds.). *Internationalizing the psychology curriculum in the United States* (pp. 307–322). New York: Springer.

Piek, J. P., Baynam, G. B., & Barrett, N. C. (2006). The relationship between fine and gross motor ability, self-perceptions and self-worth in children and adolescents. *Human Movement Science, 25*(1), 65–75.

Pine, D. S., et al. (2001). Fluvoxamine for the treatment of anxiety disorders in children and adolescents. *New England Journal of Medicine, 344*(17), 1279–1285.

Pine, K. J., & Nash, A. (2002). Dear Santa: The effects of television advertising on young children. *International Journal of Behavioral Development, 26*(6), 529–539.

Pinker, S. (2007). *The stuff of thought: Language as a window into human nature.* New York: Viking.

Pinker, S., & Jackendoff, R. (2005). The faculty of language: What's special about it? *Cognition, 95*(2), 201–236.

Pleck, J. H. (2010). Paternal involvement: Revised conceptualization and theoretical linkages with child outcomes. In M. E. Lamb (Ed.), *The role of the father in child development* (5th ed, pp. 58–93). Hoboken, NJ: John Wiley.

Plomin, R. (Ed.). (2002). *Behavioral genetics in the postgenomic era.* Washington, DC: American Psychological Association.

Plomin, R., & Spinath, F. M. (2004). Intelligence: Genetics, genes, and genomics. *Journal of Personality and Social Psychology, 86*(1), 112–129.

Plomin, R., & Walker, S. O. (2003). Genetics and educational psychology. *British Journal of Educational Psychology, 73*(1), 3–14.

Plomin, R., DeFries, J. C., McClearn, G. E., & McGuffin, P. (2008). *Behavioral genetics.* New York: Worth Publishers.

Plomin, R., Owen, M. J., & McGuffin, P. (1994). The genetic basis of complex human behaviors. *Science, 264*, 1733–1739.

Plunkett, J., et al. (2011). An evolutionary genomic approach to identify genes involved in human birth timing. *PLoS Genetics, 7*(4): e1001365. doi:10.1371/ journal.pgen.1001365.

Polivy, J., Herman, C. P., & Boivin, M. (2005). Eating disorders. In J. E. Maddux & B. A. Winstead (Eds.), *Psychopathology: Foundations for a contemporary understanding* (pp. 229–254). Mahwah, NJ: Erlbaum.

Pollack, W. (2002). Real boys: The truths behind the myths. In *The Jossey-Bass reader on gender in education* (pp. 88–100). San Francisco, CA: Jossey-Bass.

Pombeni, M. L., Kirchler, E., & Palmonari, A. (1990). Identification with peers as a strategy to muddle through the troubles of the adolescent years. *Journal of Adolescence, 13*, 351–369.

Porfeli, E. J. (2007). Work values system development during adolescence. *Journal of Vocational Behavior, 70*(1), 42–60.

Porter, R. H., Makin, J. W., Davis, L. B., & Christensen, K. M. (1992). Breast-fed infants respond to olfactory cues from their own mother and unfamiliar lactating females. *Infant Behavior and Development, 15*, 85–93.

Posner, M. I., & Rothbart, M. K. (2007). *Relating brain and mind. Educating the human brain.* Washington, DC: American Psychological Association.

Potter, D. (2010). Psychosocial well-being and the relationship between divorce and children's academic achievement. *Journal of Marriage and the Family, 72*(4), 933–946.

Pound, C. M., Unger, S. M., & Canadian Paediatric Society. (2012). The baby-friendly initiative: Protecting, promoting and supporting breastfeeding. *Paediatric Child Health, 17*(6), 317–321.

Power, T. G. (2011). Social play. In P. K. Smith, & C. H. Hart (Eds.). *The Wiley-Blackwell handbook of childhood social development* (pp. 455–471). Chichester, West Sussex, UK: Wiley-Blackwell.

Powers, P., & Bruty, H. (2009). Pharmacotherapy for eating disorders and obesity. *Child and Adolescent Psychiatric Clinics of North America, 18*(1), 175–187.

Powlishta, K. K. (2004). Gender as a social category. In M. Bennett & F. Sani

(Eds.), *The development of the social self* (pp. 103–134). New York: Psychology Press.

Powrie, R. O., et al. (2010). Special concerns for patients with advanced maternal age. In *de Swiet's Medical disorders in obstetric practice* (5th ed.). Hoboken, NJ: Wiley.

Prato-Previde, E., Fallani, G., & Valsecchi, P. (2006). Gender differences in owners interacting with pet dogs: An observational study. *Ethology, 112*(1), 64–73.

Pratt, C., & Bryant, P. (1990). Young children understand that looking leads to knowing (so long as they are looking into a single barrel). *Child Development, 61*, 973–982.

Premberg, A., Hellström, A-L., & Berg, M. (2008). Experiences of the first year as father. *Scandinavian Journal of Caring Sciences, 22*(1), 56–63.

Pressley, M., & Hilden, K. (2006). Cognitive strategies. In D. Kuhn, R. S. Siegler, W. Damon & R. M. Lerner (Eds.), *Handbook of child psychology* (6th ed.), Vol. 2, *Cognition, perception, and language* (pp. 511–556). Hoboken, NJ: Wiley.

Principe, C. P., & Langlois, J. H. (2012). Shifting the prototype: Experience with faces influences affective and attractiveness preferences. *Social Cognition, 30*(1), 109–120.

Pritchard, V., et al. (2009). Early school-based learning difficulties in children born very preterm. *Early Human Development, 85*(4), 215–224.

Provence, S., & Lipton, R. C. (1962). *Infants in institutions.* New York: International Universities Press.

Provost, B., Lopez, B. R., & Heimerl, S. (2007). A comparison of motor delays in young children: Autism spectrum disorder, developmental delay and developmental concerns. *Journal of Autism & Developmental Disorders, 237*(2), 321–328.

Pryce, C. R., Bettschen, D., Bahr, N. I., & Feldon, J. (2001). Comparison of the effects of infant handling, isolation, and nonhandling on acoustic startle, prepulse inhibition, locomotion, and HPA activity in the adult rat. *Behavioral Neuroscience, 115*(1), 71–83.

Public Health Agency of Canada. (2008). *Canadian guidelines for sexual health education.* Ottawa, ON: Population and Public Health Branch, Health Canada.

Public Health Agency of Canada. (2009). Leading causes of death, Canada, 2004, males and females combined: counts (crude death rate per 100,000). Ottawa: Public Health Agency of Canada.

Public Health Agency of Canada. (2009). Leading causes of hospitalizations, Canada, 2004, males and females combined: counts (crude rate per 100,000). Ottawa: Public Health Agency of Canada.

Public Health Agency of Canada. (2009). *HIV and AIDS in Canada. Surveillance Report to December 31,*

2008. Ottawa: Surveillance and Risk Assessment Division, Centre for Communicable Diseases and Infection Control, Public Health Agency of Canada.

Public Health Agency of Canada. (2010). Canadian Incidence Study of Reported Child Abuse and Neglect—2008: major findings. Ottawa, ON. CAT: HP5-1/2008E-PDF.

Public Health Agency of Canada. (2011). Obesity in Canada: A joint report from the Public Health Agency of Canada and the Canadian Institute for Health information. Ottawa, ON. Author.

Public Health Agency of Canada. (2011). The Chief Public Health Officer's Report on the State of Public Health in Canada 2011—Youth and young adults life in transition. Ottawa, ON: Author.

Public Health Agency of Canada. (2013). The Chief Public Health Officer's Report on the State of Public Health in Canada 2013—Infectious Disease—The never-ending threat. Ottawa, ON: Author.

Public Health Agency of Canada. (2014). Questions and answers: Gender identity in schools. http://www .phac-aspc.gc.ca/std-mts/rp/gi-is/ident -eng.php. Accessed June 3, 2014.

Puckett, M. B., Aikins, J. W., & Cillessen, A. H. N. (2008). Moderators of the association between relational aggression and perceived popularity. *Aggressive Behavior, 34*, 563–576.

Pugh, K. R., et al. (2000). The angular gyrus in developmental dyslexia: Task-specific differences in functional connectivity within posterior cortex. *Psychological Science, 11*(1), 51–56.

Pulverman, R., Hirsh-Pasek, K., Golinkoff, R. M., Pruden, S., & Salkind, S. J. (2006). Conceptual foundations for verb learning: Celebrating the event. In K. Hirsh-Pasek & R. M. Golinkoff (Eds.), *Action meets word: How children learn verbs* (pp. 134–159). New York: Oxford University Press.

Pushor, D., & Murphy, B. (2004). Parent marginalization, marginalized parents: Creating a place for parents on the school landscape. *Alberta Journal of Educational Research, 50*(3), 221–235.

Quigley, M. A., Hockley, C., Carson, C., Kelly, Y., Renfrew, M. J., & Sacker, A. (2012). Breastfeeding is associated with improved child cognitive development: A population-based cohort study. *Journal of Pediatrics, 160*, 25–32.

Quinlivan, J. A., & Condon, J. (2005). Anxiety and depression in fathers in teenage pregnancy. *Australian and New Zealand Journal of Psychiatry, 39*(10), 915–920.

Quinn, P. C. (2010). Born to categorize. In U. Goswami (Ed.), *The Wiley–Blackwell handbook of childhood cognitive development.* (2nd ed., pp. 129–152). Chichester, West Sussex, UK: Wiley–Blackwell.

Quintana, S. (2011). Ethnicity, race, and children's social development. In

P. K. Smith & C. H. Hart (Eds.), *The Wiley-Blackwell handbook of childhood social development* (2nd ed., pp. 299–316). Chichester, West Sussex, UK: Wiley–Blackwell.

Quintana, S. M. (1998). Children's developmental understanding of ethnicity and race. *Applied and Preventive Psychology, 7*(1), 27–45.

Rabasca, L. (2000). Pre-empting racism. *Monitor on Psychology, 31*(11), 60.

Raevuori, A., et al. (2009). Epidemiology of anorexia nervosa in men: A nationwide study of Finnish twins. *PLoS ONE, 4*(2), e4402.

Raikes, H., et al. (2006). Mother–child bookreading in low-income families: Correlates and outcomes during the first three years of life. *Child Development, 77*(4), 924–953.

Rakison, D. H., & Oakes, L. M. (Eds.). (2003). *Early category and concept development: Making sense of the blooming, buzzing confusion.* London: Oxford University Press.

Ramagopalan, S. V., Dyment, D. A., Handunnetthi, L., Rice, G. P., & Ebers, G. C. (2010). A genome-wide scan of male sexual orientation. *Journal of Human Genetics, 55*(1), 131–132.

Ramani, G. B., & Siegler, R. S. (2008). Promoting broad and stable improvements in low-income children's numerical knowledge through playing number board games. *Child Development, 79*, 375–394.

Ramchand, R., et al. (2009). Substance use and delinquency among fifth graders who have jobs. *American Journal of Preventive Medicine, 36*(4), 297–303.

Ramchandani, P. G., Richter, L. M., Norris, S. A., & Stein, A. (2010). Maternal prenatal stress and later child behavioral problems in an urban south African setting. *Journal of the American Academy of Child & Adolescent Psychiatry, 49*, 239–247.

Ramey, C. T., Campbell, F. A., & Ramey, S. L. (1999). Early intervention: Successful pathways to improving intellectual development. *Developmental Neuropsychology, 16*(3), 385–392.

Ramsey, J. L., Langlois, J. H., Hoss, R. A., Rubenstein, A. J., & Griffin, A. M. (2004). Origins of a stereotype: Categorization of facial attractiveness by 6-month-old infants. *Developmental Science, 7*(2), 201–211.

Randel, B., Stevenson, H. W., & Witruk, E. (2000). Attitudes, beliefs, and mathematics achievement of German and Japanese high school students. *International Journal of Behavioral Development, 24*(2), 190–198.

Rapee, R. M. (2012). Family factors in the development and management of anxiety disorders. *Clinical Child and Family Psychology Review, 15*(1), 69–80.

Rasmussen, C., Beckert, M., McLennan, L., Urichuk, L., & Andrew, G. (2010). An evaluation of social skills in children with and without prenatal alcohol exposure. *Child Care, Health, and Development, 37*(5), 711–718.

Rasmussen, K. M., et al. (2009, May 27). Institute of Medicine report. In T. Parker-Pope (2009, May 28), Study urges weight gain be curbed in pregnancy, *The New York Times online*.

Rathus, S. A., Fichner-Rathus, L., & Nevid, J. S. (2011). *Human sexuality in a world of diversity* (8th ed.). Boston: Allyn & Bacon.

Rathus, S. A., Nevid, J. S., & Fichner-Rathus, L. (2014). *Human sexuality in a world of diversity* (9th ed.). Upper Saddle River, NJ: Pearson Education.

Raudenbusch, S. W. (1984). Magnitude of teacher expectancy effects on pupil IQ as a function of credibility of expectancy induction: A synthesis from 18 experiments. *Journal of Experimental Psychology, 76*, 85–97.

Ravaldi, C., et al. (2003). Eating disorders and body image disturbances among ballet dancers, gymnasium users, and body builders. *Psychopathology, 36*(5), 247–254.

Ray, W. J. (2012). *Evolutionary psychology*. Thousand Oaks, CA: Sage.

Raznahan, A., et al. (2011). How does your cortex grow? *Journal of Neuroscience, 31*(19), 7174–7177.

Razza, R. A., & Blair, C. (2009). Associations among false-belief understanding, executive function, and social competence: A longitudinal analysis. *Journal of Applied Developmental Psychology, 30*(3), 332–343.

Reece, M., Herbenick, D., Schick, V., Sanders, S. A., Dodge, B., & Fortenberry, J. D. (2010). Sexual behaviors, relationships, and perceived health among adult men in the United States: Results from a national probability sample. *Journal of Sexual Medicine, 7*(suppl 5), 291–304.

Reichenberg, A., et al. (2006). Advancing paternal age and autism. *Archives of General Psychiatry, 63*(9), 1026–1032.

Reiersen, A. M., & Handen, B. (2011). Commentary on "Selective serotonin reuptake inhibitors (SSRIs) for autism spectrum disorders (ASDs)." *Evidence-Based Child Health: A Cochrane Review Journal, 6*, 1082–1085.

Reijneveld, S. A., et al. (2004). Infant crying and abuse. *Lancet, 364*(9442), 1340–1342.

Reis, O., & Youniss, J. (2004). Patterns in identity change and development in relationships with mothers and friends. *Journal of Adolescent Research, 19*(1), 31–44.

Reis, S. M., & Renzulli, J. S. (2011). Intellectual giftedness. In R. J. Sternberg & S. J. Kaufman (Eds.), *The Cambridge handbook of intelligence* (pp. 235–252). New York: Cambridge University Press.

Rennie, J., & Rosenbloom, L. (2011). How long have we got to get the baby out? A review of the effects of acute and profound intrapartum hypoxia and ischaemia. *The Obstetrician and Gynecologist, 13*(3), 169–174.

Renzaho, A. M. N., McCabe, M., & Sainsbury, W. J. (2011). Parenting, role reversals, and the preservation of cultural values among Arabic speaking migrant families in Melbourne, Australia. *International Journal of Intercultural Relations, 35*(4), 416–424.

Reschly, A., & Christenson, S. L. (2006). School completion. In G. G. Bear & K. M. Minke (Eds.), *Children's needs III: Development, prevention, and intervention* (pp. 103–113). Washington, DC: National Association of School Psychologists.

Rest, J. R. (1983). Morality. In P. H. Mussen (Ed.), *Handbook of child psychology*, Vol. 3, *Cognitive development*. New York: Wiley.

Rest, J., Narvaez, D., Bebeau, M., & Thoma, S. (1999). *Postconventional moral thinking*. Mahaw, NJ: Lawrence Erlbaum Associates.

Reynolds, A. J., Temple, J. A., Ou, S-R., Arteaga, I. A., & White, B. A. B. (2011). School-based early childhood education and age-28 well-being: Effects by timing, dosage, and subgroups. *Science, 333*(6040), 360–364.

Rhee, S. H., & Waldman, I. D. (2009). Genetic analysis of conduct disorder and antisocial behavior. In Y-K. Kim (Ed.), *Handbook of behavior genetics* (pp. 455–471). New York: Springer.

Rheingold, H. L., Gewirtz, J. L., & Ross, H. W. (1959). Social conditioning of vocalizations in the infant. *Journal of Comparative and Physiological Psychology, 52*, 68–73.

Rice, C. (2007). Prevalence of autism spectrum disorders—Autism and Developmental Disabilities Monitoring Network, 14 Sites, United States. *Morbidity and Mortality Weekly Report, 56*(SS01), 12–28.

Rice, F., Frederickson, N., & Seymour, J. (2011). Assessing pupil concerns about transition to secondary school. *British Journal of Educational Psychology, 81*(2), 244–263.

Richert, R. A., Robb, M. B., & Smith, E. I. (2011). Media as social partners: The social nature of young children's learning from screen media. *Child Development, 82*(1), 82–95.

Richler, J., et al. (2006). Is there a "regressive phenotype" of autism spectrum disorder associated with the measles-mumps-rubella vaccine? A CPEA study. *Journal of Autism and Developmental Disorders, 36*(3), 299–316.

Rickards, H., et al. (2011). Factor analysis of behavioural symptoms in Huntington's disease. *Journal of Neurology, Neurosurgery, & Psychiatry, 82*(4), 411–412.

Rinaldi, C. M., & Howe, N. (2003). Perceptions of constructive and destructive conflict within the family. *Infant and Child Development, 12*, 441–459.

Rizzolatti, G., & Craighero, L. (2004). The mirror-neuron system. *Annual Review of Neuroscience, 27*, 169–172.

Rizzolatti, G., & Fabbri-Destro, M. (2011). Mirror neurons: From discovery to autism. *Experimental Brain Research, 200*(3–4), 223–237.

Rizzolatti, G., Fadiga, L., Fogassi, L., & Gallese, V. (2002). From mirror neurons to imitation: Facts and speculations. In A. N. Meltzoff & W. Prinz (Eds.), *The imitative mind: Development, evolution, and brain bases*. New York: Cambridge University Press.

Roberts, A. R. (Ed.). (2007). Prologue. *Victims & Offenders, 2*(2), 103–104.

Roberts, K. C., Shields, M., de Groh, M., Aziz, A., & Gilbert, J. (2012). Overweight and obesity in children and adolescents: Results from the 2009 to 2011 Canadian Health Measures Survey. Statistic Canada, Catalogue no. 82-003-XPE. *Health Reports, 23*(3), 3–7.

Roberts, R. E., Roberts, C. R., & Duong, H. T. (2009). Sleepless in adolescence: Prospective data on sleep deprivation, health and functioning. *Journal of Adolescence, 32*(5), 1045–1057.

Robinson, J. B., Burns, B. M., & Davis, D. W. (2008). Maternal scaffolding and attention regulation in children living in poverty. *Journal of Applied Developmental Psychology, 30*(2), 82–91.

Robinson, J. R., Drotar, D., & Boutry, M. (2001). Problem-solving abilities among mothers of infants with failure to thrive. *Journal of Pediatric Psychology, 26*(1), 21–32.

Robson, W. L. M. (2009). Evaluation and management of enuresis. *New England Journal of Medicine, 360*(14), 1429–1436.

Rodkin, P. C., & Ahn, H-J. (2009). Social networks derived from affiliations and friendships, multi-informant and self-reports. *Social Development, 18*(3), 556–576.

Rodriguez, C. (2000). Culturally sensitive psychological assessment. In I. A. Canino & J. Spurlocj (Eds.), *Culturally diverse children and adolescents: Assessment, diagnosis, and treatment*. New York: Guilford.

Rodriguez, E. T., & Tamis-LeMonda, C. S. (2011). Trajectories of the home learning environment across the first 5 years: Associations with children's vocabulary and literacy skills at prekindergarten. *Child Development, 82*(4), 1058–1075.

Roebers, C. M., Moga, N., & Schneider, W. (2001). The role of accuracy motivation on children's and adults' event recall. *Journal of Experimental Child Psychology, 78*(4), 313–329.

Roelofs, J., Meesters, C., Ter Huurne, M., Bamelis, L., & Muris, P. (2006). On the links between attachment style, parental rearing behaviors, and internalizing and externalizing problems in non-clinical children. *Journal of Child and Family Studies, 15*(3), 331–344.

Roeser, R. W., Peck, S. C., & Nasir, N. S. (2006). Self and identity processes in school motivation, learning, and achievement. In P. A. Alexander & P. H. Winne (Eds.), *Handbook of educational psychology* (pp. 391–424). Mahwah, NJ: Erlbaum.

Roffwarg, H. P., Muzio, J. N., & Dement, W. C. (1966). Ontogenetic development of the human sleep–dream cycle. *Science, 152,* 604–619.

Rogers, E. E., & Piecuch, R. E. (2009). Neurodevelopmental outcomes of infants who experience intrauterine growth restriction. *American Academy of Pediatrics, 10*(3), e100.

Rogers, M. A., & Creed, P. A. (2011). A longitudinal investigation of adolescent career planning and exploration using a social cognitive career theory framework. *Journal of Adolescence, 34*(1), 163–172.

Rogoff, B. (2003). *The cultural nature of human development.* New York: Oxford University Press.

Rogowski, J. A., et al. (2004). Indirect vs. direct hospital quality indicators for very low-birth-weight infants. *Journal of the American Medical Association, 291,* 202–209.

Roisman, G. I., & Groh, A. M. (2011). Attachment theory and research in developmental psychology: An overview and appreciative critique. In M. K. Underwood & L. H. Rosen (Eds.), *Social development: Relationships in infancy, childhood, and adolescence* (pp. 101–126). New York: Guilford.

Rollins, V. B., & Valdez, J. N. (2006). Perceived racism and career self-efficacy in African American adolescents. *Journal of Black Psychology, 32*(2), 176–198.

Romans, S. E., Gendall, K. A., Martin, J. L., & Mullen, P. E. (2001). Child sexual abuse and later disordered eating: A New Zealand epidemiological study. *International Journal of Eating Disorders, 29*(4), 380–392.

Roncesvalles, M. N., Schmitz, C., Zedka, M., Assaiante, C., & Woollacott, M. (2005). From egocentric to exocentric spatial orientation: Development of posture control in bimanual and trunk inclination tasks. *Journal of Motor Behavior, 37*(5), 404–416.

Roopnarine, J. L., Krishnakumar, A., Metindogan, A., & Evans, M. (2006). Links between parenting styles, parent–child academic interaction, parent–school interaction, and early academic skills and social behaviors in young children of English-speaking Caribbean immigrants. *Early Childhood Research Quarterly, 21*(2), 238–252.

Rosario, M., Schrimshaw, E. W., Hunter, J., & Levy-Warren, A. (2009). The coming-out process of young lesbian and bisexual women. *Archives of Sexual Behavior, 38*(1), 34–49.

Rose, A. J., & Asher, S. R. (1999). Children's goals and strategies in response to conflicts within a friendship. *Developmental Psychology, 35*(1), 69–79.

Rose, A. J., Swenson, L. P., & Carlson, W. (2004). Friendships of aggressive youth: Considering the influences of being disliked and of being perceived as popular. *Journal of Experimental Child Psychology, 88*(1), 25–45.

Rose, L. Y., & Fischer, K. W. (2011). Intelligence in childhood. In R. J. Sternberg & S. J. Kaufman (Eds.), *The Cambridge handbook of intelligence* (pp. 144–173). New York: Cambridge University Press.

Rose, S. A., Feldman, J. F., & Jankowski, J. J. (2001). Visual short-term memory in the first year of life: Capacity and recency effects. *Developmental Psychology, 37*(4), 539–549.

Rose, S. A., Feldman, J. F., & Jankowski, J. J. (2004). Infant visual recognition memory. *Developmental Review, 24*(1), 74–100.

Rose, S. A., Feldman, J. F., & Wallace, I. F. (1992). Infant information processing in relation to six-year cognitive outcomes. *Child Development, 63,* 1126–1141.

Rose, S. A., Feldman, J. F., Jankowski, J. J., & van Rossem, R. (2011). The structure of memory in infants and toddlers: An SEM study with full-terms and pre-terms. *Developmental Science, 14*(1), 83–91.

Rosenbaum, D. E. (2000, May 16). On left-handedness, its causes, and costs. *New York Times,* pp. F1, F6.

Rosenstein, D., & Oster, H. (1988). Differential facial responses to four basic tastes. *Child Development, 59,* 1555–1568.

Rosenthal, R., & Jacobson, L. (1968). *Pygmalion in the classroom.* New York: Holt, Rinehart & Winston.

Ross, G., Kagan, J., Zelazo, P. R., & Kotelchuck, M. (1975). Separation protest in infants in home and laboratory. *Developmental Psychology, 11,* 256–257.

Ross, H., Ross, M., Stein, N., & Trabasso, T. (2006). How siblings resolve their conflicts: The importance of first offers, planning, and limited opposition. *Child Development, 77*(6), 1730–1745.

Rotenberg, K. J., et al. (2004). Cross-sectional and longitudinal relations among peer-reported trustworthiness, social relationships, and psychological adjustment in children and early adolescents from the United Kingdom and Canada. *Journal of Experimental Child Psychology, 88*(1), 46–67.

Rotermann, M. (2012). Sexual behaviour and condom use of 15- to 24-year-olds in 2003 and 2009/2010. Statistics Canada, Catalogue no. 82-003-XPE, Health Reports, Vol. 23, no. 1.

Rothbart, M. K., & Sheese, B. E. (2007). Temperament and emotion regulation. In J. J. Gross (Ed.), *Handbook of emotion regulation* (pp. 331–350). New York: Guilford.

Rothbart, M. K., Ellis, L. K., & Posner, M. I. (2004). Temperament and self-regulation. In R. F. Baumeister & K. D. Vohs (Eds.), *Handbook of self-regulation: Research, theory, and applications.* New York: Guilford.

Rothrauff, T., Middlemiss, W., & Jacobson, L. (2004). Comparison of American and Austrian infants' and toddlers' sleep habits: A retrospective, exploratory study. *North American Journal of Psychology, 6*(1), 125–144.

Rottinghaus, P. J., & Van Esbroeck, R. (2011). Improving person–environment fit and self-knowledge. In P. J. Hartung & L. M. Subich (Eds.), *Developing self in work and career: Concepts, cases, and contexts* (pp. 35–52). Washington, DC: American Psychological Association.

Rouse, C., Brooks-Gunn, J., & McLanahan, S. (2005). Introducing the issue. *Future of Children, 15*(1), 3–14.

Rovee-Collier, C. (1993). The capacity for long-term memory in infancy. *Current Directions in Psychological Science, 2,* 130–135.

Rowen, B. (1973). *The children we see.* New York: Holt, Rinehart & Winston.

Roxborough, H. M., et al. (2012). Perfectionistic self-presentation, socially prescribed perfectionism, and suicide in youth. *Suicide and Life-Threatening Behavior, 42*(2), 217–233.

Royal Australasian College of Physicians, Paediatrics & Child Health Division. (2006). Management of procedure-related pain in neonates. *Journal of Paediatrics and Child Health, 42*(Suppl. 11), S31–S39.

Royal Canadian Mounted Police. (2014). Cybercrime: An overview of incidents and issues in Canada. http://www.rcmp-grc.gc.ca/pubs/cc-report-rapport-cc-eng.htm. Accessed May 19, 2014.

Rübeling, H., Schwarzer, S., Keller, H., & Lenk, M. (2011). Young children's nonfigurative drawings of themselves and their families in two different cultures. *Journal of Cognitive Education and Psychology, 10*(1), 63–76.

Rubella. (2009, March 2). *The New York Times Health Guide.* Available at http://health.nytimes.com/health/guides/disease/rubella/overview.html.

Rubia, K., et al. (2006). Progressive increase of frontostriatal brain activation from childhood to adulthood during event-related tasks of cognitive control. *Human Brain Mapping, 27*(12), 973–993.

Rubin, K. H. (1982). Nonsocial play in preschoolers: Necessarily evil? *Child Development, 53,* 651–657.

Rubin, K. H., Bukowski, W. M., & Parker, J. G. (2006). Peer interactions, relationships, and groups. In N. Eisenberg, W. Damon & R. M. Lerner (Eds.), *Handbook of child psychology* (6th ed.), Vol. 3, *Social, emotional, and personality development* (pp. 571–645). Hoboken, NJ: Wiley.

Rubin, K. H., & Coplan, R. J. (Eds.). (2010). *The development of shyness and social withdrawal.* New York: Guilford.

Rubin, K. H., Coplan, R. J., Bowker, J. C., & Menzer, M. (2011). Social withdrawal and shyness. In P. K. Smith, & C. H. Hart (Eds.). *The Wiley–Blackwell handbook of childhood social development* (pp. 434–452). Chichester, West Sussex, UK: Wiley-Blackwell.

Rubinstein, S., & Caballero, B. (2000). Is Miss America an undernourished role model? *Journal of the American Medical Association, 283*(12), 1569.

Rudolph, K. D., & Flynn, M. (2007). Childhood adversity and youth depression: Influence of gender and pubertal status. *Development and Psychopathology, 19*(2), 497–521.

Rudy, D., & Grusec, J. E. (2006). Authoritarian parenting in individualist and collectivist groups: Associations with maternal emotion and cognition and children's self-esteem. *Journal of Family Psychology, 20*(1), 68–78.

Ruiz, F., & Tanaka, K. (2001). The *ijime* phenomenon and Japan: Overarching considerations for cross-cultural studies. *Psychologia: An International Journal of Psychology in the Orient, 44*(2), 128–138.

Russ, S. W. (2006). Pretend play, affect, and creativity. In P. Locher, C. Martindale & L. Dorfman (Eds.), *New directions in aesthetics, creativity and the arts, foundations and frontiers in aesthetics* (pp. 239–250). Amityville, NY: Baywood.

Russell, S. T. (2006). Substance use and abuse and mental health among sexual-minority. In A. M. Omoto & H. S. Kurtzman (Eds.), *Sexual orientation and mental health: Examining identity and development in lesbian, gay, and bisexual people* (pp. 13–35). Washington, DC: American Psychological Association.

Russo, A., Semeraro, F., Romano, M. R., Mastropasqua, R., Dell'Omo, R., & Costagliola, C. (2014). Myopia onset and progression: Can it be prevented? *International Ophthalmology, 34,* 693–705.

Russo, N. F., Pirlott, A. G., & Cohen, A. B. (2012). The psychology of women and gender in international perspective: Issues and challenges. In F. T. L. Leong, W. E. Pickren, M. M. Leach, & A. J. Marsella (Eds.). *Internationalizing the psychology curriculum in the United States* (pp. 157–178). New York: Springer.

Rutter, M. (2006). The psychological effects of early institutional rearing. In P. J. Marshall & N. A. Fox (Eds.), *The development of social engagement: Neurobiological perspectives. Series in affective science* (pp. 355–391). New York: Oxford University Press.

Sabattini, L., & Leaper, C. (2004). The relation between mothers' and fathers' parenting styles and their division of labor in the home: Young adults' retrospective reports. *Sex Roles, 50*(3–4), 217–225.

Sabia, J. J. (2009). School-year employment and academic performance of young adolescents. *Economics of Education Review, 28*(2), 268–276.

Sadker, D. (2011). More than Title IX: How equity in education has shaped the nation. *Journal of Women, Politics, and Policy, 32*(2), 167–169.

Sadker, D., Sadker, M., & Zittleman, K. (2009). *Still failing at fairness: How gender bias cheats girls and boys in school and what we can do about it.* New York: Scribner.

Sadker, M., & Sadker, D. (1994). *Failing at fairness: How America's schools cheat girls.* New York: Scribners.

Sadler, T. W. (Ed.). (2005). Abstracts of papers presented at the thirty-fifth annual meeting of the Japanese Teratology Society, Tokyo, Japan. *Teratology, 52*(4), b1–b51.

Saffran, J. R. (2009). Acquiring grammatical patterns: Constraints on learning. In J. Colombo, P. McCardle & L. Freud (Eds.), *Infant pathways to language: Methods, models, and research disorders* (pp. 31–47). New York: Psychology Press.

Sagrestano, L. M., McCormick, S. H., Paikoff, R. L., & Holmbeck, G. N. (1999). Pubertal development and parent–child conflict in low-income, urban, African American adolescents. *Journal of Research on Adolescence 9*(1), 85–107.

Saini, R., Saini, S., & Sharma, S. (2010). Oral sex, oral health, and orogenital infections. *Journal of Global Infectious Disease, 2*(1), 57–62.

Sáinz, M., & Eccles, J., (2012). Self-concept of computer and math ability: Gender implications across time and within ICT studies. *Journal of Vocational Behavior, 80*(2), 486–499.

Salami, M., et al. (2010). Change in visual experience impairs rat's spatial learning in Morris water maze. *Journal of Isfahan Medical School, 28*(111).

Salapatek, P. (1975). Pattern perception in early infancy. In L. B. Cohen & P. Salapatek (Eds.), *Infant perception: From sensation to cognition.* New York: Academic Press.

Salas, H. S., Aziz, Z., Villareale, N., & Diekema, D. S. (2008). The research and family liaison: Enhancing informed consent. *IRB: Ethics & Human Research, 30*(4), 1–8.

Salvy, S-J., et al. (2008). Peer influence on children's physical activity: An experience sampling study. *Journal of Pediatric Psychology, 33*(1), 39–49.

Salzarulo, P., & Ficca, G. (Eds.). (2002). *Awakening and sleep–wake cycle across development.* Amsterdam: John Benjamins.

Salzburger, W., et al. (2008). Annotation of expressed sequence tags for the East African cichlid fish *Astatotilapia burtoni* and evolutionary analyses of cichlid ORFs. *BMC Genomics, 9,* 96. Published online February 25, 2008.

Santonastaso, P., Friederici, S., & Favaro, A. (2001). Sertraline in the treatment of restricting anorexia nervosa: An open controlled trial. *Journal of Child and Adolescent Psychopharmacology, 11*(2), 143–150.

Saudino, K. J. (2012). Sources of continuity and change in activity level in early childhood. *Child Development, 83*(1), 266–281.

Saunders, K. W. (2003). Regulating youth access to violent video games. *Law Review–Michigan State University, 51*(70).

Sava, S., & Yurgelun-Todd, D. A. (2008). Functional magnetic resonance in psychiatry. *Topics in Magnetic Resonance Imaging, 19*(2), 71–79.

Save the Children. (2008). *State of the world's mothers 2008.* Available at http://www.savethechildren.org/publications/mothers/2008/SOWM-2008-full-report.pdf.

Save the Children. (2011). *State of the world's mothers 2011.* Westport, CT: Save the Children. www.savethechildren.org.

Save the Children. (2012). 2012 Annual Report. Retrieved from: http://www.savethechildren.ca/page.aspx?pid=389.

Savic, I., Garcia-Falgueras, A., & Swaab, D. F. (2011). Sexual differentiation of the human brain in relation to gender identity and sexual orientation. In I. Savic (Ed.). *Sex differences in the human brain, their underpinnings and implications: Progress in Brain Research, 186* (pp. 41–64). New York: Elsevier.

Savin-Williams, R. C. (2007). Girl-on-girl sexuality. In B. J. R. Leadbeater & N. Way (Eds.), *Urban girls revisited: Building strengths* (pp. 301–318). New York: New York University Press.

Savin-Williams, R. C., & Berndt, T. (1990). Friendship and peer relations. In S. S. Feldman & G. R. Elliott (Eds.), *At the threshold: The developing adolescent.* Cambridge, MA: Harvard University Press.

Savin-Williams, R. C., & Diamond, L. M. (2000). Sexual identity trajectories among sexual-minority youths: Gender comparisons. *Archives of Sexual Behavior, 29*(6), 607–627.

Savin-Williams, R. C., & Diamond, L. M. (2004). Sex. In R. M. Lerner & L. Steinberg (Eds.), *Handbook of adolescent psychology* (2nd ed., pp. 189–231). Hoboken, NJ: Wiley.

Sawady, J., et al. (2007). The National Institute of Child Health and Human Development Maternal-Fetal Medicine Units Network Beneficial Effects of Antenatal Repeated Steroids study: Impact of repeated doses of antenatal corticosteroids on placental growth and histologic findings. *American Journal of Obstetrics & Gynecology, 197*(3), 281.e1–281.e8.

Sawyer, D. J. (2006). Dyslexia: A generation of inquiry. *Topics in Language Disorders, 26*(2), 95–109.

Saxe, G. N., Ellis, B. H., Fogler, J., & Navalta, C. P. (2012). Innovations in practice: Preliminary evidence for effective family engagement in treatment for child traumatic stress—Trauma systems therapy approach to preventing school dropout. *Child and Adolescent Mental Health, 17*(1), 58–61.

Sayegh, Y., & Dennis, W. (1965). The effect of supplementary experience upon the behavioral development of infants in institutions. *Child Development, 36*(1), 81–90.

Scarr, S. (1993, March). *IQ correlations among members of transracial adoptive families.* Paper presented at the meeting of the Society for Research in Child Development, New Orleans, LA.

Scarr, S. (1998). How do families affect intelligence? Social environmental and behavior genetic predictions. In J. J. McArdle & R. W. Woodcock (Eds.), *Human cognitive abilities in theory and practice* (pp. 113–136). Mahwah, NJ: Erlbaum.

Scarr, S., & McCartney, K. (1983). How people make their own environments: A theory of genotype-environment effects. *Child Development, 54*, 424–435.

Schaffer, H. R., & Emerson, P. E. (1964). The development of social attachments in infancy. *Monographs of the Society for Research in Child Development, 29*(94).

Scharf, M., Shulman, S., & Avigad-Spitz, L. (2005). Sibling relationships in emerging adulthood and in adolescence. *Journal of Adolescent Research, 20*(1), 64–90.

Scheithauer, H., Hayer, T., Petermann, F., & Jugert, G. (2006). Physical, verbal, and relational forms of bullying among German students: Age trends, gender differences, and correlates. *Aggressive Behavior, 32*(3), 261–275.

Scherf, K. S., Behrmann, M., Kimchi, R., & Luna, B. (2009). Emergence of global shape processing continues through adolescence. *Child Development, 80*(1), 162–177.

Schmidt, L. A., et al. (2008). Shyness and timidity in young adults who were born at extremely low birth weight. *Pediatrics, 122*(1), e181–e187.

Schmidt, M. E., & Anderson, D. R. (2007). The impact of television on cognitive development and educational achievement. In N. Pecora et al. (Eds.), *Children and television: Fifty years of research*. Mahwah, NJ: Erlbaum.

Schmidt, M. E., et al. (2009). Television viewing in infancy and child cognition at 3 years of age in a US cohort. *Pediatrics, 123*(3), e370–e375.

Schmitt, D. P. (2008). An evolutionary perspective on mate choice and relationship initiation. In S. Sprecher, A. Wenzel, & J. H. Harvey (Eds.), *Handbook of relationship initiation* (pp. 55–74). New York: CRC Press.

Schmitt, D. P., et al. (2012). A reexamination of sex differences in sexuality: New studies reveal old truths. *Current Directions in Psychological Science, 21*(2), 135–139.

Schneider, S. K., O'Donnell, L., Stueve, A., & Coulter, R. W. S. (2012). Cyberbullying, school bullying, and psychological distress: A regional census of high school students. *American Journal of Public Health, 102*(1), 171–177.

Schneider, S., et al. (2012). Risk taking and adolescent reward system: A potential common link to substance abuse. *American Journal of Psychiatry, 169*(1), 39–46.

Schneider, W. (2010). Memory development in childhood. In U. Goswami (Ed.), *The Wiley–Blackwell handbook of childhood cognitive development* (2nd ed.) (pp. 347–376). Chichester, West Sussex, UK: Wiley–Blackwell.

Schonfeld, A. M., Mattson, S. N., & Riley, E. P. (2005). Moral maturity and delinquency after prenatal alcohol exposure. *Journal of Studies on Alcohol, 66*(4), 545–554.

Schoppe-Sullivan, S. J., Mangelsdorf, S. C., Brown, G. L., & Sokolowski, M. S. (2007). Goodness-of-fit in family context: Infant temperament, marital quality, and early coparenting behavior. *Infant Behavior & Development, 30*(1), 82–96.

Schraf, M., & Hertz-Lazarowitz, R. (2003). Social networks in the school context: Effects of culture and gender. *Journal of Social and Personal Relationships, 20*(6), 843–858.

Schtscherbyna, A., Soares, E., de Oliveira, F., & Ribeiro, B. (2009). Female athlete triad in elite swimmers of the city of Rio de Janeiro, Brazil. *Nutrition, 25*(6), 634–639.

Schuetze, P., Zeskind, P. S., & Eiden, R. D. (2003). The perceptions of infant distress signals varying in pitch by cocaine-using mothers. *Infancy, 4*(1), 65–83.

Schulte-Körne, G., Warnke, A., & Remschmidt, H. (2006). Genetics of dyslexia. *Zeitschrift für Kinder- und Jugendpsychiatrie und Psychotherapie, 34*(6), 435–444.

Schultz, D. P., & Schultz, S. E. (2012). *A history of modern psychology* (10th ed.). Belmont, CA: Cengage.

Schultz, D., & Shaw, D. S. (2003). Boys' maladaptive social information processing, family emotional climate, and pathways to early conduct problems. *Social Development, 12*(3), 440–460.

Schultz, L. T., & Heimberg, R. G. (2008). Attentional focus in social anxiety disorder: Potential for interactive processes. *Clinical Psychology Review, 28*(7), 1206–1221.

Schumacher, D., & Queen, J. A. (2007). *Overcoming obesity in childhood and adolescence: A guide for school leaders*. Thousand Oaks, CA: Corwin Press.

Schunk, D. H. (2012). *Learning theories: An educational perspective* (6th ed.). Boston, MA: Pearson.

Schutz, G., et al. (2008). Education policy and equality of opportunity. *Kyklos, 61*(2), 279–308.

Schwam-Harris, M. (2008). Achieving permanency in public agency adoptions: Secondary analyses of the national survey of child and adolescent well-being data. *Dissertation Abstracts International Section A: Humanities and Social Sciences, 68*(9-A), 4073.

Schwartz, S. J. (2001). The evolution of Eriksonian and neo-Eriksonian identity theory and research: A review and integration. *Identity, 1*(1), 7–58.

Schwartz, S. J., Zamboanga, B. L., Weisskirch, R. S., & Rodriguez, L. (2009). The relationships of personal and ethnic identity exploration to indices of adaptive and maladaptive psychosocial functioning. *International Journal of Behavioral Development, 33*(2), 131–144.

Scull, A. (2010). Left brain, right brain: One brain, two brains. *Brain, 133*(10), 3153–3156.

Sears, J. (2009). *Signs of being ready for solid foods*. Available at http://www.wholesomebabyfood.com/readyforsolids.htm. Accessed March 18, 2009.

Secker-Walker, R. H., & Vacek, P. M. (2003). Relationships between cigarette smoking during pregnancy, gestational age, maternal weight gain, and infant birthweight. *Addictive Behaviors, 28*(1), 55–66.

Seidah, A., & Bouffard, T. (2007). Being proud of oneself as a person or being proud of one's physical appearance: What matters for feeling well in adolescence? *Social Behavior and Personality, 35*(2), 255–268.

Seiler, C. B., Jones, K. E., Shera, D., & Armstrong, C. L. (2011). Brain region white matter associations with visual selective attention. *Brain Imaging and Behavior, 5*(4), 262–273.

Selman, R. L. (1976). Social-cognitive understanding. In T. Lickona (Ed.), *Moral development and behavior: Theory, research, and social issues*. New York: Holt, Rinehart & Winston.

Selman, R. L. (1980). *The growth of interpersonal understanding: Developmental and clinical analysis*. New York: Academic Press.

Selman, R. L., & Dray, A. J. (2006). Risk and prevention. In K. A. Renninger, I. E. Sigel, W. Damon & R. M. Lerner (Eds.), *Handbook of child psychology* (6th ed.), Vol. 4, *Child psychology in practice* (pp. 378–419). Hoboken, NJ: Wiley.

Serbin, L. A., Poulin-Dubois, D., Colburne, K. A., Sen, M. G., & Eichstedt, J. A. (2001). Gender stereotyping in infancy: Visual preferences for and knowledge of gender-stereotyped toys in the second year. *International Journal of Behavioral Development, 25*(1), 7–15.

Sex Information and Education Council of Canada. (2010). *Have teen pregnancy rates in Canada been going up, down or holding steady?* Toronto, ON.

Sex Information and Education Council of Canada. (2010). *Sexual health education in the schools: Questions and answers* (3rd ed.). Toronto, ON.

Seymour, S. C. (1999). *Women, family, and child care in India*. Cambridge, UK: Cambridge University Press.

Shamay-Tsoory, S. G. (2011). The neural bases for empathy. *The Neuroscientist, 17*(1), 18–24.

Shaw, G. M., Velie, E. M., & Schaffer, D. (1996). Risk of neural tube defect–affected pregnancies among obese women. *Journal of the American Medical Association, 275*, 1093–1096.

Shaywitz, B. A., Lyon, G. R., & Shaywitz, S. E. (2006a). The role of functional magnetic resonance imaging in understanding reading and dyslexia. *Developmental Neuropsychology, 30*(1), 613–632.

Shaywitz, S. E. (1998). Dyslexia. *New England Journal of Medicine, 338*, 307–312.

Shaywitz, S. E., & Shaywitz, B. A. (2003). Neurobiological indices of dyslexia. In H. L. Swanson et al. (Eds.), *Handbook of learning disabilities* (pp. 514–531). New York: Guilford.

Shaywitz, S. E., Mody, M., & Shaywitz, B. A. (2006b). Neural mechanisms in dyslexia. *Current Directions in Psychological Science, 15*(6), 278–281.

Sheeber, L. B., Davis, B., Leve, C., Hops, H., & Tildesley, E. (2007). Adolescents' relationships with their mothers and fathers: Associations with depressive disorder and subdiagnostic symptomatology. *Journal of Abnormal Psychology, 116*(1), 144–154.

Shepard, K. G., Spence, M. J., & Sasson, N. J. (2012). Distinct facial characteristics differentiate communicative intent of infant-directed speech. *Infant and Child Development.* doi:10.1002/icd.1757.

Sherman, J., & Bisanz, J. (2009). Equivalence in symbolic and nonsymbolic contexts: Benefits of solving problems with manipulatives. *Journal of Educational Psychology, 10*(1), 88–100.

Sherwin-White, S. (2006). Review of The social toddler: Promoting positive behaviour. *Infant Observation, 9*(1), 95–97.

Shimoni, M., Engel-Yeger, B., & Tirosh, E. (2012). Executive dysfunctions among boys with ADHD: Performance-based test and parents' report. *Research in Developmental Disabilities, 33*(3), 858–865.

Shin, H. B., & Bruno, R. (2003, October). *Language use and English speaking ability: 2000.* Washington, DC: U.S. Bureau of the Census.

Shirk, S., Burwell, R., & Harter, S. (2003). Strategies to modify low self-esteem in adolescents. In M. A. Reinecke et al. (Eds.), *Cognitive therapy with children and adolescents: A casebook for clinical practice* (2nd ed.) (pp. 189–213). New York: Guilford.

Shortt, A. L., Barrett, P. M., & Fox, T. L. (2001). Evaluating the FRIENDS Program: A cognitive-behavioral group treatment for anxious children and their parents. *Journal of Clinical Child Psychology, 30*(4), 525–535.

Shroff, H., et al. (2006). Features associated with excessive exercise in women with eating disorders. *International Journal of Eating Disorders, 39*(6), 454–461.

Shuster, M. M., Li, Y., Shi, J. (2012). Maternal cultural values and parenting practices: Longitudinal associations with Chinese adolescents' aggression. *Journal of Adolescence, 35*(2), 345–355.

Shweder, R. A., Goodnow, J., Hatano, G., LeVine, R. A., Markus, H., & Miller, P. (1998). The cultural psychology of development: One mind, many mentalities. In W. Damon & R. M. Lerner (Eds.), *Handbook of child psychology: Volume 1: Theoretical models of human development* (5th ed.) (pp. 865–937). Hoboken, NJ: John Wiley & Sons, Inc.

Shweder, R. A., Much, N. C., Mahapatra, M., & Park, L. (1997). The "big three" of morality (autonomy, community, divinity) and the "big three" explanations of suffering. In A. M. Brandt & P. Rozin (Eds.), *Morality and health,* (pp. 119–169). Florence, KY: Taylor & Frances/Routledge.

Siegal, M., & Surian, L. (2012). *Access to language and cognitive development.* New York: Oxford University Press.

Siegel, L. J., & Welsh, B. C. (2011). *Juvenile delinquency: Theory, practice, and law* (11th ed.). Belmont. CA: Cengage.

Siegel, L. S. (1992). Infant motor, cognitive, and language behaviors as predictors of achievement at school age. In C. Rovee-Collier & L. P. Lipsitt (Eds.), *Advances in infancy research,* Vol. 7. Norwood, NJ: Ablex.

Siegler, R. S., & Alibali, M. W. (2005). *Children's thinking* (4th ed.). Upper Saddle River, NJ: Prentice Hall.

Siegler, R. S., Liebert, D. E., & Liebert, R. M. (1973). Inhelder and Piaget's pendulum problem: Teaching pre-adolescents to act as scientists. *Developmental Psychology, 9,* 97–101.

Sigafoos, J., Green, V. A., Payne, D., O'Reilly, M. F., & Lancioni, G. E. (2009). A classroom-based antecedent intervention reduces obsessive-repetitive behavior in an adolescent with autism. *Clinical Case Studies, 8*(1), 3–13.

Signorello, L. B., & McLaughlin, J. K. (2004). Maternal caffeine consumption and spontaneous abortion: A review of the epidemiologic evidence. *Epidemiology, 15*(2), 229–239.

Signorello, L. B., & McLaughlin, J. K. (2008). Caffeine and miscarriage: Case closed? *American Journal of Obstetrics & Gynecology, 199*(5), e14–e15.

Silk, T. J., & Wood, A. G. (2011). Lessons about neurodevelopment from anatomical magnetic resonance imaging. *Journal of Developmental Behavioral Pediatrics, 32*(2), 158–168.

Silles, M. (2010). The implications of family size and birth order for test scores and behavioral development. *Economics of Education Review, 29*(5), 795–803.

Silva, C., et al. (2012). Literacy: Exploring working memory systems. *Journal of Clinical and Experimental Neuropsychology, 26*(2), 266–277.

Sim, T. N., & Ong, L. P. (2005). Parent physical punishment and child aggression in a Singapore Chinese preschool. *Journal of Marriage and Family, 67*(1), 85–99.

Simion, F., Cassia, V. M., Turati, C., & Valenza, E. (2001). The origins of face perception: Specific versus nonspecific mechanisms. *Infant and Child Development, 10*(1–2), 59–65.

Simmons, R. G., & Blyth, D. A. (1987). *Moving into adolescence: The impact of pubertal change and school context.* Hawthorne, NY: Aldine deGruyter.

Simonelli, A., Monti, F., & Magalotti, D. (2005). The complex phenomenon of failure to thrive: Medical, psychological and relational-affective aspects. *Psicologia Clinica dello Sviluppo, 9*(2), 183–212.

Simonton, D. K. (2000). Creativity: Cognitive, personal, developmental, and social aspects. *American Psychologist, 55,* 151–158.

Simonton, D. K. (2006). Creativity around the world in 80 ways . . . but with one destination. In J. C. Kaufman & R. Sternberg (Eds.), *The international handbook of creativity* (pp. 490–496). New York: Cambridge University Press.

Simpkins, S. D., Fredricks, J. A., Davis-Kean, P. E., & Eccles, J. S. (2006). Healthy mind, healthy habits: The influence of activity involvement in middle childhood. In A. C. Huston & M. N. Ripke (Eds.), *Developmental contexts in middle childhood: Bridges to adolescence and adulthood. Cambridge studies in social and emotional development* (pp. 283–302). New York: Cambridge University Press.

Simpson, J. L. (2000, June 1). Invasive diagnostic procedures for prenatal genetic diagnosis. *Journal Watch Women's Health.* Available at http://womenshealth.jwatch.org.

Simpson, J. L., Bailey, L. B., Pietrzik, K., Shane, B., & Holzgreve. (2011). Micronutrients and women of reproductive potential: Required dietary intake and consequences of dietary deficiency or excess. Part II—Vitamin D, Vitamin A, iron, zinc, iodine, essential fatty acids. *Journal of Maternal–Fetal and Neonatal Medicine, 24*(1), 1–24.

Sinclair, S., Dunn, E., & Lowery, B. S. (2005). The relationship between parental racial attitudes and children's implicit prejudice. *Journal of Experimental Social Psychology, 41,* 283–289.

Singh, A., et al. (2012). Physical activity and performance at school. *Archives of Pediatrics and Adolescent Medicine, 166*(1), 49–55.

Singh, K., & Ozturk, M. (2000). Effect of part-time work on high school mathematics and science course taking. *Journal of Educational Research, 91*(2), 67–74.

Sinha, M. (2012). *Family violence in Canada: A statistical profile, 2010.* Ottawa, ON: Statistics Canada. Catalogue no. 85-002-x.

Sinno, S. M., & Killen, M. (2009). Moms at work and dads at home: Children's evaluations of parental roles. *Applied Developmental Science, 13*(1), 16–29.

Skeels, H. M. (1966). Adult status of children with contrasting early life experiences: A follow-up study. *Monographs of the Society for Research in Child Development, 31*(3, ser. 105).

Skinner, B. F. (1957). *Verbal behavior.* New York: Appleton.

Skinner, B. F. (1983). *A matter of consequences.* New York: Knopf.

Skoczenski, A. M. (2002). Limitations on visual sensitivity during infancy: Contrast sensitivity, vernier acuity, and orientation processing. In J. W. Fagen & H. Hayne (Eds.), *Progress in infancy research,* Vol. 2. Mahwah, NJ: Erlbaum.

Skorikov, V. B., & Vondracek, F. W. (2011). Occupational identity. *Handbook of Identity Theory and Research,* Part 6, 693–714.

Slane, J. D., Burt, A., & Klump, K. L. (2012). Bulimic behaviors and alcohol use: Shared genetic influences. *Behavior Genetics, 42*(4), 603–613.

Slater, A., et al. (2010). Visual perception. In J. G. Bremner & T. D. Wachs (Eds.). *The Wiley-Blackwell handbook of infant development*, Vol. 1 (2nd ed.). Wiley-Blackwell, Oxford, UK.

Slater, A., & Tiggeman, M. (2010). Body image and disordered eating in adolescent girls and boys: A test of objectification theory. *Sex Roles*, 63(1–2), 42–49.

Slaughter, V. (2011). Development of social cognition. In D. Skuse, H. Bruce, L. Dowdney, & D. Mrazek (Eds.). *Child psychology and psychiatry: Frameworks for practice* (2nd ed.) (pp. 51–55). Hoboken, NJ: Wiley.

Slavin, R. E. (2012). *Educational psychology: Theory and practice* (10th ed.). Upper Saddle River, NJ: Pearson.

Slobin, D. I. (2001). Form/function relations: How do children find out what they are? In M. Tomasello & E. Bates (Eds.), *Language development: The essential readings*. Malden, MA: Blackwell.

Small, E., et al. (2010). Tobacco smoke exposure induces nicotine dependence in rats. *Psychopharmacology*, 208(1), 143–158.

Smetana, J. G. (1990). Morality and conduct disorders. In M. Lewis & S. M. Miller (Eds.), *Handbook of developmental psychopathology*. New York: Plenum.

Smetana, J. G. (2011). *Adolescents, families, and social development*. Chichester, West Sussex, UK: Wiley-Blackwell.

Smetana, J. G., Campione-Barr, N., & Metzger, A. (2006). Adolescent development in interpersonal and societal contexts. *Annual Review of Psychology*, 57, 255–284.

Smetana, J. G., Daddis, C., & Chuang, S. S. (2003). "Clean your room!" A longitudinal investigation of adolescent–parent conflict and conflict resolution in middle-class African American families. *Journal of Adolescent Research*, 18(6), 631–650.

Smiley, P. A., & Johnson, R. S. (2006). Self-referring terms, event transitivity and development of self. *Cognitive Development*, 21(3), 266–284.

Smith, J. L., Kausar, R., & Holt-Lunstad, J. (2007). Stigma consciousness in the classroom. *Sex Roles*, 57(1–2).

Smith, P. K. (1979). The ontogeny of fear in children. In W. Sluckin (Ed.), *Fears in animals and man*. London: Van Nostrand Reinhold.

Smith, R. L., & Rose, A. J. (2011). The "cost of caring" in youths' friendships: Considering associations among social perspective taking, co-rumination, and empathetic distress. *Developmental Psychology*, 47(6), 1792–1803.

Smith, W. J., & Foster, W. F. (1996). *Equal educational opportunities for students with disabilities*. Montreal, QC: McGill University, Office of Research on Educational Policy.

Smolka, E., & Eviatar, Z. (2006). Phonological and orthographic visual word recognition in the two cerebral hemispheres: Evidence from Hebrew. *Cognitive Neuropsychology*, 23(6), 972–989.

Snarey, J., & Samuelson, P. (2008). Moral education in the cognitive developmental tradition: Lawrence Kohlberg's revolutionary ideas. In L. P.

Nucci & D. Narváez (Eds.), *Handbook of moral and character education* (pp. 53–79). London: Routledge.

Snarey, J. R. (1994). Cross-cultural universality of social-moral development: A critical review of Kohlbergian research. In B. Puka (Ed.), *New research in moral development* (pp. 268–298). New York: Garland.

Snegovskikh, V. V., et al. (2011). Surfactant protein-A (SP-A) selectively inhibits prostaglandin $F_{2\alpha}$ ($PGF_{2\alpha}$) production in term decidua: Implications for the onset of labor. *The Journal of Clinical Endocrinology & Metabolism*, 96,(4), E624–E632.

Snegovskikh, V., Park, J. S., & Norwitz, E. R. (2006). Endocrinology of parturition. *Endocrinology and Metabolism Clinics of North America*, 35(1), 173–191.

Snow, K. L. (2006). Measuring school readiness: Conceptual and practical considerations. *Early Education and Development*, 17, 7–41.

Snyder, H. M., & Sickmund, M. (2006). *Juvenile offenders and victims: 2006 national report*. Washington, DC: U.S. Department of Justice, Office of Justice Programs, Office of Juvenile Justice and Delinquency Prevention.

Snyder, J., et al. (2011). The impact of brief teacher training in classroom management and child behavior in at-risk preschool settings: Mediators and treatment utility. *Journal of Applied Developmental Psychology*, 32(6), 336–345.

Sodian, B., Taylor, C., Harris, P. L., & Perner, J. (1991). Early deception and the child's theory of mind: False trails and genuine markers. *Child Development*, 62, 468–483.

Soenens, B., et al. (2007). Conceptualizing parental autonomy support: Adolescent perceptions of promotion of independence versus promotion of volitional functioning. *Developmental Psychology*, 43(3), 633–646.

Solmeyer, A. R., & Feinberg, M. E. (2011). Mother and father adjustment during early parenthood: The roles of infant temperament and coparenting relationship quality. *Infant Behavior and Development*, 34(4), 504–514.

Sommer, I. E. C., Ramsey, N. F., Mandl, R. C. W., & Kahn, R. S. (2002). Language lateralization in monozygotic twin pairs concordant and discordant for handedness. *Brain*, 125(12), 2710–2718.

Sontag, L. M., Graber, J. A., & Clemans, K. H. (2011). The role of peer stress and pubertal timing on symptoms of psychopathology during early adolescence. *Journal of Youth and Adolescence*, 40(10), 1371–1382.

Sorce, J., Emde, R. N., Campos, J. J., & Klinnert, M. D. (2000). Maternal emotional signaling: Its effect on the visual cliff behavior of 1-year-olds. In D. Muir & A. Slater (Eds.), *Infant development: The essential readings*. *Essential readings in developmental psychology* (pp. 282–292). Malden, MA: Blackwell.

Sousa, C., et al. (2011). Longitudinal study of the effects of child abuse and children's exposure to domestic violence, parent-child attachments, and antisocial behavior in adolescence. *Journal of Interpersonal Violence*, 26(1), 111–136.

Sovio, U., et al. (2009). Genetic determinants of height growth assessed longitudinally from infancy to adulthood in the Northern Finland Birth Cohort 1966. *PLoS Genetics*, 5(3), e1000409.

Specht, J. (2013). School inclusion: Are we getting it right? *Education Canada*, 53(2). Retrieved from http://www.cea-ace.ca/education-canada/issue/Spring2013 on April 3, 2014.

Spelke, E. S., & Owsley, C. (1979). Intermodal exploration and knowledge in infancy. *Infant Behavior and Development*, 2, 13–27.

Spencer, J. P., Austin, A., & Schutte, A. R. (2012). Contributions of dynamic systems theory to cognitive development. *Cognitive Development*, 27, 401–418.

Spencer, J. P. Corbetta, D., Buchanan, P., Clearfield, M., Ulrich, B., & Schoner, G. (2006). Moving toward a gran theory of development: In memory of Esther Thelen. *Child Development*, 77(6), 1521–1538.

Spencer, M. B., Dornbusch, S. M., & Mont-Reynaud, R. (1990). Challenges in studying minority youth. In S. S. Feldman & G. R. Elliott (Eds.), *At the threshold: The developing adolescent*. Cambridge, MA: Harvard University Press.

Spencer, N. (2006). Explaining the social gradient in smoking in pregnancy: Early life course accumulation and cross-sectional clustering of social risk exposures in the 1958 British national cohort. *Social Science & Medicine*, 62(5), 1250–1259.

Spieker, S., Nelson, D., DeKlyen, M., & Staerkel, F. (2005). Enhancing early attachments in the context of Early Head Start: Can programs emphasizing family support improve rates of secure infant–mother attachments in low-income families? In L. J. Berlin, Y. Ziv, L. Amaya-Jackson & M. T. Greenberg (Eds.), *Enhancing early attachments: Theory, research, intervention, and policy*. Duke series in child development and public policy (pp. 250–275). New York: Guilford.

Spittle, A. J., et al. (2010). Preventive care at home for very preterm infants improves infant and caregiver outcomes at 2 years. *Pediatrics*, 126, e171–e178.

Spitz, R. A. (1965). *The first year of life: A psychoanalytic study of normal and deviant object relations*. New York: International Universities Press.

Spitzer, R. L., Gibbon, M., Skodol, A. E., Williams, J. B. W., & First, M. B. (2002). *DSM–IV–TR casebook*. Washington, DC: American Psychiatric Press.

Sroufe, L. A. (1998). Cited in S. Blakeslee (1998, August 4), Re-evaluating significance of baby's bond with mother, *New York Times*, pp. F1, F2.

Sroufe, L. A., Bennett, C., Englund, M., Urban, J., & Shulman, S. (1993). The significance of gender boundaries in pre-adolescence: Contemporary correlates and antecedents of boundary violation and maintenance. *Child Development, 64,* 455–466.

Staff, J., Mortimer, J. T., & Uggen, C. (2004). Work and leisure in adolescence. In R. M. Lerner & L. Steinberg (Eds.), *Handbook of adolescent psychology* (2nd ed.) (pp. 429–450). Hoboken, NJ: Wiley.

Stahmer, A. C., Ingersoll, B., & Koegel, R. L. (2004). Inclusive programming for toddlers autism spectrum disorders: Outcomes from the Children's Toddler School. *Journal of Positive Behavior Interventions, 6*(2), 67–82.

Stanford University School of Medicine. (2012). *Sibling preparation classes.* Palo Alto, CA: Lucille Packard Children's Hospital at Stanford.

Stanford, J. N., & McCabe, M. P. (2005). Sociocultural influences on adolescent boys' body image and body change strategies. *Body Image, 2*(2), 105–113.

Statistics Canada. (2001). Canada Census 2001. Ottawa, ON: Statistics Canada.

Statistics Canada. (2006). Television viewing. *The Daily* (March 31, 2006). Available at http://www.statcan.ca/Daily/English/060331/d060331b.htm.

Statistics Canada. (2008). Canadian Vital Statistics, Death Database, and Demography Division (population estimates). Potential years of life lost, population aged 0 to 74, by selected causes of death and sex, Canada, provinces and territories, annual. http://www.communityaccounts.ca/SALandscape/1_8_pyll.htm#RANGE!TFtn. Accessed June 6, 2012.

Statistics Canada. (2009). *Canadian Tobacco Use Monitoring Survey, 2009: Annual, Person File.* Ottawa: Statistics Canada.

Statistics Canada. (2011). Census of Population and Statistics Canada catalogue no. 98-312-XCB, http://www.statcan.gc.ca/tables-tableaux/sum-som/l01/cst01/famil50a-eng.htm.

Statistics Canada. (2011). *Divorces and crude divorce rates, Canada, provinces and territories, annual.* Ottawa, ON, Canada.

Statistics Canada. (2012). Leading Cause of death of children and youth by age group, 2006 to 2008. http://www.statcan.gc.ca/pub/11-402-x/2012000/chap/c-e/tbl/tbl05-eng.htm. Accessed July 4, 2014.

Statistics Canada. (2012). Linguistic characteristics of Canadians—Language, 2011 census of population. Ottawa, ON. Catalogue no. 98-314-X2011011.

Statistics Canada. (2012). Low Income Lines, 2010 to 2011: Income Research Paper Series. Catalogue no. 75F0002M (No.002). Ottawa, ON.

Statistics Canada. (2012). Portraits of families and living arrangements in Canada. Families, households, and marital status, 2011 Census of population. Ottawa, ON. Catalogue no. 98-312-X2011001.

Statistics Canada. (2012). Table 282-0002—Labour force survey estimates (LFS), by sex and detailed age group, annual (persons unless otherwise noted), CANSIM (database). Retrieved from http://www4.hrsdc.gc.ca/.3ndic.1t.4r@-eng.jsp?iid=13.

Statistics Canada. (2013). Immigration and ethnocultural diversity in Canada. National Household Survey, 2011. Ottawa, ON. Catalogue no. 99-010-X2011001.

Statistics Canada. (2014). Suicides and suicide rate, by sex and by age group. Statistics Canada, CANSIM, table 102-0551. http://www.statcan.gc.ca/tables-tableaux/sum-som/l01/cst01/hlth66a-eng.htm. Accessed June 2, 2014.

Stauffacher, K., & DeHart, G. B. (2006). Crossing social contexts: Relational aggression between siblings and friends during early and middle childhood. *Journal of Applied Developmental Psychology, 27*(3), 228–240.

Steele, H. (2005). Editorial. *Attachment & Human Development, 7*(4), 345.

Steele, M., Hodges, J., Kaniuk, J., Hillman, S., & Henderson, K. (2003). Attachment representations and adoption: Associations between maternal states of mind and emotion narratives in previously maltreated children. *Journal of Child Psychotherapy, 29*(2), 187–205.

Steinberg, L. (1996). *Beyond the classroom: Why school reform has failed and what parents need to do.* New York: Simon & Schuster.

Steinberg, L. (2011). Adolescent risk taking: A social neuroscience perspective. In E. Amsel, & J. Smetana (Eds.), *Adolescent vulnerabilities and opportunities* (pp. 41–64). New York: Cambridge University Press.

Steinbrink, C., et al. (2008). The contribution of white and gray matter differences to developmental dyslexia: Insights from DTI and VBM at 3.0 T. *Neuropsychologia, 46*(13), 3170–3178.

Sternberg, R. J. (2006). The nature of creativity. *Creativity Research Journal, 18*(1), 87–98.

Sternberg, R. J., & Kaufman, S. J. (Eds.). (2011). *The Cambridge handbook of intelligence.* New York: Cambridge University Press.

Sternberg, R. J., & Williams, W. M. (1997). Does the Graduate Record Examination predict meaningful success in the graduate training of psychologists? *American Psychologist, 52,* 630–641.

Sternberg, R. J., Grigorenko, E. L., & Kidd, K. K. (2005). Intelligence, race, and genetics. *American Psychologist, 60*(1), 46–59.

Stevens, B., et al. (2005). Consistent management of repeated procedural pain with sucrose in preterm neonates: Is it effective and safe for repeated use over time? *Clinical Journal of Pain, 21*(6), 543–548.

Steward, D. K. (2001). Behavioral characteristics of infants with nonorganic failure to thrive during a play interaction. *American Journal of Maternal/Child Nursing, 26*(2), 79–85.

Steyger, P. S. (2008). Synergistic ototoxicity of noise and chemical ototoxins. *Hearing and Hearing Disorders: Research and Diagnostics, 12,* 48–54.

Stillbirth Collaborative Research Network Writing Group. (2011). Association between stillbirth and risk factors known at pregnancy confirmation. *The Journal of the American Medical Association, 306*(22), 2469–2479.

Stipek, D., & Hakuta, K. (2007). Strategies to ensure that no child starts from behind. In J. L. Aber et al. (Eds.), *Child development and social policy: Knowledge for action, APA Decade of Behavior* (pp. 129–145). Washington, DC: American Psychological Association.

Stipek, D., Recchia, S., & McClintic, S. (1992). Self-evaluation in young children. *Monographs of the Society for Research in Child Development, 57*(1, ser. 226).

Storch, E. A., et al. (2007). Peer victimization, psychosocial adjustment, and physical activity in overweight and at-risk-for-overweight youth. *Journal of Pediatric Psychology, 32*(1), 80–89.

Strategies and solutions. (2011). http://www.cdc.gov/obesity/childhood/solutions.html. Accessed August 18, 2012.

Straus, M. A. (1995). Cited in C. Collins (1995, May 11), Spanking is becoming the new don't, *New York Times,* p. C8.

Straus, M. A. (2000). Corporal punishment and primary prevention of physical abuse. *Child Abuse and Neglect, 24*(9), 1109–1114.

Strauss, J., et al. (2012). Association study of early-immediate genes in childhood-onset mood disorders and suicide attempt. *Psychiatry Research, 197*(1), 49–54.

Strayer, J., & Roberts, W. (2004). Children's anger, emotional expressiveness, and empathy: Relations with parents' empathy, emotional expressiveness, and parenting practices. *Social Development, 13*(2), 229–254.

Streissguth, A. P. (1997). *Fetal alcohol syndrome: A guide for families and communities.* Baltimore, MD: Brookes.

Streri, A. (2002). Hand preference in 4-month-old infants: Global or local processing of objects in the haptic mode. *Current Psychology Letters: Behaviour, Brain and Cognition, 7,* 39–50.

Striegel-Moore, R. H., et al. (2003). Eating disorders in White and Black women. *American Journal of Psychiatry, 160*(7), 1326–1331.

Stright, A. D., Neitzel, C., Sears, K. G., & Hoke-Sinex, L. (2001). Instruction begins in the home: Relations between parental instruction and children's self-regulation in the classroom. *Journal of Educational Psychology, 93*(3), 456–466.

Strock, M. (2004). *Autism spectrum disorders (pervasive developmental disorders).* NIH Publication NIH-04–5511. Bethesda, MD: National Institute of

Mental Health, National Institutes of Health, U.S. Department of Health and Human Services. Available at http://www.nimh.nih.gov/publicat/autism.cfm.

Strohner, H., & Nelson, K. E. (1974). The young child's development of sentence comprehension: Influence of event probability, nonverbal context, syntactic form, and strategies. *Child Development, 45*, 567–576.

Strunk, T., Simmer, K., & Burgner, D. (2012). Prematurity and mortality in childhood and early adulthood. *Journal of the American Medical Association, 307*(1). doi:10.1001/jama.2011.1952.

Strutt, G. F., Anderson, D. R., & Well, A. D. (1975). A developmental study of the effects of irrelevant information on speeded classification. *Journal of Experimental Child Psychology, 20*, 127–135.

Stupica, B., Sherman, L. J., & Cassidy, J. (2011). Newborn irritability moderates the association between infant attachment security and toddler exploration and sociability. *Child Development, 82*(5), 1381–1389.

Subbarao, A., et al. (2008). Common genetic and environmental influences on major depressive disorder and conduct disorder. *Journal of Abnormal Child Psychology, 36*(3), 433–444.

Subbotsky, E. (2004). Magical thinking in judgments of causation. Can anomalous phenomena affect ontological causal beliefs in children and adults. *British Journal of Developmental Psychology, 22*, 123–152.

Subiaul, F., Anderson, S., Brandt, J., & Elkins, J. (2012). Multiple imitation mechanisms in children. *Developmental Psychology, 48*(4), 1165–1179.

Sukhodolsky, D. G., Golub, A., Stone, E. C., & Orban, L. (2005). Dismantling anger control training for children: A randomized pilot study of social problem-solving versus social skills training components. *Behavior Therapy, 36*, 15–23.

Suldo, S. M., Mihalas, S., Powell, H., & French, R. (2008). Ecological predictors of substance use in middle school students. *School Psychology Quarterly, 23*(3), 373–388.

Sullivan, R., et al. (2011). Infant bonding and attachment to the caregiver: Insights from basic and clinical science. *Clinics in Perinatology, 38*(4), 643–655.

Sumter, S. R., Bokhorst, C. L., Steinberg, L., & Westenberg, P. M. (2009). The developmental pattern of resistance to peer influence in adolescence: Will the teenager ever be able to resist? *Journal of Adolescence, 32*(4), 1009–1021.

Sun, Y. (2001). Family environment and adolescents' well-being before and after parents' marital disruption: A longitudinal analysis. *Journal of Marriage and Family, 63*(3), 697–713.

Suomi, S. J. (2005). Mother–infant attachment, peer relationships, and the development of social networks in rhesus monkeys. *Human Development, 48*(1–2), 67–79.

Suomi, S. J., Harlow, H. F., & McKinney, W. T. (1972). Monkey psychiatrists. *American Journal of Psychiatry, 128*, 927–932.

Super, C. M. (1981). Behavioral development in infancy. In R. H. Monroe, R. L. Monroe, & B. B. Whiting (Eds.), *Handbook of crosscultural human development* (pp. 181–270). New York: Garland.

Supple, A. J., & Small, S. A. (2006). The influence of parental support, knowledge, and authoritative parenting on Hmong and European American adolescent development. *Journal of Family Issues, 27*(9), 1214–1232.

Sussman, S., Skara, S., & Ames, S. L. (2006). Substance abuse among adolescents. In T. G. Plante (Ed.), *Mental disorders of the new millennium: Public and social problems* (Vol. 2) (pp. 127–169). Westport, CT: Praeger Publishers/Greenwood.

Sutherland, K. S., Singh, N. N., Conroy, M., & Stichter, J. P. (2004). Learned helplessness and students with emotional or behavioral disorders: Deprivation in the classroom. *Behavioral Disorders, 29*(2), 169–181.

Suzuki, L. A., Short, E. L., & Lee, C. S. (2011). Racial and ethnic group differences in intelligence in the United States. In R. J. Sternberg & S. J. Kaufman (Eds.), *The Cambridge handbook of intelligence* (pp. 273–292). New York: Cambridge University Press.

Swanson, H. L., & Alloway, T. P. (2012). Working memory, learning, and academic achievement. In K. R. Harris et al. (Eds.), *APA educational psychology handbook*, Vol 1: *Theories, constructs, and critical issues* (pp. 327–366). Washington, DC: American Psychological Association.

Syed, E. C. J., et al. (2010). Effect of sensory stimulation in rat barrel cortex, dorsolateral striatum and on corticostriatal functional connectivity. *European Journal of Neuroscience, 33*(3), 461–470.

Symons, D. (1978). *Play and aggression: A study of rhesus monkeys.* New York, NY: Columbia University Press.

Takahashi, K. (1990). Are the key assumptions of the "Strange Situation" procedure universal? A view from Japanese research. *Human Development, 33*, 23–30.

Tallandini, M. A., & Valentini, P. (1991). Symbolic prototypes in children's drawings of schools. *Journal of Genetic Psychology, 152*, 179–190.

Tamis-LeMonda, C. S., Cristofaro, T. N., Rodriguez, E. T., & Bornstein, M. H. (2006). Early language development: Social influences in the first years of life. In L. Balter & C. S. Tamis-LeMonda (Eds.), *Child psychology: A handbook of contemporary issues* (2nd ed.) (pp. 79–108). New York: Psychology Press.

Tan, G. (1999). Perceptions of multiculturalism and intent to stay in school among Mexican American students. *Journal of Research and Development in Education, 33*(1), 1–14.

Tang, C. S., Yeung, D. Y., & Lee, A. M. (2003). Psychosocial correlates of emotional responses to menarche among Chinese adolescent girls. *Journal of Adolescent Health, 33*(3), 193–201.

Tanner, J. M. (1989). *Fetus into man: Physical growth from conception to maturity.* Cambridge, MA: Harvard University Press.

Tardif, T., et al. (2005). Preschoolers' understanding of knowing-that and knowing-how in the United States and Hong Kong. *Developmental Psychology, 41*(3), 562–573.

Tasker, F. (2005). Lesbian mothers, gay fathers, and their children: A review. *Developmental and Behavioral Pediatrics, 26*, 224–240.

Tasker, F., & Granville, J. (2011). Children's views of family relationships in lesbian-led families. *Journal of GLBT Studies, 7*(1–2), 182–199.

Tassi, F., Schneider, B. H., & Richard, J. F. (2001). Competitive behavior at school in relation to social competence and incompetence in middle childhood. *Revue Internationale de Psychologie Sociale, 14*(2), 165–184.

Taylor, B. (2006). Vaccines and the changing epidemiology of autism. *Child: Care, Health and Development, 32*(5), 511–519.

Taylor, H. G., Espy, K. A., & Anderson, P. J. (2009). Mathematics deficiencies in children with very low birth weight or very preterm birth. *Developmental Disabilities Research Reviews, 15*(1), 52–59.

Taylor, H. G., Minich, N. M., Klein, N., & Hack, M. (2004). Longitudinal outcomes of very low birth weight: Neuropsychological findings. *Journal of the International Neuropsychological Society, 10*(2), 149–163.

Taylor, M., & Hort, B. (1990). Can children be trained in making the distinction between appearance and reality? *Cognitive Development, 5*, 89–99.

Taylor, M., Gonzalez, M., & Porter, R. (2011). Pathways to inflammation: Acne pathophysiology. *European Journal of Dermatology, 21*(3), 323–333.

Teen pregnancy prevention and United States students. (2011, July 12). Centers for Disease Control and Prevention. Accessed September 25, 2012. http://www.cdc.gov/healthyyouth/yrbs/pdf/us_pregnancy_combo.pdf.

Tehrani, J. A., & Mednick, S. A. (2000). Genetic factors and criminal behavior. *Federal Probation, 64*(2), 24–27.

Templer, D. I. (2006). Is the evidence on ethnicity and intelligence conclusive? *American Psychologist, 61*(2), 176–177.

Tennant, P. W. G., Rankin, J., & Bell, R. (2011). Impact of maternal obesity on stillbirth and infant death: Absolute risk and temporal trends. *Journal of Epidemiology and Community Health, 65*, doi:10.1136/jech.2011.142976a.79.

Terasawa, E., et al. (2012). Body weight impact on puberty: Effects of high-calorie diet on puberty onset in female rhesus monkeys. *Endocrinology*, doi: 10.1210/en.2011-1970.

Terry, D. (2000, July 16). *Getting under my skin.* Available at http://www.nytimes.com.

Teti, A., & Zallone, A. (2009). Do osteocytes contribute to bone mineral homeostasis? Osteocytic osteolysis revisited. *Bone, 44*(1), 11–16.

Teunissen, H. A., et al. (2011). The interaction between pubertal timing and peer popularity for boys and girls. *Journal of Abnormal Child Psychology, 39*(3), 413–423.

Tharner, A., et al. (2012). Maternal lifetime history of depression and depressive symptoms in the prenatal and early postnatal period do not predict infant–mother attachment quality in a large, population-based Dutch cohort study. *Attachment & Human Development, 14*(1), 63–81.

Thelen, E., & Smith, L. B. (2006). Dynamic Systems theories. In R. M. Lerner (Ed.), *Handbook of child psychology: Vol. I. Theoretical models of human development* (6th ed., pp. 258–312). Hoboken NJ: Wiley.

Thomas, A., & Chess, S. (1989). Temperament and personality. In G. A. Kohnstamm, J. E. Bates & M. K. Rothbart (Eds.), *Temperament in childhood.* Chichester, England: Wiley.

Thompson, A. M., Baxter-Jones, A. D. G., Mirwald, R. L., & Bailey, D. A. (2003). Comparison of physical activity in male and female children: Does maturation matter? *Medicine and Science in Sports and Exercise, 35*(10), 1684–1690.

Thompson, E. M., & Morgan, E. M. (2008). "Mostly straight" young women: Variations in sexual behavior and identity. *Developmental Psychology, 44*(1), 15–21.

Thompson, R. A. (2008). Measure twice, cut once: Attachment theory and the NICHD Study of Early Child Care and Youth Development. *Attachment and Human Development, 10*(3), 287–297.

Thompson, R. A., Easterbrooks, M. A., & Padilla-Walker, L. M. (2003). Social and emotional development in infancy. In R. M. Lerner et al. (Eds.), *Handbook of psychology: Developmental psychology.* New York: Wiley.

Thompson, R. A., & Limber, S. P. (1990). "Social anxiety" in infancy: Stranger and separation reactions. In H. Leitenberg (Ed.), *Handbook of social and evaluation anxiety.* New York: Plenum.

Thompson, R. A., & Meyer, S. (2007). Socialization of emotion regulation in the family. In J. J. Gross (Ed.), *Handbook of emotion regulation* (pp. 249–268). New York: Guilford.

Thompson, V. J., et al. (2003). Influences on diet and physical activity among middle-class African-American 8- to 10-year old girls at risk of becoming obese. *Journal of Nutrition Education and Behavior, 35*(3), 115–123.

Thurstone, L. L. (1938). *Primary mental abilities.* Psychometric Monographs, 1.

Tiedemann, J. (2000). Parents' gender stereotypes and teachers' beliefs as predictors of children's concept of their mathematical ability in elementary school. *Journal of Educational Psychology, 92*(1), 144–151.

Tijms, J. (2007). The development of reading accuracy and reading rate during treatment of dyslexia. *Educational Psychology, 27*(2), 273–294.

Timmerman, L. M. (2006). Family care versus day care: Effects on children. In B. M. Gayle et al. (Eds.), *Classroom communication and instructional processes: Advances through meta-analysis* (pp. 245–260). Mahwah, NJ: Erlbaum.

Tisdale, S. (2011). Linking social environments with the well-being of adolescents in dual-earner and single working parent families. *Youth & Society,* doi:10.1177/0044118X10396640.

Tobbell, J. (2003). Students' experiences of the transition from primary to secondary school. *Educational and Child Psychology, 20*(4), 4–14.

Tobin, D. D., et al. (2010). The intra-psychics of gender: A model of self-socialization. *Psychological Review, 117*(2), 601–622.

Tomasello, M. (2010). Language development. In U. Goswami (Ed.), *The Wiley–Blackwell handbook of childhood cognitive development* (2nd ed.) (pp. 239–257). Chichester, West Sussex, UK: Wiley–Blackwell.

Tomasetto, C., Alparone, F. M., & Cadinu, M. (2011). Girls' math performance under stereotype threat: The moderating role of mothers' gender stereotypes. *Developmental Psychology, 47*(4), 943–949.

Tong, S., Caddy, D., & Short, R. V. (1997). Use of dizygotic to monozygotic twinning ratio as a measure of fertility. *The Lancet, 349,* 843–845.

Torpy, J. M., Lynm, C., & Golub, R. M. (2011). Local anesthesia. *Journal of the American Medical Association, 306*(12), 1395.

Totsika, V., & Sylva, K. (2004). The Home Observation for Measurement of the Environment revisited. Measurement issues. *Child & Adolescent Mental Health, 9*(1), 25–35.

Towse, J. N., Hitch, G. J., Hamilton, Z., & Pirrie, S. (2008). The endurance of children's working memory: A recall time analysis. *Journal of Experimental Child Psychology, 101*(2), 156–163.

Towse, J. N., Hitch, G. J., Horton, N., & Harvey, K. (2010). Synergies between processing and memory in children's reading span. *Developmental Science, 13*(5), 779–789.

Trenholm, C., et al. (2007). *Impacts of four Title V, Section 510 abstinence education programs. Final report.* Submitted to USDHHS, Office of the Assistant Secretary for Planning and Evaluation. Submitted by Mathematica Policy Research, Inc., Contract No.: HHS 100-98-0010. Available at http://www.mathematica-mpr.com/publications/PDFs/impactabstinence.pdf.

Trent, K. (2011). Too many men? Sex ratios and women's partnering behavior in China. *Social Forces, 90*(1), 247–267.

Trevarthen, C. (2003). Conversations with a two-month-old. In J. Raphael-Leff (Ed.), *Parent–infant psychodynamics: Wild things, mirrors, and ghosts.* London: Whurr.

Triandis, H. C. (2005). Issues in individualism and collectivism research. In R. M. Sorrentino, D. Cohen, J. M. Olson & M. P. Zanna (Eds.), *Cultural and social behavior: The Ontario Symposium,* Vol. 10 (pp. 207–225). Mahwah, NJ: Erlbaum.

Troxel, W. M., & Matthews, K. A. (2004). What are the costs of marital conflict and dissolution to children's physical health? *Clinical Child and Family Psychology Review, 7*(1), 29–57.

Tsui, J. M., & Maziocco, M. M. M. (2007). Effects of math anxiety and perfectionism on timed versus untimed math testing in mathematically gifted sixth graders. *Roeper Review, 29*(2), 132–139.

Turiel, E. (1983). *The development of social knowledge: Morality and convention.* Cambridge: Cambridge University Press.

Turiel, E. (1998). The development of morality. In W. Damon & N. Eisenberg (Eds.) *Handbook of child psychology, Vol 3. Social, moral, and personality development* (5th ed., pp. 863–932). New York: Wiley.

Turiel, E. (2002). *The culture of morality: Social development, context, and conflict.* Cambridge: Cambridge University Press.

Turkheimer, E. (1991). Individual and group differences in adoption studies of IQ. *Psychological Bulletin, 110,* 392–405.

Turnbull, M., Hart, D., & Lapkin, S. (2003). Grade 6 French immersion students performance on large scale reading, writing, and mathematics tests: Building explanations. *Alberta Journal of Educational Research, 49,* 6–23.

Turner, C. M. (2006). Cognitive-behavioural theory and therapy for obsessive-compulsive disorder in children and adolescents: Current status and future directions. *Clinical Psychology Review, 26,* 912–938.

Tzuriel, D., & Egozi, G. (2010). Gender differences in spatial ability of young children: The effects of training and processing strategies. *Child Development, 81*(5), 1417–1430.

U.S. Department of Health and Human Services. (2009). Sexual development of girls. http://www.4parents.gov/sexdevt/girlswomen/girls_sexdevt/index.html. Accessed October 26, 2009.

Ulijaszek, S. J. (2010). Variation in human growth patterns due to environmental factors. In M. P. Muehlenbein, *Human evolutionary biology* (pp. 396–404). New York: Cambridge University Press.

Ullman, S. E. (2007). Relationship to perpetrator, disclosure, social reactions, and PTSD symptoms in child sexual abuse survivors. *Journal of Child Sexual Abuse, 16*(1), 19–36.

Ullrich-French, S., & Smith, A. L. (2009). Social and motivational predictors of continued youth sport participation. *Psychology of Sport and Exercise, 10*(1), 87–95.

Umaña-Taylor, A. J., Yazedjian, A., & Bámaca-Gómez, M. (2004). Developing the ethnic identity scale using Eriksonian and social identity perspectives. *Identity, 4*(1), 9–38.

Underwood, M. K. (2011). Aggression. In M. K. Underwood & L. H. Rosen (Eds.), *Social development: Relationships in infancy, childhood, and adolescence* (pp. 207–234). New York: Guilford.

Underwood, M. K., & Rosen, L. H. (Eds.). (2011). *Social development: Relationships in infancy, childhood, and adolescence* (pp. 289–315). New York: Guilford.

UNICEF. (2006). *The state of the world's children: 2007*. New York: United Nations.

UNICEF. (2012). HIV and Infant Feeding. http://www.unicef.org/programme/ breastfeeding/hiv.htm. Accessed January 15, 2012.

United Nations. (2012). Department of Economic and Social Affairs. Economic and Social Development. Social Indicators. http://unstats.un.org/ unsd/demographic/products/socind/ default.htm, http://unstats.un.org/ unsd/demographic/products/socind/ childbearing.htm#tech. Accessed January 13, 2014.

United States Department of Health and Human Services. (2010). Womenshealth.gov (2010). Breastfeeding. http://www.womenshealth.gov/ Breastfeeding/index.cfm?page=home. Accessed January 15, 2012.

Upton, K. J., & Sullivan, R. M. (2010). Defining age limits of the sensitive period for attachment learning in rat pups. *Developmental Psychobiology, 52*(5), 453–464.

Urbina, S. (2011). Tests of intelligence. In R. J. Sternberg & S. J. Kaufman (Eds.), *The Cambridge handbook of intelligence* (pp. 20–38). New York: Cambridge University Press.

Vaillancourt, T., & Hymel, S. (2006). Aggression and social status: The moderating roles of sex and peer-valued characteristics. *Aggressive Behaviors, 32*, 396–408.

Valderhaug, R., Götestam, K. G., & Larsson, B. (2004). Clinicians' views on management of obsessive-compulsive disorders in children and adolescents. *Nordic Journal of Psychiatry, 58*(2), 125–132.

Valenzuela, S., Park, N., & Kee, K. F. (2009). Is there social capital in a social network site? Facebook use and college students' life satisfaction, trust, and participation. *Journal of Computer-Mediated Communication, 14*(4), 875–901.

Valkenburg, P. M., Peter, J., & Schouten, A. P. (2006). Friend networking sites and their relationship to adolescents' well-being and social self-esteem. *Cyber-Psychology & Behavior, 9*(5), 584–590.

Vallance, A., & Garralda, E. (2011). Anxiety disorders in children and adolescents. In D. Skuse, H. Bruce, L. Dowdney, & D. Mrazek (Eds.). *Child psychology and psychiatry: Frameworks for practice* (2nd ed.) (pp. 169–174). Hoboken, NJ: Wiley.

van Baardewijk, Y., Stegge, H., Bushman, B. J., & Vermeiren, R. (2009). Psychopathic traits, victim distress and aggression in children. *Journal of Child Psychology and Psychiatry, 50*(6), 718–725.

Van de Beek, C., van Goozen, S. H. M., Buitelaar, J. K., & Cohen-Kettenis, P. T. (2009). Prenatal sex hormones (maternal and amniotic fluid) and gender-related play behavior in 13-month-old infants. *Archives of Sexual Behavior, 38*(1), 6–15.

Van den Bergh, B. R. H., Mulder, E. J. H., Mennes, M., & Glover, V. (2005). Antenatal maternal anxiety and stress and the neurobehavioural development of the fetus and child: Links and possible mechanisms. A review. *Neuroscience & Biobehavioral Reviews, 29*(2), 237–258.

van der Hoorn, A., et al. (2009). Non-right-handedness and mental health problems among adolescents from the general population. *Laterality: Asymmetries of Body, Brain and Cognition.* doi:10.1080/13576500902746839.

Vando, J., Rhule-Louie, D. M., McMahon, R. J., & Spieker, S. J. (2008). Examining the link between infant attachment and child conduct problems in grade 1. *Journal of Child and Family Studies, 17*(5), 615–628.

Van Doorn, M. D., Branje, S. J. T., Hox, J. J., & Meeus, W. H. J. (2009). Intra-individual variability in adolescents' perceived relationship satisfaction: The role of daily conflict. *Journal of Youth and Adolescence, 38*(6), 790–803.

van Haren, N. E. M., et al. (2012). The genetic and environmental determinants of the association between brain abnormalities and schizophrenia: The Schizophrenia Twins and Relatives Consortium. *Biological Psychiatry, 71*(10), 915–921.

van IJzendoorn, M. H., & Hubbard, F. O. A. (2000). Are infant crying and maternal responsiveness during the first year related to infant-mother attachment at 15 months? *Attachment and Human Development, 2*(3), 371–391.

Van Norman, G. A., et al. (Eds.). (2011). *Clinical Ethics in Anesthesiology.* (pp. 49–54). New York: Cambridge University Press.

Vartanian, O., Martindale, C., & Kwiatkowski, J. (2003). Creativity and inductive reasoning: The relationship between divergent thinking and performance on Wason's 2-4-6 task. *Quarterly Journal of Experimental Psychology: Human Experimental Psychology, 56A*(4), 641–655.

Vélez, C. E., Wolchik, S. A., Tein, J-Y., & Sandler, I. (2011). Protecting children from the consequences of divorce: A longitudinal study of the effects of parenting on children's coping processes. *Child Development, 82*(1), 244–257.

Vellutino, F. R., Fletcher, J. M., Snowling, M. J., & Scanlon, D. M. (2004). Specific reading disability (dyslexia): What have we learned in the past four decades? *Journal of Child Psychology and Psychiatry, 45*(1), 2–40.

Verkuyten, M. (2009). Self-esteem and multiculturalism: An examination among ethnic minority and majority groups in the Netherlands. *Journal of Research in Personality, 43*(3), 419–427.

Verlohren, S., Stepan, H., & Dechend, R. (2012). Angiogenic growth factors in the diagnosis and prediction of pre-eclampsia. *Clinical Science, 122*, 43–52.

Verloop, J., et al. (2010). Cancer risk in DES daughters. *Cancer Causes Control, 21*(7), 999–1007.

Victor, R., et al. (2007). Correlation between high risk obesity groups and low socioeconomic status in school children. *Southern Medical Journal, 100*(1), 8–13.

Vigil, J. M., Geary, D. C., & Byrd-Craven, J. (2005). A life history assessment of early childhood sexual abuse in women. *Developmental Psychology, 41*(3), 553–561.

Vigod, S. N., Villegas, L., Dennis, C-L., & Ross, L. E. (2010). Prevalence and risk factors for postpartum depression among women with preterm and low-birth-weight infants: A systematic review. *BJOG: An International Journal of Obstetrics & Gynaecology, 117*(5), 540–550.

Villani, S. (2001). Impact of media on children and adolescents: A 10-year review of the research. *Journal of the American Academy of Child and Adolescent Psychiatry, 40*(4), 392–401.

Virji-Babul, N., Kerns, K., Zhou, E., Kapur, A., & Shiffrar, M. (2006). Perceptual-motor deficits in children with Down syndrome: Implications for intervention. *Down Syndrome: Research & Practice, 10*(2), 74–82.

Visser, M., Singer, E., van Geert, P. L. C., & Kunnen, S. E. (2009). What makes children behave aggressively? The inner logic of Dutch children in special education. *European Journal of Special Needs Education, 21*(4), 1–20.

Vitiello, B. (Ed.). (2006). Guest editorial: Selective serotonin reuptake inhibitors (SSRIs) in children and adolescents. *Journal of Child and Adolescent Psychopharmacology, 16*(1–2), 7–9.

Vohr, B., et al. (2008). Early language outcomes of early-identified infants with permanent hearing loss at 12 to 16 months of age. *Pediatrics, 122*(3), 535–544.

Volkova, A., Trehub, S. E., & Schellenberg, E. G. (2006). Infants' memory for musical performances. *Developmental Science, 9*(6), 583–589.

Volling, B. L. (2001). Early attachment relationships as predictors of preschool children's emotion regulation with a distressed sibling. *Early Education and Development, 12*(2), 185–207.

Volterra, M. C., Caselli, O., Capirci, E., & Pizzuto, E. (2004). Gesture and the emergence and development of language. In M. Tomasello & D. I. Slobin (Eds.), *Beyond nature–nurture*. Mahwah, NJ: Erlbaum.

von Gontard, A. (2011). Elimination disorders: A critical comment on DSM–5 proposals. *European Child & Adolescent Psychiatry, 20*(2), 83–88.

Vu, M. B., Murrie, D., Gonzalez, V., & Jobe, J. B. (2006). Listening to girls and boys talk about girls' physical activity behaviors. *Health Education & Behavior, 33*(1), 81–96.

Vukovic, R. K., & Siegel, L. S. (2006). The double-deficit hypothesis: A comprehensive analysis of the evidence. *Journal of Learning Disabilities, 39*(1), 25–47.

Vuoksimaa, E., Eriksson, C. J. P., Pulkkinen, L., Rose, R. J., & Kaprio, J. (2010). Decreased prevalence of left-handedness among females with male co-twins: Evidence suggesting prenatal testosterone transfer in humans? *Psychoneuroendocrinology, 35*(10), 1462–1472.

Vurpillot, E. (1968). The development of scanning strategies and their relation to visual differentiation. *Journal of Experimental Child Psychology, 6*, 632–650.

Vygotsky, L. (1978). *Mind in society: The development of higher psychological processes*. Cambridge, MA: Harvard University Press.

Vygotsky, L. S. (1962). *Thought and language*. Cambridge, MA: MIT Press.

Wagner, I. V., et al. (2012). Effects of obesity on human sexual development. *Nature Reviews: Endocrinology, 8*, 246–254.

Wakschlag, L. S., Pickett, K. E., Kasza, K. E., & Loeber, R. (2006). Is prenatal smoking associated with a developmental pattern of conduct problems in young boys? *Journal of the American Academy of Child & Adolescent Psychiatry, 45*(4), 461–467.

Wald, J., & Losen, D. J. (2007). Out of sight: The journey through the school-to-prison pipeline. In S. Books (Ed.), *Invisible children in the society and its schools* (3rd ed.) (pp. 23–37). Mahwah, NJ: Erlbaum.

Walitza, S., et al. (2006). Genetic and neuroimaging studies in attention deficit hyperactivity disorder. *Nervenheilkunde: Zeitschrift für interdisziplinaere Fortbildung, 25*(6), 421–429.

Walker, L. J (2006). Gender and morality. In M. Killen & J. G. Smetana (Eds.), *Handbook of moral development* (pp. 93–115). Mahwah, NJ: Lawrence Erlbaum.

Walkup, J. T., et al. (2001). Fluvoxamine for the treatment of anxiety disorders in children and adolescents. *New England Journal of Medicine, 344*(17), 1279–1285.

Wallen, K., & Hassett, J. M. (2009). Sexual differentiation of behaviour in monkeys: Role of prenatal hormones. *Journal of Neuroendocrinology, 21*(4), 421–426.

Wallerstein, J., Lewis, J., Blakeslee, S., Hetherington, E. M., & Kelly, J. (2005). Issue 17: Is divorce always detrimental to children? In R. P. Halgin (Ed.), *Taking sides: Clashing views on controversial issues in abnormal psychology* (3rd ed.) (pp. 298–321). New York: McGraw-Hill.

Walline, J. J., et al. (2009). Randomized trial of the effect of contact lens wear on self-perception in children. *Optometry & Vision Science, 86*(3), 222–232.

Walter, J. L., & LaFreniere, P. J. (2000). A naturalistic study of affective expression, social competence, and sociometric status in preschoolers. *Early Education and Development, 11*(1), 109–122.

Walther, F. J., Ouden, A. L. den, & Verloove-Vanhorick, S. P. (2000). Looking back in time: Outcome of a national cohort of very preterm infants born in The Netherlands in 1983. *Early Human Development, 59*(3), 175–191.

Wang, Q., Leichtman, M. D., & White, S. H. (1998). Childhood memory and self-description in young Chinese adults: The impact of growing up an only child. *Cognition, 69*(1), 73–103.

Wang, S-H., Baillargeon, R., & Paterson, S. (2005). Detecting continuity violations in infancy: A new account and new evidence from covering and tube events. *Cognition, 95*(2), 129–173.

Wang, X., Dow-Edwards, D., Anderson, V., Minkoff, H., & Hurd, Y. L. (2004). In utero marijuana exposure associated with abnormal amygdala dopamine d-sub-2 gene expression in the human fetus. *Biological Psychiatry, 56*(12), 909–915.

Ware, E. A., Uttal, D. H., Wetter, E. K., & DeLoache, J. S. (2006). Young children make scale errors when playing with dolls. *Developmental Science, 9*(1), 40–45.

Washburn, D. A. (Ed.). (2007). *Primate perspectives on behavior and cognition*. Washington, DC: American Psychological Association.

Wass, R., Harland, T., & Mercer, A. (2011). Scaffolding critical thinking in the zone of critical development. *Higher Education Research & Development, 30*(3), 317–328.

Wasserman, G. A., et al. (2000). Yugoslavia Prospective Lead Study: Contributions of prenatal and postnatal lead exposure to early intelligence. *Neurotoxicology and Teratology, 22*(6), 811–818.

Waszak, F., Li, S. C., & Hommel, B. (2010). The development of attentional networks: Cross-sectional findings from a life span sample. *Developmental Psychology, 46*, 337–349.

Waters E. (1995). The attachment Q-set. In E. Waters, B. Vaughn, G. G. Posada, & K. Kondo-Ikemura (Eds.), *Caregiving, cultural, and cognitive perspectives on secure base behavior and working models: New growing points of attachment theory and research. Monographs of the Society for Research in Child Development, 60*, 234–246.

Watson, H. J., et al. (2011). Mediators between perfectionism and eating disorder psychopathology: Shape and weight overvaluation and conditional goal-setting. *International Journal of Eating Disorders, 44*(2), 142–149.

Watson, J. B. (1924). *Behaviorism*. New York: Norton.

Watson, J. B., & Rayner, R. (1920). Conditioned emotional reactions. *Journal of Experimental Psychology, 3*(1), 1–14.

Waxman, S. R., & Lidz, J. L. (2006). Early word learning. In D. Kuhn, R. S. Siegler, W. Damon & R. M. Lerner (Eds.), *Handbook of child psychology* (6th ed.), Vol. 2, *Cognition, perception, and language* (pp. 299–335). Hoboken, NJ: Wiley.

Waxmonsky, J. G. (2005). Nonstimulant therapies for attention-deficit hyperactivity disorder (ADHD) in children and adults. *Essential Psychopharmacology, 6*(5), 262–276.

Waylen, A. E., et al. (2009). Romantic and sexual behavior in young adolescents: Repeated surveys in a population-based cohort. *Journal of Early Adolescence, 30*(3), 432–443.

Weaver, A. D., Byers, E. S., Sears, H. A., Cohen, J. N., & Randall, H. (2002). Sexual health education at school and at home: Attitudes and experiences of New Brunswick parents. *The Canadian Journal of Human Sexuality, 11*, 19–31.

Webb, P. (2007). Review of juvenile delinquency: Prevention, assessment, and intervention. *Youth Violence and Juvenile Justice, 5*(2), 211–214.

Weber, M. A., et al. (2011). Autopsy findings of co-sleeping-associated sudden unexpected deaths in infancy: Relationship between pathological features and asphyxial mode of death. *Journal of Paediatrics and Child Health, 48*(4), 335–341.

Webster-Stratton, C., Reid, J., & Hammond, M. (2001). Social skills and problem-solving training for children with early-onset conduct problems: Who benefits? *Journal of Child Psychology and Psychiatry and Allied Disciplines, 42*(7), 943–952.

Wechsler, D. (1975). Intelligence defined and undefined: A relativistic appraisal. *American Psychologist, 30*, 135–139.

Weckerly, J., Wulfeck, B., & Reilly, J. (2004). The development of morphosyntactic ability in atypical populations: The acquisition of tag questions in children with early focal lesions and children with specific-language impairment. *Brain and Language, 88*(2), 190–201.

Wegner, L., & Flisher, A. J. (2009). Leisure boredom and adolescent risk behaviour: A systematic literature review. *Journal of Child and Adolescent Mental Health, 21*(1), 1–28.

Wehkalampi, K., et al. (2008). Genetic and environmental influences on pubertal timing assessed by height growth. *American Journal of Human Biology, 20*(4), 417–423.

Weichold, K., Silbereisen, R. K., & Schmitt-Rodermund, E. (2003). Short-term and long-term consequences of early versus late physical maturation in adolescents. In C. Hayward (Ed.), *Gender differences at puberty* (pp. 241–276). New York: Cambridge University Press.

Welch, E., Miller, J. L., Ghaderi, A., & Vaillamcourt, T. (2009). Does perfectionism mediate or moderate the relation between body dissatisfaction and disordered eating attitudes and behaviors? *Eating Disorders*, in press.

Weller, E. B., & Weller, R. A. (1991). Mood disorders. In M. Lewis (Ed.), *Child and adolescent psychiatry: A comprehensive textbook*. Baltimore: Williams & Wilkins.

Wellman, H. M. (2002). Understanding the psychological world: Developing a theory of mind. In U. Goswami (Ed.), *Blackwell handbook of childhood cognitive development* (pp. 167–187). Malden, MA: Blackwell.

Wellman, H. M. (2010). Developing a theory of mind. In U. Goswami (Ed.), *The Wiley–Blackwell handbook of childhood cognitive development*. (2nd ed.) (pp. 258–284). Chichester, West Sussex, UK: Wiley–Blackwell.

Wellman, H. M., Cross, D., & Bartsch, K. (1986). Infant search and object permanence: A meta-analysis of the A-not-B error. *Monographs of the Society for Research in Child Development*, 5(3, ser. 214).

Weng, X., Odouli, R., & Li, D. K. (2008). Maternal caffeine consumption during pregnancy and the risk of miscarriage: A prospective cohort study. *American Journal of Obstetrics & Gynecology*, 198, 279.e1–279.e8.

Wentworth, N., Benson, J. B., & Haith, M. M. (2000). The development of infants' reaches for stationary and moving targets. *Child Development*, 71(3), 576–601.

Wentzel, K. R., Barry, C. M., & Caldwell, K. A. (2004). Friendships in middle school: Influences on motivation and school adjustment. *Journal of Educational Psychology*, 96(2), 195–203.

Weppelman, T. L., Bostow, A., Schiffer, R., Elbert-Perez, E., & Newman, R. S. (2003). Children's use of the prosodic characteristics of infant-directed speech. *Language and Communication*, 23(1), 63–80.

Werker, J. F. (1989). Becoming a native listener. *American Scientist*, 77, 54–59.

Werker, J. F., et al. (2007). Infant-directed speech supports phonetic category learning in English and Japanese. *Cognition*, 103(1), 147–162.

Werker, J. F., Henny, H., Yeung, & Yoshida, K. A. (2012). How do infants become experts at native-speech perception? *Current Directions in Psychological Science* 2012 21: 221 doi: 10.1177/0963721412449459.

Werner, E. E. (1988). A cross-cultural perspective on infancy. *Journal of Cross-Cultural Psychology*, 19, 96–113.

Werner, L. A., & Bernstein, I. L. (2001). Development of the auditory, gustatory, olfactory, and somatosensory systems. In E. B. Goldstein (Ed.),

Blackwell handbook of perception, Handbook of experimental psychology series (pp. 669–708). Boston: Blackwell.

Wertheim, E. H., Paxton, S. J., & Blaney, S. (2009). Body image in girls. In L. Smolak & J. K. Thompson (Eds.), *Body image, eating disorders, and obesity in youth: Assessment, prevention, and treatment* (2nd ed.) (pp. 47–76). Washington, DC: American Psychological Association.

Whalen, C. K. (2001). ADHD treatment in the 21st century: Pushing the envelope. *Journal of Clinical Child Psychology*, 30(1), 136–140.

White, C. B., Bushnell, N., & Regnemer, J. L. (1978). Moral development in Bahamian school children: A three-year examination of Kohlberg's stages of moral development. *Developmental Psychology*, 14, 58–65.

White, J. W., & Smith, P. H. (2004). Sexual assault perpetration and reperpetration: From adolescence to young adulthood. *Criminal Justice and Behavior*, 31(2), 182–202.

Whitehead, J. T., & Lab, S. P. (2013). *Juvenile justice*. Waltham, MA: Anderson Publishing.

Whitehouse, E. M. (2006). Poverty. In G. G. Bear & K. M. Minke (Eds.), *Children's needs III: Development, prevention, and intervention* (pp. 835–845). Washington, DC: National Association of School Psychologists.

Whiting, B. B., & Edwards, C. P. (1988). *Children of different worlds*. Cambridge, MA: Harvard University Press.

Whitmarsh, L., & Wentworth, D. K. (2012). Gender similarity or gender difference? Contemporary women's and men's career patterns. *Career Development Quarterly*, 60(1), 47–64.

Wilcox, W. B., & Marquardt, E. (Eds.). (2011). *The state of our unions: Marriage in America 2011*. Institute for American Values. Charlottesville, VA: University of Virginia: The National Marriage Project.

Williams, R. L. (1974, May). Scientific racism and IQ: The silent mugging of the black community. *Psychology Today*, p. 32.

Willis, J. O., Dumont, R., & Kaufman, A. S. (2011). Factor-analytic models of intelligence. In R. J. Sternberg & S. J. Kaufman (Eds.), *The Cambridge handbook of intelligence* (pp. 39–57). New York: Cambridge University Press.

Wilson-Costello, D., et al. (2007). Improved neurodevelopmental outcomes for extremely low birth weight infants in 2000–2002. *Pediatrics*, 119(1), 37–45.

Windle, M., et al. (2008). Transitions into underage and problem drinking: Developmental processes and mechanisms between 10 and 15 years of age. *Pediatrics*, 121(Suppl. April 2008), S273–S289.

Wingood, G. M., et al. (2006). Efficacy of an HIV prevention program among female adolescents experiencing gender-based violence. *American Journal of Public Health*, 96(6), 1085–1090.

Wismer Fries, A. B., Shirtcliff, E. A., & Pollak, S. D. (2008). Neuroendocrine dysregulation following early social deprivation in children. *Developmental Psychobiology*, 50(6), 588–599.

Witherington, D. C., Campos, J. J., Harriger, J. A., Bryan, C., and Margett, T. E. (2010). Emotion and its development in infancy. In J. G. Bremner & T. D. Wachs (Eds.). *The Wiley-Blackwell handbook of infant development*, Vol. 1 (2nd ed.). Wiley-Blackwell, Oxford, UK. doi:10.1002/9781444327564.ch19.

Wolchik, S. A., et al. (2000). An experimental evaluation of theory-based mother and mother–child programs for children of divorce. *Journal of Consulting and Clinical Psychology*, 68(5), 853–856.

Wolfe, D. A. (2011). Violence against women and children. In J. W. White, M. P. Koss, & A. E. Kazdin (Eds.). *Violence against women and children*, Vol. 1: *Mapping the terrain* (pp. 31–53). Washington, DC: American Psychological Association.

Wolfenden, L. E., & Holt, N. L. (2005). Talent development in elite junior tennis: Perceptions of players, parents, and coaches. *Journal of Applied Sport Psychology*, 17(2), 108–126.

Wong, F. Y., et al. (2011). Cerebral oxygenation is depressed during sleep in healthy term infants when they sleep prone. *Pediatrics*, 127(3), e558–e565.

Wood, A. C., et al. (2008). High heritability for a composite index of children's activity level measures. *Behavior Genetics*, 38(3), 266–276.

Woolfolk, A. (2008). *Educational psychology, Active learning edition* (10th ed.). Boston: Allyn & Bacon.

Woolfolk, A. (2013). *Educational psychology* (12th ed.). Upper Saddle River, NJ: Pearson.

Woolley, J. D., Phelps, K. E., Davis, D. L., & Mandell, D. L. (1999). Where theories of mind meet magic: The development of children's beliefs about wishing. *Child Development*, 70, 571–587.

Worell, J., & Goodheart, C. D. (Eds.). (2006). *Handbook of girls' and women's psychological health: Gender and well-being across the lifespan*. New York: Oxford University Press.

World Health Organization. (2003). *Global strategy for infant and young child feeding*. Available at http://www.who.int/nut/documents/gs_infant_feeding_text_eng.pdf.

World Health Organization. (2003). *Training in the management of severe malnutrition*. Geneva: World Health Organization Department of Nutrition for Health and Development. Available at http://www.who.int/nut/documents/manage_severe_malnutrition_training_fly_eng.pdf.

World Health Organization. (2011, March 16). WHO, nutrition experts take action on malnutrition. http://www.who.int/nutrition/pressnote_action_on_malnutrition/en. Accessed February 20, 2012.

World Hunger Organization. (2012). 2012 World hunger and poverty facts and statistics. World Hunger Organization Service. http://www.worldhunger.org/articles/Learn/world%20hunger%20facts%202002.htm. Accessed February 20, 2012.

Worthman, C. M. (2010). The ecology of human development: Evolving models for cultural psychology. *Journal of Cross-Cultural Psychology, 41*(4), 563–577.

Wright, C., & Birks, E. (2000). Risk factors for failure to thrive: A population-based survey. *Child: Care, Health, and Development, 26*(1), 5–16.

Wright, P., Stamatakis, E. A., & Tyler, L. K. (2012). Differentiating hemispheric contributions to syntax and semantics in patients with left-hemisphere lesions. *The Journal of Neuroscience, 32*(24), 8149–8157.

Wright, S. C., Taylor, D. M., & Ruggiero, K. M. (1996). Examining the potential for academic achievement among Inuit children: Comparisons on the Raven Coloured Progressive Matrices. *Journal of Cross-Cultural Psychology, 27*(6), 733–753.

Wynn, K. (1992, August 27). Addition and subtraction by human infants. *Nature, 358*, 749–750.

Wynn, K. (2002). Do infants have numerical expectations or just perceptual preferences? Comment. *Developmental Science, 5*(2), 207–209.

Xie, H. L., Yan, B., Signe, M., Hutchins, B. C., & Cairns, B. D. (2006). What makes a girl (or a boy) popular (or unpopular)? African American children's perceptions and developmental differences. *Developmental Psychology, 42*(4), 599–612.

Xu, L., et al. (2009). Bone and muscle development during puberty in girls—A 7-year longitudinal study. *Journal of Bone and Mineral Research*, doi:10.1359/jbmr.090405.

Xue, Y. F., Moran, G., Pederson, D. R., & Bento, S. (2010, March). *The continuity of attachment development from infancy to toddlerhood: The role of maternal sensitivity.* International Conference on Infant Studies. Baltimore, MD.

Yarrow, L. J., & Goodwin, M. S. (1973). The immediate impact of separation: Reactions of infants to a change in mother figures. In L. J. Stone, H. T. Smith & L. B. Murphy (Eds.), *The competent infant: Research and commentary.* New York: Basic Books.

Yarrow, L. J., Goodwin, M. S., Manheimer, H., & Milowe, I. D. (1971, March). *Infant experiences and cognitive and personality development at ten years.* Paper presented at the meeting of the American Orthopsychiatric Association, Washington, DC.

Yazzie, A. (2010). Visual-spatial thinking and academic achievement: A concurrent and predictive validity study. Dissertation Abstracts International: Section A, Humanities and Social Sciences, 70(8-A), 2897.

Young, D. (2006). Review of breastfeeding handbook for physicians. *Birth: Issues in Perinatal Care, 33*(3), 260–261.

Youniss, J., & Haynie, D. L. (1992). Friendship in adolescence. *Developmental and Behavioral Pediatrics, 13*, 59–66.

Yurgelun-Todd, D. A. (2007). Emotional and cognitive changes during adolescence. *Current Opinion in Neurobiology, 17*(2), 251–257.

Zajonc, R. B. (2001). The family dynamics of intellectual development. *American Psychologist, 56*(6/7), 490–496.

Zapf, J. A., & Smith, L. B. (2009). Knowing more than one can say: The early regular plural. *Journal of Child Language,* published online by Cambridge University Press. doi:10.1017/S0305000909009374.

Zaslow, M. J., Gallagher, M., Hair, E. C., Egeland, B., Weinfield, N. S., Ogawa, J. R., . . . DeTemple, J. M. (2006). Longitudinal prediction of child outcomes from differing measures of parenting on a low-income sample. *Developmental Psychology, 42*, 27–37.

Zeanah, C. H., Berlin, L. J., & Boris, N. W. (2011). Practitioner review: Clinical applications of attachment theory and research for infants and young children. *The Journal of Child Psychology & Psychiatry, 52*(8), 819–833.

Zeifman, D. M. (2004). Acoustic features of infant crying related to intended caregiving intervention. *Infant and Child Development, 13*(2), 111–122.

Zelazo, P. D., and Müller, U. (2010). Executive function in typical and atypical development. In U. Goswami (Ed.). *The Wiley-Blackwell handbook of childhood cognitive development* (2nd ed.). Wiley-Blackwell, Oxford, UK. doi:10.1002/9781444325485.ch22.

Zhai, F., Brooks-Gunn, J., & Waldfogel, J. (2011). Head Start and urban children's school readiness: A birth cohort study in 18 cities. *Developmental Psychology, 47*(1), 134–152.

Zhang, C., Solomon, C. G., Manson, J. E., & Hu, F. B. (2006). A prospective study of pregravid physical activity and sedentary behaviors in relation to the risk for gestational diabetes mellitus. *Archives of Internal Medicine, 166*, 543–548.

Zheng, L., Lippa, R. A., & Zheng, Y. (2011). Sex and sexual orientation differences in personality in China. *Archives of Sexual Behavior, 40*(3), 533–541.

Zhiqi, L., Kun, Y., & Zhiwu, H. (2010). Tympanometry in infants with middle ear effusion having been identified using spiral computerized tomography. *American Journal of Otolaryngology, 31*(2), 96–103.

Zhou, Z., Bray, M. A., Kehle, T. J., & Xin, T. (2001). Similarity of deleterious effects of divorce on Chinese and American children. *School Psychology International, 22*(3), 357–363.

Zigler, E., Abelson, W. D., Trickett, P. K., & Seitz, V. (1982). Is an intervention program necessary in order to improve economically disadvantaged children's IQ scores? *Child Development, 53*, 340–348.

Zimmerman, A. W. (Ed.). (2008). *Autism: Current theories and evidence.* Totowa, NJ: Humana Press.

Zimmerman, B. J. (2000). Self-efficacy: An essential motive to learn. *Contemporary Educational Psychology, 25*(1), 82–91.

Zimmerman, F. J., & Bell, J. F. (2010). Association of television content type and obesity in children. *American Journal of Public Health, 100*(2), 334–340.

Zimmerman, F. J., Christakis, D. A., & Meltzoff, A. N. (2007). Associations between media viewing and language development in children under age 2 years. *Journal of Pediatrics, 151*, 364–368.

Zimmermann, P., Maier, M. A., Winter, M., & Grossmann, K. E. (2001). Attachment and adolescents' emotion regulation during a joint problem-solving task with a friend. *International Journal of Behavioral Development, 25*(4), 331–343.

Zonnevylle-Bender, M. J. S., Matthys, W., Van De Wiel, N. M. H., & Lochman, J. E. (2007). Preventive effects of treatment of disruptive behavior disorder in middle childhood on substance use and delinquent behavior. *Journal of the American Academy of Child & Adolescent Psychiatry, 46*(1), 33–39.

Zosuls, K. M., Miller, C. F., Ruble, D. N., Martin, C. L., & Fabes, R. A. (2011). Gender development research in sex roles: Historical trends and future directions. *Sex Roles, 64*(11–12), 826–842.

Zuckerman, M. (2011). Personality science: Three approaches and their applications to the causes and treatment of depression. In M. Zuckerman (Ed.). *Three approaches and their applications to the causes and treatment of depression* (pp. 47–77). Washington, DC: American Psychological Association.

Zweigenhaft, R. L., & Von Ammon, J. (2000). Birth order and civil disobedience: A test of Sulloway's "born to rebel" hypothesis. *Journal of Social Psychology, 140*(5), 624–627.

NAME INDEX

f denotes figure; n denotes note; p denotes photo; t denotes table

SUBJECT INDEX

f denotes figure; n denotes note; p denotes photo; t denotes table